A
FINANCIAL HISTORY

of

MODERN U.S.
CORPORATE
SCANDALS

From

Enron to Reform

A

FINANCIAL HISTORY

of

MODERN U.S. CORPORATE SCANDALS

From

Enron to Reform

JERRY W. MARKHAM

M.E.Sharpe
Armonk, New York
London, England

Library of Congress Cataloging-in-Publication Data

Markham, Jerry W.
    A financial history of modern U.S. corporate scandals : from Enron to reform / Jerry W.
Markham.
        p. cm.
    Includes bibliographical references and index.
    ISBN 0-7656-1583-5 (hardcover : alk. paper)
    1. Corporations—Corrupt practices—United States. 2. Corporations—Accounting—
United States. 3. Enron Corp.—Corrupt practices. 4. Stock Market Bubble, 1995–2000.
5. Commercial crimes—United States. I. Title: Financial history of modern United States
corporate scandals. II. Title.

HV6769.M37 2005
364.16′8′0973—dc22

                                                                                    2005005562

Printed in the United States of America

The paper used in this publication meets the minimum requirements of
American National Standard for Information Sciences
Permanence of Paper for Printed Library Materials,
ANSI Z 39.48-1984.

BM (c)   10   9   8   7   6   5   4   3   2   1

Contents

I. The Stock Market Bubble and Enron

Financial Markets 3 • The Market Boom 3 • Raising All Boats 4 •
Run-Up in IPO Prices 5 • Structured Finance 7 • Collateralized Debt
Obligations 8 • New Instruments 9 • Commodities Futures
Modernization 11 • Traditional Markets 13 • Electronic
Communications Networks 15 • Broker-Dealers 17 • Merger
Activity 20

Fraud and Abuses 21 • Fraud Schemes 21 • Ponzi Schemes 23 •
Electronic Fraud 25 • Pump and Dump Schemes 27 • Other Problems
29 • Executive Compensation 30 • Expensing Options 33

Attacks on the Markets 34 • The First Attack 34 • The Market Reacts
35 • The Fed Reverses Course 37 • Economic Decline 37 • The
Damage Is Done 39 • Deficits and International Problems 40 • Prelude
to September 11 42 • The 9/11 Attack 42 • Restarting Wall Street 44 •
Coping With Terror 46

A Company Is Born 49 • Creating a Name 49 • Enron's Management
50 • Jeffrey Skilling 51 • Andrew Fastow 52 • Enron Values 53 •
Pipeline Operations 54 • Deregulation 54 • Trading Operations 55 •
Mark-to-Market 57 • Wind Farms 59 • Foreign Operations 59 • Foreign
Problems 60

IV. Recovery and Reform

Preface

This book examines the collapse of the Enron Corp. and other financial scandals that arose in the wake of the market downturn in 2000. Part I reviews the market boom and bust that preceded Enron's collapse. It then describes the growth of Enron and the events that led to its sensational failure. The aftermath of that collapse is described, including the Enron bankruptcy proceedings, the prosecution of Enron officials, and Enron's role in the California energy crisis.

Part II examines the role of the Securities and Exchange Commission's (SEC's) full disclosure system in corporate governance and the role of accountants in that system, like Arthur Andersen LLP, the Enron auditor that was destroyed after it was accused of obstructing justice. This part also describes several full disclosure failures such as those at Rite Aid, Xerox, and Computer Associates. Part II then turns to the development and role of fiduciary duties in corporate governance and the role of the Delaware courts in that process. Other corporate governance reforms are examined, such as the use of outside directors and the development of shareholder rights. Breaches of fiduciary duties at Tyco are also a subject of this part.

Part III reviews the meltdown in the telecom sector and the accounting scandals that emerged at Nortel, Lucent, Qwest, Global Crossing, Adelphia, and WorldCom. Other accounting scandals at AOL Time Warner, Vivendi, HealthSouth, Hollinger, and others are included in this part. Part III examines the financial scandals that appeared on Wall Street in the wake of Enron, including Martha Stewart's trial, the financial analyst conflicts, the brawl over Richard Grasso's salary, the mutual fund trading abuses, and scandals in the insurance industry. This part describes the Sarbanes-Oxley legislation that was adopted in the wake of these scandals, the burdens it imposed, and continuing flaws in full disclosure.

Finally, Part IV traces the remarkable market recovery that followed the financial scandals and the resumption of the growth of finance in America. This part addresses the flaws and myths of full disclosure and the misguided efforts of corporate governance reformers that led to the financial scandals previously described. Part IV then examines some alternatives to the present system.

Acknowledgments

I would like to express my appreciation for the assistance given by my research assistants, particularly Erin Treacy and Mistelle Abdelmagied, both law students at Florida International University. I am also grateful for the access afforded me by the British Library in London, the National Library of Scotland in Edinburgh, the National Library of Ireland in Dublin, and the London library of the Institute of Chartered Accountants of England and Wales. Finally, I would like to thank Beth Peiffer for her work on the index.

Introduction

This book is a history of the massive financial scandals that arose in the still fledgling twenty-first century, but that story actually begins with the recession in 1990–1991, an event that led to the defeat of the incumbent president, George H.W. Bush. The administration of Bill Clinton then experienced the longest period of expansion in American history and the longest bull market. That happy situation was spoiled by a market downturn in 2000 that was engineered largely through a series of punitive interest rate increases ordered by Alan Greenspan, chairman of the Federal Reserve.

The presidential election contest between Al Gore and George W. Bush created more uncertainty for the economy, and the country went into what appeared to be a recession shortly after Bush assumed office. The terrorist attacks on September 11, 2001, then delivered a devastating blow to the economy. Following on the heels of those attacks was another firestorm in the form of a financial scandal at the Enron Corp., the seventh-largest company in the United States. The collapse of that high-profile industrial giant, its massive manipulation of financial accounts, and the enormous personal profits in Enron stock by its executives led to lurid headlines and much sensationalism.

Congressional hearings on Enron's failure were conducted in an atmosphere of hysteria that rivaled the McCarthy era in the 1950s. Enron executives were paraded before cameras when they asserted the Fifth Amendment and were adjudged guilty by members of Congress before any trial. Those brave enough to testify were ridiculed and shouted down by senators and members of the House. All matter of left-wing law professors and other reformers appeared as witnesses to condemn Enron in particular and corporate managers in general. The heavily politicized scandal became a central issue in the 2002 congressional elections that decided control of Congress and was even a favorite topic during state gubernatorial contests.

The contagion spread to Enron's accounting firm, Arthur Andersen LLP, when it announced that its Houston office had destroyed large numbers of Enron documents and computer files. After a somewhat bizarre trial, Arthur Andersen was convicted of obstructing justice. Even though later reversed by the Supreme Court, that conviction spelled the end of this venerable accounting firm, and 85,000 Arthur Andersen employees lost their jobs; 28,000 of those jobs were in the United States. Two of America's largest financial services firms, Citigroup and JPMorgan Chase, found themselves embroiled in the Enron scandal after it was discovered that those banks had disguised massive amounts of loans as commodity transactions in order to keep that debt off Enron's balance sheet.

There seemed to be no limits to the Enron scandal. The Federal Energy Regulatory Commission began investigating whether Enron and other energy trading companies had manipulated the California electricity market in 2000 and 2001. During that period, electricity prices skyrocketed in California and shortages occurred, causing brownouts and bankrupting one of California's largest public utilities. Enron was found to have been exploiting inefficiencies in the California electricity market through transactions named "Fat Boy," "Get Shorty," "Death Star," and similar attention-grabbing sobriquets. This touched off another frenzy in the press and among regulators. Tapes of conversations by Enron traders contained lurid references to their trading practices, and transcripts of those conversations were posted on government Web sites and reported widely in the press.

The Enron debacle gave rise to a thirst for more financial scandals. Thanks to the market downturn, they were not long in coming. Global Crossing, a fiber-optic long network operator, saw the valuation of its stock reach $50 billion before it filed for bankruptcy, amidst controversy over its accounting practices. It was the fourth-largest bankruptcy on record in the United States. The collapse of WorldCom, the giant telecommunications firm, was even more spectacular, wresting away from Enron the title of the largest bankruptcy in history. The head of WorldCom, Bernard J. Ebbers, was indicted for fraud in connection with massive accounting malpractices that had improperly boosted earnings by as much as $11 billion.

The seventy-eight-year-old founder of another telecommunications firm, Adelphia, was arrested in a dawn raid, manacled, and frog-marched in front of news media, before being charged with looting the company. Dennis Kozlowski, the chief executive officer at Tyco International, set off another corporate scandal when it was discovered that he had not paid New York sales taxes on millions of dollar's worth of paintings. That scandal widened after Kozlowski was indicted for looting $600 million from Tyco, allowing him to spend $29 million for a vacation home in Boca Raton, Florida, and $30 million on a Manhattan apartment furnished with an instantly famous $6,000 shower curtain. Kozlowski used Tyco funds for a $2.1 million birthday party for his wife, Karen, which was held on the island of Sardinia. Singer Jimmy Buffett was imported to sing "Happy Birthday" at a cost of $250,000. That and other excesses at the party became media legend.

Accounting scandals were reaching epic proportions. Between 1998 and the first half of 2002, there were over 650 accounting restatements by public corporations: Such events had been a rarity only a few years previously. To name a few: Xerox admitted to ginning up its revenues by $6.4 billion; Reliant Resources bested that figure by announcing a restatement of earnings in excess of $7.8 billion that were the result of "round-trip" trades designed to enhance its status as an energy trader; Qwest Communications International, a telecommunications company, restated $2.5 billion in revenues between 2000 and 2001; Rite Aid restated $1.6 billion; Bristol-Myers-Squibb inflated sales figures by $2.75 billion between 1999 and 2001; Computer Associates improperly booked more than $2 billion in revenue for fiscal years 2000 and 2001; and Lucent Technologies engaged in a number of indiscretions, including improperly recognizing $1.15 billion in revenue and $470 million in pretax income for fiscal year 2000.

Executives of every stripe were under criticism for receiving hundreds of millions of dollars in compensation through options on their companies' stock, which gave them an incentive to manipulate accounting results in order to boost their compensation. The amounts of some compensation packages were simply stunning. Michael Eisner at Walt Disney Co. was paid over $750 million, largely from stock options. Larry Ellison, the head of Oracle Corp., made $706 million on his options in a year when the company's share price dropped by 57 percent. Michael Dell of Dell Computer made $233 million in one year. Sanford (Sandy) I. Weill at Citigroup made $220 million in one year and was paid a total of almost $1 billion at Citigroup.

On top of those scandals were dozens of boiler rooms selling worthless securities to the public through high-pressure sales techniques. "Pump and dump" schemes using such tactics were manipulating share prices in numerous "smallcap" stocks. Ponzi schemes, Internet touts, and other fraud schemes were rampant, reaping billion of dollars from unsuspecting investors. Alan Greenspan denounced before Congress the "infectious greed" of corporate America, but his statement failed to slow the pace of the scandals that morphed over to Wall Street. Stock analysts were found to have been secretly disparaging stocks they were touting to the public. That scandal was triggered by New York attorney general Eliot Spitzer, who revealed that a Merrill Lynch analyst, Henry Blodget, had called stocks he was promoting to public investors "crap" and a "piece of junk" in private e-mails. The analysts' scandal widened when it was revealed that Sandy Weill, at Citigroup, had his bank make a $1 million contribution to an elite preschool as a part of a Byzantine plot to gain control of Citigroup, as well as to acquire the investment banking business of AT&T. That scandal and subsequent investigations made Eliot Spitzer a national figure, and he began challenging the Securities and Exchange Commission (SEC) for supremacy of regulatory control over the securities markets.

Spitzer was attacking other Wall Street conflicts, including share "spinning" schemes in which underwriters allocated shares in hot issue initial public offerings (IPOs) to executives of large companies in order to gain investment banking business. Spitzer and other regulators reached a joint settlement with the Wall Street investment bankers over their analysts' conflicts. That global settlement totaled an incredible $1.4 billion. Those problems were followed by scandals at the mutual funds, where "market timing" and "late trading" by hedge funds were placing retail customers at a disadvantage. This was another Spitzer revelation that the SEC belatedly joined. Spitzer, the SEC, and other regulators collected over $3 billion in fines from the participants in those transactions. Media hysteria over these and other events reached a crescendo with the conviction of Martha Stewart for obstruction of justice after she lied about the reasons for her sale of stock of ImClone Systems Inc. More was to come. After Spitzer's attacks on the mutual funds waned, he then turned to the giant insurance companies such as March & McClennan and American International Group.

The problems exposed by Enron and other scandals were of such a magnitude that the entire corporate governance structure was called into question. Congress reacted with legislation in the form of the Sarbanes-Oxley Corporate Reform Act of 2002. That statute created a new oversight body for the accounting profession—the Public Company Accounting Oversight Board (PCAOB or "Peekaboo" as it is referred to by its detractors). That legislation did little to quell the uproar over supposed flaws in corporate governance, as scandals continued to play out in the newspapers. The announcement that Richard Grasso, the head of the New York Stock Exchange (NYSE), was being given $187.5 million in retirement compensation raised another storm of controversy over how such "excessive" compensation could have been authorized by the exchange's board of directors. Eliot Spitzer joined in that food fight with a lawsuit seeking to recover the compensation on the ground that a nonprofit corporation, such as the NYSE, could not pay such excessive compensation. Accounting scandals continued, with numerous more restatements and manipulated results. Particularly spectacular was the failure of Parmalat Finanziaria, a food services company, whose founders looted over $1 billion from the corporate treasury. The company's actual debt of $15.1 billion was eight times more than reported in its financial statements, and its earnings were overstated by $11 billion.

These events exposed deep flaws in the regulatory system and in corporate governance reforms imposed on corporations as remedies. Those regulatory reforms have resulted in a movement by state-sponsored union pension plans to take over corporate America, and class action lawyers are now assaulting every public corporation with massive lawsuits that have but one effect—incredible amounts in attorney fees. Ambitious prosecutors are attacking routine corporate practices for the sole reason of drawing a headline. Sarbanes-Oxley, the supposed cure for the scandals, has proved a costly failure that is undercutting America's competitive position. This book will examine those events and will describe some alternatives to this onslaught on American business.

The Stock Market Bubble and Enron

1. The Stock Market Bubble

Financial Markets

The Market Boom

The stock market boom at the end of the twentieth century was quite extraordinary. The Dow Jones Industrial Average (Dow), which was under 3000 in 1991, doubled over the following five years, the largest increase in that index's history. The Dow set other records, increasing for nine years in a row during the 1990s and registering double-digit gains each year between 1994 and 1999. The value of stocks listed on the New York Stock Exchange (NYSE) increased by 20 percent between 1998 and 1999, the period when the market upswing was at its peak. The Dow reached a record high of 11722 on January 14, 2000. The Nasdaq Composite Index exploded with the introduction of dot-com companies in the 1990s, rising from under 372.19 on January 2, 1991, to a record high of 5048 on March 24, 2000, the same date on which the Standard & Poor's 500 index reached a record high of 1527.

America seemed to be consumed by the frenzied stock market. "Money Honeys" on cable news networks were touting stocks to millions of Americans. Over one hundred new financial publications sprang up, and thousands of Web sites were devoted to financial matters on the Worldwide Web, which began operation in 1993. Over 37,000 investment clubs were meeting as the century closed. Stock ownership was said to have "become as common as the two-car garage."[1]

Business investment doubled in the 1990s, and the economy was rising with the market. February 2000 marked the longest period of economic expansion in American history, a total of 107 straight months of growth. Gross domestic product (GDP) in the United States totaled $7.2 trillion in 1997, up from about $5.8 trillion in 1992. Productivity in the United States accelerated from a 2.6 percent increase in 1995 to a 6.4 percent rate at the end of 1999, a growth rate called "astonishing" by the *New York Times.*[2] The market boom generated incredible wealth for some individuals. Between 1995 and

1997, the number of Americans with adjusted gross incomes in excess of $1 million increased by two-thirds. The top .01 percent of taxpayers in 1998 had incomes of $3.6 million and higher. Their average income was $17 million. In 1999, there were 6.5 million households in the United States that had more than $1 million in assets; 350,000 of those households had incomes of more than $2 million. The number of millionaires (defined as those having financial assets of at least $1 million, excluding their residence) reached 7.1 million in 2001, up from 27,000 in 1953. The country had journeyed a long way from the death in 1799 of its only millionaire, Elias Hasket Derby, a Salem shipowner.

The 400 richest Americans were worth over $1 trillion at the end of the century, more than the GDP of China, but those tycoons did not equal their predecessors. Andrew Carnegie was worth $100 billion in today's dollars at the height of his wealth. John D. Rockefeller would have been worth $200 billion in today's dollars. The modern-day moguls were soothing their consciences with charitable donations, as did their robber baron predecessors. The top 400 taxpayers in 2000 had incomes averaging $174 million and gave away an average of $25.3 million that year.

Bill Gates at Microsoft Corp. set up foundations that he endowed with $17 billion. George Soros, a hedge fund operator, made contributions to foundations he established that totaled more than $2.5 billion between 1994 and 2000. Ted Turner at AOL Time Warner pledged $1 billion to the United Nations, but was having trouble meeting that commitment after the stock market crashed in 2000.

Raising All Boats

The rich were not the only participants in the market boom. American households, on average, were holding 28 percent of their assets in stocks and had more of their household wealth in stocks than real estate at the end of the twentieth century. The Federal Reserve found that 52 percent of households in America owned stock either directly or through a mutual fund. This was up from 37 percent in 1992. Median stockholdings of families was $34,000, up from $13,000 in 1992. Seventy-nine million individuals owned stock, an increase from 42 million in 1983. Eighty-five percent of that stock ownership consisted of mutual fund shares.

The twentieth century was a good one for America. Real per capita income in the United States quadrupled, and the life span of the average American expanded from forty-one years to seventy-seven years during the century. Some 23 percent of all households in America had incomes of $75,000 or better as the century ended. Median household income reached $41,994 at the end of the century, increasing by 39 percent since 1990. Average income was $68,000, which was skewed upward by the wealthiest households, but inflation-adjusted per capita income doubled between 1960 and 2001. Average household net worth increased by over 25 percent between 1995 and 1998. Homeowners had an average of $122,000 in equity in their homes in 2001, up from $109,000 in 1998. The size of the average house grew from 1,520 square feet in 1982 to 2,114 square feet in 2002. The American household had an average of $5,800 in credit card debt as the twenty-first century began, but the poverty rate in the United States fell from 13.1 percent in 1989 to 12.1 percent at the end of 2002, after experiencing an interim low of 11.7 percent. This meant that some 34.6 million people were living in poverty, but the gap between the incomes of the rich and poor narrowed at the end of the 1990s. Median African-American net worth was $17,100 in 2001, a decrease of $800 from 1998, but up from $14,800 in 1992. The number of African-American households earning more than $100,000 annually during the 1990s rose from 222,000 to 415,000. Family median income of African-Americans was increasing at twice the rate of median income as a whole.

Run-Up in IPO Prices

As the new millennium began, there were about 3,000 domestic and non-U.S. companies listed on the NYSE with a capitalization of $16.8 trillion. The Nasdaq market had domestic listings of $5.2 trillion in market capitalization in 1999. Volume on the stock markets reached incredible levels in the 1990s as the market was booming. Average daily trading on the NYSE during 1999 was almost 810 million shares. Seven of the ten most active trading days on that exchange were experienced in 1999. The busiest day was December 17, 1999, when 1.35 billion shares traded, which was a record. Nasdaq dollar volume topped the NYSE for the first time in January 1999. Nasdaq daily trading volume was exceeding 1 billion shares on active days as the new century began.

Overall, the Nasdaq index rose by 80 percent in 1999. The explosive upswings in Internet companies were generating optimism in other stocks. One book predicted that the Dow would rise to over 36000 within five years and another writer was forecasting a Dow 100000. The boom on the Nasdaq market was being fueled by companies providing Internet services, often with "dot-com" in their name. These companies were selling their stock in droves to the public in initial public offerings (IPOs). The IPOs of these highly speculative Internet operations became "hot issues" that quickly traded in the secondary market at multiples of their initial offering price. Many of those companies were concentrated in the Silicon Valley area of California, causing housing prices there to increase by 45 percent in 1996 and creating a median price of $1.1 million for homes. That figure was $400,000 more than the median price of homes in Beverly Hills.

The dot-com companies were often financed by venture capital firms before their IPO in the hope that the fledgling start-up could be sold to the public at a profit. Among the better-known venture capital firms in Silicon

Valley was Kleiner Perkins Caufield & Byers. Led by partner John Doerr, that firm invested in Sun Microsystems, Compaq, Lotus, Genentech, Netscape, Amazon.com, and Handspring, all of which were hot issues and made their owners hundreds of millions of dollars. The HARM group, as a group of investment banking firms was dubbed, also handled numerous IPOs for dot-com offerings. The members of that group were Hambrecht & Quist Inc., Alexander Brown & Sons Inc., Robertson Stephens, and Montgomery Securities Inc. University and college endowment funds were a source of venture capital funds. Even the United States Defense Department was engaged in venture capitalism in the 1990s, supplying almost a billion dollars to fund various projects.

The boom in Internet stocks was said to have begun in August 1995 with an IPO by Netscape, which made a Web browser. That company went public at an offering price of $28, and the stock immediately soared to $75 before closing on its first day of trading at $58 on volume of over 13 million shares. That volume was more than the total daily average trading volume on the NYSE in 1967. Twenty-four of the twenty-five top IPO stocks were small technology start-ups in 1999. IPOs raised $70 billion in that year, which was almost twice the amount raised in 1998 and not far from the amount initially sought by President George W. Bush to rebuild Iraq after the war there in 2003.

Over 250 Internet-related IPOs occurred in 1999, and they averaged an 84 percent increase in price on their first day of trading. The price of VA Linux soared on its first day of trading from $30 to $300 in the secondary market. Priceline.com stock prices jumped from $16 to $69 on the first day and thereafter reached a high of $162. The IPO of Red Hat was priced at $14 but increased to $50 in the first hour of trading even though it reported a loss of $2 million in the prior quarter. The price of Red Hat stock eventually rose to $151. Scient's stock went from $10 to $133. eToys saw the price of its stock increase to $80 from an IPO price of $20. Internet Capital went public in August of 1999 at $6 per share. At year-end, the stock was selling for $170.

Amazon.com stock's price rose 30 percent on its first day of trading. That company did not foresee a profit for some time, but its stock tripled in price within three months. A stock market analyst, Henry Blodget, became famous for predicting that Amazon.com's stock price would rise to over $400 per share within a year. In fact, the stock passed that number within three weeks of his prediction. eBay, the Internet auction site, went public at $18, jumped to $47 before day's end, and was trading at over $240 within three months. Oxygen Holdings, an online investment firm, witnessed a twenty-nine-fold price increase on its first day of trading. Lastminute.com, an online travel group, experienced a 67 percent increase in its offering price as the Nasdaq market peaked.

Lante Corp., an Internet consulting firm, saw its stock price increase from $20 to $80 within a few weeks but then retreat, making its founder a billionaire for only a day. Commerce One, a firm providing Internet "solutions," had an increase in its stock price from $7 to $196. Capital Group's stock rose from $6 to $170. Globe.com, which was started by two Cornell college students, had an IPO price at $9 and skyrocketed to $97 within minutes, valuing the company at over $1 billion on revenues of less than $3 million. Brocade Communications Systems' stock increased to $177 from $9.50. Liberate Technologies' stock rose from $16 to $257. Redback Networks went from $11.50 to $177. Krispy Kreme's stock jumped almost 300 percent over its IPO offering price.

In the ten-year period between 1993 and 2003, more than 5,600 domestic and foreign enterprises raised a total of over $500 billion through IPOs in the United States. Starting in the 1980s through the end of the century, over 9,000 new publicly traded companies were created through their IPOs. This was more than one-half of the publicly traded companies existing at century end.

Structured Finance

The IPO market was not the only hot area of finance. "Structured finance" became a rage on Wall Street during the 1990s and formed the center of the Enron scandal. Structured finance took many complex forms, but was initially directed at the "securitization" of assets. This popular financing device involved placing assets in a special purpose entity (SPE) that sold ownership interests in itself to investors. The cash flow from the assets held by the SPE was paid out to those investors. One early such transaction was developed for the mortgage market by the Government National Mortgage Association (GNMA), a government-sponsored entity lodged in the Department of Housing and Urban Development. GNMA facilitated the ability of financial institutions to originate mortgages and then sell those mortgages to investors through the creation of "pass-through" certificates. Such certificates are, in effect, an ownership interest in a pool of home mortgages. The holder of a GNMA certificate receives an aliquot portion of all interest and principal payments of the mortgages in that pool. By 1995, there were nearly $2 trillion in outstanding mortgage and asset-backed financings in the United States.

Similar instruments were offered by two other government-sponsored entities: the Federal National Mortgage Association (Fannie Mae), which was created in 1938 (and privatized in 1968), and the Federal Home Loan Mortgage Corporation (Freddie Mac), which was chartered in 1970. Securitization spread to private banks that issued their own mortgage-backed securities that sold mortgages originated by those banks directly to investors. The proceeds of that sale were then available for lending, thereby continually increasing the amount and sources of funds available for home mortgages and increasing home ownership. Another government-sponsored entity, the Federal Agricultural Mortgage Corporation (Farmer Mac), was formed in 1988 to develop a secondary market for farm loans in a manner similar to Fannie Mae and Freddie Mac. The Student Loan Marketing Association (Sallie Mae) is still another government-sponsored organization that engages in structured finance. It provides funds to banks making student loans under the federal guaranteed student loan program. Sallie Mae purchases student loans in the secondary market and may securitize those loans.

Structured finance included collateralized mortgage obligations (CMOs), which were mortgages packaged into a SPE and sold in different tranches that might involve interest payments only from the underlying mortgages or principal payments only. The valuation of these instruments could become exceedingly complex, as seen in the following excerpt from a decision of an administrative law judge at the Securities and Exchange Commission (SEC) describing some performance characteristics of a CMO:

> "[D]uration" reflects the immediate percentage change in value a security or portfolio would experience in reaction to an interest rate change. Duration therefore is a risk indicator—an attempt to quantify the price sensitivity or "volatility" of a particular security or portfolio . . . . The record is conclusive that duration and convexity are intricately interrelated. Convexity is the rate at which duration (i.e., price volatility) changes. If duration is analogized to the speed of price changes, convexity would represent acceleration. Negative convexity indicates that a security or portfolio will increase in duration/volatility (i.e., lose value) at a faster rate as interest rates rise than the security or portfolio will decrease in duration/volatility (i.e., gain value) as interest rates fall. All things being equal, a negatively convex security or portfolio exhibits more potential to lose value than it does to gain value in an uncertain interest rate environment. Because CMO derivative securities have embedded prepayment options, they exhibit negative convexity.[3]

Collateralized Debt Obligations

A variation of the CMO was the collateralized debt obligation (CDO). These instruments involved selling debt to a SPE, which then split the debt into separate tranches like a CMO. The lowest tranche (the equity tranche) initially bore the loss of any credit defaults. If losses exceeded that tranche, then the second tranche would absorb the losses. The higher tranche was more credit-worthy and received higher credit ratings. Another related instrument was the synthetic CDO, in which credit default swaps were placed into the SPE and then interests in those swaps were sold.

Credit derivatives were valued at $2 trillion in 2002, and banks made some $1 billion in profits from credit derivatives in 2001. These instruments posed special risks to bank financial holding companies acting as dealers and having concentrated holdings in such instruments. Such holdings were closely monitored by banking regulators. These instruments did pose investment risks. In July 2001, the American Express Company announced a loss of $826 million as the result of writing down its investments in junk bonds and CDOs. Enron, one of the most innovative companies in utilizing structured finance in its operations, was among those companies trading credit derivatives. Premiums on credit derivatives for Enron's own debt jumped 20 percent in a single day when the firm began experiencing financial difficulties.

Almost any cash flow could be securitized, as demonstrated by "Bowie bonds." Those instruments were secured by the royalties of the popular singer David Bowie. He sold over $50 million of such bonds to the Prudential Insurance Co. The bonds received an AAA rating by Moody's. Other entertainers, including Rod Stewart, Ronald Isley, Dusty Springfield, and James Brown, used this financing method to sell their future earnings. The Internet wreaked havoc on these investments. Downloading of songs on the Internet through Napster, before it was curbed, and later through file sharing schemes resulted in a plunge in royalties from songs, causing the credit rating agencies to review their ratings on Bowie bonds.

Collateralized automobile receivables (CARS) were used to securitize automobile loans. The British Petroleum Co. PLC (BP) was offering interests in the BP Prudhoe Bay Royalty Trust, which was entitled to receive royalties on certain amounts of BP's production in Prudhoe Bay. A Harvard College trust was buying airline credit card receivables that it then securitized in note offerings outside the United States. Funeral home operators were securitizing their cash flows in England. States were selling lottery bonds that were secured by revenue from future state lotteries, which had become a popular revenue source for state governments. The states were also securitizing their share of the massive tobacco litigation settlements they reached with the major tobacco companies. That litigation harvested $206 billion for forty states and was to be paid over a twenty-five-year period. Another $40 billion had been garnered in earlier settlements.

New Instruments

The 1990s witnessed many other innovations in finance, including synthetic stock trading that allowed "difference" trading in stock prices, a practice banned in the nineteenth century as gambling. Synthetic stock transactions allowed traders to avoid market volatility concerns caused by their own trading and to avoid disclosures to other traders that could trade against the position, as well as avoiding margin requirements. Firms offering these synthetic products could hedge their exposures through "delta hedging" techniques that measured the sensitivity of the price of the derivative to the change in the price of the underlying asset. Citigroup was accused by a trader in one of its synthetic trading programs of hedging its risks by buying the actual securities, rather than delta trading as promised. This robbed the trader of one advantage of synthetic trading, concealing his trading strategy from the market.[4]

Tracking stock allowed investors to capture only a portion of a company's operations, allowing investors to pick and choose what operations they liked. In one such offering, Lowes Corp. sold a tracking stock for its tobacco operations, which posed some risks. The firm was fighting a $26 billion award in a class action suit brought against its tobacco operations. If upheld on appeal, that award would bankrupt the tobacco operations. Tracking stock allowed some executives to double-dip on their compensation from stock options. Two executives at Sprint made collectively $137 million on stock options from the tracking stocks for Sprint's wireless operations in 2001. An executive at Perkin-Elmer Corp., Tony L. White, made a total of almost $70 million on stock options from two tracking stocks.

Morgan Stanley created PLUS notes (peso-linked U.S. dollar secured notes) that allowed Mexican banks to move inflation-linked bonds from their balance sheets without having to record losses. A Bermuda corporation was created to issue PLUS notes backed by the Mexican inflation-backed bonds. The PLUS notes were denominated in U.S. dollars, while the inflation-backed bonds were payable in pesos to make them more salable. Another Morgan Stanley product was preferred equity-redemption cumulative stock (PERCS). That security converted into common stock on scheduled dates at ratios that varied with price. A similar product called dividend enhanced convertible stock (DECS) was created by Salomon Brothers. It allowed more profits on conversion when there was a jump in the common stock price.

The American Stock Exchange (AMEX) created something called Tracers, which were ownership interests in a trust that was composed of a basket of not less than fifteen investment-grade fixed income securities. The interest in those securities was passed through the trust to the holders of the Tracers. Morgan Stanley was selling Euro Tracers. These were tradable securities based on corporate debt from a pool of thirty European companies. The exchanges were listing something called ABS Securities, which were based on a basket of underlying corporate bonds. These were similar to equity-linked notes, except that the income for the proposed ABS securities came from a basket of investment-grade corporate bonds rather than a basket of equity securities.

JPMorgan Chase was offering tradable swap-linked notes based on a rate index of the one hundred most liquid European corporate bonds. These notes were backed by credit default swaps. Cendant Corp. was offering something called "Feline Prides," which were either Income or Growth Prides. Income Prides involved a contract under which the holder purchased a specified number of shares of Cendant common stock for $50 in cash. Cendant in turn agreed to pay the holders of the Income Prides 5 percent of the purchase price, an interest in Trust Preferred Securities paying 6.45 percent of the purchase price per year, and $50 at maturity. Growth Prides involved the purchase from Cendant of a specified number of newly issued shares of Cendant common stock. Cendant in turn agreed to pay the holders of Growth Prides 5 percent of their purchase price plus a 1/20th undivided beneficial interest in a Treasury security having a principal amount of $1,000 and maturing in 2001.[5]

In earlier years, Singapore created something called New Singapore Shares that were issued to Singapore residents and guaranteed a 3 percent return plus dividends equal to the economic growth of Singapore. More recently, Citibank arranged a $1.8 billion loan to Bulgaria. The interest rate on that loan was based on the growth rate of the Bulgarian economy. Michelin, the French tire maker, was using a $1 billion line of credit in 2000 that was contingent on GDP growth falling in its principal market. Apparently, the thought was that the drop in GDP would also reduce demand for tires and thereby create a need for the borrowing facility.

The Bank of Scotland created the shared appreciation mortgage in the 1990s under which it put back part of the price appreciation of a home as a credit against interest payments or in lieu thereof. Warren Buffett's Berkshire Hathaway was selling negative interest bonds that paid 3 percent interest, but were coupled with five-year warrants to buy Berkshire Hathaway stock at a 15 percent premium to its present stock price. The investor had to pay 3.75 percent each year to maintain the right to exercise the warrant. This resulted in a net negative rate of 0.75 percent if the warrant did not become valuable. There was a reason why such rights might be valuable. The value of Berkshire Hathaway's stock had increased by 4,000 percent since Buffett assumed management of that company in 1966. The company's A shares were pricey— $80,000 per share at one point, while the B shares were a lower $2,600.

Banks were issuing "trust preferred securities" that had characteristics of both equity and debt. They were issued through two offerings; one involved an issue of subordinated debt to a special purpose entity in the form of a trust created by the bank. The second offering was an issuance of preferred stock by the trust to investors. The result was to convert debt into equity for regulatory capital purposes. The Federal Reserve Board allowed these securities to be treated as Tier 1 Capital, which was equity that could be used by the banks in meeting their regulatory requirements. Texaco, Inc. had previously issued a form of trust preferred security called Cumulative Guaranteed Monthly Income Preferred Shares (MIPS). That offering involved the sale of preferred shares by a company organized in the Turks and Caicos Islands, the proceeds of which were loaned to Texaco. This allowed Texaco to deduct the interest payments on that offering, again converting equity to debt. Enron was also issuing MIPS. Other trust preferred securities have been issued as Quics (quarterly income capital securities), Quips (quarterly income preferred shares), Skis (subordinated capital income shares), and Tops (trust originated preferred shares).

Commodity Futures Modernization

The Chubb Corp. was the subject of claims for $350 million in "drought" insurance sold to 8,000 farmers in ten states just before and during a severe drought. The company claimed that the insurance was written by overzealous agents and that it had limited the amount of its total coverage to $30 million. The company eventually had to pay out more than $60 million. Enron took this product a step further by creating a weather derivatives market. That market began in 1996 and was valued at over $4 billion in the new century.

Weather derivatives expanded coverage to include temperature readings based on the number of days above or below normal ranges. This product became popular with oil and other energy producers, as well as construction companies that have to curb operations during cold weather. Espying opportunity, the Chicago Mercantile Exchange began trading weather derivatives. The United Nations would later consider "drought" derivatives as a way of raising funds quickly to fight such conditions. Several large corporations, including the Ford Motor Company, DuPont, Motorola, and International Paper created the Chicago Climate Exchange to buy and sell emission credits issued as a part of the effort to reduce greenhouse gases; it was officially recognized as a regulated commodity exchange in 2004.

Another product called hedge-to-arrive (HTA) contracts became popular during the 1990s. These contracts came in many forms but generally provided for the pricing of grain based on prices on the Chicago Board of Trade with adjustments for basis differences in delivery points. The contract assured a buyer of the farmer's grain, but posed the danger that the farmer would receive a price less than the current market price when the grain was eventually delivered. When farm prices did rise, farmers sold their grain at the higher market prices and rolled their HTA delivery obligations forward. The grain elevators eventually began demanding delivery on the HTAs. In some instances, the farmers had to buy grain at market price and sell at the lower contract price because their production was not sufficient to meet their delivery obligations. Dozens of suits were filed by farmers in which they claimed that these contracts were unenforceable illegal futures contracts because they allowed the farmer to defer delivery in some instances. If unenforceable, the farmers could realize the higher market prices and avoid losses they sustained from shortfalls. These claims found sympathy at the Commodity Futures Trading Commission (CFTC) but were generally rejected by the courts on the ground that, unlike a futures contract, delivery was required under these contracts even if deferred.

The Commodity Exchange Act of 1936 had been substantially revised in 1974 to extend regulation to trading on all commodity futures and options. Previously, only certain commodity futures were regulated. A ban on trading futures contracts on onions was continued and exists today; strangely, onions were the last thing that could be freely traded in Soviet Union until its fall. The Commodity Exchange Act had other anomalies, such as a requirement that all commodities be traded on a "contract market" registered with the CFTC, an agency created by the 1974 legislation. This meant there could be no over-the-counter market in instruments that were futures contracts. Similar restrictions were placed on commodity options. This resulted in a long struggle by the CFTC to stop off-exchange instruments having elements of futures or options. That effort was not successful. Over-the-counter derivatives in the form of swaps and energy contracts gave rise to exemptions for those instruments in legislation enacted in 1992.

The over-the-counter derivative problems that caused large losses at several large corporations and bankrupted Orange County, California, led an activist CFTC chairman, Brooksley Born, to seek regulation of that market, but

Congress stopped that grab for power. After the appointment of a new chairman, the CFTC moved to deregulate much of the derivatives market for large investors, and Congress approved that step in the Commodity Futures Modernization Act of 2000 (CFMA). That statute exempted most over-the-counter derivatives from regulation as long as the parties were large institutions or wealthy individuals. A provision in the CFMA also sheltered an Internet trading platform created by Enron, Enron Online, from regulation. That exemption became controversial after Enron failed.

The CFMA allowed the commodity exchanges to keep their contract market monopoly over markets in which small traders were allowed to participate. The CFTC was given authority to attack over-the-counter dealers in currency contracts after the Supreme Court ruled that the Treasury amendment in the Commodity Exchange Act precluded such regulation.[6] These currency firms were swindling unsophisticated investors of millions of dollars annually. The CFMA allowed trading in single stock futures under a strange formula in which the CFTC and SEC shared jurisdiction. Commodity markets conducting trading in single stock futures were required to adopt rules equivalent to those in the securities industry, including insider trading prohibitions that did not otherwise apply to commodity futures transactions. Margin requirements had to match those in the securities industry, a level several magnitudes greater than for futures trading. Not surprisingly, these contracts were slow to trade and had little volume.

Eurex was dominating futures trading throughout the world as the century ended, taking that position from the exchanges in Chicago, which were still clinging to open outcry trading on their floors. The Chicago Board of Trade (CBOT), which had been one of the first exchanges to use electronic price displays on its trading floor in 1967, was the most resistant to changing to electronic trading. The CBOT made a gesture in that direction by joining the Chicago Mercantile Exchange in an after-hours electronic trading system called Globex. That effort failed; the CBOT then announced a joint venture with Eurex that also fell apart. The Intercontinental Exchange (ICE) was locked in litigation with the New York Mercantile Exchange (NYMEX). ICE was accusing NYMEX of engaging in monopoly practices by excluding ICE from access to NYMEX quotations. ICE had taken over the International Petroleum Exchange in 2001. NYMEX then started trading contracts for production from the Brent Oil Field to compete with ICE. ICE was also complaining that NYMEX was offering clearing services for over-the-counter derivatives and was planning an electronic platform for trading over-the-counter energy products. ICE claimed that these services were being illegally tied to other contracts.

Traditional Markets

Competition was heating up and threatening traditional forums for trading stocks in the 1990s. The Chicago Stock Exchange, the Cincinnati Stock

Exchange, the Boston Stock Exchange and the Philadelphia Stock Exchange were either trading or planning to trade Nasdaq listed securities. Nasdaq acquired the AMEX in order to expand its offerings, but found that the acquisition was not a good match. Nasdaq then spent two years trying to sell the AMEX, but potential purchasers expressed little interest. Amex's value dropped from $700 million to $100 million before it was sold to GTCR Golder Rauner LLC, a company based in Chicago, but that sale fell through and the exchange was then sold to its members.

The adoption of decimals in 1997 for quoting securities prices as a more efficient pricing method resulted in an unexpected development. Specialists were able to increase their profits by widening their spreads slightly under decimalization. The NYSE announced the creation of an "open book" service that would allow the public access to information on the specialists' limit order book. That information provides valuable knowledge on market depth and the likely effect of market developments on prices. Such knowledge had long been an advantage to the specialist. This access was a response to concerns that the change to decimal trading made pricing stocks more difficult without such information. The open book, however, was not real time. The information entered into the open book was delayed by ten seconds, providing the specialist with a continuing edge.

As the new century began, there were about 500 Nasdaq market makers in the Nasdaq National Security Market, where the stocks of larger Nasdaq listed companies were traded. Each stock had at least three market makers; some had as many as forty. Merrill Lynch purchased Herzog, Heine & Geduld at a valuation of $900 million at the end of the twentieth century. That firm, which had been formed in 1915 as Herzog & Co., was the second largest market maker on Nasdaq. The Nasdaq market makers were seeking to change market maker compensation from spreads to other methods such as commission arrangements. As 2001 ended, Nasdaq volume was about 1.7 billion shares per day versus the NYSE's 1.2 billion shares, but NYSE listed companies still had a greater market valuation than did Nasdaq companies. The Nasdaq capitalization was $2.7 trillion while NYSE capitalization was $12 trillion, both reduced by the downturn in 2000.

The International Securities Exchange (ISE), which started operations in May 2000, was the first stock exchange to be registered with the SEC since 1973, when the Chicago Board Options Exchange (CBOE) began its operations. ISE traded options, and by late 2001 was handling about 8 percent of options trading, totaling more than 700 million contracts for the year. Merrill Lynch became a specialist and market maker at ISE. Other market makers on ISE included Morgan Stanley and Credit Suisse. The CBOE was responsible for about 40 percent of exchange-traded option volume and the AMEX 26 percent. The Philadelphia Stock Exchange and the Pacific Stock Exchange each handled about 13 percent of options volume.

Electronic Communications Networks

Electronic communications networks (ECNs) were competing with the stock exchanges for executions at the end of the century. ECNs and other alternative trading systems were then handling more than 20 percent of the orders for securities listed on Nasdaq and almost 4 percent of orders on exchange listed securities. The SEC concluded that alternative trading systems were threatening to become the primary market for some securities. Trading on an ECN is an order-driven process. This means there is no market maker or specialist that is maintaining a two-sided market in the security being traded, as is the case on Nasdaq and the NYSE. Liquidity on an ECN depends entirely on the ability to find a willing buyer or seller that has entered an opposing order or quote. Finding a counterparty through a posted bid or offer in an actively traded security on an ECN may be easy, but in less actively traded securities that task may be considerably more difficult.

ECNs operating in the market included Wit Capital, Instinet, Bloomberg Tradebook, the Attain System, the BRUT System, and the Strike System. Spear, Leeds & Kellogg was operating a routing and execution interface electronic communications network called the REDI System that was designed to process mixed-lot orders directed to it by SelectNet (another ECN) and from customer terminals. Archipelago, a rapidly growing ECN, agreed to form a fully electronic stock market with the Pacific Exchange. The latter was the fourth-largest stock exchange in the United States on the basis of trading volume. The new market planned to match customer buy and sell orders. The Pacific Exchange planned to close its trading floors in San Francisco and Los Angeles, but continued operation of its options market.

Goldman Sachs, Merrill Lynch & Co., Salomon Smith Barney, Morgan Stanley Dean Witter, and Bernard L. Madoff Investment Securities formed Primex Trading NA. It was an electronic trading system for stocks listed on the NYSE, AMEX, and Nasdaq. Primex priced stocks through an auction market. This system was available for broker-dealers, institutional investors, market makers, and exchange specialists. Primex was used to obtain securities at prices better than those posted prices in other markets. The first stocks to be traded on Primex were those in the Dow, followed by stocks in the Standard & Poor's 100 Stock Index.

By 2000, some 150 electronic communication networks were conducting bond transactions. That number would be cut almost in half over the next two years as interest rates dropped. Brokerage firms were seeking to internalize the execution of customer orders. Schwab & Co., aided by the internalization of its orders, was making about $1 billion from its market making activities. Schwab was said to be the "king of internalization" through its wholly owned subsidiary, Schwab Capital Markets. It acted as a market maker or matched many of the orders placed with Schwab. The firm used other market quotes to assure that customers received the best execution price. Several large brokerage firms, including Merrill Lynch, Goldman Sachs, and Morgan Stanley, were seeking an electronic central limit order book (CLOB), which they asserted would assure that investors received the best price available in any market. Critics claimed that the large firms were actually seeking to assure that they would retain their role as middleman, while allowing them to internalize more of their order flow. CLOB would allow those brokers to meet their best execution duties to customers by pricing off it when matching or offsetting customer orders.

Nasdaq responded to the ECN threat by developing its own electronic trading system. This was done through Optimark Technologies Inc., which was jointly owned with several Wall Street firms and Dow Jones & Co. Optimark had a supercomputer that was being used to match orders automatically. In addition, Nasdaq was considering whether it should develop an Internet trading system and was meeting with Instinet to discuss centralizing the trading of Nasdaq stocks. Nasdaq announced in December 1999 that it was entering into an agreement with Primex Trading to create an electronic auction market system to trade its issues and those listed on the stock exchanges. Nasdaq planned to expand its systems to allow the display of quotes from ECNs so that investors would have more information on available prices. The Nasdaq market thereafter began competing with the ECNs through an electronic trading program called SuperMontage, which was designed to show the best bid and ask prices and the amount of trading interest and the next four increments away from that best quote.

SEC chairman Arthur Levitt entered this debate. He contended that electronic trading should be centralized so that all orders would be displayed publicly and available to everyone. Levitt was concerned that fragmentation of the market could result in inefficient markets and executions for customers at less than optimal prices. This seemed to be a renewal of the "central market" concept that the SEC had devised after conducting a study of institutional traders decades earlier. This scheme posited that investors would be better served by a centralized trading system that would assure that every investor received the "best" execution price available for orders. The SEC was able to convince Congress to enact legislation in 1975 that made the creation of a central market a national goal, but the SEC was never able to articulate exactly how this concept would work in practice. As a result, nothing much happened to fulfill that goal except for some consolidated reporting and a link among exchange specialists. Critics of the central market system pointed out that concern with market fragmentation was really just an indication that the government did not trust competition as the best method for assuring market efficiency. After all, fragmentation was just a reflection of new centers of competition. In any event, the SEC backed off Levitt's proposal after criticism from Congress and other segments of the securities industry.

The increasing availability of computer linkages renewed some long held concerns that such systems could be used to divert volume from public exchanges, reduce market transparency, and result in disparate execution prices, as well as cause the fragmentation of markets. The SEC, under chairman Arthur Levitt, issued a concept release seeking the public's views on how the market should be structured in light of the availability of alternate electronic trading systems and whether fragmentation was a threat to competitive executions. Such "command and control" initiatives by Levitt resulted in a flood of criticism. The SEC later adopted regulations that only lightly regulated ECNs. Basically, those regulations allowed ECNs to operate without registering as a national securities exchange, as long as the ECN did not dominate trading in a security. Access to the ECN must generally be open in instances where certain volume levels are met.

Electronic trading was available after normal trading hours on the exchanges. This too raised concerns. An SEC staff study revealed wide price disparities in transactions conducted in after-hours trading. ECNs and Internet trading were, in all events, causing an upheaval at the stock exchanges. Recognizing the competitive pressure from the ECNs, the SEC allowed the exchanges to restructure themselves as for-profit organizations. Traditionally, the exchanges had been operated as not-for-profits. This change was intended to allow the exchanges to demutualize and raise capital in order to compete with the electronic markets.

The NYSE considered demutualizing but that effort bogged down, and it remained a not-for-profit organization. That decision would later cause enormous problems for its head, Richard Grasso. Nasdaq approved a $318 million private placement for the sale of a portion of that market. This restructuring was intended to make the Nasdaq market more competitive. Demutualization plans were scrapped or delayed at other stock markets. The Chicago Mercantile Exchange was the only other exchange to move forward with demutualization plans. It made an IPO of its shares in December 2002, raising $166.3 million. The IPO was a hot issue, jumping 22 percent on the first day of trading.

A seat on the Chicago Stock Exchange (formerly the Midwest Stock Exchange) sold for $135,000 in February 1999. The previous high price for a seat on that exchange had been $110,000 in August 1929. That exchange was enjoying success because it was trading NYSE, AMEX, and Nasdaq listed stocks through the Internet. This was attracting business from online brokers. The Chicago Stock Exchange began two-hour evening sessions in several NYSE and Nasdaq stocks. The Chicago Stock Exchange was then trading about 50 million shares a day. After seeing those volume figures, Nasdaq announced that it was expanding its trading hours to allow evening trading sessions.

Broker-Dealers

The securities industry had record profits of $16 billion in 1999. Executives at large brokerage firms were receiving large compensation packages. The head of Merrill Lynch, David H. Komansky, was paid $29.3 million in 1999, triple the amount he received the prior year. Merrill's chief financial officer, E. Stanley O'Neal, was paid $19.1 million. Morgan Stanley Dean Witter (now Morgan Stanley) paid its two top executives, Philip J. Purcell and John J. Mack, $26 million each in 1999.

Goldman Sachs was ranked the number one firm for merger and acquisition activity in investment banking. Merrill Lynch finished second in that category and lost its position as the leading underwriter for stocks in 2001. Merrill was beaten out by Citigroup, which had been freed of the shackles of the Glass-Steagall Act, which had limited its ability to engage in underwritings. The Gramm-Leach-Bliley Act, passed in 1999, allowed banks to engage broadly in nearly all aspects of finance.

Arthur Levitt, the SEC chairman, was critical of stockbrokers acting as investment advisers for retail customers. He claimed that small investors could monitor a short list of companies for investment by following information about those companies, allowing them to compete with professional stock pickers, a view that ignored modern portfolio theory. The bull market was raising concerns about sales practices on Wall Street. A "large firm project" conducted by the SEC staff determined that 25 percent of its broker-dealer branch office examinations resulted in referrals for enforcement actions. Levitt sought to reform the compensation system for stockbrokers, removing the commission arrangements that he claimed induced brokers to oversell securities. That was a nonstarter. An industry blue-ribbon panel, appointed by Levitt and headed by Dan Tully, the former head of Merrill Lynch, did suggest some best practices for brokerage firms.

A survey by the National Association of Securities Dealers Inc. (NASD) reviewed 663,000 registered associated persons of broker-dealers and found that within the last five years 2,751 of those individuals had three or more customer complaints and arbitrations, 216 had been subject to three or more investigations or regulatory actions, and 1,198 had been subject to two or more terminations or internal reviews based on wrongdoing. The NASD amended its rules to require special supervisory procedures for brokers with a compliance history. The firms employing such individuals must adopt heightened supervisory requirements for those individuals.

Most brokers require their customers to agree to binding arbitration of any claims they might have concerning the handling of their account. The Supreme Court, reversing earlier rulings, began enforcing such agreements, resulting in the removal of most litigation involving broker-dealers and their customers from the judicial system. The number of arbitrations filed with the NASD was up 24 percent in 2001 as a result of the market downturn. That number skyrocketed after the Wall Street scandals that followed Enron, jumping by 60 percent in 2003. Arbitration proceedings against broker-dealers are conducted by the NASD and the NYSE. Their procedures have been criticized as favoring broker-dealers due to the inclusion of industry members on the arbitration panels. California adopted a provision that allowed arbitration proceedings to be set aside when panel members were not deemed to be independent, which some NASD arbitrators would not be under the California standard. A federal district court held that the Federal Arbitration Act and the SEC oversight of the NASD arbitration programs preempted that California provision. Similar rulings occurred in connection with Florida and Massachusetts restrictions that allowed customers to opt out of NASD arbitration.

About 70 percent of arbitration claims against broker-dealers were being settled or dismissed before trial. Of the remaining claimants, about half received some award of damages from arbitrators, but those awards were generally not as much as the investor sought. Even that success rate worried the brokerage firms, as did efforts to allow punitive damages, which are not normally permitted in arbitration. Arbitration awards are subject only to limited judicial review, but customers and broker-dealers were increasingly seeking such review by claiming that unfavorable awards were in "manifest disregard" of the law.

Online trading was threatening the traditional full-service brokerage firms in the 1990s and created a new class of investors called day traders. The average commission charged by Merrill Lynch per transaction was $200 in 2000, while online brokers were allowing trades for under $10. By 1999, 110 brokerage firms were allowing customers to trade online or through "intranets." Some 5.4 million investors were using those facilities, but a study by Eliot Spitzer, the New York attorney general, in 1999 found that many online firms were not equipped to deal with the large volume of trading generated by their advertising.

The NASD and Nasdaq acted to impose more stringent margin requirements on day traders, who were avoiding margin calls because their transactions were opened and closed during the trading day and not carried overnight. The day traders faced other problems. Studies showed that more than 90 percent of all day traders lost money. At one point, 400,000 day trader accounts were in operation. Not all of them were suitable for such trading. Mark (the "Rocket") O. Barton, an Atlanta, Georgia, day trader went berserk killing his family, nine other people, and wounding twelve others before killing himself after suffering losses of nearly $500,000 from day trading.

Internet trading was responsible for 45 percent of the trading on Nasdaq in 2001 and the NYSE as well, but that volume was cut in half as the market declined. The day traders were competing with professional market makers in conducting quick in-and-out transactions. That competition was not always welcome. A number of Nasdaq market makers were charged by the SEC with colluding in setting quotations and widening their spreads. That collusion was a reaction to the so-called SOES bandits that were using the automated Nasdaq Small Order Execution System (SOES) to "pick off" market maker quotes before they could be changed in the SOES system after a market event. These problems resulted in a reorganization of the NASD, the entity responsible for maintaining and policing the Nasdaq stock market. Regulatory functions were placed in a separate unit, NASD Regulation, headed by Mary Schapiro, a former SEC commissioner; market promotion was the responsibility of another unit.

Merger Activity

Times were good on Wall Street during the 1990s. Merger activity averaged about $1.6 trillion annually between 1998 and 2000, six times the amount for mergers occurring in 1993. There were some setbacks. The Federal Trade Commission blocked a merger between Staples and Office Depot, but allowed Chevron to merge with Texaco in September 2001. Phillips Petroleum Co. merged with Conoco Inc. later in the year. Exxon had earlier been taken over by Mobil in an $80 billion merger. WorldCom Inc., which had acquired more than seventy other companies, merged with MCI Communications in 1997 in a $34.5 billion transaction. In 1999 WorldCom tried to merge with Sprint, in what would have been the largest merger in American history, but the Justice Department blocked that effort on antitrust grounds. The blocking of that merger led to the failure of WorldCom and unearthed a scandal every bit as big as Enron.

Comcast bought MediaOne in a $53 billion acquisition. Boeing acquired McDonnell-Douglas in 1997, reducing the number of large aircraft manufactures in the world to three. Airbus in Europe was one of those survivors. The pharmaceutical industry was undergoing a worldwide consolidation during the 1990s. Pfizer acquired Warner-Lambert and later purchased Pharmacia for $60 billion, making it the largest pharmaceutical company in the world, with revenues of $48 billion; GlaxoWellcome merged with SmithKline Beecham. Automobile companies were also consolidating. Daimler-Benz acquired the Chrysler Corp. Ford acquired the automobile operations of Volvo, Land Rover, Jaguar, and Daewoo Motors in South Korea. Ford ran into some difficulties with its popular Explorer, which was having rollover problems as a result of defective tires made by Bridgestone Firestone. The result was an embarrassing slanging match between the two companies over who was to blame for the tire failure. Bridgestone Firestone received a $1.3 billion infusion from its Japanese parent company to deal with the legal problems from injuries and deaths suffered in the rollovers, as well as a massive shareholder class action.

The European Commission stepped up its antitrust activities in the new century by imposing a large fine on Archer Daniels Midland for fixing food additive prices and fined thirteen pharmaceutical companies for seeking to control the vitamin market. The commission blocked the $43 billion merger of General Electric (GE) with Honeywell, although the merger had been approved by U.S. authorities, leading to claims that the Europeans were targeting American firms in order to curb their growth. That would have been the largest industrial merger in history. Honeywell had earlier merged with Allied Signal and had sought to merge with United Technologies until GE stepped in with its bid.

The European Commission seemed to be in retreat after the criticism of its rejection of the Honeywell and GE merger. It approved a $24 billion merger between Compaq and Hewlett-Packard, but then pounced on Microsoft Corp. Microsoft had been able to settle an antitrust case with the U.S. government after a circuit appeals court upheld findings that the company was a monopoly, but rejected a decision by a lower court to break the company into two parts. The appellate court removed the district court judge, Thomas Penfield Jackson, from the case after he made prejudicial remarks to the press about Microsoft. The Justice Department then settled the matter with only minor concessions being made by Microsoft. Nine of the eighteen states that had joined in the antitrust suit against Microsoft refused to agree to that settlement, but a federal appeals court approved the settlement over their objections. The competition authorities in the European Union, deeming the action by the U.S. federal court inadequate, imposed a $603 million fine on Microsoft and required it to disclose its source code. Microsoft paid the fine pending an appeal and also paid Novell Inc. $536 million to drop claims that were driving the European Union's action. Microsoft was not the only American company under attack in the European Union. Phillip Morris was required to pay the European Commission $1.25 billion for assisting the smuggling of cigarettes into the European Union in order to evade taxes. This was achieved by oversupplying countries neighboring the European Union.

Fraud and Abuses

Fraud Schemes

Fraud was burgeoning in the financial markets at the end of the century even before Enron. Popular scams involved Internet fraud, investment seminars that touted get-rich schemes, affinity group fraud in which religious or other groups were targeted for fraudulent investments, abusive sales practices, and telemarketing fraud. Some eighty companies were buying the life insurance of individuals over sixty-five who were in poor health through "viatical" contracts. The contracts were then sold to investors. Viatical contracts were not new to finance. Insurance policies on individuals who were dying or could no longer meet their premiums were sold at auction in London before our Civil War. Prospective purchasers sought to determine which of the insured marched before them was most likely to die first. An American visitor who watched such an auction at the Royal Exchange in London in 1844 remarked, "I have seen slave auctions" and "I could hardly see more justice in this British practice." In another variation, World War I veterans were given bonuses for their service overseas but those payments were not to be made until 1945 or earlier on the death of the veteran, leading the payments to be called "Tombstone Bonuses." To alleviate complaints, the Federal Reserve Board was allowed to create a guaranty program that permitted the bonus certificates to be discounted by the veterans for short-term loans in amounts of up to 90 percent of the ultimate value of the bonus. If unpaid, the guarantee was made good by the Veterans Administration. That did not stop complaints, and the routing of the Bonus Army by General Douglas MacArthur became another sad chapter of the Great Depression.

People with AIDs had been victimized through sales of their insurance policies in the twentieth century, and one retired person sold a $500,000 life insurance policy for $75,775. The SEC was pursuing fraud claims in connection with viatical contracts, claiming that they were securities under the federal securities laws. A federal judge rejected that assertion in 1996, but the SEC continued to pursue the issue. Frederick C. Brandau was returned from Colombia after being indicted in the United States for defrauding $115 million from investors in connection with viatical investment scams. Brandau had taken money from investors but failed to buy the life insurance policies. He spent the proceeds on cars, jets, helicopters, and mansions. The SEC brought another case against Mutual Benefits Corp. in Fort Lauderdale. The SEC charged that the company defrauded more than 29,000 investors who had invested more than $1 billion in purchasing such policies. The government of Tonga had been promised large profits but lost $24 million in viatical contracts by Wellness Technologies Inc. of Penngrove, California. The SEC sued that company and its president, Jesse Dean Bogdonoff, for fraud. Two individuals were convicted and three acquitted in Florida prosecution involving their sale of viatical contracts for Lifetime Capital, Inc.

Bank regulators imposed $20 million in penalties against the New York branch office of the Bank of China as a result of fraudulent loans. On another front, the Federal Bureau of Investigation (FBI) uncovered a global fraud in the new century involving metals trading that bilked various banks, including JPMorgan Chase & Co., FleetBoston Financial Corp., and PNC Financial Services Group Inc., of as much as $1 billion in aggregate. Operating out of New Jersey, the culprits were trading metals using a number of fictitious trading companies.

Jean-Claude Trichet, the president of the Bank of France, was tried for his activities while a director of the French Treasury. He was charged with helping in the early 1990s to cover up the massive financial problems at Crédit Lyonnais, which was then controlled by the government of France. Trichet was a leading candidate to head the European Central Bank (ECB). Trichet was acquitted and assumed his position at the ECB. The Executive Life Insurance Company was the center of another scandal involving Crédit Lyonnais. Executive Life's portfolio of junk bonds was sold for $3 billion to Crédit Lyonnais, a bank then owned by the French government. Crédit Lyonnais resold the bonds to a French businessman, François Pinault, a friend of French president Jacques Chirac. Pinault made large profits from this transaction, leading California and the U.S. government to claim that the arrangement was fraudulent. Those authorities also charged that Crédit Lyonnais secretly gained control of the insurance company through third parties in violation of state and federal laws. A $770 million settlement was reached with the French government and Pinault. He agreed to pay $185 million of the settlement amount. Crédit Lyonnais agreed to plead guilty to three felony charges. A related civil action brought by the California Department of Insurance was seeking a settlement for an additional $600 million payment by the French government and Crédit Lyonnais. Pinault's investment company was also a defendant in that action, and a California jury found liability. This affair led to much bitterness and resentment in the French government against American authorities.

Pinault had other problems with American justice. He held a large stake in Christie's, the famous art and antiques auction house. Alfred Taubman, the seventy-seven-year-old chairman of Sotheby's, a competing auction house, was convicted of conspiring with Christie's to fix commissions paid by sellers of art at their auctions during the 1990s. Christie's had split the role of its chairman and chief executive officer. That was a popular recommendation of corporate governance advocates, but it was not much of a reform at Christie's because those two officers were the ones creating the scheme to fix prices. Christie's, which was based in London, was not prosecuted by the U.S. government because it supplied evidence against Sotheby's chairman. Christie's chief executive officer, Christopher Davidge, was given a multimillion-dollar severance package from Christie's and was granted immunity by the U.S. government in order to get him to testify against Taubman. Dede Brooks, Sotheby's chief executive officer, was also given a deal by the government for turning on Taubman. She was sentenced to six months of house arrest in her swank Manhattan apartment. Her brother, Andrew Dwyer, had been at the center of an accounting scandal in 1992 involving the Jamaica Water Properties, which was reporting $3.6 billion in revenues before it went bankrupt. David Boies, an antitrust lawyer who would appear in the scandals following Enron, mounted a class action suit against Christie's and Sotheby's that they settled for a total of $512 million.

Ponzi Schemes

Ponzi schemes have long plagued American finance. "The term 'Ponzi scheme' is derived from Charles Ponzi, a famous Bostonian swindler. With a capital of $150, Ponzi began to borrow money on his own promissory notes at a 100 percent rate of interest payable in 90 days. Ponzi collected nearly $10 million in 8 months beginning in 1919, using the funds of new investors to pay off those whose notes had come due."[7] Ponzi conducted this scheme through his Security Exchange Company (hopefully the Securities and Exchange Commission was not named after that entity). Ponzi claimed to be investing in international postal reply coupons that paid a high rate of return. These coupons were created by the Universal Postal Union in 1906 under a treaty negotiated in Rome. The treaty allowed the sender of a letter in one country who wanted to provide return postage to include a coupon that could be redeemed in the stamps of the country of the recipient, thereby avoiding the necessity of enclosing cash that would have to be converted into the recipient's currency and then used to purchase stamps. The international reply coupons were redeemable at specified exchange rates, but after World War I several countries, including Italy, experienced devaluation in their currencies. Ponzi thought he could arbitrage the difference between the exchange rate set by the Rome treaty and the actual rate by buying the coupons with devalued Italian currency and then redeem them in the United States for a profit at the Rome treaty rate. The only problem was that the coupons were redeemable only in stamps that the Post Office refused to repurchase in cash. Ponzi was unable to solve that problem, but did not tell investors of that bar to his scheme. In fact, he was simply using the funds of new investors to pay off earlier ones, which encouraged others to invest, reaching a peak of $1 million per week, until the scheme finally collapsed.

A veritable epidemic of Ponzi schemes occurred during and after the market bubble in the 1990s. The Republic of New York Securities Corp. pleaded guilty to two felony counts of securities fraud and agreed to pay $606 million in restitution as the result of looting conducted through its facilities by Martin Armstrong. He had been running a Ponzi scheme that cost Japanese institutional investors about $700 million. The bank was charged with helping Armstrong conceal trading losses by reporting to Japanese investors that Armstrong was generating profits when in fact he was losing nearly all of their money. In another Ponzi scheme, Martin Frankel acquired funds for investment from individual investors and then used those funds to purchase insurance companies in the South. These companies provided small amounts of insurance to low-income individuals for burial policies. Frankel used the cash flow from those insurance companies to maintain a Ponzi scheme and to provide luxuries for himself and his girlfriends. He tried to conceal his activities through fictitious financial statements and claimed to be associated with a Catholic trust, a guise that he hoped would deflect regulatory inquiries. Frankel fled but was arrested in Germany with twelve passports in different names and diamonds worth millions of dollars. He and his lawyer, John Jordan, were convicted of fraud. Frankel was sentenced to seventeen years in prison.

Patrick Bennett was convicted of criminal violations in connection with one of the largest Ponzi schemes in American history. He defrauded investors of $700 million by selling securities for nonexistent office equipment leases and tax-exempt New York Transit Authority leases. Bennett used large amounts of funds for failed gambling and entertainment investments. He was sentenced to thirty years in jail. William H. Goren was running a Ponzi scheme through New Age Financial Services Inc., which took in $35 million between 1990 and 2000. Investors were given promissory notes and assured of returns ranging from 12 to 25 percent.

Federal prosecutors charged in October 1999 that a stock promoter engaged in a $300 million Ponzi scheme. The SEC filed an action against InverWorld Inc., which defrauded clients in Mexico of $475 million. Another popular fraud involved promissory notes issued by companies that would then abscond with customers' monies. Many of these operations were Ponzi schemes. State securities administrators in thirty-five states had received complaints of such activity.

Raymond Mohr's Ponzi scheme raised $3.1 million between 1993 and 2001, and a separate Ponzi scheme carried out by Lawrence Barsi raised another $2.5 million over a fourteen-year period starting in the late 1980s. Jerry A. Womack defrauded 400 investors of $19 million between 1997 and 1999. He claimed that his "Womack Dow Principle" would provide large profits and falsely claimed that he had retained brokers on the floor of the NYSE to execute his trades. This was another classic Ponzi scheme with some investors given large returns, but most of the money was used to maintain Womack's extravagant lifestyle, which included cosmetic surgery for his wife, artworks, and jewelry.

Electronic Fraud

Credit card fraud mounted to $1.3 billion as the new century began. Check fraud claimed another $19 billion, and some $64 million was stolen in bank robberies, but strong-arm robberies were down in number. Los Angeles cut the number of its bank robberies during the 1990s by 400 percent. Electronic robbery was now posing a danger. A group of criminals made off with $37 million from Citigroup in 1999. The funds were obtained through the Citigroup fund-transfer operations. Of that amount, $22 million was returned by a bank that became suspicious, but $15 million was able to be withdrawn by the individuals from a Turkish bank that received those funds.

State and federal authorities charged over 1,000 telemarketers with fraud during a thirty-month period at the end of the century. Regulators asserted that microcap stock fraud at the end of the century amounted to $2 billion a year and that investors were being defrauded of $1 million each hour. The SEC was receiving over 120 complaints a day claiming Internet securities fraud. The SEC created a special unit called the Office of Internet Enforcement to pursue those complaints and assigned 200 lawyers and analysts to this "cyberforce." The SEC filed twenty-three cases against forty-four individuals in October 1998 for activities involving fraud on the Internet. The charges included fraudulent spam messages. In May 1999, the SEC filed cases against twenty-six companies and individuals charging that the defendants had sold unregistered securities and made fraudulent profit claims through the Internet. By that time, the SEC had, in total, filed eighty cases involving Internet fraud. Many more followed. Internet chat rooms were a source of investment advice. One chat room, Tokyo Joe's Societe Anonyme, was shut down by the SEC for fraudulently touting stocks. Subscribers had paid $100 to $200 a month for the site's stock tips, which were the product of Yun Soo Oh Park. He failed to disclose that he had already bought the stocks he was touting and was profiting by the price increases that resulted when subscribers responded to his recommendations.

Abuses through the Internet included gambling through cybercasinos, unregistered offerings of stock, and unwarranted claims by brokers as to the performance of specific securities. In one case, the SEC charged that unregistered securities were sold to 20,000 investors at a cost of $3 million through the Internet. Investors were told that they could obtain large profits from a worldwide telephone lottery that would use a 900 number for payment. The lottery was falsely claimed to have receipts of $300 million. The company failed to disclose the legal, regulatory, and technical obstacles to this proposal. Internet fraud spread to Latin America. The SEC charged an individual with soliciting funds through the Web for investment in two Costa Rican companies by making false claims that the individual had major distribution contracts with the A&P supermarket chain. Another defendant was charged by the SEC with soliciting funds over the Internet for investments that were to be used to finance construction of a proposed ethanol plant in the Dominican Republic. Investors were promised a return of 50 percent. In still another Internet case, the defendants were selling bonds in a Panamanian shell company. Investors were told that they would have a risk-free investment and a guaranteed return of 11.75 percent annually. The promoters claimed that the company was providing investment capital to Latin American businesses. The company claimed to publish a magazine called the *World Financial Report* and published articles from it on the Web, which touted the bonds it was offering.

Another Internet scam involved the use of false reports. An individual in Raleigh, North Carolina, was arrested for a false report of a takeover of his employer that was supposed to have been issued by Bloomberg News. The falsified announcement was intended to drive up the employee's holdings of his company's stock. "Cyber smear" tactics were used for short sale manipulations. Presstek Inc. filed a suit in 1997 claiming that various individuals were making false statements over the Internet about the company in order to make profits as short sellers. The stock price of Emulex Corp., a fiber-optics producer, dropped from $103 to $45 in fifteen minutes on August 26, 2000, after a false press release. That release reported that the company was restating its earnings and that its chief executive had resigned.

A regulatory sweep by state and federal authorities was conducted against promissory note schemes that were targeting elderly investors. A worldwide sweep was undertaken in twenty-eight countries to track down persons committing fraud on the Internet. Governments participating included the Office of Fair Trading in England, South Korea's Fair Trade Commission, and the Federal Trade Commission in the United States. Cybercrime was reaching $266 million annually in 1999. Those efforts did not deter Internet fraud, and the SEC was criticized for its inability to deal with that burgeoning problem. Conversely, the SEC's surveillance over Web sites and chat rooms to detect securities fraud was also criticized as an invasion of personal privacy.

Pump and Dump Schemes

Pump and dump schemes were being used to manipulate the value of microcap stocks in the 1990s. An SEC official said that the Internet was becoming a new millennium boiler room. In March 2000, the SEC brought an enforcement action against some Georgetown law students, and one of their mothers, who were buying cheap stock and then pumping up the stock through rumors on the Internet. After the stock price went up, they would sell the stock. The students created a stock tip sheet known as FastTrades.com, which had more than 9,000 online subscribers. The students made almost $350,000 in trading on four stocks. In another case, two individuals were indicted in February 2000 for promoting penny stocks through thousands of e-mail messages. The securities were worthless, and the defendants were pumping up the value of the stock in order to profit on their own holdings. A fifteen-year-old boy in New Jersey was charged by the SEC in September 2000 with manipulating stock prices through a pump and dump scheme on the Internet. He agreed to return $285,000 in profits. Cole A. Bartiromo, a seventeen-year-old high school student, defrauded over 1,000 investors through an Internet pump and dump scheme. He was ordered to pay $1.2 million as a civil penalty in an SEC action.

A.R. Baron & Co. went bankrupt in 1996, but not before manipulating the prices of several stocks. The company's sales force was buying stocks for customer accounts without authorization. When customers complained, the stock was transferred to a firm error account, which bankrupted the firm when the stock declined. A.R. Baron was clearing its securities trades through Bear Stearns & Co., which paid $38.5 million to the SEC to settle charges arising from that debacle. In another case, Bear Stearns was ordered to pay $164.5 million to a Canadian investor by a jury in New York. The investor, Henryk de Kwiatkowski, was a wealthy businessman who owned Calumet Farms, the famous thoroughbred horse farm in Lexington, Kentucky. He lost $215 million trading currencies over a five-month period in 1994–1995. A federal circuit court in New York reversed the award, however, and threw out the case. Bear Stearns remained a very independent-minded firm. Its longtime chief executive officer, Alan (Ace) Greenberg, required employees to donate 4 percent of their income to charity.

Pump and dump schemes often involved more conventional boiler rooms employing hundreds of salesmen to pump up prices through high-pressure sales pitches. Market makers at such firms were used to inflate prices. A joint probe by the SEC and the Justice Department resulted in actions against sixty-three individuals in connection with microcap fraud. H.J. Meyers & Co. Inc. was one of the companies charged with pump and dump activities. The company maintained a market in the securities it was manipulating and had its sales force employ high-pressure tactics to sell the stock at ever increasing prices to customers.

The list of boiler rooms grew to include Biltmore Securities and Monroe Parker Securities. Stratton-Oakmont was a notorious boiler room that was pumping and dumping securities on unsuspecting investors. Several brokers at that firm were jailed, as was Steve Madden, who was involved in their fraud. He was a famous shoe designer and the head of a public company bearing his name. Madden was subjected to an SEC order that barred him from serving as an officer or director of any public company for seven years. Martha Stewart would be compared to Madden as an example of the downfall of the mighty, after her conviction for obstruction of justice in the wake of the Enron scandal.

The district attorney in Manhattan, Robert Morgenthau, was using the state's Martin Act to prosecute pump and dump schemes. One of the high-profile cases his office prosecuted involved a firm named A.S. Goldmen. Playing off the Goldman Sachs name—there was no Goldmen in the firm—brokers at A.S. Goldmen defrauded customers of over $100 million. A.S. Goldmen's president, Anthony Marchiano, was given a prison sentence of 10 to 30 years. His brother was also jailed, and twenty-four brokers at A.S. Goldmen pleaded guilty to criminal charges in connection with that firm's fraudulent operations.

Duke & Co. manipulated six stocks that it had sold to the public as an underwriter in IPOs for $600 million. Twenty-four brokers in that firm were convicted of felonies. Morgenthau prosecuted and convicted the chairman of the firm, Victor Wang, who was sentenced to a prison term of seven to twenty-two years. Sterling Foster & Co. was another brokerage firm that was manipulating the price of stocks underwritten by the firm through highly structured boiler room operations. Twenty-one people were given prison sentences in connection with those activities.

Organized crime was involved in the manipulation of the stock price of HealthTech International Inc. One of the individuals pleading guilty to that misconduct was a capo of the New York Genovese crime family and another individual was a member of the Bonanno crime family. Meanwhile, the Gambino crime family was suing its investment adviser for fraud. The adviser, Mohammad Ali Khan, had stolen millions of dollars from his customers, including some members of the Mafia.

In June 2000, DMN Capital Investments and 120 individuals were indicted under racketeering laws for manipulating stocks and defrauding thousands of investors of over $50 million. Prosecutors charged that DMN Capital was controlled by figures from five organized crime families who used violence and intimidation to carry out their fraudulent activities. Thomas J. Scotto, the president of the New York City police detectives union, was named as an unindicted co-conspirator in this scheme. Organized crime was not the only manipulators of stocks. The stock of Dell and other companies was the target of manipulative trading activities by traders at Morgan Stanley in 1999. Their trading affected the entire Nasdaq 100 Index computation.

Other Problems

Reliance Insurance Co. failed in 2001. This Pennsylvania insurance company was controlled by Saul Steinberg, a corporate raider of some fame who had tried, unsuccessfully, to take over Walt Disney and Chemical Bank in earlier years. Steinberg was accused of looting Reliance. The Pennsylvania Insurance Department claimed that Reliance's accounting firm, Deloitte & Touche LLP, reported publicly that the company had adequate working capital to stay solvent while privately telling representatives of Kohlberg Kravis & Roberts (KKR), a venture capital firm, that Reliance had a $350 million cash shortfall. KKR was then considering purchasing a portion of Reliance.

A scandal erupted on AMEX. Spear Leeds & Kellogg was fined a record $1 million by the AMEX for failing to supervise the activities of a managing director who was in charge of the firm's clearing operations on the exchange's floor. He had participated in trading for another firm without the approval of his employer and created fraudulent profitable stock trades for that firm by placing losing trades in another member's account. Similar problems would arise on the NYSE after Enron.

Five German banks were fined $90 million for fixing commissions on currency exchange transactions. Unilever sued Mercury Asset Management, which was owned by Merrill Lynch, for negligently managing the company's pension plan. Merrill Lynch agreed to pay $107 million to settle that claim, which was about half the damages claimed by Unilever. A Merrill Lynch broker, Tania Torruella, was the subject of much litigation after she was fired from Merrill Lynch. Merrill Lynch was paying over $18 million to customers who suffered large losses from her trading on their behalf in high-tech companies that suffered large drops in their stock prices. Victims included relatives of Torruella.

An award of $43 million was imposed against Refco Inc., a Chicago-based futures commission merchant. That liability arose in connection with the commodity trading activities of S. Jay Goldinger, a well-known money manager. The Chicago Board of Trade fined Refco $1 million and the CFTC imposed an additional $6 million penalty for Refco's association with that trader. The NYSE fined Enrique Perusquia, a broker at PaineWebber, $429 million for fraudulent activities. Frank Gruttadauria, a rogue broker at Lehman Brothers, fled after it was discovered that he looted customer accounts of $115 million over a period of fifteen years. He eventually turned himself in to federal authorities. Customers seeking damages from his conduct received mixed results. One customer was awarded $1 in damages and $700,000 in attorney fees by an industry arbitration panel.

Richard Blech, of Raleigh, North Carolina, was accused of fraud in connection with a scheme involving offshore investments in a fictitious country conducted through fake corporations and banks. Blech and his company, Credit Bancorp, were charged with swindling customers of more than $210 million. Customer funds were hypothecated and used for loans that were converted for personal use by Blech and his associates. Blech pleaded guilty to fraud charges. North Carolina officials also announced the arrest of members of a gang that had been traveling across the United States in order to conduct a massive kiting operation involving counterfeit paychecks.

Executive Compensation

The income levels of chief executive officers increased by 2,500 percent during the market boom in the 1990s, raising much criticism among corporate reformers. Median income for a chief executive at one of the larger companies was over $6 million. Executive compensation reached extraordinary levels at Enron and other companies. The SEC had long required public companies to disclose the compensation of its top four officers in their financial reports. The SEC expanded this requirement in 1992, demanding more information on stock options given to executives as compensation. The SEC required a comparison between the stock performance of the company granting options to a market index and an index of peer companies, as well as a description of the factors considered in setting the compensation of the chief executive officer.

The SEC believed that the embarrassment of announcing an excessive package would induce executives to be reasonable. The agency also thought that disclosure would pressure management to create an independent compensation committee to act as a check on executive compensation. However, the executive compensation disclosure requirement had an effect opposite to that intended by the SEC. The disclosure requirement actually legitimated even the most excessive package; after all, it was being disclosed, so there was no crime. Using an independent compensation committee composed of outside directors, who were eager to please the chief executive officer, provided more cover. Even worse, the disclosure requirement created a spirit of competition in which executives vied with each other for the largest compensation package.

Stock options emerged as a prime culprit in the greed exposed at Enron and in other scandals. Options give executives the right to buy a specified amount of the company's stock at a specified price. If the price of the stock rises above that price, the executive obtains the stock by exercising the option and then sells the stock for a profit. "The use of stock options as a form of compensation grew out of the 'shareholder value' movement of the 1980s. Options, it was said, made the interests of managers and the interests of shareholders the same. It was a seductive argument, but, as events proved, a deeply flawed one."[8] Reformers, who included Michael Jensen at the Harvard Business School (who is now repentant of that position) and Kevin Murphy at the University of Rochester, argued that an executive given only a salary had no incentive to raise the price of the company's stock, which is what shareholders most desire. The reformers contended that executives were taking their salaries, sleeping on the job, and playing golf, rather than working overtime to build the company. If options formed the greater part of the executive's compensation, it was argued, the executive would have a powerful incentive to work hard to boost the stock price, which would be in the interests of the shareholders. *Voilà*—all problems are solved.

Reformers recognized that executives in large companies might not want to give up multimillion-dollar salaries in an exchange for a gamble in their company's stock. So those executives had to be given a push in the form of the Omnibus Revenue Reconciliation Act of 1993. It prohibited corporations from deducting more than $1 million for an executive's salary or other non-incentive-based compensation without obtaining shareholder approval. This made stock options attractive to high-roller executives because there was no cap on such incentive-based compensation. The Financial Economists Round Table concluded, post-Enron, that this change in the tax laws encouraged the use of options and other "performance-based" provisions not subject to the $1 million cap. There was one drawback. The exercise of options required the executive to pay cash for the stock, which could require a massive amount of funds. That problem was readily solved by having the corporation extend a loan to the needy executive that could be paid off with the company's stock, effectively draining the treasury without calling it a salary, as was done at Enron. Another concern was that the issuance of new stock upon the exercise of stock options had the effect of diluting earnings per share and placed downward pressure on the stock price. To avoid those effects, many companies engaged in buybacks of their own stock, sometimes draining needed funds.

Options presented another advantage to management: that compensation did not have to be treated as an expense on the company's income statement. This meant that such compensation did not reduce earnings, allowing management to report higher earnings than would be the case for a large salary that would have to be expensed. Those higher earnings pushed the price of the stock higher and further boosted the value of the executive's options. By way of illustration, Cisco Systems, a high-flying Internet company, claimed a profit of $4.6 billion in one year but would have had a $2.7 billion loss if options had been expensed. Yahoo Inc., another Internet firm, announced profits of $71 million in one year, but would have had a loss of $1.3 billion if stock options had been expensed.

There was another, even darker side to this reformists' dream. The SEC requires public companies to report their earnings quarterly. Those reports are closely followed by financial analysts and money managers. Management at Enron and elsewhere became "laser focused" on their company's quarterly earnings because money managers and financial analysts demanded ever-increasing earnings each quarter or they would dump the stock, causing a precipitous drop in its price. Such a decline relieved the executives of millions of dollars in compensation in their now worthless options. Surveys confirmed that companies were forsaking long-term growth in order to meet quarterly earnings targets, but business does not normally operate on the basis of quarterly results. There will be up quarters and down quarters. As the head of Time Warner, Richard Parsons, later noted: "This is a tension that as managers we have to deal with. We're not a quarter horse. I read somewhere that the quarter horse is the fastest animal in the world in a quarter of a mile. Because of lots of dynamics, increasingly the marketplace is demanding quarter by quarter performance that has the potential to undermine the long term."[9]

Strategic business goals take years to achieve, but managers were diverted from those long-term goals by the incessant demands for quarterly results. Even worse, executives at Enron and numerous other companies began "managing" and "smoothing" the earnings to assure that their company precisely met analysts' "consensus" expectations each quarter. Many companies were meeting expectations to the penny quarter after quarter. The machinations employed to achieve that result became ever more complex and questionable when the economy began slowing.

Some 80 percent of executive compensation was paid in stock options at the end of the last century. The number of employees receiving stock options increased during the 1990s from about 1 million to 10 million. On average, corporations listed in the S&P 500 index were awarding to employees stock options valued at $170 million annually. Executive compensation increased by almost 450 percent in the 1990s, rising from an average of $2 million to over $10 million. Some of the pay packages were mind-boggling. Larry Ellison, the head of Oracle Corp., made $706 million on his options in a year when the company's share price dropped by 57 percent. Michael Eisner at Walt Disney Co. exercised options in 2000 worth some $60 million and was holding additional options valued at $266 million. That was chump change to Eisner; he made $575 million in 1998, and his compensation at Disney through 2003 was over $750 million. Sanford Weill at Citigroup bested that figure with a total of almost $1 billion. Michael Dell of Dell Computer made $233 million in one year. Charles Schwab was paid $170 million, mostly in options. Scott McNealy at Sun Microsystems weighed in at $140 million, and Irwin Jacobs at Qualcomm made $96 million. Wayne Calloway of Pepsi Co. held options worth a comparatively paltry $64 million.

Excessive compensation became the norm in the 1990s. Lawrence Coss, the head of Green Tree Financial, which became Conseco Inc., was given a bonus of $102 million in 1996 and total compensation of $200 million during his tenure, leaving a ruinous $20 billion of subprime loans on the company's books. Those high-risk loans were motivated by a desire to take advantage of accounting rules that allowed the company to report large short-term profits, while creating a time bomb that threatened the long-term prospects of the company. Megagrants of options for 1 million shares or more proliferated. Eisner at Walt Disney received options on 8 million shares in one year, while Henry Silverman, the head of Cendant Corp., received options on 14 million shares. When the price of Cendant shares dropped, he was rewarded with more options at a lower price. In total, his compensation exceeded $260 million.

John T. Chambers at Cisco Systems was paid $154 million, although the company lost $1 billion. Sir Anthony O'Reilly, the head of H.J. Heinz Co., received $182 million in compensation over a six-year period, even while the company's earnings were languishing. Jack Welch at GE received $400 million in compensation over a ten-year period; he had at least added value as well as boosting the company's stock price. Christos Cotsakos at E*Trade was paid $80 million even while the company was losing money and its stock price was plunging from $60 to $7. He was ousted and agreed to repay the company $4.6 million for unauthorized use of the corporate jet and for charitable contributions that had not been approved by the board of directors.

A survey by the *Financial Times* concluded that in the three years prior to August 2002 the top executives and directors in major business collapses then under way (e.g., Enron, WorldCom, and Global Crossing) were paid about $3.3 billion, mostly in options. Executives at some companies received "reload" options that granted new options each time an option was exercised. "Reset" options were also popular. These options lowered their exercise price when the company's stock dropped in value, allowing the executives to profit even where they were not increasing the value of the stock. Some companies allowed their executives to rescind their decision to exercise options when the stock price increased after their exercise. The SEC required those companies to disclose such practices to shareholders.

Options have special advantage for small start-up companies, like those that fueled the market boom in the 1990s. Those entrepreneurs did not have the resources to attract talented executives and staff with large salaries. They were given options instead, motivating them to succeed by garnering large profits from their options when the company went public. In one famous instance, D'Anne Schjerning was hired as a secretary for an executive at Mosaic Communications and was given stock options in lieu of a raise. She became an instant millionaire when the company went public as Netscape in 1995. Microsoft Corp. alone produced 21,000 millionaires through stock options. This was more than two-thirds of its employees.

Expensing Options

The growing size of compensation packages of executives as a result of options grants was soon raising criticism from the same reformers who had advocated the use of options in the first place. The reformers sought to curb the use of options by requiring companies to expense options given to executives and employees. That would reduce earnings and place pressure on management to limit its option grants. Otherwise, analysts' expectations would not be met, and executives would receive nothing from options, only a salary capped at $1 million.

The Financial Accounting Standards Board (FASB), an accounting industry body, had proposed in 1995 to require publicly held companies to expense options, which was long before the collapse of Enron focused public attention on this issue. This proposal met strong opposition from corporate America. Opponents "even engineered a public rally to demonstrate the grassroots support for stock options. Kathleen Brown, the California treasurer and daughter of a storied Democratic governor, shouted to a cheering crowd, 'Give stock a chance!' (It was, presumably, the first mass rally against an accounting standard since the birth of double-entry bookkeeping)."[10]

Even Arthur Levitt, the activist SEC chairman during the 1990s, came out in opposition to expensing options and pressured the accounting industry into dropping its expensing plan. Levitt reversed course after Enron's failure. He claimed that members of Congress had bludgeoned him into opposing that proposal. In any event, legislation was introduced to prohibit an expensing requirement. It received strong support from start-up companies that needed options to attract critical personnel. Senators Joseph Lieberman, Barbara Boxer, and Diane Feinstein were among the sponsors of that legislation. The U.S. Senate then passed a resolution condemning the proposal to expense options in May 1994 by a vote of 90–9. That ended the debate until Enron imploded and raised the issue once again.

An alternative to options are "stock appreciation rights" (SAR) and "phantom stock," which are incentive compensation plans that pay the executive cash in an amount equal to increases in the value of the company's stock or the value of dividends. This provides the executive with performance incentives and does not require the purchase and sale of the stock. The cash payment from an SAR, however, is immediately expensed. Restricted stock is sometimes given to executives as compensation. The executive is required to hold the stock for some extended period in order to provide long-range incentives, but most executives prefer more immediate payments and are uncomfortable with the uncertain future value of the stock.

Attacks on the Markets

The First Attack

The increase in market prices, widespread fraud and abuse, and the boom in Internet stocks raised concerns that a market bubble was developing. Alan Greenspan, the chairman of the Federal Reserve Board (Fed), had been warning of such a danger since 1994. He famously asserted in 1996 that the market was being driven by "irrational exuberance." If it was a bubble, it was a very durable one because the market simply ignored that and other warnings over the next three years. Newspapers and magazines, led by the *Economist,* continued to claim that the stock market bubble presaged a disaster for the economy, as did Yale economist Robert Shiller. Greenspan made those prophecies self-fulfilling by crushing the stock market through a series of punitive interest rate increases.

It is unclear why the stock market run-up was viewed as a bad thing. The economy was surging, productivity was up, inflation and unemployment levels were low, and national wealth was increasing. The Fed had pursued a policy of low rates since the 1980s, provided there was no risk of inflation. Although there was no threat of inflation from the stock market bubble in the 1990s, Greenspan concluded that the bubble itself was sufficient reason for raising rates. He decided to choke the economy in order to burst the market bubble. Such action, his supporters claimed, would result in a "soft landing" for the economy.

The Fed began that effort with a rate increase on June 30, 1999. That failed to slow the market, and more increases seemed to have little effect. The Dow shed 630 points during the week of October 11, 1999, its worst week ever to that date, but the market soon rallied. Greenspan then renewed his claim that the country was in the midst of one of history's "euphoric speculative bubbles." Although this statement too had little effect, Greenspan warned that he would raise rates until the bull market was broken. True to his word, more rate increases were ordered; a total of six increases were implemented. Collectively they broke the market's back, sending stock prices plunging in the new millennium. The bond market also suffered its worst setback since two historic declines that had occurred in 1994 and 1973.

After hitting a record high, the Nasdaq Composite Index began a steep plunge, dropping 25 percent during one week in April 2000 and experiencing sharp volatility thereafter. The Dow remained under pressure as well. The ten-year bull market died in 2000. That was the worst year for the market in twenty years. The Fed's actions also undermined confidence in the economy. The GDP was growing at an annual rate of 5.4 percent in the first quarter of 2000, but slowed to 2.4 percent in the third quarter and to 1.1 percent in the fourth quarter. Household wealth fell for the first time in fifty-five years.

The Market Reacts

Internet stocks were under attack. Priceline.com saw its stock fall from $162 to $1.12. Red Hat's stock price plunged from a high of $151 to $5.22. Scient stock dropped from a high of $133 to $1.75. Yahoo's IPO in 1996 had traded up from $13 to $43 on its first day. The company attained a market valuation of almost $100 billion before the market break, but then its stock price lost 92 percent of its value. Cisco Systems stock fell by $148 billion. Other big losers were EMC Networks and Oracle. The founders of Clickmango.com, a health foods business, made $5 million each from the IPO for their company in five days as the stock traded upward. The company collapsed in the downturn. InfoSpace had a market capitalization of $31 billion in March 2000 that was quickly reduced to less than $1 billion in the market downturn. The stock of a company called Theglobe.com rose over 600 percent on its first day of trading to $63.50. That stock stopped trading in April 2001 when it fell to sixteen cents per share.

Qxl.com, an online auction house, and Durlacher Corp., an online investment firm, saw their stock drop over 90 percent in value. Information technology companies were soon imploding in droves. eToys laid off 70 percent of its staff and then declared bankruptcy. More than 2,000 B2B (business-to-business) Internet companies were created in 2000 and 2001. Two-thirds of those firms were out of business two years later. Other dot-com companies that failed included Garden.com, Kozmo.com, Pets.com, Webvan, Boo.com, and PlanetRX. Amazon.com's market capitalization fell from $37 billion to $5 billion as the stock market crashed. Although Amazon.com finally became profitable at the end of 2001, posting a profit of $5 million, that result had been preceded by losses of $3 billion.

Nasdaq lost about 1,200 of its listed companies as the result of the collapse of the dot-com firms during the market retreat. This was 24 percent of the total number of companies listed on that market. Nasdaq stocks lost 70 percent of their value in the decline. The Dow was not suffering as much because its listings were concentrated in the older brick-and-mortar companies that continued to operate even in a market downturn. Still, that index was down 22 percent in 2001 from the high it reached in 2000.

Estimates of the amount of stock values lost in the overall market decline ranged as high as $8.5 trillion. The number of billionaires in the world dropped below 500. About half of the surviving billionaires had inherited their wealth, but the rest were self-made. One of the self-made men, Warren Buffett, actually saw his net worth rise by $2.4 billion to $35 billion in 2001, making him the second-richest person in the world and giving credence to claims that his refusal to invest in the Internet boom had been correct. One lost billionaire was Gary Winnick, the head of Global Crossing, which filed for bankruptcy in 2002. Microsoft's stock dropped from $120 per share to below $40 at the end of 2000. The head of Microsoft, Bill Gates, saw his fortune drop $6 billion in value in 2001, but he remained the richest person in the world with a net worth of over $50 billion.

Corporate debt defaults set a record in 1999, and bank failures were rising. The rate of unemployment nationwide was at 4.1 percent in January 2000, a thirty-year low, but that level began to rise with the market downturn, reaching 6.4 percent in 2003. That was bad, but not as bad as the recession between November 1973 and March 1975, when unemployment reached 9.2 percent. Still, some of the layoffs were massive. Procter & Gamble cut 25,000 workers. Motorola saw its stock drop $9 billion in value and laid off thousands of employees. As in the Great Depression, a concern soon arose about deflation, rather than the inflation that had plagued the economy periodically since World War II.

The Fed Reverses Course

The economy was further destabilized during the weeks of court battles over the presidential election between Albert Gore and George W. Bush, which was finally resolved by the Supreme Court. That clarification did not rally the economy, and the country was thought to be in recession just six weeks after the inauguration of President Bush. As the year 2000 ended, the Fed awakened to the damage it had wreaked on the economy by its interest rate increases. That was a reversal of the Fed's position during the 1930s. The Fed had largely stood aside as the Great Depression deepened and misery spread through society. Fed chairman Marriner Eccles had even been charged with stopping a recovery in 1936 by doubling bank reserve requirements. Although Alan Greenspan ignored the lessons of history in pushing the economy into a recession, he reversed course and began desperately slashing interest rates to levels unseen for forty-five years as the full extent of the damage from the rate increases became evident.

Greenspan's course reversal, albeit belated, seemed to be complete, and he vowed to reduce interest rates and keep them low until the economy was fully recovered. Nevertheless, the Fed's reversal on interest rates was slow to have an effect. Greenspan hinted at interest rate decreases in December 2000, but it was not until January 3, 2001, that a surprise interest rate cut was announced. That cut did little to right the economy. The Fed made five more cuts in 2001 and still more in 2002. Greenspan was walking a tightrope. Economist Milton Friedman, the Nobel Laureate, warned that an improper application of monetary policy could result in another depression if too lean or devastating inflation if too robust.

Economic Decline

The National Bureau of Economic Research concluded that the American economy was in recession from March to November 2001. The new Bush administration was contending that the recession began even earlier, during the Clinton administration. Subsequent data suggested that a recession, defined as a drop of GDP for two straight quarters, may not have occurred at all. Still, the economy shrank at an annual rate of 0.5 percent in the first quarter of 2001, rose an anemic 0.02 percent in the second quarter, and then fell 1.4 percent in the third quarter of 2001. The trade deficit ballooned to $408 billion. The net worth of the average American household fell by 14 percent over the preceding year.

On July 26, 2001, several computer companies announced that they were collectively laying off 31,000 employees. Some 6,000 of those employees were cut from Hewlett-Packard. Gateway laid off a quarter of its workforce. In August 2001, Dell Computer announced a $101 million loss after selling put options on its stock that required $3 billion to cover. This was the first loss it had experienced in eight years. Walt Disney saw its share price fall to below $20 during the year, down from a high of over $40 in 2000. Ford Motor Company announced a loss of $5.07 billion, wrote off $4 billion in assets, closed several plants, laid off 35,000 employees (10 percent of its workforce), and eliminated thousands of contractor jobs. Automobile sales were falling across the industry, but the automobile companies fought back by offering consumers zero percent financing on new car sales.

The unemployment rate was almost 6 percent by the end of 2001, its highest level in five years. Retail sales in the United States dropped 3.7 percent in November 2001, the largest monthly drop since 1992, before recovering in December. The amount of empty office space in the United States was at a record level as the economy declined, and apartment and retail rentals decreased sharply. Over 250 publicly owned companies declared bankruptcy in 2001. This was another record. Asbestos claims bankrupted Owens Corning in October 2000. The firm had over $5 billion in revenues from housing insulation sales, but the company was facing more than 460,000 asbestos claims. Polaroid Corp., one of the "Nifty Fifty" stocks in the 1950s, filed for bankruptcy in September 2001 after defaulting on nearly $1 billion in debt. It was sold to One Equity Partners, which was owned by Bank One Corp.

Corporate earnings fell 21.6 percent in the fourth quarter of 2001. The market downturn in 2000 took a heavy toll on merger and acquisition activity. The numbers of mergers and acquisitions worldwide were down 26 percent in 2002, falling in value to $1.36 trillion, down from $1.83 trillion the year before. Standard & Poor's downgraded corporate debt issued by forty-five companies in September 2001. The issues downgraded were valued at $162 billion. The number of companies having their debt downgraded had been exceeding those with upgrades since 1998. In 2001, only nine U.S. corporations had AAA ratings from the ratings agencies, down from twenty-two in 1991. In 1979, 25 percent of debt was AAA rated but in 2001 only 6.2 percent was so rated.

Some $74 billion in corporate debt defaulted in the first three quarters of 2001. Telecom defaults accounted for $31 billion of that amount. Junk bonds ("high-yield" offerings) were only about half of those in 1999, but the defaults were greater. The junk bond default rate reached 9.6 percent in August 2001, up from an 8.7 percent high in 1990. The amount of junk bonds defaulting in August 2001 was $56 billion.

Corporate debt in 2000 was 73 percent of corporate capital. This reflected a taste by corporations for leveraging their balance sheets by increasing their debt levels. Compounding this situation was the fact that some corporations, like Enron, were moving debt off their balance sheets through questionable structured finance techniques. A company borrowing funds to finance its operations only has to return principal and interest. It does not have to share profits with the lender in amounts in excess of those payments, as it would have to do if capital is raised through the sale of stock. In 2000, $146 billion was raised in new stock offerings while $935 billion was raised through debt issues. That debt figure was down from $1.2 trillion in 1998, but up from $435 billion in 1995.

The Damage Is Done

Consumer debt was a concern, having risen by $4 trillion over the previous ten years. Consumer debt as a percentage of GDP was 71 percent, a record high. Personal bankruptcies were occurring at a rate of about 29,000 per week. Consumers were spending fourteen cents of each dollar of disposable income to service their debt, but were reducing their credit card spending as the economy declined. Relieving this situation was the decline in interest rates, which allowed homeowners to refinance their mortgages. The thirty-year mortgage rate declined from 8.7 percent in 2000 to 6.5 percent in November 2001, saving homeowners on average from $150 to $200 per month in mortgage payments. Refinancing of residences was occurring at a record rate. Loan officers were nearly overwhelmed by applications. The lower interest rates set off a boom in the real estate market.

The amount of assets held in mutual funds increased from $60 billion in 1972 to $1.1 trillion in 1990. The amount held in mutual funds exploded to $5.7 trillion in 1999 (as compared to the $3.5 trillion in bank deposits), but the market downturn caused significant damage to those holdings. Mutual funds investing in equities experienced a sharp drop in value. Eighty-three percent of mutual funds in the United States had negative returns in 2001. The average stock mutual fund lost almost 11 percent in value that year. This figure reflected the fact that the stock market experienced its worst two-year period (2000 and 2001) in twenty-three years. The Dow was down 7 percent for 2001 and Nasdaq was down 21 percent. The S&P 500 Index fell by 15 percent during 2001, the second year that it had fallen more than 10 percent. The S&P Index was cut in half from its peak by the middle of 2002. New Jersey's pension fund saw the value of its investments drop by one-third. The amount of the decline in U.S. markets that followed Greenspan's interest rate increases was said to be "roughly equivalent to the destruction of all the houses in the country or the razing of many thousands of World Trade Centers."[11]

The market downturn saw the ending of the *Wall Street Journal's* annual contest pitting money managers' stock picks against those selected by throwing darts. The contest was to test the economic theories put forth by Burton Malkiel in his book *A Random Walk Down Wall Street.* Over a fourteen-year period, the professionals beat the dart throwers with an average return of 10.2 percent, while the dart-selected investments increased only 3.5 percent. Even with the stock market down, an investor with a diversified stock portfolio had an average return of 7.65 percent over the previous ten years. The Emerging Growth Fund had a 28.52 percent average return between 1989 and 1999, but lost 25 percent of its value in 2000, 27.3 percent in 2001, and 40 percent in 2002. Even so, the fund had an overall return in the ten-year period between 1993 and 2003 of 10.5 percent.

Legg Mason Value Trust was the outstanding performing mutual fund. Its manager, Bill Miller, outperformed the S&P 500 Index for twelve consecutive years from 1991 through 2002. Nevertheless, experts dismissed this performance as merely a winning streak that did not place Miller above the market theory that no one could outperform the market over the long term. Even outperforming the market sometimes meant a loss. The Legg Mason Value Trust was down almost 19 percent in 2002. In the prior year, that mutual fund lost 9.29 percent, which was not as steep as the decline in the S&P 500, but still a loss.

The Fed cut short-term interest rates eleven times in 2001 in order to reverse the situation that it had, in no small measure, brought about. Interest rates on the ten-year Treasury note dropped to 4.18 percent in November 2001. Interest rates on overnight loans between banks were 1.75 percent. This was the first time that the federal funds rate was below 2 percent in forty years. Fed chairman Alan Greenspan was receiving criticism for allowing the Internet boom to continue too long and allowing the budget surplus to slip away as a result of the downturn in the economy. Greenspan defended himself in a conference at Jackson Hole, Wyoming, in September 2002, where he asserted that it was not his fault that the stock market bubble had developed at the end of the 1990s. He contended that, if interest rates had been raised any higher, there could have been more dramatic adverse economic effects. No one questioned him on why he had raised interest rates at all when inflation posed no danger.

Deficits and International Problems

A fixture on the Avenue of the Americas in New York since 1989 was a clock showing the mounting federal debt. Between 1989 and 2000, that debt had grown from $3 trillion to $5 trillion, increasing at one point by $10,000 a second. The clock actually reversed itself in June 2000, as the debt began to be reduced as a result of government surpluses. The annual federal deficit, which had grown to massive proportions in the 1980s, was virtually eliminated by 1998. That happy circumstance changed in the new century when the deficit widened as a result of the economic downturn and the war on terror.

The economy in Argentina was coming unglued as the economic crisis in America worsened. Restrictions were placed on withdrawals from bank accounts in Argentina. Customers were allowed to withdraw only $1,000 per month in cash from their bank accounts. Argentina seized $3.5 billion in private pension fund assets to meet its obligations. The country had $155 billion in public debt outstanding, and it suspended payments on $132 billion of that amount. This was the largest sovereign debt default in history. The president of the country resigned, and the country went through five presidents in two weeks in an effort to contend with political fallout from the collapse of its economic system. The government declared a state of emergency after rioting and looting killed four people, but unlike earlier crises in Latin America, the Argentina economic crisis was not a contagion that spread immediately to other countries.

The International Monetary Fund (IMF) was withholding a $1.26 billion loan because of Argentina's failure to adhere to prior loan conditions. This held up other lending and led to much criticism of the IMF. Critics were claiming that IMF policies were undermining the economies of Mexico, South Africa, and Turkey. The IMF and the United States agreed in August 2002 to provide a bailout to Argentina and to provide $1.5 billion to Uruguay and $30 billion to Brazil as well. These problems gave rise to a proposal that would allow countries in effect to declare bankruptcy and rid themselves of debt they could not service under an IMF-administered procedure. Paul H. O'Neill, George W. Bush's first Treasury secretary, supported this proposal, but it was blocked by the large international banks that would suffer the most under such a plan. Argentina finally restructured its debt in 2004, paying about thirty cents on the dollar to debt holders.

The dollar had appreciated by some 30 percent over other major currencies in the six years before 2001. The euro, which operated under the auspices of the European Central Bank, lost almost 20 percent of its value against the United States dollar between 1999 and 2001. The euro had been introduced as a book entry currency, but became the official currency of twelve nations on January 1, 2002, when notes and coins were introduced. After the American stock markets faltered, the dollar began retreating and was selling at a discount off the euro.

The Japanese bubble economy that had collapsed as the 1990s began was still in recession and experiencing the effects of deflation. Its industrial output fell to the lowest level in fourteen years in 2001. Moody's downgraded Japan's credit rating. Japan was also criticized for its bad banking loans by the Organization for Economic Cooperation and Development. In Russia, several small groups and individuals (the "oligarchs") were controlling vast industries and reorganizing the economy. They likened what they were doing to JPMorgan's organization of trusts in America. Like Theodore Roosevelt's attacks on Standard Oil under the antitrust laws, President Vladimir Putin declared war on oil tycoon Mikhail Khodorkovsky, the head of Yukos oil, having him jailed on tax and other charges. Khodorkovsky was later sentenced to nine years in prison. President George W. Bush remarked that it appeared that Khodorkovsky had been "adjudged guilty prior to having a fair trial." The affair did much to undermine the confidence of foreign investors in Russian enterprises.

Prelude to September 11

The economy and the stock market in America were struck another blow with the terrorist attacks on September 11, 2001. The attack on the World Trade Center targeted America's dominant position in world finance, while the attack on the Pentagon was directed at another symbol of U.S. power, the military. This was not the first attack on Wall Street. The International Workers of the World had mailed bombs in 1919 to John D. Rockefeller and J.P. Morgan, who had also been shot twice by a Cornell University instructor after that individual bombed the capitol in Washington, DC. A total of thirty-six bombs were mailed and intercepted by post office officials. A bomb planted in a horse-drawn wagon loaded with steel bars and left outside J.P. Morgan's office exploded on September 17, 1920, killing thirty-three people and injuring more than 200. Despite severe damages to its premises, J.P. Morgan & Co. reopened its offices on the following day.

Fraunces Tavern, a landmark in the New York financial district and the place where George Washington gave his farewell speech to his officers at the end of the American Revolution, was bombed in 1975 by the FALN, a Puerto Rican nationalist group. That attack killed four and injured over fifty. FALN was responsible for 130 bombings in the United States in the 1970s and 1980s. That bombing campaign was stopped after a number of its members were imprisoned. Sixteen of those individuals were granted clemency in 1999 by President Bill Clinton in order to aid his wife's Senate campaign.

A terrorist attack on the World Trade Center in 1993 killed seven people and injured 1,000 others. That attack was mounted by Muslim terrorists who planted a bomb in a rental vehicle they parked in one of the towers. The participants were captured after one of their number returned to the rental agency to claim his deposit on the van. Ramzi Ahmed Yousef was the mastermind of that bombing plot. He was also convicted of planning to blow up American airliners in the Far East. Omar Abdel Rahman, a blind sheikh, was involved in the attack on the World Trade Center and was convicted, with nine others, of planning to bomb the United Nations, the Lincoln and Holland Tunnels, the George Washington Bridge, and other New York landmarks.

The 9/11 Attack

The devastation at the World Trade Center on September 11, 2001, was far in excess of the earlier attacks, indeed almost beyond comprehension. The obituaries of the more than 2,700 victims of the September 11 took several months to publish in the *New York Times*. The attack caused the collapse of seven buildings at the World Trade Center. Financial firms directly affected by that attack were Salomon Smith Barney, Credit Suisse First Boston, and Morgan Stanley. Suffering the most was Cantor Fitzgerald Securities, a bond trading firm that lost 658 of its 960 employees. Howard Lutnick, the chairman of the firm, lost a brother and was received with sympathy after he broke down during television interviews while discussing the losses suffered by his firm. That sympathy soon turned to criticism by the press, especially from Bill O'Reilly at Fox News, after the firm cut off salaries of employees killed in the attack. That criticism was muted after the firm promised to give 25 percent of its profits to the families of those killed in the terrorist attack for the next five years. Despite its losses, Cantor Fitzgerald was able to report a profit in the fourth quarter of 2001 and continued to recover thereafter, making good on its promise to share profits with the families. The company relocated its office to midtown Manhattan and within a few years had restored its workforce to over 600 employees, with plans to add 200 more. Cantor Fitzgerald brought suit against Saudi Arabia and charities in that country, charging them with responsibility for the terror attacks and seeking billions of dollars in damages.

Another firm hit hard by the terrorist attacks on September 11 was Keefe Bruyette & Woods Inc., which lost more than one-third of its employees. That firm was just recovering from a sleazy insider trading scandal involving its former head, James J. McDermott, Jr., and his porn star girlfriend, but it also bounced back, turning a profit and actually increasing its revenues while still in temporary quarters. Marsh & McLennan, the world's largest insurance broker, lost 295 employees in the attack. That company had been founded in 1871 as a response to the great Chicago fire that bankrupted many insurance companies. Marsh & McLennan set up a $22 million victims' fund for its employees but was harshly criticized when it decided to discontinue health benefits for families of victims it employed after one year. Marsh & McLennan then offered to extend that coverage to three years, but this only created more criticism because the costs were to be paid from the company's victims' relief fund rather than from other corporate revenues. That problem was straightened out, but Marsh & McLennan would become involved in some embarrassing and expensive financial scandals in the wake of Enron. Ambitious New York Attorney General, Eliot Spitzer, was the creator of that scandal. He was running for governor on a platform of reform and attack on financial institutions. His assault on Marsh & McClennan would do economic damage to that company second only to the terrorists attacks. Aon Corp., another insurance company attacked by Spitzer, also suffered tragically when its offices were hit in the South Tower of the World Trade Center by the terrorist attack. Fred Alger Management lost thirty-five employees. It too would be a target of another Spitzer crusade against mutual fund money managers. Euro Brokers lost sixty-one employees in the South Tower, most of them on its trading floor. Another firm decimated by the collapse of the World Trade Center towers was Carr Futures, which was owned by Credit Agricole Indosuez, a French company. Its trading floor was at the center of one airplane strike. That company lost sixty-nine employees.

The Morgan Stanley victims' relief fund quickly raised $15 million for families of employees killed when the company's headquarters in the World Trade Center was destroyed. Most employees had been saved by prompt evacuation orders from Morgan Stanley managers. Citigroup lost a great deal of space in the World Trade Center and laid off thousands of employees in the wake of the attacks and a declining economy. Citigroup estimated its direct losses from the September 11 attack to be some $700 million, including $500 million in loss claims at its Travelers insurance group, a venerable institution that had insured George Armstrong Custer before his death at the Little Bighorn. Another $200 million was lost as a result of business interruption. Citigroup's largest stockholder was a Saudi prince, Walid bin Talal. He had invested more than $1 billion in Citigroup in 1991 in order to save the bank when it was near failing, an investment several of his countrymen sought to destroy in the attack on September 11.

Thousands of employees working in offices damaged or destroyed in the attacks were forced to relocate to temporary or permanent offices in New Jersey, midtown New York, or elsewhere. Several law firms, including Sidley Austin Brown & Wood LLP, were forced to relocate. The World Financial Center and other adjoining buildings were damaged, forcing their evacuation. Merrill Lynch had to abandon its headquarters in the World Financial Center for several months. American Express moved 4,000 of its employees to temporary quarters. Other firms affected in the World Financial Center were Lehman Brothers, Nomura Securities, and the publisher of the *Wall Street Journal*. The New York offices of the SEC were destroyed in the attack. Morgan Stanley and Goldman Sachs announced that they would be moving significant portions of their operations out of New York City.

Restarting Wall Street

Wall Street had backup systems in place for many of its businesses as a result of the terrorist attacks on the World Trade Center in 1993, but recovery was not immediate. AMEX was forced to close for two weeks. It then transferred its options business to the Philadelphia Stock Exchange, and the AMEX specialists moved to space at the NYSE. The president of the NYSE, Richard Grasso, was able to announce the reopening of the NYSE on September 17. He would be richly rewarded for that effort, but the market set a record for the largest one-day drop on reopening, and the Dow experienced its worst single-week loss in value in percentage terms since May 1940 and the largest one-week loss in total value in history. Much of that loss was recovered in the following weeks. The Dow flirted with the 10000 mark for several days in November, and a four-day rally pushed the Dow up to 10070 on December 29, 2001. Nevertheless, the Dow had fallen for two consecutive years in a row at the end of 2001.

The September 11 attacks were estimated to have caused the loss of 1.6 million jobs in the United States; 200,000 of those jobs were lost in September alone. The attacks were particularly damaging to the airlines and other travel-related businesses. Renaissance Cruise Lines, a cruise ship operator, declared bankruptcy. American Express laid off 14,000 employees as a result of declines in its travel business. This was about 15 percent of its workforce. Airline travel dropped 25 percent in November 2001, resulting in layoffs totaling over 100,000 employees. U.S. Airways was bankrupted, and United Airlines would follow, experiencing not only losses from the attacks but also runaway expenses. United Airlines employees had been given a 55 percent ownership interest in the company in 1994. Wages and other labor costs then accelerated rapidly, making the airline unprofitable. In 2001 the Department of Justice blocked a merger of United Airlines and U.S. Airways that they needed to survive even before the attack. Both were forced to declare bankruptcy, but U.S. Airways escaped that status on March 31, 2003. The bankruptcy of United Airlines was the largest airline bankruptcy in history. Midway Airlines was already in bankruptcy and ceased business after it failed to recover from the attacks. The nine largest airlines in the United States lost a collective $11.2 billion in 2002. Congress voted a $15 billion bailout for the airlines in the form of cash for losses and loan guarantees. Southwest Airlines had a profit at the end of 2002, which made it the only major United States airline that was profitable.

AMR, American Airlines' parent company, had a loss of nearly $800 million in the fourth quarter of 2001. It avoided bankruptcy by agreeing with its unions to cut employee wages, but the press reported that AMR executives had been given large special payments for their work during the crisis. This caused an outcry at the unions, and those payments were canceled. Airlines in the United States were not the only ones affected. Air France saw a drop in operating profits of 69 percent following the September 11 attacks. Sabena, Belgium's national airline, declared bankruptcy. Swiss Air was bankrupted and stopped all flights until it received a rescue package. Air New Zealand had to be rescued by the New Zealand government, which made available more than $400 million to the company. Air Canada was in trouble and later filed for bankruptcy.

Insurance claims from the attacks on September 11 were estimated to total $20 billion. Reinsurers were liable for about two-thirds of that amount. The world's largest reinsurer, Munich Re, suffered big losses. Swiss Re, the world's second-largest reinsurer, suffered its largest loss in history as a result of the September 11 attacks. Insurance company failures increased. Over thirty insurance companies were insolvent even before the attacks. Some insurance companies received a boost from court rulings and a jury determination that the attack by the two hijacked airliners on the World Trade Center towers was a single event rather than two separate attacks. This sharply reduced the exposure of the insurance companies to the holder of the lease on the World Trade Center, a company controlled by Larry Silverstein, a wealthy real estate developer. A jury did find that one set of insurance contracts defined the event as two attacks. Nevertheless, the maximum liability of the insurance companies insuring the towers was cut from $7 billion to $4.7 billion.

Coping With Terror

The concern about future terrorist attacks resulted in increased premiums for commercial property coverage and exclusion entirely in some cases. This caused a slowdown in construction of commercial property because banks refused to finance uninsured projects. After a long fight in Congress, the Terrorism Risk Insurance Act was enacted in 2002 to provide that coverage. The federal government created a victims' relief fund managed by a special master, Kenneth Feinberg, that was to provide compensation to victims' families in amounts based on their income and assets. The families had to waive the right to sue the airlines, building managers, owners, or anyone else for other compensation in order to receive this relief. In addition, the amount of the award was to be offset by any insurance or other death payments. This raised criticism that families spending funds for insurance were being penalized for their prudence and the expense they incurred in obtaining insurance. About 97 percent of eligible families eventually signed up for the program. Awards were averaging $1.8 million per victim in 2003. The families of victims of the attack received a total of $38.1 billion from the government, insurance, and charities. Businesses received about 60 percent of that amount. The money was not always well spent. The widow of one Cantor Fitzgerald employee quickly blew through about $5 million, spending $70,000 on a Super Bowl trip and $500,000 on her wardrobe, which included handbags valued at over $5,000.

Charitable donations to families of "first responders" (police, fire, and rescue personnel) lost in the September 11 attack totaled over $350 million. More than $1 billion was raised for others affected by the attack. Criticism was directed at charitable groups such as the Red Cross and the United Way, however, for failing to provide funds promptly to families and for diverting funds donated for victims of the attacks to unrelated and sometimes dubious causes. Both charities saw a drop in contributions in the wake of that controversy. They were also the target of some 500 fraudulent claims for aid by persons falsely claiming they were victims of the attacks. Several of those individuals were charged with criminal fraud. Even worse, a number of Islamic charities in Saudi Arabia and elsewhere were the subject of investigations and orders freezing their funds because of concerns they were funneling funds to terrorists.

The SEC was concerned that advance knowledge of the attacks may have been used for insider trading. However, the commission that was appointed to report on the events leading up to the attack (the 9/11 Commission) noted: "Exhaustive investigations by the Securities and Exchange Commission, FBI, and other agencies have uncovered no evidence that anyone with advance knowledge of the attacks profited through securities transactions."[12] Two FBI agents were charged with using confidential information obtained from FBI files to manipulate stock prices by short selling schemes and by extorting cheap stock from companies who were the targets of government investigations. This scheme was discovered as a result of the inquiries into trading on advance information about the September 11 attacks. Federal investigators raided First Equity Enterprises, a firm dealing in foreign exchange for private investors. Some $100 million in customer funds had disappeared. The firm's offices had been destroyed in the September 11 attacks, and the fraud was discovered after customers began making inquiries as to the status of their accounts. In California, thirty-seven investors were defrauded of $1 million by Ross A. Rojek, who falsely claimed to have created a face recognition system to combat terrorism after the September 11 attacks.

Additional money laundering legislation was enacted in the wake of the attacks. The USA Patriot Act of 2001 required financial institutions to use due diligence in allowing foreign financial institutions to open correspondent accounts and thereby access the U.S. financial system. Financial institutions in the United States were prohibited from opening accounts for foreign shell banks that had no physical presence or affiliation with a legitimate bank. Broker-dealers were required to submit suspicious activity reports of transactions by their customers. Banks had previously been subject to that requirement. Financial institutions were required to verify the identity of their customers and establish programs in their operations to detect and prevent money laundering. The money laundering rules were extended to credit card companies and money services such as Western Union.

The September 11 attacks and a declining stock market took a toll on Wall Street firms. Merrill Lynch took a $2.2 billion restructuring charge at the end of 2001 and cut 9,000 jobs, after reporting a loss of $1.26 billion for the fourth quarter. Deutsche Bank laid off over 9,000 employees. Credit Suisse First Boston took a $450 million charge against earnings and cut 2,000 workers. It had acquired Donaldson Lufkin & Jenrette for $11.5 billion in 2000. Lehman Brothers suffered a 57 percent drop in income in the fourth quarter of 2001, while Goldman Sachs saw its fourth-quarter earnings decline by 17 percent. Investment banking firms including Morgan Stanley, Goldman Sachs, and JPMorgan Chase cut bonus payments to their employees. Charles Schwab's commission revenue fell 33 percent in the fourth quarter of 2001, largely as the result of a slump in online trading. Schwab cut 25 percent of its staff.

Banks were forced to take year-end charges against earnings because of bad loans exposed by the declining economy. FleetBoston took a $1.95 billion charge and laid off 700 people. The safe-deposit segment of the banking industry was also affected. Safe-deposit boxes recovered from the rubble of the World Trade Center at JPMorgan Chase had suffered severe damage from the heat of the fires caused by the attack. Some of the jewelry and artifacts were melted or burned beyond recognition. The bank disclaimed all liability.

The markets had absorbed shock after shock from the Fed's interest rate increases and from the devastating attacks on September 11. These blows staggered Wall Street, but another category 5 hurricane was on the way. A scandal unfolding at the Enron Corp. in Houston, Texas, would shake the financial world.

2. The Enron Corp.

A Company Is Born

Creating a Name

The Enron Corp. was the product of a 1985 merger between Houston Natural Gas Corporation and InterNorth Inc., two well-established energy companies with extensive pipeline operations. InterNorth, one of the constructors of the Alaska pipeline, was the larger of the two companies and was the purchaser of Houston Natural Gas. That purchase was aided by financing supplied by the junk bond king Michael Milken, before he was jailed. In something of a coup, Kenneth L. Lay, the head of Houston Natural Gas, emerged to head the combined firm. He then moved the headquarters of the company to Houston, rather than Omaha, where InterNorth was based.

The new name for the combined Houston Natural Gas and InterNorth companies was carefully selected. A New York consulting group considered several hundred names over a period of four months and charged more than $100,000 before coming up with a name that Ken Lay liked. It was "Enteron," but that moniker was quickly dropped after a guffawing press pointed out that this was a word used to describe an intestine, which fit nicely with the company's natural gas business. The company then opted for Enron, allowing another corporation to grab the discarded name as a perfect fit for its business profile, becoming the Enteron Group Inc., a manager of medical digital imaging services based in Chicago.

InterNorth had been the target of a notorious corporate raider, Irwin Jacobs, before the merger with Houston Natural Gas, and the fear of his attack drove InterNorth into the arms of Houston Natural Gas. Jacobs had a reputation for selling off company assets once he had control. That practice, which earned him the sobriquet "Irv the Liquidator," struck fear into the hearts of executives whose companies he targeted. Jacobs used that fear to demand "greenmail" from several companies, which paid him a premium for his holdings so that he would just go away. His greenmail victims included Kaiser

Steel Corp., Pabst Brewing Co., Walt Disney, and Borg-Warner. In a filing with the Securities and Exchange Commission (SEC), Jacobs asserted that his stake in InterNorth (and Enron after the merger) was for investment, but that his group of investors might "consider taking control." That set off alarm bells at Enron, and Jacobs was bought off with a payment of $350 million that included $13 million in greenmail. That buyout pulled badly needed funds from Enron, which was having financial difficulties at the time. Enron then had a junk bond rating from the credit agencies, but that rating would be upgraded to investment grade as Enron's fortunes improved. Enron aided that recovery by selling the shares it bought from Jacobs and Leucadia National, another large investor, to the Enron employee stock option program.

Enron's Management

Kenneth Lay, the chairman and chief executive officer of Enron at its inception and upon its demise, was a self-made man. After a humble childhood in Missouri, he had worked his way through the University of Missouri. A Navy veteran with a PhD in economics, Lay began his career at Exxon, then called Humble Oil and Refining Co. He moved from there to Washington, DC, to work for the Federal Power Commission, the predecessor to the Federal Energy Regulatory Commission (FERC). Lay moved up the bureaucratic chain when he was appointed deputy undersecretary for energy issues in the Department of the Interior. After leaving Washington, Lay began work at Florida Gas Corp., the only major natural gas pipeline owner in peninsular Florida. Lay rose through the ranks at that company to become president before becoming president and chief operating officer of Transco Energy in Houston. In 1984, Lay moved again to become chief executive officer of Houston Natural Gas.

As the head of Enron, Lay became one of the most widely respected businessmen in America. That success was not immediate and was by no means permanent. He had detractors along the way, and in 1990 *Fortune* magazine voted Lay the twelfth most overcompensated executive in the United States on the basis of a survey that correlated compensation to stock performance. That jab may have spurred Lay to push up Enron's stock price, but more of a motivation was the large grants of stock options Lay received from Enron as compensation. He was given $4 million in options after the merger with InterNorth, receiving even more in subsequent years. Lay was granted options on 1.2 million shares of Enron stock in 1994, exercisable at a price of $34 per share. Twenty percent of the option rights were to vest immediately. Eighty percent would vest almost six years later, unless Enron reported a 15 percent per year increase in annual earnings, in which case they would vest earlier. This provided a powerful incentive to meet earnings targets that would push up Enron's stock price and make the options more valuable.

Enron was generous to Lay in other ways. In 1989 he was given a five-year employment contract that provided for an interest-bearing advance of $7.5 million. That advance was to be used, at least in part, to purchase Enron common stock. Those shares, and certain personal property, were pledged by Lay as collateral for the advance. Lay was liable for only one-third of the advances, if the pledged shares proved to be insufficient to cover the liability. In 1994, Lay entered into a new employment contract that called for the repayment of his prior advances and extended to him a revolving, unsecured line of credit in the amount of $4 million. Advances on that line of credit could be paid off with Enron stock. Lay would abuse that right as Enron began its downward plunge by repeatedly borrowing $4 million from Enron and then paying off the loan with Enron stock, freeing up his line of credit each time for another drawdown and payoff with Enron stock. In an eight-month period before Enron's collapse, Lay borrowed $4 million in cash every two weeks under this line of credit, repaying those advances with Enron stock.

Lay entered into another employment contract in 1996 that provided options on another 1.2 million Enron shares. The company's generosity to Lay continued. According to a government indictment, between 1998 and 2001 Lay received $300 million from Enron stock options and restricted stock, gaining a net profit of over $217 million. He also received $18 million in salary and bonuses from the company. In 2001, the year Enron collapsed, Lay received a salary and bonus of $8 million and $3.6 million in long-range incentive payments.

Jeffrey Skilling

Another key executive receiving large amounts of compensation at Enron was Jeffrey K. Skilling. He was a graduate of Southern Methodist University and acquired an MBA from Harvard Business School, where he graduated in the top 5 percent of his class in 1979. Skilling became a partner at McKinsey & Co., a management consulting firm whose founder had stressed the value of management accounting for clients. McKinsey & Co. had been involved as a consultant in the merger that created Enron, and Skilling recommended a strategy for gas trading that led to his hiring by Enron in 1990. Skilling advocated an "asset lite" strategy for Enron that would concentrate on energy trading, rather than owning and operating hard assets such as pipelines. Lay liked that idea, and Skilling was placed in charge of Enron's trading operations when he joined the company. Skilling advanced to become Enron's president and chief operating officer in 1996. Under Skilling, Enron began calling itself a "new economy" company, asserting that, in the new economy, "[w]hat you own is not as important as what you know."[1] That same philosophy was also propelling the dot-com company boom.

Skilling's employment contract at Enron included a $1.4 million loan that was later increased to $1.6 million and made nonrecourse, which meant that Skilling was not personally liable for repayment of the debt. Instead, the loan was secured by stock options and phantom stock in Enron Gas Services Corp.; the phantom stock provided Skilling with the cash equivalent of increases in the value of the company's stock. Skilling was paid $62,000 a month as base salary in 1996, plus the phantom stock, and was granted options on 611,000 shares of Enron stock. Skilling's pay was increased over the years. According to his indictment, Skilling realized $200 million from Enron stock options and restricted stock between 1998 and 2001, resulting in a net profit of over $89 million. He was also paid over $14 million in salary and bonus during that period.

Andrew Fastow

The Enron executive most responsible for the company's collapse was Andrew Fastow, who worked his way up the ranks to become the company's chief financial officer. After graduating from Tufts, Fastow and his wife, Lea, attended and received their MBA degrees from the Kellogg School of Business at Northwestern University. Andrew Fastow started his business career at Continental Illinois Bank in Chicago, where Lea Fastow also worked. Continental Bank, as it was later named, was badly crippled in 1982 by the failure of the Penn Square Bank. Continental Bank purchased some $1 billion in loans and participations from Penn Square, most of which proved to be uncollectible. Continental Bank might have survived that blow, but other large loans in its portfolio (including credits extended to Braniff Airlines and International Harvester) had to be classified as nonperforming. These problems set off a run on the bank's deposits in 1984, and a massive rescue had to be arranged, first by Morgan Guaranty and other banks, and then by the federal government. Some $12 billion was extended to the Continental Bank in order to prevent its bankruptcy; such a failure by a money center bank would, it was feared, touch off a national panic. Continental Bank's financial position continued to deteriorate, and the federal government effectively nationalized the bank; its operations were later sold to the Bank of America.

In the interim, Andrew Fastow left Continental Bank briefly to work for CCC Information Services, an insurance industry database, but soon returned to the bank. After his return, Fastow worked on structured finance transactions that were becoming a popular part of finance in the late 1980s. One such instrument was called FRENDS (floating rate enhanced debt securities), which were ownership interests in pooled debt from leveraged buyouts. That debt was often less than investment grade, but by dividing the pool into tranches of senior and subordinated debt, the credit rating of the senior debt was enhanced. Diversification, achieved by pooling various loans, was also effective in enhancing the credit rating for this instrument, making it more attractive to investors. Another aspect of these transactions was that they removed the debt off the lender's balance sheet, a factor that would play a large role in Enron's demise. An article in the *Financial Times* of London that appeared before Fastow left the Continental Bank likened the bank's cutting-edge structured finance products to characters in the *Star Wars* movies. That theme would carry over to Enron when Fastow joined that company.

Fastow was hired by Jeffrey Skilling in 1990 to create securitization opportunities in Enron's trading operations. Fastow rose through the Enron ranks. He was admitted to senior management status in 1997 and was named the company's chief financial officer in the following year. Fastow was then thirty-six years old. In his new position, Fastow quickly made a name for himself in financial circles with Enron's often imaginative financing activities. He was given a CFO Excellence Award by *CFO* magazine in 1999.

Enron Values

Enron's management stated in its annual reports that the company's values were "respect" ("Ruthlessness, callousness and arrogance don't belong here"), "integrity," "communication," and "excellence."[2] Those claims would be derided as the company's financial structure collapsed. Enron's values included an expressed concern with the welfare of its employees. Employees were provided with generous health benefits, a gymnasium, their own Starbucks, a cafeteria (the "Enron Energizer"), and an Enron concierge service that took care of errands that might pull employees away from the office. The company opened an on-site child-care center for employees and provided backup day care for employees needing a substitute for their normal day care provider. During the summer, the children of employees could be sent to Camp Enron. These benefits were not entirely altruistic. Enron estimated that its child-care programs saved the company $870,000 in attendance losses from child-care related problems. Enron also provided employees with personal computers at home as a way to push the work envelope.

The Enron culture included a broad range of perks for executives. They were provided with the usual corporate toys, including Gulf Stream jets that came in handy for family vacations. The real corrosive feature of the Enron culture, however, was its compensation program, which tied executive pay to increases in the price of Enron's stock through stock options and other arrangements. Senior executives were given massive amounts of stock options as compensation, providing them with a strong incentive to take whatever steps were necessary to keep up the price of Enron's stock.

Another aspect of Enron was its aggressive trading culture and tough performance evaluations for employees. *Fortune* magazine ranked Enron as "No. 2 in Employee Talent" and one of the twenty-five best places to work in the United States in 1999, but it was a highly competitive environment. Under Enron's "rank and yank" rating system, employees had to be ranked in one of five categories. Fifteen percent of employees had to be ranked in the lowest category of "needs improvement." If those employees did not improve, they faced discharge.

An ironic aspect of Enron's culture was the care it gave to accounting issues. The company's own staff included 600 accountants, including some who had previously served in the highest citadels of the accounting profession's ruling bodies. Enron was shelling out over $50 million in annual auditing and consulting fees to its outside auditor, Arthur Andersen LLP, in order to ensure that its accounting practices, which were often aggressive, were in compliance with industry standards. As an institution, Enron was fastidious in complying with all required accounting standards. It reviewed several of its accounting practices with the SEC staff and obtained rulings from the Emerging Issues Task Force, which was created by the accounting industry to provide quick advice on novel accounting issues. Supplementing that compliance effort was an army of lawyers employed at Enron and some highly respected outside law firms, such as Vinson & Elkins in Houston.

Pipeline Operations

Enron was described as a "hall of mirrors within a house of cards" in a class action lawsuit brought after its bankruptcy, but that was a common misconception. Despite Skilling's "asset lite" strategies, Enron did own substantial assets throughout its existence. After the merger of Houston Natural Gas and InterNorth, Enron operated over 37,000 miles of pipeline, making it something of an "old economy" firm. Enron's pipelines were grouped into three operations, the Northern Natural Gas Company (servicing the upper Midwest), Transwestern Pipeline Company (servicing the California market), and Florida Gas Transmission (50 percent owned by Enron and servicing peninsular Florida). In 1993, Enron was transporting 20 percent of the country's natural gas. The company was also purchasing crude oil produced from 23,000 leases in 1994 and was conducting exploration for natural gas and oil through its subsidiary Enron Oil & Gas Co. (EOG), which was one of the largest independent oil and gas companies in the United States. EOG had estimated reserves of 1,772 billion cubic feet of natural gas and 20.9 million barrels of oil and natural gas liquids. Enron's principal producing areas included Big Piney, Matagorda Trend, Canyon Trend, Pitchfork Ranch, and Vernal.

Enron further expanded its operations to include the construction and operation of natural gas-fired power plants in the United States and abroad. These plants used new cogeneration technology for the simultaneous production of steam and electricity from natural gas. Enron also ventured into other areas of the energy market, including methanol, which nearly led to a disaster when an Enron methanol plant exploded in Pasadena, Texas. Fortunately, there were no fatalities, and the plant was back in operation within seven months.

Deregulation

Enron's natural gas pipeline operations were regulated by FERC under the Natural Gas Act of 1938. FERC regulated everything from rates to transmis-

sion activities for those pipelines. That regulation had traditionally been justified by its supporters on the grounds that pipelines, even if privately owned,
are public utilities that must be regulated to prevent the operator from abusing
what amounts to a monopoly on the distribution of this valuable and necessary commodity. Enron was subject to state regulation for in-state sales as
well. In Texas, regulation of intrastate sales and transportation of natural gas
was conducted by the politically powerful Texas Railroad Commission.

FERC's pervasive regulation had long been under attack by its critics for
being inefficient and discouraging competition. The oil crisis in the 1970s
added impetus to those arguments, and Congress responded in 1978 with the
Natural Gas Policy Act, which mandated that more competition be introduced
into the distribution process. FERC began that effort by trying to open up
pipeline access to all gas buyers and sellers. In 1992, FERC issued Order No.
636, which required natural gas pipelines to "unbundle" their rate charges.
This required the pipeline operators to list separately their rates for sales,
transportation, and storage charges. FERC thought that this unbundling would
increase competition by allowing customers to compare rates among pipelines. Another FERC order sought to preclude interstate pipelines from providing preferential discounts to their own marketing affiliates. Any such
discounts were required to be posted on the pipeline's electronic bulletin board
and made available to competing marketers within twenty-four hours.

Those FERC orders "significantly altered the marketing and pricing of
natural gas" in the United States.[3] Enron supported this regulatory change
and lobbied Congress and FERC to expand the deregulatory efforts for natural gas transmission. Enron also sought to create new markets in deregulated
areas of the energy industry. Enron affiliates, for example, were purchasing
natural gas and other energy products under short- and long-term contracts
and arranging financing of energy purchases marketing these products.

Trading Operations

The bankruptcy examiner for Enron would note that, before its demise, Enron
had transformed itself into "a global enterprise that was an industry leader in
the purchase, transportation, marketing and sale of natural gas and electricity,
as well as other energy sources and related financial instruments, and in the
development, construction and operation of pipelines and various types of
power facilities."[4] Enron was also engaging, as early as 1993, in "price risk
management and financing arrangements in connection with natural gas, natural gas liquids and power transactions."[5] This was simply a short form reference to Enron's efforts to become an energy trading operation, as well as a
pipeline operator.

The key to Enron's trading operations was its "gas bank" through which
natural gas was bought and sold for forward delivery, allowing Enron to make
a profit on the spread between the buy and sell prices. Enron used the bank to

buy long-term commitments from producers, sometimes paying in advance. Enron would then resell that production on a long-term basis. Enron's trading business included risk management activities for independent power producers, industrial companies, gas and electric utility companies, oil and gas producers, financial institutions, and energy marketers. These risk management activities employed financial products related to everything from interest rate risks to changes in the exchange rate with the Canadian dollar. Enron boasted that its risk management activities were producing earnings that increased by 62 percent in 1994 and by another 28 percent in 1995. Enron's earnings from related "finance" operations experienced a 138 percent increase in 1995.

Enron Finance Corp. was purchasing natural gas supplies through "volumetric production payments" and was arranging those transactions through various "financial entities."[6] The volumetric payment program involved an upfront payment to oil and gas producers for a portion of their reserves. This payment would be repaid by oil and gas delivered from the producers at fixed prices. This provided the producers with a source of cash and Enron with a source of production at a fixed price.

Enron was exposed to market risks through its forward commitments of energy products at fixed prices, which could cause a loss if prices changed adversely. Enron sought to avoid such risks through a balanced portfolio of buy and sell contracts, and it established a company policy against speculation. Enron's interest rate risks were hedged with swaps that had a notional value of $3.6 billion in 1993. That figure was in addition to $299 million in natural gas price swaps for fixed and market prices.

Enron started its trading operations through a joint venture with Bankers Trust. That relationship sought to take advantage of Bankers Trust's derivatives trading operation, which was then the industry leader. The goals of the two firms proved to be incompatible, and the relationship was terminated. Bankers Trust, not long afterward, would become embroiled in a scandal involving large losses to clients from complex instruments sold to them by the bank. Bankers Trust was sued by Gibson Greetings and Proctor & Gamble over those instruments. Bankers Trust appeared to be winning that litigation until the discovery of some tape-recorded conversations of one of its traders, whose goal was to "lure people into the calm and then just totally fuck 'em."[7] That revelation caused Bankers Trust to settle the cases. Tape recordings of Enron traders would show that they had adopted the same aggressive trading culture in their operations.

Enron's trading activities were monitored by a risk control unit operating separately from the groups that originated the transactions. Enron used a "value-at-risk" (VAR) model to measure the likely exposure of the company in the event of market movement scenarios that were based on past market activity. Such models were widely employed by derivative trading firms in the wake of losses experienced by numerous institutions in the 1990s. Enron sought to limit its daily value-at-risk from its trading operations to less than 2 percent of its income.

Enron noted in its filings with the SEC that its VAR model had inherent flaws, including the use of subjective assumptions and reliance on historical data that might not predict future performance. Enron, therefore, also used stress tests and "worst case" scenarios to measure its risks. Additionally, the company was monitoring its credit exposure from counterparties that could pose a default risk. It was clear that Enron's trading operations posed a risk that the stock market viewed with apprehension. A false rumor that the company was short of gas during an unusual cold spell and had lost millions led to a sharp drop in Enron's stock price before company executives could refute the veracity of that rumor.

A problem plaguing trading operations was the phenomenon of the rogue trader. Orange County, California, and Barings Bank were bankrupted by rogue traders. This phenomenon spread across Wall Street, causing massive problems at Salomon Brothers, Kidder Peabody, Daiwa Bank, Metallgesellschaft AG, Andre & Cie, Deutsche Morgan Grenfell, Plains All American Pipeline, TransCanada Pipeline, National Westminster Bank, and Chase Manhattan Bank. Enron too learned of the dangers of rogue traders from Lou Borget, president of Enron Oil Corp., an operation left over from InterNorth. Borget, operating out of Valhalla, New York, reported large profits from oil trading and received bonuses as a result. Borget's claims of profit, however, were fictitious. He was actually defrauding Enron by running a dual set of books and filing false reports of sham oil transactions with a group of shell companies chartered in the Channel Islands to cover his activities, a cover that Enron would later use with Chase Manhattan Bank. Borget stole $3.8 million through those transactions and was concealing large trading losses in open positions from unauthorized trading activities.

The losses on Borget's positions totaled over $1 billion, an amount sufficient to have bankrupted Enron, but market conditions improved. Enron was able to reduce that exposure down to $142 million, booking an after-tax loss of $85 million in 1987. Enron had to restate its financial statements for a three-year period to correct the shift of income by Borget's trading operation on Enron's books. Borget claimed he was simply moving profits and losses from one accounting period to the other for tax and financial reporting purposes at management's request. Enron denied that claim, and Borget was sent to prison for a year after pleading guilty to income tax violations. Another employee involved in the transactions, Thomas Mastroeni, pleaded guilty to criminal charges and was given probation.

Mark-to-Market

Enron accounted for its trading and risk management activities under the mark-to-market method in its financial reports filed with the SEC. This meant that forward and other contracts were valued at their present market value, rather than historical cost, which was the traditional way to report assets. Enron was ahead of its time in adopting this accounting method. Many critics had long contended that accounting statements were distorted by using historical cost for assets, rather than their current market value. Among those critics of the lower of cost or market approach was SEC chairman Richard Breeden, who argued in 1990 that firms dealing in marketable securities should report those assets at their current values.

Embracing that criticism, Enron sought permission from the SEC to use mark-to-market accounting on its balance sheet for its gas trading operations in 1991, and permission was granted for that line of business. Without seeking further authorization, Enron then extended that accounting method throughout its business. It was not until 1993 that the accounting profession adopted Financial Accounting Standard (FAS) 115 to require companies trading in investment securities to mark those positions to market, unless they were holding debt investments to maturity. That interpretation applied only to corporate securities that could be readily valued by published quotations on a recognized market. Enron's operations did not always fall within that standard. Enron even extended mark-to-market accounting to its merchant investments (investments in other companies), an action Enron's bankruptcy examiner would later characterize as "aggressive."[8] Mark-to-market accounting became important to Enron's success, accounting for more than one-half of Enron's profits and 35 percent of its assets in 2000.

Financial Accounting Standard 133 was adopted by the accounting profession to require mark-to-market treatment for derivative contracts. FAS 133 was issued on June 15, 1998, but was delayed in application until July 1, 2000 (January 1, 2001, for some firms), over nine years after Enron first sought permission from the SEC to use such treatment for its operations. This standard required derivative instruments to be listed on the balance sheet as an asset or a liability at fair value, as measured by earnings and the effect of hedges. Previously, there had been little disclosure on the balance sheet of such instruments, even though they could have devastating effect on a company as the result of adverse market conditions. Most companies disclosed the use of such instruments only in footnotes, which provided only vague, general descriptions that did not contain any valuations. Even so, FAS 133 was highly controversial and was opposed by many traders because of valuation issues and its introduction of further volatility into earnings. Another criticism was that FAS 133 was uncertain in scope, and it had to be clarified by another interpretation, FAS 138.

FAS 133 had a substantial effect on Enron. The company used this new standard to reclassify $532 million in "long-term debt" to "other liabilities." This methodology, as predicted by its critics, added further volatility to Enron's financial statements as energy prices fluctuated. This had both an upside and a downside. Enron could report increased earnings when mark-to-market treatment resulted in an increase in valuation, but a decline would require a charge against earnings and a reduction of asset value on the balance sheet. Mark-to-market accounting could be good for the company's managers' performance reviews when the value of its trading positions increased, but bad when they decreased. This gave managers an incentive to smooth those valuations in order to meet financial analysts' expectations and keep up the price of the company's stock.

Earnings volatility introduced by FAS 133 could be managed by hedges placed against mark-to-market positions. The hedges used by Enron, however, were not always true hedges. In addition, this process could be manipulated through the discretion available in valuing assets where there was no readily available market for comparison. Mark-to-market accounting treatment added another issue. Enron often reported increases in income from that accounting methodology without generating a corresponding amount of cash, creating a "quality of earnings" concern on the part of financial analysts. A JPMorgan analyst, for example, noted that Enron's mark-to-market accounting had the dual effect of creating "front-end-loaded earnings that bias the denominator in the P/E ratio and a timing disconnect between projects' cash and earnings effects."[9]

Wind Farms

Enron sought to enter other areas of the energy business, including renewable energy resources such as wind farms and wind turbines. Enron produced more than 4,300 wind turbines for plants in California, Germany, and Spain. This business was concentrated in the Enron Wind Corp., but certain of the wind operations were sold off to special purpose entities for accounting advantages. Those transactions would become the subject of criminal charges after Enron's bankruptcy. An Enron executive, Lawrence M. Lawyer, also pleaded guilty to failing to pay income tax on $79,000 in kickbacks he received in connection with a wind farm partnership project.

Still another alternative energy project involved a joint venture with FuelCell Energy. It was developing fuel cells that could generate electricity by using natural gas to create a chemical reaction with hydrogen and oxygen. Enron claimed that this could be a $1 billion market, but generating costs were over $5,000 per kilowatt-hour. Conventional generation costs were only a fraction of that amount.

Foreign Operations

A principal goal of Enron was to increase its activities abroad. By 1993, it had energy operations in the Philippines, Australia, Guatemala, Germany, France, India, Argentina, and the Caribbean. That list of countries was expanded in 1994 to include China, England, Colombia, Turkey, Bolivia, Brazil, Indonesia, Norway, Poland and Japan. Enron's international activities were consolidated into Enron International Inc. (EII), where Rebecca Mark was named chairman and chief executive officer. A graduate of Baylor University with a degree in international management, Mark had begun her career as a banker at the First City Bank in Houston. Like Andrew Fastow, she had been exposed to the Penn Square debacle, and she witnessed a meltdown at the First City Bank not unlike the one at the Continental Bank. She joined Houston Natural Gas before its merger with InterNorth. Mark's worldwide spending spree while she was head of EII would give her a high profile. She was featured in a 1996 *Fortune* magazine article titled "Women, Sex and Power." Unfortunately, her international acquisitions did not live up to her billing and resulted in a series of disasters that did much to contribute to Enron's downfall.

EII opened offices in London, Buenos Aires, Singapore, and Norway to conduct international commodity trading activities. Enron's international projects included pipeline and power plant acquisitions and construction. Enron owned a 42.5 percent interest in a power facility in Tesside in northeast England. EII extended Enron's operations into other parts of the globe, including Vietnam, Guam, Croatia, Qatar, Honduras, and Mozambique. Among other things, Enron constructed diesel-fired power plants for use in developing countries and managed the physical operations of several power plants located abroad. Enron owned 50 percent of two diesel engine power plants located on movable barges moored off the coast of Guatemala. Another project involved the construction of a 1,120-mile pipeline between Bolivia and Brazil at a price of $1.5 billion. A pipeline 357 miles in length was under construction in Colombia. SK-Enron was the largest distributor of natural gas in South Korea.

In Brazil, Enron acquired the Elektro Electricidade e Servicos S.A. for $1.3 billion in 1998. That same year, Enron acquired an English water company, Wessex Water, which Enron renamed Azurix. Enron valued the global water market at $300 billion and badly wanted a piece of that action. Azurix entered into a joint venture with Saur International, a French water company, to acquire Mendoza, a water company in Argentina, and Azurix also controlled the water concession in Cancun, Mexico. Azurix would not be a success and would require an enormous write-down in value that contributed substantially to Enron's woes before its bankruptcy.

Foreign Problems

There were some special risks in foreign ownership. Peru nationalized Enron's operations in that country, but Enron's losses of $200 million were covered by insurance and a settlement with Peru. One particularly large problem for Enron arose in India, where the company was a contractor for the Dabhol Power Company that was to build a gas-fired power plant and a liquefied natural gas terminal. After Enron and the consortium began construction on that power plant for the Indian state of Maharashtra, elections were held, and a new coalition government was elected that proceeded to repudiate the Enron contract. Arbitration was commenced in London and a ruling favorable to Enron was handed down.

The state of Maharashtra then agreed to continue and even expand the project from a generating capacity of 435 megawatts to 2,450 megawatts. Phase I of this project became operational in 1999. Enron agreed to provide $1.87 billion in financing for Phase II, which was scheduled for completion at the end of 2001. That schedule was not met: continuing problems with the Indian government and negative public opinion kept the plant shuttered. Phase II never became operational, and Phase I was shut down after the Maharashtra government refused to buy the electricity being generated, claiming that its cost was too high.

Another problem arose with long-term "take or pay" contracts in which Enron agreed to purchase all of the gas production of the J-Block field located in the North Sea off the English coast. Under those contracts, Enron was required to pay a fixed price for the production even if the company chose not to take delivery. Gas paid for, but not taken, could be lifted in later years. Although Enron claimed that it was not a speculator, this arrangement exposed it to a large price risk in the event spot market gas prices fell before the time for lifting gas arose under the long-term take or pay contracts. Unfortunately for Enron, that was exactly what happened.

Enron declined deliveries on the take or pay contracts but had to pay their cost anyway. Enron suffered a large loss, but claimed that it would not have a material adverse effect on its financial position. Enron filed suit in a local court in Houston, claiming that the contracts were terminated by breaches on the part of the counterparties. That proceeding was enjoined by an English court, and the defendants sued by Enron brought their own litigation in England against Enron to enforce the contracts. An English court of appeals held that Enron had no obligation to take or pay until 1997, rather than earlier dates demanded by the counterparties. Nevertheless, this was no great victory for Enron because it still remained obligated on a substantial portion of those contracts. Enron took a $463 million charge to earnings in 1997 to reflect its liabilities under the J-Block contracts.

Enron Growth

Enron Online

In 1999, Enron launched Enron Online, an Internet-based e-commerce trading platform that provided real-time quotes posted by Enron traders for wholesale customers. Those customers could contract with Enron as principal on the basis of those quotes with no human interaction. Enron Online was an unregulated exchange made possible by the efforts of the Commodity Futures Trading Commission (CFTC) to deregulate commodity transactions involving institutional investors.

Some energy trading by institutions had been exempted from regulation by legislation that was enacted in 1992 to reverse a ruling by a federal district court that transactions on the Brent Oil market were futures contracts that had to be traded on a futures exchange regulated by the CFTC. Such a requirement would have destroyed that informal market and was unnecessary because only institutions traded those contracts. Those institutions did not need CFTC regulatory protection; they could protect themselves. The exemption granted by the CFTC for energy contracts under the 1992 legislation was narrow in scope, but the agency decided to extend deregulation even further after an effort by CFTC chairman Brooksley Born to regulate over-the-counter derivatives failed. The agency adopted rules deregulating most institutional trading and that regulation was enacted into law through the Commodity Futures Modernization Act (CFMA) of 2000.

The CFMA exempted bilateral electronic trading exchanges from regulation and was quickly dubbed the "Enron exclusion" because of the benefits it provided for Enron Online. Serving on the Enron board of directors at the time the CFMA was adopted was Dr. Wendy L. Gramm, an economist who had been the CFTC chairman when the earlier energy exemption was adopted by the agency. She was married to Senator Phil Gramm, of Texas, a beneficiary of substantial Enron campaign contributions. After Enron's demise, they both came under criticism for supporting the CFMA in order to advance Enron's interests. That criticism proved to be unfounded. Apparently, the husband and wife team had, for differing reasons, nearly blocked passage of the CFMA. Senator Gramm held the legislation up until his concerns about some unrelated banking issues were resolved. Dr. Gramm, a longtime advocate of deregulating commodity trading, wanted even more deregulation.

Enron Online traded over 1,000 commodities contracts in various forms. Unlike most electronic communications networks, Enron acted as principal, as either a buyer or seller, with counterparties through Enron Online. Most electronic communications networks simply match buyers and sellers without the intercession of a market maker like Enron. There was no transparency that would allow market participants to see what other traders were doing on the Enron system. Enron initially projected that transactions on Enron Online would reach a notional amount of $40 billion by the year 2000. The company subsequently reported that it did far better than that projection, engaging in 548,000 transactions in 2000 with a notional amount of $336 billion. This made Enron the world's largest e-commerce firm in terms of notional trading amounts. Enron Online was trading about $2.8 billion per day, but that was exceeded by the $13 billion per day transacted in energy contracts traded on the New York Mercantile Exchange. Enron was also soon facing competition from other Internet exchanges, including DynegyDirect and the Intercontinental Exchange (ICE), which sought to copy Enron's success.

Electricity Market

Another market of interest to Enron was the generation and transmission of electricity. Traditionally, electricity was one of the most heavily regulated energy markets, but it was deregulated under the Energy Policy Act of 1992. To enhance competition, that legislation exempted generators selling power on a wholesale basis from traditional utility regulatory rate procedures. FERC issued orders that required electric utilities to open access to their transmission facilities to third parties at the same rates as charged when the utility was using its own transmission lines. This opened the door for competitors to enter new markets through the use of existing utility lines. That access provided an opportunity for price competition in markets previously controlled by the utilities' ability to limit access to the market, but deregulation led to volatility in wholesale electricity prices. In mid-1998, electricity prices rose in one market from $20 per megawatt hour to $7,500 per megawatt hour.

Enron sought to exploit this opening in the electricity market. It actively lobbied for additional legislation in Congress that would further enhance competition and promoted an electronic trading market for electricity. In order to impress analysts visiting its headquarters, Enron executives used some employees to create fake trading operations.

Enron sought to further expand its energy operations in the electricity segment in 1996 through the acquisition of the Portland General Electric Company (PGEC). PGEC was involved in the generation, purchase, and transmission of electricity in Oregon, California, and other western states. PGEC owned hydroelectric generating facilities, as well as a nuclear power plant that was being decommissioned. Enron was not a utility, and the lack of that status barred it from many electrical markets. The acquisition of PGEC solved that problem for Enron because PGEC was a regulated utility, thus giving Enron access to the California electricity market. Enron would exploit that access to manipulate prices and contribute to an energy crisis in California. Enron paid a 46 percent premium over market for this acquisition, but the merger made Enron the largest energy merchant in the United States. As a part of this transaction, Enron moved its corporate charter from Delaware to Oregon.

Broadband

Enron could not stand on the sidelines as e-commerce and the Internet dominated market psychology in the 1990s. The company expanded its business operations to include broadband services. Enron's broadband program sought to bypass the slower elements of the Internet and provide high-speed data delivery and even stream video through fiber-optic cable. This business was conducted through Enron Broadband Services Inc., headed by Kenneth D. Rice. Enron's broadband business involved the construction and management of a nationwide fiber-optic network. Enron marketed and promised the development of an "intelligent network platform" that would provide bandwidth management services and deliver high-quality bandwidth content.[10] The software for this intelligent network was claimed to be available for billing for broadband services based on use. Enron marketed this program abroad as well as in the United States. Enron promised its customers access to 18,000 miles of fiber-optic cable in the United States and twenty-five pooling points in the United States, Tokyo, London, Brussels, Amsterdam, Paris, Düsseldorf, and Frankfurt. Enron was also promoting its broadband services in Australia. To assure the world that Enron had the capacity to operate its system, the company had the head of Sun Microsystems announce that the Enron broadband unit was buying 18,000 routers for its system.

Enron saw a trading opportunity in bandwidth. Enron began acting as principal in bandwidth transactions and was making a market in bandwidth capacity. Enron entered into over 300 bandwidth transactions during 2000. Its first bandwidth transaction involved an "incremental contract for DS-3 bandwidth (enough for streaming video) between New York City and Los Angeles" on a network owned by Global Crossing, a company that would become another famous bankrupt.[11] As a part of its bandwidth program, Enron planned to offer structured finance, bandwidth portfolio management, and risk management products for "dark" fiber, which is optical fiber that is laid but not being used. Enron's broadband trading operations further included circuit transactions, Internet transit, private transport, and storage of information.

Enron tried to create a trading market in bandwidth in much the same way it had created a market in energy products. Enron planned to make a two-sided market in bandwidth products that would place it at the center of most transactions and provide an information advantage. Enron was accused of trying to jump-start that market by having other energy traders engage in offsetting transactions that would give the appearance of liquidity in the market, a practice called "chumming," in order to induce participation in the market by broadband-centered companies. The energy traders said to have assisted Enron denied those claims.

Enron boasted publicly of its ability to provide broadband delivery services for media, entertainment, and financial services, including live and on-demand streaming video. Enron created a stir in the media when it announced a joint venture with Blockbuster Video, a business unit of Viacom that rented movies from stores located across the nation. That joint venture was to provide video on demand to consumers in their homes, a massive market if it could be tapped. Unfortunately, this business turned out to be a financial disaster for Enron. The joint venture with Blockbuster failed to overcome several technical problems involved in streaming video, and demand turned out to be low in the test markets where it was introduced.

Enron claimed that the market for premium broadband delivery services would grow by 150 percent per year. It projected that its own broadband business would be generating $17 billion in revenue by 2005. That forecast proved to be totally unrealistic. The Enron broadband business announced a loss of $60 million in 2000, but the company claimed that it remained optimistic that the broadband market business would grow and be profitable. In fact, the whole broadband market collapsed along with the stock market in 2000, and Enron's broadband business was one of the several business units that contributed to Enron's bankruptcy. Despite its losses in broadband, Kenneth Rice, the head of that unit, was paid $47 million in 2000.

Merchant Investments

Another aspect of Enron's business was its merchant investments. Merchant investments were traditional activities that investment banks conducted in connection with their underwriting activities. The Glass-Steagall Act of the 1930s and other legislation had limited commercial banks in their ability to engage in merchant banking. The Gramm-Leach-Bliley Act of 1999, however, opened the door for this activity to commercial banks operating in a financial holding company structure, although some fairly tight restrictions were imposed by bank regulators. Those financial institutions were in competition with venture capital groups and hedge funds that were seeking to make large profits from start-up or promising enterprises.

Enron was neither an investment bank nor a commercial bank, but it wanted to mimic the venture capitalists that were in the height of their glory during the dot-com boom at the end of the twentieth century. Enron thought it could use its expertise in energy and information from its broad-based trading operations to become a merchant banker. It incorporated such activities into its business plan. The creation of Enron's merchant investment activities and its expanded trading operations were coupled with sales of some "hard" assets. Enron's investment and trading were then driving its business and earnings. By 1999, about a third of Enron employees were engaged in trading and merchant investment activities.

Enron used its merchant investments to increase its earnings by marking them to market as they increased in price. Those investments added further volatility to Enron's balance sheet because the value of those investments went down as well as up. To deal with that problem, Enron engaged in a number of complex devices to "monetize" declining assets by moving them off its balance sheet.

Financial Results

Unlike many companies, Enron paid dividends to its shareholders. The company increased its common stock dividends from an annual rate of sixty-two cents per share in 1991 to seventy-five cents per share in the fourth quarter of 1993 and to eighty-five cents per share on an annual basis in the fourth quarter of 1995. Dividends in 1996 were eighty-six cents per share, but dropped to forty-eight cents per share in 1998. In 1999 and 2000, the dividend rate leveled off at fifty cents per share on an annual basis, after a two-for-one stock split in 1999.

Enron's stock was traded on the New York Stock Exchange (NYSE), as well as the regional exchanges. The price of its common stock reached $37 in the fourth quarter of 1993, after a two-for-one stock split in August of that year. The stock rose to $47.50 in the fourth quarter of 1996, up from a high of $39 in the prior year. Enron's share price was a matter of prime concern to Enron's management. Enron executives were "laser focused on earnings per share" because that was demanded by analysts touting stocks to clients.[12] That message was sent throughout the company. When Enron's stock price passed through $50, employees were given $50 bills to mark the event.

Enron reported net income of $232 million in 1991 on operating revenues of $5.7 billion. Income increased to $306 million in 1992 on operating revenues of $6.4 billion. Operating revenues were $8 billion in 1993 and net income rose to $387 million, exclusive of a $54 million deferred tax liability. That growth continued. Net income was $453 million in 1994 on total revenues of $8.9 billion, $520 million in 1995 on total revenues of $9.1 billion, and $584 million in 1996 on revenues of $13.3 billion. In 1996, Enron's assets were reported as being valued at $16 billion, up from $10 billion in 1992. In 1997, however, Enron's net income was only $105 million on total revenues of $20.2 billion, a drop that was due largely to the charge against earnings for losses under the J-Block, take or pay contracts.

Fancy Finance

Enron employed many sophisticated financing techniques in its operations that allowed it to report the increasing revenues needed to meet analysts' expectations. One Enron subsidiary, Enron Oil and Gas Co. (EOG), operated as Enron's independent oil and gas operator. Enron sold 31 million shares of EOG to the public in 1995 through an initial public offering (IPO), realizing a pretax profit of $454 million on net proceeds of $650 million. At the same time, Enron issued $221 million of 6.25 percent exchangeable notes that were subject to a mandatory exchange in three years into shares of EOG stock. The net result of the IPO and the conversion of the exchangeable notes was to reduce Enron's ownership interest in EOG from 80 percent to 54 percent while providing Enron with $870 million in cash. In July 1999, after a deal with Occidental Petroleum fell through, Enron sold most of its EOG stock back to EOG, making the latter essentially independent. Within eighteen months, EOG's stock price had doubled, a price increase that Enron missed out on by its sale at a distress price.

Enron issued cumulative guaranteed monthly income preferred shares (MIPS) that gave investors periodic payments that were treated as interest payments for income tax purposes but were viewed by rating agencies as equity, reducing the amount of leverage on Enron's balance sheet. MIPS were thus a stock and a loan at the same time. Enron also offered collateralized debt obligations that were modeled after collateralized mortgage obligations.

Enron North America placed $324 million of notes and other instruments into such a pool. It then had Bear Stearns sell tranches in the pool to institutional investors. The tranches were rated by a rating agency. The lowest rated tranches proved to be a hard sell and had to be sold to two Enron special purpose entities (SPEs)—Whitewing and LJM2. This financing proved to be unsuccessful, and the value of the notes dropped substantially. Enron then repurchased the notes in order to protect its credit standing.

Enron created something called "credit sensitive notes" that paid higher rates of return if the company's credit rating was lowered by the credit rating agencies or lower rates in the event of an upgrade. In one such offering, Enron issued $100 million of twelve-year notes payable at 9.5 percent. If Enron's credit rating was thereafter reduced, the interest payment could go as high as 12 percent. Several other large companies, following Enron's lead, issued such notes. These notes were criticized as being cannibalistic. If the downgrade caused a higher rate to be paid, that would only worsen the financial condition of the company. The Enron offering, however, may not have been novel. Around the beginning of the twentieth century, income bonds were used to finance troubled firms. These instruments were given a debtor's preference on assets but paid a return based on the company's earnings.

In 2000, Enron held an investment grade BBB+ rating from Standard & Poor's and a Baa1 from Moody's for its senior long-term unsecured debt. The company's annual financial report for that year contained a vague but ominous warning with respect to its credit ratings:

> Enron is a party to certain financial contracts which contain provisions for early settlement in the event of a significant market price decline in which Enron's common stock falls below certain levels (prices ranging from $28.20 to $55 per share) or if the credit ratings for Enron's unsecured, senior long term debt obligations fall below investment grade. The impact of this early settlement could include the issuance of additional shares of Enron common stock.[13]

Halcyon Days

Enron was an American success story as the twenty-first century began. In 1997 Ken Lay was profiled in a *Business Week* article as a "master strategist." Enron was voted the most innovative company in America for five years running by *Fortune* magazine, which also predicted, on August 14, 2000, that Enron would be one of the top ten stocks that would last the coming decade. Enron was then the seventh-largest company in the United States and employed some 25,000 people around the world. Claiming to be the largest supplier of electricity and natural gas in North America and the second-largest marketer of electricity in the United Kingdom, Enron asserted that it was the "blue chip of the electricity and natural gas industry worldwide" and the "world's leading energy company."[14]

Enron's profits increased by over $130 million between 1993 and 1995.

This growth resulted in a tripling of Enron's stock price, and the company boasted in its financial statements that its stock was outperforming the stock market as measured by growth in the S&P 500 stock index. That claim had to be dropped in 1995, and 1996 was an even colder year, after the company failed to meet analysts' earnings expectations. Enron's mounting problems in India and the take or pay J-Block contracts were causing further concern. In 1997, Enron's profits dropped precipitously after the company announced an after-tax charge to earnings of $450 million for the J-Block transactions.

The decrease in Enron's revenues at the end of 1997 resulted in the price of its stock dropping by more than one-third. That was a traumatizing event for Enron executives whose bonuses and stock options were tied to stock price increases, but that setback was overcome, and Enron stock renewed its price climb. Enron's stock outperformed the S&P 500 Index in 1998. The stock was at $44.38 at the end of 1999, having risen almost 60 percent during the year as the bull market peaked. After a two-for-one stock split, the stock reached a high of $90.75 in the third quarter of 2000.

Financial analysts were raving about Enron and its management. *Fortune* magazine ranked Enron "No. 1 in Quality of Management" in 1999. Enron crowed that its Enron Online trading operation was "unquestionably the largest web-based eCommerce site in the world and dwarfs all other energy marketing web sites."[15] The *Los Angles Times* asserted that "companies everywhere are likely to become students of the Enron model."[16] Business schools, including Jeff Skilling's alma mater Harvard, were using Enron in case studies as a model business operation, and business school textbooks lauded the company. *CEO* magazine listed Enron's board of directors as one of the top five in the United States and praised the company's corporate governance structure. Arthur Levitt, the SEC chairman in the 1990s, invited Ken Lay to serve on an SEC advisory panel on "new economy" valuations.

Enron executives were certainly doing well as a result of the increase in the company's stock price. In 2000, the 200 highest-paid company executives all were paid more than $1 million. Collectively that year, those executives received $1.4 billion in compensation, up from $400 million in 1999. Enron executives made $1.2 billion just in stock options alone in the two years prior to the company's bankruptcy.

An Icon

Enron reported revenues for the fiscal year ended December 31, 2000, of over $100 billion. By then, Enron was an icon in Houston. It was the sponsor of a new stadium for the Houston Astros, agreeing to pay $100 million for the right to name it Enron Field. After Enron's bankruptcy, the Astros bought back that right for $2.1 million and resold it to Coca-Cola, which named the stadium after its Minute Maid division. In the meantime, Enron was announcing its plans to enter the California electricity market through advertisements broadcast on the Super Bowl.

Enron's new, fifty-story, oval-shaped office building was a defining feature of the Houston skyline. Andrew Fastow arranged for the off-balance sheet financing of Enron's office buildings through a synthetic lease that involved the sale of the building to a special purpose entity and then a lease back of the building. JPMorgan Chase led a group of banks in financing the Enron office lease arrangement. Enron budgeted $20 million for artwork to decorate its offices.

Enron constructed another large building across the street from its Houston headquarters to house its trading operations. The new building had four trading floors and cost $300 million; it would be sold in bankruptcy for a third of that amount. Reflecting Enron's obsession with its stock price, monitors in its buildings displayed the current value of the company's stock to remind employees what the company was all about. Enron's elevators streamed financial newscasts for the employees to ponder as they made their way between floors.

If imitation is the sincerest form of flattery, then Enron was indeed admired. Several other companies, such as Reliant Energy, were mimicking Enron's business model, right down to the financial newscast in elevators. Reliant even paid to have another Houston stadium named after itself, and it was there that Super Bowl XXXVIII was played. Other energy companies, including Dynegy, El Paso, and Duke Energy, were creating their own trading operations to compete with Enron. That imitation would come at a huge cost to those companies when they became embroiled in controversies over their trading practices, which in many instances had been adopted from Enron.

Enron was a civic-minded organization with a high profile. The company maintained a $10 million per year budget for community relations in Houston. In 1997 Enron hosted a reception for former Soviet president Mikhail Gorbachev, awarding him the Enron Prize for Distinguished Public Service and a $50,000 honorarium. Nelson Mandela, Nobel Prize winner and South African leader, and Colin Powell, the future secretary of state, were also given such awards. Its last recipient was Alan Greenspan, who came to Houston to receive the award just six days before Enron declared bankruptcy. Greenspan's lecture included a suggestion that success in business was accompanied by high ethical standards. Greenspan declined the Enron honorarium.

Enron endowed professorships at Rice University in Houston and the University of Nebraska, and Ken Lay did the same at the University of Houston and the University of Missouri, his alma mater. Enron and its executives were strong supporters of Houston charities, including the Houston Ballet. Ken Lay was chairman of the city's United Way campaign. His personal foundation was the recipient of Enron stock valued at $52 million in 2000, but the assets of that foundation dwindled to $2.4 million after the company's bankruptcy. Enron was even generous in its donations outside Houston. Its largesse included gifts to libraries in Oregon for "Cyber Sundays" that promoted computer literacy. Even in the midst of its collapse, Enron donated $1 million to those victimized by the terrorist attacks on September 11, 2001.

Special Purpose Entities

A strange phenomenon began appearing in the exhibits to Enron's disclosure statements that it filed with the SEC: ever-longer lists of subsidiary companies and limited partnerships. The company's 1995 Form 10-K filed with the SEC listed over 200 such entities, many of which were formed in the Cayman Islands or the Netherlands, two traditional tax havens. The number of those entities grew to exceed 3,000 and took fifty pages to list in Enron's SEC Form 10-K for year-end 2000. Despite the unusual nature of such holdings, no eyebrows were raised at the SEC. Many of these entities were limited partnerships, limited liability companies, partnerships, and business trusts that were created to serve as SPEs. They often bore exotic names (e.g., Hawaii 125–0, Cornhusker, and Ghost), but were so numerous that Enron was running out of titles, as possibly reflected by the fact that there were two SPEs named Sundance, used for different programs.

Securitizing the Balance Sheet

The use of SPEs became popular under structured financing techniques developed in the latter part of the twentieth century to "securitize" cash flows from assets placed in the SPEs. Andrew Fastow, Enron's chief financial officer, had cut his teeth on those instruments at Continental Bank, and he would employ them throughout Enron's operations. Normally in a securitization, interests in the SPEs are sold to investors and the proceeds from that sale are paid to the owner that transferred the assets to the SPE. The SPE usually has no operational role. Its only function is to hold the assets and to collect and make any required payments from the assets' income streams. Normally, an SPE's obligations are secured by the assets it holds, and those obligations are repaid by the pass-through cash flows from those assets. This provides immediate cash to the issuer and a secured obligation to the investor.

SPEs were often used to enhance the credit rating on the SPE obligations because the assets were isolated from the creditors of the entity transferring the assets to the SPE. Such isolation could be achieved, however, only if certain accounting requirements were met. Specifically, Financial Accounting Standard 140 (FAS 140) allowed the assets and liabilities of an SPE to be removed from a company's balance sheet only if an outside investor controlled, and had a substantial investment in, the SPE. The SEC's Office of the Chief Accountant opined several years before Enron's demise that, in order to achieve the required independence, the outside investor would have to have at least a 3 percent substantive equity ownership interest in the SPE. The SEC staff cautioned that a greater percentage of independent owner- ship could be required in other situations in order to ensure that the investor exercised control over the SPE. The SEC's cautionary language was ig- nored in future years, and the 3 percent ownership requirement became an unwritten rule for the independence of all SPEs in meeting accounting re- quirements. The assertion that control was given up by having an indepen- dent investor with a 3 percent ownership would be ridiculed after the fall of Enron. One commentator noted with respect to an Enron SPE: "Nobody walks away from a $1.5 billion investment and gives it to some straw inves- tor who is only putting up 3 percent. And I do not care if you get the Mes- siah to come down for a Second Coming to tell me you are giving up control, you are not giving up control."[17] Andrew Fastow was quoted as saying that the 3 percent requirement was "bullshit," because a "gardener could hold the 3 percent. I could get my brother to do it."

A related accounting requirement for SPE treatment was that the 3 percent interest of the "independent" investor genuinely had to be at risk. Enron, how- ever, engaged in numerous complex arrangements that were designed to en- sure that the SPE was not at risk from the assets it held. Those arrangements ensured that Enron retained the economic risks of the transaction. Enron's bankruptcy examiner concluded that several Enron SPEs did not have the requisite true sale status because Enron retained control of the assets and continued to have liability for decreases in their value (or profits from in- creases), as well as control over the ultimate disposition of the assets. This undermining of the true sale status of assets was accomplished through vari- ous means, including "total return swaps," put options, and circular transac- tions that returned the risk from the transaction back to Enron. In several transactions, Enron had secret understandings to protect investors from losses ("trust me equity") and used dummies as independent investors, including, in some instances, its own employees.

Another characteristic common to the securitization of assets was that the assets sold to the SPE would produce an income stream that could be used to pay back the investors buying interests in the SPE. Many of the Enron SPEs did not have income streams sufficient to meet the obligations incurred to investors. Instead, Enron provided various guarantees and swap arrangements to assure payments to the SPE investors. In entering into those arrangements, Enron was transforming the structure back to what more closely resembled a conventional loan, rather than a securitization. Enron took this whole process even farther by using SPEs for other purposes, such as removing depreciated assets from Enron's balance sheet without reflecting their loss in value under mark-to-market accountng. Enron claimed the proceeds of the "true sale" of these assets to the SPE as revenue on its financial statements, which would be improper if the assets were not properly valued or if the transaction was not a true sale.

Cactus and JEDI

One of Enron's first SPE transactions, called "Cactus," involved the creation of an SPE that purchased almost $1 billion in gas payments due Enron from producers utilizing Enron's gas bank. Enron sold ownership interests in the Cactus SPE to institutional investors such as the General Electric Co. Those investors in turn sold the gas production back to Enron, which then sold it into the market. This model was not an unusual use of an SPE, except that the return of the gas to Enron raised the issue of whether there was really a true sale of the gas to the SPE. Nevertheless, the Cactus transaction was reported publicly by Enron and was not questioned by regulators or shareholders. Andrew Fastow, who was still in a junior position at Enron at the time, helped structure the Cactus transaction. A lawsuit claimed that he had plagiarized the concept from a New York businessman.

In its 1993 filings with the SEC, Enron disclosed that it had created an entity called Joint Energy Development Investments (JEDI), an acronym taken from the *Star Wars* movies. It was formed as a limited partnership that was owned in equal amounts by an Enron subsidiary and the California Public Employee Retirement System (Calpers). This investment partnership with Calpers was a coup for Enron since Calpers was the largest retirement fund in the United States and a leading advocate of corporate governance reforms. Enron and Calpers agreed that each would invest $500 million in capital in JEDI. Enron primarily met this commitment by contributing its own common stock.

In addition to its JEDI partnership, Calpers was one of Enron's largest shareholders, holding 3.5 million Enron shares. Calpers benefited substantially from its joint venture with Enron, receiving a profit of 62 percent a year for eight years from the JEDI partnership. The market downturn that began in 2000 would give Calpers an opportunity to appreciate that profit. The pension fund's assets dropped from $172 billion to $136.6 billion in 2003, a decline of more than 20 percent.

In the summer of 1997, Enron sought to find a buyer for Calpers's interest in JEDI. Enron wanted this sale so that Calpers could invest an even greater amount in a larger partnership to be called JEDI II. Calpers set a deadline of November 6, 1997, for this buyout at a price of $383 million. That was done, albeit in a somewhat haphazard fashion, and Calpers then proceeded to invest $500 million in JEDI II. JEDI II also attracted an investment from the Ontario Teachers' Pension Plan Board, which the Enron bankruptcy examiner later concluded was accounted for by Enron in a way that allowed Enron to overstate its 1997 net income by 63 percent.

In order to buy out Calpers's JEDI interest, Andrew Fastow, Enron's chief financial officer, created a SPE called Chewco. Borrowing once again from his experiences at the Continental Bank, Fastow named this entity after the *Star Wars* movie character, Chewbacca. Fastow wanted to become Chewco's independent investor for SPE purposes. That proposal was dropped after it was determined that such participation would require Enron to disclose Fastow's involvement in its financial statements filed with the SEC because Fastow's status as an officer of the company made him a "related party." The SEC had long been concerned that related party transactions were not negotiated at arm's length, were often disadvantageous to the company's shareholders, and were frequently used to conceal losses and other problems. Public disclosure of such transactions, it was thought, would discourage their use and abuse.

To avoid disclosure, Michael Kopper, an employee working under Fastow's supervision, was chosen to be the independent investor. Since Kopper lacked officer status, transactions in which he was involved were not treated as related party transactions, and his participation need not be disclosed in Enron's public filings with the SEC. Kopper was viewed as an independent investor for purposes of the 3 percent independence requirement for SPEs on the somewhat perverse theory that he did not control Enron and, therefore, was independent. Kopper was a 1986 graduate of Duke University and subsequently attended the London School of Economics. He had previously worked at the Chemical Bank and for the Toronto Dominion Bank. Kopper joined Enron in 1994 and became a managing director in Enron's Global Marketing Group. Fastow's and Kopper's involvement in Enron's off-balance sheet activities would be fatal to the company.

Beneath the Mask

In 1998, Enron reported $31 billion in revenue and net income after expenses of $703 million. Comparable figures for 1999 were $40 billion in revenue and net income after expenses of $893 million. In 2000, the company took a $326 million charge relating to assets in Argentina as the economy there unraveled. Nevertheless, revenues in 2000 were over $100 billion and net income was $979 million. Total capitalization of Enron was $25 billion on December 31, 2000. The company then had assets valued at $65 billion, double the amount in the prior year, a clear signal of unusual activity. Some $20 billion in that incredible increase in assets was due to what Enron identified in its SEC financial reports merely as "assets from price risk management activities."

Although the company was receiving accolades in the press, Enron's financial position was deteriorating. In order to stem that decline, Enron tried to sell some of its Portland General assets to Sierra Pacific Resources for $3.2 billion (including $1.1 billion assumption of debt and preferred interests). That transaction fell through as a result of the upheavals in the California electricity market. Enron then turned to Northwest Natural Gas and reached an agreement to sell those assets for $1.9 billion in cash and stock, of which $1.5 billion was in cash.

Enron's water company, Azurix, was turning out to be another problem.

Azurix was taken public in order to relieve some of its debt. The offering was successful, but problems at Azurix continued to mount, and the company was taken private again by Enron only eighteen months later, in late 2000, for about half of its offering price. An elaborate financial arrangement was structured in order to take that looming disaster off Enron's financial statements. This involved the forming of a holding company that was jointly owned by Enron and an SPE, a Delaware business trust called Marlin Water Trust I. That SPE was funded by $900 million of debt and a small amount of independent equity. The structure was actually much more complicated than this explanation suggests. As described later in the *New York Times:*

1. Enron lent stock to a wholly owned trust.
2. The stock was used as collateral for a partnership called Marlin Water Trust I.
3. Enron created a subsidiary, called Bristol Water Trust, to manage Azurix, the water company, and later borrowed cash from Bristol.
4. Bristol pledged its future debt payments from Enron to Marlin.
5. Marlin raised money from investors.
6. Pledging its cash flow from Bristol, Marlin issued debt.
7. Enron, through Bristol, swapped Azurix for 33 percent of Atlantic Water Trust.
8. With the money it received from investors, Marlin I bought 67 percent of Atlantic Water Trust—the new owner of Azurix.
9. Some of the money invested in Atlantic by Marlin flowed through Bristol to Enron as a loan.[18]

This complicated arrangement was thought necessary because Azurix business units were performing so poorly, including its water business in Argentina, and the economy of Argentina was in free fall, causing it to default on its sovereign debt. Interestingly, the failure of the Buenos Aires Water Supply and Drainage Company had triggered the Barings Panic of 1890. The Barings Bank, one of the leading financial institutions in Europe, had invested heavily in that company and would have failed one hundred years before its death from a rogue trader were it not for the intervention of the Bank of England during that eighteenth-century panic. The debacle at Azurix resulted in the termination of Rebecca Mark, the head of Enron International, and the expense of buying back the Azurix stock required Enron to take a $326 million charge at the end of 2000. This event also moved some $1 billion in debt onto Enron's balance sheet.

Enron's investment in Elektro, the Brazilian electrical company, had soured as well, losing as much as $1 billion in value. The $3 billion power plant project in India was a disaster and was never put into operation. Enron announced that it was in talks to sell its built but nonperforming Dabhol power facility in India for $2.1 billion, but had no takers. The downturn in the Internet economy in the new century was causing huge losses at Enron Broadband Services, which was reporting a loss of $137 million. Additionally, Enron had numerous merchant investments that were plunging in value; about half were underperforming. Natural gas prices were falling, adding further to Enron's woes. These problems were being driven by an economic downturn in the United States and a falling stock market.

Some Enron executives later claimed that the declining performance of Enron's assets and the increasing need for cash that resulted in its bankruptcy might have been averted by its Project Summer. That project tried to sell Enron's foreign assets in 2000 for $7 billion to a group of Middle East investors, led by Sheikh Zayed bin Sultan al-Nahayan, president of the United Arab Emirates. The deal was nearly completed, but fell apart after the sheikh had to have a kidney transplant and suffered other problems that precluded his approval of the sale before year-end. Enron was having trouble closing other deals. It dropped out of a $25 billion natural gas project in Saudia Arabia that was being put together as a joint venture with several other energy companies. Occidental Petroleum took Enron's place.

Enron Fails

The Death Spiral

Kenneth Lay retired from Enron in February 2001 and was succeeded by Jeffrey Skilling. Skilling was a highly touted manager at Enron and Lay's expected and natural successor. Upon assuming his new role as chief executive officer, he was featured on the cover of *Business Week* and named one of the top five chief executive officers in the United States by *Worth* magazine. Despite those encomiums, the decline in Enron's performance continued unchecked, and its stock price continued to fall. Rumors were circulating that Enron was planning to cut its dividend, placing further pressure on its stock.

By this point, Wall Street was starting to question Enron's complex structure and business model. An article published in March 2001 in *Fortune* magazine was titled "Is Enron Overpriced?" and sidebars in the article stated that the company's financial statements were "nearly impenetrable" and that debt was increasing substantially while cash flow was "meager" when compared to earnings.[19] Skilling was quoted in the article as saying that these problems were due to mark-to-market accounting and that its assets could be easily securitized to generate cash.

An example of how this could be done was found in Enron's MTBE operations. MTBE was a fuel additive that was supposed to make gasoline burn more efficiently and cleanly, but several states were claiming that the chemical polluted groundwater and some states banned its use. In Congress, Republicans tried to include a provision in an energy bill that would have shielded MTBE producers from liability, while Democrats were seeking a nationwide ban on its use. That battle held up the passage of a much needed energy bill for several years. In any event, MTBE production was a suspect and declining business, and Enron sold its investment in MTBE production to an Enron SPE in a transaction called Project Timber. Enron had been trying to sell that operation for six years to independent third parties, but the best price offered was $50 million. This did not deter Enron from selling the assets to its SPE for $200 million. As a part of the transaction, Enron agreed to buy the plant's production back from the SPE and assumed any liabilities arising from the MTBE production through a total return swap. Enron booked $117 million in earnings from this transaction, which was a substantial portion of the company's second quarter earnings in 2001.

Enron's problems continued. Its lack of disclosure on SPEs was said to make it a "black box" that defied analysis. Skilling was becoming defensive. A short seller participating in an April 2001 conference call with financial analysts asked for a balance sheet for the prior quarter. Skilling replied that the balance sheet was not due for filing at the SEC for several more days. The questioner then said that Enron was the only major company that had to wait that long to produce a balance sheet. Skilling, in a much-quoted reply, said, "Thank you very much, asshole."

The declining situation at Enron turned into a crisis after Skilling unexpectedly resigned on August 14, 2001, after serving only six months as its chief executive officer. Skilling said he was resigning for "purely personal reasons" that he identified as a desire to spend more time with his family. Privately, Skilling had expressed frustration that he could not stop the drop in Enron's stock price, which had peaked at $90 per share in August 2000 and dropped to $83 at the beginning of 2001, falling to $31 after Skilling resigned. His resignation shocked Wall Street, since Skilling was still quite young (under fifty) and had been expected to run the company for several years. His resignation undermined confidence in the company, and the resulting turmoil caused Ken Lay to return to Enron.

Sherron Watkins

Upon his return, Lay, fatefully, invited employees to let him know of any concerns they might have as Enron's problems mounted. An accountant at Enron, Sherron Watkins, responded to that invitation with an anonymous note, stating that "Skilling's abrupt departure will raise suspicions of accounting improprieties and valuation issues. Enron has been very aggressive in its accounting—most notably the Raptor transaction and the Condor vehicle." Watkins's note continued: "My concern is that the footnotes don't adequately explain the transactions. If adequately explained, the investor would know that the 'Entities' described in our related party footnote are thinly capitalized, the equity holders have no skin in the game, and all the value in the entities comes from the underlying value of the derivatives (unfortunately in this case a big loss) and Enron stock and N/P." Watkins added, "I firmly believe that the probability of discovery significantly increased with Skilling's shocking departure. Too many people are looking for a smoking gun." She went on to assert, "I am incredibly nervous that we will implode in a wave of accounting scandals."

Watkins subsequently disclosed her authorship of that note and followed up with a lengthy memorandum detailing her concerns with Enron's off-the-balance-sheet use of SPE partnerships, specifically Raptor and Condor. She presented that memorandum to Lay in a meeting during which they discussed her concerns. The Raptor transactions would soon be at the center of the Enron scandal. Lay responded to Watkins's allegations by having Enron's outside law firm, Vinson & Elkins, examine the transactions that were the subject of her complaint. The law firm considered several aspects of the transactions, including Andrew Fastow's involvement in various SPEs. When the lawyers questioned Watkins, she stated that her information was not based on any firsthand knowledge; rather it was the result of rumors she had heard at the company.

Arthur Andersen LLP, Enron's auditor, advised the lawyers that it was comfortable with its disclosures in the footnotes on the transactions questioned by Watkins. Vinson & Elkins issued a report on October 15, 2001, that found no improprieties in the partnerships, although the report carefully noted that the law firm had not examined the accounting treatment for those transactions. The report further stated that the whole affair could result in "bad cosmetics" that presented "a serious risk of adverse publicity and litigation" and that Watkins's memorandum was causing Arthur Andersen to seek further assurances that the SPEs were independently controlled. The accounting firm created a working group for that purpose; that effort would trigger the events that led to Enron's downfall.

Watkins held an accounting degree from the University of Texas. She had previously worked for eight years as an accountant at Arthur Andersen, where she helped in the unsuccessful defense of Leona Helmsley (the "queen of mean" and head of the Helmsley hotel chain in New York City) against tax evasion charges. While at Andersen, Watkins audited Lou Borget's trading activities at InterNorth before the Enron merger, but discovered no wrongdoing. Watkins blamed that failure on her inexperience; she said that she had been overawed by New York, where the audit was conducted, and undercut by the shortcomings of an immature partner. Watkins had also worked as the portfolio manager for commodity backed finance assets at MG Trade Finance Corp., a subsidiary of Metallgesellschaft AG. A trader at that company entered into hedged futures positions that were showing losses of over $2 billion when spot oil prices fell below the company's futures positions. MG closed out the positions, taking the loss, and was rescued by a loan of over $2 billion that was arranged by the Deutsche Bank, which owned 11 percent of MG. The trader involved was fired, but sued MG for $1 billion for defamation and other claims. A Nobel Prize–winning economist, Merton Miller, added to the rising controversy by claiming in the *Wall Street Journal* that MG managers had panicked because they did not understand the futures markets and should have let the hedge continue and avoid losses. The managers claimed that the company would have incurred losses of $50 billion if they had not liquidated the position.

Watkins was hired by Fastow and joined Enron in 1993, just before the scandal at Metallgesellschaft hit the papers. She later expressed antipathy toward Fastow, after she became dissatisfied with her bonus. Although Watkins would emerge as a heroine in the press for her complaints to Ken Lay, she did not report her concerns to the SEC or any other regulator. She also sold $47,000 of Enron stock before its bankruptcy. Before that event, Watkins claimed that her memorandum to Lay entitled her to be included in the "inner circle" of management at Enron as the company descended into chaos. Nevertheless, with hysteria in the press mounting over the Enron and other scandals, *Time* magazine named her and other whistle-blowers as its persons of the year in 2002. Watkins then proceeded to write a book about her experiences.[20]

Accounting Disclosures

Enron reported net income of $404 million for the second quarter of 2001, but the company was stressed by a declining stock market and a slowing economy. Added to those problems were the terrorist attacks on September 11, 2001, which closed the markets for over a week in the third quarter. When the markets reopened, they experienced their largest single-week loss market values in percentage terms since 1940, when France fell to the German invaders. The attacks imposed enormous losses on the economy. Enron could not escape the effects of those attacks, but more damaging was a series of accounting disclosures that led to its bankruptcy.

On October 16, 2001, the day after receiving the Vinson & Elkins report clearing the Raptor and Condor transactions, Enron released its third-quarter earnings report that claimed a nine cent per diluted share increase in recurring earnings over that of the third quarter in the prior year. Ken Lay, in his resumed role as Enron's chairman and chief executive officer, asserted that the company was "very confident in our strong earnings outlook."[21] The third-quarter report, however, went on to record nonrecurring after-tax charges of $1.01 billion, resulting in a $618 million loss for the quarter and a $1.2 billion drop in shareholder equity.

The $1.01 billion charge was composed of $287 million from a write-down of Enron's investment in the Azurix water system, $180 million in restructuring its Broadband Services business, and $544 million in losses from investments in The New Power Holdings, certain other investments, and "early termination during the third quarter of certain structured finance arrangements with a previously disclosed entity."[22] Azurix had been the subject of the earlier write-off of $326 million at year-end 2000 when that company was taken private by Enron and its debt was moved onto Enron's balance sheet. The decline at Azurix continued, and Enron was forced to take the additional $287 million charge. Ken Lay rejected suggestions by analysts that the entire Marlin structure through which Azurix was owned posed a threat of further losses to Enron. In fact, this structure, which was supposed to have moved exposure from Azurix off Enron's balance sheet, was undermined by Enron's agreement to guarantee repayment of Marlin's debt through sales of Enron stock, or cash if the stock was insufficient. Further deterioration of Azurix's assets did expose Enron to even larger losses.

LJM

The "previously disclosed entity" referred to in Enron's public announcement on October 16 was LJM2 Co-Investment LP, which had been formed in October 1999. This entity was managed by Andrew Fastow and Michael Kopper. Fastow was the entity's general partner. LJM2 had several large institutional investors, including the Wachovia bank, GE Capital, and the Arkansas Teachers Retirement System; the latter invested $30 million. Merrill Lynch was the selling agent for the private placement of those participations. LJM2 had been preceded by LJM Cayman LP (LJM1), created by Fastow in June 1999. Credit Suisse First Boston (CSFB) and an affiliate of the National Westminster Bank (now Royal Bank of Scotland PLC) each invested $7.5 million as limited partners in LJM1.

The name LJM came from the initials of Fastow's wife, Lea, and their two sons, one of whom was named after Jeffrey Skilling. Fastow had sought, and was granted, a waiver from Enron's conflict of interest rules by the Enron board of directors so that he could act as the general partner for the LJMs. In July 2001, however, Fastow sold his interest in the LJM structure to Michael Kopper because of concern that Fastow's involvement might be questioned by analysts and reporters. A portion of the funds used by Kopper for that purchase came from Enron's purchase of Kopper's interest in Chewco. Enron's chief accounting officer, Richard Causey, agreed with Fastow that other Enron employees would be able to participate in, and profit from, the LJM structures. Fastow and Causey agreed under what they called the Global Galactical agreement that any losses to an LJM entity purchasing Enron assets would be made up in subsequent deals. Causey, who reported to Fastow, had previously been employed as an accountant at Arthur Andersen, where he worked on the Enron account. Causey did not view his role as chief accounting officer to be that of a watchman. Rather, his goal was to make sure that Enron continued to report increased earnings that would meet analysts' expectations. Causey was well rewarded for his services, receiving $13 million in stock option compensation between 1998 and 2001.

Both LJM1 and LJM2 were formed by Fastow to create a ready buyer for

Enron assets that were underperforming—to provide Enron with a way to move those assets off its balance sheet and claim earnings from their sale. The LJM2 transactions used for those purposes included the Nowa Sarzyna power plant under construction in Poland and MEGS LLC, a natural gas production operation in the Gulf of Mexico. A class action complaint later alleged that the Polish power plant was temporarily "sold" to LJM2 for $30 million. This sale allowed Enron to book a profit of $16 million, but the power plant was later repurchased by Enron from LJM2 for $31.9 million even though there was no apparent increase in the value of that operation. The LJM structure was also used to take other investments off Enron's balance sheet. These transactions bore such exotic names as Cortez, Rawhide, Sundance, Ponderosa, Firefly, JV-Company, Sequoia, Cheyenne, Cherokee, Blue Dog, Margaux, Coyote Springs, Choctaw, Zephyrus, and Fishtail.

LJM2 created four SPEs named Raptor I to IV. These entities were used to hedge the value of various Enron assets. This step was needed because, unless hedged, Enron would have to reduce the value of those assets on its balance sheet under mark-to-market accounting rules in the event of a decline. Using the Raptors, Enron was able to hedge a $954 million reduction in the value of its assets. To be hedged meant that someone else was absorbing the decline, which in this case was the Raptors. The assets of the Raptors used to absorb those losses, however, were Enron common stock and warrants on the stock of New Power Holdings, another Enron-related entity. That was a strange hedge because, in reality, Enron was offsetting losses in its assets by issuing its own stock to the Raptors. Expressed another way, Enron was hedging itself.

The declining value of Enron's stock resulted in some of the Raptors having insufficient assets to cover their obligations. In order to avoid reporting a loss of $500 million at year-end 2000, the Raptors were cross-collateralized against each other (in effect combining their assets) for forty-five days. This support arrangement used the assets in the Raptors that were still above water as collateral for those not faring as well. That emergency measure provided only temporary respite from the continuing deterioration of the Raptor vehicles' principal asset, which was Enron stock. Enron was forced to terminate the Raptors as their value continued to decline by purchasing them from LJM2. This resulted in the October 16 announcement by Enron of the loss from the Raptor related transactions in the amount of $544 million.

New Power Company

Another part of the losses announced by Enron on October 16 involved New Power Holdings Inc., which was the subject of an initial public offering for the New Power Company on October 5, 2000, at $21 per share for 24 million shares. New Power Holdings was used to hold Enron's residential retail energy business, which had never earned a profit and even lost $25 million on

$7.8 million revenue in 2000. Unrelated (non-Enron) investors had contributed $100 million in cash in exchange for stock and warrants on New Power Company stock in order to support its operations. Calpers contributed $40 million to this venture.

Enron engaged in some blindingly complex and questionable activities with respect to New Power. Enron held warrants on New Power Holdings stock. Warrants on 15 million shares of New Power Holdings were exercisable by Enron at five cents per share and warrants on another 10.3 million shares were exercisable at $9.69 per share, representing a substantial profit to Enron over the offering price of $21 per share when the New Power Company went public. Enron monetized a portion of those warrants through a series of complex transactions that involved contributing a portion of the warrants to an entity named McGarret I LLC, which was in turn transferred to the Hawaii II Trust, a Delaware business trust, for $20 million that was then distributed to Enron. That transaction was financed by a loan from a bank syndication arranged by the Canadian Imperial Bank of Commerce (CIBC).

Enron entered into a total return swap with the Hawaii II Trust in which Enron agreed to repay the amount of the financing plus interest in exchange for the amounts that might be received from McGarret I. Enron reported the $20 million it received from the Hawaii II Trust on its income statement and as cash flow from investing activities on its statement of cash flows. This process was repeated in two other transactions for an additional $55 million. A variation of these deals was then used to raise $90.9 million, of which a portion was used to repay the McGarret I loan. Enron recognized $214 million in revenue in marking-to-market the total return swaps connected with these transactions. Enron raised an additional $26.4 million in selling a part of this structure to another trust through financing provided by CIBC.

Enron was exposed to a risk of loss under its swaps should the value of the New Power Holdings stock decline. Enron created two new entities to hedge that risk. They were called Pronghorn I LLC and Porcupine I LLC. Pronghorn was a subsidiary of Enron and Porcupine was owned by Pronghorn and LJM2. Porcupine's principal assets consisted of warrants on 24.1 million shares of New Power Holdings stock. As the Enron bankruptcy examiner would later note: "Based on the $21 per share IPO offering price, those warrants had a theoretical value of about $246 million in excess of the related debt. The ability of Porcupine to meet its obligations under the hedge, however, would rapidly erode if the value of New Power Holdings declined because a decline would both increase Porcupine's obligation to pay Pronghorn and diminish its ability to satisfy the obligation," which is exactly what happened.[23] This loss was not reported because it was cross-collateralized by the Raptors before they were terminated.

The Hawaii transactions were extended to other areas and involved trusts that were used to monetize multiple assets from time to time, in effect creating a revolving line of credit. The Hawaii trusts bought assets from SPEs sponsored by Enron Broadband Services and other Enron entities in amounts totaling $436 million. The cash for these transactions was supplied by an affiliate of the CIBC at a 15 percent per year rate of return. The deals were again hedged by total return swaps that effectively entitled Enron to receive the benefit in any increase of the assets held by the SPE but also made Enron responsible for any loss in value. Because of that arrangement and other factors, the Enron bankruptcy examiner concluded that these transactions were actually loans. Nevertheless, cash from the Hawaii transactions was reported as a gain on sale on Enron's income statements and as cash flow from operating activities on its statement of cash flows.

Implosion

More bad news soon arrived. The *Wall Street Journal* and other newspapers had been intensively questioning Fastow's role in the related party transactions. This caused Enron's board of directors to examine that issue; it was only then that the directors discovered that Fastow, who claimed to have made an investment of about $5 million in the LJMs, had made massive profits from those entities. On October 24, 2001, Enron announced that Fastow was being placed on administrative leave.

Fastow's removal was a staggering blow to Enron, and its stock price went into free fall, dropping by a third in the last ten days of October. Enron's disclosures were undermining its access to the capital markets. The company could not issue more stock or long-term bonds in such circumstances and was hemorrhaging cash in amounts that threatened its continued viability. Enron's problems resulted in the credit rating agencies questioning Enron's investment grade credit rating. Those agencies placed Enron on a "credit watch," which further undercut the company's credibility and threatened its viability as cash needs mounted. Any downgrade in Enron's credit rating posed a threat to a key source of Enron's working capital—the commercial paper market, which involves the issuance of unsecured short-term promissory notes by large corporations such as Enron. Enron had some $1.85 billion in outstanding commercial paper in October 2001 that needed to be rolled over. The company's accounting revelations badly damaged its credibility in the money markets, making the rollover of its commercial paper difficult and expensive. Most large corporations have backup lines of credit available in case they are shut off from the commercial paper market for any reason. Enron was no exception. The company had access to unused credit lines totaling over $3 billion. Enron drew down those lines on October 25, 2001, using more than half of those funds to pay off its commercial paper debt. Enron added another $1 billion line of credit using a pipeline as collateral.

Kenneth Lay desperately sought salvation for Enron through a merger with Dynegy Inc., a competitor previously viewed with disdain by Enron traders. Dynegy was founded in 1984 as the Natural Gas Clearinghouse, which matched buyers and sellers of natural gas without itself taking title. Headed by Chuck Watson, its founder, Dynegy was a much smaller company than Enron, with less than half the assets, but still one of the thirty largest firms in the country. Dynegy went public in 1995 and was expanding its role in the energy industry. Dynegy's stock price had risen from $8 to $50 per share, and Watson viewed a merger with Enron as an opportunity. A $9 billion offer from Dynegy was announced to the public on November 9, 2001. The merger was to be preceded by a $1.5 billion injection of cash into Enron from Dynegy's largest shareholder, Chevron Texaco Corp. That payment now seems ironic in view of the fact that Texaco was then holding the record for the country's largest-ever bankruptcy.

On the day preceding the Dynegy merger announcement, Enron disclosed that it was restating its financial statements for the period 1997 through 2000 and for the first two quarters of 2001. That restatement reduced income in those periods by a total of $586 million, shareholder equity was cut by over $2 billion, and debt increased by $2.5 billion. The losses announced by Enron involved SPEs including Chewco Investments LP, JEDI LP, and LJM1. Enron also reported that Andrew Fastow had made $30 million from his operation of Enron SPEs. The actual amount was about twice that figure.

Chewco

Chewco was the entity that had been formed by Enron in 1997 in order to keep JEDI off its books after the Calpers buyout. Chewco had been hastily cobbled together by Enron's outside counsel, Vinson & Elkins, in forty-eight hours. A "dirty close" was used for that transaction, which meant that Enron did not have an independent 3 percent investor available for Chewco. Enron planned to correct that situation before year-end, when the transaction would have to be reported on Enron's books, if an independent 3 percent investor was not found. The transaction had to close in this manner because the Calpers deadline had not permitted time to arrange a proper SPE structure.

Chewco was funded through investments that were actually bridge loans obtained from Barclays Bank and Chase Manhattan Bank (now JPMorgan Chase). The banks advanced a total of $383 million to fund the Calpers buyout. In an apparent attempt to treat those loans as equity investments, at least temporarily, the documents for the advances resembled notes for a loan but were called "funding agreements" and "certificates" instead of loans. The banks were to be paid a "yield" that was actually an interest rate. Undermining this aura of an equity investment was the fact that the banks were guaranteed against loss by Enron.

Chewco subsequently entered into some arrangements that sought to satisfy the independent investor requirement, but that were later criticized as having failed to meet that standard. Specifically, "equity" in the amount of $11.49 million was supplied by Michael Kopper, the Enron employee who

worked for Andrew Fastow, and by William Dodson, Kopper's domestic partner. Most of the money for that 3 percent investment was obtained from
Barclays Bank through loans to entities called Big River and Little River,
which were controlled by Kopper. As security for those loans, Barclays was
given a security interest in $6.58 million in cash obtained by Chewco from
the sale of a JEDI asset. The bank was thus at risk for only about $4.9 million
of the advances it made to Big River and Little River.

The $6.58 million security interest for that advance was later charged as
having negated the independence of the outside investment in JEDI, requiring
that entity to be included on Enron's balance sheet. That shortfall of a few
million dollars was the undoing of Enron, a multibillion-dollar corporation.
Kopper and Dodson contributed only $125,000 of their own funds to become
the independent investor. Even that amount was later viewed to be
nonindependent because Kopper was an Enron employee reporting to Fastow.
Of course, such a small amount would not establish Kopper's independence
and control in any event, at least in the real world, over a deal valued at $383
million. No rational company would give up control over assets with such a
large value to an investor with such a small stake. Indeed, even an $11.49
million investment would not bestow such status in an arm's-length transaction unless there had, indeed, been a true sale.

The transaction was a lucrative one for Kopper, who received $1.5 million in
management fees from Chewco between its inception at the end of 1997 and
1999. In addition, in March 2001, Enron bought Chewco's interest in JEDI for
$35 million. Kopper and Dodson received $3 million of those proceeds in addition to some earlier payments totaling $7.5 million. They also received other
fees, including an additional $2.6 million later in the year as a "tax indemnity"
payment that Enron's inside and outside lawyers objected to at the time. In
total, Dodson and Kopper received $14.7 million, not a bad return on an invest-
ment of $125,000. Kopper paid $54,000 of those fees to Fastow's wife for work
she did for Chewco. Additional payments in the form of nontaxable "gifts"
totaling $67,000 were made by Kopper to Fastow and members of his family.

As Enron unraveled in October 2001 and Fastow's conflicts of interest
came under scrutiny, Arthur Andersen reviewed the Chewco transaction. It
concluded that Chewco did not merit SPE treatment because it did not have
the requisite 3 percent independent investor as a result of the security interest
given to Barclays for $6.58 million of the funds it advanced. These and other
problems resulted in another restatement of earnings by Enron. Issued on
November 8, 2001, this restatement increased debt by $711 million for 1997,
$561 million for 1998, $685 million for 1999, and $628 million for 2000.

Whitewing

Enron disclosed still another problem to financial analysts on November 14,
2001. This disclosure involved Whitewing LP, an Enron entity that bought

Enron merchant investments in energy projects in Europe and South America, including Elektro, the Brazilian electrical company. Whitewing was used to create a revolving credit structure for Enron through which Whitewing purchased $1.6 billion in poorly performing Enron merchant investments. This activity, called Velocity I and Velocity II, moved those investments off Enron's balance sheet and provided it with cash. The Whitewing structure was complex and involved numerous SPEs, including T'Bird, Pelican, Raven, Condor, Kingfisher, Egret, Peregrine, Blue Heron, Osprey, Merlin, Heartland, Yosemite I, Sarlux, Trakya, and Promigas.

This financing was funded by the Osprey Trust, an entity that was created by Enron and that raised $2.4 billion from institutional investors, including several mutual funds, through privately placed Osprey notes. Osprey's debt was secured by the assets transferred to Whitewing by Enron. Those assets were valued at $4.7 billion by Enron when transferred. Enron pledged 50 million shares of its own common stock and agreed to issue additional shares, if the assets securing the Osprey debt proved to be inadequate. Through this arrangement, Enron was able to keep nearly $4.2 billion in debt off its balance sheet in the year 2000 and was able to claim $418 million as cash from operations. The assets transferred to Whitewing, however, declined in value in 2001 by almost 60 percent, to less than $2 billion. The market and the economy were truly working against Enron. Payment triggers in this structure could require Enron to pay as much as $2.4 billion in the event of a decline in its credit rating and share price.

Influence Fails

As Enron approached bankruptcy, its officials reached out to the federal government for help. The government had rescued Chrysler and Lockheed when they appeared to be failing in past decades; both of those companies survived. In 1998, the New York Federal Reserve Bank pressured several large financial institutions to arrange the rescue of Long Term Capital Management, a large hedge fund, because of concern that its failure could undermine the economy, which was then under stress from foreign sovereign defaults in the Far East and Russia. Enron also had other grounds for hope that needed aid from the government would be forthcoming. The economy was under stress and approaching recession, and the stock market was in free fall. The September 11 terrorist attacks had punched holes in large segments of the economy, including the airlines, which were supplied with the necessary government support. This suggested a precedent for Enron, particularly since the failure of a company as large as Enron, with its high profile, raised concerns that a market panic could occur.

Several Enron officials were close to the Bush administration. Kenneth Lay was a personal friend of both the present and former President Bush. Lay had been offered a cabinet position in the senior Bush's administration and was cochairman of his unsuccessful reelection campaign in 1992. Lay had contributed heavily to George W. Bush's upset gubernatorial race in Texas and acted as an adviser during his transition into the White House. Their relationship was so close that, as the press later derisively reported, George W. Bush even nicknamed him "Kenny Boy." Enron's executives and its political action committee collectively made $700,000 in campaign contributions to George W. Bush and the Republican Party. Ken Lay and Enron wrote checks for a total of $200,000 for Bush's inaugural committee. Enron officers additionally contributed to the campaigns of 186 members of the House of Representatives and to seventy-one senators.

Thomas E. White, a retired brigadier general in the U.S. Army and executive assistant to the chairman of the Joint Chiefs of Staff, had been a senior Enron official before joining the Bush administration as secretary of the army. To meet ethics concerns, he sold his Enron stock, worth over $25 million, and an equal amount of options after assuming his army post, a great investment decision. There were also other relationships between Enron and the Bush administration. Lawrence Lindsey, the president's economic adviser, had been an Enron consultant and owned a significant amount of Enron stock, which he had been criticized for not selling before entering the White House. Karl Rove, the president's political adviser, had held over $100,000 in Enron stock, which he did sell after being criticized for owning stock in large companies that might seek favorable treatment from the White House. That turned out to be a fortuitous sale. Another administration official, I. Lewis Libby, Vice President Richard Cheney's chief of staff, also owned Enron stock.

On the negative side, Enron had been the subject of many newspaper articles after it was disclosed that the company had been given a say in the selection of members for Cheney's energy task force. That disclosure caused political controversy and resulted in a fight between the task force and the General Accounting Office, the congressional investigating arm, which wanted access to the task force's records in order to assess conflicts of interest. A lawsuit seeking access to those records resulted in a court order requiring some disclosures, and the issue went all the way to the Supreme Court, which sent the matter back to the lower court for further consideration.

Despite its close ties to the Bush administration, or perhaps because of them, Enron's efforts to obtain a governmental rescue were not successful. Federal Reserve chairman Alan Greenspan, Secretary of the Treasury Paul O'Neill, and Secretary of Commerce Don Evans all turned down Enron's pleas for aid. A call on Enron's behalf from Robert Rubin, a Citigroup executive and former Secretary of the Treasury in the Clinton administration, was of no avail, even though Citigroup had an immediate interest in Enron's continued viability because it had advanced hundreds of millions of dollars to the company. Even Secretary of the Army White proved to be a liability as his ties to Enron were questioned. He resigned sometime afterward, his credibility undermined by his Enron service (it was claimed in the press that the division he headed at Enron had inflated its earnings by millions of dollars) and quarrels with Secretary of Defense Donald Rumsfeld over a new weapons system.

Death Throes

Enron was able to obtain another $1 billion in cash from the banks, but more was needed. The company had consumed some $2 billion in cash in a week and was facing bigger problems as its credit ratings were lowered. Enron had several structured finance arrangements with triggers requiring payments if its credit ratings fell below investment grade. Some triggers required cash payment, while others required the additional issuance of Enron stock as collateral. These triggers had been kicking in since May as Enron's assets depreciated in value and the price of its stock dropped. One transaction called Rawhide had already been triggered by a credit rating reduction just above investment grade, requiring Enron to pay out $690 million.

On November 19, 2001, Enron made new announcements concerning its third quarter's results that showed a further decline in the company's financial position. Enron executives met that day with the company's lead banks and informed them that, in addition to the $12.9 billion of debt on its balance sheet, Enron had further off-balance sheet and other liabilities totaling $25 billion. After that announcement, the banks were unwilling to provide more funds. Ken Lay caused more controversy when it was disclosed that he would receive $60 million in severance pay upon consummation of the merger with Dynegy. The ensuing criticism led Lay to renounce that package. The merger with Dynegy, in any event, fell apart under Enron's continuing disclosures about its accounting misstatements. Enron sued Dynegy for backing out and was able to recover $88 million in settlement, but even that pittance came after Enron's bankruptcy. Dynegy would have its own massive accounting problems that would require it to restate its earnings downward for 2000 and 2001. Nevertheless, Charles Watson was allowed to keep the $10 million he was paid in those years and was awarded another $22 million in severance pay by an arbitrator.

The rating agencies cut Enron's rating to below investment grade after the Dynegy merger fell through. This triggered debt acceleration provisions in Enron's structured finance totaling almost $4 billion. Enron was forced to shut down its trading operations because counterparties would not do business with a less than investment grade (junk bond) dealer. That spelled the end of Enron. Its death throes were ugly. On November 28, 2001, Enron stock was trading for sixty-one cents a share, down from its high of $90. Enron set a new volume record for a single stock that day when 181.8 million of its shares traded.

Bankruptcy

Enron filed for bankruptcy on December 2, 2001, at the time the largest bankruptcy in American history. The prior record had been held by Texaco, which had been required to seek bankruptcy protection after being hit with a judgment of $9.1 billion for improperly breaking up a merger deal between Getty Oil and Pennzoil. The matter was later settled for $3 billion, and Texaco emerged from bankruptcy. Enron's stock was delisted from the NYSE after its bankruptcy. The outstanding Enron debt wiped out the equity of its shareholders that had been reported as $11 billion as 2001 began. Over 5,500 Enron employees were laid off upon the filing of the bankruptcy petition. They each received $13,500 in severance pay, but Enron offered $50 million to several of its executives as an inducement for them to stay on for ninety days to assist in the bankruptcy reorganization process. This led to howls of outrage in the press and from employees. The bankruptcy court did challenge several large payments to executives, in particular payments to Kenneth Lay, Jeffrey Skilling, and Andrew Fastow. The bankruptcy court, nevertheless, approved retention bonuses and severance payments to other Enron executives thought necessary to assist in the reorganization. Those amounts were $38.2 million in 2002, $29 million in 2003, and $36.2 million for 2004.

Neal Batson, the bankruptcy examiner appointed by the bankruptcy court, concluded that Enron owed its creditors more than $67 billion in debt. JPMorgan Chase and Citigroup asserted claims as creditors of more than $4 billion. Nobody expected that they would receive those amounts from the bankruptcy court because Enron simply lacked assets to pay its creditors. The bankruptcy examiner also took an aggressive approach in seeking to void or subordinate the banks' claims as punishment for their role in arranging exotic structured financing that took debt off Enron's balance sheets and disguised its true financial condition from investors and other creditors.

Enron's bankruptcy became one of the most expensive ever. By the middle of 2003, lawyers and accountants had incurred fees of $400 million to pursue creditor claims. This was more than twice the amount assessed in any previous bankruptcy proceeding. Batson and his law firm were paid $90 million for his reports on the Enron estate, which totaled over 4,500 pages and contained over 14,000 footnotes. Enron's accounting and other legal costs were expected to exceed $1 billion. Kroll Zolfo Cooper, a bankruptcy specialist firm involved in the proceeding, was seeking $63 million in fees plus a $25 million success fee. Headed by Stephen Cooper, that firm handled much of the restructuring of Enron in the bankruptcy proceeding.

Enron began gathering its assets for sale and reorganization. Among other things, the company sought refunds for tax payments made on falsified earnings. The bankruptcy examiner challenged numerous "independent" Enron SPE structures in order to have their remaining assets moved into the Enron estate for the benefit of its creditors. Recovery was limited by the fact that many Enron assets had sharply depreciated in value. For example, Enron had acquired MG PLC, a large international metals marketing firm, for $2 billion in 2000. Less than two years later, the operation was sold in bankruptcy for $145 million. UBS Warburg bought Enron's trading operation, then staffed by 650 traders, by agreeing to pay a portion of that operation's future profits to the Enron estate. That acquisition was not a success: most of the traders left despite large bonuses, and the Houston trading operation was shut down and moved to Stamford, Connecticut.

The Enron bankruptcy court was able to obtain some funds from asset sales for creditors, including $3 billion from the settlement of energy contracts and $1 billion from the sale of Enron's office buildings. Enron's pipelines in North America were sold to CCE Holdings, which was owned by Southern Union Co. and General Electric. A fight broke out over the sale of what remained of Portland General Electric to the Texas Pacific Group for $2.3 billion. Several consumer groups and businesses were protesting the sale because of concerns that electricity rates might be increased. In total, the bankruptcy examiner garnered about $12 billion from asset sales, but unsecured Enron creditors were expected to receive less than twenty cents on the dollar for their debt. Creditors of some subsidiary units of Enron would receive as much as 22.5 cents on the dollar. Yet hope springs eternal. Enron stock was trading at nine cents a share in the over-the-counter market in January 2003, up from four cents at year-end 2002.

The Powers Report

A special investigative committee was formed by the Enron board of directors to examine the conflict of interest transactions engaged in by Andrew Fastow. The committee was composed of outside directors, a standard corporate governance practice normally used to deal with breaches of fiduciary duty and to head off government investigations. That investigation continued despite Enron's bankruptcy. The chair of the committee was William Powers Jr., dean of the University of Texas law school. The actual investigation was conducted by William McLucas, a partner in the Washington, DC, law firm of Wilmer Cutler & Pickering. He was a former director of the Division of Enforcement at the SEC, where he had prosecuted Ivan Boesky and Michael Milken, two chieftans in the insider trading scandals of the 1980s.

The "Powers" report, which was actually prepared by McLucas, was submitted to the Enron board of directors on February 1, 2002, and made public. It is unclear why this investigation and report were made, especially considering the great expense it involved: more than $4 million in fees was charged for its production. The report also undermined any chance for reorganizing Enron, serving only to bounce the rubble and destroy any ongoing concern value that might have been left in Enron and its trading operations. The report stirred up more litigation against Enron and added to the increasingly hysterical climate in the media about the company.

The Powers report found that Enron's outside accounting firm, Arthur Andersen, had provided extensive advice in the accounting treatment and structuring of these transactions. "Enron's records show that Andersen billed Enron

$5.7 million for advice in connection with the LJM and Chewco transactions alone, above and beyond its regular audit fees."[24] Andersen later admitted it was wrong in concluding that LJM met the requirements for off-balance sheet treatment. It was a costly mistake for both Enron and Arthur Andersen.

Reviewing Fastow's role in LJM partnerships, the Powers report concluded that, despite approval by the Enron board, this arrangement was "fundamentally flawed" and should not have been allowed.[25] Controls over the relationship with Fastow were found to be inadequate. Further, Enron frequently had bought back assets that it sold to LJM and, in some instances, agreed to protect the LJM partnerships from loss, thereby negating a "true sale."

A key finding in the Powers report was that the "technical failure" to meet the 3 percent independent investor requirement for Chewco led to Enron's demise.[26] The Powers report could not determine why Enron failed to meet the independent investor requirements for the SPE. Enron employees acting in Enron's interest had "every incentive" to ensure that Chewco complied with those rules: "We do not know whether this mistake resulted from bad judgment or carelessness on the part of Enron employees or Andersen, or whether it was caused by Kopper or others putting their own interests ahead of their obligations to Enron. The consequences, however, were enormous."[27]

The Powers report concluded that the improper use of SPEs allowed Enron to conceal very large losses from its merchant investments by claiming that those losses were hedged, but without disclosing that the hedges were with Enron's own stock. In addition, numerous Enron SPEs were funded with Enron stock or other securities, rather than by the required independent investors. As a result, these transactions were improperly accounted for and distorted Enron's reported earnings in an amount in excess of $1 billion for the one-year period before the company's demise. The SPEs were a principal source of Enron's earnings in 2000. The company claimed $650 million in earnings in the last two quarters of 2000; the Raptor transactions provided 80 percent of that amount.

The Powers report cited the Raptors and a transaction involving Rhythms Net Connections, a company that sought to deliver high-speed Internet access through digital technology. This was one of Enron's merchant investments that was initially spectacularly successful. The Rhythms Net Connections stock rose substantially in value after its initial public offering. Enron was worried that, if the stock declined, the company would have to reflect that decrease on its balance sheet under mark-to-market accounting. Enron sought to hedge against that eventuality by having an SPE sell put options to Enron on the Rhythms stock. That SPE was funded with Enron stock in exchange for a note. Again, Enron was essentially hedging itself. The Powers report concluded that these were really "accounting" hedges, rather than economic hedges, that were intended to circumvent mark-to-market accounting for Enron's merchant investments. As it turned out, the Rhythms stock declined in value and was worthless by 2001, after which the company went out of business. This evidenced that a hedge was prudent, but the hedge employed was faulty. In order for the hedge to work, Enron stock needed to be going up while the Rhythms stock was going down. That would not happen during an overall market decline, as was the case in 2000. Enron stock was itself plummeting in value during that period.

The Powers report found that Enron was recording as income increases in value of its own stock held by JEDI, a practice not permitted by accounting rules. Further, when the Raptors were unable to meet their hedge obligations when Enron's stock dropped in value, Enron simply provided further funding in the form of $800 million in Enron stock. This allowed Enron to avoid reporting a large loss in the first quarter of 2001, but even that artifice failed as the company's stock price continued its plunge, leading to Enron's announcement of the $544 million charge to earnings on October 16, 2001.

The Powers report was especially damning of the profits made by Andrew Fastow and other Enron employees for their "passive and largely risk-free roles in these transactions."[28] In one two-month period, Fastow received $4.5 million on an investment of $25,000. Two other Enron employees each received $1 million in that transaction on an investment of $5,800. The Powers report found that several other executives, including Skilling and Lay, had not been sufficiently aggressive in supervising these transactions. The Enron board of directors was faulted for failing to supervise the LJM transactions when the board members knew of the conflicts of interest presented by Fastow's involvement. With respect to the Raptor and Rhythms transactions approved by the board, the Powers report concluded, "It appears that many of its members did not understand those transactions—the economic rationale, the consequences, and the risks."[29] Although a federal judge later ruled that the board had no liability to shareholders, several Enron outside directors agreed to pay $13 million of their own funds to settle shareholder claims. The $13 million paid by the directors was 10 percent of the profits made by those directors from their sales of Enron stock. The class action lawyer handling the case, William Lerach, had insisted on pursuing the claims despite the court's ruling. The federal appellate court overseeing the Houston district courts had by that time made clear that it would be carefully reviewing their decisions to assure maximum reach of all statutes that could apply to corporations involved in the Enron affair. Director and officer insurance paid an additional amount of $155 million and another $32 million in insurance proceeds went to creditors.

Media Circus

The Powers report fed right into the press frenzy over Enron's bankruptcy, creating a media event of unprecedented proportions in the world of business. Newspapers, magazines, and television news shows focused massive coverage on the scandal. Tens of thousands of articles were written about the company's demise and the excesses of its executives. Television networks devoted significant amounts of their news coverage to the event. Enron memorabilia, such as coffee mugs and stock certificates with Enron logos, became popular items for auction on eBay. The large Enron logo that graced its new offices in Houston sold at auction for $44,000. The Enron logo, designed for Enron's Super Bowl commercial, was in the form of a tilted E, but after the scandal broke, it was called the "crooked E."

Enron's headquarters became a tourist attraction. Jesse Jackson showed up in Houston to lead a protest seeking "social justice" for Enron employees. Congressman Richard Gephardt, then a presidential candidate, traveled to Houston to lead a protest staged by Enron employees. *Playboy* magazine jumped on the bandwagon with a "Girls of Enron" issue that featured naked former employees. CBS created a made-for-TV movie about Enron that suggested that the company's female employees were mostly ex-strippers, a claim that infuriated many employees. Other salacious accounts revealed that Louis Pai, a former senior Enron executive, was obsessed with strippers and even married one. Enron traders were said to be foulmouthed gamblers who cursed while trading and bet with each other on the trading floor. A group of Enron traders was rumored to have spent $10,000 in a single night at Treasures, a popular Houston strip club. *Newsweek* magazine claimed that the Enron corporate culture was "suffused" with sex. The *Wall Street Journal,* in a front-page article, breathlessly accused Enron executives of frequenting strip clubs and driving expensive cars and even reported with horror that one employee paid a Manhattan price of $500 a month for a parking spot (about $25 per business day). Jeffrey Skilling was faulted for marrying Enron's corporate secretary, even though he obtained board approval for his pursuit of that relationship.

The *Financial Times* of London used the Enron debacle to expand its anti-America coverage. That newspaper gleefully pointed out that making money had long been the subject of books portraying those who sought wealth as "bad" and that "businesspeople are invariably depicted as venal, corrupt, shifty, cold, emotionally stunted, superficial and unimaginative."[30] The low point was reached with a supercilious article in that newspaper by British historian Niall Ferguson, who suggested that Enron and other accounting scandals in the United States supported Karl Marx's claim that capitalism was, indeed, victimizing society.

Sadness and mystery were added to the scandal after former Enron vice chairman J. Clifford Baxter committed suicide on January 25, 2002. He had become Enron's vice chairman and chief strategy officer in 2000, after having served in other Enron affiliates since 1995. Baxter left Enron in May 2001, suffering from depression, but he seemed to be in control until the company's failure apparently pushed him over the edge. Jeffrey Skilling had noted Baxter's despondency when a neighbor supposedly compared Baxter to a "child molester" because he had worked at Enron. Baxter's suicide touched off a wave of supposition in the press on the reason for his suicide unequaled since White House counsel Vincent Foster's suicide during the Clinton administration. In the end, investigations into the reasons for Baxter's suicide revealed little, although some people still thought Baxter had taken this means to cover up more scandal at Enron. That was a common concern in regard to companies whose senior officials committed suicide, and the SEC had made it a practice to examine the books of such companies after the spectacular suicide of Eli Black, the president of the United Fruit Co. (now Chiquita Brands International) in 1974. He jumped from the forty-fourth floor of the Pan Am building in New York after being mistakenly advised that a questionable payment made by the company abroad was a bribe prohibited by United States law.

Congressional Hearings

Congress jumped into the Enron media circus by holding almost thirty Enron-related hearings within three months of that company's bankruptcy. Those hearings in many ways resembled a McCarthy-era witch hunt against suspected communists. Enron executives were likened to the terrorists who struck America on September 11, 2001. Andrew Fastow and Kenneth Lay were required to appear before television cameras to assert their Fifth Amendment rights when a letter to that effect would have done just as well. David Duncan, Enron's Arthur Andersen engagement partner, who shredded Enron documents in order to keep them out of the hands of government investigators, submitted to four hours of questioning by congressional staffers, but his attorney instructed him to take the Fifth Amendment in the televised hearings. He was then hit with a number of questions on camera that smacked of the "when did you stop beating your wife?" technique. Those loaded questions were presented as fact since the witness would no longer respond. The same tactics were employed against Fastow, even though the committee knew he was taking the Fifth. Great theater, but such histrionics had been little seen since Joseph McCarthy left the Senate.

Witnesses who did appear to testify were berated, badgered, mocked, and cut off if their answers were not what the congressional examiner wanted to hear. One member of Congress insisted on only yes or no answers to complicated, convoluted questions that assumed a guilty answer. Another member of Congress took the opportunity to disparage Jeffrey Skilling's testimony even before Skilling was called to testify. When he did appear, Skilling was assigned to a chair that would make him look smaller to the cameras, while other witnesses at the table, including his chief accuser, Sherron Watkins, were given cushions to sit on in order to make them appear more imposing.

Despite the smaller chair, Skilling held his own. He contended that Enron was in good shape when he left and that the market downturn created the storm that touched off what amounted to a run on a bank during a liquidity crisis. Skilling asserted that this run on the Enron bank was caused by the triggers in Enron credit and SPE structures making obligations payable as the result of a credit downgrade or drop in stock price. In one notable exchange during the Senate committee's pillorying of Skilling, Senator Barbara Boxer of California mocked him for having a Harvard MBA but not being able to explain when equity could be used for off-balance sheet transactions that generated income. Boxer asserted that such treatment was always improper, but Skilling responded that stock options paid as executive compensation, which were then under attack in the press for abuses at Enron, would fit that category. Skilling also noted that Boxer had herself advocated that treatment in sponsoring legislation prohibiting the expensing of stock option compensation. Interestingly, most newspapers reported only Boxer's browbeating of Skilling about his MBA and not her own complicity in his compensation arrangements or the repartee with him in which she came off looking quite foolish.

Skilling testified before SEC investigators for two days under oath, but refused to testify before the Enron bankruptcy examiner, as it became clear that he was being targeted for indictment. Skilling noted in his testimony before Congress that he continued to hold Enron shares after he left the company. Indeed, he had terminated a previous sale plan in June 2001 so that he could hold more Enron shares. Skilling generally denied knowledge of the accounting issues involving the SPEs and denied knowledge of Fastow's profiting from the partnerships. Congressional investigators were frustrated that Skilling did not sign the approval sheets for several of the deals even though there was a line left for his signature.

3. The Enron Scandal

Enron Finance

The SPEs

Neal Batson, the Enron bankruptcy examiner, filed extensive reports on the transactions that were the subject of the Powers report, as well as several other special purpose entities (SPEs). He deconstructed those transactions to compare their accounting treatment with their actual economic substance. It turned out that the two often varied. Batson found, for example, that Enron's sale of its Bammel gas storage facility to an SPE resulted in improper claims of $232 million in revenue, cash flow from operating activities of the same amount, and the omission of that figure from its reported debt. The Bammel transactions involved the sale by Enron of stored gas to an SPE that borrowed funds from financial institutions for the purchase price. A separate marketing agreement required Enron to buy the gas held by the SPE in amounts sufficient to service the SPE's debt. Enron assured the lenders that they would be protected against loss, which negated the SPE's "true sale" status.

Transactions like the Bammel sale were used by Enron to monetize declining assets by selling them to an SPE at an inflated price, but Enron had other tricks to employ. Enron used its Bammel gas storage as a part of its Project Condor, a tax scheme that utilized a "contribution-leaseback" to step up the basis on certain assets. This was accomplished by a loan of $800 million in Enron stock to Condor, an SPE. Condor then purchased the Enron assets, including the Bammel facility, but the transaction had no economic purpose beyond gaining tax benefits. Thereafter, through Project Triple Lutz, Enron sold the Bammel facility and its related pipeline business to the AEP Energy Services Gas Holding Company, an unrelated third party for $728.7 million.

Enron was utilizing something called "share trusts," which involved the issuance by Enron of its own convertible preferred stock to an SPE. The preferred shares were then sold by the SPE and the proceeds were used to satisfy the debt obligations of various Enron affiliates, thereby moving that debt off Enron's consolidated balance sheet. If the preferred stock was inadequate to meet those obligations, Enron was obligated to issue more stock to make up for the shortfall.

"Minority interest financings" were used by Enron as another means to disguise debt. These transactions involved the creation of a majority-owned Enron subsidiary, which purchased poorly performing Enron assets. The minority interest in the subsidiary was ostensibly sold for cash to a financial institution. Enron's majority interest required the subsidiary to be consolidated on Enron's financial statements, but the proceeds from the financial institution's "purchase" of the minority interest were shown as a "minority interest" on the balance sheet between debt and equity. Critically, such minority interests were viewed to be equity, rather than debt by the rating agencies. Enron used this technique to convert $1.74 billion in debt to minority interests on its balance sheet by year-end 2000. The flaw in this structure, as in other Enron structured financing, was that the financial institutions participating in these structures were guaranteed against loss by Enron, which made the transactions more of a loan than an equity investment.

The five principal minority interest structures used by Enron were called Rawhide, Nighthawk, Choctaw, Nahanni, and Zephyrus. This technique worked as follows:

> To execute the structure, the Insiders caused the creation of a subsidiary (Entity A), the majority of which Enron owned. (Therefore, Entity A was consolidated with Enron for financial purposes.) A new and allegedly independent entity (Entity B) purchased the "minority interest" in Entity A. Entities A and B were both SPEs. . . . Enron purchased its majority interest in Entity A by contributing various assets. In the meantime, Entity B took out a bank loan. Entity B then purchased its minority interest by contributing the proceeds of the loan, plus 3% equity, to Entity A. Finally Entity A loaned Enron the total amount of Entity B's contribution. At the end of the transaction, it appeared that Enron had received funds directly from an affiliate that was already consolidated with Enron for financial accounting purposes (as opposed to from the bank that loaned Entity B the money). Therefore, Enron did not have to book any debt for the transaction, and Enron's debt ratios were not affected by the loans. Additionally, Enron booked the funds as operating income.[1]

Debt and Equity

In still another method used to remove debt from its balance sheet, Enron engaged in what were called "equity forward contracts" with Lehman Brothers and Credit Suisse First Boston. Those transactions, which were valued at $304 million, involved the sale of Enron equity securities to those firms, but Enron agreed to repurchase those securities at a premium over their purchase price, a premium that could be likened to interest. In some ways, these transactions resembled a government securities repurchase (repo) transaction. A repo is, in effect, a loan secured by government securities. The Enron equity forward contracts served similar purposes, but the proceeds received by Enron from those financial institutions were not carried as debt on Enron's balance sheet.

Other Enron structured financing transactions involved sales of emission credits, "dark" optical fiber, coal leases, and other assets, and carried such names as Cerberus, Nikita, Backbone, and SO_2. These transactions generated some $1.4 billion in cash for Enron. They all followed a similar pattern in which Enron sold an asset to an SPE for cash that was obtained from a purported "equity contribution" from a financial institution that was actually a loan. The bankruptcy examiner found that, unlike a typical asset sale to an SPE that would properly remove those assets and related debt off the company's books, Enron agreed to repay the debt incurred by the SPE, continued to control the assets, and was entitled to receive any increase in the value of the assets. In some instances, this was done through a total return swap, in which Enron made payments equal to the payments due on the debt incurred by the SPE while maintaining the right to the proceeds from the ultimate disposition of the assets, after payment of the debt obligation. In many of these transactions, the assets purportedly being sold were not producing income sufficient to service the SPE's debt, leading the bankruptcy examiner to reclassify them as Enron debt. This meant that Enron's credit was being used to support the obligations, but that fact was not disclosed to investors through Enron's balance sheet or to the ratings agencies.

The Cerberus transaction involved the monetization of 11.5 million shares of Enron Oil & Gas Co. (EOG) stock that was trading at $45.25 per share on the day the Cerberus transaction was closed. At that price, the EOG shares were worth $520 million. Patterned after other Enron transactions, this deal involved the transfer of the EOG shares to an SPE called Aeneas LLC, which sold a 99.99 percent ownership interest in an Enron subsidiary called Psyche LLC, which sold that interest to the Heracles Trust for $517.5 million, which was borrowed from the Royal Bank of Canada (RBC). Enron then entered into a total return swap that retained any increase in value should the stock price rise. Enron issued a put option that required it to repurchase the EOG shares in the event of a decline to the extent necessary to repay RBC. The put option was secured by a demand note from Enron. Enron retained control over the EOG shares in order to meet certain other commitments.

The Cerberus transaction was restructured two months later to substitute a Dutch bank, the Cooperatieve Centrale Raffeisen-Boerenleenbank B.A. (Rabobank), for RBC. This was accomplished by a total return swap between those two banks, which was the equivalent of a loan assignment. In addition, the new bank entered into an equity-linked swap with Enron that set a $45 per share price for the EOG stock. The Cerberus transaction allowed Enron to claim a $31 million gain in 2000 and $517 million as cash flow from operating activities on its accounting statements. Rabobank tried to avoid its obligations to RBC under this arrangement after Enron's bankruptcy, but a settlement was reached with the RBC on the matter.

Nikita, Backbone, and Others

The Nikita transaction was entered into in September 2001, as Enron was struggling with a severe decline in the value of its assets. This transaction was designed to monetize various classes of limited partnership interests owned by Enron in EOTT Energy Partners LP, a publicly owned master limited partnership traded on the New York Stock Exchange (NYSE). An Enron entity, Nikita LLC, was the sponsor of this transaction. It transferred the EOTT interests to an SPE called Timber I LLC, which sold an interest in itself to the Besson Trust, a Delaware business trust, for $80 million. Of that amount, $71.9 million was borrowed from Barclays Bank and the balance from Credit Suisse First Boston under an arrangement requiring repayment of that amount plus 15 percent interest. The Barclays loan was supported by a total return swap with Enron. Once again, Enron claimed a gain from the transaction on its financial statements, this time in the amount of $10 million.

The Backbone transaction involved the purported sale of the right to use various strands of dark optical fiber owned by Enron Broadband Services Inc. (EBS). This asset was transferred to an SPE created by LJM2 and then later to another Enron SPE. Once again, control and the economic interest in the asset was retained by Enron through total return swaps and other arrangements. EBS initially received $100 million for the dark fiber involved in this transaction: $30 million in cash and the remainder in the form of a promissory note. The transaction was, thereafter, restructured to pay off the note through financing provided by ABN Amro Bank NV and Fleet National Bank. Later, EBS engaged in a cross-purchase sale with Qwest Communications in which EBS sold the Backbone dark fiber to Qwest and bought lit fiber in return. In this transaction Qwest gave EBS a note for $47.4 million, which was backed by a letter of credit from the Bank of America, all of which provided Enron with favorable accounting treatment for the proceeds.

The SO_2 transaction involved the purported securitization of sulfur dioxide emission credits to an SPE for $93.4 million in September and October 2001. The SPE, Colonnade Ltd., was a Guernsey company that apparently was financed by Barclays Bank. Enron entered into options and swaps that gave Enron substantial control over the emission credits and left it with the economic risks and benefits of those credits, reducing the transaction to little more than a secured loan. Interest payments were effected through the premiums paid for call options at a 0.65 percent rate over LIBOR, the London Interbank Offered Rate. In another arrangement, the Destec transaction, Enron monetized its interest in a coal lease by selling that asset to a trust for $110 million. Enron agreed to protect the trust against market risk through a series of swaps. A separate "Cash 6" transaction involved an attempt by Enron to monetize the value of an in-the-money swap it held with a nuclear facility in the United Kingdom. The cash flow from that swap was sold to an SPE created by Enron. The transaction was financed by Barclays Bank, but the bank was protected from market risk by a series of swaps with Enron.

The list of complex Enron structured finance transactions is simply too long to examine in any depth. They included Nixon (financed by Citigroup, NatWest, Barclays, and Toronto Dominion), Alchemy and Discovery transactions with the Imperial Bank of Canada, and a CLO Trust with Bear Stearns. The bankruptcy examiner found that Credit Suisse First Boston aided Fastow in profiting improperly in a transaction dubbed SAILS through the contribution of funds to an SPE (LJM) that were then paid out to Fastow.

Blockbuster

An example of Enron's abuse of mark-to-market accounting was the value assessed for Enron's video on demand deal with Blockbuster. Over $100 million in mark-to-market value was reported on Enron's financial statements even though Enron did not have the technology to deliver the movies and even though Blockbuster did not have the rights to the movies that were to be delivered. After the deal with Blockbuster fell through, Enron did not write down the project on its financial statements. To the contrary, it used that event to increase its valuation of its broadband delivery system. That action was taken on the basis of discussions with content providers on the speculative possibility of future business. Enron valued its broadband business on a mark-to-market basis at $115 million after the Blockbuster deal fell through, but within a year Enron wrote the business off as worthless.

In another transaction, Enron entered into a joint venture through an SPE (L.E. Heston LLC) with Eli Lilly Co., pursuant to which Enron was to manage and reduce Lilly's energy costs. Enron valued this transaction on its financial statements at $1.3 billion over a fifteen-year period. That value was based on the estimated payments that Eli Lilly would make to Enron for the energy cost savings that would be achieved by Enron. Enron computed that figure by obtaining an estimate of the expected cash flows on a discounted basis from this joint venture. On the basis of that estimate, Enron concluded that $38 million should immediately be recognized as revenue on its financial statements even though there had been no actual cash flows under the energy savings contract. Compounding this accrual accounting chutzpah was the fact that Enron paid Eli Lilly $50 million in advance in order to obtain the contract. Enron was not the only company engaging in such practices. Cisco Systems, a manufacturer of Internet switching equipment, was offering customers cash payments in order to induce inventory purchases. That cash and the inventory purchases were to be repaid over time by the customer with interest, but Cisco booked the transaction as revenue to itself immediately.

Business Model and Disclosure

According to Batson, the bankruptcy examiner, "Enron so engineered its reported financial position and results of operations that its financial statements bore little resemblance to its actual financial condition or performance."[2] The motivation for these transactions was to support the price of Enron's stock and to maintain its credit ratings. Enron was acutely aware of the importance of its credit ratings. In its 1999 annual report, Enron management stated that the company's "continued investment grade status is critical to the success of its wholesale business as well as its ability to maintain adequate liquidity."[3] Enron's wholesale business was the core of its operations. An investment grade rating was needed not only to keep down credit costs but also because various trigger provisions for support of the SPEs would be activated in the event of a ratings downgrade. Those triggers required issuing more Enron stock, increasing the collateral supporting structured deals, or causing a forced repurchase by Enron of various assets.

Enron's accounting machinations were often motivated by a desire to offset the effects of the company's mark-to-market accounting. By using the mark-to-market method, Enron wanted to trumpet its trading profits, but did not want to disclose its losses, so it moved declining assets off the balance sheet. As the Enron bankruptcy examiner later found, Enron also faced another quandary. It wanted a high price/earnings ratio for its stock but also needed an investment grade credit rating. Those goals conflicted with Enron's need for financing. If Enron issued more stock, its stock price would go down, reducing its P/E ratio. If Enron obtained loans instead, its credit rating would be affected. In the face of those concerns, Enron decided to have it both ways. The SPE structures took debt off the balance sheet and provided Enron with needed funds.

Had the SPE transactions been carried as debt on the Enron balance sheet, the company would have appeared to investors, analysts, and rating agencies as a much more highly leveraged company, posing risks if cash flows were unable to service the debt. That might have shut down Enron earlier and might have reduced the spike in its stock price that occurred in 2000. However, investors were not paying much attention to traditional investment ratios at that time, and Enron did make lengthy disclosures listing the thousands of SPEs it was employing. It even made disclosures concerning Andrew Fastow's involvement with the Enron SPEs. Although those disclosures were so convoluted as to be unintelligible, no one cared until Enron became a media event.

The company's proxy reports disclosed that Fastow was the managing member of LJM1 and LJM2. The Powers report concluded that those disclosures were inadequate because they did not include the amount of Fastow's compensation. The report also said that the Enron financial disclosures were "obtuse, did not communicate the essence of the transactions completely or clearly, and failed to convey the substance of what was going on between Enron and the partnerships."[4] Although the SEC has for years sought to require companies to state their prospectuses in "plain English," the following portion of the Enron disclosures concerning Fastow's involvement suggests that the SEC's goal was not attained:

In 2000 and 1999, Enron entered into transactions with limited partnerships (the Related Party) whose general partner's managing member is a senior officer of Enron. The limited partners of the Related Party are unrelated to Enron. Management believes that the terms of the transactions with the Related Party were reasonable compared to those that could have been negotiated with unrelated third parties.

In 2000, Enron entered into transactions with the Related Party to hedge certain merchant investments and other assets. As part of the transactions, Enron (i) contributed to newly-formed entities (the Entities) assets valued at approximately $1.2 billion, including $150 million in Enron notes payable, 3.7 million restricted shares of outstanding Enron common stock and the right to receive up to 18.0 million shares of outstanding Enron common stock in March 2003 (subject to certain conditions) and (ii) transferred to the Entities assets valued at approximately $309 million, including a $50 million note payable and an investment in an entity that indirectly holds warrants convertible into common stock of an Enron equity method investee. In return, Enron received economic interests in the Entities, $309 million in notes receivable, of which $259 million is recorded at Enron's carryover basis of zero, and a special distribution from the Entities in the form of $1.2 billion in notes receivable, subject to changes in the principal for amounts payable by Enron in connection with the execution of additional derivative instruments. Cash in these Entities of $172.6 million is invested in Enron demand notes. In addition, Enron paid $123 million to purchase share-settled options from the Entities on 21.7 million shares of Enron common stock. The Entities paid Enron $10.7 million to terminate the share-settled options on 14.6 million shares of Enron common stock outstanding. In late 2000, Enron entered into share-settled collar arrangements with the Entities on 15.4 million shares of Enron common stock. Such arrangements will be accounted for as equity transactions when settled.[5]

This was gobbledygook, but did flag the issue for those interested. Even the Powers report, a prosecutorial document written by a prosecutor, rejected newspaper reports that Enron's demise was due to "secret" partnerships, noting that the transactions with the LJM entities and the Raptors were all disclosed in Enron's public filings. Enron was found to have made "substantial disclosures" regarding these transactions, including their magnitude. "Any reader of these disclosures should have recognized that these arrangements were complex, the dollar amounts involved were substantial, and the transactions were significant for evaluating the Company's financial performance."[6]

Executive Bonuses and Stock Sales

Enron executives received $1.4 billion as compensation in 2000, mostly through options. Enron paid $745 million in compensation and stock awards to executives in 2001, the year of its bankruptcy. Ken Lay sold $144 million of Enron stock in the months preceding the bankruptcy. He repaid $94 million in loans from Enron with Enron stock by pulling down $4 million on his Enron line of credit every two weeks and then immediately repaying it with Enron stock that he obtained from his option grants. Jeff Skilling sold $76 million in stock and repaid $2 million in loans from Enron with Enron stock. The Enron bankruptcy examiner challenged the repayment of loans by Lay and Skilling with Enron stock, concluding that the stock was inflated in value by the accounting machinations in the SPEs. Recovery was also being sought by the bankruptcy examiner of $53 million in accelerated advances of deferred compensation to Enron executives just before its collapse. As a result of that conduct, Congress included a provision in a tax bill in October 2004 that imposed large penalties for executives who withdraw money from deferred compensation plans before normal retirement dates.

Andrew Fastow sold $30 million of Enron stock and made $45 million from his LJM partnership interests, as well as other compensation. Lou Pai, a senior executive who left Enron before the scandal, sold $270 million worth of Enron stock received as compensation for his services. Pai put the money to good use, buying a 77,000-acre ranch in Colorado that included its own mountain. Two of the businesses Pai ran resulted in staggering losses to Enron. Pai was charged in a class action law suit with aiding other Enron officers in running a Ponzi scheme with Enron by inflating profits and inducing a continual stream of new investors as the stock price rose from those manipulations. This allowed Pai, it was claimed, to accumulate large holdings in Enron stock as bonuses and to sell that stock at inflated prices. Before coming to Enron, Pai had been an economist at the SEC.

Pai had been the president of Enron Energy Services (EES) from 1997 until 2000, when he became chief executive officer of Enron Accelerator. While at EES, Pai was alleged to have approved long-term contracts for energy services that were then immediately booked as revenue even though the amounts to be received under the contracts were uncertain and no funds had been received. To meet future earnings expectations, EES was alleged to have arbitrarily adjusted the value of those contracts upward, again without any reasonable basis. A class action complaint against Pai and others at Enron further charged that the counterparties in those energy services contracts (which included such prominent entities as J.C. Penny, IBM, Quaker Oats, Starwood Properties, Chase Manhattan Bank, Eli Lilly, and the Archdiocese of Chicago) had been promised unrealistic energy savings in order to induce their participation. "Moreover, as is typical in a Ponzi scheme, the monster created required increasing funds to sustain it. EES had to attract more and more clients by more and more such fraudulent deals to keep up its artificially inflated financial reports and to make the business appear successful so that investors would continue to believe the contracts were making money and pour their money into Enron stock."[7]

Employee Losses

The Section 401(k) retirement accounts of employees at the Enron Corp. were a centerpiece of the scandal because they were concentrated in the company's own stock, which became worthless when Enron declared bankruptcy. These retirement accounts were fairly new to the financial system. The first Section 401(k) plan was offered in 1981 by the Johnson Company. By 1998, 27 percent of privately employed Americans had 401(k) accounts. Another 15 percent had 401(k) accounts through company-sponsored pension plans. The average 401(k) retirement account held just over $37,000 in 1996. That amount increased to $55,500 in 1999, but then dropped to just over $49,000 in 2001 as the stock market declined. Nevertheless, more than 50 million Americans owned 401(k) plans holding $1.7 trillion in assets as the new century began.

The number of "defined benefit" accounts at American businesses dropped by 60 percent between 1979 and 1999. These are employer-sponsored plans that seek to assure a defined amount of retirement benefits based on the employee's salary and years of service. In contrast, the Section 401(k) plan is funded by the employer's and employee's tax-advantaged contributions that will return retirement benefits based on the success of the investment of those contributions. In 1999, there were 56,000 defined benefit plans, down from 139,000 in 1979. The number of people in Section 401(k) and other defined contribution plans more than doubled between 1980 and 2000. Employees in the new century were adding more to their retirement plans sponsored by their employers than were the companies themselves. This raised concern that Section 401(k) plans, which had been intended only as supplements to employer plans, were being used by employers to reduce their contributions to employee pensions and were undermining the savings system.

Congress sought to increase retirement savings with the Economic Growth and Tax Relief Reconciliation Act of 2001 (EGTRRA). As well as cutting taxes, that legislation gradually increased contribution limits for 401(k) plans from $10,500 to $15,000 in 2006. Employees over age fifty were also allowed to make additional catch-up contributions of up to $5,000. Individuals with $15,000 or less in adjusted gross income were given a tax credit of up to 50 percent of the amount contributed to a Section 401(k) plan (up to $2,000). Reduced credits were available for those having incomes of up to $25,000. The rate of savings by individual consumers varied greatly even within the same income groups, but retirement savings were increasing on an overall basis. In 2001, 60 percent of employees had some form of private retirement account. More than $7 trillion was held in all private retirement accounts at year-end 2001.

Congress acted to encourage investor education through the Savings Are Vital to Everyone Retirement Act of 1997. That legislation authorized the secretary of labor to inform people about the importance of retirement savings. Unfortunately, that legislation did not educate the Enron employees on the investment risks of their Section 401(k) accounts. Many Enron employees concentrated large amounts of Enron stock in the Enron Corporate Savings Plan, which was a Section 401(k) self-directed retirement program. Employees additionally invested in Enron stock through the company's employee stock option plan (ESOP). At year-end 2000, 21,000 present and former Enron employees had assets valued at $2.1 billion in the Section 401(k) company accounts they maintained in the Enron Corporate Savings Plan. Additionally, 7,600 Enron employees held $1 billion of Enron stock in the company's ESOP.

Enron also provided a defined benefit plan to employees in the form of a "cash balance" program, a fairly recent innovation in finance. Officially it is a defined benefit plan but is actually a mixture of the defined benefit and defined contribution plans. A cash balance plan provides employees with a defined benefit that is equal to a percentage of the employee's salary in every year of employment, plus interest at a specified rate on the "balance" created by the yearly contributions. Companies using defined benefit plans are restricted in using their own stock to fund the plan (no more than 10 percent of the funding may be company stock). Enron employees had additional protection in the cash balance plan, even if underfunded, because such plans are guaranteed up to specified amounts by the Pension Guaranty Corporation (up to around $35,000 per year per employee).

Starting in 1998, Enron made matching grants of Enron stock as its contribution to employee Section 401(k) accounts. Employees receiving that Enron stock were required to hold it until they reached age fifty. Otherwise, the Enron employees could choose their own investment mix in their Section 401(k) accounts and could sell any Enron or other stock purchased with their own contributions at any time. Of the 14.5 million shares of Enron stock held in employee Section 401(k) accounts, 89 percent was contributed by the employees or could otherwise be sold at any time. Enron offered twenty different investment options for employee Section 401(k) plans as an alternative to investing in Enron stock, including mutual funds (such as the Vanguard 500 Index Trust, the Fidelity Magellan Fund, and the T. Rowe Price Small Cap Fund). Also available was a brokerage account that could be traded daily in any stock or other security desired by the employee. Despite those choices, the Enron Section 401(k) accounts were heavily concentrated in Enron stock. This was encouraged by the company. In 1999 the Enron benefits department assured employees that holding all their investments in Enron stock was a good idea.

Those employees holding Enron stock before the market decline saw their account values increase sharply with the run-up in Enron's stock. Of course, that buildup was reversed with the market downturn and the disclosure of Enron's problems. Indeed, the market downturn was already hammering Enron's stock before Jeffrey Skilling's resignation on August 14, 2001. His leaving caused a further drop in the company's stock price and caused employees to wonder whether they should sell the Enron stock held in their Section 401(k) accounts. Ken Lay responded to that concern when he rejoined Enron by assuring employees that Enron's third quarter in 2001 was going to be "great" and that the stock was an "incredible bargain," and he urged employees to "talk up the stock." Lay did not tell employees that he had recently sold Enron stock worth $20 million.

Lockdown

Compounding the situation at Enron was a "lockdown" in employee Section 401(k) accounts that occurred coincidentally during the critical period just before the company's collapse. The lockdown imposed a moratorium on employee sales from their 401(k) accounts during a change in the administration of the plans. This lockdown was caused by Enron's dissatisfaction with Northern Trust as the administrator for its Corporate Savings Plan. That dissatisfaction led to a decision to switch to Hewitt Associates to fill that role. To avoid bookkeeping problems during the changeover, Enron locked down the accounts until the transfer was complete. This was a common and prudent measure founded on experience, but the timing at Enron for its lockdown could not have been worse.

The Enron lockdown was first announced in an e-mail to all employees on September 27, 2001. They were notified that the lockdown would begin on October 19, 2001, and last about a month. Later, employees were advised by a letter from Enron that the lockdown would begin a week later and last for about month (the lockdown actually lasted for only eleven trading days). The difference between the start dates in these two communications was later claimed to have caused confusion on the part of employees as to exactly when the lockdown began. In any event, another notice was sent just days before Enron announced its large third-quarter loss on October 16 and began its stream of accounting abuse disclosures.

On October 25, 2001, Enron's compensation department refused employee requests to delay the lockdown, although such a delay was feasible. Claiming that the delay would be administratively difficult, the department also feared that other employees would sue if the delay locked them out of favorable market developments. Even so, Enron employees could have sold their stock after receiving notice of the lockdown and after being advised of some of Enron's very serious accounting problems. Enron's stock price dropped $3.83 during the lockdown, not a particularly large amount in the total context of the meltdown in the stock's price, but lawyers acting for the employees claimed that confusion over the start date of the lockdown increased losses. Further, Enron executives were touting the stock to employees even as it plunged in value, dissuading them from selling until it was too late. The lockdown further enraged employees when they learned that Enron executives holding stock outside their 401(k) accounts were selling millions of shares of stock. In fact, the lockout actually saved money for employees wanting to sell because there was a rally in the price of Enron stock after the lockdown was lifted. Employees were actually net buyers after the lockdown was lifted. The lawyers, however, claimed that Enron executives were touting the stock to employees even as it plunged in value, encouraging the employees to buy and dissuading them from selling until it was too late.

One employee at Enron saw the value of his 401(k) investments drop from $1.3 million to $8,200 when the company declared bankruptcy. Another retired employee with a 401(k) retirement account composed mostly of Enron stock valued at $700,000 at its peak fell to just $20,000 before she was able to sell the stock after the 401(k) lockdown. Still another employee's account dropped from $485,000 to $22,000 before she sold the stock. In total, Enron's bankruptcy was claimed to have resulted in losses of $1.2 billion to Enron employee pension plans. The employees' actual out-of-pocket loss, as measured by their personal cash contributions plus some moderate rate of return, is unknown. Some Enron employees sold their Enron stock before the lockdown. The percentage of Enron stock held in the employee Section 401(k) accounts dropped from about 63 percent of assets at year-end 2000 to 44 percent at the time of the lockdown.

The Northern Trust Corporation, which administered Enron's Section 401(k) plan before the lockdown, was the subject of lawsuits after Enron's demise. A district court ruled that Ken Lay could also be sued for fiduciary violations under the Employee Retirement Income Security Act (ERISA) as a result of his failure to safeguard employee assets. The court dismissed Jeffrey Skilling from the suit, as well as Enron's outside lawyers and banks. The complaint alleged that the Enron officers breached their fiduciary duties by allowing and encouraging Enron employees to purchase Enron stock in their Section 401(k) plans, by allowing Enron to make matching contributions in those plans with Enron stock, and by imposing age limitations on the ability of employees to sell their Enron stock in those accounts. Arthur Andersen LLP was accused of participating in those breaches by concealing Enron's true financial condition. Some of the claims made in the pension litigation were slightly ridiculous—for example, an assertion that the ESOP should not have purchased Enron stock, when that was what it was created to do.

An insurance policy for the Section 401(k) plan trustees provided $85 million to cover their liability after Enron's bankruptcy. Of that amount, $66.5 million went to 20,000 current and former Enron employees, providing on average a little over $3,000 per employee. The rest was consumed by attorney fees and costs, but Enron objected to its distribution, asserting that other creditors might also have an interest in the proceeds. The Enron directors agreed to pay $1.5 million in settlement of the employees' 401(k) claims. Of that amount, $300,000 went to the Department of Labor as a penalty.

Other 401(k) Problems

Enron employees were not alone in suffering losses from their company's stock. Some 42 million Americans held 401(k) accounts at 350,000 employers and had $2 trillion invested at the time of Enron's collapse. At the end of June 2002, the value of those accounts had dropped to $1.3 trillion. Employees at Intel, the computer chip maker, saw the value of their holdings of Intel stock drop $366 million in 2002. Lucent Corporation employees had as much as 80 percent of their assets in Section 401(k) accounts invested in that company's stock as its price declined by over 90 percent between 1999 and 2001. Forty percent of assets held in Polaroid's Section 401(k) accounts were invested in that company's stock at the time of its bankruptcy.

A survey found that many large companies had large concentrations of company stock in Section 401(k) plans, including Abbott Laboratories (82 percent of total assets in its 401(k) plans was company stock); Anheuser-Busch (83 percent); McDonald's (74.3 percent); Procter & Gamble (91.5 percent); and Coca-Cola (75 percent). On average, the Section 401(k) plans of large companies held 40 percent of their assets in employer stock. Low-wage employee accounts were the most concentrated. Employer plans having matching stock contributions also tended to be more heavily concentrated in the company's own stock.

The Enron employee losses in their Section 401(k) accounts led to calls for legislative protection from overconcentration in employer stock. Bills were introduced that would have imposed such a requirement, but Congress did not enact that legislation because opponents successfully argued that employees concentrated their stock ownership in their company in order to share in its growth. Many millionaires had been created by such stocks as Microsoft and Wal-Mart. Critics of that legislative proposal also pointed out that workers should themselves assure diversification without governmental direction. However, a survey by the American Association of Retired Persons (AARP) found that only about one-third of Americans recognized that diversification reduces investment risk.

The market downturn and Enron's problems did have the effect of educating, and reducing to some extent, the concentration of stock in employee Section 401(k) accounts across the country. At the end of 2002, such plans held only 28 percent of their assets in employer stock, down from 40 percent in 2001. Overall, the percentage of Section 401(k) retirement assets held in stocks in all companies reached its lowest level in five years at the end of June 2002 when employees held an average of 64.9 percent of their Section 401(k) portfolios in stocks, down from a high of 74.2 percent in October 2000.

The Enron employees frozen in their 401(k) accounts received particular sympathy in the press, but they were not the only ones experiencing losses. The Florida state pension fund announced that it had lost $335 million from its holdings of Enron stock. Congress questioned why large purchases of Enron stock were made by the Florida state pension fund investment manager even after it was clear that Enron was in trouble. That investment manager was Alliance Capital. Congressional investigators were quick to point out that one of its executives, Frank Savage, had sat on Enron's board of directors, but were unable to show that Savage had anything to do with Alliance's investment decision for the state pension fund. A jury later dismissed the Florida pension fund's suit against Alliance. The jury also instructed the pension fund to pay fees owing to Alliance.

Prosecution of Enron Executives

Other Abuses

The Enron executives responsible for the SPE structures were centered in the Financial Reporting Group that reported to Andrew Fastow, Enron's chief financial officer. The individuals serving under Fastow included Michael Kopper, head of special projects, as well as Jeff McMahon and Ben Glisan. McMahon and Glisan ("Fastow's field marshals") served as corporate treasurer at various times and were both former employees at Arthur Andersen LLP.

Another center for SPE activity was the accounting and tax groups at Enron that reported to Richard Causey, who in turn reported to Fastow. The 600 accountants reporting directly to Causey included some thirty accountants in Enron's Transaction Support Group who previously held management positions at Arthur Andersen or who had worked for the Financial Accounting Standards Board, the body setting generally accepted accounting principles for the accounting industry. The Enron bankruptcy examiner concluded that the individuals in Causey's group "were at the very heart of Enron SPE transactions" and were constantly seeking "larger and more aggressive applications" for those vehicles. "Moreover, because of lack of adequate understanding of the transactions by the Financial Reporting Group, the Transaction Support Group in fact determined the disclosures in the financial statements and in the notes thereto."[8]

In using the LJM structure to enrich himself, Fastow undermined the required independence of the SPEs and, more importantly, their credibility. Fastow extended this largesse to other favored Enron employees through a "Friends of Enron" program in which the supposed 3 percent independent investors in the Enron SPEs were actually friends or family members of Enron executives. Those individuals acted as mere nominees under Enron's (and Fastow's) control, rather than as independent investors with a substantial stake in the SPEs. In one transaction called RADR, the purported independent investors were Patty Melcher, a friend of Fastow's wife, William Dodson, Michael Kopper's domestic partner, and Kathy Wetmore, a Houston real estate broker used by several Enron executives for their real estate transactions. Fastow loaned Kopper $419,000 that was distributed to those friends in order that they could participate. Fastow was repaid in full, plus a profit of 15 percent for the use of his funds for four months. That was actually small change. As a federal court noted, Enron employees Fastow, Kopper, Ben Glisan, Kristina Mordaunt, Kathy Lynn, and Anne Yaeger Patel "obtained financial interests in LJM1 for initial contributions of $25,000 by Fastow, $5,800 each for Glisan and Mordaunt, and lesser amounts for the others, totaling $70,000. They quickly received extraordinary returns on their investments; on May 1, 2000, Fastow received $4.5 million, while Glisan and Mordaunt within a couple of months received approximately $1 million."[9]

The Enron Tax Group was another center for doubtful accounting practices. That group engaged in efforts to manipulate Enron's income for financial accounting purposes in transactions codenamed Teresa, Steele, Tomas, Valhalla, Valor, Tanya, Tammy I, Apache, and Cochise. The Cochise transaction deducted the cost of Enron's airplanes until they had a zero basis. Those planes were then sold to Bankers Trust for $36 million. That amount was claimed as income even though Enron had agreed that one of its affiliates would repurchase the aircraft shortly thereafter in the next accounting period.

The Tax Group increased Enron's after-tax income by $886.5 million between 1995 through 2001 through its numerous and complex tax strategies. Those schemes were at least partially responsible for the fact that Enron's tax returns for 2000 totaled thirteen volumes. Bankers Trust (later acquired by Deutsche Bank) was found to have financed several of these transactions and received $43 million in fees for its assistance. Among Enron's tax schemes were transactions structured to create "'negative goodwill' in artificial business combinations that was amortized in pre-tax income."[10] That gimmick provided $270 million in Enron's net income in 2000. Once again, Enron used SPEs to carry out these schemes.

The Enron Tax Group melded well with the Financial Reporting Group, illustrating an anomaly in accounting: companies keep several sets of books, including internal reports for management, financial accounts for investors, and another set of accounts for the Internal Revenue Service (IRS). Enron was striving desperately to make itself appear to be highly profitable to investors through its accounting statements filed with the SEC, which it dressed up even more with pro forma reports that excluded one-time adverse events. At the same time, Enron was trying to show as little income as possible to the IRS.

Enron took those common accounting practices to a new level by using tax gimmicks that generated income for financial reporting to investors and, at the same time, created losses for tax purposes. As a result of its accounting manipulations, Enron was claiming to be highly profitable on its financial accounting reports, while its tax returns painted a much different picture. Enron reported *losses* on its income tax returns filed with the IRS of $400 million in 1996, $580 million in 1997, $813 million in 1999, and over $3 billion in 2000. Comparable figures in Enron's financial reports to the SEC for those years showed *profits* (net income) of $520 million in 1996, $105 million in 1997, $893 million in 1999, and $979 million in 2000.

Andrew Fastow

The political controversy surrounding the Enron implosion required the Justice Department to take a hard line on the Enron executives. The Justice Department created an Enron Task Force that was chaired by Leslie Caldwell, a prosecutor noted for her hardball tactics that included prosecuting the elderly mothers of two drug dealers (Lorenzo "Fat Cat" Nichols and Howard "Pappy" Mason). At least one Enron executive, Andrew Fastow, would be exposed to even harsher tactics—his wife and children would be held hostage for his guilty plea.

Over thirty people were eventually charged with crimes in connection with Enron abuses, including more than twenty former Enron executives. Several individuals pleaded guilty to those charges, including Michael Kopper for his role in the SPEs used by Enron. In exchange for leniency on the length of his prison sentence, Kopper agreed to cooperate with the government by testifying against other former Enron executives, specifically Andrew Fastow, the executive who had enriched Kopper. Kopper was also the subject of charges brought by the SEC that he settled by surrendering $12 million, although he was allowed to keep more than $1 million of his assets.

Fastow, Enron's chief financial officer, was the linchpin of the government's prosecution efforts for Enron-related crimes. The prosecutors wanted to use Kopper's cooperation agreement to leverage Fastow into a guilty plea that would avoid the necessity of addressing at a trial the incredibly complex transactions used by Fastow to enhance Enron's accounts and the equally complex legal and accounting issues related to those transactions. The prosecutors' job was made harder by the fact that many of the transactions at issue were structured by an army of accountants at Enron and blessed by Arthur Andersen, various teams of in-house lawyers at Enron, and prestigious law firms. A guilty plea by Fastow would also include a "cooperation" agreement that would ensure that Fastow testified against more senior executives at Enron, including Jeffrey Skilling. Without Fastow's testimony, prosecution of Skilling would be difficult, if not impossible. The prosecutors were additionally hopeful that Fastow would help in the prosecution of Kenneth Lay.

Fastow was indicted on October 31, 2002, for wire fraud, money laundering, obstruction of justice, conspiracy, and aiding and abetting. The indictment tellingly noted that, as chief financial officer, Fastow reported "directly" to Enron's chief executive officers (Lay and Skilling). The indictment charged that Fastow engaged in various schemes to defraud by falsifying financial reports to make Enron appear more successful than it was, manipulating Enron's stock price, circumventing federal regulations for its wind farms, and personally enriching himself at the expense of Enron. Somewhat weirdly, the indictment charged that Fastow had created the "illusion of business skill and success" on the part of Fastow and other Enron executives.[11]

The indictment first focused on a RADR transaction involving Enron wind farms in California (including one called Zond). The wind farms were operating as "qualifying facilities" that were eligible for certain financial benefits under federal law if they were not more than 50 percent owned by an electric utility holding company. Enron's merger with Portland General Electric resulted in Enron becoming such a utility, requiring forfeiture of the qualifying facilities status of its wind farms. To avoid that result, Fastow had created an SPE called RADR that purchased sufficient interests in the wind farms to bring Enron's ownership below 50 percent. The indictment charged that Fastow used nominees and provided the funding through a loan from his personal bank account in the amount of $419,000 in order to reach the independent ownership requirement for the SPE. RADR was alleged to have been secretly controlled by Fastow and Michael Kopper. The indictment further charged that Fastow received profits of $188,000 as a return on the personal funds he invested in the transaction over a three-year period. These profits were distributed by Michael Kopper as "gifts" to Fastow and his wife and children in increments of $10,000.

The Chewco transaction was another part of the indictment against Fastow. The government claimed that Fastow had demanded that Michael Kopper, the individual used to supply the needed 3 percent independent equity ownership in that SPE, pay $67,224 as a kickback to Fastow through further "gifts." Fastow was also charged with approving a $2.625 million payment to Kopper when Enron purchased Chewco's interest in JEDI for $35 million. That payment was made over the objections of Enron's lawyers.

Fastow's involvement in LJM1 and LJM2 was the subject of further charges. The indictment alleged that Enron's transactions with the LJM entities were fraudulent and were used to manipulate Enron's financial results by moving poorly performing assets off its balance sheets and creating earnings through sham transactions in order to meet earning targets. Documents were backdated in order to carry out these schemes. Fastow was charged with making false statements to Enron's board of directors in order to obtain its approval for his participation in the LJM transactions.

The indictment claimed that many transactions between Enron and the LJM entities were mere "parking" or "warehousing" that allowed Enron to claim earnings and cash flow from the purported sale to the SPEs of various assets that were subsequently repurchased by Enron. The Cuiaba project was one such transaction. It involved a purported sale to an LJM entity of Enron's interest in a power plant in Cuiaba, Brazil, which was turning sour and running $120 million over budget. This allowed Enron to recognize $65 million of income in 1999 at a time when the company was having difficulties meeting its projected earnings targets. The indictment alleged that Fastow and Enron had a secret side deal in which Enron agreed to, and did, buy back the interest in the power plant at a profit to LJM.

Another count in the Fastow indictment asserted that he engaged in a complex scheme to manipulate Enron's accounts through an SPE called Talon. This vehicle was used to hedge certain of Enron's merchant investments in various start-up ventures and other companies. These holdings were required to be marked-to-market on Enron's balance sheet, and they often fluctuated widely in value, thereby posing a volatility threat to its financial statements. Enron was restricted in its ability to sell those holdings by lock-up agreements. In order to avoid reporting a decrease in the value of declining holdings, Talon locked in their value at a preset price. The government's indictment alleged that the SPE was not actually independent and that documents were backdated to achieve the desired results. Talon was funded by Enron stock, a promissory note, and LJM, which provided $30 million as the necessary 3 percent outside equity required for an SPE. Fastow entered into a secret side agreement in which Enron paid LJM $41 million to induce it to participate in the Talon transactions. This payment was disguised as a premium for a put transaction that was supposed to hedge Enron against a decline in its own stock price.

Extorting a Guilty Plea

The Fastow indictment contained a total of seventy-eight counts that would be sufficient to put him in jail for ninety years, if proved and if consecutive sentences were imposed. Reflecting the hysteria gathering around the Enron collapse, Fastow was required to post bail of $5 million after his arrest, as compared to the $3 million required of the much wealthier singer Michael Jackson for child molestation charges. Fastow and his wife were unlikely fugitives, having two small children at home, but were required to surrender their passports. Michael Jackson had his passport returned for a trip abroad at about the same time. The Fastow indictment sought forfeiture of Fastow's bank accounts, real estate, and other property totaling over $14 million. Fastow's bank accounts and other assets were frozen pending trial.

There was a reason for this sledgehammer approach. Basically, it was an extortion scheme. The prosecutors wanted to intimidate and coerce Fastow into a guilty plea in order to avoid a long, complex trial on the charges lodged against him, a contest that the government was not certain it could win. The prosecutors also needed Fastow's testimony to indict Lay and Skilling. The government was facing much criticism in the press for not indicting those two highly visible Enron executives, so no prosecutorial tactic was too unethical to assure that result. Fastow initially refused to buckle under that pressure, declaring his innocence and vowing to fight the charges. The prosecutors then obtained a superseding indictment that added twenty more counts against Fastow, upping the maximum possible jail time to 140 years. The superseding indictment also named two additional defendants: Ben Glisan Jr., the former Enron treasurer (who pleaded guilty to the charges and was the first Enron official to actually go to jail), and Dan Boyle, the former Enron vice president for Global Finance. Glisan and Boyle were added to the indictment in order to pressure them to turn on Fastow. Apparently concerned that this message might be too subtle, the prosecutors also indicted Fastow's wife, Lea, a former Enron employee who had quit the company in 1997 to raise their two children, long before the accounting abuses at Enron were in full steam.

Lea Fastow

Lea Fastow was charged with being a coconspirator with her husband and Kopper because she accepted the "gifts" from Kopper in connection with the

RADR transaction and payments from the Chewco transaction. She was also, somewhat absurdly, charged with having her father file a false tax return in connection with a breakup fee he was given after Enron counsel advised that Fastow family members could not participate in an Enron transaction. The accountants for Lea Fastow's father, at her direction, listed the fee as interest income on his tax return rather than as fees from Enron.

The crux of the charges against Lea Fastow was that the $67,224 that was "gifted" from Kopper (on which he apparently paid income tax) was not reported on the Fastows' joint tax return as income. The Fastows did report over $60 million and change in income on the tax returns in question, but the $67,224 shortfall was deemed too crucial by the IRS for mere civil action. Instead, the government used this technicality to pressure Andrew Fastow to plead guilty. The government had warned Andrew Fastow that his wife would be indicted unless he pled guilty. Even this gross abuse of prosecutorial power initially proved insufficient to elicit a guilty plea from Andrew Fastow, and the Fastows vowed to fight the charges. The trial court judge, David Hittner, in support of the government's efforts to break the Fastows, then denied the Fastows' request for a joint trial, thereby substantially increasing their legal expenses. A request that Lea Fastow's trial be postponed until the charges against her husband were resolved was also denied. The trial court ordered that she would be the first defendant in any case to be tried for wrongdoing at Enron.

The government's strong-arm tactics were successful in forcing the Fastows to submit to a guilty plea. The government agreed to an arrangement in which Lea Fastow would first serve five months in prison so that her husband could care for their children while she was gone. He would then serve ten years and pay $29 million in fines, but Judge Hittner decided he needed some additional headlines to prove he was tough on corporate criminals. The judge refused to be bound by the plea agreement and threatened more jail time for Lea Fastow. That resulted in an additional agreement that Lea Fastow would serve home detention in addition to her five months in prison. On April 7, 2004, Lea Fastow again withdrew her guilty plea and a trial was ordered after Judge Hittner objected to that arrangement. He wanted more jail time, having personally lost some $40,000 from his own investment in Enron stock, a conflict that was waived by Fastow's lawyers. The government then agreed to charge Lea Fastow with a single misdemeanor, which prevented the judge from sentencing her to more than a year in jail. She began serving her sentence in July 2004. Lea Fastow, who was not even an Enron employee at the time of the wrongdoing, was one of the first to go to jail as a result of the Enron scandal. In another vindictive act, she was sent to a maximum-security prison; the government claimed there was no room at nearby minimum-security facilities. There she was confined with two other women in a cell designed for two, kept under fluorescent lights, and denied any outdoor recreation.

Other Defendants

As a part of his guilty plea, Andrew Fastow agreed to turn on Richard Causey, Enron's chief accounting officer, and Causey was indicted for securities fraud on January 22, 2004. The Powers report concluded that many of Causey's accounting judgments were made with the concurrence of Arthur Andersen LLP, "a significant, though not entirely exonerating, fact."[12] In his guilty plea, Fastow asserted that Causey had agreed on behalf of Enron to guarantee LJM2 against loss plus an assured profit. Causey was additionally charged with insider trading as a result of his sale of Enron stock in the amount of $10.3 million at a time when he knew that the company's financial condition was other than as reported to the SEC.

David Delainey, the former chief executive officer of Enron North America and Enron Energy Services, pleaded guilty to criminal charges that he sold Enron stock during a period when he knew that the company's financial statements were overstated. He agreed to give up $4.26 million in insider trading profits and to pay $3.74 million to the SEC in civil penalties. He was barred from serving as an officer or director of a public company. Another Enron executive, Paula Rieker, managing director for investor relations and corporate secretary, pleaded guilty to selling her Enron stock at a time when she possessed inside information about losses at Enron Broadband Services. She settled civil charges brought by the SEC by paying $500,000. Her supervisor, Mark Koenig, pleaded guilty to a criminal charge and agreed to pay the SEC $1.49 million. The SEC complaint charged that, as executive vice president and director of investor relations, Koenig was responsible for drafting portions of Enron's earnings releases and analysts call scripts, but failed to disclose that Enron Energy Services and Enron Broadband Services "were not the successful business units described in the earnings releases and scripts, and as described by Enron in the analyst calls."[13] Koenig agreed to testify against other Enron executives as part of his guilty plea.

Timothy Despain, an assistant treasurer at Enron, was indicted for misleading the ratings agencies by engaging in various schemes that were designed to keep up Enron's credit rating. He pleaded guilty to those charges. The entire senior management of Enron broadband division was indicted, including Kenneth Rice and Joe Hirko, former co-chief executive officers of that group, as well as five other former officials. Federal prosecutors charged that those executives structured the sale (Project Braveheart, named after a Mel Gibson movie) of Enron's interest in the less-than-successful joint venture with Blockbuster Video for video-on-demand services. Even though there had been no actual sale, the Enron broadband division used the transaction to claim earnings of $111 million in 2001, so that it could meet its projected earnings target. The Braveheart transaction, a sale of projected revenues from the Blockbuster joint venture that never became operational, involved a sale of those revenues to an SPE called Hawaii 125–0. This transaction was structured and financed by the Canadian Imperial Bank of Commerce (CIBC). Like other Enron SPEs, however, there was a question whether the required 3 percent of independent ownership was really independent. The government further charged that there was no true sale because CIBC had been guaranteed against loss by Enron in the transaction. Kenneth Rice agreed to plead guilty to the government's charges, as did Kevin P. Hannon. They agreed to testify against the other indicted executives in that division who went on trial in April 2005. That trial was a stunning setback for the prosecutors. It lasted three months and resulted in a hung jury in July 2005 on some of the charges and acquittals on others. None of the defendants were convicted on any charge. Enron vice president Christopher Calger, however, pleaded guilty to wire fraud for his role in recognizing earnings prematurely through project Coyote Springs II and other activities.

Wesley H. Colwell, the chief accounting officer for Enron North America, faced fraud claims filed by the SEC. He was charged with misusing reserve accounts, concealing losses, inflating asset values, and using improper accounting treatment for various transactions. The SEC complaint alleged that Enron had improperly deferred more than $400 million in earnings in reserve accounts in 2000 in order to meet the expectations of financial analysts. Colwell was charged with using those reserve accounts and other activities to conceal losses of $1 billion. Other transactions were structured to avoid disclosing a $1.4 billion loss from a decline in value of pipeline assets. Colwell paid $500,000 in penalties to settle the SEC case, without admitting or denying the charges. Raymond Bowen, another Enron executive, paid $500,000 to settle SEC charges that he helped inflate Enron's earnings by overstating the value of Mariner Energy, a company owned by Enron, by over $100 million.

Kenneth Lay

The Enron bankruptcy examiner sought to recover $81.5 million from loans made to Kenneth Lay by Enron that he repaid with Enron stock. Recovery was also sought of funds paid to Lay and his wife on the surrender of annuities they held as part of Ken Lay's compensation package. The Lays were paid $10 million for those annuities by Enron, but the bankruptcy examiner contended that those contracts were worth only $4.69 million at the time of their surrender. The examiner sought payment from the Lays for the difference. The bankruptcy examiner charged that Lay and Skilling breached their fiduciary duties to Enron shareholders by approving certain SPEs, failing to supervise the use of those and other SPEs, and ignoring red flags that those structures were being abused by Fastow and Kopper.

Lay had been urging employees to buy Enron stock even while the company was collapsing and at a time when he was himself exercising options for 93,000 shares of Enron stock and then selling those shares for a large profit. A federal court allowed a class action against Lay that claimed that Enron was actually a giant Ponzi scheme and that Lay had acquired and sold stock in that scheme as part of a massive insider trading scheme. Jeffrey Skilling and other Enron officers were named in that suit as participants in the Ponzi scheme.

Lay received over $217 million in stock option profits and another $18 million in salary and bonuses from Enron between 1998 and 2001. Nevertheless, Lay's wife, Linda, announced on the *Today* television program that the Lays were in financial trouble after the collapse of Enron because their assets were still concentrated in Enron stock, which had become nearly worthless. Linda Lay claimed that she and her husband had "lost everything." Her claims of poverty were met with widespread derision, many press accounts reporting that the Lays were still living in their $7.8 million condominium in Houston. The Lays were, in fact, selling many of their assets, including their vacation homes and furnishings. Linda Lay even opened a store called Jus' Stuff that sold family possessions. Their financial problems were due to the fact that the Lays had made some very bad investments and had even borrowed $95 million from financial institutions using Enron stock as collateral.

Ken Lay exercised all his legal options in meeting the legal problems he faced, including taking the Fifth Amendment before congressional committees examining the Enron bankruptcy. Lay refused to testify anywhere else under oath but did consent to a one-day interview before the Enron bankruptcy examiner. Lay resisted SEC subpoenas for his personal financial records. He was right to do so since there was no want of prosecutorial zeal in seeking to entrap him, as demonstrated by the strong-arm tactics wielded against Andrew and Lea Fastow. Bill Lockyer, the attorney general of California, where Enron had been cited as a culprit in manipulating electricity prices, was earlier quoted as saying that he wanted personally to lead Lay to an "8-by-10 cell that he could share with a tattooed dude who says, Hi, my name is Spike, honey."[14] Jeffrey Skilling had responded to that barrage from Lockyer with a riposte of his own, cracking a joke at an industry conference to the effect that the difference between California and the *Titanic* was that the *Titanic* went down with its lights still burning.

Lay had been given a boost by the Powers report, which found no evidence that he had been told of Kopper's role in Chewco, the transaction that led to the downfall of Enron. That same report, however, faulted him for approving Fastow's involvement with the SPEs and for failing to implement sufficient controls to prevent Fastow from enriching himself and endangering Enron. The Powers report considered this an act of omission, rather than commission, noting that Lay had assigned Jeffrey Skilling management responsibility for the LJM relationship. This did not stop Lay from being indicted some thirty months after Enron's collapse. He was charged with only a limited role in Enron's accounting schemes, but was claimed to have misled investors as to the true financial condition of Enron.

The indictment claimed a conspiracy involving Lay, Skilling, and Causey that sought to manipulate earnings to meet quarterly earnings expectations of analysts. This conspiracy was alleged to have falsely touted the success of various Enron business units (including Enron Broadband Services) to analysts, masking the true extent of Enron's debt and concealing large losses. The conspiracy was said to have structured financial transactions through SPEs in a misleading manner in order to meet earnings and cash flow objectives, manipulated earnings through fraudulent use of reserve accounts, fraudulently manufactured earnings by overvaluing assets, and circumvented accounting requirements for goodwill and the true sale accounting requirements for SPEs.

Lay was further charged with lying to employees of Enron in an online forum held on September 26, 2001, during which he said the third quarter was "looking great. We hit our numbers." He claimed that the fourth quarter was looking good as well, even though he knew that Enron was facing significant losses. Lay had stated that "We have record operating and financial results," that "The balance sheet is strong," and that his "personal belief is that Enron stock is an incredible bargain at current prices." Lay further gave employees the "impression" that he had been increasing his holdings of Enron stock over the prior two months. In fact, he had bought $4 million in stock but had also sold $24 million in Enron shares. He also told a credit rating agency that Enron and Arthur Andersen had "scrubbed" the company's books and that there would be no more asset write-offs.

Lay was charged with bank fraud for obtaining loans on his Enron stock in violation of margin requirements set by the Federal Reserve Board. This was an extremely esoteric charge, suggesting that the government did not have much of a case against Lay. The government claimed that Lay had improperly used "nonpurpose" lines of credit from his banks to margin Enron stock. Such nonpurpose loans may not be used for the "purpose" of margining stock. Rather, "purpose" credit is used for margin transactions and then only up to the margin value of the stock, which in the case of Enron would be 50 percent. The nonpurpose loans were secured by Enron stock and had a loan-to-value ratio of 70 to 80 percent, which the government claimed allowed Lay to reduce the margin on his stock from the 50 percent level required for "purpose" credit.

The charges against Lay carried a maximum prison term of 175 years. Upon his arrest, Lay was handcuffed and given a perp walk for the cameras in order to humiliate him. After being freed on bail, he held a news conference in which he proclaimed his innocence, criticized prosecutors, and blamed the accounting fraud at Enron on Fastow, who was to be Lay's chief accuser. In an article in the editorial section of the *Washington Post* in 2004, Lay charged that his indictment was politically motivated and demanded a speedy trial. Lay wrote:

> Why, then, is the Department of Justice not willing to agree to an immediate and speedy trial? Could it be that my indictment—curiously issued two weeks before the Democratic National Convention—is largely political?
>
> In an article in the Aug. 16 issue of the National Law Journal, John C. Coffee Jr., a law professor and director of the Columbia Law School Center on Corporate Gov-

ernance, concludes: "To be sure, an intense political need to indict Lay may explain why prosecutors have pushed the envelope of securities and mail fraud theories to their limit. But what happens once will predictably happen again." In other words, if they can do it to me, they can do it to others.[15]

The government's response to Lay's blast was predictable. The government had learned from Lea Fastow that nothing works better than extortion with family members as hostages. Prosecutors began investigating the sale by Lay's wife, Linda, of 500,000 shares of Enron stock shortly before the company's bankruptcy. The sale was made for a family foundation and the $1.2 million in proceeds from the sale was given to charities to fulfill pledges made by the foundation. Lay's request for a speedy trial was denied, ostensibly because observing Lay's constitutional right to a speedy trial would require a severance of Lay's trial from that of Jeffrey Skilling. The government wanted them to be tried together in hope that they would point the finger at each other and in the belief that the jury could be prejudiced by the collective evidence of their large compensation packages and corporate excesses. In the event, the trial of Ken Lay and Jeffrey Skilling was postponed until January 2006. The court separated the bank fraud charges against Lay from the fraud and conspiracy charges. The government then asked that the bank fraud charges be tried in the summer of 2005, but that request was denied.

Jeffrey Skilling

Jeffrey Skilling had been faulted by the Powers report for failing to supervise the LJM partnerships properly. Enron employees claimed that Skilling had been put on notice that Fastow was acting improperly with respect to the SPEs and that Skilling approved a transaction that concealed significant losses in Enron's merchant investments. Jeff McMahon, the company's treasurer, was reported as having complained to Skilling about Fastow's LJM activities. Fastow was told of that complaint by Skilling, and McMahon was then transferred to another job at Enron. McMahon had worked at Arthur Andersen previously and with Sherron Watkins at Metallgesellschaft. They both fled to Enron when Metallgesellschaft was involved in its own trading scandal. McMahon thought that Fastow's dual roles—serving as chief financial officer and having an interest in the LJM general partnership—was "dysfunctional" and "problematic on many fronts." He also asserted, however, that those problems could be mitigated by "some pretty simple restructuring" such as taking Fastow out of the performance review process for those Enron employees with whom he was negotiating for LJM. McMahon was sued by the Enron estate after its bankruptcy to recover monies paid to him while at Enron.

On February 19, 2004, shortly after Fastow's guilty plea, Skilling was indicted on forty-two counts of insider trading and other charges. This was another case of government overkill in which the prosecutors sought a maximum of 325 years for those charges. The insider trading charges asserted that Skilling had made more than $62 million by selling Enron stock after he left the firm. Skilling had netted almost $90 million from options and another $14 million in salary and bonuses between 1998 and 2001. He was charged with conspiracy and fraud in manipulating Enron's financial statements by falsely showing growth of 15 or 20 percent annually and concealing losses and liabilities in order to meet or exceed analyst expectations. Those deceived were said to include the investing public, credit rating agencies, and the SEC.

The indictment sought seizure from Skilling of more than $50 million held in his accounts, plus his Houston home, valued at $4.7 million. Once again, the government employed strong-arm tactics to make its point by obtaining a court order freezing $50 million of Skilling's assets. Although Skilling was hardly a danger to anyone and unlikely to flee, he was brought to the courthouse in handcuffs for his perp walk and bail was set at $5 million. The government inflicts further humiliation on arrested executives by stripping them of their shoelaces, belt, and tie. Ostensibly a measure to protect against suicide, this tactic is designed to embarrass the executives by requiring them to hold up their pants and shuffle in laceless shoes. This nonsense has become so well known, even being portrayed in novels, that most executives submitting to arrest prepare accordingly: Skilling thus arrived at the courthouse sans belt and in loafers. He pleaded not guilty to the charges. Thirty additional counts were thrown in against Richard Causey for a little further overkill and to put further pressure on him to plead guilty and turn on Skilling.

The government's onslaught did have an effect on Skilling; he was taken to a New York hospital after police found him intoxicated and behaving bizarrely at 4:00 A.M. on Park Avenue. Skilling was reported to have been approaching people on the street, grabbing their clothing and accusing them of being FBI agents. Skilling claimed that he was the victim, that two men had been harassing him about Enron and refused to answer when he asked if they were FBI agents. The judge hearing his criminal case ordered Skilling to be subject to a midnight curfew, to abstain from alcohol, and to seek counseling for his drinking, which had steadily worsened as the government prosecutors focused on him. Skilling, nevertheless, put up a strong defense. He sought to make public the names of the 114 individuals named by the government as unindicted coconspirators. Those individuals apparently included many prominent members of the business and legal community, which, Skilling argued, evidenced that the government was trying to criminalize the entire business community. That motion was denied.

Bank Involvement

Prepaid Forward Transactions

Citigroup received $188 million in revenue from Enron-related transactions between 1997 and 2001. Citigroup helped structure several deals totaling over

$4.6 billion that moved debt off Enron's balance sheet and allowed Enron to claim cash flow in massive amounts from operating activities. JPMorgan Chase received $49 million in revenues from Enron between 1999 and 2000 and structured over $3.7 billion in financing for Enron between 1992 and 2001. The involvement of these and other banks in the Enron scandal resulted in criticism that the repeal of Glass-Steagall restrictions on nonbanking activities by commercial banks had been premature. There was, however, little justification for that complaint because the banking system remained sound, unlike the situation after the stock market crash of 1929 when Glass-Steagall was enacted.

The banks did have cause to regret having aided Enron's financial chicanery after its collapse. JPMorgan Chase had a fourth quarter loss at the end of 2001 of $322 million as the result of losses from Enron and Argentina. The bank disclosed that its total exposure to Enron could be as much as $2.6 billion. The value of JPMorgan Chase's own stock was cut nearly in half as a result of these problems, losing almost $3 billion in value. Citigroup's share price fell by 25 percent between January and July of 2002. By the latter date, Citigroup's stock had lost more than $11 billion in market value. Bank of America was also caught up in the Enron and other accounting scandals. Its stock lost $3.9 billion in value. That seemed to be an overreaction. Bank of America paid only $69 million to settle class action claims for its involvement with Enron.

The banks should have been forewarned by an earlier experience involving JPMorgan Chase and the Sumitomo Corp. A rogue trader at Sumitomo, Yasuo Hamanaka, lost $2.6 billion in 1996 from a failed attempt to manipulate world copper prices. The trader was assisted in that effort by financing supplied by the Chase Manhattan Bank and JP Morgan & Co. before their merger. A suit brought against those two financial institutions by the Sumitomo Corp. charged that the banks had extended $900 million in credit to Hamanaka that was disguised as copper swaps, allowing Hamanaka to leverage his positions and evade management oversight. That case was settled for a reported $125 million by the banks.

The Prepays

Undaunted by its experience with Sumitomo, Chase Manhattan (now JPMorgan Chase) engaged in a series of transactions structured as "prepaid forward" contracts in which Chase through SPEs ostensibly paid Enron in advance for the future delivery of natural gas or oil under an agreed-upon delivery schedule over a period of years. The Enron prepay transactions required the purchaser to pay the entire purchase price up front for the commodities that were supposed to be delivered by Enron in the future. As in the Sumitomo case, these transactions were claimed to be disguised loans rather than actual commodity transactions.

Forward contracts are common throughout the commodity business. They are useful in ensuring availability of commodity supplies needed by a processor or marketer and ensuring a source of sale. However, forward contracts involve risks to both parties. For example, the producer may default, requiring the purchaser to cover its needs in the market, at possibly a higher price. If the price of the contract is prepaid, the purchaser faces a loss of those funds in the event of a default. Conversely, the purchaser may default, requiring the producer to find another buyer at a possibly lower price. To protect against these risks, the parties consider each other's credit rating as a measure of their respective ability to perform. Either party may further demand collateral to assure performance and to offset damages in the event of a default.

Another risk associated with a forward contract is price fluctuations. If the price is fixed at the time the contract is entered into, the selling party must obtain the commodity for delivery whatever the price may be when delivered. If the seller does not own the commodity, it must be purchased at the market price, which may be substantially higher than the price set by the forward contract. If the seller is a producer of the commodity, it will not have to purchase the commodity at a higher price but will still receive a lower than market price under the forward contract. The purchaser also has a price risk. If the commodity price under the forward contract is higher than the market price at time of delivery, the purchaser will be required to buy the commodity at a price higher than it will receive from its resale into the market. Of course, if the parties do not want to fix their commodity prices, they can simply buy and sell at current market prices at the time they want to deliver or purchase the commodity. However, many buyers and sellers would prefer a fixed price in order to stabilize their costs or sales.

The Enron prepay transactions were structured to avoid price risk. This was accomplished through the use of Jersey Island SPEs named Mahonia Ltd., Mahonia Natural Gas Ltd. (collectively Mahonia) and Stoneville Aegean Ltd. These SPEs were created for Chase by Mourant & Co., a Jersey Island corporate chartering company operated by a law firm of the same name. The SPEs were owned by other entities that were supposed to be charitable trusts, but were managed by the same director, Ian James, and were owned by the same shareholders, Juris Ltd. and Lively Ltd. Through the use of these SPEs, the prepaid forward contracts with Enron were turned into circular transactions that negated the risks of a normal forward contract, leaving only the risks of what would otherwise be a loan. The bankruptcy examiner for Enron found that the funds used by the Jersey Island SPEs for the prepays were funded by Chase:

> The SPE received the funds from the bank on account of its own prepaid forward contract with the bank. Enron and the bank would simultaneously enter into derivative contracts pursuant to which Enron would agree to pay a fixed price for the amount of the commodity it had agreed to deliver the SPE, plus an interest factor, in exchange for the bank's agreement to pay the market price for the commodity at the times of scheduled deliveries under Enron's prepaid forward contract with the SPE.

Enron, rather than the bank or the SPE, had the risk of price fluctuation on the commodity. Enron was exposed to a floating price risk, having agreed to deliver the commodity to the SPE at specified times in the future, but had eliminated that risk by agreeing to receive the floating price from the bank in exchange for a fixed price. The bank had no commodity risk because, while it was to receive the floating commodity price from the SPE, it had eliminated that risk by agreeing to receive a fixed price (plus an interest element) from Enron in exchange for giving Enron the floating price. The SPE had no commodity price risk because it simply passed what it received from Enron to the bank.[16]

Price risk was "illusory" in several of the transactions because the commodity being delivered was sent in a round trip from Enron to one or more SPEs, or the bank itself, and then back to Enron.[17] In one such prepaid transaction entered into between Enron and Mahonia on December 28, 2000, Enron agreed to deliver natural gas to Mahonia pursuant to an agreed-upon delivery schedule. Mahonia in turn agreed to sell and deliver that same gas to Stoneville. Enron then agreed to purchase from Stoneville the identical quantities of gas and on the same dates that Enron had agreed to sell that gas to Mahonia. Any gaps or residual price risks were covered by swap contracts that put the commodity risk back to Enron.

The Sureties

A risk to JPMorgan Chase was a counterparty default on the prepaid forward contracts by Enron, a risk common to any loan transaction, but a risk that Chase did not want assume. There was a reason why Chase did not want to assume additional counterparty default risk from Enron. According to a class action suit, JPMorgan Chase had written hundreds of millions of dollars in credit default puts against Enron's long-term debt that obligated the bank to cover an Enron default on that debt. JPMorgan Chase sought to eliminate its counterparty risk from Enron in the prepay transactions, first by obtaining standby letters of credit from other banks and then by inducing insurance companies to act as sureties for the delivery of the gas and oil by Enron.

The sureties were guaranteeing Enron's delivery of the commodity, not its performance on a loan. This was an important distinction because the sureties were prohibited by New York law from acting as surety on financial transactions, as opposed to commodity deliveries. When Enron defaulted by declaring bankruptcy, the sureties refused to pay because they had discovered that the prepay transactions were actually disguised loans, rather than the forward transactions that they were represented to be when the surety bonds were obtained. The sureties claimed that such a disguise was fraudulent in inducing them to act as surety for a financial product in violation of New York law. JPMorgan Chase sued the sureties for $965 million, demanding summary judgment for that amount in the federal district court in New York. The district court refused that request and ordered a trial on the issue.[18] At the trial, JPMorgan Chase contended that the sureties were aware of the true nature of the transactions. The case was settled after it was submitted to the jury, but before the jury reached a decision. The settlement was reported as being a little over half the amount sought by JPMorgan Chase.

Before engaging the surety companies, JPMorgan Chase used standby letters of credit from other banks to guard against default by Enron on the prepay contracts. Under those letters of credit, the banks were required to pay if Enron defaulted on its delivery obligations. One of the syndicates refused to pay $165 million after Enron defaulted. JPMorgan Chase then sued the syndicate in England. The English judge, in a lengthy opinion, ruled that the prepay transactions had been properly accounted for by Enron and that U.S. securities laws were not violated by that accounting treatment. A federal court in New York also dismissed a class action on behalf of JPMorgan Chase shareholders challenging its role in the prepay transactions.

Enron obtained more than $9 billion in cash from its prepay transactions between 1992 and 2000 that it reported as operating cash flow rather than debt. The prepay transactions were designed to increase Enron's cash flows in order to match its mark-to-market earnings: "prepays were the quarter-to-quarter cash flow lifeblood of Enron," providing over half of Enron's flow of funds from operations in 2000.[19] These transactions provided almost all of Enron's net operating cash flow in 1999 and almost a third in 2000. Enron's prepay transactions were its largest source of cash in the four years before its bankruptcy.

Prepays were reported as liabilities from price risk management on Enron's balance sheet. That allowed Enron to avoid recording the amounts it received from prepays as debt, an amount that totaled over $4 billion in 2000 alone. As a result of this bit of legerdemain, "Enron's key credit ratios were enhanced significantly."[20] As the bankruptcy examiner concluded, "The prepay technique was a powerful tool employed by Enron to maintain investment grade rating."[21] Enron rejected a suggestion by Arthur Andersen that the effect of the prepay transactions be disclosed on Enron's financial statements. Andersen then concluded that Enron's financial statements would not be materially misleading if disclosure was not made.

Citigroup

Citigroup engaged in several prepay transactions with Enron, including "Project Yosemite," which involved the private placement of notes by Citigroup to institutional investors. The proceeds of those notes were then placed in "blind pool trusts" that loaned the money to Enron through prepay transactions. Citigroup paid the interest on the notes it placed with the institutional investors. Citigroup, in turn, received payments from the blind pool trusts that were receiving payments from Enron through the prepay transactions. Credit default swaps were used to provide protection to the blind pool trusts by creating an agreement to swap the prepay obligations for senior unsecured obligations of Enron. Citigroup also engaged in credit default swaps with the blind pool trusts to hedge its counterparty risk with Enron. In other transactions, Citigroup directly funded prepays, creating an SPE called Delta to mask Citigroup's role.

Even more exotic was Project Nahanni, a joint venture between Enron and an SPE created by Citigroup called Nahanni LLC. That SPE was capitalized with a $485 million loan from Citigroup and a $15 million equity contribution from a third party. That capital was used to purchase U.S. Treasury bills. Those T-bills were then "contributed" (rather than loaned) to Marengo, an Enron subsidiary, with Nahanni taking a 50 percent limited partnership interest in Marengo. Marengo sold the T-bills and loaned the proceeds to Enron, which then reported them as cash flow from operating activities. This transaction was responsible for 41 percent of Enron's total reported cash flow for 1999. The proceeds were used to pay down $500 million of Enron debt on December 29, 1999. Only three weeks later, after it closed its books on the 1999 fiscal year, Enron repaid the $500 million to Nahanni, with interest. This machination was needed to close a gap between its net income and its flow of funds from operations caused by Enron's mark-to-market accounting requirements.

Project Bacchus was another Citigroup-inspired financing program for Enron. In this structure, Enron created an SPE that was capitalized with a $194 million loan from Citigroup and $6 million in equity in order to claim independence of the SPE, as required by accounting rules. Those funds were then used by the SPE to purchase a portion of Enron's pulp and paper businesses. The $6 million equity contribution was supposed to be at risk in order to meet accounting standards, but Enron and Citigroup secretly agreed that Citigroup would not be at risk for those funds. The SEC charged that this secret agreement negated the independence of the SPE. This meant that the arrangement should have been characterized as debt on Enron's balance sheet and should not have been reported as cash from operating activities, which is how Enron characterized the payments.

Additional SPEs were created for the sale of other portions of Enron's wood product assets. They included a project called Slapshot that utilized an SPE called Fishtail LLC, which was created by LJM2. Fishtail purchased the right to future profits from Enron's wood-related futures contracts, providing Enron with cash that it could report as operating income. The Fishtail assets were later folded back into Project Bacchus through two other SPEs named Sonoma I LLC and Caymus Trust. Enron sought to refinance Bacchus and Fishtail through Citigroup, this time using an SPE called Sundance Industrial Partners LP, which was controlled by a Citigroup entity under its Salomon Brothers umbrella. Once again, that allegedly independent investor (Sundance) was determined not to have been at risk because of Enron assurances protecting against loss. True to its word, Enron redeemed the Salomon partnership interest just three days before filing for bankruptcy. That was accomplished through a loan from JPMorgan Chase of $1.4 billion that was repaid on the same day, except for the amount needed to liquidate the Fishtail and Bacchus holdings. The excess one-day amount not used for that liquidation was a part of a tax gimmick designed to avoid or evade Canadian taxes. Through these various pulp and paper projects, Enron was able to keep $375 million of debt off its balance sheet in 2001, as well as avoiding (or evading, as Enron's own counsel asserted) over $100 million in Canadian taxes.

The Enron bankruptcy examiner concluded, "Although its SPE structures were complex, Enron's primary objective was simple: (i) borrow money on what the Financial Institutions required to be a recourse basis without recording debt and (ii) record the loan proceeds as cash flow from operating activities. To accomplish those goals, Enron used its SPE structures to disseminate financial information that was fundamentally misleading."[22] The bankruptcy examiner found that Enron used its SPE transactions and other dubious accounting techniques in the year 2000 to produce 96 percent of its reported income and cut its reported debt by more than 50 percent from $22.1 billion to $10.2 billion.

Liability of Financial Institutions

By the middle of 2003, the SEC had collected $324 million in penalties from former Enron employees and institutions dealing with Enron. That figure mounted in future months, as did settlements with private litigants. Citigroup was sued by several investors in Yosemite after Enron filed bankruptcy. The suit claimed that Citigroup had sought their investments in order to reduce its own exposure from Enron. A class action suit brought on behalf of Citigroup shareholders by the Pompano Beach Police and Firefighters Retirement System attacking the bank's role in the Enron transactions was dismissed, but the Board of Regents of the University of California had better luck with its class action. Citigroup agreed to settle those claims in June 2005 for a spectacular $2 billion. That class action had already garnered almost $500 million from other institutions involved with Enron. JPMorgan Chase contributed another $2.2 billion shortly after the Citigroup settlement. The Canadian Imperial Bank of Commerce (CIBC) added another $2.4 billion to settle claims against it in that proceeding. CIBC paid another $274 million to the Enron bankruptcy proceeding. The Royal Bank of Canada also paid $25 million to the Enron bankruptcy proceeding.

On July 29, 2003, JPMorgan Chase and Citigroup agreed to pay fines totaling $255 million to the SEC for helping Enron use the prepaid forward structure to match marked-to-market earnings with cash flow from operating activities. JPMorgan Chase agreed to pay $162.5 million of that amount. JPMorgan and Citigroup agreed to pay a further $50 million to the state and city of New York in order to avoid criminal prosecution. JPMorgan announced a $387 million fourth-quarter loss in 2002 due in part to liabilities from its

Enron dealings. The bank had already taken a $1.3 billion charge to cover those problems. JPMorgan Chase paid nearly $1 billion in August 2005 to settle claims brought in the Enron bankruptcy "Megaclaims" lawsuit brought by Enron's estate in bankruptcy. That settlement included a $350 million cash payment and waiver of claims against the Enron estate valued at $660 million.

The Enron bankruptcy examiner concluded that several other financial institutions had acted improperly and were liable to the Enron estate or, at the least, that their claims in bankruptcy should be subordinated to the claims of other creditors. The Royal Bank of Scotland PLC (previously NatWest) was charged by the bankruptcy examiner with having actual knowledge of wrongdoing by Enron and with lending substantial assistance to that conduct through transactions financed by the bank. The examiner also claimed that Credit Suisse First Boston, which had received $23 million in fees from Enron in 1999, had aided other improper transactions at Enron, including a prepay totaling $150 million that was simply a disguised loan. Those transactions included the funding of a transaction called Nile that involved another one of Enron's SPE structures.

The Toronto Dominion Bank was another target of the bankruptcy examiner for its funding and structuring of prepay transactions with Enron. That bank participated in six prepay transactions with Enron totaling $2 billion. The Toronto Dominion Bank paid $350 million to settle a claim brought against it in the Enron bankruptcy proceeding. A class action complaint alleged that another form of disguised loan transaction was conducted with the Connecticut Resources Recovery Authority (CRRA) and with the Connecticut Light and Power Company (CL&P). Specifically, in March 2001, CL&P paid Enron $220 million to assume a contract to purchase CRRA's trash-generated steam electricity. Enron in turn agreed to pay CRRA $2.4 million per month for eleven years for that electricity. Those repayments were equal to repayment of the $220 million advanced by CL&P plus interest. In fact, Enron never actually purchased the electricity.

Merrill Lynch

The government charged Andrew Fastow and, in separate indictments, several other persons, including employees at the Enron Corp. and four employees at Merrill Lynch & Co., with fraud in connection with a 1999 sale of electricity-producing barges that were anchored off the coast of Nigeria. Those barges were treated by Enron as a sale to a Merrill Lynch SPE called Ebarge for $28 million when in fact there was no true sale. The government asserted that Merrill Lynch had been guaranteed that it would be bought out of the deal at a profit by Fastow in the form of a rate of return of 15 percent in less than six months.

The repurchase was financed by Enron through LJM, and the barges were later resold to a third party at a profit. The government claimed that the buyback arrangement between Merrill Lynch and Enron meant that Merrill Lynch never had the risk of ownership for the barges and that Enron had improperly booked $12 million in earnings that should have been reported as debt. Sheila Kahanek, a former Enron accountant, and Dan Boyle, an Enron vice president, were indicted in connection with this transaction. The indicted Merrill Lynch employees were Daniel Bayly, chairman of Merrill Lynch's investment banking group; James Brown, head of the Merrill's asset lease and finance group; Robert Furst, the Enron relationship manager; and William Fuhs, a Merrill Lynch vice president.

The trial began in September 2004. Although almost three years had passed since Enron unraveled, these were the first Enron employees actually to be tried for any misconduct. Ben Glisan came from his prison cell to testify that the transaction was a sham. The government declined to put Andrew Fastow on the stand although he was a cooperating witness and was claimed to have been the mastermind behind the whole scheme. As it turned out, Fastow's testimony was not needed. The jury convicted all six defendants. The government then sought an enhanced sentence for Bayly, claiming that he was responsible for the entire loss to shareholders as a result of Enron's collapse. That drew a rebuke from the Chamber of Commerce and the *Wall Street Journal*. The Chamber of Commerce asserted that the "increasingly aggressive prosecutions of white-collar crime will inflict incalculable economic and intangible harm on businesses, their employees and their shareholders." The Justice Department was seeking up to thirty-three years for what the trial judge, Ewing Werlein Jr., viewed to be a relatively "benign" crime. The judge imposed a sentence of thirty months.

Merrill Lynch engaged in several other transactions with Enron, including electricity derivative transactions that were back-to-back call options that offset each other but allowed Enron to book some $50 million in earnings to meet 1999 targets. The transactions were terminated in the following year. A Merrill Lynch broker, Daniel Gordon, pleaded guilty to criminal charges in connection with those options, and to charges that he created a bogus transaction with Merrill Lynch that allowed him to pocket a $43 million premium. (Gordon had been expelled from his high school for hacking into the school's computer and changing his grades so that he could gain admittance to an Ivy League college.) Merrill Lynch was not charged with criminal misconduct for its role in Enron's accounting ploys. In order to avoid such charges, Merrill Lynch agreed to pay the SEC a penalty of $80 million and to hire an independent auditor that would work under the supervision of a lawyer selected by the Justice Department and would review any new structured finance products.

Other Institutions

Lehman Brothers settled class action claims for its involvement with Enron for $225 million. The Canadian Imperial Bank of Commerce settled criminal charges and a civil action brought by the SEC in December 2003 for its role in various Enron transactions. The bank agreed not to engage in any structured finance transactions in the United States for three years and to pay $80 million in penalties. CIBC further agreed to be monitored for a period of three years by an independent monitor and to create an internal financial transaction oversight committee. CIBC was charged with aiding Enron in structuring thirty-four transactions that Enron improperly used to inflate its earnings by more than $1 billion and to increase operating cash flow by $2 billion. The U.S. government claimed that these transactions were actually loans totaling $2.6 billion that were not reported on Enron's balance sheet. The assets were purportedly sold to SPEs that had an independent 3 percent ownership held by the bank. In fact, Enron guaranteed the bank against loss. An SEC official called this "asset parking." Ian Schottlaender, a CIBC managing director, agreed to pay $528,750 to settle SEC charges that he helped arrange thirty-four disguised loans for Enron. Schottlaender was barred from serving as an officer and director of a public company for five years. As noted, CIBC also agreed to pay $2.4 earlier to settle class action shareholder claims on its involvement with Enron.

NatWest assisted Fastow in enriching himself through the LJM structures in a transaction that involved 5.4 million shares of Rhythms NetConnections Inc. After an initial public offering (IPO) by Rhythms, Enron was required to mark its shares to market, but was restricted from selling the stock for six months. Fastow arranged to hedge the Rhythms stock held by Enron through a put option sold by Enron to an SPE called LJM Swap Sub LP. The independent interest in this entity was funded by Credit Suisse First Boston and NatWest. After the Rhythms stock rose in value, Fastow and three employees at NatWest arranged for NatWest to sell its interest in the LJM Swap Sub at a price well below its appreciated value in a manner that allowed the three NatWest bankers to make personal unauthorized profits of $7.3 million. Another $12 million was paid to a partnership named Southampton that paid the Fastow Family Foundation $4.5 million (which was used for tax-advantaged family vacations and to hire Andrew Fastow's father, as well as a means for the Fastows to social climb). Michael Kopper received $4.5 million and five other Enron and LJM employees received a total of $3.3 million.

Andrew Fastow admitted in his guilty plea that Southampton resold to Enron for $20 million Rhythms stock that Southampton had only shortly before bought for $1 million. The three NatWest bankers, David Bermingham, Gary Mulgrew, and Giles Darby, were charged with fraud in connection with their profiting from these transactions. The U.S. government asserted that those profits should have gone to their employer, NatWest. One of the indicted NatWest bankers had "ironically" warned his bank of the suspicious nature of the Enron transactions.[23] The NatWest bankers resisted extradition from England, contending that the United States had no right to prosecute three English citizens for allegedly defrauding an English bank through activities carried out in London. An English judge ordered their extradition, but the bankers announced that they were appealing that ruling to the home secretary, Charles Clarke, but he ordered their extradition under a new antiterrorism statute. The NatWest bankers continued their fight to avoid extradition in the English courts. The Rhythms stock was not a disaster for everyone. Catherine Hapka, that company's chief executive officer, sold $21 million of the company's stock before it failed.

Barclays Bank was another financial institution caught in the web of Enron financing. Barclays, along with Citigroup, Deutsche Bank, JPMorgan, and Bank of America, acted as a placement agent for $1.9 billion of Enron zero coupon convertible bonds in February 2001. Barclays was the underwriter for $240 million of 8.75 percent obligations for Yosemite, an SPE, and the bank directly loaned more than $3 billion to Enron. A class action suit charged that Barclays was the "lead lender on a $2.3 billion debt facility to finance Enron's purchase of Wessex Water in 1998; it was co-arranger of a $250 million loan to Enron in November 1997; it participated in the September 1998, $1 billion credit facility for Enron and the August 2001, $3 billion debt facility, both used to back up Enron's commercial paper debt; it participated in a September 1998, $250 million revolving credit facility for Enron in November 1998; and it helped to arrange and participated in a $500 million credit facility for JEDI in May 1998."[24] Barclays provided the financing for several questionable transactions that kept debt off Enron's balance sheet and increased its cash flows. Sometimes the ostensible independent 3 percent owner of some Enron SPEs, Barclays was given assurances from Enron that the bank would be protected against loss. All these activities made Barclays a target for the Enron bankruptcy examiner.

H&R Block Financial Advisors was accused by the National Association of Securities Dealers, Inc. (NASD) of defrauding investors by assuring them that Enron bonds were safe investments even after Enron's disclosures of its accounting problems. Brokers at H&R Block sold $16 million of those bonds in the five weeks before Enron's bankruptcy to over eighty customers in forty states.

California Trading Scandals

Enron's problems continued to mushroom. Prosecutors and regulators attacked the company's trading operations in the California electricity market. Enron was accused of "gaming" the California energy market through trades that took advantage of regulatory inefficiencies in that market.

California Deregulates

The background of Enron's trading activities in California is complex. Congressional efforts to deregulate the natural gas market were succeeded by legislation that sought deregulation of the electricity market. The Energy Policy Act of 1992 directed the Federal Energy Regulatory Commission (FERC) to require that the states deregulate their electric utilities and provide competition in generating and transmitting electricity. Pursuant to that authority, FERC determined that vertically integrated utilities were using their market power over transmission facilities to thwart competition. In order to remedy that problem, FERC Order No. 888 required regulated electric utilities to unbundle their wholesale electric power services and to open their transmission facilities on a nondiscriminatory basis to competitors, so as to allow competitive pricing of wholesale electricity.

The FERC order required public utilities to divest themselves of a substantial portion of their generating facilities. Those public utilities could keep their transmission lines, but open access was granted on those lines to anyone wanting to open a new generation facility. This meant that new generators would not have to undergo the traditional, prolonged process for regulatory approval. FERC sought to have public utilities participate in entities called independent system operators (ISOs), which would conduct transmission and ancillary services for users of the system. The ISO would replace the system owners as the provider of those services. FERC required the ISO to be independent of market participants.

California jumped into the deregulatory effort, seeking to reduce its electricity prices, which were among the highest in the country. To encourage alternative energy sources—after all, this was California—subsidies totaling $540 million were given to wind and solar generating facilities, a boon for Enron. Under state legislation passed in 1996, California tried to implement its own deregulatory structure under the FERC order. The California legislation created the California Electricity Oversight Board (CEOB) and directed it to create the California Independent System Operator Corp. (CISOC) as a not-for-profit corporation. CISOC was to operate all electric grid facilities in the state to ensure their efficient and reliable operation. CEOB was to select the board of directors for CISOC. Those board members were required to be representatives from eleven "stakeholder" classes in the electricity market, including market participants, consumers, businesses, electricity marketers, and utilities. However, CISOC's governing structure consisting of stakeholders proved to be unworkable. The legislature, Governor Gray Davis, and FERC demanded changes, but disagreed on the makeup of a new board of directors. The legislature ordered a new five-member board appointed by the governor, while FERC demanded a seven-member body consisting of candidates selected by an independent search firm. A federal court ruled that FERC had no authority to require a public utility to replace its governing board.

The 1996 California legislation also required the creation of the California Power Exchange (PX), which began operations in 1998. It was to be a market for the trading of electricity. The PX sought to create wholesale markets for "hourly," "day-ahead" and "day-of" electricity deliveries. Most long-term contracts were prohibited. Transactions on the PX were executed through an auction process in which all purchasers paid the same market-clearing price. That price was calculated on the basis of the lowest offer price that would fill all bids, a sort of reverse Dutch auction. This created a complex market structure that was made more complex by the fact that electricity demand fluctuated broadly and quickly, while supplies could not be accurately forecast and transmission facilities were limited in meeting those fluctuations in demand.

CISOC's role was to manage the grid and schedule transmission in the "real-time" markets, which were used to meet imbalances after the PX closed for the day. Under this structure, the public utilities in California had to surrender control of the scheduling of their transmission facilities to the CISOC. That entity created something called "ancillary services" to ensure adequate supplies in times of stress. Ancillary services created reserve transmission facilities as a backup to meet imbalances. CISOC could also impose price caps in times of shortage.

Flawed System

California's three largest public utilities transferred control of their transmission facilities to CISOC and agreed to sell electricity to the PX. These public utilities were to be protected from loss as a result of their restructuring by the creation of a "stranded assets account" through which the state would reimburse the utilities for the devaluation of their assets resulting from the deregulation scheme. Most of the generation facilities divested by the California public utilities under FERC Order No. 888 were snatched up by a handful of out-of-state energy firms, including Duke Energy, Dynegy, and Reliant. Those companies had no interest in building new generation facilities until a competitive market was more fully established. Consequently, the deregulation scheme did not relieve the existing shortage of generation capacity in California. Compounding that problem was the fact that existing transmission facilities were already congested, leaving little room for new capacity. Government restrictions and environmental concerns had prevented new generation facilities from being built in California for over a decade; no incentive was given to utilities to improve or expand their transmission facilities, and they did not do so.

Another significant flaw in the deregulation effort in California was that it only targeted wholesale prices. Retail prices, for the most part, remained regulated. Retail prices in California were reduced by 10 percent and were to remain frozen (except in San Diego) until deregulation was complete. Bonds totaling $6.6 billion were to be issued by the state to fund this rate reduction. Retail prices were set at artificially low levels for political reasons (consumers wanted lower, not higher, rates, whether set by the market or otherwise). The fact that consumers would have to pay for that reduction by paying higher taxes was ignored. As one pundit noted, deregulating the electricity market at the wholesale level while fixing prices at the retail level was "based on economic principles that have made Cuba the happy, prosperous country that it is today."[25] The lower retail electricity rates undercut conservation efforts, increasing demand at a time when supply sources were under stress, creating a setting for still another perfect storm, into which Enron happily sailed.

The California restructuring led to volatility in the wholesale market and at times shortages, as demand increased and supplies tightened when generation capacity failed to increase. Brownouts and rolling blackouts were experienced in California during the summer of 2000 and were reaching a crisis stage in the winter and spring of 2001. That crisis was said to have cost the state and businesses $80 billion. Pacific Gas & Electric and Southern California Edison were two of the largest retail electric utilities companies in California. They lost billions of dollars when they were unable to pass increased wholesale electric prices on to retail consumers. Governor Davis stated that he would provide rescue funds to these utilities if they agreed to drop demands for higher rates, sell their transmission systems and provide low-cost electricity to the state for ten years. Pacific Gas & Electric then filed bankruptcy, citing unreimbursed energy costs that were increasing at a rate of $300 million per month. Southern California Edison was also in dire straits.

California sought to alleviate the shortages it was experiencing by buying electricity. Those purchases were made by the California Department of Water Resources, which became a major participant in the wholesale market. Those purchases were to be made with funds generated from revenue bonds in the amount of $12.5 billion—the largest state bond issue in history until California subsequently topped over that amount. In the interim, these purchases were made from funds already in the state treasury. This raid on the treasury and a declining economy transformed a projected California state budgetary surplus of $8 billion for 2001 to a deficit of almost $6 billion. The increased price paid by the state for electricity was not passed directly to retail electricity customers. Rather, the state's taxpayers would pay it over time in retiring the revenue bonds. This method, too, failed to encourage conservation efforts that would have reduced demand and prices.

FERC entered orders that allowed public utilities greater access to the forward market for longer term contracts (the California structure had limited them to the spot market) and removed other inefficiencies imposed by that system. FERC attempted to devise some federal controls for wholesale prices in California by sanctioning price caps and "price mitigation" orders, but their positive effects were questionable. A moderate summer, belated conservation efforts, and additional generation sources relieved the crisis. Nevertheless, the state was saddled with debt and facing a financial crisis. Perhaps worse, California entered into long-term supply contracts at a period of price peaks, assuring high electricity prices for years to come. These problems and a growing deficit in the state resulted in the recall of Governor Davis and the election of movie star Arnold Schwarzenegger as governor in 2003.

California sought refunds of $8.9 billion for claimed overcharges by wholesale generators. The state won a victory after a federal appeals court reversed a FERC order limiting the amount of refunds that could be obtained from power sellers, which could result in $2.8 billion in additional refunds. California approved a $16 billion bond offering in March 2004 as requested by Governor Schwarzenegger in order to help deal with the state's budget problems and the residue of its energy crisis. The $16 billion offering was the largest municipal bond offering ever, exceeding the $10 billion municipal offering by the state of Illinois in June 2003. California then had a $12 billion deficit and $30 billion in general obligation bonds outstanding, but that did not slow its spending. A separate $12.3 billion bond offering to improve the schools was approved in March 2004 and another $3 billion was voted for stem cell research at the request of Governor Schwarzenegger in November 2004. The governor somewhat inconsistently asked for and received approval for a proposition requiring a balanced budget. A California court struck a ballot initiative to once again regulate the California electricity market but the California Supreme Court reversed that decision.

Enron Games the Market

Enron and other large energy firms, including Dynegy, Reliant Energy, and El Paso Corp., were under attack for their role in the California energy crisis even before Enron's bankruptcy. Enron fiercely resisted a probe by a California legislative committee into its trading practices during that event. Bill Lockyer, the California attorney general, was calling for Kenneth Lay to be jailed for his stewardship during the crisis. As criticism of the company's trading mounted in the press, Jeffrey Skilling received death threats and was struck in the face by a pie thrown by a demonstrator in San Francisco.

The California electricity market was, to put it mildly, imperfect and lent itself to abuse, a fact that was obvious to all involved. Perot Systems Corp., which helped design CISOC, was accused of helping traders take advantage of its flaws. A CISOC board member asserted that gaming the California electricity market would be akin to "shooting fish in a barrel—not great sport, but lucrative."[26] Enron traders gleefully agreed to do the shooting by engaging in a number of transactions that sought to take advantage of the inefficiencies in this market. Enron increased its electricity trading revenues massively during the electricity crisis in California. In the year before that crisis, that revenue figure was $50 million but jumped to $500 million in 2000 and then to $800 million in 2001. A government report estimated that Enron made total profits of $2.7 billion from trading electricity and gas in western markets during the California electricity crisis.

Enron was accused of price gouging, including a claimed overcharge of $175 million for electricity generated by Enron wind farms. The Enron traders also developed a number of "regulatory arbitrage" trading strategies to take advantage of the imperfections in the California market. The simplest was to buy California electricity at capped prices and resell it at uncapped prices out of state when those prices were higher. Other trades, with exotic names like Ricochet, Fat Boy, Death Star, and Get Shorty, were more complex. These trades were vetted by outside lawyers before Enron's collapse, but the trades became controversial in the wake of the Enron accounting scandal, particularly when the lawyers' memoranda describing the trades were made public and posted on a government Web site. The publicity set off another Enron firestorm in the press. Later revealed were tape-recorded conversations by Enron traders, including one discussing California's demand for refunds from Enron and other energy traders for price gouging. That conversation occurred during the contested presidential election between Al Gore and George Bush in 2000:

> Kevin: So the rumor's true? They're [expletive] takin' all the money back from you guys? All the money you guys stole from those poor grandmothers in California?
> Bob: Yeah, Grandma Millie, man. But she's the one who couldn't figure out how to [expletive] vote on the butterfly ballot [in Florida that was confusing and resulted in Al Gore's challenge to the 2000 presidential election].
> Kevin: Yeah, now she wants her [expletive] money back for all the power you've charged for [expletive] $250 a megawatt hour.
> Bob: You know—you know—you know, Grandma Millie, she's the one that Al Gore's fightin' for, you know? . . .
> Kevin: Oh, best thing that could happen is [expletive] an earthquake, let that thing [California] float out to the Pacific. . . .
> Bob: I know. Those guys—just cut 'em off.
> Kevin: They're so [expletive] and they're so like totally—
> Bob: They are so [expletive].[27]

Ricochet trades or "megawatt laundering" involved buying electricity on the PX in the day-ahead or the hourly market. The electricity was then parked with a third party and reimported to California in the CISOC real-time market. This was done to avoid price caps and was an arbitrage between the PX and CISOC markets. The Get Shorty transactions involved the sale of electricity by Enron that it did not own into the ancillary services market. It would then try to buy that electricity back at a lower price, creating a short profit. There was, however, no assurance that such lower prices could be obtained.

Fat Boy transactions involved instances when Enron had supply that it could bring to California but wanted to avoid underbidding by California utilities in the PX market, which was a problem at the time. In order to shift demand from the PX market to the CISOC market, Enron inflated its scheduling in the CISOC market, allowing it to obtain more favorable real-time prices. Enron was also receiving congestion relief payments. These were payments made to energy sellers who were scheduled to send electricity over congested lines, but agreed to reroute the scheduled flow to uncongested lines in order to relieve the congestion. Enron obtained such payments through what it referred to as Load Shift. This involved overstating its loads in part of the state and understating its loads in another part. Enron thereby received payments to relieve congestion that it created solely for the purpose of receiving those payments.

Enron traders used Death Star transactions to obtain congestion relief payments by scheduling electricity over lines in the direction opposite to a congested line, purportedly to relieve the congestion. Enron then returned the electricity back to its source by using lines outside the CISOC jurisdiction, which of course did not relieve congestion. A variation of this trading was called a Wheel Out, which involved scheduling electricity to a tie point that had no capacity. The electricity was accepted by the CISOC because of a flaw in its software, a flaw that CISOC was well aware of at the time. Enron would receive a congestion payment for such scheduling when its delivery was cut back, even though Enron could not have sent the electricity over that line in any event. Enron's overscheduling also resulted in a shortage of expected electricity, causing large jumps in price.

Enron engaged in several variations of these practices in transactions nicknamed Sidewinder, Russian Roulette, Ping Pong, Donkey, and Spread Play. A question raised by this trading was whether gaming the market was illegal. Arbitrage seeks out market inefficiencies and corrects them by increasing or decreasing supply or demand, bringing the market into equilibrium. Economists gave some support for the assertion that the Enron trades were appropriate economic behavior that simply exploited a flawed market structure, which is what traders do best and what makes them so valuable in making markets more efficient.[28] There are some limits on what traders can do in exploiting market flaws. As one Enron executive stated with respect to the California market: "It's just not right: just because some moron leaves his keys in his Jaguar doesn't give you the right to steal it."[29]

Enron was not the first firm to game the energy market. Marc Rich and his companies were accused of such conduct in an indictment brought in 1984 by Rudolph Giuliani, who was then serving as the United States Attorney in New York. That indictment charged that Rich's companies engaged in a series of "daisy chain" transactions that artificially converted "old" oil from Texas that was subject to price controls of $6 per barrel imposed by the Jimmy Carter administration into "new" oil that sold at market prices that were then exceeding $30 per barrel. This allowed Rich to make massive profits, which he then concealed and evaded taxes on through a series of other transactions. Apparently, this price control evasion was a common practice among Houston oil traders, involving hundreds of millions of barrels of oil. Rich and his partner, Pincus Green, fled to Switzerland after documents that Rich was spiriting out of the United States in trunks were intercepted at the airport by federal authorities. Two Marc Rich companies pleaded guilty to criminal charges and paid $150 million in fines. Rich remained a fugitive until his controversial pardon by President Bill Clinton in 2001. It turned out that President Clinton had been given large political donations by Marc Rich's wife.

Crimes and Investigations

Various Enron traders were indicted for gaming the California market. Jeffrey Richter, the head of Enron's short-term California energy trading desk, pleaded guilty to criminal charges that he made false statements to FBI agents in connection with Enron's California trading and for engaging in improper Load Shift and Get Shorty trades. Timothy Belden, the head of Enron's trading operations in its Portland, Oregon, office, pleaded guilty to criminal charges for such trading practices. His trading desk made profits of over $250 million in a single month in 2000 and $460 million for the year. Belden was paid a bonus of over $5 million for his trading success. Another Enron trader, John Forney, was charged with eleven counts of criminal misconduct for engaging in Ricochet and Death Star trades. He pleaded guilty to one of those counts. Enron later agreed to settle claims by California and other western states over its trading during the energy crisis by paying $47.5 million in cash. The states also received claims in bankruptcy totaling about $1.5 billion, but the actual value of those claims was uncertain.

A FERC staff investigation concluded that supply and demand imbalances caused the crisis in California. It found that California's deregulatory structure was "seriously flawed" and a significant cause of the unreasonable short-term rates in the California market. That market's design created a "dysfunctional" market in California in both electricity and natural gas. FERC issued two show cause orders that charged that certain companies engaged in gaming practices and anomalous market behavior that violated the PX and ISO tariffs and the Market Monitoring Information Protocol over which FERC claimed authority.

Reliant Energy agreed to pay California customers a total of $13.8 million to settle FERC charges that it withheld supplies from the California PX over a two-day period in order to mitigate losses in an existing forward position.[30] Reliant and four of its employees were indicted for that conduct in California. Another Reliant trader was accused of aiding a BP Energy trader to use the Bloomberg electronic trading platform to "seemingly" manipulate electricity prices at Palo Verde for the purpose of aiding BP Energy in its mark-to-market accounting. BP Energy entered into a settlement with FERC pursuant to which the company agreed to donate $3 million to energy assistance programs for low-income homes in California and Arizona. FERC further charged that Reliant engaged in "churning" that substantially increased natural gas prices throughout California by quick in-and-out trades. "Churning" is a term of art in the securities and commodity futures industry that describes the excessive trading of a customer's account by a broker that controls the account. That term hardly fit what the Reliant trader was doing. Quick in-and-out trading is common in the commodity markets, where "scalpers" engage in such trades for quick profits or to limit losses, and hedgers trade rapidly to cover ever-changing commitments.

In FERC's largest-ever settlement, Reliant agreed to pay up to $50 million to settle charges relating to its economic and physical withholding and other acts. It was not clear from that settlement what Reliant had done wrong to merit such treatment. The government's charges of withholding were novel in claiming that a company could not decide when to bring product to market. Indeed, that charge turned the economic clock back to medieval days when withholding grain from the market was prohibited as the crime of "forestalling" or "regrating." Henry VIII issued proclamations in the sixteenth century that prohibited the withholding of victuals from the market in order to increase prices. Those proclamations were later enforced by the Star Chamber. Parliament dropped such restrictions in 1844 in recognition that the market was a better disciplinarian than government intervention. There were some early efforts in the American colonies to create such crimes, but those proposals never got anywhere, at least until Enron came along. This medieval crime was even more fully resurrected by a FERC administrative law judge who ruled that Sempra Energy manipulated the natural gas market in Southern California during the California energy crisis by not having sufficient gas in storage and by keeping gas in storage that could have been put on the market.

In another FERC proceeding, Duke Energy agreed to pay $2.5 million to settle charges of economic and physical withholding of supplies to the California market during the crisis there in 2000 and 2001, as well as wash trading improprieties. In accepting the settlement, FERC seemed to have largely exonerated Duke of those charges. Another settlement with Duke involved charges of gaming the California ISO market. An investigation by the California Public Utilities Commission concluded that Duke Energy, Dynegy, Mirant, Reliant, and AES/Williams withheld power from California plants during the California energy crisis. A FERC study disagreed with the extent of those conclusions.

Round-Trip Trades

Another aspect of energy trading operations in Houston that raised more scandal were "round-trip" trades, or "bragawatts" as they were sometimes called. This trading involved the buying and selling by the same traders to themselves in offsetting transactions in order to boost their trading volumes or to set prices for actual contracts. This became an industry-wide practice in natural gas. Among the firms engaged in such activities, in addition to Enron, were El Paso Merchant Energy, WD Energy Services Inc. Williams Energy Marketing and Trading, Enserco Energy Inc., CMS Energy, Dynegy, Excel Energy, Aquila Inc., and Reliant Resources.

Duke Energy, which was involved in the round trip trading, stated that the $1.1 billion in round-trip trades on its books was used to validate "real-time prices." Three Duke employees, Timothy Kramer, Todd Reid, and Brian Lavielle, were indicted for engaging in round-trip trades called "sleeves" in order to inflate their bonuses by some $7 million. Duke was subjected to an SEC cease-and-desist order for that misconduct. Duke Energy Trading and Marketing LLC agreed to pay a civil penalty of $28 million to the Commodity Futures Trading Commission (CFTC) for false reports to trade publications in order to skew natural gas indexes for the benefit of its trading positions. Duke Energy hired a new chairman and chief executive officer. The company also took a $3.3 billion charge to earnings in the fourth quarter of 2003 as part of a restructuring of its trading, international, and merchant businesses in the post-Enron era.

Other firms admitted that the round-trip trades were simply used to boost trading volumes in order to convince other traders that the round-trip trader was a big player in the market. In that context, the trades were basically innocuous because industry participants were well aware of the practice, but the CFTC thought otherwise. The Commodity Futures Modernization Act (CFMA) of 2000 deregulated much derivative trading, particularly where institutions were involved. The failure of Enron, which was a large derivatives trading corporation, resulted in calls for renewed regulation of derivatives trading. To forestall that criticism, the CFTC decided to take an expansive view of its remaining regulatory powers. The CFTC charged that these round-trip trades constituted an attempted manipulation of the commodity markets, even though a regulated commodity exchange was not involved. The CFTC charged the involved firms with making false reports of these and other trades to various industry publications, such as the *Inside FERC Gas Market Report*. So much for deregulation, and the CFTC collected over $300 million in civil penalties from several energy firms through settlements in which the respondents neither admitted nor denied the charges.

The firms charged included Williams Energy Marketing and Trading, which agreed to pay the CFTC a civil penalty of $20 million to settle charges of false reporting of price information and attempted manipulation. WD Energy Services agreed to settle similar charges for the same amount; CMS Energy Group paid $16 million, and e prime Inc. paid $16 million. Coral Energy, an affiliate of Royal Dutch/Shell Group, paid $30 million in its settlement. Reliant Energy Services Inc. paid the CFTC $18 million to settle charges that it had attempted to manipulate the market by false reports of trading and of improper trading practices. Enserco Energy Inc. and Energy-Koch Trading LP each paid $3 million as a civil penalty. Aquila Inc. and Xcel Energy Inc. paid $26.5 million and $16 million respectively to settle CFTC charges of false reporting and attempted manipulation. ONEOK Energy Marketing and Trading Company LP (OEMT) each agreed to pay $3 million; and Calpine Energy Services LP paid $1.5 million to settle lesser CFTC charges for false reporting of their trading activities in the energy market. Another settling energy firm was Mirant Americas Energy Marketing LP.

The CFTC charged fifteen natural gas traders with false reporting and manipulation. Criminal charges were brought against Michelle Valencia, a trader at Dynegy, for engaging in round-trip trades in violation of the Commodity Exchange Act. A federal court initially dismissed those charges as unconstitutionally overbroad, but the judge then reversed herself and allowed the case to proceed on a limited basis. Caught up in the Enron mania, an appellate court went further, holding that the statute was constitutional in all respects. While that case was being appealed, another indictment was entered against Valencia and four other traders from El Paso Energy, Dynegy, and Reliant Energy for submitting false data on their trading to trade publications. In addition, two other El Paso traders, Donald Guilbault and William Ham, were convicted of similar charges, and a trader at the Williams Companies pleaded guilty to such charges. Dynegy and Reliant faced SEC charges for inflating their revenues with round-trip trades and other devices.

Enron could not be left out of the CFTC's roundup. Enron and one of its traders, Hunter Shively, were charged by that agency with engaging in a manipulative scheme that involved the purchase of a massive amount of natural gas in a very short period of time through Enron Online. Enron and Shively agreed to cover any losses of other traders participating in this effort. Although the CFMA had deregulated electronic trading platforms in general and Enron Online in particular, the CFTC claimed that it was an illegal futures exchange that should have been registered with the CFTC and that trading on Enron Online affected commodity futures prices in the natural gas contracts on the New York Mercantile Exchange. Enron agreed to pay $35 million to settle those charges, which would apparently come out of the pockets of Enron's creditors. Shively agreed to pay $300,000 to settle the charges against him.

The El Paso Corp. was hard hit by the Enron scandal and the collapse of the energy trading business. A FERC administrative law judge found that the El Paso Corp. withheld supplies of natural gas to California during the crisis. El Paso agreed to pay an astonishing $1.7 billion to settle charges by FERC and California regulators that it manipulated the California electricity market during 2000 and 2001. El Paso also agreed to invest $6 million in Arizona to settle claims of manipulation of energy prices in that state. Such settlements had become a popular shakedown used by states to extort money from large corporations. In addition to that problem, the company agreed to pay $20 million to settle CFTC problems with its trading. In 2001, El Paso's trading operation had made profits of $750 million, which was about a third of the company's pretax income. In the second quarter of 2002, El Paso's trading operations lost $150 million.

El Paso lost billions on an effort to enter the broadband market through a fiber-optic network. El Paso, Duke Energy, Reliant, and others formed the Intercontinental Exchange, an online trading platform created to compete with Enron. It had been used to conduct round-trip trades, but El Paso denied engaging in any such transactions. Nevertheless, four El Paso traders pleaded guilty to submitting false information to the *Inside FERC Gas Market Report* concerning El Paso's trading in natural gas. A class action lawsuit also claimed that El Paso had improperly used SPEs to manipulate its accounts. El Paso's stock dropped 90 percent in value after all these revelations. The company began winding down its trading operations, firing 175 employees. El Paso's longtime chairman and chief executive officer, William A. Wise, resigned, but he was allowed to retain the more than $10 million in compensation and 768,000 stock options awarded to him for the $93 million in profits reported in 2001. The company actually had a loss in that year of $447 million. The company then began a massive sale of its operations abroad in order to reduce its debt load. More bad news followed in March 2004, when El Paso announced that it had overstated its proven natural gas reserves by 34 percent, requiring a write-down of its assets in an amount exceeding $1 billion and requiring a restatement of its accounting statements for the prior five years.

II

Full Disclosure and the Accountants

4. Full Disclosure

Full Disclosure Background

Disclosure History

Supreme Court Justice Oliver Wendell Holmes famously wrote in one of his opinions that a "page of history is worth a volume of logic."[1] That is certainly true with respect to the debate over corporate governance that arose after the collapse of the Enron Corp. At the heart of that debate was the concept of "full disclosure." Full disclosure is based on a theory that investors will make more informed investment decisions if management is forced to disclose all "material" information about its company. Full disclosure is also thought to discourage undesirable conduct on the part of management because exposure will embarrass executives should they engage in such activity. Those theories proved to be fallacious in the case of Enron and other accounting failures arising after the market bubble burst in 2000.

Full disclosure is a creature of the federal securities laws that were enacted during the 1930s in the wake of the stock market crash of 1929 and in the midst of the Great Depression. The disclosure requirements in those statutes were modeled after the Joint Stock Companies Act of 1844, which was enacted in England after a three-year investigation by the Select Committee on Joint Stock Companies. That Select Committee was formed at the direction of William Gladstone, the future prime minister who was then president of the Board of Trade, after a shareholder audit of the Eastern Counties Railway Co. discovered that the head of that company, George Hudson, the "Railway King," was treating costs of over £200,000 as capital and overstating profits by a then staggering £438,000. The Joint Stock Companies Act of 1844 required corporations to provide a prospectus to investors and to distribute a balance sheet at the annual meetings of shareholders. The intent of the balance sheet requirement was to assure shareholders that the company was solvent and that dividends were not being paid out of capital. This legislation also contained a provision for auditors, but they were not required to be accountants.

That legislation did not stop abuses in Great Britain. Anticipating a scandal at Tyco International Ltd. by almost 150 years, an audit by William Deloitte discovered that Leopold Redpath had purloined £150,000 from the Great Northern Railway Company in 1857. Redpath, an employee of the railroad, used those funds to maintain a luxurious lifestyle that included a magnificent country home and a mansion in London that was decorated with expensive art. Like modern corporate pirates, Redpath was known for his philanthropy, making generous contributions to Christ's Hospital and St. Anne's Society for Impoverished Gentlefolk. Redpath's theft was uncovered after questions were raised as to how he could maintain such a lifestyle on an annual salary of £300. Redpath tried to evade arrest but was captured and transported to Australia.

The English Joint Stock Companies Act of 1856 dropped the requirement for a balance sheet, but a companies act passed in 1862 contained a model balance sheet and income statement. Although the distribution of those financial statements was not mandatory, the forms encouraged their use as a default requirement in lieu of other provisions in a company's by-laws. The Joint Stock Companies Act of 1856 further provided for an audit by inspectors appointed by the Board of Trade when demanded by 20 percent of shareholders. Companies were authorized to conduct their own audits, and the auditors were to render an opinion on whether the balance sheet provided a "true and correct view" of the company. The Companies Act of 1862 also provided for an annual audit. The Companies Act of 1879, which was enacted in response to the collapse of the City of Glasgow Bank, required an annual audit of limited liability companies. In 1900, all companies registered under the Companies Act of 1879 were required to supply shareholders with an annual balance sheet audited by someone other than an officer or director of the company. The Companies Act of 1907 required all public companies to publish annual audited balance sheets. The Companies Act of 1929 additionally required an annual income statement to be made available to shareholders, but an audit of that statement was not required.

The United States was slow to adopt the approach of disclosure found in the English Companies Acts. Most corporations in the United States at the beginning of the twentieth century had little interest in disclosing their finances to the public or to shareholders. Railroads had traditionally kept their balance sheets secret. Between 1887 and 1890, the New York Central Railroad failed to supply a single annual report of its finances to shareholders. The Standard Oil Company refused independent audits on the grounds that its operations were too complex for the auditors to understand. Westinghouse Electric and Mfg. Co. did not render reports or hold shareholder meetings between 1897 and 1905. Private ledgers were the norm rather than the exception for corporations, large and small. The importance that businesses attached to formal financial statements is exemplified by the Ford Motor Company, which used its year-end bank statements as its financial statements for shareholders in the 1920s. At that time, the company had assets of more than $536 million.

Even when financial reports were given to shareholders, the information supplied usually obscured and concealed more than it disclosed, but secrecy and aversion to audits were not universal. Some railroads provided periodic financial statements with management discussions on the success of operations, but most such statements were not audited. J.P. Morgan & Co. used the services of an accounting firm to examine the books and records of corporations that were being amalgamated into a combine by that investment banker in 1897. The reorganization of the American Bell Telephone Company in 1899 was the subject of an audit that was made public. The U.S. Rubber Company, later named Uniroyal Corp., began publishing an annual balance sheet in 1893. General Electric Company published audited financial statements that year. In 1909 General Motors made public an annual report showing assets of $18 million.

Some state statutes required public disclosures of financial statements, but those requirements were usually limited to particular industries such as banks, trust companies, and insurance companies. The New York General Corporation Statute required corporations to prepare annual reports stating their paid-in capital and debt outstanding. A person falsifying corporate records was subject to fine; the successor to that statute would be used to prosecute the Tyco executives. Those disclosures were, in any event, mostly perfunctory. The New York Stock Exchange (NYSE) had sought financial information from the companies traded on its floor since 1853, but with little success. When asked for financial information by the NYSE, one large railroad responded that it "makes no report" and "publishes no statements." The *New York Times* was editorializing against speculators in 1877 and proposed that corporate directors be subjected to some "effectual and independent inspection, calculated to make . . . 'doctoring' of accounts practically impossible."[2] Beginning in that year, 1877, the NYSE required newly listed companies to file financial statements, but an audit was not required. Until 1910, "unlisted" privileges on the NYSE were extended to firms that did not want to make even unaudited disclosures. One such firm was the American Sugar Refining Company, which refused even to respond to a census questionnaire. That company was embroiled in a scandal when some members of Congress were caught speculating in its shares as debate raged over sugar tariffs.

The Industrial Commission that was formed by Congress in 1898 issued a report advocating for large corporations the use of independent accountants and annual audited accounting statements that would be made public. The Industrial Commission, which composed of ten members of Congress and nine industry representatives, thought that annual financial reports would stop manipulation of stock prices, a problem then endemic to the stock markets. Those recommendations were not implemented. Some regulation appeared likely when the Bureau of Corporations was created by Congress in 1903, during Theodore Roosevelt's administration, to monitor large companies. James R. Garfield, the son of the former president who was given the title of

Commissioner of Corporations, headed the bureau. He was authorized to investigate and subpoena any corporation engaged in interstate commerce and to gather and provide information about their operations.

The bureau's work should have set off some alarm bells on the efficacy of audits by large accounting firms. U.S. Steel Co. engaged Price, Waterhouse & Co. in 1902 to audit and certify its books to shareholders. The company even required shareholders to approve the auditor. After investigating the books of U.S. Steel, the Bureau of Corporations claimed that about one-half of its capitalized value was inflated by assets that were overvalued, but the bureau took no action. It was a somewhat toothless tiger, which never recovered from a scandal over political contributions that large corporations paid to Theodore Roosevelt's presidential campaign in order to immunize themselves against bureau investigations.

Although his Bureau of Corporations was a flop, the progressives of that era, nevertheless, found an advocate in Theodore Roosevelt. He was the "trust buster" who broke up large corporations through the antitrust laws. Roosevelt also unsuccessfully called for the creation of a federal securities commission, as did his successor, Woodrow Wilson. That task would have to await fulfillment by a Roosevelt relative.

The Panic of 1907

The Panic of 1907, during which over 2,000 firms failed, gave impetus to efforts to impose more federal regulation. New York governor Charles E. Hughes appointed a committee to conduct an inquiry into the causes of the panic. The committee's report criticized stock market speculation in general and the NYSE in particular. The committee recommended that the NYSE require financial reports, which would be made public, from listed companies. The recommended financial reports included balance sheets and income statements. The committee urged the NYSE to abolish its unlisted trading department where companies supplying little or no financial information were traded. The committee's recommendations were largely ignored, but the NYSE did abolish its unlisted department.

Federal Actions

The House Committee on Banking, chaired by Arsene Pujo, undertook an investigation of Wall Street in 1912 to determine whether there was a "money trust" controlling the American economy. The Pujo committee made sensational headlines with its finding that control of many large corporations was centered in a few groups, including financiers at J.P. Morgan, the First National Bank, and the National City Bank. That control was achieved through interlocking boards of directors.

The Pujo committee uncovered widespread speculation and stock price manipulations that were conducted through the use of "wash sales" on the NYSE, variations of which found their way into the Enron scandal ninety years later. The Pujo committee also found that corporate officers were using inside information about their companies to engage in "scandalous" trading for the officers' personal benefit. The committee wanted a federal commission to regulate the stock market and urged the NYSE to require listed companies to publish balance sheets and income statements. Despite those revelations and recommendations, Congress did not choose to regulate the securities markets. Instead, it passed the Clayton Antitrust Act and created the Federal Trade Commission as a means to stop the noncompetitive practices and abuses of interlocking directorships. The Bureau of Corporations was then folded into the Federal Trade Commission.

President Woodrow Wilson urged Congress in 1914 to allow the Federal Trade Commission to require large corporations to file uniform financial statements. That effort failed. The next serious effort to regulate securities trading arose during World War I, when the Treasury Department and the Federal Reserve Board (Fed) formed a Capital Issues Committee (CIC) to review securities offerings in excess of $100,000 to ensure that they were compatible with the war effort. The CIC, modeled after a similar committee created by the British government, was basically a way to bar speculative enterprises from tapping the capital markets. Unless approved, securities offerings could not go forward. Before concluding its operations, the CIC reported to Congress that market operators were fleecing unsophisticated individuals. The CIC opined that state laws were inadequate to deal with such problems. In response to those concerns, President Wilson asked Congress for legislation that would prevent such abuses. Congress failed to respond to the president's concerns.

Blue-Sky Laws

Some states established regulatory commissions to supervise their corporations while others assigned that duty to the secretary of state. In 1903, Connecticut required mining and oil companies to file a certificate with its secretary of state that described their finances and drilling or mining activities. Seven years later, Rhode Island required out-of-state issuers of securities to file financial reports with its secretary of state. Kansas enacted the first "blue-sky" law in 1911, a phrase coined to suggest that promoters of stock were often promoting nothing but "blue sky." The Kansas act required companies selling securities in the state to register with the bank commissioner and disclose information about their operations. Stockbrokers were required to be registered. The Kansas legislation became a model for other states. Between 1910 and 1933, blue-sky laws were adopted in all the states except Nevada.

The blue-sky laws did not require periodic full disclosure financial reports. Further, the jurisdiction of the state enacting the statute did not extend beyond its borders, and no one thought of the attorney general wolf pack concept that became so popular at the end of the last century. As a result of those limitations, the blue-sky laws proved to be ineffective in regulating corporate behavior.

New York's Martin Act, which was named after Francis J. Martin, a New York state legislator, sought to curb securities fraud scandals that occurred after World War I. That legislation was adopted by New York in 1921, but was not funded until 1923. The Martin Act authorized the New York attorney general to investigate and seek injunctions against fraudulent securities practices and manipulative activities. The Martin Act was a broad-based antifraud statute, rather than a disclosure device.

The Stock Market Crash of 1929

The 1920s have been popularly depicted as an era of excesses, but historians have found "no evidence of national overconsumption or indulgence."[3] Rather, it was then thought that technological changes and economic prosperity had created a "new economy,"[4] a refrain that would be heard again during the 1990s. The 1920s have been characterized as a period of boom, comparable to the one that lasted through much of the 1990s, but that was not quite the case. Commodity prices dropped by 50 percent or more between May 1920 and June 1921. The unemployment rate rose from 4 percent to 12 percent during that recession. Another recession occurred in 1923–1924 and a milder one in 1926. It was not until 1927 that the stock market began its historic upswing. Common stock prices increased by 37.5 percent that year, jumped another 43.6 percent in 1928, and increased by an additional 10 percent in the first quarter of 1929. That run-up in stock prices attracted many members of the public into the market.

The run-up in stock prices between 1928 and 1929 was every bit as impressive as those in the 1990s. "Since the slight flutter in March 1928, General Electric shares had jumped from $129 to $396; its competitor Westinghouse from $92 to $313; RCA from $93 to $505, and Union Carbide from $145 to $414."[5] General Motors rose from $8 to $91, AT&T went from $69 to $310; and U.S. Steel from $21 to $261. Unsophisticated investors were induced into the market on the basis of solicitations promising unrealistic returns and great wealth. Sales of near worthless securities from foreign as well as domestic sources were widespread. Pools were formed by groups of traders to manipulate stock prices.

The boom ended with the historic stock market crash in October 1929. Thousands of speculators were ruined when the value of NYSE stocks dropped from $90 billion to $16 billion. Some $50 billion in values were lost in October alone—more than the United States spent on World War I. The Dow Jones Industrial Average fell from its high of 381.17 on September 3, 1929, to a low of 41 on July 8, 1932. The bond market was also smashed.

Franklin D. Roosevelt

The Great Depression of the 1930s followed the stock market crash of 1929. The country was devastated. National income fell by more than 50 percent between 1929 and 1933. The unemployment rate rose from 3.2 percent in 1929 to 24.9 percent in 1933. A massive deflation in assets accompanied these problems. The wholesale price index fell by one-third, and commodity prices dropped by over 60 percent, imposing unprecedented hardships on farmers. Thousands of banks failed between 1930 and 1933, cutting their numbers by a third. One bank found a temporary solution for its problems by engaging in a fraudulent accounting maneuver that would be emulated by Enron. The Union Trust Co. employed "repurchase agreements" with the National City Bank and Bankers Trust Co. under which it sold doubtful loans to those entities at inflated prices and then agreed to repurchase the loans at an even higher price after its accounting period closed so that the banks would be protected from loss and compensated for the use of their funds.

New York governor Franklin D. Roosevelt exploited this economic disaster and won the presidency on a platform of blaming the Depression on the financiers and attacking Wall Street. There was some cynicism in those charges. During the 1920s Roosevelt had been himself a speculator in some rather dubious enterprises, including oil wells, a coffee substitute, a scheme to rig the lobster market, a dirigible for traveling between New York and Chicago, and machines that dispensed premoistened stamps. Roosevelt also served on the board of a company that manufactured talking vending machines. The machines said "thank you" when the customer pulled a lever to obtain a product. Unfortunately, the machines did not work very well, and the company's stock dropped from $18 to twelve cents. The company made "extravagant estimates" of earnings in order to sell its stock.[6] During the period when he was himself a speculator, Roosevelt often decried government intervention into the economy.

Even more cynically, Roosevelt attacked President Herbert Hoover for allowing stock traders to run amok, but as governor of New York Roosevelt had rejected Hoover's request to impose regulation on the stock markets in New York City, which was the center of the speculative trading then under way. Indeed, Roosevelt was the only person in the United States with the power to attack the abuses on Wall Street before the crash, since the Martin Act was in force during his governorship. Yet that statute lay untouched against the many abuses on Wall Street until this century, when an ambitious New York attorney general, Eliot Spitzer, seized control of securities regulation from the Roosevelt-created Securities and Exchange Commission (SEC) using that very statute.

Roosevelt changed course in his presidential campaign by beginning a vigorous attack on the Wall Street financiers. That platform was not an original one. He modeled his career after that of his cousin, Theodore, both having served as assistant secretary of the Navy and governor of New York. Franklin tried to emulate Teddy in every way right down to the affectation of a pince-nez. Theodore had his Square Deal and Franklin had his New Deal, which would give the poor "their fair share in the distribution of the national wealth." Theodore Roosevelt had also used attacks on the financiers to bolster his populist image, although his blasts were said to have demoralized the stock market and caused the Panic of 1907. Teddy attacked the "tyranny of mere wealth" and "malefactors of great wealth."

Franklin copied Theodore's populist attacks on the wealthy financiers, although again there was some cynicism there since Franklin lived on family wealth that surrounded him with luxury and privilege, making him a multi-millionaire. That family wealth had been gained by sometimes-speculative business operations, as well as the Chinese opium trade. Franklin Roosevelt, nevertheless, waged class warfare, pitting the poor against the wealthy and against business by claiming to support the "forgotten man at the bottom of the economic pyramid."[7] Of course, Roosevelt was drawing upon a theme long sounded in American politics, stating at one point, "The country is going through a repetition of Jackson's fight with the Bank of the United States— only on a far bigger scale."[8]

Franklin Roosevelt attacked the Wall Street financiers with ringing denunciations, including claims that the "practices of the unscrupulous money changers stand indicted in the court of public opinion, rejected by the hearts and minds of men," and that "the money changers have fled from their high seats in the temple of our civilization. We may now restore that temple to ancient truth." President Roosevelt stated in his inaugural address that dangers from abroad were "trivial" relative to the "menace of corporation control of American political institutions" and "organized greed and cunning."[9]

This populist platform found a receptive ear in a population suffering horribly from an economic malaise they could not understand and that President Herbert Hoover could not fix. Roosevelt declared a national bank "holiday" under the Trading with the Enemy Act that closed the remaining banks until they could be restarted with government backing and assurance of solvency. Federal Deposit Insurance Corporation (FDIC) insurance adopted by Congress stopped the bank runs, but created a moral hazard because bank depositors would no longer monitor the solvency of their banks. The bill on that hazard came due during the savings and loan crisis in the 1980s, costing the government and taxpayers still uncounted billions of dollars. In addition, a study found that the FDIC did not reduce the cost of bank failures between 1945 and 1994 and may have actually increased the costs associated with those failures.

Roosevelt took other steps to assure recovery in the economy, including an early precedent for the use of special purpose vehicles to manipulate accounts and avoid legal requirements. In order to inflate the currency, Roosevelt began increasing the price of gold by pegging the price at artificially high levels and then ordering government purchases at those prices. Assistant Secretary of the Treasury Dean Acheson objected to the legality of those purchases and the informality of this policy. Roosevelt then went lawyer shopping and found one at the Farm Credit Administration who would support his acts, but this still required some creative accounting. The Reconstruction Finance Corporation (RFC) was enlisted to act as a special purpose vehicle that purchased the gold at prices set by the president at morning meetings in his bedroom over breakfast. Using the gold it was purchasing as collateral, the RFC obtained the funds for this operation from the Treasury, which could not itself make the purchases. This laundering operation was too much for Acheson, who left the government, returning in later years as secretary of state under Roosevelt's successor, Harry Truman.

Laying the Groundwork for Full Disclosure

In 1914 Supreme Court justice Louis Brandeis published a book titled *Other People's Money and How the Bankers Use It,* in which he stated that disclosure of corporate finances would deter misconduct because "sunlight is said to be the best of disinfectants, electric light the most efficient policeman."[10] That was the genesis of the full disclosure system now encompassed in the federal securities laws, but Brandeis would have gone further and limited the size of large corporations, and he began a witch hunt for a "money trust" that endures today.

Brandeis was joined in his criticism of large companies by Adolf Berle and Gardiner Means in their book *The Modern Corporation and Private Property,* which was published in 1932. Berle and Means charged that large corporations had "become both the method of property tenure and a means of organizing economic life. Grown to tremendous proportions, there may be said to have evolved a 'corporate system'—as there was once a feudal system—which has attracted to itself a combination of attributes and powers, and has attained a degree of prominence entitling it to be dealt with as a major social institution." Berle and Means predicted that the corporation would grow "to proportions which would stagger imagination."[11]

Berle and Means contended that corporate powers were "powers in trust" and that large corporations were actually public institutions that should be regulated by the government to ensure that they were managed for the benefit of society. Berle and Means asserted that:

> The separation of ownership from control produces a condition where the interests of owner and of ultimate manager may, and often do, diverge, and where many of the checks which formerly operated to limit the use of power disappear. Size alone tends to give the giant corporations a social significance not attached to the smaller units of private enterprise. By the use of the open market for securities, each of these corporations assumes obligations towards the investing public that transform it from a legal method clothing the rule of a few individuals into an institution at least

nominally serving investors who have embarked their funds in its enterprise. New responsibilities towards the owners, the workers, the consumers, and the State thus rest upon the shoulders of those in control. In creating these new relationships, the quasi-public corporation may fairly be said to work a revolution. It has destroyed the unity that we commonly call property—has divided ownership into nominal ownership and the power formerly joined to it. Thereby the corporation has changed the nature of profit-seeking enterprises.[12]

Timing is everything. Berle and Means's book was published just as the debate over the need for federal regulation of public companies through federal laws was gaining steam. The effect of their book on corporate governance debates and government regulation was enormous, leading the Hoover Institution to describe the book as one of the most influential published in the twentieth century. *Time* magazine called it the "economic Bible of the Roosevelt Administration." Yet, by the end of World War II, observers of corporate activities were asserting that critics of big business were simply out of date. Peter Drucker's book *Concept of the Corporation,* published in 1946, contended that "Big Business is the general condition of modern industrial society. . . . Even to raise the question whether Big Business is desirable or not is therefore nothing but sentimental nostalgia. The central problem of all modern society is not whether we want Big Business but what we want of it, and what organization of Big Business and of the society it serves is best equipped to realize our wishes and demands."[13] Those issues would dominate the debate over corporate governance into this century.

Adolf Berle had noted the existence of a "newer and more violent discussion, reverberating through the daily newspapers, the lay magazines, and the financial chronicles" dealing "with corporate accounts; whether they should be public and to what extent; and if not, how to require publicity."[14] This was a prescient prelude to the enactment of the federal securities laws. Berle was a wunderkind, entering Harvard College at age fourteen and becoming the youngest graduate of Harvard Law School. Jordan Schwarz's biography of Berle was titled *Liberal,* but some of his views were rather radical. Notable among them was his suggestion that everyone should study the Soviet system as a "great alternative to our own system of capitalism" and that "an uncontrolled system, like our own, in the long run is headed for a smashup."[15] Yet other corporate critics went even further. In the 1930s Professor E. Merrick Dodd debated Berle on corporate governance for large corporations through back and forth articles in the *Harvard Law Review.* Dodd believed that large corporations did not belong to the shareholders or management. Rather, he argued that corporate powers should be exercised for the benefit of employees and the general public.

Harvard professor William Z. Ripley was another critic of the large corporation. His book, titled *Main Street and Wall Street,* attacked the accounting practices of public utilities during the 1920s. Ripley charged that accountants could "play ball with figures to an outstanding degree, and he complained of the 'financialization' of business." He asserted that large corporations were engaging in "deceptive and misleading financial reporting practices."[16] Ripley wanted the Federal Trade Commission to require public corporations to file financial statements. President Calvin Coolidge rejected the Ripley proposal for government-required financial reports, but George O. May, a partner in the accounting firm of Price Waterhouse & Co., urged auditors to do more in response to such criticisms. May also wanted the NYSE to demand more financial disclosures. The president of the NYSE, Seymour L. Cromwell, advocated in 1922 that public corporations file sworn financial statements, but such a requirement would not be adopted until after the Enron scandal. The NYSE did seek increased financial disclosures, and about two-thirds of its listed companies were supplying audited financial statements during the 1920s. Some 200 companies listed on the NYSE were also required to file financial reports with the Interstate Commerce Commission.

The Securities Act of 1933

The congressional investigations that followed Franklin Roosevelt's call for legislation did little more than replicate the hearings after the Panic of 1907. Both sets of hearings sought a "money trust" on which to blame the country's economic woes. Both sets of hearings focused on insider abuses, manipulation, and excessive speculation using margin. The difference was that a demoralized Congress in the 1930s was only too happy to find and punish scapegoats, and Wall Street made a nice one. After all, who could feel sorry for a financier, a class that is even less popular than lawyers.

An article in the *Ohio State Law Journal* has noted that "In the effort to galvanize public support for regulation, attention was drawn to corporate salary levels, income tax returns, and other data regarding those who appeared before the committee, even though such information had little relevance to the investigation of the causes of the stock market crash." Quoting law professor Joel Seligman, the author of that article further asserted that: "This strategy was successful in 'transforming national political sentiment from a laissez-faire ideology symbolized by the views of President Coolidge to a regulatory-reform ideology associated with Roosevelt's New Deal.'"[17] This same approach would be followed after the market bubble burst in 2000.

The result of the attacks on the financiers in the 1930s was the enactment of the federal securities laws. The first of these statutes was the Securities Act of 1933. The drafting of that legislation was done for the most part over a weekend by four members of the New Deal "brain trust": Felix Frankfurter, a Harvard law professor and future Supreme Court justice, and three of his Harvard acolytes, James Landis, Benjamin Cohen, and Tommy ("the Cork") Corcoran. Cohen and Corcoran were called Frankfurter's "Happy Hot Dogs" and the "Gold Dust Twins" for their role in the New Deal. They operated from their "Little Red House" in Georgetown, a residence that General and President Ulysses S. Grant had occupied before his own ruin from a financial scandal at a brokerage firm where he was a partner.

Cohen, the "High Priest" of the New Deal, had degrees in law and economics from the University of Chicago, did postgraduate work in law at Harvard, and clerked for Brandeis on the Supreme Court. Cohen turned a $4,000 speculation in Chrysler stocks into paper profits of more than $1.5 million by pyramiding his holdings through a margin account during the peak of the market boom in the 1920s. Those profits were wiped out in the market crash in 1929. Cohen began working in Washington in 1933 and remained in government for many years, serving in posts at the State Department and elsewhere.

James Landis would become a commissioner and chairman of the SEC and dean of Harvard Law School. He was a member of the Federal Trade Commission at the time of the hearings on the Securities Act of 1933. Tommy Corcoran clerked for Oliver Wendell Holmes on the Supreme Court and practiced corporate law on Wall Street for five years before joining the RFC in the Hoover administration after losing a significant fortune in the Stock Market Crash of 1929. Corcoran stayed on with the Roosevelt administration, withdrawing one-half of his savings from a bank after receiving inside information that Roosevelt would be declaring a bank holiday when he assumed office. Corcoran congratulated himself for having the courage to leave the other half of those funds to their fate in the bank. After the New Deal, Corcoran became a controversial and flamboyant lobbyist, secretly lobbying two Supreme Court justices for their vote in an antitrust case involving his client, the El Paso Natural Gas Corp. Many of Corcoran's unseemly lobbying tactics were exposed by FBI wiretaps of his phone.

The legislation drafted by these members of Roosevelt's brain trust was a mixture of the Martin Act in New York and the English Companies Act. The Securities Act of 1933 sought to rectify the abuses of the 1920s:

> Alluring promises of easy wealth were freely made with little or no attempt to bring to the investor's attention, those facts essential to estimating the worth of any security. High-pressure salesmanship rather than careful counsel was the rule in this most dangerous enterprise. . . . Because of the deliberate over stimulation of the appetites of security buyers, underwriters had to manufacture securities to meet the demand that they themselves had created. . . . Such conduct had resulted . . . in the creation of false and unbalanced values for properties whose earnings cannot conceivably support them.[18]

Ostensibly, the Securities Act of 1933 was based on a concept of full disclosure that sought to ensure that investors could make an informed decision before investing. The act sought to assure the investor of "complete and truthful information from which he may intelligently appraise the value of a security, and to safeguard against the negligent and fraudulent practices perpetrated upon him in the past by incompetent and unscrupulous bankers, underwriters, dealers, and issuers."[19] This was the theory of full disclosure propounded by

Louis Brandeis, who provided support and encouragement from his position on the Supreme Court as the bill moved swiftly through Congress.

President Roosevelt stated, in asking Congress for this legislation, that there was "an obligation upon us to insist that every issue of new securities to be sold in interstate commerce shall be accompanied by full publicity and information, and that no essentially important element attending the issue shall be concealed from the buying public."[20] This was a promise that would not be fulfilled for the Enron investors and other victims of failures involved in this full disclosure regime.

The Securities Act of 1933 was not supposed to mandate specific corporate governance procedures or require managers to act in any particular way, as long as whatever they did was disclosed to investors. That was misleading. As Felix Frankfurter admitted, in forcing disclosures about corporate internal affairs, the Securities Act of 1933 did seek to affect corporate governance by having an "in terrorem" effect on corporate managers and underwriters.[21] In an article in *Fortune* magazine supporting the passage of the Securities Act, Frankfurter asserted: "The existence of bonuses, of excessive commissions and salaries, of preferential lists and the like, may all be open secrets among the knowing, but the knowing are few. There is a shrinking quality to such transactions; to force knowledge of them into the open is largely to restrain their happening." Frankfurter's statement would be cited with approval by future SEC chairman William L. Cary when he turned that agency into a corporate crusader in the 1960s.[22] As will be seen, the SEC thereafter frequently used disclosure requirements to impose corporate governance reforms.

The Securities Act of 1933 added "to the ancient rule of caveat emptor, the further doctrine 'let the seller also beware.'" It put the "burden of telling the whole truth on the seller. It should give impetus to honest dealing in securities and thereby bring back public confidence."[23] President Roosevelt stated: "What we seek is a return to a clearer understanding of the ancient truth that those who manage banks, corporations, and other agencies handling or using other people's money are trustees acting for others." A House report asserted, "Speculation, manipulation, . . . investors' ignorance, and disregard of trust relationships by those whom the law should regard as fiduciaries" were "all a single seamless web."[24] Mentioned specifically were "the predatory operations of directors, officers, and principal shareholders of corporations."[25] As the Senate Banking and Currency Committee presciently warned, however, this legislation did not "guarantee the present soundness or the future value of any security. The investor must still, in the final analysis, select the security which he deems appropriate for investment."[26] That warning would go unheeded in future years.

To achieve full disclosure, the Securities Act of 1933 required the filing of a registration statement with the Federal Trade Commission (which was replaced in that role by the SEC in the following year) whenever a company made a public distribution of its securities. The registration statement required the inclusion of a prospectus fully describing material information about the company and its finances. The Securities Act of 1933 prohibited any material misstatement of fact or omission of fact that would make the information presented misleading. A twenty-day quiet period was imposed that prevented stocks from being sold under the prospectus during that period. The quiet period was intended to ensure that investors had an adequate opportunity to assess the information in the prospectus. The underwriters could conduct "road shows" during this period to showcase the stock orally to analysts, money managers, and institutional investors. Broker-dealers could also receive oral "indications of interest" from customers who might want to purchase the stock after the quiet period.

In enacting the Securities Act of 1933, Congress rejected a proposal that would have required auditors to certify the financial statements filed with the registration statement under oath because accountants asserted that they were incapable of making such an affirmation because management controlled their access to information. The Securities Act as originally introduced included a requirement that loans to officers in excess of $20,000 be disclosed, but that requirement was dropped as well.

The Securities Exchange Act of 1934

The Securities Act of 1933 was followed by more legislation. The Securities Exchange Act of 1934 created the SEC and imposed regulation over the secondary ("trading") markets in securities after their initial public offering. The Exchange Act regulated the stock exchanges and was later amended to cover the over-the-counter market. Cohen and Corcoran were the principal draftsmen of the act. Although the Exchange Act would often be cited as a measure to protect small investors, Corcoran asserted before Congress that the act was intended to keep small investors out of the market.[27]

A key aspect of the Exchange Act was its contribution to full disclosure in the form of a requirement that public companies file periodic financial reports with the SEC that would be made publicly available. This requirement was thought necessary because the disclosure requirements in the Securities Act of 1933 applied only to the initial public offering (IPO) or to subsequent stock issues, if any. That information became stale very quickly, and Congress thought that investors and traders in the secondary market should have continuing disclosures as additional protection for their investment. Interestingly, most NYSE listed companies were already publishing annual audited financial statements and over half were providing quarterly statements. As a House committee report to the Exchange Act stated, these reporting requirements were premised on an "efficient market" theory that became popular again in the 1980s:

> The idea of a free and open market place is built on the theory that competing judgments of buyers and sellers as to the fair price of a security bring about a situation where the market price reflects as nearly as possible a just price. . . . [T]he

hiding and secreting of important information obstructs the operation of the markets as indices of real value. . . . The disclosure of information materially important
to investors may not instantaneously be reflected in market value, but despite the
intricacies of security values truth does find relatively quick acceptance on the
market. . . . Delayed, inaccurate, and misleading reports are the tools of the uncon-
scionable market operator and the recreant corporate official who speculates on
inside information. . . . [28]

Initially, the periodic filing requirements applied only to exchange-listed
stocks, but the Exchange Act was amended in 1964 to extend its periodic
reporting requirements to companies in the over-the-counter market. This
action was taken after the SEC's *Special Study of the Securities Markets* in
1963 concluded that the lack of disclosure in the over-the-counter market
made it an unattractive and dangerous place for small investors.

Issuers of most publicly traded securities must now file annual reports on
SEC Form 10-K. Form 10-K was required to be signed by the corporation's
principal executive, financial, and accounting officers and by at least a majority of the board of directors, a requirement that was strengthened after Enron.
Form 10-K must include a balance sheet audited in accordance with generally
accepted accounting principles by an independent certified public accountant. Comparative statements from prior years must be included, and an income statement and a statement of cash flows are also required. The number
of shareholders must be disclosed, as well as any increase or decrease in the
number of outstanding shares during the reporting period. A description of
the parent company and subsidiaries is required, as are material changes in
the company's business, the identity of any person holding more than 10 percent of the company's stock, the names and affiliations of directors, and the
interest of management in the purchase or sale of company assets. The latter
requirement played a key role in Enron's undoing as a result of Andrew
Fastow's involvement in the special purpose entities (SPEs). The company is
required to disclose legal proceedings against it.

Form 10-K must include a management discussion and analysis (MD&A)
section. The MD&A section must discuss "any known trends or uncertainties
that have had or that the registrant reasonably expects will have a material
favorable or unfavorable impact on net sales or revenues or income from continuing operations."[29] This section was intended to provide a discussion by
management that would give context to the financial figures in the SEC-
required reports and allow investors to have access to management's views.
To that end, the MD&A requires a statement of management's views on the
company's financial condition, its capital expenditure plans, and other matters of interest. Although Harvey Pitt, chairman of the SEC during the Enron
crisis, described the MD&A as "the cornerstone of our system of corporate
disclosure,"[30] the MD&A disclosure requirement was often used by management to put its spin on the numbers and make excuses for shortfalls and problems, thereby obscuring the actual numbers.

Issuers were initially required to file an unaudited semiannual report on SEC Form 9-K. That report required disclosure of revenues, net income or loss, and a statement of any extraordinary income or losses. In an effort to assure more current information, the SEC amended its regulations in 1971 to require public companies to file quarterly financial reports on Form 10-Q. That amendment proved fateful in undermining the integrity of corporate management after financial analysts began closely following these quarterly reports. Management had to meet the "consensus" expectations of those analysts in order to keep up the stock price of their companies. A study conducted in 2004 by Thomson Financial found that over the prior five years about half the companies in the Dow Jones Index met the consensus estimates of analysts exactly or bettered those estimates by a penny. That was clear evidence of earnings management, which was a nice way of saying that accounting manipulations had become widespread because of the emphasis on quarterly reports.

Form 10-Q financial statements need not be audited because such a requirement would delay filing and thereby impair the usefulness of that information to investors. Nevertheless, in 1999, the SEC required issuers filing Form 10-Q to have those reports reviewed by their auditors before filing, even though certification was not required. The Form 10-Q report expanded the disclosures previously required in Form 9-K to include a summary of the company's capital structure and shareholder equity. Issuers must also file a Form 8-K with the SEC promptly after the occurrence of certain material events, such as a change in control of the registrant, resignations of directors, changes in accountants, and bankruptcy, ensuring that investors are advised promptly of those matters.

The Accountants as Gatekeepers

Disclosure Requirements

The federal securities laws ushered in an era of "full disclosure" that promised investors truth in the securities they bought and revelation of all "material" information that would affect their investment decisions. This was forced disclosure and came to reflect a view, as stated by the Supreme Court, that "corporations can claim no equality with individuals in the enjoyment of a right to privacy. They are endowed with public attributes. They have a collective impact upon society, from which they derive the privilege of acting as artificial entities. The Federal Government allows them the privilege of engaging in interstate commerce. Favors from government often carry with them an enhanced measure of regulation."[31]

The linchpin of the goal of full disclosure was the integrity of the financial statements of public companies. Congress proposed that government auditors should be hired to audit the books of companies selling stock to the public.

That proposal was short-lived. "As Colonel Arthur Carter, senior partner of [the] accounting firm Haskins & Sells, testifying before the assembled senators, said, 'You had better plan on some more buildings in Washington to house [the auditors].'"[32] Heeding that warning, Congress decided to rely on the accounting industry for audits. The Securities Act of 1933 required financial statements submitted with a company's registration statement to be audited by an independent public accountant. The Securities Exchange Act of 1934 further involved accountants in full disclosure by requiring an annual financial report that had to be audited and certified by independent public accountants.

The SEC was given the authority by the Securities Act of 1933 to dictate accounting disclosures and standards, but the agency decided to defer in large measure to the accounting industry in that function. Although the SEC announced in 1937 that it planned to periodically issue releases expressing its own views on appropriate standards for the accounting treatment of particular items and practices, one of those releases (Accounting Series Release No. 4) proclaimed that the SEC would normally defer to the accounting profession in setting audit standards. In that regard, the auditor's role with respect to the preparation of financial reports filed with the SEC is to determine whether those reports have been prepared in accordance with generally accepted accounting principles (GAAP) that are consistently applied. "The auditor then issues an opinion as to whether the financial statements, taken as a whole, 'fairly present' the financial position and operations of the corporation for the relevant period"[33] in accordance with GAAP. GAAP control in the absence of SEC direction otherwise.

The concept of GAAP had been developing in the accounting profession since World War I. GAAP are practices that are generally accepted by the accounting profession in determining how to account for particular items. GAAP seek to ensure that the accounting methodology properly discloses the company's financial activities and condition. GAAP are a rule-based approach memorialized in writings now totaling several thousand pages. A single GAAP standard may consume over 700 pages describing how to book a single transaction. This stands in contrast with European accounting standards set by the International Accounting Standards Board, which uses a principle-based approach that is designed to ensure reporting of the substance of transactions.

GAAP accounting standards are recorded in industry interpretations such as the *Research Bulletins* that were published between 1939 and 1959 by the Committee on Accounting Procedure. That body was formed by the predecessor of the American Institute of Certified Public Accountants (AICPA), which is now the principal professional accounting society. In 1959 the AICPA replaced the Committee on Accounting Procedure with the Accounting Principles Board (APB), which assumed responsibility for publishing opinions on financial reporting issues under general guidelines prepared by the AICPA research staff.

FASB

In 1971, the AICPA created a seven-member task force headed by Francis M. Wheat, a former SEC commissioner, to make recommendations on how better to promulgate accounting principles. The Wheat committee's members included representatives from large accounting firms, a university professor, and executives from other fields. The committee held public hearings that led to a recommendation that a full-time board should be created to set accounting standards. This led to the replacement of the APB with the Financial Accounting Standards Board (FASB) in 1973.

FASB became the prime industry standard setter for GAAP, a role recognized by the SEC in its Accounting Series Release No. 150. FASB operated under the auspices of the Financial Accounting Foundation, which was controlled by the AICPA and several other accounting profession organizations. FASB's seven full-time members were referred to in the industry as the "gnomes of Norwalk," a reference to its mystical powers and its headquarters in Connecticut. FASB was an alternative to the concept of an "accounting court" proposed by Leonard Spacek in 1957, while he headed the Arthur Andersen accounting firm. Similar accounting court proposals had been made in 1909 and 1919 by other accountants. Spacek, concerned with abuses of accounting standards, stated that "my profession appears to regard a set of financial statements as a roulette wheel to the public investor—and it is his tough luck if he doesn't understand the risks that we inject into the accounting reports." Others complained that accounting had become a game of "massaging the numbers."[34]

FASB created the Emerging Issues Task Force (EITF) in 1984 to provide prompt guidance on issues arising as the result of new instruments or structures. Enron used that body to gain approval of some of its accounting practices. A Derivatives Implementation Group was formed to aid in interpreting the application of the Financial Accounting Standard (FAS) 133, which governed the accounting treatment for derivative transactions at Enron. Other guidance was available, creating a hierarchy of precedents. At the top were FASB Financial Accounting Statements (FAS) and FASB Interpretations (FINs) and SEC Accounting Series Releases. The latter were the product of the SEC's chief accountant. Due to the agency's deference to industry standards, those SEC releases were fairly rare and were usually issued as ad hoc responses to particular problems. The SEC may also impose particular standards required for accounting statements in filings by issuers. Regulation S-X imposes various accounting requirements in public offerings. SEC Staff Accounting Bulletins may be used to provide accounting guidance. SEC Staff Accounting Bulletin 101, for example, sought to define when companies could record revenue on their books. The next levels of interpretation were FASB Technical Bulletins, AICPA Statements of Position, EITF Consensus Statements, and FASB Concept Statements.

Certification

An important aspect of auditing financial statements under the federal securities laws is that the SEC requires financial reports to be audited by an independent certified public accountant in accordance with generally accepted auditing standards (GAAS). There are thus two prongs to SEC required audits: GAAP and GAAS. The latter were produced by the Auditing Standards Board of the AICPA. One court has described the nature and application of GAAS as follows:

> The GAAS include 10 broadly phrased sets of standards and general principles that guide the audit function. They are classified as general standards, standards for fieldwork, and standards of reporting. General Standard No. 1 provides: "The examination is to be performed by a person or persons having adequate technical training as . . . auditor[s]." General Standard No. 3 provides: "Due professional care is to be exercised in the performance of the examination and the preparation of the report." Standard of Fieldwork No. 2 provides: "A sufficient understanding of the internal control structure is to be obtained to plan the audit and to determine the nature, timing, and extent of tests to be performed."[35]

An issue arising even before the creation of the SEC was the form of the auditor's certification of company financial statements. Auditors initially certified, or "attested," that the company's statements were "true." Before the creation of the SEC, an accounting industry committee headed by George May, a leading partner at Price Waterhouse, recommended that the certification be changed to an assertion only that it was the opinion of the auditors that the company's financial statements were "fairly presented" under GAAP. This approach was adopted and became the basis for future audits. Today, the "fairly presents" requirement is intended to be a check on overly technical applications of GAAP that distort a company's true financial condition. As the bankruptcy examiner for Enron noted:

> Although broad principles such as "substance-over-form" are frequently subjugated to the GAAP rules-based approach, even in those cases for which there is some authority under a GAAP rule for a particular accounting position that is inconsistent with the transaction's economic substance, both the accounting profession and the courts have acknowledged that compliance with the GAAP rules alone is not sufficient if the resulting financial statements do not "fairly present in all material respects" the financial position, results of operations and cash flows in accordance with GAAP.[36]

Early Accounting History

The auditors were given the role of "gatekeeper" for ensuring full disclosure under the federal securities laws. Once again, some history is needed to understand why the auditors assumed that role and why they were unable to live up to that billing. Modern accounting did not spring up overnight but its current processes are premised on some ancient concepts that evolved over the centuries. In that regard, bookkeeping for businesses is as old as business itself. Tokens were thought to have been used for the accounting of grain as early as 8000 BC in Mesopotamia. A knotted cord is believed to have been used for bookkeeping around 3300 BC. The ancient Babylonians were "obsessive bookkeepers."[37] The ancient Greeks and Romans had systems of accounts. Aristotle described government accountants and their auditing in some detail. Ancient Greece was said to have both internal and external accountants to audit government finances. Roman bankers were transferring credits by written notations in 352 BC. Bookkeeping was practiced in the ancient societies of Central America before Christopher Columbus arrived. Columbus was himself accompanied to America by an accountant to record the treasures he expected to find in the New World.

Many of these early bookkeeping efforts were just that—a recording of assets and debts or sales. The modern art of accounting extends beyond such mere bookkeeping. Accounting now seeks to describe and interpret the finances of the business through its assets, liabilities, capital, profitability, and flow of funds. That broader concept of the role of accounting is said to date from the development of the double entry method of accounting, which "has served as a conceptual framework for analyzing business transactions and distinguishing between capital and income."[38] One economist, perhaps in an excess of rhetoric, asserted that "double entry bookkeeping is born of the same spirit as the system of Galileo and Newton" and "discloses to us the cosmos of the economic world."[39]

Luca Pacioli, a Franciscan monk and friend of Leonardo da Vinci, published a description of the double entry method in 1494 AD. Pacioli's work, titled *Summa de Arithmetica, Geometria, Proportioni et Proportionali,* described a system of accounting that included memorials (bookkeeping records), journals, and ledgers. The accounts in this system included expense accounts, inventory, and a profit and loss account. All transactions and items were to be posted twice as offsetting debits and credits, creating equilibrium on the balance sheet. Pacioli stated that this accounting system, the "method of Venice," had been in use in Venice for over 200 years. That claim is supported by a ledger of Giovanni Farolfi's firm in Florence surviving from 1299 that contains a sophisticated double entry system.

The Gallerani firm in Siena, Italy, was using double entry accounts in its London office in 1305. The Massari ledgers from Genoa, dating to 1340, also used double entry accounting. Elements of double entry accounting have been found in the records of the Florentine banks of the Peruzzi family and Alberti del Giudice as early as 1302. The latter kept accounts of partner capital and income. The Peruzzi firm had several books of accounts including an Assets Book and a Secret Book, each of which started with a prayer for the profit and welfare of the company. The Secret Book contained an allocation of profits and losses and other summary information on the firm's operations. The Italian banks periodically (every one to five years) closed their books for inventory, after which the partners would decide whether to renew their business. The Medici banking house closed the books of all its branches on March 24 of each year, and balance sheets were then prepared for review.

The method of Venice found its way to England and Scotland before migrating from there to America. "Royal Auditors" were at work in England in the fifteenth century. Even earlier, the Royal Exchequer was audited by the "Inquest of Sheriffs." Medieval accounting by the English government was conducted in a trial-like atmosphere in which the sheriff's accounts were read aloud, apparently giving rise to the term "audit," presumably from the Latin *audice,* to hear. This process was called "charge and discharge." The exchequer or his representative would challenge each account, and the sheriff was liable for any shortfalls in accounts not proved. Where the account was accepted, the sheriff was forever discharged of liability for the period covered by the account. Accounts also had to be rendered in other areas of government, particularly the military. Those accounts included the army in Ireland and the navy, the latter illustrated by the accounts of William Soper, Keeper of the King's Ships between 1422 and 1427.

The first English text on double entry accounting was published by Hugh Oldcastle in 1543. Students were schooled in England by the seventeenth century in "casting accounts," which was business arithmetic, and of course, at some point, the "king was in his countinghouse, counting out his money." Countinghouses were widely used by commercial firms to track inventory and sales. There were also more formal governmental audits being developed. As Professor Sean M. O'Connor has noted, the audit reports of the City of Aberdeen in 1586 contained the statement: "Heard, seen, consider it, calculate and allow it by the auditors."

The Dutch East Indies Company was required to sell all its assets and distribute its proceeds every ten years as a means to ensure that its accounts were accurate. This practice was stopped in 1612. In 1673, France required commercial companies to record their transactions in records approved by government officials and to render twice-yearly accounting of their businesses. That requirement was incorporated into the Napoleonic Code in 1807. Back in England, the South Sea bubble that occurred there in 1720 resulted in a call by a special committee of Parliament (the Committee of Secrecy) for an examination of the books of a South Seas Company subsidiary, the Sawbridge Company. The Sword Blade Bank arranged for Charles Snell, "Writing Master and Accomptant," to conduct that audit. His review of the company's books was said to be the first independent audit by an accountant of a public company.

Accounting in Great Britain

Samuel Johnson cautioned in 1775: "Let no man venture into large business while he is ignorant of the method of regulating books; never let him imagine that any degree of natural abilities will enable him to supply the deficiency, or preserve multiplicity of affairs from inextricable confusion." A professional class of accountants was operating in Great Britain by the 1850s to provide audit and bookkeeping services. Many of those early accountants offered additional services such as broker, auctioneer, debt collector, writing master, actuary, and agent. They were also called on to act in insolvency proceedings, particularly after passage of the Winding Up Act in 1848.

Like England, Scotland became a prime source for the growth of accounting in America. Although Scotland was a bit slower than England in developing accounting as a profession, many Scottish children, boys and girls, were educated in the Netherlands, where they were instructed in accounting methods. More than sixty books on accounting were published in the Netherlands during the seventeenth century. Lawyers often acted as accountants in Scotland, but accounting eventually became a separate profession, and Scotland developed a "reputation as a land of accountants."[40] Around 1681, John Dickson was appointed as a "Master and Professor of Bookkeeping" by the Edinburgh Town Council. The first book on accounting was published in Scotland two years later. It was written by Robert Colinson and titled *Idea Rationaria or the Perfect Accomptant.*

The Society of Accountants in Edinburgh was created by royal warrant in 1854, and the Society of Accountants of Aberdeen was established in 1867. These societies created an examination requirement as a condition for membership and as a means of setting high professional standards. Those passing the exam were called "chartered accountants." This procedure was institutionalized in 1880 when Queen Victoria granted a royal charter to the Institute of Chartered Accountants in England and Wales, which body governs the profession in Great Britain today. That organization was an amalgamation of five accounting societies. The institute started with about 600 members, but that number would nearly triple over the next ten years.

This new breed of professional, the "accountant," was soon the target of lawsuits. An English court held in 1859 that it was an auditor's duty to discover fraud and error on the part of employees. That became the major goal of audit work until World War II.[41] The liability of accountants was clarified in another English judicial decision rendered in 1887 that stated that an auditor's duty was not just to check arithmetic but also to ensure that a company's accounting statements were a true and accurate presentation of the company's affairs. Nevertheless, the auditor was not absolutely liable for failing to discover fraud or error. Rather, the standard was that the auditor had only to use reasonable care and skill.[42]

An English decision rendered in 1886 presciently observed that the auditor is a "watchdog, not a bloodhound."[43] Still, accountants came under criticism. An English judge remarked in 1875 that bankruptcy proceedings had "been handed over to an ignorant set of men called accountants, which is one of the greatest abuses ever introduced into law."[44] There was some basis for those charges. The W.B. Peat accounting firm was sued for failing to detect that the Millwall Dock Co. had inflated its accounts receivable in 1884 by £174,000. The auditors had not verified the company's ledgers or visited its docks for a period of fourteen years.

British Accountants Move to America

The chartered accountants from Scotland and London extended their services to America. Indeed, most of the "Big Eight" accounting firms in America (now the "Final Four") trace their origins to either England or Scotland. Deloitte, Touche, Tohmatsu tracks its ancestry to Josiah Wade, who began business as an English accountant in 1780. Wade issued a certificate in 1797 stating that the accounts he audited were "Examined and Found Right." Wade's more immediate successor was the accounting firm of Tribe, Clarke & Co., which later merged with Deloitte, Plender, Griffiths & Co. William Deloitte of that firm started as an accountant in London in 1845 and became known for his audits of railroad companies. Deloitte audited the Great Western Railway in 1849 for shareholders. Four directors were forced to resign after he filed his report. This would set a precedent for internal investigation reports in America. Deloitte's firm branched into America and became Deloitte, Haskins & Sells. Touche Ross & Co. (the other part of what is now Deloitte, Touche, Tohmatsu) was founded by accountants from Scotland.

Samuel Price was an accountant in London in 1849. His firm became Price, Waterhouse & Co. in 1874. The company opened offices in America in 1890. It is now a part of PricewaterhouseCoopers. Coopers & Lybrand, the other branch of that firm, traces its origins back to Robert Fletcher in 1828 and to William Cooper, who started his accounting firm in London in 1854. A year later, Cooper described the role of an accountant as follows:

> The business of an accountant comprises the investigation and arrangement of all kinds of intricate accounts; the preparation of the accounts and balance sheets of public companies of all kinds—merchants and other partnership accounts—all accounts required in bankruptcy, and indeed the aid of accountants is always required when others lack competency in the arrangement and adjustment of their affairs. Such a profession you will perceive involves a large acquaintance with most kinds of business, and it is eminently calculated to introduce good methodical business habits.[45]

In 1926, Cooper's successors expanded to America, becoming Coopers & Lybrand. Ernst & Ernst, formed in 1903 in the United States, joined with a London firm that was founded in 1848 to become Ernst & Whinney. That firm merged with Arthur Young to become Ernst & Young. Arthur Young & Co. was started in America in 1894, but traces its origins back to James McClelland, a Glasgow accountant operating in 1824.

Peat, Marwick & Mitchell had roots both in Scotland and England, beginning with Robert Fletcher & Co., a Scottish accounting firm formed in 1867. Peat Marwick became a part of what is now KPMG after a merger with Klynveld Main Goerdeler, an international firm centered in the Netherlands. Grant Thornton, a major firm just below Big Eight status, has a Scottish branch that can be traced back to Robert McCowan's operations in the 1840s. The only Big Eight accounting firm to be founded in America was Arthur Andersen & Co. That firm survived to progress to the "Big Five" when the larger accounting firms merged at the end of the last century, but Arthur Andersen did not make it to the Final Four as a result of Enron.

Homegrown Accounting

The joint-stock companies that colonized America hired accountants to settle company accounts, leading to complaints by the Pilgrims about the competency of the accountant appointed for the Plymouth Company. Children in that colony were taught to cast accounts, and the Plymouth Colony was itself the subject of an annual audit starting in 1658. The Massachusetts Company employed accountants in London to settle accounts for its operations in America, and settlers there were appointed for the same purpose.

Accountants in colonial times in America were usually merchants engaging in bookkeeping as a sideline. Others were trained as apprentices in "compting houses." Bookkeeping in the colonies was usually limited to simple notations of expenditures and debts owed. For example, accounting records from the Salem Witch trials reveal accounts of expenses for maintaining the jailed defendants and keeping their cells "witch tight."[46] John Hancock's family business records, for a fifty-year period starting in 1724, still survive. Accounts were kept by plantation owners as part of everyday life. Those of George Washington, started at age fifteen and ending with his death, are massive in detail and constitute a description of his everyday life expressed in terms of expenditures. Thomas Jefferson also kept account books between 1767 and 1826.

By 1718, individuals were advertising their services as bookkeepers in the Boston newspapers, and in the New York papers by 1729. Double entry bookkeeping was being taught in schools in America by 1733, and accountants practiced in every major city before the Revolution. One of the earliest known audits in America involved Benjamin Franklin's sale of his interest in a printing company he owned jointly with David Hall. In 1766, James Parker audited the company for Franklin, who was then in London. Franklin appreciated the value of accounting in his business operations, remarking favorably on the accounting skills of the widow of a deceased partner who had been educated in Holland, where accounting was part of the education of both men and women.

Lawyers in America often filled the role of accountants in settling estates, but accounting evolved into a profession unto itself. Chauncey Lee published the *American Accomptant* in 1797. James Bennett published the *American System of Practical Bookkeeping* in 1814 and was operating an accounting school in New York in 1818. By that year, individuals were calling themselves "accountants" in New York, although their services still focused on bookkeeping. Before the Civil War, E.G. Folsom Commercial College was a private business school in Cleveland. Among its students was John D. Rockefeller, who began his career as a bookkeeper at age sixteen. The Bryant & Stratton School, established in 1853, took over the Folsom operation and became the leader in the creation of private business schools, which it franchised at over sixty locations. The country's numerous other accounting schools included a chain created by Silas Packard, the Packard Business College.

Over thirty books on the subject of accounting were written before the Civil War, including one by John Colt titled *The Science of Double Entry Bookkeeping*. That book was in its fourth edition in 1839, but there seems to have been some tension between Colt and the printer. Colt, whose brother brought the Colt .45 pistol to fame, was convicted of murdering his New York printer, Samuel Adams, with a hatchet. He then crated up the body for shipment to Louisiana. Sentenced to hang, Colt committed suicide in the Tombs prison in New York by stabbing himself, setting the prison on fire in the process. Crime intruded into accounting in other ways. Accounting reports of the Wells Fargo Company during the Civil War era are interesting in their attention on the income statement to losses from robberies (e.g., $2,938 from a robbery in Coulterville, Illinois in 1864) and recovered bullion from earlier holdups.

Even with the growth of accounting education, the number of professional accountants remained small. In 1850, only nineteen people identified themselves as accountants in three of the country's largest cities, New York, Philadelphia, and Chicago. That number of accountants increased to eighty-one in 1884 and then boomed to 322 in 1889. By 1885, even the distant city of Louisville, Kentucky, was able to boast of having five accountants. Many people still provided bookkeeping as a sideline, particularly for small businesses. The lack of an income tax or SEC reporting requirements meant that the aim of most accounting work was to detect employee fraud.

H.J. Mettenheim published the *Auditor's Guide* in 1869. This book reflected the increasing importance of audit work, which sought to verify accounts and act as a check against fraud and error. Audits were then used mostly to verify the work of the bookkeepers, who all too frequently abused their positions. By the 1890s, two-thirds of all audits were uncovering fraud. Accounting controls by management were emerging in the form of limitations on authority, separation of functions and cross-checking to avoid fraud.

University president Robert E. Lee, of Civil War fame, sought to include accounting in the curriculum at what is now Washington and Lee College in 1869 but died before the program could be implemented. The general was ahead of his time, but the growth in the size and complexity of commercial firms was giving rise to a need for professional accountants with academic training. In many cases, they were supplied from Scotland and England, but gradually the education of accountants in America became formalized. The first permanent accounting classes at a traditional college were offered at the Wharton School in Philadelphia in 1883. By World War I, such classes were being taught at a number of universities across the country. Today, nearly every university has an accounting curriculum, and business schools offer an undergraduate degree in accounting as well as master's and PhD programs.

Licensing Accountants

Schooling was critical, but professional societies were the key to turning accounting into a profession and establishing recognized standards, which were lacking as auditors came under increasing criticism for failing to detect employee fraud and other financial misconduct. Skepticism was even appearing in the press. *Vanity Fair* charged in the 1880s that the auditor's certificate was a "delusion and a snare."

The New York Institute of Accountants and Bookkeepers was established in 1882. It sought to ensure professionalism by examining and certifying accountants. That group was in competition with the American Association of Public Accountants, which was founded in 1887. Nine years later, New York enacted legislation titled An Act to Regulate the Profession of Public Accountants, which recognized the licensing of "certified public accountants" (CPAs). CPA exams were administered by the Regents of the University of the State of New York.

The first such exam was given in 1896 over a period of two days. No one passed the exam in that year or the next, setting a precedent for tough exams. The first woman to pass the New York CPA exam was Christine Ross in 1898, but her certificate was held up until a vote by the Board of Regents could decide whether women were qualified to practice accounting. The first African American certified as a CPA was John W. Cromwell Jr., in 1921. He sat for the CPA exam in New Hampshire, a reflection of the spread of the New York certification process to other states. Uniform testing among the states began in 1917 and was widespread by the middle of the 1920s. The CPA exam remained rigorous and is still one of the most formidable obstacles to entry for any profession. An effort to institute federal licensing of accountants was defeated by the profession before World War I.

Numerous professional societies for accountants were modeled after those in New York. They often competed with each other for prominence. The American Association of Public Accountants was largely controlled by English accountants. The Federation of Societies of Public Accountants was formed in 1902 as a national professional society. At its International Congress of Professional Accountants in St. Louis in 1904, papers were presented on how to conduct an audit and the duties of accountants. The New York societies merged in 1905 and became a nationwide organization. To further its national character, this organization unsuccessfully sought to obtain a federal charter. It changed its name in 1916 to the American Institute of Accountants in the United States of America and made another name change in 1957, becoming the American Institute of Certified Public Accountants (AICPA).

Accountants' Liability

A spur to the growth of the accounting profession in the United States was the passage of a constitutional amendment in 1913 that allowed Congress to adopt legislation imposing direct taxes in the form of an income tax. Accountants were soon devoting a significant portion of their business to advising clients on the ever-growing complexity of the Internal Revenue Code. The government gave the profession another boost when the Federal Reserve Board imposed a requirement that companies seeking to have their commercial paper qualify for discounting at a Federal Reserve Bank provide certified financial statements. The accounting profession worked with the Federal Trade Commission (FTC) in establishing standards for such statements. The accountants convinced the FTC to reject a uniform accounting system for all corporations and, instead, to adopt a program called Approved Methods for the Preparation of Balance Sheets, which the Federal Reserve Board approved and published in 1917.

As in Great Britain, the issue arose in America whether an auditor was liable when certified financial statements proved to be false. Several legal cases considered that issue. In 1925, in *Craig v. Anyon,*[47] a New York intermediate court held that an accounting firm, Barrow, Wade, Guthrie & Co., was negligent in failing to discover during its audit that a stockbroker at Bache & Co. had embezzled in excess of $1 million over a period of several years. The penalty for that failure was not particularly severe. The court required the auditors to refund their fee of $2,000.

More famous was the case of *Ultramares Corp. v. Touche,*[48] decided by New York's highest court in 1931 in an opinion written by Judge Benjamin Cardozo. The auditors in that case had certified the balance sheets of Fred Stern & Co. over a four-year period ending in 1923. The auditors knew that Fred Stern presented its balance sheets to stockholders, to contractual counterparties and to banks and others in order to obtain credit. The plaintiff had extended credit to Fred Stern on the strength of its certified balance sheets, which turned out to be inaccurate; in fact, the company was bankrupt. Although the accountants had negligently conducted their audit, missing a number of discrepancies that would have revealed the company's true condition, the court refused to subject the auditors to liability from third parties for negligence. Liability would lie only where there was some direct contract or "privity" between the third party and the auditor, or where the auditor certified accounts as being true when the auditor had no basis for such certification.

Judge Cardozo stated: "If liability for negligence exists, a thoughtless slip or blunder, the failure to detect a theft or forgery beneath the cover of deceptive entries, may expose accountants to a liability in an indeterminate amount for an indeterminate time to an indeterminate class. The hazards of a business conducted on these terms are so extreme as to enkindle doubt whether a flaw may not exist in the implication of a duty that exposes to these consequences." Later, other courts declared that they were willing to expand accountants' liability to third parties for mere negligence where it was foreseeable to the auditors that the third party would rely on the statements.[49] In England, courts held that the auditor owed no duty to subsequent shareholders and that auditors could disclaim responsibility for their opinions. The use of such disclaimers in the United States was prohibited in the audits of public companies under the federal securities laws.

Accounting Shortcomings

The passage of the federal securities laws thrust the accountant into a far broader role as the guardian of the newly implemented full disclosure requirement. That role proved to be totally unrealistic because the accounting industry was reliant on management for information and disclosure, a reality that was often frustrating to the SEC. This was a particular affront to James Landis, the former Roosevelt brain trust member, when he was SEC chairman. Landis believed that accountants should represent investors rather than management. In a 1936 speech, he charged that accountants had conflicts of loyalty between the firms paying for their engagement and investors who relied on the company's financial statements. He also complained that, while accounting was really a matter of opinion, many investors erroneously thought it was an exact science. Landis encountered some accounting problems of his own; he was jailed for failing to file his tax returns, an omission that was discovered when he was being considered for a position in the administration of President John F. Kennedy. Landis was sentenced to thirty days in jail, a sharp contrast to the one-year term given to Lea Fastow, the wife of Andrew Fastow at Enron. In any event, there seemed to be some basis for Landis's concern. An SEC investigation after World War II of companies whose stock was traded in the over-the-counter markets found a number of shortcomings in their financial statements. The agency noted that many of those companies had been audited by the large accounting firms. "In 1947, a survey by Opinion Research found that 45 percent of the public believed that companies' financial statements were untruthful and 40 percent believed that reported earnings were falsified."[50]

Accounting firms were largely self-regulated by professional societies that set GAAS or GAAP as rules for the accounting firms to follow. In the rare case where the SEC disagreed, differences were usually ironed out in negotiations between the accounting societies and the SEC. When accountants committed improper acts, discipline was left mostly to state CPA licensing procedures; rarely, the SEC would bring a disciplinary action. It was soon apparent to the SEC that auditors were not impenetrable barriers in the prevention of management misconduct. A massive fraud was discovered in 1938 at McKesson & Robbins Co., a distributor of crude drugs. The head of that company was an individual calling himself Dr. Franklin Donald Coster. He was actually a convicted criminal whose real name was Philip M. Musica. Using dummy corporations and phantom banks, Musica looted the company of $2.9 million over a twelve-year period. McKesson & Robbins claimed $87 million in assets on its accounting statements filed with the SEC, but some $20 million of those assets were fictitious. The fraud was concealed from the company's auditors, Price Waterhouse & Co., by phony inventory account receivables. The auditors examined the records of the company to verify the inventory but never actually checked the physical inventory. Faked account receivables were tested by examining shipping and other documents, but those documents had been forged in order to deceive the auditors. To carry out this fraud, Musica, assisted by his three brothers, employed massive numbers of fraudulent entries and documents. He even forged the company's credit ratings. Musica committed suicide when police tried to arrest him at his home. To settle the company's claims, Price Waterhouse agreed to return its audit fees, about $500,000.

The SEC brought disciplinary proceedings against Price Waterhouse, but a battery of experts testified that the firm had followed generally accepted procedures in its audits. As a result of that testimony, the SEC decided not to sanction Price Waterhouse, but did criticize the professional standards of the accounting profession. An earlier English case may have been right in rejecting a claim that auditors should have counted an inventory that was overstated.[51] The court there held that such an act was not an auditor's duty. Auditors traditionally (and still do) depend on management integrity. Time did not help the SEC to understand the role of the auditor. As described in a later chapter, the successor to McKesson & Robbins (McKesson HBOC) would engage in massive accounting manipulations at the end of the century.

The McKesson & Robbins case illustrated the manner in which the SEC approached its regulation of the accounting profession: it would bring disciplinary actions against accountants when an audit failed to uncover fraud, barring those accountants from practicing or appearing before it, or suspending their right to do so. This is an extreme sanction for professional accountants because much of their work is SEC-related. For that reason, the SEC was initially forgiving of accounting shortfalls, as in the McKesson & Robbins case. Another inventory shortage case was brought in 1947 by the SEC against the accounting firm of Barrow, Wade, Guthrie & Co. It too resulted in no sanctions.

The SEC took a harder line in 1952 when it imposed a ten-day suspension in the practice of Haskins & Sells, a national accounting firm, and one of its partners. That sanction was imposed because the accounting firm had certi-fied the value of an intangible asset (a patent) that the SEC believed was overvalued on the balance sheet of Thomascolor Inc. That sanction was en-tered despite the testimony of prominent experts defending the accounting firm's audit work. In another case, Touche, Niven, Bailey & Smart and two of its partners were suspended from practicing before the SEC for fifteen days in 1957. The SEC found those respondents had, ten years earlier, certified a loss reserve account that was materially inadequate to cover certain losses and contingencies of the audit client, Seaboard Commercial Corp.

The Westec Corp. engaged in various accounting maneuvers that accelerated revenues and deferred expenses in the 1960s. Two of its principals, Ernst M. Hall Jr. and James W. Williams, were convicted of manipulating the company's stock price. They were respectively sentenced to eight and fifteen years in prison. Westec's auditor, Ernst & Ernst, was the subject of an SEC enforce-ment action for certifying the company's financial statements for 1964 and 1965, which were inflated as a part of the manipulation scheme. As a sanction for that failure, an SEC administrative law judge entered an order barring Ernst & Ernst from taking on any new public company audit clients for a period of six months. The SEC reversed that order on appeal, concluding that censure was an adequate sanction. Two individual accountants at Ernst & Ernst were suspended from practicing before the SEC for periods of one year and three months.

The SEC wanted audit procedures to extend beyond merely examining records. The SEC thought that auditors should kick the tires as well—that is, they should physically examine inventory and verify account receivables di-rectly with debtors. The AICPA added these procedures to its list of GAAS. Nevertheless, shrewd criminals found creative ways around such procedures. In one of the largest financial scandals of all times (although dwarfed by Enron), Tony DeAngelis, the "Salad Oil King," faked a huge vegetable oil inventory. In order to deceive auditors, he created special chambers in storage tanks at inspection ports; the chambers contained oil while the rest of the tank was filled with water. In other instances, he pumped his limited inventory from tank to tank just ahead of inspectors. DeAngelis's failure in 1963 brought down the New York Produce Exchange and two brokerage firms, Ira Haupt and J.R. Williston & Beane. The stock market was thrown into turmoil by this massive fraud and was further staggered when President Kennedy was assas-sinated in the midst of that scandal, closing the NYSE.

The accounting profession was also facing other problems. The complex-ity of business in America continued to grow. International operations and intricate corporate structures became the norm for large corporations. Ac-countants were being called on every day to resolve complex issues in the treatment of transactions that were often unique and capable of a number of solutions under GAAP that would have dramatically different effects on the company's earnings, depending on which solution was selected. These decisions required judgment and often raised complex theoretical concerns. The accountants themselves recognized that their profession required intellect and hard work, which they sought to recognize through the creation of an Accounting Hall of Fame for its leading lights, a forum to which Arthur Andersen's founder was elected.

Accounting Problems Spread

The Securities Act of 1933 granted shareholders the right to sue auditors certifying financial statements that were not true or that were misleading. The auditors could defend on the ground that it had used due diligence in certifying the statement. The Securities Exchange Act of 1934 also imposed liability on accountants to investors relying on certified financial statements that were misleading, but the accountants could defend such claims by showing that they acted in good faith and did not know of the inaccuracy.

A 1968 decision by a federal district court in New York, *Escott v. BarChris Construction Corp.,*[52] held that the company's auditors, Peat, Marwick, Mitchell & Co. (Peat Marwick), violated the Securities Act of 1933. BarChris constructed bowling alleys, which became popular after the invention of automatic pin setters. A complaint filed under the federal securities laws charged that the company's financial statements were an accounting nightmare of Enron-like proportions. The complaint charged gross overstatements of sales, profits, and orders, understated liabilities, and failure to disclose large officer loans and customer delinquencies. Peat Marwick certified a registration statement for BarChris that failed to disclose that income from bowling alleys built by the registrant and sold to a third party had been leased back to a subsidiary of the registrant. The court held that the auditors had not used due diligence in their work or they would have discovered the failure to disclose this arrangement. The court asserted that, by certifying the company's financial statements, the auditors were falsely representing to investors that such due diligence had been done. Peat Marwick had been faulted by a court earlier, in 1966, for failing to correct the financial statements of the Yale Express System, after it was discovered that the company did not record certain liabilities on its books and was reporting uncollectible receivables as assets.[53]

Peat Marwick had grown rapidly by buying up independent accounting firms across the country. Although Peat Marwick billed itself as a national firm, those acquisitions were only loosely integrated into the firm. That arrangement led to criticism that Peat Marwick was really just a franchising operation that gave rise to some serious quality control issues. More trouble arrived at Peat Marwick after the National Student Marketing Company failed in the 1970s and its financial accounts proved to have been inflated. Peat Marwick was sued by investors for its audit work on that account. Two Peat Marwick accountants at the firm were convicted of criminal violations for their audit activities.[54] Peat Marwick was sanctioned by the SEC for its auditing of National Student Marketing, as well as a long list of other audit failures during the 1970s. One of those failures occurred at the Penn Central Company, which was the largest nonfinancial company in America when it became what was then the largest ever bankruptcy. The ruin of Penn Central came amid charges that its management had falsified company accounts to conceal losses and that the auditors were remiss in not ferreting out those activities. Another part of the SEC proceeding was Peat Marwick's audit failures for the Stirling Homex Corp., a manufacturer of modular homes that went bankrupt two years after it went public, causing great scandal. The SEC barred Peat Marwick from accepting new public company audit clients for a period of six months, and the firm was required to commission an independent review of its audit procedures. The suspension of new audit business was a severe sanction, but the sheer number of audit failures at Peat Marwick suggested there were problems at that firm, with its audit system, or both.

The SEC brought an enforcement against Arthur Young in connection with its audits of Geotek Resources Fund Inc. Geotek was controlled by Jack Burke, who was indicted for securities fraud and making false statements to the government. Burke entered into a plea bargain that resulted in a sentence of thirty months in prison. A federal district court in California dismissed the SEC's case against Arthur Young for that audit failure after a thirty-four-day bench trial. The SEC's decision to sue the auditors was criticized as politically motivated and an effort to impose controls over accounting firms not found in SEC regulations.

Flaws in Full Disclosure

Flaws in the full disclosure system were revealed long before Enron in a number of other scandals. Particularly spectacular was the discovery in the 1970s of massive numbers of payments made by public companies to foreign government officials for the purpose of obtaining business. Those multinational corporations were already under attack as a threat to the world order for avoiding regulation and undermining governments. In that regard, the ITT Corp. was accused of aiding the overthrow of the government of Salvador Allende in Chile, giving rise to the dictatorship of Augusto Pinochet. The Senate Subcommittee on Multinational Corporations, headed by Senator Frank Church, was examining that and other activities of the multinationals when it uncovered widespread payments to foreign government officials. Those payments were called "questionable payments" because U.S. law did not prohibit bribes to foreign officials at the time. However, the payments were funded from off-the-books slush funds, and the SEC contended that those accounts should have been reported on the companies' financial statements.

The SEC created an amnesty program that allowed companies making questionable payments to disclose them and thereby avoid a lawsuit by the SEC. Some 600 corporations then confessed to various bribery and record-keeping failures. Lockheed was the leader, having handed out $30 million to government officials in Japan, Germany, the Netherlands, Italy, and numerous other countries. Governments around the world toppled when those bribes were disclosed. That scandal resulted in the passage of additional full disclosure requirements in the form of the Foreign Corrupt Practices Act of 1977, which prohibited such payments. More important, the Foreign Corrupt Practices Act required public companies to make and keep books, records, and accounts that accurately and fairly reflected the transactions and dispositions of the assets of the issuer. The language of that legislation was softened in 1988 as a result of concerns that liability might be unfairly imposed; only knowing violations were made punishable, and companies were required to maintain only such accounting controls as a "prudent" person would require.

Accounting Reform Efforts

The SEC has long promoted the use of reports by public companies on their systems of accounting controls, and the agency wanted auditors to test those controls. The Foreign Corrupt Practices Act did not go that far but imposed a requirement that business transactions at public companies must be executed in accordance with management's authorization and in a manner that permits the preparation of financial statements in conformity with GAAP. Management was required to maintain a system of internal accounting controls that provided reasonable assurances of accountability for the company's assets, requiring periodic verification and limiting access only to authorized personnel. However, those standards were somewhat vague, and companies were confused as to what they meant.

The Metcalf Report

In 1973 the AICPA published a report prepared by a committee headed by Robert Trueblood, a noted accountant. The Trueblood report, titled *Objectives of Financial Statements,* urged accounting professionals to be more responsive to investors and creditors in providing information about the companies they audited. This was a reaction to the SEC's growing pressure on accountants to forsake management and serve new constituencies of investors, creditors, rating agencies, analysts, and anyone else with an interest in a company's financial statements. That proved to be an impossible goal.

Senator Lee Metcalf published a scathing report of the accounting industry in 1977 in which he charged that, while the Big Eight accounting firms were often referred to as "public" or "independent," he could find "little evidence that they serve the public or that they are independent in fact from the interests of their corporate clients."[55] Metcalf criticized the SEC's delegation of accounting standards setting to the accounting industry, noting that the SEC's decision to defer to the accounting industry in standard setting was decided by a single vote of the commissioners. Metcalf believed that the industry was disqualified from such a role by conflicts of interest.

The senator was critical that management could select an accounting method that the SEC did not approve of, as long as the effects of the use of that method were disclosed in footnotes to the company's financial statements. The SEC had ruled in 1938 in Accounting Series Release No. 4 that nonuniform accounting standards could be used as long as there was "substantial authoritative" support for the method selected. Metcalf claimed that this approach resulted in the choice of the "lowest common denominator" in the selection of GAAP for financial reporting. Metcalf pointed out that the lack of uniformity in accounting standards permitted companies to report dramatically different results from what were essentially the same operations by choosing from an array of acceptable accounting standards. Further, "creative accounting" was allowing businesses to report financial results that did not accurately portray their business. Metcalf asserted that numerous accounting scandals had led to a general belief that corporate financial statements did not accurately portray company finances. This same complaint would be made after the failure of Enron and the subsequent meltdown of several large telecommunications companies.

The Metcalf report was critical of the control exercised by the Big Eight accounting firms over the AICPA, the Financial Accounting Foundation, and FASB. The report made several recommendations to increase government control over accounting standards, including the creation of a federal board for such a purpose. The Metcalf report further suggested requiring rotation of accounting firms every few years to prevent them from becoming too cozy with audit clients. This rotation proposal was also promoted by J.S. Seidman of the Seidman & Seidman accounting firm and Professor Itzhak Sharav of the City University of New York. The Metcalf report wanted more stockholder participation in voting to approve the selection of accountants and wanted government inspections of independent auditors. Metcalf sought limitations on consulting services offered by accounting firms and encouraged the increased use of audit committees staffed by outside directors at public companies. Metcalf's charges and recommendations would set the stage for the debate over accounting after Enron.

Following the Metcalf report, Congressman John Moss sponsored a bill in the House of Representatives that would have created a National Organization of Securities and Exchange Commission Accountancy (NOSECA or "Nosey") that would register and discipline accounting firms practicing before the SEC. That effort failed, but attacks by Congress on the accounting profession continued. Metcalf sought an end to the bar on accountant's advertising. The AICPA removed that ban in 1978, leading to large-scale advertising by accounting firms and causing SEC chairman Arthur Levitt to complain that accounting firms were flooding the airports with their advertisements.

Congressional scrutiny of the accounting profession continued after publication of the Metcalf report. Between 1985 and 1988, Congressman John Dingell held over twenty hearings on what he perceived were the shortcomings of the accounting profession. Those hearings dealt with the effectiveness of auditing and with financial disclosure failures at various corporations. The hearings focused on instances in which large corporations declared bankruptcy shortly after publishing financial statements, certified by their auditors, that showed that the failing companies were in a favorable financial condition. Dingell examined the "public watchdog role" of auditors in the context of several audit failures and questioned whether auditors were failing to act as whistleblowers on their clients. The Dingell hearings also focused on the role of auditors in the savings and loan scandals. Proposed legislation flowing from the hearings, titled the Fraud Detection and Disclosure Act, would have required auditors to focus more on discovering fraud. That legislation was not adopted, but Dingell would reappear at the Enron congressional hearings where he would again attack the accountants.

The Cohen Committee

The accounting profession was finding itself involved in areas well outside its traditional role. Accountants were called on to do everything from auditing Teamster elections during the Jimmy Hoffa era to certifying the results of the Academy Awards, both of which duties were undertaken by Price Waterhouse. After World War II, accounting firms began expanding their operations in management consulting services, creating separate departments for those activities. This was in addition to existing audit and tax advice work. Management consulting was a natural niche for accounting firms, which had gotten broad exposure to systems management through their audit work. There was a long history of supplying such services. Ernst & Ernst had a consulting unit in 1908.

Consulting services grew to include executive recruitment, lobbying, marketing and product analysis, plant layout, actuarial and pension funding services, litigation support for lawyers, compliance programs required by regulators, and financial management services. In the audit arena, accountants attested to the adequacy of management's internal controls, reviewed data used by management for forecasts, assessed going concern values, and reviewed estimates for business operations. In addition, accountants advised management on systems and operations and structuring transactions for favorable tax and financial accounting purposes.

In every capacity, the auditor was a servant of management, not an adversary. The SEC, nevertheless, contended that auditors owed their loyalty to investors, while creditors claimed that auditors owed them duties as well. In 1957, the SEC noted in one of its Accounting Series Releases that "the responsibility of the public accountant is not only to the client who pays his fee but to investors, creditors and others who may rely on the financial statements which he certifies."[56] This was an impossible position for auditors; it assured that no one would be pleased and misled investors into believing that auditors had some magic method for detecting fraud and preventing the manipulation of accounts under the control of management.

A Committee on Auditors' Responsibilities, known as the Cohen committee in honor of its chairman, Manuel Cohen, a former SEC chairman, was created in 1978 to address several accounting issues. The Cohen committee's other members were representatives from academia, financial services, and the accounting industry. The committee met over a four-year period and filed an extensive report of almost 200 pages. The committee recommended that the management of public companies report to shareholders on the adequacy of their internal accounting controls. A similar recommendation was made in 1979 by a Special Advisory Committee to the American Institute of Certified Public Accountants. The SEC proposed such a rule, but later withdrew it.

The Cohen committee considered a number of other topics. The committee was asked by the AICPA to develop conclusions and recommendations regarding the appropriate responsibilities of independent auditors and to determine whether a gap existed between what the public expects and what auditors provide (the "expectations gap"). The Cohen committee concluded that such a gap did exist and recommended strengthening audit practices, including the use of periodic peer reviews. In future years, such peer reviews became an accepted practice in the accounting profession.

The Cohen committee also recommended a broader role for auditors that extended beyond a set of statements to include an overall review of the accounting period under review. The Cohen committee thought that auditors should apply a practical "smell test" to accounting statements, as well as seeking to ensure technical compliance.

The Treadway Commission

The accounting industry embraced the independent audit committee concept in a 1987 report prepared by a task force created by a group of accounting bodies, including the AICPA, which, apropos of nothing, won an award that year for its float in the Rose Bowl parade. That task force was formally named the National Commission on Fraudulent Financial Reporting, but was more commonly called the Treadway commission in honor of its chairman, James Treadway Jr., a former SEC commissioner. This body considered the need for improvements in the accounting of publicly held companies. The Treadway commission wanted auditors to take a risk-based approach in detecting fraud that would focus on high-risk areas for audit. That would be the approach followed by Arthur Andersen in its failed audit of WorldCom.

The Treadway commission recommended that public companies should be required by SEC rules to include in their annual reports to stockholders a management report signed by the chief executive officer and the chief financial officer. This proposed management report would acknowledge management's responsibilities for financial statements and internal financial controls and provide management's assessment of the effectiveness of the company's internal controls. In 1988, the SEC proposed a rule that would have required a management report on internal controls. That proposal was withdrawn in 1992, after it met stiff industry opposition. The Public Oversight Board (POB) of the AICPA, which was formed by the AICPA in response to the Metcalf report and other criticisms of the accounting profession, also recommended a management report on accounting controls, but it too became bogged down in controversy. Enron would overwhelm that opposition.

The Treadway commission noted that accountants were denying responsibility for the contents of financial statements they audited. In that regard, the commission was perceptive in focusing responsibility on company managers, concluding that they were the "key players" who bore the primary responsibility for the company's financial statements. The commission concluded that the "the tone at the top" in the management of public companies was the vital factor in assuring the integrity of financial statements. This, of course, was a truism, but also reflected the key flaw in the SEC's full disclosure model. Management controlled the financial statements, and it was management that had the incentive to manipulate those accounts and report results in the light most favorable to management. That incentive often came in the form of stock option compensation worth millions of dollars.

Despite the Treadway commission's focus on management responsibility, increasing public attention to financial statements and accounting standards was enlarging the "'expectations gap'—the gap between what was feared to be the public's perception of the auditor's role and the auditor's role in fact."[57] That gap was broadened by the SEC's continuing false assertions that auditors assured investors of full disclosure in their investments in public companies. As the SEC well knew, auditors proved time and time again through an increasingly long list of audit failures that they could not detect or prevent fraud in the complex accounting systems that were under the control of management. The AICPA tried to correct that misconception, but failed entirely. The accounting profession was only able to include in its audit certifications a statement that the "financial statements are the responsibility of the Company's management," whereas the auditor's responsibility is only to "express an opinion on these financial statements based on our audit."[58]

Another aspect of the controversy over the role of the auditor was the habit that some audit clients had of firing an auditor that objected to management accounting practices. The client would then shop for an auditor that would agree with management. Given the looseness of audit standards and the flexibility and complexity of GAAP, finding a new auditor was not usually a difficult task for the client. The SEC tried to stop this practice by requiring companies to notify the SEC promptly in a Form 8-K filing when auditors were changed, so that the issue giving rise to the firing would be exposed and management would be shamed, but management had no shame. It simply claimed that the discharge was the result of some unrelated issue such as poor service or billing issues.

Financial Scandals Embroil the Accountants

The accounting firms were facing a hostile climate from investors suffering losses. As will be seen, Arthur Andersen was the subject of several suits for its audit failures. Before 1970, Price Waterhouse, then one of the Big Eight accounting firms, had been sued only three times in connection with its audits. Five years later, that number jumped to over forty lawsuits. Peat, Marwick, & Mitchell had not been the subject of a lawsuit before 1965. Ten years later, that accounting firm had been sued over one hundred times. The number of lawsuits filed against accounting firms increased from seventy-one in 1970 to 200 in 1972.

Three accountants at Lybrand Ross & Co. were found to have certified false and misleading financial statements of the Continental Vending Machine Co. in the 1960s. The company's president, Harold Roth, was speculating in the stock market using $3.5 million in funds supplied by loans from Continental to an affiliate, Valley Commercial Corporation, that were then routed to Roth. He was unable to repay the loans after his speculations failed. Continental's auditors, Lybrand, Ross Brothers & Montgomery, agreed that if Roth posted collateral to Valley of $3.5 million, the accounting firm would not have to audit Valley's books. The collateral posted by Roth consisted of Continental's own securities, valued at $2.9 million. The auditors required Continental to disclose the loan in a footnote in its financial statements, but no details were provided.

After the Roth loans defaulted, the government brought criminal charges against Carl J. Simon, Robert H. Kaiser, and Melvin S. Fishman, the three partners at Lybrand, Ross Brothers & Montgomery conducting the audit. Experts testified at trial that the auditors had complied with generally accepted accounting principles, and the first trial ended in a hung jury. On retrial, the three partners were found guilty of conspiracy to defraud and mail fraud. The trial judge instructed the jury that the accountants could be held liable for certifying statements that did not accurately portray a company's financial condition, even if those statements were prepared in accordance with GAAP. These were the first criminal convictions of partners in a major public accounting firm in over seventy years. The convictions were upheld by the Second Circuit and review was denied by the Supreme Court, but the accountants were later pardoned by President Richard Nixon.

The collapse of the Equity Funding Corp. in 1973 revealed a massive inflation of accounts. That fraud included the use of dummy accounts, including instances where funds were routed to foreign shell companies and then sent back to Equity Funding to enhance the company's finances. The company's auditors ignored a warning from a financial analyst, Raymond

Dirks, that the company's accounts were fraudulent. Three members of the Seidman & Seidman accounting firm were convicted of criminal violations for their audit work at Equity Funding. Some 110 class actions were filed in the wake of that disaster. Seidman & Seidman had further problems when a "massive" accounting fraud was discovered at another of its audit clients, Cenco Inc. Management had inflated inventories in Cenco's Medical/Health Division between 1970 and 1975 in order to pump up the price of the company's stock. The inflated price of the stock allowed the company to buy other companies. Management used the phony inventory valuations to induce insurers to pay inflated claims for inventory lost or destroyed. "Thus, those involved in the fraud were not stealing from the company, as in the usual corporate fraud case, but were instead aggrandizing the company (and themselves) at the expense of outsiders, such as the owners of the companies that Cenco bought with its inflated stock, the banks that loaned Cenco money, and the insurance companies that insured its inventories."[59] The value of Cenco's stock dropped by 75 percent after this fraud was revealed. Cenco had accounted for a substantial portion of Seidman's total billings. The result was suits and countersuits between the company and the accounting firm in which the accountants seemed to have prevailed. Seidman & Seidman agreed to pay $3.5 million to settle class action claims against it and then sought recovery of that amount from Cenco.

The failure of Weis Securities in 1973 resulted in more claims of auditor liability. That brokerage firm had 55,000 customers and thirty branch offices. Five executives at Weis were indicted for falsifying its books and records in order to promote a public offering of the brokerage firm's own stock. Private litigants brought claims against Touche Ross & Co., the auditors for Weis, for failing to discover this fraud.[60] The case reached the Supreme Court, which held that the record-keeping requirements in the federal securities laws did not support such an action against an accounting firm.[61] This ruling was a victory for the industry, but did little to stem the growing tidal wave of litigation against accountants. Touche Ross & Co. was the subject of disciplinary action by the SEC in 1976 for failed audits of the Ampex Corp. and Giant Stores Corp. Three partners of that accounting firm—Edwin Heft, James M. Lynch, and Armin Frankel—were also named as respondents. Touche Ross challenged the SEC's authority to discipline accountants in that proceeding, but the Second Circuit Court of Appeals dismissed that claim. Touche Ross then settled with the SEC, accepting a censure and agreeing to peer review of its audit procedures.

The SEC charged David Checkosky and Norman Aldrich, accountants at Coopers & Lybrand, with audit failures for the Savin Corporation in the 1980s. They allowed Savin to treat research and development costs to be listed as "start up" costs that could be deferred rather than expensed immediately as required by GAAP. The District of Columbia Circuit Court of Appeals twice slapped down the SEC in that case and ultimately dismissed it because the

SEC failed to articulate what standard of *scienter* (degree of intent) was required for an auditor to be liable for a failed audit. That was an enormous embarrassment to the SEC, but the agency truculently amended its rule to cover all levels of intent from intentional or reckless to negligence.

Ernst & Whinney was the subject of an SEC disciplinary action in connection with its audits of United States Surgical Corp., a creator of surgical stapling devices, in 1980 and 1981. That company was inflating its revenues in order to offset the effects of increased expenses from, among other things, legal actions against competitors. An SEC administrative law judge found that Ernst & Whinney had not met its audit obligations and suspended the firm from acquiring any new audit business in the New York region for a period of forty-five days. The Supreme Court upheld a $6.1 million judgment against Ernst & Young (later Arthur Young) for its failed audits of the Co-Op, an agricultural cooperative that went bankrupt in 1984 and defaulted on demand notes totaling over $10 million that had been sold to over 1,600 investors.

The bankruptcy of ZZZZ Best led to another accounting scandal in the 1980s. That firm was headed by Barry Minkow, an entrepreneurial wunderkind who at age twenty-one built the rug-cleaning business he started in his parents' garage into a $200 million publicly traded corporation. Like the dot-com companies in the 1990s, the stock of ZZZZ Best was a hot issue. Its initial offering price increased from $4 a share to a high of $18. Minkow claimed that ZZZZ Best was the nation's largest carpet cleaner. In fact, his empire was based on inflated revenues that he used to pump up the company's stock. Among other things, ZZZZ Best claimed to have cleaning contracts for buildings that did not exist. ZZZZ Best collapsed when it was discovered that Minkow was a fraud who was using ZZZZ Best to launder money for organized crime. Minkow served seven years in prison. He became a consultant on white-collar crime after his release and occasionally appeared on television to comment on such matters, including Martha Stewart's obstruction of justice charges.

ZZZZ Best was audited by Ernst & Whinney. The firm resigned and refused to certify the financial statements for the 1987 fiscal year after discovering a fraudulent $7 million contract. ZZZZ Best then falsely advised the SEC and the public that Ernst & Whinney's resignation was not due to any disagreement over accounting policies. Believing itself constrained by client confidentiality restrictions, Ernst & Whinney did not correct that statement for some time. This episode eventually led to legislation requiring auditors to blow the whistle on their clients. The accounting firm was targeted in class action proceedings for its audits even though it never certified any ZZZZ Best financial statements.

S&L Crisis

An even larger disaster for the accounting industry was the savings and loan (S&L) debacle of the 1980s when regulatory controls first nearly bankrupted those institutions and then opened the door for fraud by endorsing some questionable accounting practices. Some 435 S&Ls failed between 1981 and 1983. In order to shore up this failing industry, the Federal Home Loan Bank Board (FHLBB) reduced capital reserve requirements and "developed new 'regulatory accounting principles' (RAP) that in many instances replaced GAAP for purposes of determining compliance with its capital requirements."[62] The use of RAP had some debilitating effects. Quoting a congressional committee, the Supreme Court noted that "'the use of various accounting gimmicks and reduced capital standards masked the worsening financial condition of the industry . . . and enabled many weak institutions to continue operating with an increasingly inadequate cushion to absorb future losses.' The reductions in required capital reserves, moreover, allowed thrifts to grow explosively without increasing their capital base, at the same time deregulation let them expand into new (and often riskier) fields of investment."[63]

RAP was allowing the S&Ls "'to defer losses from the sale of assets with below market yields; permitting the use of income capital certificates, authorized by Congress, in place of real capital; . . . allowing FSLIC members to exclude from liabilities in computing net worth, certain contra-asset accounts, including loans in process, unearned discounts, and deferred fees and credits; and permitting the inclusion of net worth certificates, qualifying subordinated debentures and appraised equity capital as RAP net worth.'" The result of these "accounting gimmicks" was "that 'by 1984, the difference between RAP and GAAP net worth at S&L's stood at $9 billion,' which meant 'that the industry's capital position, or . . . its cushion to absorb losses was overstated by $9 billion.'" Only Enron and other scandals would match this massive government-sponsored manipulation of accounts.[64]

In order to protect the Federal Savings and Loan Insurance Corporation (FSLIC) insurance fund, the FHLBB sought to encourage mergers between healthy institutions and failing ones through favorable accounting treatment. The purchase method of accounting under GAAP for mergers allowed the acquiring company to recognize goodwill (the amount paid for the acquired firm in excess of actual assets) as an asset. The FHLBB allowed acquiring S&Ls to use the purchase method. In a departure from GAAP, the acquiring S&L was allowed to use the goodwill in a manner that would generate a paper profit in the initial years after the acquisition. "The difference between amortization and accretion schedules thus allowed acquiring thrifts to seem more profitable than they in fact were."[65] The FHLBB also allowed goodwill to be counted as an asset for reserve requirements and regulatory net worth, which usually required some hard and liquid asset. This "supervisory goodwill" allowed the acquiring S&L to leverage itself further, a result sought to be limited by reserve requirements.

As the crisis heightened, Congress passed legislation that reversed the use of supervisory goodwill that had been allowed by the FHLBB. This bankrupted or caused enormous losses to the firms relying on that treatment in acquiring failed S&Ls. Some of those firms were seized and liquidated when the new requirements placed them in violation of regulatory capital requirements. Those institutions sued, claiming they had a contractual commitment from the government for that favorable treatment.[66] The Supreme Court agreed, subjecting the government to an estimated $30 billion in liability. Golden State Bancorp., which was controlled by Ronald Perelman, a corporate raider, claimed $908 million in damages as a result of that ruling. He securitized that claim by selling litigation participation certificates that gave investors a claim to the proceeds from the action. Some 120 S&Ls brought similar suits claiming damages from this change in accounting standards by the government. Glendale Federal Bank FSB, which was acquired by Citigroup, Inc., was awarded $381 million in damages in one such suit, but was denied an additional $528 million sought as "restitution." The $381 million was paid out to holders of "litigation tracking warrants" previously issued to holders of Glendale's convertible notes when it merged with Golden State Bancorp Inc. Each warrant holder was to receive .02 of a share of a Citigroup share and sixty-seven cents in cash from the $381 million settlement.

Government regulations were loosened during the S&L crisis to allow expanded investments that would provide greater returns. As Richard Breeden, a former SEC chairman, noted:

> [A]t a time when the thrift industry was economically insolvent, the . . . FHLBB encouraged the industry to grow out of its problems, hoping that growth through the accumulation of higher yielding assets would offset losses on existing mortgage assets. By greatly reducing capital requirements and continuing to make under priced federal deposit insurance available even to economically insolvent institutions, the regulators provided thrift owners with every incentive to engage in aggressive growth by speculating with taxpayer dollars. Besides causing the thrift industry to attract more than its share of fraudulent operators, this policy led to ruinous expansion that greatly increased the ultimate losses to the government.[67]

Previously unexposed to market discipline, S&L executives believed that they could use government-insured funds to obtain large returns that would allow them to live like corporate moguls with yachts, jets, mansions, expensive artworks, and other executive necessities. S&L funds were used for such things as a two-week culinary tour of France, a $148,000 Christmas party, and the services of prostitutes. One S&L employee conducted a $1 million renovation on her house on a salary of $48,000. Speculative investments included "trash-for-cash," that is, worthless assets bought from the S&Ls own executives. The services of a number of senators were purchased (the infamous "Keating Five," which included the now reformist Senator John McCain) to prevent any reforms in the deposit insurance program. The bill for the savings and loan debacle of the 1980s came due in the 1990s. Predictions for the total bill to taxpayers ranged from less than $90 billion to $1 trillion. After-the-fact cost estimates were not much better, placing the actual total cost to the Treasury at ranges reaching from $90 to $200 billion.[68]

Most of the larger failed S&Ls were public companies with audited financial statements, but full disclosure served as no check on their excesses. The SEC did require one S&L to restate its financial statements, resulting in the reporting of a $107 million loss. That restatement was required because the SEC disagreed with the accounting treatment recommended by Arthur Andersen & Co. for certain transactions. A shareholder suit against the accounting firm was dismissed. Full disclosure under the federal securities laws failed to prevent the S&L crisis, but accounting firms became the scapegoats for their failures. In a passage that would be much quoted in the wake of the Enron and ensuing accounting failures, Stanley Sporkin, federal district court judge and former head of the SEC enforcement division, lamented in a proceeding involving a failed S&L: "where were . . . the accountants and attorneys?" . . . "With all the professional talent involved (both accounting and legal)" why did not at least one professional blow "the whistle to stop the overreaching that took place in this case."[69] Accounting firms paid $800 million in legal fees to defend themselves from suits arising from the S&L crisis in 1992 alone. Ernst & Young paid settlements of $400 million and Arthur Andersen paid $79 million. Deloitte & Touche paid $312 million, and KPMG Peat Marwick paid $186 million in settlements.

Other Audit Failures

Banking failures like the Bank of Credit and Commerce International (BCCI) were blamed on the auditors. That bank was later found to be one giant criminal enterprise that bank regulators had permitted to operate globally. At the time of its failure, BCCI was the seventh-largest privately owned bank in the world. It had over 400 offices and 1.3 million customers. Clark Clifford, adviser to several presidents and former secretary of defense, and Robert Altman, the husband of Linda Carter (the television actress who played Wonder Woman), were indicted for their role in assisting BCCI to acquire an American bank through straw men. That action by the government was ill considered. Clifford could not be tried because of health reasons, and Altman was acquitted after a lengthy trial in a New York state court. Altman and Clifford did agree to pay a total of $5 million to settle charges brought by bank regulatory authorities, and they were barred from the banking business.

Accountants failed to unravel the accounting shell game utilized by the Penn Square Bank in Oklahoma that was used to sell $2.5 billion in loan participations to other banks. The failure of that shopping center bank caused a national crisis. The Federal Deposit Insurance Corporation (FDIC) sued Penn Square's auditors Peat Marwick, for failing to detect the bank's lending abuses and for certifying Penn Square's financial statements just four months before its collapse. The case was settled for a reported $18 million. Shareholder and other suits totaling over $400 million were settled by the accounting firm for undisclosed sums.

One victim, the giant Continental Bank in Chicago, which had its own auditor examine the Penn Square loans, was virtually nationalized by the government in a rescue that required the pledging of billions of dollars of government funds. That bank was where Andrew Fastow had his start in business. Ernst & Whinney, the auditor of the Continental Bank, was found not liable in a jury trial brought by shareholders who claimed that the auditor failed to warn of the bank's problems. A class action suit was also dismissed.

The accounting failures arising before the debacles of the 1990s are too numerous to catalog, but included the failure of Crazy Eddie, an electronics store, after discovery of a $45 million inventory shortage of its electronic goods. Its founder, Eddie Antar, was jailed after he was extradited from Israel, where he had fled to escape prosecution. Towers Financial Corp., a debt collection agency, turned out to be the then largest Ponzi scheme ever, with losses to investors of $460 million. It was controlled by Steven Hoffenberg, a former publisher of the *New York Post.* He was sentenced to twenty years in prison. The company was reorganized under the new name of Qualis Care by John Hall, who then proceeded to loot the company's remaining assets. Hall had previously been convicted of making false statements to the Small Business Administration; he paid a $100,000 fine to the FDIC to settle charges that he misused funds of the First City Bank in California; and he settled a claim by the SEC that he had stolen $2.1 million from a money market fund. Polly Peck International PLC was another audit failure. The company's chief executive officer, Asil Nadir, was accused in London of stealing $47 million from the company. He posted bail of $5.5 million but fled to Cyprus to avoid prosecution. Creditors received only three cents on the dollar in its bankruptcy proceeding.

Liabilities Mount

Occasional litigation victories by accounting firms did nothing to stem the growing number of lawsuits. The auditors were being sued whenever a public company had financial difficulties. Laventhal & Horwath, the nation's seventh-largest accounting firm, with 350 partners, declared bankruptcy in 1990 as the result of litigation claims and costs arising from the S&L crisis and other audit failures. At the time of its bankruptcy petition, that accounting firm was defending over a hundred lawsuits that were seeking more than $2 billion in damages. Among its audit failures was PTL, an evangelical Christian ministry of Jim and Tammy Faye Bakker. Jim Bakker was sent to prison after his 1989 conviction for defrauding 116,000 investors of $158 million that they had contributed to buy shares in Heritage USA, which was to be a vacation spot and retreat for church members. Among other things, Bakker used $265,000 of church funds to buy the silence of a church secretary, Jessica Hahn, with whom he had sex. Laventhal & Horwath, PTL's accountants, were reported to be administering a secret fund that was used to pay more than $2 million in salaries and bonuses to the Bakkers without the knowledge or approval of the ministry's board of directors.

"Data made available by the Big Six [accounting] firms revealed an astonishing $30 billion of potential liability for those firms alone at the end of 1992, roughly $3.8 million per partner. At the same time, headlines advertised not only extraordinary jury verdicts but extraordinary settlements as well. Ernst & Young's $400 million settlement with the federal government [over its S&L audits] appeared in giant headlines on the front page of the *New York Times*." Coopers & Lybrand was censured by the British government and had to pay $5 million in connection with its audits of Robert Maxwell's English publishing companies, which failed after Maxwell disappeared from his yacht and his body was found floating in the Mediterranean. An inquiry into his companies' accounts revealed that they were failing and that Maxwell had been looting employee pension funds to keep his empire afloat and to maintain his lavish lifestyle. A report on Maxwell's defalcations by the British Department of Trade and Industry was harshly critical of the audit work by Coopers & Lybrand. In the course of its investigation, the government discovered a note written by a senior partner at Coopers & Lybrand that described the accounting firm's role as an independent accountant as follows: "The first requirement is to be at the beck and call of Robert Maxwell, his sons and staff, appear when wanted and provide whatever is required."[70]

Coopers & Lybrand also came under attack for other audit failures. It settled claims arising from its audit of Barings Bank, a 300-year-old institution that was destroyed by the unauthorized trading of Nicholas Leeson, a twenty-seven-year-old trader for the bank employed in Singapore. Leeson's trading resulted in losses to Barings in excess of $1 billion. That case raised a new danger for auditors, the failure to discover a rogue trader operating in the structure of an audit client. In Leeson's case, his managers did not understand his trading practices and allowed him to control both the actual trading that caused the losses and the processing of those trades. That arrangement allowed Leeson to conceal losses until they were so large that the bank was destroyed—or almost destroyed: it was sold for £1. Coopers & Lybrand agreed to pay a reported $95 million to settle claims involving its audit work for the bank.

Coopers & Lybrand was the auditor for Phar-Mor Inc., a discount drugstore chain that filed bankruptcy in 1992 after it was disclosed that the company had included $500 million in fake inventory on its balance sheet. The company was forced to close 200 stores and lay off 17,000 employees, three times the number of jobs lost at Enron. Its president, Michael Monus, was sentenced to twenty years in prison. Phar-Mor's chief financial officer, Patrick Finn, agreed to testify against Monus and was given a sentence of thirty-three months. A jury in Pittsburgh found Coopers & Lybrand liable for failing to detect the massive fraud. Earlier, Coopers & Lybrand was caught up in a scandal involving Miniscribe Corp., a computer disk maker that filed bankruptcy in 1990 after being caught shipping bricks instead of disks to customers as a means to boost sales figures. Coopers & Lybrand and other defendants were stung by a jury verdict in Galveston, Texas, that awarded $38 million in compensatory and $530 million in punitive damages to investors that had bought $18 million of Miniscribe bonds. Coopers & Lybrand agreed to pay $50 million to settle its portion of the liability under that judgment. The experience of Frank Quattrone as a witness in that proceeding would play a role in his conviction for obstruction of justice in one of the post-Enron scandals.

Peat Marwick continued to encounter problems. The firm was the auditor for Orange County, California, which was bankrupted by the high-risk trading activities of its elected treasurer, Robert Citron, as the 1990s began. This was the largest municipal bankruptcy in history. The county lost $1.5 billion from Citron's trades, which represented about $1,000 for each resident of the county. Peat Marwick paid $75 million to settle claims that it failed to detect the amount of exposure to the county from Citron's trading. Of course, things could have been worse. Merrill Lynch settled Orange County's claims that it had acted improperly in accepting Citron's orders for the staggering sum of $400 million. Orange County's lawyers, LeBoeuf, Lamb, Greene & McRae agreed to pay $45 million to the county for failing to prevent the county's own treasurer from engaging in high-risk trades. This seems odd since Citron's election opponent had claimed that the high rate of returns experienced by the county could only come from high-risk trading.

The Supreme Court lent further credence to the claim that auditors were responsible to investors and creditors in a case involving Arthur Young:

> By certifying the public reports that collectively depict a corporation's financial status, the independent auditor assumes a *public* responsibility transcending any employment relationship with the client. The independent public accountant performing this special function owes ultimate allegiance to the corporation's creditors and stockholders, as well as to the investing public. This "public watchdog" function demands that the accountant maintain total independence from the client at all times and requires complete fidelity to the public trust. To insulate from disclosure a certified public accountant's interpretations of the client's financial statements would be to ignore the significance of the accountant's role as a disinterested analyst charged with public obligations.[71]

This misunderstanding of the role of the accountant was deceiving to an unsuspecting public that was being assured by the SEC, and now the Supreme Court, that the auditors guaranteed full disclosure under the federal securities laws, thus magically protecting the public in its investments.

Auditor liability was limited to some extent by the Supreme Court decision involving the Touche Ross audit of Weis Securities. The Supreme Court held in that case that there was no private right of action for SEC books and records violations.[72] The *scienter* requirement imposed over the objections of the SEC by the Supreme Court in *Ernst & Ernst v. Hochfelder*[73] meant that an intent to defraud had to be established in order to maintain an action under SEC Rule 10b-5 against auditors and others. This intent requirement added a cushion against liability for accountants because their failings were usually due at most to negligence, rather than any desire to deceive. Liability was sought in the case against Ernst & Ernst on the ground that it failed to detect a flaw in the system of accounting controls of the client that allowed the company's president to commit fraud. The lower courts later held that auditors have the requisite *scienter* when they prepare and certify audited financial statements that they know, or are reckless in not knowing, are false. Still another Supreme Court decision rejected aiding and abetting liability that had been the basis for seeking damages against accountants under Rule 10b-5 for failed audits.[74] Further aid was given to the accountants by the Supreme Court in disallowing claims made under the federal Racketeer Influenced and Corrupt Organization Act of 1970 (RICO) statute, which had been adopted to impose severe sanctions against organized crime and not meek accountants.[75]

These actions by the Supreme Court, although helpful, could not stem the tide of litigation against accounting firms. Arthur Andersen & Co. published a report in 1992 titled *The Liability Crisis in the United States: Impact on the Accounting Profession, A Statement of Position.* It cited a growing crisis in the accounting industry because of lawsuits by disappointed investors. The accounting profession was acting at the same time to moot criticism by establishing peer review of its audits, a practice recommended by the Cohen committee. Such peer reviews were already employed by some accounting firms even before that recommendation; sometimes those reviews were conducted as part of a settlement with the SEC.

At first, peer reviews were conducted by groups from several firms, but this arrangement proved unwieldy. In 1976, Price Waterhouse used Deloitte Haskins & Sells to conduct a peer review, and that single one-on-one review became a model for the industry. The peer review adopted by the profession called for the audit firms to review each other's work at least every three years in order to curb improper practices or undue client influence. Peer review included review of audit practices and quality control systems.

Peer review, however, did not keep Arthur Andersen out of trouble. It was given a clean bill of health by Deloitte & Touche just a few months before Enron's problems hit the press. In any event, peer review, even before Enron, did not satisfy critics, and calls for an independent accounting oversight board, that is, one controlled by the government, were ignored. The POB, created in 1977 by the AICPA, was given responsibility over the peer review process. The POB was managed by a five-member board that included nonaccountants, as well as industry professionals. The POB was succeeded in that role by the Accounting Industry Review Board.

The Independence Controversy

The SEC's full disclosure regime hinges on "independent" public accountants for integrity. The SEC states:

> Investor confidence in the integrity of publicly available financial information is the cornerstone of our securities markets. Capital formation depends on the willingness of investors to invest in the securities of public companies. Investors are more likely to invest, and pricing is more likely to be efficient, the greater the assurance that the financial information disclosed by issuers is reliable. The federal securities laws contemplate that that assurance will flow from knowledge that the financial information has been subjected to rigorous examination by competent and objective auditors.[76]

In order to ensure objective audits, the SEC requires that accountants remain independent of the management of the companies being audited. Interestingly, the SEC initially acted to weaken such independence. Before turning administration of the Securities Act of 1933 over to the SEC, the Federal Trade Commission adopted rules on auditor independence that prohibited auditors of public companies from having "any interest" in audit clients. The SEC changed that standard to "substantial interest" not long after the SEC was created.

By 1940, the SEC was pressuring the accounting industry to adopt rules to ensure greater auditor independence, but with little effect. That was an impossible dream since auditors worked for and were paid by management, a fact ignored by the SEC. In 1972, the SEC issued an Accounting Series Release that focused on auditor independence when audit firms were providing management advice through consulting arrangements. The SEC expressed concern that such consulting could impair independence, but generally allowed such activities anyway. Accountants poured into that and other areas of consulting.

The accounting firms were merging with each other, resulting in increased firm size, both domestically and internationally, and expanding into international networks. The Big Eight became the Big Five. Those survivors at the end of the twentieth century were PricewaterhouseCoopers; Ernst & Young; KPMG (an amalgamation using the initials of Klynveld Peat Marwick Goerdeler); Deloitte Touche, Tohmatsu; and Andersen Worldwide. The Big Five would have been the Final Four even before the fall of Arthur Andersen if a merger between Ernst & Young and KPMG Peat Marwick had not fallen through in 1998. The largest of the Big Five firms was PricewaterhouseCoopers. Some mid-sized accounting firms remained, including Grant Thornton and BDO Seidman.

These giant accounting firms provided legal advice, as well as other services. Indeed, by the end of the twentieth century, accounting firms found themselves listed among the largest international law firms. Landwell, PricewaterhouseCoopers was ranked as the third-largest law firm in the world at the end of 2001. Arthur Andersen Legal Services was fifth, while KPMG was ranked seventh. Ernst & Young created its own law firm by acquiring the Washington, DC, office of the Atlanta law firm of King & Spalding. These and other expanded services raised concerns that auditors were losing their independence from the companies they were auditing and now advising.

Under pressure from the SEC to address this independence concern, the

AICPA formed the Independence Standards Board (ISB) in May 1997. The ISB was dedicated to establishing rules for ensuring auditor independence. The AICPA and the SEC compromised on the makeup of the board. That compromise resulted in four persons from the accounting profession (three from the Big Five and one from the AICPA) and four persons independent of accountants sitting on the board, either side having a veto.

The AICPA was otherwise resisting pressure from the SEC to tighten standards. Despite industry studies showing that there was no logical basis or evidence supporting such a requirement, SEC chairman Arthur Levitt sought to create a new board of trustees for the Financial Accounting Foundation (which controlled the FASB) with the majority of its members drawn from outside the accounting industry. Levitt also wanted people selected for the board of trustees to be approved by the SEC. The approval proposal was rejected, but a compromise was reached on the makeup of the foundation's board. That compromise resulted in a fifty-fifty split on the board, but the standard setting process remained mired in uncertainty.

Another problem was that accountants were investing in their own clients. FASB had prohibited "material" investments in audit clients, but the material standard was defined narrowly to allow substantial investments. The SEC acted to require that auditors not own stock in their audit clients in order to ensure independence. If enforced, this rule would have kept the members of most large accounting firms out of the stock market. It was not enforced until the end of the century, when an SEC investigation of PricewaterhouseCoopers uncovered more than 8,000 violations of that rule by partners and employees of the firm. Thirty-one of the firm's top forty-three partners owned stock in audit clients. PricewaterhouseCoopers was censored by the SEC for this conduct, five partners were forced to resign, and the firm acted to strengthen its independence compliance procedures after an internal review by an independent party. These reforms did not end the SEC's concerns. In January 2002, the SEC charged that KPMG improperly invested $25 million in an investment company that the accounting firm audited. KPMG was censured for this conduct.

Consulting work continued its growth in the accounting profession. Merger and acquisition work became a lucrative field as well as other nonaudit work. By 1992, nonauditing revenues were exceeding audit revenues in the larger firms. Those accounting firms received about one-third of their revenue from management consulting in 1993. That figure increased to 51 percent by the end of the century, while audit fees fell to 31 percent of revenues in 1998. Companies in the S&P 500 Index paid auditors $3.7 billion for nonaudit services in 2000. In contrast, those same companies paid only $1.2 billion in audit fees. By 1990, Arthur Andersen's consulting services were responsible for almost one-half of the revenues of the firm.

Liabilities and litigation costs, to say nothing of reputation risks from lawsuits and SEC disciplinary actions associated with audit services, placed increased emphasis on other services. Audit work became merely an entrée to lucrative consulting arrangements made possible by knowledge gained from auditing. By the time that Enron unraveled, consulting operations of the accounting firms were producing more than 70 percent of their revenues.[77]

Other Consulting Issues

Arthur Andersen created Andersen Consulting in 1989 as a separate division of the firm. This separation of services was accompanied by the immediate and alarming fact that several hundred Andersen Consulting partners and senior staff resigned their CPA status. That once proud mark of professional honor and skill was now considered an unneeded burden. The segregation of consulting services spread to other accounting firms, but they acted as independent units that were sometimes sold off to investors. PricewaterhouseCoopers LLP agreed to sell its audit and consulting business to IBM for $3.5 billion. KPMG initially sold an equity interest in its consulting operations to the Cisco Corp. and thereafter spun off its consulting group through a public offering that raised $2 billion. The KPMG consulting group then changed its name to BearingPoint Inc. Deloitte Consulting announced that it was breaking off from the auditors at Deloitte Touche, Tohmatsu, but later, in 2003, the two operations agreed to stay together. Ernst & Young sold its consulting operations in February 2000 to Cap Gemini SA, a French firm, for $11.3 billion. Grant Thornton sold off its e-business consulting operations.

The increased role of consulting services had raised alarm bells at the SEC before these split-offs, and the SEC decided to revise its auditor independence rules. In so doing, the SEC noted the changing nature of the accounting industry, concluding that, far from being policemen, accounting firms were becoming primarily business advisory service firms as they increased revenues from nonaudit services. Accounting firms were entering into business relationships, such as strategic alliances, co-marketing arrangements, and joint ventures, with audit clients and were offering ownership of parts of their practices to others, including audit clients. Audit clients were found to be hiring an increasing number of accounting firm partners, professional staff, and their spouses for high-level management positions.

The SEC adopted rules to reflect these changes. Among other things, those rules clarified the circumstances under which an auditor would retain independence in light of investments by auditors or their family members in audit clients, employment relationships between auditors or their family members and audit clients, and the scope of services provided by audit firms to their audit clients. The rules identified certain nonaudit services that could impair the auditor's independence. The SEC rules established four broad standards for measuring whether activities would impair auditor independence. For example, acting as an advocate for an audit client or performing outsourced management duties would raise a concern that the auditor's independence was impaired. Standards for determining whether nonaudit services would impair independence were specified.

Despite industry studies showing there was no basis for such a requirement, SEC chairman Arthur Levitt sought the complete separation of audit and consulting services. Levitt met opposition from Congress in that effort. He approached Senator Trent Lott, the Senate majority leader, for support, asserting that the *New York Times* and *Washington* Post were supporting his proposal. Lott famously responded that "I'm not familiar with what you're proposing to do, but if those liberal publications are in favor of it, then I'm against it." Levitt was particularly concerned with audit firms providing consulting advice to audit clients on information technology. The SEC independence rules, as adopted, did not contain such a bar. Instead, the SEC defaulted to its full disclosure model by requiring the audit committees of public companies to report whether the consulting activities of their auditor were impairing its independence. As in other instances where the SEC sought to implement corporate governance through full disclosure, this technique proved to be a failure.

The SEC moved to limit the accounting firms from providing internal audit services for audit clients because the auditors would effectively be auditing themselves. The SEC limited internal audit services by an outside auditor to 40 percent of its work for the client. Arthur Andersen was then using an "integrated" audit process for Enron that included an integration of outside and inside audit work. Kenneth Lay at Enron protested that the SEC's rule would interfere with that program. The two firms, Arthur Andersen and Enron, were indeed integrated. Arthur Andersen had one hundred employees devoted to the Enron account in Houston. Andersen even maintained offices at Enron's headquarters, where a full floor was set aside for the Andersen auditors.

The tax advisory services of accountants threatened their auditor independence in another way. As noted, public companies actually keep several sets of books: (1) internal, nonpublic reports for management; (2) financial reports for the SEC and investors; (3) pro forma reports for the analysts; and (4) tax accounts for the Internal Revenue Service. As was the case at Enron, companies frequently show a profit in their reports to the SEC while at the same time claiming much lower earnings or even a loss on their tax returns. A General Accounting Office report found that between 1996 and 2000 more than 60 percent of all corporations in the United States paid no federal income tax. The number of large public companies not paying taxes was lower, about 45 percent, but this was during a period when the economy was booming and many of those companies were showing record profits in their SEC reports and even larger profits to analysts in pro forma reports. Even fewer foreign corporations were reporting taxable income from their U.S. operations as a result of transfer pricing techniques that involve accounting manipulations that transfer U.S. earnings to a country that has a lower tax rate.

Accountants as Policemen

Despite their shortcomings as investigators, members of Congress acted to expand the role of accountants in the full disclosure process by adopting legislation on auditor independence. That legislation sought to force accountants into the role of policemen, no matter how ill-equipped they might be for such a role. The Private Securities Litigation Reform Act of 1995 set forth audit requirements for accountants certifying the statements of public corporations. Those auditors were required by that statute to comply with GAAP and GAAS standards. This legislation additionally required auditors to investigate any possibly illegal acts they might encounter during an audit and to inform management. This was the result of the ZZZZ Best scandal. Under this legislation, if management did not act, and the matter was material, the auditor was required to report the issue to the board of directors. The board must then inform the SEC of the issue. If the board did not act, the auditor was required to inform the SEC or resign the engagement. The resignation would also have to be reported to the SEC, as well as the reasons for resignation. This legislation made the accountant a professional informant, which was then a unique role for professionals.

The SEC played a more activist role during the 1990s in seeking auditor liability for management misconduct. SEC chairman Arthur Levitt claimed that, if private industry prevented the SEC from guiding the accounting process, the result would be an undermining of the capital raising process. In a speech titled "The Numbers Game" delivered in September 1998 in New York, Levitt stated that a "culture of gamesmanship" had developed over accounting practices. He warned that the SEC would aggressively prosecute accounting abuses. Levitt was most concerned with "smoothing" earnings by management in order to meet analysts' expectations, but also asserted that auditors are the "public's watchdog in the financial reporting process. We rely on auditors to put something like the Good Housekeeping Seal of Approval on the information investors receive."[78] Actually, the chairman's assertion of what accountants could deliver was as misleading as Enron's financial statements. The effect was that investors believed themselves relieved from any responsibility for due diligence in monitoring management, as owners of a business or piece of property normally would be expected to do. Levitt also sought to strengthen audit committees, a concept he had opposed when he was the head of the American Stock Exchange. The SEC adopted a rule in 1999 requiring disclosures of audit committee activities, another attempt at shaming management into strengthening those committees.

A phenomenon arising as the century closed was an astonishing number of restatements by public companies of accounting statements previously filed with the SEC. At the request of the SEC, the POB commissioned a study to examine the increasing number of those restatements. That study was conducted by the Panel on Audit Effectiveness, which was headed by Shaun F.

O'Malley, the former head of Price Waterhouse LLP (the O'Malley commission). On August 31, 2000, the panel issued a report that made several recommendations to improve the audit process, but found that it was still fundamentally sound. One recommendation was that audits should concentrate more on fraud detection. In making that recommendation, however, the panel noted that auditors were ill equipped to perform such a role, lacking the power to subpoena records or witnesses.

These efforts had little effect on accounting problems. The SEC filed thirty cases involving accounting fraud in September 1999 and that number would balloon after Enron. In one case, Ernst & Young agreed to pay $185 million to settle claims arising from its consulting activities for Merry-Go-Round Enterprises Inc., a Maryland retailer in bankruptcy. This was the second-largest settlement in Maryland history. The accounting firm had been advising Merry-Go-Round on its restructuring while in bankruptcy.

The LLPs

Auditors were trying to limit their liability by forming limited liability partnerships (LLPs). Previously, the SEC had required accounting firms (and stockbrokers) to be general partnerships that imposed unlimited liability on partners for any wrongdoing by any partner or employee. The SEC removed the partnership restriction on stockbrokers in order to allow them to tap the capital markets for equity, after the whole industry nearly foundered in the paperwork crisis at the end of the 1960s. One of the last holdouts was Goldman Sachs & Co., but it too succumbed to the market bubble at the end of the last century. The Goldman partners were well rewarded for their patience. Senior partners received payouts from the firm's initial public offering ranging between $125 and $150 million. Junior partners received a relatively paltry $50 to $60 million. The only other holdout, Lazard, an investment banking partnership founded in 1848, went public in 2005, but the terms and enthusiasm for that offering were disappointing.

Incorporation by lawyers and accountants was also prohibited by state legislators on the theory that those professionals owed special fiduciary duties to the public and should not be allowed to hide behind a corporate shield. Those prohibitions were eased initially by allowing lawyers and accountants to become "professional corporations." That status allowed them to have the advantages of various tax-advantaged retirement programs available to corporate employees, but members of these professional corporations remained personally liable for all the activities of the partnership. The savings and loan debacle of the 1980s resulted in numerous lawsuits seeking massive damages from accounting and law partnerships. Those claims would have bankrupted individual partners in those firms, even though they had not participated in any way in the alleged wrongdoing. In 1991 the Texas legislature responded to such concerns with the creation of the "limited liability partnership," which allowed limited liability for professionals such as lawyers and accountants.

The Texas statute was the result of liabilities incurred by Jenkens & Gilchrist, a large Dallas law firm, and its many partners, including some retired partners, as the result of alleged misconduct by a single partner in connection with the savings and loan problems. The firm was able to settle its problems with the FDIC for $18 million without admitting any wrongdoing, but damages could have been many times that figure had the case been successfully prosecuted. More than 1,200 Texas law firms changed their status as general partnerships to LLPs when the LLP legislation was enacted. By 1997, forty-eight states had adopted similar legislation.

The litigation arising from the S&L crisis against law firms also led to pressure on state legislatures to provide some limited liability to partners in accounting firms, which was done. By 1994, four of the Big Six accounting firms reorganized themselves from partnerships into LLPs. These reorganizations took place under state laws that varied in their terms. For example, in Illinois, where Arthur Andersen became an LLP, the LLP statute extended limited liability to partners for malpractice claims against other partners. Such limited liability did not include ordinary commercial debt, a distinction that would be raised in the legal proceedings against Arthur Andersen after its collapse. Like the stockbrokers, the next logical step for the accounting firms would be to sell themselves to the public to raise capital. KPMG announced in 1998 that it wanted to sell a portion of itself through an initial public offering. KPMG could not obtain regulatory approval for that offering until 2001, at which time it went public.

5. Arthur Andersen and Other Scandals

Arthur Andersen & Co.

Background

The Enron scandal was at its heart an accounting scandal, and Enron's auditor, Arthur Andersen LLP, was soon drawn into the maelstrom. The accounting firm had given unqualified opinions on all of Enron's annual financial reports. Those opinions concluded that Enron's financial statements were prepared in accordance with generally accepted accounting principles (GAAP) and that Arthur Andersen had not detected any material flaws in Enron's systems of accounting controls and procedures. In particular, the annual report filed with the Securities and Exchange Commission (SEC) by Enron for the year ended December 31, 2000, stated that Arthur Andersen was of the opinion that Enron's accounting and financial disclosures were correct in all material respects. Since Enron was being portrayed in the press as the biggest accounting scandal ever, questions were quickly raised as to how Arthur Andersen could give such a certification, and the Powers report on Enron's failure opined that Arthur Andersen failed to provide objective accounting judgment that would have prevented Enron's accounting manipulations. Arthur Andersen then became the subject of numerous lawsuits and government investigations. As often the case in financial scandals, irony abounded because Arthur Andersen was the force that destroyed Enron by requiring it to restate its accounts and disclose Andrew Fastow's conflicts of interest.

Early Years

Arthur Andersen LLP was the only Big Eight (and later Big Five) accounting firm that was of solely American origin. Its founder, Arthur Andersen, was described as "stern, erect, somewhat ascetic, exceedingly proper—and an unrepentant maverick."[1] He was born in 1886 and orphaned at age sixteen. To help pay for his schooling, Andersen worked as a clerk and later as an assistant controller at Fraser & Chalmers, a part of Allis-Chalmers Mfg. Co. He attended night school at Northwestern University, where he studied accounting. After graduating, he worked at Price Waterhouse and Joseph Schlitz, a brewery, and taught accounting classes at Northwestern. In 1915 Andersen became a full professor at Northwestern, where he wrote a textbook titled *The Complete Accounting Course*. Two years earlier, at age twenty-eight, Andersen had joined with Clarence M. DeLany to purchase a firm called the Audit Company, after its owner's death. The new firm was initially named Andersen, DeLany & Co., but became Arthur Andersen & Co. in 1918, after DeLany's departure.

Andersen insisted on hiring only college graduates to serve as accountants in his firm, a requirement not universal at the time. He required his accountants to dress and act like professionals and to go out every day for lunch in order to meet possible new clients and to expose the world to his firm. He wanted his accountants to "dig behind the figures to understand their underlying significance to a business."[2] Andersen told his accountants to "think straight and talk straight."[3] He advocated "common sense accounting" rather than theory. He also introduced the concept of specialization of accountants in particular industries, so as to better understand the client's operations. Andersen favored extending accounting services (beyond mere audit work and tax advice) into consulting.

Andersen placed much emphasis on the internal training of accountants. They were schooled in an audit approach that was used throughout the firm. This education had the dual goal of ensuring quality and of integrating the firm's many offices into a single culture. The effort to mold the company's accountants into a single image was successful over the years, and those emerging from the Arthur Andersen training program were referred to as "Androids" for their monochromatic dress and mannerisms. Arthur Andersen's principal training center was eventually located in St. Charles, Illinois. That campus covered over 150 acres, contained several buildings for classrooms, and even had dormitories. The facility was staffed by 500 full-time employees, offered over 400 courses, and was training 68,000 individuals annually as the twenty-first century began.

Andersen set an example of integrity for his firm by refusing to certify doubtful accounts, even when pressured to do so by large clients. His firm was chosen to provide audit and accounting services to the Insull companies that were reorganized after their leader, Sam Insull, fled the country to escape charges that he had manipulated the price of his companies' stock during the market run-up in the 1920s. Insull created two investments trusts called the Insull Utilities Investment Company and the Corporation Securities Company. These special purpose entities were used to purchase large amounts of stock issued by the Insull companies. The trusts borrowed from banks to obtain funds by using the Insull securities as collateral, a very Enron-like procedure. The banks were in danger of a default when the Insull securities declined sharply in value. Arthur Andersen was retained to monitor the situation and to review expenditures by the Insull companies under a "stand still" agreement with the banks. The Insull engagement much enhanced Andersen's reputation and provided his firm with expertise in public utilities and energy generation. By the time of his death in 1947, when he was sixty-one, Andersen was said to be "perhaps the best-known and most respected American accountant."[4]

The Arthur Andersen firm grew over the years. By 1928, the firm employed 400 people, which increased to 700 by 1940. Leonard Spacek, who took over management of the firm after its founder's death, expanded operations worldwide and pioneered consulting activities in computer services. Arthur Andersen's offices rose in number from sixteen to over ninety under Spacek's leadership. Revenues increased from $8 million to $190 million. Like Andersen, Spacek was an independent-minded individual. He wanted more complete disclosure on balance sheets of sale and leaseback transactions, but there was a cross-current in the Andersen culture that grew over the years. By the 1970s, Arthur Andersen & Co. was considered the most aggressive of the Big Eight accounting firms in promoting its views and those of its clients. It had a maverick image that reflected a disdain for the more conservative views of others. That viewpoint would align it nicely with Enron's corporate culture.

Andersen Audit Problems

By the end of the century, Arthur Andersen had over 300 offices located in eighty-four countries. It employed 85,000 people worldwide; 28,000 of those employees worked in the United States. Arthur Andersen was generating $9.3 billion in revenue when the Enron scandal broke and was serving over 100,000 clients. However, even before Enron, Arthur Andersen had been involved in a number of major accounting problems that were undermining the firm's reputation. The go-go years of the 1960s witnessed numerous scandals, perhaps the largest of which was the implosion of Investors Overseas Services (IOS), the giant offshore mutual that was looted by Robert Vesco. Arthur Andersen was the auditor for a key portion of the IOS mutual fund structure and was targeted by investors as a deep pocket following Vesco's flight. After a fifty-five-day trial and two weeks of deliberations, a jury entered an award of $80 million against Arthur Andersen & Co.[5]

The collapse of the Four Seasons Nursing Centers of America Inc. in 1970 resulted in claims that Arthur Andersen, its auditor, failed to disclose that the company's financial statements were not accurate. Another failed audit involved Frigitemp Corp., which subsequently defaulted on its loans. Four banks sued Arthur Andersen under the federal securities laws for certifying inaccurate financial statements of Frigitemp. That suit was dismissed by an appellate court on the grounds that a security was not involved. In 1975, in response to continuing criticism of its role in various other auditing scandals, Arthur Andersen hired an independent "public review board" to review the firm's operations.

Not surprisingly, that report praised Arthur Andersen's audit procedures. Peat, Marwick & Mitchell, which was also under fire, took a different approach and hired Arthur Young & Co. to conduct a "quality review" of its operations.

Between 1980 and 1985, Arthur Andersen had additional problems with failed audits and paid out a total of $137 million to settle litigation claims. One audit failure, in 1981, involved the DeLorean automobile company, which made a stylistic car with gull-wing doors that was less than a commercial success. The British government barred Arthur Andersen from government contract work for failing to detect and report fraud at DeLorean, which resulted in large losses to the British government as a result of funds it supplied to DeLorean in order to boost British jobs. The company's founder, John Z. DeLorean, a former General Motors executive, was reported to have diverted $17 million of company funds into a Swiss bank account, some of which was for his personal use. An Arthur Andersen internal memorandum reported that, if knowledge of that diversion became public, "the game will be up." A jury in New York entered a verdict of over $100 million against Arthur Andersen; $35 million went to the British government for its losses from DeLorean. The U.S. government failed in its prosecution of John DeLorean for trying to buy and distribute fifty-five pounds of cocaine in order to save his automobile company. The sale was set up through a government sting operation that the jury thought went too far in entrapping DeLorean.

Arthur Andersen paid $20 million to settle a suit involving the failure to detect unauthorized trading of bonds at Marsh & McLennan Co. Arthur Andersen was found to have made misrepresentations in accounting statements in connection with the failure of Drysdale Securities Corp., a firm dealing in repo transactions. Arthur Andersen paid $45 million to settle claims made by Chase Manhattan Corporation, which had been clearing the Drysdale account. Arthur Andersen was not alone in these problems. The failure of another repo dealer, ESM Government Securities Inc., caused a savings and loan crisis as the result of its fraudulent dealings. One of its auditors, Jose L. Gomez, was convicted of taking a $250,000 bribe to falsify the firm's accounting statements. He was sentenced to twelve years in prison. Gomez was employed at the accounting firm of Grant Thornton, which agreed to pay $80 million to settle cases brought after that fraud was revealed.

Arthur Andersen was caught up in the scandal involving Penn Square, the shopping center bank in Nebraska that originated and sold over $2.5 billion of largely worthless oil patch loan participations to other banks in the 1980s. William G. Patterson, the loan officer at Penn Square responsible for generating most of those participations, was noted for his flamboyant partying—including drinking liquor out of his cowboy boots—with clients. Seafirst National Bank, an Arthur Andersen audit client, suffered massive losses from that debacle. The rain of audit failures continued. Arthur Andersen agreed to pay $79 million to settle claims arising from the savings and loan failures of the 1980s. It paid another $17 million to settle a lawsuit involving audit work for the

Financial Corporation of America. Arthur Andersen, Coopers & Lybrand, and Grant Thornton paid $30 million to settle claims by the Illinois insurance commissioner for failed audit work on the Reserve Insurance Company, which was bankrupt while the auditors were certifying accounting statements showing the opposite. Arthur Andersen was the target of litigation in connection with the bankruptcy and ensuing scandal at Nucorp Energy, a seller of oilfield equipment. Arthur Andersen was found not to be liable for that failure after a trial in a class action suit brought on behalf of Nucorp shareholders.

Gibson Greetings fired Arthur Andersen as its auditor after suffering large losses from derivatives sold by Bankers Trust. The rogue trader scandal at Metallgesellschaft AG, a German company, and its American subsidiary, MG Refining and Marketing Corp., embroiled Arthur Andersen, its auditor. That company was where Sherron Watkins worked after leaving Arthur Andersen and before joining Enron. Arthur Andersen certified profits of $31 million using American GAAP for Metallgesellschaft's operations in the United States. At that time, a rogue trader had positions showing some $2 billion in losses. KPMG was hired to review Arthur Andersen's work. KPMG found even larger profits under GAAP, but German accounting requirements would have shown a $291 million loss.

Arthur Andersen was involved in a giant fraud in the 1990s involving Procedo, a German factoring firm, and Balsam, a manufacturer of sports playing surfaces. Those firms had been using false invoices, purportedly certified by Arthur Andersen's St. Louis office. Another Arthur Andersen client, Supercuts Inc., was booking franchise revenue for salons still under construction after workers on-site were given a "construction cut," that is, a construction worker's hair was cut so the company could claim that the shop was in operation. The company's chief executive officer, David Lipson, was fined $2.84 million for insider trading after he sold Supercuts stock before the company announced a decline in its earnings.

The state of Connecticut sought the revocation of Arthur Andersen's license to practice as a result of its audits of the Colonial Realty Company, a Hartford company that sold tax-advantaged investments in real estate. The firm collapsed after it was discovered to be running a Ponzi scheme that utilized exaggerated valuations of its properties. An Andersen auditor was given $200,000, three cars, a cruise, and other benefits in exchange for disregarding Colonial Realty's problems. Arthur Andersen employees were accused of destroying audit documents for Colonial Realty under the ruse of complying with Arthur Andersen's document retention policy. Arthur Andersen and its insurers eventually paid over $100 million to settle lawsuits arising from that scandal.

Andersen's Problems Mount

The Arizona attorney general filed suit against Arthur Andersen on behalf of 13,000 investors, many of them elderly, who lost some $600 million in a

Ponzi scheme involving real estate promoted by the Baptist Foundation of Arizona, an Arthur Andersen audit client. Arthur Andersen entered into a settlement in that litigation pursuant to which it agreed to pay investors $217 million. The audit partner for that account had also been involved in Arthur Andersen's audits of Charles Keating's Lincoln Savings & Loan, which gave rise to one of the worst of the savings and loan scandals in the 1980s. A court considering claims against Arthur Andersen arising from the Enron failure noted with respect to Andersen's work for the Baptist Foundation:

> As was typical of accounting in the Enron debacle, the (Baptist) Foundation used off-balance-sheet entities to hide significant losses in real estate investments from investors. The Foundation sold real estate at inflated prices to a company known as ALO, a related-party controlled by the Foundation, in exchange for an IOU rather than cash. Although several outside accountants and professionals warned the Arthur Andersen auditors for two years that they were suspicious of fraudulent accounting at the Foundation, Arthur Andersen paid no heed. Review of public records of ALO revealed that it had a negative worth of $106 million and was not capable of making good on its debt to the Foundation. From the first warning until the Foundation failed, Arthur Andersen issued two more unqualified opinions that permitted the Foundation to raise another $200 million of investor savings.[6]

Arthur Andersen was caught up in the accounting scandal at the Sunbeam Corp., which had improperly shifted revenues among accounting periods in order to inflate income. The SEC filed an injunctive action against Philip E. Harlow, the engagement partner for Arthur Andersen on the Sunbeam account, charging that he had failed to use "professional skepticism." Harlow was barred from acting as an auditor of a public company for a period of at least three years. Arthur Andersen agreed to pay $110 million to settle shareholder lawsuits in connection with Sunbeam's problems. The firm was again accused of improperly destroying documents involving its Sunbeam audits.

Waste Management Inc., a large waste removal firm, announced in February 1998 that it was restating $3.5 billion in earnings improperly claimed through changes in the depreciation schedule for the company's garbage trucks. Waste Management paid $457 million to settle a class action securities suit that was filed in the wake of that disclosure by the Connecticut Retirement Plans and Trust Funds. The company's statements had been audited by Arthur Andersen's Houston office. Arthur Andersen agreed to pay a $7 million penalty to settle SEC charges that it had failed to detect and report the accounting change for the garbage trucks. That was then the largest civil penalty ever imposed on an accounting firm by the SEC. Four Arthur Andersen partners were sanctioned by the SEC, paying fines ranging from $30,000 to $50,000 and barred from practice before the SEC for periods ranging from one to five years. After his return to the firm, one of those partners was promoted to Arthur Andersen's risk management group. Arthur Andersen agreed to settle shareholder lawsuits arising from the Waste Management case for $220 million in 1998.

The Waste Management case illustrated the sometimes cozy relationships between auditors and clients. Waste Management's chief accounting and chief financial officers had all been auditors at Arthur Andersen. Andersen had been Waste Management's auditor since 1971. In the six years prior to this scandal, Arthur Andersen had billed Waste Management $7.5 million in audit fees and $18 million for consulting and tax advisory services. Arthur Andersen's liability in the Waste Management case had been predicated on documents that had been retained by Arthur Andersen beyond any required regulatory time period. Thereafter, Arthur Andersen updated its record retention policy in order to ensure that documents were not kept any longer than necessary. That policy was put in place not long before Enron's problems began.

Arthur Andersen was the auditor for the Boston Market Trustee Corp., which operated Boston Chicken, a chicken franchising operation that filed for bankruptcy in 1999, after suffering $900 million in losses. The company was subsequently sold to McDonald's Corp. Before its bankruptcy, Boston Chicken restated $300 million in revenue from loans made to franchisees and start-up costs that the company had treated as revenue. Losses were kept off the company's books by parking transactions at affiliates. Arthur Andersen agreed to pay $10.3 million to settle a class action suit challenging its audit work at Boston Chicken.

Another Arthur Andersen audit problem involved the McKesson Corp., a pharmaceutical distributor that acquired HBO & Co. in 1999 for $14 billion, becoming McKesson HBOC. McKesson HBOC was the successor to McKesson & Robbins, the firm that had set the bar for auditor liability in the 1930s after a failed audit by Price Waterhouse. McKesson HBOC had to restate $300 million in revenues in 1999 for the prior two years, resulting in a $9 billion drop in market value as the company's stock fell almost 50 percent. The chairman, president, chief executive officer, and chief financial officer of the company were all fired or resigned. Richard H. Hawkins, the company's chief financial officer, was indicted for making false statements to the government and conspiring to commit securities fraud. In another setback for the government, Hawkins was acquitted of all charges. Six other executives at McKesson were also indicted in connection with its accounting problems. Four of those executives pleaded guilty to those charges. McKesson agreed to pay $960 million to settle class action claims over these problems. The SEC charged an Arthur Andersen partner, Robert A. Putnam, with securities fraud for approving false financial reports of the company that were inflated by, among other things, backdating revenues.

Arthur Andersen agreed to settle claims involving its audit work for a company called Department 66 for $11 million. Still another problem for Arthur Andersen was its work for American Tissue Inc., the fourth-largest paper maker in the United States. That company was defrauding its creditors through fake account receivables carried on its balance sheet. Creditor losses totaled $300 million after the company went bankrupt. American Tissue's chief financial officer pleaded guilty to criminal charges and the chief executive officer was indicted. An Arthur Andersen auditor, Brendon McDonald, was indicted for obstruction of justice for destroying e-mails and shredding documents to cover up the fraud. Those acts took place on September 4, 2001, only a few months before Enron's problems surfaced. Qwest Communications International was inflating its revenues by $2.5 billion in 2000 and 2001. Its auditor was Arthur Andersen, and questions were raised as to the accounting firm's responsibility in certifying Qwest's statements. Arthur Andersen was fired from the engagement and replaced by KPMG. Qwest later agreed to settle SEC accounting charges for $250 million.

Accenture

One of Arthur Andersen's pioneering consulting efforts was the development of a payroll management system for General Electric's plant in Louisville, Kentucky. Such consulting services became an increasingly important part of Arthur Andersen's business mix, resulting in the creation of Andersen Consulting in 1989 as a separate division of the firm. Accounting, audit, and tax services remained with Arthur Andersen & Co. The two units (the auditors and the consulting group) operated under the umbrella Andersen Worldwide. Andersen Consulting acted quickly to establish its own image by a massive advertising campaign that included the de rigueur Super Bowl advertisements for the breakout of a growing firm.

Tension soon developed between the audit group and Andersen Consulting. A disparate number of partners in Andersen Worldwide were auditors, but the members of the Andersen Consulting group were contributing an equal amount of revenue. A revenue-sharing agreement was reached, but that did not ease friction for long because Andersen Consulting was required to transfer over $1 billion annually to the auditors under the formula set by that agreement. This caused resentment at Andersen Consulting, but the disparity between the two groups also caused turmoil at the audit unit, as concerns arose over its future profitability. In 1992, several partners were eased out of the audit group because they were not producing sufficient revenues. Lost in that group were several partners who had added stability and conservatism to the firm.

As the situation between the consulting and audit groups continued to deteriorate, both sides instituted arbitration proceedings claiming various breaches of their agreements on sharing business and other issues. Finally Andersen Consulting sought complete separation. The audit group demanded compensation of 150 percent of the consulting group's revenue—an amount the audit group claimed totaled almost $15 billion—as the price for agreeing to a split-off. That demand was based in a provision in the partnership agreement that applied to partners leaving Arthur Andersen. The arbitrator selected to settle this dispute was Guillermo Gamba from Colombia, a graduate of Harvard Law School who had acted as an arbitrator in only one other proceeding. He resolved the dispute in 2000 by ordering a split into independent audit and consulting firms. The auditors' demand for $15 billion was rejected. Instead, the arbitrator awarded only $1 billion after the two sides could not agree on terms.

The now separate consulting group carried on its business as Accenture. The timing of this breakup could not have been better for the consulting business or worse for the auditing side. Accenture walked away from Andersen with a very valuable business purchased for a song, while the auditors were left with the less profitable and high-risk audit business that would spell their doom. Accenture later made a public offering, selling about 12 percent of the firm for $1.67 billion. Accenture's stock was listed on the NYSE, and the group then began worrying about meeting analysts' expectations in order to keep the stock price moving upward. That was a small problem compared with the bullets it had dodged. Accenture had a new name unsullied by Enron and the numerous other audit problems at Arthur Andersen. The new company avoided the billions of dollars of liability from Arthur Andersen's audit problems and escaped the effects of the government's prosecution of Arthur Andersen. What a hat trick for the consulting group and what a disaster for the auditors! Accenture was happily using Tiger Woods, the golfer, to promote its consulting business in airports and elsewhere after Arthur Andersen met its doom.

Enron Erupts

On top of its sea of auditing troubles, Arthur Andersen was reeling from its break with Accenture as the new century began. At the time of the breakup, Arthur Andersen's audit business was the smallest and slowest growing of the Big Five. The audit group was also facing declining margins, massive liabilities, and increased competition for audit services. It could ill afford any more audit failures with their resulting liabilities and regulatory problems. A new chief executive officer, Joseph Berardino, was appointed to head Arthur Andersen not long before Enron unraveled. He called a meeting of Andersen partners in October 2001 in New Orleans in order to begin rebuilding the firm. It was there that he was advised of Enron's impending problems. The focus of the firm soon changed from rebuilding to survival.

Arthur Andersen earned $52 million in fees from Enron in 2000. Of that amount, $27 million was for consulting, and the remainder was for audit work. Enron was an important client, and its bankruptcy and the accounting abuses that caused it ensured that Arthur Andersen would be a major target of private litigation and government investigations. Predictably, any collapse of a public company was immediately blamed on its auditors, but here the heat would be even more intense because of the aggressive accounting tactics employed by Enron.

Berardino tried to defend Arthur Andersen in the press and even published an article on the editorial page of the *Wall Street Journal,* but the storm of controversy soon overwhelmed his efforts. Arthur Andersen's senior officials were grilled at length before congressional committees. Their frustration at being accused of responsibility for Enron's failure was evident. As Berardino stated in his testimony, "Arthur Andersen blessed the accounting for the transactions. We don't bless the economic viability of a company. It's the result of management's decisions that determines whether a company succeeds or it doesn't." Enron was "a company whose business model failed." Berardino noted that Enron's stock price had been falling throughout 2001 and had lost much of its value before the accounting disclosures made headlines in October. He asserted, "There's a crisis in my profession. But I think that there's a crisis in terms of our whole capital markets reporting model."

In the midst of the controversy over its role in auditing Enron, Arthur Andersen announced that its Houston office had destroyed large amounts of Enron documents and deleted computer files and e-mails. The London, Portland, Oregon, and Chicago offices of the firm had also destroyed documents. The shredding occurred after the engagement partner on the Enron account in Houston, David Duncan, ordered the implementation of Arthur Andersen's somewhat euphemistically named "document retention policy." That policy sought to ensure that documents were destroyed after the retention period required by the SEC or other regulators so that the documents would not fall into hands of class action lawyers. Duncan, a Texas A&M graduate, had become an Arthur Andersen partner at age thirty-five and was placed in charge of the Enron audit team two years later. That audit team was a large one that practically lived with the Enron accountants. Duncan was personally close to Richard Causey, Enron's chief accounting officer.

Senior Arthur Andersen personnel notified the SEC and Congress of the shredding as soon as it came to their attention. Duncan was placed on leave and then fired for bad judgment. Outside counsel was ordered to investigate the event, and former senator John C. Danforth was retained by Arthur Andersen to review its document retention policies. The shredding of the Enron documents caused concern that Arthur Andersen would be the subject of criminal action and lawsuits that would destroy it. That concern was well placed. David Duncan was indicted, pleaded guilty to obstruction, and agreed to testify against his old firm.

The Indictment of Arthur Andersen

Arthur Andersen was indicted on March 7, 2002, for obstruction of justice as the result of Duncan's acts. That indictment caused many large clients, including Sara Lee Abbott, Brunswick Corp., and FedEx, to switch auditors. A successful criminal prosecution would prevent Arthur Andersen from continuing its audit activities for even the clients remaining loyal and would result in the elimination of the jobs of 28,000 Andersen employees in the United

States alone. Arthur Andersen's future was clearly in doubt. A rally organized by the firm in Chicago to raise employee morale had little effect in stemming defections, despite the participation of the Reverend Jesse Jackson, and only served to anger the Justice Department.

Arthur Andersen tried to save itself through a merger with Deloitte Touche but that effort failed. Arthur Andersen's lawyers proposed a settlement under which the firm would be reorganized and procedures established to ensure the quality of audit work, including a special monitor to ensure compliance. All individuals involved in the destruction of Enron documents were to be fired. Paul Volcker, the former chairman of the Federal Reserve Board, was hired as a special consultant by Arthur Andersen to effect a settlement with the Justice Department. Volcker was given extraordinary powers of control over Arthur Andersen as a condition of his involvement. He proposed a plan to save the firm that included several accounting reforms such as rotating partners on client accounts at least every five years, prohibiting partners from accepting employment from a client for at least one year after working on the client's account, and eliminating bonuses to auditors for generating consulting business. In return, Volcker asked the government to dismiss the indictment against Arthur Andersen. That request was rejected by the Justice Department.

An effort was made by Arthur Andersen's lawyers to reach a settlement in which prosecution of Arthur Andersen would be deferred if it engaged in no further misconduct; that was the deal given to Christie's in the price-fixing scandal with Sotheby's. That offer was also rejected. Compounding the situation for Arthur Andersen was the collapse of several other large Arthur Andersen audit clients. Global Crossings, a long-distance telecom carrier, filed for bankruptcy protection on January 28, 2002. Adelphia Communications Corp. filed for bankruptcy on June 25, 2002. The nation's sixth-largest cable company, Adelphia was at the center of a storm over disclosures in its financial statements. Another seismic event was the bankruptcy of WorldCom on July 21, 2002, another Andersen audit client. WorldCom admitted to over $8 billion in accounting irregularities. In deciding not to settle with Arthur Andersen, the Justice Department considered the fact that investor losses from the accounting failures at various Arthur Andersen audit clients totaled over $300 billion.

The Trial of Arthur Andersen

The trial of Arthur Andersen, which lasted almost a month, proved highly controversial, and the verdict bordered on the bizarre. The jury concluded that David Duncan, the Andersen partner who ordered the destruction of the documents, really had not caused Arthur Andersen to obstruct justice, despite his own testimony admitting that he had done exactly that. To be sure, Duncan somewhat undermined his own confession on cross-examination when he admitted that he did not have any intent to commit a crime when he ordered that the documents be destroyed. Duncan testified that it took several months for him to conclude that he might have obstructed justice by his actions. He said that he believed that it was legal to destroy documents until an SEC subpoena was received and that he had ordered employees to destroy only those documents allowed to be destroyed by the Arthur Andersen document retention policy. In addition, Arthur Andersen's lawyer, Rusty Hardin, was able to establish that copies of the files were still available through backup sources.

Rather than Duncan, the individual found guilty of obstruction of justice by the jury in the Arthur Andersen case was a company lawyer, Nancy Temple. She was an unlikely obstructer. An honors graduate of the Harvard Law School, Temple had been a litigation partner at Sidley & Austin, one of Chicago's largest and most respected law firms, before moving to Arthur Andersen's headquarters in Chicago in July 2000. Temple developed a reputation for honesty and integrity as a lawyer, but came under attack after the Enron failure for sending an e-mail on October 12, 2001, reminding the Enron engagement team about Arthur Andersen's document retention policies: "It will be helpful to make sure that we have complied with the policy." Government prosecutors argued that this was code for ordering a destruction of documents in order to frustrate future investigations.

Duncan told congressional investigators before he took the Fifth Amendment that Temple had asked him in conference calls that took place before that e-mail was sent whether his engagement team was in compliance with the firm's document retention policies and that he had responded: "At best, irregular." Duncan did not react immediately to those calls or that e-mail but, at a later meeting with other audit partners, they concluded that Temple's inquiry was a suggestion that Enron documents not required to be retained by Andersen's document retention policy should be shredded. His group did not start that shredding until October 23. Temple was unaware of that activity.

Temple concluded by October 9 that some SEC investigation was "highly probable," and Arthur Andersen retained outside counsel, Davis Polk & Wardwell, a well-known New York law firm, on that date to provide advice on how to respond to Enron-related issues. Temple consulted with that law firm on October 16. To that point, no litigation had been filed against Arthur Andersen and no subpoenas had been served on the firm. Unknown to Temple, the SEC staff had made an informal inquiry to Enron on October 17, but the SEC staff was not at that time authorized by its commissioners to conduct a formal investigation or to issue subpoenas. Such informal inquiries are made routinely by the SEC staff and may or may not result in a formal investigation and charges, although the growing Enron hysteria made a formal investigation a certainty and prosecution highly likely. In any event, no additional action for preserving Enron documents was deemed necessary after Temple's consultation with Davis Polk on October 16. As a result, Arthur Andersen's normal document retention and destruction plan remained in effect.

Temple learned of the SEC staff's informal inquiry to Enron on October

23. She was then told that the Arthur Andersen engagement team in Houston was assisting Enron to comply with an informal SEC document request by gathering Enron-related documents. The SEC did not start a formal investigation of Enron until October 31, at which point the SEC staff was authorized to issue subpoenas to gather information. Arthur Andersen did not receive a formal subpoena from the SEC for Enron documents until the close of business on November 8, 2001. Temple notified employees of its receipt by voice mail. Her voice mail message apparently triggered Duncan's secretary's to issue what became an infamous order, "No more shredding." The Davis Polk law firm drafted a memorandum describing what steps Arthur Andersen personnel should take to preserve Enron records. That memorandum was distributed to the Enron engagement team on November 10, 2001.

Temple testified nervously and at length before Congress on her activities and seemed to have had a bona fide basis for her actions. She stated that, in reminding the auditors on the Enron engagement of the Arthur Andersen document retention policy, she was seeking to ensure compliance with firm policy and not obstruction. This may have been naive on her part, but she hardly appeared cynical in testifying on this point before Congress. Nevertheless, after the Justice Department saw its principal witness, David Duncan, go up in smoke on cross-examination, the department claimed that Temple was obstructing justice by her e-mail, but the jury was not able to find that the e-mail was obstruction.

The Justice Department claimed that Temple engaged in an additional act of obstruction during a telephone conversation in which she suggested to David Duncan that he remove a passage in a memorandum addressed to "The Files." That memorandum described a conversation Duncan had with Richard Causey, Enron's chief accounting officer. Duncan stated in the memorandum that he had advised Causey that a proposed Enron news release on its third-quarter results, which stated that large charges against income were "non-recurring," could be misleading. Causey responded that the release had been reviewed by Enron lawyers and would retain the reference to "non-recurring."

Temple was copied on Duncan's memorandum, which included references to her discussions with Duncan. She responded with an e-mail that recommended deletion in his memorandum of discussions with Arthur Andersen counsel and with her specifically. This was a commonsense and appropriate bit of legal advice, since she did not want a waiver of attorney client privilege or to become a witness. Temple consulted with Davis Polk on this issue before making that recommendation to Duncan. She further suggested that the reference to the Enron news release as being misleading should be deleted because there were serious issues as to whether it was in fact misleading.

Temple advised Duncan that Arthur Andersen's outside legal counsel (Davis Polk) was determining whether the accounting firm had an obligation under the Securities Exchange Act of 1934 to notify Enron that its characterization of "non-recurring" was inappropriate. If such notice was made and Enron did not correct its statements, Arthur Andersen would then have an obligation to notify the SEC of its concerns. Temple told the Enron engagement team that they could not delete a reference to the fact that Arthur Andersen had provided Enron with some incorrect accounting advice in the first quarter of 2001. This all hardly sounded like obstruction. Rather, it was the work of a careful lawyer. In any event, Duncan removed the reference to "misleading."

Temple testified before Congress on her conversations with Duncan on his memorandum and presented what appeared to be a believable explanation. She was prevented from testifying at the Arthur Andersen trial, however, because the Justice Department threatened her with prosecution before the trial, forcing her to plead the Fifth Amendment, if called by Arthur Andersen to testify in its defense. Since she had testified at length before Congress, there is no reason to think she would not have testified at the trial before that prosecutorial threat. Once the threat was issued by the Department of Justice, however, no lawyer worth his salt would have allowed her to testify, and she did not.

In the absence of an explanation, the jury found that Temple's advice on changing the Duncan memorandum was obstruction. Government strong-arm tactics thus secured a conviction, but the means used were hardly laudable. Class action claims brought against Nancy Temple for her role in preparing the memorandum were later dismissed by the federal court in Houston. No indictment for obstruction was ever brought against Temple, and a leading legal ethics expert and vice dean of New York University Law School, Stephen Gillers, opined in the *New York Times* that Temple's advice was routine for any lawyer: "'Don't put it in writing' is advice lawyers give every day to protect clients from creating documents that may be used, or often misused, to their detriment."[7] Gillers pointed out that federal obstruction of justice statutes exempt from their reach bona fide legal advice, which was exactly what Temple was rendering. Arthur Andersen's lawyer Rusty Hardin stated, "If I could have called Nancy Temple to the stand, Andersen would never have been convicted. The jury had to make a character judgment abut someone— worst of all, a lawyer they'd never seen before."[8]

Conviction

Aiding the prosecution was the fact that the judge hearing the Arthur Andersen case, Melinda Harmon, was biased in favor of the government. That attitude would spread through the judiciary as hysteria over the Enron scandal broadened. Harmon entered ruling after ruling that worked to ensure conviction. Among other things, she allowed Arthur Andersen's earlier audit transgressions to be brought up to smear the firm even though virtually all of those actions had been settled without a finding of guilt. Harmon's jury instructions were tailored to favor the government. The judge told the jury that Arthur Andersen was liable for the acts of Duncan even if his acts were contrary to the partnership's instructions; presumably this applied to Temple as well. This means that any employee, anywhere, at any level, even when acting against the firm's policies, can destroy a company with a single wrong or merely questionable act. That single act could throw tens of thousands of employees out of a job in a time of economic weakness and destroy the wealth of a firm accumulated over decades.

Even so, it was a close-run thing. The jury appeared to be hung after extended deliberations that lasted seven days, but the judge kept sending in instructions favorable to the government, including an "Allen dynamite charge," which is the instruction the judge gave to pressure the jury into a conviction. She even told the jury members that they did not have to agree with each other about which Enron employee (Duncan or Temple) obstructed justice as long as they all agreed that someone did. This meant that Arthur Andersen could be convicted even if no one person was identified as the one who had committed a crime. The jury finely came back with a verdict of guilty of obstruction of justice on June 15, 2002.

Arthur Andersen was fined $500,000 and put on five years probation as its sentence for the obstruction of justice conviction. That was a mere wrist slap compared to the financial fallout from the conviction, which was that venerable firm's death knell. Arthur Andersen lost its CPA licenses with the conviction, and clients could no longer use it as an auditor after the SEC barred it from auditing public companies. As a result of the conviction, 85,000 Arthur Andersen's employees were thrown out of work worldwide, 28,000 in the United States, a total far outnumbering the 5,000 employees at Enron that were similarly affected.

Arthur Andersen's conviction was upheld on appeal; it appeared that no judge wanted to be on the wrong side of the Enron hysteria, but the Supreme Court intervened and issued a writ of certiorari to allow it to review the conviction. Thereafter in a stunning decision the Supreme Court unanimously reversed the Arthur Andersen conviction. The court held that the trial court had erred in instructing the jury on what constitutes obstruction of justice. The Supreme Court ruled that it was not inherently wrong for a corporation to direct employees to destroy documents. The Supreme Court also faulted the trial judge for instructing the jury that, even if Arthur Andersen "honestly and sincerely believed that its conduct was lawful," the jury could still find it guilty. The Supreme Court's decision was handed down well over two years after the Arthur Andersen conviction and came too late for the Enron employees and partners.

Even worse, the Arthur Andersen conviction badly damaged Enron investors. Arthur Andersen had proposed a settlement of $750 million for its Enron-related liabilities that was to be paid substantially out of future revenues. That offer was turned down by the plaintiff's attorneys, presumably because it was only an opening bid. After the company was indicted, the settlement offer was reduced by Arthur Andersen to $375 million. Compounding the situation, Arthur Andersen's liability insurer, Professional Services Insurance Co. Inc., a Bermuda-based insurer that was expected to cover most of the Baptist Foundation loss, declared that it was unable to do so. Arthur Andersen agreed to pay the $217 million due in that settlement from its own funds. Its conviction, however, meant that the 13,000 Baptist Foundation investors, many of them elderly, would be left holding an empty bag with Arthur Andersen's other creditors after the accounting firm ceased business as a result of the conviction.

Arthur Andersen's settlement offer for Enron was taken off the table entirely after the conviction. Plaintiffs then negotiated a $60 million settlement from the Arthur Andersen parent company, of which $20 million was to go to general creditors. The foreign affiliates of Arthur Andersen agreed to pay $40 million to settle their liabilities. Those firms had operated under the name Andersen Worldwide Société Cooperative, a Swiss entity that acted as a holding company for Arthur Andersen operations abroad. Additional amounts from Arthur Andersen were problematic. The criminal conviction had destroyed the going concern value of the firm and killed any ability to fund a settlement from future billings.

Rusty Hardin, Arthur Andersen's attorney, charged that the prosecution of the company was "one of the greatest tragedies" in the history of the criminal justice system. That was an understatement. Tens of thousands of innocent Andersen employees lost their jobs, the lifework of thousands of partners was destroyed, and even more thousands of investors were shut off from any hope of recovery by the excessive prosecutorial zeal. Another immediate result of the Enron disaster was the opportunity for the surviving Big Four accounting firms to raise their fees and to limit the scope of their engagements. With greater market power following the demise of Arthur Andersen, they were able to threaten clients with resigning their audit engagement if the higher fees were not paid. Those increased costs would be passed onto investors.

Full Disclosure Fails

Enron was not an isolated incident of accounting fraud or miscreant executives, and Arthur Andersen was not the only accounting firm that had an audit failure. Public companies were hemorrhaging accounting frauds in the wake of Enron's collapse. Some of the individuals and companies involved would become legends in financial history, including the likes of L. Dennis Kozlowski at Tyco, Gary Winnick at Global Crossing, the Rigas family at Adelphia, and Bernard and Ebbers at WorldCom.

SEC Role

Restatements of financial reports were rare before 1995 (there were only two restatements in 1977 and 1978 and only one in 1979), but that number rose sharply during the market run-up at the end of the century. The numbers of such restatements varied according to the reporter, but one source reported 116 restatements in 1998, and the SEC cited a report identifying 234 restatements in 1999, 258 in 2000, and 305 in 2001. This massive increase was made worse by the fact that the number of publicly traded firms decreased by 20 percent since 1997. Before its demise, Arthur Andersen conducted a study of 723 restatements between 1997 and 2000. It found that most were due to overstating earnings; next in line was the correction of the extent of the liabilities shown on the balance sheet. The miscreants included the Kimberly-Clark Corporation, Vista 2000 Inc., Teltran International Group Ltd., Aura Systems Inc., Manhattan Bagel Inc. Latin American Resources Inc., Aurora Foods Inc., FLIR Systems Inc., the Seaboard Corp., Unify Corp., and Quintus Corp.

Accounting abuses reflected in such restatements were said to have cost investors $88 billion between 1993 and 2000. Most of those losses occurred in the last three years of the twentieth century. A *Wall Street Journal* survey concluded that market losses to investors after restatements of financial results totaled $17.7 billion in 1998, $24.2 billion in 1999, and $31.2 billion in 2000. Cited in Congress were the following overstatements: Waste Management—$1.32 billion; Enron—$500 billion; Informix—$200 million; Sunbeam—$60 million; Microstrategy—$66 million; and Critical Path—$20 million. There were many others.

The increase in restatements did not pass unnoticed by regulators. In his speech at New York University's Stern School of Business in September 1998, SEC chairman Arthur Levitt decried the fact that quarterly earning reports were becoming a "numbers game" in which executives manipulated financial accounts to show a "smooth earnings path" in order to meet the consensus earnings estimates of financial analysts. Levitt stated that accounting "trickery" was used to obscure the normal volatility that occurs in earnings. "Managing may be giving way to manipulation. Integrity may be losing out to illusion." He warned that the SEC would aggressively prosecute accounting abuses. Levitt followed that warning with an accounting enforcement sweep that involved charges against almost seventy individuals and companies. Clearly, something was happening with earnings reports to provide an appearance of smooth growth. "In fact, between 1992 and 1999, the number of companies that beat quarterly earnings projections by one penny quadrupled."[9] That figure was too convenient to be happenstance.

Accrual Versus Cash Accounting

An issue debated before World War I was whether accountants should be mere clerks who verify entries or professionals who apply judgment in presenting company financial statements, and whether accounting should be "scientific," requiring a uniform accounting system. Those stressing the importance of the auditor's judgment noted that it is not a one-size-fits-all world: "Accounting is not precise or scientific. It is an art, and a highly developed one."[10] Each industry and each company within an industry is different and requires judgment in how best to present financial results, but the GAAP rules were applied broadly and interpreted across industry lines.

Before World War I, the judgment of auditors was limited by the accounting doctrine "anticipate no profits and provide for all possible losses."[11] This principle of conservatism required assets to be carried on the balance sheet at their historical cost. This historical cost or book value approach replaced the use of par value as the measure for valuing companies. The par value of a company's stock often had no relation to the value of the company's assets or operations and was often "watered" as the result of stock being issued to insiders in exchange for assets that were vastly overvalued. The historical cost method posed similar problems and raised other concerns. The use of historical costs, while conservative, often masked the actual financial condition of companies, particularly those with assets that had changed in value over time. That problem gave rise to calls for mark-to-market accounting such as that employed, and abused, by Enron.

Another concern was that the balance sheet was often of limited use in valuing an ongoing business operation, especially service companies that have few assets, but generate much income that values the company far above its assets. The shortcomings of the balance sheet led the accounting profession to shift its focus in later years to the income statement. The principle of conservatism was initially applied to the income statement by "cash" accounting, which recorded revenue only when received and expenses only when paid. Many accountants argued that such cash accounting was misleading because the receipt of cash might occur in an accounting period after the sale was made, thereby distorting the actual profitability of the company during the relevant period. Similarly, an expense might be paid in an accounting period after it was incurred, further distorting the company's income statement. Those concerns led to a general acceptance of the concept of "accrual" accounting.

Accrual accounting requires a corporation to recognize revenues when earned and liabilities when incurred. This method matches income with associated expenses even if the two are actually paid or received in different reporting periods. The SEC states: "The accrual method of accounting requires that revenue be recognized when the earnings process is complete and an exchange has taken place, as opposed to the 'cash' method of accounting, which allows for revenue recognition only when a cash payment is actually received."[12] To illustrate, say a computer was sold for $2,500 and delivered to a customer on December 15, 2004. The customer was billed, but payment was not actually received until January 1, 2005. Under the cash method, the sale occurred on January 1, 2005, while under the accrual method, the sale occurred on December 15, 2004. The accrual theory is that to record the sale on January 1, 2005, would distort the corporation's accounting picture, that is, shareholders would think that the sale was actually made in 2005 rather than 2004, thereby understating sales in 2004 and overstating sales in 2005.

Accrual accounting tries to provide a more accurate picture of profitability, but it too has some serious deficiencies. As one commentator notes: "The rub is that accrual-basis accounting affords a great deal of flexibility and judgment in the timing of income and expense recognition. Will American Airline's new airplanes be serviceable for thirty years or should they be depreciated over just twenty? Should research and development expenses be charged to earnings as they are incurred, or should some portion be capitalized and charged only over time? And so on."[13]

That accrual accounting is readily susceptible to aggressive interpretation is illustrated by IBM's accounting practices in recent years. Louis Gerstner Jr., the former head of American Express, was hired by IBM to bring it back from a near-death experience that stemmed from the company's prolonged defense of the antitrust suit brought by the Justice Department and bitter competition over the sale of personal computers. IBM posted a loss of $4.6 billion in 1992, the largest loss in all corporate history at the time. Gerstner ruthlessly cut expenses, discharged 100,000 employees, and was successful in returning the company to profitability. Aggressive accounting practices were employed to post some profits at IBM. Among other things, the company used the proceeds of a sale of an Internet business to offset operating costs. The SEC objected to that treatment, but IBM refused to accede to the agency's views. The SEC then issued one of its accounting bulletins to prohibit such treatment in the future.

Although IBM had other disputes with the SEC over its accounting practices, it was not sued by that agency; apparently IBM's stalwart defense of the Justice Department's antitrust suit over a decade discouraged the SEC. In the event, IBM's aggressive accounting treatment showed double digit increases in earnings, while sales were only increasing by about 5 percent per year. The result was that IBM met or exceeded analysts' expectations in every quarter between 1997 and 2001. In 1999, IBM generated gains in operating income of $800 million as a result of the restructuring of its pension plan and increases in the value of pension fund assets caused by the market bubble. The company was buying back its stock, which increased earnings per share by reducing the number of shares outstanding, but also increased the company's debt levels. In January 2002, IBM announced that it had beat 2001 fourth-quarter estimates, but that performance was due to the sale of a business unit that generated more than $300 million.

Motorola was recognizing income on an accrual basis from $2.9 billion in long-term receivables in 2001. Of that amount, $2 billion was due from a single customer in Turkey, which proceeded to default on a $728 million payment due to Motorola under their financing arrangement. The flexibility allowed by accrual accounting is further illustrated by Citigroup's $239 million gain in the third quarter of 2002 as a result of changes in estimates on the timing of revenue recognition from securitizations. Nine-month results that year were aided by another $128 million from an increase in the amortization period for direct loan origination costs. SBC Communications, which paid its chief executive officer, Edward Whitacre Jr., $82 million despite the fact that its stock dropped for twelve straight quarters, was assuming a long term rate of return on its pension fund assets of 9.50 percent in 2001 and 2002. This allowed it to free up earnings, but the actual returns were losses in both years. General Mills assumed a 10.4 percent return on pension plan assets, allowing it to claim an additional $2.657 million in after-tax income between 2000 and 2003. Pension fund raids became a favorite way to gin up earnings as the upswing in the stock market resulted in overfunded plans. Fortune 500 company pension plans were overfunded by $250 billion in 1998 but were underfunded by about the same amount in 2002 as the result of the stock market crash.

Another flaw in accrual accounting is that it does not disclose whether a company has the cash to pay its bills as they come due. In the earlier example, accrual accounting would require recognition of the computer sale immediately even though cash was not received until the next year. Yet there would be no cash available to pay bills in the year of the sale recognized under accrual accounting. In the case of mark-to-market accounting, that lack of cash could carry forward over a considerable period of time, until the asset was liquidated. That gap was filled by the statement of cash flows, which was a measure of actual liquidity because it was essentially cash basis accounting. That statement allowed analysts to see cash in and cash out, the old-fashioned way of determining whether a company was viable.

Secret Reserves

Increased merger activity in the 1960s was accompanied by earnings manipulations by management that was designed to boost stock prices to aid in acquisitions. The "big bath" involved a large write-off in one accounting period in order to rid the company of prior losses that were a drag on earnings. Those write-offs were often blamed on old management, or labeled as one-time events, in order to exonerate present management and allow it to report higher earnings in the future. "Quasi-reorganizations" of a corporation's business were another way to write off accumulated losses and, in effect, to start over again. These big baths and reorganizations were said to be misleading because new shareholders looking at the company's financial statements would not know of past losses. The SEC took steps to stop such abuses, but many companies—Pepsi Co, for example—were still using the big bath device in the 1990s.

Another concern was the use of reserve accounts to smooth earnings. Initially, "secret" reserve accounts were tapped to increase earnings during difficult times. In Europe, earnings management was traditionally and widely carried out through the use of such secret reserves. This was considered an accepted and prudent practice there, much akin to saving for a rainy day or keeping a stash of cash in a cookie jar for unexpected household needs. The Board of Trade in England created a Company Law Amendment Committee in 1929 that considered the use of secret reserves to smooth earnings. Most witnesses appearing before this committee defended such reserves as a prudent practice. One witness claimed that there would have been no solvent businesses in England after an economic downturn in 1921 if secret reserves had not been available. The Council of the Law Society asserted that using secret reserves was a sound business practice. Nevertheless, there were critics who contended that secret reserves allowed companies to conceal a declining business. That claim was given support by the bankruptcy of the Royal Mail Steam Packet Co., which had used its secret reserves to conceal its business problems until it was bankrupt.

The use of secret reserves was common from about 1890 to 1920 in America, but it was criticized after World War I as misleading to investors who sold their shares without knowledge of that valuable asset; few were otherwise concerned with their use in smoothing earnings. World War II witnessed the use of "special war reserves" in the United States that were supposed to cover unexpected contingencies arising from the war, but became the basis for smoothing earnings.

Cookie Jar Reserves

Saving for a rainy day is generally considered prudent, but not in the strange world of full disclosure mandated by the SEC. The SEC tried to limit the use of secret reserves after World War II, and the FASB, under pressure from the SEC, announced in 1990 that it would require the disclosure of contingency reserves in footnotes to financial statements.

The ban on secret reserves was easily evaded through the use of "disclosed" reserve accounts. Reserve accounts are required under accrual accounting methodology to reflect expected losses in the future from current transactions. For example, a reserve account is required to offset expected uncollectible account receivables from current sales that are reported as current revenue. By overstating the amount of the expected losses in the reserve account during a particularly robust period of sales, management could reduce earnings in that period to match the expectations of financial analysts. In a quarter where sales are not up to expectations, management can "discover" that uncollectible receivables are less than expected and then dip into the reserve and treat the excess reserves as revenue and thereby meet expectations. This practice was popularly referred to as "cookie jar" reserves.

Cookie jar reserves became a common practice by public companies in the United States despite the SEC's opposition. Microsoft Corp., the giant computer software company, admitted to holding large amounts of cookie jar reserves during the 1990s. Those reserves were created for the purpose of smoothing earnings in the event of revenue declines. W.R. Grace, a Florida chemical company, was sued by the SEC in 1998 for holding $20 million in reserves created years earlier for future use in smoothing earnings. PricewaterhouseCoopers was fined $1 million for its audit work for SmarTalk TeleServices Inc., a prepaid phone card company that went bankrupt. The accounting firm allowed SmarTalk to create a $25 million restructuring reserve in 1997 when there were no related structuring charges. That reserve allowed the company to smooth earnings in future years. The auditors at PricewaterhouseCoopers changed their work papers to cover up their involvement in that activity when they learned of a shareholder suit against the company. Philip Hirsch, the audit partner on the account, was barred from practicing before the SEC for one year.

Channel Stuffing

"Channel stuffing" is another way to manipulate accounts and manage earnings. This practice involves sending a customer unneeded goods that can be booked as sales and revenue under the guise of accrual accounting. Usually there is a right of return for the unneeded items, which meant that the goods would be returned at a later date, requiring a reversal of the sale entry in a later period. This was a temporary expedient caused by the incessant demands of financial analysts for continuing revenue increases in every quarter. Such manipulation accelerated as the economic slowdown at the end of the last century cut actual sales.

One early channel stuffing case involved Bausch & Lomb, which required its distributors to purchase $25 million in contact lenses at inflated prices in 1993 just before year-end. The distributors were not required to pay for the lenses until sold, most of them were not, and the company incurred large losses in the following year when the lenses were returned. Bausch & Lomb had to lower its earnings estimates three times, causing the price of its stock to be cut in half. The amount of the overstated profits was some $18 million. Bausch & Lomb Inc. was the subject of a shareholder lawsuit that charged that the company inflated its earnings in 1999 and 2000. Bausch & Lomb settled that lawsuit for $12 million.

Other public companies in the United States engaged in channel stuffing by pushing sales of seasonal goods through discounts or incentives that would induce distributors to purchase product immediately, even though it might not be sold until the next season. Donnkenny Inc., a women's apparel company, went so far as to book revenue from shipments placed in storage at a warehouse. Microdyne Corp. engaged in channel stuffing by pushing products with a right of return for unsold goods that were unneeded. The SEC charged executives at Cylink Corp., a Santa Clara, California, firm producing cryptographic software, with inflating sales in a single quarter by almost $1 million through a scheme in which customers were sent product and allowed up to three months to return it.

Sunbeam Corp. was one of the worst channel stuffers. Albert (Al) Dunlap had been hired to revitalize Sunbeam, as he had previously revived Scott Paper Co. Dunlap earned the nickname of "Chainsaw Al" for his willingness to close or sell off unprofitable operations at Scott Paper. Such strong-arm tactics proved inadequate at Sunbeam, so the company adopted the use of cookie jar reserves to improve earnings and started channel stuffing furiously. The channel stuffing at Sunbeam was carried out under an incentive program that involved the sale of Sunbeam's outdoor gas barbecue grills at a steep discount. An obstacle to that program was the distributor's unwillingness to purchase more grills than they could sell during a single season. Otherwise, the excess grills would have to be stored for some considerable period of time. To overcome that concern, the distributors were allowed to have Sunbeam hold this merchandise until needed.

This channel stuffing succeeded in boosting sales figures in 1997, but caused a shortfall in 1998. That shortfall, in turn, led to even more desperate accounting gambits. The company artificially increased revenue by inducing sales with provisions for a right of return that amounted to simply parking the merchandise only for the accounting period. Merchandise return authorizations were then deleted from the company's computer. This resulted in long delays in resolving the right of the customers to returns, which allowed the company to defer recording those returns on the company's records and thereby delayed the effect of the returns on the company's earnings. After these machinations came to light, Dunlap was fined $500,000 and banned permanently by the SEC from serving as an officer in a public company. One Sunbeam investor, Ronald Perelman, lost $680 million after Sunbeam collapsed and filed for bankruptcy. Perelman sued Morgan Stanley, Sunbeam's investment banker, in a Florida state court, claiming that it misled him as to Sunbeam's finances when he made his investment. Morgan Stanley was sanctioned by that court for failing to produce documents concerning its role in that transaction. The sanction was that Morgan Stanley was not allowed to present a defense to the suit. The jury eventually awarded Perelman a total of $1.45 billion in compensatory and punitive damages, and the judge added another $130 million for lost interest.

Bristol-Myers-Squibb, the giant pharmaceutical company, announced that it was restating $2.75 billion in inflated sales figures between 1999 and 2001 and inflated earnings of $900 million. The earnings were pumped up through various means, including cookie jar reserves in the form of restructuring charges. The company was also channel stuffing by giving incentives to distributors to load up on unneeded drugs so that the company could meet analysts' projections. Wholesalers were paid incentives to buy more drugs from the company than they needed. A class action suit was filed by the Retirement System of Louisiana and the General Retirement System of the City of Detroit challenging those practices. A federal district court dismissed the case, but the pension funds appealed. Fearing an adverse result from the lingering

Enron hysteria, Bristol-Myers agreed to settle the suit for $300 million even before the appellate court ruled—a heavy price for a case that had been won in the lower court. Bristol-Myers also agreed to settle an SEC action involving its accounting problems for another $150 million.

Peter Dolan, chief executive officer at Bristol-Myers-Squibb, filed a sworn certification that the company's financial statements were accurate in August 2002, a requirement imposed by the SEC after the failure of Enron. Dolan had to recant that certification after announcement of the company's problems. He and other executives were the targets of a criminal investigation by the Justice Department. The company's chief financial officer, Frederick Schiff, and Richard Lane, an executive vice president, were indicted for their role in the accounting manipulations. The company paid another $300 million under a deferred prosecution agreement to settle that probe. The company further agreed to split the role of its chairman and chief executive officer, in keeping with a current corporate governance fad, after previously hiring retired federal judge Frederick Lacey to act as a monitor over its financial reports. Despite these problems, it appeared that Dolan was a good manager of his executives' time, making sure they could get about the country efficiently by spending $100 million for executive aircraft. The accounting treatment for those aircraft also had to be restated. These events did not result in accurate financial statements in the future. On March 15, 2004, Bristol-Myers-Squibb announced that it was restating its financial accounts once again, but this time it was increasing revenue in 2003 by over $200 million and net income by $154 million. The increase was good news, but did little to evidence that the company's financial statements were very dependable.

Statement of Cash Flows

Dynegy Corp. was charged by the SEC with engaging in improper accounting techniques in its statement of cash flows that involved special purpose entities (SPEs) that did not meet the 3 percent independent investor requirement. Those transactions, called Project Alpha, were created in order to meet concerns by financial analysts that there was a widening gap between Dynegy's net income and its operating cash flow resulting from mark-to-market accounting principles used for its forward contract positions. This was the same problem that Enron had encountered. To close that gap, Dynegy created a complex group of SPEs that were used to increase 2001 operating cash flow by $300 million. The SEC charged that, in reality, the $300 million was a disguised loan. The SEC stated that this was "particularly significant for two reasons: first, analysts view operating cash flow as a key indicator of the financial health of energy trading firms such as Dynegy; and second, historically, the Statement of Cash Flows has been considered immune from cosmetic tampering."[14]

Dynegy settled civil charges with the SEC over this conduct. The price of

Dynegy's stock dropped from $28 to less than a dollar within a few months after these revelations. Dynegy subsequently agreed to pay $468 million to settle a class action shareholders lawsuit brought by the University of California over the Project Alpha transaction. As part of that settlement, the company also agreed to elect two individuals to its board selected by the university, a requirement that would become a favored tactic by that institution in its class action cases against firms having accounting problems. Sim Lake, a federal judge in Houston, handed out a stiff sentence to a Dynegy executive for his role in the company's accounting problems. Jamie Olis, Dynegy's senior director of tax planning, was convicted after a trial and sentenced to over twenty-four years in prison, placing him up there with second-degree murderers. Before Enron, he would have served at most a few years, but the judge cited a desire by Congress for stiffer punishments in imposing that sentence. A court of appeals later ruled that sentence was excessive. Two other Dynegy accounting executives, Gene Shannon Foster and Helen Christine Sharkey, pleaded guilty to fraud charges, assuring them of a lesser sentence.[15]

Pro Forma Results

Another accounting abuse involved the misuse of pro forma results. These were accounting statements prepared by management that did not conform to GAAP because one or more nonrecurring events were excluded from the results for the period under review. Pro forma results allowed management to claim that, but for such nonrecurring events, the company's core business was profitable and doing well. This was useful information to investors and analysts, but pro forma results could be abused. Trump Hotels & Casino Resorts Inc. claimed in its pro forma results that it exceeded analysts' earnings expectations, if a one-time charge were excluded. The company failed to disclose, however, that it was including a one-time $17.2 million gain in order to reach that figure. Trump settled an action brought by the SEC over that omission by agreeing to cease and desist from such conduct in the future.

Ashford.com, an online jewelry company, misstated its pro forma financial results in March 2000 in order to beat analysts' expectations. That was done by improperly deferring $1.5 million in expenses under a contract with Amazon.com. In September of that year, Ashford.com misstated its pro forma results again by changing the classification of certain expenses on its income statement from "marketing expenses" to "depreciation and amortization." This change inflated its pro forma results because those statements did not take depreciation and amortization into account.

Rite Aid

The market downturn in 2000, a decline in economic activity, and, in some cases, overcapacity induced executives to use a variety of accounting maneuvers to disguise the effects of those events on the financial condition of their companies. One company that encountered difficulties as the result of its accounting manipulations was Rite Aid Corp. Headquartered in Camp Hill, Pennsylvania, Rite Aid was the third-largest retail pharmacy chain in the United States. Its accounting problems were triggered by a whistleblower, Joe Speaker, the company's new chief financial officer. In June 1999, Rite Aid restated its revenues for the period 1997–1999. That announcement was tempered by the company's assertion that it was cutting revenues in those periods only by a few million dollars. Later in the year, however, the company disclosed a further restatement, totaling a staggering $1.6 billion. That was then the largest restatement in United States history, although that record would later be bested several times.

Rite Aid's stock dropped by 87 percent after that restatement was announced. Martin Grass, Rite Aid's chief executive officer and the son of its founder, was forced to resign and pleaded guilty to criminal charges, as did two other executives. Aptly named federal district court judge Sylvia Rambo refused Grass's plea bargain for a maximum eight-year prison sentence. She wanted more jail time, a disease that was spreading around the judiciary. The judge later backed off, and Grass was sentenced to eight years in prison and fined $500,000. The judge later knocked off a year from Grass's sentence after the Supreme Court held that federal sentencing guidelines were invalid. Rite Aid's seventy-five-year-old chief counsel and vice chairman, Franklin Brown, was found guilty by a jury of making false statements to the SEC, obstruction of justice by tampering with a witness, and other misconduct. He had left retirement in order to help the company through the crisis but faced the possibility of a prison sentence as long as sixty-five years. He was given only ten years but that was surely a life sentence. Five other executives were also convicted, including Franklyn Bergonzi, the company's chief financial officer. Judge Rambo gave him two years and four months. Eric Sorkin, an executive vice president, was sentenced to five months in prison. The company fired its auditor, KPMG, and settled shareholder lawsuits for $200 million. KPMG also agreed to pay $125 million to settle shareholder class action claims, which was then the largest recovery against an auditor in action under the SEC's antifraud rule. The lawyers bringing the case received 25 percent of that recovery.

Computer Associates

Computer Associates International, a software company based in Islandia, New York, was the fifth-largest computer software company in the world when its accounting manipulations came to light. Those problems surfaced after the head of the company, Charles Wang, and two other executives received $1.1 billion in incentive compensation based on increases in the price of the company's stock. Wang's share of that loot was $700 million. This episode set a record for the highest executive compensation ever paid. Two months after handing out those bonuses, Computer Associates announced that it was not meeting analysts' expectations, and its stock price plunged. Wang then removed himself from operations and quickly retired. One of the outside directors serving on the board of Computer Associates was Richard Grasso, the head of the New York Stock Exchange (NYSE). Grasso would later have some compensation issues of his own.

Computer Associates improperly booked customer contracts in order to meet analysts' expectations at the end of its reporting quarters. Although it took more than two years to correct its records, Computer Associates finally admitted in April 2004 that it had booked more than $2 billion in unearned revenue for its fiscal years 2000 and 2001. Another $560 million had been improperly booked in prior years. Computer Associates was counting some sales twice and booking contracts as sales before the contracts were signed. Fourteen executives were fired after these revelations, including Ira Zar, the company's chief financial officer. Zar subsequently pleaded guilty to criminal charges concerning his manipulation of company accounts, as did two other executives, David Rivard and David Kaplan. Another executive, Lloyd Silverstein, pleaded guilty to a criminal charge of obstruction of justice, as did Steven Woghin, the company's general counsel. The company's new chairman and chief executive officer, Sanjay Kumar, resigned and was indicted for his role in these problems. Stephen Richards, the company's top sales executive was fired and then indicted. Computer Associates agreed to pay $225 million under a deferred prosecution agreement with the Justice Department, and arrangement that had been denied to Arthur Andersen. This allowed the company to escape criminal charges. The $225 million was to be used as a restitution fund for injured investors, but those investors expressed little or no interest in seeking restitution from the fund in the months following the settlement. One institutional investor, the California Public Employees Retirement System (Calpers), said it was waiting for the government to call before seeking reimbursement for its members.

John Swainson was hired to become the new chief executive officer of Computer Associates and given an $8.6 million compensation package. But the company's troubles continued in October 2003. Its stock price dropped 10 percent over concerns on how widespread were its accounting problems, and 5 percent of the company's employees were laid off. A shareholder proposal asking the company to sue the discharged executives and obtain return of the bonuses they were paid was defeated after management objected to the proposal.

Xerox

Xerox Corp. had been struggling for some time but appeared to have turned itself around at the end of the century, as revenues increased and its stock price doubled. Unfortunately, those revenue increases were achieved by accounting manipulations. Xerox confessed on May 31, 2001, that it had "misapplied" accounting rules and was restating its accounts for the prior three years as a result of problems in a Mexican subsidiary. That was only the beginning of the debacle. Xerox eventually restated a total of $6.4 billion in entries for the years 1997–2001, resulting in a decrease in income of $3 billion. The company had been boosting revenues each quarter through "close the gap" exercises that included "topside" accounting entries (entries directed by management). A whistleblower at the company, James Bingham, was fired for objecting to these accounting practices. The price of Xerox's stock dropped by 90 percent after the extent of the company's accounting abuses was revealed.

Xerox was fined $10 million by the SEC and six of its executives paid another $22 million to settle SEC charges for their accounting abuses. Xerox agreed to pay all but $3 million of those fines for the executives. The SEC charged that two chief executive officers at Xerox, Paul Allaire and G. Richard Thoman, "set a 'tone at the top' of the company, which equated business success with meeting short-term earnings targets," while Barry Romeril, the chief financial officer, directed personnel "to make accounting adjustments to results reported from operating divisions to accelerate revenues and increase earnings."[16] Romeril, an English accountant, was permanently barred from practicing as an accountant before the SEC. Gregory B. Tayler, a Canadian accountant and Xerox's director of accounting policy, was suspended for three years. The company's accounting firm, KPMG, and five of its partners were the subject of SEC charges that they too "meekly" audited Xerox.[17] KPMG also had other problems; it had paid $75 million to settle claims involving its audit work for Oxford Health in 1997. Oxford Health paid $300 million to settle a class action suit over its medical claims malpractices. That suit was brought by the Colorado Employees Retirement Association. By then labor union pension funds were suing after every corporate scandal or setback. KPMG later settled the SEC's charges over its Xerox audit work by accepting a censure and paying $22.5 million. That figure included the return of its audit fees plus interest. KPMG also agreed to set up a review procedure for its audit practices and to set up a whistleblower procedure.

Critical Path and Others

Critical Path, a San Francisco–based e-mail software maker, restated about $20 million for two quarters in 2000. The company had created fictitious sales contracts, concealed contingencies affecting revenue recognition, and backdated software licensing agreements in order to increase revenues. The president of the company and former PricewaterhouseCoopers auditor, David Thatcher, pleaded guilty to securities fraud charges. He was fined $100,000 but was allowed to keep the $8.6 million he made from sales of Critical Path stock. Another Critical Path executive, Timothy Ganley, was indicted for selling $32,000 of Critical Path's stock after he learned that the company was not going to meet analysts' earnings expectations. The price of Critical Path stock dropped from a high of $113 to $1.85 after these revelations, cutting the company's valuation from $3.8 billion to $192 million.

Conseco Inc., an insurance and financial services provider based in Carmel, Indiana, was charged by the SEC with accounting fraud. The company was required to mark-to-market securities held in inventory, but failed to mark down securities that had declined in value in 1999. That failure was motivated by a desire to avoid an adverse effect on the company's stock price. Conseco declared bankruptcy and tried to sell Greentree Financial for $1.01 billion, a considerable discount from the $6.44 billion that Conseco had paid for that company in 1998. Rollin Dick, the company's chief financial officer, and James Adams, the chief accounting officer, were charged by the SEC with responsibility for the accounting misconduct. Both resigned from Conseco. The SEC asserted that they were motivated by loans from the company totaling $100 million, which they used to purchase Conseco stock.

Conseco was a serial payer of excessive compensation to its executives. Conseco paid its chief executive officer, Stephen Hilbert, $170 million even though the company disintegrated on his watch and had to file for bankruptcy. He was given $74 million as severance in 2000. More large payouts would be made in later years to Conseco executives despite its continuing financial problems. Hilbert's successor, Gary Wendt, was given $53 million after serving in the job for only two years. Wendt was followed by William Shea, who was given a severance package of $13.5 million after two years on the job. The firm's chairman, R. Glenn Hillard, was given a $20 million compensation package in 2003.

The Interpublic Group of Companies Inc. restated $181.3 million in earnings improperly added to its accounting statements between 1997 and 2002. On August 5, 2002, it announced that it was delaying the release of second-quarter Form 10-Q. That resulted in a 35 percent drop in its stock price. Interpublic settled class action and derivative suits for its accounting manipulations by agreeing to pay 6.5 million of its own shares and $20 million in cash, with a total value of about $96 million. The cash was to be used for attorney fees and expenses. The company further agreed to hire Pinkerton Compliance Services to act as a third-party investigator of any reports of accounting misconduct at the company for a period of five years.

PNC Financial Services Group Inc. was required to restate its earnings twice for 2001. Those restatements reduced earnings by $377 million, a reduction of about one-third of the earnings previously reported. PNC transferred a portfolio of distressed loans to three special purpose entities in order to take them off its books. PNC agreed to pay $115 million in restitution and penalties under a deferred prosecution deal with the Justice Department for this activity. American International Group Inc. (AIG), the giant insurance company, was charged by the SEC with facilitating accounting fraud at PNC by allowing bad loans to be moved off the bank's books and onto those of an AIG subsidiary. AIG was caught up in other scandals as well.

Bankers Trust pleaded guilty to federal criminal charges that senior officers illegally diverted $19.1 million to the bank's books from unclaimed checks and other credits that were supposed to escheat to the state of New York. That diversion was used to improve the bank's financial performance from 1994 to 1996, a time when the bank was mired in a scandal over its sale of complex derivatives that caused losses at Gibson Greetings and others. Bankers Trust agreed to pay a $60 million fine to the Justice Department and a separate fine of $3.5 million to New York authorities to settle charges for this scheme. One Bankers Trust executive, B.J. Kingdon, pleaded guilty to criminal charges, but a jury acquitted two other executives at the bank. Bankers Trust later merged with Deutsche Bank AG. More adroitly, Bank of America transferred problem loans to a subsidiary in a tax-free transaction in exchange for stock ownership of the subsidiary. The subsidiary wrote down the value of the loans, triggering a write-down by Bank of America in the value of the subsidiary's stock and creating a tax loss for Bank of America on its investment in the subsidiary. The result was $418 million in tax savings and a substantial reduction in the company's tax rate for the quarter in which the transaction was completed.

MCA Financial Corp., a mortgage brokerage firm, was charged by the SEC with inflating its accounts in 1998 by overvaluing mortgages and failing to write off uncollectible debts. The company's auditor, Grant Thornton, agreed to pay $1.5 million to settle SEC charges that it aided and abetted those accounting misrepresentations. In another case, an Ernst & Young audit partner, Thomas C. Trauger, was arrested for changing work papers in order to obstruct an investigation by the Office of the Comptroller of the Currency (OCC) and the SEC into how NextCard Inc. booked credit card defaults. NextCard's stock price dropped by more than 80 percent after that revelation. Trauger told another partner that they needed to "beef up" their work papers in order to assure that the files would not be combed over by "some smart-ass lawyer." Another auditor at Ernst & Young, Oliver Flanagan, pleaded guilty to criminal charges for his participation in this scheme.

The failure of Superior Bank FSB in Oak Brook Terrace, Illinois, in July 2001 was the largest bank failure in over ten years. Losses to the Federal Deposit Insurance Corporation (FDIC) were expected to exceed $500 million. Superior Bank was a subprime lender that extended loans to individuals with poor credit histories. Its losses arose from securitized subprime mortgage loans that were experiencing large defaults. The bank was jointly owned by Alvin Dworman, a New York real estate developer, and the wealthy Pritzker family in Chicago, which also owned the Hyatt chain of hotels. The Pritzkers agreed to pay depositors $460 million over fifteen years to settle claims from the bank's failure. The FDIC filed a $2 billion suit against Ernst & Young, the bank's auditors, for failing to audit its books and records, properly resulting in a "gross misstatement of Superior's assets." That suit was dismissed because the FDIC had signed a mandatory arbitration clause with Ernst & Young in its capacity as a receiver for the bank. Ernst & Young later agreed to pay $125 million to settle the FDIC claims. The Pritzker family was to be given $31 million of that amount. It was needed because a family quarrel had resulted in a splitting of its wealth. Stephen Snyder, the lawyer handing the case for the FDIC, also won a $276 million award for Steele Software Systems Corp. in an action brought against First Union Corp. for misappropriating an automated title search system. However, the court reduced that figure by $100 million. Snyder then began a $1 million advertising campaign in the *Wall Street Journal* and the *New York Times* that was soliciting clients to bring him a $1 billion lawsuit. Interestingly, the Office of Thrift Supervision, which regulated the Superior Bank, had rated the bank highly in its supervisory ranking system until Ernst & Young required the bank to write off some of the securitized subprime mortgage loans.

The Hamilton Bancorp Inc. was closed by the OCC in 2002. Its chairman, Eduardo Masferrer, executive vice president, Juan Carlos Bernace, and senior vice president, John M.R. Jacobs, were the subject of SEC charges that they made manipulative trades with other banks to hide the bank's losses. The transactions at issue were swaps involving "adjusted price trades." This was the second-largest U.S. bank failure in over ten years, placing second behind the Superior Bank collapse. Household International Inc. was inflating its accounts between 1994 and 2002, reporting "dramatic" and continuous increases in income and earnings. The company's stock rose in response, but dropped even more rapidly after Household announced it was restating its accounts. The restatement reduced income and equity by $386 million. Household had other regulatory problems in its lending practices, and its stock price dropped from $63.25 to $28 in less than three months. The company had been audited by Arthur Andersen & Co.

The chief financial officer for North Face Inc. was barred by the SEC from serving as an officer or director of a public company for five years for misstating the company's financial results between 1997 and 1998. Among other things, he was improperly claiming revenue on barter and consignment sales. Richard Fiedelman, the audit partner for North Face at Deloitte & Touche LLP, was barred from audit work at public companies for at least three years, but he had already retired at the time of the entry of that order by the SEC. The chief financial officer at Leslie Fay was given a nine-year prison sentence for accounting fraud that inflated the company's earnings. Leslie Fay subsequently declared bankruptcy. Some less imaginative executives at another company, FLIR Systems, a maker of thermal imaging products, simply listed expenses as assets and overstated accounts receivable. Three executives at that company were indicted for their role in that accounting fraud.

Indictments were filed in 1999 against two former executives of Livent Inc., a producer of Broadway plays, after it was discovered that the company's accounts had been inflated by $325 million. One of those executives, Garth Drabinsky, had been the producer of the wildly popular musical *Phantom of the Opera*. He fled to Canada to avoid prosecution in the United States, but was arrested by the Royal Canadian Mounties and charged with fraud in connection with his Livent activities. The fraud at Livent was discovered after the company was sold to a group of investors led by Michael Ovitz, a short-time Walt Disney executive whose severance package had become the epitome of excess in corporate compensation.

In 1997, Informix Corp., a Menlo Park, California, producer of database software, announced that it was restating its 1996 revenues, reducing them by $200 million. That turned a reported profit of $97 million for the year into a loss of $73 million. Among other things, Informix had booked revenue from multimillion-dollar contracts with various companies, including Hewlett-Packard and Fujitsu. Those companies were given side agreements allowing them to cancel the deals. The price of Informix's stock dropped from $12.20 to $6.25 after disclosure of these manipulations, losing $900 million in market capitalization. Informix's chief executive officer, Phillip E. White, made $3.2 million from Informix stock sales in 1996. He was indicted and pleaded guilty to a securities fraud felony count. The company and its auditors, Ernst & Young, settled class action lawsuits from shareholders for $142 million. Informix sold its software operations to IBM.

A subsidiary of the Seaboard Corp., which was involved in shrimp farming, was found to have understated expenses between 1995 and 2000 in order to increase earnings. The Edison Schools settled charges that nearly half of its reported revenues were actually expenses paid by school districts to third parties on Edison's behalf. The effect of that improper accounting treatment was to increase revenue dramatically, boosting the price of Edison's stock. Lesser restatements occurred at Restoration Hardware as the result of improper booking of furniture sales.

Just For Feet was the subject of another accounting scandal. Based in Birmingham, Alabama, this company operated a large number of shoe stores, including those acquired from its purchase of Athletic Attic. The company had become known for a racially offensive Super Bowl advertisement not long before its bankruptcy. Thomas Shine, president of Logo Athletic Inc., pleaded guilty to charges that he misled Just For Feet's auditor, Deloitte & Touche, by falsely confirming a $700,000 receivable purportedly owed to Just For Feet. Jon Epstein, the president and chief executive officer of Fila USA, pleaded guilty to aiding Just For Feet in its accounting manipulations by allowing it to record $1.4 million in nonexistent accounts receivable from Fila. Executives from Adidas, Converse, and Logo Athletic pleaded guilty to similar charges.

When the accounting problems at Just For Feet were disclosed, the price of its stock plunged, destroying over $700 million in capitalization. Just before that announcement, the company sold $200 million in notes; those note holders were left with claims in bankruptcy. The company's executives managed to sell $50 million in stock before the disclosure of those accounting manipulations. The son of the founder of the company, Don-Allen Ruttenberg, pleaded guilty to criminal charges for his role in that accounting fraud. Just For Feet's comptroller, Peter Berman, agreed to pay a civil penalty and disgorgement of $52,000 to settle SEC charges for his role in the fraud. He was also barred from serving as an officer or director of a public company. Just For Feet's auditor, Deloitte & Touche, was charged in a class action lawsuit as having a conflict of interest as a result of its efforts to obtain a consulting contract from Just For Feet. The accounting firm settled those claims and paid $375,000 to settle SEC charges. Deloitte auditor Steven Barry was barred from audit work by the SEC for two years and Karen Baker was barred for one year.

Still More Problems

Spiegel Inc., a catalog retailer since 1905, acquired the Eddie Bauer outdoor clothing outfitter in 1988 and entered into online sales during the Internet boom in order to update its business. The company was 90 percent owned by Michael Otto, a German businessman. The rest of the stock was owned by public shareholders, mostly in America. Sales performance was deteriorating in 1999, and executives at Spiegel created an operation dubbed "easy credit to pump up sales." That program involved extending credit card sales to subprime credit risks. Those receivables were then securitized and moved off the balance sheet, but the downturn in the economy resulted in unexpectedly large defaults that were about to trigger payoff requirements under the securitization program that would have bankrupted Spiegel. Spiegel executives then acted to misstate the calculation for those performance triggers, which kept the company going for another two years. The company's condition continued to deteriorate, and it quit filing reports with the SEC for fifteen months before it filed for bankruptcy in 2003. Otto asserted that he decided not to file those reports in order to save the company and the jobs of its 7,700 employees. Otto thought that the failure to file would result only in a fine. He ended up paying $104 million to settle claims made in bankruptcy by Spiegel creditors. Those creditors also took the remainder of Spiegel's assets.

A Belgian company called Lernout & Hauspie Speech Products was listed on Nasdaq and had a market valuation of $10 billion before it declared bankruptcy in a sea of allegations of accounting fraud. The SEC charged that the company falsified some 70 percent of its accounts between 1996 and 2000 by treating loans as sales, using round trip transactions with shell companies to inflate revenues, and creating fictitious customer accounts. The company, which made speech recognition software, was outed by Marc Cohodes, a short seller managing a hedge fund called Rocker Partners. While purchasing software for his son, he discovered that the company was shipping products that had not been ordered. The company's auditor, KPMG-Belgium, fiercely resisted efforts to make it produce documents in a federal court in the United States that was hearing claims brought by disappointed investors against the accounting firm. KPMG tried to enlist the aid of the Belgian courts to fend off discovery demands from the U.S. court, but later agreed to pay $115 million to settle the class action suit. KPMG remained under attack from bankruptcy courts in the United States and Belgium. Collectively, they were seeking over $700 million from the accounting firm. One suit brought by the company's trustee was dismissed on the grounds that the company was in *pari delicto* with any misconduct by KPMG.

Sport-Haley Inc. was charged with manipulating its accounts by misstating work-in-process inventory, understating losses, and wrongfully capitalizing costs. Based in Colorado, the company distributed golf apparel. An accountant, Kenneth R. LeCrone, was the subject of SEC charges for certifying the Sport-Haley financial statements. He was employed by the accounting firm of Levine, Hughes, and Mithuen Inc., which destroyed and altered its work papers after learning of the SEC investigation. The accounting firm settled with the SEC by agreeing to pay a fine of $50,000 and was barred from practice before the SEC for at least three years.

Raytheon Company, a manufacturer of airplanes and military equipment, agreed to pay $410 million to settle a class action law suit brought by the New York state retirement plan. The complaint charged that Raytheon manipulated its financial accounts between 1998 and 1999, failing to take losses on contracts that could not be completed and claiming revenues on anticipated contracts that were not yet signed. PricewaterhouseCoopers, a defendant in that action, was reported to have paid $50 million to settle those claims. Raytheon paid the SEC $12 million to settle charges over its accounting practices and discharged its chief financial officer, Edward S. Pliner. The company also paid $39 million to settle another shareholder lawsuit over the sale of some assets in 2000. PricewaterhouseCoopers had other problems. It paid another $50 million to settle claims over its audit work at U-Haul International owned by Amerco Inc.

Gateway, Inc., the computer manufacturer, was charged by the SEC with misleading analysts on its computer sales by manipulating earnings in 2000. The company settled that case with the SEC without admitting or denying the charges. Three of the company's executives were charged with misconduct in connection with that episode. Gateway was claiming that it was doing fine in a saturated personal computer market. In fact, its computer sales were declining, producing very little of the company's net income in 2000. Instead, Gateway's income was the result of nonrecurring items and inflated accounts. The SEC charged Gateway with misleading investors by this conduct and with failing to disclose the effects of subprime loans to high credit risk customers for peripheral sales. That credit was extended in amounts totaling $112 million in order to meet analysts' expectations in the second quarter of 2000. The company additionally sold $50 million in high-quality consumer loans on its books to another company so that it could claim that income in the second quarter. To accomplish that sale, Gateway had to loan the purchasing company $50 million. Through such machinations, Gateway was able to exceed analysts' expectations by a penny.

The gap between expectations and actual results was even bigger in the third quarter of 2000 at Gateway. The company then began extending credit to even riskier consumers through a program dubbed DDS, which stood for "deep, deep shit." Losses on those loans were expected to exceed 50 percent but were made anyway in the amount of $84 million. At the same time, Gateway reduced its loan loss reserves in order to further boost income. Another measure used to meet analysts' expectations for the third quarter was a $21 million sale of computers to a vendor. That sale was booked as revenue even though the vendor had a right of return for any unsold computers and was not óbligated to purchase the computers until they were actually shipped to customers. Several other manipulations used to meet the expectations gap included the reduction of reserves set aside for potential liabilities from patent infringement claims. The SEC issued only a cease and desist order as the sanction for this misconduct, a stark contrast to the severe sanctions imposed on other firms.

A Dallas software company, i2 Technologies Inc., admitted to misstating $1 billion in revenues between 1997 and 2002. The company agreed to pay $10 million to settle SEC charges for that misconduct. Among other things, the company improperly claimed $44 million in barter transactions in software licenses, recorded income from software that was not yet functional, and accrued income before being earned.

Eleven persons were indicted at Peregrine Systems Inc. for inflating accounts between 1999 and 2001 in order to push up the company's stock price. The defendants used fictitious quarter-end transactions involving software sales with third-party vendors who sometimes were bribed to acknowledge the sales or provided side agreements that made the transactions nonbinding. Not surprisingly, those customers failed to pay, causing Peregrine's receivables to balloon. Peregrine then sold the receivables to banks and removed them from the company's balance sheet even though the sales were on a recourse basis. Several of the receivables were based on fake invoices, including one for a purported $19.58 million sale. Several executives pleaded guilty to criminal charges. One executive vice president bragged to others about the transactions, asserting that he was planning to start a company called "Quartermaker Inc." Executives at Peregrine made several million dollars selling their stock while this scheme was being carried out.

Round Trips

The SEC brought an action against Reliant Resources Inc., the energy firm that had been sanctioned by the Commodity Futures Trading Commission

(CFTC) for engaging in "round-trip" trades. The round-trip trading attacked by the CFTC became the target of the SEC because such transactions inflated revenues on financial statements disseminated to the public. The round-trip trades were offset by the same amount of expenses, but stock analysts focused on increased revenue as well as income. The fact that the trading hurt the company's profit margins was largely ignored.

The SEC further charged that Reliant structured "swing-swap" transactions to move greater than expected earnings to subsequent years. The swing-swaps involved four financially settled natural gas swap transactions that moved about $20 million from 2000 to 2001. "The 'legs' of the two December swap transactions were a sale (or fixed cash inflow) of 1,500,000 million British thermal units ('mmbtu') at $26.50 per mmbtu and a purchase (or fixed cash outflow) of 1,500,000 mmbtu at $39.85 per mmbtu, with the counter party's legs perfectly offsetting, resulting in a $20 million pre-tax loss. The legs of the two January swap transactions were a purchase of 3,100,000 mmbtu at $13.215 per mmbtu and sale of 3,100,000 mmbtu at $19.6747 per mmbtu, again with the counter party's legs perfectly offsetting."[18] Reliant announced in July 2002 that it was restating its earnings for a three-year period as a result of an artificial inflation of its revenues by more than $7.8 billion by round-trip trades. Reliant settled SEC charges without admitting or denying the allegations. The sanction in this case was limited to a cease and desist order.

Other energy firms were targeted by the SEC, including CMS Energy Corp., which had inflated its revenue by $5.2 billion through round-trip trades with Reliant and Dynegy. The SEC charged Dynegy with inflating its balance sheet by engaging in such conduct through its electronic trading platform, Dynegydirect. Specifically, the SEC charged that, on November 15, 2001, Dynegy entered into two massive round-trip trades of electricity on Dynegydirect in which Dynegy simultaneously bought and sold power at the same price, terms, and volume, resulting in neither profit nor loss to either party. At that time, Dynegy was trying to enhance the industry's view of the liquidity on its electronic trading platform, but the round-trip trades also resulted in $236 million inflation of revenues. Dynegy settled the SEC case without admitting or denying the charges. Dynegy's chief executive officer resigned after these disclosures, and the company closed its energy-trading operations. Dynegy's auditor, the defunct Arthur Andersen firm, later agreed to pay $1 million to settle claims for its failed audit work.

A pre-Enron scandal arose at Cendant Corp., a marketer and hotel franchiser that owned the Days Inn chain of motels and Century 21, the large real estate broker. Cendant inflated its revenues by more than $500 million. Investors in the company saw the price of their stock drop from $35 to $19 after that revelation, reducing the capitalization of the company by $19 billion; $14 billion of that amount was lost in a single day. That was the largest accounting fraud up to that date, but that title was lost to Enron and others. Cendant agreed to pay investors $3.5 billion to settle claims involving its accounting manipulations. This was the largest such settlement in history. The lead plaintiff in that class action suit was the California Public Employee Retirement System (Calpers). As a part of the settlement, Cedant was forced to make certain corporate governance changes, including the election of a majority of outside directors to its board and allow only outside directors on the audit, nominating, and compensation committees. Cendant also agreed to drop its staggered election of directors and prohibit the repricing of employee stock options after their grant, except with the approval of a majority of voting shareholders. Three company officers pled guilty to criminal fraud charges. They were Cosmo Corigliano, the company's chief financial officer, Anne Pember, controller, and Casper Sabatino, a company accountant.

The chairman of Cendant, Walter A. Forbes, was indicted for selling $11 million of Cendant stock before the announcement of these accounting problems. Forbes and Cendant vice chairman Kirk Shelton were charged with inflating the company's revenues. Shelton was convicted of twelve counts, but a mistrial was declared for Forbes after the jury was unable to reach a verdict on the charges lodged against him. Much of this fraud occurred at CUC International, a company that was part of the merger that formed Cendant. CUC had been inflating its accounts since 1983, the year the company went public. Cendant's auditors, Ernst & Young, paid $335 million to settle charges for failing to detect this fraud. Cendant was suing and seeking billions more from Ernst & Young. The SEC barred two Ernst & Young partners from auditing public companies in the future. Cendant recovered from this scandal and rewarded its chief executive officer, Henry Silverman, with a $13.8 million cash bonus for 2003. His total compensation for that year was $60.1 million.

Microstrategy Inc., a software firm, issued a restatement of its accounts that showed losses from 1997 to 1999, rather than the large profits claimed in its SEC filings. Microstrategy's stock price fell from $140 to $86.75 after that restatement. The founder of the company, Michael J. Saylor, experienced a $6.1 billion drop in his net worth as a result of that decline. PricewaterhouseCoopers, the auditor for Microstrategy, agreed to pay $55 million to settle claims arising from its audit work. Warren Martin, the audit partner on the account, was barred from practice before the SEC for a period of two years. Another problem faced by PricewaterhouseCoopers arose from audits of Mid-American Waste Systems, a NYSE firm that went bankrupt in 1997. A federal judge certified a class action suit against the firm for its audit failure.

Ernst & Young was the subject of litigation for its auditing of Fruit of the Loom Inc. That company was accused of, among other things, engaging in a "pull-forward" program that used early shipments to increase sales so that analysts' expectations could be met. Deloitte & Touche agreed to pay $24 million to settle claims arising from its audit work on Medaphis Corp., an Atlanta company that provided management software and services. Medaphis had to restate its accounts for 1995–1997. Pearson PLC, the owner of the *Financial Times* and Penguin Books, took a huge charge to earnings after it was discovered that Penguin had not been deducting discounts given for prompt payments, inflating earnings over a six-year period by $163 million.

Mercury Finance disclosed that it overstated earnings in 1995 and 1996 by 100 percent. The chief executive officer and controller resigned. Rent-Way Inc., which operated over 1,000 rent-to-own stores, restated $110 million in revenues in 2000 as a result of overstatements of inventory and treating expenses as assets. Fabri-Centers, the owner of the JoAnn fabrics chain, was charged by the SEC with failing to disclose that it was underestimating the cost of goods sold in its quarterly financial reports. The company agreed to pay $3.3 million to settle those charges.

Kmart

Kmart was another American business icon that was in trouble after the economy began its decline in the new century. As concern arose about Kmart's continued viability, its share prices dropped dramatically, falling 70 percent in a single week. Formerly known as S.S. Kresge, Kmart's stock was underwritten by Merrill Lynch & Co. during the 1920s, along with other chain stores such as Western Auto. That underwriting laid the groundwork for Merrill Lynch's future underwriting business and became a model for the securities industry.

Kmart filed for Chapter 11 bankruptcy on January 22, 2002, just as the Enron scandal was in full bloom. This was the largest retail bankruptcy in history. The prior holder of that title was Federated Department Stores, which failed early in the 1990s. Kmart followed Enron as the largest bankruptcy of any kind at the time. Kmart reported almost $40 billion in annual sales before that filing. The Kmart bankruptcy was another shock to the faltering economy. Congressman William (Billy) Tauzin of Florida, nevertheless, claimed that the Kmart failure was something of a victory for the concept of full disclosure because the company's financial statements had tracked its downward flight. That was poor comfort for shareholders.

The federal government subsequently indicted two Kmart executives for securities fraud and other violations in connection with the Kmart bankruptcy. The government charged that those executives lied to Kmart's accountants concerning various transactions. The charges were later dropped because the government did not think it could establish evidence sufficient to prove its claims, giving rise to the question of why the executives were indicted in the first place. Claims against Kmart's auditor, PricewaterhouseCoopers LLP, were dismissed by a federal judge. The SEC brought charges against three Kmart executives for inflating the company's revenues by $24 million through accelerated booking of vendor allowances in the last quarter of 2000. Executives at PepsiCo Inc., Eastman Kodak, and Coca-Cola Enterprises Inc. were also charged by the SEC with aiding Kmart in that manipulation. PepsiCo engaged in similar conduct with Fleming Co., a grocery distributor that would have its own accounting and bankruptcy problems.

Kmart survived but closed hundreds of stores. One of its important lines of business was the marketing of Martha Stewart brand products. That line of products, called Everyday, had a strong image that Stewart made popular with consumers. Stewart's marketing value took a beating after her indictment for obstruction of justice, but Kmart stayed with her during the public furor over that event, even using her in advertisements during the World Series. Kmart merged with Sears, Roebuck & Co. in November 2004. The combined firm was the third-largest retailer in the United States.

The Tyco Scandal

The Growing of Tyco

Tyco International Ltd. (not to be confused with Tyco Toys, which is owned by Mattel Inc.) was a high-flying conglomerate that acquired over 1,000 companies in the span of a few years. Originally headquartered in Exeter, New Hampshire, Tyco moved its operating headquarters from New Hampshire to New York in 1995, and its charter was transferred to Bermuda in 1977. The latter move reduced Tyco's tax bracket from 34 percent to 25 percent.

Tyco continued to be controlled in the United States by its chief executive officer Dennis Kozlowski, a Seton Hall graduate with a degree in finance. Kozlowski began his career as a financial analyst, but decided operations were more to his liking and eventually moved to Tyco. After sixteen years at Tyco, he became the company's president and chief operating officer. Kozlowski was soon promoted to the role of chairman and chief executive officer. Known as a daredevil, Kozlowski flew his own helicopter, was a blue-water sailor, and rode a motorcycle. He pursued a higher profile as Tyco grew, buying the racing yacht *Endeavor,* which required a crew that was paid $200,000 in salaries annually. Kozlowski, through Tyco, sponsored a sailboat in the round-the-world Volvo Ocean Race and bought an interest in two sports teams in New Jersey, the Nets and the Devils. He was given a seat on the board of the Whitney Museum, after Tyco made a $4.5 million qualifying contribution. Kozlowski had estates in Nantucket, New Hampshire, and Boca Raton and an expensive apartment in New York that were paid for by Tyco. He began collecting art and antique furniture. Living the life of a corporate titan would be his undoing.

Tyco Business

Starting out as a seller of fire protection systems decades earlier, Tyco expanded its reach in the 1990s into other lines of business that the company claimed were complementary to its traditional operations. Between 1993 and 1996, Kozlowski acquired sixty-five companies for Tyco, and Tyco's stock rose 30 percent each year during that period. One acquisition was Kendall

International Inc., a maker of disposable medical products, which was acquired in 1994 through a $1.4 billion stock swap. Other acquisitions included Inbrand Corp., which manufactured disposable products for adult incontinence, ADT Ltd., an electronic security systems company, and Keystone International Inc., a manufacturer of industrial valves. Tyco also acquired the underwater telecommunications cable operations of AT&T Corp.

The pace of Kozlowski's purchases accelerated in 1997. During that year, Tyco made twenty-eight acquisitions valued at $10.7 billion. Its share price jumped 50 percent, a result that was aided by an announcement from Kozlowski that the firm's earnings estimates were being revised upward. Kozlowski was granted more than $50 million in Tyco options as a reward for his efforts. Kozlowski continued on his acquisition binge. In his first six years as chief executive officer of Tyco, Kozlowski made 110 acquisitions. Between 1997 and 1999, he made $30 billion in acquisitions. One large purchase involved AMP Inc., which was acquired by Tyco for $11.3 billion in 1998, after a bidding war with Allied Signal. This acquisition boosted Tyco's revenues to $22 billion in 1999. By then, Kozlowski was becoming a corporate legend for his ability to cut costs and increase earnings, while successfully digesting the company's many acquisitions.

Tyco's Problems Emerge

One analyst likened Kozlowski to a corporate Babe Ruth, and he was said to have a cultlike following among investors. Kozlowski was noted for his conservative earnings projections at Tyco. One analyst, however, was questioning Tyco's accounting practices as early as 1998. In October 1999, a money manager in Dallas, David W. Tice, criticized Tyco's financial reports, claiming that the company was taking excessive charges in order to manage future earnings and that it was concealing a decline in cash flow by delaying payments. That caused Tyco's stock to drop 10 percent before its trading was halted temporarily on the New York Stock Exchange (NYSE). After trading resumed, Tyco's stock fell nearly another 10 percent. Tyco then announced that it was buying back 20 million of its own shares, which was a popular device for management to support a declining stock price, but one that drained the corporate treasury. That effort failed to rally the stock, which dropped another 23 percent on volume of 114 million shares after the company disclosed that the SEC had begun an informal inquiry of its accounting practices. By then, Tyco had shed some $40 billion in its stock valuation.

In order to restore faith in the company's management, Kozlowski declared that future option grants to executives would be tied to earnings increases, as well as to the company's stock price. It is doubtful whether this change had much effect on the company's performance, but the situation stabilized in June 2000, after Tyco announced that it was restating some of its financial accounts at the request of the SEC. Those changes had little effect on the company's results, and the fact that the SEC brought no formal charges was viewed by many as exonerating Tyco. Tyco's general counsel, Mark A. Belnick, was given a $12 million bonus by Kozlowski for convincing the SEC not to file suit, thereby rallying the company's stock price. Kozlowski was also well rewarded for dealing with the crisis. His compensation for 2000 was $205 million, and he was given $485 million in restricted stock to boot.

Tyco resumed its acquisition binge by acquiring Mallinckrodt Inc., a health care company, for $3.24 billion in stock and C.R. Bard, a maker of medical devices, for $3.13 billion. Tyco purchased the CIT Group, a commercial finance company, for $9.2 billion in cash and stock. The Dai-Ichi Kango Bank of Japan was paid $2.49 billion of that amount for its holdings in the CIT Group. The bank insisted that it be paid in cash rather than Tyco stock. A Tyco outside director, Frank E. Walsh, was paid $10 million for helping to arrange this acquisition. A charity for which he acted as trustee was given another $10 million by Tyco. Walsh was on Tyco's compensation committee and was a friend of the head of the CIT Group, Albert Gamper Jr. The CIT purchase was a surprise to Wall Street because it was outside Tyco's line of business, and Kozlowski had long touted his acquisition strategy of not going outside Tyco's core business structure.

Tyco spent $19 billion in 2001 on 350 acquisitions. At the end of 2001, Tyco had 270,000 employees worldwide and reported revenues of $36 billion for the year. Its widespread operations were carried out through 2,342 subsidiaries. Among other things, Tyco was one of the world's largest suppliers of undersea fiber-optic cable and had agreed to lay a fiber-optic system across the Pacific to Japan for Global Crossing, another financial disaster then in the making.

Tyco's Problems Grow

Renewed questions concerning Tyco's accounting were raised as 2001 ended. David Tice continued his criticism, and short sellers were focusing on how Tyco treated goodwill from its acquisitions. Those traders claimed that Tyco was inflating its goodwill accounts. Tyco treated almost the entire cost of its acquisitions as goodwill on its balance sheet, an amount totaling $30 billion. That criticism, and the reduced earnings announced by the company as 2002 began, caused a 20 percent drop in Tyco's stock price. In an effort to rescue the situation, Kozlowski announced on January 23, 2002, that Tyco would be split into four separate companies and that the CIT Group acquired in the prior year would be sold off. This plan of attack was being used by other companies in financial trouble as the economy declined.

This announcement caused a further sharp drop in the price of Tyco's stock, which fell by 43 percent during January 2002. Kozlowski claimed that the company's stock price decline was the result of fallout from the Enron scandal, which was then in full bloom. Although Kozlowski stated that he rarely sold his

Tyco stock, he and the company's chief financial officer, Mark Swartz, sold $100 million in Tyco stock during the company's fiscal year ending in 2001. Kozlowski returned Tyco shares valued at $70 million to satisfy a portion of the $88 million loaned to him by the company. The shares sold back to the company by these two executives were replaced with more stock options. That raised further concerns about the company when disclosed in January 2002. Kozlowski and Swartz then announced they were buying back 500,000 Tyco shares with their own money because it was a great value at its reduced price.

Tyco faced more trouble as February began. The ratings agencies reduced its credit rating, which shut the company off from the commercial paper market. That raised concern that the company would be faced with a liquidity crisis, and the company's stock resumed its free fall. At that point, Tyco's stock had lost 50 percent of its value for the year. Kozlowski then disclosed that Tyco had drawn down $7.4 billion on its credit lines, but asserted that the company would have plenty of cash left over after paying off its commercial paper obligations, which could not be rolled over as the result of the ratings downgrade. The company also admitted that its earnings would not meet projections. Further disclosures came to light concerning stock sales by Kozlowski and Swartz. They had sold Tyco stock totaling over $500 million over the last thirty months. Kozlowski took home $330 million of that amount. He had claimed a few months before this disclosure that his entire net worth was in Tyco stock.

In April 2002, Kozlowski announced that the plan to break up the company into four independent concerns was being abandoned, but that Tyco would continue to try to sell the CIT Group. Kozlowski conceded that this aborted plan was a mistake on his part. The sale of the CIT Group was later accomplished through a public offering, as a result of which Tyco had to take a $6 billion charge against earnings. Tyco laid off 7,000 employees. Kozlowski was now becoming a subject of unfavorable press, losing his Babe Ruth image.

The Scandal Begins

The Tyco scandal commenced in earnest at the beginning of June 2002 when the company reported that Kozlowski was under investigation for evading $13 million in New York sales taxes on paintings that he had purchased for a Fifth Avenue apartment that was maintained for his personal use by Tyco. That apartment cost Tyco $18.5 million. The paintings included a Monet and a Renoir. The purchase price of the Monet was $3.9 million. The paintings were bought in New York and sent to Tyco's headquarters in New Hampshire in order to avoid paying New York sales tax, which was inapplicable to goods sent out of state. The paintings were then returned to the New York apartment. In some cases, empty boxes were sent to New Hampshire, and the paintings were taken directly to Kozlowski's apartment. Kozlowski resigned on June 3, 2002, after he was informed that the district attorney's office in Manhattan would be indicting him for evading more than $1 million in sales taxes.

The sales tax scheme used for Kozlowski's paintings was not new. In the 1980s, some high-end jewelers, Bulgari, Cartier, and Van Cleef & Arpels, were charged with sending empty jewelry boxes out of state so customers could evade the sales taxes on items they had purchased. Revillon Inc., a high-fashion furrier, was charged with shipping empty boxes out of state that were supposed to contain fur coats purchased by customers. Revillon was required to pay $2 million in taxes and penalties for this conduct, and two employees were fined small amounts ($250 and $500). Van Cleef & Arpels paid $5 million; Cartier paid $2.2 million; and Bulgari $1.9 million. No one was sent to jail and prosecutions were brought only against the stores responsible for collecting the tax, rather than the customer. With the Enron mob in full cry, however, all rules were off.

The Scandal Broadens

Tyco's stock fell to $16.05 after Kozlowski's resignation, down some $60 for the year. As the scandal broke, Tyco retained the services of William McLucas at the law firm of Wilmer Cutler Pickering in Washington, D.C. McLucas and his law firm were the ones who prepared the Powers report, which machine-gunned the dead body of Enron. McLucas was shoved aside from such a role at Tyco, however, after Tyco's general counsel, Mark Belnick, resigned on June 10, 2002. David Boies was hired by a special committee of the board to replace McLucas as the company's Inspector Javert.

The Tyco board of directors announced that Tyco was suing Belnick for taking a $20 million bonus not approved by the board of directors and for drawing down loans totaling over $14 million through a Tyco program set up to aid employees who moved from New Hampshire to New York when the company moved its headquarters. Belnick, who already lived in New York, used $10 million from those loans to buy a vacation home in Utah and $4 million for a Central Park apartment. Before coming to Tyco, Belnick had been a well-respected partner in the New York law firm of Paul, Weiss, Rifkind, Wharton & Garrison. Belnick worked for Arthur Liman at that law firm, assisting in the unsuccessful defense of Michael Milken, the 1980s junk bond king, as well as Liman's work for the congressional committee investigating the Iran-Contra affair during the Reagan administration.

Edward Breen, the former president of Motorola, was appointed to take over the management of Tyco. Breen was paid $3.5 million to rescue Tyco and was promised large stock option grants if he was successful. But the rain of bad news at Tyco continued with the announcement on July 23, 2002, that the company had lost $2.32 billion in the prior quarter. Most of that loss was attributable to Tyco's sale of CIT Group. After being on the job for less than a week, Breen fired Mark Swartz, Tyco's chief financial officer. Swartz received a severance package valued at $44.8 million, but had to give up an additional $91 million he was due under his employment contract with Tyco. The firing of Swartz resulted in widened investigations of Tyco's financial statements and further undermined confidence in the company. More credibility was lost with Kozlowski's widening problems.

Kozlowski's Indictment

Kozlowski's indictment for sales tax evasion was scandalous but that was only the beginning. He was subject to a further indictment a few weeks later for tampering with evidence. The Manhattan district attorney widened his investigation to examine whether Tyco had been paying for Kozlowski's personal expenses. That inquiry proved fruitful, and Kozlowski was indicted on September 12, 2002, charged with looting $600 million from Tyco. Those funds allowed him to purchase a $29 million vacation home in Boca Raton, Florida, a $7 million apartment to settle divorce claims from his ex-wife, and expensive jewelry from Tiffany's and Harry Winston, including a $5 million diamond ring. The New York apartment used by Kozlowski had needed furnishing and refurbishment, which was paid for by Tyco. Those purchases included an instantly famous $6,000 shower curtain, a $2,200 wastebasket, a $15,000 "dog" umbrella stand, a $17,000 antique traveling toilet box, a $6,300 antique sewing basket, two sets of sheets on sale for $5,960, and a pincushion for $445. Included in the indictment was the purchase of $2,900 worth of coat hangers for the New York apartment. This last purchase was doubly disloyal since Tyco controlled some 80 percent of the plastic clothes hanger market. In total, Tyco spent $30 million to buy and decorate the apartment for Kozlowski. This included the cost of the paintings on which sales tax was not paid. His lawyers contended that Tyco properly paid for the apartment and furnishings because Kozlowski used it for business. He needed the apartment to impress other executives with whom he was negotiating multibillion acquisitions for Tyco.

Kozlowski used Tyco funds for other expenditures, including $2.1 million spent on a birthday party for his wife, Karen, a former waitress he met at a restaurant near Tyco's offices. That party was held on the island of Sardinia, and singer Jimmy Buffett was imported for her entertainment at a cost of $250,000. That bacchanal included paid models dressed in Roman togas and an ice sculpture of Michangelo's *David,* from which Stolichnaya vodka flowed through his famous organ for guests to fill their glasses. A twenty-minute video of that party was shown at Kozlowski's trial, causing a sensation in the press. The cost of the party totaled $70,000 per person, and Kozlowski charged one-half of its costs to Tyco, on the theory that the guests included employees and a board meeting for a subsidiary was held during the six-day event. The board meeting, however, was largely attended by speakerphone because many board members were not on the island.

Kozlowski was further accused of giving millions to charity in his own name even though Tyco supplied the funds. In a bit of silliness, the indictment accused Kozlowski of exchanging gifts of wine with Phua K. Young, a Merrill Lynch analyst who was friendly to the company. Kozlowski even used Tyco funds to hire private investigators at Kroll & Associates to investigate Young's fiancée in order to assure Young that she was worthy of him. Young, who was paid a salary of $4.5 million by Merrill Lynch, was accused of misconduct by the National Association of Security Dealers (NASD) for, among other things, accepting champagne from Kozlowski and for taking rides on the Tyco jet. Merrill Lynch executives testified that Merrill Lynch had been given lead underwriter status in a $2.1 billion bond offering by Tyco after it hired Young, who had been promoting Tyco stock. Young was fined $225,000 by the NASD and suspended from the securities business for one year.

Mark Swartz was indicted along with Kozlowski on September 12, 2002. He and Kozlowski were charged with stealing $170 million from Tyco by taking bonuses that were not approved by the board of directors. Both executives were charged with larceny for realizing $430 million in stock sales that were inflated in price because the defendants had not properly disclosed the company's finances. Mark Belnick, Tyco's general counsel, was indicted for not disclosing his loans from Tyco on the Tyco officers' and directors' questionnaire that called for disclosure of nonroutine transactions. The indictment charged that this omission violated a New York statute prohibiting falsification of business records. A subsequent indictment charged that the $12 million bonus received by Belnick after he convinced the SEC not to bring charges was theft because it had not been authorized by the board of directors.

Although they posed no physical danger to anyone, all three of the former Tyco executives were given their perp walk and arraigned in handcuffs. Despite the fact that their flight risk was less than zero, bail was set at a whopping $100 million for Kozlowski and $50 million for Swartz, which meant that they had to post 10 percent of that amount with a bail bondsman to remain free. The government sought to keep the defendants jailed by claiming that their assets were all looted funds that should be frozen pending trial. This required Kozlowski's ex-wife to bail him out, and Swartz's family put up the money for him. Piling on is not prohibited by prosecutorial ethics, so federal prosecutors jumped in and charged Swartz with tax fraud for failing to report the forgiveness of $12.5 million in loans from Tyco as income. At the same time, Tyco's new management had decided to "reverse" forgiveness of those same loans and was demanding repayment from Swartz even though his assets were frozen.

Restructuring

Several members of the Tyco board of directors resigned or were replaced. Former outside director Frank Walsh admitted that he violated the New York Martin Act by accepting the $20 million finder's fee for the CIT Group acquisition. He agreed to repay that money from his own funds, including the amount that went to the charity, and was fined $2.5 million. An internal report filed by David Boies charged that Tyco had been manipulating its financial results under Kozlowski. Although Boies had earlier asserted that Tyco did not have other significant accounting irregularities, the company announced that it was restating $382 million in earnings in prior years. The Boies report faulted the company's internal controls and corporate governance procedures. He could not resist adding a further piece of sensationalism, disclosing a $110,000 hotel bill for Kozlowski during a two-week trip to London.

Tyco had more bad news. Its new chief executive officer, Edward Breen, announced lower than expected earnings after he cleaned house. Breen said there would be a further write-off for the company's fiber-optic network, bringing such charges for that network to over $4 billion. The company was able to raise $5.25 billion in January 2003 through a sale of convertible bonds in a private placement and through an additional line of credit, but continued to have problems as earnings declined by 50 percent in the prior quarter. A charge of $265 million was taken for the company's fire and security operations, and the head of that unit was fired. Tyco was further embarrassed in May 2003 when it disclosed $1.2 billion more in accounting problems, and several more executives were fired. In June 2003, the company made a further restatement of $528 million and conceded that it might have to restate $630 million more. In November of that year, the company began cutting 7,200 jobs and closing 200 facilities and sold its undersea fiber-optic network for $130 million, which was $3.5 billion less than what Tyco had paid for it.

A shareholder proposal to move the company's official headquarters back to the United States from Bermuda was defeated. The Tyco shareholders did pass a motion requiring their approval of any executive severance packages, a response to the deal with Swartz and a slap at Breen's management. The shareholders voted to retain PricewaterhouseCoopers as the company's auditors, but the accounting firm replaced the audit partner on the account, Richard Scalzo. The SEC permanently barred Scalzo from auditing public companies. The SEC charged that he knew that Tyco maintained a general reserve fund to meet unanticipated expenses and to smooth earnings. Scalzo was also charged with not requiring disclosure of the bonuses paid to Kozlowski.

Tyco was struggling with all this bad publicity, but its stock price doubled after its plunge from the announcements of Kozlowski's sins. The new executives at Tyco were given large bonuses in 2004 for their success, amounting to many millions of dollars. Tyco was then listed as number fifty-two in the list of the world's largest companies. The now famous apartment used by Kozlowski was sold by Tyco in 2004 for $21 million, shower curtain not included.

The Trial

The New York district attorney's office deferred prosecution of Kozlowski on the sales tax charges pending trial on the grand larceny counts. The prosecutors also conceded in court that PricewaterhouseCoopers had approved the handling of many of the transactions that were the subject of the grand larceny indictment and had advised Tyco executives that the transactions need not be disclosed in filings with the SEC. The government prosecutors had some difficulty in articulating the theory of their case in the light of those revelations, resorting to sensationalism and delighting the media for days by reveling in Kozlowski's excesses. The showing of the Sardinia film in particular caused quite a stir in the press. Two Tyco employees called as witnesses were forced to confess that they had had affairs with Kozlowski. Yet even these tawdry disclosures seemed to wear thin after a time.

Kozlowski did not testify at his trial, but Swartz gave an impassioned nine-day defense of his actions when he took the stand. Swartz asserted that Kozlowski and the board of directors had approved his actions. David Boies was brought in to undercut Swartz's testimony on the $12.5 million bonus that Boies had discussed with Swartz. Boies testified that Swartz had admitted that the payment was a "mistake," which conflicted with Swartz's claim that the transaction had been properly approved. Swartz then resumed the stand to try to explain away Boies's testimony. The judge in the case dismissed organized crime charges brought against Kozlowski and Swartz at the close of evidence. Those were the most serious charges in the case, but multiple counts of other charges remained, including grand larceny.

The trial of Kozlowski and Swartz lasted six months. The jury deliberations soon turned into another media circus after a juror complained that the other jurors were not being open-minded about the innocence of the defendants. The judge was given a note from the jury that said the atmosphere was "poisonous." Juror No. 4 was holding out for a not guilty verdict. She was identified in the press as Ruth Jordan, a seventy-nine-year-old former teacher and law school graduate. Jordan, according to one juror, had stated during deliberations that a "Waspy" board of directors at Tyco had turned on Swartz and Kozlowski and served the "Polack and the Jew on a platter for a D.A. eager to make an example of somebody—anybody—for the corporate greed of the late 90s."[19] Jordan ignited further controversy in the press when she apparently made an "OK" hand gesture to the defendants when leaving the courtroom after the jury met with the judge. That gesture was given full front-page coverage in the *New York Post*.

The defendants demanded a mistrial, contending that Jordan was being put under pressure to vote for a guilty verdict. The judge denied that motion and sent the jury back for more deliberations. A mistrial was finally declared after Jordan became the subject of heated attacks on the Internet and anonymous communications by phone and letter, evidencing the hysteria of the Enron era. In interviews afterwards, the jurors expressed themselves as being unimpressed by Kozlowski's excesses. Rather, they were focused on accounting issues. Jordan was interviewed on the CBS *60 Minutes* program and expressed the view that the defendants were innocent. The trial judge set a retrial date for Kozlowski and Swartz in 2005. The judge excluded the sales tax charges from that trial, noting that such charges were historically brought only against the companies that failed to charge and pay the tax. Shortly before his retrial, Kozlowski gave an interview that was reported on the front page of the Sunday *New York Times*. He protested his innocence and claimed that he was unaware of the $6,000 spent on the shower curtain.

Belnick's Trial

Mark Belnick was tried not long after Kozlowski and Swartz's mistrial. Belnick presented an aggressive defense in a trial that lasted several weeks. He testified that Kozlowski had authorized the payments he received. This raised a technical issue of common law as to whether Kozlowski had the "apparent" authority to grant such bonuses and other compensation. The payments to Belnick, while quite large, did not on their face appear extraordinary in the context of a multibillion-dollar company where large compensation packages were being given to other executives. Further, Belnick's action in heading off the SEC's investigation had saved the company's shareholders hundreds of millions of dollars in losses from the sharp drop in the price of their stock that would have followed such an action, to say nothing of the millions of dollars of attorney fees and fines that would have resulted. In that context, the bonuses and loans were within the range of reasonable. With respect to the charge of not disclosing his Tyco loans on the officers' and directors' questionnaire, Belnick asserted that Mark Swartz advised him that the loans need not be disclosed because they were routine.

After five days of deliberation, the jury acquitted Belnick of all charges. A derivative suit against Tyco that had sought money from Kozlowski and other Tyco officers and its auditor, PricewaterhouseCoopers, was dismissed. The judge concluded that the law of Bermuda, the place of Tyco's incorporation, did not allow such suits. A class action suit that sought damages on behalf of shareholders was allowed to proceed.

The retrial of Dennis Kozlowski and Mark Swartz began on January 18, 2005. The prosecutors presented a more restrained case, only briefly mentioning the birthday party on Sardinia serenaded by Jimmy Buffett, the long-time friend and uncertain relative of Warren Buffett. The $6,000 shower curtain also seemed to have disappeared, perhaps because Tyco had made a profit on the sale of the apartment. The prosecutors focused their case on showing that the defendants had not received appropriate board approval for large payouts they received. Several directors testified for the government on that point One witness, Donna Sharpless, Tyco's director of executive compensation, also testified that Swartz and Kozlowski had deferred large amounts of their cash bonuses between 1998 and 2001 into retirement plans and into insurance policies, which had the effect of reducing the amount of compensation that Tyco reported to shareholders in its proxy statements. An auditor for PricewaterhouseCoopers testified, however, that he had been informed of the bonuses paid to Kozlowski and Swartz. There was some other good news for Kozlowski. A New York court ruled that Tyco's director and officer insurance coverage was responsible for paying his legal bills.

In a surprise move, Kozlowski took the stand in his own defense, testifying that the compensation committee had approved his payouts and denying any wrongdoing. Kozlowski asserted that he had overlooked the omission of $25 million in loan forgiveness from his income tax records. After eleven days of deliberations, the jury convicted Kozlowski and Swartz on nearly all counts. One juror was a holdout but finally succumbed to pressure from her peers. The basis for the verdict was proclaimed in a front page headline in the *New York Times* on June 19, 2005: "Big Paychecks Are Exhibit A."

6. Fiduciary Duties and Corporate Governance Principles

Corporate Governance

The looting of Tyco International Ltd. was a failure of the full disclosure system mandated by the federal securities laws, but it also raised questions as to the efficacy of corporate governance standards created by state law. A review of the development and regulation of corporations by the states is necessary to understand those issues.

Joint-Stock Companies

The American corporation traces its history to the English joint-stock companies that were modeled after the joint-stock schemes for the Irish plantations and that were used to America and explore much of the rest of the world beginning in the sixteenth century. Financial historian John Gordon has asserted that: "Next to the nation-state itself, the joint-stock company was the most important organizational development of the Renaissance and, like the nation-state, made the modern world possible." Corporate governance concerns soon arose with those companies. They were feared as monopolies in colonial times because the royal charter or patent under which a joint-stock company operated excluded competition in defined areas of the world. Another problem, and one that lingers today, was that sales of stock in the joint-stock companies were often accomplished by less than truthful advertising, the London Company being one example of a company known for such practices.

The concept of a corporation as a separate juridical entity raised further concerns. John Pollexfen, a member of Parliament, complained in the 1690s that corporations "have bodies, but it is said they have no souls; if no souls, no consciences." The South Sea Bubble in 1720 was an occasion that aroused special concern about corporate governance. Antipathy for the speculation that occurred during that bubble haunts finance in America even today. The bubble began after the South Sea Company took over the public debt of England in exchange for the exclusive right to conduct trade with South America. That plan excited much speculation in the stock of the South Sea Company and provided an opportunity for John Blunt, an English merchant, and the Sword Blade Bank to manipulate its share prices upward. The price of South Sea stock rose from £128 to £1,050 in less than a year. Similar success was sought by other enterprises, many of which were of a speculative nature and included everything from dubious funeral and insurance schemes to a business "for carrying on an undertaking of great importance, but nobody to know what it is."[1] The Mississippi Bubble was engineered in France at about the same time by John Law. It involved speculation in the stock of the Compagnie des Indes, which had control over the Louisiana territory. Both bubbles burst, causing much scandal and large losses to speculators who had previously reaped large profits.

In order to limit the growth of the speculative enterprises appearing during the South Sea Bubble, Parliament passed legislation prohibiting the operation of corporations unless they held a charter granted by the crown, a prerogative that Lord Coke had claimed in 1612 resided with the king. This legislation resulted in the pricking of the South Sea Bubble. Share prices dropped dramatically from £1,050 to £150 over a four-month period, ruining many prominent investors, including Sir Isaac Newton. The chancellor of the exchequer was sent to the Tower of London and the postmaster general took poison for his role in promoting the South Sea Company. The directors of the South Sea Company were arrested and their assets were seized, a process that would be applied to the mangers of Enron and other firms involved in the scandals arising after the bursting of the stock market bubble in 2000. The English bubble act did not stop market manias, as evidenced by a canal bubble that occurred late in the eighteenth century. The bubble act was repealed in England in 1825, paving the way for more speculative operations. As noted by Lord Henry Cockburn, there was a joint-stock company "epidemic" in England in 1826 that included the creation of a company that was formed for the purpose of organizing and promoting joint-stock companies. That event was followed later in the century by a railroad mania.

The South Sea Bubble Act was imposed on the American colonies in 1741. That gave rise to controversy over which colonial authorities had the power to issue corporate charters. As a result, colonial charters were limited mostly to government units, charities, libraries, and educational institutions like Dartmouth, William and Mary, Yale, and Harvard. As Supreme Court justice Louis Brandeis later noted, "Although the value of this instrumentality in commerce and industry was fully recognized, incorporation for business was commonly denied long after it had been freely granted for religious, educational, and charitable purposes by corporations."[2] Several real estate ventures, such as the Virginia, Ohio, and Loyal companies, were given land patents during the colonial period. There were also some pre-Revolution fountain societies for providing drinking water, companies that built toll bridges and roads, and some fire insurance and manufacturing schemes that acted in a corporate capacity, but most commercial firms operated as partnerships or proprietorships. In all, there were about forty commercial corporations in America before the Revolution, but they were "puny institutions," in the words of Professor Eugene Rostow at the Yale Law School.[3] The Revolution freed the states to issue their own charters. By 1800, over 350 commercial corporations had been chartered, some of which remain in existence today, including the Bank of New York and the Revere Copper Company.

Early Corporate Governance Concerns

Philosophers were questioning the role of business and the pursuit of wealth as the corporation appeared on the scene in America:

> In the late 18th century, when Utilitarianism was still young, there were a group of "Christian Utilitarians" who . . . mixed their utilitarian concerns with religion. Led by Archdeacon William Paley, the Anglican author of many influential treatises in the 19th century, they forged a theological link between orthodox Christianity and vulgar utility with its secular preoccupation with human happiness. (Our own Thomas Jefferson expressed a common concern by rendering John Locke's "pursuit of property" into "the pursuit of happiness.") However, most of the classical Utilitarians were followers of David Hume, Jeremy Bentham, and, later, John Stuart Mill, all of whom were ardent secularists as well as materialists. As such, they distinguished sharply between the religious, moral, natural, and political sanctions, focusing their attention on the latter. Today, their descendants are members of the Law and Economics movement (though they speak of "costs and benefits" rather than "pleasures and pains").[4]

Corporate governance was elevated as an area of academic study in 1776 with the publication of Adam Smith's *An Inquiry Into the Nature and Causes of the Wealth of Nations*. Smith described the business of a joint-stock company as being managed by a "court of directors," the equivalent of a modern board of directors. Those directors were subject to "the control of a general court of proprietors," a reference to a meeting of the shareholders.[5] Smith notes that a reform measure then recently passed by Parliament had extended the term in office of the twenty-four-member court of directors of the East India Company from one to four years. Those terms were staggered so that six new directors were elected each year, and those leaving office could not be reelected in the following year. This assured that board positions did not become an entitlement. Today, about 60 percent of modern American corporations have staggered boards of directors, but their purpose is the opposite that of the East India Company. Staggered boards are now used to entrench management by assuring that control will be relinquished only over a term of years when a hostile takeover is attempted.

The East India Company had other issues. The Boston Tea party was a protest over the monopoly given to that company for the importation of tea into America. In 1783, the government in England fell after the House of Lords rejected a bill that would have "improved" the East India Company's corporate governance structure by replacing its private management with a board of seven commissioners appointed by Parliament. William Pitt, the younger, led the opposition to that legislation in the House of Commons and became prime minister after he charged that the act was an illegal seizure of private property and an "exercise of tyranny."

Adam Smith raised some practical concerns about the governance of corporations. He noted that corporate directors "being the managers rather of other people's money than their own, it cannot well be expected, that they should watch over it with the same anxious vigilance with which the partners in a private copartnery frequently watch over their own," and that "negligence and profusion, therefore, must prevail, more or less, in the management of the affairs of such a company."[6] This concern would be echoed by American observers of corporations. In 1833, William Gouge asserted that corporate officers managed the affairs of their company more carelessly and expensively than an individual proprietor did. Gouge asked, "[W]hat would be the condition of the merchant who should trust everything to his clerks, or the farmer who should trust everything to his laborers?"[7] The law and economics school of thought that developed late in the twentieth century also focused on these "agency costs."

The American courts had to struggle with the role of the corporation as a separate legal entity. This issue was resolved by 1819 when that role was defined by Justice Joseph Story in his concurring opinion in *Trustees of Dartmouth College v. Woodward:*

> An aggregate corporation at common law is a collection of individuals united into one collective body, under a special name, and possessing certain immunities, privileges, and capacities in its collective character, which do not belong to the natural persons composing it. Among other things it possesses the capacity of perpetual succession, and of acting by the collected vote or will of its component members, and of suing and being sued in all things touching its corporate rights and duties. It is, in short, an artificial person, existing in contemplation of law, and endowed with certain powers and franchises that, though they must be exercised through the medium of its natural members, are yet considered as subsisting in the corporation itself, as distinctly as if it were a real personage. Hence, such a corporation may sue and be sued by its own members; and may contract with them in the same manner as with any strangers.[8]

Charter Wars

The United States Constitution left the power to charter corporations to the state legislatures. President George Washington's cabinet split over whether the federal government retained the "reserved" power to issue a federal charter to incorporate a business after Alexander Hamilton recommended such a charter for the Bank of the United States. That dispute pitted Hamilton against

Thomas Jefferson. Hamilton prevailed, but the issue created much enmity and uncovered a fault line in American politics that exists today between opponents and proponents of big business.

The chartering of the Manhattan Company furthered the political rift and created bad feelings between Aaron Burr and Hamilton. Hamilton wrote the charter for the Bank of New York (BONY) and led a fight in the New York legislature over its approval, a process that took seven years. Hamilton assisted Burr in obtaining a charter for the Manhattan Company, which Burr claimed was being formed to supply pure drinking water to the city as a measure to suppress yellow fever epidemics. That was a ruse but served to speed approval of the charter for the Manhattan Company, even while the BONY charter languished before the legislature.

An obscure provision in the Manhattan Company charter allowed the company to use its excess capital to engage "in the purchase of public or other stocks, or in any money transactions or operations not inconsistent with the laws and the constitution of the State of New York."[9] Under that authority, the Manhattan Company opened an "office of discount and deposit"—in other words, a bank. Both institutions survive today. BONY, which started as a private bank in 1784, is still listed on the New York Stock Exchange (NYSE). The Manhattan Company merged with the Chase National Bank in the twentieth century to become the Chase Manhattan Bank, now JPMorgan Chase, the institution that played a key supporting role in the Enron scandal.

Fear of corporate power was widespread in nineteenth-century America. As explained by Supreme Court justice Louis Brandeis, himself a leading critic of large corporations:

> There was a sense of some insidious menace inherent in large aggregations of capital, particularly when held by corporations. So at first the corporate privilege was granted sparingly; and only when the grant seemed necessary in order to procure for the community some specific benefit otherwise unobtainable. It was denied because of fear. Fear of encroachment upon the liberties and opportunities of the individual. Fear of the subjection of labor to capital. Fear of monopoly. Fear that the absorption of capital by corporations, and their perpetual life, might bring evils similar to those which attended mortmain.[10]

The British Mortmain Act of 1736 referred to by Justice Brandeis restricted transfers of land to the church and other charitable organizations in order to prevent property from being removed forever from heirs and public use. Early corporate charters in America reflected a similar concern by limiting the life of corporations to fixed terms of between twenty and fifty years. Such a restriction gave rise to the epic political battle between Henry Clay and President Andrew Jackson over the renewal of the charter of the second Bank of the United States (BUS) in the 1830s. Jackson was influenced by the South Sea Bubble in opposing renewal of the charter. He stated that "ever since I read the history of the South Sea Bubble I have been afraid of banks." He thought BUS was a threat to the American economy, even calling it a "monster." Jackson feared the "concentration of money,"[11] a refrain heard periodically throughout American history, right down to the 2004 Democratic convention in Boston. Banking was especially suspect in the early years of the republic. Robert Potter, a North Carolina legislator who had castrated two men he mistakenly thought were having an affair with his wife, sought to stop banking altogether in that state in 1829. His proposal was defeated only by a tie vote in the North Carolina legislature.

Jackson was concerned with corporate governance at BUS. It had a large number of foreign shareholders. Those shareholders could not vote, and Jackson feared that this would place control of this powerful institution into the hands of a small group of Northern financiers. Henry Clay came to the defense of the bank, but lost this bitter fight with Jackson after the Senate sustained Jackson's veto of the bill chartering the bank. Jackson then transferred federal deposits from BUS to the "pet" banks owned by his supporters. Clay had the Senate censure Jackson for that action, but Jackson protested and the censure was expunged, handing Clay a defeat that ended his own presidential aspirations. Daniel Webster, a preeminent corporate lawyer as well as senator and statesman, had come to the aid of Clay and BUS during the fight over its charter. He defended corporations eloquently, asserting that they tended "not only to increase property, but to equalize it, to diffuse it, to scatter the advantages among the many, and to give content, cheerfulness, and animation to all classes of the social system."[12] Of course, Webster's eloquence did not save the bank or Clay's career.

General Incorporation Laws

Another restriction on corporations was that they could perform no business that was not defined in their charter. Any acts outside the scope of the charter were considered to be ultra vires and void. The strictness of the application of that doctrine is well illustrated in a North Carolina case in which certain of the shareholders claimed that the Greenville and Raleigh Plank Road Company was acting ultra vires in purchasing stage coaches and seeking a contract to deliver the mail over a plank road being built by the company. The corporation had been chartered by the state legislature in 1850 for "the purpose of effecting a communication by means of a plank road from within the limits of Greenville in Pitt County, to the city of Raleigh," plank roads then being a national mania. The court found this charter did not permit a stagecoach or mail business. The court said that, if the power of building the road were to imply the power for such activities, the corporation could engage in all matter of dangerous activities such as "buying and selling horses, cattle, or produce, under the suggestion that the road would be subservient to these purposes."[13]

In response to concerns that charters were being granted or denied through corrupt practices in the state legislatures, a concern well illustrated by the chartering of the Manhattan Company, the states gradually began moving the chartering process away from the legislatures. This removal was accomplished through "general" incorporation laws that allowed incorporation without a special charter from the legislature. New York passed such an act in 1811, but it was limited in scope. In 1822, the New York constitution was amended to require the consent of two-thirds of each house to issue a charter. That constitution was amended again in 1846 to remove the process entirely from the legislature. Other states followed the New York approach. "By 1850 a general law permitting incorporation for a limited business purpose had become common; and after 1875 extension of the privilege to every lawful business became so."[14]

The ultra vires doctrine remained a problem, so corporate lawyers attempted to describe every conceivable business in corporate charters. This resulted in prolix and sometimes ridiculous charters. Consider this excerpt from just one of twenty similar paragraphs in the charter of the Uniroyal Corporation, a company best known for its tire manufacturing:

> The objects for which said company is formed are:
> 1. To manufacture, formulate, construct, grow, raise, produce, mine, develop, purchase, lease, buy or acquire in any other manner, import, export, convert, combine, compound, spin, twist, knit, weave, dye, grind, mix, process, introduce, improve, exploit, repair, design, treat or use in any other manner to lease, sell, assign, exchange, transfer or dispose of in any other manner, and generally to deal and trade in and with any or all of the following:
> (a) rubber, balata, gutta percha, all other related or unrelated natural gums, artificially prepared rubber, reclaims of such rubbers and other gums; raw or processed natural latex, artificially prepared aqueous dispersions of crude or reclaimed rubber, aqueous dispersions of synthetic rubber or of rubber-like or other materials, and equivalents, derivatives and substitutes of any of the foregoing, whether now or hereafter known or used in industry, and all other commodities and materials competent to be put to any use similar to any of the uses of any of them, and articles, goods or commodities produced in whole or in part from any thereof or from the use of any thereof. . . .

By 1875, many states were allowing corporation for any "lawful purpose," obviating most concerns with ultra vires, but early state laws also imposed limitations on the size of corporations. New York initially limited the maximum authorized capital of corporations to $100,000, raising that amount to $5 million in 1890. In Massachusetts, the maximum amount of capital for some businesses was initially set at $5,000. Capital restrictions placed on corporate charters were gradually lifted or removed entirely as states began to compete for corporate business.

Large corporations were still constrained by state statutes that prohibited one corporation from holding the stock of another corporation. The Standard Oil Company, which was chartered in Ohio, tried to circumvent that restriction by creating a trust in which a board of trustees was assigned control of the stock of several companies, allowing those companies to be operated as a single unit. The trustees were elected by the holders of certificates of ownership in the trust, including John and William Rockefeller and Henry Flagler. However, an Ohio court ruled in 1892 that this trust arrangement was improper because it required Standard Oil to surrender its corporate authority to the trustees. Fortunately for Standard Oil, an alternative had recently been enacted in another state.

Modern Corporate Law

In order to raise revenues, New Jersey enacted a corporate law in 1888 that allowed its corporations to own the stock of other companies, giving rise to "holding" companies that could operate in several states. New Jersey announced that it was dedicated to making its corporate laws as friendly as possible to corporations. This led to a mass chartering of businesses from other states in New Jersey, particularly those from New York. New Jersey's flexible corporate laws encouraged enough chartering activity to allow the state to pay for its operations almost entirely from corporate franchise fees. West Virginia tried to compete for that business but lost out when it increased its franchise fees. The New Jersey statute came at a most opportune time. The American economy was a national one by the end of the nineteenth century and giant business combinations were being formed to service it, but those combinations were under assault from critics fearing their size. New Jersey's liberal corporate laws solved many of those problems.

New Jersey lost its position as the place of choice for incorporation after Governor Woodrow Wilson adopted his so-called Seven Sisters reform legislation, which prohibited holding companies. The New Jersey corporations then reincorporated in Delaware where the expressed policy of the legislature was to make corporate life as unrestricted as possible. After Wilson became president, the New Jersey legislature repealed his holding company reform, but it was too late. Delaware had gained prominence as the desired place of incorporation by large corporations, and it would not relinquish that position. Today, New Jersey taxes are among the highest in the country, while Delaware's have been historically low because of franchise fees. Delaware received another revenue boost when the Supreme Court ruled that abandoned funds held by financial institutions would escheat to the state of the place of incorporation of the institution holding the funds. Since many of those financial institutions were Delaware corporations, those funds went to Delaware, rather than to other states, particularly New York, where large amounts of abandoned funds are held.

Justice Brandeis charged in 1933 that the "race" for charters among the states by easing restrictions "was one not of diligence but of laxity."[15] The competition to attract corporate charters gave rise to reform efforts advocating the creation of a federal chartering requirement that could be used to regulate large corporations. Strangely, this "progressive" idea seems to have originated with John D. Rockefeller, who supported such a requirement while testifying before the Industrial Commission, which was formed by Congress in 1898. Possibly anticipating the growth of the modern attorney general wolf packs, Rockefeller wanted such a charter in order to avoid multiple state regulation and restrictions, but the idea got nowhere. The Bureau of Corporations, which was created by Congress in 1903 and located in the Department of Commerce and Labor, advocated such a proposal during Theodore Roosevelt's administration. Presidents Wilson and Taft also unsuccessfully sought such a reform. William O. Douglas raised the idea again when he was chairman of the Securities and Exchange Commission (SEC) before World War II. He too failed.

Still, the idea would not die. Another proponent of federal chartering was William Cary, a law school professor at Columbia and chairman of the SEC during the 1960s. Cary thought that "we are tending toward a managerial, rather than a capitalist society—thanks in large part to the shift of authority to management."[16] Cary wanted federal control through a "Corporate Uniformity Act" that would stop the "race to the bottom" of ever less stringent state corporate laws. His proposal would have established federal fiduciary duties and minimum corporate governance standards for large corporations. Cary's federal charter proposal found little support in Congress, but corporate law professors, including Professor Donald Schwartz at the Georgetown Law School, continued to seek such a requirement late into the twentieth century.

Some reformers shifted their aim by seeking more restrictive legislation through uniform state corporate laws. That process resulted in a Uniform Business Corporation Act in 1928, but it was not widely accepted. Another model act, created in 1950, was adopted by several states. By 1999, about half the states were using the Revised Model Business Corporation Act. That legislation was a disappointment to reformers because it copied many of the liberal provisions of the Delaware law. It also failed to unseat Delaware as the leading place of incorporation for large companies.

Delaware and the Model Business Act

Delaware corporate law and the Model Business Act vary in several ways but not dramatically. Both provide that corporate existence begins with the filing of a charter with the secretary of state. Under the Model Business Act, the corporation is presumed to have the power to engage in any lawful business, unless the charter filed by the corporation states otherwise. Delaware requires an affirmative statement of the corporate purpose but allows that to be "any lawful purpose," which pretty much eliminates the ultra vires doctrine.

State corporate laws allow corporations to incur debt and issue stock to equity owners with such rights as may be stated in the charter. This permits a broad range of equity vehicles, including common stock that may be voting, nonvoting, or weighted; convertible stock that may be exchanged under specified conditions for debt or other instruments; preferred stock that may have cumulative dividend rights; or even tracking stock that provides ownership interest in only a specified segment of a company's operations.

Varying dividend and liquidation preferences can be created, as illustrated in the following chart of the capital structure of the Axton-Fisher Tobacco Company in the 1940s.

Class A Stock	Class B Stock	Preferred Stock
Dividends		
Cumulative dividend of $3.20, and share any additional amounts with Class B	$1.60 dividend, and share any additional amounts with Class A	$6 cumulative dividend
Liquidation Preferences		
Twice amount received by Class B after payment of creditors and preferred stock liquidation	One-half amount received by A	Liquidation of $105 plus accrued dividends
Conversion and Call Features		
Convertible to B and callable at $60 plus accumulated dividends	None	None
Voting		
No votes unless four dividends missed	Sole voting rights	Same as Class A[17]

The Transamerica Corp. saw a financial opportunity from this structure after discovering that Axton-Fisher's tobacco inventory was carried on its books at cost (book value) of $6.3 million. The actual market value of the tobacco was $20 million. Transamerica bought up over 80 percent of Axton-Fisher's Class B stock and two-thirds of the Class A stock. Afterwards, Transamerica caused Axton-Fisher to redeem the remaining Class A shares and pay the cumulative dividends due to that class. The company was then liquidated by paying off the preferred shareholder liquidation rights and cumulative dividends. The result was that the Class A shareholders who were redeemed were paid $80.80 per share, instead of the $240 they would have received if they had not been redeemed. A federal court agreed that the Class A shareholders were wronged by not being notified in advance of Transamerica's plans.[18] The court, nevertheless, ruled that the redeemed Class A shares would not have the double liquidation rights of that class. Rather, the court concluded that, if they had been notified of the plan to redeem, the Class A shareholders would have had no choice but to convert to Class B with its lower liquidation right.[19]

State laws govern dividend payments. The traditional role of those statutes was to allow dividend payments only from profits; otherwise the company would be in liquidation and impair creditor rights. Corporate lawyers were able to avoid many of the dividend restrictions through such devices as a revaluation of assets or changes in par value, an early illustration of how accounts could be manipulated to avoid legal restrictions. State "fraudulent conveyance" statutes also prohibited sales of corporate assets at less than their fair value. Those statutes were directed at the common practice of selling the assets of a failing corporation at a bargain price to managers, who would then restart the business under another name, leaving the old company creditors with nothing.

The Board of Directors

State corporate statutes provide that the board of directors is responsible for managing the affairs of the corporation, not the shareholders. The peculiar relationship between the shareholders and the board of directors is illustrated by the 1880 decision of a New Hampshire court that the shareholders had no power to appoint an individual to act as a committee with the board of directors in winding up the affairs of the company. The court ruled that the power to manage the company lay with the board of directors and could not be usurped by the shareholders.[20] If shareholders were displeased with the acts of the board, their remedy was to replace the directors at the next election.

Constraints may be placed on the board of directors by corporate bylaws that typically include provisions for calling stockholder meetings and other such housekeeping requirements. This sounds mundane but can become strategically important in fights over corporate control. Failure to follow procedural requirements can also invalidate corporate actions. Moreover, at least after Enron, criminal charges may be brought against executives who fail to obtain board approval for personal expenditures such as the use of the corporate jet for personal jaunts or, in the case of Tyco, expensive shower curtains. The theory in such prosecutions is that, absent board approval, using corporate assets for personal use is larceny.

In the absence of bylaw provisions, state corporate laws may have default provisions for quorum, notice, and other requirements. These statutes seek collegial decision making on the part of the board. The board members must meet together as a group, unless unanimous agreement is reached in writing on a particular matter. In order to preserve collegial decision making, state corporate statues may prohibit quorum requirements of less than one-third. When a quorum is present, an affirmative vote of a majority of the board members present will constitute corporate action, unless otherwise provided in the bylaws.

The board of directors appoints officers of the corporation to manage its day-to-day affairs. The board sets policy while the officers implement that policy. The Model Business Act states that the business of the corporation is managed "by or under the direction of" the board, a recognition that the board of directors may act as an overseer, rather than as a manager. Generally, the board of directors is expected to hire and oversee management, approve financial and business objectives, review the adequacy of internal financial controls, and select and recommend to shareholders candidates for the board of directors. State statutes may require an expression of the board's views to guide shareholders on certain strategic matters, such as a merger, that the shareholders are being asked to approve.

Outside Directors

Directors may be officers of the corporation or they may be "outside" directors that are not managers. A popular corporate governance reform has been to encourage or require the use of a majority of outside directors on corporate boards and on certain committees. Outside directors were not always viewed as valuable. In an article titled "Directors Who Do Not Direct," published in 1934, William O. Douglas criticized the hiring of prominent individuals to serve on boards in order to give the company credibility. Douglas charged that those individuals often played no real part in directing the company. Decades later, Harvard law school professor Victor Brudney noted that there were limits on what outside directors could accomplish and cautioned against placing too much reliance on outside directors as a check on management. The outside director bandwagon, nevertheless, gained much momentum after the Enron scandal. Even before that event, most large public companies had boards of directors that were composed of a majority of outside directors, including Enron.

The SEC, early on, sought to guide corporate governance standards in public corporations through its full disclosure requirements. One area in which the SEC played a particularly prominent role was its advocacy of adding more outside directors, particularly on the audit committees that oversee corporate auditors and the auditing process. The audit committee, staffed with at least some outside directors, was introduced into the American corporate governance system in the 1930s, and the NYSE was advocating their use before the SEC (the SEC signed on to that reform in 1940), but without much effect. The theory behind this reform was that outside directors would be less prone to try to cover up problems than management.

In the 1970s, Senator Lee Metcalf, a frequent critic of the accounting industry after a series of audit failures in the 1970s, advocated the use of audit committees staffed only with outside directors to act as a check on management and the auditors. Arthur Levitt, then head of the American Stock Exchange (AMEX), opposed Metcalf's audit committee recommendation, at least for small public companies like those listed on the AMEX because of the attending expense. In 1978, the NYSE required its listed companies to create an audit committee staffed with outside directors. An accounting industry task force subsequently made recommendations that focused on strengthening the audit committee, including giving them a greater role in monitoring the process of preparing quarterly reports. The audit committee movement was given statutory recognition by the Federal Deposit Insurance Corporation (FDIC) Improvements Act of 1991. It required large FDIC-insured banking institutions to have audit committees staffed by outside directors and to provide them with independent legal counsel.

After becoming SEC chairman, Arthur Levitt began seeking reforms in the accounting industry, including further strengthening audit committees, with which he apparently now found himself compatible. In response to that pressure, the Blue Ribbon Committee on Improving the Effectiveness of Corporate Audit Committees was formed by the SEC, National Association of Securities Dealers (NASD), and NYSE in 1998. That body was called the Whitehead committee in honor of its cochairman, John C. Whitehead, a partner at Goldman Sachs. The Whitehead committee recommended greater oversight by the board of directors in the audit function and tried to set some standards for assuring that outside directors were truly independent. Nasdaq and the NYSE adopted those reforms in 1999. The audit committees of companies listed on the NYSE or traded on Nasdaq with a capitalization of more than $200 million were required to be composed entirely of outside directors, who were required to be "financially literate." The SEC also adopted disclosure requirements that required public corporations to report on the nature and role of their audit committees, but those reforms failed to catch or stop the accounting abuses at Enron and elsewhere.

The use of outside directors on the board and on other committees, particularly the compensation and nomination committees for board members, grew with these regulatory efforts. The individuals serving as outside directors were often academics, former high-level government officials, or prominent business leaders. Despite their inevitable brilliance, they rarely had operating knowledge about the company's business or sufficient contact with the company to act as a check on management. Another source of outside directors was the pool of personal friends of the chief executive officer or people who were nominated as a form of patronage doled out by that executive.

The reform movement for more outside directors proliferated after the Enron scandal. The NYSE adopted a rule requiring a majority of board members of companies listed on the exchange to be outside directors. This rule required that all members of the audit, compensation, and nominating committees be outside directors. There was, however, no evidence that outside directors assured good management. Academic studies found that companies with independent boards (boards of directors staffed by at least a majority of outside directors) did not perform better than firms having a majority of inside directors. A case in point is the Eastman Kodak Co., possibly the worst managed company in America. For decades, shareholders there were pummeled by management blunders. The company first lost out to foreign producers of camera film and then completely misjudged the digital revolution in cameras. The price of Eastman Kodak stock dropped from $76 in 1999 to $25 in April 2004, after the company cut its dividend from $1.80 to fifty cents and slashed 16,000 jobs, three times those lost at Enron. That was in addition to the 22,000 employees laid off at Kodak since 1998. Dropping film manufacturing as its core business, which accounted for 70 percent of its revenues, Kodak turned to digital cameras and equipment. The company was taking accounting charges of over $1.3 billion and was dropped from the list of stocks included in the Dow Jones Industrial Average in the new century.

Even with its gross mismanagement, Eastman Kodak was among the 1 percent of companies receiving a perfect score for corporate governance in a survey of public corporations by an international governance rating body. Kodak's board of directors consisted of eleven outside directors and only one inside director. Those outside directors included such luminaries as Paul H. O'Neill, the tell-all secretary of the treasury in the second Bush administration who also served on the board of Lucent Technologies, which had been manipulating its accounts on a massive scale; Bill Bradley, former senator and professional basketball player; Martha Layne Collins, former governor of Kentucky; Laura D'Andrea Tyson, former chair of the President's Council of Economic Advisors; and Delano E. Lewis, former ambassador to South Africa. Brilliant as they were, none of those individuals was in a position to manage Eastman Kodak and did nothing discernible to improve its fortunes. The company even had its own "chief governance officer," as well as a "Senior Executive Diversity and Inclusion Council" and a gay Web site to further its political correctness and shield the company from criticism for its poor performance. Those reforms all failed; even the Diversity and Inclusion Council could not avert a massive class action suit charging racial discrimination in promotions and a hostile work environment for African-Americans. More embarrassment came when Kodak had to restate its financial reports for 2003 and 2004 because of accounting failures. Its auditor also expressed an adverse opinion on the internal financial controls of the company. That opinion appeared to be justified because the company had to delay reporting its 2004 results, which when filed showed earnings of $93 million less than previously announced. Kodak then experienced a rating downgrade in $2.3 billion of its debt, pushing it below investment grade and into junk bond territory. A first quarter loss of $142 million in 2005 resulted in another downgrade in the company's debt rating. More job cuts followed and Daniel Carp, Kodak's chief executive officer and chairman, announced that he would be taking an early retirement. These problems did not prevent Carp from receiving compensation of $4.4 million in compensation for 2004. After a second quarter loss in 2005 of $146 million, Carp announced the layoff of another 10,000

Kodak employees, twice the number who lost their jobs in the Enron bankruptcy. The company also decided to shut down or get rid of about two-thirds of its manufacturing assets.

Kodak was embroiled in more scandal. That company is based in Rochester, New York, which like other upstate New York communities have some of the highest taxes in the nation, crippling their economies and discouraging new enterprises. A Kodak executive, Mark S. Camarata, came up with a solution to Kodak's massive property tax bill. He hired an appraisal firm owned by John Nicollo to seek a reduction of Kodak's assessments. Nicollo was paid by Kodak on the basis of the amount of property taxes he saved Kodak. According to a government indictment, Nicollo then bribed Charles A. Swab, a local government assessor, to lower the Kodak assessment. Nicollo kicked back part of the millions of dollars he received from Kodak for that reduction to Camarata. It looked like a real win-win situation for everyone, but government prosecutors were not amused. The government claimed that other taxpayers were required to pay more in taxes because of this scheme, but Kodak filed a lawsuit claiming that its properties were overassessed because of the scheme and were still overassessed. The company conceded there were some large holes in its internal financial controls. Among other things, two Kodak executives approved over 160 unauthorized contracts and payments without any documentation to support them.

In contrast, Berkshire Hathaway, which is controlled by Warren Buffett, is one of the most successful companies in the country in recent years, but had one of the most politically incorrect boards of directors. The members of its board included Buffett, his wife (before her death), his son, his longtime business partner, and an insider who was a coinvestor. Ironically, Buffett was himself becoming a corporate reform advocate for businesses (other than his own) after Enron, and was becoming a reformist icon for probity and high ethical standards in business. That seems strange in light of his politically incorrect governance structure at Berkshire Hathaway. In fact, Berkshire Hathaway itself exists at all only because of a loophole in the Investment Company Act of 1940, administered by the SEC. Were it required to register as an investment company, Berkshire Hathaway's decidedly nonindependent board would have to be restructured and its operations terminated. "Berkshire Hathaway escapes the 1940 Act only by folding its strategic investment activities into an insurance subsidiary, and exploiting Nebraska's permissive insurance statute in a fashion that no other company can be expected to duplicate."[21] In addition, Buffett had problems with the SEC in the 1970s involving claims of misleading investors through sales of fraudulent insurance policies by insurance agents and manipulating stock prices through Blue Chip Stamps, a company that awarded consumers with prizes for buying groceries, and his company was being investigated in 2004 by Eliot Spitzer, the New York attorney general, for some of its insurance practices. General Re, owned by Buffett's Berkshire Hathaway, was also under investigation by the SEC for selling insurance products to public companies that could be used to smooth earnings by the purchasers of those policies, and to boost reserves. Buffett was directly involved in at least one such transaction.

In all events, the evidence strongly suggests that outside directors are powerless to stop scandals. Enron is a case in point. It had an audit committee staffed with outside directors. Eleven of the fourteen directors on Enron's board were independent outside directors at the time of its collapse. These experienced and notable executives, academics, and former government officials included Robert Jaedicke, professor of accounting and former dean of the Stanford University graduate school of business; Charls Walker, former deputy secretary of the Treasury; John Mendelsohn, president of the University of Texas; John Wakeham, former secretary of state for energy in the United Kingdom and leader of both the House of Lords and House of Commons; Norman Blake Jr., secretary general of the U.S. Olympic Committee; and Dr. Wendy Gramm, an economics professor at George Mason University in Virginia and former chairman of the Commodity Futures Trading Commission (CFTC). The board also included present or former senior executives at General Electric, Penn Central Corp., Gulf & Western Industries Inc., Alliance Capital Management, and the State Bank of Rio de Janeiro.

Another firm with a massive accounting failure was Xerox. Its board of directors had a majority of outside directors, including several prominent individuals such as Vernon Jordan, a Washington power broker, and former senator George Mitchell. Global Crossing, the center of another colossal scandal, had a board laden with prominent outside directors, including Maria Elena Lagomasino, cohead of JP Morgan Private Bank; Pieter Knook, a senior Microsoft executive; William E. Conway Jr., a managing director of the Carlyle Group; and Steven J. Green, former ambassador to Singapore. The outside director chairing the audit committee at Waste Management, where massive accounting fraud occurred, was Roderick M. Hills, a former SEC chairman. His wife, Carla Hills, the former U.S. trade representative, served on the boards of Lucent and AOL Time Warner, two more companies with massive accounting problems.

Clearly, outside directors were unable to prevent the accounting manipulations that led to the corporate scandals after the stock market bubble burst. What value, then, do outside directors provide? The answer is considerable. Outside directors are useful in providing wisdom, differing perspectives and, yes, contacts that can be used to further business, but their usefulness is limited in preventing management abuses. Outside directors, by definition, are not involved in the day-to-day management of the company, and they are controlled by information flows from management. As the American Law Institute has noted: "As a practical matter, the initiation and formulation of major corporate plans and actions must depend in large part on an intimate knowledge of the business of the corporation, and this knowledge is more likely to be possessed by the senior executives than by the board."[22]

More Board Reforms

Although outside directors have proved to be unable to police corporations, reformers continue to cling to the dream, even demanding more. They now seek at least a majority of outside directors on nominating committees. Those committees often perpetuate management in office by nominating friendly candidates for election to the board of directors that management can control. Reformists also advocate a number of other measures for better corporate governance, including reducing the size of boards. Some large companies use boards of twenty or more directors, making decision making at the board level unwieldy. Another reform is to have a "lead" outside director who will have a separate power base where a majority of the board is composed of outside directors, creating a board within a board. Accompanying that reform is a demand that the outside directors periodically meet with each other without management being present. Separate counsel and access to other experts have also been urged for outside directors.

Reformers seek to split the role of chairman of the board of directors and the chief executive officer. Chief executive officers like to hold both positions because it allows them to maintain control of the company and the board, the latter being particularly important for entrenchment purposes. Reformers believe that having an outside director serve as chairman will make the board less subservient to management and give outside directors greater independence. The Conference Board Blue Ribbon Commission on Public Trust and Private Enterprise, which was created after the Enron scandal and chaired by John Snow, later the secretary of the Treasury, recommended that all public companies should split those roles. This proposal met with opposition. Critics claimed that this would undercut the authority of the chief executive officer and make that post less effective. Notably, the roles of chairman and chief executive officer were split at WorldCom, perhaps the biggest accounting scandal of all. Enron also divided the role of chairman and chief executive officer between Jeffrey Skilling and Kenneth Lay before the company came unglued, another corporate governance reform that added little or not protection to shareholders.

Confidential voting has been widely urged to prevent undue management pressure, and boards have been urged to adopt codes of ethics to be signed by all executives and employees. The contents of the codes are largely anodyne exhortations to do the right thing, but may include restrictions on outside employment and business that might conflict with the company's interests. Ethics officers, risk managers, and diversity executives are also being hired in large numbers. Staggered boards used by management to fend off unwanted takeovers and to retain control in the unlikely event of a shareholder revolt are another target of corporate reformers. Institutional investors at Gillette mounted an attack on its use of a staggered board in 2004 and obtained a shareholder vote in which 68 percent of the shareholders sought its termination. The Gillette management ignored the vote. Sears, Roebuck & Co. and Federated Department Stores Inc. refused to drop their staggered boards even after shareholder majorities voiced support for such a change. The California Public Employee Retirement System (Calpers) led another successful vote against the use of staggered boards at Ingersoll Rand, but management resisted that demand. Management at Procter & Gamble Co. did agree in 2005 to drop its staggered board of directors as a result of pressure from corporate reformers.

Calpers had better success in challenging the controversial head of Walt Disney, Michael Eisner, whose board of directors failed all corporate governance tests. The outside directors on the Disney board included such luminaries as the principal of the elementary school attended by Eisner's children, his personal lawyer, his architect, and the president of Georgetown University, which had been the recipient of large donations from Eisner. Eisner sent copies of board memos to his wife as well as to large investors. The Disney board was restructured after several massive blunders by Eisner that led to criticism by some of Eisner's hand-picked outside directors. Those directors were removed in that restructuring. In a singular bit of chutzpah, Eisner asserted that their removal was required as a measure to upgrade Disney's corporate governance. He claimed that those outside directors were no longer independent because of various ties to Disney. Yet, another "outside" director who remained friendly to Eisner was left on the board even though his spouse was receiving $1.35 million from a Disney related channel.

Roy Disney, a nephew of Walt Disney and a director who was very critical of Eisner, was forced off the board because of a Disney mandatory retirement rule that had been waived for other more friendly directors such as actor Sidney Poitier. The rebelling directors were replaced with toadies more subservient to Eisner, including former senator George Mitchell. Eisner then failed to obtain the approval of 43 percent of the shareholders in a vote of confidence on his performance. That seemed like a large percentage as compared to other management-sponsored initiatives, but the opposition of Roy Disney, the poor performance at Disney while Eisner was taking hundreds of millions of dollars in compensation, and a scandal over the amount of compensation paid to Michael Ovitz, a short-lived Disney executive, had left Eisner vulnerable. The vote, in any event, had little effect. Eisner resigned as chairman but kept his chief executive officer role. Several state pension funds, including Calpers and the New York State retirement plan, continued to seek his removal from that position. As a way to defuse that opposition, Eisner announced that he would be retiring in two years, allowing him to remain firmly entrenched until then, as evidenced by Roy Disney's decision to drop efforts to reorganize the Disney board.

Comcast announced a $48.7 billion offer for Disney on February 11, 2004, but withdrew the offer in May after facing resistance from Eisner, who rejected the offer before consulting with the Disney board of directors. Eisner then disclosed that he was interested in becoming Disney's chairman after his term as chief executive officer was concluded. He was also able to draw the support of 94.6 percent of Disney shareholders in his reelection to the board in 2005, despite Calpers opposition to his reelection.

Roy Disney and Stanley P. Gold, another rebelling director who had been removed from the Disney board, attacked Eisner after the publication of *Disney Wars,* a best-selling book that was highly critical of Eisner's reign. Disney and Gold took out a full-page advertisement in the *Wall Street Journal,* which charged that Eisner was trying to appoint Robert Iger as his successor without board involvement and that Senator George Mitchell was refusing to investigate claims in the *Disney Wars* book concerning mismanagement. Disney and Gold said the board was putting its "head in the sand" and that if claims made in the book were true the board should require a return of the bonuses given to Eisner and others. Eisner responded by immediately having the Disney board appoint Iger as chief executive officer, succeeding Eisner a year earlier than originally planned. Eisner asserted that he was retiring from Disney in September 2005. Disney and Gold sued in the Delaware court's claiming that the Disney board had lied to shareholders in asserting that they would conduct a worldwide search for a successor to Eisner and that external candidates, not just Iger, Eisner's hand-picked successor, would be considered. A Delaware Chancery judge refused to dismiss that lawsuit. Before Enron such claims would have been dismissed out of hand. The suit was settled after Roy Disney was hired as a consultant and made a director emeritus. Eisner's tenure had resulted in decidedly mixed results. He increased Disney's market value from $1.8 billion in 1984 when he took over control to $57 billion in 2005, but Eisner lost billions of dollars in the Euro Disney theme park and other misadventures, and the company's stock price continued to lag.

The SEC weighed in (years after the issue of governance at Disney was first raised) with a lawsuit claiming that the company failed to disclose that it had hired children of outside directors and provided other benefits. Among those receiving undisclosed benefits were Roy Disney and Stanley Gold, his financial adviser and attorney, both of whom had sought to unseat Eisner. The company also failed to disclose that another director received a car and driver and an office to work from.

Corporate Officers

State corporate laws initially specified certain officers that had to be appointed by the board of directors, but modern statutes leave that decision largely to the bylaws. In earlier years, the president was the principal corporate officer, but today that position has been superseded by the title of "chief executive officer." Similarly, the importance of the corporate treasurer has been downgraded in favor of the "chief financial officer"; many of the latter were charged with accounting fraud in the wake of Enron. Corporations generally have a corporate secretary to authenticate corporate records, but from there the list of executive positions is endless. Today, large corporations have a bewildering array of officers. Even positions with the same name might entail varying degrees of responsibility at different corporations. For example, the position of vice president may be a powerful one at a manufacturing concern, but only titular at some financial services firms. Chief operating officers, executive vice presidents, group vice presidents, senior vice presidents, and managing directors all have roles that may vary in importance at individual firms.

Officers are agents of the corporation, but they have only the authority to carry out such duties as may be authorized by the board of directors. An officer cannot bind the corporation without the authorization of the board of directors, but that authorization may be "actual" or "apparent." The former is created by a board resolution that expressly or by implication authorizes the action. Authority may be present even in the absence of actual authority when the board of directors clothes someone with "apparent" authority through some act that would reasonably lead a third party to believe that the actor has been given express authority. Appointment as an officer of the corporation may clothe someone with such apparent authority. For example, the president of a company has the apparent authority to enter into an employment contract on behalf of the corporation, unless the contract is extraordinary in nature, as in the case of an employment contract for life. If not extraordinary, the employment contract is enforceable, even if the president did not have actual authority from the board of directors. These rules played a significant role at Tyco and in other prosecutions charging corporate looting.

Shareholder Responsibilities

State corporate statutes allow limited liability for shareholders. This means that the shareholders are not responsible for the debts of the corporation beyond their investment. When a corporation becomes bankrupt, creditors will have claim to all assets of the corporation until their debts are satisfied. If corporate assets are not sufficient to cover those debts, shareholders have no obligation to pay the unsatisfied amounts, securing their personal assets from creditor claims.

Limited liability for shareholders raised concerns about creditor protection. As a creditor protection provision, earlier state corporate statutes imposed minimum capitalization requirements before the corporation could commence business. "One may start a business on a shoestring in Kentucky, but if it is a corporate business the shoestring must be worth $1,000."[23] Most of those requirements have since been abandoned as insufficient or arbitrary because some businesses require more capital than others. Creditors can protect themselves in any event by securing their debt or making their own assessment of the creditworthiness of the corporation. More practically, at least in small corporations, creditors may require "recourse" against the shareholders by requiring them to guarantee the corporation's debt.

The courts have occasionally "pierced the corporate veil" to hold share-holders personally liable when the corporate structure has been abused, but those cases are rare, and no court has ever pierced the veil of a public corporation. The veil piercing cases usually involve an involuntary creditor. This would include instances in which someone sustains injury or death from the act of a corporate employee, and the assets of the corporation are inadequate to provide compensation. In one famous case in 1961, a corporate veil was held not to shield a lawyer from personal liability for the drowning of a child. The lawyer acted as a temporary officer and director and had nominal owner-ship of "qualifying" shares in the Seminole Hot Springs Corporation. He acted in those capacities in order to qualify the corporation under California law. The company managed a swimming pool that it leased, the child drowned, and a judgment of $10,000 was obtained. Justice Roger Traynor, a famously liberal California jurist, held that shareholders of the corporation could be held personally responsible because the company did not observe the for-malities of its corporate structure and had inadequate capital to conduct its business.[24]

Shareholder Rights

At common law shareholders were given "preemptive rights" to purchase shares in new issues of stock in amounts sufficient to prevent dilution of their percentage of ownership. For example, assume that a corporation has autho-rized 1,000 shares of common stock, of which 100 shares have been sold to the existing stockholders. Shareholder A owns forty of the outstanding shares, but the board of directors subsequently votes to sell the remaining authorized but unissued 900 shares. Preemptive rights would entitle Shareholder A to buy at 360 of those shares in order to retain his status as a 40 percent share-holder. Absent such a right, Shareholder A's proportional amount of owner-ship would be reduced dramatically when the shares are sold to other shareholders or to a third party. Today, state statutes usually deny preemptive rights, unless required by the corporation's charter. This is important for large public companies because contacting millions of existing shareholders for exercise of their preemptive would be cumbersome.

State statutes usually provide for an annual meeting of shareholders, where directors are elected, and establish housekeeping requirements such as quo-rum and notice requirements for those meetings. These housekeeping require-ments are often default provisions that may be varied by the bylaws, at least in some areas. Only those shareholders listed on the books of the company on the record date set by management or the bylaws will be allowed to vote. Shareholder approval usually is reached when a quorum is present and a plu-rality of those voting approve. Delaware has a provision in its corporate stat-utes that allows shareholder action to be taken without a meeting, if shareholders with enough votes to pass the action approve in writing.

Shareholders are usually given some limited inspection rights to company books and records. Although shareholders are the owners of the corporation, unlimited inspection rights could harm the company. For example, if unrestrained access were allowed, a competitor could buy a share of Coca-Cola stock and then demand the right to inspect the formula for Coke. That would harm the company, since the formula is not patented. Generally, shareholders are given a right of access to a list of the shareholders so they may communicate with each other on company matters. Even that access has raised concerns that shareholder lists will be obtained for use as marketing tools.

Political activists have bought a few shares of stock and then sought access to corporate records to further their causes, raising issues about the limits of inspection rights. A case in point involved an effort by an antiwar activist to obtain corporate records of Honeywell Inc. that involved its production of weapons for use in the Vietnam War. The activist had only a nominal holding in the stock of Honeywell. He was working with a group of war protesters on what they called the Honeywell Project, which sought to convince the company's shareholders to approve a demand that Honeywell stop making armaments. A Minnesota court denied such inspection,[25] but other courts have allowed activists in other causes to gain access to at least some corporate records. Several states amended their statutes to discourage such efforts by requiring shareholders seeking inspection to own a stated minimum amount of stock for at least a specified period of time.

Shareholder Voting

Corporate voting is mostly carried out through shareholder proxies, which are the corporate equivalent of absentee ballots in a political election. Incumbency is even more important in corporate elections than in political campaigns because management controls the proxy machinery in a public company. Management usually selects the nominees who will stand for election for membership on the board and makes recommendations for other shareholder votes. Most shareholders will vote for management's nominees and recommendations, if they vote at all. This is because, at least until recently, most shareholders voted with their feet by selling their shares if they did not support management. When shareholders of a public company do seek to oppose management in a proxy vote, they usually lose. Even successful campaigns conducted by large shareholders are monumentally expensive.

Control by management of the proxy machinery has been a concern of reformists for many years. In 1912, the House Committee on Banking found that public shareholders in the United States were largely powerless and took little initiative to seek to control or influence management policies. The committee was unable to find a single instance in which stockholders in a public corporation voted out existing management. Illustrative of why that was the case was the American Telephone & Telegraph Company. It was one of the largest corporations in America with over 700,000 individual shareholders, but no single shareholder held more than 1 percent of the company's stock. This meant that there was simply no power base to oppose management.

Concerns about management control were renewed in the 1932 by Adolf Berle and Gardiner Means in their seminal work on this subject, *The Modern Corporation and Private Property*. Berle and Means found that management exercised varying degrees of control, which they separated into three categories:

1. Majority control: One shareholder or group owns or controls 35 percent or more of the company's stock. Even when a majority vote is required for shareholder action, the holder of at least 35 percent of the stock will likely be able to obtain the support of the small percentage of shareholders needed for victory.

2. Management control: The largest block of the stock owned in these companies does not exceed 5 to 10 percent of the outstanding shares of company. Because management controls the proxy machinery, and most shareholders are passive, management will have almost complete control of the company. Management of publicly held corporations rarely lose proxy battles. Even with regard to election of directors, management controls the process, that is, management-sponsored proxy materials set forth the management slate of directors in these corporations.

3. Minority control: In these companies, a single shareholder or group controls somewhere between 10 and 35 percent of the company's shares. If the holder of this block of stock is not participating in management, then control is shared between that shareholder and management. They will usually work together, since each is in a position to win a contested proxy fight: on the one hand, management has control of the proxy machinery, but on the other hand, the large stockholder controls a large amount of stock and will likely have the resources to wage a campaign to convince other shareholders to vote actively against management.[26]

Most large public companies fall within the second category identified by Berle and Means, presenting the danger that the managers will manage for their own benefit, rather than for shareholders. This will mean large compensation packages for executives, a fleet of executive jets and every form of perquisite, from swank Manhattan apartments to extravagant parties on a tropical island. Actually, each of the other control scenarios identified by Berle and Means poses corporate governance problems. In the first, the majority shareholder may sell its control for a premium, to the exclusion of other shareholders. The majority shareholder may take actions that will benefit the majority shareholder personally to the exclusion of other shareholders—for example, signing a favorable contract with another company owned by the majority shareholder. The third form of control relationship identified by Berle and Means is essentially a standoff between management and the large minority shareholder, but their alliance may result in detriments to the other shareholders, as when the large minority shareholder is given lucrative contracts, employment, or other advantages.[27]

A growing phenomenon that postdated Berle and Means is the institutional investor that gained control of a majority of all outstanding stock in public corporations as the 1990s began. Those institutions include public and private pension plans, insurance companies, trusts managed by banks, mutual funds, and hedge funds. Traditionally, these institutional investors were passive investors; they sold their stock when displeased with management, but that approach was criticized by reformists. For example, Bernard S. Black's 1992 law review article titled "Agents Watching Agents: the Promise of the Institutional Investor Voice" urged institutional investors to drop their normally passive investment stance. Black, a professor at the Columbia Law School, where Adolf Berle had taught, wanted institutional investors to have a "voice" on the board. He advocated the creation of an elaborate "monitoring" structure in which employees, executives, board members, and institutional investors would all watch each other for any sign of misconduct, a sort of Soviet-style business community.[28]

Most institutions continued their passive role, but several public pension plans did become active investors and aggressive advocates of corporate governance changes. The leaders of that movement were the California Public Employee Retirement System (Calpers), the largest retirement fund in the United States, and the New York State government retirement plan. Those institutions often withhold their votes from management's choices for board positions and proposed "good" corporate governance proposals for shareholder votes. To aid their cause, Calpers and Institutional Shareholder Services Inc. (ISS), a corporate governance reform organization, developed a database of outside directors, like the one maintained by the British Institute for the Promotion of Non-Executive Directors, that could be used to select their own candidates for board positions.

The pension funds were rarely successful in having their candidates elected or corporate governance proposals approved, but they continued their efforts. ISS now provides advice on how institutional investors should vote their proxies. According to its Web site in 2004, that company was "the world's leading provider of proxy voting and corporate governance services. ISS serves more than 950 institutional and corporate clients worldwide with its core business—analyzing proxies and issuing informed research and objective vote recommendations for more than 10,000 U.S. and 12,000 non-U.S. shareholder meetings each year." It is unclear how ISS arrives at such "informed" decisions.

Proxy Votes

Despite the reality of disenfranchisement, an elaborate legal structure governs proxy votes at both the state and federal levels. State law controls the voting process and rights of shareholders to vote. Those statutes include requirements for shareholder votes on certain matters such as mergers. State legislatures are sometimes flexible in the application of those provisions, as illustrated in a takeover battle between SunTrust Banks Inc. and First Union Corp., which were both seeking control of the Wachovia Corp. in 2001. First Union and Wachovia were based in North Carolina, while SunTrust Banks operated from Georgia. To assure that Wachovia stayed at home, the North Carolina legislature passed special legislation to prevent SunTrust from calling a meeting to ask shareholders to approve bylaw changes that would have provided an opportunity for SunTrust to gain control. The battle was also fought in the North Carolina Business Court, and First Union prevailed in the end. The fight was, in all events, a costly one. SunTrust spent over $30 million in its losing proxy fight, which raises the question of how small shareholders could ever hope to win a campaign against management.

A reformist measure popular in the middle of the last century was "cumulative" voting requirements in state statutes and constitutions that allowed shareholders to concentrate their votes on one or more directors, instead of the normal plurality process in which only one vote per share per director is permitted. Cumulative voting seeks to provide a greater opportunity for minority representation on the board of directors. That goal was largely defeated by using staggered boards, with only a small percentage of the directors elected each year. A staggered board thus made it mathematically harder for minority shareholders to elect a director. For example, in an election of three members of a nine-member board, about 250 percent more cumulative votes are required to elect a single director than would be needed if all nine were elected at once. In addition, the ever-increasing dispersion of stock ownership, and the ability of shareholders to simply sell their shares when displeased, meant that cumulative voting was of little interest to most shareholders. States such as Pennsylvania and Illinois repealed mandatory cumulative voting rights requirements, making such provisions discretionary.

One popular method for more completely disenfranchising shareholders was the use of two classes of stock, one voting and the other a nonvoting class that had a greater dividend right than the voting class. The dividend feature attracted nonmanagement shareholders and assured control to an individual or group willing to forgo the larger dividend in exchange for control. In addition, in the event of a sale of the corporation, management would capture any premium for control. Reformists objected to this "disenfranchisement" of shareholders even though those shareholders made their own voluntary choice. The NYSE has mandated one vote, one share structures since 1926, and the SEC tried to prohibit nonvoting class arrangements in the late twentieth century, but a federal court ruled that the agency had no authority to impose such a prohibition under its full disclosure authority.[29] Nasdaq subsequently acted to prohibit such nonvoting classes from trading through its facilities, but several such companies still exist.

Proxy Fights

Proxy fights are rare in large public companies, but occasionally a battle will break out among large shareholders or during corporate acquisitions, and some of them have been epics. One such struggle occurred in the 1950s when Louis B. Mayer tried to take over control of Loew's Inc., which owned Metro-Goldwyn-Mayer Inc. (MGM). Mayer had controlled Loew's for decades and in 1940 was paid the then princely salary of $670,000. Mayer's interests turned to horse racing, and he was ousted after the company lost millions of dollars. Joseph Vogel, who headed Loew's in 1956, came under attack when Mayer tried to regain control of the company by forming an alliance with Joseph Tomlinson, Loew's largest shareholder. In order to avoid a proxy fight, Vogel agreed to a compromise that created a thirteen-member board of directors. Six members were to be selected by Vogel and six by Tomlinson, with the thirteenth to be agreed upon by both sides. The compromise fell apart after two of the six Vogel-selected directors resigned, as did the neutral director and a Tomlinson director. The Tomlinson directors asked for a special board meeting to fill the vacancies; since they were a majority, they planned to elect their candidates and take over control. The Vogel directors refused to attend, preventing a quorum. A Delaware court ruled that the Tomlinson faction could not fill the board vacancies because there was no quorum at the meeting.

Vogel launched his own counterattack by calling a special meeting of the shareholders for the purpose of expanding Loew's board from thirteen to nineteen directors, to elect new directors to fill vacancies, and to remove Tomlinson and one of his supporters from the board. Vogel prevailed in the resulting shareholder vote, electing all but one of his candidates. A Delaware chancery court judge ruled that the bylaws authorized Vogel to call the special meeting and that the shareholders could fill the vacancies on the board. The removal of Tomlinson and his supporter from the board was found to be improper, however, because they were not given an opportunity to present their defense to the shareholders before proxies were solicited by management.

A critical aspect of this case involved the question of who controlled the company when the lack of a quorum prevented action by the board. The court ruled that management (the Vogel faction) was in control even though the Tomlinson group had a majority on the board. This meant that Vogel could use corporate funds to wage the proxy battle with the Tomlinson group. Vogel was unable to use his reacquired control to remove Tomlinson from the board because of a cumulative voting provision in the company's charter. Tomlinson soon renewed his assault, and Vogel responded by successfully seeking elimination of the cumulative voting right, paving the way to remove Tomlinson from the board.

This did not end the battle for control of Loew's. Vogel's successor, Robert H. O'Brien, who was paid a most un-Enron-like salary of $20,000, was the target of another fight in 1967 for control that was launched by Philip J. Levin, a real estate developer owning a substantial block of the company's stock. Levin was joined by other large shareholders. They sought to oust the management directors. That was no easy task. Levin's group sought to have a federal court enjoin O'Brien and other management directors, charging that they were "paying for the services of specially retained attorneys, a public relations firm and proxy soliciting organizations, and, in addition, have improperly used the offices and employees of MGM in proxy solicitation and the good-will and business contacts of MGM to secure support for the present management."[30] The injunction was denied, but Levin prevailed in the shareholder vote, electing his director candidates.

Not long afterward, in the 1960s, the company was the subject of another contest for control that was initiated by Time, Inc. and Edgar Bronfman, the head of Seagram Co. Levin sold MGM to those interests. It was subsequently sold to Kirk Kerkorian in 1969, a well-known corporate raider who bought and sold MGM more than once. One of those sales was to Ted Turner at CNN in 1986 for $1.5 billion, which crippled Turner's finances. Turner resold MGM back to Kerkorian three months later for $300 million, but Turner kept its film library and colorized the films, making many movie buffs angry. In 1990, Kerkorian sold MGM to Giancarlo Parretti and Florio Fiorini, two Italian businessmen later accused by federal authorities of engaging in massive fraud in acquiring control of American companies. Kerkorian sold MGM again in 2004 to Sony for $4.9 billion.

Another notable proxy fight involved a shareholder vote approving the merger of Hewlett-Packard and Compaq in 2002. Walter B. Hewlett, a son of one of the company's founders, challenged that merger after an exceptionally close shareholder vote. Both sides spent millions on the proxy battle preceding that vote, taking out full-page advertisements in the *Wall Street Journal* and other papers. Hewlett charged that management's proxy materials were misleading and that Carelton (Carly) Fiorina, Hewlett-Packard's chief executive officer, bought votes by threatening Deutsche Bank with a loss of considerable Hewlett-Packard business if its money mangers did not vote the stock they controlled in favor of the merger. Fiorina had previously been an executive at Lucent Technologies Inc., but managed to escape before that company imploded. The money managers at Deutsche Bank, under some slightly irrational theory of fiduciary duties, were planning to vote Compaq shares under their management in favor of the merger, while voting the Hewlett-Packard shares they managed against the merger. That course had been recommended by ISS, the organization that advises institutions on how to vote their proxies in a politically correct manner. By voting both ways, however, the money managers were acting contrary to the interests of both those clients holding Compaq shares and those holding Hewlett-Packard shares.

Traditionally, state courts have prevented shareholders from selling their votes, equating the process to a political campaign, which it is not. A share of stock is an ownership interest in a piece of property on which an investment return is sought, so what is wrong with increasing that return by selling your vote? Recognizing that reality, at least one court has concluded that the common-law rule on vote buying is outmoded. In any event, the Delaware court found that Walter Hewlett had failed to prove his charges, even though evidence showed that Fiorina had left a voice message on the telephone of one of her subordinates telling him to "call the guy at Deutsche again first thing Monday morning. And if you don't get the right answer from him, then you and I need to demand a conference call, an audience, etc. to make sure that we get them in the right place. . . . get on the phone and see what we can get, but we may have to do something extraordinary for those two to bring 'em over the line here." After leaving that message, Fiorina called the Deutsche Bank officials, and they switched their vote on seventeen million of the twenty-five million shares they had under management in favor of the Hewlett-Packard-Compaq merger.

The judge found no misconduct in that call, which had been taped without Fiorina's knowledge. The SEC was not so forgiving; it fined the investment advisory unit of the Deutsche Bank $750,000. The SEC claimed conflicts of interest because the advisory unit failed to disclose that it had worked for Hewlett-Packard and that it was intervening in the voting process. This did not help Walter Hewlett, who experienced the realities of the business world. Carly Fiorina refused to allow him to be renominated to the company's board of directors as punishment for bringing the lawsuit challenging her conduct. Hewlett spent millions of dollars of his own money in this unsuccessful, quixotic campaign. Carly Fiorina had a few years to savor that victory, but the merger was a failure. Fiorina was ousted in February 2005 in a boardroom coup that occurred after she resisted efforts by the board to limit her operational role. Her pain was eased somewhat by a $42 million severance and retirement package. She was replaced by Mark Hurd from NCR Corp. He then cut 14,500 jobs, three times the number lost at Enron, and reduced the benefits of retirees.

SEC Proxy Regulation

In 1934, William O. Douglas referenced a report in one of his law review articles that had been prepared by an investigating committee of the Texas Corporation. That report read like the Powers report, which was compiled after Enron. Among other things, the officers of the Texas Corporation had the board they controlled approve their large bonuses and extended themselves huge loans to meet margin calls on their personal stockholdings. As a cure for such abuses, Douglas wanted to prevent the board of directors of large corporations from being nominated by the company's managers. He wanted a majority of the board to be composed of stockholders who were not managers. To accomplish that goal, Douglas sought to have the proxy machinery taken out of the hands of management. By regulating the proxy process, Douglas thought that control could be taken from management and transferred to the shareholders. Of course, as noted by David A. Skeel Jr., a law professor at the University of Pennsylvania, "Douglas had his eye on the Supreme Court, and in the New Deal, such aspirations required an unquestioned commitment to governmental control of business and finance."

Douglas's attack on the proxy process became a popular reformist refrain that was embodied in the federal securities laws. The Securities Exchange Act of 1934 thus granted the SEC authority to regulate proxy solicitations by public companies. The SEC also adopted rules requiring management to provide shareholders with an annual report on the company's operations, including audited financials. That report must be delivered to the shareholders as part of the proxy solicitation for the annual meeting of shareholders at which directors are elected and other action taken. The required information is taken from the SEC Form 10-K and wrapped in a fancy cover with pictures of management and smiling employees. This report failed to fulfill the SEC's goal of full disclosure. Instead, it provided management with an opportunity to downplay any problems or disasters, which management inevitably called "challenges," and to put its spin on the financial statements.

The SEC proxy rules contain an antifraud prohibition for statements made in proxy materials and require access by shareholders to a shareholders list so that they may communicate with each other, supplementing state laws on this topic. Proxy statements must be filed with the SEC's Division of Corporate Finance for review before being mailed out to shareholders, but that review is cursory, at best. The SEC adopted another rule designed to encourage shareholder democracy through proxy solicitations. That rule requires management to submit shareholder proposals for a vote by the shareholders. Management must include the proposal and a supporting statement from the proposing shareholder of not more than 500 words in its proxy statement. To be eligible to have such a proposal included, the investor's holdings must be worth at least $2,000 or constitute 1 percent of the securities to be voted at the meeting. The SEC's shareholder proposal rule has been used extensively by proponents of "shareholder democracy," to seek votes on proposals relating to management compensation, conduct of annual meetings, shareholder voting rights, and similar matters. Activists opposed to the Vietnam War, discrimination, smoking, pollution, and other social issues have also used this rule to seek changes in company policies that affect their causes.

The SEC allows management to exclude proposals in defined areas. For example, a proposal that seeks to require something that is not legal under state law need not be included in the proxy. This allows management to exclude matters that seek to require the corporation to undertake a certain act because state law vests that determination in the discretion of the board of directors. A proposal is proper if it merely requests board action or seeks a bylaw change to require it. Another excludable category is for matters that are not significant enough to materially affect the company's business. In one case, a court ruled that management had to include a proposal to stop a company's sales of pâté because of the cruelty to geese from the forced feeding required to engorge their livers, a process described as follows:

> Force-feeding usually begins when the geese are four months old. On some farms where feeding is mechanized, the bird's body and wings are placed in a metal brace and its neck is stretched. Through a funnel inserted 10–12 inches down the throat of the goose, a machine pumps up to 400 grams of corn-based mash into its stomach. An elastic band around the goose's throat prevents regurgitation. When feeding is manual, a handler uses a funnel and stick to force the mash down.[31]

After reading that horrifying description, the judge concluded that the matter was material, even though pâté sales constituted only a minuscule part of the company's business. He ruled that the matter had "ethical and social significance" and should be considered by shareholders.

Exclusion is permitted for proposals that involve personal grievances. The author's personal favorite in this category involves the following proposal for inclusion in the proxy materials of the Orbital Sciences Corporation:

> To my fellow shareholders:
> As long as I can remember, I have wanted to work on rockets. Some people want to be firemen or policemen. I wish to work on rockets. Keeping to my dream, I earned a University of California degree in physics. I sent out 917 resumes looking for work related to rockets. I was not offered one interview.
> Out of all the companies I sought interviews with, the one company that I know is capable of fulfilling my goals is Orbital Sciences Corporation. I sent my resume to [the] Chief Executive Officer, and to the human resource department, and once again was rejected without an interview.
> I have purchased stock in Orbital Sciences Corporation and as a fellow shareholder have come to you to plead my case. I ask you as fellow shareholders to help me get a job with Orbital Sciences Corporation.
> Shareholder proposal
> Whereas R—— F——, a resident of Bellevue, Washington, did try to obtain employment through proper channels at Orbital Sciences Corporation and was not given an interview;
> Now therefore we the shareholders do hereby direct the Chief Executive Officer to give R—— F—— a job in the Advanced Projects Group, as either an assistant to the engineers, a technician, or any other suitable position utilizing R—— F——'s knowledge, skills, and abilities. The job is to start no later than December 31, 1996 and is to pay a starting salary of no less than $19,200 per year.

One of the most controversial topics for shareholder proposals involves discrimination issues. In 1992, the SEC staff announced a per se approach that would allow the exclusion of discrimination proposals concerning religion, race, sex, or sexual orientation. The SEC reversed that per se rule six years later, announcing that it would use a case-by-case approach on these issues. In 2005, for example, the SEC staff required Bank of America Corp. to include a shareholder proxy proposal requiring that at least 50 percent of its board members be minorities. The staff reversed that position one week later and allowed the bank to exclude the proposal.

Reformists and protestors of various stripes have used the SEC proxy provisions to push other causes ranging from opposition to smoking, protests against the war in Vietnam, and environmental issues. More recently, the SEC staff required ExxonMobil Corp. to include a shareholder proposal in its proxy that would require the company to disclose its views on global warming and the effects of drilling for oil in Alaska parkland and other protected areas.

When a company wants to exclude a proposal, it petitions the SEC staff to allow exclusion under one or more of the categories recognized by the SEC rule. This process consumes thousands of hours of SEC staff time, diverts resources from detecting fraud, and is a distraction for corporate management. Exclusions of proposals are sometimes challenged in court even when the SEC staff allows exclusion. In one case, the SEC allowed the Dow Chemical Company to exclude a shareholder proposal that sought to amend the company's charter to prohibit the company from selling napalm for use in Vietnam. The proponent of this proposal was the Medical Committee for Human Rights, which was using a small holding of Dow shares to promote its opposition against the war. The committee claimed that, by manufacturing napalm, Dow was discouraging recruitment of young workers and that the company's global business was being harmed by the negative publicity from the sale of napalm.

A federal appeals court held that the SEC's determination that the proposal could be excluded was subject to judicial review. The court further held that the proposal should be submitted to shareholders because the company was asserting that its "manufacturing and marketing of napalm was made not because of business considerations, but in spite of them; that management in essence decided to pursue a course of activity which generated little profit for the shareholders and actively impaired the company's public relations and recruitment activities because management considered this action morally and politically desirable." The court held that such an approach should be subject to a shareholder vote.

The Supreme Court agreed to review the issue but dismissed the petition as moot after Dow included the proposal in its proxy statement and less than 3 percent of shareholders voted in favor for the proposal.[32] Under SEC rules, this meant that the proposal was ineligible for resubmission for a vote for a number of years. This illustrated another problem with this process, virtually all of the proposals submitted under this SEC rule failed to receive a significant number of shareholder votes without management support. Even in those rare instances in which a proposal was passed over management opposition, management often ignored the demand because it was only a request, such as was done in recent shareholder votes demanding an end to staggered boards of directors.

Fiduciary Duties

Trustees

Another aspect of corporate governance is the application of "fiduciary duties" to the acts of officers, directors, and controlling shareholders. This concept of fiduciary duty was borrowed from the law of trusts that was developed under English law and transplanted to the United States. The law of trusts involves principles of "equity" developed in the chancery courts of London. "Of all the exploits of equity, the largest and most important is the invention and development of the trust."[33] As Professor Frederic W. Maitland has stated: "If we were asked what was the greatest and most distinctive achievement performed by Englishmen in the field of jurisprudence, I cannot think that we could have any better answer to give than this, namely, the development from century to century of the trust idea."[34]

Trusts were, indeed, important in England. Some 20 percent of the capitalized value of all English assets was held in trust at the beginning of the twentieth century. The trust migrated to America. By 1929, banks in the United States were managing more than 100,000 trusts and more than 1,000 millionaires were using trusts to dispose of their estates. The trust concept places the management of one person's assets into the hands of another party, the trustee, who manages those assets for the beneficiary of the trust or the *cestui que trust.* That relationship is ripe for abuse because the beneficiary is completely dependent on the trustee to use proper care in the investment of the trust funds and to avoid self-dealings that benefit the trustee, but harm the beneficiary.

The chancery courts in England imposed special duties on trustees in order to protect trust beneficiaries. "The most fundamental duty owed by the trustee to the beneficiaries of the trust is the duty of loyalty."[35] That fiduciary duty prevents the trustee from profiting at the expense of the beneficiary in dealing with the trust. In addition, "[i]f the fiduciary enters into a transaction with the beneficiary and fails to make a full disclosure of all circumstances known to him affecting the transaction, or if the transaction is unfair to the beneficiary, it can be set aside by him."[36]

A second fiduciary duty is that of "care." Trustees were held to strict standards under that duty in selecting investments for trust funds. Although chancellors in equity proceedings initially allowed trust funds to be invested in joint-stock companies, including the East India Company, losses from common stocks during the South Sea Bubble in 1720 caused the English chancery court to reconsider such investments. The chancery courts then restricted trust investments in securities to government issues. A much cited 1830 decision by a Massachusetts court in *Harvard College v. Amory* ruled that trustees must use "sound discretion" in investing trust assets. Trustees must act in the same manner as "men of prudence, discretion and intelligence manage their own affairs, not in regard to speculation, but in regard to the permanent disposition of their funds, considering the probable income, as well as the probable safety of the capital to be invested."[37]

The courts in the United States differed on whether this "prudent man" rule allowed trustees to invest in corporate stocks, and other uncertainties abounded. State legislatures stepped in to provide guidance through so-called legal lists of instruments approved for trust investments. Those lists initially did not include common stocks but were expanded in the twentieth century to allow some percentage of trust assets to be held in such investments. Still later, those restrictive legal lists were undercut by studies showing that long-term investors in common stock did better than investors in other instruments. The legal lists were further undermined in the last quarter of the twentieth century by "modern portfolio theory," which stresses diversification. Under this theory, the portfolio is assessed as a whole, allowing the introduction of risk elements, even futures and options, to achieve diversification. Modern portfolio theory was given a boost when the Department of Labor ruled that pension plan administrators could meet their prudent man investment obligations by employing that theory in their investment programs for defined benefit retirement plans regulated by the Employee Retirement Income Security Act (ERISA).

The fiduciary concept was borrowed from trusts and applied to corporations in order to fill what the judiciary perceived were gaps in state corporate statutes. The separation of ownership from control recognized by Berle and Means created a demand for protection of shareholders from the self-interest of management. "Courts and legislatures have met this need by treating management, directors, and controlling shareholders as 'fiduciaries' who owe certain legally enforceable duties to the firm."[38] "The corporation is a human enterprise, subject to human failings, and the goal of the law has been to prevent, correct, or rectify those failings when necessary. The bulk of these adjudicative mechanisms come under the general heading of fiduciary duty."[39]

The Business Judgment Rule

The application of fiduciary duties to corporations began in England in the eighteenth century. Lord Hardwicke concluded in 1742 that the members of a corporate board were employed in a trust relationship for shareholders. That concept was recognized in a few judicial decisions in America at the end of the nineteenth century, but did not achieve much recognition until after World War I. Fiduciary standards for corporate directors and officers then became popular. There are, however, some deep-seated differences between the supervision of a trust and the management of a corporation. The trustee of a trust is allowed to invest in only "prudent" investments and forbidden to incur risk, modern portfolio theory being only an example of how reduced risk is the goal of a trustee. The opposite is often the case for a corporate venture: The greater the risk, the greater the reward.

Managers of a corporation are expected to incur risk in order to obtain rewards in the form of profits. Were it otherwise, no pharmaceutical company would ever invest billions of dollars, often fruitlessly, in the search for new drugs. The start-up companies that transformed the economy through the Internet would never have incurred those risks. Computer chip makers would not have sought to improve their product, lest they fail, and so on. Society will not progress unless corporate managers are free to incur risk, sometimes reckless risks. Treating a corporation as a strict trust would stop that risk taking because a breach of fiduciary duty results in personal liability for managers, exposing them to billions of dollars of personal liability in a large corporation.

Another difference between the trust and a corporation is that trustees are not allowed to profit at the expense of the trust, receiving only moderate compensation for their services. In contrast, corporate managers seek to maximize their profits and obtain lucrative compensation through their corporate offices. That compensation is the key incentive for employees to fight their way through the ranks and perform most ably. Removing lucrative compensation incentives would decrease competition, breed caution and laxness, and harm the economy as a result.

The courts have sought to paper over the differences between a trust and a corporation through something called the "business judgment rule." That rule posits that the courts will not second-guess the business judgment of management, even if management proves to be wrong and the company is destroyed, but the courts will not defer to the business judgment of management when it breaches a fiduciary duty. An often cited application of the business judgment rule involved the lighting of Wrigley Field in Chicago for nighttime baseball. A minority shareholder brought suit in 1967 charging that Philip Wrigley, the president and majority stockholder of a Delaware corporation that owned the Chicago Cubs, was acting improperly by refusing to light Wrigley Field so the Cubs could play at night. Nighttime baseball had been played since 1935, and well over one-half of all professional baseball games were being played at night by the middle of the 1960s. The Cubs were losing money, and the plaintiff complained that revenues were hurt substantially by the lack of nighttime games. Wrigley was claimed to be acting on a personal belief that baseball was a daytime game and from an unwillingness to disturb the neighborhood with traffic from night games, matters that were alleged to conflict with the interests of the shareholders.

The court dismissed the complaint, holding that under Delaware law it is not the function of the courts "to resolve for corporations questions of policy and business management. The directors are chosen to pass upon such questions."[40] The court deferred to the board of directors on whether night baseball would be profitable and ruled that the board could properly conclude that it was in the long-term interests of the corporation to protect the neighborhood. In a postscript, the Chicago Cubs management did try to add lights to Wrigley Field in 1982, but neighborhood opposition led to a legislative ban on nighttime baseball at the field. A compromise was reached in 1988 that allowed the Cubs to light the field, but only for eighteen night games per season. The lights did not bring the Cubs a World Series title; their last being won in 1908.

Fiduciary Duty of Care

Interest in the corporate fiduciary duty of care had grown with a Supreme Court decision written in 1920 by Justice Oliver Wendell Holmes in *Bates v. Dresser*.[41] In that case, the court held that the president of a bank breached a fiduciary duty of care to shareholders when he ignored some warning signals concerning a clerk who was stealing from the bank's accounts. Justice Holmes stated that "some animals must have given at least one exhibition of dangerous propensities before the owner can be held," and he conceded that the clerk had created a unique scheme to loot the bank that could not have been uncovered "except by a lucky chance." Nevertheless, the warning signals were held to be sufficient to put the president on notice that something was amiss. They included a missing package containing $150 and some shortages in a few accounts that were blamed on the wrong employee. The clerk involved in the fraud was living beyond his means; he was making only $12 a week but had been "supporting a woman" and had "set up an automobile," and he may have been speculating in copper stocks. The bank's examiners failed to uncover the fraud, but the president was held personally liable for the defalcations even though he was a victim of the fraud; his own account had been looted. Outside directors were relieved of liability because they received no such warnings.

Another respected jurist, Learned Hand, ruled in 1924 that a director breached the fiduciary duty of care when the director paid little attention to the affairs of the company. Judge Hand examined the role of a board member:

> While directors are collectively the managers of the company, they are not expected to interfere individually in the actual conduct of its affairs. To do so would disturb the authority of the officers and destroy their individual responsibility, without which no proper discipline is possible. To them must be left the initiative and the immediate direction of the business; the directors can act individually only by counsel and advice to them. Yet they have an individual duty to keep themselves informed in some detail, and it is this duty that the defendant in my judgment failed adequately to perform.[42]

The director in this case was a mere "figurehead." He had spoken with one Maynard, the manager of the company, while commuting to New York City from Flushing and on social occasions, but only general information was given to the effect that the business looked promising, when in fact it was failing.

The director had invested a substantial amount in the enterprise but relied entirely on Maynard to direct the company. Judge Hand thought more was required of a director, but could find no damages. Even if the director had been informed of the personnel problems that caused the company to fail, it was not clear that he could have resolved those issues, which were "slowly bleeding it to death." This was not entirely just a pyrrhic victory for fiduciary duties because future courts would more carefully search for damages from a breach of the fiduciary duty of care.

Delaware Duty of Care

The duty of care became a way by which courts could sit in judgment on the process by which corporate decisions were made by a board of directors, setting aside any decisions the court thought were made too hastily or without enough information. The most virulent example of such second-guessing was a 1985 decision of the Delaware Supreme Court in *Smith v. Van Gorkom*,[43] which was so extreme that the legislative reaction was to allow corporations to eliminate the fiduciary duty of care. There, in a fulsome opinion, the Delaware Supreme Court ruled that the board of directors of the Trans Union Corporation breached its fiduciary duty of care in approving a merger on short notice and without adequate consideration. Trans Union was facing a somewhat unique problem that was driving the board to seek a merger. The company had investment tax credits that it could not use before they expired, which meant that a valuable asset was being dissipated. Trans Union's chief executive officer and chairman, Jerome Van Gorkom, could not convince Congress to make those credits refundable. He then arranged to sell the company to Jay A. Pritzker, a wealthy corporate takeover specialist, for $55 per share. The board met on short notice and approved the transaction in a twenty-minute meeting. They considered no documents, had no presentation from investment bankers, and did not even read the merger agreement.

The Delaware Supreme Court held that this hasty approval violated the board's fiduciary duty of care. The court refused to credit that the board had been discussing the tax problem ad nauseam and that the merger, at a large premium, was a heaven-sent solution to the tax credit problem. The court's ruling was something of a surprise since the members of the Trans Union board of directors included several outside directors who were prominent members of the business community and collectively had over a century of business experience, as opposed to little or none on the Delaware Supreme Court. The court conceded that "Trans Union's five 'inside' directors had backgrounds in law and accounting, 116 years of collective employment by the Company and 68 years of combined experience on its Board. Trans Union's five 'outside' directors included four chief executives of major corporations and an economist who was a former dean" of the graduate school of business at the University of Chicago and chancellor of the University of Rochester.

"The 'outside' directors had 78 years of combined experience as chief executive officers of major corporations and 50 years of cumulative experience as directors of Trans Union."[44] In the court's view, however, these experienced directors provided no value to the decision-making process because of the haste in which the decision was made.

The court demonized Van Gorkom in the opinion, while the directors undoubtedly thought he was a hero for arranging this deal. If serious people indulge in such acts, the Trans Union directors probably exchanged corporate high fives with Van Gorkom when he disclosed the transaction at the board meeting. After all, the stock had been trading at less than $40 in the public markets, the company had run out of solutions for solving its tax credit problems, and the sale to Pritzker was a clean cash deal that would give the shareholders a premium of at least $15 per share over the market high, an increase of over one-third. Yet the board members found themselves facing personal liability and charges that they had breached their fiduciary duties. The court asserted that greater care might have led to a higher price, but a search that included solicitation of over 150 companies by Salomon Brothers failed to uncover another suitor. That prominent and aggressive investment banking firm was given substantial incentives by Trans Union to make that search a successful one, but no buyer appeared, a fact the court sought to avoid by suggesting that Van Gorkom had discouraged buyers.

The Trans Union board was faulted by the Delaware court for not consulting with an investment banker and failing to read the lengthy merger agreement. The court wanted the board to make decisions as a court does, with briefs, arguments, and extended deliberations, a very formal, ritualistic, and time-consuming decision-making procedure. This demand overlooked the realities of the business world. Business decisions often have to be made quickly or an opportunity will be lost. In the case of Trans Union, there was a downturn in the industry after its sale. As a result of the board's decisive action, the shareholders received a large premium for their stock instead of a loss. The court's demand for top price for shareholders is, in any event, a very dangerous business approach. Any investor that seeks to hold out only for the top of the market will die poor because no one is able to predict that event. The Rothschilds achieved fame in their financial dealings on the strength of their view that "only fools set out to make the highest returns."[45] The Delaware court was also hopelessly disconnected from reality in faulting the directors for not reading the merger agreement. There was nothing to read. It was an all-cash deal. It was up to the well-paid and skilled lawyers employed by Trans Union to prepare the fine print and assure that the price would be obtained in that agreement. The directors had no interest in reading the turgid pages of the lengthy agreement needed to reach that simple result.

The Trans Union litigation was later settled for a reported $23.5 million that was paid in part by the directors' liability insurance and in part by Pritzker. As a result of the *Van Gorkom* decision, director and officer liability insurance costs rose 360 percent in a single year and became almost impossible to obtain by many corporations. Criticism of the *Van Gorkom* decision was widespread, described as "ludicrous" in one instance. Delaware and some thirty other states enacted legislation that allowed corporations to remove directors from any liability for a breach of the fiduciary duty of care. A survey subsequently found that the shareholders of 90 percent of Delaware corporations responded by relieving their directors from the duty of care. Those proposals were approved by large majorities of the shareholders, evidencing either affirmative approval or a lack of interest in following management's recommendations on the issue. As for Jerome Van Gorkom, he continued to act as chairman of the Chicago Lyric Opera Society, became an undersecretary at the State Department, and served as the deputy director of a Catholic relief organization, acting as a volunteer personally distributing food to the needy. He bailed the Chicago school system out of a dire crisis and served (less successfully) as the head of the Chicago Housing Authority. Van Gorkom was appointed to serve on two federal advisory commissions that sought reform of the nation's Social Security system.

The Delaware statute allowing a corporation's charter to eliminate the fiduciary duty of care after the *Van Gorkom* case did not limit the liability of a director for a breach of the director's fiduciary duty of loyalty, actions taken in bad faith, or intentional misconduct. The Delaware Supreme Court, unrepentant, used those provisions to nullify waivers of the duty of care. The court held that, notwithstanding any such waiver, it would review the "entire fairness" of transactions when there was a lack of care on the part of the board of directors. This was completely confusing and undermined the legislative provision for waivers.

The Delaware Supreme Court seemed to retreat a bit from its expansive application of fiduciary duties in a case challenging a decision by Michael Eisner to hire Michael Ovitz as the president of the Walt Disney Company. Eisner was the incredibly well-compensated chairman and chief executive officer of Walt Disney. Ovitz was his longtime friend and a Hollywood talent broker. Eisner gave Ovitz a five-year employment contract that provided for a $1 million per year salary plus options on five million shares of Walt Disney stock. The Disney board of directors approved this contract even though Ovitz had no experience in running a public company. Fourteen months later, after quarrelling with Eisner, Ovitz was terminated. Ovitz's employment contract entitled him to a severance package worth $140 million. Shareholders sued in a Delaware court, claiming that the Disney board had breached its fiduciary duties in approving that employment contract. The complaint charged a breach of the fiduciary duty of care even though Disney had eliminated that duty after the *Van Gorkom* decision.

The complaining shareholders asserted that the Disney board breached their fiduciary duties by agreeing to a contract that allowed Ovitz to walk away with such a vast sum for so little time on the job or addition of value. The complaint charged that Eisner was rewarding a friend when he entered into the Ovitz contract, rather than acting in the best interests of the shareholders. The outside directors who considered the contract were also attacked because they were said to be cronies or otherwise beholden to Eisner and had acted to please him, rather than protecting the shareholders. The plaintiffs further charged that a number of corporate governance features favored by reformists were missing at Walt Disney. The company's outside directors did not own much stock, they did not hold a regular "retreat," or meet separately from management, and they did not give Eisner a written assessment of his performance as was common at other companies. However, the court concluded:

> All good corporate governance practices include compliance with statutory law and case law establishing fiduciary duties. But the law of corporate fiduciary duties and remedies for violation of those duties are distinct from the aspirational goals of ideal corporate governance practices. Aspirational ideals of good corporate governance practices for boards of directors that go beyond the minimal legal requirements of the corporation law are highly desirable, often tend to benefit stockholders, sometimes reduce litigation and can usually help directors avoid liability. But they are not required by the corporation law and do not define standards of liability.[46]

The Delaware Supreme Court held that the business judgment rule protected the directors. It treated the case as one involving a breach of the fiduciary duty of care even though Disney shareholders had waived that right. The court concluded that the board was protected by its reliance on a compensation expert in approving the Ovitz employment agreement. The court said: "Due care in the decision making context is *process* due care only. Irrationality is the outer limit of the business judgment rule. Irrationality may be the functional equivalent of the waste test or it may tend to show that the decision is not made in good faith, which is a key ingredient of the business judgment rule."[47] So the Disney board of directors that was composed of Eisner cronies was allowed to approve a compensation agreement without realizing that Ovitz would walk away with almost $140 million if Eisner got mad at him, a not uncommon practice for Eisner. In contrast, the renowned board members at Trans Union were personally liable for obtaining a premium of one-third over the market for shareholders and saving them millions from the subsequent market downturn. Those results hardly seem consistent or even rational.

The fight at Disney was not over. On remand, the plaintiffs amended their complaint to claim further breaches of fiduciary duties, and the action was allowed to go to trial by a chancery judge on the grounds that the directors "consciously and intentionally" disregarded their responsibilities, which the judge opined would take them outside of the protection of the charter provision waiving the duty of care.[48] That formula seems to mean that directors will be liable unless they meet a duty of care that was supposedly waived. In any event, Ovitz was hammered at the trial on his wayward management at Walt Disney. He claimed that he was frustrated at every step by Eisner. The trial lasted thirty-seven days and generated almost 10,000 pages of testimony.

In a 175–page opinion, the Delaware chancery judge ruled that, while the actions of the Disney board did not meet ideal corporate practices, they did not rise to the level of a breach of fiduciary duties. That opinion was rendered in August 2005, long after the Enron scandal; but, in a rare instance of judicial restraint, the judge concluded that fiduciary duty standards should not be changed by that event and other scandals. He also noted that imposing overly high standards of care could result in risk avoidance by corporate managers that could cripple the modern corporation and hurt society as a whole.

The Ovitz contract was not the biggest such disaster at Disney. Another executive, Jeffrey Katzenberg, was forced out by Eisner before Ovitz's arrival. After his own hiring, Ovitz negotiated a settlement of Katzenberg's severance claims for $90 million, but Eisner refused to pay. Disney did not fare well in the subsequent litigation over Kazenberg's claims. Eisner turned down several settlement proposals that would have resolved that litigation for considerably less than the $285 million Disney ultimately had to pay Katzenberg.

The Fiduciary Duty of Loyalty

The fiduciary duty of loyalty achieved prominence principally as the result of decisions written by Judge Benjamin Cardozo of the New York Court of Appeals during the 1920s. Cardozo would succeed to the Supreme Court seat of Oliver Wendell Holmes, the promoter of the fiduciary duty of care. In 1928, while still on the New York bench, Judge Cardozo ruled in *Meinhard v. Salmon,* that a partner in a joint venture breached a duty of loyalty to his partner by not sharing a new business opportunity.[49] Cardozo concluded that this was an opportunity that belonged to the partnership and not to the individual partner, despite the fact that the new venture would commence after the termination of the partnership. In much quoted words, Cardozo stated that, where a fiduciary duty of loyalty is owed, the ordinary "morals of the market place" are not sufficient. "Not honesty alone, but the punctilio of an honor the most sensitive, is then the standard of behavior." Cardozo's extreme sensitivity to the morals of the marketplace reflected the fact that his own father had been removed from the New York bench for misconduct in connection with the judicial assistance he rendered to robber barons Jay Gould and Jim Fisk. That assistance allowed them to avoid the disastrous effects of their failed gold corner in 1869.

Another opinion rendered by the younger Cardozo held that an outside director breached a duty of loyalty to the company on whose board he served by entering into a one-sided contract with another company that he controlled.[50] In that case, John F. Maynard was both the president of Globe Woolen Co. and a director and chairman of the executive committee of Utica Gas & Electric Co. An engineer at Utica had tried to convince Maynard to electrify Globe Woolen's operations, but Maynard refused unless he could be guaranteed a saving over his present costs. The Utica engineer assured Maynard there would be a saving, and contracts to that effect were approved at a Utica executive committee meeting. Maynard attended that meeting, but did not participate or vote. Globe Woolen spent $21,000 to convert to electricity, but the contract quickly became a losing one for Utica because the engineer had miscalculated. Maynard also increased Globe Woolen's dyeing operations that consumed twice as much electricity as an alternative process ("slubbing"). It appeared that Utica would lose $300,000 on this contract if it were to be enforced.

Cardozo likened Maynard to a trustee in his role as a director of Utica, stating that a trustee "cannot rid himself of the duty to warn and to denounce, if there is improvidence or oppression, either apparent or on the surface, or lurking beneath the surface, but visible to the practiced eye." Cardozo asserted that, by attending the Utica executive committee meeting, Maynard was implicitly assuring the other committee members that it was a just and equitable contract. "Faith in his loyalty disarmed suspicion," and the contract was held to be voidable by Utica.

Cardozo did not have the last word on the ability of a director to contract with the corporation on whose board he sits. That issue was the subsequent subject of state corporate laws. In 1931, California amended its laws to allow such transactions if the transaction was fair to the corporation or approved by a majority of disinterested directors or shareholders. That approach was followed by other states and was adopted in the Model Business Act, but the expansion of fiduciary duties cannot be stopped by mere legislation. A California court ruled that compliance with the voting provisions of that statute was not enough; the transaction had to be inherently fair to the corporation even with a favorable vote.[51] The Delaware court made a similar ruling with respect to its statute, stating that the statute "merely removes an 'interested director' cloud when its terms are met and provides against invalidation of an agreement 'solely' because such a director or officer is involved. Nothing in the statute sanctions unfairness . . . or removes the transaction from judicial scrutiny."[52]

The PGA Tour was to find out that such a statute did not even remove the "cloud" referred to by the Delaware court. The tour had passed a rule banning use of so-called square or *U* grooved clubfaces by players in favor of *V* grooves. The Tour believed that the *U* groove clubs spun the ball excessively, allowing too much control out of the rough and taking away the advantage of landing on the fairway. The player members on the board recused themselves from the vote on the rule because of a perceived conflict of interest from their sponsorships of various club manufacturers, some of which did not make or promote *U* grooves. Instead, the outside directors approved the rule. A bylaw of the tour, however, required a majority vote of player representatives before an equipment rule could be passed. After being challenged on that issue in court, the tour had the entire board approve an amendment to its bylaws, allowing approval of an equipment rule by the disinterested board members, which they proceeded to give once again. This process complied with an interested director statute like that in California and Delaware. That action was challenged, however, and a federal appeals court in California ruled that complying with a state statute on interested director transactions did not preclude the application of fiduciary duties. The court believed there was a cloud over the decision-making process because the player members of the board knew that the bylaw change would result in the same decision that had not been properly approved previously.[53]

Another aspect of the fiduciary duty of loyalty involves the usurpation of a corporate opportunity by an officer or director. This concept was made famous by a 1939 decision of the Delaware court in *Guth v. Loft.*[54] In 1931 Pepsi-Cola was in bankruptcy after suffering large losses from speculations in sugar futures; it had guessed wrong on the effect of World War I on sugar prices. Loft Inc. had been purchasing Coca-Cola syrup for its stores in large amounts, but Charles Guth, the president of Loft, became dissatisfied with Coca-Cola because it would not give him a discount. Guth began negotiating with Pepsi and was able to purchase its trademark and formula for a small amount. Guth used Loft funds without the permission of its board to make the purchase for a company he owned. Guth then used Loft facilities and employees to manufacture and advertise Pepsi and used Loft stores for distribution. After Pepsi became popular and very valuable (it was worth millions at the time of the suit), Loft sued Guth, claiming that he had breached his fiduciary duty of loyalty by usurping a corporate opportunity. Without splitting any infinitives, the Delaware Supreme Court agreed:

> Corporate officers and directors are not permitted to use their position of trust and confidence to further their private interests. While technically not trustees, they stand in a fiduciary relation to the corporation and its stockholders. A public policy, existing through the years, and derived from a profound knowledge of human characteristics and motives, has established a rule that demands of a corporate officer or director, peremptorily and inexorably, the most scrupulous observance of his duty, not only affirmatively to protect the interests of the corporation committed to his charge, but also to refrain from doing anything that would work injury to the corporation, or to deprive it of profit or advantage which his skill and ability might properly bring to it, or to enable it to make in the reasonable and lawful exercise of its powers. The rule that requires an undivided and unselfish loyalty to the corporation demands that there shall be no conflict between duty and self-interest.[55]

The court went on to identify a hazard of the fiduciary duty concept: "The occasions for the determination of honesty, good faith and loyal conduct are many and varied, and no hard and fast rule can be formulated. The standard of loyalty is measured by no fixed scale."

Charles Guth raised some defenses that are common to corporate opportunity cases. He unsuccessfully claimed, among other things, that the Pepsi opportunity was out of Loft's line of business and that the opportunity had come to him in a personal capacity and not as an officer or director of Loft. When such claims are raised, the courts may look to whether there was an "expectancy" on the part of the corporation for the opportunity, whether, in fairness, the transaction belonged to the corporation, and whether the opportunity was disclosed to the corporation. Merely because the corporation could not afford the opportunity may not be a defense because the corporation could possibly borrow the money on the strength of the opportunity.

Executive Compensation

Efforts have been made to use fiduciary duties to curb excessive executive compensation. In *Rogers v. Hill,* the Supreme Court held that an incentive plan for executives of the American Tobacco Company was an improper waste of corporate assets.[56] That compensation program was contained in a bylaw approved almost unanimously by the shareholders in 1912. It was devised by James Duke, the benefactor of Duke University, who controlled and was retiring from the company at the time he proposed the compensation plan. Duke offered his executives 10 percent of any amount the company earned over its current earnings so that they would have a stake in increasing profits. He believed this to be fair to shareholders like himself since they would be receiving 90 percent of any increases.

Tobacco sales expanded quickly during the 1920s, and the executives at the American Tobacco Company were receiving what then amounted to massive amounts of compensation. The president, George W. Hill, received total compensation of $592,000 in 1929, which jumped to over $1 million in 1930. At the time, economists were advocating a ceiling on executive compensation and it was popularly thought that "no man can be worth $1,000,000 a year."[57] The federal circuit court of appeals in New York upheld the compensation arrangement in a 2–1 decision, but it was later discovered that one of the judges voting to support the bonuses, Martin T. Manton, had been given a "loan" that was arranged by an American Tobacco Company lawyer in the amount of $250,000. That loan was never repaid. The judge was convicted of accepting a bribe and the lawyer was disbarred. The Supreme Court took up the matter, holding that, while the percentage of the bonus was not excessive, the absolute amounts rendered by the enormous expansion of the company's business became unreasonable at some point. The court directed the trial court to decide to what extent the payments were excessive, but the shareholders then ratified the payments.

Another challenge was made to payments under the American Tobacco Company's compensation scheme in subsequent years. The payments continued to be massive. For example, Hill's son was receiving compensation of $230,000 at age thirty-two, after being on the job for only three years. But the stockholders again ratified the payments in 1940, and a New York state court judge, after examining the value of the services provided and the expansion of the company's business, refused to find that the compensation was excessive. Although courts continue to assert that there is some outer limit for executive compensation, this decision pretty much put an end to challenges to excessive executive pay under the fiduciary duty concept, paving the way for the incredible compensation packages paid out to Enron and other executives.

Close Corporations

Fiduciary duties have found their most expansive application in the context of "close" corporations, which are small companies that have no market for their stock and that are owned by only a few shareholders who are often employed in the business. The close corporation is frequently family-owned, which only intensifies the battles over control that frequently take place in these enterprises. In a public corporation, shareholders who disagree with management, or believe themselves to be oppressed, are able to sell their stock. No such opportunity exists in a close corporation.

Minority shareholders are subject to the whims of the majority in a close corporation and often find themselves squeezed out by being denied access to the corporate treasury. That can occur in a number of ways, but most common is for the majority shareholder to be paid most or all of the corporation's profits as a salary, leaving little or nothing for dividends that would give minority shareholders some return on their investment. The minority shareholders may be denied jobs while relatives of the majority shareholder are given employment. The courts have tried to remedy the plight of minority shareholders in close corporations through a broad application of fiduciary duties. In fact, there are now two sets of fiduciaries duties imposed on corporations: one for shareholders in public corporations and one for those in close corporations. Both sets of laws were created from whole cloth by the judiciary.

In one case, a Massachusetts court held that Harry Rodd, a majority shareholder in a close corporation, breached a fiduciary duty of loyalty when he had the corporation buy back a portion of his stockholdings as a part of a retirement and estate plan. This was found to have been unfair to John Donahue, a minority shareholder who was not given a similar opportunity to sell back his stock to the company. Rodd had been the driving force behind expansion of the company, making an initial investment of $10,000 and loaning money to the company for its expansion, mortgaging his house in the process. Donahue was a nonmanagement employee in the company, but he was promoted through the ranks after he invested $1,000 in the enterprise at Rodd's urging. Donahue also received a benefit from the purchase of Rodd's shares because that transaction increased the percentage of Donahue's ownership interest, diluting the ownership of Rodd in the process. The court, nevertheless, thought the access to the corporate treasury given to Rodd by the purchase of his shares should be made equally available to Donahue.[58]

The protection of minority shareholders in close corporations reached its apex when some state courts ruled that any act by a majority shareholder was a breach of fiduciary duty if it defeated the "reasonable expectations" of a minority shareholder. In a North Carolina case, *Meiselman v. Meiselman,*[59] a father had build up a chain of theaters into a very valuable business. He left the shares of the company on his death to his two sons, but the younger son, Ira, was given a greater amount than the older son, Michael. Michael's relegation to a subordinate role was apparently the result of family concerns over whom he was dating, since he had brought "a non-Jewish woman" to a family function. Further friction developed after Ira failed to invite Michael "to a football game to which all of the males in the family traditionally had been invited." Michael's shares were initially placed in a trust subject to his father's control until he married a Jewish woman. Despite these problems, Michael was employed in the family enterprises until he brought suit against Ira for usurping a corporate opportunity involving the handling of ticket sales. Ira then fired Michael and took away his corporate credit cards. Michael sued again to protest his discharge.

The North Carolina Supreme Court held that majority shareholders in a close corporation owe special fiduciary duties that prohibit them from engaging in activities that would defeat the "reasonable expectations" of minority shareholders. In this case, the court concluded that Michael might have reasonable expectations of continued employment, access to the corporate credit cards and other fringe benefits, and even participation in management decisions. The court rejected Ira's claims that Michael should have only the rights of an ordinary shareholder—that is, to vote his minority shares. In a separate opinion, however, one judge noted that Michael had little expectation of anything since the shares were a gift from his father. Michael had not used his own funds to buy the stock, and his father had clearly wanted Ira in control.

Then there was the Galler family corporation in Illinois, which was created by two brothers as equal owners. The illness of one brother led to a shareholders' agreement providing that the family of each brother would be given equal control and equal access to corporate profits through required dividends and payments. When one of the brothers, Benjamin, died, the other brother, Isadore, and his family refused to carry out the agreement, cutting off payments to Benjamin's widow and refusing to pay the amount of the dividend set by the shareholder agreement. An Illinois court ordered the agreement to be enforced and required the Isadore Galler family to account for all monies it had received from the corporation while the case was pending. Isadore's family then refused to make the payments due Benjamin's widow unless she agreed to give up her demand for an accounting.[60] The court stepped in again and required the Isadore Galler family to repay $300,000, but it took over twenty years to resolve this dispute through the courts.

The Galler decision was representative of a number of decisions involving shareholder agreements that sought to allocate control of a close corporation but were subsequently challenged by one side or the other. The Delaware courts handed down a number of confusing decisions on the enforceability of such agreements. In one case, the court considered an agreement between two members of the Ringling circus family, Edith Ringling and Aubrey Haley, the former wife of Edith's brother. The agreement defined how their proxies should be voted so as to ensure that control of the circus was kept away from John Ringling North, who they feared would mismanage the company. The agreement provided that an arbitrator would be given a proxy to vote their shares if the two women could not agree on whom to vote for as directors. The agreement worked for three years, but in 1946 Edith Ringling and Aubrey Haley quarreled. Haley then refused to vote her shares as directed by the arbitrator.

The Delaware Supreme Court held that their voting agreement was valid but was not specifically enforceable because it was not "coupled with an interest," an arcane legal principle involving agency law.[61] This meant that the court would not order the shares to be voted as agreed, but money damages for the failure to vote as agreed could be sought. In the case of the Ringling voting agreement, however, damages could not be shown from the mere loss of control, making the agreement worthless. The result was to allow John Ringling North to obtain control of the corporation from the other two Ringling family members. He would bankrupt it in 1956.

The court in the Ringling case ruled that the agreement was valid even though it did not comply with a Delaware statute for voting trusts; those trust arrangements were specifically enforceable. Subsequently, a group of oil companies owning a majority interest in the American Independent Oil Company (AIOC), a Delaware corporation exploring for oil in the Middle East, entered into a voting agreement that sought to keep control of that company away from other participating oil companies. The lawyers structured the agreement as a voting trust in order to make it enforceable and avoid the specific enforcement problem raised by the Ringling decision. At the same time, the lawyers were relying on the Ringling holding that shareholder agreements need not comply with the voting trust statute, which required that the stock be transferred on the company's books to the trustees and set limitations on the term of the trust. The Delaware court admitted that, "if read literally," the Ringling decision supported the views of the lawyers drafting the agreement. Nevertheless, the court held that the agreement was void for not complying with the Delaware voting trust statute because it was in all essential terms a voting trust.[62] However, a later Delaware case held that a shareholders' agreement that was in the form of a voting trust was not void. The court distinguished the AIOC case on the grounds that the agreement in the case before it was known to the other shareholders, while the AIOC agreement was not.[63]

In desperation, another set of lawyers took a different approach with even more disastrous results for Giant Food Inc., a large grocery chain based in the Washington, DC, area. Giant was a public company, but the common stock sold to the public was nonvoting. This allowed the company to be controlled in equal parts by the Cohen and Lehrman families. The Cohen family held the company's Class AC stock and the Lehrman family held its Class AL stock. Each class could elect two members of the four-member board. A third class of stock was added after some family squabbling in order to prevent a deadlock on the board. This Class AD stock was entitled to elect one member to the board to serve as a tiebreaker in the event of a deadlock. The single share of stock for this class was set at $10 par value. It had no right to dividends or to share in distributions on liquidation beyond its par value. The share of Class AD stock was issued to Joseph Danzansky, the company's corporate counsel.

This arrangement seemed to have worked well between 1950 and 1964, but then Danzansky voted in favor of a Cohen proposal in which Danzansky replaced a Cohen family member as president of the company. The AD and AC shares were voted in approval of that proposition, the AL shares against. Danzansky selected his successor to the AD stock, who then proceeded to ratify Danzansky's employment contract. The Lehrman family cried foul and tried to have the Delaware court declare that the Class AD stock was an illegal voting trust. The court declined to do so, concluding that Delaware law allowed as many classes of stock as desired by a corporation.[64] This meant that the Lehrman family lost its equal position upon Danzansky's defection, which undercut the whole purpose of the arrangement.

New Business Structures

Late in the twentieth century, new forms of corporate structure appeared that challenged the traditional application of fiduciary duties for close corporations. This movement started with concerns over liabilities from traditional general partnerships in which all members were liable personally for the debts of the partnership. Such unlimited liability meant that, if partnership assets were inadequate to pay a liability, the partners were jointly and severally liable for that debt to the full extent of their personal assets. In contrast, shareholders in a corporation are protected by the corporate "veil" from such personal liability.

Most business enterprises were incorporated in order to avoid the personal liability associated with the partnership, but the traditional corporate governance structure was often too unwieldy for small businesses. To deal with that concern, a new form of limited liability enterprise was created, the "limited liability company" (LLC), an entity that seems to be modeled after the German GmbH. The state of Wyoming was the first to enact legislation allowing such entities, in 1977, and other states soon followed. The LLC authorized by those statutes allowed complete flexibility in capital structure and management, while also allowing limited liability. One concern was double taxation. A corporation is taxed on its earnings and then shareholders are taxed on dividends when those profits are distributed. The Internal Revenue Service (IRS) had alleviated some of that hardship for small corporations by allowing them to elect "Subchapter S" status, which did not include a tax at the corporate level. Nevertheless, qualification for such status was limited and did not allow multiple classes of shareholders. The IRS subsequently recognized favorable pass-through tax treatment for the owners of LLCs and adopted a "check the box" approach for other corporations that allowed much more flexibility in obtaining pass-through treatment even for Subchapter S corporations.

The interests of the members of the LLC were not represented by traditional stock that was governed by the corporate laws of the state of incorporation. Rather, their ownership rights were spelled out in an "operating agreement" that governed the operations and management of the LLC. This innovative structure was just in time for the wave of entrepreneurs seeking to exploit the Internet. The LLC was popular with many other small business owners wanting to run their businesses as partnerships but with the limited liability available to owners of a corporation. The operating agreement could be quite detailed on how the affairs of the company were to be managed, allowing management structures outside the traditional board of directors. Minority interests could be protected by contract, including such things as "tag-along" provisions requiring a purchase of the minority's interest equal in proportion to a sale by the majority.

More Fiduciary Duties

Fiduciary Duties of Controlling Shareholders

Another area of corporate governance to which fiduciary duties have been applied involves the activities of controlling shareholders. In one case, the Delaware court held that a controlling shareholder of the Sinclair Oil Company had to show that its decision not to enforce a contract between Sinclair and another controlled subsidiary was not "intrinsically" unfair to minority shareholders.[65] More extreme was a decision by Justice Roger Traynor in California, which held that a controlling shareholder of H.F. Ahmanson & Company breached a fiduciary duty by creating a market in the stock of a savings and loan association (S&L) that excluded minority shareholders. The S&L had only a few shares outstanding and had no interest in making a public offering. The United Financial Corp. bought 85 percent of those shares. United then sold its own stock to the public, raising large sums for its owners and creating an active market in United stock, but not that of the S&L. United made an offer to the remaining minority shareholders in the S&L, but it was badly underpriced. Justice Traynor held that exclusion of the minority shareholders from the market for the United stock violated a fiduciary duty to minority shareholders of the S&L, rejecting a claim that the minority was seeking a free ride on the expense, effort, and risk taken by United to create that market.[66]

Another corporate governance issue involving controlling shareholders has been the premium commonly paid over market prices when control stock is purchased. The premium is paid because control can bring all the perquisites of management, including changing business plans, large compensation packages and, of course, the corporate jet and a Manhattan apartment. Adolf Berle posited in 1932 that such a premium was a corporate asset. The courts have not adopted that theory in its entirety, but on occasion will require surrender of the premium. One instance in which Berle's corporate asset theory was adopted involved the sale of a controlling interest of the Newport Steel Corp. for a premium during a period of steel shortages caused by the Korean conflict. Steel prices were frozen, but the premium was paid for the right to allocate the steel production of Newport. A federal appeals court held that this was the impermissible sale of a corporate asset.[67] The seller in this case was required to give up his control premium. He had previously blocked a merger that would have benefited all shareholders.

The facts of the Newport case were peculiar, and the Berle doctrine has not otherwise been applied broadly, but it does occasionally raise its head. Another occasion in which a control premium is improper is when control is sold to someone the seller knows will loot the corporation. A control premium paid for a corporate office is also improper. When more than 50 percent of the stock is sold, the courts allow the parties to agree that the existing directors will resign and be replaced with the purchaser's candidates, as replacement is a foregone conclusion. The courts become concerned when a premium is paid for less than 50 percent of the stock because it may be for the sale of a corporate office. As Adolf Berle pointed out, however, working control of a large public company may be obtained with less than 50 percent of the stock because most shareholders will vote for management's candidates in all events.

When does a position become so small that it cannot justify a claim of control and becomes an illegal sale of an office? The limit seemed to have been reached by Roy Cohen, Senator Joseph McCarthy's notorious assistant and controversial lawyer. Cohen owned only 3 percent of the stock of the Lionel Corp., but controlled seven of the ten positions on the board. Cohen sold his stock for a premium under an agreement in which he agreed to have his directors resign and replace them with the purchaser's candidates. The court voided the sale of those offices.[68]

Derivative Suits

Another device entering the corporate governance debate is the "derivative suit" that is brought by a shareholder on behalf of the corporation. There was no such right of action at common law, but one was recognized by Lord Chancellor Lyndhurst in the English courts of equity in 1828. That right of action migrated to the United States not long afterwards. As the United States Supreme Court describes it:

> The common law refused . . . to permit stockholders to call corporate managers to account in actions at law. The possibilities for abuse, thus presented, were not ignored by corporate officers and directors. Early in the 19th century, equity provided

relief both in this country and in England. Without detailing these developments, it suffices to say that the remedy in this country, first dealt with by this Court in *Dodge v. Woolsey,* 18 How. 331 (1856), provided redress not only against faithless officers and directors but also against third parties who had damaged or threatened the corporate properties and whom the corporation through its managers refused to pursue. The remedy made available in equity was the derivative suit, viewed in this country as a suit to enforce a *corporate* cause of action against officers, directors, and third parties. As elaborated in the cases, one precondition for the suit was a valid claim on which the corporation could have sued; another was that the corporation itself had refused to proceed after suitable demand, unless excused by extraordinary conditions.[69]

The derivative suit is now recognized in state and federal courts. These proceedings are popular with lawyers because attorney fees may be awarded and the corporation can often be coerced into settlement in order to avoid a trial before a fact finder that might have an antibusiness bias. As the Supreme Court noted, however, the shareholder has some hurdles to overcome. The action must be one affecting the corporation generally, not simply a claim involving the status of an individual shareholder. Normally, demand must first be made on the board of directors to bring the suit before the shareholder can sue derivatively.

The demand requirement has raised fiduciary duty issues. Once demand is made, the board may decide not to bring the case for any number of reasons. For example, the cost of the suit might be far greater than any potential recovery. In such a case, the business judgment rule will apply, barring the shareholder from bringing the action unless there is a breach of fiduciary duty. Where there is a breach of fiduciary duty, however, demand need not be made on the corporation before filing suit. Demand is excused on the theory that it would be futile. That is the situation preferred by plaintiff lawyers. The board of directors will try to avoid that result by appointing a special committee of the board of directors composed of outside directors unaffected by the claimed conflict or breach of fiduciary duties of management. That arrangement allows the corporation to climb back under the shelter of the business judgment rule.

This was done by General Motors (GM) after it agreed to buy back the holdings of H. Ross Perot, the failed-third party candidate in the 1992 presidential election. Perot's GM holdings were acquired when he sold his company, Electronic Data Systems (EDS) to GM. Perot served on the GM board of directors and soon became a thorn in management's side, making such criticisms as "Until you nuke the old GM system, you'll never tap the full potential of your people." Perot wanted to be bought out, and management was happy to oblige, paying him a "giant premium" for his GM tracking stock covering EDS operations, but Perot had to agree as a part of the buyout that he would cease his criticism of GM management. The premium was paid at a time when GM was having financial difficulties, and a derivative action claimed that payment of the premium to Perot was "hush mail" designed to entrench management, creating a conflict of interest and a breach of fiduciary duties.

The Delaware Supreme Court held that the decision to pay Perot a premium was protected by the business judgment rule because a committee of independent directors had recommended its approval by the GM board, which was composed of a majority of outside directors. The court stated that a board of directors with a majority of outside directors acts as "overseers of management. So viewed, the Board's exercise of judgment in resolving an internal rift in management of serious proportions and at the highest executive level should be accorded the protection of the business judgment rule absent well-pleaded averments implicating financial self-interest, entrenchment, or lack of due care," all of which were lacking here.[70] Other courts were not always as deferential to special litigation committees formed to hear demands from shareholders seeking to bring a derivative action. They became concerned that the special committees were being used as smoke screens to cover management's involvement in improper conduct.

The use of special committees to handle fiduciary duty concerns spread to other areas of corporate decision making, including opposition to hostile takeovers in which management might be charged with entrenching itself. Those committees were also used to investigate corporate wrongdoing through an internal investigation. Afterwards, the committee traditionally provided a report exonerating management and trumpeting how the company had cleaned up the matter by firing low-level employees or taking other corrective actions. That report was then shared with prosecutors as an often successful means of convincing them not to bring an action against a company or its present management. That shield would become a sword in the Enron era when special committees began hiring former SEC officials and prosecutors to conduct these investigations. They vied with each other for producing the most explosive reports, which then became the basis for wrecking the company and ruining its management.

Fiduciary Duties Redux

Although the Delaware legislature had sought to create a corporate-friendly environment, the Delaware judiciary embraced fiduciary duties for corporate officers and directors in a manner hostile toward the management of large public companies. The acceptance of fiduciary duties was a natural step for the Delaware chancery court, which has the responsibility for resolving corporate disputes. The chancery courts had traditionally adjudicated matters involving trusts and acted as a court of "equity" that tried to resolve disputes "equitably" without regard to strict legal standards. The Delaware courts were initially reluctant to find breaches of fiduciary duty. Columbia Law School professor and former SEC chairman William Cary charged in 1974 that the Delaware courts had "contributed to shrinking the concept of fiduciary responsibility and fairness, and indeed have followed the lead of the Delaware legislature in watering down shareholders' rights."[71] That situation changed in the 1980s when the Delaware court began taking a more activist approach, the *Van Gorkom* decision being one example. The fiduciary duty principle allowed the Delaware courts effectively to superimpose themselves over the decision-making processes of the board of directors of large public corporations during takeover battles. Those decisions were often conflicting and not well reasoned, triggering a "sharp debate" among law professors and practitioners.[72]

In *Weinberger v. UOP, Inc.,* the Delaware court examined a situation in which Signal Companies Inc. initially purchased 50.5 percent of UOP (formerly known as Universal Oil Products), giving it control.[73] Three years later, Signal made a tender offer for the remaining stock of UOP at $21 a share without disclosing to the UOP board that an internal evaluation by two Signal officers had viewed the stock as a "good investment" at a price up to $24 per share. The Delaware Supreme Court found this a breach of fiduciary duty because Signal dominated the UOP board but did not disclose the $24 figure to directors who were not in Signal's management. The court criticized the hurried nature of the decision making in the transaction, the whole event playing out over four days. Signal defended that claim by noting that UOP had obtained a "fairness" letter from an investment banking firm, Lehman Brothers, opining that a price of $20 or $21 was fair. The court derided that opinion because it had been hurriedly prepared over three days. The Lehman partner in charge of the project was off skiing while due diligence for the letter was being conducted. The partner was given a draft of the letter in which the price was left blank until the UOP board meeting. The court suggested that Signal might have met its duties without disclosure if it had had UOP appoint a committee of independent directors to negotiate at arm's length. However, that seems absurd when the facts are considered. The remaining UOP stock was trading on the market at about $14.50 per share. In a truly arm's-length negotiation, Signal would have offered an independent committee, say, $16, instead of $21, and the independent committee would have had to take it because no one else would pay a premium for a minority interest.

A major topic of interest in the 1980s was the use of defensive measures, such as poison pills, to fend off hostile takeovers. Those takeovers created a conflict of interest for management because there was often a strong likelihood that it would be replaced if the takeover was successful. Management, therefore, had an incentive to entrench itself by fending off the takeover, even if the merger was in the best interests of the shareholders. Some corporate theorists argued that management should be passive and let the shareholders decide whether to accept the hostile tender offer. Others argued that management should be active and ensure that the shareholders received the best value possible before allowing a takeover. In *Unocal Corp. v. Mesa Petroleum Co.,*[74] the Delaware Supreme Court held that management need not be passive. The court ruled that the defensive tactics used by Unocal to fend off a hostile takeover bid were permissible, as long as they were not designed to entrench management in breach of its fiduciary duty of loyalty. Any such defensive tactics were required to be reasonable in relation to the threat posed to the corporation by the takeover.

In the *Unocal* case, Mesa made a tender offer for 64 million of Unocal shares at $54 per share, a substantial premium over market. Unocal responded with an exchange offer of its own providing that, if Mesa was able to buy 64 million shares, then Unocal would buy back the remaining 40 percent of its own outstanding securities at $72 per share. This had the effect of discouraging shareholders tendering into the Mesa $54 share offer because everyone hoped that the other shareholders would go first and take the lower price, creating a form of prisoners' dilemma. Moreover, in the event that there were enough willing victims to trigger the Unocal exchange, then Mesa would be left owning a company with a huge debt and would have been forced to pay $72 per share for the remaining 40 percent of the company. This effectively thwarted Mesa and prevented the shareholders from receiving any premium for their stock. The court rejected claims that action was taken in order to entrench management because a majority of the board was outside directors, and they had met separately with advisers before recommending approval by the full board.

The turmoil created by the hostile takeovers of this era led to the entry of the SEC into the regulation of acquisitions by public companies. Those takeovers were often carried out through tender offers to the public shareholders of the target company. Hostile takeovers were bitterly opposed by the management of the target corporation, and those contests often resulted in confusing, coercive offers to the shareholders. The Delaware courts initially dealt with those takeovers under their fiduciary duty doctrines, but adverse publicity from the hostile takeovers soon aroused congressional interest. Before his conviction on bribery and conspiracy charges, Senator Harrison Williams of New Jersey introduced legislation to deal with the corporate raiders who were threatening some venerable enterprises, firing existing management and shutting down unprofitable operations attended by massive layoffs. Williams viewed this as "industrial sabotage," but his legislative proposal was claimed by its sponsors to be neutral in regulating takeovers. In fact, the act was intended to discourage hostile takeovers. In application, however, it had the opposite effect, legitimating hostile takeovers by their regulation. The regulatory purpose thus failed, and hostile takeovers are now an accepted part of finance.

The SEC's rules under the Williams legislation require anyone acquiring 5 percent of a class of stock of a public company to file a form with the SEC identifying themselves and stating their intentions—for example, when the stock is being acquired for investment or control and what their plans for the company are. Their source of financing must be disclosed. This requirement was intended to give incumbent management a heads-up so that a raider could not make a stealth takeover. The SEC's rules further require that a tender offer must be held open for at least twenty business days following the date the offer is first published, sent, or given to security holders. Ostensibly, this rule was intended to allow shareholders an adequate opportunity to consider the terms. Its actual intent was to allow incumbent management an opportunity to put its defenses in place. The SEC also adopted a rule that effectively reversed the decision of the Delaware court in *Unocal* insofar as it allowed a self-tender offer from incumbent management to discriminate by excluding a corporate raider. The SEC rule requires offers to be open to all shareholders on the same terms, and in the event of oversubscription the offer must be prorated. This measure was a rare instance where the full disclosure regime and fiduciary duties conflicted.

Back to Delaware

The Delaware courts were soon flooded with cases challenging whether various poison pills were reasonable in relation to the threat posed by a takeover. Those challenges involved such things as no-shop provisions, sales of company "crown jewels," and various rights plans that were designed to pay out large amounts to shareholders and burden the company with debt, making it unattractive for takeover and assuring that shareholders would receive no premium for their stock. Golden parachute severance packages were given to incumbent management that were paid out in the event of a takeover, enriching the executives and reducing corporate assets for the acquirer. Impediments to changes in management were adopted that prevented the proponent of a hostile takeover from replacing the board of directors. These provisions were variously called "dead hands," "no hands," "slow hands," and "numb hands." Poison pills that entrenched management were soon being protested by corporate governance advocates, but the Delaware legislature responded with an antitakeover statute that made it easier for management to fend off unwanted takeovers.

Another controversial decision by the Delaware Supreme Court was *Revlon, Inc. v. MacAndrews & Forbes Holdings, Inc.*[75] That case involved the takeover of Revlon by Ronald Perelman, a corporate raider who headed Pantry Pride, a supermarket chain. Perelman began the bidding at $42, but met determined resistance from Revlon, which adopted a poison pill and repurchased 10 million of its own shares, paying for them in part with the issuance of notes to the tendering shareholders (the "Revlon notes"). To assure that the Revlon notes had credibility, the company restricted the amount of debt it would take on in the future; additional debt would be allowed only if approved by the company's independent directors. Perelman continued the fight, and Revlon sought a "white knight" in the form of Forstmann Little & Co., a venture capital firm. Forstmann offered to top the Perelman bid, which had been increased to $47.50, but required a waiver of the restrictions on additional debt, which sent the price of the Revlon notes plunging. Perelman responded to this intervention by raising his offer to $53 and then to $56.25, which was bested by a counteroffer from Forstmann of $57.25. Perelman then said he would top any future Forstmann bid by a fraction. At that point, Revlon decided to sell the company to Forstmann because it agreed to support the price of the Revlon notes at par.

In judging the conduct of the Revlon board of directors, the Delaware Supreme Court announced a new fiduciary duty rule. Directors could no longer use defensive measures when it appeared that the company was going to be sold off. In such a case, the directors become auctioneers and are required to do everything possible to obtain the highest price. The Revlon board was found to have breached that new fiduciary duty because they made a price concession to Forstmann in order to obtain its agreement to support the Revlon notes at par. The court said that creditors, in this case the holders of the Revlon notes, were owed no fiduciary duties. Creditors are protected only by the terms of their contract. This seemed rather harsh since the tender in which the Revlon notes were issued caused Perelman to raise his bid. As a result of its strategies, the Revlon board obtained $57.25 for shareholders, rather than the $42 opening gambit by Perelman or his initial hostile offer price of $47.50. At the same time, the board protected the Revlon note holders who had been an essential part of that strategy. The cost of providing that protection was a minuscule amount offered by Perelman over the Forstmann bid.

The Delaware Supreme Court in *Revlon* once again tried to dictate corporate decision making through the guise of fiduciary duties. The SEC jumped in with a claim against Revlon, charging that the board had not made full disclosure of its negotiations with Forstmann. Revlon would struggle on over the years, heavily burdened with the $1.6 billion in debt needed to finance the acquisition. In addition, one of Revlon's outside directors, Martha Stewart, was forced to resign from the board after her conviction for obstruction of justice. Perelman went on to live the life of a corporate mogul. He married actress Ellen Barkin and was able to sell his house in Palm Beach for $70 million, which was the highest price ever paid for a single-family residence. As for Forstmann, it lost another famous takeover battle that pitted it against Kohlberg, Kravis, Roberts & Co. in the acquisition of RJR Nabisco.

The Delaware Supreme Court was heavily criticized for its ruling in *Revlon* and sought to retreat in a subsequent case involving Time Inc., the publisher of *Time* magazine.[76] In 1989, Time Inc. announced that it was merging with Warner Communications through an exchange of securities that was intended to be a "merger of equals." Paramount Communications, formerly known as Gulf & Western, then made an unexpected competing tender offer of $175 per share in cash for Time, Inc. This valued Time at almost $11 billion. Time then agreed to purchase half of Warner's shares for $70 per share. Time planned to merge Warner into Time after it acquired the rest of the

Warner shares. Paramount responded by raising its offer to $200 for each Time share, which Time rejected.

Inevitably, the matter found itself in the Delaware Supreme Court. That body held that Time could properly enter into the merger agreement with Warner even though a much higher price could have been obtained by selling the company to Paramount. This conflicted with its decision in *Revlon,* but the Delaware court found that Time's strategy of long-term growth justified the merger notwithstanding the higher offer. The result was that Time shareholders, who were not given a vote on the issue, lost the opportunity for a 100 percent profit. As for long-term strategies, the price of Time stock fell below $100 after the merger, although the executives at Time and Warner made millions. Steve Ross at Warner made almost $75 million from the merger, plus $121 million in compensation as an executive at the combined firm.

The combination of Time and Warner did not prove successful in preserving the Time culture. N.J. Nicholas Jr., of the Time management group was forced out as chief executive officer of the merged company and replaced by Steve Ross of the Warner Brothers group. He in turn was replaced on his death by an executive in Time's cable division, Gerald Levin, who then began a series of acquisitions, including Turner Broadcasting (CNN) and America Online (AOL). The AOL Time Warner merger became somewhat infamous for the $54 billion it had to write off its books to reflect the diminished value of the combined enterprise in 2002. This was the largest write-off in corporate history. Levin's acquisitions also made *Time* magazine only a small part of the overall enterprise that was soon struggling. The *Time* magazine staff was slashed, "changing the culture" in "radical ways."[77]

The Delaware Supreme Court changed course once again in a subsequent case.[78] Beaten in its quest for Time Inc., Paramount Communications sought a "strategic alliance" with Viacom Inc. that would frustrate a takeover by QVC Network. Paramount sought the protection of the rule laid down in the *Time* case that long-range objectives could overcome concerns of gains from an immediate sale. The Delaware court blocked Paramount from adopting defensive measures that were designed to stop QVC. The court ruled that the situation was really a sale and that *Revlon* duties applied.

Delaware Excesses

The Delaware court was forsaking the directive of its legislature to make Delaware corporate-friendly. That trend accelerated in the 1990s, as the Delaware court began routinely second-guessing business judgments, becoming in effect an appellate court for management decisions. As noted in one press report: the "pro-management slant" of the Delaware court of chancery attracted many large companies to Delaware. "But since the late 1990s, amid the increasing importance of corporate and growing clout of institutional investors, the court has become liberal toward shareholders."[79]

Corporate matters in Delaware are handled by chancery judges steeped in the tradition of fiduciary duties for trusts and equitable concepts that judges freely make up as they go along. Some states, like North Carolina and Florida, have created special business courts to handle corporate disputes without the attending chancery baggage. North Carolina, in particular, has tried to stop the spread of Delaware's expansive application of fiduciary duties by passing a statute rejecting the auctioneer duties requirement imposed by the Delaware Supreme Court in its *Revlon* decision.[80] The North Carolina business court had this to say about the Delaware court's review standards for management's actions during a takeover battle:

> First, the number of standards of review has become confusing and contributes to an inability of practitioners to advise their clients appropriately. Second, the use of categories of transactions to which standards of review are applied has been perceived as outcome determinative. . . . Third, the Delaware Supreme Court has erroneously blended the duty of care standard and the test of entire fairness creating confusion in the bar. As a result, the original benefits of the circumstance specific application of the business judgment rule in duty of care cases and the application of the entire fairness test in duty of loyalty cases have been lost. . . . Fourth, the straight application of either the business judgment rule or the entire fairness test does not work to resolve the tensions between the conflicting requirements of shareholders and directors in transactions or board actions affecting the shareholders' right to sell or vote. The use of some other review process is required. Failure to provide a meaningful review process will remove a critical tool and much needed flexibility in resolving the inherent conflict between the internal requirements of our corporate system. Fifth, the intermediate standards adopted in Delaware are confusing and perhaps not internally consistent. The focus on "entrenchment" may be part of the problem. The necessity for courts to evaluate "threats" and "proportional responses" starts to sound a lot like nondeferential judicial review of business decisions.[81]

Although the North Carolina judge was highly critical of the Delaware court's application of fiduciary duties, he then proceeded himself to find a breach of fiduciary duty for a "numb hands" provision in a merger agreement that extended the terms of the agreement for five months beyond any shareholder vote disapproving the merger. The term would have the effect of delaying the takeover by a third party, in this case SunTrust Banks, which was battling with the First Union Corp. to take over the Wachovia Corp. It thus appears that judges are institutionally unable to keep their hands off corporate transactions and management decision making.

For Whom Does Management Manage?

For whom does management manage? This question has long been the subject of debate in corporate governance circles. An early case addressing that issue involved Henry Ford's efforts to turn the Ford Motor Company into an eleemosynary organization. Ford owned 58 percent of the stock of that company, allowing him to completely dominate its affairs and select its other directors. Ford announced in 1916 that the Ford Motor Company would no

Kenneth Lay. The head of Enron who went from celebrated head of Enron to one of the most notorious corporate executives of all times. *(Nick Adams, photographer, Getty Images©)*

Jeffrey Skilling and his accuser Sherron Watkins (side by side). Skilling's resignation touched off the events that led to the collapse of Enron. *(Mark Wilson, photographer, Getty Images©)*

Lea and Andrew Fastow. The wife held ransom by government prosecutors for her husband's guilty plea. *(Courtesy of the Houston Chronicle©)*

Adolf Berle. The Columbia law professor who led the assault on large corporations and their management. *(Bob Landry, photographer, Getty Images©)*

Nancy Temple. This mild-mannered lawyer became a pawn in the prosecution of Arthur Andersen. *(Nancy Temple by permission of Getty Images, Alex Wong, photographer©)*

Gary Winnick (on the far right). The founder of Global Crossing and former confidant of Michael Milken. *(Alex Wong, photographer, Getty Images©)*

John Rigas. The head of Adelphia, a cancer victim, was handcuffed in a dawn raid on his home. *(Spencer Platt, photographer, Getty Images©)*

Bernard Ebbers. The head of WorldCom is given his "perp" walk for the benefit of the press. *(Stuart Ramson, photographer, Getty Images©)*

Richard Breeden (second from right). He was the "Corporate Monitor" who was given control of WorldCom after its bankruptcy. He imposed a Fabian corporate governance system on the company. *(Courtesy of the Securities and Exchange Commission Historical Society)*

Byron D. Woodside   William L. Cary   Edward N. Gadsby   J. Allen Fear, Jr.

William Cary (second from left). This activist SEC chairman created the crime of insider trading. *(Courtesy of the Securities and Exchange Commission Historical Society)*

Martha Stewart. Her success made her a target for government entrapment. *(Stephen Cherin, photographer, Getty Images©)*

Jack Grubman. His efforts to have his children enrolled in a prestigious pre-school program led to a scandal of immense proportions. *(Mark Wilson, photographer, Getty Images©)*

Frank Quattrone. He was targeted for prosecution solely by reason of his prominence as an investment banker being paid $120 million per year. *(Chris Hondros, photographer, Getty Images©)*

Arthur Levitt (second from right). He became a full-disclosure gadfly after the massive scandals that arose on his watch as an activist SEC chairman. *(Courtesy of the Securities and Exchange Commission Historical Society)*

Harvey Pitt (seated in the middle). The hard-working SEC chairman who became another target of the hysteria surrounding Enron. Seated to the right of Pitt is **Harvey Goldschmid**. He undermined Pitt and served as Arthur Levitt's surrogate on the SEC. *(Courtesy of the Securities and Exchange Commission Historical Society)*

longer pay special dividends to its shareholders, although it had over $50 million in cash on hand, a staggering sum at the time. The company would only pay a regular 5 percent dividend totaling $2 million each year. Ford stated that the remainder of the cash would be used to expand production and decrease the cost of Ford automobiles while increasing their quality. Ford was already carrying out that plan by buying iron mines, building ships to carry the ore, and constructing steel smelters on the River Rouge in Dearborn, Michigan. As a Michigan court concluded, Henry Ford thought that "the Ford Motor Company has made too much money, has had too large profits, and that, although large profits might still be earned, a sharing of them with the public, reducing the price of the output of the company, ought to be undertaken."[82]

John and Horace Dodge, two minority shareholders holding about 10 percent of Ford's stock, objected to Henry Ford's generosity and sued to compel a special dividend and to stop his expansion plans, which would consume the company's cash. The Michigan court ruled that only the directors of a corporation have discretion as to the timing and amount of dividends, not the stockholders. The court stated that it would not interfere unless the directors were acting fraudulently or were refusing to declare a dividend when it was clear that the corporation had such a large surplus of profits that refusal to declare a dividend amounted to an abuse of discretion. The court examined Ford's plans, which included reducing the price of Ford cars to $360 from $440 and increasing employee wages to unheard-of levels: Ford would shock the world by offering wages of $5 per day. After carefully considering the broad discretion given to the board of directors, the court concluded that it would not interfere with Henry Ford's pricing and expansion plans, but did order a special dividend to be paid. That dividend allowed the Dodge brothers to start their own company, which is now a part of DaimlerChrysler, but their ending was a sad one: they both received fatal doses of alcohol poisoning on a drinking binge in New York City during prohibition. Ford Motor Company would also experience difficulties in the 1920s on matters ranging from labor strife to a cash shortage from its massive expenditures, which led the company to engage in a check kiting scheme to cover shortfalls. Nevertheless, though still struggling, the Ford Motor Company survives even today.

The decision in the *Ford* case did not end the debate over whether corporate managers could use their corporations for philanthropic purposes. One issue was whether corporations could make charitable donations. An often cited New Jersey court decision upheld a contribution of $1,500 made to Princeton University in 1951 by the A.P. Smith Mfg. Co. over the objections of a shareholder. The court spent much ink describing the history of corporate giving:

> When the wealth of the nation was primarily in the hands of individuals they discharged their responsibilities as citizens by donating freely for charitable purposes. With the transfer of most of the wealth to corporate hands and the impo-

sition of heavy burdens of individual taxation, they have been unable to keep pace with increased philanthropic needs. They have therefore, with justification, turned to corporations to assume the modern obligations of good citizenship in the same manner as humans do. Congress and state legislatures have enacted laws that encourage corporate contributions, and much has recently been written to indicate the crying need and adequate legal basis therefore. In actual practice corporate giving has correspondingly increased. Thus, it is estimated that annual corporate contributions throughout the nation aggregate over 300 million dollars with over 60 million dollars thereof going to universities and other educational institutions. Similarly, it is estimated that local community chests receive well over 40% of their contributions from corporations; these contributions and those made by corporations to the American Red Cross, to Boy Scouts and Girl Scouts, to 4-H Clubs and similar organizations have almost invariably been unquestioned.

During World War I corporations loaned their personnel and contributed substantial corporate funds in order to insure survival; during the depression of the '30s they made contributions to alleviate the desperate hardships of the millions of unemployed; and during World War II they again contributed to insure survival. They now recognize that we are faced with other, though nonetheless vicious, threats from abroad that must be withstood without impairing the vigor of our democratic institutions at home and that otherwise victory will be pyrrhic indeed. More and more they have come to recognize that their salvation rests upon sound economic and social environment, which in turn rests in no insignificant part upon free and vigorous non-governmental institutions of learning. It seems to us that just as the conditions prevailing when corporations were originally created required that they serve public as well as private interests, modern conditions require that corporations acknowledge and discharge social as well as private responsibilities as members of the communities within which they operate. Within this broad concept there is no difficulty in sustaining, as incidental to their proper objects and in aid of the public welfare, the power of corporations to contribute corporate funds within reasonable limits in support of academic institutions.[83]

Of course, it was not made clear why Princeton needed the funds more than the shareholders, especially since its endowment was undoubtedly larger than the economies of many countries. Also missing from this panegyric was a discussion on how corporate executives used charitable contributions from their corporations for their own social climbing. Dennis Kozlowski at Tyco took that practice to new heights.

State statutes, including the Model Business Act, allow corporate political contributions, but a federal statute, the Tillman Act, prohibits such contributions. That statute was passed after allegations that the Bureau of Corporations had stopped investigations of businesses making large campaign donations to Theodore Roosevelt's presidential campaign in 1904. Contributors included J.P. Morgan, who gave $150,000; Henry Clay Frick, who gave a meager $50,000; George Gould, the son of a notorious speculator, who gave $500,000; and Chauncey Depew, chairman of the New York Central, who gave $100,000. Roosevelt was most seriously embarrassed by a $100,000 campaign donation from the Standard Oil Company, which he was seeking to break up. He returned that cash.

Social Responsibility

The *Ford* decision was a frustration for corporate governance advocates who wanted corporations to act for the greater benefit of society. E. Merrick Dodd Jr., a Harvard Law School professor, wrote an article in that school's law review in 1932 entitled "For Whom Are Corporate Managers Trustees?" Dodd rejected the view that corporations exist for the sole purpose of making profits for shareholders. He wanted to expand fiduciary duties to require corporate managers to protect employees and the public in general, not just investors.[84] In more recent years, Milton Friedman, the Nobel Prize–winning economist from the University of Chicago, rejected that theory, asserting that corporate managers should have as their exclusive goal to make as much money as possible for shareholders, while conforming to legal and ethical standards of society. Dodd's views did not gain much acceptance by the courts, but over one-half of the have states adopted "other constituency" statutes. That legislation allows the board of directors to consider interests other than maximizing shareholder wealth in making corporate decisions without breaching its fiduciary duties. Only one of those statutes requires the board to consider interests other those of shareholders, and only a few of the statutes state that other interests may be considered equally with those of shareholders.

Another model for corporate governance that incorporates another constituency is "codetermination," which is used in Germany. The German Federal Codetermination Act of 1976 mandates that in firms with 2,000 or more employees (AGs), one-half of the members of the supervisory board be worker representatives. The shareholders select the other half. The board's chairman and vice chairman are elected by a two-thirds majority of the supervisory board, with the chairman having the decisive vote in the event of a labor-shareholder split. That system led to much corruption at Volkswagen AG where union officials were plied with junkets and prostitutes by management in order to gain their favor. In America, the relationship of management and labor has been historically adversarial, and that is codified into federal labor law in order to oust management-controlled unions. Although some labor representatives have served on boards of U.S. companies, there seems to be little interest in such representation on the part of labor or management.

The issue of the social responsibility of corporations arises in the context of union pension plans promoting social responsibility. Two of the leaders of that movement are Calpers and the New York City retirement system. As one court noted, the latter uses its shareholder status as a bully pulpit for pursuing liberal social causes.[85] Calpers made the news in 1991 when it rejected applications by dozens of money managers that did not measure up to the California affirmative action program. Calpers pursues a course of socially responsible investing, eschewing tobacco and other stocks that it views as politically incorrect. However, there is a problem with such social investing: nearly every large company will have a product line or operation that offends someone. A film company may have an objectionable line of R-rated movies, while an orange juice company uses pesticides. Automobile companies pollute the air, pharmaceutical and cosmetic companies use animals to test products, hospitals provide abortions, airplanes create noise pollution for those living close to the airport, grocery stores sell meat, and computer companies enrage Luddites.

The Contractarians

The application of fiduciary duties as a way to control business has come under attack from a school of thought that arose in the last quarter of the twentieth century. It was based on Nobel Prize winner Ronald Coase's famous work *The Nature of the Firm,* published in 1937. Coase deconstructed the corporation and concluded that it was simply a mechanism to reduce transaction costs. He theorized that a corporation will undertake an activity whenever it is cheaper for it to do so than to contract for the activity from an outside vendor.[86] Expanding that theory, Michael Jensen and William Meckling posited in 1976 that the corporation is a business relationship, rather than a trust, and that monitoring management was an agency cost.[87] The so-called Chicago school of law and economics then posited that business relationships are governed by contractual agreements, making the corporation simply a "nexus of contracts," rather than a fiduciary relationship. The Chicago theorists believed that market forces would ensure that managers do not overreach in negotiating those contracts; otherwise no one would buy the company's stock. Leaders in this school of thought included Richard A. Posner and Frank H. Easterbrook, professors at the University of Chicago law school and now federal appellate court judges, and the dean of that law school, Daniel R. Fischel. These theorists were dubbed "contractarians."[88]

The contractual theorists placed reliance on the market for discipline instead of fiduciary duties created by jurists with no knowledge or experience in business. Under the contractual theory, shareholders are assured only of rights they might have under a contract with the corporation. The courts would not be called upon to create rights that the parties themselves did not establish by contract. As Easterbrook noted when he became an appellate judge: "Because the fiduciary duty is a standby or off-the-rack guess about what parties would agree if they dickered about the subject explicitly, parties may contract with greater specificity for other arrangements. It is a violation of duty to steal from the corporate treasury; it is not a violation to write oneself a check that the board has approved as a bonus."[89]

The contract theorists did not have an easy time in challenging the by-then-conventional wisdom of the importance of a fiduciary model. Corporate law theorists adhering to this contractual view were ridiculed by other law professors inculcated with fiduciary standards for their entire careers. That hostile attitude gradually diminished and contractual theory is now taught in nearly every law school. The contractarians have not been as successful in having the courts consider their views. Delaware and other states have effectively blocked the application of this theory, even when desired by shareholders, by decreeing that the fiduciary duty of loyalty cannot be waived. Although the duty of care is subject to waiver, the Delaware courts have undermined even that waiver by its "entire fairness" standard of review. As a result, the courts, and not the owners, continue to decide how corporations should be managed. In all other business relationships, the parties decide themselves what protections are needed. That is the approach taken by the courts for debts. Bondholders, for example, are not protected by fiduciary duties, except in some rare and extreme instances. The contractarians ask why shareholders should fare any better.

III

Full Disclosure Fails

7. Telecoms and WorldCom

Telecommunications

Meltdown

The telecommunications industry was thrown open to competition after the entry of a consent decree in 1982 in an antitrust suit brought by the Justice Department against AT&T. Aided by an irascible federal district court judge, Harold Greene, AT&T was forced to agree to its own breakup, and Judge Greene assumed control of the company during that process. At that time, AT&T held the title of the largest company in the world and accounted for about 2 percent of gross domestic product (GDP) in America. The consent decree required AT&T to spin off 80 percent of its operations worth $80 billion into seven regional operating companies, which were dubbed "baby bells." The baby bells were allowed to keep their local service operations, but were barred from providing long-distance services outside their regions. This opened the door for many new entrants into the field of long-distance communications.

The Telecommunications Act of 1996 went even further in encouraging competition by abolishing local telephone monopolies, requiring existing telephone companies to provide interconnection to their networks, and encouraging free entry into other areas of telecommunications. These actions had further disastrous effects on AT&T, which reduced the size of its workforce of 1 million employees in 1984 to 61,000 in 2004, but a revolution in communications took place after competition was opened to all. Cable, microwave, satellites, and wireless phones became new and driving forces in the telecommunications field. The opening of the Worldwide Web in the 1990s was an advance that required a massive restructuring of communications networks. Fiber-optics was another leap for the industry, and telecommunications companies began racing with each other to develop fiber-optic networks. Over 80 million miles of fiber-optic cable was laid in the United States between 1996 and 2001.

Telecommunications firms had spent heavily to rewire the country for cable and then turned to fiber-optics for broadband, an investment that would not be recovered before the stock market collapsed and the recession hit. In total, the telecom companies borrowed over $2 trillion to fund this explosion of growth, but the downturn in the economy and overcapacity turned that industry into a disaster. The meltdown of the telecoms was said to have resulted in losses of up to $4 trillion in market capitalization, and 600,000 employees lost their jobs. Twenty-three telecom companies declared bankruptcy.

The economic downturn also resulted in a massive number of accounting irregularities by the telecommunications firms. Accounting restatements and scandals soon popped up at several telecom companies, including AT&T, which lost 15 percent of its stock value in a single day in May 2000 when it announced a 5 percent decrease in projected earnings. AT&T later confessed that it had overstated earnings for 2001 and 2002 because employees had circumvented accounting controls and increased revenue improperly. AT&T settled a class action lawsuit for $100 million that charged accounting manipulations. That lawsuit claimed that AT&T and its chief executive officer, C. Michael Armstrong, inflated earnings projections in 1999 in order to keep its stock price up while buying the MediaOne Group Inc. and while completing a public offering of its wireless operations. After those transactions were completed, the company slashed its projections, resulting in a sharp drop in the price of its stock and that of its wireless operation. AT&T had other problems. Among other things, it acquired a controlling interest in the AtHome Corp., which had to take a $6 billion write-off and went bankrupt. AT&T had also sold put options on that stock in connection with its acquisition, requiring AT&T to pay $3 billion when AtHome's stock plunged after that write-off.

The accounting manipulations of AT&T paled in comparison to those at other telecoms. Indeed, several world records would be set for the size of accounting restatements, investor losses, and other marks of distinction in the increasingly grim world of full disclosure.

Nortel

Nortel Network Corp., a communications equipment supplier headquartered in Brampton, Ontario, with significant operations in the United States, was particularly hard-hit by the downturn in the economy. The company, which traces its origins back to 1895, had decided to focus its business on wireless and Internet communications and the booming fiber-optic network business. Nortel was reporting revenues of $30 billion as the century ended, up from $10 billion five years earlier. Nortel engaged in an acquisition spree between 1997 and 2000 that expanded its operations in Latin America, Asia, and Europe, as well as North America. The purchase of Alteon WebSystems, a maker of Web server equipment, for $7.8 billion proved to be Nortel's high-water mark. Nortel's stock began a sharp decline after that acquisition, falling by over 75 percent by year-end.

Like other major companies, Nortel was resorting to various gimmicks to boost earnings. The company increased sales by loaning billions of dollars to customers so that they could buy Nortel products, a demand creation program that could not be sustained indefinitely. The free fall in Nortel's stock price was assisted by a November 2000 announcement that the company was restating its financial accounts to reduce revenue by $125 million. Nortel's stock plunged even further after it disclosed a loss of $19 billion for the fourth quarter of 2000. This tied with the same amount reported by General Motors in 1992 as the largest quarterly loss ever reported by a corporation to that date. That record was punctured on July 27, 2001, when JDS Uniphase, a manufacturer of telecommunications components, announced a $44.8 billon loss from write-downs of its acquisitions.

Nortel laid off over 30,000 employees as its problems mounted in the glutted telecommunications market. More thousands were cut over the following months. The company's workforce eventually dropped from 95,000 to 35,000, as compared to the mere 5,000 jobs lost at Enron. Revenues fell by $20 billion. Nortel's stock price lost $140 billion in market capitalization, a decline of some 90 percent. *Maxim* magazine noted that, if an investor had invested $100,000 in Nortel stock in July 2001, at a time when the stock was soaring, that same stock would have been worth only $5,483 in December 2001. In contrast, if the investor had invested $100,000 in Budweiser beer, the investment would be worth $10,000 in empty returnable bottles.

As was the case for other faltering companies, executive compensation at Nortel came under criticism after it was revealed that Nortel's executives had been awarded $2.5 billion in stock options. Nortel's chief financial officer, Terry Hungle, was forced to resign in February 2002 as a result of some questionable personal investments involving the trading of retirement funds. Nortel continued to experience difficulties in 2002. The company was forecasting a drop in its sales, which proved to be reality, but a new chief executive officer, Frank Dunn, promised a turnaround. Nortel reported a profit in the first quarter of 2003, allowing large cash bonuses to be paid to its executives, but that turned out to be another accounting deception. This time accrued liabilities were manipulated to provide the profits, a cookie jar reserve scheme. Those practices were uncovered by an internal investigation conducted by William McLucas, the former Securities and Exchange Commission (SEC) enforcement chief who prepared the Powers report at Enron. Dunn was fired, along with the company's chief financial officer, Douglas Beatty, and the company's controller, Michael Gollogly. In total, seven executives, who had received large bonuses under the company's "return to profitability" program, were fired. Nortel sued Dunn and other executives seeking a return of their bonuses. Some of those directors agreed to return their bonuses. Chubb Corp. sued to have the Director and Officer insurance policies it issued to Nortel to be declared invalid because of the fraud at the company.

Nortel disclosed on October 23, 2003, that it was restating its financial statements for the last three years to correct $1 billion of improperly recorded expenses and revenue, but asserted that those restatements would reduce losses previously reported for those periods. The price of Nortel stock dropped 44 percent in the wake of these revelations. Nortel became something of a poster child for full disclosure failures. It restated its revenues for 2003, cutting net income for that year in half. Criminal investigations were under way in the United States and Canada and another 3,500 employees were laid off. The company issued a profit warning for the third quarter of 2004 and disclosed that major new problems had been discovered in its financial reports, requiring it to restate over $3 billion in results for 1999 and 2000. The company reported in December 2004 that net income for 2003 would probably have to be reduced by at least 28 percent and that other years would have to be restated. The company filed no annual report for the year 2003 and no financial reports with the SEC in 2004. Nortel was only able to "estimate" its current accounts. It announced in January 2005 that it had discovered further misstatements in its accounting reports for the years 1999 through 2001 that involved, among other things, wrongly booking a $200 million transaction with Qwest Communications International Inc. Twelve Nortel executives agreed to repay $8.6 million in bonuses received as a result of those accounting manipulations.

Lucent

Equally shocking were the events at Lucent Technologies Inc., a company that was spun off from AT&T on October 1, 1996. The new company considered 1,100 names before deciding on Lucent and then spent $100 million to advertise its new name and status. Lucent's stock was a high flyer, rising from around $9 to $75 in 1996. Based in Murray Hill, New Jersey, Lucent became a leader in the telecommunications equipment market but lost that position as the industry shifted from voice to data transmission. Lucent tried to enter the Internet networking business, but was delayed because it could not use a favorable merger accounting technique for some few years after its split from AT&T. That delay was costly in the fast-growing Internet business where even a few months lead was a tremendous advantage. When that accounting restriction was lifted, Lucent began aggressively expanding its reach into telecommunications. Over three years the company made eighteen acquisitions that totaled $43 billion, including the purchase of Ascend Communications for $24 billion in 1999.

Lucent's stock price jumped by 30 percent after the company met analysts' expectations for fifteen straight quarters. Those results were no accident. Lucent was managing its earnings by, among other things, immediately writing off $2.5 billion in research and development so that those costs would not be a drag on future earnings. However, as with other companies, accounting gimmicks could not conceal the effects of a declining business for long, and Lucent followed Nortel in a downward plunge when the telecom market collapsed. The beginning of 2000 brought bad news when Lucent disclosed that it was not meeting analysts' earnings expectations. Its stock price fell 25 percent, eliminating $63 billion in shareholder value in a single day. Lucent warned that it would not be meeting analysts' earnings projections in subsequent quarters. Such reports, which would become common on Wall Street, were referred to as "profit warnings," a term frequently heard in the London market and soon common here as well. Lucent, which would make four profit warnings in 2000, was slashing the size of its workforce by thousands.

Lucent restated its financial accounts, reducing revenues by $125 million in October 2000. That number was revised upward in the following month to reduce revenues by $679 million for the fiscal year 2000. Lucent's stock price was down 80 percent for the year following that announcement. Its credit ratings were cut four times as the bad news trickled out. Lucent dismissed its chief financial officer, Deborah Hopkins, on May 6, 2001. The outside director that chaired Lucent's audit committee was Paul Allaire. His full-time job was to serve as chairman of the Xerox Corp., which experienced its own accounting debacle, and he became a target of SEC charges for allowing the manipulation of that company's accounts. On July 24, 2001, Lucent disclosed that it had lost $3.2 billion in the prior quarter and was laying off another 20,000 employees, bringing the total number of layoffs to over 60,000. That number was increased by more than 10,000 over the next year. Lucent stated in its July announcement that it was planning to take up to $9 billion in restructuring charges. The company lost $16 billion in 2001, and its stock fell in value by almost $250 billion between 1999 and 2001.

Lucent engaged in accounting manipulations to conceal its declining business from the market. In total, Lucent concealed more than $20 billion in losses. Lucent had desperately sought to meet analysts' expectations through weekly "gap closure" calls to the nationwide sales force that sought to find revenue to meet the gap between those analysts' expectations and orders in hand. Long-term goals were ignored for those quarterly exercises. Like other telecoms, Lucent engaged in some high-risk vendor financing that involved the financing of equipment sold to customers with weak credit ratings who would have had difficulty obtaining financing from a bank. Instead, the default risk was assumed by Lucent. It was willing to take that risk since the sales funded by the loans increased revenues under accrual accounting requirements to the levels demanded by the financial analysts, but extending that financing to high credit risks was compared to "high yield heroin."[1] Lucent wrote off over $500 million in receivables for 2000 and was owed another $700 million from Winstar Communications Inc., which had declared bankruptcy.

Lucent inflated earnings by shipping unfinished products and even shipping goods to customers that had not been ordered. The company was channel stuffing by booking equipment sales as revenue when those goods had a right of return. Lucent employees asked customers to take nine months of product in a single quarter so that the sales staff could meet their revenue targets. Lucent raided its pension funds by claiming they were overfunded (based on more aggressive assumptions on rate of return), claiming a $1.3 billion gain in 1999 from that adjustment.

Over fifty lawsuits were filed against Lucent as a result of its accounting practices. Lucent settled these lawsuits through payments of cash and securities that were valued at $653 million. The lead plaintiffs included Teamsters Locals 175 and 505. The lawyers handling the suit were awarded $88 million in attorney fees. The SEC charged Lucent and ten of its executives in May 2004 with misstating the company's financial reports. The SEC claimed that Lucent improperly recognized $1.15 billion in revenue and $470 million in pretax income for fiscal year 2000. Lucent agreed to pay a civil penalty of $25 million to settle the SEC action, a figure that was swelled by the company's lack of cooperation with the SEC.

The price of Lucent's stock dropped to 5 percent of its high, and its debt was downgraded to junk bond status. Lucent spun off Agere Systems Inc. in an effort to bolster its financial position. Lucent required underwriters in that offering to supply $1.1 billion in loans as a condition for receiving Lucent's investment banking business. Many traditional underwriters did not want to undertake such a commitment, but the commercial banks, which were freed from the Glass-Steagall Act underwriting restrictions, were happy to participate on those terms.

Lucent's problems continued. The company announced in October 2002 that it was cutting 10,000 more jobs and taking a $4 billion restructuring charge. By 2003, Lucent was valued at less than $10 billion, down from its peak market capitalization of $258 billion. Lucent rehired Patricia Russo to serve as its chief executive officer. She had left seventeen months earlier to assume that position at Eastman Kodak, another troubled company. Lucent's problems with full disclosure continued into 2004. Two Lucent executives were discharged for bribing Chinese government officials and not properly accounting for those payments.

Qwest

Qwest Communications International Inc., a telecommunications company that went public in 1997, was manipulating its financial accounts like a veteran at the end of the century. Based in Denver, Colorado, Qwest's telephone and wireless operations serviced fourteen states. The company expanded its domestic network by such devices as digging trenches and burying cable along railroad rights-of-way (a legacy of the robber barons) and bridging connection gaps by purchasing capacity from other networks. Qwest became a telecommunications giant in 1999 when it acquired U.S. West, a former baby bell. That acquisition was accompanied by a merger with the Frontier Corp., a $66 billion transaction. Qwest's stock price doubled in 2000, jumping from $20 to $40 and rising at one point to $50. Qwest was soaring with the other telecoms until the economic downturn and a glut in fiber-optic capacity took its toll. Qwest began eliminating 4,000 jobs in September 2001. As in the case of other telecoms, this was a signal that the company was faltering.

Qwest first came under criticism for immediately recognizing income from contracts for services that covered periods as long as twenty-five years. If such income were spread over the life of the contracts as required by generally accepted accounting principles (GAAP), the company's financial statements would have reflected much lower revenues. Qwest had to write off $950 million of the value it had claimed for those contracts and admitted that its revenues had been inflated by $2.5 billion in 2000 and 2001. Qwest's auditor was Arthur Andersen LLP. The name of that unfortunate accounting firm continued to surface even as it was being destroyed in a courtroom in Houston.

Four relatively low-level executives at Qwest were indicted and tried in Colorado on fraud and conspiracy charges in connection with a $100 million project to link the Arizona public school system to the Internet. The executives were alleged to have accelerated equipment sales in that project in an amount totaling $34 million in order to meet earnings targets. Two of those individuals, John Walker and Bryan Treadway, were acquitted by the jury of all charges. The jury acquitted the other two executives, Thomas Hall and Grant Graham, of some charges and deadlocked on the remaining counts. The SEC brought a related civil action that charged those and other defendants with improperly booking revenue from transactions with Genuity Inc., a telecommunications company. The SEC claimed that the defendants inflated revenues by more than $140 million.

Qwest bolstered its financial results by engaging in "capacity swaps" for phone connections with other companies that it then listed as revenue. One of the companies involved was Global Crossing. The capacity swaps looked a lot like "round-trip" transactions that simply routed capacity in a circle. Qwest had to restate the revenue from those capacity swaps. Qwest accelerated the publication of its Colorado Springs phone directory in order to increase revenues in the fourth quarter of 2000 and even manipulated its accounting treatment for employee vacation time. Qwest engaged in other accounting irregularities, including a failure to disclose that $299 million in gains was due to a one-time adjustment in employee pension plan funding. Qwest inflated revenues from "flash sales" for its Internet service, a practice that involved grossly overestimating by 60 to 70 percent the number of minutes new customers would use under their contracts and then immediately recognizing revenue on the basis of the inflated estimate. The company agreed to settle the SEC's charges over its accounting manipulations for a staggering $250 million.

Qwest's stock, which had reached a high of $50, fell to $2.79 after these revelations. Congress expressed outrage that Qwest executives had sold $640 million in the company's stock between 1997 and 2001. Joseph Nacchio,

Qwest's chairman and chief executive officer, sold Qwest shares worth $235 million. In total, Nacchio received over $216 million in compensation. After settling with Qwest, the SEC charged that Nacchio and several other executives at Qwest were responsible for the company's massive accounting fraud, which amounted to over $3.8 billion. The defendants in the SEC action included Robert Woodruff and Robin Szeliga, former chief financial officers; Gregory M. Casey, executive vice president; and Afshin Mohebbi, Qwest's chief operating officer. The SEC complaint charged that Nacchio created a "culture of fear" at Qwest that was based on "meeting its numbers." Nacchio was quoted as saying that: "The most important thing we do is meet our numbers. It's more important than any individual product. . . ." Nacchio, Woodruff, and Szeliga were also charged with insider trading because they allegedly sold shares while knowing that the company's accounts were inflated. The SEC further asserted that this fraud had facilitated Qwest's merger with U.S. West. The SEC sought a return of the $300 million in compensation received by these executives, including Nacchio's $216 million. Szeliga later pleaded guilty to a criminal charge of insider trading in realizing a profit of $125,000 upon the exercise of its options.

A grand jury was investigating Qwest in connection with the allocation of hot issues in initial public offerings to Qwest executives by small equipment companies. The grand jury was seeking to determine whether equipment bought from these companies was purchased by Qwest for business reasons or merely to gain access to the shares. On October 1, 2002, Eliot Spitzer, the New York attorney general, jumped into the fray by asserting his *parens patriae* authority through a lawsuit against executives at various telecoms, including Philip Anschutz, Qwest's founder. Spitzer claimed that the defendants had improperly profited by more than $1.5 billion from shares given to them in hot issues as an inducement for them to direct their company's business to the investment banking firm of Salomon Smith Barney. This practice was called "spinning."

Spitzer sought to reclaim $4.8 million in profits made by Anschutz from those hot issues. Spitzer charged that the allocations had been made to Anschutz by Salomon Smith Barney to obtain the investment banking business of Qwest. Anschutz settled those charges by agreeing to donate $4.4 million to charities of Spitzer's choice, a move that was valuable to Spitzer's future political ambitions. Ironically, Dennis Kozlowski, the convicted former head of Tyco, was accused of using charitable contributions made by Tyco for just such a purpose. In any event, the contribution was hardly a strain for Anschutz; he had a personal fortune estimated at $5 billion, down from $16 billion before the market downturn. After his resignation, Anschutz began producing general entertainment movies, including one with Walt Disney Co.

Qwest's troubles continued. The company suffered a $766 million loss in the second quarter of 2004. That loss was largely due to the costs of unwinding a tax shelter that had been challenged by the IRS. Qwest also confessed that it had overstated the number of its long-distance lines for the fourth quarter of 2003. Qwest and Verizon were under investigation for that practice by both the SEC and the Federal Communications Commission. Verizon admitted that it had overstated the number of its long-distance lines by over 1.5 million in the first quarter of 2004.

Other Telecom Troubles

Cisco Systems, a manufacturer of Internet switching equipment based in San Jose, California, passed Microsoft as the largest capitalized company in the United States in 2000 after an acquisition spree. Cisco, which was audited by PricewaterhouseCoopers, was notable for its $1 billion investment in KPMG's consulting operations. That stake was repurchased when KPMG Consulting went public. Cisco was generous with employee stock options, and its stock price raced upward as it met financial analysts' expectations for twenty-five consecutive quarters. Lower-level employees at Cisco Systems received 80 percent of that company's options grants, and they made a total of $19 billion by exercising those options before the company's stock plunged.

Cisco's stock price peaked on March 27, 2000, at $80.06, just three days after the Nasdaq market index topped out. Cisco was experiencing large losses, writing down more than $2 billion of its reported inventory in the following year. Cisco's stock price dropped sharply, falling from its $80 high to $11.24 in September 2001. The company's stock lost $148 billion in value, as the firm laid off 8,500 employees. Cisco wrote off $2.5 billion in inventory. Like Lucent and other telecommunication equipment manufacturers, Cisco was lending its customers money on favorable terms to buy its products. Some of those customers were high credit risks. That financing, which was carried out through a subsidiary, Cisco Systems Capital, amounted to over $2.4 billion.

Other telecoms were also encountering hard times. Charter Communications, a cable company, overstated revenues by some $300 million. Two Charter executives pleaded guilty and two other officers, including the company's chief financial officer, Kent Kalkwarf, were indicted for failing to disconnect thousands of delinquent subscribers in order to inflate revenue numbers for funds that were supposed to be coming from those subscribers. After entering guilty pleas, the four executives were given sentences that ranged from fourteen months in prison to two years probation. The company settled SEC charges for that conduct by agreeing to the imposition of a cease and desist order. No fine was imposed. Teligent Inc., a firm founded in 1997 by Alex J. Mandel, a former senior executive at AT&T Corp., was created to provide wireless telephone and Internet access through microwave transmitters mounted on leased building roof space ("roof rights"). The company, based in Vienna, Virginia, made an initial public offering that became a hot issue, trading up from its offering price of $21.50 to $37.50 and reaching $45 two years later. Teligent's stock soared after it announced a partnering with the German phone service company Mannesmann, reaching a high of $100 in 2000. The company had other large institutional investors, including Nippon Telephone and Telegraph.

The market downturn and overcapacity soon turned Teligent's happy situation into a disaster. In May 2001, the company announced that it was laying off 40 percent of its workforce and struggling to meet debt payments. Mandel resigned shortly after that announcement, and the company declared bankruptcy. The price of the company's shares was then at fifty-six cents. Teligent's principal competitor, Winstar Communications Inc., filed for bankruptcy at about the same time as Teligent. Winstar's shares had peaked at $56 in the prior year and dropped to forty cents before the bankruptcy filing. Jack Grubman, a financial analyst at the Smith Barney unit of Citigroup, maintained a buy rating on its stock until just before its bankruptcy.

Level 3 Communications announced a $535 million loss in the first quarter of 2001, resulting in the layoff of 2,000 employees. Corning Glass increased its telecommunications revenue by $2 billion between 1999 and 2000, mostly through sales of fiber-optics. The bottom then dropped out of that market, badly damaging Corning, which was already suffering from a mass of asbestos litigation claims. The company laid off thousands of employees and took a $5.1 billion charge on its books. Corning suspended dividends for the first time in its history. Corning stock reached a high of $113.10 in September 2000, only to fall to $1.10 by October 2002. A federal district court dismissed an employee class action lawsuit complaining of investments made by the company pension plan in Corning stock. Other suffering companies such as Enron, WorldCom, the Williams Companies, and Kmart were not so lucky. Courts found that the pension schemes of those companies did impose fiduciary responsibilities that made their own stock a bad investment.

Global Crossing

Global Crossing Ltd., a large fiber-optic long network operator, filed for bankruptcy protection on January 28, 2002. That was then the fourth-largest bankruptcy in U.S. history, setting off a new sensation in the press, which was already in frenzy over Enron. Global Crossing was a Bermuda company managed from Beverly Hills, California. Founded in 1997, the company went public on August 13, 1998, and the price of its stock rose from $6.50 to $25.50 on its first day of trading on Nasdaq. Global Crossing moved its listing to the NYSE on November 6, 2000. There, the stock's price continued to rise, spurred by a prediction from the Commerce Department that Internet traffic would be doubling every hundred days.

Global Crossing's chairman, Gary Winnick, had worked at the side of Michael Milken at Drexel Burnham Lambert for seven years before founding Global Crossing. Milken, the "junk bond king" of the 1980s, had made $1.1 billion between 1984 and 1987. Winnick, who was in charge of Drexel's convertible bond department, was granted immunity from prosecution by the government after he agreed to testify against Milken. Winnick was spared the role of a rat when Milken later pleaded guilty. Winnick invested $15 million to start Global Crossing. That investment grew to be valued at $6 billion after Global Crossing went public. One of Global Crossing's major stockholders was the Canadian Imperial Bank of Commerce (CIBC), which paid $41 million for a 25 percent stake in the company. CIBC syndicated a $482 million loan to Global Crossing and loaned it an additional $850 million. CIBC also acted as Global Crossing's underwriter and performed other investment banking services. Global Crossing was a bonanza for CIBC, at least until its failure.

Global Crossing was created for the purpose of laying a fiber-optic cable across the Atlantic Ocean. To fulfill that goal, the company purchased the largest independent undersea cable-laying firm in the world. At the time of its bankruptcy, Global Crossing had 100,000 route miles in its fiber-optic network that translated into 1.7 million fiber-optic miles, reaching twenty-seven countries and 200 major cities on four continents. Global Crossing's expansion plans included a 12,000-mile undersea cable to Japan and a 10,000-mile undersea and terrestrial cable to South America. The company expanded its operations to include domestic telecommunications. Global Crossing became a force in that market after merging with the Frontier Corp., a long-distance carrier, through a $10 billion transaction.

Global Crossing tried to acquire US West Inc., a regional Bell company, but lost that effort in a fight with Qwest Communications. Global Crossing was successful in its effort to acquire Ixnet, which was renamed Global Crossing Financial Markets and used to provide network connections to financial services firms in the form of high-speed transmission of data, processing of financial information, and conducting electronic trading. Global Crossing also provided bandwidth for media and entertainment uses that included digital production, animation, and special effects.

Accounting Manipulations

Global Crossing spent $15 billion laying fiber-optic cable before being hard-hit by the glut of overcapacity, after competitors rushed into this business. That competition resulted in reduced prices for access to high-speed lines that were far below the profit margin needed by the telecommunications firms to sustain their growth. The market downturn caught up with Global Crossing in 2001. The company wrote off $17 billion in assets that year.

Worse trouble was on the way. The SEC and Federal Bureau of Investigation (FBI) began an investigation of Global Crossing after one of the company's executives, Roy Olofson, a former vice president of finance, complained that revenues were being booked improperly. He charged that the company boosted revenue by reporting sales while keeping the expenses related to those sales off its income statement. This was accomplished by designating those expenses as capital expenditures that were amortized over time, instead of being expensed immediately. This was still another example of how accrual accounting could be manipulated for advantage. According to the company, Olofson complained only after he was denied a multimillion-dollar severance package that he had demanded for wrongful termination after he returned to work from a leave he took to deal with lung cancer. Gary Winnick called Olofson an "extortionist."[2]

The transactions under review by the government involved something called indefeasible rights of use (IRUs) that allowed Global Crossing to pump up revenues. An IRU is the right to use a specified capacity or bandwidth over a designated line for a specified period of time. IRU revenues totaled over $700 million at Global Crossing in 1999 and constituted about one-half of the company's revenue. A class action suit contended that, in order to meet analysts' projections, Global Crossing improperly recorded as immediate income amounts due under the IRUs that should have been booked over the entire term of each IRU, a period of up to twenty-five years.

An internal e-mail at Global Crossing provided fodder for lawsuits over the company's accounting practices. The e-mail stated that "prices are dropping fast and to some extent we are our own worst enemy. When saddled with an unreasonable revenue expectations [sic] we do the crazy deals at the end of the quarter. This, in turn, causes prices to drop which makes it more likely that we'll need to do another deal at the end of the next quarter."[3] One such crazy deal involved capacity swaps with other telecommunications companies, including 360 Networks. These transactions involved reciprocal capacity agreements that required each company to pay the other for offsetting capacity, another form of "round-tripping." The effect was that the actual cash payments by each party were offset by a payment from the counterparty, but Global Crossing treated the cash paid out as a capital expenditure that was amortized over time. Another internal e-mail at Global Crossing stated that this "swap crap is going to kill us in the long run,"[4] but a special committee appointed by the company's board of directors concluded, after an internal investigation by the Coudert Brothers law firm, that the transactions were legitimate, an approach somewhat different from that of the Powers report at Enron.

Global Crossing was, in all events, another accounting failure of massive proportions. The company's financial statements failed to disclose that Global Crossing had losses of $25.7 billion in 2000 and 2001. Those losses would not be reported until December 2003, long after the company was bankrupt. Global Crossing was audited by Arthur Andersen LLP, which had to withdraw from that engagement after its criminal conviction. A criminal investigation of Global Crossing stalled without any charges being filed. This seems strange in light of the general hysteria of the time, but the answer may lie in the fact that there were even greater failings in the offing that would overshadow Global Crossing.

The SEC settled charges against three Global Crossing executives, including Dan Cohrs, chief financial officer, and Joseph Perrone, chief accounting officer. Gary Winnick had agreed with the SEC staff to pay a $1 million fine, but the SEC commissioners in a 3–2 vote concluded that Winnick should not be held liable because he was only the company's chairman and not an executive officer. Thus the reformist goal of splitting the role of chief executive officer and chairman appears to have backfired on its proponents.

Bankruptcy

Global Crossing's bankruptcy wiped out shareholder value that at one point exceeded $45 billion. As at Enron, insiders at Global Crossing made huge profits, totaling $5.2 billion, before the company's fall. Gary Winnick sold $735 million of his Global Crossing stock and used a controversial tax shelter marketed by the BDO Seidman accounting firm to shield his profits from taxes. Winnick still held large amounts of the company's stock at the time of the company's bankruptcy filing, cutting his prior net worth by several billion dollars and pushing him off *Forbes* magazine's list of the 400 richest individuals in the United States. Yet he remained ensconced in his $94 million mansion in Beverly Hills; its purchase price set a new record for the highest ever paid for a single family home in the United States.

Global Crossing borrowed $2.5 billion from a bank syndicate led by JPMorgan Chase & Co. just two months before its bankruptcy. Those banks sued Winnick and twenty-two other Global Crossing executives over the loan, claiming that the defendants had engaged in a "massive scam" to conceal Global Crossing's true financial condition from the bank consortium. Citigroup, another Global Crossing banker, was on the receiving end of a class action lawsuit for its involvement with that company. Citigroup agreed to pay $75 million to settle that litigation, which charged that the bank had undisclosed conflicts of interest and that research reports issued by its analysts inflated the value of Global Crossing as an investment. Some ninety other lawsuits were filed in response to the failure of Global Crossing, including one brought by an organization called Judicial Watch against former President Bill Clinton. That suit alleged that Clinton had conspired to pump up Global Crossing's stock price by allowing the awarding of a favorable Defense Department contract in exchange for the $1 million contribution the company made to his presidential library. That suit was dismissed on the grounds that the former president was immune from such claims.

Another political figure profiting from Global Crossing stock before its failure was Terry McAuliffe, the chairman of the Democratic National Committee. He received $100,000 of Global Crossing shares for introducing Winnick to President Clinton in 1997. McAuliffe garnered $18 million in profits after the company made its initial public offering. A close associate of Clinton, McAuliffe was among the shrillest of the voices condemning Enron executives and corporate America in general for greed in receiving excessive profits. McAuliffe was unembarrassed at his own rate of return from his political connections, which exceeded even that of Hillary Rodham Clinton's famous $100,000 profit from a $1,000 investment in commodity futures contracts.

Anne Bingaman, a former Clinton administration official, was paid $2.3 million as a lobbyist for Global Crossing. She was the wife of Democratic senator Jeff Bingaman of New Mexico—closing the circle with Senator Phil Gramm and his wife, Wendy, at Enron. On the other side of the aisle, former President George H.W. Bush took $80,000 in Global Crossing stock in lieu of a fee for a speech he gave at the company. That stock was valued at over $14 million at its peak. Senator John McCain received a $31,000 campaign donation from Global Crossing for helping it with the Federal Communications Commission. Both political parties received over $500,000 for their 2000 conventions. Perhaps as a result of the offsetting involvement of these high-level political figures and their political parties, the bankruptcy of Global Crossing seemed to pass unnoticed at the time that the frenzy over Enron was at its height, despite many similarities, including a whistleblower, large political contributions, and claims of improper accounting treatment. Congress held hearings on Global Crossing's failure, but WorldCom and other failures overshadowed that show.

Accounting Failures

Before its demise, Global Crossing created a loan program for its executives to borrow up to $7.5 million each so they would not have to sell their Global Crossing stock as its price began dropping in 2001. Those loans were to be drawn from a $1 billion line of credit maintained by the company. The executives needed this arrangement because they held their Global Crossing stock in margin accounts and had been borrowing against it. As the price declined, those executives were receiving margin calls for additional funds to secure those loans.

Like Enron workers, Global Crossing employees had the majority of the holdings in their Section 401(k) retirement accounts invested in Global Crossing stock at the time of its bankruptcy. Several of these disappointed investors showed up to testify before Congress. Facing criticism from those employees when he testified before Congress, Gary Winnick agreed to cover their losses by donating $25 million of his own funds, which delighted the congressional inquisitors. One congressman even described Winnick's gesture as "magnanimous. It is one of leadership. And I think you have just shocked a lot of people, and you ought to be proud of that."[5] As the chairman of the committee noted, however, those employees were not the only ones needing assistance: other investors had been decimated as well.

Reorganization

As part of its bankruptcy reorganization, Global Crossing sold a 61.5 percent ownership in itself to Singapore Technologies Telemedia for $250 million, wiping out what had once been $40 billion in shareholder stock value and $12 billion in debt. Winnick was a defendant in seventy lawsuits, but a $325 million settlement was reached with Global Crossing's former officers and Simpson Thatcher, the company's New York lawyers. Most of that amount was to be paid by their insurance companies. Simpson Thacher agreed to contribute $19.5 million to the settlement even though it had not been sued. Winnick paid $55 million out of his own pocket and agreed to give another $20 million to employees. A suit brought on behalf of employees holding Global Crossing stock in their Section 401(k) accounts was settled for $79 million, with Winnick contributing his $25 million and insurance companies kicking in the rest.

The whole Global Crossing affair reached comic proportions when, shortly after the company emerged from bankruptcy, it announced the largest quarterly profit in American history. That $24.88 billion profit had little to do with the company's revenues, which were $719 million for the quarter, while earnings were a minuscule $13 million. Instead, this monstrous profit was the result of accounting changes in the bankruptcy proceeding. Those changes included the reduction or elimination of liabilities in bankruptcy, elimination of equity obligations, and "fresh start" accounting adjustments from the IRUs that were changed to reduce liabilities under those contracts. That bizarre profit announcement caused a dramatic 38 percent drop in the price of new shares issued by the company when it emerged from bankruptcy. Nevertheless, billionaire investor Richard Rainwater bought a 7.5 percent interest in Global Crossing, viewing it as a value.

The SEC later charged Global Crossing with accounting manipulations through capacity swaps with other telecom companies, but no fine was imposed. Three Global Crossing executives agreed to each pay fines of $100,000 to settle SEC charges for that conduct. They were Thomas J. Casey, chief executive officer; Dan Cohrs, chief financial officer; and Joseph Perrone, executive vice president. Incredibly, as noted, the SEC rejected a recommendation by its staff that an action be brought against Gary Winnick.

Adelphia

Adelphia Communications Corp. was another scandal of gigantic proportions. It was the nation's sixth-largest cable company before its bankruptcy, providing cable television, high-speed Internet access, and local telephone service to customers in twenty-nine states. Adelphia went public in 1986 with two classes of stock. Its class A shares were given one vote per share, while the class B shares had ten votes per share. The class A shares were sold to the public. The class B shares were owned by Adelphia's founders, John Rigas and his family in Coudersport, Pennsylvania. They also owned 12.5 percent of the class A shares, giving them control of the company. Lest there be any doubt, the class A shares were allowed to elect only one of the nine directors on the Adelphia board. Five Rigas family members served on the board. The other four directors were outside directors.

Adelphia was founded by John Rigas and a brother, Gus, in 1952. They were the sons of Greek immigrants and used the Greek word for brothers as the name of their company. Devoted to family programming, Adelphia was an unexciting venture until the late 1990s. The company then expanded quickly through the acquisition of three other cable companies for $10 billion. Those acquisitions increased Adelphia's subscriber base from 2.2 million to over 5 million despite the dropping of *Playboy* and other adult entertainment channels from the offerings of the acquired companies. Although debt more than doubled to $9.7 billion, the company's stock price quadrupled between 1998 and 1999, reaching $86 per share. In order to fund its acquisitions, Adelphia issued large amounts of class A stock. The Rigas family also purchased large amounts of Adelphia B shares at the same time in order to maintain its control position. The funding of those purchases became the target of newspaper stories on March 28, 2002. Those reports revealed that Adelphia had engaged in "co-borrowings" of $2.3 billion with the Rigas family. Under this co-borrowing arrangement, either Adelphia for the business or the Rigas family personally could draw down on various lines of credit and other lending arrangements with financial institutions. Both Adelphia and the Rigas family were liable for repayment of any amounts drawn down by the other.

The co-borrowing arrangement was disclosed to Adelphia's outside auditors, Deloitte & Touche, and the existence of this arrangement and the maximum amount that could be borrowed was disclosed to investors, but not the amount actually drawn down. The SEC was also advised of the co-borrowing arrangement. Deloitte & Touche had recommended disclosure of the amount of the drawdowns, but did not insist on such disclosure. The Pittsburgh law firm of Buchanan Ingersoll acquiesced in Adelphia's decision not to disclose the actual amount of the drawdown. Under GAAP, disclosure was required only if there was a reasonable possibility of a loss. As the Enron scandal mounted, Deloitte & Touche did finally insist on a footnote disclosure of the Rigas family's borrowings in the company's SEC Form 10-K annual report due on March 31, 2002. That disclosure caused a stir among analysts. That response and the ongoing hysteria over Enron caused Deloitte & Touche to withhold its certification of the company's audit. That action in turn triggered defaults in Adelphia loan covenants and caused the SEC to investigate.

These revelations were followed by a cascade of other problems. Adelphia announced that its cash flow and revenue in the years 2000 and 2001 had been inflated by more than $500 million. The company had also inflated the number of its cable subscribers. One technique reported to have been used by Adelphia to increase cash flow was to purchase large numbers of digital boxes from its suppliers, Motorola and Scientific Atlanta, for $125 even though they normally cost only $100. The additional $25 was then kicked back to Adelphia by the suppliers as a fee that went into cash flow. These revelations shocked the financial system, already staggered by Enron, and forced Adelphia into bankruptcy on June 25, 2002. That filing came just ten days after Arthur Andersen's conviction of obstruction of justice, giving rise to more concern that the full disclosure system had broken down completely.

The SEC filed civil charges against the Rigas family and others, asserting that they had committed "one of the most extensive financial frauds ever to take place at a public company" by failing properly to report the co-borrowings. The SEC charged that the defendants had falsified operations reports and inflated earnings to meet analysts' expectations. Specifically, the defendants were charged in the SEC complaint with falsifying information that was "crucial to the 'metrics' used by Wall Street to evaluate cable companies." That information involved the number of the company's "basic" cable subscribers, the extent of its cable system upgrades, and its earnings before interest, taxes, depreciation, and amortization (EBITDA). The SEC claimed that the defendants had concealed "rampant" self-dealing.[6]

Internal Investigation

David Boies was hired by a special committee of Adelphia directors to conduct an internal investigation that resulted in what was becoming a ritual: trashing of management and providing assistance to those bringing litigation against the company. Boies, who performed a similar role at Tyco, had attained fame for his supporting role in IBM's epic defense against antitrust charges in a case that lasted from 1969 until 1982 and involved several years of trial. His success in defending CBS in a libel suit brought by General William Westmoreland was followed by some stunning losses. Boies represented the government in its losing effort to break up Microsoft; he was the Al Gore lawyer that lost the challenge to the outcome of the 2004 presidential election in the Supreme Court; and he was Napster's lawyer in its losing effort to stay in the business of facilitating the stealing of copyrighted songs.

The Rigas family was ousted from Adelphia by the special committee at Boies's direction, and the company was then placed in bankruptcy. Criminal investigations into self-dealing by the Rigas family were quickly launched. The founder of Adelphia, John Rigas, seemed to be an unlikely target for the government. He never sold a share of his Adelphia stock and never received stock options. The family used $1.4 billion to buy Adelphia B shares in order to keep their interest in the company undiluted as more class A stock was issued. That stock was purchased on margin and would require large borrowings to support when the market began its downward plunge. Funds borrowed under this program were also used to support the family's privately owned cable operations. An additional $150 million was loaned to the Buffalo Sabers, a hockey team owned by John Rigas, and $45 million went to his other business operations. Another $3 million went to a movie, *Songcatchers,* financed by John Rigas's daughter.

Adelphia and the Rigas family drew down a total of $5.6 billion under the co-borrowing arrangement. Those loans were syndicated by Wachovia Bank, the Bank of Montreal, and the Bank of America and sold to numerous other financial institutions. In exchange for their syndication efforts, those three banks were promised investment banking business from Adelphia, including underwriting its stock sales. Commercial banks had been excluded from such underwriting activities by the Glass-Steagall Act until its erosion and eventual repeal at the end of the twentieth century. The investment banking fees to the three banks totaled $230 million.

Criminal Charges

James Brown, Adelphia's vice president for finance, and Timothy Werth, its accounting director, pleaded guilty to criminal charges of concealing the company's financial condition in the accounting reports filed with the SEC. Michael Mulcahey, an executive in Adelphia's accounting section, pleaded innocent to charges that were filed against him. John Rigas was arrested on July 24, 2002. He was the subject of a 103-page indictment charging him with looting Adelphia and concealing its true financial condition and its business dealings with the Rigas family from shareholders. Rigas's two sons, who lived at home with him, were also arrested. One son, Michael, was Adelphia's executive vice president for operations and the other, Timothy, its chief financial officer.

The Rigas arrest was dramatically staged with a Gestapo-like dawn raid on their New York apartment. The government handcuffed 78-year-old John Rigas, a cancer patient, and frog-marched him in front of waiting television cameras for the now familiar perp walk ritual. Rigas's tie, shoelaces, and belt were taken away from him when he was arrested, purportedly to prevent suicide but actually to embarrass him during processing. The manacling and parading of the elderly, nonviolent Rigas before the assembled press and cameras was a particularly obscene bit of grandstanding by government prosecutors. The abuse was so bad that it even drew a protest from the New York Civil Liberties Union, an organization not normally concerned with the rights of white-collar criminal suspects.

In contrast to the treatment given Rigas, Enron executives, and other white-collar defendants, a federal judge held the New York City government in contempt in 2002 for handcuffing inmates for transportation, even those previously found with weapons. Inmates could be handcuffed only if a hearing was first held to determine whether such manacling was necessary and whether it might be harmful to the inmates' health. Fines imposed on the city for violating those requirements were to be credited to the inmates' own accounts. In 2002, in another case, a federal judge found that a burglary suspect had been improperly subjected to a perp walk in handcuffs by New York authorities. The city settled that case for $250,000. The U.S. Supreme Court subsequently set aside a death penalty because a violent defendant had been shackled in front of the jury during the sentencing phase, after being convicted of robbing and murdering an elderly couple. The court held such restraints could be used during the guilt and sentencing phases only where there is some strong security interest. That ruling came just a few weeks after a violent offender killed his trial judge and three others after being uncuffed in a Georgia courthouse before being brought before a jury. Apparently, no such rights are available to high-roller executives who pose no danger to anyone, except possibly from their errant golf shots.

The Rigas family members were charged in the indictment with treating company assets as their own and with misleading the rating agencies. John Rigas had to miss court on several occasions to obtain cancer treatments at the Mayo Clinic, and the trial did not start off well for the government prosecutors. They were scolded by the federal judge, Leonard Sand, for putting on a witness who gave "mistaken testimony." The judge called that an "egregious error." Nevertheless, the government proceeded with what would become a familiar litany of corporate excesses.

Adelphia maintained a fleet of three aircraft and had seven full-time pilots. The Rigas family was accused of using the company's Gulfstream for personal trips. This was a favorite way to embarrass executives, after Henry Ford II was found to have used company planes to pick up his wine and to fly his mother's cats and dogs in the 1970s. The Rigas family was charged with using those aircraft for personal jaunts, including shopping trips by John Rigas's wife, golf outings by other family members, and several trips to obtain Christmas trees, one of which was too short, requiring a second flight for a replacement. Timothy Rigas had a company plane fly to the Caribbean to pick up an actress friend, Peta Wilson, who starred in a television series called *La Femme Nikita*. She testified at the trial of the Rigas family that she flew on the jet at least eight times and had not reimbursed the company for that expense. The indictment further charged that Adelphia paid for an African safari for the Rigas family.

Never shying from overkill, the prosecution presented evidence that Tim Rigas had Adelphia pay for a shipment of one hundred slippers that he liked after wearing them at a hotel. That made great press, reminiscent of the large numbers of shoes found in the closet of Imelda Marcos, the former first lady of the Philippines, after her husband was deposed from office. The slippers sought by Tim Rigas could only be bought in bulk, however, and cost a grand total of $268, hardly an amount that justified a high-profile criminal prosecution. He was also charged with having Adelphia pay for a $1 million condominium and $700,000 for a membership at the Briar Creek Golf Club in South Carolina. Adelphia spent $13 million on a golf course being built by John and Timothy Rigas near Coudersport. The total budget planned for the course was to be a whopping $40 million. Another $26 million went to purchase timber rights on the Rigas family ranch.

The Rigas trial lasted for months and resulted in convictions of John and Timothy Rigas on some, but not all counts. The jury deadlocked over the charges against Michael Rigas, resulting in a mistrial. Michael Mulcahey was acquitted of all charges. The Rigas family troubles continued. Adelphia sued them for looting the company. Targeted as well were Deloitte & Touche, for failing to require disclosure of the amount of the Rigas borrowings, and Adelphia's banks, which were charged with misconduct for agreeing to the co-borrowing arrangement. PricewaterhouseCoopers replaced Deloitte & Touche as the company's auditor.

Adelphia filed a reorganization plan in its bankruptcy proceedings on February 25, 2003. Under that plan, ownership of the company was to be turned over to Adelphia's unsecured creditors, leaving shareholders with nothing but some class action suits that would undoubtedly be settled for a relatively small amount that would be further reduced by the lawyers' contingency fees. Adelphia's headquarters were moved from Pennsylvania to Greenwood Village, Colorado. A consortium of banks agreed to supply $8.8 billion in financing to restructure the company, which went on the auction block for $17.5 billion. Time Warner and Comcast prevailed over Cablevision in that auction. In December 2004, Adelphia announced that it had failed to report losses before 2001 in amounts totaling $1.7 billion. Adelphia also disclosed that it lost over $13 billion following its bankruptcy, largely as a result of asset write-offs. The company offered the SEC and the Justice Department $700 million to settle its accounting problems, up from $425 million from its original offer. Adelphia eventually agreed to settle its problems with the SEC and the Justice Department by paying $715 million into a victims compensation fund. At the same time, the Rigas family agreed to forfeit about $1.5 billion in assets to Adelphia. This left the family with about $80 million in operations unconnected with Adelphia. Deloitte & Touche LLP agreed to pay $65 million to settle SEC charges over its audit work at Adelphia. The Rigas family contribution did little to assuage government zeal and overreaching. Prosecutors asked for 215-year sentences for John and Timothy Rigas. The judge was more lenient giving Timothy Rigas twenty years and John Rigas fifteen years, but still probably a death sentence for him. The judge did leave an out that would let Rigas out of prison under a somewhat God-like formula that permitted Rigas to be released after serving two years if he could show that he had only three months to live. Michael Rigas later pleaded guilty to a single count of altering business records.

WorldCom

The Company

If there are any doubts about the inadequacy of full disclosure and other corporate governance reforms, the bankruptcy of WorldCom Inc. should lay them to rest. It was another colossal failure for every aspect of corporate governance. WorldCom's demise set a record for the largest bankruptcy in the world, shoving Enron aside for that honor. Headquartered in Clinton, Mississippi, WorldCom was the second-largest long-distance telephone provider in the United States, the largest international telephone carrier, and the world's largest Internet carrier at the time of its bankruptcy. Its operations spanned six continents and some hundred countries where the company serviced 20 million customers. WorldCom had reported revenues of $30 billion and more than 60,000 employees before its bankruptcy.

WorldCom had been built through the efforts of Bernard J. Ebbers, the son of a traveling salesman from Canada. Ebbers spent some formative years on a Navajo Indian reservation in New Mexico and worked variously as a milkman and a bouncer. After attending college in Canada without much success, Ebbers transferred to Mississippi College, a private liberal arts college in Clinton, Mississippi, where he was given a basketball scholarship. After his graduation, Ebbers worked as coach at a Mississippi school before becoming a distribution manager at the Stahl-Urban Company, a garment factory in Brookhaven, Mississippi. After five years at that company, Ebbers bought the Sand's Motel and Restaurant in Columbia, Mississippi, which was described by some as a "dump," but which Ebbers made profitable. He invested with others in more motels, developing a chain and becoming a millionaire in the process.

In 1983, Ebbers invested in a company called LDDC (Long Distance Discount Company), one of the many long-distance carriers formed after the breakup of AT&T by the Justice Department. He took charge of the company in 1985 in order to prevent it from failing. He soon made LDDC profitable and began growing it with acquisitions, totaling seventy-five over the next fifteen years. LDDC became a public company in 1989 through a merger with Advantage Companies Inc., a Nasdaq listed company. LDDC's revenues were then exceeding $100 million. Ebbers expanded its markets in the United States and abroad through a series of acquisitions.

By 1994, LDDC's revenues reached $2.2 billion. The company's name was changed in 1995 to WorldCom to reflect its growing global business. That reach was extended with the acquisition of MFS Communications Inc. for $12.4 billion in stock in 1996. This merger created the first integrated local and long-distance company since the breakup of AT&T and provided an entrée for WorldCom into fiber-optics and Internet services. At that point, WorldCom was the fourth-largest long-distance telephone company.

In 1996, the *Wall Street Journal*'s "Shareholder Scoreboard Survey" awarded WorldCom its number one ranking, out of 1,000 companies, for best ten-year performance. The company was added to the S&P 500 Index that year. WorldCom expanded its operations in the Internet market in 1997 with the purchase of Compuserve from H&R Block for $1.2 billion. At the same time, WorldCom restructured its operations and entered into a joint venture with America Online. WorldCom bought Brooks Fiber Properties for $2.4

billion, a provider of communications services that allowed businesses to bypass local phone networks. WorldCom's growth was not always smooth or well-thought-out. WorldCom's $6 billion acquisition of Digex Inc. from Intermedia Communications Inc. was arranged after a thirty-five-minute conference call made on less than two hours' notice. This acquisition was negotiated without the knowledge or approval of WorldCom's board of directors. Compounding this casual approach to corporate governance mandates, WorldCom announced the deal before seeking the after-the-fact approval of the board and falsified the board minutes to cover up that lack of prior approval. Ebbers managed to renegotiate the deal downward a bit after Intermedia's stock value dropped, but that required him to pay greenmail to some Digex shareholders opposing the deal.

MCI

WorldCom shocked the stock market in October 1997 when it announced a surprise $30 billion bid for MCI Communications, a large long-distance carrier. The MCI acquisition was like the fish swallowing the whale because MCI's revenues were some 250 percent greater than WorldCom's. To obtain control of MCI, WorldCom had to outbid British Telecommunications, as well as another competing bid made by GTE, the third-largest local phone company. GTE tried to fend off WorldCom with an antitrust suit, claiming that a merger with MCI would reduce competition in the Internet backbone service area. WorldCom avoided that issue by agreeing to sell off the Internet business to Cable and Wireless. WorldCom also raised its offer, prevailing with a winning bid of $36.5 billion in cash and stock.

Antitrust authorities in the United States and Europe closely scrutinized the MCI merger because both firms provided Internet services in competition with each other, but the regulators let the merger proceed. The Reverend Jesse Jackson, called a corporate shakedown artist by one biographer, appeared at WorldCom's shareholder meeting to speak out in opposition to the merger, claiming that it would have an adverse effect on workers. Jackson used the Telecommunications Act of 1996 to oppose telecom mergers before the Federal Communications Commission, claiming they would unfairly affect workers. At the same time, Jackson told the involved companies that he would drop his opposition if they made monetary payments to his causes and implemented diversity programs in the form of minority set-asides. MCI and WorldCom refused to make such payments, despite Jackson's threats of a boycott.[7]

The WorldCom shareholders overwhelmingly approved the MCI/WorldCom merger. The combined firm had 79,000 employees and $27 billion in annual revenues. As a result of this merger, WorldCom became a major global communications provider. Its services were extended to the government as well as to private consumers. Among other things, WorldCom provided services for a million Social Security beneficiaries, data network services for the post office, network management for the Pentagon, and communications services for Congress and many government agencies.

This merger was, at the time, the largest in American history. The company changed its name briefly to MCI WorldCom before switching back to WorldCom. The combination gave WorldCom a new high profile that was exploited by its management, which sponsored a PGA Tour tournament and recruited basketball star Michael Jordan to serve as WorldCom's spokesman. WorldCom's stock was soaring, increasing by two-thirds in 1997. WorldCom had a market valuation of $115 billion when its stock price peaked at $64.50 per share in 1999. The company was then the fourteenth-largest company in the United States. MCI reported a fourth-quarter loss before its merger with WorldCom was complete, but a few months later WorldCom reported that its first-quarter earnings were up tenfold, before one-time charges.

Bernard Ebbers continued his efforts to grow WorldCom. He acquired SkyTel, a paging service, for $1.8 billion. A deal to acquire Nextel fell through, but WorldCom then tried to acquire Sprint Corp. for an incredible $129 billion. The WorldCom bid for Sprint appeared to be successful until the Justice Department brought suit to stop it in June 2000. Attorney General Janet Reno claimed that such a combination would re-create the AT&T monopoly broken up by Judge Green in 1982. That charge seemed a bit absurd since there was intense competition in the residential long-distance market, and a Sprint/WorldCom merger would have faced even greater competition from other Internet providers. Perhaps more important, the merger would have reduced the glut of capacity in the telecommunications market that was then appearing. In the event, WorldCom backed down and withdrew its bid for Sprint. This crippled both WorldCom and Sprint.

WorldCom encountered other obstacles. In 1999 a computer glitch shut down its Internet connections for several large businesses and banks, as well as the Chicago Board of Trade, for ten days. Ebbers blamed that problem on Lucent Technologies. WorldCom had to settle "slamming" complaints (switching customers from other providers without their permission) for $3.5 million.

WorldCom Accounting

WorldCom was a laboratory for the accounting world. Between 1996 and 2000, WorldCom reported earnings of $16 billion on its financial reports filed with the SEC, while claiming less than $1 billion in taxable income. That probably made sense to an accountant, but to the rest of the world it looked like a cooking of the books, a cooking sanctioned by the government. The SEC did block the company from writing off large sums in research and development costs immediately after the merger with MCI. WorldCom wanted to use those write-offs to pump up future earnings. After discussions with the SEC, WorldCom had to settle for one-half the amounts it sought.

WorldCom met analysts' earnings expectations to the penny for the third quarter of 2000 before one-time charges, but the company announced on October 26, 2000, that it was writing off $685 million of receivables from bankrupt customers, causing a sharp drop in its stock price. WorldCom disclosed in November that it would not meet analysts' expectations for the fourth quarter. The company was in an apparent panic as the telecommunications market melted down. Ebbers then proclaimed that WorldCom was splitting its operations into four units, copying similar plans announced by AT&T and Tyco. Mimicking another AT&T tactic, WorldCom created two tracking stocks, including one for its declining long-distance business. Those announcements were not viewed favorably in the stock market. WorldCom's stock price dropped by 20 percent and was down 75 percent from its high. In January 2001, WorldCom began laying off 10,000 employees, which was 13 percent of its workforce.

The downturn in the economy placed much pressure on WorldCom management to increase performance. In the world of full disclosure, that meant manipulating financial accounts in order to prop up earnings in the hopes of an improvement in the economy that would rescue the company. An SEC complaint charged that "as the economy cooled in 2001, WorldCom's earnings and profits similarly declined, making it difficult to keep WorldCom's earnings in line with expectations by industry analysts."[8] The company then began manipulating its accounting reports on a massive scale to conceal the true depth of that decline.

Bernard Ebbers

Bernard Ebbers was given the largest grants of stock options for any executive during any five-year period. Ebbers sold $60 million of his stock before 1995, but then stopped his sales and started accumulating WorldCom stock. Ebbers became a bull on the company and closely monitored his executives to discourage them from selling their WorldCom stock. He reportedly even fired an executive for selling WorldCom stock. Ebbers held onto his own WorldCom shares right through its bankruptcy. Ebbers's net worth reached $1.4 billion in 1999, but he presented some interesting contrasts. Although Canadian by birth, he became an American citizen and strove to be a "good ole boy" from the South, often appearing at work in jeans and cowboy boots, long before dress down-days became popular. Ebbers drove an old pickup truck, hung out in poolrooms, ate in local restaurants unvisited by Zagat, and opened WorldCom board meetings at the Western Sizzlin' steakhouse with a prayer. He lived relatively simply in Mississippi, maintaining his residence in a double-wide trailer while building a $1.8 million home, which was not extravagant by most executive standards. A lodge built by Ebbers on a nearby lake was more expensive but not obscene. He was a generous supporter of his community, but in a low-key way, taught Sunday school, and even worked in a local homeless shelter.

This laid-back lifestyle and his informal dress at work were in stark contrast to some of Ebbers's toys, which included a 130-foot yacht called *Aquasition*. Ebbers's portfolio included the ownership of a yacht-building company and a hockey team, the Bandits, that he bought and moved to Mississippi. Another ego purchase was the Douglas Lake Ranch in British Columbia, which Ebbers bought for $66 million. The ranch covered 164,000 acres and had access to 350,000 acres of government land on which he could graze his 22,000 head of cattle. Ebbers joined in the purchase of another 460,000 acres of timberland in Alabama, a trucking company, a rice farm in Louisiana, a building in Chicago, a marina, and several motels. Ebbers's assets were largely acquired through bank loans that he secured with WorldCom stock. WorldCom also made a fleet of executive jets available to him, including a $30 million Gulfstream IV.

Scott Sullivan

Scott Sullivan was considered Ebbers's right arm on financial matters at WorldCom. Sullivan provided a polished appearance on Wall Street, a role that Ebbers eschewed. Sullivan was a graduate of the State University of New York (SUNY) at Oswego, where he received a degree in accounting and became a certified public accountant. He joined KPMG, the giant accounting firm, after graduation and was a manager on that firm's General Electric engagement. Sullivan then moved to General Electric and worked for a time at Telus Communications in Florida and at the Advanced Telecommunications Corp. He joined WorldCom after WorldCom acquired the latter company. Sullivan became a leader at WorldCom through his work on the MCI deal and was given a chief financial officer Excellence Award in 1998 by *CFO* magazine. Andrew Fastow, at Enron, would receive that accolade the following year. Sullivan was the highest-paid chief financial officer in the United States in 1998 with compensation of $19 million. Over the next four years, he received a total of $45 million in compensation. He commuted to WorldCom's headquarters in Clinton, Mississippi, each week from his home in Boca Raton, Florida, on a company jet.

Free Fall

WorldCom's stock started dropping in early 2000, along with the rest of the telecommunications industry. On June 30, 2000, the company's stock price was less than half its price one year earlier. By year-end 2000, WorldCom's stock price had more than halved once again and continued to slip during 2001. WorldCom tried to buck the market by reporting profits of $1.4 billion in 2001 and $130 million in the first quarter of 2002. In fact, the company was losing money during those periods.

Scott Sullivan was called on to conceal WorldCom's actual financial condition from financial analysts as the telecommunications market collapsed. In order to meet analysts' expectations, Sullivan ordered that operating costs be changed to capital expenses to increase earnings. Sullivan used reserves to boost earnings by over $800 million. Refund payments were delayed in order to improve cash flow and earnings. These machinations concealed the full extent of WorldCom's problems, but the market continued to hammer WorldCom's stock as the Enron scandal reached its peak and accounting questions continued with respect to WorldCom.

One opportunity could have saved WorldCom. In November 2001, Verizon made an offer for WorldCom at a premium of 40 percent over the market price of WorldCom stock at the time. Ebbers viewed the offer as too low and advised the WorldCom board that he did not plan to pursue it. The board concurred in that judgment. WorldCom then began its own effort to merge with a stronger company, but was stymied by constant questions about its accounting methods. That concern was raised to a new level when the company reported that the SEC had started an investigation of its financial reports, driving the stock down even further. The declining market price of WorldCom's stock raised concern that its executives might soon start bailing out by seeking employment with competitors. To solve that problem, Ebbers was given the authority by the WorldCom board to hand out $238 million in retention bonuses in 2000. Of that amount, Ebbers and Sullivan each received $10 million. Ebbers was actually authorized to draw $30 million, but chose to take a lower amount.

Ebbers was in a perilous financial situation because he had borrowed $679 million from the Travelers Insurance Company, before its merger with Citigroup. His total debt was about $900 million, all of which was secured by WorldCom stock. The market downturn required him to provide large sums to maintain the stock at the required margin level. Ebbers was slated to receive $2 million per year in dividends from the WorldCom tracking stock, but that was not enough to save him from margin calls on loans he had secured with his WorldCom stock. To fill that gap, Ebbers borrowed $61 million from WorldCom, and WorldCom guaranteed another $100 million of his debt in 2001. Ebbers continued to borrow from the company, as the value of his stock declined and margin calls increased. By February 2001, Ebbers owed WorldCom $374 million. The loan amounts, which would grow to $408 million, were provided on very favorable terms, including an attractive interest rate of around 2 percent. The loans were justified by the board on the ground that the company's stock price, which was already falling, would be further undermined by reports that Ebbers was selling his stock. Those loans were not disclosed in the company's financial reports, and Ebbers used some of the loan proceeds from WorldCom for personal expenses, including $1.8 million for his home, and he wrote a check for $2 million to his ex-wife.

Ebbers had acquired some seventy companies and increased the company's stock by 7,000 percent before its free fall, but that was yesterday. Ebbers was forced to resign from WorldCom on April 30, 2002. His dismissal was the result of a palace revolt by WorldCom board members who were having second thoughts about the loans made to him and his lack of cooperation in giving up all his assets to secure them. The board members also thought that Ebbers had lost his strategic direction, focusing on cutting costs, sometimes by petty methods, and that he was ignoring customers. Perhaps more important, the directors thought that Wall Street had lost faith in Ebbers's leadership. Although he then owed WorldCom over $400 million, Ebbers was given a severance package that included a payment of $1.5 million annually for life as long as he met payments on his loans. That payment would cause much outrage in Congress and in the press as the extent of the company's problems became known.

WorldCom's credit rating was cut shortly after Ebbers's resignation, being downgraded to junk bond status. The price of WorldCom stock dropped to $2 from its high of $96.76 reached on June 30, 1999. Layoffs were ordered that exceeded 20,000 employees. The company reversed its tracking stock structure and recombined the tracking stock with its common stock and eliminated the annual tracking stock dividend of $284 million. Scandal exploded on June 25, 2002, after the company announced that it was restating its earnings. WorldCom admitted that it had improperly accounted for $3.9 billion in costs that made the company appear to be profitable when it was not. The accounting manipulations at WorldCom principally involved the reduction of WorldCom's "line costs," but revenues were inflated as well. A line cost was the expense of carrying communications traffic (voice or data) from one point to another. Those costs accounted for about one-half of WorldCom's total expenses. Capitalizing those costs reduced line costs. Revenues were inflated by using accounts titled "Corporate Unallocated" that added revenues from nonoperating sources that were ginned up in amounts exactly needed to meet analysts' expectations. Accrual accounting reserves were used to create cookie jar reserves, although those reserves eventually ran out. In one transaction, WorldCom claimed $225 million in revenue from a billing to Cherry Communications that was disputed by that company, which was, in any event, in bankruptcy.

These manipulations were blamed on the pressure Ebbers placed on subordinates to meet analysts' earnings expectations: "the emphasis on revenue was 'in every brick in every building.'"[9] The WorldCom board fired Scott Sullivan on June 25, 2002, because of his use of questionable accounting practices. Sullivan tried to convince the board that his accounting treatment was proper, submitting a white paper detailing his arguments, but by this point there was no chance that his justifications would be considered. The company's stock then dropped to nine cents per share. Sullivan had sold most of his WorldCom stock while he was the company's chief financial officer, making about $30 million.

The amount of WorldCom's inflated accounts continued to rise. On August 8, 2002, the company disclosed that another $3.3 billion had been improperly accounted for, bringing the total to more than $7 billion. An SEC investigation charged that WorldCom had actually misstated its earnings by $9 billion and others claimed that the misstatements were as much as $11 billion. WorldCom also wrote off a whopping $79 billion in assets and goodwill. A federal district court judge said this was "perhaps the largest accounting fraud in history." WorldCom filed for Chapter 11 bankruptcy on July 21, 2002, wiping out $180 billion in shareholder equity. WorldCom was delisted from Nasdaq.

Internal Investigations

William McLucas, the Enron inquisitor who had been pushed out of the Tyco inquiry, was hired to conduct an internal investigation of WorldCom for a special committee of the board of directors. That special committee was chaired by Nicholas deB. Katzenbach, who had been attorney general during the Lyndon Johnson administration. The special committee hired PricewaterhouseCoopers to assist in preparing a 340-page report (the Katzenbach report). Another report filed by WorldCom's bankruptcy lawyer, Richard Thornburgh, another former attorney general of the United States, totaled a relatively paltry 118 pages. These reports, and one prepared by former SEC chairman Richard Breeden, in his role as a corporate monitor appointed by a federal court in an SEC action, were a feast for plaintiff lawyers.

It is unclear why three reports were needed. They added no little expense and drained funds that might have been better used for creditor claims, as judged by the $715 an hour charged by McLucas and the total of $13 million charged by his firm. Thornburgh's law firm, Kirkpatrick & Lockhart, charged $8 million while his report was being prepared. The cost to WorldCom of all this lawyerly tongue clucking was more than $50 million and the meter was still running. The corporate monitor announced in April 2004 that he was going to stick around for another two years to oversee corporate governance at WorldCom at a rate of $800 per hour. He had already received $2.3 million for his work over the prior twenty-one months. The total fees requested by these and other advisers in the bankruptcy proceeding exceeded $600 million.

The Katzenbach report did not spend much time on the events that caused the collapse of WorldCom. It did note in passing that Ebbers's strategy of "growth through acquisitions" was dependent on a continuing increase in WorldCom's stock price and that Ebbers was frustrated by the government through its blocking of the merger with Sprint. Ebbers seemed demoralized by that event, and the company was left "drifting" when he lost his "strategic sense of direction."[10] The declining price of WorldCom's stock precluded such a strategy in any event. The Katzenbach report did consume much scarce timber on its description of the misuse of corporate jets by WorldCom executives and at least one board member. Usually good for headlines, those revelations fell a bit flat this time.

Despite its expense, the Katzenbach report was rather thin in establishing culpability by Ebbers. The report's best shot was its charge that Ebbers sold $70 million in WorldCom stock in September 2000 before a disappointing accounting report was filed. Less convincing was attributing the accounting fraud to Ebbers because "he was the source of the culture, as well as much of the pressure, that gave birth to this fraud."[11] He was said to have been aware that "financial gimmickry" was being used to meet analysts' earnings expectations. Ebbers was faulted for promoting WorldCom's stock to analysts and crowing about the company's double-digit revenue growth. He was also found to have closely followed WorldCom's "MonRev" reports. These were internal reports that summarized revenues from the company's various units and the company's reserve accounts that could be released to increase revenues. This was evidence of another failing in full disclosure requirements. Executives do not use the SEC required financial reports to manage their business. Instead, they use internally generated financial reports that are not made public.

The only other substantive evidence of Ebbers's involvement in the accounting manipulations was a voice mail message from Sullivan to Ebbers in which Sullivan said an accounting report had "fluff" in it in the form of "all one time stuff or junk."[12] Although there was no proof that Ebbers had ever listened to the message or that "fluff" meant something sinister, the Katzenbah report could not resist repeating the message at least twice. Missing were the kind of explosive e-mails that were by then a common part of every financial scandal. This was because Ebbers did not like to use e-mail or computers, even though he was the head of one of the largest Internet providers in the world. Most damning of all, the Katzenbach report disclosed that Ebbers had referred to efforts at WorldCom to create a corporate code of conduct as a "colossal waste of time."

The Katzenbach report got a dig in against Scott Sullivan, noting that he had used a portion of one of his bonuses to give gifts of $20,000 each to seven employees he thought had helped him obtain that bonus. Unlike Andrew Fastow's wife at Enron, those employees were not indicted for not claiming those gifts as income. Ebbers had also loaned various WorldCom executives several hundred thousand dollars. The Katzenbach report kicked the dead body of Arthur Andersen, WorldCom's former auditor, for failing to detect and prevent the company's accounting manipulations. There seemed to be little purpose in that condemnation since Arthur Andersen was bankrupt when the reports were filed. The criticism was, in any event, pretty weak, asserting that the auditor "appears to have missed several opportunities" to discover the fraud.[13] Katzenbach also faulted the WorldCom board even though his report conceded that the company had the proper corporate governance structure, including a majority of outside directors. The report concluded that no board members (other than Ebbers and Sullivan) knew or should have known of the fraud. Instead, the report stated that it was "possible" that the board members "might have" questioned trends at the company had they been more familiar with was happening in the company's operations. This seems strange since outside directors by definition are not involved in operations of the company they are directing.[14]

Thornburgh's report added little to the mix even though he hired a "forensic" accountant to assist him. Thornburgh did focus a bit more on the failure of the business plan at WorldCom, which appears to be the actual cause of its problems. The report traced the almost incredible growth of WorldCom under Ebbers, an individual with no experience in the telecommunications industry. "Within 15 years, it had become a global telecommunications giant and one of the largest companies in the world. Few companies in the annals of American business have grown so large and so fast in such an intensively competitive marketplace."[15] The company had disclosed its strategy in SEC filings, which Thornburgh summarized as follows:

- "Competition and capital requirements in the telecommunications industry would result in consolidation of competitors to a few dominant companies;
- To survive, WorldCom needed to grow its services, customer base and facilities rapidly and continually;
- The most effective means to grow was the acquisition of existing telecommunications companies with desirable shares of geographic or service markets; and
- Investment in new technologies was critical to reducing marginal costs, attracting customers and meeting their demand for new and better services."[16]

Thornburgh criticized this approach, saying that WorldCom had no corporate planning bureaucracy to guide its growth and that the company was largely grown by the force of Ebbers's personality. The Thornburgh report found that Ebbers "dominated" WorldCom in creating this complex communications giant by acquisitions. That growth was not bureaucratically defined but was "opportunistic" and caused difficulty in integrating its diverse components.[17]

Ebbers had led the company while it engaged in over sixty acquisitions during a fifteen-year period. Thornburgh's report noted that some of those acquisitions were the largest of their time in the industry. They included Metromedia Communications Corp. and Resurgens Communications Group Inc. ($1.25 billion), Williams Technology Group Inc. ($2.5 billion), and MFS Communications Company Inc. ($12 billion). Starting with annual revenues of $1 million in 1984, Ebbers increased that number to over $17 billion by 1998.

The Thornburgh report was remarkably candid in discussing the role of the outside auditor, in this case Arthur Andersen, noting that an "audit is not intended to provide a guarantee regarding the accuracy of the financial statements" and that "ultimately, a company's financial statements are the responsibility of management."[18] In that regard, Thornburgh was critical of WorldCom's management and its corporate governance, noting that an outside director sitting on the compensation committee had been given a sweetheart deal on a lease on a WorldCom jet. Thornburgh was further outraged that Ebbers's severance package included use of a corporate jet. By this time, corporate jet use and executive perks were replacing concerns with accounting failures.

Corporate Monitor

As the result of an action brought by the SEC, a federal district court appointed Richard Breeden, a former SEC chairman, to act as a corporate monitor for WorldCom, giving the government effective control over the company. According to the court, Breeden was to act as a "financial watchdog" over WorldCom assets and create a model of corporate governance for other companies to follow. Breeden filed a 150-page report on WorldCom's corporate governance practices. One paragraph of the report was devoted to what actually caused WorldCom's bankruptcy, namely, "acquisitions at profligate bubble era pricing" and failure to integrate those companies. Another factor was the "industry wide downturn in revenues," which Breeden acknowledged was "a global problem not unique to WorldCom."[19] Nevertheless, Breeden argued that it was a failure by the "gatekeepers" (board members, auditors, and lawyers) at WorldCom that was to blame for the company's demise.

Breeden was politically correct on most aspects of the corporate governance structure he imposed on WorldCom, but proved to be out of step on the use of poison pills. Those devices are used by management in many companies to fend off unwanted takeovers and entrench themselves, frustrating acquisitions that might be in the shareholders' best interests. Breeden noted the dangers of poison pills but thought that the company might have a need for them when it emerged from bankruptcy. He contended that competitors might try to wreck the company and buy it at a cheap price. As support for that concern, Breeden cited a newspaper report stating that a WorldCom competitor had "indirectly" funded the "Grey Panthers," an "intergenerational advocacy organization" seeking "social justice," to make public protests against WorldCom. He did not admit to the possibility that he was trying to entrench himself or his hand-picked managers.

Breeden's World

WorldCom, the largest accounting failure of all time, had a board with a majority of outside directors before its failure. Indeed, the company had more outside directors than most other large public companies. Some 80 percent of

WorldCom's board members were outside directors while Bernard Ebbers was in control. Although Breeden asserted that some of those directors were friends and cronies of Ebbers, there were some prominent outside directors who were independent, including Judith Areen, the dean of the Georgetown Law School. She served on the board and on the audit committee, apparently proving that, despite their advocacy for reforms, law professors do not have any special insight in preventing accounting failures. Another outside director serving on the WorldCom board was Gordon Macklin, the former president of the National Association of Securities Dealers (NASD), the body charged with regulating the Nasdaq market where WorldCom's stock was traded. Those individuals were powerless in detecting or preventing the accounting fraud at the company.

WorldCom under Ebbers had all of the correct committees (audit, compensation, etc.) demanded by corporate governance advocates, and those committees were correctly staffed with outside directors. WorldCom was also one of the few corporations in the United States that had adopted the practice of separating the roles of chairman and chief executive officer, the reformist proposal that became the rage after Enron failed. "WorldCom had the recommended committees, and in outward form conducted itself in accordance with most if not all formalities suggested by governance checklists."[20]

After condemning the "arrogance of power" at WorldCom, Breeden's report set forth seventy-eight recommendations that were "intended as a blueprint for action."[21] He required WorldCom to restructure its board so that eleven of its twelve members were outside directors. Breeden limited the number of boards that WorldCom's outside directors could serve on and placed a term limit of ten years on board members and auditors. Board members were required to attend annual indoctrination sessions on their responsibilities. Nominations for board positions had to be solicited from holders of at least 15 percent of the company's shares. Breeden required WorldCom to hold electronic "town hall meetings" in which shareholders could propose resolutions for shareholder votes without restriction. This kind of vote is not even available in most governmental units, at least since the days of the ancient Greek plebiscites.

Breeden hired a "corporate restructuring officer" for WorldCom who was a "certified fraud examiner," and a chief financial officer who was a "certified insolvency and reorganization accountant." Breeden also created a "restatements group." Apparently, this meant that restatements were to become a permanent part of the corporate world. Breeden had the company hire 400 additional employees for finance and accounting positions. A dividend target of 25 percent of annual net income was set, and Breeden placed strict limitations on executive compensation. Breeden wanted to limit the maximum amount that could be paid annually to any executive to $15 million. Severance packages were limited; in the case of a chief executive officer, that limit was three times base pay or $10 million, whichever was greater. Stock options were barred for five years and permitted thereafter only with share-holder approval.

The only thing missing from Breeden's corporate governance utopia was a Cambodian reeducation camp. He sought to correct that deficiency by requiring WorldCom to provide sensitivity training to employees on the importance of full disclosure and business ethics. New York University and the University of Virginia developed those programs for WorldCom. Employees and executives were required to sign ethics codes containing pledges of adherence to full disclosure and loyalty oaths that would have done the House Un-American Activities Committee proud. Executives at Breeden's WorldCom were to be trained in ethics and were to "set the tone at the top." Although Ebbers had always set a strong moral tone from the top, starting board meetings with prayer and establishing high corporate governance standards, that did not stop WorldCom from collapsing in the market downturn. Breeden also recommended that racial diversity issues be addressed, not because race played any role in WorldCom's demise, but because Breeden believed that the culture created by Ebbers had given short shrift "to respect for individuals, as it focused on the ability of Ebbers and his lieutenants to issue commands and to obtain immediate obedience."[22]

Breeden replaced the entire board of directors at WorldCom and hired a new chief executive officer, Michael Capellas, the former chief executive officer of Compaq Computer Corp., who sold that company to Hewlett-Packard and became its president before moving to WorldCom. WorldCom renamed itself MCI after its bankruptcy and moved its headquarters to Ashburn, Virginia. WorldCom filed a reorganization plan in its bankruptcy proceedings pursuant to which creditors were to receive about thirty-six cents on the dollar, while shareholders received nothing. Some creditors experiencing possible losses were holding collateralized debt obligations, including WorldCom's, that were backed by different junk bonds and high-risk borrowings, which provided a high yield and a high risk of default.

Some competitors, including Verizon and AT&T, wanted WorldCom liquidated because they claimed it would have an unfair competitive advantage after emerging from bankruptcy and shedding much of its debt. That protest failed. Some good news appeared when Leucadia National Corp. sought to purchase 50 percent of MCI's stock after reorganization, but Breeden's reforms seemed to have little effect on WorldCom's recovery. The company announced a first quarter loss in 2004 of $388 million. In May 2004, the company began laying off 7,500 workers, a third more than those that lost their jobs after Enron perished. The third quarter was an even bigger disaster. MCI announced a $3.4 billion loss after taking a $3.5 billion write-off on assets, and the company was facing hundreds of millions of dollars in tax claims from the states.

"Vulture" investors that had bought up WorldCom debt now owned a large portion of the company. They were demanding board representation, but

Breeden allowed only four of the company's largest shareholders to be represented on the board and was seeking to impose restrictions on the ability of those directors to sell their stock—so much for shareholder rights. Two of those investors gave up board slots rather than accept restrictions on their rights as shareholders. MCI also had other management problems, despite its new corporate governance structure. A power struggle broke out almost immediately after the company emerged from bankruptcy. Richard R. Roscitt, the company's new president and chief operating officer, was forced out after only seven months on the job. He was given an $8.1 million severance package along with other benefits. Michael Cappellas took control. He was given a $20 million compensation package that included bonuses based on the accuracy of MCI's financial statements and compliance with its code of ethics.

MCI continued to split the role of the chairman and chief executive officer. This split in roles had been demanded by Breeden in keeping with the current fad for the division of those offices. Nevertheless, Cappellas was assured that he would receive no interference from the new chairman, eighty-two-year-old Nicholas deB. Katzenbach. Katzenbach's appointment was a direct violation of a Breeden reform requirement that no director serve who was older than seventy-five. Apparently Breeden's rules do not apply to retired government officials. Even Katzenbach, who apparently had not read Breeden's report, was candid enough to admit that he was too old to be a board member and that he viewed his role as largely passive.

The new corporate governance structure at MCI was not without cost. Advisers in its reorganization were seeking fees in excess of $600 million. The judge who appointed Breeden as corporate monitor threatened sanctions against MCI for not obtaining Breeden's permission before paying $25 million in legal and other professional fees. MCI continued to have performance problems, experiencing a $71 million loss in the second quarter of 2004. Despite that loss, the company stated that it was continuing its plans to pay a forty cent per share dividend from cash on hand. Although dividends are supposed to be paid out of profits, MCI management thought that the dividend would attract investors to its stock, distracting them from the company's continuing losses.

Like Enron

There were many parallels between the scandals at WorldCom and Enron. Arthur Andersen had audited both. As it had for Enron, *Playboy* published a "Women of WorldCom" issue in December 2002, probably making the best case for full disclosure in the whole disaster. WorldCom had a whistleblower accountant, Cynthia Cooper, who was named a "Person of the Year" by *Time* magazine in 2001, along with Sherron Watkins at Enron. Cooper worked in the internal audit division of WorldCom. She was informed by John Stupka in WorldCom's Wireless Division that $400 million had been moved out of his division in order to boost company revenues. Cooper reported this to WorldCom's chief financial officer, Scott Sullivan, and to the firm's outside auditors, Arthur Andersen & Co., which was then under attack for its Enron audits. Sullivan directed her to back off, but she then complained to the WorldCom audit committee. Cooper began her own investigation of WorldCom's books. Working at night, she discovered several million dollars in improper accounting entries. Like Watkins at Enron, Cooper defended the head of the company, asserting that she did not believe that Bernard Ebbers knew about these transgressions.

The WorldCom revelations resulted in more congressional hearings. Ebbers and Sullivan were called to testify before the House Committee on Financial Services. The committee had been advised in advance that Ebbers and Sullivan would assert their Fifth Amendment privilege and would not answer any questions posed by committee members. Sullivan's attorney asked that his client not be required to appear at the committee hearing to make that assertion. Under Justice Department guidelines, such appearances were not required before grand juries when counsel advised that the client would be taking the Fifth. Sullivan's lawyer also noted that many people consider it unethical for congressional examiners to pose questions after a witness makes it clear that he or she would assert the Fifth.

That plea fell on deaf ears in Congress, where another media circus was staged through televised hearings in which Ebbers and Sullivan were pummeled and ridiculed for asserting their Fifth Amendment rights and subjected to inflammatory questions that assumed their guilt. Ebbers, in his own clever bit of theater, made a lengthy statement asserting his innocence and then declaring that he would be taking the Fifth Amendment in response to any questions. In the course of this statement, Ebbers stated that he was "proud" of his work at WorldCom and predicted that "no one will conclude that I engaged in any criminal or fraudulent conduct during my tenure at WorldCom."[23] Ebbers asked the committee members to respect the Constitution and not to ask inflammatory questions they knew he would not respond to because of his assertion of the Fifth Amendment privilege. This upstaged and outraged the committee members who had come well armed with just such inflammatory questions, knowing that Ebbers would not respond.

Various members of the committee wanted to have Ebbers held in contempt or be declared to have waived his Fifth Amendment rights in making his statement. Nothing came of that effort, and predictably committee members used the assertion of the Fifth Amendment as an admission of guilt by Ebbers and Sullivan, something no court would allow a prosecutor to do. Stephanie Tubbs Jones, a democrat from Ohio told Ebbers that "the fact that you appear here just to say that you're exercising your fifth amendment right doesn't make you look any better in the eyes of the public who have been damaged by the activities of your company and corporation."[24] California democrat congresswoman Maxine Walters demanded that this "cowboy capitalism must stop."[25]

The WorldCom engagement partner for Arthur Andersen, Melvin Dick, was hailed into the hearing. Dick claimed that WorldCom executives, who assured him that there were no "topside" entries, had lied to Arthur Andersen. Dick described the role of the auditors for a public company in the following words:

> The fundamental premise of financial reporting is that the financial statements of the company, in this case WorldCom, are the responsibility of the company's management, not its outside auditors.
>
> WorldCom management is responsible for managing its business, supervising its operational accounting personnel and preparing accurate financial statements. It is the responsibility of management to keep track of capital projects and expenditures under its supervision. The role of an outside auditor is to review the financial statements to determine if they are prepared in accordance with generally accepted accounting principles, and to conduct its audit in accordance with generally accepted auditing standards, which require that auditors plan and perform . . . the audit, to obtain reasonable assurance about whether the financial statements are free of material misstatement.[26]

Dick went on to note that Arthur Andersen had developed some sophisticated software to test WorldCom's accounts and that it used a risk-based audit method to focus on particular areas where fraud was likely to occur. That method, which relied on assessments of management integrity, was popular with other audit firms and was used at HealthSouth Corp., where another giant accounting fraud was unfolding. Dick advised the committee, to the dismay of the committee members, that there was no way to design a fail-safe system against management misconduct. Dick reported that Arthur Andersen's fees from WorldCom totaled $16.8 million in 1991. Of that amount, $4.4 million was for audit work. The rest was for tax and other services.

Jack Grubman, an analyst who had been touting WorldCom stock, was called to testify in the WorldCom hearings. He worked for Salomon Smith Barney (which became a unit of Citigroup). Grubman, considered the leading telecom analyst on Wall Street, was "renowned for his shoot-from-the-hip opinions and polemical research reports."[27] Grubman had recommended that investors "load up the truck" with WorldCom stock. He continued to tout WorldCom stock as it plunged toward bankruptcy, even though other analysts at Smith Barney Salomon were backing away from it.

Grubman's involvement with WorldCom and other activities would put him at the center of the analysts' scandal on Wall Street in future months. Among the companies touted by Grubman, in addition to WorldCom, were Qwest, Global Crossing, XO Communications, and Windstar Communications, all of which were disasters for investors when their stock plunged. Grubman argued in his congressional testimony that many investors had made money on his recommendations while the market was trending upward. He expressed remorse that he had not predicted the downturn in the telecom industry, but denied that he had done anything wrong.

Grubman readily conceded that he had been paid huge sums as an analyst and that he had sat in on WorldCom board meetings to aid Salomon Smith Barney's investment banking business. He had advised on the MCI merger and the aborted merger with Sprint, which was not the usual role of an independent analyst. Nevertheless, Grubman assured Congress that he did not use any inside information from WorldCom in his published analyses. Grubman further claimed that his role as an analyst depended on his reputation and that, therefore, he did not let his firm's interest in obtaining investment banking business interfere with his independence as an analyst. He pointed out that an independent research firm had recommended WorldCom as a buy right up to its bankruptcy. The Thornburgh report also noted that between 1996 and 2002, there were 884 analysts' reports on WorldCom by sixty-one different firms and none had spotted the company's accounting problems.

Grubman decried the fact that the stock market had become "short-term oriented":

> Broadly speaking, the market which is not just Wall Street firms, it is the mutual funds and pension funds and money managers out there who are getting graded every quarter, Morningstar, and all these guys put stars against funds. And so the pressure comes all the way up and down the supply chain. . . . But that pressure to perform quarter in and quarter out doesn't stop and start with Wall Street. It goes all the way through the supply chain of who manages money, and each client at each turn of the corner puts increasing pressure to perform on a quarterly basis. So it is a big issue.[28]

Grubman also tried to shift blame back to the auditors, asserting that analysts were dependent on audited financial statements: "Our judgments are only as good as the public statements."[29] This was too much for one congressman who seemed to have become unhinged at the passing of the buck by Grubman to the auditors and those auditors passing that buck to Ebbers and Sullivan, who were taking the Fifth. In venting his frustration, democratic representative Michael Capuano from Massachusetts stated:

> If this wasn't real, I really think this is great for Monday afternoon TV. This is the worst soap opera I have ever heard. The only unfortunate part is it's real.
>
> We have 17,000 laid-off employees, probably 100,000 people in the pension systems who are now losing their money, not to mention the millions of other people who have invested in this company.
>
> We've got a CFO who, according to all reports, again has cooked the books to the tune of $4 billion in a lie that anyone who is taking introduction to Accounting 101 knows how to avoid.
>
> We have a CEO who made hundreds of millions who apparently didn't have any idea what was going on in the financial world of his own multi-billion-dollar corporation. I guess all he did know was how to borrow $400 million from the corporation.
>
> We have an auditor who apparently can't audit, somehow missed that simple $4 billion lie.
>
> And we have an independent analyst who is neither independent nor a very good analyst. Apparently, you don't analyze anything. You take what the auditors say, and they take what the CFO says.[30]

Litigation

The reports filed by Thornburgh, Katzenbach, and Breeden further undermined confidence in WorldCom and provided much ammunition in the numerous class action lawsuits filed against the company. The usual suspects brought that litigation, including the California State Teachers' Retirement System, which was offering its lawyers a bonus for any personal assets recovered from WorldCom executives. The California Public Employee Retirement System (Calpers) was also claiming losses of $565 million from WorldCom's demise. Alabama's pension system lost $1.1 billion and the New York state retirement system, which lost $300 million, filed an eye-aching complaint over 250 pages long.

WorldCom employees holding stock of the company in their Section 401(k) accounts also sued WorldCom, Ebbers, and Sullivan, claiming that they were responsible for encouraging employees to hold WorldCom stock at a time when Ebbers and Sullivan knew the stock was overvalued because of improper accounting practices. The defendants in that suit agreed to pay $51 million to settle those claims, most of which was paid by WorldCom's insurance policies. A federal district court judge threw out a suit against the WorldCom Section 401(k) plan trustee Merrill Lynch. The court found that Merrill Lynch had no duty to advise employees to sell WorldCom stock out of their Section 401(k) accounts. WorldCom's banks were being sued, and AT&T claimed that WorldCom had defrauded it and other telecommunication firms by fraudulent access and other charges. On May 20, 2003, WorldCom, by then renamed MCI, agreed to pay $750 million to settle SEC claims for its accounting practices, the largest settlement in the agency's history. That money was to be given as restitution to former shareholders, but it had to be taken from creditors, reducing their rights in bankruptcy.

A wolf pack of state attorneys general from fourteen states planned charges for tax evasion, claiming that WorldCom manipulated its accounts to evade state taxes. Those tax programs had been designed by KPMG, which replaced Arthur Andersen as WorldCom's auditor. The attorneys general petitioned to have KPMG removed as the company's auditor, but the bankruptcy judge denied that motion. The states were demanding that KPMG forfeit the $162 million it had charged WorldCom for its work.

Criminal and Other Charges

Federal prosecutors ordered the arrest of Scott Sullivan and David F. Myers, the company's controller. They were released on bail of $10 million and $2 million, respectively, after their perp walk. Myers pleaded guilty shortly afterward, asserting that he had been instructed to change company records by "senior management." Myers was given a one-year prison sentence. Another WorldCom employee, Buford Yates Jr., WorldCom's director of general accounting, pleaded guilty to falsifying accounts, declaring that the instructions to do so had come from the highest levels of the company. Two other WorldCom accountants, Betty Vinson and Troy Normand, also entered guilty pleas. Vinson was given a prison sentence of five months and Normand probation for three years.

The government charged that, starting in the first quarter of 2001 as revenues declined, the defendants changed the accounting treatment for WorldCom's line costs from operating expenses to capital expenses. Employees referred to these manipulations as "close the gap" exercises. The defendants also used reserve accounts at the company to reduce line costs by crediting those costs and debiting reserve accounts. The indictment charged that this manipulation was done in order to meet analysts' expectations and to substantiate management's prior "guidance" to those analysts. Entries into reserve accounts had the effect of reducing line costs by $828 million in the third quarter of 2000 and by $407 million in the fourth quarter. By the end of the first quarter in 2001, line costs converted into capital costs totaled $3.8 billion. Overall, these entries increased the company's reported earnings by $5 billion. The government charged that Sullivan and other WorldCom executives concealed these topside entries from Arthur Andersen.

Ebbers was a target of Eliot Spitzer's "spinning" suit involving allocations in initial public offerings (IPOs) that were hot issues to telecom executives by Salomon Smith Barney in order to obtain the investment banking business of their firms. Jack Grubman supplied Ebbers with stock in hot IPOs being handled by Salomon Smith Barney so that Ebbers would send investment banking business Grubman's way. Between 1996 and 2000, Grubman supplied Ebbers with over 800,000 shares of hot IPOs from which Ebbers made profits of over $11 million. Among the shares allocated to Ebbers were Qwest Communications and Teligent Inc.com. Another winning allocation was Rhythms NetConnections, which caused so much trouble at Enron. In return, WorldCom used the investment banking services of Salomon Smith Barney in its bid for MCI. WorldCom paid that investment banker $32.5 million upon successful completion of that merger. During the period when Ebbers received IPO shares in twenty-one offerings, Salomon Smith Barney received $107 million in investment banking fees from WorldCom.

In August 2003, the Oklahoma attorney general, W.A. Drew Edmonson, filed criminal charges against WorldCom and six former executives for state securities law violations, claiming that state pension funds lost $64 million from their investments in WorldCom stock. The defendants included Ebbers and Sullivan. They were freed on $50,000 bail. That prosecution threatened the ability of the federal prosecutors to proceed against Ebbers, so the Oklahoma attorney general dropped the charges against him, but threatened to indict again after federal prosecutors brought charges and set a deadline for the federal government to act.

Oklahoma's action raised the danger that corporate executives could be subject to fifty different prosecutions in the fifty states, even when, as in the case of Oklahoma, a state had only a tangential relationship with the corporate activity. After its bankruptcy, WorldCom settled the Oklahoma charges by agreeing to cooperate in future prosecutions of Ebbers and other executives. The company further agreed to create 1,600 jobs in Oklahoma over the next ten years. Stephen Gillers, the New York University law professor who had come to the defense of Nancy Temple at Arthur Andersen, asserted that the Oklahoma settlement was an abuse of the justice system because "[t]he criminal law isn't meant to be used for economic leverage."[31] Nevertheless, such settlements would undoubtedly become the shakedown of choice by other attorneys general.

A federal district court refused to dismiss fraud charges in a class action brought against Arthur Andersen for its role in auditing WorldCom. Arthur Anderson was bankrupt, but that did not stop the New York State Common Retirement Fund from continuing its class action claims against that accounting firm for its audit work on WorldCom. After five weeks of trial, Arthur Andersen agreed to pay $65 million to settle those claims. Claims against the two audit partners on the engagement, Melvin Dick and Mark Schoppet, were dismissed. That class action was spearheaded by Alan G. Hevesi, the New York State comptroller on behalf of the New York State Common Retirement Fund, which claimed it had been defrauded by Arthur Andersen's failure to disclose the line cost treatment by WorldCom. The pension fund argued at trial that Arthur Andersen should have been more alert because it had classified it as a maximum risk client because of WorldCom's many acquisitions and billing systems. The class action lawyers used a professional actor to portray Scott Sullivan, which they were allowed to do because Sullivan was claiming the Fifth Amendment in that trial. The actor read to the jury excerpts of Sullivan's testimony from his criminal trial. Citigroup was named as a defendant in that action as a result of Grubman's activities, and it agreed to settle those claims for a stunning $2.58 billion, of which $141.5 million went to pay attorney fees. JPMorgan Chase paid another $2 billion in a settlement entered into just before a trial in the class action was about to commence, which was about $630 million more than what the matter could have been settled for earlier in the proceeding. Bank of America paid $460 million in settlement of the same charges. Lehman Brothers paid $62.7 million and Credit Suisse First Boston, Goldman Sachs, and UBS each paid $12.5 million as extortion to avoid facing a jury hostile to big business in general and Wall Street in particular. Another $428 million was thrown in by ABN Amro Holding NV, Mitsubishi Securities International, Mizuho International, and BNP Paribas Securities Corp. These investment banks were accused of failing to make a proper investigation of WorldCom's finances before underwriting its bonds.

Ten WorldCom directors agreed to pay $54 million to settle charges that they failed in their fiduciary duty to oversee the company's finances. Hevesi, on behalf of the New York Common Retirement Fund, insisted that those directors pay $18 million of that amount from their personal funds, which was 20 percent of their aggregate net worth. The balance was to be paid from officers' and directors' insurance policies. A federal judge rejected the settlement after other defendants objected to provisions in the agreement limiting the directors' liability, but eleven of the WorldCom directors then agreed to pay $20 million from their own funds in settlement. Bert Roberts, the former chairman of the WorldCom board, contributed another $4.5 million from his own assets. The insurance companies providing director and officer liability insurance for WorldCom kicked in an additional $36 million. Critics noted that capable outside directors now have a powerful incentive not to accept such posts or to insist on much higher remuneration to cover this new risk. A New York newspaper also revealed after this settlement that Hevesi was receiving large campaign contributions from tort lawyers. In a separate action brought by the Retirement Systems of Alabama, which claimed to have lost $165 million as a result of WorldCom's failure, Citigroup, JPMorgan Chase, and Bank of America agreed to pay $111 million in settlement.

Ebbers's Indictment

The federal government was slow in indicting Bernard Ebbers, waiting over two years before finally charging him in the midst of the Martha Stewart trial. Ebbers had assured his fellow parishioners that "you aren't going to church with a crook," but John Ashcroft, the attorney general of the United States, thought otherwise. Ashcroft personally announced Ebbers's indictment by federal authorities in Manhattan on March 2, 2004. The location of the indictment was a little strange, since WorldCom and Ebbers were headquartered in Mississippi at the time of the conduct in question. There was a quarrel, however, between the Mississippi and Manhattan U.S. attorney offices over who should prosecute the case. Apparently, the Justice Department was concerned that Ebbers remained popular in Mississippi and that prosecutors there did not have the expertise to handle the case. The prosecutors were prescient. As will be seen, a prosecution against Richard Scrushy, the head of Health South, that was brought in Alabama rather than New York backfired on the government.

The Ebbers indictment came shortly after Scott Sullivan agreed to plead guilty and to testify against Ebbers. Although he had previously claimed that Ebbers had no knowledge of the accounting manipulations, Sullivan changed his tune in the plea agreement in order to reduce his sentence. Sullivan settled an SEC enforcement action, agreeing to a lifetime bar from serving as an officer or director of a public company. Ebbers pleaded not guilty and was released on $10 million bail. Federal prosecutors filed additional charges against Ebbers in May 2004, asserting that he made false filings at the SEC.

Scott Sullivan, the former chief financial officer for WorldCom, was the principal witness against Ebbers. The Ebbers's trial began with Sullivan's claim that he had personally informed Ebbers of the fraud. Sullivan further testified that Ebbers had rejected the Verizon takeover bid because he was afraid the ongoing accounting fraud at WorldCom would be uncovered in the due diligence investigation required for such an acquisition. Somewhat ironically, Verizon was again in the process of trying to acquire MCI as Sullivan's testimony was being given in court. That merger would allow Michael Capellas, MCI's chief executive officer under its new politically correct structure, to receive a $22 million bonus even though the company's revenues had declined dramatically under his leadership.

Sullivan had some other nuggets, including a charge that some WorldCom board members were literally asleep during board meetings, but the sum of evidence against Ebbers at the conclusion of the government's case was Sullivan's accusations against Ebbers. There was little or no corroborating evidence of those charges, and Ebbers's attorneys attacked Scott Sullivan's deal for a reduced sentence in exchange for his testimony against Ebbers. They also focused on Sullivan's marital infidelities and long-term and frequent use of cocaine and marijuana.

Ebbers called Cynthia Cooper to testify. She was the whistleblower who broke the case in the first place. Cooper testified that Arthur Andersen LLP, WorldCom's auditors, had signed off on the company's statements and had endorsed management's treatment of its accounts. The defense argued that if the accountants would not detect any problems, Ebbers, a nonaccountant, was in no position to do so. Cooper also testified that Sullivan had said to her that "I want to make it clear that this was my idea and I'm responsible for this." Cooper offered further support for Ebbers, stating that after Sullivan ordered her to delete adverse information being given to the audit committee Ebbers told her to "tell the audit committee what you need to tell them." Bert Roberts, the WorldCom chairman, then testified that Scott Sullivan had stated just before Sullivan was fired that Ebbers was unaware of the improper journal entries.

Ebbers, in a surprise move, took the stand. He portrayed himself as a self-made man who was a physical education major in college and unsophisticated in finance. Despite the fact that he was the head of one of the world's largest telecom companies, Ebbers testified that "I know what I don't know . . . I don't to this day know technology. I don't know finance and accounting." Ebbers said his role was that of a coach, which is what he had been trained to do in college. "I always thought I was a pretty good coach and coaching and supervising sales people and marketing people is really like coaching." Ebbers asserted that: "I didn't know there was such a thing as line-cost capitalization." He denied Sullivan's accusations, stating that if Sullivan had informed him of the fraud "we wouldn't be here today."

Ebbers testified that he used the last of his cash to buy three million WorldCom shares shortly after he was forced out of the company. His lawyer, Reid H. Weingarten, argued that Ebbers would not have made that investment if he were aware of the fraud because he would have know that his successors would uncover a fraud of such magnitude. The prosecutors responded by calling Ebbers a "liar" in closing arguments and mocked his posture of an "aw shucks" country boy who left accounting and day-to-day management of the company to others. They argued that Ebbers's decision to cut off free coffee to employees to save $4 million made it unlikely that he would not have been aware of the massive manipulations of the accounts of WorldCom by Sullivan. Ebbers had testified that the decision to eliminate the coffee was made by a cost-cutting task force at WorldCom.

Barbara S. Jones, the federal judge assigned to the trail, assured a conviction by instructing the jurors that they need not find that Ebbers committed fraud himself, but only that he "deliberately closed his eyes to what was otherwise obvious" and that "direct proof" was not required to show that Ebbers was guilty. That fitted nicely with the government's argument that Ebbers had to be aware of Sullivan's manipulations simply because of their sheer size, a claim that overlooked the fact that apparently no other senior executives or board members had suspected the fraud carried out by Sullivan. The judge further crippled Ebbers defense by refusing to grant immunity to witnesses that were refusing to testify on his behalf because of concern that they were targets of Justice Department investigations. That was the same tactic that had been used by the Justice Department to obtain a conviction of Arthur Andersen. In the event, it took eight days of deliberation before the jury convicted Ebbers on all counts. Members of the jury asserted that Ebbers had hurt himself by testifying, and they gave little weight to Sullivan's testimony. Rather, they concluded that even without proof, the accounting manipulations were so enormous that Ebbers simply had to know of them. The jurors also focused on the adjustments by Sullivan that were disclosed in documents sent to Ebbers.

Ebbers was sixty-three and suffering from heart problems. Government prosecutors, nevertheless, demanded a life sentence, a fate usually reserved for murderers. Unable to resist a headline, Judge Barbara Jones sentenced Ebers to twenty-five years, even though she conceded that was likely a life sentence. Ebbers also forfeited his remaining assets. Those assets were down to a relatively paltry $40 million. Ebbers's sentence was clearly skewed by the hysteria over the Enron, WorldCom, and other financial scandals. Consider the prison term imposed on Ahmed Ressam just a few weeks after Ebbers was sentenced. Ressam was intercepted at the Canadian border with one hundred pounds of explosives in the trunk of his car that he planned to use to blow up the Los Angeles airport to mark the beginning of the new millennium. Ressam had attended one of Osama bin Laden's terrorist training camps in Afghanistan. Ressam refused to cooperate with the government after his arrest in identifying the terrorists assisting him in his attempt at mass murder. Nevertheless, Ressam was given a prison sentence of twenty-two years, and he will be eligible for release in fourteen years. Considering Ressam's age, thirty-eight, and health, the actual effect of his sentence is perhaps less than one-third that given to Ebbers.

If further proof was needed as to just how arbitrary was Ebbers's sentence, Scott Sullivan provided it. Judge Jones sentenced Sullivan to five years in prison despite her conclusion that he was the "architect" of the accounting manipulations at WorldCom and the "day-to-day manager" of that fraud. Sullivan was forty-three at the time of his sentencing, twenty years younger than Ebbers. The judge believed that the comparatively light sentence given to Sullivan was justified because his testimony against Ebbers, who played at most a passive role in the fraud, assured Ebbers's conviction.

More Problems

More accounting problems surfaced at WorldCom (now MCI) in March 2004. MCI again restated WorldCom's accounts, reducing pretax income by an incredible $74.4 billion for 2000 and 2001. This converted the company's claimed profit in 2000 of $4.6 billion into a loss of $48.9 billion. The claimed profit of $2.1 billion in 2001 was converted into a loss of $15.6 billion. Many of the amounts restated were for assets that had dropped in value, but almost $11 billion was for fraudulent accounting that improperly reduced expenses. In October 2004, MCI wrote off another $3.5 billion of assets.

The SEC was investigating whether members of WorldCom's creditors' committee in the bankruptcy proceeding, including Blue River LLC, had improperly used inside information. MCI was accused of defrauding other carriers by avoiding the payment of network access fees. More bad news followed. MCI posted a fourth quarter loss of $32 million in 2004 as revenues dropped by 10 percent. Two months later, the company restated that loss, increasing it to $145 million. Despite Breeden's reforms, MCI announced that it had discovered another weakness in its financial controls. MCI's auditor, KPMG also expressed an adverse opinion on the company's financial controls, a requirement that was imposed by Congress as the direct result of WorldCom's failure. MCI further disclosed that it expected an even greater reduction in earnings for 2005. MCI was then being sold for less than its market capitalization after emerging from bankruptcy.

Accounting Problems in the Entertainment Industry and Elsewhere

AOL Time Warner

Accounting problems were spreading throughout the economy. AOL Time Warner had some particularly troublesome problems. America Online acquired Time Warner in 2000, creating the world's largest media company. By then, Time Warner was carrying more than $15 billion in debt, and the company's finances were so complex that the annual financial report filed with the SEC was almost 900 pages long. Although initially portrayed in the press as the "deal of the century," that merger was not a success. Time Warner was already floundering under the leadership of Gerald Levin, and the acquisition in 1995 of Ted Turner's Turner Communications, which owned CNN, had proved to be another failure. Turner, a colorful adventurer and sailor, was given enough Time Warner stock to make him an eccentric billionaire.

Time Warner appeared to have missed any opportunity to take advantage of the new Internet economy before merging with AOL. In contrast, AOL had seen its share price explode from $2 to $40 between 1997 and 1998. More than 2,000 employees at AOL were millionaires, and four of its executives were worth more than $650 million, Steve Case topping the list at $1.5 billion. Although operationally a much smaller company, AOL's market capitalization was nearly double that of Time Warner. AOL agreed to purchase Time Warner in an exchange of stock valued at $112 billion. Consummation of the merger was delayed for a year while the Justice Department considered its antitrust implications. The deal pushed the value of Ted Turner's stock from $7 billion to $10 billion, leading Turner to remark to a gathering of students that it was like having sex for the first time. That value would soon sink to less than $2 billion as the economy declined. AOL was particularly hard-hit by the bursting of the Internet bubble. Its advertising revenues went down and the number of subscribers declined as the result of competing Internet access services. That decline resulted in a massive write-down of AOL Time Warner's assets.

Goodwill

A matter of some financial concern in mergers had, for years, been the accounting treatment for the entities being combined. Two methods had been employed—the purchase method and the pooling of interests method. Under the purchase method, the premium paid over the book value of the assets of the acquired entity was treated as goodwill required to be amortized as a charge against earnings over a period of no more than forty years. The effect of this method was to reduce earnings. Under the alternative pooling of interests method, the balance sheets of the two merging companies were combined at book value. No premium for goodwill was recognized and there was no reduction of earnings or amortization. This made the pooling of interests method more desirable for companies wanting to boost their share prices but was criticized as distorting the actual condition of the new company.

In the 1970s the SEC attempted to require the use of the purchase method, but was frustrated in that effort, after being challenged in court for failing to use proper procedures in adopting the requirement. The SEC continued its efforts, and the accounting industry's Financial Accounting Standards Board (FASB) proposed in 1999 that the pooling of interests method should be eliminated and that the purchase method should be required. FASB further proposed that the maximum amortization period for goodwill under the purchase method should be reduced to twenty years. This proposal touched off a storm of controversy, and FASB then adopted an approach that eliminated the pooling of interests accounting treatment from mergers occurring after June 30, 2001. This change recognized goodwill on the balance sheet but eliminated the requirement that goodwill from mergers be amortized over any specific period. Nevertheless, goodwill must be reviewed annually or more often if necessary, and reduced as a charge against earnings, if it is found to be impaired. This would mean that an unsuccessful merger would have to be acknowledged by write-offs.

FASB's new rule had disastrous effects at several companies suffering from the decline in the economy, reintroducing the "big bath" phenomenon. WorldCom Inc. and Qwest Communications International were forced to take massive write-offs of goodwill. Nortel Networks and JDS Uniphase Corp. collectively wrote off billions of dollars of merger goodwill. The AOL Time Warner merger also proved unsuccessful, and the FASB rule forced the company to announce in 2001 that it would be taking a staggering $54 billion charge against earnings in 2002.

Cooking the Books

Gerald Levin and Steve Case acted as coheads of AOL Time Warner after the merger. Both were committed to high corporate values and maintaining the public's trust but that did not stop accounting fraud or the internecine warfare between the two. AOL was cooking its books before the merger with Time Warner. In order to meet analysts' expectations and to keep its stock price up, AOL manipulated its financial accounts through a number of accounting maneuvers. Among other things, AOL settled long-term contracts with struggling Internet companies in a way that gave AOL an immediate cash boost while covering up its declining business. A senior executive at AOL was discharged for engaging in round-trip transactions with Homestore.com, a company in which Cendant was the largest shareholder. Those circular transactions allowed Homestore.com to inflate its revenues. AOL was the reciprocal beneficiary of such transactions. Jeffrey R. Anderson, an executive at PurchasePro.com Inc., pleaded guilty to criminal violations of the securities law as a result of transactions that improperly boosted AOL's income by $15 million in the fourth quarter of 2000. Another PurchasePro executive, Scott Miller, pleaded guilty to obstruction of justice charges for destroying documents connected to the government investigation, a by now familiar reaction to accounting investigations. Subsequently, two other AOL executives and four executives at PurchasePro were indicted for this conduct. Among those indicted was Charles "Junior" Johnson, the former chief executive officer of PurchasePro. His wealth had increased to $1 billion as that company's stock skyrocketed, but he rode it all the way down as the market collapsed, losing all of it and $5 million of his own money as well.

AOL engaged in other manipulations. It treated current marketing expenses involving the sending of CD disks to potential customers for possible subscription as an asset rather than an expense. This had a favorable short-term effect, but pushed those costs into future years. To avoid that problem, AOL simply took a one-time write-off of $385 million. AOL sold advertisements for eBay Inc. and booked that revenue as its own. In order to accelerate advertising revenues that were accounted for by the number of advertisements sent on AOL, the company jammed computer lines with advertisements that were supposed to have run over an extended period of time. In one transaction, AOL agreed to settle a $28 million arbitration award against Wembley PLC by having that company purchase $23 million in advertisements for its 24dogs.com Web site, where users can gamble on greyhound races. AOL then flooded its subscribers with advertisements for those dog races in order to gain immediate income.

The SEC charged AOL in 2000 with misrepresenting its accounts by deferring advertising expenses. The company settled that action by agreeing to a cease and desist order. AOL announced a restatement of its accounts in 2002, reducing revenues by $190 million, and another $400 million was in doubt. Those problems would appear minor as AOL Time Warner had to face the effects of a declining stock market and economy. The situation was worsened by a $1.3 billion buyback of the company's own stock in 2001. During the period of that repurchase, top executives at AOL Time Warner sold over $500 million of their stock in the company, which began sharply dropping in price in the second half of the year. AOL Time Warner's announcement that it would not be meeting analysts' projections for the third quarter sent the stock price in a further free fall to a level of about one half of its price in May.

Accounting Problems Expand

Debt levels at AOL Time Warner reached $28 billion and revenues continued to decline. Worse news was ahead. After an exposé of AOL's financial accounting shenanigans in the *Washington Post* in July 2002, AOL Time Warner's stock dropped further. The company's stock price was down 85 percent over the prior year, evaporating over $200 billion in shareholder stock value. The company renamed itself Time Warner in 2003, dropping AOL from its name. The *New York Times* called that merger "one of the biggest blunders in corporate history."[32] In August 2005, Time Warner agreed to settle a class action shareholders' lawsuit over the merger for $2.4 billion. That litigation was brought by the Minnesota State Board of Investment, which administers that state's pension funds for public employees. Time Warner reserved another $600 million to settle other claims stemming from that debacle.

Ted Turner resigned as vice chairman of the company. His net worth dropped by $5 billion in 2001 and was soon below $2 billion, making it difficult for him to meet a pledge of $1 billion he had made to the United Nations. Turner started a chain of restaurants, called Ted's Montana Grill, that he hoped would allow him to meet that pledge. The restaurants specialized in buffalo burgers.

Gerald Levin, the cohead of AOL Time Warner, was paid $148 million while the company was melting down. Steve Case, the other cohead, received $128 million. Case, nevertheless, fell out of the billionaire's club as a result of that company's stock price being cut in half, leaving him with a net worth of a mere $600 million.

AOL Time Warner announced a $45 billion loss for the last quarter of 2002. The company had a total year loss in 2002 of $98.7 billion. That was the largest loss in the history of the United States. The company began selling off assets, including a 50 percent ownership interest in Comedy Central, which was sold to Viacom for $1.2 billion, and its Warner Music Group, which was sold to a group of investors led by Edward Bronfman Jr. for $2.6 billion. Accounting problems persisted. Time Warner conducted an internal investigation of accounting practices by its AOL unit in Europe in 2004. The company announced in November 2004 that it was reserving $500 million for costs from its AOL accounting problems and that it was restating more of its results for 2000 and 2001. Thereafter, Time Warner agreed to pay $210 million to settle criminal charges under a deferred prosecution agreement with the Justice Department regarding its accounting problems. The company also agreed to restate its accounts for 2001 and 2002 for the third time in an amount totaling $430 million and to hire an independent examiner to review the accounting treatment of various other transactions between 1999 and 2002.

Time Warner settled accounting charges brought by the SEC for $300 million, a fine that was second to only the $750 million paid by WorldCom. The SEC charged that the company overstated online advertising revenues and the number of subscribers to its AOL service. The SEC noted that stock prices of Internet-related businesses declined precipitously in 2000 as sales of online advertising declined and subscriptions flattened. In order to offset that problem, AOL used fraudulent bulk sale and round-trip transactions to increase its online advertising revenues. The SEC also charged that Time Warner engaged in that and other accounting frauds in violation of a prior cease and desist order against AOL. Wayne Pace, chief financial officer, and two other executives were subject to cease and desist orders for approving the transactions, but were allowed to keep their jobs, unlike the fates of executives at other companies. In a separate action, Jason Smathers, an AOL engineer, pleaded guilty to stealing 92 million AOL user names that he sold to spammers who sent those customers an estimated 7 billion unwanted solicitations.

Vivendi

Vivendi Universal SA, a French entertainment company, announced a loss of $13 billion for 2001. That was followed by a $25 billion loss for 2002, besting the loss of $23 billion posted by France Telecom. Vivendi wrote down over

$12 billion of assets in the form of corporate goodwill after FASB changed its rule for merger accounting. Vivendi was audited by Arthur Andersen before its demise.

Vivendi had started as a French water and sewer company, then named Générale des Eaux, before it became a worldwide multimedia conglomerate as a result of a series of acquisitions engineered by its chairman, Jean-Marie Messier. His largest acquisition was Seagrams, which also owned Universal Studios. Vivendi paid $42 billion for that purchase and another $50 billion to acquire 3,000 other companies. This acquisition binge made Vivendi second only to AOL Time Warner in the entertainment field and the largest private sector employer in France. Among its holdings were Canal Plus, a European pay television company, and Houghton Mifflin, the American publishing house that was bought for $2.2 billion. Vivendi Universal was listed on the New York Stock Exchange (NYSE) after adopting U.S. accounting methods and Messier became a member of the NYSE board of directors, where more scandal was brewing.

By the conclusion of his acquisition binge, Messier had become a French icon and an international society figure. He also proved, if proof were needed, that executive excesses have no limits. Vivendi operated a fleet of aircraft for its executives that included four Gulfstreams and an Airbus A319 complete with shower. Messier spent much of his time in the company's $17.5 million apartment in Manhattan, which was modestly decorated for another $3 million. The company also maintained a residence for Messier in London and a chateau in France that included a miniature rain forest.

Vivendi Problems

When the market downturn ravaged Vivendi's share price, the company began the familiar path of shoring up that price by stock buybacks and accounting manipulations. Messier had Vivendi spend some $11 billion of badly needed funds on its stock buybacks, but the stock still dropped in value by $6 billion. Vivendi sold puts on 23 million shares of its stock, causing a further loss of $1 billion. On April 24, 2002, Vivendi shareholders, in an extremely rare act by the shareholders of any public company, rejected a proposal to grant the company's executives options worth $2 billion. The embarrassed Messier claimed that the vote was the result of either a malfunction or a hacker's penetration of Vivendi's electronic proxy voting system, which used remote handheld devices. That claim was a bit too fortuitous, and Messier's already diminished credibility was further undercut.

Messier was forced out of Vivendi in July 2002. He was given a termination package valued at over $23 million ($25 million with interest). The company's new management refused to comply with the agreement, but an arbitrator ordered it to be enforced. New management additionally discovered that the company's debt had been badly understated, reaching $37 billion, $8 billion more than reported publicly. The company's problems continued to mount after the French police raided its offices in December 2002. The homes and offices of board members were also searched. The Commission des Opérations de Bourse (later renamed the Autorité des Marchés Financiers), which was the French equivalent of the SEC, began an investigation. Messier was detained by French authorities for questioning by a magistrate in an investigation of manipulation and insider trading at Vivendi. Messier and Vivendi agreed to pay $1.34 million to settle charges of publishing misleading financial information in action that was later filed by the Autorité des Marchés Financiers.

Messier settled a case brought by the SEC for $50 million. The SEC forced him in that litigation to drop his claim to the $25 million severance package that he had negotiated just before he was turned out of Vivendi and that the arbitrator had ordered to be enforced. The SEC took that action under new legislation adopted after Enron's collapse. Messier was barred from serving as an officer or director of a public company in the United States for ten years. The SEC action charged that Vivendi and Messier had concealed the company's cash flow and liquidity problems, had used reserve accounts to meet earnings targets, and had failed to disclose various financial commitments.

Vivendi had a loss of $2.28 billion in the first half of 2004, but appeared to be recovering. The company sold 80 percent of its interest in Universal entertainment properties to General Electric, which combined those properties with its NBC operations.

HealthSouth

Full disclosure scandals resumed after a Justice Department raid in March 2003 on the offices of the HealthSouth Corp. in Birmingham, Alabama. HealthSouth was one of the country's largest providers of outpatient surgery, diagnostic imaging, and rehabilitation services, operating over 1,800 locations and reporting revenues of $4 billion. The company's management improperly accounted for some $2.7 billion of assets and earnings. Seventeen HealthSouth executives agreed to plead guilty to various charges in connection with this massive accounting fraud. All five of the company's chief financial officers over a fifteen-year period were among those pleading guilty. Three executives pleaded guilty to filing false oaths as to the accuracy of the company's financial statements, the first such prosecutions under legislation adopted after Enron. The Justice Department appealed the sentences of five of the defendants who pleaded guilty, claiming that the judge had been too lenient.

Richard Scrushy, the company's founder and chairman, was paid $260 million by HealthSouth between 1996 and 2002, mostly through stock options. Scrushy started his career as a gas station attendant before obtaining a degree in respiratory therapy from the University of Alabama's Birmingham campus. He was said to be a control freak who hired armed private body-guards and detectives to monitor employees. The company's offices were under televised surveillance; employees' e-mails were reviewed and their phones tapped. HealthSouth kept a fleet of seven corporate aircraft available for Scrushy's use. He used company funds to invest in personal ventures, including $1 million on "Third Phase, a girl band that he hoped would be the next Destiny's Child."[33] The band's career was furthered by a grant of 250,000 HealthSouth stock options to Tony Mottola at Sony Records, who then gave the band a recording contract.

One executive finally balked at filing false financial reports with the SEC. HealthSouth's chief financial officer, William Owens, became a government informant and secretly recorded conversations with Scrushy in order to supply the government with ammunition. In earlier years, Owens and Scrushy had been fellow members of a band called "Proxy," but that did not prevent Owens from becoming a government informer. Scrushy was indicted on eighty-five counts of accounting and other fraud. The government charged that he had induced his executives to commit the accounting fraud through threats, intimidation, and large pay packages. The government charged that Scrushy and his executives were manipulating the company's accounts in order to meet analysts' expectations, a process the HealthSouth employees called "filling the gap." The company boasted in its financial reports that it had met analysts' expectations for fifty straight quarters, the second-longest streak of any Fortune 500 company.

In a related civil action, the SEC charged Scrushy with falsely certifying the company's financial statements and for overstating its earnings. When it became clear that the financial manipulations were unraveling, Scrushy and other executives covered up their fraudulent accounting entries by blaming the company's problems on a change in Medicare reimbursements for group therapy. This event was called "Transmittal 1753" and was claimed to require an immediate and annual charge of $175 million. HealthSouth had previously settled a claim of overbilling Medicare for $7.9 million.

Scrushy mounted a strong defense. He noted that HealthSouth had been rated in the top 10 percent of companies in a national survey of good corporate governance procedures. Internal investigations by the law firm of Fulbright & Jaworski before the scandal broke seemed to have cleared Scrushy of wrongdoing, and claims of document destruction (shredding) were discounted. Scrushy defended himself on the *60 Minutes* television program, but took the Fifth Amendment four days later at the inevitable congressional hearings that investigated the accounting problems at HealthSouth. Scrushy was bombarded at the hearing with the now-expected when-did-you-stop-beating your wife questions. Like Bernard Ebbers, Scrushy managed to get in an opening statement even though he was taking the Fifth, leading to howls of outrage among committee members.

Scrushy began hosting a talk show in which he interviewed people pilloried in the press. Among his profiles was one on Judge R.M. Moore, the Alabama judge who had been removed from the bench in 2003 for refusing to remove a sculpture containing the Ten Commandments from the courthouse. Scrushy underwrote the cost of the show, which was aired in Birmingham, Alabama, where Scrushy's trial was to be held. Scrushy, a white man, joined a local black church in Birmingham, apparently seeking to ensure that he was friends with everyone who might appear in the jury pool. Scrushy blamed the fraud on subordinates. His impertinence was met with more charges filed against him by the Justice Department, a now-common practice for executives that refuse to plead guilty.

The government indicted James Bennett, HealthSouth's president, for accounting fraud as the Scrushy trial opened. The Scrushy criminal trial began with a stream of HealthSouth executives testifying that Scrushy had participated and ordered the accounting manipulations. Those witnesses included five former chief financial officers at HealthSouth, one of whom stated that Scrushy had said that "All public companies fudge their numbers." The testimony of those witnesses was somewhat suspect since they all pleaded guilty to fraud charges and were trying to reduce their sentences. They were unable to produce a single document or e-mail tying Scrushy to the fraud. The government claimed that this was because Scrushy had ordered a massive shredding of documents, even expressing anger when he discovered that some documents had been mistakenly left on a loading dock instead of being shredded.

One witness, William Owens, the former HealthSouth chief financial officer, wore an eavesdropping device that was sewn into his tie so that government investigators could record his conversations with Scrushy over the company's accounting practices, but those conversations were often inaudible or too cryptic to ascertain what was being discussed. One executive testifying against Scrushy was accused of being on a "mood-altering drug" by Scrushy's attorney. That witness, Michael Martin, admitted that he had been taking an antidepressant drug for two years, but stuck to his story that Scrushy knew of the fraud.

The government employed its usual tactic of prejudicing the jury against wealthy executives by showing that Scrushy was a big spender. The jury was shown pictures of some of his purchases, including a $300,000 boat that he called *Monopoly,* a 360-acre farm in Alabama, and two SUVs. That failed to convince Judge Karen O. Bowdre that this justified a money-laundering charge, which she dismissed. The judge had already reduced the number of counts against Scrushy from eighty-five to fifty-five. Three counts were dismissed because of misconduct on the part of the SEC and the Justice Department, but Judge Bowdre backed off that decision after the Justice Department threatened an appeal. Another federal judge had unfrozen Scrushy's assets because of similar misconduct on the part of those prosecutors. More counts were dismissed at the government's request at the close of its case. The judge thereafter cut even more charges, including some Sarbanes Oxley charges, leaving

Scrushy to face thirty-six counts. The government was receiving other setbacks. In total, fifteen HealthSouth executives had pleaded guilty to criminal charges. Ten of those individuals had been sentenced by the conclusion of Scrushy's trial. Only one was given a jail sentence and that was only for five months, but the court of appeals ruled that the sentences of two of those defendants were too lenient. Two other HealthSouth executives were acquitted in a separate trial while the Scrushy jury was deliberating. They had been charged with violations of the Foreign Corrupt Practices Act for making payments to a consultant that were used to obtain a contract in Saudi Arabia. Those payments eventually reached members of the royal family in that country.

The government tried to frustrate and prejudice Scrushy's defense by bringing up Enron during cross-examination of a Scrushy witness. The judge cut off that attack as being improper and sanctioned the government by denying further cross-examination of that witness. Scrushy's lawyers toyed with having Scrushy testify, but in the end decided to keep him off the stand. The jury found itself unable to reach a verdict after several days of deliberation on the seventy-eight pages of jury instructions given to them by the judge. They asked the judge for instructions in layman's terms but that request was refused. It seems that being a criminal is a complicated process. The judge sought to resolve the impasse with an Allen Dynamite charge, but the jury seemed to have lost interest in the trial, meeting only intermittently over a period of more than a month to consider the charges. The government then sought to further prejudice the jury by announcing a $100 million settlement by HealthSouth with the SEC. After more than a month of deliberations, an ill juror had to be replaced, requiring the jury to start its deliberations all over again. Another effort was then made to prejudice the jury through an announcement that HealthSouth was restating its financial statements to report a loss between 2000 and 2002 of over $1 billion, rather than the profit of $210 million originally claimed. It was all for naught. After the addition of the alternate juror, a verdict was reached quickly. Scrushy was acquitted of all counts, which meant that he would not go to jail or forfeit his $300 million in assets. He could also seek indemnification of his attorney fees from HealthSouth and was even threatening a wrongful discharge suit.

Scrushy still faced a mountain of civil lawsuits, including one brought by the SEC. Government prosecutors were also not graceful in defeat. They initially appealed the earlier dismissal of some of the counts against Scrushy in order to regain something from this enormously shameful debacle. After Scrushy's lawyers pointed out that the Constitution bars double jeopardy, the government concluded that they were only in for more embarrassment, and the appeal was dropped. Ironically, on the same day that the government decided to drop its prosecution of Scrushy, Bernard Ebbers was sentenced to life in prison for his relatively passive role at WorldCom. It appeared that justice had lost all meaning in the nebulous world of full disclosure.

HealthSouth fired its auditor, Ernst & Young LLP, which, as was pointed out in Congressional hearings, had used a risk-based auditing approach like that used at WorldCom, concluding that HealthSouth management had generated reliable financial information and that the company had "designed an environment for success." The auditors limited the scope of their audit in view of those findings. Among other things, the auditors did not examine additions of less than $5,000 to individual assets on the company's books. That loophole was where much of the fraud occurred. HealthSouth settled Medicare fraud charges with the Justice Department for $325 million in January 2005. HealthSouth also entered into an "Integrity Agreement" with the Office of Inspector General of the Department of Health and Human Services that required HealthSouth to adopt a Code of Conduct and to create a Corporate Compliance and Ethics Program. The company estimated that it spent $350 million to correct its accounts for the SEC.

HealthSouth tried to boost its corporate governance after these problems by appointing Less S. Hillman as an outside director and the chairman of its audit committee. Hillman was a former audit partner at Ernst & Young and described himself as a "numbers guy." He appeared to have turned around the faltering fitness center business of Bally Total Fitness Holding Corp., where he served as chief executive officer and president. Hillman, however, had to resign from the HealthSouth board in the middle of the Scrushy trial after Bally Total Fitness announced that it was suspending Hillman's severance payments and restating its earnings as a result of accounting irregularities that occurred while he was in charge of the company. Federal prosecutors were conducting a criminal investigation of Hillman's role in those problems.

Freddie Mac and Fannie Mae

The Federal Reserve Board was expressing concern in the new century with the Federal National Mortgage Association, now known as Fannie Mae and the Federal Mortgage Corporation, known as Freddie Mac, two government-sponsored enterprises (GSEs). Those entities bought mortgages as an investment, using borrowed funds obtained cheaply as a result of their government status and implied government guarantee. These two GSEs were behemoths, with combined assets and off balance sheet obligations totaling more than $2.4 trillion at the end of 2000. They had outstanding collective debt of $1.7 trillion in 2004, of which about one-third was held by foreign investors. Freddie Mac's mortgage portfolio had grown tenfold since 1994 to $600 billion. The GSEs claimed that they were hedging their risks from interest rate changes, but a study of mortgage hedges discovered that such transactions were increasing moves in long-term interest rates by up to 30 percent, creating market turmoil.

Fannie Mae and Freddie Mac were succeeding in their mission of supplying home mortgages to America. These two entities financed more than 70 percent of all middle-income family mortgages in 1999. They held nearly as many residential mortgages as all commercial banks. Critics feared, however, that these organizations would run out of a market. In Richmond, Virginia, for example, home ownership was at 76 percent of families in 2002, as compared to 62 percent in 1997. Critics were also concerned that the two GSEs were lowering lending standards to the danger point and that adequate disclosure was not being made with respect to their accounting policies.

Freddie Mac and Fannie Mae faced further criticism in Congress for the advantages they enjoyed over other lenders as a result of their government-sponsored status and implied government guarantee, which lowered their funding costs. A report prepared by the Federal Reserve Board staff on the role of Fannie Mae and Freddie Mac concluded that the implicit subsidy in the form of reduced interest rates, which was based on a general belief that the government would not allow those entities to fail, was worth at least $119 billion and perhaps as much as $164 billion. This constituted a significant part of the market value of both GSEs.

Alan Greenspan, chairman of the Federal Reserve Board, advocated that Congress restrict the growth of Fannie Mae and Freddie Mac. He stated that they were posing a systemic risk to the financial system because of the large amount of mortgage-backed securities bought back for their own portfolios. This caused a sharp drop in the price of their shares. Fannie Mae also experienced a 50 percent drop in net income at the end of the third quarter in 2002, while interest rates were falling. Fannie Mae confessed on October 29, 2003, that it had mispriced the value of its mortgages. Fannie Mae had to restate its financial accounts by increasing the value of its mortgage holdings by $1.1 billion, increasing stockholder equity in that amount. This restatement did not affect earnings, but the error caused further concern about Fannie Mae's operations.

Fannie Mae had other problems. Its holdings of mortgage-backed securities on mobile homes and manufactured housing were declining in value. Some 24 percent of those securities were rated as junk by credit agencies, down from investment grade ratings in 2002. This was the result of a large number of defaults by mobile home purchasers. Fannie Mae wrote off $237 million from those mortgages during the first three quarters of 2003. That was small change compared to Fannie Mae's subsequent announcement that it had lost $6.9 billion from derivative transactions.

As a result of these problems, Fannie Mae was having difficulty meeting its regulatory capital requirements, falling more than $4 billion below required amounts. Despite that shortfall, Fannie Mae agreed to increase its capital, requiring it to seek additional funding. Fannie Mae adopted corporate governance reforms in April 2004 that included splitting the role of its chairman and chief executive officer, Franklin Raines, a bow to the newest fad in corporate governance. Raines was to give up one of those roles by 2007. Fannie Mae stated that it would begin making current public reports on its finances, but proved unable to do so.

The Office of Federal Housing Enterprise Oversight (OFHEO), an independent entity within the Department of Housing and Urban Development, was the designated regulator for Fannie Mae. OFHEO claimed that Fannie Mae had been smoothing its earnings through cookie jar reserves and boosting executive bonuses by deferring expenses. In one instance, Fannie Mae executives delayed recognizing $200 million in expenses in order to meet the earnings target for the highest executive bonus to the penny. Fannie Mae was not accounting for its hedges and derivatives in accordance with GAAP. A criminal investigation was triggered by those disclosures.

Fannie Mae executives were hauled before a congressional committee for the usual pillorying, but they hotly defended their accounting treatment and denounced the OFHEO report. They demanded a review of their accounting by the SEC. Fannie Mae stated that it would have a $9 billion loss if the SEC agreed with the OFHEO conclusions. Unfortunately for Fannie Mae, the SEC's chief accountant later agreed with OFHEO, which meant a massive restatement was required, and Raines and his chief financial officer, J. Timothy Howard were forced to resign. OFHEO then challenged their multimillion-dollar severance packages. Fannie Mae also announced that its financial statements for the last three years could no longer "be relied upon."

Daniel Mudd, appointed to replace Raines on an interim basis, announced a $5 billion issuance of preferred stock to shore up Fannie Mae's capital position. This did not stop OFHEO from expanding its attack. It advised Congress that both Fannie Mae and Freddie Mac were using their government-sponsored role to charge excessive fees to homeowners. The Federal Reserve Board weighed in with a report that Fannie Mae and Freddie Mac had a "negligible" effect on stabilizing and maintaining low mortgage interest rates, which was supposed to be one of their main missions.

Fannie Mae fired its auditor, KPMG, but judging from its audit fees that accounting firm was only lightly auditing Fannie Mae, averaging about $2 million per year for the period 2001–2003. Another embarrassment emerged in December 2004. Fannie Mae agreed to forfeit $7.5 million that was the proceeds of fraudulent loans received from the First Beneficial Mortgage Co., in Charlotte, North Carolina. After discovering that the loans were fraudulent, Fannie Mae allowed them to be resold to the Government National Mortgage Association (GNMA). In response to these revelations, Fannie Mae agreed to upgrade its corporate governance by creating an "Office of Compliance and Ethics" and directed its general counsel to report any wrongdoing to the board and to OFHEO. Fannie Mae also agreed to raise its capital level by 30 percent, but its problems were not over. OFHEO found further improprieties in its accounting statement relating to losses on derivative instruments and other problems that were expected to result in an additional $2.8 billion in write-offs. OFHEO discovered that Fannie Mae employees were forging signatures on financial legers and altering accounting records and more questions were raised on how it was accounting for the trusts it creates for mortgaged-backed securities. OFHEO directed Fannie Mae to adopt policies that would prevent such conduct. OFHEO additionally proposed a regulation that would have required the separation of the offices of chief executive officer and chairman, but that met opposition from the Bush administration, which did not want to dictate corporate governance structures. The problem was solved in any event because both Fannie Mae and Freddie Mac agreed to separate those offices.

Fannie Mae remained under attack from OFHEO, which was criticizing its accounting treatment for the trusts in which it held its mortgages. OFHEO further claimed that Fannie Mae was cherry-picking by keeping the best mortgages for itself in order to boost earnings and selling the less lucrative mortgages to investors ("keep the best and sell the rest"). Alan Greenspan continued his criticism of Fannie Mae and Freddie Mac. In the meantime, Fannie Mae stockholders were taking a beating from all of this regulatory scrutiny, the stock dropping by 25 percent. With all of these problems, Fannie Mae remained as the second-largest financial institution in the United States, second only to Citigroup.

Meanwhile, the other government-sponsored mortgage provider, Freddie Mac, was smoothing its earnings by shifting profits to other accounting periods. Earnings management was needed because the adoption of Financial Accounting Standard (FAS) 133 by the FASB concerning valuation of derivatives required a huge bump-up in its earnings that would result in decreased returns in future years. Salomon Smith Barney helped Freddie Mac shift some of that income forward through transactions called "Coupon Trade-Up Giants." These transactions created over $700 million in losses for Freddie Mac that were used to offset gains in derivative positions. Morgan Stanley also engaged in similar transactions for Freddie Mac. Another method for managing earnings was through the use of "linked swaps," which allowed Freddie Mac to defer earnings into later periods because changes in swap values were amortized. Another tool involved using historic rather than current volatility measures for valuing Freddie Mac swaptions. Blaylock & Partners LP, a broker-dealer, was used as cover for some of Freddie Mac's accounting manipulations. Tape recordings of conversations by Blaylock's traders revealed that they knew that the transactions being conducted for Freddie Mac had no economic substance and were for accounting purposes only. In total, Freddie Mac moved $5 billion of revenue into future periods.

Freddie Mac was audited by Arthur Andersen LLP, which Freddie Mac had fired after the Enron controversy arose. Freddie Mac spent $175 million in auditing and legal fees to restate its accounting statements. The president of Freddie Mac, David Glen, was discharged after its accounting problems emerged, and Freddie Mac agreed to pay a $125 million civil penalty to its regulator, OFHEO. Freddie Mac's chairman, Leland Brendsel, and its chief financial officer, Vaughn Clarke, were forced to resign. Brendsel sued Freddie Mac, seeking $60 million in stock option compensation that was withheld by OFHEO. A federal judge ordered those funds to be paid to him, holding that

OFHEO was overreaching its regulatory powers in ordering the funds to be withheld. Freddie Mac appointed a new chief executive officer, Gregory J. Parseghian, but he too had to resign after an internal investigation by a special committee of the board, conducted by James R. Doty, a former SEC general counsel and a partner at Baker Botts LLP, revealed that Parseghian had been involved in the transactions used to manage earnings. Richard Syron, the former head of the American Stock Exchange, replaced Parseghian. Freddie Mac experienced a 52 percent drop in income for 2003 and was having difficulty in releasing its financial statements on a timely basis. Legislation in Congress that sought to increase regulation over Fannie Mae and Freddie Mac bogged down, but OFHEO, acting on its own, decided to increase regulatory restrictions and provide for a government takeover in the event of failure.

Another government program, the Federal Home Loan Banks, was causing concern. Located in twelve districts in the United States, these institutions are owned by commercial banks and other financial institutions. The Federal Home Loan Banks issue debt securities that provide funding to their members. The Federal Home Loan bank in New York announced that it was suspending dividend payments at the end of September of 2003 as the result of $183 million in losses from mobile home loans. The Federal Home Loan Bank of Pittsburgh was also having problems. It had an 82 percent decrease in second-quarter earnings as the result of multimillion-dollar losses from derivatives and investments in the third quarter of 2003. The Chicago and Seattle Federal Home Loan Banks were subject to loan restrictions by their regulator, the Federal Housing Finance Board. Two directors on the Seattle bank board of directors were later removed and banks there were required to repurchase over $70 million in improperly issued stock. These events resulted in calls for additional regulation of the Federal Home Loan Bank system. The Federal Agricultural Mortgage Corp. (Farmer Mac), another lender with a federal charter that supplied credit to farmers, was also receiving criticism. Farmer Mac was seeking its first ever credit rating in 2004 after criticism from its regulator, the Farm Credit Administration. A disappointing second quarter in 2001 resulted in an 18 percent drop in Farmer Mac's share price.

Lord Black

Conrad Black, an English lord (Lord Black of Crossharbour) and conservative newspaper publisher, was the subject of charges that he was looting Hollinger International Inc., a newspaper company that publishes the *Chicago Sun Times,* the *London Daily Telegraph,* and the *Jerusalem Post.* Scandal broke out after published reports claimed that Black and another executive received unauthorized payments of over $32 million, as well as $180 million in management and "noncompete" fees that were paid to entities controlled by Black. That information was inadvertently disclosed by Hollinger in a filing with the SEC.

Lord Black had just published a lengthy hagiography of Franklin Roosevelt and was accused of using company funds to purchase some of Roosevelt's private papers for $8 million to aid his research. Those papers were subsequently sold by Hollinger for $2.4 million. Black resigned as chief executive officer after these revelations, resulting in a jump in the company's stock price. He agreed to repay certain of the challenged amounts, but later refused to make a $7.2 million payment under that agreement and was then removed as chairman by the board.

The revelation of the payments to Black touched off a fight for control of Hollinger. A special committee of the board was formed to attack him. That committee hired Richard Breeden of WorldCom fame to conduct the investigation. Black counterattacked by hiring his own junkyard dog lawyer, David Boies. Black also sued Breeden and the special committee for defamation in Canada, seeking $644 million in damages. Breeden's lawyer called the suit "ridiculous." Similar claims had been made in the United States against former U.S. attorney general Griffin Bell by a stockbroker who was the subject of an internal report prepared by Bell for E.F. Hutton. The report described a massive check-kiting scheme by E.F. Hutton for which it was indicted on 1,000 counts. Bell blamed the problem on low-level managers, including the plaintiff, and exonerated the firm's principal executives. Bell had to go to trial on the defamation claim but ultimately prevailed. Defamation law in Canada, however, made such claims more easily provable than in the United States.

The special committee at Hollinger responded with further charges of self-dealing by Black, asserting that a company he controlled had bought newspapers from Hollinger at less than their fair market value and that various payments had been made to Black and others without proper board authorization. Hollinger had two classes of stock that gave Black 73 percent of the voting rights even though he owned less than 15 percent of the company's equity. This was made possible by a class B issue of stock that had ten to one voting rights, as compared to the class A stock that was largely held by the public. Black tried to sell his controlling interest in Hollinger to the Barclay brothers, who owned newspapers, hotels, and other properties in England. The Barclays offered $316 million for Black's control shares in Hollinger. In seeking that sale, Black failed to take into account the very flexible fiduciary duties imposed by Delaware judges. Black was blocked by a Delaware court from selling his majority interest in Hollinger. The Barclay offer was then withdrawn.

The Delaware chancery court judge found a breach of fiduciary duty on Black's part because he had voted to support an effort by the Hollinger board of directors to sell some of its properties to relieve the company's financial problems. Black then began negotiating separately to sell his controlling ownership interest, undercutting the board's efforts. The chancery judge thought that Black's action had breached a "tag-along" promise that would allow the class A shareholders to convert their A shares into Bs in the event of a merger, giving them some of the premium from a sale of control. The chancery court also ruled that Black's fiduciary duties on the board required him to invoke a poison pill that would prevent him from selling his own shares.

Black was stripped of the right to remove directors as the result of the settlement of an SEC action charging books and records violations. Under the consent decree in that action, Black agreed that a special monitor would be appointed over the company if Black used his power to remove the outside directors. That special monitor was to be Richard Breeden. Breeden issued a 500-page report accusing Black of "corporate kleptocracy." The report contained the customary list of misuse of corporate funds: "Food, cell phones, perfume, and other routine living expenses, including tips by Mrs. Black while on shopping trips, were expensed to Hollinger." Black was reimbursed by Hollinger for such items as "handbags for Mrs. BB ($2,463), jogging attire for Mrs. BB ($140), exercise equipment ($2,083), T. Anthony Ltd. Leather Briefcase ($2,057), opera tickets for C&BB ($2,785), stereo equipment for the New York apartment ($828), silverware for Blacks' corporate jet ($3,530), Summer Drinks ($24,950), a Happy Birthday, Barbara dinner party at New York's La Grenouille Restaurant ($42,870), and $90,000 to refurbish a Rolls Royce . . . for Black's personal transportation." Numerous charitable contributions were also made in Black's name by Hollinger.

Breeden was particularly outraged by the party at La Grenouille where "eighty guests including Oscar de la Renta, Peter Jennings, Charlie Rose, Barbara Walters and Ron Perelman enjoyed dinner at $212 a plate, including Beluga caviar, lobster ceviche, and 69 bottles of fine wine. Black personally paid an additional $20,000 toward the cost of the evening. At least Black's choice of venue for his wife's birthday was less expensive than Dennis Kozlowski's party for his wife on Sardinia that was charged in part to Tyco."[34] Three dinner parties for Henry Kissinger cost another $28,000, and Black's wife, Barbara, a journalist, was paid $1.1 million for what was claimed to be a "no-show" corporate job. Black did lead the life of a corporate tycoon with palatial residences in Palm Beach, Toronto, London, and New York, to which he commuted on Hollinger jets, which were also used for travel to places as exotic as Bora Bora. The Hollinger jets cost the company $24 million to operate over a period of about six years.

More significantly, Breeden claimed that Black and another executive, David Radler, looted more than $400 million from the Hollinger companies in order to support Black's business empire. A federal judge dismissed racketeering charges brought against Black by Hollinger, but the SEC weighed in with a suit against Black and Radler claiming that they improperly removed $85 million from Hollinger, much less than the amount claimed by Breeden, but still considerable. Among other things, the SEC suit charged that Black and Radler arranged for the sale of some Hollinger publications at a below market price to a company they controlled and that they invested $2.5 million of

Hollinger money in a venture capital fund they controlled without obtaining approval of the audit committee.

The Hollinger board of directors was another target of Breeden. "Black named every member of the Board, and the Board's membership was largely composed of individuals with whom Black had longstanding social, business or political ties. The Board Black selected functioned more like a social club or public policy association than as the board of a major corporation, enjoying extremely short meetings followed by a good lunch and discussion of world affairs."[35] The Hollinger board was composed of several prominent independent directors, including Henry Kissinger, the former secretary of state; Richard Perle, a former senior executive at the Pentagon; Richard Burt, former ambassador to Germany and arms negotiator; Robert Strauss, former ambassador to the Soviet Union and Democratic Party leader; Alfred Taubman, the chairman of Sotheby's who had been jailed for price fixing; and Dwayne Andreas, the head of Archer Daniels Midland Co., which had its own price fixing problems. Hollinger had an international advisory committee that included such stalwarts as William F. Buckley Jr. and George Will.

Hollinger also had a politically correct audit committee. The head of the committee was James R. Thompson, a former governor of Illinois, crusading U.S. attorney in Chicago, and a member of the commission investigating the 9/11 terrorist attacks. As U.S. attorney in Chicago, Thompson had aggressively pursued government corruption, even jailing another former Illinois governor and federal appellate judge, Otto Kerner, for bribery and mail fraud in connection with his role in the purchase and sale of stock in a horse racing track. Thompson was voted one of the hundred most influential lawyers in America, but those credentials did not allow him to pierce Black's machinations. Also serving on Holliger's audit committee were Richard Burt and Marie-Josee Kravis, an economist and wife of Henry Kravis, the famous entrepreneur. They had largely deferred to Lord Black in the management of the company and were accused of being "ineffective" and "inert" in their roles on the audit committee.

Henry Kissinger received some improper payments from the company, but agreed to repay them. Outside director Richard Perle was accused of a breach of fiduciary duties in approving unfair related party transactions. Breeden wanted Perle to return $3 million, included a $2.5 million investment in his venture capital company and undisclosed salary payments. Black resigned from Hollinger in November 2004. That was the first step in a plan to take Hollinger private and escape the rigors of full disclosure by purchasing the 22 percent of common stock not already owned by Black. In the meantime, class action suits were filed against Black and Hollinger by the Teachers' Retirement System of Louisiana and the Washington Area Carpenters Pension and Retirement funds. Hollinger also filed a $520 million suit against Black in an apparent effort to keep him from taking control once again, and the Ontario Securities Commission weighed in with similar claims. The outside directors of Hollinger paid $50 million to settle claims against them. That payment was covered by the company's insurance.

Black had been roundly criticized for the two-tier stock structure that gave him control of Hollinger, but that structure was common to the newspaper business. The *Wall Street Journal* is owned by Dow Jones & Co. that is controlled by the Bancroft family under a provision that allows them to hold 7.5 million class B shares to maintain control over the company. Despite their support for corporate governance reform and attacks on other businesses, the New York Times Co. and the Washington Post Co. have similar structures.

There were other troubles in the news business. The *New York Times* upgraded its corporate governance structure by hiring a "public editor," Daniel Okrent, to act as a monitor over the quality of the paper's reporting. That position was created after it was discovered that reporter Jayson Blair had plagiarized and even made up numerous stories published in the *Times*. Blair had been promoted on the basis of his African-American race rather than merit and left unsupervised. The newspaper's two leading editors, Howell Raines and Gerald M. Boyd, were forced to resign. Reporters at the *Times* were shortly complaining that the new public editor was interfering with their work.

CBS News appointed Richard Thornburgh, the former attorney general, and Louis D. Boccardi, a former Associated Press executive, to investigate the use of forged documents by anchorman Dan Rather to attack President George W. Bush's service in the National Guard. That attack was aired on *60 Minutes* at a critical point in the 2004 presidential campaign. Rather announced that he was stepping down as anchorman in advance of Thornburgh's report. When filed, the Thornburgh report took the once traditional path for such internal reports. It exonerated Dan Rather and CBS News president Andrew Heyward of any political bias and blamed the fiasco on overzealous reporting by underlings, who were fired or forced to resign.

The Tribune Co., owner of the *Chicago Tribune, Newsday,* and other publications, took a quarterly charge of $35 million in 2004 as a result of the fact that *Newsday* and a Spanish language publication had been overstating circulation figures. Those figures determined advertising rates, and the $35 million charge was to cover the cost of settling with advertisers who had overpaid based on the inflated circulation figures. Two publishers resigned. A further restatement of those figures was required a few months later, resulting in an additional charge of up to $60 million. The SEC began a broad-scale investigation of newspaper circulation figures after disclosure of these problems.

Grocery Store Accounting

Kroger Co., the Cincinnati-based supermarket chain, announced in March 2001 that it was restating its accounts for the years 1998–2000. That action was the result of earnings smoothing at Ralphs Grocery, which had been acquired by Kroger a few years earlier. Chris Hall, the chief accounting officer for Ralphs Grocery, left that company before the Kroger restatement announcement to become the chief financial officer at Rite Aid. He was reassigned by Rite Aid management after his involvement in the Ralphs Grocery problems became known.

ConAgra Foods reduced its reported earnings for 1998–2000 by $123 million as the result of faked sales and earnings in its farming division, United Agri Products. Those manipulations involved $287 million in accounting entries. Con Agra sold that and other divisions in order to turn itself entirely into a food distribution company. A federal appellate court reversed a decision to dismiss a class action lawsuit over those improprieties.

The Great Atlantic & Pacific Tea Co. Inc. (A&P) was investigating the timing of the recognition of allowances and accounting for inventory by certain of its operating regions. A&P restated its income statements for fiscal years 1999 and 2000 and the first three quarters of fiscal year 2001 and fired ten executives. A class action complaint against the company was dismissed on the grounds that the plaintiff failed to establish intent to defraud on the part of A&P, despite claims that management was smoothing earnings in order to meet analysts' expectations.

Royal Ahold NV, a Dutch company that was one of the largest grocery distribution firms in the world, disclosed in February 2003 that it was restating $500 million in earnings between 2001 and 2002. That restatement directly affected American investors because the company's American depository receipts (ADRs) were traded on the NYSE. ADRs represent an ownership interest in foreign securities held on deposit, often with a bank. They allow trading in foreign securities when direct ownership is not practical. The price of the Ahold ADRs dropped 60 percent after the company's restatement announcement. Later, Royal Ahold reported that it had further accounting irregularities that would cause a $1.41 billion loss for 2002. On October 20, 2003, Ahold announced a revised and larger $5.02 billion loss for 2002.

Royal Ahold owned large food chains in the United States, including Stop & Shop, Top Markets, and the Giant supermarket chain. The company operated more than 3,600 stores worldwide and had 280,000 employees when the scandal broke. Most of Ahold's problems were concentrated in its U.S. Foodservice division. That unit increased earnings through inflated rebates supposedly paid by food producers to encourage the promotion of their products.

Howard Schilit, a financial analyst at the Center for Financial Analysis, claimed that Royal Ahold had been engaging in dubious accounting practices for some two years before it went public with its disclosures of abuses. Royal Ahold's chief executive officer, Cees van der Hoeven, resigned. He had built the company from a small Dutch grocer into the world's third-largest retail firm through the acquisition of companies valued at almost $20 billion in over thirty countries. The company's chief financial officer, Michael Meurs, and other top management officials were removed. Ahold fired the chief executive officer at U.S. Foodservice. Two other executives resigned when it was discovered that they had inflated supplier rebates in order to increase earnings.

Dutch investigators staged a raid on the company's offices and those of its auditor, Deloitte & Touche. The investigators were looking for evidence that revenues from joint ventures had been improperly claimed. Royal Ahold, thereafter, announced that it was changing its accounting treatment for those joint ventures, resulting in a reduction in revenue of $24.8 billion. Royal Ahold faced investigations from a plethora of regulators, including the U.S. Department of Justice, the SEC, the NYSE, the NASD, the Office of the Dutch Public Prosecutor, the Euronext Amsterdam Exchange, and the Dutch Authority for Financial Markets.

In the United States, Timothy J. Lee, an executive vice president at the Ahold U.S. Foodservice unit, pleaded guilty to criminal charges, as did William Carter, a vice president for purchasing. The chief financial officer for that unit, Michael Resnick, and Mark Kaiser William, an executive vice president for purchasing, were indicted. In January 2005, seven executives at U.S. Foodservice Inc. were indicted by the Justice Department and charged by the SEC for their role in the accounting fraud at Ahold. An executive at Tyson Foods and one at General Mills were also charged. The company itself settled with the SEC, but no fine was imposed because of the "extraordinary" cooperation of the company with the SEC investigation.

Royal Ahold's problems triggered investigations into other large food distributors including General Mills, Nash Finch Co., Sara Lee Corp., and Tyson Foods. Fleming Companies Inc., of Lewisville, Texas, America's largest food distributor, filed for bankruptcy in April 2003. An accounting scandal had hurt the firm, but a more critical problem was the loss of its largest customer, Kmart, which declared bankruptcy after Fleming demanded payment on a large number of invoices that had not been paid. The SEC settled an action against the company charging that Fleming overstated its earnings in 2001 and the first half of 2002. Fleming used "initiatives" to create an illusion of growth and financial strength for financial analysts at a time when it was suffering from the loss of Kmart as a customer. Fleming used the initiatives to bridge the gap between Wall Street expectations and disappointing actual operating results. The initiatives included side letters from suppliers that were used to justify accelerated recognition of up-front payments the suppliers made to secure forward-looking contracts. Also settling were three Fleming suppliers and seven of their employees. The suppliers included Dean Foods Company, Kemps LLC, and Digital Exchange Systems Inc. Fleming was not fined, but the suppliers and their employees agreed to pay civil penalties that totaled $1 million.

Italy also was facing grocery problems. Cirio, an Italian food company, defaulted on $1 billion of its bonds in 2002. Another grocery store accounting scandal on a massive scale arose at Parmalat Finanziaria SpA, an Italian dairy company. Parmalat had been a small operation until its founder and chairman, Calisto Tanzi, who started out as a ham and tomato paste salesman, went on an acquisition binge. He built Parmalat into the world's largest dairy company, with thirty subsidiaries and large operations in the United States. Parmalat held an investment grade credit rating for its debt from the rating agencies. Suspicions were aroused, however, after Parmalat withdrew a $360 million Eurobond offering in February 2003, claiming that market conditions were not favorable. The withdrawal was widely viewed as a sign that the company was in trouble. Parmalat had been reporting strong earnings, but an accounting report revealed in 2003 that the company had been falsifying its financial statements for thirteen years. That report asserted that Parmalat's actual debt of $15.1 billion was eight times more than reported in its financial statements. The company had overstated its earnings by 500 percent in just the first nine months of 2003, and the total for that and prior years exceeded $11 billion.

The scandal burgeoned after Parmalat was forced to admit that a $4.83 billion deposit on its books that was supposed to be held at the Bank of America did not exist. A forged confirmation for those funds had been given to the company's auditors in order to certify its statements. A Bank of America official in Italy admitted that he took $27 million in a kickback scheme from Parmalat. In addition, Parmalat confessed that its public announcement that it had bought back $3.6 billion of its own bonds was a lie. The scandal widened after Tanzi was found to have looted $1.1 billion from the company. Much of that amount was funneled into Parmatour, a tourism company controlled by the Tanzi family, but it too was missing $2 billion. The Parmalat scandal shocked the Italian political system, through which Tanzi had made political contributions totaling $120 million.

Parmalat employees were caught shredding falsified documents and destroying computers with hammers in order to frustrate prosecutors. Tanzi and several others, including his son, Stefano, and brother, Giovanni, were arrested by Italian authorities. Parmalet's outside counsel and ten of its executives, including its chief financial officer, pleaded guilty to criminal charges in Italy, but none of their jail terms exceeded thirty months. An action against the Bank of America in the United States was dismissed, but claims against Deloitte & Touche LLP and Grant & Thornton LLP were allowed to go forward.

Prosecutors in Italy also sought the indictment of twenty-nine other individuals, the Bank of America, and Parmalat's auditors, Grant Thornton (Italaudit) and Deloitte & Touche. Several of the individuals for whom indictments were sought were employees of those institutions. Prosecutors in Italy also charged that officials of Citigroup, Morgan Stanley Deutsche Bank aided Parmalat's fraud while acting as investment bankers for the company. Citigroup responded with a lawsuit in New Jersey, which claimed that it was a victim of Parmalet's fraud. The SEC brought fraud charges against Parmalat, asserting that it violated U.S. securities laws by misrepresenting its financial condition while selling notes valued at $1.5 billion in this country and privately placing ADRs. The SEC called the scandal "one of the largest and most brazen corporate financial frauds in history."[35]

Enrico Bondi, a court appointed administrator for Parmalat, filed suit against Deloitte and Grant Thornton in U.S. courts seeking $10 billion in damages. Deutsche Bank AG and UBS AG were targets of other suits by Bondi, which charged that Deutsche Bank arranged debt that overburdened the company and that UBS wrongfully seized Parmalat funds when the company was bankrupt. Similar charges of grabbing funds were levied against Citigroup, but that bank responded with its own lawsuit against the Italian government, claiming that its rights as a creditor were being violated. Credit Suisse First Boston was another target. The administrator was seeking $306 million in damages in Italy from that firm for arranging disguised loans for Parmalat. An affiliate of the Banca Intesa SpA in Italy agreed to pay the Parmalat administrator $197 million to settle claims arising from its financing of Parmalat.

8. Analysts and Insider Trading Scandals

The Martha Stewart Case

History of Insider Trading

In the beginning, there was no such crime as insider trading. A New York court ruled in 1868 that directors of a corporation owed no duty to disclose nonpublic information about their company before buying or selling its stock.[1] That rule was a long-lived one. As held in the leading case of *Goodwin v. Agassiz,*[2] decided by a Massachusetts court in 1933, officers and directors of a corporation had no duty to disclose the existence of a favorable copper mining report before purchasing company shares. This was the majority rule under common law, at least in non-face-to-face transactions or where special circumstances might require disclosure. Nevertheless, Adolf Berle, the Columbia law professor, advocated in the 1920s that insider trading should be prohibited. Drawing on the earlier work of other professors, Berle argued that a requirement of full disclosure, coupled with imposing fiduciary duties on directors, should be adopted to preclude insider trading. His advocacy would lay the groundwork for the imposition of that requirement some thirty years later.

William O. Douglas, then a professor at the Yale Law School and later chairman of the Securities and Exchange Commission (SEC) and Supreme Court justice, complained in 1934 of insider trading and some very WorldCom and Enron-like practices:

> Recent court records and Senate hearings are replete with specific and illustrative material—secret loans to officers and directors, undisclosed profit-sharing plans, timely contracts unduly favorable to affiliated interests, dividend policies based on false estimates, manipulations of credit resources and capital structures to the detriment of minority interests, pool operations, and trading in securities of the company by virtue of inside information, to mention only a few. These are not peculiar to recent times. They are forms of business activity long known to the law.[3]

As witnessed by Enron and other recent scandals, nothing has changed since Douglas's lament. Douglas himself engaged in insider trading while serving on the Supreme Court. His brother, Arthur, tipped Douglas in 1953 on an impending change in control of the Statler Hotel chain. Douglas made a profit of $8,000 from that inside information, an amount equal to about a third of his annual salary on the court.

Congress considered abuses involving trading by insiders during the hearings that led to the adoption of the federal securities laws. Echoing Adolf Berle, a Senate committee reported that among "the most vicious practices unearthed" in congressional hearings was "the flagrant betrayal of the fiduciary duties by directors and officers of corporations who used their positions of trust and the confidential information, which came to them in such positions, to aid them in their market activities."[4] The committee decried the "unscrupulous employment of inside information" by officers, directors, and "large stockholders who, while not directors and officers, exercised sufficient control over the destinies of their companies to enable them to acquire and profit by information not available to others."[5] Despite these protestations, the resulting legislation adopted only a very narrow prohibition on insider trading. The Securities and Exchange Act of 1934 required certain insiders (defined as officers, directors, and persons owning 10 percent or more of the company's stock) to report their transactions in their corporation's stock to the SEC and to forfeit any short-term profits (defined as profits made in any six-month period). Those profits were forfeitable even if the insider was not acting on inside information. Otherwise, in accordance with the common law rule, anyone could trade on inside information, at least until a new chairman arrived at the SEC in the 1960s.

SEC Creates a Crime

The new chairman was Professor William Cary from the Columbia Law School, where one of his colleagues was the long-lived Adolf A. Berle. Taking up the cudgels for Berle, Cary succeeded where Berle had failed in creating an insider trading prohibition where none had been before. Cary did not seek legislation from Congress for the enactment of this controversial prohibition. Instead, he simply made it up in 1961 through an opinion in an SEC administrative proceeding entitled *In re Cady Roberts & Co.*[6] This proceeding was an uncontested settlement in which Chairman Cary asserted that a stockbroker receiving nonpublic "inside" information from a director of a company violated SEC Rule 10b-5 when he sold securities based on that information for his own account and for the accounts of customers. Although Rule 10b-5 had been adopted some twenty years earlier, no court had held that it prohibited insider trading—nor had the SEC made such an argument. Nevertheless, Cary asserted in that opinion that "the securities acts may be said to have generated a wholly new and far-reaching body of federal corporation law." The federal securities law created "many managerial duties and liabilities unknown to the common law. It expresses federal interest in management-stockholder relationships which heretofore had been almost exclusively the concern of the states." Cary contended that Rule 10b-5 provides "stockholders with a potent weapon for enforcement of many fiduciary duties."

The *Cady Roberts* decision was a surprise to corporate lawyers and a shock to the world of corporate executives. More was to follow. In 1968, the Second Circuit Court of Appeals in New York upheld an SEC suit charging that several executives employed by the Texas Gulf Sulphur Company violated Rule 10b-5 when they purchased the company's stock on the basis of knowledge of a nonpublic favorable mining report. The SEC contended, and the Second Circuit agreed, that Rule 10b-5 required "relatively equal access to material information."[7] This reversed the common law rule set forth in *Goodwin v. Agassiz*. The Second Circuit's decision meant that executives of a company possessing nonpublic information about their company's stock could not trade until the information had been fully disseminated to the public.

The SEC's invention of this crime called insider trading was based on the moralistic ground that it was unfair to allow people to profit simply because they have privileged access to information. The SEC argued that the markets were demoralized by such practices and that capital-raising efforts were made harder by insider trading. Not everyone was convinced by that claim. Professor Henry G. Manne, an early and persistent critic of the SEC's insider trading prohibition, published a book in 1966 that attacked the SEC's decision in *Cady Roberts*. He noted, among other things, that there was no economic basis for asserting that trading by insiders is harmful to the markets. Similarly, Professor Daniel Fischel, a law professor and later dean of the University of Chicago School of Law, noted with respect to the *Texas Gulf Sulphur* decision that there was "no evidence that investors had less 'confidence' in our securities markets before" *Texas Gulf Sulphur* than after and that insider trading can actually be "beneficial" by rewarding success.[8]

In fact, markets function on a principle exactly opposite to the equal access doctrine invented by Chairman Cary. People trade in the stock and other markets on the basis of their view that they have unequal information or special insight that will allow them to profit, while others without that information or insight will lose. Economists call this "asymmetric" information. Critics of the SEC's insider trading theory also note that trading volume is so high in many publicly traded companies that insider trading has no discernible effect on other investors, individually or in the aggregate. That would be particularly true in the case of Martha Stewart whose transactional saving was less than $50,000, assuming of course that what she did was insider trading, a matter of some doubt, as will be seen.

Critics of the SEC's insider trading charges further claim that, even when an inside trader moves the market substantially, such trading is a good thing, making the markets more efficient in pricing a stock for its real value, ahead of the delayed reports in SEC-required disclosures. The profits made by the inside trader ensure that the price of the stock is accurate, reflecting all information, some of which the company may otherwise want to delay publishing, particularly bad news. Arguments have also been made that trading on inside information prepares the market in a stock for large corrections. The stock price is moved gradually by the inside traders, avoiding sharp price fluctuations that create panic or uninformed investment decisions that cause greater injury to public investors. "Of course, there is also the practical argument that there is no such thing as a secret and that the information will in all events leak into the market selectively, so why bother?"[9]

The Supreme Court Responds

In *Chiarella v. United States,* the Supreme Court rejected the "equal access" theory propounded by the SEC.[10] That case did not involve the "classic" insider trading by an executive in the stock of his own company. Rather, a "mark-up" man who selected type fonts and page layouts for a printing company was trading on nonpublic information obtained from tender offer materials being printed for law firms handling acquisitions. The lawyers disguised the identity of the target companies, but Vincent F. Chiarella became adept at identifying the companies. He was aided by the fact that the level of disclosure required in the proxy materials by the SEC was too detailed to disguise the target completely. The Supreme Court, in rejecting the SEC's equal access theory, held that Chiarella owed no duty of disclosure to the target companies' shareholders. Chiarella was spared prison by the Supreme Court's decision, but he had given up his profits to the SEC and wandered from job to job until an arbitrator restored him to his printing position.

The SEC had also argued before the Supreme Court that, even if there was no equal access requirement, Chiarella could still be held liable under SEC Rule 10b-5 for "misappropriating" the information from his own employer and its clients. The Supreme Court rejected that argument because it had not been raised in the lower court and, therefore, could not be considered on appeal, a basic requirement of appellate practice. Undaunted, the SEC continued with its new misappropriation theory and thereafter was able to convince the Second Circuit Court of Appeals in New York to uphold findings of Rule 10b-5 violations against another printer under the misappropriation theory.[11]

The Justice Department brought a criminal case in the 1980s under the misappropriation theory against a *Wall Street Journal* reporter, R. Foster Winans. He was running an insider-trading ring based on information that would have market effect when disclosed in the newspaper's "Heard on the Street" column. This case wound its way to the Supreme Court, which held that such conduct constituted mail and wire fraud, but the justices split evenly (4–4) on whether the misappropriation theory had validity. Under the rules of the Supreme Court, in the event of such a split, the decision of the appellate court below is upheld.[12] In this case, the court below (the Second Circuit Court of Appeals in New York) had upheld the theory. Winans went to prison and wrote a book about his experience.

Most other lower courts supported the misappropriation theory, except for the Fourth Circuit Court of Appeals, which rejected it, asserting that Rule 10b-5 did not support criminal liability for what amounted to a breach of fiduciary duty, a matter previously handled civilly. The Supreme Court in *United States v. O'Hagan* finally decided the issue in 1997.[13] There, the Court held that the misappropriation of nonpublic information constituted a criminal violation of Rule 10b-5 even though the information was not obtained from the target company. In this case, a lawyer, James O'Hagan, misappropriated "outside" information about a proposed tender offer for Pillsbury Company from a client of his law firm that was planning the tender. The lawyer bought large amounts of options on Pillsbury stock, making profits of over $4.3 million when the tender offer was announced.

The application of the SEC's insider trading theory through the assistance of the judiciary has left some interesting issues. What if the *Wall Street Journal* had given its reporter permission to trade? In that case, there would be no misappropriation. What about the case of Barry Switzer, the famous Oklahoma football coach who overheard some boosters talking about inside information while he was sunbathing in the stands? A court held that his trading on that information did not violate Rule 10b-5.[14] Contrast that decision with the criminal conviction of a psychiatrist who traded on nonpublic information supplied during therapy by a client concerning her husband's business activities. That client was the wife of Sanford Weill, who later became the head of Citigroup and who would have his own full disclosure problems in the analysts' scandals on Wall Street that arose after the fall of Enron.[15]

Tippers and Tippees

Another leak in the full disclosure system for insider traders was the so-called tippee. This is someone who is not an insider but is tipped by an insider on nonpublic information on which the tippee then trades. The SEC asserted that its equal access doctrine prevented the tippee from trading. That theory was put to the test after the SEC brought an insider trading case against Raymond Dirks, a financial analyst who sold out the positions of his institutional clients in the stock of Equity Funding Corp. after he was tipped by an Equity employee on a massive accounting fraud at that company. Dirks conducted an intensive investigation of those allegations and concluded they had substance. Dirks told his clients, and anyone else who would listen, about these disclosures. Dirks's clients sold their Equity funding securities in response to that information, saving themselves more than $16 million.

Dirks tipped the *Wall Street Journal,* urging a reporter there to write a story on the fraud. The reporter ignored this recommendation but told the SEC about Dirks's allegations. At first the SEC did nothing. A court considering Dirks's action later noted that the "SEC had a history of failing to act promptly in the Equity Funding case," closing an earlier inquiry without taking action.[16]

The SEC eventually got involved and sued Dirks for tipping his clients with this "inside" information. Again rejecting the equal access to information doctrine propounded by the SEC, the Supreme Court threw out the SEC's case against Dirks.[17] The Supreme Court held that Dirks owed no duty to anyone not to trade on that information. It also ruled, however, that a tippee could be held liable for a violation of Rule 10b-5 if the insider would benefit personally from the disclosure to the tippee.

The *Dirks* decision has led to some inconsistent results. In one instance, a federal appellate court held that Donna Yun, the wife of the president of Scholastic Book Fairs Inc., could be found guilty of insider trading after she allowed a coworker to overhear a conversation with her attorney in which she disclosed confidential information about her husband's company.[18] The coworker, without her knowledge, then traded on that information. The wife was held to have misappropriated the information even though she did not trade or profit herself or encourage her coworker to do so. The case had to be retried because an appellate court held that the trial judge had not properly instructed the jury on how the misappropriation theory was to be applied. The *Dirks* decision saved a barber and his client in another case. A federal district court dismissed insider-trading charges brought by the SEC against David W. Maxwell, a senior executive at Worthington Foods Inc., and his barber, Elton L. Jehn, who was tipped by Maxwell on an agreement by the Kellogg Company to acquire Worthington. The court dismissed the case because Maxwell did not personally benefit from the tip.

Insider Trading Scandals

SEC chairman William Cary's activist policies attracted a counterreaction in the form of objections by the business community to what was being perceived as the SEC's overregulation of the securities markets. In response to that criticism, the administration of President Richard Nixon, in which William J. Casey served as SEC chairman, started an effort to deregulate the securities markets. That effort was frustrated by the Watergate scandal that led to Nixon's removal from office.

After Ronald Reagan was elected president, Republican deregulatory efforts were renewed. Stanley Sporkin, the aggressive head of the SEC's Division of Enforcement, was moved over to the Central Intelligence Agency (CIA), where he became that agency's general counsel under CIA director William J. Casey, the former SEC chairman under Nixon. The SEC began cutting back its enforcement, but sought to avoid criticism that it was going easy on business by pursuing insider trading cases. The new chairman of the SEC, John Shad, announced that he was going to "come down with hobnail boots" on insider trading.[19] True to his word, several such cases were brought by the new head of the SEC's Enforcement Division, John Fedders, who had been a partner in the Washington, DC, law firm of Arnold & Porter. The SEC assumed that these cases would not unduly disturb Wall Street, but Fedders was forced to resign after being accused of physically beating his wife, a story that was broken by the *Wall Street Journal* after Fedders embarrassed that publication by charging its reporter, R. Foster Winans, with running an insider trading ring. Fedders's family life was then turned into a television movie. Despite that setback, the SEC continued its insider trading program, bringing a number of high-profile cases that caused the decade of the 1980s to be characterized as an era of base greed, a title that the 1990s would also claim.

In one insider trading case in the 1980s, Paul Thayer, deputy secretary of defense, was found to have given his mistress inside information that he had obtained when he was chairman of the LTV Corporation and an outside director of Anheuser-Busch. Dennis Levine, a managing director at Drexel Burnham, Lambert, who was paid $1 million a year as compensation, was the head of an insider-trading ring that reaped millions. Its members included young investment bankers at Lazard Frères, Shearson Lehman Brothers, and Goldman Sachs & Co. Another member of that ring was Ilan Reich, a partner in the New York law firm of Wachtell Lipton Rosen & Kartz, which specialized in mergers, providing access to some significant inside information. Using information obtained through his firm and from his coconspirators, Levine traded in over fifty stocks and made profits of $12 million.

Levine concealed his trading through an anonymous account in the Bahamas branch of Bank Leu International, a Swiss bank. He was caught after an anonymous letter sent to Merrill Lynch from Venezuela revealed that Merrill Lynch brokers were piggybacking on the always profitable trades in the Bank Leu account just before merger announcements. Merrill Lynch referred that complaint to the SEC, which sought information from Bank Leu on the identity of its client. The SEC was concerned that the account was trading on insider information because it always made money, something that would not ordinarily occur in a securities account no matter how professional the trader. The bank responded that such information was confidential under Bahamian law. The SEC then advised Bank Leu that it would be charged with insider trading unless it identified its client. The bank was represented by Harvey L. Pitt, a partner in the law firm of Fried, Frank, Harris, Shriver and Jacobson, a former SEC general counsel and future SEC chairman during the height of the Enron scandal. Pitt worked out a deal whereby the attorney general of the Bahamas waived the bank secrecy laws so that Bank Leu could identify Levine. Ironically, Levine had recommended Pitt to the bank, hoping that Pitt's knowledge of the SEC and his contacts there would allow him to frustrate the agency's investigation.

Levine was arrested on May 12, 1986, and pleaded guilty to four felony charges. In order to lessen his prison term, Levine implicated Ivan Boesky, a Wall Street arbitrageur and corporate raider made famous by his remark to a group of students at the University of California that "greed is healthy." Boesky was represented by Harvey Pitt, the same lawyer who had represented Bank

Leu. Although Boesky was barred from the securities business and agreed to pay a fine of $100 million, Pitt made sure that Boesky was given the opportunity to select his own very lenient sentencing judge, and Boesky served only twenty months. Pitt embarrassed the SEC when the press found out that the plea agreement negotiated by Pitt permitted Boesky to sell his stock before the public announcement of his arrest. That inside information allowed Boesky to avoid the sharp drop in stock values for that stock that occurred after the announcement.

As a means to reduce his own prison sentence, Boesky confessed that he had received inside information on takeover targets from Martin Siegel, another highly paid investment banker at Drexel Burnham, Lambert. Siegel pleaded guilty to felony charges of insider trading, was sent to prison, and paid $9 million to settle SEC insider trading charges. Siegel implicated others, including two arbitrageurs: Timothy Tabor, who was arrested in his home at night, and Richard Wigton, who was handcuffed in his office and frog-marched out in tears to face television news teams tipped off to the arrest by the U.S. attorney in Manhattan, Rudolph Giuliani, later to become mayor and a political hero after the terrorist attacks on September 11, 2001. Apparently with tongue in cheek, Giuliani claimed that the raids and handcuffing of these mild-mannered and completely harmless executives were necessary in case they had a knife or other weapon. Charges against both Tabor and Wigton were subsequently dropped. Another victim of Siegel's effort to receive a reduced sentence was Robert Freeman, the head of the arbitrage department at Goldman Sachs. Freeman pleaded guilty to trading on inside information provided to him by Bernard ("Bunny") Lasker, a floor broker on the New York Stock Exchange (NYSE). Lasker told Freeman that a takeover of Beatrice Foods was rumored to be experiencing problems. Freeman confirmed that information with Siegel, who was involved in the transaction and told Freeman that "your Bunny has a good nose." The rumor about Beatrice Foods proved to be inaccurate, but Freeman was imprisoned and fined $1 million.

The scandals of that era peaked with the indictment of Michael Milken in March 1989 on ninety-eight felony counts of securities violations, mail and wire fraud, and racketeering. The charges brought against Milken involved the "parking" of stock and some complicated manipulation claims. Although Milken is popularly thought of as an insider trader, no insider trading charges were filed against him. Milken's real crime was his popularization of junk bonds, which were controversial because of their use in highly leveraged takeovers. There was no law against such securities, so Milken had to be demonized by some dubious allegations made by Ivan Boesky as part of his own guilty plea. An effort to entrap Milken by wiring Boesky for a meeting at the Beverly Hills Hotel failed. Lacking proof against Milken, the government turned to extortion, as they did later with Lea Fastow, by indicting his brother, Lowell Milken. FBI agents were sent to question Milken's ninety-two-year-old grandfather in order to add further intimidation.[20] Milken folded under this onslaught, pleading guilty to six felony counts and agreeing to pay a fine of $600 million. The government agreed in turn to drop the charges against Milken's brother and stopped its harassment of other family members. Milken was sentenced to a then astonishing ten years in prison by an "inexperienced judge playing to the headline writers calling for blood."[21] The sentence was later reduced, but Milken's firm, Drexel Burnham, Lambert was forced to plead guilty to felony charges and agreed to pay a fine of $650 million. This crippled the firm and it later failed, sending its employees to the unemployment lines, a precursor of the indifference shown by the government to such considerations in its prosecution of Arthur Andersen.

There were some serious issues about Milken's guilt, as described in a book by Daniel Fischel titled *Payback: The Conspiracy to Destroy Michael Milken and His Financial Revolution.* Fischel contended that Milken was a victim of resentment in the press for his success and the political ambitions and zeal of Rudolph Giuliani. Like Thomas Dewey before him, Giuliani was seeking to parlay high-profile prosecutions into political capital that would make him the mayor of New York. Giuliani in turn created a model for New York Attorney General Eliot Spitzer. Fischel's accusations against Giuliani were not couched in the usual turgid, convoluted prose of academia. Fischel claimed that Giuliani was "unscrupulous" in his corporate "reign of terror" that employed "the same anticapitalist greed-bashing rhetoric used so successfully in Communist countries."[22] According to Fischel, Giuliani's prosecutorial zeal turned technical regulatory violations into criminal fraud charges, all based on a bogus claim that the government was preserving investor confidence in the market.

As Fischel noted, Milken's real problem was that he made a lot of money, a fact that was pointed out in detail in the indictment in order to prejudice the press and a jury against him, while the crimes that were charged were, at worst, technical regulatory infractions and more accurately "routine business practices common in the industry."[23] After being released from prison, Michael Milken donated millions to cancer research, and he became a czar of for-profit education investments. Meanwhile, a new SEC chairman had been appointed by President George H.W. Bush. That appointee, Richard Breeden, was soon crowing that insider traders caught by the SEC would be "left naked, homeless and without wheels."[24] Breeden went on to become the crusading corporate monitor for WorldCom and Hollinger.

Insider Trading Legislation

Congress acted to strengthen sanctions for insider trading by enacting the Insiders Trading Sanctions Act of 1984 and the Insider Trading and Securities Fraud Enforcement Act of 1988. That legislation allowed the SEC to seek a penalty from inside traders equal to three times the profits they made or the losses they avoided by their trading. Persons "controlling" the inside trading of another could be fined up to $1 million. Informants exposing insider trading were eligible for a bounty of up to 10 percent of any penalty recovered by the SEC. Insider traders were liable to stockholders trading contemporaneously opposite the transactions of the insider. Persons conveying inside information were subject to criminal penalties, and fines for violations were increased from $100,000 to $1 million.

This legislation did not define insider trading, leaving much doubt as to what is actually prohibited. Such a definition was not difficult to formulate. The European Union Commission adopted a directive defining the term, although that prohibition was only rarely enforced by its member states. Harvey Pitt, the future SEC chairman, and others lobbied Congress for a definition to provide certainty for those involved in the market. The SEC did not want to specify such a definition for fear that it would give traders a roadmap that would allow them to take advantage of information asymmetries that the SEC might not like. The SEC would rather define the practice after the fact, thereby providing the *in terrorem* effect sought by Justice Frankfurter and discouraging innovative trading that might lead to greater market efficiencies.

More Insider Trading Issues

The SEC's insider trading theory continued to raise complexities in its application, particularly since the crime remained undefined. Consider the case of Robert Chestman, a stockbroker who was tipped on the takeover of Waldbaum Inc. by one of his clients, Keith Loeb.[25] Loeb's wife, Susan, was the niece of the president and controlling shareholder of Waldbaum. Her mother, Shirley, tipped her on that takeover. Each of the family members had been pledged to secrecy, but Loeb informed Chestman of the potential takeover. Chestman traded personally for his own account, making a profit. The Second Circuit, normally a court that kowtows to the SEC's expansive theories, held there was no violation of Rule 10b-5, but that decision came in an unusual 6–5 en banc vote of the court. Keith Loeb was found not to have owed any fiduciary duty to keep the information confidential under Rule 10b-5. Nevertheless, because the nonpublic information involved a takeover, Chestman was found to have violated SEC Rule 14e-3, which applied to anyone with such information no matter how attenuated the source. Had the information not involved a takeover, Chestman would have walked away from the SEC charges.

The SEC tried to fill the hole in its Rule 10b-5 insider trading program rent by the Chestman case by passing another rule that defines relatives as having a duty of confidentiality when they receive nonpublic information. That rule also covered instances in which people agree to keep information confidential even if they are not relatives. Before the adoption of that rule, a member of the Young Presidents Organization was indicted for trading on information provided in confidence by a fellow member.[26] This organization was composed of corporate presidents under the age of fifty, and the members were pledged to maintain the confidence of information imparted by other members. A federal district court ruled that the breach of that confidence was not a misappropriation and was not a breach of a legal fiduciary relationship that would give rise to an insider trading claim. Although the SEC's new rule would have subjected the defendant to liability, that rule was passed after he had profited and did not apply to his conduct.

A gap appeared in the SEC's insider trading prosecutions under Rule 10b-5 in the form of a "use and possession" doctrine that, like the *Dirks* case, would have broad implications in the Martha Stewart prosecution. The SEC contended that an insider possessing inside information violated Rule 10b-5 even if that person would have bought or sold the stock anyway because of prior investment plans or commitments. For example, say that an executive had a long-standing loan payment due that would require her to sell stock on a specific date. Before the stock sale, but long after the commitment, she became aware of inside information that would undercut the value of the stock after she sold it. The SEC contended, under its possession theory, that such a sale violated Rule 10b-5 because she possessed inside information even though she did not use it as the basis for her sale. The courts rejected that claim,[27] and the SEC acquiesced in that rejection by adopting still another rule. The new rule allowed insiders to trade even if they were in possession of inside information, provided they had a preexisting plan in place to trade before coming into possession of the inside information.[28] This rule would be the crux of the prosecution's case against Martha Stewart, who was accused of falsely claiming that she had such a plan. It was also a key factor in Kenneth Lay's sale of millions of dollars of Enron stock before his company's demise.

Insider Trading Continues

In the meantime, insider trading continued unabated on Wall Street even as full disclosure was collapsing at Enron, WorldCom, and elsewhere. Particularly salacious were the news reports of the charges filed in 1999 against pornographic film actress Kathryn Gannon, who used the stage name Marilyn Starr. She had been tipped by her paramour, James J. McDermott Jr., the former head of Keefe, Bruyette & Woods. Gannon and another boyfriend made $170,000 from those tips, including a merger transaction involving Barnett Banks and NationsBank. McDermott's conviction was overturned on appeal, but he was convicted again after a retrial and sentenced to eight months in prison, even though he did not himself trade or profit. Gannon was sentenced to three months after she agreed to give up her extradition fight from Canada. This love triangle case was dubbed "Wall Street's Dirty Deal."[29] Earlier, in the 1990s, seventeen executives at the AT&T Corp. were charged with trading on the basis of inside information on four AT&T acquisitions between 1988 and 1993. Their profits totaled $2.6 million. Most of the defendants pleaded guilty, including the two ringleaders, Charles Brumfield and Thomas Alger. The prosecutor in that case would prosecute Martha Stewart.

Lionel Thotam pleaded guilty to trading on tips received from Davi Thomas, a post office employee. Thomas read the column "Inside Wall Street" from *Business Week* magazine to Thotam over the telephone when the magazine reached his postal facility in advance of being distributed to the public. Thotam made $77,000 from his trading, while Thomas made $154,000. Thomas and his wife, Soni Jos, were arrested for this conduct. That was not the only inside trading on that column. Two employees of the company printing the magazine were tipping two of their friends on information in the column. The friends made $1.4 million from their trading, paying the two printing plant employees $50 per week for the tips, later increasing that amount to $200. All four pleaded guilty to insider trading charges.

Goldman Sachs traded on inside information about the Department of the Treasury's decision to discontinue temporarily the thirty-year bond that was announced to the public on October 31, 2001. The firm had been tipped by a political consultant, Peter J. Davis, who had attended an "embargoed" Treasury press conference describing the change. Davis phoned the information to a senior economist at Goldman Sachs, John M. Youngdahl, twenty-five minutes before the embargo on disclosure of the information was lifted, but only eight minutes before a Treasury official inadvertently posted the announcement online. During those seventeen minutes, Goldman Sachs bought $84 million in thirty-year bonds and bond futures covering another $233 million, resulting in profits of $3.8 million.

Youngdahl pleaded guilty to charges of inside trading and other misconduct for misuse of this information. He was sentenced to two years and nine months in prison and paid the SEC a civil penalty of $240,000. Goldman Sachs agreed to pay $9.3 million to settle charges brought by the SEC. An executive at the Massachusetts Financial Services Company, Steven Nothern, was tipped by the same political consultant on the embargoed information and traded $65 million in bonds for portfolios he managed. Massachusetts Financial Services agreed to pay a penalty of $200,000 and to reimburse $700,000 to the company selling the Treasury bonds.

Raymond Evans, a Long Island attorney, agreed to pay $850,000 to settle charges that he sold shares of Hirsch International Corp. after receiving inside information that this client was having a bad quarter. He also bought shares of Periphonics Inc. after receiving confidential information from that client. Mark Kelly was charged by the SEC with tipping two friends with inside information on the acquisition of Golden State Bancorp by Citigroup in 2002. David M. Willey, the chief financial officer at Capital One Financial Corp., was charged with trading on inside information that bank regulators were about to downgrade Capital One's supervisory assessment. That change had an adverse effect on the bank's stock price; it fell by 40 percent. The SEC charged that Willey made several million dollars from his trading. Rick Marano, an analyst for Standard & Poor's, was indicted in 2004 for insider trading in the stock of companies under review at his firm. Marano and others that he tipped made more than $1 million from that information. A laid-off invest-ment banker at JPMorgan Chase agreed to pay $200,000 to settle SEC charges that he traded on inside information about the shares of Panamerican Bever-ages, Inc. before it was acquired by Coca-Cola Femsa SA. He made a profit of $79,000.

The husband of a legal secretary at Skadden Arps Slate Meagher & Flom LLP was tipping a friend on mergers being handled by Roger Aaron, the part-ner his wife worked for at the law firm. The husband and the individual he tipped pled guilty to insider trading and other criminal charges. John Free-man, a temporary word processor, was charged with tipping at least ten others on mergers that were being handled by Goldman Sachs while he worked there. The individuals he tipped then tipped others, bringing the number of people charged to nineteen. Freeman also carried out such activities at Credit Suisse First Boston. This gang made profits of over $1 million. Freeman pleaded guilty to criminal charges.

George P. Matus, senior vice president of marketing and investor relations at the Carreker Corp., tipped his brother on a decline in the company's earn-ings. The brother was a broker and traded put options on Carreker, making profits of $200,000. Both brothers were indicted for insider trading and for making false statements to the SEC. E. Garrett Bewkes Jr., a director at Inter-state Bakeries, told his son Robert, who was a broker at UBS, to sell Interstate stock before a poor earnings announcement. Robert sold that stock for his family and client accounts in amounts totaling $230,000. Robert Bewkes was barred from the securities industry for five years and agreed to pay $137,306 to settle the case. His father paid $67,517 in settlement. Interstate Bakeries, the maker of Twinkies, later filed for bankruptcy, and the company was under investigation by the SEC for its accounting treatment of reserve accounts.

Diane C. Neiley, an executive assistant at BetzDearborn Inc., tipped her boyfriend, Joseph Doody IV, who tipped his father, on a proposed merger of her company with Hercules Inc. The word spread quickly, and the SEC sued a total of eighteen people for trading on that information. Patricia Bugenhagen, an executive secretary at BetzDearborn, tipped a friend, who tipped his brother, who tipped his fellow investment club members. Another secretary at the company tipped her husband, who tipped his accountant. Olga S. Litvinsky, a secretary at JPMorgan Chase & Co., tipped her future husband Felix Litvinsky on the acquisition. The defendants were required to repay $4 million.

ImClone

More spectacular were the criminal charges against Martha Stewart, the doyenne of good living. The Martha Stewart scandal began with the arrest of Dr. Samuel D. Waksal on June 12, 2002. Waksal was a founder of ImClone Systems Inc. and the company's president and chief executive officer. ImClone had under development and review a new drug called Erbitux, for the treatment of irinotecan-refractory colorectal (colon) cancer. Colon cancer is one of the most deadly cancers, taking the lives of over 56,000 Americans annually. The drug was promising because it could kill malignant cancer cells without harming normal cells. Erbitux looked so promising that Bristol-Myers Squibb made a $2 billion equity investment in ImClone on September 19, 2001, and agreed to co-market and help develop the drug. ImClone touted Erbitux as a drug that would become ImClone's lead product, providing large future revenues.

While vacationing in the Caribbean during the holidays late in December 2001, Waksal learned that the Food and Drug Administration (FDA) was planning to announce its refusal to review ImClone's application for a license to sell Erbitux to the public. Although the FDA's concern was the manner in which a trial for the drug had been conducted, and not with the drug itself, the delay required for further trials would have an obvious adverse effect on the company's stock price. Waksal was in a desperate situation, reportedly owing more than $80 million on loans secured by his ImClone stock. He tried to sell his ImClone stock, as well as that of his father, Jack Waksal, and his daughter, Aliza, an actress. Those accounts were all held at Merrill Lynch. Jack Waksal was able to sell $8 million in ImClone stock, and Sam sold $2.5 million of ImClone stock for his daughter but was blocked from selling his own shares by lawyers at Merrill Lynch who were concerned with his insider status at ImClone. Sam Waksal then purchased put option contracts on over 20,000 ImClone shares through a Swiss brokerage account that he thought would conceal his involvement because of Swiss bank secrecy laws.

These transactions occurred before the public announcement of the FDA's action on December 28, 2001. Sam Waksal's brother, Harlan, the cofounder of ImClone, had sold $50 million in ImClone stock earlier in the month and escaped prosecution. Timing is everything, but Harlan was one lucky guy when it came to legal problems. He had previously been arrested for trying to smuggle two pounds of cocaine into the country, but that charge was dropped after a judge found that the search was illegal. Sam Waksal was not so lucky. He was indicted for insider trading and was handcuffed in a dawn raid on his fashionable SoHo loft and marched in front of media cameras. Waksal's bail was set at $10 million, which had to be posted in cash. When it was discovered that he had ordered the shredding of documents relating to his activities, Waksal was additionally charged with obstruction of justice.

Waksal vowed to fight the charges, but the government threatened prosecution of his eighty-year-old father, a Holocaust survivor, and his daughter, Aliza. This was by now a familiar government extortion tactic used to obtain a guilty plea. Once again, it worked. On March 7, 2003, Samuel Waksal pleaded guilty to various counts of perjury, obstruction of justice, and securities fraud. He was subjected to a lifetime ban on serving as an executive of a publicly traded company, sentenced to over seven years in jail, and fined $3 million. The federal judge imposing that stiff sentence, Judge William H. Pauley, could not resist a bit of showboating by giving a lecture at Waksal's sentencing on the importance of full disclosure. Waksal's father and daughter were not indicted, but the father was sued by the SEC and settled by paying $2 million.

Waksal was pilloried in the press. Among other things, it was reported that he had failed to pay sales taxes amounting to more than $1 million on paintings he bought from a New York art gallery—shades of Tyco. The press also pointed out with glee that an ImClone director, Dr. John Mendelsohn, had served on the board at Enron and was a member of the Enron audit committee. Congressional hearings were held on Waksal's sales, revealing the usual executive abuses such as Waksal's use of his corporate credit card to pay for bottles of wine and tickets to sports events. Those hearings also spotlighted that Martha Stewart had sold her ImClone stock at about the same time as Waksal. More fallout came after Bristol-Myers Squibb was hit with a class action from state and municipal pension funds claiming that it had been too optimistic with respect to its massive investment in ImClone. That claim was included in the $300 million settlement with those pension funds over Bristol-Myer Squibb's accounting manipulations.

Martha Stewart

Martha Stewart started her career as an advertising model ("Tareyton smokers would rather fight than switch") before becoming a stockbroker at the firm of Pearlberg, Monness, Williams & Sidel. She left that profession after the market downturn in the 1970s cut equity prices in half. Stewart then started a catering business that led to the publication of her bestseller book, *Entertaining.* From there she began developing a media empire that consisted of more books, magazines, including *Martha Stewart Living,* a syndicated newspaper column, and her own television program. Stewart was signed on to promote Kmart products that she helped design, and she did a CBS special with then first lady Hillary Clinton.

Stewart's products were initially sold through Time Warner, the giant media company, until she purchased the rights to those products for $85 million. That transaction was structured so that Stewart had to pay only $18 million in cash. Stewart moved those products to Martha Stewart Living Omnimedia, Inc., which went public in 1999 and was listed on the NYSE. Omnimedia was dedicated to marketing Martha Stewart's image as the diva of domestic living through books and magazines, television programs, and merchandising programs. Omnimedia's initial public offering (IPO) on October 19, 1999, was a hot issue priced at $18 but almost immediately traded up to $37. Omnimedia had two classes of stock, one of which controlled the company's voting power and was largely owned by Stewart. She also owned 61 percent of the company's equity. Stewart was a billionaire, at least on paper, after Omnimedia went public. She was Omnimedia's chief executive officer and also an outside director of the NYSE.

Stewart presented a disciplined but benign persona in her television programs and magazine articles. Some exposés, however, demonized her as a control freak and as contemptuous of others, shouting at employees and being rude to those she came into contact with during her working day. Stewart was portrayed as a spoiled member of high society who nearly crushed a landscaper with her car, cursing and screaming at him in anger over a fence placed near her property. At about the time of that incident, a *National Enquirer* reporter wrote a book depicting Stewart as a lying, scheming, conniving bundle of meanness, asserting among other things that she was temperamental, had attempted suicide, and engaged in self-mutilation.[30] The *National Enquirer* followed up on the book with the headline "Martha Stewart Is Mentally Ill." Stewart responded with a libel suit seeking $10 million in damages, but the suit was later dropped.

Those press attacks should have alerted Stewart that she would be the target of government prosecutors, who read newspapers and see a headline for themselves in targeting high-profile public figures, particularly those with a persona of arrogance. Michael Milken had learned that lesson. His demonization as the "junk bond king," a completely legal and now respectable area of finance, led to his prosecution. Arrogant women were particularly susceptible to prosecutions that were designed to put them in their place. A case in point was Leona Helmsley, the original "queen of mean," who earned her title by petty tirades and insults to employees and others around her. She was the wife of billionaire Harry Helmsley, a hotel magnate in New York. Leona Helmsley was portrayed in advertisements as an elitist who ensured only the highest quality in the Helmsley hotels. She was convicted of 333 counts of tax evasion in 1989, after her husband was found mentally incompetent to stand trial. Her defense was not helped by her reported remark that "only the little people pay taxes." Prison did not seem to leaven Helmsley's vitriol. She was hit with a $10 million punitive damage award by a jury for firing the manager of her Park Lane Hotel because he was gay. A court reduced the verdict to $500,000, noting that the jury had reacted so harshly because of their dislike for her queen of mean personality and insensitivity. Harry Helmsley was treated less harshly after his death. A large memorial was erected in his honor on Broadway in the financial district in New York.

Bess Myerson, the former Miss America, socialite and New York's cultural affairs commissioner, was arrested for shoplifting and accused by then U.S. Attorney Rudolph Giuliani of bribing a judge by giving the judge's daughter a job with the city. Myerson was acquitted of the bribery charge after a two-month trial, but still received much criticism for the telephone harassment of a former boyfriend and for engaging in various dubious financial schemes. Another overbearing woman who would be demonized and then stood in the dock was Imelda Marcos, the former first lady of the Philippines. She became infamous for the thousands of pairs of shoes in her closet, leading the press to characterize her as a "world-class shopper." After her husband's death,

Giuliani's office charged her with fraud and racketeering for having helped her husband loot the Philippine treasury of over $220 million. She was tried with Adnan Khashoggi, a wealthy Saudi Arabian businessman who had been embroiled in the questionable payments scandals involving Lockheed in the 1970s. Khashoggi was charged with helping the Marcoses conceal their ownership of four buildings in New York. The government tried to convict Imelda Marcos on the basis of her extravagant lifestyle, but the jury acquitted her and Khashoggi of all charges, one juror even calling the government's case "silly."

Martha Stewart's Crime

Martha Stewart sold 3,928 shares of ImClone stock before the public announcement of the FDA's action on Erbitux. Stewart was a friend of Samuel Waksal, and she shared a common broker with him at Merrill Lynch. That broker, Peter Bacanovic, had previously worked at ImClone. Waksal had dated Stewart's daughter, and Martha Stewart socialized with him and Bacanovic. Waksal, Stewart, and Bacanovic were all society figures in New York, which made the story an even bigger media event.

Martha Stewart quickly became a target after the SEC began its inquiry into Waksal's transactions. Stewart told government investigators that she had previously given Peter Bacanovic what amounted to a stop-loss order that mandated he sell her ImClone stock if its price dropped to $60. She claimed that it was that preexisting order, not knowledge of Waksal's sales, that triggered her sales when ImClone stock dropped below that figure. This was important because, under SEC insider trading rules, a preexisting plan to sell stock would not be actionable as insider trading. A stop-loss order would constitute such a plan.

Bacanovic supported Stewart's testimony on this point, as did Douglas Faneuil, Bacanovic's assistant at Merrill Lynch, when questioned by SEC and FBI investigators. Faneuil and Bacanovic were later fired by Merrill Lynch when the firm's lawyers found conflicts in their stories over what had happened with Stewart's ImClone sock sale. Faneuil then pleaded guilty to a misdemeanor charge that he had lied to government investigators in supporting Stewart's story. Faneuil claimed that Bacanovic agreed to pay him a percentage of Bacanovic's bonus and to give him extra vacation time and airplane tickets to support the stop-loss story and to deny discussing Waksal's sales with Stewart. As a part of his guilty plea, Faneuil agreed to testify against Stewart and Bacanovic.

After Faneuil's guilty plea, Stewart and Bacanovic were indicted for making false statements to the government, obstruction of justice, and securities fraud. Stewart resigned as chairman and chief executive officer of Omnimedia and stepped down from her position as a director of the NYSE. Stewart also had to give up her regular guest appearances on the CBS *Early Show*. Omnimedia's share price dropped by 65 percent in the two months after this scandal broke out.

Peter Bacanovic was charged with trading on inside information on the ground that he had misappropriated information from Merrill Lynch about Waksal's sales that he then gave to Stewart. Martha Stewart was not indicted for insider trading, apparently because the law was not clear on whether the tippee of a misappropriater would violate Rule 10b-5. Moreover, Stewart had not spoken directly to Waksal, and it was not clear why Waksal was selling his stock. The SEC was not so shy, charging Stewart with insider trading in a related civil suit. The government indictment did make a claim, described in some reports as a trumped-up charge, that Stewart had made up the stop-loss order story in order to support the stock of her own company, which would be hammered in the market if she were found to have engaged in insider trading. This was a completely novel legal theory. Such novel theories are not normally made in criminal prosecutions, but all rules were off in the post-Enron hysteria.

The Stewart Circus Begins

The Martha Stewart investigation was certain to draw headlines, and that prospect was too tempting for Congress to resist. Congressional committees began intensive investigations of this massive less-than-$50,000 fraud, if it was fraud. The chairman of the House Committee on Energy and Commerce, W.J. ("Billy") Tauzin from Louisiana, demanded that Attorney General John Ashcroft pursue the case. Tauzin noted that congressional investigators had learned that Stewart had left a message with a secretary at ImClone for Waksal immediately after her conversation with Faneuil. The message read: "Something is going on with ImClone and she wants to know what. She is on her way to Mexico." That Mexican vacation was showcased at the trial when the government lawyers pointed out that Stewart wanted to deduct its $17,000 cost as a business expense, although that fact had nothing to do with the charges.

Stewart's indictment was a media circus. Her attorney, Robert Morvillo, complained that she was being targeted because of her high profile, asking: "Is it because she is a woman who has successfully competed in a man's world by virtue of her talent, hard work and demanding standards?" *Newsweek* magazine noted ominously that "Manhattan jurors have historically taken great glee in bringing down powerful arrogant women," citing the cases of Imelda Marcos, Bess Myerson, and Leona Helmsley.[31] The government denied claims that Stewart was being targeted because of her success. Stewart opened her own Web site to use as a medium to defend herself from the press and declared her innocence in a full-page advertisement in *USA Today*. She stated that she had simply returned a call from her broker and that the "government's attempts to criminalize these actions make no sense to me."[32] Stewart ducked questions on the case in a television interview conducted by Barbara Walters.

The government placed a woman, Karen Patton Seymour, in charge of Stewart's prosecution to neutralize the gender bias charge. Stewart was also spared the handcuffed perp walk because that might have engendered sympathy for her, evidencing just how cynical the government is in these arrests. Stewart appeared for her arraignment in what was breathlessly reported in the press as an "off-white trench coat and matching umbrella."

The Government's Case

Stewart was tried with Bacanovic in a federal courtroom in lower Manhattan, where the judicial system and courtroom sketch artists were almost overwhelmed with other full disclosure and corporate governance cases. The Adelphia trial was getting under way, the Tyco trial was in its sixth month, and Bernard Ebbers at WorldCom was brought in for his perp walk after being indicted during the Stewart trial. According to the government's indictment, Bacanovic had handled Waksal's ImClone stock sales from Florida, where Bacanovic was on vacation. Bacanovic, with Faneuil on the line, called Martha Stewart on December 27, 2001, to tell her about Waksal's sales. Stewart was on vacation, en route to Mexico in a private jet, and could not be reached. Faneuil left a message that Bacanovic had called and that he thought ImClone's stock price was "going to start trading downward."

During a refueling stop in San Antonio, Texas, Stewart was given Bacanovic's phone message by her New York assistant, Ann E. Armstrong. Stewart had Armstrong connect her to Merrill Lynch to speak to Bacanovic, but he was in Florida. Stewart then spoke to Faneuil and was told that Waksal and his daughter were trying to sell all of their ImClone stock. Stewart asked about the stock price twice in the call, and Faneuil said that the price was $58. She told Faneuil to sell all of her ImClone shares. This spared her some $46,000 in losses when the ImClone stock price dropped after the FDA's action was publicly announced. For billionaire Stewart, this was chump change, but it would be her undoing.

At this point, Stewart could be criticized for her sales, but wrongdoing would have been difficult to prove under the SEC's insider trading rule. It was her subsequent statements to government investigators that got her into trouble. Irony would abound in this case, but of particular note is that Stewart was under no obligation to speak to those investigators. She could simply have advised them that she was exercising her Fifth Amendment privilege. Had she done so, the SEC would have been left with a doubtful insider trading claim that probably would have been settled, been dismissed on motion or on appeal, or, at worse, resulted in a fine that would have been inflated by her celebrity status but not lethal.

Stewart was interviewed by investigators from the SEC, FBI, and the U.S. attorney's office. That level of attention should have alerted her that she was a high-profile target. An average insider trader avoiding losses of $46,000 would not have attracted that kind of attention. No formal record of her interview was made, but the investigators testified that Stewart said that she had agreed with Bacanovic on December 20, 2001, during a review of possible sales in her portfolio for year-end tax sales, that he should sell her ImClone shares if the price dropped to $60. Bacanovic supported this statement, asserting that he had urged her to sell the shares on December 20, when ImClone stock was trading at $64, but Stewart thought that the new ImClone drug would be a success and did not want to sell. Bacanovic claimed he persuaded her to enter the stop-loss order as a precaution.

Stewart denied knowledge of Bacanovic's phone message that was relayed to her on December 27 concerning ImClone's stock trading down. According to the investigators, she said that she had spoken to Bacanovic about selling her ImClone stock on that day, telling him to sell it because she did not want to be bothered on her vacation. In fact, she had spoken to Faneuil, not Bacanovic, and they had discussed Waksal's sales. Stewart said that she and Bacanovic had discussed Omnimedia's and Kmart's stock in that call when in fact she had not spoken to him at all. The government indictment charged that this was part of a conspiracy between Stewart and Bacanovic to conceal what had actually happened. Stewart denied knowing that Waksal had an account with Bacanovic and said she had no recollection of being told that the Waksals were selling their ImClone shares.

The government charged that Bacanovic altered a worksheet containing a list of Stewart's stocks held at Merrill Lynch on December 21, 2001. He had made some notes on that worksheet about Stewart's holdings, including an entry stating "@ 60" next to her ImClone holdings, which suggested support for Stewart's claim that she had earlier given a stop-loss order at that price for the ImClone stock. The indictment claimed that this entry was in an ink different from that of other entries. According to the government, this evidenced that the entry was made after the others and was a further part of the conspiracy to conceal the actual events. This entry resulted in an extended battle between experts for both sides over what the ink differences meant. A questioned documents examiner, Larry Stewart (no kin to Martha), testified on this issue for the government. He was the director of the U.S. Secret Service crime laboratory and claimed to be the only real expert in the world on such matters. However, the jury was unable to conclude that the "@60" notation was added to cover up what actually happened.

Faneuil managed to provide evidence of Stewart's meanness by testifying about her abruptness on the phone and her complaints about the music played on the Merrill Lynch phone system. He said that Stewart sounded "like a lion roaring underwater."[33] The defense lawyers hammered at Faneuil's credibility by focusing on his drug use and the sweetheart deal given to him by prosecutors after he agreed to implicate Stewart, but he stuck to his second story. More damaging testimony came from Stewart's assistant, Ann Armstrong. She testified that, after the government started its investigation, Stewart changed the phone log of the message left by Bacanovic on December 27 to read "Peter Bacanovic re imclone," cutting out a statement that

Bacanovic thought ImClone would be trading downward. Reconsidering that action, Stewart shortly afterward had Armstrong change the log back to its original wording. Armstrong began crying on the witness stand while describing this incident, which made the whole episode look especially damning. The government argued that this act evidenced consciousness of guilt on Stewart's part.

The testimony of Mariana Pasternak, Stewart's companion on her Mexican vacation, was sometimes uncertain and reluctant, but she let drop a nugget by asserting that Stewart had said, "Isn't it nice to have brokers who tell you those things?"[34] Under cross-examination, Pasternak admitted that she was not certain that Stewart had actually used those words, but the damage was done nonetheless. Pasternak's husband had sold 10,000 shares of ImClone on the day after his wife learned of Stewart's sales.

There was good news for Stewart at the trial. The federal judge hearing the case, Miriam Goldman Cedarbaum, threw out the charge that Stewart had committed securities fraud by lying to the government in order to support the price of Omnimedia stock. That charge would have carried the most jail time—ten years. Buoyed by that victory, Stewart's attorneys put on only a cursory defense. One witness, Heidi DeLuca, Stewart's business manager, testified that she had discussed the stop-loss order with Bacanovic, but Bacanovic had denied such a conversation when interviewed by government investigators before the trial. The government pointed out that Stewart gave DeLuca a $20,000 raise, which the prosecutors claimed was a reward for supporting Stewart's testimony. The defense rested its case without either Stewart or Bacanovic testifying.

Stewart was criticized in the press for some of the finery she wore to the trial, including expensive designer handbags and a mink scarf. Every article of visible clothing that Stewart wore was described in detail in press reports. Stewart did receive support at the trial from some celebrities, including comedian Bill Cosby, who sat behind her at the trial. This was an old trial lawyer's trick, employed most successfully by Edward Bennett Williams, the Washington, DC, lawyer. In 1957 he brought in Joe Louis, the famous African-American boxer, to sit behind James Hoffa, the legendary head of the Teamsters Union who was being tried for bribery, in front of a largely black jury hearing the government's case against Hoffa. That tactic was effective and Hoffa was acquitted.

Stewart took the celebrity parade a bit too far with the appearance of Rosie O'Donnell, the actress and talk show hostess. O'Donnell had just finished her own stalemated trial that involving charges and countercharges of mismanagement of the magazine *Rosie,* named after herself. Like Stewart, O'Donnell rose to fame on a persona of niceness, but that trial exposed a mean streak and abusive behavior toward underlings. O'Donnell could not stay for Stewart's entire trial because she had to fly to California to participate in a mass of gay marriages then drawing headlines in San Francisco. California Governor

Arnold Schwarzenegger ordered his attorney general to stop the issuing of those licenses, and the marriages were annulled by the California Supreme Court. After delivering their verdict, the jurors in the Stewart trial asserted that the celebrity appearances did not leave a favorable impression.

After three days of jury deliberations, both Stewart and Bacanovic were found guilty of the remaining charges. At age sixty-two, after a lifetime of achievement and obstacles overcome, Martha Stewart was a convicted felon. In addition to prison, she would lose her right to vote and would be barred from further serving as an officer of a public company. By the time of the trial, Stewart had lost $400 million in the declining value of her Omnimedia shares. Public shareholders in Omnimedia were battered as well. Omnimedia's stock dropped 23 percent after the guilty verdict, all for a trade that saved her $46,000.

Aftermath

The Martha Stewart case abounded with irony. There would have been no prosecution if Stewart had not talked to investigators. The fact that she failed to take that basic precaution is inexplicable, particularly since she was represented by Wachtell, Lipton, Rosen & Katz, a high-profile law firm, during the interviews. Surely, her lawyers were aware of the entrapment techniques commonly used by government investigators, a technique borrowed from the "perjury trap" prosecutions of mobsters in the 1950s. Numerous insider trading cases have been referred by the SEC to criminal authorities when inside traders deny, as they almost inevitably do, that they traded on inside information.

Dr. Waksal would be saving no further lives from his jail cell, but Erbitux was approved by the FDA in September 2003, after showing very promising results against colon cancer. The drug was expected to generate over $1 billion in sales annually for ImClone, although initial sales proved to be a little slower than expected because the average treatment cost was $160,000. Interesting is the fact that, while Waksal and Stewart were selling their ImClone shares, Carl Icahn, the corporate raider, was buying ImClone shares and had profits in his position of $250 million in May 2004 when ImClone stock rose to over $70.

Robert Morvillo, Martha Stewart's attorney at trial, came under criticism for refusing to put Stewart on the stand to testify and for turning down some plea deals that might have kept her out of jail. Alan Dershowitz, the gadfly Harvard law school professor, was especially vociferous in his criticism of Morvillo. In an article on the editorial page of the *Wall Street Journal,* Dershowitz also criticized the lawyers at Wachtell, Lipton for allowing Stewart to be interviewed by government investigators before her indictment. Dershowitz was in turn blasted by Michael F. Armstrong and other prominent defense lawyers for second-guessing Morvillo's judgment that Stewart should not testify. They pointed out that Dershowitz did not know what facts Morvillo was dealing with in making that decision. The plea deals were apparently turned down because prosecutors could not assure that Stewart would receive any less jail time than that which she was subject to after the trial. In any event, it turned out the time she was given was no more than that in the plea deals.

More drama arose from the discovery that a juror had lied on his questionnaire concerning prior misconduct. The judge denied a defense motion for a new trial on the basis of that information. Raising another issue was the indictment of Larry Stewart, the government's handwriting expert, for perjury. He was charged with falsely testifying at the Stewart trial about what he did to ascertain that the "@60" notation was added at a later date. The defense again sought a new trial, but the government opposed that motion because the jury had not convicted on the "@60" issue on which that witness had testified. A jury also acquitted Larry Stewart of the perjury charges, concluding that his false statements did not affect the Martha Stewart jury. The judge agreed with the government and denied a new trial.

Stewart was sentenced to five months in prison and five months of house arrest and fined $30,000. Bacanovic received the same prison sentence but was fined only $4,000. Douglas Faneuil, as a reward for his testimony, was fined only $2,000 and given no jail time. In a statement made immediately after the sentencing, Stewart lamented that this "small personal matter" had been "blown all out of proportion" in an "almost fatal circus" in the media.[35] She noted its devastating effect on the shareholders of her company and that 200 employees had to be laid off. In perhaps the unkindest cut of all, Stewart's former friend, Senator Hillary Rodham Clinton, publicly announced that she was donating to charity the $1,000 campaign contribution that she had received from Stewart.

Omnimedia's stock rose by almost 40 percent after Martha Stewart's sentencing. Stewart hit the talk show circus seeking to restore her public image and the fortunes of her shareholders. She then decided to serve her sentence without awaiting the outcome of her appeal and was assigned to "Camp Cupcake," a minimum security prison in West Virginia. Before surrendering, Stewart signed a new employment contract with Omnimedia under which she would receive an annual salary of $900,000, an expense allowance of $100,000, a bonus that could range from $500,000 to $1.35 million, and a signing fee of $200,000. The value of Omnimedia jumped sharply after the announcement of the merger of Kmart and Sears.

Martha Stewart's emergence from prison in March 2005 set off another media storm. Her picture graced the cover of *Newsweek* magazine, as well as a full-page advertisement by CNBC in the *Wall Street Journal* trumpeting a program about her. Stewart also announced while still in prison that she would be hosting a variation of the *Apprentice* television program made popular by Donald Trump and which involved the cold-blooded firing of individuals competing for a job with his organization. The price of Martha Stewart Living Omnimedia Inc. stock quadrupled while she was in prison, pushing her fortune up to the $1 billion mark before retreating. Stewart even turned her imprisonment into a fashion statement, wearing a poncho in public appearances that was knitted by a fellow inmate. Stewart's house arrest was extended for three weeks for some infraction of the rules governing her confinement, possibly an unauthorized snowmobile ride.

The government indicted two other individuals who sold ImClone stock in December 2001 after allegedly being tipped by Sam Waksal. One of those defendants did not appear to be a particularly dangerous criminal. He was Dr. Zvi Y. Fuks, chairman of the Department of Radiation Oncology at the Memorial Sloan-Kettering Cancer Center. The government did not explain the long delay in bringing those indictments or their timing after Stewart's release, but speculation arose that Sam Waksal was trying to cut his sentence so he could get back on the social circuit with Stewart by ratting out others.

Analysts' Scandals

The Role of the Analyst

The full disclosure system sought to impose "gatekeeper" status on financial analysts. The analysts were supposed to examine the complex and lengthy financial statements that public companies filed with the SEC and then issue a report providing the public with the analysts' views on the desirability of the stock as an investment. Analysts "followed" particular companies after their initial report so that investors were kept up to date. The analysts set targets ("expectations") for a company's future growth for each quarter and reviewed the company's cash flows, debt burden, and other financial measurements. The analysts used various "signals" to alert investors about the stock, including "buy," "hold," or "sell."

Several analysts might follow the same stock, and their "consensus estimate" was the bar that the management of a company had to meet for favorable recommendations. Failure to meet those targets in even a single quarter would cause a sharp drop in the price of the company's stock as "momentum" investors rushed to abandon that company and move on to another investment. Mutual funds and other money managers were also quick to dump a stock because they were graded on their quarterly results. Adding to this vicious cycle, company executives, rather than pursuing long-term business goals, were motivated by their stock options to produce the ever-increasing quarterly results demanded by analysts; otherwise, the price of their stock would drop, rendering their options worthless. This led to earnings management or "smoothing," as it was sometimes euphemistically called, through cookie jar reserves, channel stuffing, and other tactics. If product growth was lagging behind analysts' expectations, management bought another company to improve the numbers immediately, whatever the cost. If debt was too high, management moved it off the balance sheet in order to improve the numbers immediately. If cash flows were not meeting analysts' expectations, structured finance was used to provide the funds as disguised debt. Enron and other scandals revealed such activity on a massive scale.

Professional stock analysts have long been the subjects of criticism. As Benjamin Graham and David Dodd noted in their classic 1940 book *Security Analysis,*

> The advance of security analysis proceeded uninterruptedly until about 1927, covering a long period in which increasing attention was paid on all sides to financial reports and statistical data. But the "new era" commencing in 1927 involved at bottom the abandonment of the analytical approach; and while emphasis was still seemingly placed on facts and figures, these were manipulated by a sort of pseudoanalysis to support the delusions of the period.[36]

Graham and Dodd noted that analysts could not ensure investor profits, particularly in a speculative market where luck played as much of a role as the insight provided by an analyst whose "position in the speculative field is at best uncertain and somewhat lacking in professional dignity. It is as though the analyst and Dame Fortune were playing a duet on the speculative piano, with the fickle goddess calling all the tunes."[37] Graham and Dodd further cautioned:

> It is a matter of great moment to the analyst that the facts are fairly presented, and this means that he must be highly critical of accounting methods. Finally, he must concern himself with all corporate policies affecting the security owner, for the value of the issue which he analyzes may be largely dependent upon the acts of the management. In this category are included questions of capitalization set-up, of dividend and expansion policies, of managerial compensation, and even of continuing or liquidating an unprofitable business.
>
> On these matters of varied import, security analysis may be competent to express critical judgments, looking to the avoidance of mistakes, to the correction of abuses, and to the better protection of those owning bonds or stocks.[38]

The analysts at the end of the twentieth century would provide none of those services; instead, they engaged in the "pseudoanalysis" that Graham and Dodd decried.

Supervising the Analyst

Most of the best-known financial analysts work for large broker-dealers and investment bankers with underwriting operations. That relationship creates a conflict of interest because the investment bankers do not want one of their own firm's analysts disparaging the stock of a client. Further, analysts might have access to nonpublic information from their investment banking cohorts that could be used to aid their analysis. For decades, these conflicts of interest were alleviated by sealing off the analysts from the investment bankers by a "Chinese wall," which isolated information flows. Analysts could be "brought over" the Chinese wall to aid investment bankers in connection with a client the analyst was covering. In such an instance, the analyst had to cease coverage of the stock until the investment banking activity was disclosed to the public or became nonmaterial. In addition, "restricted lists" were used to prevent analysts from issuing reports on clients with ongoing initial public offerings so that those reports were not used to manipulate the offering. Another device, "watch lists," were used to identify investment banking clients that might have a conflict with analysts' opinions, in which case extra supervision was applied to prevent abuse.

These arrangements were supported by the SEC, but raised some interesting issues, such as whether analysts should continue to promote a stock after the investment bankers received nonpublic adverse information about the issuer. Presumably, the Chinese wall would prevent the analysts from learning that information, but clients relying on a report urging them to buy or hold the stock would be rather unhappy when prices dropped. In addition, analysts' compensation depended, at least in some measure, on how well their employer firm performed as a whole. A large component of that performance was often investment banking business. For that reason, an analyst would be reluctant to disparage an investment banking client.

Market Solution

A market solution to these conflicts appeared in the form of "discount brokers," which appeared in large numbers after the SEC unfixed brokerage commissions in May 1975, an event that came to be known as May Day on Wall Street. Brokerage commissions had first been fixed under the so-called Buttonwood agreement, which was signed, as legend has it, under a buttonwood tree in 1792 by a group of brokers trying to control the then fledgling stock market in New York and became the basis for the creation of the NYSE. The unfixing of commissions by the SEC allowed the creation of discount brokers that charged reduced commissions, made possible in part because they did not provide expensive research. Brokerage firms employing analysts to do research and provide investment advice became known as full-service firms. Charles Schwab & Co., a leading discount broker, built itself into one of the largest broker-dealers in United States on the basis of its claims that research in the full-service firms was conflicted and did not justify their higher commissions. As the Supreme Court noted, "Schwab is known as a 'discount' broker because of the low commissions it charges. Schwab can afford to charge lower commissions than full-service brokerage firms because it does not provide investment advice or analysis, but merely executes the purchase and sell orders placed by its customers."[39]

The existence of the discount broker seemed to solve the problem of analysts' conflicts. Investors picking individual stocks could go to Schwab or some other discount broker and trade cheaply without the assistance of conflicted research, or they could use the much more expensive services of a full-service firm that provided conflicting advice. The doctrine of unintended consequences intervened to limit that solution. In fact, the creation of the discount broker only worsened the analysts' conflicts. Full-service brokers were forced to place increased emphasis on their investment banking and trading activities because their commission business was declining as a result of competition from the discount brokers. The analysts then shifted their activities to become supporters of the investment banking side of the business, which was more lucrative than the commission business in any event. Equally interesting, Charles Schwab, which for a time had a capitalization greater than Merrill Lynch, began providing advice to customers during the market run-up in the 1990s.

Regulation FD

The Securities Act of 1933 prohibited secret compensation or benefits from issuers to analysts in order to induce them to tout the issuer's stock. That proved ineffective in preventing analysts' abuses. Arthur Levitt, chairman of the SEC during the market run-up in the 1990s, wanted more regulation of analysts. In a speech before the Economic Club of New York in October 1999, he described a "web of dysfunctional relationships" on Wall Street. Among other things, Levitt contended that many financial analysts were "a bit too eager to report what looks like a frog is really a prince." Levitt renewed his criticism after the Enron scandal, noting that, even after Enron's stock collapsed to seventy-five cents a share, twelve of seventeen analysts covering that stock were still rating it as either a hold or a buy. In fact, after the departure of Skilling and the October 16 revelations that sent Enron's stock into a free fall, sixteen of seventeen securities analysts covering Enron still rated it a "strong buy" or "buy." Levitt asserted that unsophisticated investors could not understand the role of analysts or what the analysts' signals meant, while more sophisticated investors did. The analysts' "signals" were indeed confusing. Salomon Smith Barney, for example, used a five-category rating system for stocks: buy, outperform, neutral, underperform, and sell. Other firms used different signals, and even when signals were the same their definitions varied among firms.

Financial analysts did, for a time, add value in the shaky world of full disclosure. While that value depended to some degree on their ability to analyze the often inflated financial reports filed with the SEC, the real value they added was their ability to obtain information that was not generally available to the public. Some analysts were aggressive in looking behind the numbers published by the companies in their SEC reports. Those analysts would befriend management and cultivate relationships with individual employees to obtain "color" and other "soft" information on the company's operations. In the case of Raymond Dirks, the analyst who exposed a massive fraud at Equity Funding in the 1970s, those contacts allowed him to make that exposure.[40]

The information being sought through these channels was not available from management press conferences touting the company's stock or from the dry, dated reports filed with the SEC. This effort to seek information outside the filed reports raised questions of whether this soft information was undermining the SEC's full disclosure system because of the unequal access to information gained by analysts in their investigations. The SEC lost its attempt in the case against Raymond Dirks to prevent analysts from obtaining information from company executives. As a consequence, analysts continued to meet with, and be briefed by, management and employees. The SEC has a long memory, however, and years later its activist chairman, Arthur Levitt, sought to reverse the Supreme Court's decision through a regulation somewhat laughably called SEC Regulation FD, the FD standing for "full disclosure." This regulation prohibited analysts from obtaining information from the officers of companies they were following unless the information was supplied to the press at the same time.

Regulation FD was a slap at the Supreme Court, but more importantly it choked off the only independent sources of information available to analysts. In a bit of twisted government logic, the SEC concluded that the market should not receive information that will efficiently value a company unless everyone has the information at precisely the same time. Levitt claimed that, after its adoption, Regulation FD and technology were providing investors with an information bonanza. In fact, that bonanza proved to be information supplied only by financial statements that had been massively manipulated, as demonstrated by the hundreds of restatements made by public companies at the end of the last century. Moreover, a study by the National Bureau of Economic Research concluded that Regulation FD had resulted in a significant loss of analysts' coverage for small companies, making it harder for them to market their stock. Regulation FD resulted in a 17 percent drop in the analysts' coverage of small companies and a 5 percent drop in coverage of midsize companies.

In one of its first prosecutions under Regulation FD, the SEC charged that Richard J. Kogan, the chairman and chief executive officer of Schering-Plough Corporation, met privately with analysts and portfolio managers and "through a combination of spoken language, tone, emphasis and demeanor, Kogan disclosed negative and material, nonpublic information regarding Schering's earnings prospects, including that analysts' earnings estimates for Schering's 2002 third-quarter were too high, and that Schering's earnings in 2003 would significantly decline."[41] Apparently, full disclosure now extends to facial expressions. One company, Siebel Systems Inc., was caught twice violating Regulation FD. The first time, its chief executive officer, Tom Siebel, was charged with making selective disclosures at an investor conference. The company was fined $250,000 for that slip. In the second instance, company officials were privately providing money managers optimistic outlooks that were inconsistent with their public statements of pessimism. The U.S. Chamber of Commerce was supporting Siebel Systems in claiming as a defense to its disclosures that Regulation FD was an unconstitutional infringement of free speech. Not surprisingly, a group of law professors filed a brief in opposition to the Chamber and in support of Regulation FD. They support free speech everywhere except in corporate America. The federal district court judge hearing the case, George Daniels, then embarrassed the SEC by throwing out the case and criticizing the agency for being overly aggressive. The judge noted that the SEC's interpretation of the rule could prevent the dissemination of relevant information needed by investors. In another bizarre case, the SEC charged Flowserve Corp. and its chief executive officer C. Scott Greer, as well as another executive, for repeating to analysts a forecast that had previously been made publicly. The defendants settled the case by agreeing to pay the SEC $400,000.

Stock Touts

Denied any informational advantage as a product they could sell, analysts were left to tout stocks like snake oil salesmen. A *Wall Street Journal* article in 1998 noted that analysts had become "cheerleaders" for their company's investment bankers. Mary Meeker was given the title of "queen of the net" by *Barron's* magazine in 1998 for her hyping of initial public offerings by Internet companies that were underwritten by her firm, Morgan Stanley. Many of those stocks turned out to be disasters for investors. One of the stocks that Meeker was recommending as a buy, even as its stock was plunging, was Priceline.com. The price of that company's stock reached $134 per share in May 1999 but dropped back down to single digits. Those recommendations did not seem to affect Meeker's standing in the industry since she was named Morgan Stanley's coleader of tech sector research in 2004. Another bullish analyst during the bubble was Abby Joseph Cohen at Goldman Sachs. She too was undeterred by the collapse of the market that had damaged investors so badly. In February 2004, Cohen was predicting that the Dow would hit 11,800 within a year. That would exceed the highest peak of 11,722 that the Dow had reached during the bubble that ended in 2000. Cohen's view seemed reckless at the time, but the Dow was coursing toward that level after the elections in 2004. The Dow was just under 1000 points short of reaching that record in February 2005, but it was still not a bad recovery from the low points reached after the bursting of the bubble in 2000 and the terrorist attacks on September 11, 2001. The Dow was showing further strength in March 2005, reaching 10940 on March 5.

The enthusiasm of analysts for recommending stock purchases demonstrated that they had dropped their role as analysts and become mere touts. Most analysts did not make underperform or sell recommendations until a company was in bankruptcy. The analysts were mostly buy side only. Eliot Spitzer, New York's attorney general, noted that Salomon Smith Barney gave no sell and only fifteen underperform ratings for over 1,000 stocks, many of which had plunged in value. Another study found that in the year 2000 there was a buy-to-sell ratio on analysts' recommendations of 100 to one. A separate SEC examination found several analysts at eight of the top Wall Street firms recommending shares as a buy while their own firms were selling the stock. Sixteen analysts at those firms issued buy recommendations for stocks that they themselves bought in initial public offerings. This might evidence they had a belief in their own research, but also raised concerns that they were "scalping" by making the recommendations in order to increase the profits from their personal holdings.

Conflicts Grow

The analysts became allied with their investment banking colleagues, despite the Chinese walls at the firms, as their analytic value diminished. Analysts became promoters for the stock of their firm's investment banking clients. The compensation of the analysts was tied to the profits of the investment bankers, giving them a stake in ensuring that the investment banking clients were kept happy by positive recommendations for their stock. Analysts were subject to dismissal if their reports offended investment banking clients. Marvin Roffman, an analyst at Janney Montgomery Scott, found that out the hard way after he criticized Donald Trump's Taj Mahal gambling project in 1990. Trump had him fired. Roffman sued and settled for $750,000 from his employer and an additional amount from Trump.

The SEC's general counsel, David Becker, declared before Enron's collapse: "Let's be plain. Broker-dealers employ analysts because they help sell securities. There is nothing nefarious or dishonorable in that, but no one should be under the illusion that brokers employ analysts simply as a public service."[42] Another problem was the herd mentality that existed among Wall Street analysts. The concept of "consensus estimates" suggested a degree of uniformity. Wall Street tends to go in one direction until the market change is too dramatic to ignore. This means that when the stock market is going up, the herd assumes it will continue to rise until after the downturn has long since become apparent to the rest of the world. Similarly, when interest rates are low, Wall Street assumes they will stay that way and enters into strategies that will cause losses when rates rise. Analysts, like reporters, read each other's reports and often adopt each other's views. A study found that analyst recommendations were at their most positive as the stock market peaked in 2000 and that optimism continued into 2001, long after the market downturn had become apparent to other market watchers.[43] The analysts also had other flaws. They were often wrong. Studies showed that analysts' predicted corporate earnings were off by 50 percent on average during the first half of the 1990s. Management sought to correct that problem in the second half of the decade by managing earnings to meet analysts' expectations.

Citigroup

Sandy Weill, as head of Citigroup, was elected to the board of directors of the Federal Reserve Bank of New York in 2001—a great honor—but he was discovering that leading a diversified financial services firm had its downsides. Weill and a Citigroup unit, Salomon Smith Barney, were under attack from Eliot Spitzer, the New York attorney general, for abuses resulting from the conflicts of interests between investment analysts and investment bankers in that group.

Jack Grubman, who worked at Salomon Smith Barney, was said by the NYSE to be "the preeminent telecom analyst in the industry." Salomon Smith Barney received almost $800 million in investment banking fees from firms covered by Grubman's reports. He claimed an even higher figure in internal messages at his firm, asserting that he was involved in obtaining over $1.1 billion in investment banking revenues while posing as an independent analyst. Grubman was well rewarded for his work, being paid $20 million annually between 1998 and 2001. This made him one of the most highly paid analysts on Wall Street, even though he was ranked as the worst of Salomon Smith Barney's over 100 analysts by the firm's own retail sales brokers. One broker said that Grubman was a "poster child for conspicuous conflicts of interest," and another said, "I hope Smith Barney enjoyed the investment banking fees he generated, because they come at the expense of retail clients."[44]

Between 1998 and 2002, Grubman covered up to thirty-six stocks. "The stock prices of many of those companies dropped dramatically and 16 went bankrupt. Yet, . . . Grubman never issued any Sell ratings and assigned only two Under Perform ratings."[45] Grubman admitted in an internal e-mail that he wanted to downgrade several of the companies that he was rating, which were heading toward bankruptcy, but got a "huge pushback" from the investment bankers. Grubman's e-mails contained several cynical comments which evidenced that he was rating stocks to keep the clients happy and not on the basis of any fundamental or technical analysis. In one e-mail, he called a company a "pig" and warned that its stock was going to zero, even though he had just published a positive research note on the company. Analysts at Salomon Smith Barney were told to adjust their earnings expectations downward for investment banking clients so that the companies would meet projections and thereby experience an increase in their stock price as investors responded.[46]

More spectacular was the change in Grubman's views on AT&T. Grubman had maintained a neutral recommendation on AT&T, which was actually a quite negative view in the bubble era. Sandy Weill, the head of Citigroup, was a member of AT&T's board of directors, and AT&T managers complained to him about Grubman's position.[47] The AT&T managers expressed particular offense that Grubman had not included AT&T in his list of the most important telecommunications companies of the future at an industry trade show. Grubman wrote a letter of apology for that omission. Weill asked Grubman to take a "fresh look" at AT&T for a possible upgrade, which Grubman proceeded to do, conducting an apparently thorough review. Weill continued to press Grubman on his fresh look as that process was under way. In updating Weill on his progress, Grubman sought Weill's help in getting Grubman's children admitted to the 92nd St. Y preschool program, which in the world of the New York elite was equivalent to an Ivy League admission. After noting that there are "no bounds for what you do for your children," Grubman issued a thirty-six-page report upgrading AT&T's stock. That enabled Salomon Smith Barney to become lead underwriter and joint book manager on a $10.62 billion tracking stock underwriting by AT&T. That role produced $45 million in investment banking fees for Citigroup.

Later e-mails from Grubman stated that he had been pressured to upgrade his rating on AT&T by Weill and that he "used Sandy to get my kids into 92nd St. Y pre-school (which is harder than Harvard)." Grubman also noted that the chief executive officer of AT&T served as an outside director on Citigroup's board. Weill needed that director's vote in a showdown over control with John Reed, who had shared power with Weill at Citigroup after the merger of Citibank and Travelers Insurance. Reed was shouldered aside by Weill in a tense confrontation before the Citigroup board of directors. Grubman gleefully boasted that he and Weill had played AT&T "like a fiddle."

For his part, Weill called a board member of the 92nd St. Y and said he would be "very appreciative" if the school admitted Grubman's children. The board member understood that his appreciation would be expressed in the form of a contribution to the school. Not surprisingly, Grubman's children were allowed to matriculate at this little Harvard, and as a thank you, Citigroup donated $1 million to the 92nd St. Y. Grubman's gratitude did not last long. "On May 17, 2000, three weeks after the [AT&T] IPO, two months after his children were admitted to the 92nd St. Y preschool, and after AT&T announced disappointing earnings, Grubman issued a research report in which he compared AT&T with WorldCom," which was then in its death throes.[48]

Eliot Spitzer, the New York attorney general, broke this story to the press, setting off another media frenzy. Grubman later claimed that he had made up the story about his children's admission to the 92nd St. Y, but that assertion did not dispel the massive regulatory problems for Citigroup that resulted from those disclosures. The Grubman e-mail messages were more exhibits of the effect on Wall Street of the Internet. Often unguarded and written in casual and exaggerated language common to traders and others working on Wall Street, these messages proved to be a bonanza for prosecutors. Salacious e-mails sent to Grubman by Carol Cutler, who was trying to persuade Grubman to leave his wife, also became required reading for regulators. Interns hired by Spitzer pawed through thousands of e-mail messages searching for any scrap of dirt. Regulators even forced the large brokerage firms to develop search engines to uncover inflammatory messages in the billions of internal e-mails generated by their employees that could then be used against the firms in their prosecutions.

Deleting e-mails was not an option. In December 2002, five brokerage firms—JP Morgan Securities Inc. later agreed to pay $2.1 million to settle such charges. Citigroup-Smith Barney, Deutsche Bank AG, Goldman Sachs Group, Morgan Stanley, and U.S. Bankcorp, Piper Jaffray Inc.—agreed to pay fines totaling $8.25 million for failing to retain e-mail messages.

Spitzer additionally targeted Merrill Lynch after he discovered that an analyst at Merrill Lynch was recommending shares publicly in order to assist the firm's investment banking business even though he was disparaging the same shares privately in e-mails. The center of that investigation was Henry Blodget, a well-known Internet analyst who headed Merrill Lynch's Internet research group. Blodget became famous after predicting that Amazon.com's stock would increase to $400, which seemed incredible at the time. That prediction came true even much sooner than Blodget had predicted. Blodget claimed in internal e-mails that various stocks that he had recommended to the public were actually "crap," "a dog," and "a piece of junk." He received an e-mail from an institutional client asking what was good about GoTo.com, other than investment banking fees. Although Blodget was publicly touting the stock at the time, he replied "nothing" and called the stock a "powder keg." Blodget referred to the stock of Internet Capital Group Inc. as a disaster in an e-mail message at a time when Merrill Lynch was favorably recommending it in research reports.

Spitzer fined Merrill Lynch $100 million after Blodget's e-mails were discovered. Merrill Lynch agreed to state in its research reports whether it has an investment banking relationship with a corporate client and provide other information concerning the independence of its recommendations. According to Kurt Eichenwald, a *New York Times* reporter who wrote a book on Enron, Merrill Lynch fired John Olson, an analyst who was rating Enron negatively before its demise. That firing came after Andrew Fastow complained of that coverage and threatened to withhold Enron's investment banking business. Enron's rating by Merrill Lynch's analysts was then upgraded. Fastow imposed a similar punishment on Don Dufresne, an analyst at Salomon Smith Barney. The firing of Olson was in addition to the embarrassments from Phua Young, the Merrill Lynch analyst who exchanged expensive wine gifts with Dennis Kozlowski at Tyco and had Tyco investigate his fiancée. A federal judge dismissed investor suits against Merrill Lynch on statute of limitations and other grounds. In another action, the NYSE fined Merrill Lynch $625,000 after one of its analysts, Peter Caruso, told selected clients in advance that he was downgrading his views on Home Depot Inc. This was said to be a violation of SEC Regulation FD. Another Merrill Lynch employee, Janina Casey, was fined $150,000 for leaking the same report in advance of publication to selected institutional clients. Those clients sold several million shares of the company's stock. Two Merrill Lynch analysts in London were suspended in 2004 pending an investigation of whether they had selectively leaked their research report on J. Sainsbury PLC before its public release.

IPO Abuses

By this point, Eliot Spitzer was becoming a national figure. He was selected as the "Crusader of the Year" by *Time* magazine, and the London *Times* designated him as its "Business Person of the Year." Spitzer was a graduate of Harvard Law School and an editor of its law review. He clerked for a federal judge and then worked at the same New York law firm where Mark Belnick of Tyco had been a partner. Spitzer then moved to the Manhattan district attorney's office before running a losing campaign for New York attorney general in 1994. Undaunted, he ran for that post again in 1998 and beat the incumbent, Republican Dennis Vacco, by a narrow margin. Spitzer could claim no humble beginnings. Spitzer reported as income of almost $1 million in 2002. His wealthy father contributed $9 million to Eliot's two campaigns, giving rise to charges that Spitzer was evading New York laws limiting campaign contributions. That did not deter him from becoming scolding businesses and indicting those who engaged in any practice even slightly questionable. Spitzer's wife, Silda A. Wall, also a lawyer, gave up practice to run their own foundation, which mixed nicely with Eliot's political ambitions.

Eliot Spitzer charged investment bankers with "spinning" shares to clients from hot issue IPOs in order to obtain their investment banking business. Spinning was not a new invention. Such allocations were part of the abuses in the 1920s, when JP Morgan & Co. had "preferred" lists for its hot issue allocations that included politicians, corporate executives, and other prominent figures. Among the honorees were Calvin Coolidge, the former president; General John Pershing, leader of American forces during World War I; William Woodin, who would become secretary of the Treasury; F.H. Ecker, president of the Metropolitan Life Insurance Co.; Albert Wiggin, chairman of Chase National Bank; Charles E. Mitchell, president of National City Bank, which had its own preferred list; Richard E. Whitney, an official at the NYSE; and Charles Lindbergh, the famous flyer.

The spinning schemes attacked by Spitzer were actually encouraged by SEC regulations. Under SEC rules, all shares in a public offering must be sold at the offering price set by the investment banking firm acting as the lead underwriter, whatever the actual market price of the stock. In order to ensure a sale of all shares, the underwriter sets the offering price just below the estimated market value of the stock. If underwriters underestimate demand, the issues may be underpriced and oversubscribed. These "hot" issues trade up immediately. The underwriters may select the buyers who may purchase the shares, providing an almost automatic, certain, and large profit to the recipient in a hot issue. The underwriters perceived that some value could be gained by allocating the shares to officers of other companies who could direct business their way. Allocations in hot issues were usually extended to favored customers of the underwriters, "a practice popularly known as 'friends and families,'"[49] and later as "spinning." Eliot Spitzer deemed that rather common business practice wrongful.

The SEC conducted a study of hot IPO issues in 1959 and another in the 1970s. The SEC expressed concern that the public was receiving insufficient information about such issues, which often plunged in value as quickly as they had risen during the offering. To deal with concerns that executives working for underwriters were grabbing hot issue allocations for their own account, the National Association of Securities Dealers Inc. (NASD) issued a "Free Riding and Withholding Interpretation" that prohibited IPO allocations to underwriters and their "affiliated persons" (employees or their relatives) in a hot issue. This interpretation further prohibited hot issue allocations to money managers in a position to direct that business to the underwriter. Such practices had been the subject of an article in 1984 by Jay R. Ritter.[50]

This did not stop the spinning of shares to investment banking clients. In one such transaction in 2000, Michael Dell, the head of Dell Computer, demanded 150,000 shares of an IPO by the Corvis Corp. The SEC was on notice that spinning was occurring even before Spitzer attacked. In an action brought against Stuart James Co. in 1993, the SEC charged that firm with providing favored customers with allocations in hot issues. Those shares were sold to other customers who were induced to buy through high-pressure sales pitches. The SEC and NASD were investigating other such practices in 1997, long before Spitzer jumped in, but they apparently were not too concerned even though they had primary jurisdiction over such issues. This left the door open for Spitzer, and he shouldered his way in with his litigation against the telecom executives.

Eliot Spitzer's suit against Bernard Ebbers at WorldCom and Philip Anschutz at Qwest for spinning targeted other telecom executives, including Stephen Garofalo, founder of Metromedia Fiber Network Inc.; Clark McLeod, founder of McLeodUSA Telecommunications, which provided Internet access and long-distance telephone service in twenty-five states; and Joseph Nacchio, another executive at Qwest. These executives maintained "private wealth management" accounts at Salomon Smith Barney. Collectively, they made over $1.5 billion in personal profits from these allocations. Spitzer's action, which was brought under New York's Martin Act, charged that Salomon Smith Barney was also supplying favorable research recommendations on the stock of companies as an inducement for their investment banking business. Federal prosecutors later indicted Marc B. Weisberg, a Qwest executive, for using "friends and family" IPO allocations for his personal benefit that were intended for Qwest. He demanded those allocations in exchange for Qwest contracts and made profits of $2.9 million. Among the IPO allocations he received were those of Redback Networks Inc. and Akamai Technologies.

A gang of forty state regulators joined Spitzer in investigating the practices of stock analysts and their recommendations for IPOs that were being underwritten by their firms. Goldman Sachs Group was under investigation by the state of Utah after it was disclosed that executives of twenty-one large United States companies received shares in IPO hot issues from Goldman Sachs.

Goldman Sachs must have been astonished to find itself placed under the regulatory control of the Mormon state; it was a long way from Wall Street. The reason for that scrutiny was bizarre. Utah had drawn Goldman Sachs as a target when the state attorney generals drew lots to attack particular investment bankers. The recipients of the IPO allocations from Goldman Sachs gifts included executives at the Ford Motor Company and eBay, Inc., the online auction firm. William Ford Jr., chairman of the Ford Motor Company, received 400,000 Goldman allocated shares. The Ford Motor Company and Goldman settled a shareholder lawsuit over that allocation by agreeing to pay $13.4 million, $10 million of which was to be given to a Ford charity; the rest went to the lawyers.

Another IPO underwriting practice under attack was restrictions on "flipping." Those restrictions seek to prevent individuals from purchasing shares in an IPO and then quickly reselling those shares in order to take a quick profit. The underwriters managing an offering do not like flipping because, if there are too many such sales, completion of the underwriting may be delayed or disrupted. The managers, therefore, impose measures to limit flipping, including penalties that allow the underwriter to reclaim underwriting fees from the firms whose customers sold the stock. Another restriction involved the revocation of offering privileges, which means that those firms would not be given allocations in future offerings. These antiflipping measures were enforced through computer programs established with the Depository Trust Corporation, which handled and tracked the transfer of stocks. The antiflipping restrictions were no secret. Newspapers reported throughout the 1990s that brokers were pressuring customers not to flip IPO stocks until the underwriting was completed. These antiflipping practices were claimed to be anticompetitive in a class action lawsuit, but a federal appellate court rejected that claim because those practices were permitted by SEC rules.[51]

Morgan Stanley and Goldman Sachs each paid $40 million to settle SEC charges that they had required customers receiving IPO allocations at the offering price to buy additional shares in the secondary market once the stock began trading. That requirement was imposed to push up the prices of the IPOs. A $1 billion settlement was reached with some 300 companies with failed IPOs from the Internet era boom in a class action lawsuit that also targeted their underwriters. Under the terms of the settlement, the issuing companies would not have to pay anything if more than $1 billion was subsequently recovered from the underwriters. The issuers would be liable for any shortfall in recovery from the underwriters in an amount less than $1 billion.

Frank Quattrone

Credit Suisse First Boston (CSFB) earned more than $200 million between 1998 and 2001 in connection with its investment banking activities for IPOs of technology companies. CSFB would later regret receiving those fees. Analysts at CSFB were found to have been subject to evaluation by investment banking personnel, and analysts' bonuses were tied to investment banking revenues. The firm agreed to pay $100 million to regulators after it was charged that CSFB had rigged initial public offerings of high-tech companies by allocating shares to favored customers in return for profits paid out through inflated commission payments. The state of Massachusetts also charged CSFB with having its analysts promote stocks that they were privately disparaging. CSFB analysts issued research reports for Digital Impact Inc. and Synopsys Inc. that made positive recommendations for those stocks while they were being criticized internally. Research reports on two other companies, Numerical Technologies Inc. and Winstar Communications Inc., were found to lack a reasonable basis in fact and made unwarranted claims because the CSFB stock analysts were pressured to tout those stocks in order to obtain investment banking business. A research report for New Power Holdings Inc., the Enron spin-off, was tainted by conflicts because the analysts had ownership interests in that company.

Frank Quattrone was another problem for CSFB. Quattrone was a Wharton Business School graduate with an MBA from the Stanford Business School. He originally developed an investment banking business for Morgan Stanley in the tech sector, but moved most of his staff to the Deutsche Bank before moving again to CSFB in 1998. There Quattrone became the head of the technology development area, which became a firm-within-a-firm that provided investment banking and research services from Quattrone's office in Palo Alto, California. Quattrone was successful and was paid $120 million in 2000 by CSFB.

Quattrone was the investment banker for Amazon.com Inc. and Cisco Systems Inc., two of the hottest of Internet stocks. One of the services offered by his group was to provide private investment accounts for officers of investment banking clients. Quattrone was found to have allocated hot issue IPOs to those private client accounts (referred to internally as "Friends of Frank"), providing each of them on average $1 million in profit. One of the allocations involved VA Linux Systems, which saw its stock price increase by almost 700 percent on its first day of trading, giving Quattrone's clients a $10 million gain.

Quattrone was using CSFB analysts to pump the stock of his investment banking clients. Those analysts were given bonuses based on the investment banking deals on which they worked. An internal evaluation praised one analyst because she played a critical role in acquiring a particular investment banking client and remained "a supporter of the stock despite difficult Internet environment." Prospective clients were assured of positive coverage from CSFB analysts if they signed on with Quattrone. An unwritten rule for analysts at CSFB was "if you can't say something positive, don't say anything at all" and to "go with the flow of the other analysts, rather than try to be a contrarian."[52] Positive ratings were maintained for some stocks even though CSFB institutional investors were being cautioned privately about them.

In another government "gotcha" case, Quattrone was arrested for obstruction of justice and tampering with witnesses in connection with an e-mail he had forwarded in December 2000.[53] The e-mail was from Richard Char, CSFB's global head of execution, who was an attorney. A draft version of the e-mail of which Quattrone received a copy on December 4, 2000, stated that, as a result of the collapse of securities markets, the plaintiffs' class action bar could be expected to mount an "all out assault" on IPOs in the tech sector. The draft e-mail further suggested that "in the spirit of the end of the year (and the slow down in corporate work), a memorandum should be sent to members of Quattrone's group reminding them of the firm's document retention policy" and suggesting that before employees left for the holidays, they should catch up on file cleanup. "Today, it's administrative housekeeping. In January (after subpoenas are received), it could be improper destruction of evidence." Quattrone sent a response to that e-mail, stating, with respect to the last remark, "You shouldn't make jokes like that on e-mail."

Less than two hours later, Richard Char sent a modified form of the original e-mail to Quattrone's group. The e-mail was headed: "Time to clean up those files." The new e-mail eliminated the offending reference, quoted the firm's document retention policy, and referenced a firm Web site for its full text. Quattrone also added a warning that the firm's normal document retention policy would be suspended once a lawsuit was filed "(since it constitutes destruction of evidence)."

Shortly after sending his e-mail on December 4, 2000, Quattrone prepared another e-mail to the same recipients that began with a statement that he had previously been a witness in a securities litigation case, but Quattrone decided not to send the message. On the next day, Quattrone was advised by CSFB that he needed to retain his own counsel in connection with a grand jury investigation of CSFB underwriting practices. Late in the evening on that day, after the close of business, Quattrone completed the e-mail he had began the day before and sent it out to his group. The e-mail sent by Quattrone on December 5 was headed "time to clean up those files." It attached the text of the e-mail that was sent on December 4 and stated: "having been a key witness in a securities litigation case in south texas i strongly advise you to follow these procedures." That case involved Miniscribe Corp., the computer disk maker that filed for bankruptcy in 1990 after being caught shipping bricks instead of disks to customers as a means of boosting sales figures. The company was also reporting nonexistent inventories in foreign locations.

Five minutes after Quattrone sent that message, Richard Char sent an e-mail to Quattrone saying that CSFB had suspended its normal document retention policy at the request of the NASD. On the following morning before the opening of business in California, counsel for CSFB advised Quattrone's group that the "editing process" urged in Quattrone's e-mail had to be suspended because of a "routine regulatory inquiry." Because of the timing, it is unlikely that anyone destroyed any documents as a result of Quattrone's December 5 e-mail, but documents had been destroyed in response to the December 4 e-mail of which Quattrone had received a copy.

The indictment charged that at the time he forwarded the December 4 e-mail, Quattrone knew that the NASD was investigating CSFB's handling of an IPO for VA Linux. The indictment further charged that Quattrone knew that the SEC had commenced an investigation of CSFB's equity underwriting process that had been allocating hot IPO shares to clients on the condition that they pay exorbitant commissions on other trades. That practice became the subject of a grand jury investigation of which Quattrone was aware.

The government's case at trial was less than impressive, despite having a judge heavily biased in its favor. That octogenarian jurist, Richard Owen, disparaged Quattrone and his lawyers throughout the trial and ruled at every opportunity for the government. He allowed the prosecutors to show that Quattrone received $120 million in total compensation for the two-year period 1999–2000, which had nothing to do with the charges and everything to do with trying to prejudice the jury. Unlike Martha Stewart, Quattrone took the stand at his trial. He was by all accounts a horrible witness for himself, denying at one point that he had anything to do with allocating IPOs, which the government pounced on to undercut his credibility. Just in case the jury did find him believable, Judge Owen instructed the jury in essence that they should ignore Quattrone's testimony because he had an interest in the outcome of the case. The judge even refused a jury request to have testimony favorable to Quaattrone read back. That testimony was from a CSFB investment banker who had stated that the recipients of the Quattrone e-mails did not have possession of the documents that were under investigation.

The jury was unable to reach a verdict despite an "Allen dynamite charge" from Judge Owen. Such a charge pressures the jury to reach a decision despite disagreements and usually results in a verdict for the government, as was the case in the Arthur Andersen verdict. Despite that charge, Quattrone's trial ended in a hung jury, and a mistrial was declared in October 2003. Jurors voting for a guilty verdict stated afterward that they would have voted to acquit Quattrone until he took the stand. CSFB could have certainly used him at his desk. The company reported a loss of $2.4 billion in 2002.

The government demanded a retrial of Quattrone after plea negations fell through. As a result of the publicity concerning the Tyco juror, who was threatened after she hung the jury in the first Kozlowski trial, the judge ruled that the names of the jurors selected on retrial should remain anonymous, but a federal appeals court later held that ruling was in error and violated the First Amendment rights of the press. The defense in the Quattrone retrial used records of cell phone calls and hundreds of e-mails received and sent by Quattrone during the days in question, suggesting that the message was an off-the-cuff response and not a grand conspiracy. Judge Owen continued his one-sided rulings against Quattrone, some of which were met with derision by spectators at the trial. He, nevertheless, assured a conviction of Quattrone on all counts on May 4, 2003. Owen then sentenced Quattrone to sixteen months in prison, which was well above federal sentencing guidelines. The probation department had recommended five months of prison time and five months of supervised release. For good measure, Owen denied bail pending appeal, but an appeals court reversed that ruling. Quattrone received some unexpected help in his subsequent appeal of the conviction. The National Association of Criminal Defense Lawyers and other groups representing public defenders filed an *amicus curiae* brief that sought reversal because of the obvious bias of Judge Owen. They called Quattrone's conviction a "judicial mugging."

Analysts' Settlement

Salomon Smith Barney agreed on December 24, 2002, to pay a $5 million fine to the NASD for allowing its analysts to tout Winstar Communications Inc., the telecom company that later became bankrupt. JPMorgan Chase settled a case for $25 million in which it was charged by the SEC with allocating hot issues during the tech boom to preferred customers. The institutional customers were given allocations in IPOs, provided that they agreed to purchase additional shares in the aftermarket in order to support the market price. This practice was called "laddering." This was all small change. In December 2002, ten investment banking firms agreed to a $1.4 billion settlement with Eliot Spitzer and other state, federal, and self-regulatory organizations in an action challenging analysts' conflicts.

Among the investment banks included in the settlement were Citigroup and Salomon Smith Barney, CSFB, Morgan Stanley, Goldman Sachs, Lehman Brothers Holdings Inc., UBS AG Deutsche Bank, and Bear Stearns Co. Jack Grubman, the Citigroup analyst, agreed to pay $15 million for his indiscretions and was barred from the securities business for life. No worries, though—Grubman had been given a $19.5 million severance package when he resigned from Salomon Smith Barney. Grubman became a consultant to Distinctive Devices Inc., a maker of devices for digital television abroad, causing a sharp jump in the price of that company's stock. Grubman's problems were not over, however. He was defending over 1,000 arbitration claims that had been filed against him. Henry Blodget, the Merrill Lynch analyst, was fined $2 million and barred from the securities industry for life. Blodget then began working as a freelance writer for an online magazine called *Slate* that was owned by Microsoft. He covered the Martha Stewart trial for that publication.

The regulators gave Sandy Weill, the head of Citigroup, a pass, agreeing not to sue him in light of the generous contribution by Citigroup to the settlement to the tune of $400 million, which far exceeded the $200 million paid by CSFB and the $200 million paid by Merrill Lynch for its analysts' problems. Weill agreed not to stand as an outside director for the NYSE, which was having problems with other directors, including Martha Stewart. A chagrined Sandy Weil announced that he did not want cash or stock bonuses from Citigroup in 2002, but he was given $14.5 million anyway.

Under the settlement, the investment bankers agreed to separate their research and investment banking businesses physically and through different reporting lines. The two groups were to have separate legal and compliance staffs and separate budgets. "Firewalls" were to be created between the investment bankers and the analysts. Investment bankers were to have no say in what companies should be covered by the analysts. Analysts were barred from investment banking sales presentations or road shows showcasing IPOs before their issuance. Analysts' compensation could not be based on investment banking revenues or input from investment banking personnel. Rather, their compensation was to be computed on the basis of the quality and accuracy of their reports. Ridiculously, the SEC demanded that a lawyer be present whenever discussions occur between analysts and investment bankers. One bank had to hire fourteen of these chaperons, who did little but listen to dull conversations at a cost of more than $1 million annually. In total, some fifty such chaperons were employed on Wall Street to meet this requirement.

Each settling firm agreed to hire an "independent monitor" to conduct a review eighteen months after the settlement in order to measure compliance. The settling firms agreed to make publicly available ratings and price target forecasts by their analysts and disclose their investment banking relationships with covered firms that might create a conflict of interest. The firms agreed to create Web sites showing their analysts' performance. The settlement banned allocations of IPO shares to corporate executives (spinning). Most startling, the settlement required the firms to spend $450 million to purchase research from at least three independent firms for a period of five years and to make those reports available to retail investors in order to allow them to better assess stock recommendations. Seven of the settling firms agreed to pay a total of $85 million to fund "investor education funds" to be created by the states and the SEC. Those funds would be used to alert investors to investment risks. The investor education program set up by the SEC under this part of the settlement proved to be a farce. The program was still not off the ground as 2005 began, and its director, George G. Daly, resigned. The fund failed to provide quarterly financial reports to the court overseeing the settlement and was criticized for trying to lease expensive office space from one of the settling firms. The chairman of the fund, Charles Ellis, and several directors also later resigned, throwing the whole program into further disarray. The states made a grab for the funds allocated to the SEC after this fiasco, but they were having their own problems. The Investor Protection Trust created by several states to spend settlement monies for investor education was experiencing losses in its own portfolio from overly aggressive investments.

The regulators involved in this settlement were not always on the same page. The NASD and Spitzer spent some time quarreling over the language in the settlement agreement. Spitzer sought to tone down the accusatory language, while the NASD was trying to make the situation look as dire as possible. Other investment bankers settled charges similar to those included in the $1.4 billion settlement. U.S. Bancorp Piper Jaffray agreed to pay $25 million in fines and to make structural changes as a result of charges of securities analyst conflicts. Deutsche Bank Securities Inc. and Thomas Weisel Partners LLC agreed to pay $87.5 million to settle SEC and state claims of conflicting research. Piper Jaffray settled charges that it used IPO allocations to obtain business for its investment banking business. The company was fined $2.4 million for that conduct. JPMorgan Chase paid $6 million in fines to the NASD for claims made against Hambrecht & Quist, which had been a popular investment banking firm for high-tech companies before being purchased by JPMorgan Chase. Hambrecht & Quist had been charging customers excessive commissions for IPO allocations, which the NASD likened to sharing in customer profits, a prohibited practice. Morgan Stanley, Bear Stearns, and Deutsche Bank were collectively fined $15 million for such conduct. FleetBoston Financial paid $28 million to settle claims by the SEC and the NASD for excessive commissions charged to customers of the Robertson Stephens securities arm of the bank. Another $5 million was paid to settle charges that a Robertson Stephens analyst had been promoting a stock in which he had a significant position without disclosing that fact to his clients.

Nations Bank Montgomery Securities was allocating IPO issues to clients in order to encourage more business from their firms. The SEC sanctioned an investment adviser receiving such allocations. The SEC charged several broker-dealers with failing to disclose that they had received payments for providing research coverage of public companies. The respondents collectively paid $3.65 million to settle those charges. Those firms were Needham & Company Inc., Janney Montgomery Scott LLC, Prudential Equity Group LLC, Adams Harkness Inc., Friedman, Billings, Ramsey & Co. Inc., and SG Cowen & Co. LLC.

A $432 million settlement fund was created to compensate investors who had bought stocks from broker-dealers whose analysts were hyping such stocks as Ask Jeeves Inc., WorldCom, Global Crossing, and Level 3 Communications. The settlement terms were being criticized because many investors bought the same stocks from other firms, but would receive no compensation. As it was, even those entitled to compensation seemed little interested. The court had to approve a nationwide advertising campaign to find those affected.

The SEC also adopted Regulation AC (Regulation Analyst Certification) that requires analysts to certify that their reports accurately reflected their personal views and to disclose whether any compensation they received were for the views expressed in their reports. Certifications were also required for public appearances.

The NASD tightened its hot issue rule to prohibit spinning, but left a gap for investment bankers, allowing them to allocate shares to accounts in which they held a less than 10 percent interest. The NASD prohibited analysts from issuing "booster shot" research reports and required them to publish a final research report when they terminate coverage of a company. Analysts were prohibited from soliciting investment banking business and from seeking approval of their reports or recommendations from the companies being reviewed, although analysts could seek guidance on whether factual statements were correct. Analysts were required to disclose whether they own any stocks of the companies they cover. Firms were required to disclose the percentage of their recommendations that are buy, sell, hold, and so on. Analysts and their families were prohibited from trading in a stock covered by the analyst thirty days before publication of a research report or five days after its publication. Gary Davis, an analyst at Jesup & Lamont Securities Corp., quickly acted to violate those rules by selling shares he owned during this "quiet period" in companies he was recommending a "strong buy" or "buy." Davis sold over 200,000 such shares and made profits in excess of $100,000. He was fined and suspended from acting as an analyst by the NASD.

Despite the huge settlement with Spitzer and other regulators, private litigants were losing most of the arbitration and other cases that sought to cash in on those charges. Nevertheless, an arbitration panel ordered Merrill Lynch to pay Gary Friedman and his wife $1 million for failing to disclose its analysts' conflicts. Additional perils awaited the analysts. Several firms were accusing each other of plagiarizing research reports. A French court penalized Morgan Stanley $38 million for disparaging remarks made by one of its analysts, Claire Kent, about the stock of LVMH, the fashion house for labels such as Louis Vuitton, Moet, and Hennessy. The court found that her remarks had unfairly destroyed shareholder value. Citigroup's Smith Barney unit encountered a similar problem. Jonathan Litt, one of its real estate analysts, criticized Peter Munk for his corporate governance practices at Trizec Canada Inc., a company controlled by Munk. Litt said that Munk needed "to wake up to the new world of corporate governance" and that Munk should turn on his television and observe the arrest of WorldCom executives. Litt then announced that he was turning his findings of misfeasance over to Eliot Spitzer and other regulators. Trizec and Munk sued in Canadian court claiming defamation. Citigroup settled that case by apologizing and making a $1.6 million contribution to a charity selected by Munk.

CKE Restaurants Inc., which operates Hardee's, was the target of an analyst who wanted a consulting contract as a condition for ceasing negative reports on the company. That analyst, C. Clive Munro, was caught in a FBI sting operation set up with the cooperation of the company. Munro pleaded guilty to one count of extortion. He had previously been the subject of a $1.6 million judgment for publishing false and misleading research about another company.

Another problem was that corporate earnings were becoming increasingly volatile in the new century. This was making profit forecasts by those companies and the analysts covering them more difficult. Even so, newspapers reported that analysts were still touting stocks even after the $1.4 billion settlement. Several analysts were predicting growth that appeared unlikely to be achieved. The SEC conducted an investigation focusing on conflicts of interest between the bond trading operations of broker-dealers and their fixed income research reports. There was some good news. A study conducted in 2005 found that Wall Street analysts' reports were becoming more reliable.

Congressional Hearings

Charles Schwab & Co. sought to take advantage of the analyst scandals through an advertising campaign that disparaged the Wall Street full-service firms. The CBS television network refused to run one of those advertisements, which portrayed the office manager of a brokerage firm telling brokers to sell a stock he calls a "pig." The manager instructs the brokers to "put some lipstick on this pig."

Congress held hearings that sought to determine why analysts had not exposed Enron's accounting problems and were even recommending the stock as the company plunged into bankruptcy. The analysts were attacked in Congress on the high number of favorable recommendations for Enron stock less than a month before its bankruptcy.[54] One independent analyst had questioned Enron's financial statements more than six months before its collapse, as did an article in *Fortune* magazine. The analysts defended their continuing support for Enron on the grounds that the company's core business remained profitable, even while its broadband services were having trouble. Further, even after Enron announced its accounting irregularities, the prospective merger with Dynegy appeared to create an environment favorable for Enron's recovery, especially since Chevron Texaco was willing to provide capital to support the merger. One analyst claimed that he was misled by Enron's faking of trading activity during a conference held by the company for over one hundred analysts at its headquarters.

Those excuses might cover Enron, but there were other analyst failures. According to an analyst at Motley Fool, thirty-two of thirty-eight analysts covering Lucent Technologies were recommending it as a buy even while the company was in free fall. None of those analysts had a sell recommendation.[55] Members of Congress and witnesses noted that less than 2 percent of analysts' recommendations were to sell stock. Analysts called as witnesses claimed that they made few sell recommendations because they only selected stocks to recommend that they believed would be long-term performers, thereby weeding out sell stocks.

Senator Joseph Lieberman defined analysts as "watchdogs" who were supposed "to keep the stock markets fair and to give them [investors] accurate information to help them decide where to put their money and with it their hopes for economic advancement and retirement security."[56] Analysts appearing as witnesses at the congressional hearings countered by noting that they were completely dependent on the audited financial statements of the companies they covered for their analysis because Regulation FD prevented access to independent sources. Those financial statements were said to be the "bedrock" of any analysis.[57] A witness from the Consumers Union, Frank Torres, testified with now familiar frustration:

> This situation is amazing. No one seems to know anything about what these companies do or how things operate. Analysts point to the auditors. The auditors say Enron wasn't forthcoming. I am waiting for Enron to blame the investors for investing in their own company's stock. Where is this going to end? Who is going to be accountable and who is going to be the watchdog for investors?[58]

Mutual Fund Scandals

Eliot Spitzer, the New York attorney general, was soon leading another attack on Wall Street. An informant tipped Spitzer's office that mutual funds were engaging in trading practices that were claimed to be detrimental to retail customers. The ensuing scandal was everything that Spitzer could have hoped for, putting him back in the news, and making the SEC again look incompetent, and giving Wall Street another black eye. The mutual fund industry he attacked was a big target, holding some $7.5 trillion in customer assets.

Some History

Mutual funds trace their history back to the Société Générale de Belgique, a trust originally created in 1822 by King William of the Netherlands, which allowed beneficiaries to hold interests in government loans. Even earlier, in 1664, the East India Company had purchased its shares from existing shareholders at book value, providing some elements of a mutual fund. Other trusts in the 1830s were used to sell the stocks held by a bank that were acquired from defaulting borrowers. In France, in 1852, the Société Générale de Crédit Mobilier (no relation to the Credit Mobiler railroad construction company that caused much scandal in America later in that century) used shareholder funds to invest in the operations of other companies, including the dynamite business of Alfred Nobel.

Investment companies were being formed in London in the 1860s. Those entities used investor funds to finance the purchase of shares of other companies. They included the London Financial Association and the International Financial Society, both of which failed. The Foreign and Colonial Government Trust purchased the securities of several foreign firms. Formed in the 1870s, the Submarine Cables Trust invested in the securities of telegraph companies. Its own stock traded on the London Stock Exchange. Robert Fleming founded the Scottish American Investment Trust in 1873. It had over 500 investors and used a professional board of advisers to select investments.

In America, the Massachusetts Hospital Life Insurance Company (MHLIC), originally formed in 1818 as an insurance company, operated a trust in which it invested the commingled funds of beneficiaries. Around 1845, some Boston friends of Daniel Webster contributed $37,000 to MHLIC for Webster's account while he was secretary of state. This slush fund provided him with an income of about $1,000 annually, but "someone remarked that the proposition was 'indelicate' and he wondered how Mr. Webster would take it? 'How will he take it?' snorted [Harrison Gray] Otis. 'Why, quarterly, to be sure!'"[59]

The United States Mortgage Company formed in 1871, and the New York Stock Trust, formed in 1889, had aspects of an investment company. The Boston Personal Property Trust, which was formed in 1893, invested its funds in a group of diversified securities, but it was a tontine scheme. These early efforts to create investment companies in America did not spread quickly. The real growth of investment companies in America would have to await the stock market boom that occurred in the 1920s. Then a "veritable epidemic of investment trusts inflicted the Nation."[60]

Investment Company Act of 1940

By 1929, an investment company was being formed every day in America. About 10 percent of all investors held investment company shares before the stock market crash of 1929. The companies' allure was the result of claims of diversification and expert management. Investors were told that the investment company allowed them to make a small investment that would be pooled with other investor funds and used to purchase a broad range of securities issued by other companies. Expert managers were to select those stocks based on a professional analysis. The stock market crash was a disaster for those investors. The Goldman Sachs Trading Corporation, an investment company, obtained over $100 million from investors for its operations. Its shares traded at one point before the crash at $326. They were selling for $1.75 in 1932. Another investment company saw its share prices drop from $100 to sixty-three cents.

After its creation in 1934, the SEC conducted a study of the operations of investment companies, discovering a number of abuses. Those abuses included speculative investments, failure to diversify as promised, undue leverage obtained from bond sales, the purchase of stock on margin, and self-dealing on the part of the organizers of the investment companies. The SEC study resulted in the passage of the Investment Company Act of 1940, which has been called "the most intrusive financial legislation known to man or beast."[61] It "places substantive restrictions on virtually every aspect of the operations of investment companies; their valuation of assets, their governance and structure, their issuance of debt and other senior securities, their investments, sales and redemptions of their shares, and, perhaps most importantly, their dealings with service providers and other affiliates."[62]

The Investment Company Act contained several corporate governance reforms. Forty percent of the directors of the mutual fund were required to be "outside" directors independent of the fund's investment adviser, and transactions with affiliated persons were restricted. Investment companies were prohibited from issuing debt securities or preferred stock that would allow them to leverage their market positions.

Mutual Funds

Most of the investment companies in the 1920s were "closed-end" companies that invested in stocks instead of making something, like automobiles. Before the Investment Company Act of 1940, closed-end investment companies obtained funds by issuing their own common and preferred stock to investors and by borrowing through bond issues, providing the common shareholders with leverage. The stock of closed-end companies traded in secondary markets and was even listed on the stock exchanges.

The "open-end" investment company, or "mutual fund," as it is now called, first appeared in 1924 but did not have time to develop before the market crashed in 1929. The mutual fund was invented by Edward G. Leffler in Boston. Such companies continually sell and redeem their shares at their net asset value. This means that an investor wishing to liquidate his or her investment simply notifies the company of that desire, and the company will return the investor's aliquot portion of the total fund based on its net asset value at the close of business on the day of redemption.

Scandals and Abuses

The Investment Company Act did not stop mutual fund abuses. "Letter stock" was purchased by mutual funds from speculative operations and then valued at unrealistically high prices in the 1960s. Letter stock involved an agreement to purchase stock once it was registered with the SEC at some time in the future. One mutual fund saw its value drop 93 percent after it was discovered that its letter stock had been vastly overvalued. The letter stock scandal spread quickly through the securities industry, even ensnaring Justice William O. Douglas and the actress Jill St. John when Parvin-Dohrmann's letter stock ran into problems.

A massive scandal arose in the wake of the collapse of Investors Overseas Services (IOS) in the 1960s. IOS was a giant offshore mutual fund that had been structured to avoid regulation by the SEC. IOS was founded by Bernard Cornfeld, a colorful jet-setting playboy. IOS managed a "fund-of-funds" that invested in the shares of other investment companies. Such fund-of-fund schemes were prohibited by the SEC in the United States until recently. IOS was supposed to operate only offshore in order to avoid regulation by the SEC, but some sales were made to U.S. investors. Those sales were accompanied by ill-considered investments of mutual fund investor funds. The SEC then attacked, and Cornfeld eventually folded, selling IOS to Robert Vesco, who proceeded to loot the company of hundreds of millions of dollars. Vesco fled to the Caribbean where he remained a fugitive, but was eventually jailed in Cuba for another fraud.

Notwithstanding those problems, mutual funds became popular investment mechanisms, replacing the closed-end fund as the vehicle of choice. By 1980, some 500 mutual funds held $100 billion in assets in the United States. Peter Lynch, the portfolio manager for Fidelity Investments Magellan Fund, was said to be the most successful manager of the era. When he retired in 1990, the Magellan Fund had more than 1 million investors, $14 billion in assets, and an average annual return of almost 30 percent.

Mutual fund growth was spurred by the invention of money market funds that allowed investors to receive a return on their liquid funds. By 1993, there were 3,800 mutual funds holding about $1.6 trillion in investor funds. In 2001, there were 8,200 mutual funds holding about $6.6 trillion in assets for 95 million investors. The number of mutual funds exceeded the number of stocks listed on the NYSE and Nasdaq in the new century. In 2002, mutual funds held 18 percent of all publicly traded equity securities in the United States. The amount of funds held in mutual funds exceeded those held in bank accounts. Banks were even selling their commercial loans to mutual funds.

Mutual Fund Investment

Mutual funds are sold by their sponsors through broker-dealers, acting as underwriters, or directly by the fund itself. Mutual funds are managed under a contract with an investment adviser that trades the fund's assets in accordance with the investment objectives set forth in the mutual fund's prospectus. Over the years, investors were given every conceivable form of investment opportunity in mutual funds. Specialized funds could be found for everything from telecom stocks to government bonds. An investor seeking to invest in fixed income instruments could choose among mutual funds investing in money market instruments, municipal securities of most states and many subunits, federally insured bonds, mortgage-backed securities, and corporate bonds, with subchoices of convertible bonds, global bonds, differing maturities, and rating grades down to and including junk bonds. Equity investors could pick from index funds on a broad range of indexes, funds that invest in a particular business sector, option funds, growth funds, and aggressive growth funds. Funds for contrarians trade against popular investment views; for the internationally inclined, there are global equity funds and emerging market funds for stocks of companies in lesser developed countries. Balanced funds (with varying balances) invest in both fixed income and equity securities, while "quant" funds use computer programs to make stock picks, and vulture funds invest in failing companies. There are even mutual fund portfolios for politically correct investors that invest in environmentally friendly companies and avoid tobacco stocks. For those interested in politically incorrect investments, the Vice Fund invested in tobacco, alcohol, gambling, and other sin stocks.

Mutual funds were the investment of choice of many small investors. More than one-half of all households in the United States owned mutual funds in 2001. Mutual funds were very active traders; their average annual turnover rate was 122 percent in 2000, but, depending on the manner of calculation, several studies found that mutual fund performance was lagging that of the overall market. Some studies showed that lag to be severe, while other more favorable calculations showed that the gap was smaller but still lagging. About 6.5 percent of equity mutual funds were closed each year after the turn of the century. Closure usually meant that the fund's trading strategy had failed. By closing an unprofitable fund, mutual fund complexes could better their track records.

Market Timing

Abuses were occurring in mutual funds sold in the United States, despite the intrusive provisions of the Investment Company Act of 1940. Usually, those problems involved commissions or loads charged by the funds. NASD rules limited the amount of the sales load that could be charged on mutual fund sales. In most instances, that maximum sales load was 7.25 percent, which was still a large piece of the investor's funds. An abusive sales practice arose to evade even that limitation. Called "switching," this practice involved moving investors in and out of different mutual funds in order to generate commissions, while promising profits from trading opportunities. Another related abuse was to encourage retail customers to engage in "market timing" transactions that seek to anticipate favorable market moves and make quick profits. Market timing trading is not appropriate for small investors because of loads, the time and place advantages of professional traders, and the skill required to profit from market timing transactions.

Switching and market timing were prohibited and punished by the SEC where retail investors were charged excessive commissions. The SEC charged Market-Timing Technologies LLC and David A. Perry of Atlanta, Georgia, with soliciting investment advisory clients through Internet Web sites that advertised asset management programs that identified market timing opportunities in shifting client funds among various mutual funds within a fund family, which would not result in a load charge. The defendants claimed that their models produced historical average annual returns of 9 percent or more but failed to disclose that these return rates were based primarily on hypothetical investments.

Market timing transactions in mutual funds by professional traders was not viewed by the SEC as a matter of concern since the professionals could look after themselves. A barrier to using mutual funds for market timing even by professionals was the fact that mutual fund shares can only be liquidated at the net asset value of the fund as measured by prices at the end of the trading day. That restriction was thought to be a practical bar that would generally prevent even professional investors from using market timing because they could open or close a position only once every twenty-four hours.

Competition

Following the bursting of the market bubble in 2000, mutual fund advisers sought ways to bolster their advisory fees. Those fees were based on the net asset value of assets under management, which were dropping in value during the market downturn. In addition, many investors withdrew from mutual funds as the market plunged, further reducing the amount of assets under management. Mutual funds trading equities experienced a multitrillion-dollar drop in assets between March 2000 and December 2002. During December 2002, over $100 billion dollars was withdrawn from equity mutual funds in the United States, a record for a single month. The average stock mutual fund in the United States dropped 22 percent in value during 2002. This was in excess of declines in 2001 and 2000.

Mutual funds faced competition that further threatened their market. Closed-end funds had record years for attracting investor funds in 2002 and 2003 and were heading toward another record in 2004. Those securities could be traded anytime a market was open anywhere in the world. Exchange traded funds (ETFs) were also becoming increasingly popular. These were essentially investments that tracked the value of a particular index. The first of these contracts appeared in 1993 and were called SPDRs (Standard & Poor's Depository Receipts) or "spiders." They were the equivalent of a diversified mutual fund but allowed intraday trading. Spiders quickly became popular. After several more such vehicles became available, they took on a new name: ETFs. The ETFs provided competition to the mutual funds because of their greater flexibility. ETFs could be market-timed during the trading day. By 2004, there was $211 billion invested in ETFs, an increase of some 50 percent from the year before. The number of ETFs increased from thirty in 1999 to 143 in 2004. Barclays Global Investors offered 97 different ETFs to its customers. The holdings in those funds grew to $87 billion in the course of a few years. ETFs were first used mostly by institutional investors and active traders, but later attracted individual investors as well. They became popular even for employee Section 401(k) retirement plans and were expanded to include actively managed investments as well as passive indexes. ETFs even expanded into commodities, including streetTRACKS Gold Shares, which traded gold.

In order to meet this competition, as well as declining fees as net asset values dropped, mutual funds advisers began allowing hedge funds and other professional traders to engage in market timing and "late" transactions. Even the SEC recognized that market timing was "not illegal per se," unless an unsophisticated investor was induced to use market timing to increase commissions for the salesman. Market timing transactions, nevertheless, increased transaction costs for the mutual fund, required it to maintain higher amounts of liquidity, and could dilute holdings of other shareholders if the funds shares were overpriced when the market timer liquidated. Late trading, in which traders were allowed to enter liquidation orders after the close of trading (after 4 PM), was another matter. This allowed those traders to take retroactive advantage of market movements.

Market timing by professional traders had been occurring for some time. Professor Frank Partnoy at the San Diego Law School traced such practices back to the 1920s, and some such trading was occurring in the early 1990s. Market timing and late trading had been studied by several professors. David Dubofsky had been studying the effects of such trading since the stock market crash of 1987, after being tipped by a student. The SEC was well aware of the market timing engaged in by institutions as early as 2001. The SEC staff had urged the mutual funds industry to curb such practices, but proposed no new regulations and did not assert that such activity was illegal.

Spitzer's Charges

Eliot Spitzer, the New York attorney general, took a more aggressive approach. In September 2003, Spitzer charged Edward J. Stern and a hedge fund he managed, Canary Capital Partners, with improperly late trading mutual fund shares. In order to make that charge, Spitzer claimed that this conduct violated the New York Martin Act. Edward Stern was the son of Max Stern, who owned the pet food empire at Hartz Mountain Corp. and was a real estate magnate in New York. Canary Capital Partners was required to pay $40 million to settle this case, part of which was to be used for restitution to the mutual funds. Edward Stern agreed not to trade in mutual funds or manage any public investment funds for ten years.

Security Trust, a bank used to transfer mutual funds, was charged with helping Canary Capital and other hedge funds to late trade mutual funds. The bank was ordered dissolved by banking regulators. Nicole McDermott, an executive at Security Trust, pleaded guilty to charges in New York that she had facilitated improper mutual funds trading in overnight transactions entered after the close of the market. Her hedge fund customers made $85 million while Security Trust made $5.8 million in profits. Another institution allowing late trading by Canary Capital Partners was Bank of America's mutual fund complex that operated under the name of Nations Funds. Those funds had imposed a 2 percent redemption fee to discourage market timing transactions but waived the fee for Canary Capital Partners. Several Bank of America employees were fired following that revelation. JPMorgan Chase was also under investigation for financing Canary's trading.

The SEC was severely embarrassed by Spitzer's suit and his claim that late trading and market timing abuses were widespread in the mutual funds industry. In an effort to reclaim some of its lost regulatory ground, the SEC started filing its own suits, claiming that late trading arrangements were not properly disclosed under its full disclosure regimen. The SEC asserted that market timers were profiting from time zone differences in foreign markets where securities held in a mutual fund's portfolio traded after the cutoff time for net asset value pricing in the United States. The trader could profit by purchasing the mutual fund shares on the basis of events occurring after the foreign market closing prices were set, but before the mutual fund calculated its net asset value. The market timer would then sell his mutual fund shares the next day when the net asset value reflected the events on which the trader bought shares. This conduct was not itself illegal, but the SEC could always claim that it had not been properly disclosed. In addition, the SEC charged that late trading violated the Investment Company Act of 1940 because orders received after 4 PM were supposed to be executed at the closing price on 4 PM on the next day. In fact, the Investment Company Act of 1940 contained no such provision. It only specified the manner of computing net asset values of investment funds; it did not set the time for that computation. In any event, the SEC charged that late trading allowed traders to profit from market events occurring after 4 PM that were not reflected in the net asset value computed at that time. This assured the trader a virtually risk-free profit when he obtains information with market effect after the 4 PM pricing. Late trading also involved conditional trades placed before the 4 PM cutoff but with the right to cancel the trade after the cutoff period.

Lawyers at large law firms had advised mutual funds that they could trade as late as 5:45 PM Eastern Time because, even though mutual funds were supposed to price funds at 4 PM, the funds did not actually report their pricing until 5:30 PM, or later. The lawyers thought that a 5:45 PM cutoff would prevent anyone from taking advantage of information to profit from knowledge of the fund pricing and events occurring after the close of trading. After the issue hit the press, the SEC proposed a rule for a "hard" cutoff at 4 PM.

Theodore Charles Sihpol III, an employee of Bank of America Securities LLC, was the subject of SEC charges for time stamping mutual fund order tickets for hedge funds in advance of a 4 PM cutoff so that the orders would appear to have been entered before that time. Spitzer brought criminal charges against Sihpol, complete with tape recordings of transactions in which he was beating back requests to allow late trading after 5 PM. This was the only one of the lawsuits brought by Spitzer to go to trial by late 2005. In a stunning reversal of fortune for Spitzer, the jury found Sihpol not guilty of most charges. The jury hung on a few counts, but even on those charges the vote was overwhelmingly in favor of acquittal. Spitzer, nevertheless, announced that he would retry Sihpol on the counts that hung the jury, an act the *Wall Street Journal* called "petty." Spitzer then dropped further prosecution.

Pimco funds, operated by Allianz AG, a German insurance company, their chairman Stephen Treadway, and others were the subject of SEC charges for allowing Canary Capital Partners to market time. That trading was allowed in exchange for an agreement by Canary to keep $27 million invested in the funds on a long-term basis, a requirement called "sticky assets." Canary was allowed to make 108 market timing transactions over a period of a little more than one year. The funds had prohibited other investors from making more than six in-and-out transactions over a one-year period. The Pimco funds settled charges by the SEC by agreeing to pay $50 million, $10 million of which was to be used for restitution to mutual fund investors.

Bill Gross was managing $350 billion in fixed income assets at Pimco, which was 2 percent of the United States bond market. His Pimco Total Return bond fund was the largest in the country. New Jersey charged Gross with improper conduct for market timing, but those charges were later dropped, apparently because no harm had been incurred by the funds. PA Fund Management, PEA Capital, and PA Distributors agreed to pay $50 million to settle SEC charges for market timing Pimco funds and paid another $18 million to New Jersey.

Three FleetBoston Financial Corp. mutual funds were allowing professional traders to engage in market timing transactions. The SEC and Spitzer charged that traders for FleetBoston's Columbia Funds engaged in a total of $2.5 billion in market timing transactions between 1998 and 2003, including $355 million in such trades in the Columbia Young Investors Fund, a mutual fund for children. As a condition for being allowed to market time, traders were required to maintain sticky assets in the mutual funds. For example, Ilytat LP, a hedge fund based in San Francisco, agreed to leave $20 million in sticky assets if it were allowed to engage in in-and-out market timing transactions in the Columbia Funds. Ilytat then made 350 in-and-out trades in those mutual funds.

Columbia Funds agreed to pay $140 million in restitution and penalties to settle actions brought by the SEC and Spitzer challenging these trading practices. The Bank of America and FleetBoston later merged and jointly settled their mutual fund problems by paying $675 million to regulators. Of that amount, $160 million was to be used to reduce fees charged to mutual funds investors. Spitzer insisted that fee reduction, which was highly controversial because it made him the regulator of mutual fund fees, a matter that Congress had placed in the SEC's bailiwick.

Bank One Corp., which sponsored the One Group mutual fund complex, allowed Canary Capital Partners to late trade in its mutual funds. Bank One settled charges for this activity by agreeing to pay $90 million, including mutual fund fee reductions totaling $40 million. Mark Beeson, the head of the One Group funds, was barred from the mutual fund industry for two years. Richard Strong, founder and chairman of Strong Capital Management, which was the adviser to the Strong Capital complex of mutual funds, resigned after the SEC learned that he and his family made $600,000 in profits from market timing trades. Richard Strong agreed to pay $60 million in restitution and civil penalties and was barred for life from the securities industry. Anthony D'Amato, executive vice president at Strong Capital Management, paid $750,000 to settle charges against him. The Strong mutual funds agreed to pay $175 million in settlement. The funds were then sold to Wells Fargo & Co. at a considerable profit to Strong.

Mark Whiston, the chief executive of the Janus funds, resigned after market timing charges were raised. Janus Capital Management LLC agreed to a settlement with Spitzer totaling $225 million plus $1 million to the Colorado attorney general. A separate settlement with the SEC cost Janus another $100 million. The mutual fund complex agreed to reduce its fees by $125 million over a five-year period and to appoint independent chairmen to its mutual funds boards of directors. Janus lost, as a result of redemptions, almost one half of the $320 billion in assets it had under management before the scandal.

The Problem Spreads

Alliance Capital Management LP, owned by the French Insurance Company AXA SA, entered into a joint settlement with the SEC and Spitzer, agreeing to pay $250 million in penalties and disgorgement of improper profits from late trading. Alliance agreed with Spitzer to reduce its mutual fund fees by 20 percent, pushing the total cost of the settlement up to $600 million. Gerald Malone and a fellow executive at Alliance were suspended for allowing rapid trading transactions in mutual funds. Other sales executives were asked to resign. Alliance Capital Management had other problems. It had been a money manager for Florida state pensions, which lost $250 million as a result of its investments in Enron Corp. purchased for it by Alliance. The Florida pension fund board sued Alliance charging that it had been misled by Alliance and that Alliance had conflicts of interest because an Alliance board member, Frank Savage, also served on the Enron board. A Florida jury rejected that claim.

Massachusetts Financial Services Co., which was owned by Sun Life Financial Inc., agreed to pay $225 million to settle charges brought by Spitzer, the SEC, and the New Hampshire Bureau of Securities. The company agreed to cut its fees by $125 million. An employee at the firm had presented a chart to management titled "Market Timing Wheel of Terror." He stated that long-term investors were being penalized by market timers. Spitzer claimed that investors had lost up to $175 million. Sanctions were imposed against officers of Massachusetts Financial Services, including a three-year ban on serving as a director or officer of a mutual fund imposed on its chief executive officer, John Ballen. He was suspended for nine months from serving in the securities industry in any position.

The SEC settled further charges against Massachusetts Financial Services for failing to disclose that it was engaged in a practice called "directed brokerage." This involved using commissions from brokerage operations trading mutual fund assets to provide additional compensation to brokers for selling its funds. TD Waterhouse agreed to pay the SEC $2 million to settle charges that it made undisclosed payments to investment advisers as an inducement for them to recommend TD Waterhouse to their clients. The SEC, thereafter, adopted a rule prohibiting the use of directed brokerage.

Gary Pilgrim was accused by Spitzer and the SEC of making market timing transactions in the Pilgrim Baxter mutual funds that he managed with Harold Baxter through Pilgrim Baxter & Associates. Those mutual funds had $7.4 billion under management. Pilgrim Baxter conducted that trading through Appalachian Trails, a hedge fund in which Pilgrim had an interest. Harold Baxter was tipping Alan Lederfeind, a friend, on nonpublic information about portfolio transactions of the Pilgrim mutual funds. That information was used for market timing transactions by Lederfeind, who managed the brokerage operations at Wall Street Discount Corp. Spitzer sought disgorgement of $250 million in management fees that the defendants received while they were engaged in market timing transactions. Appalachian Trails made about $13 million from its 120 market timing transactions. Gary Pilgrim earned about $3.9 million of that amount. Both Baxter and Pilgrim resigned from Pilgrim Baxter Associates. They agreed to pay $160 million to settle the charges brought by Spitzer and the SEC, and they were barred from the securities business for life. Pilgrim Baxter & Associates agreed to pay another $100 million in settlement and changed its name to Liberty Ridge Capital to avoid the stigma of market timing abuses.

Putnam Investments, owned by Marsh & McLennan, was engaging in market timing transactions. Lawrence Lasser, the chief executive officer of Putnam Investments, resigned. He was paid $35 million before his resignation and was given another $78 million after he threatened litigation over his severance pay. Two Putnam managers were charged with civil fraud for failing to stop market timing transactions that were used to take advantage of predictable trading patterns of foreign share prices following U.S. market trends. Those two employees were highly compensated by Putnam, one receiving $14.3 million and the other $8.7 million in 2000. The Putnam market timing investigation widened after Putnam announced that it was discharging six money managers who had engaged in market timing trades in international mutual funds for their own accounts. Nine more employees were later fired.

Massachusetts securities regulators charged Putnam Investments with allowing market timing by the Boilermakers Local Lodge No. 5 as a favor to that pension fund and to encourage it to pay more fees. Ten members of the union made $2 million in profits from market timing transactions, and the union was receiving rebates of fees totaling $40,000 per year from the Putnam funds. The market timing at the Putnam funds was carried out despite the fact that those funds had created a department to monitor such trading, the "market timing police." The department was not successful, and Putnam Investments agreed to pay the SEC and the Massachusetts Securities Division a total of $110 million in penalties plus $10 million in restitution to customers. A subsequent investigation revealed that investors lost over $108.5 million from late trading and other abuses at Putnam, ten times original estimates. Under the terms of the settlement agreement, this meant that Putnam had to pay an additional $83 million in restitution. Marsh & McLennan, the Putnam funds' parent, was already under attack for its corporate governance structure, and the company agreed to nominate a director selected by its institutional investors. That director was a former federal prosecutor, but his appointment failed to prevent a subsequent scandal involving Spitzer and Marsh & McLennan.

The SEC and Spitzer charged Invesco Funds Group Inc. with improperly allowing market timing transactions in its mutual funds. Invesco and Aim Investments agreed to pay Spitzer and the SEC $450 million to settle those charges. Raymond Cunningham, the head of Invesco Funds, paid a civil penalty of $500,000 and was barred from the securities industry for two years. Three other executives at that fund settled SEC charges by paying $340,000 and were barred from the mutual fund industry for one year.

More Disclosures

The list of market timers continued to grow. The SEC charged Security Brokerage Inc., a Las Vegas brokerage firm, with improperly generating $175 million in profits from late trading and market timing of mutual fund shares. The SEC brought civil charges and Spitzer brought criminal charges under the New York Martin Act against Steven B. Markovitz, a senior trader for Millennium Partners LP, a hedge fund that was late trading mutual funds. Three Merrill Lynch brokers were fired for assisting that trading. Davenport & Co. LLC also agreed to pay the NASD $450,000 to settle market timing charges, and paid another $13.5 million to settle charges brought by the states of New Jersey and Connecticut for the same conduct.

Franklin Resources Inc. was charged by Massachusetts regulators with fraud for allowing market timing transactions in mutual funds by a Las Vegas investor, Daniel G. Calugar, the president of Security Brokerage Inc. In exchange for investing $10 million in a Franklin Templeton hedge fund, Calugar was allowed to market time transactions valued at $45 million in the Franklin Small Cap Growth Fund. Those charges were settled for $5 million, but the Massachusetts regulators brought another action after Franklin Templeton claimed that it did not admit wrongdoing in its settlement with the state. Calugar was charged by the SEC with making profits of $175 million from market timing and late trading of mutual funds managed by Alliance Capital Management and Massachusetts Financial Services Co. Fred Alger Management suspended three employees, and the firm's vice chairman, James P. Connelly Jr., pleaded guilty to obstructing an investigation into market timing practices in the Fred Alger mutual funds. Connelly, who had tried to conceal trading arrangements with Calugar at Security Brokerage Inc., was given a prison term of one to three years.

Franklin Advisers paid $50 million to settle charges that it allowed thirty traders to engage in market timing transactions in the funds it advised, including Franklin Templeton. Paul Flynn, executive director of equity arbitrage trading at the Canadian Imperial Bank of Commerce, was improperly trading mutual funds for the hedge fund clients of the bank and was disguising that trading. Spitzer and the SEC charged Flynn with stealing more than $1 million from a mutual fund through a late trading scheme. Flynn provided financing to hedge funds that he knew were engaging in market timing and late trading of mutual funds. The Canadian Imperial Bank of Commerce paid $125 million to settle SEC late trading and market timing charges.

The Empire mutual fund admitted that employees had engaged in late trading. Charles Schwab & Co. admitted that its U.S. Trust unit allowed hedge funds to late trade mutual fund shares. Schwab agreed to pay $350,000 to settle SEC charges arising from that activity. Federated Investors allowed late trading and market timing transactions in its mutual funds. J. & W. Seligman & Co. agreed to waive certain fees and repay $3.7 million to funds it sponsored that allowed market timing trades.

Bear Stearns fired six employees in connection with abuses in mutual fund trading. Later, three more employees in its clearing unit were dismissed for facilitating improper mutual fund transactions. Loomis Sayles & Co. was found to have allowed market timing transactions. UBS AG fired two of its brokers and disciplined others for violating mutual fund trading rules. A trader for Millennium Partners LP, a hedge fund, pleaded guilty to trading mutual funds after the market closed.

The SEC charged Mutuals.com Inc. and three of its officers and two broker-dealers with illegally aiding hedge funds and institutional investors in engaging in market timing and late trading in mutual funds. This conduct occurred after the late trading scandals were already in the headlines. The Pershing unit of the Bank of New York was under investigation for aiding that trading. State Street Research Investment Services Inc., a Boston firm, agreed to pay $1.5 million to the NASD to settle charges on market timing transactions. Kautilya Sharma and Neal Wadhwa at Geek Securities in Miami pleaded guilty to criminal charges of allowing late trading in mutual funds. They had set a time stamp machine to record orders as having been entered before 4 PM. RS Investment Management LP paid $25 million to settle SEC market timing charges, and agreed with Eliot Spitzer to reduce its fees by $5 million. Two employees at Kaplan & Co. Securities in Boca Raton, Florida, agreed to pay $750,000 to settle SEC charges that they allowed clients to market time and late trade mutual funds. They also pleaded guilty to criminal charges filed by Eliot Spitzer under the Martin Act. Bean Murray & Co. was fined $150,000 for allowing late trading by Canary Capital and other hedge funds. Bear Stearns was also accused of aiding such trading.

Wachovia Securities acquired a majority interest in Prudential Securities in July 2003. That timing was not good. The SEC and the Massachusetts Securities Division charged that Prudential brokers in the firm's Boston office had improperly market timed trades amounting to $1.3 billion. The SEC alleged that the brokers used false identification numbers and misspelled their own names in order to evade Prudential's restrictions on such trading. The trades were made by the brokers for hedge fund clients and involved several major mutual funds.

The publicity and panic surrounding these late trading and market timing scandals caused investors to flee from mutual funds. They withdrew $54 billion from Putnam Investments alone in the fourth quarter of 2003. That was too bad because they had to pay entry and exit costs as a result of that liquidation. Many investors liquidated their mutual fund shares and parked their money in money market funds, receiving little return and missing the market upswing that was then under way. Some investors moved their money to other longer-term mutual funds, incurring additional charges in the process. These activities were encouraged by Morningstar Inc., a mutual funds rating service, which announced that it would be rating mutual funds based on corporate governance scores. Performance was apparently a secondary consideration. Morningstar itself was making an IPO and planned a politically correct board. Nevertheless, its founder, Joe Mansueto, was to retain complete control of the company. Morningstar was under investigation by the SEC for overstating returns of the Rock Canyon Top Flight Fund and failing to take prompt corrective action after being notified of the error. Eliot Spitzer was also investigating Morningstar for possible conflicts of interest in its pension consulting activities. The SEC then commenced an investigation of that activity.

Other Mutual Fund Issues

Mutual funds often have multiple classes that charge differing loads (sales charges): some are front-end loaded, others are back-end loaded, and some have no loads. A longtime concern with those arrangements is that customers are often steered to the class having a higher load. In other instances, customers are steered to a mutual fund that provides special incentives to salespersons, who recommend that fund over funds with similar objectives but lower charges.

Morgan Stanley agreed to pay the SEC $50 million to settle charges in connection with its sale of mutual funds. Among other things, the firm was directing customers to mutual funds based on commissions paid for those funds, rather than the appropriateness of the investment for the customer. Certain "preferred" funds paid higher commissions to Morgan Stanley's registered representatives as an incentive to push those products. The Morgan Stanley sales force also failed to disclose at the point of sale that its class B shares of certain of its proprietary mutual funds charged higher fees for large transactions. The Massachusetts securities regulator dismissed charges against Morgan Stanley, which had asserted that the firm falsely denied that it was paying special commissions on certain mutual funds in order to encourage their sale without regard to investor interests. Morgan Stanley paid another $435,000 to New Hampshire authorities for giving brokers extra benefits for selling Morgan Stanley proprietary funds. The rewards included a "steak-a-thon" in which brokers were given steaks for such sales. American Express sued the state of New Hampshire from sanctioning it for incentives given to salesmen for promoting in-house mutual funds. The suit claimed that the state's laws were preempted by the federal securities laws.

Many mutual funds have "breakpoints" that provide a discount on the loads paid by customers who invest specified amounts in the funds, and many mutual fund complexes administering funds with differing objectives allow customers to switch among the funds in the complex without charging additional loads. Purchases of more than one fund in a complex are usually accumulated and given the advantage of breakpoints. This too opened the door to abuse. In order to increase their commissions, unscrupulous sales personnel urged customers to divide their investments among separate funds just under the breakpoints, thereby avoiding the breakpoint discount. To prevent such abuses, regulators required customers to be given a "breakpoint letter" describing the discounts available.

The SEC charged that a registered representative in Prudential's Wilkes-Barre, Pennsylvania, office sold customers class B mutual fund shares without informing them that they were eligible for breakpoints on class A shares. The registered representative received higher commissions from the sale of the class B shares. Twelve brokers and managers at Prudential resigned as a result of such mutual fund abuses. Similar charges were brought against Kissinger Advisory Inc. and others. Fifteen brokerage firms agreed to pay $21.5 million to the SEC and NASD to settle charges that they failed to provide breakpoint discounts for mutual fund customers. Among the firms included in the settlement were Wachovia Securities LLC, UBS Financial Services, American Express Financial Advisors, Raymond James Financial Services, Legg Mason Wood Walker, Lehman Brothers, and Bear Sterns & Co. Thereafter, the SEC and the NASD directed 450 securities firms to notify their customers that they might be due refunds because those firms had failed to provide breakpoint discounts on their class A shares. Appropriate breakpoint discounts were not given in one out of every five transactions.

The SEC also investigated whether mutual funds were paying retirement planners to recommend their clients to the funds and whether mutual fund advisers were directing brokerage business to brokers providing them with lavish entertainment and gifts. Heartland Advisors Inc., an adviser to mutual funds, and its founder and president, William Nasgovitz, were charged with overstating the value of municipal bonds held in the portfolio of its funds. Nasgovitz was additionally charged with insider trading for tipping a friend on the pricing problem before it was made public. Four other individuals were also charged. FT Interactive Data, a service that priced assets owned by the Heartland mutual funds, settled charges that it had mispriced the mutual funds portfolios by adjusting values downward in small increments in order to avoid showing a sudden large loss. Piper Capital Management was censured by the SEC and an adviser to its funds was fined $2 million and had its investment adviser registration revoked for mispricing collateralized mortgage obligations held in one of Piper's mutual funds. The risks of those obligations were not disclosed properly to investors.

Bridgeway Funds and its chief executive officer, John Montgomery, agreed to pay $5 million to settle SEC charges that the funds were charging performance fees that were based on the wrong asset levels. Montgomery had been a strong advocate of corporate governance reforms for mutual funds, even testifying before Congress on those issues. His funds were highly rated by Morningstar as being protective of investor interests. First Command Financial Services was charged by the NASD with defrauding military personnel by selling them a high-priced Franklin Resources mutual fund without disclosing that 50 percent of the first twelve payments would be used to pay commissions. The firm agreed to pay $12 million to settle those charges, and Franklin Resources discontinued the fund. The SEC investigated other mutual fund managers to determine if they were improperly receiving rebates from commissions paid by mutual funds for the execution of trades. Quick & Reilly and Piper Jaffray were fined by the NASD for pushing mutual funds to customers that were paying those brokerage firms commissions and other payments for preferential treatment.

Citigroup Global Markets Inc. paid the SEC $20 million to settle charges that its Smith Barney sales force failed to disclose payments received from some seventy-five mutual funds to provide "shelf space" for their products in making recommendations to investors. Marsh & McLennan's Putnam Investments paid $40 million to settle charges that it made such payments to brokers. American Express Financial Advisors paid $13 million and JPMorgan Chase & Co. paid $2 million to settle SEC charges concerning their mutual fund sales practices. Capital Research & Management, which manages the American Funds complex of mutual funds, sued California attorney general William Lockyer seeking a court order that the SEC had exclusive jurisdiction over its mutual funds sales practices. Lockyer responded immediately with a suit charging those funds with fraud for failing to shelf space payments.

Edward D. Jones & Co. paid $75 million to settle SEC and NASD charges that it failed to disclose to investors that it was receiving payments from mutual funds recommended by its sales force. The sales force was given points toward European and Caribbean vacations for selling those funds. California attorney general William Lockyer demanded hundreds of millions more from the firm to settle charges he might bring as a result of that activity. Edward D. Jones had published newspaper advertisements decrying the mutual fund late trading and market timing scandals, but later had to confess that it had itself allowed thousands of late trading transactions.

Fidelity Investments disciplined sixteen traders for accepting gifts from Jefferies Group Inc., which acted as a broker for Fidelity. The gifts included expensive wine and travel on private jets to the Super Bowl and Wimbledon. Expenses were also paid for the bachelor party of Thomas Bruderman, a Fidelity trader who was marrying the daughter of Dennis Kozlowski of Tyco fame. Those expenses included private jets, a cruise, women, and entertainment that included a dwarf. Some golf outings with the Bank of America Corp. were also under investigation. Fidelity Investments had other problems that involved its use of "fair value pricing" to set prices for investments in its international funds. That pricing method was used to prevent traders from arbitraging its funds based on differing closing times in foreign markets, but critics claimed that such pricing was arbitrary, and the SEC began a study of fair value pricing and demanded more disclosures on its use. The SEC also charged Garrett Van Wagoner, a popular mutual funds manager, with improperly using fair value pricing to improve his funds' performance. Van Wagoner agreed to pay $800,000 to settle those charges. Although he continued to advise his mutual funds, he was barred from serving as a director for seven years.

Variable Annuities

Regulators were examining variable annuity investments for late trading and market timing. Variable annuity investment programs operate much like a mutual fund, but are used as a retirement plan. Variable annuities initially became popular because of their tax advantages, but the reduction in federal capital gains taxes equalized competition with mutual funds. At the end of 2002, $800 billion was held in variable annuity accounts, a fraction of the amount held in mutual funds.

The SEC charged Gregory P. Waldon at FASCO International Inc. with switching investors in and out of variable annuity contracts in order to boost his commissions. A joint study of the variable fund industry by the SEC and NASD found that customers were being sold variable annuities that were not suitable for them. The NASD then sought to impose additional regulation over variable annuities. Conseco Inc., the troubled insurance firm that was under assault for accounting and other problems, was targeted by regulators for allowing variable annuity holders to engage in frequent trades in their accounts. This trading was being conducted by large investors. Conseco and Inviva Inc. agreed to pay a total of $20 million to settle charges brought by Eliot Spitzer and the SEC for that trading activity. One market timing trader sued the life insurance companies for cutting him off from such trading. He claimed that he had been promised that he would be allowed to engage in such transactions in his variable annuity account.

One More Media Event

Spitzer and the SEC collected over $3 billion in fines and restitution from mutual funds that settled late trading and market timing cases, with more to come. Some investors were given refunds exceeding any conceivable losses they might have sustained. Some investors were given payments even though they were not invested in mutual funds at the time the late trading or market timing occurred. That overreaching was criticized by Dennis Vacco, a Republican and former New York attorney general, who had been turned out of office by Spitzer. Vacco contended that Spitzer was being overly aggressive in attacking the mutual funds.[63] Vacco had actually begun the effort by New York to take over regulation of Wall Street from the SEC by "expanding the criminal justice role of this office, from prosecuting cop killers to busting drug gangs, but also being more aggressive in using our criminal justice authority to go after scam artists in the marketplace."[64]

Lawyers engaged in food fights in seeking lead counsel status in the class actions brought against the mutual fund and other firms involved in the market timing and late trading scandals in 2003. Congress held more hearings, and legislation was proposed to increase regulation and require more disclosure of fees, compensation, and other matters. The SEC did not await that legislation before proposing new rules that would, among other things, require more disclosures on fees and portfolio investments. Mutual funds were required to create compliance programs and hire compliance officers. The SEC adopted rules requiring investment advisers to establish a code of ethics and to disclose the effects of market timing transactions and the policies of the mutual fund concerning such trading.

One particularly controversial rule adopted by the SEC required that the office of the chairman of a mutual fund board had to be separate from the chief executive officer and that outside directors had to constitute at least 75 percent of mutual fund boards. Those outside directors would have to meet in separate sessions at least quarterly. This rule had been approved by a split 3–2 vote of the SEC, despite a study showing that mutual funds with nonindependent chairmen charged lower fees than those with an independent chairman. Further, boards with management chairmen performed better on average in their investments. This study was conducted by Stephen Ferris and Xuemin Yan, two finance professors at the University of Missouri. They examined some 450 mutual fund families and concluded that mutual funds with independent chairmen were no less likely to be involved in scandals and had higher expenses because of additional support needed for chairmen with no knowledge of the funds they manage. The U.S. Chamber of Commerce sued the SEC to block implementation of this rule, but a federal court refused to enjoin enforcement. The Chamber did not believe that the government should be dictating how business should be managed in America. The Chamber of Commerce eventually prevailed in its action against the SEC. A court of appeals ruled that the SEC had not adequately considered the costs of the rule or an alternative presented by two Republican commissioners. William Donaldson had, in the interim, announced his resignation, but he had the commission readopt the rule after only a one-week review because he knew his successor would not vote for such a requirement. That arbitrary act set off a storm of controversy and did even further damage to the already tarnished reputation of the SEC. In response to this SEC rule, Congress enacted legislation requiring the SEC to conduct a study of whether companies with independent chairmen actually perform better. This was an effort to shame the SEC into reversing its rule.

The new SEC rules and programs were expected to increase the costs of mutual fund management and stifle the creation of new funds. The increased costs were to be borne by mutual fund investors, once the fee reduction agreements expired. This was deeply intrusive government regulation, dictating how private businesses should be managed, a matter that government has shown no familiarity with in the past. In addition, the SEC was proposing a mandatory 2 percent redemption fee on mutual funds purchased and sold within five days, which was designed to make market timing costs prohibitive. The SEC later decided to allow mutual funds to use their discretion in imposing such fees. The SEC and Congress were additionally considering restrictions on "soft dollar" arrangements, which involve using commissions paid to broker-dealers to be transferred in part to mutual fund investment advisers to compensate those advisers for research reports or other services.

Hedge Funds

Hedge funds numbered over 6,000 and held over $600 billion in assets as the new century began. Some of those hedge funds were at the center of the Wall Street mutual fund scandal. The hedge funds' reputation had already been besmirched by the collapse in 1998 of Long Term Capital Management (LTCM), a hedge fund created by John W. Meriwether, a former vice chairman of Salomon Brothers whose reckless style was made famous in a book by Michael Lewis called *Liar's Poker.* Meriwether had been forced to leave Salomon Brothers as a result of a scandal over a corner in the Treasury note market. Meriwether's next venture was LTCM, which lost 90 percent of its capital in September 1998 from "convergence" trading. In a scene reminiscent of J.P. Morgan's saving of the market after it crashed in 1907, LTCM had to be rescued by a group of investment banks at the behest of Peter Fisher, a senior official at the Federal Reserve Board Bank in New York. Merrill Lynch, Goldman Sachs, Morgan Stanley, JP Morgan, and others supplied $3.6 billion to shore up the hedge fund and avoid a market panic.

Tiger Management, a hedge fund that had $23 billion in capital, lost $2.1 billion of that amount in September 1998. It lost another $3.4 billion in October, including $2 billion that was lost through currency trading on a single day. Tiger Management, which was managed by Julian H. Robertson, continued to lose heavily and was closed in March 2000 after its capital fell from $22 billion to $6.5 billion. Another hedge fund experiencing trouble in October 1998 was Ellington Capital Management in Greenwich, Connecticut. That fund was managed by Michael Vranos, a former mortgage-backed security trader at Kidder, Peabody. He was forced to dump the fund's huge position in mortgage-backed securities in order to meet margin calls.

Two "convertible-arbitrage" hedge funds lost $315 million in 2001, 40 percent of their value. These funds were arbitraging between convertible bonds and the shares into which they could be converted. Kenneth Lipper, the manager of those convertible funds, was sued by some of his investors. His clients included Michael D. Eisner, the head of Walt Disney, and Julia Roberts, the actress. Lipper was a former deputy mayor of New York and a movie producer. Edward J. Strafaci, portfolio manager for Lipper's convertible hedge funds, was indicted by the Justice Department for overstating the value of convertible bonds and preferred stock held in four of the funds. Lipper had to write down $315 million in value of convertible bonds held in his portfolio as a result of that overpricing, cutting their value nearly in half. Strafaci pleaded guilty to criminal charges.

George Soros's $20 billion Quantum Group suffered large losses when the Russian government defaulted on its debt in August 1998. Soros shut down his $1.5 billion emerging markets hedge fund, which was a member of his Quantum Group. His Quantum Fund was down by 21 percent at the end of the twentieth century. In total, Soros's hedge funds dropped by $7.6 billion in value, down from $22 billion in August 1998. Soros was the infamous hedge fund manager who knocked Great Britain out of the exchange rate mechanism that was being used to achieve currency convergence with other European countries in the 1990s. Soros was said to have made $2 billion from that operation. Soros was found guilty of insider trading by a French court in 2002. That conviction related to his purchase, some fourteen years earlier, of four formerly state-owned companies in France for his Quantum Endowment Fund. Soros was fined $2.3 million by the French court. These were not the first regulatory problems encountered by Soros. In 1986 he had been sanctioned by the Commodity Futures Trading Commission (CFTC) in 1986 for violating trading limit rules. He had also been charged with stock manipulation by the SEC in 1979 for selling shares in Computer Sciences Corp. before its public offering. Soros covered the short sales by acquiring the stock in the initial public offering at a lower price. Soros was permanently enjoined from engaging in such conduct in the future.

A $200 million hedge fund in Japan, the Eifuku Master Fund, lost almost all of its capital over a seven-day period in January 2003. Some companies were claiming that negative research by hedge funds was hurting their stock prices. The complaining companies included MBIA Inc., the Federal Agricultural Mortgage Corp. (Farmer Mac), and Allied Capital Corp. A hedge fund fraud scheme involving the Manhattan Investment Fund, which was managed by Michael Berger, resulted in losses of $350 million. In Naples, Florida, David Mobley's Maricopa Index Hedge Fund turned out to be a Ponzi scheme that defrauded some 300 wealthy investors of over $120 million between 1993 and 2000. Mobley claimed to have a "predator system" that assured large trading gains. In fact, he was using the money for personal extravagances, including expensive real estate in Naples and a fleet of luxury automobiles. Mobley was sentenced to seventeen years in prison. An arbitration proceeding brought against Morgan Stanley to recover those losses was dismissed. Mobley had supposedly kept the client's money at Morgan Stanley.

The Internal Revenue Service was investigating hedge funds that were keeping their investments offshore in order to avoid taxes. One hedge fund had sheltered $192 million in funds offshore. The CFTC charged Tradewinds International, a hedge fund, with fraud for overstating the value of its assets. The hedge fund claimed assets of over $18 million when the actual amount was $1.1 million and gains of 12 percent when the fund was actually experiencing losses. The fund's manager, Charles L. Harris, sent investors videos that contained a movie of himself confessing to improper trading while fleeing in his yacht. He was later captured.

NorthShore Asset Management LLC, a Chicago hedge fund, reported that $37 million had been stolen from the fund, but an SEC investigation concluded that the partners managing the hedge fund had lost the money in investments in speculative securities. KL Financial Group, a hedge fund servicing the wealthy in Palm Beach, Florida, closed after suffering losses that were estimated to range up to $400 million. The FBI and SEC were trying to ascertain what happened to the investors' funds. Another hedge fund manager, Steven A. Cohen, was apparently doing much better. His net worth was estimated to be over $2 billion, and he was earning over $350 million per year. A front-page article in the *New York Times* reported that this success allowed Cohen to amass an incredible art collection and become a force in that market.

Hedge funds operated under an exemption in the Investment Company Act of 1940 that excluded regulation of investment companies catering to wealthy individuals, but some hedge funds reduced their minimum investment amounts to as low as $25,000. That encouraged the less wealthy to participate. Mutual funds were investing in hedge funds, providing even small investors with backdoor access to the hedge funds. As these less wealthy investors entered these funds in an attempt to snare the huge gains previously experienced only by the wealthy, they began to realize that the risks were commensurate with the rewards. A hedge fund, particularly in difficult market conditions, could provide sharp losses as well as profits.

Citigroup agreed to pay the NASD $250,000 to settle charges that it supplied hedge fund investors with a targeted rate of return that was not substantiated. The NASD warned broker-dealers managing hedge funds that they were responsible for assuring that investments in hedge funds were suitable for their customers. The NASD conceded that hedge funds were becoming a mainstream investment, but noted that they posed huge risks for investors.

The SEC began an attack on the hedge funds after disclosure of the Canary Capital mutual fund trading. Hedge funds had been previously unregulated, but after conducting a study of hedge funds in 2003, the SEC staff recommended that the managers of hedge funds should be required to register with the SEC as investment advisers under the Investment Advisers Act of 1940. This recommendation aroused intense opposition in the industry, even though about half of the larger hedge funds were already registered as advisers. Despite the opposition, SEC chairman William Donaldson forced the adoption of the proposal as a way of showing his regulatory toughness. It was adopted by a 3–2 vote of the SEC. A hedge fund manager sued to stop the implementation of the rule.

The government did not await new rules before suing the hedge funds. The SEC charged a hedge fund official with failing to supervise employees, even though the hedge fund was not registered with the SEC. Such failure to supervise claims had previously been limited only to firms and employees registered with the SEC. Eliot Spitzer and the SEC investigated hedge funds to determine if they were manipulating stock prices through short selling. There was even talk of curbing short selling because of such activities. This was a throwback to earlier eras when short sellers were accused of causing market downturns. Interestingly, short sellers were one of the few interests on Wall Street that actually act as an effective gatekeeper by remaining skeptical of full disclosure and closely examining company operations for flaws being covered up by managers in their accounting statements.

Hedge funds were seeing drops in the value of their assets, but investors were still contributing funds. In total, hedge funds numbered almost 7,000 and had over $850 billion under management in 2004. This was a considerable increase over the $1.5 billion held by 200 hedge funds in 1969 and the $400 billion under management in 2000. Some hedge fund managers were more successful than others. Stephen Cohen at Sac Capital Advisors was managing $4 billion in hedge fund assets. During the prior twelve years, he increased hedge fund assets by 40 percent a year and was paid performance fees of 50 percent of that increase.

Permal, a $20 billion hedge fund, announced that it was creating a Sharia-compliant Islamic hedge fund. Some venture capitalists disinvited the University of California from participating in their funds because of a court ruling in California that required the university to disclose the performance record of the venture capital funds in which the university system was invested. Many of those hedge funds were intensely private groups that objected to any such disclosure. Some states were considering legislation to negate such disclosure requirements.

9. More Scandals and Reform

Sarbanes-Oxley

Arthur Levitt

Full disclosure reform proved to be an empty promise to many investors after the stock market bubble burst in 2000, but its defenders became even more aggressive in propounding its supposed benefits. Former Securities and Exchange Commission (SEC) chairman Arthur Levitt was the leader of that pack. After he left the agency, he wrote a self-serving book that blamed the collapse of the markets on everything but his own stewardship. Levitt claimed that he had been frustrated by Republicans, plus Democrat Senator Joseph Lieberman, and a group of legislators that Levitt derided as "New Democrats" with "probusiness positions." Levitt claimed that "powerful special interest groups" on Wall Street were another barrier that kept him from stopping abuses in the market.[1] Those coconspirators included the Business Round Table, the Securities Industry Association, the United States Chamber of Commerce, and the National Federation of Independent Businesses. Democracy was, indeed, a terrible thing for full disclosure. Levitt did not, in any event, explain why the vast powers already given to the SEC were inadequate to stop even the grossest of accounting frauds. Indeed, the number of investigations and enforcement actions actually declined during several of the years that Levitt served as chairman of the SEC.

Levitt advocated more regulations even though the federal securities laws and SEC regulations already filled volumes. None of the scandals or schemes during the market bubble were particularly novel, but Levitt's posture appeared to be that, if a lot of regulation does not work in assuring full disclosure, add a lot more. Levitt wanted to make the already draconian sanctions in the federal securities laws more punitive and require that anyone even loosely connected with the process become enforcers and informants in the guise of being "gatekeepers."

A New Chairman Arrives

Harvey Pitt was appointed by President George W. Bush to replace Arthur Levitt as chairman of the SEC. Pitt arrived after the market bubble burst, leaving him to clean up the problems that arose on Levitt's watch. Pitt appeared to be an ideal choice for reforming the agency, having served both at the SEC and in the private sector. A graduate of Brooklyn College and St. John's University law school, Pitt started his career as a bottom-rung lawyer in the SEC Office of General Counsel in the 1970s, working his way up the ranks to become the agency's general counsel. In that role, Pitt unsuccessfully tried to engineer a takeover of jurisdiction from the Commodity Futures Trading Commission (CFTC) for financial derivatives. Still, Pitt developed a reputation at the SEC for brilliance and integrity, and his long working hours were legend, as were his demands on the staff he supervised.[1]

During his tenure on the SEC staff, Pitt witnessed scandals that should have warned him of the dangers of filling the position of chairman. William Casey, while SEC chairman, came under fire after he refused to turn over investigative papers that a congressional committee was seeking in connection with the Watergate scandal.[2] Casey sent the papers to the Department of Justice, which could claim executive privilege to shield the papers from congressional scrutiny; the SEC was a creature of Congress and could claim no such privilege. The papers were delivered to John Dean at the Department of Justice; he later became White House counsel and a key player in the Watergate scandal. Unknown to Casey, an SEC attorney had kept complete notes on the papers, which had to be surrendered to Congress.

Casey left for the State Department after that controversy, serving years later in the Reagan administration as the director of the Central Intelligence Agency (CIA). Casey was replaced as SEC chairman by G. Bradford Cook, the SEC's general counsel and Harvey Pitt's supervisor. Cook's tenure was short-lived. He had to resign from the agency after it was revealed that he had changed the wording in an SEC complaint filed against Robert Vesco, the fugitive financier who looted the Investors Overseas Service (IOS) mutual funds. Before the complaint was filed, Cook removed allegations about campaign contributions made by Vesco to Republican candidates.

Pitt left the SEC to enter private practice. He rose to fame during the insider trading scandals of the 1980s and proved a skillful negotiator in his representation of Ivan Boesky. Pitt represented a broad spectrum of financial institutions, including banks, broker-dealers, accounting firms (Arthur Andersen was on that list), and executives having problems with financial regulators. Pitt represented industry trade groups such as the Investment Company Institute (the lobbying group for mutual funds), the Securities Industry Association (the lobbying group for broker-dealers), and the American Institute of Certified Public Accountants (AICPA). Pitt represented the accounting industry in negotiating with the SEC when the Independence Standards

Board (ISB) was formed by the AICPA under pressure from the SEC. He was the author of an AICPA white paper presented to the ISB that accused the SEC and Chairman Arthur Levitt of trying to create "command and control" regulations over the accounting industry. Levitt boycotted the ISB's first meeting at which the white paper was presented.

While in private practice, Pitt was frequently referred to in the press as a "prominent" securities lawyer and was quoted as saying, "some of my clients say the worst penalty is paying my fees. They can be very expensive." Pitt had an intellectual bent, publishing numerous thoroughly researched articles on securities industry issues and a treatise on the regulation of financial institutions. Although Pitt was sometimes critical of particular SEC policies, he venerated the agency and was the president of an SEC historical society composed of SEC alumni. That society reflected another phenomenon associated with full disclosure. The SEC was known for the high rate of turnover in its personnel, creating a revolving door into private industry. Once there, those individuals became strong advocates of the full disclosure system. Those alumni cherished their service at the SEC and held heavily attended reunions periodically in Washington, DC. At one such reunion, Supreme Court Justice William O. Douglas, a former SEC chairman, described his varied career and his travels, including a trip to Russia with Robert Kennedy, making the point that he had met every class of person around the world. The justice then opined that with that broad experience it appeared to him that stockbrokers were the lowest breed of individual on earth, a pronouncement that was greeted with raucous shouts and applause from the gathered SEC alumni.

Harvey Pitt retained an ambition to become SEC chairman, an opportunity he seized after George W. Bush won the 2000 election. Pitt's timing was most unfortunate. He assumed office right in the middle of the market downturn and only a few months before the Enron scandal broke. Even so, Pitt's background, experience, and intellect seemingly made him an ideal candidate for the job. By all accounts, Pitt served his country well in dealing with the near panic in the markets after the terrorist attacks on September 11, 2001, only a few weeks after he assumed office. Pitt also promised a kinder and gentler SEC enforcement policy for accountants. He wanted companies to work with the agency in resolving compliance problems, eschewing more splashy enforcement actions. Those words would come back to haunt him when Enron failed and the press began hounding anyone who had ever supported the business community.

Pitt tried to create a more workable relationship with the accounting industry as a substitute for the contentious policies of Arthur Levitt that had proved a failure in preventing either the market bubble or abuses. Pitt sought to curb the number of restatements of financial results, suggesting that investors were being inundated with conflicting information. The timing of that announcement could not have been worse, coming just as Enron was restating its accounts. Pitt proposed the creation of a new regulatory body dominated by public members with expertise in accounting and with the power to discipline accountants and maintain quality control standards. This appeared to be what Levitt had sought and Pitt had frustrated in private practice.

Pitt acknowledged that "[t]he development of rule-based accounting standards has resulted in the employment of financial engineering techniques designed solely to achieve accounting objectives rather than to achieve economic objectives."[3] He began advocating "current" or real-time disclosure of financial information, a then current reformist fad. Pitt noted that many corporations were already announcing earnings in advance of their filing with the SEC. Pitt's proposal for accounting oversight was met with much criticism. The members of the Public Oversight Board (POB), created in 1977 to review the quality of audits and oversee peer reviews, resigned in May 2002, believing that the Pitt proposal of a new oversight board had undermined its position and made it a lame duck. The POB was managed by a five-member board that included nonaccountants, as well as industry professionals. Pitt responded that the issues at stake were "too important for the POB simply to walk away."

Pitt created another furor when he suggested that his role as chairman be elevated to cabinet status, a proposal that had been rejected in the 1970s when Pitt was a staff attorney at the SEC. The press somewhat superciliously claimed that Pitt was trying to increase his pay by about $35,000 a year in seeking cabinet status, but Pitt was already a multimillionaire, and he was quick to point out in testifying before Congress that he had taken a 99 percent pay cut to come to the SEC. Pitt's proposal also had some merit. The Chicago Mercantile Exchange had unsuccessfully urged in 1993 that Congress consolidate financial regulation into a single cabinet-level department to cut down overlap and inefficiencies imposed by the morass of regulators in the United States. That path of single regulation was followed by other countries, including Great Britain, Japan, and Germany. Great Britain appeared to have success with that approach at the time Pitt floated his proposal.

Pitt did a flip-flop on the expensing of options paid as compensation, resisting the idea at first but backing off, as it became a contentious issue in the Enron hearings before Congress. Pitt was then embarrassed by New York attorney general Eliot Spitzer's attack on the securities analysts. The SEC looked ineffective as a result, and Pitt was unsuccessful in co-opting Spitzer. More criticism came with the disclosure that Pitt had met privately with Eugene D. O'Kelly, the head of KPMG at a time when that accounting firm was under investigation for its audit of Xerox. O'Kelly bragged in a memorandum sent to KPGM employees that he had discussed the case with Pitt, who denied that claim and was recused from the case in any event because of his prior representation of KPMG. Pitt was further criticized for not announcing his recusal from the Enron matter quickly enough in the press, and he was blamed for the Enron failure in his role as counsel to the accounting industry.

As criticism of Pitt's policies mounted the *Wall Street Journal* and the *New York Times,* an unusual combination, called for his resignation. They were soon joined by Senator John McCain of Keating Five fame, and others. Soon, Pitt was a pariah in the press. The White House added more trouble for Pitt with the appointment of Harvey Goldschmid to fill a Democratic commissioner slot on the SEC. Goldschmid was a Columbia University law professor who was seeking to preserve the legacy of Adolf Berle and his colleague William Cary by imposing more strangling regulation on large corporations. Goldschmid, who had drafted of Regulation FD while serving as SEC general counsel under Arthur Levitt, remained loyal to Levitt and became a harsh critic of Pitt, undermining his administration.

Election Issues

Control of the Senate was up for grabs in 2002, and Enron and other corporate scandals became a centerpiece of the election. Each party tried to out-Enron the other. The Democrats were stymied in criticizing the president over the war on terror, which left the economy and corporate scandals (led by Enron) as issues. The president preempted the Democrats on the economy by calling for more tax cuts to aid recovery from the economic downturn. Democrats turned to Enron and tried to claim that the Republicans were responsible, even though the company had come to prominence while President Bill Clinton was in the White House. The Republicans, nevertheless, were tarred with the problem, and their strategy was to simply outshout the Democrats in their denunciation of corporate management. That would prove a difficult task, as demonstrated by Senator John Kerry's assertion that comparing Enron executives to the Corleone family in the *Godfather* movies about the mafia was an insult to the Corleones. It was later revealed, however, that Kenneth Lay, the head of Enron, had served on the board of trustees of the Heinz Center, an environmental advocacy group created by Kerry's wife, Teresa Heinz Kerry.

President Bush quickly bent to political pressure and personally delivered an attack on Wall Street. Alan Greenspan, the Federal Reserve chairman, joined him in asserting that accounting scandals could undermine investor confidence in the stock market and threaten the economy. President Bush's Wall Street address in July 2002 sought to assure the American people that corporate miscreants, such as those at Enron, would be punished severely. He announced a ten-point action plan to improve full disclosure and requested harsher penalties for corporate executives caught cooking the books. The president reported that the Department of Justice was creating a corporate fraud task force, headed by a deputy attorney general, that would act as a "financial crimes SWAT team." Included on the task force were representatives from the SEC, the CFTC, and the Treasury Department. The president's tough speech was not well received in the press. Many commentators expressed the view that his proposals were not strong enough to stop corporate fraud. In fact, that speech set off a witch hunt at the Department of Justice that endorsed and employed all manner of hardball tactics against corporate executives and their families, as Lea Fastow found out to her dismay. Within a year, the task force had charged over 350 defendants with corporate fraud and obtained over 250 convictions, mostly through guilty pleas, including twenty-five chief executive officers.

President Bush tried to further an image of toughness and quell hysteria in the press by directing the SEC to require the chief executive officers and chief financial officers of about 1,000 of the largest publicly traded companies based in the United States to certify personally, under oath, the accuracy of their company's financial statements. This loyalty oath to full disclosure would have done the McCarthy era proud. A total of sixteen companies were unable to certify the accuracy and completeness of their reports and filed explanations. Peter Dolan, chief executive officer at Bristol-Myers Squibb, had to recant the sworn certification of his company's financial statements when it restated its financial statements later in the year. The loyalty oath did not encompass foreign companies such as Tyco and Global Crossing, which were based in Bermuda.

The president was himself under fire for having accepted $180,000 in loans from Harken Energy Corporation before he became president. Harken had purchased an oil company Bush had organized, and he used the proceeds of that loan to buy shares of Harken stock. The president was being criticized for having sold 212,140 Harken shares in 1990, two months before that company announced an unexpected $23.2 million quarterly loss. Mr. Bush received $848,000 from that sale, with the stock then trading at about $4 per share. Its price dropped to $2.37 after the invasion of Kuwait by Iraq threatened a large oil exploration contract Harken had in Bahrain. The stock dropped further after the announcement of the quarterly loss, but later recovered. Bush used the proceeds of the stock sale to pay off a loan used to acquire his interest in the Texas Rangers. He subsequently sold that holding for $15 million, which also outraged his opponents.

Critics alleged that Harken had been using improper accounting procedures in booking some transactions while Bush was on its board, and the company's chief executive officer admitted that its financial statements were "a mess."[4] This issue had been raised in earlier Bush campaigns and had not gained much traction. Nevertheless, Enron and other burgeoning financial scandals were creating political opportunity to renew that criticism. President Bush, as he had in the past, pointed out that the Harken stock recovered and several months later was trading at twice the price he had received for his sales. He had also filed with the SEC a notice of his intention to sell his stock before doing so, although the SEC report of the sale itself was filed eight months late. Bush was cleared of insider trading charges by the SEC investigation. The agency also brought no charges as a result of the late filing of the form.

Vice President Richard Cheney was under criticism for his stewardship at Halliburton Corporation, a Houston energy company that was one of the world's largest oil field service and construction companies. Cheney had served as chairman and chief executive officer of that company from 1995 to 2000. It was now clear that anyone having any connection with a public company would forever be tainted by the full disclosure system. A lawsuit brought by Judicial Watch, a private interest group, sought to prove that Cheney conspired to defraud investors by questionable accounting practices at Halliburton, implemented with the assistance of Arthur Andersen, that resulted in inflated income and earnings of over $500 million in a four-year period. The lawsuit claimed that Halliburton had booked income from such things as construction project overruns even though the amounts of those overruns were still in dispute and had not been received. A federal district court dismissed the suit.

Halliburton settled for $12 million an SEC action, which charged that the company had failed to disclose a change in its accounting procedures in 1998. The company's controller agreed to pay a $50,000 fine for that conduct. The change in accounting procedure was appropriate but, because it was not disclosed, the SEC claimed that the federal securities laws had been violated, a novel theory of full disclosure. A class action suit went further, charging Halliburton with "serial accounting fraud" in inflating its revenues between 1998 and 2001. A federal judge rejected a $6 million settlement of that litigation, concluding that the settlement was inadequate. Halliburton then came under attack for overcharging during the Iraq war and for exclusive contracts given to the company to rebuild Iraq after the war. Halliburton admitted that one of its employees had received a $6 million kickback from a Kuwaiti contractor.

Sarbanes-Oxley Is Enacted

The hearings in Congress on Enron's failure did not result in broad support for new securities laws, but the demise of WorldCom renewed congressional interest. An early focus in the hearings on post-Enron legislation was the use of derivatives, which had been deregulated by the Commodity Futures Modernization Act of 2000 (CFMA) and were thought to have played a role in Enron's demise. The International Swaps and Derivatives Association, however, published a study that concluded that internal control failures rather than derivatives caused the collapse at Enron. The CFTC began actively investigating the energy firms for market manipulation despite their deregulation by the CFMA, resulting in large settlements of false price reporting by energy trading firms such as Duke, Dynegy, and Reliant. The law had to be stretched and bent a bit to obtain those results, but the CFTC's effort did have the effect of forestalling further regulation of derivatives.

Examples of retirees who lost their savings were trotted out again after WorldCom's demise, but little discussion was given to the fact that those savings had been wildly and artificially inflated by the misuse of the full disclosure system. Attention shifted again to stock options granted to executives as compensation, but that effort stalled in the face of arguments that stock options had beneficial effects for start-up companies and had provided wealth to many. Similarly, blaming the accounting scandals on the Republicans did not have any staying power, since they too were on the attack. Instead, the accountants became the principal target, as the public rage that had been whipped up by the press and members of Congress had been only partially vented in the prosecution of Arthur Andersen. After several audit failures were found, the Federal Reserve Board and other bank regulators weighed in by threatening to bar accounting firms from auditing banks.

The pressure for more regulation proved too much after the failure of WorldCom. Legislation in the form of the Sarbanes-Oxley Corporate Reform Act of 2002 was passed in Congress and signed into law by President Bush on July 30, 2002. The president stated: "This law says to corporate accountants: the high standards of your profession will be enforced without exception; the auditors will be audited; the accountants will be held to account." Sarbanes-Oxley created a new government oversight board over the accounting industry that would not "just slap around a few accountants." Rather, it would be given "massive power, unchecked power, by design."[5]

Republican senator Mitch McConnell had tried to kill this legislation through an amendment that would have required labor unions to be audited by public accountants. McConnell pointed out numerous frauds by labor officials who had stolen or misused union funds. He mocked the revelations of corporate executive excesses at Enron by pointing out that one labor union official had been given huge kickbacks to direct union funds into a Ponzi scheme that resulted in losses of $355 million to union members. Another union official embezzled millions of dollars from a union that he used to buy, among other things, eight cars, two boats, three jet skis, a riding lawnmower, and 108 collectable dolls. McConnell noted that directors of a union-owned insurance company had been sold stock in Global Crossing at a bargain that allowed them to realize large profits as an inducement for investment of the insurance company's reserves into Global Crossing, resulting in large losses. Apparently, unions play a little rougher than corporate boardrooms because Senator McConnell cited as another example several union officials who had been charged with bombing the home of a dissenting union member's home and stabbing another worker. McConnell asserted that union corruption was epidemic and should be dealt with in the same manner as corporate crime as proposed in the pending legislation.

McConnell's amendment might have been offered tongue in cheek, but it aroused the ire of Senator Edward Kennedy, who called the McConnell amendment a "poison pill" because the Republicans knew that the Democrats would never agree to the imposition of full disclosure requirements on their core constituency, the labor unions. Phil Gramm, the Republican senator from Texas, was uncharacteristically muted in supporting the McConnell amendment. After he and his wife had been tarred by Enron, Gramm announced that he would not be running for reelection, and he lost his fervor for opposing government regulation of the markets. Instead, other senators were left to cite the old anodynes that "our economic system is based on transparency" and that "we have to expect that public accounting firms are acting as corporate watchdogs over corporate financial statements."[6]

The signing of this legislation helped the Republican Party in the 2004 elections. The Republicans regained a narrow majority in the Senate, kept control of the House, and claimed a number of governorships. Still, full disclosure came with a steep price tag. To comply with its edicts, corporations had to pay hundreds of billions of dollars in the form of audit expenses, litigation costs, lawyers' fees, and lost executive time. The SEC itself became an ever-rising cost. In August 2002, President Bush proposed an increase in the SEC budget of 77 percent, an increase of $300 million, pushing the SEC's budget to over $700 million. This was to allow the agency to hire 800 more lawyers, accountants, and investigators. The SEC budget would increase in future years, peaking at $888 million for the 2006 fiscal year. Its sister agency, the CFTC, saw its budget grow to $99 million in that year.

PCAOB

One unique proposal floated in the congressional hearings by two accounting professors, Joshua Ronen and G.A. Swanson, would have created audit insurance that would be paid for by the public companies to insurance companies. The insurance companies would then be authorized to commission audits of those companies in order to reduce their exposure. This proposal assumed that management would not be even more emboldened to hide the ball from the auditors and that the insurance companies would not then refuse coverage for fraud. Congress opted instead for another layer of regulation that was closely modeled after the proposal by Harvey Pitt for a new accounting oversight body.

The centerpiece of the Sarbanes-Oxley legislation was the creation of a new public regulatory organization to set accounting standards for the industry. Called the Public Company Accounting Oversight Board (PCAOB), it quickly became known as "Peekaboo." Sarbanes-Oxley directed that PCAOB be formed as a federal corporation governed by the not-for-profit laws of the District of Columbia. PCAOB was to be funded by issuers of securities, adding further to the cost of doing business in America and inflating the costs of goods to consumers since these fees would be passed onto them through increased prices. Fines collected by PCAOB for infractions were to be used to fund scholarships for accounting students, since no one in their right mind would otherwise want to become an auditor with all of this regulatory scrutiny. Accounting firms that audit public companies were required to register with PCAOB. Registration laid the groundwork for other intrusive and expensive regulation, such as establishing books and records requirements, setting auditing standards and inspections, creating ethics rules, and sanctioning auditors. Foreign accounting firms were subjected to these requirements when they certified statements for public firms.

PCAOB was not ungenerous with its own budget ($152.8 million for 2005), its own staff (300 employees), or its own executive compensation. Its members awarded themselves salaries of $450,000 per year, and the chairman of PCAOB received $560,000, to be paid for out of fees assessed against public companies based on their market capitalization. This was far in excess of salaries given to officials at other government agencies, such as the Treasury Department and the SEC. PCAOB planned to inspect accounting firms and assess how they compensate partners and set the "tone at the top," a now familiar and broken refrain. PCAOB rejected a suggestion by one of its members that it should rotate its own auditors every five years. In a bit of irony, PCAOB headquarters in Washington, DC, were located in space that had been vacated by Arthur Andersen.

The Financial Accounting Standards Board (FASB) retained control over the setting of generally accepted accounting principles (GAAP), but the SEC was ordered by Sarbanes-Oxley to conduct a study of "principles-based accounting" such as that used by the International Accounting Standards Board (IASB). FASB was already considering the adoption of principle-based accounting standards, rather than the rule-based GAAP. The SEC issued a concept release in 2000 that sought comment on the development of a set of broad standards for determining whether an international accounting method met the SEC's goals of full disclosure. The European Commission was requiring companies listed on stock exchanges in the European Union to replace their national financial rules with international accounting standards by 2005. As a result of that requirement, and because many foreign companies began delisting in the United States as the result of Sarbanes-Oxley requirements, the SEC announced in April 2005 that it planned to move forward on allowing foreign companies to use international accounting standards in filing financial reports in the United States. In the meantime, almost 100 countries, including all of Europe, had adopted IASB standards rather than U.S. GAAP standards. In addition, European corporations report only semiannually. An effort to have corporations report quarterly was blocked by England and the European Union. The European Union dropped plans for a U.S.-style full disclosure system after Enron and other scandals.

The SEC, after consulting with the chairman of the Federal Reserve Board and the secretary of the Treasury, was authorized to appoint the five members of PCAOB. Terms were limited to five years and only two of the board's members could be certified public accountants. Paul Volcker, the former chairman of the Federal Reserve Board, turned down the position as chairman of PCAOB, believing that it should be only a part-time job. SEC chairman Harvey Pitt was then pressured by some Democratic members of Congress and Harvey Goldschmid, the Democrat SEC commissioner, to appoint John Biggs for that position. Biggs had been the head of TIAA-CREF, an activist institutional shareholder that had been an early advocate of an independent agency for regulating accountants. According to Goldschmid's supporters, Pitt had agreed to hire Biggs, but then decided to appoint William H. Webster, the former head of the CIA and FBI and a former federal appeals court judge.

Webster had been brought into the CIA and FBI to lend integrity to those agencies. Webster was viewed as a model of rectitude, but he failed to account for the long arm of full disclosure or the ennui of Goldschmid over the failure to appoint Biggs. According to a subsequent Government Accountability Office (GAO) (formerly known as the General Accounting Office) report, Pitt had been advised that Webster had been the chairman of the audit committee at U.S. Technologies Inc., an Internet company that was having financial difficulties. Pitt was not told that the audit committee had fired the company's auditors, BDO Seidman LLP. The accounting firm then reported to the SEC that there were material weaknesses in the accounting controls at U.S. Technologies. Webster said that the accounting firm was fired because of its high fees and not because of its criticism of management.

The GAO noted that Pitt had assigned the chief accountant at the SEC, Robert Herdman, the task of vetting Webster's background. Herdman learned of the problems at U.S. Technologies but did not consider them important enough to report to Pitt. Nevertheless, when that information was disclosed in the press, Goldschmid used the ensuing scandal to administer the coup de grâce to Harvey Pitt right in the middle of the 2002 elections. Goldschmid claimed a lack of full disclosure on the part of Pitt in submitting Webster's name for a vote in which the SEC commissioners approved Webster by a 3–2 straight party line vote (by law only three commissioners could be from the current administration's party).

The GAO report faulted all the SEC commissioners, including Pitt, for not being more diligent in their background check on Webster, who was never charged with any wrongdoing. Unaccustomed to the ugly politics of full disclosure, William Webster resigned from the PCAOB post after only three weeks on the job. Pitt resigned as SEC chairman on November 5, 2002. Robert Herdman also resigned, and the disclosure of the problems at U.S. Technologies led to a flurry of government investigations. C. Gregory Earls, the chief executive officer at U.S. Technologies, was subsequently indicted for misappropriating $15 million of the company's funds. The SEC sought an injunction to stop him from using his own funds to keep the company afloat for the benefit of its shareholders. A jury later convicted Earls of fraud in connection with USV Partners LLC, a company he created to solicit investments in U.S. Technologies. Earls was sentenced to over ten years in prison and was ordered to pay $22 million in restitution to victims who included parents of some Harvard students he met through his child who was attending that university.

Harvey Pitt was replaced by William H. Donaldson, a former chairman of the New York Stock Exchange (NYSE) and head of Donaldson Lufkin Jenrette, a Wall Street brokerage firm that was the first broker-dealer allowed to go public by the NYSE and the SEC. That firm was acquired by the Equitable Life Insurance Co. in 1985 and later sold to Credit Suisse First Boston for $11.5 billion. Donaldson had described Levitt's Regulation FD as "crazy" but toned down that criticism during his confirmation hearings. Bowing to pressure, Donaldson began urging more and more regulation even in areas not regulated before, such as the hedge funds. The SEC took some time to find a new PCAOB chairman. Finally, on April 15, 2003, William J. McDonough, the former president of the Federal Reserve Bank of New York, was appointed to the position. He lasted only two years in that position.

Sarbanes-Oxley tried to restrict many of the consulting services offered by audit firms. This latter-day Glass-Steagall provision applied to consulting services that brought in revenues of more than 5 percent of the total audit fees paid by the client and included such things as bookkeeping, financial information systems design, internal audit services, actuarial services, appraisal or valuation services, fairness opinions, management and human resource selection functions such as executive recruitment, broker-dealer or investment adviser or investment banking services, legal services, and any other expert services unrelated to the audit function. The auditors were allowed to keep their tax planning operations, after the SEC agreed not to bar the use of those services. The result of the SEC restrictions was that some large companies were employing as many as three of the Big Four accounting firms for auditing and consulting and other services.

Many accountants employed by the Big Four accounting firms as consultants were soon leaving for other jobs, giving rise to claims by those firms that their employees were being improperly raided. Twenty percent of the accountants at the Big Four accounting firms left in 2003. The number of more experienced accountants leaving was an even higher 25 percent. One survey found that over 50 percent of accountants viewed their profession to be less attractive than it was five years ago.

Sarbanes-Oxley did not require auditor rotation, a long-advocated reform, but did require the lead audit partners to be rotated every five years. Junior partners had to be rotated after seven years but could return after two years. The rotated lead audit partner and review partner could come back after five years. The GAO was directed to study whether complete auditor rotation should be required. Sarbanes-Oxley prohibited audit firms from providing audit services to companies whose chief executive officers or chief financial officers had been employed by the audit firm during a one-year period before the audit. Sarbanes-Oxley ordered the GAO to conduct a study of the factors that led to the consolidation of the Big Eight accounting firms into the "Final Four" and whether that consolidation had led to less competition and higher costs.

The Sarbanes-Oxley legislation required disclosure of off balance sheet transactions and contingent obligations. The SEC was directed to study the use of special purpose entities and to report to Congress whether additional legislation was needed to regulate them. The SEC was directed to adopt regulations governing the use of pro forma disclosures. In compliance, the SEC required such statements to be reconciled with generally accepted accounting principles, resulting in a decrease in the use of pro forma accounting by publicly held companies. Another study was ordered to determine whether investment banks had aided public companies in manipulating their earnings through structured finance transactions, naming specifically derivatives at Enron and the capacity swaps at Global Crossing.

The SEC was directed to consider real-time disclosures, and the agency subsequently accelerated the time period in which financial statements must be filed after the close of an accounting period, cutting that filing time by a third. The SEC delayed implementation of those accelerated periods until the end of 2005 for large companies and smaller companies were exempted for an ever longer period. The reach of Form 8-K was expanded to require additional disclosures between the filing of quarterly and annual reports. Those additional disclosures included termination of material agreements, director and officer resignations and appointments, and changes to bylaws. These increased disclosure requirements were expected to double the number of 8-K filings, which previously numbered about 80,000 annually.

The SEC was directed to adopt rules requiring management to implement internal controls for financial reporting and to assess the effectiveness of those controls. This proved to be an extremely expensive exercise and caused much complaint. Issuers were additionally required to adopt codes of ethics and any waiver of those code provisions had to be publicly disclosed, a rule adopted specifically in response to Enron's waiver of its conflict rules so Andrew Fastow could act as general partner in the LJMs. It was that conflict of interest that brought down Enron. The role of the audit committee was strengthened: it now had the authority to hire its own advisers, hire and fire the company's auditors, and resolve any disputes between management and the auditors over accounting issues. Audit committees were required to be composed entirely of outside directors, one of whom had to be a "financial expert." Audit committee members were prohibited from receiving consultation or other fees from the company. The auditors were required to make certain reports to the audit committee independent of management. Nasdaq and the NYSE adopted rules that sought to assure that outside directors were truly independent and not conflicted. However, Michael Eisner, the chief executive officer at Walt Disney, used those rules to remove directors that were becoming critical of his management blunders. The rules also had several loopholes that allowed various conflicts.

More Regulation

Sarbanes-Oxley enacted the Bush administration's loyalty oath into law by requiring all chief executive officers and all chief financial officers of publicly traded companies to certify that the financial reports of the company are accurate. Knowingly false violations or certifications were subject to prison terms of up to twenty years and penalties of up to $5 million. If the reports were inaccurate, the chief executive officer and the chief financial officer had to reimburse the company for any bonus or equity-based compensation received for the accounting period covered by the inaccurate report and disgorge any profits realized from sales of the company stock by those officers during that period.

The SEC was authorized to seek a court order freezing "extraordinary" payments made to executives at companies with accounting problems. This might be viewed as the Bernard Ebbers amendment in recognition of the extraordinary compensation package he received on his termination from WorldCom. One of the first victims of this statute was Jean-Marie Messier, the former chairman of Vivendi Universal. The SEC forced him to give up his $25 million termination package, which an arbitrator had ordered to be paid. A federal appeals court in California held that payments of $37.6 million in cash and 6.7 million shares of stock to two executives at Gemstar-TV Guide Inc. were not "extraordinary," which meant that those payments could not be frozen pending an SEC action charging the executives with inflating accounts. The court agreed to review that ruling after criticism was received. The appeals court sitting *en banc* thereafter reversed its panel's decision, concluding that the payments were "extraordinary." One of the executives receiving those payments, Henry C. Yuen, the chairman of Gemstar, later pleaded guilty to criminal charges that he obstructed the SEC's investigation into the company's accounting problems.

The Sarbanes-Oxley legislation provided for protection for whistleblowers that included collection of attorney fees and damages resulting from their whistleblowing activities. Whistleblowers working in foreign subsidiaries of American companies, however, were not protected under Sarbanes-Oxley. Strangely, the Occupational Safety and Health Administration (OSHA) was given the task of assuring protection to accounting whistleblowers. OSHA investigators are not skilled in accounting issues and have no subpoena authority to verify employer claims that a discharge was unrelated to accounting issues. That did not stop the filing of over 300 whistleblower claims in the United States, creating a whole new genre of lawsuits. In one of the first of these cases, an administrative law judge for the Department of Labor, where OSHA resides, required Cardinal Bankshares to rehire David Welch, its former chief financial officer who had been fired after he refused to sign the company's financial statements and then refused to cooperate with the company's lawyers. A subsequent investigation revealed that there was no basis for his claims, but he was awarded back pay and attorney fees anyway. That decision was appealed to a federal court.

Document retention requirements were increased to require auditors to retain their audit work papers for five years. Persons destroying documents or tampering with documents or obstructing an investigation of an audit could be subject to prison terms of up to twenty years. The statute of limitations for securities fraud was lengthened. The U.S. Sentencing Commission was ordered to determine whether sentencing guidelines should be increased for obstruction of justice. The maximum penalties for mail and wire fraud were increased from five to twenty years. Congress did not go so far as to require amputation of limbs, mutilation, removal of ears, or even the death penalty, as was the case for financial crimes during the colonial period.

Sarbanes-Oxley prohibited companies from making loans to executives, a problem in the 1920s but only the subject of regulation in response to the loans at Enron. Another requirement was that sales of stock by insiders be reported more promptly to the SEC. Still another Enron-generated provision in the Sarbanes-Oxley Act prohibited officers and directors from purchasing or selling the issuers' securities during any blackout period for pension fund programs. Profits from such sales were recoverable by the corporation or shareholders. Plan administrators were required to give thirty days' notice of any blackout period and the reasons for the blackout.

Attack of the Law Professors

Corporate governance standards under the federal securities law have been driven over the years by leftist law professors claiming special knowledge on how to manage a corporation. The Enron scandal brought those professors out in droves. Joel Seligman, the dean of the Washington School of Law in St. Louis, asserted before Congress: "A deterioration in the integrity of our corporate governance and mandatory disclosure systems may well have advanced, not because of a novel strain of human cupidity, but because we had so much success, for so long, that we began to forget why fundamental principles of full disclosure and corporate accountability long were considered essential."[7] This seemed to suggest that the problem was that full disclosure had been taken for granted. Columbia Law School professor John C. Coffee weighed in with an article titled "Understanding Enron: 'It's About the Gatekeepers, Stupid.'" For the benefit of the stupid people, Coffee identified, among others, financial analysts and lawyers as gatekeepers responsible for ensuring full disclosure. Apparently, Congress did not want to be thought stupid, so it adopted various gatekeeper provisions as part of the Sarbanes-Oxley legislation, including a requirement for a study of gatekeepers.

A number of law professors focused particularly on the role of lawyers as gatekeepers. They pointed to the law firm of Davis Polk & Wardwell for its role in advising Nancy Temple on the document issues that led to the downfall of Arthur Andersen. Davis Polk was used as an example even though no one in that firm had been found guilty of any misconduct or even charged with wrongdoing. Vinson & Elkins was another source of the law professors' wrath. Although no charges had been proven that any lawyer at Vinson &

Elkins had engaged in wrongdoing, the law professors strongly condemned the lawyers in that firm.

As Enron's lead corporate counsel, Vinson & Elkins was certainly learning the perils of gatekeeper status. The firm was criticized in the Powers report for failing to bring a stronger, more objective, and more critical voice to Enron's public disclosures. A federal court in Houston refused to dismiss a class action suit that challenged Vinson & Elkins' representation of Enron, but did dismiss out a large Chicago law firm, Kirkland & Ellis, which represented Andrew Fastow and LJM. The Enron bankruptcy examiner was seeking cash from Vinson & Elkins and Andrews & Kurth, another Enron outside law firm.[8] In-house lawyers at Enron were also targeted by the bankruptcy examiner for breaching their fiduciary duties to Enron by failing to oversee Enron's use of special purpose entities.

The law professors made frothing denunciations of Enron's lawyers. Professor Robert Gordon at Yale, apparently unschooled in the concept of due process, claimed that the Enron lawyers were bad people who had succumbed to something called "libertarian antinomianism, for which there is no known cure."[9] He cited the Vinson & Elkins investigation of Sherron Watkins's complaint at Enron as evidence of the lawyers' guilt. Professor Susan Koniak at Boston University was even more vociferous in her condemnation of lawyers in an article in the *Columbia Law Review*. She charged that executives committing crimes "had lawyers showing them the way."[10] Koniak cited as evidence of the Enron lawyers' guilt her belief that O.J. Simpson, the famous football player who slashed the throats of his ex-wife and her friend, was really guilty of murder despite his acquittal. That apparent non sequitur was supported by Koniak's assertion that Enron's lawyers, like Simpson, were going to escape punishment because the issues were complicated and they had a lot of money. At least one member of the bar thought these charges were the result of "hysteria," intemperate and a reminder of McCarthy era abuses.[11]

Disciplinary Proceedings

Lawyers have traditionally been regulated by their own bar associations or the courts in which they are admitted to practice. Misconduct may result in a suspension or revocation of the lawyer's license to practice law. The SEC has in the past tried to discipline lawyers practicing before it by barring or suspending their representation of clients in connection with SEC business. That could be a death sentence for a corporate lawyer's practice. There was also a conflict of interest in such cases: the SEC was an adversary in court cases brought against the lawyer's clients, which destroyed its neutrality in sanctioning the lawyers. The SEC also had a vested interest in seeking to bar or suspend lawyers because this would intimidate them from offering aggressive advice to their corporate clients that might conflict with the often overly expansive interpretations of the federal securities laws taken by the SEC.

The SEC adopted a rule in 1935 that allowed the agency to discipline lawyers practicing before it. No lawyer was disciplined under that rule (Rule 2(e)) until 1950 and only five such cases were brought in the next decade. In the 1970s, however, the SEC brought over eighty-five such proceedings against attorneys. That set off a sharp debate at the SEC and in the legal community. Roberta Karmel, an SEC Commissioner, was particularly critical of such proceedings. Nevertheless, Theodore Sonde, a senior SEC staff member, likened corporate lawyers whose clients were committing securities laws violations to a taxicab driver ignoring the rape of a passenger in the backset. This comment caused no small amount of consternation in the corporate bar. The SEC enforcement staff even wanted to bar lawyers from practicing before the agency when the staff disagreed with their arguments in court, an effort that was stopped by the SEC's office of general counsel.[12] The SEC staff, nevertheless, asserted that lawyers should be required to report violations of the federal securities laws by their clients to the SEC. That was not a normal role for lawyers and raised serious issues about the attorney-client privilege.

During the 1970s, the SEC charged two prominent law firms (Lord, Bissell & Brooks and White & Case) and certain of their partners with securities law violations in connection with their representation of a merger transaction by the National Student Marketing Corp. The SEC claimed that the lawyers had aided and abetted securities laws violations by that company and its officers by failing to require them to disclose some negative comments made by an accounting firm, Peat Marwick, in a "comfort letter" concerning the company's financial condition. The lawyers counseled disclosure by their client but were ignored. The SEC argued that the lawyers had an obligation to stop the merger and even to report the problem to the SEC. This case set off a storm of controversy. White & Case and its accused partner, Marion J. Epley III, settled with the SEC. Lord, Bissell & Brooks and its two accused partners went to trial before a federal judge. The judge found violations, but he refused to enjoin the lawyers as requested by the SEC. While acknowledging the debate engendered by the SEC's complaint, the judge provided little guidance on the role and responsibilities of lawyers in such instances.

ABA Response

In the wake of that case, the American Bar Association (ABA) changed its rules to obviate any ethical obligations that might be thought to support the SEC's view that lawyers should act as whistleblowers on their clients. The ABA claimed that lawyers were advisers, not police officers. Nevertheless, the SEC brought similar charges against two other lawyers and their law firm in 1978, but this time the action was brought as an agency administrative proceeding presided over by the SEC itself, the same agency that brought the charges. The respondents were Charles J. Johnson and William R. Carter, partners in the New York law firm of Brown, Wood, Ivey, Mitchell & Petty. Both were graduates of Harvard Law School. An administrative law judge at the SEC concluded that Johnson and Carter had aided and abetted violations of the federal securities laws by their client, National Telephone Company, when they failed to require the client to disclose information concerning the effects of the terms of a loan commitment on the future of the company. The lawyers had counseled disclosure, but did not resign when disclosure was not made.

The SEC administrative law judge suspended their right to practice before the SEC. That decision set off much criticism of the agency by the legal profession, and Carter and Johnson appealed to the SEC. Concluding that no express rule or norm governed the lawyers' conduct, the SEC let the lawyers off, but then proposed a rule making lawyers liable for not preventing securities law violations by their client. The ABA reacted harshly once again, and the SEC then folded its hand on this issue. The rule was not adopted; the SEC announced that, as a policy matter, it would not aggressively pursue such cases, and it did not bring such actions after its Carter and Johnson decision. That posture would be changed by statute after the Enron scandal.

S&L Problems

The savings and loan debacle of the 1980s provided another opportunity for a government attack on lawyers for counseling financial institutions that commit fraud and fail. The Office of Thrift Supervision brought an enforcement action against the New York law firm of Kaye, Scholer, Fierman, Hays & Handler, claiming that lawyers there had made false and misleading statements in documents filed in connection with their representation of Lincoln Savings & Loan. That institution was operated by Charles Keating Jr., himself a lawyer. Keating looted the company, paying himself and his family $34 million while he was driving Lincoln into bankruptcy. The Office of Thrift Supervision demanded $275 million in restitution from Kaye, Scholer and directed that 25 percent of the law firm's earnings be frozen pending resolution of the litigation. The law firm folded under that onslaught and agreed to pay $41 million to settle the case.

The action against Kaye, Scholer raised a storm of controversy because lawyers were not normally viewed as guilty of their clients' misconduct. The "Keating Five" members of Congress (which included the now reformist Senator John McCain) received $1.3 million in campaign contributions to run interference for Keating with regulatory agencies. None of those members of Congress were charged. Two law professors, Jonathan R. Macey and Geoffrey P. Miller, claimed that the attack on Kaye, Scholer was actually an effort to divert attention from the regulatory incompetence of Daniel Wall, the head of the Federal Home Loan Bank Board, who had protected Keating from regulatory scrutiny. Moreover, Keating's convictions were overturned by a federal appeals court, and a $4.3 billion judgment obtained by the government against him was set aside. Keating then pleaded guilty to reduced criminal charges for time already served. Charges against his son were also dropped, evidencing another instance where government prosecutors targeted family members in order to force a guilty plea. More successfully, the SEC brought disciplinary proceedings against Keating's old law firm that he retained after assuming control of Lincoln. The SEC sanctioned that firm and asserted that a law firm has a duty to disclose to the SEC all material facts about a client within the firm's knowledge.

The government's extortion scheme worked against other law firms. Sidley & Austin paid $7.5 million to settle charges concerning its representation of Lincoln Savings & Loan. In another instance, Jones, Day, Reavis and Pogue paid $51 million to settle regulatory actions for its representation of S&Ls. Paul Weiss, Rifkin, Wharton & Garrison shelled out about $40 million in settlements of charges in connection with its legal advice to other thrifts. Few law firms could stand up to this government onslaught that threatened large judgments or even freezing their assets as in the case of Kaye, Scholer. The California-based law firm of O'Melveny & Myers was an exception. It successfully fought the Federal Deposit Insurance Corporation (FDIC) to the Supreme Court over the law firm's representation of the American Diversified Savings Bank (ADSB). O'Melveny represented ADSB in two real estate syndications that had to be rescinded after it was discovered that two individuals controlling the bank had "fraudulently overvalued ADSB's assets, engaged in sham sales of assets to create inflated 'profits,' and generally 'cooked the books' to disguise the S&L's dwindling (and eventually negative) net worth."[13] The law firm's victory was short-lived. On remand, the Ninth Circuit Court of Appeals in California thumbed its nose at the Supreme Court and reaffirmed its prior opinion.

Legislation

The lawyers-as-gatekeepers bandwagon reached its peak when a group of forty law professors wrote a letter to Harvey Pitt at the SEC asking him to adopt a rule for attorney responsibilities in the wake of Enron. The rule demanded by the professors required attorneys representing public corporations who observe a possible violation of the federal securities laws to "climb the corporate ladder" by reporting the violation to supervisors, all the way to the board of directors if necessary, to correct the violation. Pitt assigned the matter to his general counsel, David Becker, and Becker responded that the SEC had abandoned the disciplining of lawyers in 1981.

Deeming that response inadequate, the law professors turned to Congress. Legislation designed to achieve the law professors' goals was then introduced by Senator John Edwards from North Carolina, who was preparing for a presidential bid that would embrace an antibusiness platform. Senator Mitch McConnell could not resist again goading the Democrats with an amendment to that bill that would have created a client's rights program, requiring lawyers, among other things, to refrain from soliciting clients during a "bereavement" period of forty-five days after an event causing the client injury. Among the abuses cited by McConnell was a lawyer disguising himself as a priest in order to gain access to victims. This proposal mocked Edwards, who had obtained much wealth as a trial lawyer in personal injury actions against doctors and hospitals. McConnell's ploy failed, and the Sarbanes-Oxley Act directed the SEC to adopt such a rule.

The legislation required lawyers to climb the ladder and report violations up the chain of command through the company's in-house lawyers, through the audit committee, and all the way to the board of directors, if necessary. The SEC decided to take that requirement a step further. As noted by Thomas Hazen, a law professor at the University of North Carolina, the SEC's proposed rules were "calling for a noisy withdrawal from representation and notification to the SEC if the attorney is not satisfied that the course taken by the client would correct the wrongful conduct."[14] The noisy withdrawal proposal met widespread opposition and was scrapped by the SEC, perhaps only temporarily because the agency continued to consider such a requirement. The SEC did require lawyers to climb to the top of the corporate ladder if employees or executives were about to violate the securities laws. Thus was enlisted still another policeman in the full disclosure model. In the process, the attorney-client relationship, so basic to American rights, was undermined. That relationship was turned from one of trust, confidence, and dispassionate advice into an adversarial, investigative role.

The attorney-client privilege was under further attack from the Department of Justice. After Arthur Andersen LLP was demolished, companies had to face the possibility that their business would be destroyed or crippled by criminal charges for full disclosure failures. Taking advantage of that fear, the Department of Justice began demanding that, in order to avoid criminal prosecution or to obtain leniency in sentencing, corporations had to show extraordinary cooperation in the government's investigations. This was a powerful threat, since "in the history of the U.S. financial markets, no major financial-services firm has survived an indictment."[15] Among other things, such cooperation would require the companies to waive the attorney-client privilege for communications between company lawyers and employees and the work product doctrine for the lawyers' notes concerning representation. Frank Quattrone was indicted and convicted on the basis of such a waiver. Companies were required to deny any assistance to "culpable" executives, including the payment of attorney fees, even when the company was bound by law and contract to make such payments. Termination of employees being investigated by the government was also viewed favorably, before conviction or even charges.

Role of the Rating Agency

The ratings agencies have come to be viewed as another gatekeeper in the corporate governance structure erected by the full disclosure system. These agencies review the finances of large companies and issue a report on their credit-worthiness. The company under review requests and pays for this report and uses it to convince creditors to extend credit. Because the report is an assessment of the likelihood of default, it will play a large role in determining the interest rate to be paid by the company when credit is extended. "The greater the risk, the higher the reward" is an immutable rule of finance. This means that the higher the credit rating, the more likely that credit will be extended, particularly on an unsecured basis, and the lower will be the interest rate.

The two leading ratings agencies are Moody's and Standard & Poor's. Their ratings are as follows.

Moody's	S&P/Others	Meaning
Aaa	AAA	Highest quality
Aa1	AA+	High quality
Aa2	AA	
Aa3	AA-	
A1	A+	Strong payment capacity
A2	A	
A3	A–	
Baa1	BBB+	Adequate payment capacity
Baa2	BBB	
Baa3	BBB–	
Ba1	BB+	Likely to repay; ongoing uncertainty
Ba2	BB	
Ba3	BB–	
B1	B+	High-risk obligations
B2	B	
B3	B–	
	CCC+	Vulnerable to default, or in default
Caa	CCC	
	CCC–	
Ca	C	In bankruptcy, or default[16]

Some History

The ratings agencies trace their history back to 1837, after Lewis Tappan's business as a silk merchant failed in the Panic of 1837. A former editor of the *Journal of Commerce,* Tappan founded the Mercantile Agency, which reported on the credit of individuals and businesses. This was a valuable service to those extending credit, and the concept spread. Tappan's firm was bought by Robert Dun in 1859 and was renamed Dun, Boyd & Co. It supplied information on the "character, capacity and pecuniary condition of persons asking credit." The firm was said to be "an indispensable adjunct to the trade of the country" and a "great conservator of credit."[17] A lawyer, John M. Bradstreet, founded Bradstreet's, another credit reporting firm, in 1849. That company merged with Dun's firm in 1933 to become Dun & Bradstreet.

In the nineteenth century the credit agencies employed some 10,000 correspondents to provide credit information on individuals and firms. Included among those reporters were U.S. Grant, William McKinley, Grover Cleveland, and Abraham Lincoln. The credit agencies did not always get it right. One report asserted that John D. Rockefeller was a poor businessman. Credit reporting grew as the economy expanded. *Poor's Manual* was published in 1890 and was analyzing bond issues in 1916. John Moody began rating bonds in 1909 and started Moody's Investors Service in 1914. That firm was later acquired by Dun & Bradstreet, but was spun off at the end of the century. Financial World and Brookmire Economic Service provided rating services. Standard Statistics Co. rated bonds in 1922. It joined with Poor's Publishing Co. to become Standard & Poor's. Fitch Publishing Co. joined the business in 1924 with its own bond ratings.

Poor's initially used a "three-thirds" rating system that was based on past financial performance, current financial condition, and expected future performance. By the end of the 1920s, the rating agencies were using ratings based on letter grades with subcategories that ranged through investment grade down to what were called junk bonds in the 1980s. The credit information business gradually developed into two branches: a credit reporting service for consumer credit and a rating system for corporate debt. The consumer credit reporting agencies were subject to regulation as part of the consumer protection laws passed in the late twentieth century. The corporate credit rating agencies were not similarly regulated.

The corporate rating agencies proved to be fallible. The collapse of the Penn Central Railroad in 1970 and its default on $82 million in commercial paper caught the rating agencies unawares. A lawsuit brought against Dun & Bradstreet, which had given a "prime" rating to Penn Central's commercial paper, was dismissed.[18] Standard & Poor's and Moody's gave Orange County, California, their highest rating before its collapse in 1994. One rating agency was sued for overrating Orange County's debt. A bankruptcy judge held that the ratings were protected by the First Amendment and that the plaintiff would have to show knowledge of falsity and actual malice to establish liability for a bad rating. This is an exceptionally high standard of proof that bars liability from claims of mere misjudgment.[19]

Expansion of the Rating Agency's Role

The SEC was traditionally wary of the ratings agencies. It was not until 1981 that the SEC changed its policy of prohibiting disclosure of a company's credit rating in prospectuses and other disclosure documents filed with the agency. It then allowed, but did not require, disclosure of ratings. Earlier, the role of the rating agencies was expanded with the creation of federal insurance for customers of bankrupt broker-dealers through the Securities Investor Protection Corporation (SIPC). The SEC adopted a "net capital" rule to assure broker-dealer liquidity and to act as a protective device to cut losses in the event of insolvency. This net capital rule is complex beyond comprehension but includes a requirement for a reduction in value (a "haircut") on bonds held in inventory based on their rating by a rating agency. Regulators relied on ratings from the rating agencies for other regulatory requirements. Money market funds were restricted in their ability to invest in bonds other than those rated in the highest categories. In addition, bank regulators used ratings to define valuation standards for so-called Type III securities, which must be at least investment grade to be held in a bank portfolio. Securitizations held by banks were risk-weighted for capital requirements based on their credit ratings. A proposed revision in bank capital requirements by the Basel Committee would risk-weight corporate loans based on their credit ratings. Standard & Poor's and Moody's, interestingly, opposed that proposal, stating that ratings were not designed for that purpose.

Critics argued that the reliance by federal agencies on private rating companies was giving those rating agencies a quasi-governmental role and creating an artificial demand for rating agency services. That view was enhanced by the SEC's requirement that it would recognize ratings only by those agencies it designated as a "nationally recognized statistical rating organization" (NRSRO). The oligarchic nature of the ratings business led to further criticism. At the end of the century, the key rating agencies for fixed income instruments in the United States were Moody's, Standard & Poor's, Fitch, and Duff & Phelps. The SEC recognized Dominion Bond as another credit-rating agency that would hold NRSRO status in 2003. Standard & Poor's was rating over $2 trillion of debt worldwide and controlled 41 percent of the market for ratings; Moody's held 38 percent and Fitch 14 percent.

Like the accountants, rating agencies were paid for their services by the companies they rated. This created the appearance of a conflict of interest, which critics were quick to point out whenever a highly rated company failed. The opportunity for more criticism arose with the demise of Enron. Moody's had received over $1.5 million annually from Enron to rate its debt. Moody's and Standard & Poor's were still rating Enron's debt as investment grade four days before its bankruptcy. Enron's stock price had been steadily dropping during the prior months, plunging from over $20 per share to $1 before the rating agencies downgraded its debt to junk bond status. Enron's bonds dropped from $85 to $35 in the two weeks preceding their downgrade to junk status.

Ratings agencies came under scrutiny as gatekeepers, almost solely as the result of the efforts of Frank Partnoy, a law professor at the University of San Diego. In his congressional testimony, Partnoy criticized the quasi-regulatory role of the ratings agencies under SEC regulations. He charged that their NRSRO designation had given the ratings agencies a "monopoly lock on their business." He asserted: "If we got rid of those legal rules and made credit ratings a competitive business, we would not have these issues where it is dramatic if you get downgraded below BBB. . . . Why does it matter if Standard & Poor's, this private agency, downgrades you below BBB? Because you are toast in financial markets if you are below BBB. It is much more expensive to borrow."[20]

In response to Partnoy's charges, the ratings agencies insisted that they were blameless because they were dependent on the audited financial statements of the companies they rated and conducted no independent audits of their own, thus shifting blame to the accountants, who shifted it onto management. This was the same defense raised by the analysts, and it provoked more cries of outrage from members of Congress, who wanted to know what value the rating agencies added if all they did was read published financial statements. The rating agencies did meet privately with management to assess its credibility and were given an exemption from Regulation FD to allow such contacts. Nevertheless, that information flow was controlled by management. The rating agencies, like the analysts, also defended their tardy downgrade of Enron to their belief that the proposed Dynegy merger supported Enron's value. They noted that the merger had been backed by Chevron-Texaco and had gained the support of major banks that injected $1.5 billion into Enron before those negotiations collapsed.

The Sarbanes-Oxley Act directed the SEC to study the rating agencies and determine if they should be deputized as gatekeepers for the full disclosure system. The European Union was also pressuring the United States to regulate credit rating agencies. The SEC responded with a concept release that sought public comment on whether the agencies should be subject to some form of regulation. The SEC announced that it intended to examine the anticompetitive practices of the large rating agencies and the potential conflicts of interest raised by the fact that rating agencies are paid by the companies whose debt they are rating. The rating agencies were also expanding their services to provide consulting advice, raising concerns of conflicts of interest when rating consulting clients.

The SEC later concluded that it did not have the authority to regulate the rating agencies, and Congress then held more hearings on the role of the ratings agencies. SEC chairman William Donaldson testified in those hearings that self-regulation by the rating agencies was inadequate and that more legislation might be needed. The SEC then adopted a definition of NRSRO that would give it a handle on imposing affirmative regulation. The SEC's actions dissatisfied Eliot Spitzer, the New York attorney general, and he began his own investigation of Moody's ratings of mortgage-backed securities and of reinsurance companies.

In Europe, the German parliament called for IOSCO (the international organization of security commissions) to create an international code of conduct for the ratings agencies that would provide for an issuer right of appeal from the rating it receives. IOSCO published a report in 2004 on the ratings agencies and principles they should follow. It was also working on a code of conduct. The European Parliament got in on the act by passing a resolution asking the ratings agencies to improve the transparency of their ratings and to avoid conflicts of interest.

Responding to this pressure, the rating agencies began tightening rating standards and threatened downgrades of several companies in the wake of the Enron failure. The tightening of those ratings resulted in increased borrowing costs for the affected firms. Standard and Poor's also announced that it would no longer rate structured finance transactions. Standard & Poor's was particularly concerned with home loans from Georgia because the Georgia Fair Lending Act, which was passed to stop predatory lending practices, allowed borrowers to sue those involved in securitizing the loan.

Sarbanes-Oxley Is No Panacea

More Costs

SEC chairman William Donaldson claimed in a speech to commemorate the seventy-fifth anniversary of the stock market crash of 1929 that Sarbanes-Oxley had helped prevent another Great Depression and that it was "valuable government intervention." Actually, the economy had recovered well before the intervention of Sarbanes-Oxley, and the additional regulation added by that legislation provided no greater protection to investors. Indeed, the number of restatements actually increased after the adoption of the legislation. Sarbanes-Oxley only added more expense to the already burdensome full disclosure system. Hank Greenberg, the head of American International Group Inc. (AIG), the giant insurance company that was in trouble with the SEC for accounting manipulations and with Eliot Spitzer for other financial transgressions, complained that his company was spending $300 million a year to meet Sarbanes-Oxley requirements. Public companies in the United States with revenues under $1 billion were facing an average increase in auditing and accounting costs of 130 percent after the passage of that legislation. Public companies were expected to incur over $5.5 billion in costs annually as a result of Sarbanes-Oxley. Audit fees increased by 50 percent, costs to companies going public for the first time increased substantially, and the cost of director and officer insurance skyrocketed. Many highly qualified chief executive officers were limiting the number of boards on which they sit because of liability concerns, denying their expertise and experience to companies that needed it. Some chief executive officers were even prematurely retiring in order to avoid concerns of liability should their company encounter any financial difficulties. Sarbanes-Oxley also did nothing to make financial statements more reliable. The number of restatements hit a new record of 414 in 2004, up from 330 in 2002.

Eastman Kodak was perhaps the most politically correct company in

America on corporate governance, but its chief executive officer, Daniel Carp, complained post-Sarbanes-Oxley that "these rules have run amok," "we are taking good money out of our corporations and investing it in accounting requirements," and "that's money I'm not spending in research and development or I'm not spending in advertising or I'm not training my people."[21] One company saw its earnings cut by 10 percent as the result of such costs. That company complained that its legal fees alone had increased by 105 percent in the first quarter of 2004. Business leaders complained that Sarbanes-Oxley did not increase investor confidence and was impeding economic growth because managers were becoming too timid in their business operations.

A backlash in Delaware occurred as Sarbanes-Oxley intruded deeply into what was formerly the province of state courts. Delaware vice chancellor Leo Strine was also critical of efforts to increase the number of independent directors because it simply thrust more power into the hands of the chief executive officer. John Thain, the new chief executive officer of the NYSE, noted in an editorial published in the *Wall Street Journal* that foreign companies were refusing to list their stock in the United States because of the increased costs of regulation, driven principally by the Sarbanes-Oxley requirement for reports and assessment of internal controls. Almost no European issuers made offerings in the United States in 2004, and complaints concerning the costs of Sarbanes-Oxley led the SEC to consider the adoption of a rule that would allow existing foreign registrants to withdraw their registration of existing offerings. Sarbanes-Oxley was posing other problems. The number of companies missing their deadlines for filing financial reports with the SEC doubled in the third quarter of 2004.

Congress sought through Sarbanes-Oxley to create an adversarial relationship between auditors and their clients, but that will in all likelihood result in fewer, not more, disclosures from management to auditors. The nature of an adversarial relationship is that management will not respond unless asked, but accountants have no way of knowing what to ask. The effect of this new relationship is already apparent in the increased number of auditor changes after Sarbanes-Oxley was enacted. In the first six months of 2004, some 900 companies changed auditors, either at the auditor's request or because the auditor was dismissed by management. That was nearly equal to the entire number of auditor changes for 2003. Those statistics suggest that relationships between auditors and management were becoming troubled, as well as adversarial. Among those switching auditors was American Express Co., dropping Ernst & Young LLP, which had been auditing American Express since 1975. American Express was Ernst & Young's best audit client, accounting for $23 million in audit fees. By 2004, the Big Four accounting firms were dropping clients at triple their rate two years earlier. Many of the companies turned loose were small firms that had to scramble for other audit services, often at an enormous increase in costs. BDO Seidman, a second-tier auditor, was able to increase its fees in some instances by 100 percent.

A backlash was growing against PCAOB and its broad-ranging powers. Peter Wallison, a former Treasury Department general counsel, counsel to President Ronald Regan, and a resident scholar at the American Enterprise Institute, charged that PCAOB had no oversight of its own and was urging Congress to fold it back into the SEC. Wallison further asserted that Sarbanes-Oxley was impairing "the collegiality that once prevailed between directors and management, and may be impairing the management risk-taking that is an essential element of economic growth." This touched off a fight at the SEC where two commissioners tried to demand greater scrutiny of PCAOB and the FASB before approving their budgets.

The attack on the analysts was also backfiring. SEC commissioner Harvey Goldschmid complained in September 2004 that money had been withdrawn from investment research, declining as much as one-third at some large brokerage firms. That reduction in coverage was hitting small companies the hardest. This did not deter the SEC staff from seeking more "gatekeepers." The head of the SEC Division of Enforcement, Stephen Cutler, advocated that corporations hire an ombudsman to act as a "private inspector general," another step in turning large corporations into government bureaucracies that use such inspector generals. Such a requirement was imposed on Qwest Communications International in its settlement with the SEC over accounting manipulations.

Executive Compensation

The provision in Sarbanes-Oxley requiring public companies to recover bonuses given to executives based on earnings that proved to be wrongly stated was largely ignored. The compensation for chief executive officers continued to rise even after Enron and the passage of Sarbanes-Oxley. A survey of the salaries of the chief executive officers of sixty-nine of the largest companies in the United States in 2002 saw a rise of 15 percent. Their total direct median compensation was $3 million. The median cash bonus was $605,000. Seventeen chief executive officers saw their restricted stock grants increase by 73 percent. A survey of compensation paid to chief executive officers in 2003 saw another increase, to an average of $8.6 million.

Reuben Mark at Colgate Palmolive Co. received $141 million in compensation, mostly from options, in 2003. Steven Jobs at Apple Computer received $74 million, George David at United Technologies received $70 million, and Henry Silverman at troubled Cendant received $54 million. Larry Ellison at Oracle Corp. was at it again, making $40 million in 2003. Harvard University paid the two lead money mangers for its endowment fund $35 million each in 2003, but reduced their compensation by $10 million each in 2004. John F. Antioco at Blockbuster Inc., a troubled company that had partnered with Enron on broadband, was paid $19 million in salary between 1999 (when the company went public) and 2004, in addition to uncounted millions in stock options. In October 2004, Antioco received options on 1.7 million shares of the company's stock plus restricted stock worth $12 million. Meanwhile, Blockbuster lost $3 billion.

Bank of America announced in 2004 that, despite its lackluster performance, its retiring chairman, Charles Guilford, would be receiving a severance package of $16.36 million plus another $8 million or so in "incentive" payments, plus $3.1 million per year for his life and $2.3 million to his wife for each year she survives him. Lucent Technologies Inc. paid its chairman and chief executive officer Patricia Russo $13.6 million in 2004, doubling her prior year's compensation. Tyco paid its new chairman and chief executive officer, Edward Breen, $10.7 million in 2004 for his work in restoring confidence in the company. Walt Disney gave its beleaguered head, Michael Eisner, a $7.25 million bonus. Walt Disney did announce some compensation reforms that would give executives more restricted stock rather than options and require those executives to hold Disney company shares in an amount equal to at least three times their base salary.

Abuses continued to surface. The government charged David C. Wittig, chief executive officer of Westar Energy Inc., with spending millions of dollars in company funds without board approval. This scandal was called the "Enron of the Midwest." Wittig's excesses included $6.5 million on the renovation of his office, requiring a $29,000 television cabinet, and profligate use of the corporate jet that included a family jaunt to Europe. He was paid millions for relocation expenses but never moved. Wittig upgraded his Kansas residence, the former home of failed presidential candidate Alf Landon, with $111,000 in window treatments and a $1,200 bronze alligator. Wittig had chutzpah; he and another fired executive sought $189 million in deferred compensation and severance pay after their dismissal. The company spent $9 million on an internal investigation conducted by the New York law firm Debevoise & Plimpton to determine if Wittig had manipulated the company's books. The lawyers could find no accounting fraud, but did uncover the lavish spending. Wittig was convicted of bank fraud and was tried for other violations involving his alleged looting of the company, but the jury could not reach a verdict and a mistrial was declared. He and Westar's chief strategy officer, Douglas Lake, were later convicted of looting the company. They were ordered to forfeit their assets. Wittig had previously been featured on the cover of *Fortune* magazine for the size of his salary at Salomon Brothers.

Options Again

An academic study found that companies often granted options as compensation just prior to releasing positive information or just after the disclosure of negative information. Outside directors often shared in those grants. The SEC also examined derivative transactions set up to allow executives to receive the value of their stock even though there was no sale. This strategy could be used to avoid the short-term profit prohibitions contained in the Securities Exchange Act of 1934.

Some voluntary restrictions on options compensation were imposed after Enron. IBM announced in February 2004 that its top 300 officers would receive stock options that they could exercise only if IBM's shares rose by 10 percent or more. Some companies adopted politically correct pay standards such as capping executive compensation at some multiple of the average worker's pay. Coca-Cola stopped providing projected earnings and began expensing options granted to its employees and executives. The company still found itself under investigation by the SEC for its accounting practices. Coca-Cola was shipping excess product to Japanese bottlers in order to overstate its revenues. That channel stuffing, or "gallon pushing" as it was called by Coca-Cola employees, was disclosed by a whistleblower, Matthew Whitley. Coca-Cola settled the SEC charges stemming from its Japanese operations by agreeing to strengthen its internal accounting controls and to create an Office for Ethics and Compliance. The Department of Justice decided not to bring charges. The company also paid Burger King $21 million to settle claims that Coca-Cola used teenagers to skew a product test in Burger King restaurants. Meanwhile, Coca-Cola's earnings remained under stress. A new chairman, Neville Isdell, was hired with a compensation package that could exceed $17 million if certain conditions were met. Between 1999 and 2004, Coca-Cola paid out $200 million to a small group of executives as compensation.

Citigroup, Procter & Gamble, General Electric, and General Motors followed Coca-Cola with announcements that they too would be expensing options. Winn-Dixie and Boeing had been expensing options for some time before Sarbanes-Oxley. By 2004, 500 publicly traded companies decided to expense options, but only 21 percent of companies whose profits would be reduced by less than 1 percent agreed to expense options voluntarily. Many companies involved in information technology refused to expense their options, stating that they would do so only if required by law. The Conference Board Blue Ribbon Commission on Public Trust and Private Enterprise recommended the expensing of options. One of its members, Paul Volcker, the former Federal Reserve Board chairman, advocated the elimination of options altogether as executive compensation.

FASB became more aggressive after Enron and the creation of PCAOB. FASB announced several more rigorous accounting requirements. Among other things, it changed the independent ownership requirements for special purpose entities (SPEs), such as those employed by Enron. The new FASB rule created a rebuttable presumption requiring that an outside independent investor provide at least 10 percent of the SPE's capital, an increase of 7 percent over the prior rule. This rule mimicked a proposal that Arthur Andersen made before Enron collapsed. The FASB did not require operating leases to be included on the balance sheet. This allowed the 500 largest companies to exclude almost $500 billion of those obligations from their balance sheets.

The FASB did not appear enthusiastic in addressing the options expensing issue. The International Accounting Standards Board decided in February 2004 that it was requiring companies using international accounting standards to expense stock options starting in 2005, and the European Union subsequently adopted such a requirement. This put further pressure on the FASB to adopt that concept. The FASB announced in April 2004 that it was proposing to require the expensing of options under generally accepted accounting principles. That proposal, predictably, met much opposition, but FASB moved ahead. It also decided to treat stock options as equity, rather than liabilities, when expensed, raising more controversy, and announced it was seeking more disclosures on stock buybacks that were being used to negate the dilution effects of option grants. The FASB announced in October 2004 that it was delaying implementation of this requirement for an additional six months. A bill was approved in the House in July 2004 that sought to block the FASB proposal requiring expensing of options, except that the FASB would be allowed to require expensing of options granted to a company's top five executives. New companies could delay expensing even for those executives for a three-year period. The FASB proposal did not apply to options vested before its effective date. Acxiom Corp. exploited that loophole by vesting large amounts of employee options immediately. Other corporations were expected to follow suit.

The effect of expensing options could be dramatic. Microsoft Corp. reported that its earnings had been reduced by six cents per share in the fourth quarter of 2003 as the result of its decision to expense options granted to employees and executives. Microsoft therefore decided that it would no longer issue stock options to employees as compensation and incentive. Instead, employees were to be given restricted stock that would require them to remain with the company for specified periods before vesting. The outstanding options of Microsoft employees, which were out-of-the-money, were to be purchased by JPMorgan Chase & Co. Options had made millionaires out of thousands of employees at Microsoft, but that opportunity was denied to future workers. Several other companies decided to stop granting options to employees as a result of the expensing requirement, including Time Warner, Charles Schwab, and Aetna.

The List Grows

The number of restatements set another record in 2003, up 13 percent from 2002. The leading causes for those restatements were errors in balance sheet reserves and contingencies. Levi Strauss & Co., the jeans maker, announced in October 2003 that it had overstated its 2001 net income by $26 million. Its third-quarter 2003 results were also overstated, being almost $5 million lower than reported. Levi Strauss & Co. closed its last U.S. factory and laid off 21 percent of its workers on September 11, 2003. The SEC charged Gateway, the computer manufacturer, and three of its executives with improperly booking revenue and profits on phony transactions. Goodyear restated its net income for the years 1997 to 2003, reducing net income during that period by $65 million.

The SEC sued Donald Fitzpatrick, chief operating officer at Liberate Technologies Inc., for inflating the accounts of that company by 17 percent in 2002 and 2003 through round-trip transactions in which customers were provided funds to buy Liberate products. Investors lost more than $40 million as a result of that conduct. Fitzpatrick was indicted and another executive, Thomas Stitt, settled SEC charges for his role in this scheme. The company filed for bankruptcy, but a judge ruled that the company was not bankrupt. Lucent Technologies Inc. and Cisco Systems Inc. had made substantial investments in Liberate.

The Royal Dutch/Shell Group confessed to having overstated its proven oil and natural gas reserves by 20 percent or 4.35 billion barrels. This reserve restatement was the result of accounting regulations that were created in 1992. Those rules required disclosure of estimates of proven oil and gas reserves and their present value based on the cash flow that was expected to be received when those reserves were sold, which at best was an educated guess. There were also varying methods by which this information could be reported. Shell was forced to restate its reserves four times. In one such announcement, on May 24, 2004, the company restated and reduced its earnings by $400 million for the period 2001–2003. Eventually, Shell reported that its oil and gas reserves had been overstated by 41 percent. The company's chairman, Philip Watts, was let go, but gently, with a $1.9 million severance payment. Shell's auditors were sued over the problems, along with various executives. Shell settled charges by regulators in the United States and England for this overstatement by agreeing to a penalty of $150 million, but the Department of Justice decided not to bring criminal charges. The company settled a class action claim brought by its pension funds for the reserves overstatement for $90 million.

Pension funds based in the Netherlands holding Shell stock were seeking corporate governance changes, mimicking America. They were joined by two union pension funds in the United States that were suing to require Shell to drop its two-tier board of directors governance structure, under which a small group of managers filled the top-tier board, a structure that had existed since 1907. Shell gave into that pressure, merging its British and Dutch units and creating a single board of directors.

The problems at Shell rippled through the industry. British Petroleum Co. PLC (BP) reduced its estimates of oil and gas reserves by 2.5 percent on March 11, 2004. BP later wrote off $2.3 billion in assets. The El Paso Corp. announced that it too had overstated its oil and natural gas reserves by more than $1 billion, requiring a restatement of its prior five years of financial reports. An internal review conducted by an outside law firm only made the matter worse, and another restatement was announced in August 2004 for natural gas hedges. El Paso disclosed that, as a result of its restating for those hedges, shareholder equity would be reduced by $1 billion and charges would be taken for $1.6 billion for the period 1999–2003. The scandal over these reserves gave rise to another gatekeeper, independent firms specializing in auditing such reserves. Concern was expressed, however, that at least some of those firms had conflicts from their consulting services to the oil companies. Dynegy Inc. had another problem. It settled charges of violations of the Clean Air Act brought by the Environmental Protection Agency by agreeing to spend $545 million to improve its emission controls in Illinois.

MetLife Inc. restated its accounts for 2003 as the result of a manipulation of deferred expense accounts at its New England Life Insurance Co. unit. The SEC staff recommended filing charges against the company for that misconduct. Metropolitan Mortgage and Securities stopped making interest payments on securities sold to over 35,000 investors. Its auditor, Ernst & Young, resigned, stating that there had been material misstatements in the company's financial reports for the prior three years. Metropolitan Mortgage filed for bankruptcy on February 4, 2004, and investors lost some $600 million. Red Hat disclosed in July 2004 that it was restating its accounts for the prior three years, causing a 24 percent decline in its stock price. The company's chief financial officer resigned.

Electronic Data Systems (EDS) was under scrutiny for its accounting practices. EDS had been founded by H. Ross Perot, the eccentric billionaire who sold EDS to General Motors and became a third-party candidate for president in 1992; his campaign resulted in the defeat of George H.W. Bush and the election of Bill Clinton. EDS chairman and chief executive officer Richard Brown was dismissed, and the company reported a loss. EDS restated revenues in October 2003, eliminating $2.24 billion in prior profits. The company's credit rating was cut to junk bond status. More problems surfaced in 2004 involving the overvaluing of assets, and the company was unable to produce its third-quarter results on time. Delphi Corp., thereafter, admitted that it had improperly booked various transactions with EDS.

Delphi Corp., the largest maker of auto parts, inflated its cash flow by $200 million in 2000 by selling materials in one accounting period to an accommodating customer and buying them back in the next accounting period. The company also overstated its revenues in 2002 and 2003 by improperly deferring expenses. The company terminated the employment of its chief financial officer, Alan S. Dawes. Delphi's chairman and chief executive officer J.T. Battenberg resigned, as did its chief accountant Paul Free. The company was reporting huge losses in 2004 and was expecting more losses in 2005. General Motors disclosed that it had engaged in two questionable transactions with Delphi including one that increased General Motors's income by 19 percent in 2000 and allowed the company to beat analysts' expectations. Delphi then announced further accounting problems involving off balance sheet debt.

Two more Delphi executives then resigned, and the company restated its results for 2001 and 2002, reducing earnings for those two years by $300 million. Delphi was then targeted by class action suits brought by state employee pension funds in Oklahoma and Mississippi. Two foreign mutual funds also saw a chance to increase their returns and joined in the litigation. Delphi filed for bankruptcy on October 8, 2005, an action that placed the jobs of its 185,000 employees in jeopardy. The company's labor costs were out of control, and the company was considering massive wage cuts. General Motors had spun off Delphi but retained some of its obligations. A few days after Delphi's bankruptcy filing, another auto parts supplier, Dana Corp., announced that it was restating its financial statements for the prior six quarters. Another auto parts maker, Collins & Aikman Corp., delayed its financial statements for 2004, announcing that it would be restating results. That disclosure resulted in a 24 percent decline in its stock price. General Motors also announced a restatement and laid off 30,000 employees.

The SEC required SunTrust Banks Inc. to restate its earnings for three years and reduce its loan loss reserve account by $100 million before the SEC would grant approval to SunTrust's merger with Crestar Financial Corp. The SEC alleged that SunTrust's loan loss reserves were artificially high and had been inflated by SunTrust to meet the quarterly earnings expectations set by financial analysts. The bank was inflating its earnings by reducing the amount allocated in the current quarter to loan losses and relying on money placed into its loan loss reserve cookie jar to cover any expected loan losses. This created some tension with bank regulators who preferred loan loss reserves as large as possible in order to protect the FDIC insurance fund. SunTrust fired three executives for misusing loan reserve accounts.

The SEC charged that Soulfood Concepts and its chief executive officer, Markova Campbell, filed false financial statements for the periods covering 2001–2003. The defendants copied prior filed reports, changed their dates, and included a fictitious auditor's report. Soulfood's auditor had previously resigned. Safescript Pharmacies Inc., formerly known as RTIN Holdings Inc., was an electronic prescription technology company based in Longview, Texas. Safescript, its chief executive officer, Stanley L. Swanson, and others were charged by the SEC with inflating reported revenues in 2002 and 2003 by selling franchise agreements to start-up franchisees in exchange for worthless stock and promissory notes that were immediately recognized as revenue, despite the inability of the franchisees to pay those obligations. The defendants also presented a fictitious certificate of deposit to the company's auditors.

The chief executive officer, chief financial officer, and vice president for sales at Medi-Hut Co. Inc., a drug wholesaler headquartered in New Jersey, were sentenced to over forty months in prison for inflating company revenues and earnings and for making false statements to SEC investigators. Paul H. Bristow, the chief financial officer for eFunds Corp., and another executive,

Nikhil Sinha, settled SEC charges that they allowed eFunds to improperly recognize $2.1 million in revenue from a payment by an affiliated entity that eFunds had agreed to reimburse through future consulting fees. They were fined and enjoined from further such conduct.

Executives at DPL Inc., which owns Dayton Power & Light Co., were sued by that company after they were paid $33 million in cash at the end of 2003. The company claimed that they had misled the compensation committee in obtaining approval of the payouts. The executives were countersuing, seeking an additional $50 million. Seven executives at Symbol Technologies Inc. were indicted for channel stuffing and other practices that inflated the company's earnings by $200 million between 1998 and 2003 in order to meet analysts' expectations. Based in Holtsville, New York, the company was the leading maker of bar code scanners, as well as wireless networks. The indicted executives included its president, Tomo Razmilovic, and chief financial officer, Kenneth Jaeggi. Razmilovic fled the country. He was declared a fugitive from justice and placed on the postal inspectors' most wanted list. The company paid restitution and fines in an SEC action totaling $139 million. Brian Burke, the company's chief accounting officer, pleaded guilty to criminal charges for his role in the fraud.

Four executives at Enterasys Network Systems Inc. pleaded guilty to criminal charges for accounting fraud. Among those defendants was Enrique P. Fiallo, the company's chief executive officer. The company was involved in computer networking. A $20 million dollar shortfall in meeting analysts' expectations had led the defendants to fill that gap by sending funds secretly to other companies who then purchased Enterasys products through distributors. Enterasys then claimed those sales as revenue. Two Enterasys executives, including its chief financial officer, pleaded not guilty. One of the company's outside directors and the head of the audit committee was the former governor of New Hampshire, Craig Benson.

John Brincat, the chief executive officer for Mercury Finance Co., was indicted for manipulating the company's earnings by keeping bad loans on the books. John Howard Dawes, chief financial officer for Cylink Corp. in Santa Clara, California, was sentenced to three years probation and six months home confinement for falsifying that company's records, requiring a restatement of results for 1997 and 1998. A similar sentence was given to Thomas Butler, Cylink's vice president for sales.

OfficeMax Inc. fired four of its executives and forced the resignation of its chief financial officer, Brian Andersen, who had been in that position for only two months. Christopher Milliken, the company's chief executive officer, later resigned. That action was taken after a vendor complained that $3.3 million in sales had been falsified in the last quarter of 2004. The company was reviewing its records for the prior two years for similar practices, requiring it to delay its financial reports. A planned merger between Mylan Laboratories Inc. and King Pharmaceuticals Inc. was endangered by a restatement of King's financial statements. Corporate raider Carl Icahn was also trying to frustrate the merger, claiming that King was overvalued.

Some companies cut retirement benefits in order to improve their financial statements. Those changes could be posted immediately or used as cookie jar reserves. Six large corporations were under SEC investigation for such practices in October 2004. They included Delphi Corp., the auto parts maker, Ford Motor Co., General Motors Corp., and Northwest Airlines. Employee benefits were a growing problem. Bank of America was under investigation by the IRS for its accounting treatment of its cash balance pension funds. Employees had filed a class action lawsuit claiming that the bank was arbitraging the fund by encouraging employees to roll their Section 401(k) accounts into the cash balance plan. The bank, it was claimed, then invested those assets at a return higher than what would be paid under the cash balance plan, allowing Bank of America to keep the difference. A federal appellate court held that Xerox was liable for several millions of dollars for miscalculating the benefits due under its cash balance plan. In another case, IBM was held to have violated age discrimination laws because older workers were paid less than younger workers with the same seniority under its cash balance plan, resulting in a $300 million settlement by IBM. IBM thereafter announced that employees would no longer be given access to cash balance plans; instead, they would be offered only Section 401(k) plans.

More Audit Failures

An August 2004 report of its review of the Final Four accounting firms conducted by the Public Company Accounting Oversight Board (PCAOB) reported that those firms had all missed significant audit issues. Generally accepted accounting principles were being misapplied and audit independence efforts were lacking. PCAOB was further concerned with the quality control systems of the accounting firms. KPMG agreed to pay the shareholders of Gemstar-TV Guide International Inc. $10 million as a part of an SEC settlement for failed audit work. KPMG was also censured by the SEC in October 2004 and later agreed to pay an additional $25 million to settle a class action over the same audit problems. The accounting firm had treated the matters as quantitatively immaterial, but the SEC charged they were "qualitatively" material, a theory the SEC had been pursuing for years under its full disclosure model without much success, at least until Enron opened the door for any disclosure theory. KPMG was the smallest of the Big Four accounting firms in the new century, with 100,000 employees in over 700 offices in 152 countries. KPMG's worldwide revenues were $10.7 billion in 2002, of which $3.4 billion was generated in its operations in the United States. Tax services were responsible for about $1.2 billion of that revenue. KPMG had a 13 percent increase in global revenues for fiscal year 2003. KPMG, which maintained its headquarters in Switzerland, was experiencing strong growth in audit services, driven by acquiring business from Arthur Andersen and increased audit demands in the United States.

The SEC charged Grant Thornton LLP and one of its partners, Peter M. Behrens, with failing to audit properly MCA Financial Corp.'s financial statements. MCA had used related party transactions in order to overstate its income. Another accounting firm, Doern Mayhew & Co. PC, and one of its directors, Benedict Rybicki, were also charged in that case. The two accounting firms were jointly auditing MCA. This was part of a program promoted by Grant Thornton under which it partnered with small accounting firms to audit clients jointly, giving the audit more credibility with Grant Thornton's national name and providing Grant Thornton with access to the clients of the small firms. Grant Thornton settled the SEC charges by agreeing to provide fraud detection training to its entire audit staff and to pay the SEC a civil penalty of $1.5 million.

PricewaterhouseCoopers was censured by the SEC in 2004 for its audit of Warnaco Group Inc., one of the largest apparel manufacturers in the United States. The accounting firm was charged with allowing Warnaco to announce in a restatement of its financial results that a portion of the erroneous charges was due to start-up-related costs. In fact, the reason for the restatement was an inventory overstatement. An appellate court upheld a $12 million award against Coopers & Lybrand in favor of a community college, which charged that the accounting firm failed to detect improper investments by the college's treasurer. PricewaterhouseCoopers was slammed with a $182 million judgment in 2005 for Coopers & Lybrand's audit work for the Ambassador Insurance Co. The wheels of justice do grind slowly. That company went bankrupt twenty years earlier. The accounting firm was also being investigated by the SEC for car rental agreements that it had with the Hertz Corp., an audit client. The SEC was seeking to determine whether those arrangements affected the accounting firm's independence. Hertz had just been sold for $15 billion.

Thomas Trauger, a partner in the accounting firm Ernst & Young, pleaded guilty to obstruction of justice charges in connection with destruction of the audit papers of NextCard. That company had issued credit cards to individuals with high credit risks and was bankrupted from the resulting defaults. Ernst & Young agreed to pay $1.5 million to settle charges made by the U.S. attorney in Philadelphia that it advised hospitals to submit over 200,000 Medicare claims for unnecessary blood tests between 1991 and 1997. Quovadx, a business software company, announced that its chief executive officer and chief financial officer had resigned as a result of an SEC investigation of its accounting practices. The company had been recognizing revenues before receiving assurances of payment. Quovadx's accounting firm, Ernst & Young, was also under attack.

Ernst & Young was the subject of an enforcement action by the SEC over its consulting relationship with PeopleSoft that the SEC claimed undercut Ernst & Young's independence as an auditor. Ernst & Young was paid $425 million for implementing PeopleSoft software for third parties. Between 1994 and 1999, Ernst & Young received a mere $1.7 million in audit fees from PeopleSoft. An administrative law judge at the SEC ordered Ernst & Young to disgorge those audit fees and to accept no new clients for a period of six months. This was the harshest sanction imposed on a large audit firm since the case involving several audit failures by Peat Marwick in the 1970s. The California Board of Accountancy fined Ernst & Young $100,000 for this conduct and placed the company on probation. Ernst & Young gave up its consulting practice after the PeopleSoft charges were filed. The SEC was also investigating whether Ernst & Young breached independence rules for auditors by entering into a profit-sharing arrangement with American Express Co.

The government's effort to separate audit and consulting services was showing up in the numbers. In July 2004, a little over 40 percent of fees paid to audit firms were for nonaudit services, down from 55 percent in the prior year and well below the 72 percent paid in 2001. Deloitte Touche Tohmatsu, the giant accounting firm, had a 21 percent increase in global revenue for its fiscal year ending May 31, 2003. About a third of the firm's revenue came from consulting. The firm announced that it was selling its consulting services unit, but reversed that decision in 2003, leaving it as the only major accounting firm with a consulting service operation. Deloitte remained under pressure from the government to sell those services. Deloitte had other problems. It was the defendant in a lawsuit seeking $2 billion in damages. That suit was brought by two Japanese insurance companies that suffered large losses when their North Carolina aviation reinsurer, Fortress Re Inc., failed. Fortress Re was a Deloitte audit client that had used fraudulent accounting methods to conceal liabilities and misstated the nature of the coverage. Two Fortress Re executives were slapped with a $1 billion judgment in arbitration for that misconduct and had to relinquish $400 million in personal assets, including a jet, to settle the claim. Deloitte paid a reported $250 million to the claims brought by the Japanese companies. The problem involved something called finite insurance, a product that was being used by other companies to manipulate their financial results. Deloitte continued to face liabilities from its audits of Parmalat SpA and Adelphia Communications Corp.

Travel and Taxes

Clients were challenging the travel billing practices of the accounting firms. One lawsuit charged that PricewaterhouseCoopers kept rebates from airlines and hotels, rather than passing them back to audit clients who had been billed in full for the travel charges. The accounting firm settled that lawsuit for $54.5 million. KPMG was also sued for keeping discounts that it had obtained for travel for employees working on client accounts. KPMG agreed to pay $34 million to settle those claims, one-third of which went to the lawyers for the plaintiffs. The plaintiffs themselves were paid with certificates that would give them credit toward future accounting services or they could receive cash worth 60 percent of the face value of the certificate. Ernst & Young LLP agreed to pay $18 million to settle a class action over its travel billing practices, and the Department of Justice was investigating that conduct.

The Enron scandal gave the government leverage to invade the accounting firms' tax advisory practices. Instead of seeking legislation to close tax loopholes, as has been the tradition in this country, the government simply asserted that they were illegal and attacked the accounting firms for advising clients to minimize their taxes. KPMG, Arthur Andersen (before its demise), BDO Seidman, and Ernst & Young LLP sold tax shelters with such names as FLIPS, OPIS, COBRA, BLIPS, and CARDS. PricewaterhouseCoopers promoted a tax shelter program called BOSS (bond and option sales strategy) and Son of Boss. These strategies had been vetted by prominent law firms as well as by the major accounting firms but, in the post-Enron era, that only fueled attacks on their use. A congressional study of KPMG shelters asserted that 240 individuals had claimed $5.8 billion in losses resulting in tax savings of $1.4 billion. KPMG was marketing over 500 tax products through its Tax Innovation Center in its Washington, DC, office. Class action law firms then got into a dogfight over the spoils from KPMG's mea culpa. They were further aided by a deferred prosecution agreement reached by KPMG with the Department of Justice. Using that agreement as leverage, class action lawyers forced KPMG and the law firm of Sidley Austin Brown & Wood to pay $225 million to settle claims over their role in the marketing of certain of these tax shelters. The class action lawyers were to receive $30 million in fees.

KPMG dismissed Richard Smith, the head of its tax services. Some thirty other partners were also required to leave the firm. The Department of Justice was considering an indictment of the accounting firm itself, but was having doubts after the reversal of the overturning of Arthur Andersen's conviction. KPMG was desperately apologizing and begging the government to avoid that result, which would be the firm's death knell. The SEC was in all events preparing for the contingency of a "Big Three" accounting environment.

After its misjudgment in the Arthur Andersen case, the Department of Justice had finally woken up to the fact that the indictment of a major accounting firm would only result in its destruction with a loss of thousands of jobs. Nevertheless, the Department of Justice can use its leverage to extort money and impose what it perceives as good corporate governance reforms. In the case of KPMG, the price paid to the government for a deferred prosecution agreement was $456 million. KPMG agreed to hire an "independent monitor" who was none other than Richard Breeden of WorldCom fame.

Nineteen senior partners at KPMG were indicted for their role in marketing tax shelters. One of those accountants, David Greenberg, was denied bail by Andrew J. Wistrich, an overly zealous magistrate, and was ordered to be transported in custody to Manhattan from Los Angeles. Two Stanford law school professors, Robert Weisberg and David Mills, broke ranks with their fellow professors' disdain for the rights of white-collar defendants. In a *Wall Street Journal* op-ed piece, Weisberg and Mills called the indictments "very strange" because the prosecutors were trying to legislate tax policy through the criminal courts. The authors also noted that the conduct at issue normally would not be considered criminal.

Ernst & Young paid $15 million to settle IRS claims for its role in marketing tax shelters. Ernst & Young had previously come under scrutiny for selling tax shelters to executives at Sprint Corp., allowing them to shelter $100 million in stock option sales and leading to their dismissal. Deutsche Bank AG was embroiled in this controversy for its role in selling currency options used to generate losses for COBRA shelters. Deutsche Bank was also involved in OPIS (offshore portfolio investment strategy) shelters.

The government continued its strong-arm prosecutorial tactics against those accused of financial crimes. In order to assure that they would not be properly represented, the government forced KPMG to agree not to pay the attorney fees for KPMG employees under indictment. An e-mail at KPMG stated that one of the partners testifying before Internal Revenue Service investigators had decided his best course would be to feign forgetfulness and claim he was not in the loop. The e-mail called this "the rope-a-dope/Enron defense."

Sarbanes-Oxley had, nevertheless, been good to KPMG. Its earnings in fiscal 2005 were up 16 percent over the prior year and had experienced a 14 percent growth in the prior year. KPMG's troubles were not over. The Public Company Accounting Oversight Board (PCAOB) claimed that one in four of KPMG audits were flawed. Deloitte & Touche LLP fared even worse. PCAOB claimed that half of the audits it reviewed for that firm resulted in restatements. Clearly, the accounting profession was unable to live up to the expectations that they would act as full disclosure policemen for the government, a failing that had become painfully obvious over the last half century.

PCAOB decided to extends its reach by enacting rules prohibiting accounting firms from auditing companies to which they sold tax shelters that the IRS determined were abusive. In addition, audit firms were prevented entirely from selling tax shelters to executives of audit clients. The SEC and PCAOB also prohibited contingency fees that were based on cost savings resulting from consulting or tax advice by audit firms. The IRS granted an amnesty to users of abusive shelters, allowing them to avoid some penalties. About 1,500 taxpayers accepted that amnesty by July 2004. The Son of Boss amnesty program alone yielded over $3.2 billion in taxes and penalties. The General Accounting Office estimated that the total amount of taxes sheltered by the entire accounting firm programs ranged from $11 to $15 billion annually between 1993 and 1999. Fortune 500 companies were claimed to have used tax shelters to avoid $3.4 billion in taxes between 1998 and 2003. An IRS study also found that there was an annual gap of over $300 billion in what taxpayers owe and what they pay.

The IRS demanded that Sidley Austin Brown & Wood LLP, a large law firm that provided 600 legal opinions for tax shelters, to supply the names of its clients. The law firm resisted that action, but the partner in charge of the program, R.J. Ruble, was dismissed by the firm, and he was then indicted by the government. Jenkins & Gilchrist, the Texas law firm that had found itself in trouble during the savings and loan crisis in the 1980s, was the target of other suits for its role in developing tax shelters. A federal judge ordered that law firm to disclose the names of clients using those shelters. The law firm later agreed to pay $75 million to settle lawsuits with clients who had invested in tax shelters suggested by Jenkins & Gilchrist and which the IRS later challenged.

In another tax avoidance measure, corporations took out life insurance policies on the lives of their employees, with the company listed as the largest beneficiary. The tax advantage to such insurance was that the benefits upon death were not taxed. Some members of Congress questioned whether such tax advantages were appropriate. The IRS was also concerned with tax avoidance that involved the transfer of options granted to highly compensated executives to family partnerships in an exchange for a promissory note. The partnership then cashed out the options without paying taxes on the profits. The IRS estimated that such devices had been used to avoid paying as much as $700 million in taxes. An amnesty was offered by the IRS for those disclosing their involvement in such transactions. Almost one hundred executives and thirty-three companies accepted that amnesty by July 2005, agreeing to pay taxes, interest, and a 10 percent penalty.

Walter Andersen was indicted for evading $210 million in income taxes, a new record for an individual. He earned the money on which the tax was not paid through the sale of Mid-Atlantic Telecom. He was also charged with failing to pay sales taxes in the District of Columbia of $250,000 for purchases of art, jewelry, and wine, including works by Salvador Dali and Rene Magritte. That charge was only a faint echo of the $13 million of unpaid sales taxes by Dennis Kozlowski.

Executive Issues

Boeing Co. was under fire for hiring Darleen Druyun, a U.S. Air Force officer working on a $23 billion Boeing proposal to upgrade the air force's tanker fleet and other defense contracts. Druyun was fired by Boeing after it was revealed that she had discussed the contract with Boeing's chief financial officer, Michael Sears, and had also sought jobs for her daughter and son-in-law. Druyun pleaded guilty to criminal charges for that violation of procurement procedures after prosecutors threatened her daughter with criminal charges. Druyun then admitted that she and Sears had tried to cover up their discussions. Druyun was sentenced to nine months in prison. Sears was fired by the company and pleaded guilty to criminal charges, resulting in a four-month prison sentence. Phillip Condit, the head of Boeing, resigned from his position as chairman and chief executive officer.

Boeing was involved in another scandal after it improperly acquired documents of a competitor, Lockheed Martin Corp., causing the government to revoke $1 billion in Boeing contracts. A Boeing employee pleaded guilty to purloining those documents, which related to rocket development. Boeing agreed to a government demand that it hire an independent monitor that would report violations of Boeing's ethics code to the government. The monitor supervised over 100 Boeing employees who were dedicated to the task of ensuring compliance with Boeing's code of ethics. The company opened "ethics hotlines" on which employees could report ethics violations. Problems continued at Boeing. The company agreed to pay $72.5 million to settle sex discrimination litigation. Still other problems surfaced on its $100 billion contract to aid in the modernization of the U.S. Army. Boeing was suspended from doing business with the air force for twenty months as a result of its misdeeds, costing the company an estimated $1 billion. Shortly after that suspension expired, Boeing announced that its current chief executive officer, Harry Stonecipher, was resigning because he was having a consensual extramarital affair with a female executive. That affair was revealed by an anonymous tip from the company's ethics hotline, and such conduct was found to be a violation of the company's ethics code. Stonecipher was given a bonus of $2.1 million as a sendoff, but the publication of his affair triggered an expensive divorce action from his already estranged wife of over fifty years. Boeing was negotiating with the government to pay a penalty reported to be as high as $500 million in order to avoid criminal prosecution over its misdeeds.

Boeing was not the only government contractor having difficulties. Titan Corp. pleaded guilty to bribing an African official in violation of the Foreign Corrupt Practices Act and paid fines totaling $28.5 million, the largest ever under that statute. That problem caused Lockheed Martin Corp. to drop plans to merge with Titan. InVision Technologies, a General Electric Co. subsidiary that makes airport explosive detection machines, paid $1.1 million to settle SEC charges that its agents were making payments in Asia in violation of the Foreign Corrupt Practices Act.

The chairman of Smith & Wesson Holding Corp., Joseph Minder, resigned after it was revealed that he was the "Shotgun Bandit" who had escaped from prison after being convicted of numerous armed bank robberies and holdups in Michigan. Those indiscretions had occurred decades earlier during his youth, and after being recaptured and serving his time, Minder began working with juveniles. As a part of his rehabilitation, Minder obtained both a masters and a bachelor of arts degree from the University of Michigan. Minder became a model citizen, but that did not save his job from the hysteria arising from Enron. Executives continued to be targeted for excessive compensation. Jack Welch, the retired head of General Electric, came under attack in September 2002 after his wife filed for a divorce and disclosed that he was receiving a large number of retirement perks from GE. Welch had spent his entire career at the company, starting at an entry-level position and rising to chairman and chief executive officer, a position he held from 1981 to 2001. During Welch's tenure, GE's market capitalization increased by over 3,600 percent to more than $150 billion. He built GE into a massively profitable enterprise, increasing its market value, and was generally viewed as a model executive.

The perquisites given to Welch by GE included use of an expensive New York apartment, unlimited access to a private jet, membership at an exclusive golf course, a leased Mercedes Benz and driver, bodyguards, and tickets to the opera and sports events. The total value of all the perks was $2.5 million in 2001, which was considerably less than the value that Welch continued to bring to GE. Responding to media criticism in an editorial in the *Wall Street Journal,* Welch declared that he was renouncing several of those benefits in order to quell the furor. Welch could have taken cash instead of those perks and avoided that criticism. The SEC censured GE for failing fully to disclose those perks. General Electric subsequently announced that it was restating its operating cash flows for 2002 and 2003 by a total of over $2.2 billion because of improper accounting treatment for vendor financing. General Motors Corp. and Ford Corp. also announced that they were revising their operating cash flow treatment for such financing. General Electric was continuing to expand its financial services business, agreeing to buy Aegon's commercial finance business in Europe and the United States for $5.4 billion. GE Capital also bought the consumer finance operations of Abbey National for $1.3 billion.

State regulators were pursuing full disclosure failures against businesses, but had problems of their own. On July 31, 2003, the SEC charged James Kerasiotes and the Massachusetts Turnpike Authority with failing to disclose to municipal bond investors that the "Big Dig" highway and tunnel project in Boston had $1.4 billion in cost overruns and was facing billions more when it was discovered that the tunnel was leaking. Twelve individuals were indicted in Philadelphia in a pay-to-play case involving payments made to the city treasurer, Corey Kemp, for directing business to financial service firms. Among those indicted were employees of JPMorgan Chase & Co. and Commerce Bancorp. The payments included a new deck for Kemp's house and a trip to the Super Bowl. Kemp and two executives at Commerce Bancorp were convicted of some of the charges.

More Fraud

Pump and Dump Schemes

The pump and dump schemes of the 1990s continued to surface after passage of Sarbanes-Oxley. The SEC warned in 2004 of pump and dump schemes in which callers left messages containing an insider's stock tip on answering machines that sounded as if the message had been left at the wrong number. Michael Pickens, son of T. Boone Pickens, the famous corporate raider, was arrested for sending "blast" faxes that appeared to be sent to the wrong address but contained an apparent hot tip on a stock Michael Pickens was manipulating. He was also charged with growing marijuana.

Eli and Ari Dinov and David Rubinov were charged with using spam e-mails to tout the stock of Discover Capital Holdings Corp., obtaining $1.1 million from investors in the process through a private placement. Stephen Thomas raised over $8 million from 1,400 investors through "pre-IPO" offerings of stock that he claimed would be hot issues, but no initial public offering ever occurred. In one pump and dump scheme, Steven Wise, the chief executive officer of Marx Toys & Entertainment Corp., was charged by the SEC with bribing brokers to pump his company's stock, so that he could sell his holdings at a profit. The bribes were paid in shares of the company.

Great White Marine & Recreation Inc. was the center of a $10 million pump and dump scheme orchestrated by Alvis Colin Smith Jr. In another scheme, $4.2 million in unregistered stock of American Automation Inc. was sold to 450 investors across the country by Kendyll and Hazel Horton. The SEC tried to have Hazel Horton evicted from her home for violating an asset freeze order, but a Texas court refused that request. David I. Namer was sentenced to twenty-nine years in prison, which was one of the longest white-collar sentences ever handed down, for his involvement in an Internet pump and dump scheme. Namer sold fraudulent corporate notes to hundreds of investors, raising $35 million. He claimed that the notes were insured.

A broker at Kirkpatrick, Pettis, Smith, Polian Inc. ran up the price of the stock of Creative Host Inc. by 3,618 percent, from seventy-eight cents to $29, reaping commissions of $1 million in the process. The stock of Orex Gold Mines Corp. was the subject of a pump and dump scheme using high-pressure, boiler room sales tactics. Jeanette B. Wilcher and the Life Foundation Trust defrauded investors out of more than $3 million in a pump and dump scheme involving the stock of Hitsgalore.com Inc. Wilcher was indicted for her role in that scheme. The SEC had her held in contempt of court for failing to disgorge $1 million in profits that she made in the scheme. Wilcher was then jailed and subjected to a fine of $1,000 per day that would be doubled every day thereafter that the disgorgement was not paid. Wilcher failed to comply with that order.

Even more brazen were the promoters of Pixelon, who made an initial public offering and then celebrated with a $60 million party in Las Vegas that consumed 80 percent of the financing. The party entertainers included the Who, the Dixie Chicks, and Tony Bennett. The chief executive officer of the company, Michael Fenne, whose real name was David Kim Stanley, became a fugitive from justice; he was captured and imprisoned. Brokers at Nationwide Securities Corp. were manipulating the stock of Thermo-Mizer Environmental Corp. after its IPO in 1996. Four of those brokers were given prison terms ranging from eighteen months to over four years.

David Melillo, the president of Euro-Atlantic Securities Inc., was charged with manipulating the stock of Hollywood Productions Inc. He was convicted of bribing brokers to push the stock. After an unknown terrorist mailed anthrax to congressional offices and to news reporters in 2001, seven individuals, including accountants and lawyers, were indicted for falsely promoting the stock of 2DoTrade on the strength of claims that it had developed an antianthrax drug. That assertion pushed the price of the company's stock up by 400 percent.

A seventeen-year-old student, Benjamin Synder, was charged by the SEC with planting false news stories on the Internet, where he posted prices for the stock of Viragen International Inc. The teenager claimed that the company was producing a drug that could be used to treat anthrax. Synder used the name of a Bloomberg reporter to provide support for his stories, which he posted through a computer in a public library in Lawrenceville, Georgia. The teenager owned about $500 of stock in the company.

Synder was not the youngest offender. Jonathan Lebed of Cedar Grove, New Jersey, was sued by the SEC when he was fifteen for engaging in pump and dump activities. He bought low-priced, illiquid securities and then made false claims as to the company's performance on the Internet that pushed up their prices, allowing him to profit. The teenager had to repay $285,000 of gains. The SEC also brought an action against a seventeen-year-old California student who had raised $1 million through an Internet securities offering for an online betting operation.

Anthony Elgindy was charged with manipulating stock prices by spreading negative information on companies through his Web site, allowing him to profit from short sales. This case raised some novel legal theories because at least some of the information was true. Elgindy was additionally charged with receiving confidential information from Jeffrey Royer, an FBI agent. Royer was a defendant in that criminal prosecution. The SEC charged several firms with offering investors the chance to exchange worthless stock they had purchased in earlier pump and dump schemes for blue chip stocks, provided that the investors paid a large "advance fee." The firms never delivered the blue chip shares, but kept the fees. The scheme was operated from the Dominican Republic from 2002 to 2004. Six firms were sued by the SEC for these activities, including Crescent Financial Group Inc. and Berkshire Tax Consultants Co.

A federal court enjoined Sara Jane Peck, Larry Grabarnick, Marc David Shiner, and Donald LaBarre and ordered them to pay over $7 million in disgorgement, prejudgment interest, and civil penalties. The defendants were running an Internet boiler room that promoted investments in unregistered LLP units through bulk e-mails and Internet Web sites. Investors were told they would benefit from the deregulation of the electricity market in California. More than 580 people nationwide invested over $10 million in this scheme.

Joseph J. Wozniak and others touted the stock of Aqua Vie Beverage Corp. through millions of false and misleading tout sheets faxed to homes and businesses. From November 2002 through May 2003, Wozniak offered millions of shares of unregistered Aqua Vie common stock. In another case, Phoenix Telecom LLC was enjoined from selling investments in pay telephone leasebacks using insurance agents and the Internet. Some 2,000 elderly investors lost $74 million in this fraud. Global Health, which claimed to be a biotechnology company that had developed a cancer treatment, issued letters to investors on FDA letterhead stating that Global Health's cancer treatment has been approved by the FDA. Those letters were forgeries.

Emission Controls Corporation and its president and chief executive officer, Syd Cooke, were charged by the SEC with using manipulated test results to convince a group of investors that the company had invented a device that lowered vehicle emissions to near-zero levels. A false press release to that effect was issued by defendants on January 3, 2003.

The SEC announced that it was planning a new enforcement program that would result in a rapid suspension of trading in stocks attacked by spammers. The SEC had been previously rebuked by the Supreme Court in the use of that suspension authority, which was supposed to last for only ten days but had been rolled over in some cases by the SEC for years.

Courtney Smith was indicted in Los Angeles by a federal grand jury for accepting $1.3 million in cash and stock of GenesisIntermedia Inc. in exchange for touting that company's stock on CNN, CNBC, and Bloomberg television. The money was funneled through his girlfriend. Smith had previously marketed the "Ab Twister" and a "relationship" product called "Men are from Mars, Women are from Venus" through television infomercials. Richard Hines was sentenced to twelve years in prison and ordered to pay some $6 million in restitution for running a boiler room operation using the name Satellite Capital Group. Among other things, Hines and his partner John Temple were using Tom Bosley, the star of the popular television program *Happy Days*, to promote one of their investment products.

Ponzi Schemes

Sarbanes-Oxley had no discernible effect on the operation of Ponzi schemes. Global Express Capital Real Estate Investment I LLC ran a $48 million Ponzi scheme in 2003 that promised profits of 12 percent annually from investments in mortgage loans. J.T. Wallenbrock & Associates sold promissory notes to over 6,000 investors, raising over $230 million between 1999 and 2002. The company claimed that the money was to be used in a "factoring" business involving receivables purchased at a discount from Malaysian latex glove manufacturers. In fact, it was a Ponzi scheme. Larry T. Osaki was indicted for continuing to operate a Ponzi scheme after he had been enjoined by a court in an SEC proceeding brought in connection with the J.T. Wallenbrock scam. Osaki pleaded guilty to the federal criminal charges.

Starcash Inc., a Florida firm, was selling payday loan investments promising returns of 30 to 42 percent. Investors lost over $7 million in an eight-month period from that operation. James Malbaff and Thomas Gregory Cook were selling bank instruments they claimed returned 1,300 percent. They raised $825,000 from thirty investors before being stopped by the SEC. Federal prosecutors charged in another case that a stock promoter had engaged in a $300 million Ponzi scheme. Reed E. Slatkin bested that fraud with a $600 million Ponzi scheme that involved 800 investors in his Reed Slatkin Investment Club LP. Over $250 million of that amount could not be recovered. Slatkin was sentenced to fourteen years in prison for criminal charges that included obstruction of justice. Kevin Leigh Lawrence pleaded guilty for his involvement in a $100 million Ponzi scheme. D.W. Heath & Associates Inc. and others defrauded some 800 elderly investors out of $60 million. Those investors were sold promissory notes that were claimed to be safe and secure. A scam reported in the *Ladies' Home Journal* involved a pyramid scheme called Women Helping Women. Under this program, women agreed to buy a plate at a "dinner party" for $5,000 or share that plate with other women. Thereafter, the women buying that plate would receive the proceeds of future dinner party plate sales. The magazine estimated that 500,000 women had been defrauded by this scheme. Losses were estimated to total over $12 million.

Heartland Financial Services Inc. took in $60 million from some 1,000 investors through a Ponzi scheme. David Mobley carried out this fraud by telling investors he was running a hedge fund with $450 million under management. The funds he did not spend on maintaining his lavish lifestyle were lost through bad investments, but he did contribute $3.5 million to charities. Thomas McCrimmon and others were convicted of engaging in a Ponzi scheme they called the Hammersmith Program. That program was supposed to have involved European currency market transactions that were purportedly backed by U.S. Treasury bills. In fact, it was a Ponzi scheme and investors lost over $60 million. John Aptt and Douglas Murphy ran a Ponzi scheme through their Financial Instruments Corp. that obtained $14 million from investors by promising them that they would double their money. Aptt and Murphy were sentenced to nine and eight years in prison, respectively.

Eric Stein defrauded 1,800 investors of $34 million through a Ponzi scheme targeting those over age fifty. Stein became a fugitive from justice, but was caught and sent to prison for eight years. Lloyd Benton Sharp sold investments to retired investors in ornamental Japanese paulownia trees. Those investments were made through Pension Plans of America Inc., which was controlled by Sharp. He told investors that this investment was as good as "gold in Fort Knox" and that he had a firm contract with another company to buy the trees when they matured for $81.8 million. Sharp had a prior criminal conviction for securities violations and was the subject of various SEC actions.

Even bigger was the sale by Kenneth Kasarjian of over $800 million in lease assignments that had already been assigned or which did not exist. The private placement memorandum used to sell these instruments contained false financial statements that were inflated by fictitious year-end transactions and false claims made to the auditors. Enrique E. Perusquia, a broker at UBS PaineWebber Inc., lost $68 million in client funds through speculative mining property investments from which he received kickbacks. He stole client funds and engaged in unauthorized margin transactions.

Kevin Lawrence obtained $91 million from 5,000 investors through claims that his company, Znetix Inc., was about to make a highly profitable IPO. No such offering was made. Lawrence and two of his colleagues pleaded guilty to criminal charges. Lawrence was sentenced to twenty years in prison. The SEC was able to recover a $330,000 diamond engagement ring from Lawrence's fiancée. Assisting Lawrence was Clifford G. Baird, the author of a book called *Power of Positive Self Image.* His company was touting Znetix stock as based on "rock solid financial statements." In California, MX Factors LLC ran a Ponzi scheme that claimed it returned 12 percent in sixty to ninety days. Investors lost $33.5 million.

Edward Jung was charged in February 2004 with defrauding fifty-five investors of $21 million through an options trading scheme. Four Star Financial Services promised returns of 18 percent per year from fees charged on 900 number telephone calls. Five hundred investors lost some $140 million. "Prime bank" schemes were popular scams that involved promises of large returns on risk-free investments involving complex loan funding mechanisms. In one such fraud, Rayvon Inc. promised investors returns of over 6 percent monthly, which translated to over 72 percent per year.

Another prime bank scheme drew prison sentences for five individuals who defrauded investors of $11 million. Those sentences ranged from six to fifteen years. William R. Kerr's China Investment Group Ltd. defrauded investors of $12 million through a prime bank scheme. Kerr claimed that he controlled a $200 million trust that he could leverage to make profits of 13,000 percent and that he was supervised by the World Bank. Terry L. Dowdell was the mastermind of a $120 million scheme involving what he claimed were foreign bank trading instruments that provided a return of 160 percent. Dowdell sold those instruments through the Vavasseur Corp., a Bahamian company he owned. David and James Edwards and others raised $98 million from 1,300 investors through a prime bank scheme. An even bigger fraud involving the Credit Bancorp. Ltd. (CBL) caused investor losses of $210 million. That scheme, masterminded by Richard J. Blech, involved two programs (the CBL Insured Credit Facility and the CBL Insured Securities Strategy) that promised large returns and low risk. Nicholas Roblee, aka Nicholas Richmond, was sentenced to five years in prison for defrauding investors of over $2 million in a prime bank scheme.

Gregory Best was sentenced to nine years in prison for his role in a Ponzi scheme that defrauded investors of over $24 million. Philip Gratz, a Florida broker, was sentenced to seven years in prison for defrauding investors of $9 million. He had promised them annual gains of between 25 and 50 percent but used the money for jewelry, artwork, vacations, and a luxurious home. Gratz had previously been convicted of securities fraud in 1995.

Other Scandals

The CFTC and SEC brought actions against numerous firms that were acting as boiler rooms in the sale of currency contracts to unsophisticated investors. Hundreds of millions of dollars were lost from those investments. On November 19, 2003, the FBI and the U.S. Attorney's Office in New York arrested forty-seven individuals in "operation wooden nickel," a sting conducted in connection with currency trading abuses. The arrests were the culmination of an eighteen-month undercover operation. Several of the arrested traders had been rigging trades so their employers lost money to a counterparty that kicked back money to the traders. Among the firms victimized by this conduct were JPMorgan Chase & Co., UBS AG, Société Générale SA, the Alliance Group AG, and the Israel Discount Bank. Daniel Gordon, a Merrill Lynch trader, pleaded guilty to criminal charges of embezzling $43 million from the firm during the year 2000. He created an offshore company and engaged in fictitious transactions in energy products to carry out that scheme.

One questionable trading practice was called "spoofing." A trader placed a buy order through an electronic communications network at a price that moved the current market offer. The trader then sent an opposing order at the same price to a market maker on Nasdaq or an exchange specialist and canceled the first order, leaving the market maker with a loss and the trader with a profit. The SEC brought several actions against traders engaging in such practices. Knight Trading Group, which was sold to Citigroup in 2004, agreed to settle an SEC case for $79 million that charged the firm with front-running the orders of institutional customers. Included among its customers were the Putnam funds owned by Marsh & McLennan, which had its own regulatory problems with late trading and market timing. Other customers were Fidelity Investments and T. Rowe Price Group Inc.

Goldman Sachs agreed to pay a $2 million penalty for selling IPOs before they were approved by the SEC. The NASD fined eight brokerage firms, including Merrill Lynch, Morgan Stanley, and Charles Schwab, a total of $610,000 for overcharging customers buying and selling municipal bonds. Citigroup, Goldman Sachs Group, Deutsche Bank AG, and Miller Tabek Roberts Securities LLC agreed to pay $20 million to the NASD to settle claims that they charged excessive markups and markdowns on bonds sold to institutional customers. Those markup rules sought to fix broker-dealer fees as a measure to protect small investors but were now being extended to institutions with enough bargaining power to negotiate their own prices. Citigroup paid $275,000 to settle NASD charges that it sold investments in two commodity funds to unsuitable retail investors. The securities industry had earlier extended its suitability rule for small retail customers to protect institutions after they suffered a series of losses from derivative transactions in the early 1990s.

Morgan Stanley was charged by the SEC with inflating the value of mark-to-market assets on its own balance sheet in 2000 and was required to restate its accounts in 2003 as a result of other accounting discrepancies. That broker-dealer encountered more charges from the SEC for improperly valuing aircraft in its aircraft leasing business. Morgan Stanley agreed to a cease and desist order to settle those charges. Carlos H. Soto, a Morgan Stanley broker in Puerto Rico, was arrested on February 19, 2004, for stealing more than $50 million of clients' funds. His scheme was to tell investors that they were investing in conservative investments, such as mortgage-backed securities. He then took the money, invested it in risky instruments in the hopes that he could make profits, and kept the difference between the profits and what the investors had been promised. He had faked account statements in order to carry out this scheme. Philip Cummings, an employee of Ex-Teledata Communications Inc., a credit-reporting firm, pleaded guilty to identity theft affecting 30,000 individuals. Three other persons were charged in the case.

ChoicePoint Inc. disclosed that a group of individuals hacked into its computer base to obtain personal information on some 400,000 individuals that had been gathered for background checks. That disclosure caused a drop in the company's stock of some 18 percent. The chief executive officer and the president of ChoicePoint collectively sold over $16 million of the company's stock just before public disclosure of this problem, touching off an SEC investigation. Hackers also stole personal information on 30,000 individuals from the LexisNexis Group. HSBC PLC thereafter announced that the security of 180,000 of its MasterCard holders had been compromised and MasterCard later conceded that the security of millions of cardholders had been breached.

Todd Eberhard, chairman of Park South Securities LLCV and a well-known financial analyst, pleaded guilty to fraud charges for stealing customer funds and churning their accounts, causing millions of dollars in losses. Kevin O. Kelley, a money manager and former broker at Royal Alliance (which was owned by the American International Group), was arrested by postal inspectors for defrauding clients of millions of dollars. One of his alleged victims was Carol Raybin, a schoolteacher who had inherited a large sum of money from a relative killed in the collapse of the World Trade Center towers.

A jury found that Asensio & Company Inc., an investment adviser and short seller, violated the federal securities laws in making disparaging statements about the stock of Chromatics Color Sciences International Inc., which made a device that could nonintrusively detect the level of bilirubin in babies. The short seller's campaign was effective; the price of Chromatics stock dropped, but later recovered. Because of that recovery, the jury awarded no damages. That verdict was upheld on appeal.

Insider trading cases continued to surface. An AT&T employee and others agreed to disgorge $578,000 in profits from insider trading in the stock of Intelefilm Corp. That trading concerned information about a new company being developed by Intelefilm and AT&T called Intelsource.org. Another example of insider trading led to SEC charges against Derrick McKinley, who shorted the stock of his company, Gilatech Inc., after learning of medical problems with a drug it was marketing. Eric Tsao, an executive at MedImmune Inc., pleaded guilty to criminal charges of insider trading on information concerning his company's acquisitions. He made $150,000 from that trading.

Evan S. Collins, a former senior financial officer for Network Associates, Inc., now known as McAfee Inc., traded on inside information concerning fraudulent accounting practices that were about to be disclosed. Collins was also charged criminally for that conduct. His profits from the trading totaled $253,000. The SEC brought insider trading charges against three employees at LendingTree Inc., a financial services firm located in Charlotte, North Carolina. Mark P. Mead (vice president of national accounts), Michael J. Ricks (senior director of strategy and sales), and John H. Woody (senior director of sales and product management) purchased LendingTree stock just prior to the announcement on May 5, 2003, of a merger with USA Interactive, which caused LendingTree's stock to jump by 41 percent. Two other executives at Lending Tree were also charged with engaging in the same misconduct. All six executives agreed to settle the SEC charges and one executive, Brian Paquette, pleaded guilty to criminal charges of obstruction of justice.

Russell and Thomas Bradlee, Louis P. Stone IV, and Angela DelVacchio settled SEC charges of trading on inside information concerning the acquisition of F&M Bancorp in March 2003 by Mercantile Bankshares Corporation. James Jensen, a financial consultant to Crown Resources Corp., traded on inside information of that company. Four executives at Golden State Bancorp were charged with trading on inside information of its acquisition by Citibank in 2002. They used options to garner $250,000 in profits.

The SEC was investigating Chaunce Hayden, a gossip columnist for *Steppin' Out* magazine, after he stated that Howard Stern, the controversial disc jockey, might move to satellite radio. Shortly afterward, Stern did announce that he was leaving Viacom for Sirius satellite radio in a deal valued at over $100 million. That announcement resulted in a big jump in Sirius stock. Hayden was a frequent guest on Stern's show, but he denied receiving any inside information. An investigation by the NASD sought to determine whether the decision of Lehman Brothers Holdings Inc. to include Fitch Ratings into its bond index had been leaked in advance of its announcement. The inclusion of that rating in the index bumped up the stock price of General Motors because it would aid its credit rating. There was an increase in grading General Motors stock in the days before the Lehman announcement. John J. Amore, a day trader, was being investigated for trading off "squawk box" information that was broadcast to sales forces of broker-dealers on analysts' tips and confidential trading information about activity by institutional investors, which would have market effect. Thomas J. O'Connell, a Merrill Lynch broker in the firm's Garden City, New York office, was arrested for that conduct. Benjamin D. Grimaldi, the Merrill Lynch office manager for that branch, was charged with tampering with a witness in that investigation. He pleaded guilty to that charge. Brokers at Citigroup and Lehman Brothers were also indicted for accepting payments from day traders for access to their squawk boxes, which announced large customer orders that the day traders would then front run. A Citigroup broker, Ralph D. Casbarro, pleaded guilty to one such charge.

The SEC was examining other Wall Street firms to determine if they were tipping their customers with inside information on large institutional customer sales that might push down prices. The SEC was also investigating the practice of brokerage firms buying up stock for their own accounts in order to fill customer orders and then marking that stock up to fill the order. A unit of the Knight Trading Group agreed to pay $79 million to settle SEC charges over such conduct.

Robert Goehring, the communications director at Gerber Scientific Inc. settled SEC charges of insider trading in his company's stock. He was both buying and shorting the company's shares in advance of various announcements by the company that had market effect. He was barred from serving as an officer or director of a public company. Goehring, who had also been tipping a friend, Armund Ek, was charged criminally for that conduct. Previously, two executives at a Gerber subsidiary were charged with insider trading on merger and other corporate activities. In still another case, a Gerber executive settled charges of insider trading by buying and selling Gerber stock in advance of announcements concerning the company.

Frank R.V. Loomans, manager of investor relations at Cox Communications Inc., was charged with insider trading through his father's account. Loomans transferred his profits, which totaled $285,000, outside the country and fled to Brussels, Belgium, after the SEC began its investigation. Seven employees of Seven Flower Foods Inc. in Georgia agreed to pay a collective amount of $115,000 for trading on inside information that caused the company's stock to jump sharply when publicly disclosed. A trader at Fidelity Investments was charged with front running firm trades through transactions he conducted in his mother's account.

Adrian Alexander (aka Adrian Antoniu) agreed to pay $420,000 to settle SEC charges that he traded on inside information about a plan by Luxottica SpA to take over U.S. Shoe Corp. He was tipped by his girlfriend, Susi Belli, manager of investor and public relations for Luxottica. In another case, Linda Ensor and her husband Stephen settled SEC charges that they traded on inside information in advance of a negative announcement by TALX Corp., where she worked as an executive assistant. The SEC charged three California brothers, Anthony C. Sudol III, Michael G. Sudol, and Richard J. Sudol, with insider trading. Anthony Sudol was an employee of Cisco Systems Inc. and he tipped his brothers with nonpublic information on Cisco acquisitions plans.

Thom Calandra, a founder of CBS Market Watch, agreed to pay $540,000 to settle SEC charges that he was scalping stocks that he touted in a market newsletter without disclosing that he owned the stocks and was profiting as readers responded to his recommendations. The SEC charged Guillaume Pollet, a managing director at Société Générale's SG Cowen, with short selling on information he obtained from his trading desk, which handled private investments in public equities (PIPEs). Pollet later pleaded guilty to a felony count for that conduct. Hillary Shane, a hedge fund manager, agreed to pay $1 million to settle SEC charges that she sold CompuDyne Corp. stock short on the basis of inside information about a PIPE transaction.

Min Ma and his girlfriend Joyce Ng were charged with trading on inside information obtained from their jobs as desktop publishers at Merrill Lynch's offices in San Francisco. A federal appeals court ordered Robert Happ to pay $85,000 for insider trading in the shares of Galileo Corp., and the SEC was ordered to pay him $87,000 in attorney fees as a result of misconduct by the agency in the proceedings. In Rocky River, Ohio, Peter Wilson, pretending to be an employee of Nasdaq, directed companies with a price spike to make an announcement that there was nothing to justify the market action. Wilson sold the stock short, profiting when the stock dropped in price after the announcement. He was fined $22,000 and was barred from trading securities in the future.

The SEC investigated "exchange funds" in which executives of large companies pooled their stock with each other in order to diversify their holdings. The SEC was concerned that executives had used those funds to reduce their exposure during the market downturn at the end of the century without disclosing that fact to shareholders. Another SEC investigation sought to determine whether executives at Analog Devices and other companies were being awarded stock options just in advance of favorable news that would ensure them profits.

The SEC was embarrassed by its premature release of company filings in November, several of which contained news with market effect. The SEC did not sue itself for that error. Another leak was discovered in the full disclosure system. Proxy solicitation firms were plying clerks at broker-dealers and banks with gifts for disclosing the confidential holdings of institutional investors. Stock surveillance firms were engaging in similar conduct. Those firms supply corporate officers with information on what institutions are buying and selling their company's stock. In one instance, clerks at CIBC Mellon Trust Co. received tickets to sporting events and cash tips of $50 to $100 for supplying that information. Other clerks were given $50 gift certificates and boxes of steaks. The SEC sought to determine whether such information was used for inside trading.

Fraud Abroad

The number of class action lawsuits filed against foreign companies listing their stock in U.S. markets rose to twenty-one in 2003, while a total of 175 such suits were filed in U.S courts against all issuers. In Germany, executives at Mannesmann AG were tried in a criminal court for breach of fiduciary duty for taking $70 million in bonuses after that company was acquired by Vodafone PLC in 2000. That $208 billion merger was the largest in history. A German court rejected the criminal charges but concluded that the payments were improper. Kirk Kerkorian sued Daimler Chrysler, charging that the announcement that the two firms would combine as a merger of equals was false because Daimler took over the control of the business. Kerkorian had been a large holder of Chrysler stock. That lawsuit was subsequently dismissed by a federal judge. In the meantime, Daimler Chrysler agreed to pay $300 million to settle class action suits over the merger with Chrysler. Kerkorian was himself the subject of insider trading charges in a class action suit for selling $661 million of the company's stock in advance of some adverse news. Daimler had other problems. The SEC opened an investigation of the company after a whistleblower claimed that it was maintaining secret accounts to bribe foreign government officials.

Inflated accounting statements were not just an American phenomenon. Kim Woo-Choong, the founder of Daewoo Enterprises in South Korea, was accused by South Korean authorities of inflating Daewoo's assets by $30 billion. The chairman of the SK Corporation in South Korea was convicted of engaging in a $1.32 billion accounting fraud and for insider trading. He was sentenced to three years in prison. Carl Cushnie, the founder of the Versailles Finance Group in London, was convicted of accounting fraud in connection with accounting misstatements amounting to £100 million between 1992 and 2000. Fred Clough, the company's finance officer, was also convicted. The trial was conducted American-style, featuring the lavish lifestyle of the defendants.

Joyti De-Laurey, a secretary in the London office of Goldman Sachs, stole $7 million from the private accounts of her bosses without their missing it. She wired the funds to an account in Cyprus and wrote a prayer asking God to help her with the theft. A London judge sentenced her to seven years in prison. Edward Canale and Michael Connolly, two executives in the New York office of BNP Paribas, pleaded guilty to stealing $12 million from the bank by diverting assets to shell companies they owned.

Martin Marcus, the deputy chairman of Queen Moat Houses, was fined £250,000 in 2004 for his stewardship of the company during the early 1990s when it posted one of the largest losses in British history. His license as a chartered accountant was revoked. The firm's auditor, Bird Luckin, was fined £17,000.

Ernst & Young faced a massive negligence claim in Great Britain from its audits for Equitable Life, an insurer in financial trouble. Audit firms in the United Kingdom were seeking legislation that would limit their liability from audit failures, and the government has proposed such legislation. Austria and Germany had already set liability limits for auditors, and other European countries allowed auditors to set liability limits contractually with clients. Australia was considering assessing auditor liability based on the auditor's proportional contribution to losses.

The National Australia Bank disclosed in January 2004 that rogue traders at the bank had lost $458 million in foreign currency trading. Chinese Aviation Oil Corp. (Singapore), a Chinese jet fuel company, lost $550 million in speculative oil derivative transactions. Chinese officials arrested sixty-nine government officials and bank employees charged with stealing $900 million from the Industrial & Commercial Bank of China. The Chinese government was considering a cap on executive salaries as a way of curbing greed and corruption, which undoubtedly would have the opposite effect. The Irish banks were having difficulties. Allied Irish Banks lost $750 million in 2002 as the result of a rogue currency trader in its Baltimore office, John Rusnak. The bank faced another scandal in 2004 and was being investigated by the new Irish Financial Services Regulatory Authority for overcharging customers some $30 million in foreign exchange conversions. The Irish revenue authorities were also investigating some offshore tax shelters for executives at Allied Irish Banks. Michael Soden at the Bank of Ireland resigned after it was discovered he had used his office computer to visit a Web site for Las Vegas escorts just before a planned trip to the United States.

The increasing activist role of institutional investors was spreading to Europe. The European Union urged more disclosures of executive compensation, a matter that had traditionally been treated as private in Europe. A survey of European managers discovered widespread skepticism that corporate governance reforms provided any real investor protection. The British company Marks and Spencer was being strong-armed by institutional investors to change its management as a condition for support in opposing a hostile takeover effort being mounted by Philip Green. Green eventually dropped this takeover attempt. The Financial Services Authority (FSA), Great Britain's financial services regulator, required companies there to adhere to a Combined Code on Corporate Governance. Following a report by Sir Derek Higgs, FSA was considering a proposal that would require auditors to review the internal controls of audit clients, a requirement already invoked in America.

Japanese regulators were notoriously lenient in regulating Japanese financial institutions even after a revamping of the regulatory structure. That leniency did not extend to foreign firms. Credit Lyonnais, Bear Stearns, Deutsche Bank, and Nikko Salomon Smith Barney were charged in 2002 with engaging in short sales that were driving down the market. Morgan Stanley, charged with manipulating a stock through short sales, was barred from trading for five weeks. The foreign firms claimed that the Japanese regulators were themselves trying to manipulate the market by stopping short sales. The Japanese regulator's efforts to restrict short sales reflected a long abandoned belief in the rest of the world that short sellers were responsible for market declines. Massachusetts had prohibited short sales in 1836 and Pennsylvania in 1841, but those restrictions accomplished nothing. The Industrial Commission formed by Congress in 1898 unsuccessfully sought to stop short selling as a means to prevent market declines. Congress investigated short selling after the stock market crash of 1929, but only some insider restrictions on short selling were imposed. The SEC adopted a "tick test" to curb short sellers from driving down markets, but it proved ineffective; the SEC was rethinking that restriction after Enron. Short selling restrictions were rejected altogether in the commodity markets in the 1930s even though farmers claimed that short sellers were driving prices down below the cost of production.

The Tokyo branch of Credit Suisse was excluded from engaging in the derivatives business in Japan after several abuses in 1999. The Japanese regulator denied claims that it was discriminating against foreign firms but continued to act against them. Citigroup was under investigation by Japanese authorities in 2004 for misleading statements concerning private placements of structured bonds. The Japanese government required Citigroup to close its private banking business in Japan, charging that it was being used for money laundering, misleading clients, and engaging in illegal tying arrangements. Citigroup dismissed its vice chairman, Deryck Maughan, and two other executives for failing to prevent that conduct. Citigroup closed down its trust unit in Japan after discovering more problems there. Citigroup was having other problems with a manager for private equity investments in Brazil and the bank severed that relationship. The NYSE fined Citigroup $350,000 for allowing a broker to send e-mails to customers promoting short sale strategies that contained erroneous information about the target companies, which included Guess Inc., the jeans maker. Citigroup announced in the midst of these problems that it was creating a five-point plan to bolster its ethics that would include annual ethics training for all employees. This did not satisfy the Federal Reserve Board, which prohibited Citigroup from making further acquisitions until it solved its compliance problems, which appeared to be out of control.

Citigroup was in trouble in Europe for a trading strategy that involved massive trading in European government bonds on several electronic communications networks. This strategy was called "Dr. Evil," a reference culled from the Austin Powers spy movie spoofs. German prosecutors later dismissed the case concluding the trades were not illegal manipulation. Other European regulators continued to investigate, but the Eurex found no violation. The Financial Services Authority in London did plan to fine Citigroup for failures in its internal controls that allowed the transaction. Citigroup later paid $25 million to settle those charges. The MTS Spa, the electronic trading platform through which the transaction was conducted, suspended Citigroup's trading privileges. Citigroup was fined $10,000 by the Reserve Bank of India for allowing a forgery ring to operate an account at the bank. The Indian government arrested more than a hundred individuals who had forged financial documents valued at more than $600 million.

In China, corporate governance advocates were receiving more press play. Professor Larry Lang was becoming a latter-day Ralph Nader as a number of financial scandals surfaced. The government of China seemed to take corporate governance a bit more seriously than even its most zealous advocates in America. In September 2004 four employees, including two employed at state-owned banks, were executed for corruption that totaled $15 million. Liu Jinbao, the chief executive officer for the Bank of China, was also given a death sentence for accepting bribes totaling $170,000 and embezzling about $3 million, but that sentence was suspended for two years.

Scandal at the New York Stock Exchange

Richard Grasso

The NYSE was beleaguered with competition from electronic communications networks and Nasdaq as the new century began. Concern with that competition led to merger talks between the NYSE and Nasdaq in December 2003. Nasdaq denied it was engaged in such negotiations, but other officials confirmed the discussion, which in any event did not progress. The NYSE was embarrassed by Martha Stewart's resignation from its board after her indictment. Sandy Weill from Citigroup withdrew as a candidate for the board after his run-in with Eliot Spitzer, and other directors were in regulatory hot water. More troubling was the $187.5 million retirement package given to the head of the NYSE, Richard Grasso. That disclosure created a storm of controversy when revealed in the press.

Grasso tried to deflect criticism by agreeing to give up about $48 million of his compensation, but that effort failed. In reaction to media criticism, the NYSE board of directors, which had approved the compensation package, required Grasso to resign on September 17, 2003. The NYSE also disclosed that six other of its top executives had received annual compensation over a five-year period that exceeded $140 million. More eyebrows were raised when it was reported that the two chief operating officers at the NYSE had accumulated retirement benefits of $30 million each and that its recently appointed copresidents, Robert Britz and Catherine Kinney, would each receive $19 million in benefits should they retire at age fifty-five, birthdays that would occur in the next three years.

Grasso was replaced by John Reed, the former head of Citibank who had been ousted in the power struggle with Sandy Weill after the merger of Citibank and Travelers. Reed agreed to accept total compensation of $1, but the exchange paid $3.7 million to a search firm to secure his services. The NYSE then adopted several corporate governance reforms, including reducing the number of board members from twenty-seven to ten, none of which would be NYSE members. An "advisory" panel of NYSE members was created to provide advice to the board. A new chief executive officer, John Thain, was named, splitting the roles of chairman and chief executive officer that had been held by Grasso. Thain was the former president of Goldman Sachs Group Inc. He came on board at the NYSE for a mere $4 million per year, and Reed then largely played only a passive role at the exchange. A former senior staff member at the SEC, Richard Ketchum, was hired to become the NYSE's chief regulatory officer.

Reed demanded that Grasso return a substantial portion of his benefit package. Grasso rejected that request, causing Reed to unleash Eliot Spitzer, who welcomed more headlines and the opportunity to take over regulation of the NYSE from the SEC. Spitzer began an investigation to determine whether the payments to Grasso violated the New York not-for-profit corporate law. Yes, the NYSE is a not-for-profit corporation that reported a profit of $50 million in 2003. Grasso hired his own junkyard dog, Brendan Sullivan, a partner at the law firm of Williams & Connolly in Washington, DC. Sullivan had become famous for his remark that he was not a "potted plant" in response to a congressional committee's request that he remain silent during the testimony of his client Oliver North, the architect of the Iran-contra scandal. Sullivan completely flummoxed the Senate investigating committee by not allowing it to interview North in advance and then having North take an aggressive defense of his actions. An appeals court dismissed North's conviction on criminal charges for shredding documents, obstructing Congress, and accepting an illegal gratuity in the form of a security fence. North lost a race for a congressional seat in 1994 but became a talk show host and popular war correspondent for the Fox cable news network. Sullivan's defense of North was considered comparable to pitching a no-hitter in the major leagues.

Spitzer filed suit against Grasso on May 24, 2004. Kenneth Langone, the prior head of the NYSE compensation committee, was additionally named as a defendant. Spitzer claimed that Grasso and Langone misled the NYSE board on the amount of Grasso's compensation. Spitzer further charged that Grasso had intimidated the very powerful Wall Street executives that sat on the NYSE board into approving his compensation package. Omitted from Spitzer's suit was Carl McCall, the former New York State comptroller and a powerful Democrat whose support was needed by Spitzer for his planned run for governor. McCall had served as the head of the NYSE compensation committee after Langone and at the time when it approved the massive retirement package for Grasso. Langone had the bad luck of being a Republican, but Spitzer claimed that McCall had been misled while Langone was culpable. McCall returned the favor by threatening the career of a popular Long Island politician who was considering a challenge to Spitzer for the Democratic nomination for governor.

Langone and Grasso both blasted Spitzer in editorials in the *Wall Street Journal,* and both vowed to fight. Grasso countersued the NYSE for the $40 million he had been willing to forgo previously. Grasso sued Reed for making false and defamatory statements. That claim was dismissed by a New York judge, but an appellate court reversed the judge, concluding that Grasso had pleaded an adequate cause of action. Grasso's lawyer removed Spitzer's suit to federal court. Spitzer then had to seek removal back to state court, a motion that was granted after a delay of some few months. The *Wall Street Journal* weighed in with an editorial that detailed documents given to NYSE board members that fully evidenced that they had not been misled about Grasso's compensation. McCall in particular had been given exact details on the package from a compensation expert. The NYSE responded with an internal report that portrayed Grasso as a Machiavellian manipulator of the NYSE corporate governance system. It also disclosed that Grasso's executive assistant was paid $240,000 per year, that he had two drivers who were each paid $130,000 per year, and that Grasso was given access to a private jet. Omitted from the report, which was prepared by Dan Webb, the former United States attorney from Chicago, were accolades from prominent NYSE board members about Grasso's leadership and statements from directors exonerating him of any improprieties in the setting of his pay. Those comments were discovered only after Grasso's lawyers asked the judge hearing that case to grant them access to the work papers behind the Webb report. The judge granted that request. The *Wall Street Journal* also obtained access to the materials and, in a nearly full-page editorial, derided Spitzer's lawsuit. The editorial noted that witnesses had testified that McCall had been responsible for any failures to inform the board. The reason for the large cash payment to Grasso was also exposed. The NYSE could not issue stock options; were it a public company, directors testified that Grasso's compensation would have been as high as $500 million from options. More controversy followed when McCall's lawyers advised the court that a tape recording of his interview in the Webb investigation had been erased or otherwise malfunctioned.

The odd thing is that Grasso probably deserved the compensation. Unlike Michael Ovitz, who contributed very little to earn his $140 million compensation package for fourteen months' work, Grasso was a longtime employee of the NYSE who had worked his way through the ranks without even the benefit of a college education. Grasso was a successful executive, keeping the NYSE competitive in the face of severe threats from Nasdaq, electronic communications networks, and international trading. NYSE market share in the stocks it listed for trading was 85 percent under Grasso even though it was still using the outmoded specialist system, which had the benefit of providing members with profits of $2.12 billion between 1995 and 2000. The price of NYSE memberships nearly doubled during Grasso's tenure and trading volume was at a level scarcely believable when he assumed command. Average daily trading volume on the exchange increased from 179 million shares in 1991 to about 1.4 billion shares in 2000. Grasso had also acted heroically in reopening the NYSE after the September 11 terrorist attacks, sending an important message to the world that American markets were robust and undeterred by that wanton destruction. In a further petty act, the NYSE ordered the removal of a plaque on the exchange's building commemorating the victims of the September 11 terrorist attack because it bore Grasso's name.

NYSE Problems

The NYSE announced that it was closing its lunchroom for lack of interest, a once important Wall Street meeting place. Specialists' revenue dropped by 60 percent and profits fell by 50 percent after Grasso left. The NYSE's market share of stocks it listed for trading dropped below 80 percent for the first time ever and was down to about 75 percent in January 2004. A NYSE seat sold for $1.35 million in October 2003, a five-year low and down over 60 percent from prices in 1999. In July 2004, the price of a NYSE seat fell to $1.25 million, down from the $2 million paid for seats under Grasso's reign and below the price of seats on the smaller New York Mercantile Exchange (NYMEX), the energy exchange in New York. Lease rates for NYSE seats were at their lowest levels in eleven years in October 2004. NYSE seats reached a nine-year low in January 2005 with a sale at $975,000. Another blow was struck when Charles Schwab announced that it was selling its NYSE seats, concluding that their prestige was now lost and that access could be gained at a lower cost. The price of NYSE seats did experience rebound over the next few months reaching $1.54 million in March 2005 after it appeared that the SEC was adopting a rule that would assure that the exchange's monopoly over its listed securities would be maintained. The NYSE had been profitable under Grasso, but was facing losses in its operations after he left as the result of legal costs from the attack on him and changes in corporate governance. Compensation expenses were higher than those under Grasso, despite his large pay packet.

The NYSE was plagued by a series of trading scandals on its floor. Independent floor brokers, or $2 brokers as they are sometimes called, were engaged in "flipping" or "trading for eights." This practice involved the purchase or sale of a security for a customer followed by the sale or purchase of the same security for a profit of one-eighth of a point, the then spread between the bid and ask prices. This allowed floor brokers to receive both a commission for the trade and profits from the spread. The government claimed that at least sixty-four people had received $11 million in profits from such conduct. Seven of the floor brokers were concealing their trading through the Oakford Corp., splitting their profits with that firm. Nine floor brokers and one clerk pleaded guilty to reduced charges after the government admitted it could not determine the amount of their profits or even which trades were illegal. Two of the brokers were given one-week prison terms. Charges were dropped entirely against one floor broker. A court of appeals set aside a SEC decision upholding NYSE sanctions against one floor broker involved in this scandal. The court concluded that the SEC had given little or no attention to the facts of the case and had merely copied language it used in other cases to support the sanctions. Two floor brokers sued the NYSE, claiming that the exchange knew of and condoned the trading while William Donaldson was NYSE chairman. Another future SEC chairman, Harvey Pitt, had successfully represented the NYSE in a lawsuit brought against it by one of the floor brokers involved in these activities.

Of course, profiting from the spread between the bid and ask price was exactly what the NYSE specialists did legally throughout the trading day, but they too were in trouble. An SEC report found that NYSE specialists were mishandling and trading ahead of customer orders. The SEC study concluded that investors were bilked out of at least $155 million by this activity and that the NYSE did not have effective means to detect such violations. When violations were found, the NYSE usually did not take any serious action. The SEC investigation, which covered the period 1999–2003, found that large numbers of trades that could have been matched with other customer orders were instead taken by the specialists as principal, allowing them to profit at the expense of customers. The specialists were "interpositioning" themselves between buy and sell orders of customers, profiting on the spread. In addition, the specialists were "trading ahead" of customers by engaging in transactions for their own account at a favorable price while holding a customer order that could have been executed at that price. Specialists were also helping customers to "mark the close," which involves setting an artificial closing price, usually for margin purposes.

The SEC charged that these practices violated the duty of the specialists to maintain a "fair and orderly" market. Several specialist firms on the NYSE agreed to pay an astonishing $241 million to settle claims that they were improperly executing customer orders. The settling firms included Bear Wagner Specialists LLC, LaBranche & Co. LLC, Fleet Specialist Inc. (owned by FleetBoston Bank), Van der Moolen Specialists USA LLC, and Spear, Leeds, & Kellogg Specialists LLC (owned by Goldman Sachs). Todd Christie was dismissed as chief executive officer of Spear, Leeds. Christie had been nominated to the NYSE board of directors before that dismissal. Seven smaller specialist firms agreed to settle similar charges with fines totaling $10.2 million. The SEC charged the NYSE with failing to supervise its specialists, and fifteen traders working for the specialist firms were indicted. The NYSE settled the SEC charges by agreeing to hire an independent monitor to audit its self-regulation at a cost of $20 million. The exchange also agreed to create a monitoring system for specialists that would involve filming and tape recording their activities. Full disclosure, it seemed, needed George Orwell to make it work.

In the wake of those cases, the SEC proposed corporate governance reforms for stock exchanges that would separate regulatory and marketing functions and require that a majority of the governing board be outside directors and that 20 percent of the directors represent member interests. Nominating, governance, audit, compensation, and regulatory oversight committees would be required and all of the members of those committees would be outside directors. The NYSE went a step further allowing nominations for one board seat by the public on its Web site. Ellyn Brown was the nominee selected. She was a former Maryland securities regulator.

The California Public Employee Retirement System (Calpers) brought a class action against the NYSE and seven of its specialist firms, seeking damages from the conduct attacked by the SEC. More problems surfaced for the NYSE. Frank J. Furino was arrested for tipping off Andover, a day trading firm, on impending trades that would have a market effect. Furino was a clerk on the floor of the NYSE employed by Lawrence Helfant LLC, which was later acquired by the Jefferies Group. The trader made $300,000 by front running those trades, which included transactions in the stock of the Enron Corp. and Computer Associates. Fidelity Investments called for the NYSE to be reorganized and the role of the specialist eliminated. Fidelity wanted the NYSE structure modified to become an electronic communications network. John Thain did seek changes that would devalue NYSE seats even further by requiring more electronic trading. The specialists were concerned that the proposal would cut them out of the order flow. Despite its problems, the NYSE remained a powerful institution. Its average daily trading volume in 2003 was 1.4 billion shares, up from 16 million shares in 1970. Program trading accounted for about 40 percent of volume, which suggested that professional traders were dominating the market.

Lest there remain an institution in the securities industry that had not been sued by the SEC, charges were brought against the American Stock Exchange (AMEX), the Philadelphia Stock Exchange, and the National Stock Exchange. The SEC claimed that those exchanges had failed to ensure that specialists were not trading ahead of customer orders and withholding pricing information. The combined daily trading volume on those exchanges was about 600 million shares. Three AMEX officials were also targeted. Another SEC probe sought to determine if customers were being denied "best execution" of their orders by Nasdaq market makers that were receiving orders by reason of payments for order flow.

Another challenge appeared after the SEC announced that it was seeking to restructure the securities markets by modifying its National Market System rules, which require that customers receive the "best execution price available" on any of the markets trading the security being bought or sold. This rule had favored the NYSE in the past, forcing much business there. The SEC proposal would have created an exception to this best price requirement for "fast market" conditions. Market makers could ignore better quotes on other markets under such conditions, as long as the execution was within a stated amount of the best price. The SEC was considering a cap on market access fees and expressed a desire to regulate the formula used for distributing market data revenue, which is revenue based on quotation and last sale price reporting dissemination to market participants. This effort to impose a kind of public utility regulation over the markets was opposed by the exchanges. The SEC also proposed to prohibit the quoting of stocks in increments of less than one penny except for shares trading under one dollar. The NYSE opposed this proposal because the exceptions to the best execution rule would hurt its market, and the SEC announced it was revising those rules to once again favor the NYSE by expanding the "trade through rule" that forced executions onto the NYSE and away from electronic communications networks. William Donaldson was being accused by the *Wall Street Journal* as supporting his old employer, the NYSE, over other markets in pushing this proposal. The Nasdaq market has no trade through rule and was receiving only about 20 percent of activity in its shares because of competition from other sources. In contrast, the NYSE's regulatory protection from the trade through rule allowed it to maintain an 80 percent share of transactions in its listed securities. The trade through revision was passed by a 3–2 vote of the SEC. The dissenting votes were by the two Republican commissioners. They had some strange bedfellows in their opposition, including the two leading advocates of corporate reform—Calpers and TIAA-CREF. The revised rule continued to protect the NYSE and extended its reach to Nasdaq, which would centralize that market and make it less competitive.

Centralization came faster than anyone expected. The NYSE announced shortly after the adoption of the trade through rule that it was merging with Archipelago Holdings Inc., a Chicago-based electronic communications network that was executing about 25 percent of volume in Nasdaq stocks. Archipelago had begun operations in 1997 as an electronic communications network. In 2000 it joined with the Pacific Exchange Inc. to create the first open all-electronic stock market in the United States. Archipelago took out some whimsical full-page advertisements in the *Wall Street Journal* to announce the opening of that exchange. One of those advertisements was a bizarre, but nonetheless amusing, promotion for a spray paint for bald men that "looks completely natural from a distance of just over 40 feet." Another advertisement contained a test to determine if an individual qualified for trading on the exchange. The applicant was required to answer such questions as "Did a female give birth to you?" "Are you a cat?" and "Do you keep getting older?"

The merger was intended to provide the NYSE with competitive access to Nasdaq stocks and allow it to enter the market for electronic executions. The new company was named NYSE Group Inc. The merger would convert the NYSE into a public for-profit company. NYSE seat holders were to receive $300,000 each in the merger plus stock controlling 70 percent of the merged company, valuing their seats at about $1.8 million. The merged operation was valued at $3.5 billion in its entirety. The NYSE operations accounted for about $2.4 billion of that amount. The deal pushed NYSE seat prices up to $3.5 million.

The NYSE merger raised some interesting questions for the Spitzer suit against Grasso since any recovery would be paid to the now-for-profit owners of the NYSE. Spitzer's suit had already met much derision because any funds obtained in judgment from Grasso would be given to the multimillionaire holders of NYSE seats. They hardly needed the attorney general to protect their interests. Spitzer tried to duck that criticism by advising the court that he would request that any recovery be paid to the NYSE regulatory section. More irony was added after Kenneth Langone, the former NYSE board member and cofounder of Home Depot, presented a proposal for a counterbid for the NYSE. He thought the exchange was being undervalued and charged that Goldman Sachs, which advised both the NYSE and Archipelago and owned 15 percent of the latter, had a conflict of interest in putting that deal together. Goldman Sachs's role had particularly angered E. Stanley O'Neal at Merrill Lynch. If Langone's proposal had borne fruit, he would have been in effect a plaintiff in the suit brought by Spitzer against Grasso and himself. Spitzer was spared the embarrassment of facing that issue since the Grasso trial was postponed until after the election for New York governor. In the meantime, the price of Archipelago stock jumped, but William Higgins, a member of the NYSE, sued to stop the merger, claiming that member seats were being undervalued. A New York judge denied a motion to dismiss that suit, concluding that the complaint properly alleged conflicts of interest and breaches of fiduciary duty. The court found the allegations of personal and business ties by six NYSE board members to Goldman Sachs was, "simply put, impressive." John Thain was even more closely tied to Goldman and would profit personally from the merger. An NYSE member threatened Higgins with a car bombing if the Archipelago merger was blocked.

Kenneth Langone was lobbying members to vote against the merger. Langone also leveled another blast against Spitzer on the editorial pages of the *Wall Street Journal.* Langone disclosed that depositions of other NYSE directors who had approved Grasso's compensation all revealed that they believed they had been fully informed on the compensation package and that Langone had acted properly in presenting the package to the board. Langone called Spitzer a "bully" and again noted that any recovery by Spitzer in the suit would go to the members of the NYSE who were already multimillionaires. In the meantime, while multiple attorneys were working on the case in the attorney general's office, Spitzer was claiming that he did not have enough attorneys to prosecute Medicaid fraud.

The post-Grasso NYSE was still devoted to good corporate governance. Just one hour before trading was to begin in the stock of Life Sciences Research Inc., the NYSE announced that it was refusing the listing because animal rights organizations had demanded that the exchange send these "puppy killers," aka researchers, back to the pink sheets. NYSE members were also up in arms over a plan by the NYSE staff, beefed up by adding a former SEC official, to fine over twenty broker-dealers millions of dollars for submitting incomplete trading data. The NYSE staff was also seeking to stop the practice of "shredding," which involved splitting customer orders in order to gain additional revenue. The SEC, nevertheless, was threatening to sue some NYSE staff members personally for failing to enforce exchange rules aggressively enough—regulators suing regulators.

Nasdaq responded to a competitive threat from the NYSE merger with an announcement that it was acquiring Instinet from Reuters for $1.9 billion.

Another exchange, the New York Mercantile Exchange, was also in play with the Blackstone Group leading an effort to buy a 20 percent stake in that exchange. The Chicago Board of Trade later conducted an IPO of a minority ownership stake in its operations that became a hot issue, climbing over 50 percent on its first day of trading. The regional stock exchanges also responded to these developments by selling ownership stakes in their operations to large broker-dealers. The Philadelphia Stock Exchange sold stakes to, among others, Merrill Lynch UBS AG, Morgan Stanley, and Citigroup. The Boston Stock Exchange was opening an electronic exchange in a joint venture with Credit Suisse First Boston, Citigroup, Fidelity Investments, and Lehman Brothers.

Spitzer Again

SEC chairman William Donaldson had, somewhat embarrassingly, sold millions of dollars of his own stocks when he joined the SEC and placed the proceeds into mutual funds involved in the late trading and market timing scandals. That certainly gave him a stake in those investigations. Donaldson was attempting to replicate Arthur Levitt's proregulation stance in order to seize power back from New York attorney general Eliot Spitzer, but that effort failed. Spitzer continued to taunt Donaldson in public speeches over the SEC's failure to uncover the market timing scandals, noting that hedge fund prospectuses had prominently boasted of that trading. Internal and external reviews concluded that the SEC was too cautious an agency, causing it to lose out in the regulatory race with Spitzer. Conceding defeat, Donaldson announced a "joint initiative" with state regulators to consider protocols and coordination among regulators.

California authorized its attorney general, William Lockyer, to pursue violations by firms involved in the securities business, including broker-dealers and mutual funds. Lockyer, politically ambitious, was trying to rival Spitzer in his efforts to obtain headlines through probes of securities industry firms. California also enacted legislation that paid bounties to employees bringing actions against employers for labor violations even if the employee was not injured by the practice. In another effort to become the next Eliot Spitzer, Denise Nappier, the state treasurer of Connecticut, sued the investment banking firm of Forstmann Little for placing the state in investments that were too risky, resulting in a loss of $125 million. The jury refused to award any damages because the state was well aware of the nature of the investments and had acquiesced in Theodore Forstmann's conduct. That verdict was of some solace to Forstmann but did not reimburse his lost time or attorney fees. He also had to deal with $3 billion in his firm's failed investments in the telecom sector.

Spitzer expanded his investigations into other areas. Among other things, he took on the Office of the Comptroller of the Currency (OCC), the federal regulator for national banks. Spitzer sought control over national banks operating within New York, while the OCC claimed exclusive jurisdiction over those institutions. The federal bank regulators were much less timid than the SEC in protecting their turf. They made it clear that they would fight any Spitzer incursions on their turf throughout the federal court system. In October 2005, a federal district court judge, at the request of the OCC, permanently enjoined Spitzer from investigating the consumer loan practices of national banks. Spitzer began looking elsewhere for headlines, even meeting with dairy farmers in upstate New York to see if he could further their complaints about low milk prices. That appeared to be a nonstarter when prices began to rise. Spitzer then turned to the insurance industry and launched an attack on the fees paid to brokers for recommending policies to clients. Those fees had been a routine part of the insurance brokerage business, but Spitzer charged Marsh & McLennan Corp., the world's largest insurance broker, with defrauding its large corporate clients by accepting fees from insurance companies in exchange for directing business to those companies. Spitzer further charged that Marsh & McLennan had engaged in bid rigging. That touched off another scandal in the press.

Marsh & McLennan's chairman and chief executive officer, Jeffrey W. Greenberg, was forced to resign. The company's general counsel, William Rosoff, was anther victim. Those resignations were required by Spitzer as a condition for the company to avoid criminal charges. Four other executives were dismissed. A new corporate governance structure was created. The inside directors were required to resign, and the Marsh & McLennan board was restructured to be composed of only outside directors, plus the company's new chief executive officer, Michael G. Cherkasky. The company also separated the roles of chairman and chief executive officer.

Marsh & McLennan agreed to pay $850 million to settle Spitzer's claims, and the company was forced to issue a public apology for its conduct. The groveling demanded by Spitzer in that statement included an admission that the company's conduct was "unlawful" and "shameful." The Connecticut attorney general, Richard Blumenthal, weighed in with another suit against Marsh & McLennan charging that it had concealed payments that increased the costs on workmen's compensation insurance. The U.S. Department of Labor and the Pension Benefit Guaranty Corp. were also investigating the company with respect to its pension fund advisory business. A Marsh broker, Robert Stearns, pleaded guilty to criminal charges, as did five others. Several insurance companies were named as participants in Marsh & McLennan's activities.

Zurich Financial suspended a number of employees. Ace Ltd., a Bermuda insurance company, was embroiled in this scandal and dismissed two employees. The number of guilty pleas grew. Kathryn Winters, a former managing director at Marsh & McLennan, pleaded guilty to criminal charges brought by Spitzer. Two other Marsh & McLennan executives and three from American International Group Inc. (AIG) pleaded guilty to criminal charges for their role in those payments. Spitzer indicted a total of twenty-five individuals for their role in the activities he disliked; included in that number were sixteen March & McLennan executives. Seventeen of those defendants pleaded guilty. Spitzer used those guilty pleas to launch an assault in the press against the U.S. Chamber of Commerce, which had been critical of his attacks on Wall Street. Spitzer claimed that those guilty pleas evidenced widespread corruption that only he could root out.

Hank Greenberg, the head of AIG, had asked the New York insurance commission whether such payments were legal some two years before Spitzer's attack, but received no reply. AIG had earlier encountered problems in assisting PNC Financial Services Group Inc. to manipulate its accounts. In addition, AIG was sued by the SEC and was under investigation by criminal prosecutors for marketing insurance policies that posed little risk, but provided a disguised loan to the seller through an up-front payment of the policy proceeds. The loan was repaid through periodic premium payments, allowing the seller to claim the up-front policy proceeds as income rather than a liability. AIG allowed Brightpoint Inc., a telephone distributor, to conceal losses through such a fraudulent life insurance policy. AIG agreed to pay the SEC and the Department of Justice a total of $136 million to settle the PNC and Brightpoint cases. AIG was also required to accept the appointment of an independent monitor to review its accounts for other improprieties. Greenberg was under investigation for calling on Richard Grasso at the NYSE to have the specialists keep up the price of AIG's stock in order to reduce the cost of a merger with American General Corp.

Seventy-nine-year-old Maurice (Hank) Greenberg was eventually forced to resign from AIG. That resignation came after AIG auditors reported that the company's financial controls were seriously flawed. Howard Smith, AIG's chief financial officer, was also forced to resign. Greenberg was replaced as chairman by Frank G. Zarb. Zarb had been the head of Nasdaq at a time when that market was attacked by regulators for allowing market makers to engage in collusive practices that allowed them to widen spreads and reduce competition. Zarb brought his old friend Arthur Levitt, the former SEC chairman, on board as an adviser to the AIG board of directors. Greenberg joined the unemployment line with his son Jeffrey who had been ousted by Spitzer as the head of Marsh & McLennan. Another Greenberg son, Evan, the head of Ace Ltd., a Bermuda insurer, was also being investigated by Spitzer. That insurance company subsequently restated its financial statements for the period 2000 through 2004 as the result of its use of finite insurance.

The inevitable internal investigation at AIG discovered several other questionable transactions that had been used to manage earnings. This stream of revelations pushed down the price of AIG stock by some 25 percent. AIG announced on March 30, 2005, that it was reducing its net worth by $1.7 billion as a result of various accounting manipulations. They included a secret $1.1 billion agreement to protect investors in Union Excess, a Barbados reinsurance company. This placed AIG shareholders and the company's

93,000 employees in danger of a government indictment that would destroy the company.

The price of AIG's stock dropped by 30 percent as a result of the uncertainty created by these investigations. The company was embroiled in further problems after it was discovered that documents were being destroyed. Starr International Co., which was controlled by Hank Greenberg and which owned 12 percent of AIG shares, responded to Greenberg's dismissal from AIG by ousting the AIG directors from its board. The reason for that action was said to be conflict of interest concerns because that company set the pay for AIG executives, but this only created more turmoil at AIG. The relationship between Starr and AIG had been cleared by PricewaterhouseCoopers and by two prominent New York law firms, but the Teachers Retirement System of Louisiana in Delaware brought suit in Delaware claiming a breach of fiduciary duty. Greenberg was being referred to as an "imperial" chief executive, a title used for Bernard Ebbers as well, and which was obviously a takeoff on the "imperial presidency" label given to the administration of President Richard Nixon after his downfall. The prosecutors tried to set a perjury trap for Greenberg, a veteran of the Normandy invasion and Korea, by refusing to allow him to review any documents they were questioning in connection with their investigation. Greenberg, who had been voted chief executive officer of the year in 2003, had headed the company for forty years and built it into a $100 billion enterprise employing thousands. He rightly wanted to refresh his recollection on the events at issue, which comprised only a small part of his stewardship, before testifying under oath and subjecting himself to perjury charges for any error. One of Greenberg's lawyers, the ever-present David Boies, was too experienced to fall for such gutter tactics. He directed Greenberg to take the Fifth Amendment in response to investigator questions and explained why in an op-ed piece in the *Wall Street Journal*. Boies was testifying against Mark Swartz in the Tyco retrial when that piece was published.

Spitzer's gubernatorial campaign staff linked AIG Web searches to the Web site promoting his run for governor. Spitzer also proclaimed in a television interview that AIG was a "black box," that Greenberg committed "fraud," and the only issue was whether Greenberg's conduct should be sanctioned by civil or criminal charges. The *Wall Street Journal* responded to that sally with an editorial taunting Spitzer to indict Greenberg and actually go to trial if he really thought Greenberg was guilty of a crime. The paper also pointed out that finite insurance was "a virtual necessity in this era of runaway tort actions" and that the accounting treatment for such products was complex and subject to judgment. John C. Whitehead, former chairman of Goldman Sachs, also weighed in with an op-ed piece in that paper defending Greenberg as "one of America's best CEOs and most generous philanthropists." In opposition, the *New York Times* ran a headline story on its business page entitled "An Industry Bully Gets Its Comeuppance."

In the event, Greenberg appeared to take the Fifth Amendment in front of fifteen regulators at Spitzer's office. They included representatives from the SEC, the Department of Justice, and the New York Insurance Department. Greenberg was accompanied by two of his lawyers, Robert Morvillo, Martha Stewart's attorney, and Kenneth Bialkin, an experienced securities lawyer. More headlines followed after it was disclosed that Greenberg transferred 2.3 billion AIG shares to his wife of sixty years in order to protect his assets from lawsuits. Jim Petro, the Ohio attorney general, filed a class action suit against AIG and asked the court to require Greenberg's wife to return her shares to him. The normally unrepentant Greenberg later decided to unwind that transaction.

The company's comptroller, Michael Castelli, was placed on leave after he began cooperating with Spitzer, and the company's internal investigation then discovered another $1 billion in accounting problems, which were blamed on Greenberg. Spitzer filed suit in May 2005 against AIG, Greenberg, and the company's chief financial officer, Howard I. Smith. The complaint asserted that Greenberg's personal wealth was increased by $65 billion each time the company's stock increased by one dollar. Spitzer charged that Greenberg was intensely interested in changes of the price of AIG stock and often sought to support its price with large purchases. The charges contained little that had not already been reported in the press. Spitzer did additionally claim that Greenberg was aware that the company was improperly gathering workman's compensation premiums because he did not want to hire forty more employees who would be required to comply with government requirements for the treatment of such premiums.

Greenberg was denied access to personal assets and files left at the company by the company's new management. He responded with a letter to the board of directors on his eightieth birthday decrying the "vile accusations" being made against him and asking for an opportunity to respond to those allegations. The company retaliated by turning over tapes to prosecutors in which Greenberg was said to have urged purchases of the company's stock as it declined, which then became a centerpiece of the Spitzer charges. Greenberg's lawyers responded to his dismissal by the board with a fifty-page white paper that asserted that AIG's auditors, PricewaterhouseCoopers, had been aware of the transactions for which he was fired. Frank Zarb and other executives still at AIG were aware of and involved in challenged transactions. The lawyers further claimed that the restatement of the company's reserves was itself an attempt to manipulate the company's accounts by excessive write-offs that would later be reclaimed to increase earnings and make new management look good, which actually happened in 2005. The lawyers' efforts proved to be unavailing. AIG even filed suit to require Greenberg to give up his controlling interest in AIG.

AIG restated its accounts in May 2005, reducing shareholders' equity by 2.7 percent (about $500 million less than expected) and profits for the period 2000 to 2005 were reduced by $ billion. The company's board had failed to uncover those shortfalls or the accounting gimmicks used at AIG before Spitzer began his attacks. Once again, the existence of luminary outside directors did not prevent scandal. The AIG outside directors included Richard Holbrooke, a former ambassador to the United States, William Cohen, a former senator and Secretary of Defense, and Carla Hills, the former U.S. trade representative.

The SEC and Spitzer launched an extensive investigation into such practices by other insurers. General Re, owned by Warren Buffett's Berkshire Hathaway, was under investigation by the SEC for selling insurance products that could be used to smooth earnings. Elizabeth A. Monrad, the chief financial officer for the corporate governance reform advocate TIAA-CREF, was a target of the SEC for her former work at General Re. Joseph Houldsworth, an executive at General Re, pleaded guilty to a criminal charge of conspiring to help falsify AIG's financial statements. The SEC asserted in a separate action that Richard Napier, a General Re senior vice president, was speaking with AIG chairman Greenberg daily about a finite insurance transaction designed to aid AIG's earnings picture, and hide the faltering financial condition of Reciprocal of American from regulators and policy holders.

Warren Buffett was personally under security from the government for his role in AIG's accounting manipulations that were conducted in General Re. The media was reporting that Buffett was being questioned by government investigators on his briefing and approval of a transaction with AIG that moved $500 million in claims from General Re to AIG along with $500 million in premiums. This allowed AIG to increase its reserves by $500 million and book $500 million in revenue. The increase in reserve levels was needed because Greenberg had been criticized by some large stockholders for having reserve levels too low for its business. The issue raised by regulators was whether there was any risk to AIG in the transaction. AIG later admitted that this transaction was improper. The *Wall Street Journal* reported that it was Warren Buffett who ratted out Hank Greenberg in order to appease regulators and turn their attention away from Berkshire Hathaway's indiscretions. Buffett was treated tenderly by investigators when they interviewed him; he was not even placed under oath and was invited to supply the regulators with some of his folksy wisdom. One rating service was not so forgiving. Fitch Ratings downgraded Berkshire Hathaway's debt from stable to negative because of concern over the company's regulatory problems and Buffett's age. The SEC staff was also recommending enforcement actions against Buffett lieutenants, Ronald Ferguson and Joseph Brandon at General Re, for their role in aiding the accounting manipulations at AIG. Five other General Re executives were also targeted.

Another Berkshire Hathaway insurance unit, National Indemnity Co., paid $2 million to the liquidator for the HIH Insurance Ltd. in Australia because of a questioned transaction with that company. Australian investigators were also questioning another transaction between General Re and FAI Insurance. Platinum Underwriters, a Bermuda reinsurer, unwound a "finite" insurance contract with a Berkshire Hathaway subsidiary because of accounting concerns that side agreements negated the passing of risk. That product allowed purchasers to pay for losses with deductible insurance premiums in transactions that were structured to prevent the insurer from having any risk, thereby taking on aspects of a loan. In other words, the purchaser of the insurance paid extraordinarily high premiums over the life of the policy. Any funds paid in excess of actual claims were returned at the end of the contract period.

Axa Re, Munich Re, and Zurich Re sold $170 million in "retroactive" reinsurance to MBIA Inc., in order to protect that insurance company's reserves after it suffered a large loss on a credit default bond. The retroactive insurance was paid for over time, allowing MBIA to cover up the magnitude of its loss and tap the capital markets for more funds.

The Municipal Bond Insurance Association (MBIA) that was formed in 1973 created a popular insurance product that insured holders of municipal securities against default. That product and its offshoots were insuring some $2 trillion in municipal and asset back securities in the new century. MBIA had to restate its financial statements for seven years, starting in 1998, because of improper treatment of reinsurance agreements. MBIA had previously complained that negative research by hedge funds was hurting its stock price. MBIA had to later disclose that it covered up a $170 million loss under an arrangement in which other insurance companies absorbed the hit in response to a promise from MBIA of future business. Renaissance Re announced that it was restating its financial accounts for the years 2001 through 2004 as a result of its accrual accounting treatment for payments made and received on its insurance contracts. CNA Financial Corp. restated three years of its accounting results as a result of Spitzer's attacks on insurance industry accounting practices. General Electric Co.'s insurance activities were also under attack from the SEC. Hannover Re AG in Germany was another target.

The McCarran-Ferguson Act that was passed in 1945 sought to oust the SEC and the federal securities laws from regulating insurance companies. The SEC found a way around that bar by arguing that various insurance products were actually securities. An even bigger gap in that preemption was the SEC's use of full disclosure claims against insurance companies that issued publicly traded securities.

Spitzer used the New York Donnelly Act to pursue the insurance companies; it was passed in the nineteenth century and copied the federal Sherman Antitrust Act. New York statutes have a very long reach. Spitzer brought suit against a California insurance company, Universal Life Resources, charging that it was referring clients to insurance companies without disclosing the fees received for the referrals. Among the firms making those payments were MetLife Inc., Prudential Financial Inc., and Unum Provident Corp. Spitzer further charged that the founder of Universal Life, Douglas P. Cox, engaged in self-dealing transactions with the company. Spitzer had thus expanded his reach to become a nationwide regulator of all corporate and financial activity.

Spitzer was actually beaten to the punch by William Lerach, a leading class action lawyer who filed suit against UniversalLife in advance of Spitzer. The state of California had already hired Lerach to pursue the insurance agencies involved in the Spitzer probe. California insurance commissioner John Garamendi brought suit against UniversalLife shortly after Spitzer and additionally sued the insurance companies making the payments. Spitzer denied that he was coordinating his actions with Lerach or California.

Ohio weighed in with subpoenas against Chubb Corp., another large insurer. Congress began holding hearings, providing Spitzer an opportunity to demand federal regulation of the insurance industry, something Congress had refused to do throughout American history. At the same time, Spitzer demanded that Congress take no action that would preempt his attacks on the industry.

An op-ed piece in the *Wall Street Journal* asserted that at least some of the insurance activities targeted by Spitzer were common and necessary business practices. An editorial in that paper stated: "there is something troubling about a public official unilaterally deciding that an industry's business model must change—especially when other regulators have blessed it for years." The *Journal* also criticized the tandem actions of class action litigants with Spitzer. It charged that Spitzer had created "a climate of fear because he charges into industry after industry and criminalizes long standing practices."[22] Eighty percent of those responding to a *Wall Street Journal* e-mail poll thought that the regulatory climate in the United States was hurting business and Spitzer was playing a prominent role in creating that perception.[23]

Professor Henry G. Manne asserted in a *Wall Street Journal* op-ed piece:

> In an era of general acceptance of deregulation and privatization, Mr. Spitzer has introduced the world to yet a new form of regulation, the use of the criminal law as an *in terrorem* weapon to force acceptance of industry-wide regulations. These rules are not vetted through normal authoritative channels, are not reviewable by any administrative process, and are not subject to even the minimal due-process requirements our courts require for normal administrative rule making. The whole process bears no resemblance to a rule of law; it is a reign of force. And to make matters worse, the regulatory remedies are usually vastly more costly to the public than the alleged evils.[24]

Arthur Levitt, the former SEC chairman, contributed his own op-ed on the same page seeking "modest regulation" to end this "culture of CEO dominance and board pliability" and "build up a culture of accountability and oversight."[25]

In any event, Spitzer and California were doing no favors for employees of Marsh & McLennan. The company laid off 3,000 employees after its earnings dropped 94 percent as a result of Spitzer's attack. Marsh & McLennan reported a fourth-quarter loss in 2004 of $676 million after the company's settlement with Spitzer. Another 2,500 jobs were lost, and the company cut its dividend in half, increased its fees, and cut unprofitable clients. The number of jobs lost from Spitzer's assault on March & McLennan nearly equaled those lost after Enron's failure and the economic effects on the company transcended those of the September 11, 2001, terrorist attacks, not exactly a positive outcome. Employee holdings of company stock in Section 401(k) accounts were devastated by Spitzer's attack on the Putnam Funds owned by Marsh & McLennan and then by the insurance broker charges. The $1.3 billion value of Marsh & McLennan stock held in those employee accounts was cut in half after Spitzer filed the insurance charges. In total, the stock of Marsh & McLennan lost $11.5 billion in value as a result of Spitzer's attack. This raised the question of who was benefiting from these attacks, especially since none of the $3 billion collected by Spitzer in his assaults had been returned to the supposed victims. Undeterred, Spitzer took his insurance probe international, joining with the SEC to investigate foreign reinsurance companies to see if they had been used to manipulate financial results of American companies.

Mike Hatch, the Minnesota attorney general, tried to get in on the act by charging Willis Group Holdings, the third largest insurance broker, with refusing to cooperate in its investigation of its insurance sales practices and commission payments that steered business to the insurers paying the highest commissions to Willis. Spitzer then entered the fray after finding a random e-mail that described a contingent fee arrangement for steering business to particular companies. Willis paid $50 million to settle Spitzer's charges.

Aon Corp. was the subject of a suit in which it was claimed that brokers were induced to send business to insurance companies by being allowed to keep premiums for months at a time in order to earn interest on the float. A California judge dismissed that claim, but the plaintiff's lawyers appealed the ruling and sought the aid of Eliot Spitzer. Spitzer was happy to oblige and Aon Corp. agreed to pay $190 million to settle charges brought by Spitzer and attorney generals from Connecticut and Illinois that the company had steered clients to insurance products paying the highest commissions. Aon then found itself under investigation by the U.S. Department of Labor on other matters.

First USA agreed to pay $1.3 million in settlement with New York and twenty-seven other states over its telemarketing practices. AOL was the target of an attorney general wolf pack from thirty-six states in the 1990s after it changed its pricing to allow unlimited Internet access for a flat fee, but did not have the capacity to handle the response. Another attorney general wolf pack filed suit against five electric utilities claiming that they were causing global warming. Scientists, however, questioned the data used to support the global warming theory and found it defective. To stop such scientific attacks, some members of Congress tried to slip a provision into legislation that would have prohibited the collection of data by the government on the veracity of the global warming theory. The green movement was being rejected in Congress, so it turned to the banks and pressured them to adopt their theory. They found a receptive audience. In order to burnish their tarnished images, JPMorgan Chase & Co., Bank of American Corp., and Citigroup Inc. agreed to adopt policies limiting lending to industries that contribute to global warming. JPMorgan Chase also agreed to lobby Congress in support of limiting greenhouse gas emissions. General Electric announced that it was curbing its own greenhouse emissions and published a seventy-five-page *Citizenship Report* on its efforts to appease corporate governance reformists. Spitzer sued an Ohio power plant for building such tall smoke stacks that pollution was carried into New York by the jet stream. He also attacked online gambling and spamming operations located in Colorado and other places outside New York and even, in some cases, outside the United States.

Spitzer charged Sony BMG Music had made payments to radio stations (payola) to induce them to play its music. Sony paid $10 million to settle those charges, but critics in the music industry were questioning why it should be illegal to pay someone to play your music. Time Warner agreed to pay Spitzer $1.25 million to settle charges that its AOL unit had tried to frustrate customers from canceling its Internet service. Spitzer led a mob of fifteen attorney generals in a suit against the U.S. Department of Energy, claiming that the department failed to adopt proper energy savings standards for small appliances. Perhaps Spitzer's greatest contribution to law and order was his $300,000 settlement with Emmis Communications for sponsoring of a "Smackfest" contest on its radio station. This event featured women contestants who took turns slapping each other in the face as hard as possible for prizes. Spitzer claimed that such activities violated a New York state law governing combative sports.

Spitzer attacked Express Scripts Inc., a company that managed pharmacy benefits for New York state employees. His suit claimed that the company had kept over $100 million in drug rebates that should have been passed back to the state. Smelling fresh meat, the attorney generals for nineteen other states joined in the pursuit of that company. Spitzer brought sensational charges against GlaxoSmithKline, claiming that the pharmaceutical company had concealed negative results from trials for an antidepression drug, Paxil, when used by children. The fact that the drug was not approved for use by children and was not promoted for use by anyone other than adults did not deter Spitzer. Glaxo settled the case brought by Spitzer by agreeing to pay $2.5 million and to publish a summary of all its drug trials. Spitzer then turned on three other drug companies, McKesson Corp., Cardinal Health Inc., and AmerisourceBergen Corp., with an investigation of their drug resale practices.

The attorney general wolf packs attacked other companies. Bristol-Myers Squibb agreed to a global settlement of $670 million in litigation brought by thirty-seven states and territories charging that drug manufacturer with illegally inhibiting generic drug competition. Pharmaceutical companies had other problems. Pfizer agreed to pay $430 million to settle claims that it had improperly marketed its Neurotin drug for unapproved uses. That action was the result of a whistleblower, David Franklin, who received $24.6 million as payment for his disclosures. Pfizer had to pay another $430 million to settle asbestos claims against one of its subsidiaries. Schering-Plough agreed to pay $350 million to settle charges that it overcharged Medicaid for drugs. Bayer AG paid $257 million to settle similar charges. Elan Corp., an Irish pharmaceutical company, agreed to pay $15 million to settle SEC claims that it had misled investors on the condition of its finances.

Merck, another pharmaceutical company, was having problems with tax accounting. The company faced tax liabilities of more than $2 billion for deductions disallowed by the Internal Revenue Service. Merck was hit with a disaster later in the year when it was forced to pull Vioxx, a popular drug for arthritis pain, off the market because of adverse health effects. The company was then targeted by a lawsuit by the New York comptroller, Alan G. Hevesi, who had become a serial plaintiff in actions against corporations experiencing problems, including Bayer AG, MCI Inc., McKesson Corp., Raytheon Co., and Cendant Corp. It seemed that county sheriffs and dogcatchers were about the only officials not targeting corporations for litigation. A wrongful death action in Texas resulted in a jury verdict of $24.5 million in actual damages and $229 million in punitive damages to the widow of one user of Vioxx, a Merck painkiller drug. Texas law capped the punitive damages at $1.6 million, but the award gave a boost to numerous other cases filed against Merck relating to the side effects of Vioxx. The company was receiving unfavorable treatment in court from Carol E. Higbee, a New Jersey judge hearing the first of several of those cases lodged in her court. The judge found herself engaged in a shouting match with Diane Sullivan, a Merck lawyer, after one particularly strong-arm ruling. In the end, the judge was not able to force a guilty verdict from the jury. It found that Vioxx was not responsible for the plaintiff's heart attack. Even while being portrayed in court as a selfish business seeking profits at the expense of patients, Merck announced that it had discovered a vaccine that will prevent certain cervical cancers, a drug that will save an untold number of lives. Nevertheless, Merck's Vioxx problems led to the loss of 7,000 jobs.

Not to be outdone by state functionaries, the SEC launched an investigation into payments made by money management firms to retirement planners for referring pension fund clients. Business was also under attack from private litigants. The Supreme Court held that a $145 million punitive damage award imposed against State Farm Insurance Company was excessive. ExxonMobil was ordered to pay $11.9 billion to Alabama in a case in which the state claimed that the company had underpaid royalties due on leases for gas fields in Mobile Bay. Another Alabama case resulted in an award of $1.28 billion against Tyson Fresh Meats for its practice of buying cattle for forward delivery rather than on the spot market. The plaintiff claimed that this practice resulted in a decrease in cattle prices to producers and was anticompetitive in violation of the Packers and Stockyards Act of 1921. The complaint asserted a claim of monopsony, meaning that a firm has enough market power to push down prices from suppliers, as opposed to the normal monopoly, where it is seeking to raise prices for products that it is selling. The trial judge set the jury verdict aside. Tyson had other problems. The SEC was investigating it for failing to disclose $1.7 million in perks, which apparently included use of the corporate jet, to Donald Tyson, its retired chief executive officer. Tyson repaid the funds when the payments were questioned by a committee of outside directors. Tyson Foods and Don Tyson agreed to pay $1.7 million to settle SEC charges for failing to disclose those perks. The SEC charged that the amount of those benefits were much higher than originally disclosed. They totaled $3 million and included theater tickets, jewelry, art works, oriental rugs, the use of the corporate jet and expensive vacation homes by his family and friends, and $84,000 in lawn care. Tyson was not ungenerous with others. Not long after the SEC charges were filed, Tyson made a $7.6 million gift to the University of Arkansas.

The automobile industry had also felt the lash of the attorney general wolf packs. Ford Motor Company paid $51.5 million to settle charges over rollovers of its popular SUV *Explorer* that were caused by defective Firestone tires mounted on those vehicles, causing the deaths of some 270 passengers. The attorney generals used more than half of that settlement to fund an advertising campaign featuring a hairy monster that warns young drivers on the dangers of driving SUVs. The Insurance Institute for Highway Safety called the ad campaign a "complete waste of money." Ironically, Bridgestone later agreed to pay Ford $240 million to settle Ford's claims over those tires.

IV

Recovery and Reform

10. Market Recovery

The Economy

Demographic Changes and Finance

Ironically, while the full disclosure system was being circumvented by nearly every market participant during the 1990s, the country was experiencing unprecedented prosperity. Even after the bubble burst, there was no Great Depression like that experienced in the 1930s. Despite the collapse of the stock market, and in the face of Alan Greenspan's crippling interest rate increases, a terrorist attack of previously unimaginable magnitude, wars in Afghanistan and Iraq, and numerous financial scandals, the recession associated with those events turned out to be perhaps the mildest ever. Indeed, data examined in 2004 raised questions as to whether there had been a recession at all, as typically defined by a decline in gross domestic product (GDP) for two straight quarters. There had been drops in GDP in two quarters in 2001, but not consecutively.

Even people still contending that a recession had occurred admitted that the downturn was much milder than first believed. Consumer spending on automobiles and other durable goods reached a fifteen-year high in the fourth quarter of 2001. The economy actually grew in that quarter, albeit at an anemic 0.2 percent annual rate, but at least it was not a decline. Despite the market drop, Americans had increased their assets by $20 trillion over the prior ten years. The housing market was actually booming during the recession. Rising home prices and the large number of sales even raised concern that a real estate bubble was under way. New home construction in 2000 rose at the fastest rate since 1986, and mortgage refinancing was a growth business in an era of low mortgage rates. Mortgage refinancing cut the cost of home ownership for millions of households, freeing up consumer funds for use elsewhere in the economy. Banks and online firms pushed these loans to consumers by offering quick application processes, as well as low interest rates. The dollar value of home equity loans (second mortgages) was climbing toward $1 trillion in 2002, an increase of 20 percent from the prior year.

The Enron scandal did have some direct effects on the economy. Insurance premiums for director and officer liability jumped significantly. Enron's bankruptcy and credit problems at other large companies caused a squeeze on commercial paper issuers, shrinking the size of that market by hundreds of billions of dollars. JPMorgan Chase was a leader in arranging credit lines as a backup for firms having difficulty raising working capital in the commercial paper market. This presented a danger, however, because lack of access to the commercial paper market might signal an impending bankruptcy. More significantly, after-tax corporate profits declined 15.9 percent during 2001, which was one of the worst declines since World War II. Household income fell in both 2001 and 2002, also for the first time since World War II. Income dropped on average by 5.7 percent in 2002 to a total of $6 trillion from $6.35 trillion in 2000. The income of Americans in the highest ninety-fifth percentile was $150,000 in 2002, which was a drop of almost $3,000 from 2001. Incomes in the twentieth percentile dropped to $17,915 from $18,256. The number of Americans who earned more than $100,000 fell in 2002.

Health care insurance costs were increasing, and many employers reduced coverage. The number of people without health insurance comprised more than 15 percent of the population, totaling 43.6 million in 2003, but many of those individuals were young persons who did not want to incur the cost of health insurance. There were no figures available on how many of those individuals were being denied essential care or whether self-insurance was more cost-beneficial than insurance for those individuals.

About 48 percent of individuals between the ages of thirty-five and sixty-four in the United States earned less than $30,000 a year as the new century began. The percentage in that age group earning less than $15,000 a year was about 25 percent. Those living in poverty in America rose from 11.7 percent in 2001 to 12.1 percent in 2002 and to 12.5 percent in 2003. This meant that in 2002 there were about 34.6 million poor people, up about 1.7 million from the prior year. Household income among the poorest families was an average $14,232, while incomes among the wealthiest families averaged $155,527. However, those data were somewhat misleading. When immigrants, who usually start at the bottom and work their way up, are factored out of income data, the gap between rich and poor declines. Household income was also spread over fewer persons than in prior years. Today, the average household is composed of 2.6 persons versus four persons only twenty-five years ago. Still, there were disparities. For example, the average black household net worth was $6,100 in the new century while the figure for the average white household was $67,000. The number of minority families owning their own homes was just over 50 percent, while overall home ownership stood at about 70 percent.

The concept of being poor was also changing. Studies showed that over 40 percent of the poor owned their own homes, and most had central heating, air conditioning, washers and dryers, at least one automobile (70 percent of the poor), and the vast majority owned color television sets and VCRs. A book titled *The Progress Paradox* detailed the advances in society in recent generations, contrasting the plight of the poor today with that of past generations. Deaths from many diseases had declined drastically or ceased altogether, and the living conditions of most of the poor were undreamed of even by the middle classes of earlier years. Yet many Americans were unhappy with their condition and believed themselves to be disadvantaged.[1]

The average adult had grown by one inch and picked up twenty-five pounds over the last forty years. This reflected the remarkable fact that even poor Americans were facing a danger to their health that was inconceivable at the beginning of the twentieth century. Hunger had always been the traditional defining measure of poverty, but as the twenty-first century began the adverse effects associated with overeating was a plague on society. An estimated 64 percent of Americans were overweight, and more than one in fifteen adults in the United States was obese, meaning more than one hundred pounds overweight. A study found that 38 percent of public school students in Arkansas were overweight. The adverse health effects from that increased weight were the second leading cause of death in the United States in the new century. The poor were especially hard-hit by this phenomenon. They were literally eating themselves to death.

Economic Conditions

Energy prices fell dramatically in the fourth quarter of 2001 as a result of increased production and favorable weather conditions in the United States. To counter that decline, the Organization of Petroleum Exporting Countries cut production by 1.5 million barrels a day. The Federal Reserve Board announced on January 30, 2002, that it would maintain the low interest rate policy introduced after the market collapse for the near future. During that month, the Standard & Poors 500 and the Dow Jones Industrial Average increased about 20 percent over their December lows. Although the Dow tracked back through 10000 on February 14, 2002, the markets weakened and volume dropped in February as hysteria mounted over Enron. Twenty percent of the stocks on major U.S. stock exchanges had plunged in value by more than two-thirds since the beginning of the year.

President George W. Bush appeared to be facing a declining economy. Sales of everything from computers to automobiles were down. Also declining were capital spending, corporate profits, consumer confidence, personal income, and job creation, while inventories shot up. The Nasdaq index was down 62 percent from the prior year. The president knew full well the political dangers associated with a declining economy; a recession had led to his father's defeat even while his leadership was acclaimed for expelling Saddam Hussein from Kuwait. The new president was determined to avoid that obstacle to his reelection in four years, but efforts to pass a stimulus package in

Congress fell apart over partisan bickering. A huge subsidy bill for farmers was passed through Congress in a replay of New Deal efforts to support farm prices. That legislation provided for as much as $180 billion in subsidies to farmers over a period of several years, reversing the prior course of Congress in eliminating farm subsidies.

President Bush called an economic conference in Austin, Texas, to promote his plan for tax cuts. Just after that meeting, the Federal Reserve Board announced that the economy was in trouble and facing the possibility of a serious decline. Bush then focused his recovery efforts on tax cuts. He had clashed with the Democratic candidate, Vice President Al Gore, over tax cuts during the presidential campaign. Gore wanted to balance the budget and pay off the national debt, rather than enact tax cuts. The Democrats claimed that the wealthiest 1 percent of taxpayers would be the primary beneficiary of Bush's tax cut proposals. Republicans then accused Democrats of a desire to "soak the rich" with taxes, launching charges of class warfare that smacked of the Franklin Roosevelt era during the Great Depression.

Although the Gore Democrats claimed that the wealthy were not paying their share of taxes, there were statistics to suggest that the tax burden had already been shifted to the wealthy. The top 1 percent of taxpayers paid 37.4 percent of federal income taxes for 2000, up from 25 percent in 1991. The top 1 percent of taxpayers included those with an adjusted gross income of over $313,000, and they collectively received about 21 percent of all adjusted gross income. Another survey showed that the top 5 percent of income earners were receiving 34 percent of adjusted gross income and were paying 55 percent of personal federal income taxes. The top 10 percent of taxpayers received 44.9 percent of adjusted gross income and paid 66.5 percent of total personal federal income taxes. The top 10 percent of taxpayers in 2002 were those making over $81,000. Moving further down the chain, the top 25 percent of taxpayers paid 84 percent of income taxes in that year. This group included persons making at least $55,000 per year. The top 50 percent of income earners received 86.8 percent of adjusted gross income and was paying 96 percent of all taxes. The bottom 50 percent of income earners received 13.2 percent of adjusted gross income and paid only 4 percent of taxes. In 1998, families with children and household incomes of less than $10,000 were paying no income tax.

The declining economy gave impetus to the Bush administration's demand for tax cuts totaling $1.6 trillion, but the president still faced some obstacles to that proposal. The Democrats opposed the cuts, again claiming that they would result in a large deficit and benefit mostly the wealthy. An interesting aspect of this debate was the reversal of the position taken by both Democrats and Republicans in the 1960s when President John F. Kennedy had sought a tax cut. He rejected claims that a tax cut would lead to large deficits and inflation. Kennedy stated that "the soundest way to raise revenues in the long run is to cut rates now." Republicans of that era feared that a large tax cut without assurance of a balanced budget would be "morally and fiscally wrong."[2]

Before the election of George W. Bush, control of the Senate rested with the Republicans, with a 55–45 split. That majority was whittled down in the election held in 2000, and control was lost in May 2001 when Senator James Jeffords defected to the Democrats. The president was able to deliver on his campaign promise for tax cuts despite Jeffords's defection. Aided by some Democrats, Republicans managed to pass a watered-down version of Bush's tax cut proposals in June 2001. That package was said to total $1.35 trillion in cuts, but those reductions were spread over several years, dampening their ability to help the economy immediately. Income tax reductions were phased in over a period that would end in 2006, while the estate tax was phased out over a period ending in 2010. The estate tax would be reinstated in full in 2011. Some cash was immediately handed out in the form of a $600 rebate to each family. Although savings rates were otherwise negative, Americans saved most of those rebates, diminishing their hoped-for effect on the economy.

Bush avoided some of the worst of the New Deal errors, such as increasing taxes, that kept the country mired in depression. Nevertheless, he did provide some unnecessary protection to U.S. producers from steel imports in a mini–Smoot-Hawley protective measure. That "escape clause" proceeding cost consumers an estimated $680 million as steel prices increased by 30 percent over the next few years, and critics claimed that 200,000 American jobs were lost as a result of those price increases. The World Trade Organization ruled that the president's action violated its rules, allowing the European Union to impose retaliatory measures of more than $2 billion on U.S. exports to Europe. In the face of that onslaught, Bush dropped the tariffs.

Raising Capital

Efforts to raise capital continued. U.S. Eyecare, a subsidiary of Nestlé, made a public stock offering in March that raised $2.3 billion. Aeropostale, a clothing retailer, made an initial public offering (IPO) in May 2002 that was a hot issue. Aeropostale share prices increased by more than 50 percent during its first trading day. That company had been owned by Federated Department Stores but was sold to Bear Stearns in 1998. Time Warner Inc. sold $6 billion of global debt in April 2002. This was $2 billion more than originally planned.

The economy was growing at a 6.1 percent annual rate in the first quarter of 2002. Manufacturing and construction spending were increasing and productivity in the United States was rising at the fastest rate in twenty years, but economic data suggested in 2002 that the recovery was slowing, and some alarmists were claiming (wrongly) that the recession was actually deeper than previously believed. Those concerns were relieved a bit after consumer confidence rose rapidly in March 2002.

Amtrak was about to shut down before the Bush administration provided emergency funding of $100 million. The United States was bumping against its debt ceiling as the summer began. President Bush warned that the United

States could default on its bonds unless the ceiling was raised. Previously, in 1995, the Treasury Department had borrowed $40 billion from government employee pension funds when the debt ceiling was reached, causing much consternation at the time. On May 16, 2002, the Treasury Department replicated that raid by borrowing $42 billion from the Government Securities Fund of the Federal Employees Retirement System. The government borrowed another $2 billion from the Civil Service Retirement and Disability Fund before Congress provided the needed funding.

Volatility continued in the stock markets in April as economic news and the ongoing crisis in the war on terror threatened investor confidence. The Dow was at 10249 on April 8, 2002. Trading volume was down, and the Dow experienced volatility that sometimes saw drops of over 500 points a day. Gold prices had been rising since October 1997, but began dropping in June 2002. The price of gold closed at $322.10 on June 6, 2002.

The stock markets were drifting down in June. The S&P 500 Index dropped to its lowest level since September 27, 2001, but was still 5 percent higher than its September 21 bottom in the wake of the reopening of the markets after the September 11 attacks. The Nasdaq 100 index also fell to its lowest point since September 2001. That index had fallen 36 percent in the prior six months. The Nasdaq market was down by $4 trillion from its high in 2000, a drop of 72 percent. The Dow was down a relatively smaller 22 percent from its high that was reached in 2000.

The Nasdaq index was at 1400 on July 1, 2002. This was the lowest point in five years. Nasdaq was retrenching, dropping plans to engage in joint ventures in Europe and Japan. The Dow fell almost 700 points during the week that began on July 8, dropping by more than 100 points on every day but Thursday of that week. The Dow was at 8813.5 on July 11, 2002, down from its high of 11722.98 on January 14, 2000. The S&P Index was down to 927.37. Its high had been 1527.46 on March 24, 2000. The Nasdaq Composite Index had fallen from its high of 5408.62 on March 10, 2000, to 1374.43 on July 11, 2002. The markets in Europe were dropping. The CAC40 index was down 24 percent in Paris and the Frankfurt Xetra DAX was off 20.5 percent.

The Dow plunged 439.66 points on July 15, 2002, before rallying in an hour and a half of trading by 400 points. The Dow had the worst two weeks since the stock market crash of 1987 in the weeks preceding July 19, 2002. The Dow fell to 8019.26 on July 19, a day when New York Stock Exchange (NYSE) trading volume reached 2.63 billion shares. This was the largest daily trading volume in history on that exchange. Stocks lost $1.41 trillion in this two-week period. The Dow dropped to 7784.58 on July 22, bringing that average to its lowest point since October 1998. This was the fourth-heaviest trading day ever. The Dow fell again on July 24, to 7702.34, but clawed back 488.96 points on July 25 on NYSE volume of 2.77 billion shares, a new record. Adding to this volatility was the fact that in July 2002 program trading that followed computer models that predict market behavior was becoming the principal way in which stocks were being bought and sold, accounting for 51 percent of average daily trading volume on the NYSE.

Infectious Greed

Alan Greenspan testified before Congress in July 2002 that "infectious greed" had invaded corporate America, but he asserted that the economy was recovering. The five-year Treasury note fell to the lowest yield ever on August 7, 2002. That was good news for the government because the U.S. budget deficit was growing. Treasury Inflation Protected Securities (TIPS) were sold in a Treasury auction that sought to raise $9 billion in those ten-year notes on July 10, 2002. TIPs have a rate of return indexed to the Consumer Price Index. Some $125 billion of these securities had been sold in previous auctions.

The stock market rebounded rather dramatically on July 29, 2002 with a 447-point gain in the Dow, which closed at 8711.8. This was the second major surge in a four-day period, the largest percentage increase since 1933 and the largest gain ever for such a period in terms of points. The Dow was still down 26 percent from its peak in January 2000. The Dow increased by 1,009.54 points in just four days, but volatility continued. The Dow dropped by 229.97 points, falling to 8,506.62 on August 1, 2002. It fell again on Friday, August 2, dropping by 193.49 points, closing at 8,313.13. The Dow shed another 269.50 points on August 5, but sprang back by 230.46 points on Tuesday, August 6. The Dow went up another 182.06 points on August 7, closing at 8456.15. The Dow rose more than 250 points on August 8. That was the third session in a row with triple-digit increases. The total rise in the three sessions of Tuesday, Wednesday, and Thursday that week was almost 670 points. The Dow jumped over 8 percent over this three-day period. This was the largest increase over any three-day period since 1987. The week of August 19 saw further volatility, but the Dow finished above 9000 on Friday, August 23, 2002. This was the first close over 9000 since July 9. On September 3, however, the Dow took another hammering, dropping 355.45 points to 8408.05. That average fell by more than 200 points on September 12, 2002, to close at 8379.41.

The airlines continued to lose billions of dollars. US Airways declared bankruptcy, and American Airlines announced that it was laying off 7,000 workers. Northwest Airlines disclosed that its pensions were underfunded by $3 billion. United Airlines pension plans were also underfunded. They had been 100 percent funded in January 2000, but the decline in the stock market and low interest rates resulted in a drop in coverage. United Airlines estimated that it would have to make $4.2 billion in pension contributions through 2008 and later stopped contributions to employee retirement plans. The Pension Benefit Guaranty Corporation (PBGC) took over the United Airlines pension plan deficits in 2005. Those plans then had a deficit of $9.8 billion. United Airlines agreed to provide the government $1.5 billion in notes and preferred stock, but the company had a $1.1 billion loss in the first quarter of

2005. The PBGC was receiving large stockholdings in other bankruptcies as a condition for taking over pension obligations, raising concerns that this would allow governmental intrusion into the management of those corporations. Delta Airlines disclosed a $3.15 billion deficit in its pension funding. The amount of pension underfunding at U.S. airlines totaled over $21 billion. Complete exposure to the PBGC from faltering defined benefit plans at all U.S. companies was estimated to be almost $100 billion, much of which was concentrated at automobile companies. Another festering sore was the multiemployer-defined benefit plans, which were underfunded by $150 billion as 2005 began.

Mixed Signals

The Dow continued to suffer in September 2002, falling below 8,000 on Thursday, September 19, down over 20 percent for the year. The Nasdaq index dropped to 1184.93 on September 24. This was its lowest level in six years. The Dow lost 295.67 points on September 27 and was down to 7591.93 on September 30, 2002. That was the average's lowest point in four years. The plunge in the market in the third quarter of 2002 was again the worst since 1987. The market's decline and volatility were scaring investors. They pulled a record $50 billion out of U.S. equity mutual funds in August 2002. This was the largest monthly net outflow ever recorded to that date.

Online trading had declined by the spring of 2002 by more than 25 percent from its peak. At the height of the market boom in the 1990s there had been 400,000 day traders, a number that was reduced to 7,500 in the fall of 2002. Ameritrade sought to pay $1.29 billion to acquire Datek Online Holdings Corporation, another online trader. This would make the combined firm the largest online trader in the business. Several large day trading firms agreed to pay $70 million in fines to the Securities and Exchange Commission (SEC) to settle claims that they had been manipulating trades on the Nasdaq stock market. Datek agreed to pay $22.5 million of that amount.

Online bond trading received a cold reception. Among the online bond dealers was J.W. Kurth, which operated a Web site called Shop4Bonds.com. General Motors Acceptance Corp. was selling bonds to retail investors through various broker-dealers. A new online discount brokerage firm, OptionsXpress, focused on trading options. Started in 2001, this firm had 70,000 customers and revenues of $50 million in 2003.

Morgan Stanley made a note offering in April 2002 that brought in $7.3 billion for the firm, which had been losing money for six straight quarters. Global underwriting volume fell by 5.1 percent in 2002. The total amount for underwritings in 2002 was $3.9 trillion, down from $4.1 trillion in 2001. Underwriting fees dropped even more sharply. FleetBoston Financial Corp., the seventh-largest bank in the United States, closed its Robertson Stephens unit after a leveraged buyout effort by its managers failed. Robertson Stephens, based in San Francisco, was the underwriter for the IPO for Sun Microsystems Inc. and E*Trade Group Inc., as well as a leader in the dot-com IPOs of the late twentieth century.

Japanese Operations

Nomura Securities, the leading broker-dealer in Japan, fell behind Citigroup Inc. in the underwriting of Japanese stocks in 2001, but the American firms were having difficulty selling stocks to individual investors in Japan. Merrill Lynch purchased Yamaichi Securities but was forced to scale back its operations after its Japanese operations lost $500 million in fiscal year 2001. Charles Schwab ended its efforts to introduce its discount brokerage operations to Japan through a joint Internet brokerage arrangement with a Japanese insurance company. DLJ-Direct, E*Trade, and Monex continued to maintain operations in Japan.

The economic situation in Japan was of concern. The valuation of the Nikkei 225 fell below the Dow in February 2002 for the first time in forty-five years, setting an eighteen-year low. Japan had its credit rating downgraded by two levels by Moody's in June 2002. The Bank of Japan announced in September 2002 that it was planning to buy stock held by Japanese banks. This plan was thought to be an effort to push the stock market up as well as shore up the banks that were faltering. That announcement, however, resulted in a loss of confidence in the Japanese government, which was unable to sell out a ten-year bond auction. The eight largest banks in Japan announced a total loss of $40 billion in 2002. Mizuho was responsible for $20 billion of that loss, a record for Japan. The world's largest bank, with $1.2 trillion in assets, Mizuho was the result of a combination of Fuji Bank, Dai-Ichi Kangyo, and the Industrial Bank of Japan. Mizuho incurred another $16.5 billion loss in the third quarter of 2003.

Whistlewood Holdings, a hedge fund, was buying distressed Japanese assets. This firm managed by Tim Collins was a $4 billion private equity fund. There were plenty of distressed assets available. Among other things, it purchased the Long Term Credit Bank of Japan in 1999, which was renamed Shinsei Bank and was taken public. Whistlewood bought Japan Telecom for $2.2 billion in another transaction. Interest rates in Japan dropped below zero, and the Japanese economy did improve in 2003, growing at a 3.9 percent rate in the second quarter of 2003. The Japanese stock market rose by 40 percent later in the year. The operations of American investment bankers had encountered many difficulties in Japan, but this did not deter them from entering the Chinese markets. Goldman Sachs and Morgan Stanley announced joint ventures there, pushing Merrill Lynch into following their lead.

Banking and Insurance

Bank of America added over 500,000 new checking accounts in 2002. It had 28 million customers and 4,226 branches in twenty-one states. That bank introduced Saturday banking, which other banks quickly mimicked. The federal government was pressuring subprime credit card businesses to increase their loan loss reserves and change their marketing practices in order to restrict the amount of credit being extended in these risky loans. First Alliance Mortgage Corp. agreed to settle predatory lending charges brought by the Federal Trade Commission for $60 million. The questioned loans, made to over 18,000 individuals, involved claims that high fees and interest charges were concealed from borrowers.

Merger and acquisition activity was off in 2002 in the United States, falling behind that in European companies. Merger transactions in 2000 in the United States amounted to $1.7 trillion. In contrast, in the first six months of 2002 there was only $400 billion in mergers and acquisitions. This was the slowest period in years for that activity. There were, nonetheless, some big deals. Willamette was acquired by Weyerhauser for $6.11 billion on January 22, 2002, and Northrop acquired TRW for $7.8 billion in a hostile takeover. Northrop had begun the bidding at $5.9 billion.

Gruntal Financial announced that it was being acquired by Ryan, Beck & Co., a New Jersey broker-dealer, in April 2002. Ryan, Beck was an affiliate of BankAtlantic Bancorp in New Jersey. Gruntal had been founded 122 years before. The easing and eventual repeal of bank branching prohibitions and Glass-Steagall restrictions on investment banking activities of commercial banks as the twentieth century closed allowed nationwide banking and consolidation of financial services. The growth of Nations Bank and its merger with the Bank of America exemplified the former, and the merger of Citicorp with Smith Barney and Travelers Insurance the latter. This consolidation went one step further with the merger of J.P. Morgan and Chase Manhattan, turning the clock back to the heyday of the 1920s when commercial banks operated their own investment banking arms. Morgan Stanley remained an investment bank and brokerage firm after its merger with Dean Witter. The consolidation of banks assured that there would be no banking crisis such as that suffered during the Great Depression, when branching restrictions resulted in small "unit" banks with little capital to withstand an economic decline. Canada, which had no such restrictions, had suffered no bank failures in the 1930s, while thousands of banks in the United States failed.

Banks continued their intrusion into the insurance industry. The BBT Corp., a bank based in North Carolina, acquired over seventy insurance agencies. Banks were not immediately interested in purchasing insurance underwriting operations even though allowed to do so by the Gramm-Leach-Bliley Act. Many large life insurance companies were demutualizing and turning themselves into full-service financial services firms as bank and broker-dealer competition threatened their historical markets. Among those demutualizing were Equitable, MetLife, and the Mutual Life Insurance Company of New York. The John Hancock Insurance Company, founded in 1862 and named after the great patriot, demutualized in 2000, becoming John Hancock Financial Services Inc. The company was sold for $1.7 billion in the demutualization offering, but was acquired for about twice that price in September 2003 by Manulife, a Canadian insurance company.

Prudential Financial was able to make a successful IPO that demutualized the company. The company raised about $3 billion in its IPO. A spin-off of Travelers Property and Casualty by Citigroup was to be conducted in part by a 20 percent sale of the company through an IPO that sought to raise over $4 billion. The demutualization process was a reverse of the regulatory efforts at the beginning of the twentieth century. Then, a New York state legislative committee (the Armstrong committee) sought to force the Equitable Life Assurance Co. to mutualize as a result of the excesses of its controlling shareholder, James Hyde. The committee may have been onto something. David F. D'Alessandro, the chief executive officer at John Hancock, was paid $21.7 million two years after the company was demutualized, despite the fact that John Hancock's stock price had fallen by 32 percent. That was seven times more than he had earned when the company was owned by its policyholders.

Anthem purchased WellPoint for $16.4 billion. This created the biggest managed care firm in the United States. WellPoint executives were to be paid $200 million upon the consummation of that merger. WellPoint's chairman and chief executive officer was to receive $82 million of that amount, which caused the California Public Employees Retirement System (Calpers) to oppose the merger and led to another corporate shakedown by state officials. California insurance commissioner John Garamendi grabbed a headline by announcing that he would not approve the merger, while the California Department of Managed Health Care, which had a greater interest in the transaction, approved it. Anthem was then forced to pay $265 million for various state programs to buy off Garamendi, but that led other states to seek similar payments, including the Georgia insurance commissioner, John Oxendine. He withdrew his prior approval of the merger and extracted $126 million from Anthem that was to be used to pay for rural health care in Georgia.

Blue Cross and Blue Shield of North Carolina were seeking to convert from mutual companies into profit-making ventures. Prudential Financial Inc. offered $690 million in 6.75 percent equity security units in February 2002. The lead underwriter was Goldman, Sachs & Co. Prudential Financial Inc. made a public offering of $3.4 billion in common shares early in 2002. Prudential was selling a total of 126.5 million shares of common stock in this offering. That money was needed because Prudential Securities Inc. was slammed with a $250 million punitive damage award by a jury in a class action suit involving its securities sales.

Prudential purchased the variable annuity business of Sweden's Skandia Insurance for $1.27 billion. Prudential and the Wachovia bank merged their securities brokerage operations as 2003 began. Wachovia owned 62 percent of this joint venture and Prudential owned the remaining 38 percent. The combined workforce of these two firms totaled 12,500 brokers, behind the 14,000 employed at Merrill Lynch and the 12,699 employed at Citigroup Inc. through its Salomon Smith Barney brokerage. Morgan Stanley, at the time, had 12,546 brokers. The merger of Prudential and Wachovia ran into problems in September 2004 when a new joint computer system went into operation and failed for several days.

Insurance companies were managing more than $3 billion in charges for asbestos and other claims, and life insurers were suffering from the market downturn. Some of the larger companies were downgraded by the credit rating agencies. Those downgraded included Metropolitan Life, Hartford Life, Guardian, Jefferson Pilot, and Manufacturers Life. AXA SA bought MONY Group Inc. in 2003, but some shareholders resisted that acquisition, and AXA had to sweeten its offer. Executives at MONY were to receive payouts of $90 million as a result of the merger, but gave up $7 million of that amount after shareholders protested. In order to finance this deal, AXA sold convertible bonds that were to be repaid in cash plus interest if the deal fell through. If the deal was successful, the bonds could be converted to AXA shares at a substantial profit. Travelers Insurance Company and St. Paul agreed to merge. That merger was valued at $15.4 billion. Travelers was the spin-off of the property and casualty insurance business that Citigroup had acquired. United Health acquired Mid Atlantic.

Reparations for Slavery

Several insurance companies were still charging some black policyholders higher premiums than whites in 2000. Rates in the 1960s for blacks had been as much as 25 percent more than for whites because of longevity differences, but that disparity was dropped for new policies after civil rights activists protested against it. Some of the insurance companies failed to reduce the premiums for existing policies; those payments continued right into the year 2000. Chicago, Detroit, Philadelphia, and Los Angeles adopted ordinances requiring firms contracting with those cities to disclose any links they might have had with slavery before the Civil War. Lehman Brothers had to disclose that one of its original brothers was a slaveholder and JPMorgan Chase had to reveal that it had some tangential ties with the Citizens Bank of Louisiana that accepted slaves as collateral for loans.

Insurance companies and other financial institutions were asked to pay for some old sins. Lawsuits were filed against FleetBoston, Aetna and CSX, New York Life Insurance Company, Lehman Brothers, Norfolk Southern Railway, Liggett (the tobacco company), and Lloyd's of London, among others, seeking reparations for their having exploited slaves before the Civil War. The precedent cited was that 80,000 Japanese-Americans interned during World War II had been paid $1.6 billion in reparations, and Germany made reparation payments to individuals held as slaves during World War II.

The reparations suits for the pre–Civil War slaves sought damages from existing firms that had profited from slavery earlier in their history. The damages sought were in dollars that were to be time valued, so that each dollar that should have been paid to a slave would now be worth over $400,000. There was criticism that such damages would be difficult to prove and that identifying descendants would pose hurdles. The suit against the New York Life Insurance Company, called the Nautilus Insurance Company before the Civil War, involved its practice of insuring the lives of slaves. One Virginia slave owner paid a premium of $5.81 to insure the life of a slave for $412, which would be worth about $8,800 today. Large newspapers were accused of having published advertisements for return of escaped slaves. FleetBoston, which traces its beginnings to Providence Bank, which was chartered in 1791, was under attack because it had been controlled by a slave trader, John Brown, at the time it was founded. Lehman Brothers was charged with having been started by family members who owned slaves. Brown Brothers was accused of making loans to plantation owners and executing judgments against slaves and other assets when loans were defaulted. Various railroads were accused of using slave labor to build their roadbeds. Westpoint Stevens, a textile maker, was claimed to have made rough clothing purchased by slave owners for their slaves. A federal judge in Chicago dismissed the reparations claims. Victims of the Holocaust in World War II had better luck in an action in the United States courts against the Swiss banks for holding looted assets of Jewish victims. Paul Volcker, the former Federal Reserve Board chairman, negotiated a settlement in that suit for $1.25 billion.

Stock Market Reaction

A lockout of unions in the west coast ports during the fall of 2002 cost the economy $1 billion a day. President Bush moved to have that action stopped by injunctive proceedings under the Taft-Hartley Act. This was the first time that the Taft-Hartley Act had been so used in twenty-four years. Corporate bond defaults reached a record $140 billion for the year in September 2002. There were fifty fallen angels in that group during this period as well. These were companies whose bond ratings dropped from investment grade to junk bond status.

The Dow rose 346.86 points on October 1, 2002, but fell back again, dropping to 7755.61 at the close of trading on October 2. The Dow closed at 7501.49 on October 8. Merrill Lynch then announced that it would no longer make a market in 70 percent of the smaller stocks traded on Nasdaq. This left about 2,400 stocks on Nasdaq that it would be trading. The Dow dropped to 7286.27 on October 9. That average was then down 38 percent from its high more than two years previously, signaling the worst bear market since 1974. The S&P 500 stock index lost almost half of its value, which made it the worst bear market for that index since the 1930s.

The Dow experienced a rally on Thursday and Friday, October 10 and 11,

2002, rising to 7850.29 at the close of trading on that Friday. The average jumped 316 points during the day. The stock market climbed again on Tuesday, October 15. The Dow had its biggest seven-day rally in almost thirty years during the seven-day period ending on October 19, 2002. It reached 8538.24 on October 21. By then investors had regained $2.2 trillion of the $7.4 trillion they had lost in their net worth since the bubble burst. Adding more juice to the market, the Federal Reserve Board cut interest rates by .05 percent on November 6, 2002. The federal funds rate was then at 1.25 percent, its lowest rate in decades.

Industrial output dropped 0.2 percent in December 2002. Output was up less than 1 percent for the year, the lowest growth rate since 1983. The trade deficit was widening. Nevertheless, the economy expanded at a 0.7 percent annual rate in the fourth quarter of 2002, and the housing market remained strong, even while the stock market was faltering. Low interest rates transferred into high home sales during 2002, and new home sales set a record that year. The average interest rate on a thirty-year fixed rate mortgage was 6.07 percent. The average price of a new home was $218,900, a 5.8 percent increase during the year. The savings levels of Americans continued to raise concern. The shortfall in savings needed by the baby boomers for retirement was predicted to be between $28 billion and $36 billion a year.

Gold reached $351.20 per ounce at the end of 2002 and closed at $360 an ounce on January 22, 2003. This was a six-year high. Daily trading volume on the NYSE was hovering around 1.5 billion shares. The Dow closed on December 31, 2002, at 8341.63, experiencing its worst annual loss since 1977. Nasdaq shares lost nearly a third of their value during the year, falling 614.89 points to close at 1335.51. The S&P 500 Index lost 23.4 percent of its value during 2002, closing at year-end at 879.82.

The amount of securities outstanding reached a staggering amount even with the market downturn. There was $18.1 trillion in stock outstanding in 2002. That was in addition to $9.7 trillion in corporate loans and another $4.8 trillion in corporate bonds. The entire bond market (including government debt and mortgage-backed securities) was valued at over $20 trillion. The "buy" side of the market in bonds was composed largely of investors, usually institutional investors. On the "sell" side of the market were the broker-dealers and firms dealing in fixed-income instruments. The bond market was having some problems. A record $157.3 billion of debt defaulted throughout the world in 2002, exceeding the previous high of $117.4 billion in 2001.

United Airlines declared bankruptcy on December 9, 2002. Such disasters had an adverse effect in the credit derivatives market, which offered derivative contracts that would protect against credit defaults. Although the credit derivatives market did not immediately suffer any undue adverse effects from the Enron bankruptcy, that situation changed with the bankruptcies of WorldCom and other large firms. The credit derivatives market appeared to be thin by year-end. Prices varied widely. Firms were charging $140,000 to

$200,000 for each $10 million of default protection on the credit risks from CommerzBank AG, a large German bank. The credit derivative market was estimated to be close to $2 trillion in 2002, up from $180 billion in 1997. That number would rise to $5.44 trillion in 2005.

McDonald's Corp., the giant hamburger chain, announced a 2002 third-quarter loss of $390 million. This was the first quarterly loss since the company went public thirty-seven years previously. That loss eliminated McDonald's earnings at the end of 2002, but the company later returned to profitability and even increased its dividends. McDonald's also won a lawsuit that sought to hold the company liable for the increasing level of obesity in America. Several states passed laws to stop such nonsense. McDonald's did agree to pay $8.5 million to settle a class action law suit that charged that the company failed to inform customers in delays in its announced plan to switch to reduced fat cooking oils for its French fries. Krispy Kreme, the doughnut seller and hot issue of the bubble era, saw its stock drop 10 percent when newspapers reported that the company had a synthetic lease on a $30 million plant. That arrangement was proper under generally accepted accounting principles but was characterized in the press as an off-balance-sheet trick like those employed by Enron. Krispy Kreme unwound the transaction and moved the liability back onto the balance sheet, but faced further accounting problems from an SEC investigation of its accounting treatment for franchise repurchases. Krispy Kreme disclosed more franchise accounting problems for franchise repurchases and restated its earnings after disclosing that it had been inflating shipments in order to conceal declining earnings. The price of its stock dropped 15 percent after that announcement. Krispy Kreme fired its chief executive officer, Scott Livengood, and replaced him with Stephen Cooper who was acting as the chief executive officer for Enron during its bankruptcy reorganization. Krispy Kreme employees and other investors filed class action suits claiming that they had been misled by the company into investing in Krispy Kreme stock. Krispy Kreme announced a fourth-quarter loss in 2004 and stated that its prior accounting manipulations were even worse than previously reported. The company conducted an internal investigation by a special committee of newly appointed outside directors, one of whom, Michael Sutton, had been a former chief accountant at the SEC. Those two directors later ordered the discharge of six senior executives.

The restaurant industry was drowning in a sea of restatements over their restaurant leases. In addition to Krispy Kreme, the restaurant chains restating or reviewing their lease accounting included Wendy's International Inc., Jack in the Box, Applebee's International, CKE Restaurants (Hardee's), Darden Restaurants (Red Lobster and Olive Garden), Ruby Tuesday, and Brinker International (Macaroni Grill and Chilis). This problem spread, producing in an avalanche of over 250 companies restating their financial results as the results of their accounting for leases. Wendy's took another hit after a customer, Anna Ayala, claimed that she had bit into a human finger in chili that she bought from a Wendy's outlet in California. Ayala threatened to sue Wendy's. The resulting publicity caused a sharp drop in sales at Wendy's restaurants before Ayala was arrested and charged with attempted larceny for faking the incident in order to extort money from Wendy's. ConAgra Foods paid $14 million to settle a class action shareholder lawsuit involving fictitious sales and inflated earnings at a subsidiary that sold products under the names of Chef Boyardee and Marie Callender. Conagra Foods was restating its results because of tax errors totaling over $200 million.

Visteon Corp., an automobile parts supplier, was restating its earnings for the years 2002 through 2004. Dow Chemical experienced a fourth-quarter loss in 2002 in the amount of $809 million. A dot-com company with a perennial loss was Amazon.com, but it experienced a quarterly profit at the end of 2002, the second quarterly profit in its history.

The New Year—2003

Taxes

Treasury Secretary Paul O'Neill was forced from office at the end of 2002. He had been a controversial figure in the Bush administration, having been too often guilty of speaking before thinking. O'Neill had opposed President Bush's tax cuts and made a spectacle of himself with a trip to Africa accompanied by Bono, the lead singer for U2. O'Neill would seek revenge with a book highly critical of President Bush just as the 2004 election cycle was under way. Lawrence Lindsey, the director of the National Economic Council and White House economic adviser, resigned from the Bush administration. He had been a former consultant to Enron.

President Bush announced plans for further tax cuts at the beginning of 2003. This proposal included a plan to accelerate tax cuts previously approved and to eliminate taxes on dividends, as well as accelerating depreciation. The president's proposal sought tax cuts of $670 billion in total over ten years. This plan spurred the Dow to a record for the first three days of the new year, but tax cut legislation was not passed until May 2003 by an evenly divided vote in the Senate that was broken by Vice President Richard Cheney. Even that victory was muted because the legislation reduced taxes less than the amount sought by Bush and was full of gimmicks, including the expiration of some of the tax cuts if not renewed by Congress in future years.

Significantly for the market, the rate on long-term capital gains was reduced to 15 percent. Marginal income rates were cut, reducing the top bracket for marginal rates to 35 percent. The effect of the cut was actually to increase tax revenues as the economy expanded from the additional investment and expenditures allowed by reduced taxes and interest rates. Nevertheless, spending was outpacing revenues. The Bush tax cuts did not eliminate taxes on dividends, but did reduce their taxation rate to 15 percent. Bond fund dividends were still taxed as ordinary income. This legislation had the immediate effect of increasing the dividend rate by many companies already paying dividends, and a number of companies announced that they would begin paying dividends for the first time. One company did not need that incentive. The Bank of New York has paid a dividend every year since 1785. A Cato Institute study found that companies in the S&P 500 Index increased their dividends by $33 billion during a one-year period starting in May 2003. Microsoft began paying dividends after the Bush tax cut and went further in 2004 with a special dividend of $32 billion, amounting to about $3 per share.

Stock market volatility continued as 2003 began. The Dow closed at 8369.47 on January 24, 2003, but dropped to 7945.13 at the end of the month. Consumer confidence was at its lowest level since 1993, and the stock market drifted downward as war with Iraq approached. A sharp rally occurred on Monday, March 18, 2003, the day before the president gave Saddam Hussein forty-eight hours to get out of town. The Dow jumped 282.21 points and rose 8.4 percent before the war, which was the largest rise in a comparable time period in twenty years. The Dow fell by 327.29 points on Monday, March 21, 2003, when the war actually began, but promptly bounced back as it became apparent that the American forces were ripping through the Iraqi opposition. Congress sought to provide $3 billion to the airlines after their bookings dropped sharply with the Iraq war. American Airlines was facing bankruptcy. The airlines were not the only ones having problems. Goodyear announced a $1.11 billion loss for the first quarter of 2003.

The dollar was under attack. The euro exceeded parity with the U.S. dollar for the first time on July 15, 2002. Between February 2001 and December 2002, the dollar fell 26 percent against the euro. This was more a reflection of the weakness of the dollar than any strength in the euro. The dollar lost 8.8 percent of its value against a basket of nineteen other currencies during 2002. Nevertheless, the U.S. dollar remained popular around the world, even among the country's enemies. Several hundred million dollars in U.S. currency was found in sealed containers that were hidden in dog kennels at a Saddam Hussein palace in Baghdad after the city was liberated by American forces. The cache totaled $650 million in sequentially numbered $100 bills. That currency had been shipped from the United States to three banks under a Treasury program called "Extended Custodial Inventory." That program was designed to monitor and control the international distribution of U.S. currency, but it apparently needed a little refining. Saddam Hussein had additional large sums of American dollars when he was later captured hiding in a concealed hole in the ground.

The stock market rallied at the end of May 2003 as a result of growing strength in the economy. The Dow was 8,850.26 on May 30, 2003, and closed above 9,000 on June 4, 2003, the first time that had occurred since the prior August. The Dow reached 9318.96 on June 16, 2003. Treasury bond yields were then at their lowest levels in forty-five years. The interest rate on thirty-year mortgages dropped to 5.54 percent. This was the lowest rate in more than forty years, but the ratio of owner equity to residence value for personal residences was at a record low, suggesting that consumers were leveraging their residences.

The inflation rate in the United States was at a thirty-seven year low in May 2003. The Federal Reserve Board cut interest rates again on June 27, 2003. The cut was twenty-five basis points and reduced interest rates to 1 percent, the lowest interest rate in forty-five years. This was the thirteenth cut by the Federal Reserve Board since January 3, 2001. Interest rates had been reduced from 6.5 percent to 1 percent over that two-and-a-half-year period. Those cuts were not without cost. Bond losses in the three-month period ending July 2003 were the worst in any such period since 1927. The effects of the market downturn lingered. The unemployment rate was 6.4 percent, the highest since 1994. Instability in the economy was blamed on the corporate scandals.

Trading Places

Trading on the NYSE was disrupted on October 2, 2002, when an order for $4 million to sell a basket of S&P 500 stocks was mistakenly entered as an order to sell $4 billion. The order was canceled after $622 million had been filled. This was not the only large error. Such events were being called the "fat finger" syndrome. UBS Warburg faced potential losses of millions of dollars after a trader mistakenly entered a sell order for 10,000 Dentsu shares at ¥16 each, instead of sixteen shares at ¥610,000 each. The trader ignored a signal from the computer system questioning the trade. In 2004, Lehman Brothers overstated an order for a short sale of Viacom Inc. stock by $1 billion, and a Morgan Stanley trader caused the Russell 2000 index to move by 2.8 percent after he entered an order for a basket of stocks in an amount of several billions of dollars over what he had intended. The stock of Corinthian Colleges dropped 32 percent in eight minutes on December 5, 2003, as the result of an erroneous order. Nasdaq halted trading in the stock and canceled hundreds of trades made during the eight-minute period when the glitch occurred. Electronic communications networks (ECNs) halted trading briefly but started trading again in this stock before the Nasdaq halt, causing complaints.

Island ECN, an electronic communications network in New York, was bought by Reuters PLC, the owner of the Instinet Group, for $500 million. Island and Instinet were merged and accounted for about 22 percent of volume in Nasdaq listed stocks before Instinet was sold to Nasdaq. Charles Schwab, Fidelity Investments, DLJdirect, and Spear, Leeds & Kellogg developed MarketXT Inc. It offered an evening trading session for the 200 largest stocks on the NYSE and Nasdaq. Bridge Trader allowed Internet institutional order entry and permitted orders to be routed to multiple brokers through its trading network. This information system provided quotes, watch lists, and order book market data. Before the announcement of its plans to merge with the NYSE, Archipelago Holdings operated ArcaEx, the largest ECN, and purchased the Pacific Exchange for $50 million.

Cantor Fitzgerald, recovering from its devastating losses in the attack on the World Trade Center, found itself in competition with BrokerTec Global LLC, an electronic bond trading network owned by several financial firms. A jury ruled that a Cantor Fitzgerald patent for its electronic bond trading system was invalid. Two ECNs trading bonds, Thomson TradeWeb and MarketAxess, received a surge of business in 2004. The BRASS Utility System was an ECN that provided automatic execution, clearance, and settlement of trades in Nasdaq stocks. Subscribers were broker-dealers, but their institutional customers could be given direct access to the system. The Attain System was an ECN that provided an alternative method by which market makers could handle their requirements to display customer limit orders to the public pursuant to SEC order-handling rules. It also allowed matching of orders of subscribers as well as displaying a book of orders on Nasdaq. The system sought to provide matching without unnecessary intermediation by market makers. Knight Trading Group in Jersey City, New Jersey, which was sold to Citigroup in 2004, paid brokers for order flow in order to capture their customers' business for execution on its ECN. Knight was handling about 20 percent of the volume of the most active Nasdaq stocks. Liquidnet, an ECN that allows anonymous trading by institutions, began trading in 2001 and was valued at $1.8 billion in 2005. That amount exceeded the capital value placed on the NYSE and Nasdaq.

Nasdaq was planning to trade funds that would track international stock indexes and compete with exchange-traded funds. The Nasdaq called these funds Baskets of Lifted Depository Receipts (BLDRs). Single stock futures were being traded by OneChicago and Nasdaq-Liffe as a result of the passage of the Commodity Futures Modernization Act of 2000 (CFMA), which allowed such trading for the first time. OneChicago was a joint venture of the Chicago Board of Trade, the Chicago Mercantile Exchange, and the Chicago Board Options Exchange. OneChicago traded 270,000 single stock futures contracts in its first three months of trading. Trading on the Nasdaq-Liffe Exchange had been about 200,000 contracts during the same period. These amounts were disappointingly small, fewer than ten thousand contracts a day. That lack of interest was apparently due to the fact that SEC margin requirements were imposed on these contracts, which were magnitudes higher than those for commodity futures contracts regulated by the Commodity Futures Trading Commission (CFTC). A product that proved immediately popular was options on spiders—exchange traded funds—that began trading in 2005.

Nasdaq was authorized by the SEC to begin trading through its own electronic trading platform, which was named SuperMontage. The AMEX began electronic trading in its options products in 2004. The SEC approved the creation of the Boston Options Exchange (BOX), a new all-electronic options exchange. BOX, created by a group of investment banks, offered a "price improvement" program that allowed firms to trade internally when they could improve the price over that quoted on the exchanges.

The Merchants Exchange, which was founded in 1836 to trade in buffalo skins and whiskey, began operating an energy futures exchange in the new century. The exchange was designed to allow energy traders to negotiate block trades bilaterally and then to post and clear the transactions electronically, an arrangement made possible by the CFMA. The exchange's clearinghouse provided a guarantee against default on contracts cleared through its facilities. The Merchants Exchange was in competition with the New York Mercantile Exchange and the London International Petroleum Exchange. The Department of Justice was investigating possible antitrust violations by FXall, an electronic exchange owned by seventeen financial institutions, including Citigroup Inc., JPMorgan Chase Corp., Goldman Sachs, and Deutsche Bank. The Department of Justice's concern was that the members of this electronic exchange were told not to work with competing online services such as Currenex.

The Pentagon disclosed in July 2003 that it was studying the creation of an online futures exchange that would offer investments in the possibility of terrorist attacks or other political events within a particular time period. The proposed exchange was designed after the electronic market for election campaigns created by the College of Business at the University of Iowa. The Iowa market offered participants an opportunity to bet on the outcomes of political elections in a futures-style trading atmosphere. The new Pentagon market was called the Policy Analysis Market. The Pentagon spent about $750,000 to study the creation of this market and sought $8 million from Congress to support it. Once made public, however, the idea was met with a storm of criticism in Congress and derided in the press. The Defense Department then dropped the idea. Retired Admiral John Poindexter, who was in charge of the project, was forced to resign. Poindexter had been national security adviser to President Ronald Reagan and was at the heart of the Iran-contra scandal that arose during Reagan's administration. His criminal convictions for his role in that affair were set aside by an appellate court. More conventionally, Goldman Sachs, along with the Deutsche Bank, created an "economic derivatives market" that traded synthetic options for such things as nonfarm payrolls, retail sales, and confidence indexes.

The Chicago Mercantile Exchange (CME) demutualized in November 2000 and became a shareholder-owned company, selling about 15 percent of itself in a public offering in January 2003. The CME renamed itself, becoming Chicago Mercantile Exchange Holdings Inc. after it went public. The CME agreed with Bloomberg, and later Reuters, to allow traders on those systems to access trading in CME currency futures contracts. The CME was planning to trade an index instrument on residential housing prices. The chief executive officer of the exchange, James McNulty, resigned in August 2003 after creating dissatisfaction among members because he was pushing electronic trading too hard. Ironically, the CME's net income would jump by 54 percent in the first quarter of 2005, largely as the result of increased electronic trading. Searching for revenues and cost savings, the CME agreed to clear trades made on the Chicago Board of Trade (CBOT). The CBOT then dropped the use of its own clearing body, CBOT Clearing Corp., which had been formed in 1926. This left the CBOT Clearing Corp. without a mission, so it sold 15 percent of itself to Eurex, the world's largest derivatives exchange.

Eurex was owned in equal shares by the Deutsche Börse AG and the Swiss Stock Exchange (SWX). Eurex had volume of 801 million contracts in 2002. Eurex was in need of a clearinghouse in the United States because it was planning to start trading here through its electronic EurexUS Exchange. Eurex met stiff resistance from the U.S. exchanges in seeking approval from the CFTC for the EurexUS Exchange. Eurex sued the CBOT and CME for antitrust violations, charging that those exchanges were trying to prevent it from entering the U.S. market. The Chicago exchanges responded with counter-charges claiming that Eurex was planning to pay its brokers for order flow to the new exchange. The Federal Reserve Board and the Treasury Department supported the Eurex application over the opposition of the Chicago exchanges. The CFTC approved that application on February 4, 2004.

Liffe, the London futures and options exchange, was acquired by Euronext, the Paris-based exchange that was formed by the combination of the Dutch and Belgian exchanges. The London Stock Exchange (LSE) and the OM Stockholm Exchange created a jointly operated derivatives exchange. The LSE had been the target of an unsuccessful takeover attempt by OM. The Deutsche Börse offered to buy the LSE in 2004 for $2.5 billion, but that effort failed. The International Securities Exchange claimed that it was the first "fully electronic" options market in the United States. Electronic trading did not assure success. BrokerTech stopped trading in November 2003. This was the only all-electronic futures exchange in the United States at that time.

The CBOT lost its ranking as the world's largest futures exchange, falling to fifth place in the new century as the result of electronic competition from Eurex and others. The CBOT had dominated futures trading in the world since its inception just before the Civil War. The CBOT- defended its old-fashioned open outcry trading system, while traders were expressing a preference for electronic trading. In order to curb its decline, the CBOT started a new electronic trading system provided by Euronext-Liffe. The new system was called Liffe-Connect. Previously, the CBOT used an electronic trading system linked with Eurex, but that arrangement fell apart and led to Eurex starting operations here. About 80 percent of the U.S. Treasury bond and note futures contracts traded through the CBOT were being executed electronically and the remainder in the open outcry pits while the CBOT was working with Eurex. On an overall basis, electronic trading on the Chicago futures exchanges grew from less than 8 percent in 1999 to about 60 percent by 2004. New all-electronic exchanges included CBOE Futures Exchange, HedgeStreet, NQLX,

OneChicago, and U.S. Futures Exchange. An effort by NYMEX to introduce open outcry trading in London was meeting resistance from the Europeans who were expressing a preference for electronic trading.

More on the Market

The economy increased by a surprising 3.3 percent in the second quarter of 2003. Economists were forecasting growth of as much as 5 percent or more for the third quarter. Consumer spending increased 0.8 percent in August 2003. The Dow was rising, reaching 9300 on August 14, 2003. The Dow reached 9545 on September 17 and hit a fifteen-month high during the week of September 19, but prices retreated during the last week of September 2003. Nasdaq dropped by 6 percent, which was its worst week since April 2002. The Dow and the S&P 500 also fell. Their decline was not as great, but it was their worst performance for six months. The Dow closed at 9380.24 on September 29, 2003. Nasdaq closed at 1824.56.

The Dow hit its highest point in over fifteen months during the week of October 6, 2003. The Dow had fallen to a five-year low on October 9, 2002, but jumped by 33 percent over the next year. The Dow closed at 9674.68 on Friday, October 10, and reached 9748.31 on October 29, 2003. This was a 17 percent increase for the year. The highest point for the year for the Dow was 9812.98, reached in the middle of October. The Nasdaq Bulletin Board, normally a market for illiquid securities, was heating up with 41 billion shares traded in September. That figure exceeded the 40 billion shares traded on the Nasdaq National Market for stocks with higher capitalization. It also exceeded the 29 billion shares traded on the NYSE.

The Federal Reserve Board announced on October 28, 2003, that it had no plans to increase interest rates and that it expected rates to remain low "for a considerable period." The number of employed people in the United States increased by 126,000 in October 2003, giving hope that the unemployment situation was improving. Unemployment claims were at an eight-month low. Productivity in the United States rose at an 8.2 percent annual rate in the third quarter of 2003. This was the largest growth rate in twenty years. Productivity had been expanding at an annual rate of 5 percent since the country came out of recession in November 2001. One report suggested that productivity gains were due to the fact that Americans were working longer hours, increasing their time on the job by 20 percent between 1970 and 2002. This contrasted with a drop of 24 percent in working hours in France during that same period.

Citigroup Inc. reported an all-time record high of $4.69 billion in earnings in the third quarter of 2003. JPMorgan Chase reported $1.63 billion in net earnings for that quarter. Collectively, U.S. corporate profits rose 30 percent in the third quarter of 2003 over the prior year. This was the largest rise in nineteen years. The annual pace of corporate earnings was then over $1 trillion, which was the first time this ever occurred. Third-quarter GDP increased by 8.2 percent. Manufacturing activity was at its highest level in twenty years in the fourth quarter. Consumer expenditures as a percentage of GDP reached a fifty-four-year high in that month, but the dollar continued to fall against the euro. At year-end, the dollar had reached a record low, closing at $1.2555 against the euro.

Existing home sales increased by 3.6 percent in September 2003, a record rate. About 68.4 percent of all U.S. households owned their own homes in the third quarter of 2003. About 46 percent of Hispanic households and 48 percent of African-Americans were in that category. The median age of homeowners in the United States was just over fifty. Household wealth was on average $385,000 per family, but that wealth was concentrated, skewing its distribution. The deficit in the federal budget for the fiscal year ending September 30, 2003, was $374 billion, which was less than expected, but was still the largest in history. The deficit for 2002 had been $158 billion. The government was expecting a deficit of $480 billion for 2004. The Treasury was selling $57 billion in notes in early November 2003. This was smaller than the expected $61 billion funding that the Treasury was thought to be placing. The November offering was for three-, five-, and ten-year notes.

The Nasdaq market reached a twenty-one-month high on November 6, 2003. The Dow rose above 9900 on December 5, 2003, the first time that that this level had been reached in eighteen months. The Dow broke through 10000 during the following week, but fell back to 9923.42. The Federal Reserve Board announced on December 10, 2003, that it considered the risk of inflation a possibility but stated that it planned to continue its policy of maintaining low interest rates. Nevertheless, the suggestion of inflation caused the market to fall back below 10000. The capture of Saddam Hussein in Iraq was accompanied by the Dow piercing the 10000 mark again, reaching 10278.22 on December 19, 2003.

The number of unemployment claims again declined at the end of 2003, reaching their lowest level in three years. Corporate profits set an all-time record in the fourth quarter. The economy grew at a rate of 4 percent in that quarter. This was a slowdown from the summer pace but still quite strong. Consumer spending continued to grow, and exports increased by almost 20 percent. The growth rate for the American economy in the fourth quarter was twice that of Japan and three times that of Europe. Consumer spending accounted for some two-thirds of the economic activity in the United States.

Retirement Concerns

Retirees were becoming a central concern in the securities markets as the twentieth century closed. They experienced a double hit when the market bubble burst in 2000, resulting in a declining stock market for their equity holdings and dropping interest rates that undermined their fixed income investments. In 2001, only 53 percent of workers thought they had enough money to live comfortably in retirement, a decrease from 72 percent in 2000. Only about one-fourth of workers over age fifty-five had $100,000 or more in retirement savings, and one-third of the workers in that age group had less than $50,000 in retirement savings.

Traditional defined benefit plans were outperforming Section 401(k) accounts after the market crashed in 2000, but that situation was expected to reverse as the market surged upward. The average balance in employee Section 401(k) balances at the end of 2003 was $76,809, up from $59,510 at year-end 2002 and even above the $65,572 average at the end of 1999. Participation of eligible employees in Section 401(k) plans dropped to 60 percent in 2003, down from 80 percent in 2002.

Consumer debt set a new record in December 2003. More than 1.6 million people filed for bankruptcy in the fiscal year ending September 30, an increase of 7.8 percent over the prior year. Bankruptcies by families had increased by 400 percent over the last twenty-five years, and many of the bankrupts were baby boomers approaching retirement. Housing foreclosures increased over 350 percent during that period.

The Pension Benefit Guaranty Corporation (PBGC), which insures defined benefit plans for 44 million individuals, had a $3.64 billion deficit for fiscal year 2002. That was somewhat shocking since the PBGC had a $7.7 billion surplus in 2001. That agency experienced further difficulties as 2003 began and had a staggering $23.3 billion deficit in 2004. Despite a rising market, there was still a $259 billion shortfall in pension funding by the 500 largest U.S. companies at the end of 2003. General Motors disclosed that its liabilities to retired employees for health care costs were $63.4 billion. General Motors made a $17 billion debt offering, which was the largest such offering ever made by a company in the United States in order to fill deficits in its pension funds. United Airlines announced that it was discontinuing its employee pension plans, and Delta changed its defined benefit plans to cash balance plans in order to reduce costs.

Social Security

Social Security as a retirement mechanism was in need of repair. In earlier years, 8.6 workers were supporting each retiree receiving Social Security benefits. By 1998, there were only 3.4 workers for each recipient, and it was projected that there would be only two workers per beneficiary in the year 2030. In addition, life expectancy increased from 68.2 years in 1950 to 77.3 in 2002 and was continuing to increase, placing even more demands on the reduced number of workers. The Social Security Commission warned that the Social Security system would be paying more in benefits than it collected in taxes within the next fifteen years. In its annual report to workers the Social Security Commission stated that "Without changes, by 2042 the Social Security Trust Fund will be exhausted. By then, the number of Americans 65 or older is expected to have doubled. There won't be enough younger people working to pay all of the benefits owed to those who are retiring." The Social Security Trust Fund held about $1.2 trillion in 2001 but needed $10 trillion to pay the baby boomer benefits that were expected in future years.

The Social Security system is a very bad investment. The average male worker born in 2000 could expect a return of only 0.86 percent on his contributions. That figure was negative even for those paying the maximum amounts of contributions. Social Security has other flaws. It is an annuity; therefore, life expectancy as well as contributions determines the amount of benefits received. Under that formula, male African-Americans have had a negative rate of return from Social Security for the last forty years. Black males were receiving on average $13,400 less in Social Security benefits than they paid into the system. A Rand Corp. study conducted in 1996 found that Social Security was transferring on average $10,000 from African-Americans to more affluent whites with a longer life expectancy. The average black male collects less than one year of Social Security while the average white male collects seven years of such benefits. The increasingly higher retirement age under Social Security was worsening this situation.

Social Security's reform has long been blocked by politics, but the increasing gap in Social Security coverage and retirement needs, and the changing demographics that were inevitably bankrupting the system, gave rise to reform efforts. In January 1997, a federal advisory council divided over the issue of whether to allow private Social Security accounts, but seven of its thirteen members wanted to require compulsory saving through individual accounts. Another federal advisory committee unanimously recommended the use of private accounts to supplement Social Security. The 2000 presidential election focused further attention on the issue of whether Social Security should be privatized.

As a presidential candidate, George W. Bush broke the political taboo on criticizing the Social Security system. After his election, he appointed a commission on Social Security reform that released a report suggesting differing models for reforming the Social Security system. One proposal would allow individuals to invest 2 percent of their payroll tax contributions in individual accounts in an exchange for reduction by a similar amount of their Social Security benefits. Another proposal would allow employees to invest 4 percent of their payroll tax contributions with a reduction in benefits. Still another proposal would allow a reduction in payroll taxes, provided that the employees invested an additional amount in their private retirement accounts. These proposals were nonstarters in a declining stock market and a volatile political climate. Nevertheless, Alan Greenspan, chairman of the Federal Reserve Board, asserted that budget deficits could lead to Social Security cuts. Greenspan also suggested cutting back Medicare benefits. Rather than cutting back on Medicare, President Bush signed legislation that expanded it by providing prescription drug benefits.

Housing Market and Millionaires

Home ownership reached a record 69.2 percent in 2003. Critics worried that a real estate bubble might be developing, but Alan Greenspan discounted that possibility. The inflated housing market and rising stock prices did increase the total net worth of United States households to $44.41 trillion at the end of 2003. This was a record. American households owned more than $14 trillion in real estate assets. New housing construction in December 2003 was the highest since 1978.

Sales of existing homes set a record in 2003, exceeding $6.1 billion. The earlier record had been $5.57 billion, set in 2002. Over 7 million homes were sold in 2003, including 1.09 million new homes, which was an all-time record. Home prices were increasing at a rate of 7.4 percent annually. One thing spurring home sales was the fact that 40 million Americans were moving each year. Reverse mortgages were becoming popular in the new century. These mortgages allowed individuals to take out a loan on their house that was secured by the increased equity from the run-up in residential prices. Reverse mortgages were particularly popular for elderly people who needed large amounts of cash to pay for health care and other expenses.

The number of millionaires in America declined in 2003. A millionaire was defined as someone with more than $1 million in investable assets, which excluded the person's home. A Federal Reserve Board study found that the number of homes valued at over $1 million was increasing in the United States, but those mansions still accounted for only 0.6 percent of the housing market. California contained forty-one percent of the over $1 million homes. New York had 7.1 percent and Florida 5.8 percent. The heaviest concentration of over $1 million homes was in Cambridge, Massachusetts, with 11.6 percent, and San Francisco with 7 percent. The Fed study found that one in seventy-two white homeowners had a million-dollar house, while only one out of 762 minority homeowners owned such a home. Thirty-one percent of those owning a house valued at more than $1 million paid for their houses in cash, and many were planning renovations.

The Nasdaq index was up 50 percent for 2003. That index closed the year at 2006.48. It had not reached that level for almost two years. The Standard & Poor's 500 Index increased by 26.4 percent to 1111.92 during 2003. The Dow rose 25.3 percent in 2003 to close year-end at 10453.92. The Russell 2000 Index increased by 45.4 percent, reaching 556.91. The price of gold went over $414 an ounce at the end of December. This was the first time in eight years that price had been reached.

Without Enron to create a competitive market, natural gas prices began a precipitous rise in 2003 and were at record levels. The CFTC investigated to determine if those prices were being manipulated by some unknown and mysterious source, but could find no culprit. Instead, the agency concluded that natural market forces had caused the price spike. Cattle futures prices dropped after a mad cow was discovered in the United States in December 2003. It turned out that the cow had been brought in from Canada before quarantine restrictions had been imposed after an outbreak of mad cow disease in Alberta. The CFTC investigated to determine whether cattle futures traders had received advance word from government officials that the cow had tested positive for mad cow disease.

Financial Services

Some 700,000 brokers were selling securities at about 5,500 brokerage firms in the United States in 2003. About 30 percent of investors with $5 million in investable assets were using full-service brokers. That number had been 41 percent in 2001. About 15 percent of investors were using investment advisers. That number was 8 percent in 2001. Seventeen percent of investors were using financial planners in 2003. A survey found that 22 percent of individuals with investments worth more than $5 million did not use any investment adviser or broker for advice. Former SEC chairman Arthur Levitt claimed that investors with less than $50,000 did not need a stockbroker to guide their savings because mutual funds were available. That recommendation overlooked a very basic problem. Most investors did not know what mutual fund to select, often basing decisions on past returns that were random events.

Merrill Lynch faced problems in its business operations after the bursting of the stock market bubble. That firm cut the number of its brokers by 37 percent. The firm closed 150 of its 750 offices and its operations in Japan and Canada. E. Stanley O'Neal, who was placed in charge of that restructuring, laid off 23,000 employees and fired nineteen senior executives. Two of O'Neal's supporters, Thomas H. Patrick and Arshad Zakaria, were dismissed after they clashed with him over the reorganization. As a reward for his efforts, O'Neal was appointed Merrill Lynch's chairman and chief executive officer in December 2002, replacing David H. Komansky. O'Neal, the grandson of a slave, was one of the first African-Americans to achieve such a high position on Wall Street. Black Americans had been largely excluded from Wall Street until the 1960s, and even then, they were hired only sparingly. In 1964, June Middleton, a stockbroker at Hornblower & Weeks & Hemphill, was believed to be the only black woman employed at a NYSE firm. Merrill Lynch hired its first black stockbrokers in 1965. Goldman Sachs named its first black partner in 1986.

Stanley O'Neal proved to be a tough manager. He restructured the firm's operations, employing call centers, rather than individual brokers, in order to cut costs. This seemed to be borrowing from the playbook of Charles Schwab, the discount broker. It also seemed to work. In February 2004, Merrill Lynch announced that it was seeking to hire additional brokers, but the National Association of Securities Dealers (NASD) later began an investigation into complaints that the call centers were mistreating customers. The firm reported a $4 billion profit for 2003 and began buying back as much as $2 billion of its own common stock. Merrill Lynch then had a market value of $54.4 billion with almost 950 million shares outstanding. Merrill's earnings for the fourth quarter rose 10 percent, to $1.08 billion. As a result of this success, O'Neal saw his pay double to $28 million. David Komansky, O'Neal's predecessor, had been paid $32.5 million, but O'Neal's pay was still among the highest on Wall Street. Besting him was James Cayne at Bear Stearns Co., who was paid $27 million in 2003 plus stock valued at $12.3 million.

O'Neal's efforts were not a complete success. Merrill Lynch was losing out to the banks in underwritings and merger advisory activities that had been traditional Merrill strongholds. Merrill's stock was down 20 percent at one point in 2004, but the company posted record earnings for the year, and announced a $4 billion buyback of its own stock. Merrill Lynch was having some success in defending lawsuits and arbitrations brought as a result of its analyst scandal that led to the large settlement with the SEC and Spitzer. A district court also dismissed a complaint that charged that Merrill Lynch had failed to meet its duties as a directed trustee of the WoldCom Inc. 401(k) plan. It continued to have regulatory problems, receiving a fine of $250,000 from the NASD for failing to produce documents in arbitration cases. Citigroup and Morgan Stanley were each fined the same amount for such failures. In a separate action, Morgan Stanley was fined $2 million for failing to report promptly customer complaints to regulators. Fidelity Brokerage Services LLC was fined $2 million by the SEC and NYSE for destroying and altering documents to cover up the fact that required records had not been kept. A New York appeals court set aside a $27 million arbitration award against Waddell & Reed Financial Inc. in a case in which a financial adviser had charged that the firm smeared his reputation in order to keep his customers when a dispute arose and he left the firm.

Wall Street profits were estimated to be $15 billion for 2003, a 100 percent increase from 2002. Wall Street traders were back to their big spending ways, chartering jets and indulging in other extravagances as their bonuses grew with the uptick in the stock market. Edward Jones, a St. Louis based brokerage firm, was having difficulty selling stock to clients. Douglas Hill, the company's managing partner was forced to resign after the firm's mutual fund practices came under attack from regulators. He paid $3 million to settle those charges and the brokerage firm paid another $72 million. Research analysts were not coming up with any winners and prior picks had dropped, causing unrest among the sales force, as well as customers.

Charles Schwab, the founder of the discount brokerage firm named after himself, was number fifty-one on *Forbes*'s list of the richest Americans. His wealth was estimated at $3.2 billion in 2003, but his firm was struggling. The company dropped its "fund of funds" program allowing investment in mutual funds that were made up of other mutual fund shares. Unlike Bernard Cornfeld's Fund of Funds that imploded in the 1960s, this fund of funds failed to attract much interest. Conditions at Schwab continued to decline in 2004, and Charles Schwab was recalled to his post as chief executive officer, replacing David Pottruck. Charles Schwab Corp. reduced the number of its offices to 286, down from 400 at the height of the market bubble. The firm laid off 245 employees and sold its research operations to UBS, the large Swiss bank. That sale returned Schwab to its origins as a discount broker that did not provide investment advice.

Information services on Wall Street were having mixed results. Bloomberg LP, the firm created by New York's mayor before he entered politics, had 171,350 subscriptions for its screens as 2003 began. It had revenue of $2.75 billion. Reuters was running into difficulty in its financial data services. The 152-year-old company was said to be undergoing a "crisis," reporting its first yearly net loss since it went public in 1984. The loss was expected to be almost $500 million. Instinet, which was majority owned by Reuters, was also hurt by declining trading volumes in Nasdaq stocks. Reuters planned to cut 1,000 jobs and to take a $234 million restructuring charge, and it sold Instinet to Nasdaq for $1.9 billion. Some good news arrived. Reuters and JPMorgan Chase agreed that Reuters customers would be given access to the JP Morgan electronic trading platform. Reuters also announced that it was creating an online currency options trading platform.

Time Warner closed its CNNfn financial news cable network, as the fad in financial news diminished after the market downturn. The *Wall Street Journal* revamped its layout in 2002, the biggest visual change to that paper in sixty years. The *Journal*'s revenue was dropping, however, falling 34 percent during the market downturn. *USA Today* was the nation's leading distributor of newspapers, the *Wall Street Journal* was second, and the *New York Times* third in circulation. The London *Financial Times* was hit with a $418 million judgment in England for libeling a brokerage firm, Collins Stewart Tullett PLC.

Financing Resumes

General Motors made a $4 billion convertible bond offering in June 2003. Its GMAC unit tried to sell its commercial mortgage business to Deutsche Bank for $1 billion. The General Motors offering was topped by a $5.6 billion issue by a German bank in July 2003 that was convertible into shares of another company. Deutsche Telekom issued $2.3 billion in euros in mandatory convertible bonds. These instruments expired after three years and holders were required to convert the bonds into the common shares of Deutsche Telekom. This was an effort to boost the company's credit ratings. The mandatory conversion feature meant that the company would not have to repay the principal borrowed in cash. Rather, it could simply issue more of its common stock. "Pfandbriefs" were being issued in Germany. These were highly rated instruments given preferential treatment in bankruptcy. Only certain mortgage banks and issuers were allowed to sell these instruments. The market in German

Pfandbriefs approached $1 trillion, and efforts were made to sell these instruments in the United States.

The IPO market revived in 2003. Ten IPOs were conducted in October, the busiest month in more than a year. Those IPOs raised $1.26 billion. IPO offering prices rose 33 percent in 2003 over those in the prior year. Orbitz LLC was among the companies planning to go public in 2003. Merger activity was picking up, and Goldman Sachs was leading Wall Street in merger advisory activities. The size of the acquisitions it advised was nearly twice that of the second-place finisher, Morgan Stanley. Citigroup was third; Merrill Lynch was seventh, just ahead of J.P. Morgan, but behind Bank of America and Credit Suisse First Boston.

Ford announced that it was eliminating 12,000 jobs in September 2003. Standard & Poor's cut its credit rating on Ford Motor Company's $180 billion of debt to the lowest level considered investment grade in November. Ford was able to have a shareholder lawsuit dismissed that was complaining that the company had lost $953 million in trading palladium contracts. Ford was anticipating a price rise in palladium that is used for emission controls, but prices actually fell by more than 50 percent. Chrysler was planning to eliminate thousands of positions. Philips announced a $287 million restructuring charge for its consumer electronics operations. The printing company R.R. Donnelley & Sons agreed to acquire Moore Wallace, one of the world's largest printers of business forms and labels, for a price of $2.8 billion. Berkshire Hathaway had a market value of $118 billion in November 2003. It was holding $24 billion in cash because Warren Buffett did not see sufficient opportunities in the marketplace. Nevertheless, he made some large acquisitions, including Clayton Homes for $1.7 billion and McClane Co., a food distributor, for $1.5 billion. Buffett also took an interest in HCA, a hospital chain.

R.J. Reynolds Tobacco Holdings (RJR) reported a $3.45 billion loss in the third quarter of 2003. RJR and Brown & Williamson thereafter announced they were merging. BAT Industries PLC would be the largest shareholder in this firm. RJR agreed to buy the American cigarette operations of British American Tobacco for $2.6 billion in October 2003. Altria Group was the former Phillip Morris companies. It was the victim of a $12 billion judgment in a tobacco suit. The company was required to post a bond in that amount in order to appeal the verdict but had difficulty raising the money. Some thirty states then passed statutes limiting the amount required to be posted on bond for appeals, fearing that such large bonds could bankrupt the tobacco companies that had become cash cows for the states as a result of the tobacco litigation settlements. The tobacco companies paid the states $6.2 billion in 2004 as part of their $246 billion settlement with the states that was to be paid over a twenty-five-year period. The states securitized about $20 billion of that settlement through bond sales, suggesting that Enron was not the only entity that enjoyed the use of structured financing. The federal government went to the well one too many times. An appeals court threw out a $280 billion claim lodged against the tobacco companies by the attorney general. The Supreme Court refused to review that decision.

The Illinois Supreme Court gave some hope for relief from punitive jury awards by setting aside a $1 billion verdict against the State Farm Insurance Company for its use of allegedly lower quality generic auto parts in repairing automobiles of insured clients. That decision threatened the award imposed against the Altria Group for its cigarette business because both decisions were based on similar reasoning in granting class action status.

Banking

Credit Cards

Check payments accounted for 85 percent of all noncash payments in 1979, but the number of checks written in the United States decreased by 37 percent between 1997 and 2002. Credit and debit card transactions were exceeding payments by checks and cash. President Bush sought to make check clearing more expeditious by approving legislation called Check 21. That statute allows banks to transfer facsimiles of checks electronically, rather than actually moving the physical documents for clearing purposes. This was designed to cut the time for clearing of checks from days to hours. The banks had been hiring fleets of airplanes to fly checks to the clearinghouses; the new legislation would save that expense. The faster payment system also meant that customers would have less time to cover checks they had written without sufficient funds in their account, which was expected to increase bounced check fees for banks.

The number of households with payment cards increased from 16 percent in 1973 to 73 percent in 2003. Payments on those cards nearly tripled over the prior ten years to $2.2 trillion, constituting 20 percent of GDP. First USA bank was the nation's largest issuer of Visa credit cards in 2003. Citigroup bought the credit card and financial products business of Sears Roebuck for $3 billion. Citigroup abandoned Visa in favor of MasterCharge and began "slamming" its Visa customers into converting to MasterCharge. MBNA Corp. agreed to stop similar practices of switching customers into American Express cards. American Express was allowing other financial institutions to issue its cards in order to compete with Visa and MasterCharge. The largest seller of smart cards in terms of revenues was Schlumberger, with annual sales of $700 million.

The Department of Justice sought to block the acquisition of Concord ESS Inc. by First Data Corp., which also owned Western Union. This would have been a $7 billion acquisition and would join two of the largest debit card networks. In its lawsuit, the Department of Justice stated that customers purchased more than $150 billion in goods and services through those networks. A settlement totaling $3 billion was reached in litigation brought against Visa

USA Inc. and MasterCard International Inc. for charging differing fees for debit card and credit card transactions. Of that amount, $220 million went to the lawyers, but they had requested twice that amount. The disparity in fees was ostensibly on security grounds. Actually, the banks did not like debit cards because the money for the charge was immediately removed from the bank and there were no lucrative financing charges, as when a balance is carried on a credit card. That litigation was filed by large retail firms including Sears Roebuck & Co. and Wal-Mart Stores Inc.

Visa had an operating loss of $1.4 billion at the end of its fiscal year, September 30, 2003, but more trouble lay ahead. The competition authorities at the European Commission charged that Visa was improperly excluding competitors from its network. A California court also held that Visa and MasterCard should refund $800 million in fees charged on currency exchanges for transactions conducted abroad that were not properly disclosed.

The market share of the American Express credit card dropped from 32.7 percent in 1970 to 19.8 percent in 2002. American Express sued Visa and MasterCard and several banks that prohibited the issuance of credit cards through American Express. The American Express Black Card, which was issued by invitation only, carried with it a $1,000 annual fee, which was increased to $2,500 in 2002. Qualifications for receiving the credit card were uncertain but it was thought that its holders were expected to charge at least $150,000 a year. Individuals holding American Express cards since the 1960s also qualified. The company dropped its green American Express Card, which was a classic in the credit card industry. Starting out with a cardboard card, American Express had switched to the green plastic card in 1959. American Express announced it was selling its financial advisory unit as it retreated from its plan to become a financial supermarket. Regulators in New Hampshire then charged that the advisory unit was providing special incentives to the sales force for selling proprietary mutual funds that were often performing poorly. Included among the prizes for selling in-house funds was a one-year lease on a Mercedes-Benz.

Banking Consolidation

Banking services in the United States were increasingly concentrated among a few banks. The ten largest banks in the country held 17 percent of bank assets in 1990, increasing to 44 percent in 2003. There was concern that this consolidation would cause a danger to the economy in the event that one of these banks failed. The government in the past had, sometimes, adopted a "too big to fail" policy, as in the case of the Continental Bank in Chicago, rescuing big banks while letting smaller ones fail.

HSBC Bank bought Household International, a consumer finance company, for $16.15 billion. BB&T, a large North Carolina bank, snagged First Virginia Bank for $3.3 billion in February 2003. Bank of America acquired

FleetBoston for $43 billion on October 27, 2003. This created the second-largest bank in the United States. After that merger, Bank of America controlled 9.8 percent of the nation's bank deposits, had assets totaling $966 billion, and operated 5,700 branches nationwide. The bank began eliminating 12,500 jobs after the merger. It was forced to make over $400 million in loans to the poor as an extortion payment required by the state of Massachusetts as a condition for approval of the merger. At the federal level, the Community Reinvestment Act (CRA) was used by community groups to extort payments from banks engaging in mergers; those groups would agree not to oppose the merger once payment was made. Senator Phil Gramm included a provision in bank legislation in 1999 that was designed to stop such "CRA extortion" by requiring reports to be filed that disclosed such payments.

BNP Paribas, one of the larger European banks, found itself in trouble over its role in the massive oil-for-food scandal in Iraq that was sponsored by the United Nations. Over $20 billion was looted from that program by Saddam Hussein and various other individuals. That scandal gave every evidence of exceeding the corporate scandals of the Enron era. Marc Rich, the fugitive oil trader pardoned by President Bill Clinton, was said to be involved in the scandal, as was Kojo Annan, the son of the United Nations (UN) Secretary General Kofi Annan. Copying the corporate scandals in America, Paul Volcker, the former chairman of the Federal Reserve Board and unsuccessful rescuer of Arthur Andersen, was hired to conduct an internal investigation of the scandal for the UN. That investigation was then used by the UN as the basis for refusing requests for information on the scandal from the U.S. Congress. The Volcker investigation borrowed a page from the American corporate scandal book of yesteryear. It exonerated Kofi Annan, the head of the UN, and was generally a white wash of UN officials, leading to the resignation of two investigators working on the investigation. The Department of Justice was more aggressive, indicting David Bay Chalmers Jr., a Houston oil trader, and his company Bayoil U.S.A., which had been assisted in purchasing the oil from Iraq by the Enron Reserve Acquisition Corp. Also indicted was Tongsuon Park, the South Korean lobbyist who was a key player in the "Koreagate" scandal in the 1970s. Park had bribed several members of Congress in that earlier scandal with envelopes stuffed with cash. Park's Georgetown Club, as well as his parties and a $32,000 stereo system had become instantly famous as that scandal unfolded, but criminal charges against him arising from that event were later dropped. Park had been trained and mentored by Thomas Corcoran ("Tommy the Cork"), one of the principal authors of the federal securities laws who was himself a controversial lobbyist. Several other companies and individuals were later indicted in the oil-for-food scandal, including Oscar Wyatt Jr., an eighty-one year old Texas oilman. Wyatt was caught discussing bribes he paid for Iraqi oil on Enron era tapes made by oil traders at the El Paso Corp. Paul Volcker let the UN off lightly but found that over half of the 250 or so companies purchasing oil under the oil-for-food program paid kickbacks to obtain allocations. Those companies making such payments included Siemens, Volvo, and DaimlerChrysler. Even worse, some 2,250 companies paid kickback to the Hussein regime to obtain the "humanitarian" contacts in Iraq that were the basis for allowing the oil sales. Not wanting to be left out of any more financial scandals, the SEC began investigating Tyco International Ltd., El Paso Corp., and others to determine whether their participation in the oil-for-food program violated full disclosure requirements.

Foreign banks were growing. Banco Santander Central Hispano SA, a Spanish financial institution, offered $14.6 billion for Abbey National PLC in England. Credit Agricole SA in France acquired Credit Lyonnais SA, Europe's third-largest bank, in December 2002 for $20 billion. Credit Lyonnais had been the center of several financial scandals. Other European giant banks included Barclays Bank PLC in Great Britain, ABN Amro Holding NV in the Netherlands, and Deutsche Bank AG in Germany. Deutsche Bank announced that it was taking an $800 million write-off as 2005 began and cautioned that further losses could be expected. HSBC announced on October 28, 2003 that it was buying the Bank of Bermuda for $1.3 billion.

A merger was sought between Mitsubishi Toyko Financial Group and UFJ in Tokyo in 2004 that would create the largest bank in the world, with assets of $1.746 trillion. A competing bid was made by Sumitomo Mitsui, which was partially owned by Goldman Sachs. This was Japan's first takeover fight involving a bank. Mitsubishi Tokyo Financial Group ultimately prevailed with a bid of $29 billion. Thereafter, the Japanese government allowed Daiwas Securities Group to merge with Sumitomo-Mitsui as a form of consolation prize. UFJ lost $6.5 billion in the first half of 2004 while Mitsubishi Toyko Financial Group's earnings dropped by 43 percent. The Royal Bank of Canada bought Centura Bank, based in Rocky Mount, North Carolina. The Toronto-Dominion Bank bought Waterhouse Securities Inc. (renamed TD Waterhouse), a discount broker.

Another large merger occurred when Wachovia bought SouthTrust Corp. for $14.3 billion. Wallace D. Malone Jr., the chief executive officer for SouthTrust, was given a $59 million severance package plus a pension of $3.8 million. Bank One Corporation, a large Midwest bank and credit card distributor, was on the hunt. It purchased the U.S. life insurance operations of Zurich Financial Services in May 2003 for $500 million. This made Bank One the second-largest bank insurance underwriter, Citigroup being the leader. Bank One was headed by Jamie Dimon, formerly Sandy Weill's protégé at Citigroup. Dimon left for Bank One after a series of disputes with Weill, including a fight over the employment of Weill's daughter at the bank.

Bank One agreed to sell its trust operations to JPMorgan Chase for $720 million in July 2003. Banking consolidation had reduced the number of trust service managers from 4,000 to 3,000 over the prior ten years. Subsequently, on January 14, 2004, Dimon announced that Bank One would be merging with JPMorgan Chase, a $58 billion merger. He would succeed to control of the combined operation in 2006, after JPMorgan Chase's head, William B. Harrison, stepped down. Harrison had been in charge of JPMorgan Chase during its dealings with Enron and other failures. This merger was one of a continuum. JPMorgan Chase was an amalgamation of the Chemical Bank, which had merged with Manufacturers Hanover Corp. in 1991, then with Chase Manhattan Corp. in 1996 and JP Morgan in 2000. The bank also acquired Robert Fleming, the Beacon Group, and Hambrecht & Quist.

The merger with Bank One resulted in the layoff of 10,000 employees. The combined operations of JPMorgan Chase and Bank One made the new institution the second-largest bank in the United States, with more than $1 trillion in assets, behind Citigroup but ahead of Bank of America. The upswing of the economy helped make the merger successful. JPMorgan Chase announced a profit of $1.86 billion for the last quarter of 2003, and other banks, including the Bank of New York, also reported large increases in earnings. JPMorgan Chase later spun off its private investment operation, JP Morgan Partners LLC, because of conflict on interest concerns with other clients.

The merger of Bank One and JPMorgan Chase struck a blow to Chicago as a banking center. Bank One was one of the largest banks in that city. Previously, the Continental Bank in Chicago had been acquired by Bank of America Corp., after Continental suffered numerous regulatory and business problems. One of the banks remaining in Chicago was the Northern Trust Corp., with $41 billion in assets, compared with Bank One's $290 billion. The Harris Bank in Chicago was owned by the Bank of Montreal. Another Chicago bank still existent was LaSalle Bancorp., but it was a subsidiary of ABN Amro Holding NV, a Netherlands company.

Regions Financial Corp. and Union Planters Corp. announced a $6 billion merger on January 23, 2004. This would make that combined operation the nation's fourteenth-largest bank holding company based on deposits. The new entity was to be called Regions Financial Corp. Sovereign Bank acquired Seacoast Financial, a Massachusetts bank holding company, for $1.1 billion. The National City Bank offered $2 billion to buy the Provident Bank. Both banks were in Ohio. North Fork agreed to buy Greenpoint, and SunTrust Banks acquired National Commerce Financial Corp. in a transaction valued at $7 billion, making SunTrust the seventh-largest bank in the United States. Fifth Third Bank acquired First National Bankshares in Florida for $1.57 billion.

The banks were using their ability to make commercial loans to attract investment banking business. Citigroup Inc., JPMorgan Chase & Co., and Bank of America Corp. had a combined total of 22 percent of equity underwritings in 2003. This was an increase from 12 percent in 2000. This market share was being taken from Goldman Sachs Group, Morgan Stanley, Merrill Lynch & Co., and other traditional investment bankers. The percentage of equity underwritings by those firms dropped from 37 percent in 2000 to 30 percent in 2003.

The banks were the subject of competition from automobile companies, including General Motors, BMW AG, Volkswagen, and Toyota. Those companies were offering savings accounts, certificate of deposits, money market accounts, and even online banking. Nordstrom Inc. had its own federal savings bank. Wal-Mart had been blocked by regulators from acquiring a bank because of concerns that it would outcompete the commercial banks. Wal-Mart was, nonetheless, offering banking services in one hundred stores through a partnership with a U.S. subsidiary of Toronto-Dominion Bank. Wal-Mart also planned to offer check cashing, wire transfers, and money order services that could be provided without owning a bank.

Banking Problems

The Office of the Comptroller of the Currency and other bank regulators proposed regulations that would require banks to identify transactions that have heightened reputational and legal risks and to scrutinize those transactions more closely. The SEC and bank regulatory authorities assembled a task force in 2004 to consider structured finance products sold by banks that were being used to manipulate financial results. The goal of the task force was to develop rules that would make the banks responsible for such abuses by their clients, eliminating the claims made by banks that they were not responsible for their clients' accounting treatment of those transactions.

A jury determined that the Bank of America had misapplied Social Security deposits to pay for bank fees. A jury decided to give each affected depositor $1,000, which would total up to $1 billion. The Riggs Bank was having difficulty with its foreign diplomatic business, long a mainstay of the bank. Riggs was fined $25 million for failing to file suspicious financial activity reports required by regulators to prevent and detect money laundering and terrorist activities. Additional concerns of money laundering were raised with respect to the transfers totaling $800 million, including some suspicious transfers from officials in Equatorial Guinea, where oil production was providing opportunities for graft. Riggs also allowed General Augusto Pinochet, the controversial former Chilean dictator, to conceal his identity on accounts holding more than $4 million. Riggs was acquired by the PNC Financial Services Group in July 2004, which had itself been the subject of some embarrassing financial restatements. PNC used Riggs' subsequent guilty plea to a criminal charge for failing to file suspicious activity reports as leverage to reduce the offering price. Riggs then sued asking that PNC be required to complete the merger, but the matter was quickly settled with a $134 million drop in the offering price. Riggs agreed to pay $16 million to settle the Department of Justice charges and paid another $8 million to Spain for failing to freeze Pinochet's assets as ordered by a Spanish court. Riggs paid a further $3.8 million to settle shareholder lawsuits over these issues. A Senate report later found that Pinochet and his family had over 125 accounts in the United States at eight banks including Citigroup, Bank of America, and the Espirito Bank in Miami.

AmSouth, a Florida bank, was fined $50 million for failing to file a suspicious activity report with bank regulators that would have disclosed a Ponzi scheme that fleeced elderly investors of $10 million. That scheme was carried out by Louis Hamric and Victor Nance through Mutual of New York (MONY). The bank was given a deferred prosecution deal from the Department of Justice and was forced to incur an additional $6 to $9 million in compliance costs annually. Critics claimed that the Department of Justice was trying to hijack bank regulation and criminalize even modest regulatory violations. Banco Popular, a Puerto Rican bank, was fined $21.6 million for failing to file suspicious activity reports and money laundering failures under a deferred prosecution deal with the Department of Justice.

ABN Amro Holding NV severed relations with almost one hundred correspondent banks in Russia and Eastern Europe because of money laundering concerns by bank regulators in the United States and Europe. UBS AG, the largest bank in Europe, was fined $100 million by the Federal Reserve Board for allowing funds to be sent to Cuba, Libya, Iran, and Yugoslavia, which were subject to sanctions by the United States and for which money transfers were prohibited. The Arab Bank PLC was ordered by the Office of the Comptroller of the Currency to close its operations in the United States as the result of money laundering activities by Palestinian charities linked to terrorists. Bank of America was under investigation for transferring funds tied to the drug trade in Uruguay. JPMorgan Chase was at the center of a probe into millions of dollars transferred by a small ice cream shop in Brooklyn to Al Qaeda supporters in Yemen. The Bank of New York was negotiating a fine of over $20 million with regulators for failing to file suspicious activity reports. Several banks entered into agreements with federal regulators to improve their anti-money laundering efforts. Those banks included Deutsche Bank, Standard Chartered PLC, and UnionBanCal Corp.

Money

The number of U.S. households banking online grew from about 500,000 in 1998 to over 20 million in 2003. Some $160 billion in mortgages were obtained through the Internet in 2001. Many people were paying their bills on the Internet; 60 million people used the Internet to prepare their tax returns; and 8.5 million persons filed their returns electronically in 2002. Software was available for consumers to compute their taxes, manage their money, and plan their retirement. Brokerage firms were particularly eager to provide investment planning assistance through Internet software programs. Merrill Lynch entered into a partnership with HSBC Holdings PLC to offer Internet banking, but that joint venture attracted few investors. The unit had about 100,000 accounts and net assets of only about $109 million when it was discontinued in 2002. Merrill Lynch and HSBC had contributed $1 billion each to this venture. Credit unions were becoming more active in online banking, finding that they were able to compete with banks in this service area.

Despite the growth of electronic payments, coins and bills were still in use. The release of commemorative quarters for all the states had proved popular initially with coin collectors and the public in general, but interest waned as the number of these coins increased. Of all coins minted, more than two-thirds were pennies. By the beginning of this century, the United States Mint had produced since its inception almost 289 billion pennies, which if lined up edge to edge would circle the globe over 130 times. Some coins were worth more than others. An 1895 Morgan dollar sold for $145,000. The Treasury Department issued a new nickel in 2004. This was the first change to that coin in sixty-six years. The coin showed the Louisiana Purchase on the back; Thomas Jefferson remained on the front. Another nickel was minted to commemorate the Lewis and Clark expedition. The Treasury planned to put 180 million of these new nickels into circulation. The mint was making 900 million for eventual future use.

The Department of the Treasury was considering the elimination of the use of paper for the U.S. savings bond, making it a book entry security. A redesigned twenty-dollar bill was printed in 2003. This was the first redesign for notes since the 1920s. The bill had background colors of green, peach, and blue, the first use of color beyond green in American currency. The fifty- and one-hundred-dollar bills were redesigned for issuance in 2004 and 2005. The use of digital scanners and color printers was making it easier to counterfeit money. Police in Colombia confiscated $200 million in counterfeit U.S. currency in 2000 and an additional $41 million in December 2001. The newly designed U.S. currency used several tricks to frustrate counterfeiters, including a plastic security thread that would show up under ultraviolet light. One proposal for stopping counterfeiting was to integrate radio frequency identification tags that could be added to currency to authenticate bills. The European Central Bank was seeking to use such tags to authenticate euro notes by 2005.

The Year 2004

The Recovery Strengthens

The Nasdaq index reached a thirty-month high on January 12, 2004, closing at 2111.78. The Dow closed at 10485.18 on that day and jumped to 10702.51 on January 26. The S&P 500 Index reached 1139.09 in February 2004. This was up 2.4 percent for the year. The dollar continued to fall against the euro. On January 13, it reached a new low of $1.2782. The trade deficit for the United States grew to a record $43.06 billion in January 2004, and total federal debt pushed past $7 trillion in February. The Dow hit a two-and-a-half-year high on February 11, reaching 10737.70 before backing off. The Nasdaq index dropped thirty points on February 23, 2004. This brought it to levels that it had been trading as the year began. The Nasdaq average dropped below 2000 on March 9, 2004.

The number of IPOs increased in 2004. There were twenty-two such offerings through February 15, 2004. This was double the amount in the first six months of 2003. B&G Foods Holding Corp. conducted an offering of $565 million of an equity-debt security called an enhanced income security (EIS). Each EIS entitled the holder to one share of the common stock of the company and a portion of a debt security. This would give the holder two streams of income, which would include a quarterly dividend from the common share and a quarterly interest payment from the debt interest. The instrument was designed to minimize tax effects, with the dividend being taxed to the recipient at 15 percent. The interest payment could be deducted by the company. A similar instrument called an income deposit security (IDS) was developed by the Canadian Imperial Bank of Commerce, which had been barred from engaging in structured finance in the United States for three years as a result of its Enron involvement. Offerings of those instruments were made by Volume Services American Holdings Inc. and American Seafood Corp. Collectively, those two companies sought to raise $700 million from such instruments.

The U.S. economy continued to strengthen in the first half of 2004. The unemployment rate was 5.6 percent in March. Some 1.4 million jobs had been recovered in the prior year while inflation-adjusted retail sales grew by 3 percent. Real GDP increased at a 6.1 percent annual rate in the first two quarters of 2004, which was the fastest in twenty years. Manufacturing activity was at its highest level in twenty years in the first quarter of 2004. Non-farm productivity grew by 5.4 percent in the prior year, which was the fastest growth rate in twenty-three years. Overall productivity was a more anemic 2.9 percent, but interest rates remained at a forty-five-year low. The prime rate was at 4 percent, the discount rate was 2 percent, and call money was 2.75 percent. Short-term London Interbank Offer Rates were 1.1 percent. Treasury bills were selling at a discount rate of 0.95 percent for twenty-six weeks. The overnight repo rate was 0.97 percent. On March 10, 2004, the average rate for a thirty-year fixed rate mortgage was 5.4 percent.

Alan Greenspan expressed the view that the risk of deflation from a declining economy had lessened, a problem encountered during the Great Depression and a worry while the recession was under way in 2001. The Fed had received criticism that its concern with deflation had been overwrought. Greenspan opposed tax increases as a means to cut the deficit and claimed victory over the economy, asserting that the reduced interest rates had aided recovery. Greenspan did not take credit for causing the recession through the increases that had crippled the stock market. Not long after Greenspan declared deflation was not a danger, concerns were raised that inflation might be appearing, requiring an interest rate rise if that were the case. Several financial firms began offering bonds with returns based on inflation rates, copying the TIPS issued by the Treasury Department.

Daily volume in the foreign currency market reached $1.9 trillion in 2004. A district court held that Federal Reserve Board officials were immune from liability under the Securities Exchange Act of 1934. The complaint in that case alleged that those officials had manipulated the price of gold through the Bank of International Settlements.

Market Activities

Exxon Mobil Corp. was the world's largest company by sales volume and had annual revenues that exceeded the GDP of all but twenty of the 220 countries in the world. Large multinational corporations formed fifty-three of the 100 largest economies in the world in 2004. Troubling was the fact that the number of U.S. companies among the Fortune 500 largest companies based on market capitalization dropped from 240 to 227. There were other concerns. Mirant Corp., an electricity generator, announced a $1.57 billion loss that eliminated all shareholder equity before it declared bankruptcy.

A high-profile takeover battle was being waged between Vodaphone and Cingular, both of which sought to buy AT&T Wireless. The two companies initially bid $38 billion. The fight concluded on February 17, 2004, with victory by Cingular after it agreed to pay $41 billion for AT&T Wireless. AT&T Corp. was struggling; its credit rating was lowered to junk status by one rating agency after failed investments amounting to $100 billion in cable and wireless by its former chief executive officer C. Michael Armstrong. The company began laying off 7,000 employees in October 2004, bringing the total for the year to 12,000 and 60,000 less than were employed in 2000. AT&T also wrote off $11.3 billion in assets.

The Dow fell to 10128.23 on March 11, 2004, after terrorist bombings in Spain killed almost 200 people. The Dow changed the makeup of its index on April 1, 2004. Added were American International Group Inc., Pfizer, and Verizon Communications Inc. Dropped from the index were AT&T Corp., Eastman Kodak Co., and International Paper Co. The average life of a company in the S&P 500 Index was approaching ten years. Only seventy-four of the companies listed in that index in 1957 remained there when the century ended. Six large companies, including Hewlett-Packard and Schwab, agreed to dually list their shares on the NYSE and Nasdaq.

The Russell 2000 stock index, which is composed of small cap stocks, reached a record high on April 5, 2004. The Dow rallied strongly to exceed 10500, and the S&P 500 Index was near a two-year high. A spike in oil prices, however, pushed gasoline prices above $2.00 per gallon and was accompanied by a market downturn in which the Dow dropped below 10000. The Dow bounced back and was trading at 10242 on June 4, 2004. The Dow then proceeded to drift in a range between 10300 and 10450. Oil prices remained a concern, reaching a twenty-one-year high of $48.70 a barrel on August 19, 2004, and trading through $50 a barrel in September.

Politics and the Economy

Although it had recovered from the Enron era scandals, the economy played a large role in the 2004 presidential campaign. The jobless rate had fallen to a two-year low by January 2004, but President George W. Bush was coming under sharp criticism from the eventual Democratic candidate for president, Senator John Kerry. The senator claimed that the economy under the Bush administration was worse than that under President Herbert Hoover during the Great Depression because 3 million jobs had been lost while Bush was in office, more than those under Hoover's administration. Of course, 3 million jobs in the 1930s were in no way comparable to the same number in the 2004 economy. The population of the United States had increased vastly in the interim as had the total number of jobs as the economy expanded. Two income families, now common, were virtually unheard of in the 1930s. The Democrat's claims also omitted the fact that the employment rate was 5.6 percent in 2004 versus almost 25 percent during the Great Depression. Senator Kerry was seeking higher taxes on the wealthy even though his multimillionaire wife Teresa Heinz Kerry, was using every available tax loophole to keep her tax rate below 12.5 percent.

Howard Dean, the former governor of Vermont and at one point the leading Democratic contender for the presidency, used the Internet to raise $50 million in political contributions, mostly from small donors in amounts of less than $100. Dean's campaign rhetoric included claims that the administration of President George W. Bush is "of the corporations, by the corporations, for the corporations."

Some dinosaur financiers were advocating some seemingly strange positions given their backgrounds. Felix Rohatyn, a renowned investment banker who had saved New York City from a financial crisis in the 1970s, claimed on the editorial pages of the *Wall Street Journal* that increased regulation of American markets was necessary. Jon Corzine, the former chairman of Goldman Sachs, won a Democratic Senate seat in New Jersey and became a leading left-wing speaker for the Democratic Party, asserting antibusiness positions.

George Soros and Peter Lewis, another billionaire, supported efforts to unseat President Bush in the 2004 elections through a flaw in the recently passed McCain-Feingold Act which sought to curb undue influence by wealthy contributors. Soros, a multibillionaire hedge fund manager, undermined that goal by exploiting a loophole that allowed "political organizations" exempted from tax by section 527 of the Internal Revenue Code to spend unlimited funds to oppose a candidate. Soros formed a 527 political organization called Moveon.org. He contributed millions of dollars to that organization to create nasty attack advertisements smearing Bush. That effort backfired when another 527 political organization, SwiftVets.com, attacked Kerry's Vietnam war record, which he had made a centerpiece of his presidential campaign.

The swift boat veterans had served with Kerry on small boat patrols in Vietnam. They were funded with only a few hundred thousand dollars, but drew blood in their attacks. The Kerry campaign cried foul even though it had welcomed Soros's support for many months before it felt the sting of the swift boat veterans. Soros continued his anti-Bush campaign with a book and a two-page advertisement in the *Wall Street Journal*. Soros and his candidate lost the presidential election, and a French appeals court upheld Soros's insider trading conviction a few months later.

Retail sales increased in March of 2004 and job growth was at a four-year high. Government figures indicated that 308,000 jobs were added to the economy in that month and more in April and May. Outsourcing of jobs to foreign countries where pay scales were low was another concern of the Democrats. Call centers were being moved to India, and many companies were examining cheaper production in countries from Asia to Central America. Democrats blamed this trend on the Bush administration, claiming that he was giving away jobs. Republicans asserted that outsourcing was beneficial by reducing costs and making America more competitive.

Wealth

The recovery of the stock market and growth in the American economy were generating more wealth. The number of millionaires was up by 14 percent in 2004. By then, one in every 125 Americans was a millionaire. The number of millionaires and their growth in the United States and Canada was outstripping the combined numbers of millionaires in Europe, Asia, the Middle East, and Latin America. A comparative study by a Swedish think tank found that average GDP per capita in the United States was 32 percent higher than the average for the European Union, allowing the average American to spend $9,700 more per year on consumption than the average European. The category of low-income families, those with incomes of less than $25,000, was 25 percent of households in the United States, as compared to 40 percent in Sweden.[3] A study by the European Union in 2004 concluded that it would not achieve its goal of surpassing the United States as the world's most competitive economy by 2010.

Women in America were making inroads into business. The number of businesses in which women held at least a 50 percent stake increased from 5 percent in 1977 to nearly half in 2004. The *Wall Street Journal* showcased a list of fifty women holding senior positions in corporations around the world. However, concerns with discrimination persisted in the securities business. Statistics showed that men constituted two-thirds of all executives in that industry. Morgan Stanley agreed to pay $54 million in July 2004 to settle claims that it had discriminated against its women employees. A nationwide class action against Smith Barney was settled with an agreement by that firm to spend $15 million on diversity programs. That action claimed gender discrimination, sexual harassment, and retaliation. Smith Barney was hit with renewed claims of sex discrimination in 2005. UBS was the recipient of a $29 million verdict by a New York jury for sex discrimination claims by Laura Zubulake, one of its executives. The verdict included $20 million in punitive damage claims. Merrill Lynch was also the subject of discrimination charges by women employees that received widespread press coverage in the United States. An English court dismissed a sexual bias case against Merrill Lynch, but found that the plaintiff had been treated unfairly. Merrill Lynch did win an arbitration case in which the plaintiff claimed that her broker did not describe her account value in a way that a person with dyslexia could understand.

Big Business

General Motors (GM) was the defendant in a class action lawsuit that charged that its dealer lending practices discriminated against minorities in setting auto loan rates. This financing was conducted through the General Motors Acceptance Corporation (GMAC). GMAC had allowed dealers to increase their quoted interest rates without telling buyers and keep the difference. Nissan settled similar charges. GM could not be too upset with GMAC since it generated 70 percent of GM's profits. H&R Block, a tax preparation service, was subjected to protests for the fees and interest that it was charging on tax refund loans. In some instances, the fees for these loans were as much as 150 percent on an annualized basis. H&R Block was also restating its financial statements for 2003 and 2004.

Bank of America was hedging its exposure from mortgage defaults through structured bonds called real-estate synthetic investment securities, which provided a rate of return based on the risk of default. Trading in the debt and equity of the scandal-marred companies from the bubble era was popular in 2004. Those issues included Enron, HealthSouth, WorldCom, and Adelphia Communications Corp. The convertible bonds of Adelphia had increased 25 percent and its equity stock was up 52 percent.

Enron shares were a popular novelty item even though they were valueless. Enron had been crippled by its overoptimistic predictions of broadband usage, but its predictions were proving true, albeit belatedly. Broadband was used by more than 50 percent of online users in 2004. General Electric Co. (GE) acquired Ionics, a water company, for $1.1 billion in November 2004. GE thought water was a growth business worth some $360 billion. That growth came too late for Enron, which had anticipated that market development by several years. GE also increased its dividend by 10 percent and announced plans to buy back $15 billion of its own stock.

Harrahs acquired Caesars Entertainment for $5.2 billion. Wallace Barr, the chief executive officer of Caesars, was to receive over $20 million as a result of that transfer of control, drawing protests. Oracle encountered stiff opposition when it tried to acquire PeopleSoft, both of which were software companies. PeopleSoft had been known for spending $2 million a year to provide free bagels for its staff. PeopleSoft's revenues increased from $113 million in 1995 to $1.4 billion in 1999. Oracle made an offer for PeopleSoft in June 2003 and continued to bid for the company late in 2004, increasing its offer from $16 a share to $24. The Department of Justice tried to block the merger on antitrust grounds, and Oracle dropped the price of its bid for PeopleSoft, decreasing it to $21 a share or a total of $7.7 billion as the antitrust trial was about to begin. The judge hearing the case dismissed the Department of Justice's claims. PeopleSoft then fired its chief executive officer, Craig Conway, and the board rejected the Oracle bid despite its approval by 61 percent of the PeopleSoft shareholders. The merger was approved in December 2004 after the offer was sweetened. The combined company then announced a 9 percent reduction in its workforce totaling 5,000 jobs, the same number of jobs that had been lost at Enron.

Quarterly Results

GDP grew at an annual rate of 2.8 percent in the second quarter of 2004. Corporate profits were down on an overall basis in the second quarter, but results were mixed. J.P. Morgan Chase posted a $548 million loss in the second quarter of 2004 as a result of a $2.3 billion charge it took for its Enron and WorldCom liabilities. The company then dropped the periods in its name, becoming JPMorgan Chase. Citigroup saw its profits fall by 73 percent in the second quarter, after taking a charge of $4.95 billion for litigation expenses from its many Enron and other bubble era problems. Washington Mutual Inc. experienced difficulties, closing its fifty-three commercial banking offices and laying off 33,400 employees, but still operating 1,800 retail branches.

Pharmaceutical companies were having mixed results. Pfizer and Roche had a good second quarter, while Merck, Glaxo, and Schering-Plough had disappointing results. General Motors had a near 50 percent increase in income. Conoco Corp. had a 75 percent jump in its earnings. Time Warner experienced a 27 percent reduction in income as compared to the second quarter of the prior year. Corning was surviving on the strength of its popular liquid crystal display (LCD) screens, but continued to suffer large losses from its fiber-optics operations and asbestos claims. Halliburton agreed to pay $4.2 billion to settle its asbestos litigation. After his reelection, President George W. Bush sought legislation to limit such claims, which were appearing in ever-increasing numbers.

Cisco had a 41 percent increase in income, and Walt Disney's net jumped by 20 percent in the second quarter. Tyco reported a 63 percent increase in its income for the quarter, after reducing its debt by 10 percent. Qualcomm had a strong showing, as did Verizon Communications, Vodafone Group, and Ericsson. Sprint and Nextel had a good quarter and later sought to merge. Lucent could claim four straight profitable quarters, but Qwest had a disastrous quarter.

Cablevision Systems Corp. lost $187 million and Charter Communications lost $416 million. Charter's chief executive officer Carl Vogel resigned after losses continued in later quarters. Microsoft reported an 81 percent increase in net income in the second quarter, but still disappointed analysts. The company planned to spend $30 billion to buy back a portion of its stock. McDonald's earnings increased by 25 percent. Amazon.com declared a profitable second quarter. Boston Scientific earned $313 million for the quarter, and American Express recorded a record $876 million in income, but laid off 2,000 employees in December 2004. U.S. Steel reported a $211 million profit.

Exxon Mobil had record income of $5.79 billion. BP, Chevron-Texaco, Tysons Foods, and Xerox all doubled their earnings from the previous year and beat analysts' expectations. Xerox received a credit upgrade and raised $500 million through a bond offering. JP Morgan Securities Inc. and Citigroup Global Markets Inc. placed that debt through senior unsecured bonds maturing in seven years. Despite its ethics problems with the government, Boeing experienced a $607 million profit. Northrop had a 51 percent increase in earnings as defense work soared. Goodyear had a profitable quarter, its first in almost two years. Even Eastman Kodak had a good quarter, despite a continuing decline in film sales.

More Growth

Investors were purchasing record amounts of foreign securities in 2003 and 2004. Sales of existing housing set an all-time record and new home starts were the second highest in history in June 2004, the record having been set in the previous month. Consumer spending fell in June, but bounced back in July, and consumer confidence reached a two-year high in July. The Federal Reserve Board reported solid economic growth; GDP was rising at a rate of 3 percent. As a consequence, Alan Greenspan began raising interest rates with a 0.25 percent increase in short-term rates on Fed funds from 1 percent to 1.25 percent on June 30, 2004. That rate hike destabilized the market once again. The Dow dropped to 10163.16 on July 16, 2004, its lowest close since May. The Dow fell below 10000 on July 23, 2004, dropping to 9962.22. The Nasdaq average was at 1849.09 on that date, the lowest point since October of the prior year. The markets sprang back a bit later in July with the Dow going back through 10000 before falling below that mark in August. A bad jobs number in July pushed the Dow down to 9815 on August 6.

The terrorist threat remained. On Sunday, August 1, 2004, Tom Ridge, secretary of the Department of Homeland Security, elevated the terrorist threat level, citing strong intelligence that terrorists were planning an attack on several financial institutions, including Citigroup headquarters in New York, the NYSE, and the Prudential building in Newark, as well as the International Monetary Fund in Washington, DC. American finance remained as a key symbol of America's dominance in the world.

Google Inc., the Internet search engine, went public in August 2004 after much fanfare. Google had announced in April 2004 that it was planning a $2.7 billion IPO through a Dutch auction in order to assure small investors a better opportunity of participating. That IPO turned into a farce when actually attempted later in the year. The company's Dutch auction was unpopular with institutional investors and investment bankers, causing the size of the offering to be cut back drastically at a price substantially lower than predicted. The SEC and the Department of Justice had long sought a competitive auction process for securities underwritings. Seeking to require competitive bidding for shares, the Department of Justice had charged several leading underwriters with monopoly practices in the 1950s. Federal district court judge Harold Medina threw that case out of court, and it was clear from the Google offering that traditional underwriting methods remained dominant even into the new century. Nevertheless, Google's stock soared, reaching $126.86—nearly 50 percent more than its offering price—on September 28, 2004. That was only the beginning. Google's stock price went over $400 in 2005. The company issued another $4 billion in stock in September 2005, but this time used a traditional fixed price underwriting, abandoning the auction process. Although the company agreed to give $265 million to charity from the offering, the explosion in Google's stock price pushed Google's two cofounders well up onto the list of billionaires in America. They promptly sought a new excess in corporate perks through a lavishly outfitted Boeing 767 passenger jet. Notwithstanding Google's problems, Morningstar, the politically correct mutual fund rating service, announced in 2005 that it was planning to auction its IPO as a way of ensuring access to its shares by small investors. The offering was successful, except that it too was under priced, rising some 55 percent over the next two months.

Google was under investigation for some options and stock transactions that were conducted without registration at the SEC. Google and its general counsel were charged by the SEC with failing to register $80 million of stock options under the federal securities laws. That complaint was settled without significant sanctions. The company's founders had also given an interview to *Playboy* that raised concerns of possible violations of the "quiet period" before its IPO, under the Securities Act of 1933, but the SEC later proposed a loosening of that restriction. Google's corporate governance structure was also criticized. Institutional Shareholders Services ranked Google lower than any company in the S&P 500 Index for its corporate governance structure. Among other things, Google had two classes of stock, one of which had weighted voting rights and was controlled by insiders. Google was not expensing options granted to employees and executives, and insiders were given reset options that allowed them to lower the exercise price of their options, if the company's stock dropped in value.

Although there was little threat of inflation, Alan Greenspan raised interest rates by another 0.25 percent on August 10, 2004, pushing the Fed rate to 1.5

percent. That action was accompanied by a triple-digit jump in the Dow, but that market move was only temporary, and the Dow resumed its drifting. The economy appeared to be cooling in the third quarter, after the Federal Reserve Board's two interest rate increases in quick succession. The Dow was at 10181.74 on August 26, 2004. The housing market was slowing as existing home sales fell in July by 6.4 percent from the prior month and the median price of homes did not increase. The unemployment rate dropped to 5.4 percent in August and 144,000 jobs were added. Stating that the economy "appears to have regained some traction," the Federal Reserve Board raised rates again by one quarter of a point on September 21, 2004. The Dow closed on that day at 10244.93 but slid to 10109.18 on the following day. Oil closed at $49.90 a barrel on September 28 as a result of hurricane in Florida, turmoil in Russia, and production concerns in Nigeria. Conoco Corp. then announced a $2.36 billion investment in Lukoil, a Russian oil company.

The third quarter in 2004 saw resurgence in the economy. Construction reached a record high in August and manufacturing activity was strong. The interest rate on fifteen-year mortgages was around 5 percent. Consumer spending was rising and productivity was at 4.6 percent. Household wealth was up 11 percent over the year. After-tax profits were almost 20 percent. Capital investment by businesses had increased by 14 percent over the year, while increased spending for machine tools was up 54 percent. Inflation was low, but oil hit new highs for five straight days in October, going through $54 a barrel.

The Dow closed at 10192.65 on October 1, 2004. Although 96,000 jobs were created in September, Democrats claimed it was not enough. The unemployment rate remained at 5.4 percent. Congress passed a corporate tax bill in October that removed an export subsidy tax declared to be in violation of GATT standards by the World Trade Organization, but the bill added some $100 billion in other corporate tax relief. Banks were competing for funds by offering customers gifts that ranged from flat-screen televisions to automobiles. Community Bancorp. in New York offered a Cadillac to purchasers of a certificate of deposit in the amount of $400,000, but paying only 1 percent interest for a five-year term. Comparable instruments, sans Cadillac, were paying 3.51 percent, the difference being greater than a lease payment on such a vehicle, proving, once again, that there is no free lunch on Wall Street.

October proved volatile in the markets. The Dow hit an eleven-month low on October 25, but then rallied by 250 points over the next two trading days, reaching 10002.03. Oil prices closed at $55.15 per barrel, a record, but dropped to $50.13 on November 2. Natural gas prices were soaring, and gold closed at $429 per ounce on that day. Third-quarter results were disappointing, with a 2.4 percent drop in corporate profits from the prior quarter, but almost two-thirds of the companies included in the S&P 500 Index met or exceeded analysts' earnings estimates. United Airlines and US Airways were still in serious trouble with large losses. American Airlines had a large loss, and Delta was facing bankruptcy. JetBlue had a sharp drop in earnings. Computer Associates had a $96 million loss as a result of its accounting problems. Lucent had a profit, but BellSouth had a drop in earnings. Exxon Mobil's earnings increased by 56 percent. Royal Dutch/Shell Group had similar results as oil prices soared. DaimlerChrysler AG had profits of $1.21 billion, and eBay's income rose by 52 percent. Dynegy issued a profit warning in December 2004 and projected a large loss for 2005.

The market dropped sharply when exit polls on Election Day wrongly suggested that Senator John Kerry was leading in key states in the presidential election. The reelection of President George W. Bush resulted in a stock market rally, the Dow reaching 10391.31 on November 8, 2004. Oil prices dropped to $46.87 on November 15, but the dollar was dropping against the euro, the euro rising to $1.2987. Gold was up to $430.10 per ounce on November 4, 2004, a sixteen-year high. Job growth was strong. That good news was met by another interest raise by Alan Greenspan, the fourth such increase since June, pushing overnight discount rates at the Federal Reserve Banks to 2 percent. Greenspan later testified before Congress that federal budget deficits were "unsustainable" and he was perplexed by the failure of long-term interest rates to rise in tandem with short-term rates. The market continued to climb, reaching 10550.24 on November 15, 2004, a seven-month high. Consumer spending was on the increase, and the personal savings rate was a near-record low in December 2004. The savings rate in the United States fell from 8 percent in the 1980s to about 1 percent in 2004.

Exxon-Mobil reported a record-setting fourth quarter profit of $8.42 billion. Vivendi Universal reported its first quarterly profit in four years. AIG, the insurance company, had a 12 percent increase in net income despite its regulatory problems. That good news was followed by subpoenas from the SEC and Eliot Spitzer, which knocked down AIG's stock price and dragged down the Dow. Ahold Nv was recovering from its accounting scandals, posting a large fourth quarter profit. Ahold had been saved from bankruptcy by loans totaling $4 billion. Its U.S. Foodservice subsidiary in the United States, which had been the center of the scandal, continued to struggle and its future was in doubt. The stock of Parmalat SpA, the giant Italian food company that had also been the subject of a multibillion dollar scandal, resumed trading in its stock in October 2005, and it was then the target of a takeover effort. The company's founder, Callisto Tanzi, was still on trial in a Milan courtroom for his role in the fraud. At the same time, five executives at Fleming Co. Inc., the failed wholesale grocery distributor, were belatedly accused by the SEC of manipulating accounts at that business in 2001.

Personal income increased by a record 3.7 percent in December, boosted by Microsoft's $32 billion dividend. Although the trade deficit hit a new record in November, the economy was growing at a rate of 4 percent. Defaulted loans at national banks were at a six-year low, and manufacturing increased in December for the nineteenth straight month. Some 157,000 jobs were added in December, bringing the total job additions for the year to 2.2 million, which replaced many of the jobs lost after the market downturn. Industrial output increased for the first time in four years, raising concerns with inflation. The Dow jumped to 10676.45 and passed through 10800 on December 23, but the dollar fell to a new low of $1.3640 against the euro. Venture capital investments were up in 2004, the first increase in four years. The number of IPOs exceeded 250, an increase from eighty-five in 2003. Merger and acquisition activity in December 2004 was the highest ever for any one month and underwriting volume for the year was $5.7 trillion, also a new record. Mergers and acquisitions increased for the year by 50 percent over 2003, the largest annual increase since 1998.

Some giant mergers were in the works, including a $57 billion merger of Proctor & Gamble and Gillette that would result in a windfall to Gillette's chief executive officer, James Kilts, of over $150 million. That merger provided a large profit to Warren Buffett's Berkshire Hathaway, which held large amounts of Gillette stock. Berkshire Hathaway's earnings had fallen in 2004. That company was sitting on $40 billion in cash and Warren Buffett was lamenting the lack of opportunities in the market. The merger with Gillette met opposition from William Galvin, secretary of state for Massachusetts, who claimed that the price for Gillette was inadequate. This was a startling attempt to take over merger negotiations by a state functionary, and Procter & Gamble sued him claiming that such issues were preempted by the federal securities laws. Galvin continued his effort and opened a new front in the prosecutorial war against Wall Street by attacking the fairness opinions of Goldman Sachs and UBS, the investment bankers in the deal. Fairness opinions on the valuation of a company in a merger had long been criticized as saying whatever the party paying for the opinion asked.

The telecom industry was consolidating. AT&T was bought by SBC Communications for $16 billion, resulting in a loss of 13,000 jobs. MCI was the target of an offer from Qwest for $6.3 billion, but Verizon entered the fray, and its bid of $7.6 billion was accepted by MCI. That was substantially less than an increased Qwest bid and less than its market capitalization after MCI emerged from the bankruptcy court. The acceptance of that bid appeared to conflict with the auction requirements of Delaware law. The acceptance of the Verizon offer also presented some irony since Bernard Ebbers' rejection of Verizon's earlier bid had doomed WorldCom at a time when it was valued at around $180 billion, Qwest responded with another bid, pushing its bid up to $8.9 billion, which was about 19 percent higher than the bid accepted from Verizon. That too was rejected and Qwest responded with an even higher bid of $9.74 billion that MCI again refused after Verizon raised its offer. Qwest then quit the battlefield, but vowed to fight on by seeking to have antitrust authorities stop the deal. The Verizon offer accepted by MCI was still 13 percent less than Qwest's. That offer was accepted even though Verizon had argued before the bankruptcy court that MCI was the fruit of the WorldCom "criminal enterprise" that should have been liquidated to prevent competition with Verizon. Michael Capellas, the MCI chief executive officer, announced that he was leaving the company after the merger and was taking nearly $40 million with him.

Viacom announced a write-down in goodwill totaling $18 billion. Global Crossing posted a fourth quarter loss. Adelphia was in play. Time Warner Inc. and Comcast Corp. were competing with Kohlberg Kravis Roberts (KKR) and Providence Equity Partners over Adelphia with bids being submitted in the $17 billion range. William R. Huff, a manager of a junk bond hedge fund holding large amounts of Adelphia debt, was seeking a higher buyout figure. KKR and Bain Capital Partners were also purchasing Toys 'R' Us for $5.7 billion.

The Dow closed the year at 10783.01, up 3.1 percent for the year. The S&P 500 Index was up by 9 percent over the year, and the Nasdaq composite index was up 8.6 percent, closing at 2175.44. Despite regulatory problems in the mutual funds industry, diversified equity-based mutual funds had an average return of 12 percent for the year, beating the indexes. Bill Miller at Legg Mason out performed the S&P 500 Index for the fourteenth straight year.

President Bush was on the offensive. He appointed a blue ribbon panel to propose changes that would simplify the tax code. He also continued his push for reform of Social Security and of abusive tort litigation brought against businesses. The economy had apparently come full circle with Alan Greenspan's addition of still another one-quarter increase in interest rates on December 14, 2004. The Federal Reserve Board stated then that it would continue to raise rates at a "measured" rate. The ten-year Treasury note was then yielding 4.22 percent.

GDP increased by 4.4 percent during 2004, the highest rate of growth in five years, and productivity grew in the last quarter to 2.1 percent. Exports set a record in December, but the trade deficit for the year also set a record, reaching $666 billion. Employee Section 401(k) retirement accounts were up 10 percent on average in 2004. Household net worth was at a record $48.53 trillion. The number of millionaire households (excluding the value of their homes) increased in 2004, reaching a record 8.2 million but consumer debt was reaching $2.12 trillion, another record. Congress then tightened the bankruptcy laws to provide more protection to debtors from defaults. Senate Democrats failed to block passage with a "poison pill" amendment directed against antiabortion protestors.

Corporate profits increased by 13.5 percent in the fourth quarter of 2004 over those in the third quarter, the strongest growth rate since 1992. The bull market on Wall Street was twenty-seven months old in January 2005, but concerns were being raised that it would not last, and January was a weak month for the market. Alan Greenspan piled on with another interest rate increase on February 2, 2005, but IPOs in the first six weeks of 2005 reached a record $8.4 billion and housing starts reached a twenty-one-year high in January. This gave rise to a wave of newspaper articles claiming that another bubble was under way. Of particular concern were interest-only mortgages that did not require any principal payments on a monthly basis. New homes sold at a record pace in April 2005, and their median price hit $230,800. Alan Greenspan weighed with a statement that there was "froth" in the real estate market and that the boom was not sustainable. He stopped short of claiming a national market bubble, but did say there were several local bubbles.

WellPoint Inc. had a 12 percent drop in its fourth quarter earnings after its merger with Anthem Inc., but Cedant Corp. had a 24 percent increase in its earnings for the quarter. Cedant's chief executive officer, Henry Silverman was rewarded with $24 million in compensation. Smithfield Foods took out a full-page advertisement in the *Wall Street Journal* to point out that for an investor holding $100 in its stock on April 8, 1975, when Joseph W. Luter III became chief executive officer, that stake would have been worth $105,600 on Valentines Day in 2005. Terry Semel at Yahoo! Inc. received $120 million in compensation in 2004, mostly in options. Three executives at Viacom Inc., including Summer Redstone, each received over $50 million in compensation for 2004. Another winner was Ann Mulcahy, chairman and chief executive officer at Xerox, which was recovering from its accounting scandals. She saw her pay increase by over 50 percent in 2004, reaching $8.2 million. That extra incentive did not appear to do much good. Xerox had a disappointing second quarter in 2005 and announced the layoff of 2,600 employees. Michael Jefferies, chief executive officer at Abercrombie & Fitch Co., agreed to forgo a $12 million bonus after a shareholder lawsuit was filed challenging that award. He also agreed to forgo any option grants for two years.

Wall Street was celebrating with large pay packages to its chief executive officers. Stan O'Neal was paid $32 million. Henry Paulson Jr. at Goldman Sachs garnered $29.8 million, James Cayne at Bear Stearns received $24.7 million, and Richard Fuld at Lehman was on the receiving end of $26.3 million. Pay packets were down at Citigroup, but Sandy Weill and his top two lieutenants all took home more that $16 million. Kenneth Lewis received $19.3 million as chief executive officer and chairman of the Bank of America despite the fact that the bank had paid out more than $1 billion in settlements from scandals arising at the bank.

Morgan Stanley's chief executive officer, Philip Purcell, received $22 million despite criticism from former executives from the old Morgan Stanley side of the firm (who owned about 1 percent of Morgan Stanley stock) who were claiming that the company's stock was lagging because of poor management. As a sop to those criticizing Morgan Stanley's corporate governance, Purcell had the shareholders approve a provision eliminating its use of a staggered board of directors. That was not enough for eight former Morgan Stanley executives who wrote the board of directors urging Purcell's replacement. Purcell responded by appointing two of his lieutenants, Stephen Crawford and Zoe Cruz, as copresidents, causing two other senior managers from the old Morgan Stanley side of the business to resign. More defections followed including Joseph R. Perella, a high-profile investment banker. Purcell was tied closely to the retail side of Morgan Stanley that was intensively regulated by the SEC, but he was not exactly a politically correct member of the world of full disclosure. Purcell had been previously quoted as saying that the "career regulator is the scariest animal I've ever met in my life."

In order to stem criticism, Purcell announced that he would try and sell Morgan Stanley's Discover Credit card business, but that did not satisfy the old Morgan Stanley investment bankers. They recruited the New Jersey public pension funds to attack Purcell and Calpers then joined the attack, as did the American Federation of State, County, and Municipal Employees. Another group, the Council of Institutional Investors, expressed opposition to Purcell after control of that organization was taken over by labor representatives. Morgan Stanely was also facing a large judgment in the Florida courts in a suit brought by Ronald Perelman over its investment banking work for Sunbeam Corp. The trial court judge denied Morgan Stanley any defense because of its failure to produce e-mails in a timely fashion. That trial was thrown into further disarray after three jurors were mysteriously approached by a client of Perelman's lawyer. The jury eventually awarded Perelman a total of $1.45 billion in compensatory and punitive damages, and the judge added another $130 million for lost interest. That exceeded a verdict of $1.3 billion upheld by the Supreme Court against the Exxon Mobil Corp. for failing to pay promised discounts to gas stations.

Purcell subsequently announced his resignation and was replaced by John Mack who Purcell previously forced out of the firm. Mack was enticed on board with a $60 million compensation package for his first two years at the company. Purcell walked off with another $43.9 million plus an annual pension for life of $250,000. Morgan Stanley also agreed to contribute an additional $250,000 each year to charities of Purcell's choice. Purcell picked up another $40 million in selling about 20 percent of the Morgan Stanley shares and options he had acquired from the company. A protégé of Purcell's Stephen Crawford, had been in his job as copresident for less than four months, but he received a $32 million severance package as a going away present. This set off another round of criticism in the press and three labor union pension funds began an attack on the company's board. Mack then renounced his compensation package in favor of one that would be based on his performance. Plans to sell the Discover credit card operations were dropped even though Purcell's failure to sell that business had been one of the chief points of criticism against him. The change in management also did not stop the firm's regulatory problems. The SEC was threatening to fine Morgan Stanley $10 million for failing to retain e-mails relating to various SEC inquiries.

The securities industry was employing about 790,000 individuals servicing 93 million investors, producing revenues of $210 billion in the United States. Merrill Lynch, Morgan Stanley, and Piper Jaffray announced that they would no longer pay brokers' commissions generated from customer accounts holding less than $50,000. This eliminated any incentive to service those accounts. The NYSE warned the brokerage community against their use of "sweep" accounts that paid less than money market rates on cash held in customer accounts.

More Fraud

The year 2005 began with the trials of Bernard Ebbers, Dennis Kozlowski, and Richard Scrushy. The trials of Kenneth Lay and Jeffrey Skilling were postponed until January 2006, over five years after Enron's demise. The scandal at Marsh & McLennan was winding down to be replaced by the one at the American International Group Inc. Martha Stewart's emergence from prison in March 2005 set off a media storm of publicity that Stewart took advantage of through a number of celebrity appearances and promotions. Stewart quickly produced a new book, *The Martha Rules,* and she inked a new deal with Sirius Satellite Radio for a Martha Stewart channel. Stewart was soon dominating the airwaves with celebrity appearances and through her *Apprentice*-style program, which was receiving unfavorable reviews. KB Homes announced that it was having Stewart design homes that the company would build and sell in North Carolina. On one night Stewart was being favorably interviewed on *Larry King Live* while a made-for-TV movie about her trial and imprisonment was playing on another channel. The producers of that movie had carefully selected a most unattractive actress to play Stewart. Stewart also encountered some difficulties when she tried to travel to Canada. Authorities there denied her admittance because she was a convicted felon.

In contrast to the punishment inflicted on Stewart, two friends of Samuel Waksal agreed in November 2005 to pay $2.77 million to settle insider trading charges over their sales of the stock of Imclone Systems Inc. The government agreed to drop criminal charges. One of those individuals was Zvi Fuks, chairman of radiation oncology at Memorial Sloan-Kettering Hospital in New York. He had sold after Waksal tipped him on the Food & Drug Administration's action against the Imclone cancer drug, the same event that led to Stewart's incarceration.

Another celebrity emerging from jail, Steve Madden, was greeted by a widespread advertising campaign from his old company, Steve Madden Ltd., heralding his return from imprisonment for stock fraud. Thomas Coughlin, Wal-Mart vice chairman, was forced to resign after it was discovered that he had falsified his expense reports in amounts totaling more than $100,000. He was being paid more than $6 million annually at the time. Coughlin claimed that the expenses were to reimburse him for funds he spent on fighting union organizers. That revelation led to a grand jury investigation. Robert E. Brennan, the former penny stock king at First Jersey Securities Inc., was continuing a more than twenty-year battle with the SEC and federal prosecutors over his fraudulent activities that involved some 500,000 customers. He had been ordered to pay $75 million in disgorgement, but sought to conceal his assets by various fraudulent maneuvers. He was convicted of bankruptcy fraud, but a sentence for contempt of court was set aside by an appellate court in 2005.

Accounting problems continued. Office Depot Inc. restated its earnings for 2002 through 2004 because of improper treatment of its accounting for leases, a problem that was being experienced at other companies including Target Corp., May Department Stores, and Kohl Corp. ConAgra was restating its earnings because of accounting errors and Saks Inc., the high-end department store chain, was delaying its financial results because of improper "mark-down" allowances from vendors. Three senior executives were fired after an internal investigation of those problems. Best Buy and Circuit City separately delayed reporting their results because of accounting problems.

JPMorgan Chase & Co. was back in the news with the disclosure that it was conducting an internal investigation of Michael Weinberg, an executive in its real estate department and a close associate of the bank's president, Jamie Dimon. The inquiry focused on his relationship with J.T. Magen Co., a construction firm that did work on Weinberg's apartment as well as work for the bank. The construction company was also under investigation by the Manhattan district attorney for kickbacks allegedly made to a Citigroup executive, Thomas Moogan, who was subsequently indicted by the Manhattan district attorney's office. He must not have been cooperating because his wife was indicted as well for filing false tax returns.

Citigroup was under investigation by Eliot Spitzer for its predatory lending practices. It had earlier paid a $70 million fine and restitution to settle Federal Reserve Board charges over such conduct. The hapless Citigroup encountered more problems with its Smith Barney mutual funds, agreeing to pay the SEC $208 million for out sourcing its transfer services in exchange for investment banking business. In desperation, Citigroup hired Michael Schell, a partner in a prominent New York law firm, to become the vice chairman of its Global Banking division, and Lewis Kaden, a partner at another large New York firm, was hired to fill another vice chairman slot. It was appearing that businessmen were no longer capable of running financial services firms. This hiring was accompanied by Citigroup's $2 billion settlement in the Enron class action brought by the Board of Regents of the University of California. Citigroup had turned itself into an ATM machine for regulators and class action lawyers.

Citigroup threw in the towel for its asset management group, swapping those operations for the brokerage business of Legg Mason Inc. That swap effectively put an end to what was left of the once venerable Salomon Brothers. Sandy Weill tried to bail out of Citigroup, but the severance package he initially demanded was too much for his board. They were especially concerned with his demands for access to the corporate jet and other perks because of the bad publicity generated by the retirement packages of Richard Grasso at the NYSE and Philip Purcell at Morgan Stanley. The board was also reported as not being too happy with Weill's plans to compete against some Citigroup businesses. Charles Prince, Weill's ordained successor, was changing the Citigroup business plan from expanding the business to concentration on ethics and internal controls.

Full Disclosure Continues to Fail

Apparently, the consultants at Bearingpoint left their auditing skills behind when they left KPMG. Bearingpoint announced in April 2005 that its financial reports could not be relied on by investors and that it would not be publishing any financial results for the first nine months of 2005. Nine executives left the company, which was expected to be writing down some $400 million in goodwill carried as an asset on the company's books. PCAOB concluded that all of the Big Four accounting firms were conducting flawed audits and the smaller firm of BDO Seidman LLP received a similar report card. It seems there is no such thing as a good audit. The accounting firms were using their bargaining power, which was strengthened by the demise of Arthur Andersen LLP, to require audit clients to submit claims over audit failures to arbitration and to waive punitive damages.

The Interpublic Group of Companies was unable to issue its financial results. Interpublic, an advertising firm, later restated its financial statements by reducing revenues by over $500 million for the period from 1999 to 2004. Tommy Hilfiger Corp. was manipulating its financial accounts and announced a restatement for the years 2001 to 2004. Three executives at iGo Corp. were charged by the SEC with overstating that company's revenues by millions of dollars. Limited Brands Inc. took a $61 million charge to correct its prior accounting for leases. Taser International Inc., the maker of stun guns, announced that its accounting statements for 2004 should not be relied upon by investors.

Huntington Bancshares Inc. paid $7.5 million to settle SEC charges over the inflation of its earnings by almost $100 million between 1997 and 2003. Three officers agreed to return their bonuses, including the company's chief executive officer, Thomas Hoaglin. Kenneth Winger, the chief executive officer at Safety-Kleen Corp., and Paul R. Humphreys, the company's chief financial officer, were hit with a $200 million judgment in April 2005 for accounting manipulations at that company between 1997 and 1999 that inflated earnings by some $500 million. The Safety-Kleen outside directors paid another $36 million in settlement. The company's auditor, PricewaterhouseCoopers paid $48 million to settle charges for failing to detect those problems.

The Dollar General Corp. agreed to pay $11.5 million to settle SEC charges that it manipulated its accounts for the period 1998 through 2001. James E. Reid, a sales executive at Firepond Inc., was accused of fabricating sales contracts of more than $5 million in order to inflate company revenues in 2002 and to increase his commissions and salary. The SEC was considering changes to its rules that would increase the number of restatements even further, but did let MetLife Inc. off the hook for a $31 million accounting error in the second quarter of 2003.

Mehdi Gabayzadeh, the chief executive officer for American Tissue Inc., was convicted of securities fraud for a $300 million scheme that was designed to keep the company out of bankruptcy. A Delaware court cleared Oracle Corp.'s chief executive officer Larry Ellison and its chairman Jeffrey Henley of insider trading charges arising from shareholder claims that those two individuals sold Oracle stock in 2001 before an adverse earnings report. The plaintiffs' lawyer, Joseph Tabacco Jr., then vowed to pursue the claim in California where he thought the law might be more favorable. Larry Ellison then agreed to pay $100 million to the charity of his choice to settle that suit. The judge hearing the case in California balked at awarding the lawyers bringing the case $22.5 million in fees that would be paid by Oracle shareholders. The case making the same charges against Ellison had been dismissed in Delaware because the court there concluded that no rational judge or jury could find him guilty of the charges. In the midst of the California settlement, Ellison announced that Oracle was buying Siebel Systems for $5.85 billion. Ironically, a federal district court judge had just thrown out a high profile case brought by the SEC against Thomas Siebel, the head of Siebel Systems. Siebel had been charged with violating SEC Regulation FD, which prohibits the leaking of information by executives to analysts.

Nabil Hanna, the top scientist at Biogen Idec Inc., agreed to pay $375,000 to settle SEC charges that he traded on inside information about a cancer treatment that showed much promise. Marisa Bardis, an attorney for Smith Barney and later Morgan Stanley, was tipping Jeffrey Streich on confidential merger information. Streich passed that information onto Robert Breed who then tipped his mother, brother, and wife. They then traded on that information. Gary Taffet, a New Jersey politician, settled SEC charges that he had traded on inside information received from a law firm secretary who had tipped her husband Fiore Gallucci. He tipped Taffet and another friend. Shades of ImClone: the SEC charged that Richard B. Selden, the chief executive officer for Transkaryotic Therapies Inc., sold his holdings in the company's stock after learning that the Food and Drug Administration would not approve a drug that the company was touting.

The beat went on. Scandals in the "pink sheets," where illiquid stocks trade, were becoming widespread. Vincent Montagna, a hedge fund manager for Tiburon Asset Management, was arrested for overstating returns and for stealing client funds that he used for personal expenses, including a mink coat. The SEC charged Michael O'Grady with running a pump and dump scheme that left thousands of messages from "Debbie" with hot stock tips. O'Grady had been given $40,000 in cash delivered in a duffel bag from a Florida promoter to carry out this scheme. John S. Lipton and seven others were arrested for running a Ponzi scheme that defrauded over 1,000 investors of more than $80 million. Thomas Noe, a Republican official in Ohio, was under investigation after an exotic $13 million investment in rare coins by the state's workman's compensation fund went missing. Noe was also charged with violating federal campaign contribution limits by funneling payments to the

George W. Bush presidential campaign through other persons. Alberto Vilar, a well-known patron of the opera, was arrested for stealing $5 million that he used for his contributions to the opera, as well as for personal expenses. Roys Poyiadjsis, the co-chief executive officer of AremisSoft Corp., agreed to pay $200 million to settle SEC claims that he was inflating the company's revenues while selling millions of his own shares before the company went bankrupt. Gary Van Waeyenberghe was charged by the SEC with stealing $24 million from over 600 clients in connection with the sale of Enhanced Automobile Receivables (EARs) and Reality First Mortgages (RFMs).

The NASD entered into a $34 million settlement with fourteen brokerage firms for receiving undisclosed payments from mutual funds to give those funds "shelf space," which meant those funds would be given preference in recommendations. An internal investigation at MassMutual Financial Group, the eleventh largest insurance company in the United States, led to the firing of Robert J. O'Connell, the company's chairman and chief executive officer, for inflating his retirement benefits by millions of dollars and for protecting his son and a son-in-law from company disciplinary action. Other personal activities were questioned, and several other executives were terminated as well. O'Connell was ratted out by his wife who was angry over the fact that he was having an affair with a female executive at the company.

Bank of America paid $35 billion for MBNA Corp., the leading credit card distributor. Adidas, the athletic shoemaker, bought competitor Reebok for $3.8 billion. That sale would give Reebok's chief executive officer, Paul Fireman, a gain of over $800 million. Sonja Anticevic, a sixty-three-year-old woman from Croatia, and nine others with connections to her were charged by the SEC with making more than $4 million in illegal profits on inside information concerning that merger. The defendants purchased out-of-the-money call options to leverage their profits. In another case, Hubert A. Jeffreys pleaded guilty to charges that he had lied to investors concerning a possible merger between his skateboard company, Earthboard Sports USA Inc. and an unnamed "major" footwear company.

Senator Bill Frist, the Republican majority leader, made a fortuitous sale of stock in HCA Inc., a large hospital company founded by his family. The stock was supposed to be in a blind trust but Frist ordered his family's holdings to be sold shortly before a bad earnings announcement that caused a precipitous drop in the stock's price. Frist claimed that he sold the stock in order to avoid the appearance of a conflict of interest in proposing legislation that would affect hospitals. The *New York Times* editorial page demanded a government investigation. The U.S. attorney in Manhattan and the SEC quickly obliged.

Another Enron?

Refco Inc., a commodity brokerage, made an IPO in August 2005 that attracted over $580 million. Refco's stock was listed on the NYSE where it traded for two months before the company became embroiled in a scandal that was being compared to the one at Enron. Refco was originally named Ray E. Friedman & Co., after its founder who started it in 1969. The firm's name was shortened to just his initials (Refco) after it was taken over in the 1970s by his stepson, Thomas Dittmer. Dittmer, an aggressive speculator in cattle and other futures contracts, was known for handing out gold watches after making winning trades.

Refco achieved notoriety after Robert Bone, a broker in its Springdale, Arkansas office, provided Hillary Rodham Clinton with a short-term profit of $100,000 on a $1,000 investment in commodity futures in 1978 and 1979. That was her first venture into the commodity futures markets and that profit became the target of criticism during her husband's presidential campaign. Just after Clinton took her profit, Bone's other customers lost large sums in the futures markets when cattle prices declined. Bone was suspended from supervisory and sales positions by the Chicago Board of Trade and the Chicago Mercantile Exchange and he then became entangled in litigation with Refco. A jury found that Thomas Dittmer had used Bone and his Refco customers to run up cattle prices and that Dittmer then shorted the market, causing cattle prices to fall sharply. The decline in cattle prices ruined Bone's customers and caused hardship on cattle farmers who had to sell their livestock at reduced prices. That jury verdict was set aside by a federal appellate court because of insufficient evidence to sustain the manipulation charges, sparing Dittmer from paying a massive amount of damages. Nevertheless, Dittmer was suspended from trading by the Chicago Mercantile Exchange for six months as the result of regulatory problems at Refco.

In the years following those problems, Refco grew into one of the largest commodity futures merchants regulated by the CFTC. That growth was largely fueled by the acquisition of other faltering firms, and it developed a reputation as an aggressive firm in trading and dealing with customers. Refco expanded into over-the-counter derivatives as deregulation took hold. The firm experienced large losses in 1999 as a result of customer defaults, and Dittmer left the firm. He viewed Refco to have little value at the time, allegedly leading him to promise Edwin L. Cox 50 percent of the value of Refco if Cox would assist him in saving the company. Cox was a Texas businessman who had been convicted and imprisoned for bank fraud before being pardoned by President George H.W. Bush. Cox had invested with Dittmer at Refco investor, and Dittmer's alleged promise of 50 percent of the firm led to much litigation between Cox and Dittmer after Refco staged a recovery. Dittmer appears to have prevailed in that litigation.

Refco encountered several regulatory problems with the CFTC, settling one action brought by that agency by paying a civil penalty of $6 million. The CFTC also fined Refco $1.25 million for filing false reports on its net capital position, which was below the agency's early warning levels. The CFTC further charged that Refco's accounting system was inadequate. A Refco subsidiary was found to have allowed fictitious wash sales by a customer. In still another case, the CFTC concluded that Refco had failed to supervise its employees, allowing a fraudulent order allocation scheme to occur. Refco was also the subject of a number of private actions brought by disgruntled customers. Refco hired Dennis Klejna, the head of the CFTC Enforcement Division, to be its general counsel in order to deal with those kinds of problems, but the expansion of the firm's business led to other issues. Refco operated a broker-dealer that was regulated by the SEC. Santa Maggio, a president of that unit, was the target of an SEC investigation involving a short sale manipulation of the stock of Sedona Corp., a software firm that was destroyed in the process. Maggio agreed to settle planned SEC charges by accepting a suspension of one year from any supervisory role at Refco. That agreement was reached just before an even larger scandal occurred at the firm.

Tone Grant took over control of Refco when Dittmer retired in 1999 and rebuilt the company. Phillip Bennett succeeded Grant. Bennett, a boyish looking fifty-seven year old, was a British citizen who graduated from Cambridge University and was hired to work at Refco by Dittmer in 1981. In 2005, Bennett arranged the sale of a majority stake in Refco to Thomas H. Lee Partners, a hedge fund. Several large pension funds were investors in Thomas H. Lee Partners, including Calpers, which put up $200 million. Thomas H. Lee Partners had become famous for a large profit made on its purchase and resale of Snapple, the beverage company. In August 2005, shortly after the transaction with Thomas H. Lee Partners, Bennett arranged for Refco's IPO. Insiders at Refco, including Bennett and Tone Grant, were said to have pulled more than $1 billion from Refco as a result of its sale to Thomas H. Lee Partners and its subsequent IPO. Bennett retained a substantial stake in Refco after the IPO.

Scandal exploded on October 10, 2005 after Refco placed Bennett and Maggio on leave and announced that its SEC required financial statements could no longer be relied upon by investors. The NYSE immediately suspended trading in Refco's stock. The reason for Bennett's suspension was that a new employee discovered that Bennett had assumed $720 million of loans due Refco through a company he controlled. Those loans were the result of uncollectible receivables owed by former customers. Those customers were reported to include Victor Niederhoffer, a hedge fund manager who incurred large losses during a financial crisis in the Asian markets in 1997. Apparently, Bennett was using his company to take loans off Refco's books just before the end of each quarter and replacing them at the beginning of the succeeding quarter in order to conceal the fact that the loans were uncollectible. Bennett was assisted in that process by Liberty Corner Capital Strategy LLC, a New Jersey hedge fund. If those debts had been written off Refco's books as uncollectible, Refco would have been operating at a loss, which would have precluded its IPO.

After being confronted by the Refco board with his involvement in the $720 million loan, Bennett agreed to pay Refco the outstanding balance of $430 million in cash plus interest. He obtained that money from Bank fur

Arbeit und Wirtschaft P.S.K. (Bawag), a trade union bank in Austria that had previously invested in Refco. Bawag tried to stop the payment after the scandal broke, but that effort came too late. The U.S. attorney in Manhattan, in another fit of excess zeal, arrested Bennett thirty-six hours after Refco publicly disclosed the Bennett loan arrangement. The U.S. attorney claimed that haste was needed because wiretaps on Bennett's phone revealed that he was planning to flee to Europe. In fact, Bennett had booked a European wine tasting tour. Santa Maggio was not immediately indicted. He had found it in his interest to become a cooperating witness for the government against Bennett.

Refco was a highly leveraged firm, and Bennett's indictment caused a run that undercut the firm's viability. Refco was forced to shut down parts of its operations and declared bankruptcy, proving once again that an indictment of a financial firm, or in this case its chief executive officer, is a death sentence for the business. The Refco bankruptcy was the fourth largest on record, at least for a time because a subsequent filing by Refco reduced the size of its estate considerably. A Russian hedge fund, VR Global Partners, was Refco's largest creditor. It was owed $620 million. Commodity funds managed by James B. Rogers had $362 million on deposit with Refco. Rogers was co-founder of the Quantum Fund with George Soros, the billionaire hedge fund manager who had become a leading advocate for extreme left wing causes. Rogers was also a popular business talk show commentator who had written a book advocating commodity investments as a profitable alternative to stocks and other investments. Published before the Refco bankruptcy, the book noted that his funds were up 165 percent and included the best performing index fund in the world in any asset class. It was unclear what effect the Refco bankruptcy would have on that boast, but Rogers sued Refco claiming that the monies in his funds should have been held at the CFTC regulated arm of Refco where they would be immune from claims of other Refco creditors.

After declaring bankruptcy, Refco desperately sought to sell its remaining operations. A tentative deal was struck with J. Christopher Flowers to sell Refco's regulated commodity futures business for $768 million. Flowers had become famous as a turnaround artist for his successful rescue of the Long Term Credit Bank of Japan, which he renamed as the Shinsei Bank. Flowers's offer led to a bidding war for the regulated Refco business. Such competition in a bankruptcy fire sale suggested that there was value at Refco that had been destroyed for shareholders by the government's indictment. One brokerage firm saw another opportunity in the scandal. Interactive Brokers Group LLC placed full-page advertisements in the *New York Times* that solicited Refco customers to move their accounts to that firm. Interactive Brokers claimed that it obtained about $120 million in Refco customer accounts from that campaign, and it made a bid of $858 million in the bankruptcy proceeding for the remainder of Refco's CFTC regulated business. Other competing bidders showed up to bid for that business. The Man Group LLP won that auction.

Enron had become the gold standard for scandals and the one at Refco was almost immediately compared to it in the press. One widely reported Associated Press article twice likened the Refco scandal to the one at Enron Corp. The press was again focusing on the Commodity Futures Modernization Act of 2000 as a culprit. That legislation had deregulated a significant portion of Enron's and Refco's operations, allowing sophisticated investors to trade in a broad range of over-the-counter derivative transactions. However, critics could point to no unregulated activity that contributed to the Refco scandal. Instead, the loans in question clearly fell within the SEC's jurisdiction and were another full disclosure failure. Like Andrew Fastow's activities at Enron, the related party transactions involving Bennett were not disclosed properly on Refco's SEC filings. Despite Sarbanes-Oxley and the doubling of its budget, the SEC had failed to detect those loan arrangements or any other problem at Refco when it allowed the company to go public just a few months earlier.

The Public Company Accounting Oversight Board (PCAOB), which had been created by Sarbanes-Oxley as another layer of regulation to prevent such scandals, also had done nothing to assure that Refco's auditors would prevent or discover such activity. An editorial in the *Wall Street Journal* jokingly suggested that a new regulator should be created to oversee PCAOB. Still, one reporter suggested that the debacle was the result of a loophole in Sarbanes-Oxley that did not require certification of IPO financial statements by the chief executive officer as if that would have caused Bennett to structure the loans any differently.

Attacks were launched against the gatekeepers after the Refco failure. The rating agencies tried to avoid those attacks by immediately downgrading Refco to junk bond status. Refco's auditor, Grant Thornton LLP was not so nimble. It had noted in its audit of Refco that there were significant flaws in that company's financial reporting systems, but did not discover the arrangement with Bennett. That failure led to Grant Thornton being the target of multiple class action lawsuits that were filed almost immediately after Bennett's suspension. In a parallel to the criticism of Enron's law firm, Vinson & Elkins, the *Financial Times* weighed in with a front page report that breathlessly announced that the well respected law firm of Mayer, Brown, Rowe & Maw had prepared some of the documents used for the Bennett loan transaction. The law firm had also acted as counsel to Refco in its IPO. Goldman Sachs Group Inc. was being criticized for acting as an underwriter in the Refco IPO and acting as an adviser for the proposed sale of Refco assets in bankruptcy to J. Christopher Flowers, a former Goldman partner.

The usual cast of characters on the investor side was present for the Refco scandal. Among those investing directly in the Refco IPO were Calpers, TIAA-CREF, and the New York and Pennsylvania state employee retirement systems. Arthur Levitt, the former chairman of the SEC, was hired as an adviser by Refco after the scandal broke, but he quickly resigned when it became clear that he would have no role to play in the bankruptcy. Robert Morvillo,

Martha Stewart's attorney, was hired to represent Robert Trotsen, Refco's former chief financial officer. Trotsen had suddenly resigned in the months before the Refco IPO and was given a $54 million severance package.

Unlike Enron, Refco faded quickly from the front pages of the newspapers. It was an off year in the election cycle and, therefore, Congress had little interest. A money laundering charge for campaign contributions brought against House majority leader Tom DeLay by a local Texas prosecutor was also diverting their attention. Moreover, at least for the moment, the public seemed to have sated its appetite for financial scandals.

Fraud continued elsewhere. The SEC charged Humatech Inc., a fertilizer and animal feed business, with improperly booking sales to an affiliated distributor in England that were contingent on the products being sold by that distributor. The company's chief executive officer, David Williams, and its chief financial officer, John Rottweiler, were also charged. Six executives at Impath Inc., a bankrupt medical diagnostics firm, were indicted for creating $64 million in phony revenues for the company between 1999 and 2003. This allowed the company to report large profits while it was actually losing money. Four executives agreed to plead guilty. The two remaining defendants were Anuradha Saad, the company's chairman and chief executive officer, and Richard Adelson, president and chief operating officer. Navistar International Corp. was under investigation by the SEC after the company restated its earnings for the years 2002 to 2004.

The SEC charged Pension Fund of America LC and PFA Assurance Group Ltd. (PFA) in Coral Gables, Florida, with defrauding $127 million from over 3,400 investors through the sale of "retirement trust plans" that combined life insurance and investments in mutual funds purchased through U.S. banks and broker-dealers. This was a variation of the scheme carried out by Equity Funding in the 1970s. PFA had a network of over 500 sales agents deployed throughout Central and South America. PFA failed to disclose that up to 90 percent of funds invested were used to pay exorbitant commissions and fees. In another case, the FBI charged that an elaborate fraudulent medical insurance scheme had defrauded insurance companies of $1 billion and involved thousands of patients who had been sent to California for unnecessary operations and procedures.

Market Development

The Dow was showing some strength as the new year began, reaching 10940.55 on March 5, 2005 but this was still below its high of 11722.98 on January 14, 2000. The Nasdaq index was 2070.61 on March 5, still almost 60 percent below its high of 5048.62 that was reached on March 10, 2000, but well above its low on October 9, 2002, of 114.41. The Federal Reserve Board continued its rate increases, pushing federal fund rates to 2.75 percent on March 22. Some former stock stars were still lagging. Microsoft stock was down 50 percent from its peak and Cisco Systems was down 75 percent. General Motors announced large losses in March 2005, causing a dramatic drop in its share price and a cut in its credit rating to just above junk bond status.

Oil prices were setting new records, reaching over $58 per barrel in April. The Federal Reserve Board disclosed that it planned to push interest rates to much higher levels and did so on May 3, 2003, setting short-term rates at 3 percent. That threat, the continuing attack by Spitzer on large businesses, and disappointing first quarter results for IBM sent the market reeling. IBM had tried to obscure its earning shortfall by revealing just before the posting of its results that it was accelerating the date for the expensing of employee options. IBM then announced a stock buy back of $5 billion and took a charge of over $1.3 billion as part of a cost-cutting effort that would eliminate 10,000 jobs, mostly in Europe.

The Dow fell nearly 400 points during the week of April 15, closing at 10087.51. The Nasdaq average fell to 1908.15. Sears lost $9 million in the first quarter as a result of $90 million accounting adjustment. General Motors added more bad news with a loss of $1.1 billion in the first quarter of 2005, and the company subsequently announced that it was laying off 25,000 employees, five times the number of jobs lost at Enron. Both General Motors (GM) and Ford then had their debt rating reduced to junk bond status. Kirk Kerkorian, the octogenarian corporate raider, undaunted by his losses at Daimler Chrysler, sought to acquire some 5 percent of GM's stock. GM indefinitely suspended further stock sales by its executives, completing their transformation from entrepreneurs into bureaucrats. That did little good. GM had a $1.2 billion loss in its North American operations in the second quarter of 2005 and a $1.63 billion loss in the third quarter. The company was being throttled by its union. Those union members were among the highest paid workers in the country and were the beneficiaries of $5.6 billion in annual health care payments from the company. GM slashed those benefits in October 2005. A $1.07 billion loss at Delta Airlines further staggered the market, but the Dow rallied by over 200 points on April 22, 2005.

ImClone stock was up after it beat analysts' expectations even though revenue was down from the prior year. Nortel experienced a 75 percent drop in revenue in the first quarter of 2005. Gary Daichendt, its president and chief operating officer, resigned after less than three months on the job, but Nortel did manage to triple its profits in the second quarter of 2005. Tyco had a similar decline, as did Marsh & McLennan. Tyco was conducting an internal investigation to determine whether employees violated the Foreign Corrupt Practices Act. Edward Breen, who took over from Dennis Kozlowski at Tyco, received a $200 million compensation package after tripling the price of Tyco's stock, but Tyco stock dropped back 10 percent in August 2005 after a poor quarter. Kozlowski and Mark Swartz, his former chief financial officer, were finally sentenced in September for identical terms of a minimum of eight years and a maximum of twenty-five. They will be eligible for parole after a little more than six years. Kozlowski was ordered to pay $167 million in fines and restitution. Swartz was ordered to pay a total of $85 million. Swartz and Kozlowski were led away in handcuffs after their sentencing for assignment to a maximum security prison. MCI announced a sharp drop in revenue just after accepting Verizon's final bid for a merger. It also settled a $1 billion tax claim from the State of Mississippi for $100 million. Computer Associates was back in the news with a decline in earnings and the announcement of further accounting problems that might require a restatement.

The Senate was considering legislation that would require chief executive officers to certify their companies' tax returns as well as SEC financial reports. An SEC investigation found conflicts of interest on the part of pension plan consultants, which left no one in the financial services industry without a taint. The U.S. House of Representatives declared April as financial literacy month. Small investors were dropping their efforts to pick stocks. Only about 34 percent of equities were owned by individual investors. The rest were owned by institutions. Only six public companies in America were holding triple A debt ratings. The collateralized debt obligation market was booming, reaching $120 billion as 2005 began. Employee income was up in the first quarter of 2005 and the GDP was increasing at a rate of 3.5 percent. Nearly 275,000 jobs were added to the economy in April 2005, but consumer debt was continuing to rise, reaching $2.127 trillion in March.

Corporate jet demand was up by 30 percent in 2005 and their executives continued to make headlines. The *Wall Street Journal* even ran a front-page article identifying the worst abusers. Leading the pack was Barry Diller, the media mogul, who ran up a $832,000 bill on the company jet in 2004. The IRS responded with a ruling that made it harder for corporations to deduct the use of their aircraft when used for executive jaunts. No worries for Diller though. Vivendi Universal Entertainment announced that it was buying out his holdings in that company for $3.4 billion. This article must have hit a responsive chord because the *Wall Street Journal* followed it up a few months later with another front-page article on the same subject. Featured this time were executives using corporate aircraft to fly to Florida for golf outings at exclusive private resorts. Among the culprits were Raymond LeBoeuf, chief executive officer of PPG Industries, Nicholas Chabraja, chief executive officer at General Dynamics, Edward Zander, chief executive officer at Motorola, James Rohr, chief executive officer at PNC Financial, and Albert Lord, chairman of Sallie Mae.

Merger activity continued as the bidding war over MCI concluded and the NYSE and Nasdaq began acquiring ECNs. Valero Energy acquired Premcor, a refiner, for $8.7 billion. DoubleClick Inc. went for $1.1 billion and General Electric sold a self-storage business for $2.5 billion. Forstmann Little bought 24-Hour Fitness for $1.6 billion. Neiman Marcus was sold for $5 billion. E*Trade Financial offered to buy Ameritrade Holdings for $5.5 billion. An SEC administrative law judge ruled that the $6.6 billion merger of America

Electric Power Co. with Central & South West Corp. violated the Public Utility Holding Company Act of 1935, another dinosaur piece of New Deal legislation that would soon be history; it was repealed shortly afterward. Duke Energy Corp. bought Cinergy Corp. for $9.1 billion, and a Berkshire Hathaway unit bought PacifiCorp. for $5.1 billion and assumed $4.3 billion of the debt of that company. Internationally, Unicredito Italiano SpA was acquiring HVB Group in Germany for $20 billion, while Washington Mutual paid $6.45 billion for Providian Financial.

Wellpoint purchased WellChoice for $6.5 billion, making the combined firm a mega giant in health insurance. Lincoln National Corp. acquired Jefferson-Pilot Corp. for $7.5 billion, creating the fourth largest insurance company in the United States. The European Commission announced in September 2005 that it was conforming its antitrust review procedures for mergers to those of the United States. That action came too late to save the Honeywell and General Electric merger that had been approved by U.S. authorities several years earlier but was then blocked by the European Commission.

The market bounced back in the middle of May. The dollar was strengthening, the Euro was down, and the Bush administration took protective action against the import of Chinese textiles, thereby assuring a price increase for American consumers. A glitch on Nasdaq resulted in the mispricing of several shares, one was overpriced by almost $1,000. June 2005 witnessed good economic news and the economy seemed to be fully righted from the downturn in 2000, but oil prices were still volatile, exceeding $70 per barrel in August 2005 after hurricane Katrina, which was estimated to have caused $200 billion in damages. Gas prices at the pump were exceeding $3.00 per gallon. The oil companies reported record profits for the third quarter of 2005. Exxon Mobil Corp. alone reported a $9.9 billion profit for the quarter. This led to calls for price controls and "windfall" profit taxes, which had never worked in the past and had only exacerbated shortages. Even less familiar with the basics of Economics 101, Bill O'Reilly, the populist firebrand news commentator on the Fox cable news channel, did not want government price controls. Instead, he wanted to force the oil companies to cap their profits "voluntarily" in order to stop his nightly assaults on their management. Much of the increased demand for oil was being blamed on China. A Chinese oil company, CNOOC, supported that view with an $18.5 billion offer for Unocal, setting off a political storm over concern that the Chinese might be trying to take over America, the same concern that had been raised with Japan while its economy was booming in the 1980s. A competing offer was made by Chevron for $17.8 billion and CNOOC withdrew its offer.

The economy had grown by a strong 3.8 percent in the first quarter of 2005, but the poverty rate had risen to 12.7 percent and the top 20 percent of households were receiving 50.1 percent of all income. Alan Greenspan continued his interest rate increases at the Federal Reserve Board. The tenth increase came in August 2005, pushing short-term rates to 3.50 percent, up from 1 percent in the prior year. Greenspan was also continuing his warnings that Freddie Mac and Fannie Mae portfolios were so large as to prevent those entities from hedging all their risks. Fannie Mae aided his cause after government investigators discovered more accounting problems at that entity, including the overvaluation of assets and the use of finite insurance to cover up losses. Fannie Mae was expected to report that it was restating $11 billion in profits between 2001 and 2004.

Corporate earnings were generally high, but Kimberly-Clark Corp. had disappointing results, causing it to lay off 6,000 employees. The unemployment rate was down to 5 percent in June and fell to 4.9 percent in August. Nevertheless, the *New York Times* was still complaining of slow job growth, suggesting that Enron, WorldCom, and other companies involved in scandals were to blame. The Dow reached 10705.55 on July 29, 2005, still off its record high of 11722, and it retreated even more to 10397.29 on August 26. The S&P 500 and Nasdaq hit four-year highs in July.

Sales of existing homes set a record in June and that bubble continued to burgeon during the summer. In a replay of the stock market bubble of the 1990s, the *Economist* and other publications were warning that the bubble would be bursting and wreaking havoc. Alan Greenspan then warned that investors were unrealistically assuming that the economy was permanently less risky, setting the stage for continuing his assault on the real estate market with higher interest rates. Greenspan also noted that consumers were borrowing against their home equity to fuel an additional $600 billion in spending. The median sales price for a home was a pricy $220,000 in August 2005, but increased interest rates were having an effect on the market. The estimated dollar value of mortgages to be issued in 2005 was a paltry $2.78 trillion, down from $4 trillion in 2003.

Household net worth in the United States was approaching a record $50 trillion, but Delta and Northwest airlines filed for bankruptcy in September 2005, joining United and US Airways. U.S. auto sales fell by 14 percent in October and hurricanes Katrina and Rita were a disruption to the economy. Those problems did not deter Greenspan from raising rates on September 20, 2005 to 3.75 percent and to 4 percent on November 1. The latter was the twelfth consecutive increase in interest rates since June 2004. The Fed asserted that hurricanes Katrina and Wilma had increased inflationary pressures and more rate increases seemed likely. The Dow fell to 10238.76 on October 10, 2005, but strong third quarter growth, 3.8 percent, pushed it back up to 10402.77 on October 28 and to 10931.62 during Thanksgiving week. Gas prices dropped to under $2 per gallon during that holiday, but gold was approaching $500 per ounce. The housing market was then showing signs of cooling, leading the Federal Reserve Board to hint that it might slow further interest rate increases.

Enron Continues

Enron was gone but not forgotten. Lea Fastow emerged from prison in June 2005 to serve her last month of confinement in a halfway house. A docudrama about Enron (of the Fahrenheit 9/11 ilk) was released at about the same time. It was insipid, containing a reenactment of the suicide of Clifford Baxter, delving into what it portrayed as sinister ties between Enron and the Bush administration and displaying some unrelated archived footage of strippers designed to spice up things. Even a reviewer for the *New York Times* was led to conclude that the producers "stretch the limits of documentary technique." Another film, *The American Ruling Class,* attacked the wealthy and included a statement by former CBS anchorman Walter Cronkite supporting that attack. A Broadway play titled *Privilege* focused on the effects on the children from their father's insider trading scandals.

Fallout from other Enron era scandals continued to make the news. The managers in the Enron bankruptcy awarded themselves large bonuses in July 2005. By then, sixteen former Enron officials had pleaded guilty to criminal charges, but the first Broadband trial had resulted in no convictions (the jury was hung on some charges and acquitted on others), raising concerns that the trial of Jeffrey Skilling and Kenneth Lay might not be the slam dunk anticipated by the government. The Toronto-Dominion Bank announced that it was reserving $238 million to settle class action claims in the Enron shareholder litigation. The defunct Arthur Andersen accounting firm agreed to pay $25 million to settle claims over its auditing of Global Crossing. Reliant Energy agreed to pay $460 million to settle charges relating to its exploitation of the California energy crisis during 2000 and 2001, but California was again hit by rolling blackouts in August 2005. Duke Energy Corp. took an $883 million charge in the third quarter of 2005 to shut down its western wholesale energy operations that had embroiled it in the earlier California energy crisis.

Henry Blodget, the Merrill Lynch analyst who had promoted stock to the public that he was privately disparaging, was repentant and was being rehabilitated by the press. Turning to writing, his articles appeared in the *New York* magazine and on the op-ed page of the *New York Times.* A profile in the business section of the *New York Times* even asked that his sins be forgiven. The Supreme Court gave Blodget another boost by refusing to review the dismissal of a class action suit against him and Merrill Lynch that claimed that they had made overly optimistic claims about the performance of the stock of 24/7 Real Media and Interliant. The Supreme Court agreed to review another appellate ruling that allowed a class action to proceed against Merrill Lynch where the claim was made that the plaintiffs had not sold stock because of inflated research reports. Another financial analyst, Paul Johnson, was found guilty by a jury of SEC charges that he failed to disclose his holdings in the stocks he was promoting.

The government could not accept defeat in its case against Richard Scrushy at HealthSouth, so they indicted him on other charges, along with former Alabama governor Don Siegelman. The government claimed that Scrushy paid Siegelman $500,000 for an appointment to the Alabama Certificate of Need Review Board, a body that approves new hospital construction in the state. Aaron Beam, one of the HealthSouth chief financial officers, who testified unsuccessfully against Scrushy, was sentenced to three months in prison for his role in the fraud at HealthSouth. Another former chief financial officer, Weston Smith, was given twenty-seven months, the longest term given any HealthSouth executive. He had been the prime whistleblower exposing the fraud. The SEC refused to drop its suit against Scrushy after his acquittal, and a federal judge ordered the case to be sent to mediation. Ironically, a jury convicted another HealthSouth executive, Hannibal Crumpler, of the accounting fraud that was the subject of the Scrushy trial.

Ahold NV, the failed Italian grocer, agreed to pay $1.1 billion to settle shareholder lawsuits over its accounting manipulations. MCI was reported as having reached a settlement with several states over charges of tax evasion by WorldCom amounting to over $750 million. MCI was to pay $315 million to settle those claims. MCI was also given a deferred prosecution agreement by the Department of Justice as a result of the company's record $750 million settlement with the SEC. The Department of Justice expressed sympathy for the company's employees and "legitimate bystanders" in deciding not to prosecute. MCI's reformist management structure was still struggling. It posted a 12 percent decline in sales in the third quarter but did manager to turn a profit just before completing its merger with Verizon. The class action lawyers continued to add to the settlements from its bond underwriters. Citigroup and JPMorgan Chase agreed to pay Calpers and other state pension funds $651 million in October 2005. This was in addition to the over $4.5 billion paid by those institutions in earlier settlements with the New York State Common Retirement Fund. The New York City pension funds had opted out of the class action against WorldCom and were able to demand a $78 million settlement from the underwriters of WorldCom bonds, which erased most of the losses of those pension funds.

Bernard Ebbers was appealing his conviction for the WorldCom accounting manipulations. Ebbers's lawyers were claiming that the government had employed the same tactic used to gain the conviction against Arthur Andersen LP that was set aside by the Supreme Court. In the Andersen case, lawyer Nancy Temple had been kept off the stand by the government by threatening her with prosecution. In the WorldCom case, Ronald Beaumont, WorldCom's chief operating officer was named as an unindicted coconspirator to keep him off the stand and to allow out-of-court hearsay statements to be used against Ebbers. Ebbers's lawyers had sought to have the lower court require Beaumont to testify, asserting that his testimony would be exculpatory of Ebbers.

The lawyers for Kenneth Lay and Jeffrey Skilling were making similar claims against prosecutors heading their prosecution. They claimed that the government had named over one hundred individuals as coconspirators and so intimidated potential witnesses that almost no one would even talk to the defense lawyers. The situation was bad enough that Sim Lake, the federal judge handling the case, sent letters to thirty-eight potential witnesses advising them that they could talk to defense lawyers. Judge Lake had reason to be concerned with fairness. He had sentenced Dynegy executive Jamie Olis to twenty-four years in prison for manipulating the accounts of that company, a sentence previously reserved for second-degree murder. A federal appeals court ruled in October 2005 that Judge Lake had overvalued the losses sustained by the California Retirement System in determining that such a lengthy sentence was warranted.

Qwest Communications agreed to pay $400 million to settle shareholder claims over its accounting manipulations. The government was still trying to garner some more publicity from the Adelphia scandal. Although he was already on death row, the government indicted John Rigas and his son Timothy in October 2005 for tax evasion. The charges were based on a convoluted claim that the loans they took out from Adelphia were income because Rigas did not intend to repay them. Gregory Dearlove and William Caswell, two auditors at Deloitte & Touche, were accused a few weeks earlier by the SEC of assisting the fraud at Adelphia. More startling, David Boies was asked by Adelphia to resign his position as special counsel for corporate ethics at that company because he had failed to disclose a conflict of interest. Adelphia discovered that Boies' children partly and indirectly owned a company called Amici LLC, which had been paid over $5 million by Adelphia to store and manage its legal documents. The founder and managing director of Amici was William Duker, a lawyer formerly associated with Boies. Duker had pleased guilty to felony charges in 1997 and served a prison sentence for defrauding the federal government. Duker had submitted inflated legal bills in a case brought by the FDIC against Michael Milken, the junk bond king of the 1980s. Boies and Duker were representing the FDIC and the Resolution Trust Corp. in that litigation.

The relationship between the Boies family and Amici was discovered as the results of complaints that Amici's document management was incompetent. A lawyer at Sullivan & Cromwell, Boies' old law firm, complained that the database created by Amici was padded with phone books, menus, shoe catalogues, and cookbooks in order to run up costs. Two other Boies clients that had been involved in massive corporate scandals, Tyco and Qwest, were also paying Amici millions of dollars for document management. Dennis Kozlowski and Mark Swartz were claiming that their defense had been impaired by Boies because he had withheld millions of Tyco documents from their lawyers until their trial was over, preventing their use by the defense. The scandal spread after it was discovered that Boies' law firm had been sending clients to Legal & Scientific Analysis, a firm partially owned by his children and Duker, that provides expert witness testimony.

David Radler, the business partner of Conrad Black at Hollinger International, was indicted and agreed to plead guilty to charges that he authorized $32 million in disguised bonuses for himself and others. Radler agreed to cooperate with the government, which meant that he would be testifying against Conrad Black in exchange for a sentence of twenty-nine months and a small fine. Also indicted was Hollinger general counsel, Mark Kipnis. The government's overly zealous tactics continued. The U.S. attorney in Chicago seized $8.9 million that was owed to Conrad Black after he sold a Manhattan apartment. Black was later indicted. The charges included the now predictable and boring claims of unauthorized party expenses and jet travel, including a trip to the South Pacific with his wife.

Dean L. Buntrock, the founder of Waste Management Inc., and three other company executives agreed in September 2005 to pay a total of $30 million to settle SEC charges over the massive accounting fraud at that company, which had occurred over a five-year period between 1992 and 1997. An arbitration panel found that Charles Conway, Kmart's former chief executive officer and chairman, had engaged in no misconduct during the collapse of that company that resulted in bankruptcy. The SEC almost immediately responded to that ruling by charging Conway with fraud in failing to reveal that the company had excessively built up its inventories and was delaying payments to vendors in order to remain liquid. The SEC also charged John T. McDonald, the former Kmart chief financial officer with the same misconduct.

Eastman Kodak Co. announced another 1,000 layoffs, bringing the total of lost jobs at that company since 2001 to 25,000, five times the job losses at Enron. The situation was actually much worse than even that large number. Despite the near perfect corporate governance scores given to Kodak by reformists, the company had lost an astonishing 100,000 jobs since 1988. That downward spiral continued with the announcement of a third-quarter loss in 2005 of $1.03 billion.

Corporate governance, nevertheless, seems to sell. The SEC charged Apollo Publications Corp. with falsely claiming that it had the world's best board of directors, including Fed chairman Alan Greenspan and former presidents George H.W. Bush and Jimmy Carter. Shareholders were said to include Tony Blair, Vladimir Putin, and many of the leaders of other countries. The Apollo Web site asserted that its mission is "to unify the world Language, History and Culture, to form all documents of Law on IOE (The Imperial of the Earth), . . . to issue the new and only Notes of Currency and Stamp on IOE, . . . to consolidate Globe School Textbooks, to World Wide Web Customers OnLine purchasing, schooling, banking and charting, etc."

More Problems

The NASD continued to impose large fines for late trading and other mutual fund offenses. In October 2005, eight broker-dealers were fined $7.75 million for shelf space payments that were given as incentives to promote certain mutual funds. Janney Montgomery Scott LLC and First Allied Securities Inc. agreed to pay $3 million to settle NASD market timing charges. That trading was conducted by traders for two hedge funds between 2000 and 2003. Federated Investors Inc. agreed to pay $100 million to settle charges brought by the SEC and Spitzer for late trading and market timing and agreed to turn over control of its board to outside directors. Pimco, a firm involved in the late trading and market timing mutual fund scandals, was the target of a government investigation that sought to determine whether it caused a squeeze in the market for Treasury securities. That action was an apparent reply of a manipulation of the Treasury market by Paul Mozer at Salomon Brothers in the 1990s, an act that nearly destroyed that firm. Two executives at the Security Trust Co., which had also been involved in the late trading and market timing mutual fund scandals, pleaded guilty to criminal charges brought by New York attorney general Eliot Spitzer. They were Grant Seeger, the company's chief executive officer, and William Kenyon, president.

Bayou Securities LLC, a hedge fund, was found to be missing several hundreds of millions of dollars after its founder, Samuel Israel III, announced his retirement at age forty-six in order to spend more time with his family. Israel and his chief financial officer, Daniel Marino, pleaded guilty to criminal charges of fraud. Hedge fund fraud was spreading. The SEC brought over fifty cases against hedge fund managers in the new century that caused investor losses of an estimated $1 billion. Still, that was only a small percentage of the $870 billion managed by over 7,000 hedge funds in the United States.

The FBI wrapped up some old business by killing Puerto Rican nationalist Filiberto Ojeda Rios, age seventy-two, in September 2005. He was a fugitive from an indictment for the robbery of $7.2 million from a Wells Fargo depository in West Hartford, Connecticut. Rios fled to Puerto Rico in 1990 after cutting off an electronic tracking device that he had been fitted with pending his trial. Martha Stewart did not go that far but was laughing on television about the tracking device she had to wear. Her entire staff showed up one day wearing mock tracking devices on their legs that were provided by Stewart. She even fitted her dog with one.

DreamWorks Animation SKG was under investigation for trading that occurred in its stock before its first quarter reports in 2005. The height of regulatory absurdity was reached in an SEC settlement with Ford Motor Credit Co., over a securities offering. Ford agreed to pay $700 million to settle those charges even though there was no harm done to investors. So much for "no harm, no foul," and the fine did not help Ford investors with the deepening financial crisis at that company. Ford's North American operations experienced a $700 million loss in the second quarter of 2005, causing the company to project layoffs of more than 10,000 white-collar workers, twice the number of employees losing their jobs at Enron.

Excessive executive entertainment continued unabated. Robert Greifeld, the head of Nasdaq, hosted a family reunion at an Irish castle at a cost of some $500,000. The exact cost was in doubt because Greifeld was suing the organizer, claiming that he had been overcharged. Walt Disney appeared to have reformed its compensation practices after the debacle over compensation paid to Michael Eisner and Michael Ovitz. The new chief executive officer, Robert Iger, was being paid a relatively paltry $17.25 million per year. A scandal broke out at Mercury Interactive Corp. over the misdating of options given to employees as compensation. The misdating was used to allow lower strike prices in order to assure greater profits when the options expired. Three executives at the company resigned after that disclosure.

Government prosecutors were cashing in their chips for more lucrative employment. John Ashcroft, the attorney general at the time of the Enron scandal, started a consulting firm to provide advice on conducting corporate internal investigations. Assistant Attorney General Michael Chertoff, who was responsible for the prosecution of Arthur Andersen, used the fame he gained from that ruthless act to lever his way into becoming secretary for Homeland Security before the Supreme Court reversed the accounting firm's conviction. Bad judgment apparently is no bar to advancement in government, but the cost was high as Chertoff proved as head of Homeland Security by bungling rescue efforts after hurricane Katrina and causing the loss of a number of lives. Christopher Wray, the chief the Department of Justice's criminal division and one of the overseers of the Enron era prosecutions, left government to join the law firm of King & Spalding. James Comey, who as deputy attorney general and former U.S. attorney in Manhattan spearheaded several of the financial scandal prosecutions, announced he was leaving government. The head of the SEC's enforcement division, Stephen M. Cutler, returned to the private sector. He was replaced by Linda Thomsen, who had been in charge of the SEC's Enron task force.

Prosecutors continued to undermine the attorney-client privilege by having former executives plead guilty to charges of obstruction of justice because they lied to lawyers conducting an internal investigation of Computer Associates International, the computer firm that had been racked by accounting scandals. The government claimed that the executives should have known that their company's lawyers would turn over their statements to the government. Computer Associates had to restate its earnings again in 2004 and 2005 as the result of prior manipulations.

Eliot Spitzer was in full campaign mode in 2005 for his run at the governorship in New York. He promoted that effort with an investigation of discriminatory lending practices by HSBC Holdings PLC and Citigroup Inc. That led to another turf war with the Office of the Comptroller of the Currency (OCC), the regulator for national banks. Unlike the SEC, Julie Williams, the acting head of the OCC, was not backing down from confrontation with Spitzer. Williams blasted Spitzer in a news release in which she rejected his claims that federal regulators had been "beaten down," "neutered," or "sapped of the desire" to regulate. Williams then had Spitzer permanently enjoined by a federal district court from further investigating those banks. The OCC also pushed California Attorney General Bill Lockyer back in his efforts to regulate national banks through a federal court decision in Lockyer's home state.

Undaunted by the OCC's feistiness, Spitzer renewed his criticism of the SEC, saying that the agency's failures were not due to a lack of resources. Rather, he asserted that the SEC lacked "willpower" and "drive." Spitzer got his comeuppance in the trial of Theodore Charles Sihpol III, the employee at Banc of American Securities who was criminally charged by Spitzer with allowing late trading in mutual funds. The jury found Sihpol not guilty on twenty-nine counts and were hung (11–1 in favor of acquittal) on four other counts. Most major financial institutions were afraid to challenge Spitzer's claims that accepted business practices were criminal merely because he disapproved of them. Sihpol had no money to buy his way out so he had to fight. He did so even though his employer had cut off his attorney fees in order to please Spitzer. Sihpol's lawyers showed the jury that late trading was a recognized practice and did not violate ay law.

Spitzer churlishly announced that he would retry Sihpol, the mutual fund late trader, on the charges on which the jury could not reach a verdict even though the vote had been overwhelmingly in Sihpol's favor on those charges and were unanimous on acquittal on the other charges. Obviously intended to blunt the adverse publicity from the acquittal of Sihpol on most charges, the decision to retry Sihpol was a clear abuse of prosecutorial discretion. After much criticism for that decision, Spitzer agreed to drop the charges against Sihpol, using a settlement by Sihpol with the SEC as a cover for his retreat. In the SEC settlement, Sihpol was fined $200,000 and barred from the securities industry for five years. Spitzer also dropped criminal charges for mutual fund trading abuses that he had lodged against Paul Flynn, a managing director of the Canadian Imperial Bank of Commerce. In fact, the Sihpol verdict so thoroughly routed Spitzer that he even agreed not to bring criminal charges against Hank Greenberg at AIG.

One company was also fighting back. Spitzer had demanded that J. & W. Seligman & Co. settle market-timing fees, but the company refused. Spitzer then tried to extort the company by threatening to attack the company's advisory fees as being excessive if it did not settle the market timing claims. J. & W. Seligman again refused and sued Spitzer, claiming that he had no authority to investigate advisory fees charged to mutual fund customers because that matter was in the exclusive province of the SEC. Spitzer retaliated with claims that the company had engaged in more market timing transactions than previously disclosed.

By October 2005 the SEC had been able to distribute less than 1 percent of the billions of dollars it collected as shareholder restitution after the Enron and other scandals appeared in the press. The SEC's efforts to distribute funds to investors from the massive financial analysts' settlement reached comedic proportions. The agency was too incompetent to distribute the funds or even determine who was injured so it appointed a Distribution Fund Administrator for the task. That administrator then placed an advertisement in the *New York Times* seeking proposals from "banks and financial institutions" on how to distribute the funds obtained by the settlement. The advertisement asked that institutions submitting bids have no conflicts of interest with the settling parties.

The SEC was also harshly criticized in a *Wall Street Journal* op-ed piece for endangering the public by discouraging drug manufacturers from stockpiling flu vaccines to prevent a possible pandemic. The SEC was refusing to allow those companies to treat government payments for that stockpiling as revenue until the vaccine was actually distributed. One company, Aventis, refused to participate in a program for stockpiling children's vaccines for the same reason.

In the meantime, the SEC was involved in its own mini-scandal of a budget shortfall of $50 million despite the incredible increases in its budget by Congress after the Enron scandal. The SEC blamed the problem on cost overruns for the leasing of new office space. Even more embarrassing, a GAO investigation found "ineffective management controls" at the SEC for its own accounting and that the SEC had "material weaknesses" in its own internal controls for the preparation of its accounting statements. No one was jailed, but some unnamed employees were disciplined. The Chamber of Commerce noted that, if the SEC were a public company, the agency and its commissioners would have been the target of multiple government investigations and class action lawsuits. SEC chairman William Donaldson announced his resignation shortly afterward.

President Bush quickly nominated Christopher Cox as chairman of the SEC as Donaldson's replacement. Cox was a former congressman who had worked with House Speaker Newt Gingrich to enact the Private Securities Litigation Reform Act of 1995 that sought to curb abuses in class action lawsuits brought under the federal securities laws. Cox, himself a victim of one such suit, had sought even stronger legislation than the bill that was adopted. Even so, Cox's opponents were using the fact that he had been sued as a reason for attacking his nomination. Cox's nomination met with an attack on the front page of the *New York Times,* which charged him in a headline with the very serious crime of being a "Friend to Corporations." The Cox nomination also set off howls of rage at the AFL-CIO and several other large labor unions that were seeking to gain control over corporate management through their pension holdings. Another outraged critic was Phil Angelides, the California treasurer who oversees Calpers and Calstrs, the largest public pension fund in the United States. Smarting from that criticism, and learning from Harvey Pitt's experience as head of the SEC during the Enron collapse, Cox was soon pandering to the full disclosure crowd by promising continued strong enforcement, refusing to back off most of the controversial Donaldson "reforms" and demanding more disclosures on executive compensation.

The *New York Times* also tried to push back a developing backlash from the reversal of the Arthur Andersen conviction and the rising tide of resentment against Sarbanes-Oxley. That once proud paper responded to those events with an article suggesting that Arthur Andersen and its 28,000 employees deserved its destruction with or without a conviction. The *New York Times* Sunday edition of June 5, 2005, was devoted largely to attacking every aspect of Wall Street. The front page led off with a highly alarming article about how the "hyper-rich" were taking over Nantucket Island, a report that surely must have spread cries of anguish and fear across Middle America. The article further charged that the Bush tax cuts had set off a dangerous epidemic in the number of wealthy people, who were increasing at an exponential rate. The business section then led off with an attack on Citigroup for its settlement with the SEC over its mutual fund distribution practices. The paper claimed that those obscure charges justified the restrictive regulations imposed on Wall Street. Another lead article in the business section triumphed Ronald Perelman's legal victory over Morgan Stanley. As a corporate raider, Perelman made an unlikely hero. These reports were only a warm up for the *Times* Sunday Magazine on June 5. It was devoted to a series of articles attacking hedge funds, real estate investments, derivatives, corporate mergers, and discrimination against women on Wall Street. One article featured Carl Icahn, another dinosaur corporate raider who was now being portrayed as a hero. The magazine's contents reached its nadir with a remarkably crude cartoon series belittling the management fight at Morgan Stanley, but they were effective. Philip Purcell announced his resignation shortly afterward.

11. Reforming the Reforms

The Myths of Full Disclosure

Reforms and Power

Corporate reform efforts have been passionately pursued by generations of law professors, self-styled reformers like Ralph Nader, state pension plans, members of Congress, the Securities and Exchange Commission (SEC), and wolf packs of attorney generals. Those reform efforts surfaced most stridently during the New Deal, but blossomed again in the 1960s with the arrival of William Cary at the SEC. This reform movement accelerated in the 1970s with Ralph Nader's populist attacks on large corporations. He charged that "these massive institutions create serious adverse consequences for consumers, workers, shareholders, taxpayers, small businesses, and community residents." Nader wanted corporations to become more "sensitive" and sought alternative "consumer-owned private enterprises at the community level."[1] He wanted to curb the power of large corporations, which he blamed for all societal failures, and he wanted to end "corporate welfare," which apparently meant that all corporate profits should be seized.

The reformers claim purity in their motives, which have encompassed a wide range of causes, including protecting investors, increasing auto and worker safety, preserving the environment, and opposing war. The reformers want to divert the economic power of corporations for their causes, which requires them to cripple management that currently controls that power. This power grab has not passed unnoticed by management. As noted in a 1977 speech by Otis M. Smith, vice president and general counsel for General Motors:

> I submit that the real corporate governance issue today is not so much one of honesty or of ethics, but of *power*. A lot of people seem to believe that even scrupulously honest corporate managers have too much of it. A.A. Sommer, Jr., an SEC Commissioner, summarized this viewpoint well at a recent conference on Federal and state laws regulating corporate management:
> "... the real name for what has been feared has been power: the power of certain people to do certain undesirable things to other people.... Corporations as such

have no power; the people who control them—whatever that means—have the power
to decide whether a plant will be closed, thus impoverishing a community; to decide
to curtail production, thereby adding massively, in some instances, to the rolls of the
unemployed, thus creating a problem for the political bodies; to blunder and thereby
harm the interests of those depending upon the prosperity of enterprise for jobs,
dividends, security. . . ."

The debate over governance, accordingly, is no longer confined to lawyers practicing in the corporate and securities area. It has engaged the attention of environ-
mentalists, consumerists, and also people interested in the enforcement of the antitrust
laws. For example, a leading government official recently stated publicly that the
antitrust laws are concerned with "centralization of wealth and economic and political power in the hands of an unelected and an unaccountable few," by which he
means corporate managers. This, interestingly enough, is how many business people
would describe some of the appointed government regulators.[2]

This struggle for power takes many forms. At its most extreme, terrorists
want to destroy the corporate power that produces so much of the nation's
wealth. Pension funds seek to acquire control over management in order to
further the labor movement and implement their social goals. The cadre of
law professors that periodically flock to Washington seeking more regulation
want to transfer power from management to the courts and to the lawyers.
That effort is working as seen by the deep intrusion by the Delaware courts
into corporate decision making. Directors are now afraid to make a decision
without consulting a lawyer, as illustrated by the request of the outside directors for their own lawyers before deciding the fate of Hank Greenberg at
American International Group Inc. The attorneys general want headlines and
random taxes in the form of huge settlements. All want to harness corporate
power for their own purposes, but none of them are willing to pay for the cost
of acquiring that control in the market place. Rather, they want the government to seize that control and turn it over to those special interest groups free
of all charges.

Full Disclosure

Government regulators have been quite willing to act as enforcer for the reformers. In the process, they have criminalized common business practices
and created crimes of full disclosure out of whole cloth where there had been
none before. This activity made for great theater and lurid headlines that furthered the political ambitions of prosecutors, but it was certainly not at all
helpful to the economy. Corporate governance reforms affect every aspect of
life in America when they impose unneeded restrictions on management, and
the full disclosure system is the most burdensome of all. SEC regulations
govern every aspect of securities trading, from the initial offering and the
underwriting process to the secondary markets.

The pervasive full disclosure regulations reflect a belief that the market is
not sufficiently efficient to provide investor protection and that the market
does not respond quickly enough to abuses. Supporters of full disclosure be-

lieve that a handful of bureaucrats are smarter than the millions of participants in the stock market. Yet it was those market forces that destroyed Enron
years before anyone in Enron management ever went to jail. In fact, it is
doubtful that there would have been any prosecutions if the market had not
lost faith in Enron's management. The SEC's full disclosure system did not
prevent or even detect the accounting abuses at Enron, which are now considered the most scandalous of all times. The SEC also failed to uncover the
massive accounting frauds at dozens of other companies, including WorldCom
and Tyco.

Compliance with the failed full disclosure system has required the employment of hundreds of thousands of accountants and tens of thousands of
lawyers. It has consumed massive amounts of executive time, required vast
expenditures of corporate funds, and, in the end, failed. Regulation piled on
regulation, statute on statute, judicial decisions by the thousands, all at an
appalling cost, but without any success in fulfilling the goal of ensuring full
disclosure or even good corporate governance.

Even worse, the financial system has been gamed by full disclosure participants even more cynically than the Enron traders gamed the California
electricity market. Corporate managers gamed the system by inflating quarterly reports to push up the value of their stock options. Accountants gamed
the system by creating imaginative accounting practices to allow those results. Banks gamed the system by making disguised loans in order for their
clients to obtain improper accounting treatment. Analysts and investment bankers gamed the system to push out hot issues. Investors and their lawyers gamed
the system to sue whenever a company experienced a business reverse. Prosecutors gamed the system to gain fame by high-profile prosecutions that should
never have been brought. Judges gamed the system by unfair rulings and long
prison sentences that sought headlines that would pave the way for promotion
to the next higher bench. Fraudsters gamed the system by taking advantage of
the myth of protection offered by full disclosure. Congress gamed the system
with more legislation for partisan political purposes.

Myth Revealed

Numerous companies played the short-term earnings game created by the full
disclosure system administered by the SEC by managing their earnings through
various and sometimes dubious means. That effort increased as overcapacity
and other problems affected corporate revenues and income. Those accounting machinations could be sustained only so long; reality eventually caught
up with the fiction, particularly as the economic slowdown bit into operations
and sales at the end of the century. That slowdown exposed those accounting
tricks and resulted in a flood of announcements by public companies that
they were restating prior earnings reports or other financial accounts.

In most instances, the SEC read about the scandals in the newspapers before acting. The reason for that failure is self-evident. The SEC simply does not have the resources or ability to ensure the integrity of the full disclosure system. At the time Enron was imploding, the SEC's staff of about 3,000 was divided into various divisions and several offices. One of the SEC divisions was responsible for enforcement, one for regulating mutual funds, and another for oversight of the stock exchanges and broker-dealers. None of those divisions stopped the scandals under their jurisdiction.

Another division, the Division of Corporate Finance (Corp Fin), was responsible for reviewing financial statements filed with the SEC by public companies. Corp Fin was responsible for reviewing the quarterly Form 10-Q reports, the annual Form 10-K reports, and the special circumstances reports required on Form 8-K filed by over 12,000 public companies and additional thousands of offerings of securities and proxy proposals. Corp Fin did not have resources adequate to review any of the financial reports filed with it to ensure that they were accurate. Some 300 individuals were employed in Corp Fin, too few to review all filings. Instead, a screening process was used to select particular statements for "review," but only the filed document was examined. Corp Fin did not conduct a full or even partial audit of the company to test the accuracy of the filed documents selected for review. It only questioned particular transactions that appeared suspicious on their face from the disclosures in the filed documents selected for review.

Before Enron, Corp Fin had a goal of reviewing each company's annual report at least once every three years. That goal was not met. Only 53 percent of public companies filing with the SEC had their annual reports reviewed in the three years preceding Enron's collapse. Interestingly, Corp Fin did review the annual reports filed by Enron in 1991, 1995, 1996, and 1997. The division also conducted full reviews of Enron's proxy statements in 1993 and 1994, as well as documents submitted for a merger and acquisition of some subsidiaries in 1996 and 1997. Corp Fin conducted full reviews of two securities offerings by Enron in 1992 and 1998 and undertook partial reviews on particular issues of seven other Enron offerings. No serious problems were revealed in any of those examinations.

Enron exposed another problem: the information it filed with the SEC was stale. Even if the SEC had been alerted by Enron's last annual report, that document was not filed at the SEC until April 2, 2001. "Allowing the SEC staff time to initiate and conduct a review in accordance with its ordinary timetables, it is unlikely that any revelations its review brought about would have come early enough to do more than hasten Enron's demise."[3] Although the Enron financial reports were raising some eyebrows on Wall Street as a result of its rapid growth, changes in its business operations, and widespread use of special purpose entities, no one at the SEC was concerned. The SEC had planned to review Enron's 2001 annual report after concerns over its accounting were raised in the press, but Enron's bankruptcy mooted the issue, and no report for that period was ever filed by Enron.

After Enron's failure, Sarbanes-Oxley required the SEC to review the financial statements of all public companies at least every three years, one-third each year. The SEC was able to conduct a cursory review of only 23 percent of filings in 2003 and had trouble finding staff to do more, filling less than a third of its vacancies in the first half of fiscal 2004. A Government Accounting Office report also found that the SEC was lagging behind in computer technology to aid in its mission.

Accountants as Bloodhounds

Even with increased staff and more sophisticated computers, the accounting practices and statements of the thousands of public companies regulated by the SEC will be too massive and too complicated to permit anything other than a cursory review by the SEC of some small percentage of the thousands of financial statements it receives each year, unless its staff is increased by a million or more. That means that the agency, as a practical matter, will never have the resources to look behind the financial reports filed by management. Lacking the hundreds of thousands of auditors and even greater numbers of supporting staff that would be required for it to conduct any meaningful review of financial statements filed with it, the SEC has shifted the burden of reviewing those financial reports to the accounting profession. The SEC proclaimed that default in ringing tones:

> Independent auditors have an important public trust. Every day, millions of people invest their savings in our securities markets in reliance on financial statements prepared by public companies and audited by independent auditors. These auditors, using Generally Accepted Auditing Standards ("GAAS"), examine issuers' financial statements and issue opinions about whether the financial statements, taken as a whole, are fairly presented in conformity with Generally Accepted Accounting Principles ("GAAP"). While an auditor's opinion does not guarantee the accuracy of financial statements, it furnishes investors with critical assurance that the financial statements have been subjected to a rigorous examination by an impartial and skilled professional and that investors can therefore rely on them. Providing that assurance to the public is the auditor's over-arching duty.
> Investors must be able to put their faith in issuers' financial statements. If investors do not believe that the auditor is truly independent from the issuer, they will derive little confidence from the auditor's opinion and will be far less likely to invest in the issuer's securities. Fostering investor confidence, therefore, requires not only that auditors actually be independent of their audit clients, but also that reasonable investors perceive them to be independent.[4]

According to the SEC, the accountant is supposed to ensure that the actual results of public companies' operations are accurately reported and portrayed. In the eyes of the SEC, the accountant is the cop on the beat who will protect investors from all investment risks. In reality, the auditor can only certify that the corporation's financial statements were prepared in accordance with GAAP. That certification is based on the auditor's review of the company's records and some verification of their accuracy through sampling, confirmation, or observation. The audit process has been described as follows:

> In a typical audit, a CPA firm may verify the existence of tangible assets, observe business activities, and confirm account balances and mathematical computations. It might also examine sample transactions or records to ascertain the accuracy of the client company's financial and accounting systems. For example, auditors often select transactions recorded in the company's books to determine whether the recorded entries are supported by underlying data (vouching). Or, approaching the problem from the opposite perspective, an auditor might choose particular items of data to trace through the client's accounting and bookkeeping process to determine whether the data have been properly recorded and accounted for (tracing).
>
> For practical reasons of time and cost, an audit rarely, if ever, examines every accounting transaction in the records of a business. The planning and execution of an audit therefore require a high degree of professional skill and judgment. Initially, the CPA firm plans the audit by surveying the client's business operations and accounting systems and making preliminary decisions as to the scope of the audit and what methods and procedures will be used. The firm then evaluates the internal financial control systems of the client and performs compliance tests to determine whether they are functioning properly. Transactions and data are sampled, vouched for, and traced. Throughout the audit process, results are examined and procedures are reevaluated and modified to reflect discoveries made by the auditors. For example, if the auditor discovers weaknesses in the internal control system of the client, the auditor must plan additional audit procedures which will satisfy himself that the internal control weaknesses have not caused any material misrepresentations in the financial statements.[5]

This process provides only minimal assurance that the records are actually accurate or that all information needed by the investor has been disclosed. As one court noted, auditors are "not detectives hired to ferret out fraud"[6] or, as a nineteenth-century English decision noted, an "auditor is a watchdog, not a bloodhound."[7] That view was echoed in a more recent opinion of the California Supreme Court where it was observed that:

> As a matter of commercial reality, audits are performed in a client-controlled environment. The client typically prepares its own financial statements; it has direct control over and assumes primary responsibility for their contents. . . . The fundamental and primary responsibility for the accuracy [of financial statements] rests upon management. The client engages the auditor, pays for the audit, and communicates with audit personnel throughout the engagement. Because the auditor cannot in the time available become an expert in the client's business and record-keeping systems, the client necessarily furnishes the information base for the audit.[8]

The SEC has refused to accept this practical limitation on the role of the auditor. The SEC claims that auditors really are bloodhounds, but the fact remains they have no noses with which to smell. An accountant is not an investigator or prosecutor. An accounting firm does not have subpoena power; it cannot offer immunity to recalcitrant witnesses or tap their phones. Unlike the Justice Department, accounting firms cannot offer plea bargains or indict the wives of executives to force their husbands to assist in their investigations. An auditor does not have paid informants, surveillance teams, or search warrants.

More practically, auditors do not have the time or resources to investigate every annual report of clients for fraud before their certification. Those reports must be filed within a relatively short period of time after the close of the accounting period. Even that brief period is being reduced by the SEC from ninety to sixty days following the Enron scandal. It is absurd to even suggest that auditors could uncover a complex fraud scheme in such a short period of time. At most, an audit provides creditors and investors with some limited third-party verification of the finances of the company, which is a very narrow function. In the best of circumstances, an audit does not ensure management integrity and certainly is not a promise of investor wealth or an insurance policy against management failures or market downturns.

Auditor Liability

As noted, the SEC and the Justice Department have broad powers to investigate that far exceed those of the auditors, but SEC and Justice Department investigations, for even a limited reporting period, take years and the resulting prosecution even more years. A case in point is Enron. Even after the disclosure of its problems, the government with all its powers took years to indict Enron's top executives, using some strong-arm tactics that might be abhorrent to the rest of the civilized world. Even then, no senior executive's trial was set to commence until well over four years after Enron's collapse. Those trials will take months to conclude with no assurance of success. In contrast, Arthur Andersen had only a few months to review those same figures and was limited to a few cursory tests for verifying data.

It was the SEC's job to detect the accounting frauds at Enron and elsewhere, but it failed completely, despite having all the powers of the government. That authority included the power to direct Enron to provide any information desired by the SEC. The SEC could have subpoenaed the officers and directors of Enron to testify under oath on the company's finances before its collapse and could have had them prosecuted by the Justice Department if they lied. If the SEC with all its powers failed, then how can auditors that have no such powers be blamed for an audit failure? Yet Arthur Andersen did receive just such blame and was destroyed in the process.

As a result of the federal securities laws, "Caveat emptor was replaced by caveat auditor."[9] Private litigation against a public company, its officers, and its auditors is now a given whenever there is any hiccup in the earnings of a public company. Any accountant becoming an auditor faces the continual danger of reputational attack, SEC civil prosecutions, monetary penalties, employment bars, and even criminal charges from the government and loss of personal assets from private litigation whenever there is an audit failure. Accountants at the Big Four accounting firms are well paid, but the risks out-weigh those gains, especially if there is a more lucrative and less risky alternative available in the form of consulting services.

The effect of attacks from private and government litigation is reflected in the decline in the numbers of individuals seeking to become auditors. The number of accountants who were members of the American Institute of Certified Public Accountants (AICPA) (which included about 85 percent of all accountants in the United States) grew to 320,000 in 1995, up from 95,000 in 1973. The growth rate of membership in the AICPA dropped from above 10 percent in 1983 to less than 2 percent in 1994 and is now negative.

According to former SEC chairman Arthur Levitt, the number of candidates sitting for CPA exams decreased from 55,763 in 1993 to 38,573 in 1999, which was a period when the number of public companies needing audits was growing rapidly. The percentage of students majoring in accounting dropped from 4 percent in 1990 to less than 2 percent in 2000. What happens when the SEC runs out of accountants to prosecute? Ironically, the adverse publicity from the Enron and other scandals resulted in a surge of applicants to the accounting schools—apparently there is indeed no such thing as bad publicity. Yet the number of accounting degrees awarded in 2003 was still 10,000 below the number granted in 1995, and AICPA membership was declining even as the demands for accounting services was increased dramatically by the Sarbanes-Oxley Act.

Accountants Work for Management

The accounting fraud at Enron and other large companies, as well as the flood of restated earnings, put paid to claims that full disclosure protects investors from fraud or excessive speculation. Those failures proved beyond peradventure that corporate governance reforms implemented over the years were hollow promises of protection from management overreaching.

A bit of reality ignored by corporate governance advocates is the fact that accountants work for and report to management. Even with the increased burdens placed on auditors by Sarbanes-Oxley, the immutable fact remains that management not accountants, is responsible for disclosure. SEC claims and much legislation to the contrary notwithstanding. Arthur Andersen earned $52 million in audit and consulting fees from Enron in the year prior to its demise. That made Enron's management an important client for the auditors assigned to that engagement, and a demanding one. Accountants by and large are decent and honorable professionals, but there is a strong inclination to trust and aid the client whenever legally possible. It is not an adversarial relationship, such as when the SEC or other government agency investigates a perceived wrongdoer.

Still another flaw in the logic of the SEC's full disclosure model is its failure to recognize that accounting statements are supposed to be management tools but SEC-required financial statements are now used by management to obtain credit or to induce investment, rather than to track their business operations. Strong evidence of just how worthless those SEC-mandated reports are is the fact that nonpublic internal reports are used to manage most businesses, not SEC-required reports. Management views SEC financial statements as a management presentation that should put the company in the most favorable light, just as its advertising does. Managers control those reports, and they have every incentive to present the data favorably, especially when their compensation is affected.

Another troublesome bit of reality is that full disclosure gives off an aura of real-time financial information when in fact most of it is quite stale, as well as inflated. As one senior government official noted, accounting provides backward-looking information, particularly trailing quarterly earnings. He also noted that the accounting professor "is driven by accounting standards that are a function of habit and history, of often archaic and abstract principle, and of a shortsighted conviction that it is better to obscure rather than illuminate the real source of earnings."[10]

The concept of real-time disclosure was adopted in the Sarbanes-Oxley Act, but the doctrine of unexpected consequences will no doubt intervene. Soon we can expect that managers will effectively be managing newsrooms reporting on the company, rather than spending time actually managing the business. Real-time disclosures will encourage short-term stock manipulations, place retail investors at a further disadvantage with professional traders when the information is actually accurate, and engender even more litigation when it turns out that the real-time disclosure was wrong, as happens for many first reports.

The Perfect Storm

The full disclosure system was supposed to ensure management integrity, but investors learned otherwise when the market bubble burst in 2000. The theocracy of full disclosure proved an empty promise, but that should have already been apparent even before Enron. Accounting failures cost investors $88 billion between 1993 and 2000. That number expanded exponentially in the wake of Enron and other scandals, evaporating trillions of dollars in shareholder stock values and resulting in the loss of millions of jobs. The Brookings Institution estimated that the effect on the American economy from the accounting scandals equaled a $10 per barrel rise in the price of oil. That was an understatement.

What factors led to the perfect storm of accounting failures at Enron and elsewhere after the market bubble burst? Congress blamed it on the auditors. Unfortunately, the real culprits appear to be the corporate reforms that encouraged stock options as compensation and the quarterly earnings reports required by the SEC. That effort backfired badly, creating a vicious cycle that demanded ever-increasing profits and revenues in each and every quarterly report filed with the SEC.

Full disclosure became a tool for management abuse, allowing executives to manipulate accounting results to meet analysts' expectations. Few managers could resist the temptation of the fabulous wealth produced by that structure. Full disclosure even allowed management to rationalize abuses. Presumably, there is no fraud if disclosure is made, so management justified dubious practices and exorbitant compensation through disclosures. Some of those disclosures were confusing and unintelligible, as in the case of the related party transactions at Enron, but management believed itself absolved if at least some disclosure was made.

Although the SEC was turned into a regulatory icon over the years by corporate reformists, that image was badly tarnished by its failure to prevent or detect the massive accounting frauds. The SEC's reputation and the goals of full disclosure were revealed by Enron and other failures to be supported by nothing more than myths. The congressional testimony of Paul Volcker, the former chairman of the Federal Reserve Board and would-be rescuer of Arthur Andersen, shows just how deeply those myths had penetrated into the regulatory realm. Shocked by the breakdown in full disclosure during the 1990s, Volcker testified:

> We have long seen our markets, and our accounting systems, as models for the world, a world in which capital should be able to move freely to those places where it can be used most effectively and become a driving force for economic growth and productivity. In fact, a large portion of international capital now flows through our markets. We have been critical of the relative weakness of accounting and auditing standards in many other countries, arguing that those weaknesses have contributed to the volatility, inefficiency, and breakdown of the financial systems of so-called emerging economies.
>
> How ironic that, at this point in economic history when the performance of the American economy and financial markets has been so seemingly successful, we are faced with such doubts and questions about a system of accounting and auditing in which we have taken so much pride, threatening the credibility and confidence essential to well-functioning markets.[11]

Volcker's perplexity stems from a widespread belief that America owes its dominant place in finance to the SEC's full disclosure system, but that belief is pure urban legend that bears no relation to reality. The United States gained financial dominance in the world well before the adoption of the federal securities laws. Long before the creation of the SEC, Andrew Carnegie was crowing that America could afford to buy the entire United Kingdom, which had previously dominated world finance, and settle its debts in the process. The United States was the largest industrialized country in the world as the twentieth century began, more than three decades before the federal securities laws arrived. At that time, it was producing 24 percent of all manufactured goods in the world, a figure that increased to 33 percent by 1913.

Pre–Full Disclosure Finance

The investment bankers of that earlier era were consolidating whole industries into nationwide enterprises, making them more efficient and competitive and laying the groundwork for an economy that was unparalleled in the world. That was done without any assistance from the SEC. Between 1897 and 1904, more than 4,000 firms merged into 257 surviving entities. During that period, 319 railroads combined. The 100 largest companies quadrupled in value as a result of combinations, controlling 40 percent of the industrial capital of the United States. U.S. Steel was the largest of those combinations. It accounted for 7 percent of the gross national product (GNP) for the entire country and operated some 160 steel plants that produced more steel than Great Britain and Germany combined. U.S. Steel's total capitalization of $1.4 billion was nearly three times the annual revenues of the federal government at the time. A syndicate composed of 300 underwriters distributed the securities used to finance that amalgamation without the aid of any SEC regulations.

The financiers on Wall Street controlled vast amalgamations of capital and raised enormous sums for investment through sophisticated underwriting methods that are still in use today. That skill proved handy when the European nations turned to America to fund their armies as World War I began; the United States became a net creditor after the outbreak of the war. Wall Street provided what was then an astonishing $7.3 billion in financing to allies during World War I and another $2.2 billion after the war for recovery. Wall Street provided that capital while at the same time allowing America to field its own forces when it was drawn into the conflict. The United States proved dominant in that war and was recognized as the financial and political center of the world at its conclusion. The Herculean efforts needed to finance that massive conflict were in no way aided by SEC-mandated full disclosure.

Another Myth

Full disclosure advocates also placed their support for the federal securities laws on the myth that the stock market crash of 1929 caused the Great Depression. Those reformers claimed that the SEC and full disclosure would prevent future market bubbles. Without a bubble, they contended, there could be no further depressions or recessions. If that was its raison d'être, then why did the SEC fail to prevent the market bubble that occurred in the 1990s? The agency had over sixty years to prepare for and prevent that bubble, but the SEC and full disclosure were powerless to prevent or stop that event.

John Kenneth Galbraith, the Harvard economist, perpetuated the myth of a speculative bubble as the cause of economic downturns. His book, *The Great Crash, 1929* blamed the Great Depression of the 1930s on the speculative orgies in the securities markets that occurred between 1927 and 1929.

Galbraith became a constant predictor of doom and gloom over the years and, unlike the mythical Cassandra, was widely believed and feted by corporate reformers. His credibility was undercut considerably by his somewhat hysterical and baseless prediction before a congressional committee that a market run-up in the 1950s threatened economic disaster. Galbraith's congressional testimony and book, which were timed for the twenty-fifth anniversary of the Stock Market Crash of 1929, did accompany a market reverse that resulted in a loss of $7 billion in market capitalization. Galbraith's biographer, Richard Parker, notes that a subsequent FBI investigation of that event cleared Galbraith of participating in a communist plot to undermine the market, but the FBI concluded that Galbraith was "conceited, egotistical and snobbish." Galbraith's *The Affluent Society* and *The New Industrial State* attacked the large corporations and their demand creation that was supposedly brainwashing consumers. He went further in *Economics and the Public Purpose* with a call for socialism that would include the nationalization of large companies. Galbraith proclaimed in 1985 that Communism in the Soviet Union was superior to capitalism in America, but by then he had been marginalized to the loony left. Galbraith reemerged to gloat when the market crashed in 2000, but the long-lived economist went mute again after the recession proved mild.

Panics, depressions, and recessions have long been a part of the American economy. Recessions occurred as early as 1765. A collapse of the British credit system in 1772 caused large-scale failures in New York businesses, and another financial crisis arose in 1784. A panic in 1792 landed William Duer, former assistant secretary of the Treasury under Alexander Hamilton, in debtors' prison after his massive speculation in bank and other stocks failed. Robert Morris, the "financier" appointed by Congress to restore the nation's finances at one of the darkest hours of the Revolution, met the same fate as Duer. Morris was ruined by a downturn in the economy and the failure of a scheme to sell plots of land in the new capital at Washington, DC.

A financial panic in 1819 turned into a depression that resulted in a massive deflation of prices, ruining numerous firms and bankrupting many individuals, including Thomas Jefferson. Another recession was experienced in 1829, but more serious was the Panic of 1837, which was followed by a depression that lasted until 1843, again causing much hardship. Other notable panics and downturns occurred in 1857, 1873, 1884, and 1893. The Panic of 1893 was followed by a depression so severe that it was called the "Great Depression" until that title was ceded to the one that occurred in the 1930s.

Many of these events occurred after periods of speculation and were often accompanied by sensational business failures. For example, the Ohio Life Insurance and Trust Company failed in the 1857 panic as a result of speculative operations and embezzlement by its cashier. Jay Cooke & Co. failed in the Panic of 1873. That failure resulted in lurid newspaper headlines because

Jay Cooke was the underwriter for a vast amount of the Union debt during the Civil War and a financier of considerable stature afterward. Another sensational failure was that of Grant & Ward in the Panic of 1884. One of its partners was the former president and general, U.S. Grant. The firm was the victim of another partner's defalcations and a confidence game that he was running. The Panic of 1893 was touched off by the failure of the Philadelphia & Reading Railroad Co.

Speculation during those early economic downturns was roundly condemned, but those events were classically viewed as the result of the business cycle that regularly produced boom and bust periods in the economy. The Panic of 1837 was blamed on the economic policies of Andrew Jackson that first destroyed the Bank of the United States and then curbed liquidity with the issuance of his Specie Circular. The Panic of 1857 was attributed to the end of the Crimean War that resulted in a glut on the wheat market in America as exports declined when Russia reentered the market. The panics regularly occurring at the end of the nineteenth century were the result of a continuing farming crisis, the overbuilding of railroads and localized economies that were not competitive and subject to failure in times of stress. Other contributing factors were the Civil War–era laws that prevented state banks from issuing notes to expand the money supply during a panic. The Panic of 1907 was also attributed to faults in the money market, as well as Theodore Roosevelt's attacks on business. However, the stock market crash of 1929 was blamed by reformists as the cause of the Great Depression, rather than more deep-seated economic problems and regulations that weakened the banking system. That view was based on the common logical fallacy of post hoc, ergo propter hoc (it comes after, it therefore comes because). Today, most economists believe that the stock market crash of 1929 "was probably an event of relatively minor significance" in causing the Great Depression.[12] Even the left-leaning *Economist* magazine, which had been screaming about the dangers of a bubble in the 1990s years before it burst, conceded that the Great Depression of the 1930s "was caused by wrong-headed monetary and fiscal policy, combined with the Smoot Hawley tariffs, and not by happenings on Wall Street."[13] Milton Friedman, the Nobel Prize–winning economist, placed particular blame on the failure of the government to expand the money supply during the 1930s, thereby preventing recovery and prolonging the depression.

Recessions and depressions are now attacked by expanding the money supply, cutting taxes, and reducing interest rates. Alan Greenspan, who had caused the downturn through massive interest rate increases, even more quickly slashed them when he realized the extent of the damage he had wreaked. President George W. Bush in no small measure aided that rescue with tax cuts. Even so, as reflected in his support of the Sarbanes-Oxley legislation, the president reverted to the popular misconception that the stock market causes recessions.

Still Another Myth

Another myth supporting full disclosure is that the federal securities laws rescued the economy and pulled the country out of the Great Depression and into prosperity. In fact, the federal securities laws only discouraged new stock offerings for fear of the penalties that could be imposed. Although a nascent recovery appeared to be under way in 1936 as Wall Street adjusted to those statutes and resumed capital-raising efforts, President Franklin Roosevelt undermined that effort through renewed attacks on the financiers. His still famous "rendezvous with destiny" speech that was written by Thomas Corcoran, a principal architect of the federal securities laws, blamed economic "royalty" for the country's problems. Roosevelt claimed that these "privileged princes of these new economic dynasties" and business "mercenaries" had created a "new despotism" and an "economic tyranny" that caused the Great Depression. "And as a result the average man once more confronts the problem that faced the Minute Man: For too many of us life was no longer free; liberty no longer real; men could no longer follow the pursuit of happiness." The president claimed that his assault on the corporate chieftains was a "war" that was being fought over the "survival of democracy."[14] In other remarks, Roosevelt called businessmen "a stupid class."[15] A tax bill introduced in 1935, called the "soak-the-rich" bill, was another part of Roosevelt's effort to attack the wealthy in America. None of this encouraged businessmen to risk their fortunes in the market, so capital went back into hiding.

Roosevelt used more than just words to attack the financiers. He had the Justice Department seek an indictment against Andrew Mellon under the tax laws. Mellon was a political opponent and wealthy businessman who was a former secretary of the Treasury. Roosevelt sought Mellon's destruction, but Mellon placated Roosevelt and bought off further attacks with a donation of his art collection to what is now the National Gallery. Another target was Moses Annenberg, a newspaper publisher who had been attacking Roosevelt's economic programs. Roosevelt wanted Annenberg "for dinner." In a foreshadowing of prosecutorial excesses following Enron, Annenberg was threatened with criminal tax charges that would result in a prison sentence of 147 years. Annenberg, who was dying from a brain tumor, responded that, like Nathan Hale, he did not "have enough years to give to my country." Annenberg finally broke under pressure when the government advised him, in a very Lea Fastow–like move, that his son Walter would also be indicted. Moses Annenberg pleaded guilty to a single count of tax evasion and was sent to prison even though he was dying. His son, Walter, went on to become the U.S. ambassador to London and a wealthy and respected publisher.[16]

The economy seemed to be recovering in 1936 before the attacks from the Roosevelt administration, but the stock market dropped by almost 40 percent between August and October of 1937, and the economy slumped once again. This period was called "a depression within a depression." The Dow Jones

Industrial Average was just under 100 in 1938. It had reached 194.40 in 1937. Roosevelt had truly frozen capital. New private investment in the middle of the 1930s was only about one-third of that in 1929. Roosevelt claimed that the slowdown in investments was an effort to undermine his authority. He called it a "capital strike." The existence of a capital strike was never proven, but as Walter Wriston observed while heading Citibank: "capital goes where it is welcome and stays where it is well treated."[17]

Roosevelt launched another attack on the wealthy by creating a Temporary National Economic Committee to study the concentration of economic power, including that of the Mellon and Du Pont families. Its findings were less than impressive and had little effect. The chairman of the Federal Reserve Board, Marriner Eccles, was considered by many economists to have provided additional help in sending the country back into recession during 1937 and 1938. At that time, the Fed doubled reserve requirements for the banks. The Fed was also doing little to provide liquidity to the economy by expanding the money supply, and the newly enacted Social Security tax was draining money from the economy. Franklin Roosevelt tightened fiscal policy during this period, even while consumer spending was dropping.

Attacks on Business

The themes sounded by Franklin Roosevelt were not new to American politics. Thomas Jefferson, opposing Alexander Hamilton, was concerned that northern merchants would centralize power through banks and other financial institutions. The concern over corporate power drove the fight between Andrew Jackson and Henry Clay over the charter of the second Bank of the United States. The attacks on "concentrated" wealth by the populists and reformers at the beginning of the twentieth century sought to limit the power of large corporations like the Standard Oil Company. The efforts of Ida Tarbell, the muckraker, Louis Brandeis, the reformist justice, Adolf Berle, the crusading law professor, and the naked aggression of Franklin Roosevelt against business during the New Deal had everything to do with attacking the power of big business and little to do with economics or protecting shareholder values.

In 1893, William Jennings Bryan, echoing Andrew Jackson, asserted that "on one side stand the corporate interests of the United States, the moneyed interests, aggregated wealth, and capital, imperious, arrogant, compassionless" while "on the other side stand an unnumbered throng, those who gave the Democratic Party a name and for whom it is assumed to speak."[18] That rhetoric was pulled from the dustbin by Vice President Al Gore, who campaigned on an antibusiness theme in the presidential election in 2000. Senator John Kerry attacked the rich and promised extra taxes for them in his presidential campaign in 2004. That platform was somewhat incongruous in view of the fact that the senator's wife, Teresa Heinz Kerry, had a net worth valued in the hundreds of millions of dollars and was using every available tax avoidance scheme to keep her tax rate equal to that of a middle-class family. In another populist refrain, Kerry's running mate, John Edwards, himself a multimillionaire trial lawyer before retiring to the Senate, portrayed himself as the son of a poor mill worker and insisted he would stand up for the rights of the poor and middle-class. That recalls the gibe launched by the Roosevelt campaign to counter similar claims by Wendell Wilkie, referring to him as just a poor, "simple, barefoot Wall Street lawyer." Edwards was a vociferous opponent of Social Security reform during the campaign, but was accused by opponents of avoiding several hundred thousand dollars in Social Security and Medicare tax payments by treating payouts from his law practice as dividends instead of salary.

Former president Bill Clinton launched another attack on "concentrated wealth" at the 2004 Democratic convention, despite having just received $10 million for his memoirs while his wife, Hillary Rodham Clinton, received another $8 million for hers. Senator Ted Kennedy, whose vast wealth was protected from taxes by various schemes, also made an appearance at the convention, citing Franklin Roosevelt as a prelude to bashing President George W. Bush as a supporter of the advantaged.

In any event, the federal securities laws did not resurrect the stock markets and the economy by restoring investor confidence and making it safe to renew capital-raising efforts in the 1930s, as claimed by their adherents. The demands of full disclosure only added further burdens on businesses. The enactment of the Glass-Steagall Act, which separated commercial and investment banking activities, further ensured that the investment bankers would be too weak to lead a recovery. The markets were then cut off from the financial strength previously provided by Wall Street. The cumulative effect of those laws was to freeze capital for years.[19]

The Great Depression ended only when World War II broke out in Europe. As war approached, Roosevelt stopped his assaults on the financiers and even denied in a graduation address at the University of North Carolina that he "breakfasted on a dish of grilled millionaire."[20] Roosevelt then dropped his New Deal antibusiness programs and became the wartime commander in chief who brought numerous business leaders into his administration to aid the war effort. The New Deal and full disclosure did nothing to right the economy. The GNP in the United States did not reach 1929 levels until 1940, when unemployment still stood at 14.6 percent. The economy only recovered from the Great Depression as a result of orders for military supplies related to the war in Europe.

The SEC and New Deal legislation played no positive role in that recovery. The SEC was even declared a nonessential agency during World War II and was shipped off to Philadelphia. The stock markets continued to languish even after the war as the sword of Damocles in the form of full disclosure continued to hang over the underwriters on Wall Street. It was not until November 17, 1954, that the market returned to its 1929 high under a more business-friendly Eisenhower administration and a favorable court opinion dismissing a massive antitrust suit against Wall Street underwriters. The Dow Jones Industrial Average tripled during the 1950s, while the SEC lay somnolent and unthreatening.

The SEC Fails

Fraud Before the SEC

Still another myth circulated by the supporters of full disclosure is that the SEC has been a guardian over the markets, preserving their integrity and stopping widespread fraud. Historical evidence suggests otherwise, but a reminder is needed that the financiers of the pre–full disclosure era were no angels. The depredations of the robber barons, including the likes of Jim Fisk and Jay Gould, are legends in American finance. The machinations employed by Enron and other large corporations during the market bubble in the 1990s, although unequaled in their complexity, are not novel in their goals; they smack of the abuses of earlier eras.

An accounting scheme used during the 1890s, called "office boy" loans, involved a large "loan" to a clerk of a bank. The clerk would use the loan proceeds to purchase depreciated assets at an inflated price from a company that needed to report a higher value for the assets on its accounting statements. The company guaranteed repurchase at the inflated price in the next accounting period. In one case, a clerk who was making $15 a week was loaned $661,491 by a trust company. The proceeds from that loan were used to buy depreciated assets from the Western National Bank of New York. The New York Life Insurance Co. went even further, loaning more than $4 million to a messenger in order to fund one of these transactions. That clerk was then being paid a salary of $600 a year.[21]

These transactions were conducted in a more sophisticated manner after the turn of the century. In 1903, George Perkins, a partner at J.P. Morgan & Co., arranged for the New York Life Insurance Co. to sell depreciated railroad bonds at par to the New York Security and Trust Co. in order to inflate the insurance company's balance sheet at year-end. The insurance company claimed on its financial records that this was a "sale" of those bonds, but the trust company making the purported purchase listed the transaction as a collateralized loan on its own books. Perkins was indicted for that conduct, but the case was dismissed after the bonds recovered substantially in value. J.P. Morgan & Co. engaged in a similar operation for the New York Life Insurance Co., agreeing to buy depreciated bonds at year-end, only to resell them at the beginning of the next year at the same price.

The insurance companies engaged in other year-end accounting chicanery. These schemes involved efforts to inflate profits when a company was having difficulty or, conversely, cutting or deferring profits artificially in order to avoid paying dividends to policyholders. The Equitable Life Assurance Co.

concealed large advances made to agents in the 1890s by funneling those loans through compliant trust companies. This was a regulatory arbitrage in which the company was trying to avoid insurance regulation restrictions on such advances. In 1904, Equitable withdrew over $20 million from various trust companies in order to avoid regulatory restrictions on business relations with trust companies in which directors were also stockholders. The funds were returned early in the following year after year-end reporting was completed. Another scheme involved reciprocal loans to the executives of participating banks in order to avoid government restrictions on loans by a bank to its own officers.

A parallel to the Internet boom in dot-com companies in the last decade of the twentieth century was the plank road mania that broke out in the 1850s. Some 300 plank road companies were created after George Geddes of New York claimed that the planks would last eight years. In fact, they only lasted four, and the plank road companies quickly folded in favor of the makers of more durable road surfaces. Jay Gould, the future robber baron, was a builder on one plank road and it was there that his disdain for the law first became evident. When told that an injunction was being sought to halt construction on a portion of the road, Gould had his lawyers delay the proceeding while his crews worked around the clock to complete construction before the injunction could be served. P.T. Barnum, a financier as well as the manager of his circus, criticized a petroleum mania after the Civil War in terms that also might have been applied to the dot-com mania of the 1990s:

> Every Sham, as has often been said, proves some reality. Petroleum exists, no doubt, and is an important addition to our national wealth. But the Petroleum humbug, or mania, or superstition, or whatever you choose to call it, is a humbug, just as truly, and a big one, whether we use the word in its milder or bitterest sense.
>
> There are more than six hundred petroleum companies. The capital they call for is certainly not less than five hundred million dollars. The money invested in the notorious South Sea Bubble was less than two fifths as much—only about $190,000,000.[22]

The American Ice Company

Still, one has to go back many years to find a financial scandal to match Enron in drama. That candidate is the American Ice Co. scandal. Like Enron, the American Ice Co. made large contributions to politicians and engaged in questionable accounting practices. It was the fifth-largest company in the United States before it was consumed in scandal as the twentieth century began. Although ice machines had already arrived, they were crude and not widely available. Most ice was cut from rivers and ponds and shipped to the cities. The American Ice Co. sought to exploit the demand for ice by creating a monopoly through the combination of the Consolidated Ice Co. of New York and the Knickerbocker Ice Co. of Maine. Other ice companies in Boston, Philadelphia, Richmond, and Washington were brought under the company's umbrella, giving the combination effective control of all ice business along the Atlantic coast. Its tentacles even stretched to St. Louis and Chicago.

To frustrate any would-be competitors in New York City, the American Ice Co. gained the favor of the city dock commissioners through some well-placed gifts of stock. The commissioners ensured that competing supplies would be turned back or melted by delayed landings. The ice fields of competitors were smashed with steamships. The American Ice Co. lowered prices, or even gave away ice, to the customers of independent ice dealers. As many as 500 independent deliverymen were forced out of business by these tactics. In 1900 after the competition was destroyed, the American Ice Co. increased its ice prices by well over one hundred percent.

Outrage at the increases imposed by the American Ice Co. was widespread. As the *New York Times* reported, "It is talked of everywhere, from the slums to the clubs, in Wall Street and on the street cars." Other financial shenanigans increased the notoriety of the American Ice Co. It was capitalized at a then massive $60 million, but reaching that figure took considerable imagination. A lawsuit claimed that this valuation was an accounting fiction. Charles W. Morse, the president of the company, was said to have personally received $15 million in stock in exchange for property worth less than $800,000. Morse made a profit of an estimated $12 million, a massive fortune at the time.

William R. Hearst launched an attack on the American Ice Co. through his newspapers. The scandal quickly widened. The mayor of New York, Robert Van Wyck, and his brother, a Democratic Party gubernatorial nominee, were found to have received American Ice Co. stock valued at almost $900,000. Mayor Van Wyck was spotted vacationing in Maine with Morse, the so-called Ice King. Several other prominent New York politicians on both sides of the aisle were found to have received large amounts of stock in exchange for their support. Like Wall Street in the wake of the Enron affair, the American Ice Co. was the target of a crusading New York attorney general, J.C. Davis, who commenced proceedings to bar the company from doing business in New York. Charges of conspiracy were also brought by a New York magistrate against officers of the company.

Governor Theodore Roosevelt joined the fray as the Republican national convention approached, attacking the American Ice Co. as part of his campaign. In response, Tammany Hall, whose politicians had been well greased with American Ice Co. stock, threw its support in the presidential race to William Jennings Bryan. Roosevelt, of course, won the presidency and began his crusade against large corporate combinations. Tammany Hall lost the confidence of the city when its citizens saw the greed exposed by the American Ice Company and other scandals. Its leaders were soon in flight. The American Ice Co. even had to roll back its prices, settling for a comparatively paltry 30 percent increase over its pre-monopoly prices.

Like Enron, the American Ice Co. scandal had legs. In 1906, the company was indicted in Washington, DC, after an "ice famine" in that city. New York continued its pursuit of the company. Roosevelt's successor as governor, Charles Evans Hughes, ordered criminal charges to be brought against it. The company was convicted after a trial that compares to that of Enron's accounting firm, Arthur Andersen. Unlike Arthur Andersen, however, the American Ice Co. was not destroyed by a conviction. The company simply shrugged off the $5,000 fine imposed and continued its ten-year war against the New York attorney general's efforts to keep it from doing business in New York. The American Ice Co. did finally agree to discontinue its operations in New York in 1911, but on the company's own terms. Its natural ice business was assumed by the old Knickerbocker Ice Co. The company's fledgling artificial ice plants were transferred to a new entity, the Ice Manufacturing Co. The American Ice Co. continued to operate elsewhere until 1961, when it changed its name to American Consumer Industries Inc. In the meantime, Governor Hughes moved on to other things. He became a Supreme Court justice and political candidate, losing the presidential election of 1916 in an Al Gore–like close finish.

It was rightfully said of Charles Morse that his "activities in the banking and industrial world had been of an extreme character, even when judged by American speculative standards."[23] After being removed from the American Ice Co., Morse acquired control of a chain of banks that nearly failed during the Panic of 1907. The New York Clearinghouse refused to save those banks until Morse agreed to retire from banking. Morse was sentenced to fifteen years in prison for stealing from one of those banks. That sentence was extremely harsh for white-collar crimes at the time, but Morse's imprisonment lasted only a few years as the result of a controversial pardon by President William Howard Taft. The president was told that Morse had only a few weeks to live and was suffering horribly. To demonstrate that Morse was not receiving special treatment, another dying inmate was also pardoned. The other inmate died quickly as promised, but Morse failed to keep his bargain. Claims were later made that Morse swallowed soap chips to stimulate internal bleeding as a means to convince government physicians that he was suffering a terminal illness. One of Morse's fellow inmates was Charles Ponzi who would go on to even greater crimes after his own release.

After being freed, Morse went to Europe for the cure and returned in robust good health, outliving President Taft by three years. Morse had promised his attorneys $100,000 for his pardon, but he refused to pay them after he was released. That omission was not forgotten by one of those lawyers, Harry Daugherty, who became attorney general of the United States under President Warren G. Harding. Daugherty indicted Morse for fraud in 1922 in connection with some ship construction contracts, but Morse was acquitted. Daugherty was himself caught up in the Teapot Dome scandal and was forced to resign his post as attorney general, only narrowly avoiding criminal charges. The secretary of the interior, Albert Fall, was not so lucky. He had arranged to lease government-owned oil fields to private developers in exchange for $250,000 in bribes and was jailed.

Other Pre-SEC Scandals

The American Ice Company scandal was succeeded by others. The Pujo committee, which investigated Wall Street after the Panic of 1907, found conflicts
of interest widespread on Wall Street. Numerous abuses were identified, including sweetheart loans to insiders, inordinate speculation, insider trading,
and manipulation. The Capital Issues Committee (CIC) created by the Federal Reserve Board to review stock offerings during World War I, wanted to
regulate securities offerings after the war because of fraudulent sales campaigns that the CIC claimed were causing a loss of "morale" and "confidence" that could be preserved only by federal regulation.[24] Like the market
downturn in 2000, the stock market crash of 1929 revealed numerous corporate excesses. Kreuger & Toll, which controlled over 90 percent of the world's
match production, was looted by its founder, Ivar Kreuger (the "match king")
through forgery, fictitious accounts, and other skullduggery. In 1929 the securities of Kreuger & Toll were the most widely held in the United States. Kreuger
was listing his match monopoly rights as assets and treated bribes he paid for
those rights as goodwill, giving a whole new meaning to the term.

Kreuger saved the French currency with a loan to the government of $75
million and was awarded an honorary degree by Syracuse University on the
same occasion when it granted that same honor to Franklin Roosevelt. President Hoover even invited Kreuger to the White House for advice on how to
respond to the stock market crash. Like some of the financiers caught up in
recent scandals, Kreuger was socially prominent, squiring Greta Garbo to
events and befriending politicians and other business tycoons. Like the executives at Enron, he was lionized in the press as a successful businessman,
even making the cover of *Time* magazine in 1929 during the very week that
the stock market crashed. Kreuger committed suicide in 1932, and it was then
discovered that his companies were bankrupt. Claims against his bankrupt
firm exceeded a then astonishing $1 billion. An audit conducted by the Price
Waterhouse accounting firm after Kreuger's suicide found that $250 million
of assets claimed by Kreuger were fictitious.

Another disaster with Enron-like overtones was the collapse in the 1930s
of the Alleghany Corp., a company that owned a vast network of railroads and
was valued at $3 billion. The Van Sweringen brothers acquired control of that
empire with an investment of just $1 million through a highly leveraged hold-
ing company structure. Its collapse made headlines. The brothers had sold
stock in the enterprise through J.P. Morgan & Co., and preferred customers of
that investment banking firm were given preferential access to the stock before it reached the public, mimicking the share "spinning" schemes under
attack by Eliot Spitzer in the recent scandals on Wall Street.

The Insull Utility Investments scandal in the 1930s was an even closer
parallel to Enron. It was a highly leveraged operation that generated some 10
percent of the country's electric power through a pyramid of a hundred hold-

ing companies that controlled over 250 operating companies. Investors lost hundreds of millions of dollars when this business collapsed. Once again, preferred customers, including several prominent politicians, were given preferential access to offerings of Insull stock in order to gain their favor. The head of that empire, Samuel Insull, was indicted for misleading investors and manipulating the company's stock price by wash sales. Insull had been Thomas Edison's secretary and was involved in the development of what became the General Electric Co. before moving to Chicago and creating his own electricity empire there. Insull fled to Greece and was captured after some Keystone Cop adventures. He was eventually acquitted of all charges by a jury after five minutes of deliberations, but died impoverished in a Paris subway. Historian Sir Harold Evans has asserted that Insull "was not a crook" and that Insull's prosecution was a "politically motivated witch hunt," again very reminiscent of the Enron era prosecutions. In the meantime, Arthur Andersen became the auditor for the Insull companies.

On the SEC's Watch

Fraud was thus no stranger to finance. That being said, history also evidences that full disclosure under the federal securities laws did not stop such abuses, as evidenced by Enron, WorldCom, and the mass of other accounting manipulations. Charles Ponzi's operations in 1919 were replicated on a massive scale in the 1990s despite the onerous regulation imposed by the federal securities laws. The schemes of concern to the CIC had their counterparts in the penny stock boiler rooms that were promoting stocks from the 1950s to the 1990s. Investors poured $10 billion into penny stocks in the 1980s. Hundreds of thousands of those investors were then thoroughly swindled by the likes of Blinder Robinson and First Jersey Securities. Additional legislation was enacted to deal with the penny stock frauds, but those scams would be succeeded with but little interruption by the microcap pump and dump schemes of the 1990s.

Much has been written about other abuses in the markets in the 1920s that were used to justify the enactment of the federal securities laws. Once again, nearly every misdeed of that pre–full disclosure era has its counterpart in scandals arising during the market bubble in the 1990s but with greater magnitude. Stock touts were making recommendations in the 1920s that were as equally conflicted and baseless as those made in the analysts' scandals of the 1990s. Investment company problems were as prevalent then as now, and the SEC has been powerless over the years to stop them despite its enormously intrusive regulations. The SEC's creation changed nothing. The only thing missing from the earlier schemes was the phony quarterly earnings reports at the center of today's scandals.

Enron was not the first sensational fraud on the SEC's watch. The career of Edward Gilbert, the "Boy Wonder of Wall Street," during the 1960s had some

Enron-era parallels of looted corporate funds and lavish living. Gilbert acquired control of the E.L. Bruce Co., a large manufacturer of hardwood flooring, and amassed a fortune estimated at $25 million, a then enormous sum. He became known for an opulent lifestyle, which included a sumptuous apartment on Central Park, a villa in France overlooking Monte Carlo, a museum-grade art collection, and expensive jewelry for his wife, who was said to be "one of the world's best dressed women." Gilbert appeared frequently in the newspaper society columns with celebrities. His downfall came when he "borrowed" $2 million from E.L. Bruce to meet margin calls on stock he owned in the Celotex Corp., a manufacturer of building materials. Gilbert had purchased those shares as part of a plan to have E.L Bruce take over Celotex, but a sharp market downturn in 1962 resulted in large and unexpected margin calls.

Gilbert took the funds without seeking approval of the E.L. Bruce board of directors. The merger fell through and Gilbert suffered further losses in the market. He then confessed to his board of directors and secured the loan with personal assets. Gilbert asked the board to ratify the loan, but John Cahill, a lawyer representing one of the outside board members, gave a speech before the board charging that Gilbert's unilateral act in taking the funds was felonious. Cahill further asserted that, if the directors approved Gilbert's loan, they could be in breach of their fiduciary duties to shareholders and be held personally liable. Gilbert then fled to Brazil, which was one of the few countries that did not have an extradition treaty with the United States at the time.

Gilbert joined the ranks of other financiers seeking refuge from American securities laws, including Lawrence McAfee Birrell, Earl Belle, Ben Jack Cage, Serge Rubinstein, Virgil Dardi, and Alexander Guterma, who destroyed seventy-five public companies with losses over $100 million in the 1950s. Gilbert's flight was front-page news across the nation in 1962. *Life* magazine carried a lengthy article and pictures of him in exile. Charles Kuralt interviewed him for CBS News, a segment that also contained an interview with Attorney General Robert F. Kennedy about government plans to prosecute Gilbert should he return to the United States.

Five months later Gilbert did return to face charges in both federal and state courts in Manhattan, after Brazil denied him permanent residence status. He was then targeted for prosecution by Robert M. Morgenthau, the U.S. attorney in Manhattan at the time. Frank Hogan, a crusading district attorney in New York, also brought criminal charges in state court against Gilbert, presaging the rivalry between Eliot Spitzer and federal prosecutors in this century. Ironically, Hogan was succeeded by Robert M. Morgenthau as the Manhattan district attorney. Morgenthau would stay in office for decades, even living long enough to direct the prosecution of executives at Tyco and other corporate miscreants after the market bubble burst in 2000.

Gilbert was charged with larceny for "borrowing" the $2 million from his company and for failing to file an information form required by the SEC concerning his stock sales, an oversight that President George W. Bush had been guilty of at Harken. Pleading guilty to the state and federal charges in 1957, Gilbert served a little over two years in both state (Sing Sing) and federal prisons. Gilbert had been blocked from repaying the $2 million by an IRS jeopardy assessment, a factor that played a large role in his prosecution and incarceration. A federal appeals court ruled in 1977 against the IRS on its jeopardy assessment, concluding that Gilbert had not stolen the money and had intended to repay the loan. Gilbert's problems, however, were not over. He was convicted of manipulating the price of the stock of the Conrac Corp., a maker of communications equipment, and sent back to jail. His lost his case on appeal despite the efforts of his lawyer, Alan Dershowitz, a voice that was heard in the Martha Stewart scandal. Gilbert emerged from prison, repaid his creditors, and built a successful real estate empire that included 180 properties in twenty-five states valued at $1.5 billion.

Other financial scandals also demonstrated similarities between past and present problems that the SEC could not prevent. The SEC's proudest moment in the 1930s was its forced reorganization of the New York Stock Exchange (NYSE) after one of the exchange's leading lights, Richard Whitney, was found to have embezzled large sums. That scandal has its modern counterpart, only in greater magnitude, in the massive sums paid to Richard Grasso, the head of the NYSE as the new century began. Although Grasso was no embezzler, according to Eliot Spitzer, Grasso illegally siphoned those sums from the exchange despite the SEC's pervasive oversight.

The 1960s, which became known as the "go-go" years in the stock markets, began with a massive scandal involving specialists on the American Stock Exchange. That scandal has its counterpart in the specialists scandals on the NYSE revealed in this century. Even Eliot Spitzer's effort to take over the SEC's faltering regulatory role is not new. Dennis Vacco, Spitzer's predecessor as New York's attorney general, held public hearings and reported on a mass of boiler room operations that were defrauding investors of millions of dollars. Even earlier, a study by a New York attorney general in 1969 found that the full disclosure approach to the regulation of new securities issues was proving totally ineffective, a finding that was proved again in the dot-com offerings in the 1990s.

A scandal involving Louis E. Wolfson had overtones of the prosecution of senior executives in the Enron era scandals, such as Bernard Ebbers, who claimed that they left accounting issues to others. Wolfson became famous for his losing fight to take over Montgomery Ward in the 1950s. Sewell Avery won that battle but then was forced to resign as the head of that company by institutional investors who were displeased with his autocratic leadership. That was the height of Wolfson's glory. In 1958, the SEC charged in a civil action that Wolfson issued a false press release claiming that he had sold one-fourth of his holdings in American Motors. In fact, he had sold the entire position and even went short. Thereafter, Wolfson was convicted of selling securities without registering them with the SEC. His defense was that he "operated at a level of corporate finance far above such 'details' as the securities laws" and was "too busy with large affairs" to concern himself with such "minor matters" that should have been handled by subordinates. The Second Circuit Court of Appeals in reviewing Wolfson's conviction stated that: "Obviously in finding the appellants guilty the jury rejected this defense, if indeed, it is any defense at all."

Wolfson was indicted for another scheme in which he had a third party secretly purchase hundreds of thousands of shares of Merritt-Chapman Scott, a company controlled by Wolfson. The company could not buy the shares in its own name because of loan restrictions, but Wolfson thought the shares were a bargain, hence the subterfuge. The indictment also charged Wolfson with lying to the SEC and filing false reports. A jury found Wolfson guilty, but the conviction was reversed on appeal. Two retrials of Wolfson deadlocked because the juries and judge could not agree on the charges. The matter was settled with a nolo contendere plea in which Wolfson was given a suspended sentence and fined $12,000. A Delaware court thereafter held that Wolfson was entitled to indemnification from Merritt-Chapman Scott for all his expenses and attorney fees, plus interest. Those fees and expenses were considerable since he was represented by Edward Bennett Williams, the famous trial lawyer and owner of the Washington Redskins. This did not end the Wolfson scandal. *Life* magazine reported in 1969 that Supreme Court Justice Abe Fortas was being paid $20,000 a year under a lifetime annuity purchased for him by the Wolfson Family Foundation. Fortas was then a candidate for the Chief Justice slot, but he resigned from the bench after this revelation set off a storm of controversy.

The 1970s saw abuses ranging from the Investors Overseas Service (IOS) mutual fund collapse and its later looting by Robert Vesco to the highly publicized accounting frauds at National Student Marketing and Four Seasons Nursing Centers and the pyramid sales schemes of Glenn W. Turner. The questionable payments made by Lockheed and other large corporations to foreign government officials in order to obtain business resulted in the fall of several foreign governments when revealed in the 1970s. The Equity Funding scandal in that decade involved the cooking of that company's books on a massive scale.

There were numerous financial scandals in the 1980s. The collapse of the Penn Square Bank (the strip mall bank), the unveiling of the Bank of Credit and Commerce International SA (BCCI) as an international criminal enterprise, and the savings and loan debacles threatened the entire financial system. The insider trading scandals of the 1980s involved the likes of Ivan Boesky and the prosecution of Michael Milken, the "junk bond king." The bankruptcy of Baldwin United Corp., a firm that went from selling pianos to controlling insurance companies, resulted in investor losses totaling some $9 billion. Baldwin United presaged some aspects of Enron, including abuses of mark-to-market accounting that were exposed when a market change undermined the company's business plans.

Accounting Scandals New and Old

Accounting scandals folded in nicely with politics even before Enron. The Wedtech Corporation, an ostensibly minority-owned enterprise, was charged in the press as constituting one giant accounting fraud in the 1980s. Rudolph Giuliani, then the U.S. attorney in Manhattan, prosecuted and convicted various individuals associated with Wedtech. The convictions of three of those defendants were set aside on appeal after the Second Circuit found that testimony presented by government prosecutors was false, a contrast with the false testimony given by a government witness in the Martha Stewart trial. An independent special prosecutor, James C. McKay, spent $3 million to obtain a conviction of Lyn Nofziger, a political adviser to President Ronald Reagan, in connection with his lobbying for Wedtech. That conviction was also thrown out on appeal.

The savings and loan (S&L) crisis in the 1980s led to a hysterical reaction that resulted in substantially more regulation and enhanced fiduciary duties, causing banks to "cut back on their lending. The flow of capital dried up—as did, gradually, the U.S. economy itself."[25] The result was the 1991 recession that cost George H.W. Bush a second term. Moreover, that regulation did nothing to prevent the Enron-era abuses, but presaged the reaction of adding more regulation to the already burdensome structure. As one law professor noted:

> In the 1980's and early 1990's, courts second-guessed financial institution decisions with respect to a new range of loan activities that had previously gone unquestioned. As a result, bank and thrift directors now face common-law negligence liability for loans that are inadequately secured, for over reliance on risky types of collateral, for pre-funded interest clauses, for failures to perfect security, and for rollovers of delinquent loans. In addition, for the first time ever, irrespective of statutes or by-laws, courts held financial institution directors liable for defective internal controls. The most important recent holdings in this regard penalize directors for eschewing or ignoring loan underwriting standards, for not analyzing borrower credit profiles, and for lax administration of loans and other investments. Thus, in banking, the common-law duty of care has significantly reduced board discretion to approve bank loans.[26]

Despite their pervasive regulation, including full disclosure for publicly owned institutions, over 1,000 thrifts and over 1,600 banks failed between 1984 and 1994. The government responded with a massive effort to liquidate those institutions and to find scapegoats such as Charles Keating, the head of the failed Lincoln Savings & Loan Association. His case was eventually thrown out of court, but not before he had been jailed for some time. In one strange case, a federal judge found that the FDIC had brought a baseless $1 billion claim against Charles E. Hurwitz, a wealthy Texas businessman who owned stock in a failed savings and loan association. The judge found that the FDIC had prosecuted the suit with the encouragement of Vice President Al Gore in order to force Hurwitz to turn a 4,400-acre forest of ancient redwood trees owned by one of his companies into a park through a "debt-for-nature" swap. In a scathing opinion, the judge ordered the FDIC to pay Hurwitz's litigation costs. Despite the failure of earlier legislation, Congress went further after the savings and loan crisis and criminalized mere business mistakes:

> Few offenses bring forth the public's wrath more than those of a dishonest banker. The high-profile prosecutions of those at the helm of large failed institutions fed the hunger of the news media, politicians, and social commentators. It follows that after the public had been provided a steady diet of bank and savings institution failures during the 1980's, coupled with several high-profile prosecutions, the next leap was a mere step for the political establishment. That leap was the assumption that the financial institution industry had been populated by criminals. While numerous theories have been advanced to explain the banking debacle of the 1980's, no empirical data has been presented that would suggest that widespread criminal behavior was the primary cause. However, the assumption of widespread criminality carried little political risk. No rational elected official, officer of the court, or legal scholar wants to be perceived as "soft on crime." Therefore, Congress, with the support of the President, enacted a series of laws that represented a radical departure in the way the criminal justice system viewed the banking and thrift industries. This becomes significant due to the unique nature of banking. Our banking process is complex, and Congress' regulatory system is enormous.
>
> The compliance burden challenges the acumen of the most thorough compliance system designers. Even under ideal circumstances, some loans will go unpaid and some accounts will be overdrawn. One must acknowledge that even the most talented individual with the best technological support can make an occasional mistake. Some reports will be completed incorrectly. Some regulations will be violated. In all but the rare case, these mistakes and violations will result from an oversight, innocent mistake, or possibly a mistake in business judgment. This business reality becomes more relevant due to the changes in the law outlined herein because the potential punishment is enormous. Coupling this with banking's evolving role as an instrument of law enforcement through anti-money laundering legislation, one finds a massive body of potential criminal penalties available for use against bank officers and directors.[27]

The stock market crash of 1987 proved once again that the SEC and full disclosure do not stabilize a market or prevent precipitous declines. The 1987 crash set a new record for the most severe one-week decline in history, exceeding that of the stock market crash of 1929. The SEC blamed the 1987 market break on the speculative excesses of commodity futures traders operating on low margins in stock index futures contracts. The commodity futures markets, according to the SEC's own reports, had become "synthetic" stock markets and were being used to price stocks. In other words, the commodity markets were viewed as more efficient than the stock markets, but how could this be possible? There was no full disclosure concept in the commodity markets, yet those markets were more efficient than the SEC-regulated full disclosure markets!

The SEC was vigorous during the 1990s under chairman Arthur Levitt, but was equally ineffective in stopping fraud through full disclosure. Overall earnings by Standard & Poor's 500 companies were estimated to be inflated by 20 percent or more as the century closed. Between 1998 and 2002, public companies made over 860 accounting restatements that were the result, in many cases, of efforts to inflate earnings or cut losses. The number of restatements increased by 53 percent during Levitt's reign, while the number of public companies decreased by 14 percent.

Prosecutions

Attorney General John Ashcroft boasted in March 2004 that the Justice Department had indicted more than 600 executives and obtained more than 200 convictions as a result of Enron and other financial scandals. The number of convictions had increased to over 500 by the end of the year. With such statistics, full disclosure was starting to sound more like the drug trade and less like a sound basis for regulating bona fide financial markets. Everyone involved in the securities industry was facing the risk of prosecution or personal liability for any perceived disclosure failure on the basis of twenty-twenty hindsight. In order to make full disclosure work, seemingly every public company was to be sued periodically by the SEC, and their executives must all be indicted whenever there was a business failure.

The SEC and the Justice Department criminalized even the most trivial of corporate housekeeping failures. An executive who does not have a corporate board resolution for every ride on the corporate jet is now a criminal. Executives awarded bonuses by the chief executive officer are felons, unless they demand a board resolution before accepting the money. A corporate executive seeking to rally employee morale by talking up the company will face years in jail, if the company subsequently fails. Breaches of fiduciary duty now result in prison terms as long as those for murderers. Risk taking must be encouraged if society is to advance, and that presents a paradox that reformers seem unable to grasp. Enron was an exciting new business model that brought several innovations in energy trading and exposed vast flaws in the energy markets in California and elsewhere. The Enron "asset light" model ultimately failed in the market downturn, but that should not stop others from reforming and revising that model to make it work. No entrepreneur will do so, however, if his or her every step is haunted by a criminal prosecution that will impose draconian sanctions equal to those imposed on violent criminals.

The massive number of prosecutions against corporate executives has resulted in a demand for former prosecutors and regulators as outside board members, particularly in those companies with regulatory problems. The companies adding such members include Lockheed Martin Corp. (former Manhattan U.S. attorney James Comey who prosecuted Martha Stewart and Frank Quattrone); Bristol-Myers Squibb Co. (former FBI director Louis Freeh who was selected for that role by the U.S. attorney as a part of a settlement with the company); Adelphia Communications Corp. (former SEC commissioner

Philip Lockner Jr.); Computer Associates International Inc. (former SEC commissioner Laura Unger); American International Group Inc. (former SEC chief accountant Michael Sutton) Marsh & McLennan (former U.S. attorney in Brooklyn Zackrey Carter); and United Technologies Corp. (former deputy attorney general Jamie Gorelick). Former SEC chairman Richard Breeden and former U.S. attorney general Nicholas Katzenbach were assuming complete control of large corporations with disclosure problems. None of those individuals had qualifications for managing a business. Their only role will be to demand caution and avoidance of risks.

The litigation statistics in Ashcroft's prosecution boast reflect another disturbing aspect of full disclosure: it is corrupting the government as well as businesses. Government prosecutors have lost their integrity in enforcing full disclosure. Using family members as pawns in extorting guilty pleas, staging dawn raids on executives' homes, and handcuffing the suspects for press photographs make for great theater but at the cost of basic fairness, decency, due process, and, in the case of Arthur Andersen, the loss of 28,000 jobs in the United States. Equally troubling was the fact that when the government was actually put to the test of a trial the prosecution often failed as in the case of the Enron broadband trial, the prosecution of Theodore Sihpol and the reversal of the Arthur Andersen LLP verdict on appeal. The high profile convictions that were obtained (such as those of Bernard Ebbers, John Rigas, and Frank Quattrone) were often accompanied by judicial and prosecutorial misconduct and appeals to jury prejudice against the wealthy. Also distributing was the developing pattern of giving chief executive officers lenient treatment in exchange for their testifying against the chief executive officer of their company. The chief financial officers were the architects of the accounting manipulations that were at the heart of the Enron era scandals. They were the ones who sold the executive officers on those practices. The chief executive officers at worst were mostly passive in their involvement in the schemes, but were being given life sentences for their passivity.

The SEC and federal prosecutors created dubious full disclosure crimes by always finding something else that should have been disclosed. When that failed, they threatened family members, as in the case of Michael Milken, Andrew Fastow, and Samuel Waksal. Perjury and obstruction traps can be sprung on executives who will inevitably purge their files when they perceive threats of government prosecution. Pursuing phony charges against executives like the one dismissed against Martha Stewart and criminalizing general business practices like those exposed in Eliot Spitzer's crusades provide headlines for ambitious prosecutors but add nothing to the economy. Rudolph Giuliani rode to fame on the back of his Wall Street prosecutions even though many of them were overturned on appeal. Drawing on that model, Eliot Spitzer made financial cases the basis for his quest for higher office, obtaining billions of dollars in settlement and drawing lurid headlines before ever having tried a single case. Spitzer was clearly trying to mimic other New York prosecutors like Giuliani and Thomas Dewey who had risen to higher political office on the strength of high profile prosecutions. Spitzer even went so far as to copy the attacks on the insurance industry that occurred at the beginning of the twentieth century. Charles Evans Hughes was counsel to the Armstrong committee, which conducted that investigation, an effort that boosted him into the governor's office and led to a near miss at the presidency.

The National Association of Security Dealers (NASD) announced the collection of a record number of fines for 2004, a total of $102 million, and investor arbitration awards at the NASD reached a record $194 million. The SEC reported that the number of its enforcement cases increased by 40 percent between 2001 and 2004. The penalties imposed by the SEC in 2004 reached $2.68 billion, up from $1.39 billion in 2002. About 20 percent of the SEC's financial fraud cases involved Fortune 500 companies. Those fines only drained corporate funds and served the interest of no one. Indeed, the Government Accountability Office found that most of the fines and restitution imposed in these high profile cases were not collectable. Such uncollected amounts doubled in the three years after Enron, reaching $25 billion. Still, the announcement of a large fine, even if uncollectible, guaranteed headlines. Even some SEC commissioners were choking on the excess prosecutory zeal of the post-Enron era. Two commissioners at the SEC objected to a settlement with the Wachovia bank, which agreed to pay $37 million to settle SEC charges that it had not disclosed that it purchased $500 million of First Union stock during its takeover battle with SunTrust Bank. Those two commissioners believed that the amount of the fine was excessive and only served to punish shareholders, not the management responsible for the conduct. They also objected to the $250 million fine imposed against Qwest Communications International Inc. Thereafter, the SEC, in a 3–2 party line vote, rejected a staff recommendation that an action be brought against Gary Winnick, the head of Global Crossing, even though he had agreed to pay a $1 million fine. SEC chairman William Donaldson joined in that vote after coming under much criticism for his excessive regulatory zeal, having often sided with the Democratic commissioners against his fellow Republicans, commissioners Cynthia A. Glassman and Paul S. Atkins. Perversely, the basis for that vote was the assertion that Winnick should not be held liable because he was only the company's chairman and not an executive officer with operational responsibilities. The reformist goal of splitting the role of chief executive officer and chairman thus saved Winnick from sanctions even though he had founded and controlled the company.

Donaldson was also backtracking on several pending rule proposals and enforcement actions before he retired from the SEC. Democratic commissioner Harvey Goldschmid then announced plans to step down from the SEC, another apparent recognition of the rising backlash against increased regulation. That retreat nearly turned into a route after an appellate court threw out the SEC rule requiring mutual funds to split the role of chairman and chief executive officer and to increase the number of their independent directors. The court concluded that the SEC had not adequately considered the effects of the rule. Donaldson had announced his resignation before that decision, and he knew that his successor would not approve of such an unjustified requirement. Usually, such rules take months or years to be reformulated, but in an unseemly display of arrogance Donaldson rammed the rule back through the SEC within a week so that he could assure its passage on the day before he left office. This seemed to have annoyed the appellate court because Donaldson had not even awaited the mandate from the court before readopting the rule. The court stayed the implementation of the readopted rule pending another appeal by the U.S. Chamber of Commerce. One SEC commissioner, Cynthia Glassman, apologized to the court for Donaldson's unseemly haste.

Donaldson was bolstered by a later survey which concluded that hiring additional independent directors and an independent chairman was not proving to be overly costly. Nevertheless, Donaldson's act severely undercut what little was left of the SEC's image of a nonpartisan institution. The *Wall Street Journal* reported that, in a further petty act, the SEC had leaked the fact that it was investigating Edward Johnson, the ultrarich head of Fidelity mutual funds complex, for the heinous crime of accepting free tickets to a figure skating event at the 2002 winter Olympics. It just happened that Johnson was one of the more severe critics of the mutual fund corporate governance rule and had published a study that evidenced the rule was unjustified.

SEC commissioner Harvey Goldschmid furthered the appearance of partisan politics at the SEC by announcing that he was delaying his departure so that the Republican commissioners could not repeal any of the Enron-era "reforms" after Donaldson left. Even so, two Arthur Andersen partners were saved by a 2–2 vote of the SEC commissioners after Donaldson's departure. The two Republican members voted to affirm dismissal of charges that those auditors acted improperly in their audit of Spectrum Information Technologies Inc. The Democratic members on the commission voted to find guilt even though an administrative law judge had found no misconduct. The split vote resulted in the affirming of that decision.

Two unlikely bedfellows, former senators Bob Dole and Tom Daschle, made an appeal on the editorial page of the *Wall Street Journal* for a revision of the costly Sarbanes-Oxley requirements. The SEC also granted small companies another year to comply with the internal controls reporting requirement. Since the requirement had been delayed so long, it was unclear why it was needed at all. The economy recovered quite nicely without it. SEC treasury secretary John Snow weighed in with an appeal that prosecutors not criminalize every mistake by a business and that prosecutorial decisions be more balanced. He appointed an advisory committee to study the effects of Sarbanes-Oxley on small businesses. That action was taken after it was reported that the number of companies delisting their stock tripled in 2003 and that many businesses decided not to become public companies because of the costs associated with that legislation.

This created a boon for private equity investors as start-up firms were driven from the public markets. A new term, "going dark," was coined for those companies deciding to delist their stock. The requirement that companies review and opine on their internal controls was particularly costly and was diverting corporate resources from production to auditors. The costs for compliance with the internal controls requirement were continuing to skyrocket reaching an average $4.36 million for large companies, 40 percent more than estimates of just a year earlier. Another survey found that those compliance costs were actually much higher, on average $7.8 million. Small firms were carrying an even bigger burden in terms of the percentage of such costs to their revenues. Total costs were estimated to be $35 billion, twenty times what the SEC had originally forecast. Average audit fees nearly doubled in 2004. Annual costs in 2005 were expected to exceed $6 billion, and it was charged that a not insignificant portion of that work was being outsourced to India as just one more drain on the economy. With all that cost, there were 227 restatements of financial reports in the first half of 2005 as compared to 282 for the entire year in 2004. The SEC and the Public Company Accounting Oversight Board (PCAOB) then claimed that the increased costs were the fault of the auditors who were interpreting Sarbanes-Oxley too strictly. Of course, if auditors interpreted the act otherwise, they would go to jail. In order to further deflect criticism, the SEC announced that it would seek to reduce the burdens of Sarbanes-Oxley. The SEC also overruled the FASB and delayed the options expensing requirement for six months, but denied a petition by Cisco Systems to use a market approach for valuing its employee options.

Companies were hiring compliance officers to train employees on SEC legal requirements, which required additional training staff and massive loss of employee time for such training. The *New York Times* reported that Sun Microsystems was estimating that it would spend $6 million a year on such training. Another cost was the fees paid to PCAOB, which were over $2 million per year for some public companies. Sarbanes-Oxley did have a supporter (beyond Messers. Sarbanes and Oxley) in Alan Greenspan who came out with an unsupported claim that the legislation had proved to be useful. The actual results were disheartening. The number of late filing companies doubled because of the requirements of Sarbanes-Oxley. Some 500 companies reported flaws in their internal controls for meeting unrealistic SEC full disclosure requirements, including Eastman Kodak and SunTrust Banks Inc.

Studies by RateFinancials Inc., an independent research group, found that one third of the companies in the S&P 500 index were not reporting their financial statements accurately in 2004. Forty percent of those companies were engaging in related party transactions, which was how Andrew Fastow brought down Enron. Other studies by that firm found that 75 percent of the companies it studied were still engaging in off–balance sheet financing and 64 percent were making unrealistic assumptions in funding their pensions. The SEC brought an action in July 2005 that charged twenty public companies with failing to file any financial reports. Sarbanes-Oxley was also doing nothing to encourage the entrepreneurial spirit in America. A study headed by Professor Paul F. Reynolds at Florida International University found that the number of new businesses had decreased by 20 percent between 2003 and 2004.

Full disclosure was being reduced in other ways. The number of public companies providing forecasts on their earnings and other aspects of their finance declined by 17 percent in 2004. The decline in forecasting by the largest companies was almost 20 percent, and a survey revealed that a further 10 percent of public companies planned to restrict forecasts. Successful executives were retiring prematurely in order to escape securities fraud claims in the event of future problems or economic downturns. Chief financial officers were retiring in droves. The number of those executives leaving their position increased by 23 percent in 2004. One executive was fighting back against the reformers. Peter Brabeck at Nestle SA was seeking to combine the roles of chairman and chief executive for himself, reversing the division of those roles at Nestle.

Donaldson at the SEC had responded to the growing criticism over the worst of the "reforms" (requiring annual management opinions on internal controls) by seeking comment on the problems it raised and advocating delays in implementing that requirement for smaller firms and foreign companies. As a sop to the reformers, Donaldson was urging more disclosures on executive compensation, but Sarbanes-Oxley reforms appeared to have failed in that area. Bonuses awarded to chief executive officers increased substantially in 2004 and executive perks were on the increase. A survey of almost 200 public companies found an increase of 12 percent in compensation to chief executive officers. They were receiving on average about $10 million. Another survey found that the ratio of compensation for chief executive officers to that of the average worker increased from 301–1 in 2001 to 431–1 in 2004. One of the winners was Michael Eisner at Walt Disney who received a $7.25 million bonus despite the unprecedented no-confidence vote given to him by shareholders. Retirement benefits were exploding as executives retired from the threats of prosecution and harassment from regulations. Vance D. Coffman received $31.5 million upon his retirement as chief executive officer at Lockheed Martin. Henry McKinnell Jr. was given $6.5 million per year after his retirement at Pfizer. Lee Raymond at Exxon Mobil, Edward Whitacre Jr. at SBC Communications, and William McGuire at the United Health Group all were being paid in excess of $5 million per year upon their retirement.

One study did show that companies with higher rankings in the financial sophistication of their audit committee members tended to perform on average in the stock market better than those that did not, which seemed intuitive. Yet, the audit committee of the premier performer in the market, Warren Buffet's Berkshire Hathaway, was ranked very near the bottom in that survey. In order to meet NYSE requirements for a majority of outside directors, Buffett appointed Bill Gates, the monopolist founder of Microsoft, onto the Berkshire

Hathaway board. His fellow board members then included Donald Keough, the former head of Coca-Cola, and Water Scott from Level 3 Communications Inc. Several Buffett cronies, including his lawyer, a partner from that same firm, and one of Buffett's sons, Howard, remained on the board. The *Wall Street Journal* reported that despite Warren Buffett's frequent criticism of hedge funds, Berkshire Hathaway invested about $500 million in a hedge fund managed by the son of a Buffett friend. In any event, the reformers were not giving up. Among other things, they wanted chief executive officers to have degrees in liberal arts from Ivy League schools, a change from the current concentration of degrees in business from state schools and lesser private colleges.

Even Eliot Spitzer tried to be more business friendly as a warm-up for his upcoming New York gubernatorial bid, but overplayed his hand in a press interview in December 2004. Spitzer remarked to a reporter that a "re-energized" SEC lessened the need for any more aggressive regulatory actions on his part. Spitzer said in that interview that investigations by fifty different states could balkanize regulations. That interview and comment appeared on the front page of the *New York Times* on December 25. Spitzer quickly claimed that he had been misquoted after his remarks were criticized as an all too blatant appeal for business support in his campaign and the *New York Times* issued a retraction. To prove his toughness, Spitzer threatened more spectacular charges in 2005, launched another attack on the insurance industry, and indicted James Zimmerman, the chief executive officer of Federated Department Stores, for perjury in connection with an antitrust investigation. That drew criticism from the business community. Tom Donohue, president of the U.S. Chamber of Commerce, accused Spitzer in widely quoted remarks of acting as "the investigator, the prosecutor, the judge, the jury and the executioner." A *Wall Street Journal* editorial mocked Spitzer for trying to keep any chefs from serving on the board of the James Beard Foundation, a New York culinary institute, after its head was indicted for stealing from the foundation. Spitzer claimed that the chefs had a conflict of interest that would bar them from serving on the board because they were involved in the food preparation business.

Attorney General Wolf Packs

Another unnecessary burden on corporations is the state attorney general wolf packs that attack everything from tobacco, drugs, banks, and financial analysts to mutual funds. Eliot Spitzer and seven other state attorney generals were even suing utility companies located outside their states on the ground that those companies were contributing to the yet unproved theory of global warming by their emissions. The suits sought to require those utilities to reduce the amount of their carbon monoxide emissions by 3 percent over the next decade. The state attorney generals were emboldened by the giant tobacco litigation settlements. Those settlements were also a boon to private lawyers assisting the states in that litigation. The legal fees amounted to billions of dollars collectively and were riddled with abuses. Dan Morales, a former Texas attorney general, and Marc Murr, a Houston attorney, were jailed for trying to steal millions from the $17 billion Texas settlement through improper fee claims. Among those claiming fees from the tobacco settlement was Hugh Rodham, the brother of then First Lady Hillary Clinton, even though he had no experience in such litigation. The attorney generals used and encouraged private attorneys to pursue litigation on behalf of the states represented by the attorney generals. That relationship had some insidious benefits for both. The private attorneys could seek contingency fees that were not available to the attorney generals and the private attorneys could in return make political contributions to the attorney generals. A U.S. Chamber of Commerce study noted several such arrangements, including a total of $150,000 paid to California attorney general Bill Lockyer by the lawyers in Milberg Weiss Bershad & Schuman, a large class action firm often associated with Lockyer's causes.

The state attorney generals, and then numerous other state officials, began to cast their nets wider after their tobacco success, as exemplified by California attorney general Bill Lockyer's suit against McDonald's and other fast food restaurants that seeks to require labels on their French fries warning that such fare may cause cancer. Flying the tattered populist banner of class warfare and antibusiness attacks, the state attorney generals were seeking to set national policy and impose their own self-designed regulations through lawsuits, bypassing Congress in the process. Stalwart liberal and former secretary of labor under Bill Clinton, Robert Reich hailed this as a new era of "regulation by litigation." The *New York Times Magazine* was even portraying Spitzer's tactics as a way for the Democrats to stage a strategic comeback through attacks on Republicans. Ronnie Earle, a local Democratic prosecutor for Travis County, Texas decided to put the strategy advocated by the *New York Times* into practice. He indicted Tom DeLay, the ultraconservative House Republican majority leader, for money laundering in connection with corporate campaign contributions. The charges were convoluted and of doubtful propriety, but the effect was the immediate removal of DeLay from his leadership post, a feat that could not be accomplished at the polls.

DeLay charged that the indictment was an effort by the Democrats to criminalize his conservative politics. Any doubt as to whether the Democrats would try to capitalize on Earle's partisan prosecution was removed when Democratic House minority leader Nancy Pelosi placed a link to the arrest warrant obtained by Earle on her Web site. To Delay's further dismay, the judge assigned to the case was Bob Perkins, a Democrat who was a contributor to Moveon.org, the liberal organization founded by George Soros who was one of Delay's chief critics. Delay's lawyers sought to have Perkins removed, but he resisted that effort and another judge had to order his removal. Delay was also outraged by the fact that Ronnie Earle had settled cases against Sears Roebuck and Cracker Barrel, two of the corporations making the donations in question by simply requiring them to make large contributions to the School of Public Affairs at the University of Texas, which is located in Earle's hometown of Austin. Those donations were to be used to fund a program on the role of corporate money in politics.

Although the relative obscurity of the attorney general office and now local officials has provided cover for their activities, the attacks they are making on the political process and the threat they pose to business by their random and politically motivated attacks are reaching a proportion that can no longer be ignored. An effort has begun to rein in the state attorney generals. Richard Grasso and Kenneth Langone at the NYSE have been fighting Eliot Spitzer's politically motivated suit, even mocking him in the press. The only defendant tried by Spitzer in the mutual funds scandal resulted in an embarrassing loss to the attorney general. Perhaps a more serious challenge is a suit by the Competitive Enterprise Institute that challenges the state tobacco settlement that is administered by the National Association of Attorney Generals as an illegal cartel in violation of the antitrust laws. The attorney generals were also accused of violating the "compact clause" of the Constitution that prohibits the states from entering into compacts with each other. Still another consideration is the commerce clause that assigns to Congress the right to regulate interstate commerce.

Led by Eliot Spitzer, the attorney general wolf packs are even now attacking every aspect of business with particular emphasis on finance. Most recently, Connecticut attorney general Richard Blumenthal announced that he would be pursuing his own regulatory agenda for hedge funds. Blumenthal was displeased with the SEC's limited regulation of those operations and was seeking help from other states to impose a separate regulatory structure. Such litigation generates billions for the states and had now become an essential part of state finance, but it is an unrepresentative and random tax on businesses. The state attorney general wolf packs sued everyone standing around Enron in order to recover the $1.5 billion in losses from Enron stock owned by thirty-one state pension funds. Other corporate failures such as WorldCom met the same response. The headlines generated by such actions have now become a way for these minor government officials to advance to higher office. As a result, the states have taken over much of the regulation of public companies, marginalizing the SEC in the process. The National Securities Markets Improvement Act of 1996 had sought to preempt most state securities regulation over large public companies, but there was a loophole that allowed state actions for fraud. That loophole proved big enough to drive a truck through for Spitzer and other state officials.

This situation is the result of the fact that financial regulation in the United States is based on a "functional" approach, which allows various agencies to oversee particular aspects of the operations of a financial services firm. Functional regulation actually made some sense at one time. Financial services in the United States were once offered in discrete industries that could be regulated separately. Broker-dealers handled securities and were regulated by the SEC, banks handled deposits and lending and were regulated by bank regulators (state banking commissions or the Office of the Comptroller of the Currency, the Federal Reserve Board, the Office of Thrift Supervision, and the Federal Deposit Insurance Corporation), insurance companies sold insurance and were regulated by the state insurance commissioners, and futures commission merchants marketed commodity futures contracts and were regulated by the Commodity Futures Trading Commission (CFTC). That sensible division was lost when financial institutions started offering all these products under the same umbrella as the Glass-Steagall barriers were gradually pulled down and finally repealed.

The result of the unification of financial services is that the SEC now regulates the securities operations of bank affiliates and insurance companies, as well as traditional broker-dealers. The CFTC regulates commodity futures activities of bank affiliates and all other market participants, and bank regulators regulate banking activities of many diversified financial institutions. The fifty states and the District of Columbia superimpose their own banking, insurance, and securities rules over the same financial service firms, resulting in a mass of redundancy and inefficiency and hordes of regulators vying for headlines with every financial scandal. Yet, even with all this regulation, it appears that there are never enough tools in the regulatory drawer. Each scandal requires more legislation, more regulations, and even more regulators, most recently the PCAOB.

Other countries take a unified approach to financial services regulation. In England, the Financial Services Authority (FSA), created in 1997 after a series of financial scandals, assumed the duties of nine regulatory agencies governing everything from stocks, futures, insurance to banking and funeral planning. The FSA immediately began work on a "single rule book" for all financial services. Japan and Germany opted for single regulators for financial services. The United States could well follow that example by curbing the number of regulators that compete for prosecutions against corporations and impose layer after costly layer of regulation. There is, however, a danger from a single regulator. In Japan, the government was using its single regulator, the FSA, to continue its command and control over the economy. The FSA in England was also flexing its muscles in an apparent effort to mimic the SEC in America. The FSA was fining companies for disclosure failures, including Pace Micro Technology PLS, which was fined a record £450,000.

The Government Accountability Office (GAO) issued a report in 2004 asking Congress to consider whether the existing functional approach to financial regulation has continued merit in light of the amalgamation of financial services into giant companies. The report noted that jurisdictional fights and lack of coordination were a problem and that information sharing was lacking. The GAO asked Congress to consider the single regulator models in England and elsewhere. Thereafter, in August 2005, the Congressional Research Service prepared a white paper that contrasted the functional approach to regulation in the United States with that of single regulators abroad and noted possible benefits from the single regulator model.

Private Securities Litigation

Another problem in need of reform is the mass of private litigation that is choking corporate America. The federal securities laws contain some provisions that provide an express right to sue for violations by those injured. Those statutes have not spawned an undue number of lawsuits. Rather, the mass of litigation has been brought under the SEC's ubiquitous Rule 10b-5, a broad antifraud provision that was rather casually adopted in 1942 after it was discovered that the president of a company was buying up company shares at a low price by misrepresenting the company's financial condition. Although that rule has no attending statutory provision authorizing private rights of action for violating its terms, a federal district court ruled in 1946 that there was an "implied" private right of action for violations.[28]

Other courts followed that decision, and the Supreme Court recognized such an implied right of action under Rule 10b-5 in *Superintendent of Insurance v. Bankers Life & Casualty Co.*, a decision rendered in 1971.[29] Four years later, the Supreme Court began tightening its standards for implying private rights of action under federal laws. In *Cort v. Ash,* the Court refused to find an implied private right of action for violations of a criminal law prohibiting corporate campaign contributions.[30] The Supreme Court subsequently noted in *Cannon v. University of Chicago,* that it had deviated from its standards for finding implied private rights of action in its decision in *Superintendent of Insurance.*[31] The Court decided, however, to acquiesce in the then twenty-five-year-old practice in the federal courts of allowing private rights of action under Rule 10b-5.

Between 1946, when it was first held that a private right of action existed under SEC Rule 10b-5, and 1968, when the first federal appellate case on insider trading was decided, federal court decisions citing Rule 10b-5 numbered just 284. Since that latter date, Rule 10b-5 has been cited in over 11,000 federal court decisions. That number, which does not include SEC administrative proceedings or thousands of arbitration proceedings involving broker-dealers, is about equal to the number of public companies reporting to the SEC. That punishing figure was pushed up by a 60 percent increase in class actions filed against public companies in 2001. The companies that were defendants in those suits lost more than $2 trillion in market capitalization after those suits were filed. The amount of settlements in securities class actions reached $5.4 billion in 2004 and was rising as the suits filed during the Enron era scandals were being settled. The mean settlement amount for securities class actions in 2004 was $27 million, up 33 percent from the prior year.

Settlements after the adoption of Sarbanes-Oxley were frequently including requirements for changes in corporate governance. The *Wall Street Journal* called this "Governance at Gunpoint." A settlement involving the Cendant Corp. had started that trend. That restructuring was not successful. Cendant announced in October 2005 that it was splitting itself into four separate companies. Sprint agreed in one such settlement to create the position of lead independent director. HCA Inc., the company founded by Senator Bill Frist, agreed to rotate its auditors and add more independent directors, but that did not stop an insider trading scandal at the company that involved the senator. Hanover Compressor Co. agreed to rotate its auditors. Ashland Inc., an oil company, agreed to increase the number of outside directors and appoint a lead director to settle an action brought by the Central Laborers' Pension Welfare and Annuity Fund. No damages were paid and the only beneficiary of the suit appeared to be the lawyers. A federal prosecutor went even further in coercing a deferred prosecution agreement from Bristol-Myers Squibb over its accounting problems. The company was required by U.S. Attorney Christopher J. Christie to employ a nonexecutive chairman (James Robinson III, the former chief executive officer of American Express), to add former FBI director Louis Freeh as an additional outside director and to appoint Frederick Lacey, a former federal judge, to monitor the company and report periodically to Christie's office. Christie also required the company to endow a chair in business ethics at his alma mater, the school of law at Seton Hall University. That was in addition to the $300 million he required the company to pay into a shareholder compensation fund, a payment that brought the total paid by Bristol-Myers at the demand of prosecutors to $839 million.

Investors were receiving little benefits from the massive post-Enron settlements. By July 2005, only two cents of every dollar paid in those settlements had reached investors. A fifty-member operation headed by Richard Breeden was working to pay WorldCom investors settlement funds with little success but at a cost of over $3 million and growing.

Abuses in class action litigation brought under Rule 10b-5's private right of action were endemic to the process. Aggressive plaintiff lawyers vied with each other to sue first whenever there was some corporate bad news so that they could lay claim to massive fees. Those abuses included the use of "professional plaintiffs" that held small amounts of stock in numerous companies, enabling their allied class action lawyer to sue immediately whenever the press reported an event out of the ordinary. The enormous costs and exposures associated with those lawsuits often resulted in large settlements, regardless of the merits of the claims. Settlements were forced by using the corporate fear of antibusiness bias on the part of juries. Those settlements provided little benefit to shareholders, indeed drained corporate funds, but were a lucrative source of attorney fees, often amounting to millions of dollars.

One law firm, Milberg Weiss Bershad Hynes & Lerach LLP, was lead counsel in 55 percent of the class action lawsuits involving securities claims in the

1990s. William Lerach of that firm was paid $13.6 million in 1998, but was himself the target of a lawsuit that resulted in a whopping $50 million judgment. Lerach had started the problem by suing Lexecon Inc., a Chicago consulting firm, for its role in preparing reports supporting the financial position of the Lincoln Savings & Loan before its notorious collapse. Lexecon settled the claim for $700,000. Also named in the suit was Daniel Fischel, a part owner and expert witness for Lexecon, which defended corporations from securities litigation, such as those brought by Lerach's firm. Fischel was the University of Chicago law professor and later dean of that institution who wrote a book defending Michael Milken. Fischel believed that the lawsuit was brought by Lerach in order to undermine Fischel's credibility as an expert in future securities litigation. Lerach did make disparaging remarks about Fischel after the settlement and attacked Fischel's credibility as a witness in a suit brought against Apple Computer. After that case was concluded, a lawyer from Lerach's law firm was reported as having said of Fischel: "That little shit is dead, and he'll never testify again." Fischel and Lexecon then sued Lerach for defamation and malicious prosecution.

Fischel's lawsuit looked like a long shot in light of the Lexecon settlement and appeared to be finished at several points, but he pursued it relentlessly for nearly a decade. Fischel made a successful appeal to the Supreme Court to have the case returned to Chicago from Arizona, where it had been sent for consolidated discovery. The judge there had severely limited the scope of the case and was preparing to decide the remainder of the issues himself, rather than send it back to Chicago for trial. The Supreme Court ordered the judge to return the case to Chicago, where a jury awarded Fischel and Lexecon $45 million in actual damages before beginning its deliberations on punitive damages. Lerach then agreed to settle the claim for $50 million, but Fischel made him wire transfer the funds immediately before calling off the jury.

Lerach continued his class action cases, including one against Enron when that scandal broke and one against Lucent Technologies. His law firm split up in 2004 after an acrimonious quarrel between Lerach and another senior partner. That did not slow Lerach. Among other things, he was lead counsel in the $100 million AT&T accounting manipulation settlement and was hired by California to pursue the insurance companies involved in the bid rigging practices uncovered by Eliot Spitzer. Lerach's new law firm received a setback from the Supreme Court in a class action suit against Dura Pharmaceuticals Inc. The Court ruled in that action that, in order to recover, the plaintiffs had to prove that any alleged misrepresentations by the company had to be shown to have actually caused the company's losses rather than other market events. This did not discourage the Lerach law firm, which vowed to simply replead its claims and continue its action. Lerach was also receiving millions of dollars in settlements obtained in the Enron litigation, which totaled almost $5 billion by June 2005.

Private securities litigation grew to become an industry unto itself. Even where disclosure was faithfully made, the federal securities laws set the stage for litigation after any dip in a stock's price, providing a bonanza to the class action bar and battalions of defense attorneys. In those cases, the plaintiff shareholders, as a class, were essentially suing themselves, since it was their company that engaged in the alleged wrongdoing. Also targeted were executives, directors, auditors, and anyone else standing around corporate headquarters. Settlements were extorted from those defendants in amounts that provided little benefit to shareholders but staggering sums to the lawyers. Studies found that securities class actions were not being settled on the basis of the merits of the actions. Rather, fears of juries and litigation costs were what drove settlements.

Former House leader Newt Gingrich's "Contract with America" sought litigation reforms in the federal securities laws, resulting in a bill titled the Common Sense Legal Reforms Act of 1995. That bill would have imposed the "English rule" for attorney fees in securities class actions. Under the English rule, the loser in litigation pays the other side's attorney fees. Under the "American rule," each side bears its own attorney fees, except in class actions, derivative suits, and a few other instances where the defendants must pay the other side's fees when the plaintiff prevails. There is no reciprocal payment when the derivative or class action plaintiff loses. Imposition of the English rule on both sides would stop frivolous actions and require professional plaintiffs to consider carefully whether their suit has merit.

PSLRA

The proposed Common Sense Legal Reforms Act was opposed by the same reformers that caused the problem. "A petition circulated by the author and Columbia Law School Professor [and later SEC commissioner] Harvey Goldschmid . . . urging rejection of the initial H.R. 10 was signed through February 10, 1995, by seventy law professors who collectively concurred, 'that the bill, in its current form, would effectively end most federal securities class actions, would generally threaten the viability of all private securities litigation, and would, therefore, threaten basic protections for investors and for our capital markets.'"[32] As a result, the provision for attorney fees was removed from the Private Securities Litigation Reform Act of 1995 (PSLRA).

The PSLRA did seek to restrict overreaching by lawyers in securities litigation through several provisions, including requirements of detailed pleading describing the conduct claimed to be fraudulent and the presence of intent by the defendants. This legislation was opposed by the powerful trial lawyers' bar and was vetoed by President Bill Clinton, who received much support from those lawyers. Congress overrode that veto, the only Clinton veto that was not sustained. Still, the litigation reform effort failed because the plaintiffs' bar simply moved its activities to the state courts. Congress responded with more legislation, the Securities Litigation Uniform Standards Act of 1998, that sought to close that loophole by allowing removal of claims brought for stock fraud in state court to a federal court.

Unfortunately, these legislative acts failed to curb abusive securities litigation. The number of securities-related lawsuits more than doubled in 2001 over the prior year, and settlement costs were up over 20 percent. The number of securities class action suits increased by 31 percent between 2001 and 2002. The number of class action lawsuits increased by 16 percent in 2004 over the prior year. Before the PSLRA, there had been only a few cases settled for over $100 million. After the enactment of that legislation, some twenty cases were settled for more than that amount, some even running into billions of dollars. The PSLRA actually worsened the situation by having the courts appoint, as lead plaintiff in securities class actions, the shareholder with the largest financial interest in the claim. This inevitably meant that an institutional investor, rather than a professional plaintiff holding only a few shares, would be appointed as lead plaintiff. That institutional plaintiff was given the presumptive right to select the lawyers handling the class action.

The class action bar experienced a shock in June 2005 with the indictment of Seymour M. Lazar, a long time client of the law firm of Milberg Weiss Bershad & Schuman. The government charged that Lazar received $2.4 million in kickbacks from the law firm over a twenty-year period as payment for acting as the firm's dummy plaintiff in over fifty class action lawsuits. William Lerach and Melvyn Weiss were targets of the continuing criminal investigation into the activities of their law firm. Prosecutors were having statute of limitations problems, however, because many of those payoffs were made to the individual private plaintiffs before the adoption of the PSLRA in 1995.

This investigation did not slow the Milberg Weiss law firm. Only days after the Lazar indictment, the law firm announced a $90 million shakedown of the Royal Dutch/Shell Group for overstating its reserves, and Lerach had collected over $7 billion from financial institutions in the Enron litigation. Lerach was also scouring Europe for class action plaintiffs. Milberg Weiss did receive a setback when a Delaware judge dismissed an action brought by that firm over the firing of Michael Ovitz at Walt Disney Co., but the law firm quickly recovered. A federal appeals court reversed the dismissal of a class action suit brought by Milberg Weiss under the antitrust laws against underwriters engaging in the IPO abuses of the 1990s such as "laddering" to increase the after-market price of the IPO securities. Milberg Weiss was also receiving the lion's share of the $30 million in attorney fees from the class action settlement with KPMG and Sidley Austin Brown & Wood over their role in marketing tax shelters.

Most institutions had little interest in pursuing litigation over a failed investment or management error. That was not true, however, for the state pension funds, and they soon were themselves professional plaintiffs in securities class action lawsuits. The state pension funds were investing in nearly every stock in the market, allowing them to claim injury whenever a stock dropped in price. Such diversification is the means by which investors protect themselves from management and other company-specific risks. Under such a strategy, investment losses from particular companies are expected, but the state pension funds could not accept an investment loss of any kind. They perceived litigation as a means of improving their performance results and full disclosure under the federal securities laws as an insurance program that protected them from any market loss. With their large holdings, the state pension funds were given lead plaintiff status in numerous cases. Soon, these union retirement programs were demanding larger and larger settlements. They were also offering bounties for recoveries from the personal funds of executives. Business executives were being hunted like animals. The massive contingency fees given to the class action lawyers further fueled the abuses, a process that even the moderate Supreme Court Justice Sandra Day O'Connor cited as a flaw in our judicial system in a speech given some six months before the Enron scandal.

The California Public Employee Retirement System (Calpers), the largest retirement fund in the United States, became the leader in this abusive litigation, but other state government pension funds, such as those in New York, also joined the game. The University of California was the lead plaintiff in the class action suit brought against Enron's banks and others. This situation reached the point of absurdity when the Pompano Beach Police and Firefighters Retirement System brought a class action lawsuit against Citigroup, claiming that the bank should reimburse its own shareholders for losses in the value of Citigroup's stock as a result of its involvement with Enron, a forced dividend. The pension funds were also appointing lead counsel on a political basis, even demanding political contributions from those lawyers.

Pension Funds as Managers

The SEC interjected itself further into corporate governance issues after the Enron and WorldCom scandals. The agency amended its regulations in 2003 to require money managers to vote proxies for the stock they manage and to disclose their voting practices. Many money managers had been passive investors, choosing to sell the stock if they did not approve of management. The SEC rule nixed that approach, raising several concerns in the process. Many money managers are in no position to substitute their judgment for that of corporate management. They manage broad-scale holdings and cannot inform themselves on every corporate vote. There are also conflict concerns when money managers have different strategies for different customers. The SEC asserted that these problems could be avoided by relying on the advice of independent services that promote good corporate governance, which apparently means that business should not be judged by success, but by politically correct governance standards.

The issue remains a serious one since institutional investors own 68 percent of stocks. A cottage industry sprang up to rate corporations on their governance standards. Those ratings groups included Institutional Shareholders' Services, the Corporate Library, GovernanceMetrics International (which approved the governance practices of only 34 of the 3,220 companies it reviewed), Moody's, and Standard & Poor's. A *Wall Street Journal* editorial pointed out that Institutional Shareholders' Services was ranking corporations on their corporate governance standards at the same time that it was charging those companies consulting fees for advice on how to improve their ranking. That firm was hardly ideologically neutral. Its chairman, Robert C.S. Monks, was an advocate for far left causes; including an advertising campaign he conducted that accused John Roberts, then candidate for the position of Chief Justice of the United States, of being the "Latest Face of Extremism." Monks' father, Robert A.G. Monks, was the corporate activist who had started the effort in the 1990s to separate the role of the chairman and chief executive office in public corporations. Law and business schools were also seeking to set corporate governance norms through various classes and institutes. Their efforts were dealt a setback when Florencio Lopez-de-Silanes, the head of the Yale Institute for Corporate Governance, was forced to resign in 2005 after it was discovered that he had double-billed some $150,000 in travel expenses to the institute.

The SEC was proposing another reform to give Calpers and other state pension plans more control over corporate management by allowing them to nominate individuals to the board of directors of public companies. The rule proposed by the SEC would allow shareholders holding at least 5 percent of a company's shares to make nominations for the board of directors, providing institutions like Calpers with an opportunity to take over the boardrooms of American corporations. California was considering legislation that would adopt an even lower threshold of 2 percent nomination rights for corporations doing business there. The pension plans want outside directors that they can control and who will promote union interests. This effort reflects nothing less than an effort to socialize the markets. That would be the death knell for American financial dominance and the economy. Outside directors should not be used for such purposes. The SEC had rejected such a rule in 1942, after members of Congress claimed it was communist in nature. The idea was revived and rejected again in 1992. The SEC's proposal of such a requirement after Enron also set off a storm of controversy. The agency was flooded with some 16,000 comment letters on the proposal. Even Evelyn Davis, the longtime corporate gadfly, was against turning control over to the labor unions. Fortunately, the SEC was split over this proposal even after Enron, and its adoption was in question. Nevertheless, the SEC staff was examining other ways to achieve the same result, and SEC commissioner Harvey Goldschmid attacked SEC chairman William Donaldson in the *New York Times* for backing away from this proposal.

The SEC staff reversed itself and allowed Walt Disney Co. to exclude a shareholder proxy proposal that would have authorized Calpers to nominate board directors. In announcing that change in position, the SEC staff noted that the SEC had yet to vote on the issue, which seemed to signal a recognition by the SEC that turning over control of corporate America to the labor unions might not be such a good idea after all. In a policy reversal announced with the shareholder nomination proposal, the SEC staff had stated that it would require companies to include shareholder proxy proposals allowing them to nominate directors. The staff reversed that position after Donaldson backed off the proposed rule, allowing Halliburton, Qwest, Walt Disney Co., and Verizon to exclude such proposals. Several liberal Democrats in the U.S. House of Representatives, led by John Dingell, then wrote to the SEC protesting this most recent change in policy. Trying to please everyone, the SEC staff required Citigroup to have its shareholders vote on a proxy proposal by the United Brotherhood of Carpenters pension fund that sought to require a majority vote for directors, rather than the plurality provided for under state law. That proposal had been submitted by the Brotherhood of Carpenters and other labor unions to some seventy companies. Despite the SEC's apparent abandonment of its proposed rule on shareholder nominations, the American Federation of State, County, and Municipal Employees used the problems at American International Group (AIG) to launch a lawsuit demanding that AIG allow the union pension fund to nominate directors.

The efficacy of the SEC nomination proposal was in all events suspect since the Enron bylaws had a quite liberal provision for allowing shareholder nominations for board positions. Nevertheless, several companies, including Pfizer, Walt Disney, Microsoft, and United Technologies, adopted a form of majority vote requirement for elections in which a director receiving a plurality would not be elected if a majority of votes were marked as "withheld."

Gretchen Morgenson, a business columnist and corporate governance scold for the *New York Times,* compared the rights of shareholders in corporations that do not require a majority vote for the election of directors to those of citizens in the USSR. Presumably, she was exaggerating for effect. Otherwise, that claim demonstrates a disturbing lack of knowledge of both the Soviet Union and voting rights in the United States. Voters were given no choice in Soviet elections and dissidents were sent to a Gulag, or worse. In corporate America, shareholders may vote as they please, for or against management. They can oppose management in a proxy fight and even elect their own slate of directors, if they have sufficient votes and funds to finance a campaign. An even more efficient way to vote against management where an investor is displeased with management for any reason is to simply sell the stock. The proceeds can then be placed in one of the millions of the investment alternatives available in America.

As for the requirement of a majority vote, the Soviet Union demanded near unanimity, which is apparently what Morgenson and other reformists are seeking for public corporations. Yet, in America, Bill Clinton was elected in 1992 with only 43 percent of the popular vote. Abraham Lincoln did not even do that well, receiving only 39 percent. More interesting is the fact that the majority vote required in the Electoral College resulted in the election of four presidents, including George W. Bush, who actually lost the popular vote.

State pension plans did not await SEC rules to mount an attack on corporate America. A group of those plans managing $1 trillion in assets announced that they would be working together to improve integrity of management in public corporations. That cabal included representatives of fourteen states and cities. The AFL-CIO boasted in 2004 that mutual funds were following its recommendations on votes for executive compensation in 55 percent of cases. That organization was supported by Arthur Levitt's bizarre claim that the AFL-CIO should earn accolades for being a supporter and protector of individual investor causes. More embarrassing was an effort by the Communications Workers of America to unseat Robert A. Stranger from the board of Citizens Communications. Unfortunately, Stranger died some six weeks before that campaign was launched. Stranger had headed the company's compensation committee that approved a generous compensation package for the chief executive office, Leonard Tow. It was that approval that aroused the ire of the Communication Workers.

TIAA-CREF, the pension fund founded by Andrew Carnegie for destitute college professors, with about $290 billion under management claimed that corporate governance in America was faulty and that boards of directors should be restructured to allow more public representation. TIAA-CREF even had its own senior vice president and chief counsel for corporate governance, Peter Clapman. He was seeking to force large companies to tighten the manner in which they granted stock options. This was at a time when TIAA-CREF's chief executive officer, Herbert M. Allison Jr., was being paid $9 million per year to manage the funds of struggling, underpaid professors. Allison also proved to be less than a stalwart reformer when it came to his own stewardship. He failed to inform his own board (one of whose members was former SEC chairman Arthur Levitt) of a business arrangement between two TIAA-CREF trustees and Ernst & Young to jointly market a valuation for stock options needed by corporations under the new option-expensing requirement. That arrangement was a violation of the SEC's auditor independence requirements. The two trustees resigned at the demand of the SEC staff. A subsequent internal investigation by Nicholas Katzenbach, the former attorney general and WorldCom inquisitor, criticized Allison for not promptly notifying the TIAA-CREF oversight board of this proposal and urged a change in its corporate governance structure that would eliminate the board of overseers over the boards of TIAA and CREF. TIAA-CREF also resorted to a trick used by many corporations it was criticizing. That is, it was hiring proxy solicitation firms to help pass unpopular shareholder measures. In the case of TIAA-CREF, that was the passage of a proposal to quadruple fees on some of its mutual funds at a time when other mutual funds were being forced by Eliot Spitzer to reduce their fees. That effort failed, but TIAA-CREF resubmitted the proposal for another shareholder vote. So much for shareholder democracy!

After Enron, Calpers announced that it was withholding votes for directors of 2,700 companies in the United States because Calpers claimed that the directors on the board were not sufficiently independent. Calpers additionally targeted Walt Disney, Coca-Cola, Royal Dutch/Shell Group, Emerson Electric Co., and Maytag Corp. for corporate governance reforms. Calpers was withholding support from the reelection of several Citigroup directors, including Sanford Weill and Charles Prince. Calpers launched another initiative in November 2004 against excessive executive compensation seeking more disclosures concerning compensation and targeting specific companies having what Calpers viewed as the worst compensation practices. In an effort to appease Calpers and other reformist critics, Christopher Cox, the new and supposedly conservative chairman of the SEC, was supporting their efforts to have more full disclosure on executive compensation. According to Cox, shareholders receiving such information could mount a proxy fight against those executives receiving excessive compensation. In response to that claim, Professor Henry G. Manne, the former dean of the George Mason University School of Law and a leading critic of the SEC full disclosure regime, asserted in a *Wall Street Journal* op-ed piece that: "Only in the make-believe world of SEC regulation could anything like the proxy fight be seen as a significant solution to the . . . problem of exorbitant salaries."

Calpers also required the investment managers handling its funds to set their compensation based on performance and required external money managers and consultants to adhere to Calpers's code of ethics as a condition for doing business. Beyond weird, Calpers was seeking an investigation of the Abu Ghraib prison abuses in Iraq on the strength of its $12 million investment in CACI International, a company that employed three translators that worked at the prison. That effort was spearheaded by Philip Angelides, the California treasurer and a trustee at Calpers, who is expected to run for governor in 2006. A new and more dangerous tactic has been to force the election of board nominees through class action litigation. Dynegy thus agreed, in addition to paying $468 million, to elect two individuals to its board who were selected by the University of California, the lead plaintiff in the litigation. Cendant Corp. agreed to elect a majority of outside directors to its board in a settlement with Calpers.

More frightening was the political attack on the Sinclair Broadcast Group during the 2004 presidential election. That company was planning to air a documentary critical of Senator John Kerry's antiwar activities after he returned from service in Vietnam. The broadcast was pulled after William Lerach, the class action lawyer and a Democrat, threatened a shareholder lawsuit if the program was run. Lerach claimed that the broadcast would result in a loss of revenues to the company because some advertisers might pull their accounts. The New York comptroller, Alan Hevesi, a Democrat, then made a similar threat of a class action suit on behalf of the state's pension funds. Full disclosure was now being turned into a weapon for lawyers, unions, or anyone else with a political agenda. Havesi was making no idle threat. As the sole trustee for the New York Common Retirement Fund, he held sway over $120 billion in assets, making him the largest investor in the United States. Hevesi was not all that successful in his investments for the fund, which were underperforming and causing New York taxpayers to make up massive deficits. The annual report for the retirement fund cheerily dismissed those problems and provided excuses that would do a faltering dot-com company proud. Hevesi was also seeking legislation that would allow him to increase his bets on more risky investments in order to achieve higher investment returns. Earlier, another New York comptroller, Carl McCall, had used his office to demand that the SEC investigate Congressman Rich Lazio for insider trading. Lazio had made a profit of $13,500 by trading options on the stock of Quick & Reilly in 1997, a discount brokerage firm whose principals were supporting his political career. There was no apparent reason why the New York comptroller would have any interest in such a matter, except that Lazio just happened to be running against Hillary Rodham Clinton for the Senate at the time. Clinton was receiving renewed criticism for her miraculous short-term profit of $100,000 on a $1,000 investment in commodity futures made years before through the Refco brokerage firm. McCall sought to neutralize that problem with an SEC investigation of Lazio. Just to make sure it received proper attention, McCall also sent the letter to the *New York Times*. Lazio had disclosed the trades on his congressional financial disclosure forms, and the SEC could find no violations. Nevertheless, the attack put Lazio on the defensive in the Senate race. McCall was himself immune from full disclosure attacks as witnessed by Eliot Spitzer's decision to exclude McCall from the Richard Grasso lawsuit.

Reform efforts have not been particularly successful in other areas. Calpers objected to excesses in executive pay in the early 1990s, but the result was only that compensation increased. Each year Calpers published a list of companies that, in its view, were not performing as they should. This resulted in what became known as the "Calpers effect." The companies that Calpers listed as underperforming thereafter outperformed the S&P 500 Index and other companies in their industry. Nevertheless, Calpers claimed that its investments in companies with good corporate governance standards were outperforming its other investments in 2004. Actually, Calpers own investments dropped in value by $27 billion between 1999 and 2003, and its performance was lagging behind similar institutions. California taxpayers were making up the shortfall.[33] Calpers was undeterred by such problems. It was seeking in 2005 a new rule that would prohibit investment banking firms from offering opinions on the fairness of mergers and other acquisitions in which the investment banker was a participant.

Calpers Governance

Interestingly, the public pension plans were not themselves paragons of corporate virtue. Calpers was heavily involved in one of Enron's special purpose entities and could be fairly accused of setting the ball in motion that led to Enron's ultimate collapse. Calpers was even then billing itself as an aggressive guardian of its interests as a shareholder and investor. "But in the case of the Enron Corporation, Calpers was the watchdog that did not bark."[34] It was not the only one. The *New York Times* led the pack in attacking the accounting practices at Enron and other financial "shenanigans," but had itself engaged in a "newsprint" swap with Enron that was used as a "cash flow hedge."

Calpers's own independence was questioned by the *Wall Street Journal,* which noted that eleven of Calpers's thirteen board members were dependent on union funds in one way or another. There appeared to be clear conflict of interest when Calpers sought to unseat Steve Burd as chairman of Safeway, the giant food company, after a bitter strike by the United Food and Commercial Workers union (UFCW). Calpers's president, Sean Harrigan, was an international vice president of UFCW. That effort was at all events less than successful. Calpers could persuade only 16.7 percent of shareholders to oppose Burd's reappointment, despite a lagging stock price. Harrigan also used his Calpers position to pressure California supermarkets to settle a union strike.

A reaction to Calpers's extremes seemed to be setting in as witnessed by the removal of Harrigan as president in December 2004. He had received much criticism for his use of Calpers to support his union's strike against Safeway. Still, Calpers remained dominated by trustees with labor union and liberal Democratic ties, who vowed to maintain their attacks on corporate management even as they claimed that Governor Arnold Schwarzenegger was seeking to replace them with more moderate representatives. In any event, Calpers may have overplayed its hand because legislation was introduced to convert Calpers from a defined benefit plan to a Section 401(k) format, which would shift control of the investment accounts to employees. Governor Schwarzenegger was seeking a constitutional amendment to allow such a transformation. Calpers's union members began picketing and organizing demonstrations against Schwarzenegger because of that proposal. California Attorney General Bill Lockyer torpedoed the Schwarzenegger proposal by including some totally extraneous language in the ballot initiative asking if the voters approved eliminating death and disability benefits for police and firemen. Schwarzenegger then announced that he would drop the proposal and seek alternate remedies. One such Schwarzenegger ballot initiative would require state employee unions to have written permission from its members to use union funds for political purposes. Similar initiatives in Utah and Washington had nearly dried up such funding. The state employee pension funds in California, however, successfully managed to portray Schwarzenegger's initiatives as an unfair and brutal attack on nurses and teachers.

The *Wall Street Journal* and others also advocated a Section 401(k) format for Calpers as was done for the Florida retirement system. This move would take Calpers and its ilk out of the money management business, in which they had no expertise and were using only to advance a political agenda. However, Calpers supporters, such as the *New York Times,* noted that Nebraska dropped its conversion to Section 401(k) accounts after those accounts performed more poorly than defined benefit arrangements. Nevertheless, like Florida, a dozen or so states were allowing workers to maintain their own investment accounts, reflecting the need to cover a nationwide shortage in state- and municipal-defined benefit pension plan obligations. This was worse than the now increasingly unpopular defined benefit plans of corporate employers. Forty-five states are affected by such shortfalls. In thirteen of those states unfunded pension obligations exceed the states' annual general revenues. California taxpayers were paying $2.6 billion to state pension plans. New York City was paying $2.3 billion to its employee plans in 2004, more than triple the amount paid in 2000. Health benefit costs are expected to double for those workers by 2008. West Virginia state employee plans are underfunded by $5 billion, and the state fund has only about 20 percent of the assets needed to meet its pension obligations. Even worse, Illinois has a $38 billion shortfall in its state pension funds. The total amount of underfunding by state and local pensions is estimated to exceed $450 billion. That amount was about $200 billion more than the total underfunding of private defined benefit plans.

Six members of San Diego's municipal pension fund voted to increase city pension benefits by hundreds of millions of dollars. They were later arrested for that vote, which had the effect of substantially increasing their own pensions. San Diego had other issues. Valerie Stallings, a council member, pleaded guilty to receiving some gifts from the owner of the San Diego Padres, which was seeking $170 million from the city for its new ballpark. Another scandal arose after it was discovered that the city's pension fund had a $1.1 billion shortfall. As now customary, the city sued its financial advisers, in this case Callan Associates, claiming that they had undisclosed conflicts of interest. In fact, the pension fund's troubles stemmed from the fact that benefits had been increased for the fund's beneficiaries without providing any means to pay for those increases. The city was forced to restate its financial reports in amounts totaling over $600 million.

The ensuing scandal forced the mayor from office and resulted in investigations by the SEC, the Justice Department, and others. The city hired the law firm of Vinson & Elkins of Enron fame to prepare a report on what happened. KPMG, which had been hired to audit the city's books after the scandal arose, was dissatisfied with that probe and refused to certify the city's financial statements, cutting it off from the bond markets. An audit committee appointed by the city was causing further confusion. It was headed by former SEC chairman Arthur Levitt. The drama grew after the election of a new city attorney,

Michael Aguirre, who immediately began seeking his own headlines and interfering with the other investigations already under way. Aguirre was the
lawyer who had previously sued SEC chairman Christopher Cox for violations of the federal securities laws. This affair was referred to by the *Wall
Street Journal* as an "Enron by the Sea."

Calpers was refusing full disclosure of the management and advisory fees
it paid to money managers and was being sued by a news organization to
force disclosure. After that litigation was filed, Calpers agreed to make those
disclosures. Among other things, it paid advisory fees of $8.1 million to an
adviser with a 2 percent rate of return, as compared to an industry average of
9.7 percent. Calpers had been forced by earlier litigation to disclose its performance results. According to the *Wall Street Journal,* those disclosures revealed that Calpers had invested in Yucaipa Companies despite negative returns.
That company had ties to two powerful Calpers board members. Several similar
conflicts were also revealed.

Two Pennsylvania state pension funds were suing Time Warner and Royal
Dutch/Shell Group over their accounting problems. Those state funds had
lost 25 percent of their value, amounting to $20 billion, over the previous
few years, while paying $250 million in management fees. The Pennsylva-
nia state treasurer, Barbara Hafer, was resisting an investigation of those
fees. The Louisiana state teachers' retirement system, which had lost as
much as $2 billion from risky ventures, was the plaintiff in sixty class ac-
tion suits against companies in which it invested, including one in which
the retirement fund had only a $30,000 stake. Although the fund's trustees
were sticklers for compliance with corporate governance at the companies
they were suing, they seemed less concerned about their own activities. The
trustees had been receiving various gifts from a money manager that had
been given $900 million to manage for the state fund. "If the Louisiana and
Pennsylvania pension funds were private entities, their trustees might well
be the target of a lawsuit themselves for being so lackadaisical about their
fiduciary duty."[35]

Moreover, the unions' own corporate governance has not proved to be particularly successful, as shown by Senator Mitch McConnell's efforts to require union audits. Even before that event, Jimmy Hoffa, the head of the
Teamsters before his imprisonment and later disappearance, had turned the
looting of union pension funds into an art form through his connections to
organized crime. Given protected status by a series of New Deal laws, unions
became a center for corruption. The Norris-LaGuardia Act of 1932 had stacked
the deck in favor of the unions. That situation was sought to be rectified by the
Taft-Hartley Act in 1947, but unions were still able to cripple significant portions of the economy with exorbitant wage and benefit demands, including
the automobile and airline industries.

Ullico, a union-owned insurance company, was the center of a scandal in
2002 after it was disclosed that its board of directors, composed of union

officials, were given stock at artificially low prices and was bought back by the company at a higher price, even after the price of the stock plunged. An internal investigation by James Thompson, former governor of Illinois and federal prosecutor and chairman of the Hollinger audit committee, resulted in the dismissal of Ullico's president and chief executive officer, Robert Georgine. Georgine had received more than $20 million in compensation over a four-year period. A Senate report revealed that seventeen of the company's directors participated in this plan, receiving cumulative profits of over $10 million, and that Georgine spent $4 million to discredit Thompson's report, including a counterreport prepared by another law firm. Like the Rigas family, Georgine made liberal use of the corporate jet to visit Switzerland, Fiji, and Italy, and he put four relatives on the payroll.

More recently, four officials of the American Maritime Officers Union were indicted for embezzling union funds and rigging elections. Those charged included the union's president, Michael McKay. In Chicago, two lawyers were indicted for seeking a kickback of $850,000 from a money manager seeking to handle investments for the Teachers Retirement System of Illinois. Stuart Levine, a trustee for the pension fund, was also indicted and an unidentified "high ranking" public official was said by the indictments to be involved in this scheme. Reporters were questioning whether that official was Illinois governor, Rod Blagojevich.

A reaction was setting in to some of the worst litigation abuses. Congress adopted additional legislation that sought to require class actions in federal rather than state courts that were being used to forum shop for the state with the largest jury verdicts. That reform was not expected to be successful. An earlier statute, the Securities Litigation Uniform Standards Act of 1998, had sought to remove state class actions in securities law cases to the federal courts, but that act had little effect on reducing the number of class actions or reducing litigation abuses. More is needed such as imposing the English Rule for attorney fees, especially on institutional plaintiffs like Calpers who have the resources to pay for the cost of ill-founded litigation.

Repealing the Federal Securities Laws

The Securities Laws

The New Deal full disclosure regime that was supposed to provide investor protection did not work as claimed. The federal securities laws were supposed to protect small investors as large institutional investors were believed to be able to fend for themselves. Instead, a study by the U.S. Chamber of Commerce concluded that it was the large investors who were being benefited through litigation under the federal securities laws. Unlike many small investors, those institutions were diversified in their investments. That diversification offsets the effects from inflated accounting at one firm. By allowing the institutions to claim more from litigation, however, the institutions are allowed to improve their returns at the expense of those not sharing in the settlements.

Patching the full disclosure system and adding even more layers of regulation has not made it structurally sound. Repeal or massive revision is needed. Of course, such corrective action will be fiercely resisted by Calpers and the cadre of law school professors who, like a murder of crows, will flock to Congress with dire predictions of economic ruin and investor losses should full disclosure be repealed. Anyone criticizing the full disclosure concept will be branded as a reactionary, but repeal of some SEC-administered legislation has already occurred or is under way.

The Chandler Act was repealed years ago. That statute was passed in 1938 after a massive study of protective and reorganization committees conducted by the SEC under William O. Douglas and Abe Fortas before those two ethically challenged individuals rose to the Supreme Court. It revealed that corporate insiders were using those committees for their own purposes and to the determent of creditors. To rectify such abuses, the Chandler Act gave the SEC supervisory authority over corporate reorganizations. The SEC broadly exercised that power until that act was repealed by the Bankruptcy Reform Act in 1978. There have been few, if any, complaints that repeal of the Chandler Act has had any adverse effect on investors. Indeed, David A. Skeel Jr., a law professor at the University of Pennsylvania, has called the period that the Chandler Act was in effect "in many respects the dark ages of U.S. bankruptcy law" and that its repeal "almost completely repudiated both the SEC and the New Deal vision of bankruptcy" that had sought to exclude management, their lawyers, and Wall Street investment bankers from corporate reorganizations.

The Public Utilities Holding Company Act of 1935 (PUHC), another statute administered by the SEC, was long the subject of repeal efforts in Congress. PUHC is a dinosaur piece of legislation that was enacted largely in response to the failure of the Insull holding companies in the 1930s. The statute sought to simplify the corporate structures of public utilities, but failed, as even a cursory review of the special purpose entities listed in Enron's financial statements would evidence. An energy bill pending before Congress in 2004 contained provisions for repealing PUHC. That bill was passed by the House of Representatives over the opposition of Ralph Nader and his advocacy group, Public Citizen. Although the bill stalled in the Senate over other issues, a majority of senators were in favor of repealing PUHC, and appeal was achieved in August 2005 with the signing into law by President Bush of a long delayed energy bill.

Other New Deal financial legislation that proved unworkable has been targeted for repeal. Even Social Security, the most sacred of all New Deal cows, is under attack by President George W. Bush's administration. The Glass-Steagall Act, which hamstrung commercial banks for decades, was watered down by bank regulators and then repealed through the Gramm-Leach-Bliley Act in 1999. Another New Deal statute, the Commodity Exchange Act of

1936, was amended in 1974 to create the Commodity Futures Trading Commission (CFTC) as an analogue to the SEC for derivatives. Congress had second thoughts about that regulation in the new century. The Commodity Futures Modernization Act of 2000 deregulated vast segments of derivatives trading. Although there was some initial bleating that this deregulation contributed to Enron's problems, no such connection was ever made.

The failure of the full disclosure system as the century ended makes a strong case for repealing the federal securities laws, but their repeal will not end the need to prosecute and prohibit fraud. Corruption inhibits legitimate business activity. Gross evidence of that fact is found in the gangsters of the prohibition era, the drug lords of Colombia, and the Russian mobsters. Consequently, there is a need for some type of antifraud rule and prosecution. There is, nevertheless, a danger in employing a fraud prohibition. The government will certainly use it to overreach and to create affirmative regulations of the command and control variety. That is what the SEC did with Rule 10b-5. The SEC used that rule to create a broad range of new regulatory requirements by defining activities as fraudulent even when they were common industry practices: not the least of this genre is the previously nonexistent crime of insider trading.

As Professor Henry Manne has asserted:

> Insider-trading regulation has its primordial introduction in the muck of New Deal securities regulation, which was itself justified on the trumped-up theory that full disclosure was the best way to deal with corporate fraud and deception. Over the years the benign-sounding idea of passive regulation in the form of full disclosure has morphed into a morass of active regulation. Full disclosure now wraps around— and regulates—corporate governance, accounting, takeovers, investment banking, financial analysts, corporate counsel, and, not least, insider trading.[36]

Professor Manne has also correctly noted in one of his periodic op-ed pieces in the *Wall Street Journal* that "the regulatory philosophy of full disclosure has been tried for over seventy years and has been found sadly wanting as a way to protect shareholders from corporate and financial abuses."

The SEC can be expected to continue to attempt to create substantive regulations through antifraud actions raising "novel" legal theories. The SEC does not even need the assistance of the courts to carry out that process. The agency has a long history of creating new regulations through uncontested settlement agreements in its disciplinary proceedings. Those agreements are not subject to judicial review and avoid the often lengthy process of promulgating a formal rule, which can then be challenged in court. It was in such a proceeding that the crime of insider trading was created from whole cloth by William Cary. A former SEC commissioner, Roberta Karmel, decried the use of such settlements to create law in a book titled *Regulation by Prosecution: The Securities and Exchange Commission vs. Corporate America.* Her criticism, however, did not inhibit the SEC from continuing that practice.

The SEC was also able to convince the courts to reduce many traditional standards for fraud in its actions. The standard of materiality for determining whether a statement is fraudulent was lowered to include about anything that would interest a shareholder, even if the information would not have changed the investment decision that caused the loss. The SEC is continuing to seek a reduction in even this low threshold by claiming that "qualitative" information must be disclosed even if the amount at issue is too small to be "quantitatively" material, such as taking a ride on a corporate jet to a vacation spot or giving an analyst a bottle of wine. Even without that extension, reliance on omitted material is presumed, and the Supreme Court adopted a "fraud-on-the-market" theory in *Basic Inc. v. Levinson*[37] that relieved plaintiffs from showing any reliance on false statements in company press releases they claimed were false. Under that theory, the plaintiff need not have even read or heard of the information claimed to be false. Rather, the court presumed reliance because in an efficient market the price of the stock would reflect all information, including the information alleged to be false. The effect of the false information, theoretically speaking, would be transmitted to the plaintiff through changes in the price of the company stock.

The fraud-on-the-market theory, of course, presumed that the market was efficient and that the statements had not been discounted by the market, if it were indeed efficient. As Justice Byron White pointed out in a separate opinion, dissenting in part to the majority's ruling in the *Basic* case, "while the economists' theories which underpin the fraud-on-the-market presumption may have appeal of mathematical exactitude and scientific certainty, they are, in the end, nothing more than theories which may or may not prove accurate on further consideration." He also noted that the "the fraud-on-the-market theory is at odds with the federal policy favoring disclosure" because it seeks market discipline instead of government regulation and that "some of the same voices calling for acceptance of the fraud-on-the-market theory also favor dismantling the federal scheme which mandates disclosure."[38]

Justice White was right to be concerned. Within a decade, the efficient market hypothesis was under attack from all quarters as being overly simplistic and even wrong. Even its strongest proponents conceded that the theory was riven with flaws. Eugene Fama, the father of the efficient market hypothesis, was among those conceding its shortcomings. A new school of "behavioral economics" led by Richard Thaler attacked the efficient market theory: although "conventional finance theorists assume that only 'rational' behavior affects equity prices, behavioral finance theorists argue that how people actually behave makes a difference to stock prices. Specifically, behavioral finance is based on the observation (based on cognitive psychology and decision theory) that in some circumstances humans make systematic errors in judgment and that these behavioral biases affect equity prices."[39]

As has also been noted:

> During the last three decades, while law faculties across the nation were succumbing to the brilliant simplicity of the Coase theorem and the analytical force of the law and economics movement, social scientists in other departments were discovering evidence that should have given pause to even the most ardent legal economic positivist. Those scientists—cognitive psychologists, behavioral researchers, probability theorists, and others—were discovering powerful evidence that the rational actor model, upon which the law and economics project depends, is significantly flawed. In place of the rational actor model, those scientists were developing a human decisionmaker model replete with heuristics and biases, unwarranted self-confidence, a notable ineptitude for probability, and a host of other nonrational cognitive features.[40]

All of these theorists presume too much. The market is neither perfectly efficient nor completely inefficient. Rather, to paraphrase Winston Churchill, free market discipline is the worst possible system, except for any other.

Manipulation

Manipulation prohibitions are another ever-growing intrusion into business. In the words of the SEC: "A fundamental goal of the federal securities laws is the prevention of manipulation. Manipulation impedes the securities markets from functioning as an independent pricing mechanism and undermines the fairness and integrity of those markets."[41] Manipulation classically involves trading practices, such as wash and other rigged trades, that artificially boost or depress the price of a stock. The SEC sought to expand the reach of manipulation prohibitions by applying the term to simple breaches of fiduciary duty, a problem historically regulated only by the states under their common law. That effort was beaten back by the Supreme Court in *Santa Fe Industries Inc. v. Green,* in which the Court stated, "'Manipulation' is 'virtually a term of art when used in connection with securities markets' . . . The term refers generally to practices, such as wash sales, matched orders, or rigged prices, that are intended to mislead investors by artificially affecting market activity."

The Court in the *Santa Fe* decision reined the SEC in a bit, but also stated, "Section 10(b)'s general prohibition of practices deemed by the SEC to be 'manipulative'—in this technical sense of artificially affecting market activity in order to mislead investors—is fully consistent with the fundamental purpose of the 1934 Act 'to substitute a philosophy of full disclosure for the philosophy of *caveat emptor.*'"[42] Under this guise of full disclosure, the SEC was allowed to adopt expansive antimanipulation regulations that created command and control directives over much market activity. SEC Regulation M, for example, contains a series of complex rules with detailed requirements for every aspect of underwriter stabilizing activities during a distribution of securities into the market.

A critical element in manipulation cases is a requirement that the defendant acted with the specific intent to create an artificial price. "So long as the investor's motive in buying or selling a security is not to create an artificial demand for, or supply of, the security, illegal market manipulation is not established."[43] That raises the concern of what constitutes the requisite intent. Consider the following account of trading through Cantor Fitzgerald, a prime dealer and "blind broker" in the U.S. government bond market:

> Dealers would watch bond prices move across a screen on their desk. When they liked what they saw, they'd call their Cantor broker and make a trade or ask questions. Most important, they could trade without giving away their position. For example, if Merrill Lynch wanted to sell 200 million U.S. Treasury bonds, they wouldn't call up Goldman Sachs and declare their intentions. They'd enter the Cantor marketplace and no one would know it was them. Or they might put up a bid for the bonds to convince competitors there was a big buyer out there, only to sell in the bond futures pits of Chicago. They could trade through Cantor to take a position or to get out of one.[44]

Few market participants would claim such behavior was improper, but what separates that conduct from the gaming of the electricity market by the Enron traders? Usually that question is answered by the existence of fictitious transactions that have only the purpose of moving the market. One court has noted:

> Liability for manipulation wholly independent of fictitious transactions in fact raises interesting questions. Without such transactions, the core of the offense can be obscure. It may be hard to separate a 'manipulative' investor from one who is simply overenthusiastic, a true believer in the object of investment. Both may amass huge inventories and place high bids, even though there are scant objective data supporting the implicit estimate of the stock's value. Legality would thus depend entirely on whether the investor's intent was 'an investment purpose' or 'solely to affect the price of [the] security.'[45]

Mulheren's Prosecution

The court's concern was not theoretical. "In the late 1980's a wide prosecutorial net was cast upon Wall Street. Along with the usual flotsam and jetsam, the government's catch included some of Wall Street's biggest, brightest, and now infamous—Ivan Boesky, Dennis Levine, Michael Milken, Robert Freeman, Martin Siegel, Boyd L. Jeffries, and Paul A. Bilzerian—each of whom either pleaded guilty to or was convicted of crimes involving illicit trading scandals. Also caught in the government's net was defendant-appellant John A. Mulheren, Jr., the chief trader at and general partner of Jamie Securities Co., a registered broker-dealer."[46] Mulheren had been indicted as the result of testimony from Ivan Boesky, who cooperated with the government in order to reduce his own jail term. Learning of that treachery, Mulheren became enraged and went after Boesky. He was stopped by police who found a loaded assault rifle in the back of his Mercedes Benz. Mulheren was indicted by the U.S. attorney in Manhattan, Rudolph Giuliani. The indictment charged that Mulheren had manipulated the stock of Gulf & Western Industries Inc. (G&W)

by purchasing 75,000 shares of G&W common stock on October 17, 1985, for the purpose of raising its price to $45 per share.

The jury convicted Mulheren, but like many of Giuliani's prosecutions, that conviction was set aside on appeal. Boesky, who had been trying to take over G&W, had tipped Mulheren that the stock was a good buy and also stated that it "would be great" if the G&W stock traded at $45. Mulheren subsequently entered an order at that price. The Second Circuit Court of Appeals found these facts to be too ambiguous to support a finding of manipulative intent on the part of Mulheren, particularly since he lost money in the process. The court noted that none of the usual indicia of manipulation, such as wash trades, were present in Mulheren's trading. His successful appeal allowed Mulheren to remain in the securities business. The assault charges against him were also dropped; he asserted that his anger was the result of a stomach problem that prevented him from taking the lithium prescribed for a manic-depressive condition. Mulheren then turned to running a successful stock trading company named Bear Wagner Specialists LLC, which controlled about 17 percent of average daily trading volume on the NYSE. Mulheren died of a heart attack in 2003 at age fifty-four.

CFTC

The Mulheren prosecution evidenced the dangers of manipulation charges. Any trading activity that the government does not like can be labeled as intending to have an improper market effect, just as the flapping of a butterfly's wings in Africa can be charged with starting the forces that result in a hurricane in Florida. The CFTC adopted this butterfly approach in the charges it filed against Duke and other energy traders following the downfall of Enron. Those claims were based on charges of attempted manipulation, not actual manipulation. Previously, the CFTC had almost always charged actual manipulation, which requires the government to establish four elements: (1) the ability to move market prices, (2) the specific intent to create an artificial price, (3) the existence of an artificial price, and (4) that the accused caused the artificial price. Demonstrating elements (1), (3), and (4) required complex market evaluations, resulting in long and costly litigation that the CFTC usually lost.

The CFTC adopted its new approach of charging only "attempted manipulation" in order to spare itself the burdensome task of proving that the trader had the ability to influence prices, that an artificial price occurred, and that the trader caused the artificial price. The CFTC was emboldened by tape recordings of traders' conversations that contained much cursing and loose talk as traders sought to take advantage of market conditions, even calling their trading activities manipulation. A complete examination of those transcripts reveals, however, that the traders were acting competitively in trying to take advantage of market disparities or inefficiencies. That is what traders do, and it is a valuable service, even if their language is coarse and their desire to "manipulate" the market results in aggressive trading.

Under the CFTC's novel attempted manipulation doctrine, the agency needed to prove only an overt act (such as a false report to a trade publication) and manipulative intent, even if there was no significant market effect. It is particularly unfortunate that this new doctrine was created through uncontested settlements. In contrast, where it was claimed that false reports were used to manipulate prices in a contested case, a district court required that all the traditional elements of manipulation be proved. The alleged false reports had to be shown to be part of a scheme to manipulate prices.[47] The CFTC's newly minted approach puts traders in jeopardy for after-the-fact second guessing of aggressive trading practices. Timid traders will lead to worse, not better or more efficient price discovery.

Two professors from the University of Chicago, Daniel Fischel and David Ross, have argued that "the concept of manipulation should be abandoned altogether. Fictitious trades should be analyzed as a species of fraud. Actual trades should not be prohibited as manipulative regardless of the intent of the trader."[48] In light of the government's overreaching in charging manipulation for every practice it dislikes, that recommendation is sound.

Market Discipline

As a result of reformist efforts in the last century, laissez-faire economics became a term of derision embraced by the liberal left and even kept at arm's length by the conservative right. Adam Smith's invisible hand was rejected in favor of full disclosure in the 1930s, but the failure of the full disclosure model suggests that those reformist imprecations are misplaced. Market discipline has proved a more powerful regulator than full disclosure. The "Chicago school of law and economics" has been attacking the devotees of regulation for some time. That Chicago group questioned the full disclosure system mandated by the federal securities law even before the market bubble in the 1990s began. As Professors Easterbrook and Fischel noted in 1984:

> What does a mandatory disclosure system add to the prohibition of fraud? The implicit public-interest justification for disclosure rules is that markets produce "too little" information about securities when the only rule is one against fraud. . . . All we can say is that after fifty years, the proponents of regulation have *no* scientifically-acceptable evidence of a favorable cost-benefit ratio for any disclosure rule that rests on the benefits of reducing fraud or increasing confidence. . . . No matter what the disclosure laws say, the "average investor" who gets disclosure statements through the mail will always be too late to take advantage of any bargains available to those who use information first.[49]

The authors did admit that, while they could not assert that the federal securities laws were beneficial, they were not confident that the laws replacing an antifraud standard would be more effective in stopping abuses. That is undoubtedly true, but the massive costs associated with full disclosure would be avoided, and the false implication that full disclosure protects investors would no longer mislead the public.

Public companies were spending over $12 billion annually in audit fees even before Sarbanes-Oxley, to say nothing of all the executive time and lawyer fees required to manage disclosure and litigation expenses from full disclosure claims. Additional costs are incurred by diversions and schemes required to chase quarterly profits. Even those costs pale in light of the losses experienced by investors who believe that full disclosure in some way protects them from investment losses. How many trillions of dollars have been lost by investors in proving the opposite is true? In that regard, Professor Stephen Choi at the Boalt Hall law school at Berkeley has advocated regulating investors rather than the issuers of securities. Under that approach unsophisticated investors would be protected from themselves while more sophisticated investors would be free to contract for investment services without regulatory interference.

Disclosure in a Free Market

The SEC full disclosure system is one based on moral claims of what businesses should do in an ideal world. In that regard, the creation of the SEC and the adoption of Sarbanes-Oxley after the Enron scandal are the result of what law professor Jose Gabilondo has identified as being the result of "moral panics." Normally, such panics are associated with witch hunts, as in Salem, or some other hot button issue that is perceived to threaten social or moral order in society. Such panics start with some incident or outrage that is then blown completely out of proportion by sensationalism and lurid press reports that exploit anxieties such as fears about economic insecurity that occur in a market downturn. Those reports in turn result in populist outrage that is directed at demonizing particular individuals, such as Kenneth Lay, Jeffrey Skilling, and Bernie Ebbers. That reaction in turn results in prosecutorial misconduct, as well as legislative and judicial responses in the form of ill thought out legislation or draconian sentences. During a moral panic, no voice of moderation is allowed and the most extreme claims are accepted without question. The market discipline model is more measured. It looks at the actual cause and effects of the downturn and punishes those whose business model failed.

In a market discipline model, management is free to refrain from publishing financial statements. Some companies may choose not to disclose their finances. Investors must then decide whether to invest without that information. Some investors will elect not to invest. Others may value the company as a random event, investing only if there is a high risk-reward ratio, the method by which lotteries and other gambling enterprises operate. If the information is needed to sell the company's shares, management will have an inducement for providing information. The veracity of the disclosure will then be assessed by the market, and not by a handful of bureaucrats at the SEC that do not have time to make a meaningful review in any event.

If management chooses to disclose, it must ensure that it does not defraud investors by false claims. Absent fraud, the rule of caveat emptor would require investors to take responsibility for their own investments. Investors would have a duty to protect themselves by thoroughly researching an investment. If adequate and reliable information is not available, or if the investor is otherwise incapable of making such a judgment, that individual has no business picking stocks. Instead, the investor should stick to government guaranteed instruments or indexed stock holdings.

This does not mean that accounting statements will no longer have any value. They will be worth exactly what they provide: a statement by management of the company's financial position with some minimal verification by a third-party auditor paid for by the persons being audited. If that information is not satisfactory, then investors may invest elsewhere or, if they have the bargaining power, engage their own auditor and demand access to the books and records of the company for an audit they commission and control.

Relying on the market for discipline has another dimension. Financial information is a commodity. It is the basis for many business and investment decisions and, as such, has value. Under the full disclosure regimen mandated by the federal securities laws, the government seeks to force management to give away this valuable proprietary information for free and at great cost to the business owning the information. Management naturally resists that demand. The government also tries to command the time and place for publication of corporate information, ignoring the nature of this very valuable commodity. Information is like air. It will seep through every crack and crevice and escape through every open door. It is unrealistic to think that information, any more than air, can be contained except in a closed environment that cannot exist in an open society.

As Professor Henry Manne noted in 1966 in his criticism of the SEC's then recent creation of the insider trading prohibition, "Information is one of the most easily transmitted of all commodities. To prevent its rapid dissemination while it has exchange value is extremely difficult. Any attempt to regulate or police a market in information confronts two obstacles. The first is the extremely difficult one of knowing which transactions to prevent. The second is the actual job of policing once the undesired transactions are identified."[50] Manne was correct. Information about securities has value and should be bought and sold just like any other commodity. The government should not require that this commodity be given away for free or that it be distributed in some particular manner, as is now required by the federal securities laws.

The CFTC conducted a study early in its history to determine whether SEC insider trader prohibitions should be applied to commodity trading. The CFTC decided not to adopt such a prohibition because it would impair the efficiency of the commodity markets. This principle of treating information as a commodity was laid down much earlier by Chief Justice John Marshall in a Supreme Court decision titled *Laidlaw v. Organ*.[51] In that case, a New Orleans merchant received knowledge from the British fleet that the Treaty of Ghent had been signed, concluding the War of 1812. He then bought a large amount of tobacco. The seller of the tobacco, who was not similarly informed, retook possession of the tobacco by force after news of the treaty became generally known, the publication of which caused tobacco prices to increase by 30 to 50 percent. The purchaser sought to recover possession of the tobacco, but the seller claimed he was misled by not being informed by the purchaser of the signing of the treaty. It was argued for the seller that "[s]uppression of material circumstances within the knowledge of the vendee, and not accessible to the vendor, is equivalent to fraud, and vitiates the contract." However, Justice Marshall, for the Supreme Court, ruled there was no duty to disclose the purchaser's knowledge of the treaty:

> The question in this case is, whether the intelligence of extrinsic circumstances, which might influence the price of the commodity, and which was exclusively within the knowledge of the vendee, ought to have been communicated by him to the vendor? The court is of opinion that he was not bound to communicate it. It would be difficult to circumscribe the contrary doctrine within proper limits, where the means of intelligence are equally accessible to both parties. But at the same time, each party must take care not to say or do any thing tending to impose upon the other.[52]

This is a simple standard that has equal applicability to stocks. If there is no required disclosure or equal information opportunity for tobacco or other farming commodities, why is such a rule needed for stocks? Although the SEC and its supporters continually assert that there is something special and overridingly important about the capital-raising functions of the stock market that demands full disclosure, there is no evidence that those claims have any merit. Farming is the largest business enterprise in America. It is vital to our economy and our very lives, but full disclosure is not mandated for persons buying, selling, and producing agricultural commodities. The second-largest industry in the country is construction. It too is vital to our daily lives and commerce, but there is no SEC-type mandated disclosure for construction. Nearly 70 percent of families in America own their own homes, and those purchases were made without SEC-style disclosures or accounting opinions. Instead, a contractual approach is used for home purchases that requires the purchasers to sign dozens of documents that are unreadable and contain many lawyer-driven disclosures. Although inefficient, this system operates much more smoothly then SEC mandated full disclosure where everyone involved becomes a crook. Further, as Easterbrook and Fischel have noted, most individuals of moderate means have a greater interest in being protected from fraud in the sale of education than they do in buying securities. Yet there is no full disclosure law for such investments. The justification for the full disclosure model now is said to be market efficiency rather than fairness to customers. This seems strange, if one views information as a commodity. Pricing and distribution of a commodity in the marketplace are more efficient than a government program that forces the commodity to be given away, using threats of jail as the only incentive for disclosure. Moreover, if free information is more efficient, then why not require newspapers to make full disclosure and give their information away for free?

Commodity Model

A commodity-based model applied to the regulation of securities would, as noted by Justice Marshall, continue to prohibit fraud. This requirement is essential to any commodity transaction, and common stocks and tobacco are no different in that regard. In a commodity model system, companies could use their advertising to sell their stocks to the public. As in all advertising, puffery will be used and consumers will have to deal with that problem, as they do with other advertising. Where there are fraud and deceit, then carefully circumscribed private remedies and government prosecution should be available.

Insider Trading

Insider trading poses a more difficult issue. In the commodity model, there is really no such thing as inside information. If you have information unavailable to others, you may trade on that information. Indeed, such trading is thought to be desirable because it makes markets more efficient. No one begrudges a reward to those bringing this information to market. Say a farmer discovers a wheat rust in his field that will damage the entire region's crop when it spreads. The farmer is entitled to trade on, and profit from, that information. The result will be to increase prices and signal to the market that there will be a shortage of wheat. Alternate supplies can then be arranged or other adjustments made. The discoverer of that information makes the market more efficient and should be rewarded by profits from his trading.

Inside information about a corporation does not exactly fit the commodity model identified by Justice Marshall because commodity-based information is usually equally available, at least in theory, to everyone. Nevertheless, giving advantage to insiders at corporations will assure more efficient pricing by providing a reward for bringing that information to the market. Insider trading, of course, has become a moral issue that the SEC has used since the 1960s to expand the full disclosure concept. That banner is frayed but could be adapted to a commodity model for its adherents. The misappropriation theory would fit a commodity-based regulatory model. Theft of information held privately could be prohibited. After all, commodity theft (e.g., cattle rustling) is prohibited, and that prohibition is everywhere applauded. Financial information could be treated in the same manner.

Indeed, the CFTC and the U.S. attorney in Manhattan used the misappropriation theory to prosecuted futures trading by two individuals based on information they purloined from their employer. In that case, Thomas Edward Kelly, a trader at John W. Henry & Co. in Boca Raton, Florida, and his friend, Andrew David Rhee, made $4.7 million by "front running" John W. Henry orders. That company traded large orders for clients in the commodities markets and its orders had obvious market effect. Owned by John Henry who also owned the world champion Florida Marlins baseball team, the firm managed $2.2 billion in assets for clients. Kelly and Rhee were sentenced to thirty-three months in prison for their activity.

Labeling Versus Full Disclosure

The pure market approach in commodity trading and construction is clouded a bit by labeling laws that require content disclosures on food items and warning labels on dangerous consumer goods such as tobacco and alcohol. Even so, those warnings are concise, and no accountant's certification is required. Many states also impose simple disclosure requirements for the sale of a residence, but those disclosures cover only basic items and in many states are voluntary.

Labeling, instead of full disclosure, is used in the commodity markets regulated by the CFTC under the Commodity Exchange Act of 1936. That agency mandated a one-page risk disclosure statement that must be given to customers trading commodity futures or option contracts. These are highly sophisticated instruments that pose immense speculative risks to investors, but there is no elaborate full disclosure requirement such as that contained in the federal securities laws. That summary risk disclosure requirement was adopted after the CFTC rejected full disclosure and the "suitability" rule used in the securities industry that prohibits a broker-dealer from recommending a security that is not suitable in light of the particular investment needs of the customer. The CFTC risk disclosure tells customers that they, rather than their futures commission merchants, should decide whether commodity futures trading is suitable for their own investment interests. That document contains generic risk disclosures that describe the risks of trading commodity futures and options in general terms. The CFTC disclosure documents do not address the risks of particular commodities being traded and do not purport to provide a certified accounting statement for the pork bellies or the S&P 500 Index that trade in these markets.

Of course, government being what it is, even a disclosure form can easily become so complicated and convoluted that customer protection is lost, as in the case of SEC-mandated prospectuses and financial reports. A good example is found in the disclosure statement required for single stock futures. The SEC was given joint regulatory control with the CFTC over single stock futures, and the disclosure statement for those instruments immediately became a long, complex, miniprospectus, negating its value as a warning to unsuspecting investors. What should an SEC-mandated disclosure form contain? Certainly, investors should be warned that certification of a corporation's financial statements by an accountant does not ensure their accuracy.

A disclosure requirement should preempt state laws. The Supreme Court ruled in *Cipollone v. Liggett Group, Inc.* that the warnings required by federal law on cigarette packages preempted any state law requirement for additional warnings. The court went on to conclude, however, that the federal labeling requirement did not preempt state law claims based on breach of warranty, false advertising, fraudulent misrepresentations, or concealment of facts concerning the health risks of smoking.[53] That latter ruling opened the way for the states to pursue the tobacco companies and obtain their massive settlements. That loophole should be sealed by complete preemption of states in bringing financial disclosure–related suits, absent express permission from the SEC. As it stands now, Eliot Spitzer, an otherwise minor state government official, was able to assume command of financial regulation for the entire country. His power is so great that he was even able to obtain an order from a U.S. magistrate directing the SEC not to dispose his witnesses in a market timing case until he was done with them.

Another concern is governmental efforts to undercut the value of disclosure documents. The CFTC risk disclosure statement proved a formidable defense to claims by customers that their commodity brokers had misled them, especially since the customer was required to sign the form. The CFTC then undercut the statement's value by ruling that the effect of a risk disclosure statement is negated by oral misrepresentations by brokers. Of course, every lawsuit now contains such a claim of oral misrepresentations. Interestingly, a federal appeals court ruled that a sophisticated investor in securities was bound by written disclosures, despite oral misrepresentations made by the defendant.[54] The same court, however, later ruled that unsophisticated investors were not so bound under a CFTC disclosure form.[55] Another federal appellate court ruled that investors could not close their eyes to an oral statement that conflicted with a CFTC disclosure document.[56] This situation should be clarified. The disclosure statement should be treated like any other contract. Consumers sign contracts every day for everything from cars to houses, but rarely are able to contend that the written terms of the contract should be ignored in favor of a salesman's exaggerated claims.

Conclusion

Corporate governance began as an effort to more efficiently marshal capital and diversify risks among those contributors. That effort was a success, creating a British empire that stretched from the American colonies to India and beyond. The joint-stock companies also settled America, but fear of monopoly power prevented their use as commercial enterprises until after the Revolution. Even then, restrictions on their size and the need to obtain a charter from a state legislature inhibited their use. Those restrictions reflected a long-standing division in American politics between business and its opponents, a split that first appeared between the northern merchants and southern planters after the Revolution.

Gradually, business prevailed in removing the restrictions on corporate charters. In particular, the last quarter of the nineteenth century witnessed the adoption of more liberal corporate statutes that allowed broad corporate purposes and holding company structures. Those statutes were timely since the country was being transformed from scattered local markets into a national economy that required massive concentrations of capital and giant enterprises to build. There followed a consolidation of businesses and the creation of giant combines, resulting in a counterreaction among populists and reformers who perceived large businesses both as a threat and a source of wealth that should be shared.

Despite a number of market crashes, recessions, and depressions, the populists and reformers gained little traction until the stock market crash of 1929 and the Great Depression that followed. That opened the door for Franklin Roosevelt's New Deal and the adoption of the federal securities laws, which were premised on Louis Brandeis's concept that forced disclosures would prevent corporate misconduct. That proved to be an empty promise.

Other corporate reforms, such as fiduciary duties, were an effort to shift the power of corporate management to the courts. There were certainly corporate abuses that needed checking, but the courts were soon aggregating to themselves corporate decision making for which jurists had no experience or expertise. More reforms followed in the form of demands for outside directors and staffing of audit and other committees with such directors. Proxy and other requirements were added that sought to dilute the power of management. Those efforts were met with failure. Reformers next sought to align management's interests with those of shareholders through stock options. That reform was coupled with a new requirement for quarterly financial reports. Those two reforms converged to create the perfect storm that led to the Enron and other scandals. Management inflated accounts to meet the expectations of analysts each quarter in order to profit from stock options.

In another "reform," financial analysts were forced from their role as corporate monitors by Regulation FD and were stuck with the management-generated quarterly reports as their only source of information. The analysts lost all integrity in the process and became mere shills for their investment banker cohorts. Other reforms cratered. The invented crime of insider trading only spread with each prosecution. Mutual funds were subject to massively intrusive corporate governance requirements, which nevertheless failed to prevent the scandals that arose from market timing and late trading practices.

Under the guise of reform, every common business practice that any state functionary disliked was instantly criminalized or used to shake down large corporations, creating a random tax unsupported by legislation. Class action lawyers filed suit immediately after every press report of a corporate problem. Those suits were used to extort ever greater sums from businesses. Such extortion was even used for the partisan political purpose of stopping a television broadcast critical of a presidential candidate. Then came the state pension funds, which tried to grab power from the corporations for their own causes.

The libraries are now filled with volumes of laws and strangling regulations attacking every aspect of corporate governance. Each was adopted in response to one financial scandal or another. Those perpetuating the scandal were in jail or had long since fled the country, with the result that the ensuing regulations served only to trap and punish the innocent and unwary, who must bear their cost into eternity. After a scandal, there is the inevitable hysteria in the press. Something must be done—anything—without regard to its efficacy or cost. The result is a pile of regulations compiled with little rhyme and no reason, liable to be interpreted in any way that will further the political ambitions of an aggressive prosecutor or provide fodder for the class action lawyers.

Something more than this haphazard and costly approach to regulation is needed for an economy as complex as that of the United States. Regulations should be passed only after reflection on their cost and benefit, rather than on the strength of unsupported claims by those with an agenda. Behind most of these reforms has been a horde of law professors with little or no experience in business. They have been given great deference by state legislatures and Congress because of their knowledge of esoteric corporate laws. That deference continues despite the failure of the reforms they advocate, resulting in a never-ending cycle of reform, failure, and then more regulations. Sarbanes-Oxley is the most recent example. This failed approach has only added costs to the economy and enriched the lawyers.

A new look is needed without the hysteria of an Enron or other scandal. Whatever path is taken for reform of corporate governance, some basics should apply. The courts and government bureaucrats are ill-equipped to second-guess management decisions under the guise of full disclosure or any other precepts of corporate governance. They are equally unable to substitute regulations for market discipline. The economy is simply too complex for the government to manage. The role of the courts and the government is to curb corruption that undermines confidence in the market and sends capital elsewhere. That should be done by attacking real corruption and not criminalizing every business practice the government may find objectionable.

Notes

Chapter 1

1. Arthur Levitt, *Take on the Street,* p. 245.
2. *In re Piper Capital Management, Inc.,* 2000 WL 1759455 (S.E.C. 2000), affirmed, 2003 WL 22016298 (S.E.C. 2003).
3. *Caiola v. Citibank, NA,* 295 F.3d 312 (2d Cir. 2002).
4. *In re Cendant Corp. Prides Litigation,* 51 F. Supp. 2d 537 (D.N.J. 199), vacated in part, 243 F.3d 722 (3d Cir.) *cert. denied,* 534 U.S. 889 (2001).
5. *Dunn v. Commodity Futures Trading Commission,* 519 U.S. 465 (1997).
6. *United States v. Masten,* 170 F.3d 790, 797 n. 9 (7th Cir. 1999).
7. Joseph E. Stiglitz, *The Roaring Nineties,* p. 122.
8. Ken Auletta, *Media Man,* p. 131.
9. Roger Lowenstein, *Origins of the Crash: The Great Bubble and Its Undoing,* p. 44.
10. National Commission on Terrorist Attacks, *The 9/11 Commission Report,* p. 172.

Chapter 2

1. Enron Annual Report 1999, p. 2.
2. Enron Annual Report 1998, p. 71.
3. SEC Form 10-K, Annual Report for the Fiscal Year Ending December 31, 1994, of the Enron Corp., p. 26.
4. Neal Batson, Court-Appointed Examiner, First Interim Report, *In re Enron Corp.,* p. 1.
5. SEC Form 10-K, Annual Report for the Fiscal Year Ending December 31, 1993, of the Enron Corp., p. 4.
6. Ibid., p. 42.
7. Frank Partnoy, *F.I.A.S.C.O.,* p. 33.
8. Neal Batson, Court-Appointed Examiner, Second Interim Report, *In re Enron Corp.,* p. 28.
9. Ibid., p. 26.
10. SEC Form 10-K, Annual Report for the Fiscal Year Ending December 31, 2000, of the Enron Corp., p. 1.
11. Enron Annual Report 1999, p. 15.
12. Enron Annual Report 2000, p. 2.
13. Ibid., p. 3.
14. Enron Annual Report 1998, p. 4.
15. Enron Annual Report 2000, p. 9.
16. James Flanigan, "Enron E Commerce Success Exemplary, Unsettling," *Los Angeles Times,* January 28, 2001.
17. "Enron: What Went Wrong," p. S16.
18. Diana B. Henriques, "The Brick Stood Up Before. But Now?"
19. Bethany McLean, "Is Enron Overpriced?" p. 122.

20. Mimi Swartz with Sherron Watkins, *Power Failure: The Inside Story of the Collapse of Enron.*

21. Batson, First Interim Report, p. 2.

22. Ibid., p. 3.

23. Ibid., p. 33.

24. Report of Investigation by the Special Investigative Committee of the Board of Directors of Enron Corp., p. 5.

25. Ibid., p. 9.

26. Ibid., p. 5.

27. Ibid., p. 7.

28. Ibid., p. 16.

29. Ibid., p. 23.

Chapter 3

1. *In re Enron Corp., Complaint*, Ch. 11, Case No. 01–16034 (AJG).

2. Neal Batson, Court-Appointed Examiner, Second Interim Report, *In re Enron Corp.*, p. 15.

3. Enron Annual Report 1999, p. 15.

4. Report of Investigation by the Special Investigative Committee of the Board of Directors of Enron Corp., p. 17.

5. Enron Annual Report 2000, p. 48.

6. Report of Investigation, p. 187.

7. Neal Batson, Court-Appointed Examiner, Third Interim Report, *In re Enron Corp.*, p. 33.

8. *In re Enron Corp.*, 235 F. Supp. 2d 576, 617 (S.D. Texas 2002).

9. Batson, Second Interim Report, p. 40.

10. *In re Enron Corp.*, 2003 U.S. Dist. LEXIS 7632 (S.D. Texas).

11. *United States v. Fastow Indictment.* Cr. No. H-02–0665 (S.D. Tex., October 31, 2002).

12. Report of Investigation, p. 21.

13. *Securities and Exchange Commission v. Koenig*, Cir. No. H-04-3370 (S.D. Tex. 2004), complaint.

14. James L. Sweeny, *The California Electricity Crisis*, p. 192. Lockyer's rhetoric makes one wonder whether he might be the descendant of Robert Lockyer, the "known agitator" executed by a firing squad in front of St. Paul's Cathedral in 1649 on the order of Oliver Cromwell. Trevor Royle, *Civil War*, p. 511.

15. Kenneth Lay, "The Politics of My Trial."

16. Batson, Second Interim Report, p. 45.

17. Ibid., p. 58.

18. *JPMorgan Chase Bank v. Liberty Mutual Insurance*, 189 F. Supp. 2d 24 (S.D.N.Y. 2002). The author acted as an expert for the sureties in this proceeding and for the Enron bankruptcy estate in the Megaclaims Litigation over the failure of Enron.

19. Batson, Second Interim Report, p. 45.

20. Ibid., p. 45.

21. Ibid., p. 62.

22. Batson, Third Interim Report, p. 25.

23. Neal Batson, Court-Appointed Examiner, Final Report, *In re Enron Corp.*, p. 69.

24. *In re Enron Corp.*, 235 F. Supp. 2d 576, 652.

25. Ann Coulter, *How to Talk to a Liberal*, p. 133.

26. Bethany McLean and Peter Elkind, *The Smartest Guys in the Room: The Amazing Rise and Scandalous Fall of Enron*, p. 266.

27. Richard A. Oppel Jr., "Enron Traders on Grandma Millie."

28. DeCesaris et al. "Energy Trading Strategies in California: Pro-Competitive or Market Manipulation?"

29. Mimi Swartz with Sherron Watkins, *Power Failure: The Inside Story of the Collapse of Enron*, p. 264.

30. The author has acted as an expert for Reliant in connection with certain aspects of its trading.

Chapter 4

1. *New York Trust Company v. Eisner,* 256 U.S. 345, 349 (1921).

2. "Another Wall Street Lesson," *New York Times,* April 14, 1977.

3. Allan H. Meltzer, *A History of the Federal Reserve,* p. 464.

4. Ibid., p. 253.

5. Conrad Black, *Franklin Delano Roosevelt: Champion of Freedom,* p. 199.

6. Ibid., p. 152.

7. H. Paul Jeffers, *Diamond Jim Brady: Prince of the Gilded Age,* p. 96.

8. Black, *Franklin Delano Roosevelt,* p. 309.

9. Jerry W. Markham, *A Financial History of the United States: From J.P. Morgan to the Institutional Investor (1900–1970),* p. 177.

10. Louis D. Brandeis, *Other People's Money and How the Bankers Use It,* p. 4.

11. Adolf A. Berle and Gardiner C. Means, *The Modern Corporation and Private Property,* p. 3.

12. Ibid., p. 7.

13. Peter Drucker, *Concept of the Corporation,* p. 5.

14. Adolf A. Berle Jr., "Publicity of Accounts and Directors' Purchases of Stock," p. 827.

15. Jordan A. Schwarz, *Liberal: Adolf A. Berle and the Vision of an American Era,* p. 64.

16. William Z. Ripley, *Main Street and Wall Street,* p. 37.

17. Elisabeth Keller and Gregory A. Gehlmann, "A Historical Introduction to the Securities Act of 1933 and the Securities Exchange Act of 1934," p. 338.

18. H.R. Rep. No. 73–85, p. 2.

19. S. Rep. No. 73–1455, p. 153.

20. H.R. Rep. No. 73–85, p. 2.

21. George E. Barnett, "The Securities Act of 1933 and the British Companies Act," p. 18.

22. Felix Frankfurter, "Securities Act—Social Consequences," p. 55.

23. H.R. Rep. No. 73–85, p. 2.

24. H.R. Rep. No. 73–1383, p. 6.

25. S. Rep. No. 73–1455, p. 68.

26. Ibid., p. 153.

27. Willian Lasser, *Benjamin v. Cohen, Architect of the New Deal,* p. 92.

28. H.R. Rep. No. 73–1383, pp. 11–12.

29. 17 C.F.R. § 229.303(a).

30. Committee on Financial Services, "Hearing on Accounting Under Sarbanes-Oxley: Are Financial Statements More Reliable?" p. 1068.

31. *United States v. Morton Salt Co.,* 338 U.S. 632, 652 (1950).

32. Mike Brewster, *Unaccountable: How the Accounting Profession Forfeited a Public Trust,* p. 9.

33. *United States v. Arthur Young & Co.,* 465 U.S. 805, 832 (1984).

34. Ralph Nader, Mark Green, and Joel Seligman, *Taming the Giant Corporation,* p. 164.

35. *Bily v. Arthur Young & Co.,* 834 P.2d 745, 750 (Sup. Cal. 1992).

36. Neal Batson, Court-Appointed Examiner, Second Interim Report, *In re Enron Corp.,* p. 53.

37. Michael Chatfield, *A History of Accounting Thought,* p. 5.

38. Michael Chatfield and Richard Vangermeersch, eds., *The History of Accounting: An International Encyclopedia,* p. 4.

39. Ibid.

40. Michael J. Mepham, *Accounting in Eighteenth-Century Scotland,* p. 1.

41. Nichol's Case, 3 Deg. & J. 387 (1859).

42. Leeds Estate, 36 Ch. D. 787 (1887).

43. *Kingston Cotton Mills Co.,* [1886] 2 ch. 279, 288.

44. Richard P. Brief, *History of Public Accounting in the United States,* pp. 14–15.

45. Ibid., pp. 2–3.

46. Gary J. Previts and Barbara Dubis Merino, *A History of Accountancy in the United States: The Cultural Significance of Accounting,* p. 19.

47. *Craig. v. Anyon,* 212 A.D. 55, 208 N.Y.S. 259 (N.Y. App. Div., 1st Dept. 1925).

48. *Ultramares Corp. v. Touche,* 255 N.Y. 170, 174 N.E. 441 (N.Y. Ct. App. 1931).

49. The development of common law liability for auditor negligence is described in *Bily v. Arthur Young & Co.,* 834 P.2d 745 (Sup. Cal. 1992).

50. Previts and Merino, *A History of Accountancy in the United States,* p. 333.

51. *Kingston Cotton Mills Co.,* [1886] 2 ch. 279, 288.

52. *Escott v. BarChris Construction Corp.,* 283 F. Supp. 643 (S.D.N.Y. 1968).

53. *Fischer v. Kletz,* 266 F. Supp. 180 (S.D.N.Y. 1967).

54. Staff of the Senate Subcommittee, *The Accounting Establishment,* p. 4.

55. Previts and Merino, *A History of Accountancy in the United States,* p. 335.

56. Michael R. Young, "The Liability of Corporate Officials to Their Outside Auditor for Financial Statement Fraud," p. 2159.

57. Ibid.

58. *United States v. Simon,* 425 F.2d 796 (2d Cir. 1969), *cert. denied,* 397 U.S. 1006 (1970).

59. *Cenco, Inc. v. Seidman & Seidman,* 686 F.2d 449, 454 (7th Cir.), *cert. denied,* 459 U.S. 880 (1982).

60. *Resnick v. Touche Ross & Co.,* 470 F. Supp. 1020 (S.D.N.Y. 1979).

61. *Touche Ross & Co. v. Redington,* 442 U.S. 560 (1979).

62. *United States v. Winstar Corp.,* 518 U.S. 839, 846 (1996).

63. Ibid.

64. Ibid., at 847.

65. Ibid.

66. Ibid.

67. Richard C. Breeden, "Thumbs on the Scale," p. 71.

68. Jim Powell, *FDR's Folly: How Roosevelt and His New Deal Prolonged the Great Depression,* p. 57.

69. *Lincoln Savings and Loan Association v. Wall,* 743 F. Supp. 901, 920 (D.D.C. 1990).

70. John Plender, "Tame Pussies, Watchdogs and Siamese Twins: Broker Abacus Needs Attention," *Financial Times* (London), April 8, 2002.

71. *Arthur Young & Co.,* 465 U.S. at 818.

72. *Touche Ross & Co.,* 442 U.S. 560.

73. *Ernst & Ernst v. Hochfelder,* 425 U.S. 185 (1976).

74. *Central Bank v. First Interstate Bank, N.A.,* 511 U.S. 164 (1994).

75. *Reves v. Ernst & Young,* 494 U.S. 56 (1990).

76. Securities and Exchange Commission, "Revision of Auditor Independence Requirement," Securities Exchange Act Release No. 43602.

77. Brewster, *Unaccountable,* p. 11.

78. Arthur Levitt Jr., "The Numbers Game."

Chapter 5

1. Michael Chatfield and Richard Vangermeersch, *The History of Accounting: An International Encyclopedia,* p. 44.

2. Ibid.

3. Susan E. Squires et al., *Inside Arthur Andersen: Shifting Values, Unexpected Consequences,* p. 31.

4. Chatfield and Vangermeersch, *The History of Accounting,* p. 45.

5. *Fund of Funds, Ltd. v. Arthur Andersen & Co.,* 545 F. Supp. 1314 (S.D.N.Y. 1982).

6. *In re Enron Corp.,* 235 F. Supp. 2d 576 (S.D. Tex. 2002).

7. Stephen Gillers, "The Flaw in the Andersen Verdict."

8. Pamela Colloff, "The Trick Is Not to Act Like a Lawyer," p. 218.

9. Mike Brewster, *Unaccountable: How the Accounting Profession Forfeited a Public Trust,* p. 195.

10. Louis Lowenstein, "Financial Transparency and Corporate Governance: You Manage What You Measure," pp. 1345–1346.

11. *Space Controls, Inc. v. Commissioner,* 322 F.2d 144, 148 (5th Cir. 1963).

12. *In re Clinger & Co.,* Securities Exchange Act Release No. 39390.

13. Lowenstein, "Financial Transparency and Corporate Governance," pp. 1345–1346.

14. *Securities and Exchange Commission v. Dynegy*, Inc., SEC LEXIS 2415 (S.D. Texas Sept. 25, 2002).

15. Holman W. Jenkins Jr., "Should the Stock Market Be the Sentencing Judge?"

16. SEC News Release 03–70.

17. Adrian Michaels, "KPMG Accused of Ignoring Xerox Warnings."

18. *In re Reliant Resources*, Inc., Securities Exchange Act Release No. 47828.

19. Mark Maremont et al., "Mistrial Scuttles Possible Jury Verdicts in Tyco Case."

Chapter 6

1. Louis Loss, *Securities Regulation*, p. 4.

2. *Louis K. Liggett Co. v. Lee*, 288 U.S. 517 (1933).

3. Ralph Nader et al., *Taming the Giant Corporation*, p. 33.

4. Calvin Woodward, "Listening to the Mockingbird," p. 584.

5. Adam Smith, *An Inquiry Into the Nature and Causes of the Wealth of Nations*, p. 800.

6. Ibid., p. 800.

7. William M. Gouge, "A Short History of Paper Money and Banking in the United States," p. 41.

8. *Trustees of Dartmouth College v. Woodward*, 17 U.S. (4 Wheat) 518 (1819).

9. John Donald Wilson, *The Chase: The Chase Manhattan Bank, N.A. 1945–1985*, p. 58.

10. *Louis K. Liggett Co.*, 288 U.S. 517.

11. A.S. Colyar, *Life and Times of Andrew Jackson*, 2: 634.

12. Robert Remini, *Daniel Webster: The Man and His Time*, p. 597.

13. *Wiswall v. The Greenville and Raleigh Plank Road Company*, 56 N.C. 183 (1857).

14. *Louis K. Liggett Co.*, 288 U.S. 517 (1933).

15. Ibid.

16. William L. Cary, "Federalism and Corporate Law: Reflections Upon Delaware," p. 670.

17. Thomas L. Hazen and Jerry W. Markham, *Corporations and Other Business Enterprises: Cases and Materials*, p. 462.

18. *Zahn v. Transamerica Corp.*, 162 F.2d 36 (3d Cir. 1947).

19. *Speed v. Transamerica Corp.*, 135 F. Supp. 176 (D. Del. 1955).

20. *Charlestown Boot & Shoe Co. v. Dunsmore*, 60 N.H. 85 (1880).

21. Ronald J. Gilson and Reinier Kraakman, "Investment Companies as Guardian Shareholders," p. 1003.

22. American Law Institute, *Principles of Corporate Governance* § 301, comments.

23. *Tri-State Developers, Inc. v. Moore*, 343 S.W.2d 812 (Ky. 1961).

24. *Minton v. Cavaney*, 364 P.2d 473 (Cal. 1961).

25. *State ex rel Pillsbury v. Honeywell, Inc.*, 291 Minn. 322, 191 N.W.2d 406 (1971).

26. Berle and Means, *The Modern Corporation and Private Property*.

27. Ibid.

28. Bernard S. Black, "Agents Watching Agents: The Promise of the Institutional Investor Voice."

29. *Business Roundtable v. Securities and Exchange Commission*, 905 F.2d 406.

30. *Levin v. Metro-Goldwyn-Mayer, Inc.*, 264 F. Supp. 797 (S.D.N.Y. 1967).

31. *Lovenheim v. Iroquois Brands, Ltd.*, 618 F. Supp. 554 (D.D.C. 1985).

32. *Medical Committee for Human Rights v. Securities and Exchange Commission*, 432 F.2d 659 (D.C. Cir. 1970), *vacated as moot*, 404 U.S. 403 (1972).

33. Austin W. Scott, "The Progress of the Law, 1918–19: Trusts," p. 688.

34. Austin W. Scott, "The Trust as an Instrument of Law Reform," pp. 462–463 (quoting Frederic W. Maitland).

35. Austin W. Scott, *The Law of Trusts*, p. 856.

36. Austin W. Scott, "Liabilities Incurred in the Administration of Trusts," p. 725.

37. *Harvard College v. Amory*, 26 Mass. (9 Pick) 454 (1830).

38. Kenneth E. Scott, "Corporation Law and the American Law Institute Corporate Governance Project," p. 927.

39. Lawrence E. Mitchell, "The Death of Fiduciary Duty in Close Corporations," p. 1675.

40. *Shlensky v. Wrigley*, 237 N.E.2d 776 (Ill. App. 1968).

41. *Bates v. Dresser*, 251 U.S. 524 (1920).

42. *Barnes v. Andrews*, 298 F. 614, 615 (S.D.N.Y. 1924).

43. *Smith v. Van Gorkom*, 488 A.2d 858 (Del. 1985).

44. Derek Leebaert, *The Fifty-Year Wound*, p. 642.

45. *Brehm v. Eisner*, 746 A.2d 244 (Del. 2000).

46. Ibid.

47. *In re Walt Disney Company Derivative Litigation*, 825 A.2d 275 (Del. Ch. 2003).

48. *Meinhard v. Salmon*, 249 N.Y. 458, 164 N.E. 545, 546 (N.Y. Ct. App. 1928).

49. *Globe Woolen Co. v. Utica Gas & Electric Co.*, 121 N.E. 378 (N.Y. 1918).

50. *Remillard Brick Co. v. Remillard-Dandi Co.*, 241 P.2d 66 (Cal. 1952).

51. *Fliegler v. Lawrence*, 361 A.2d 218 (Del. 1976).

52. *Gilder v. PGA Tour, Inc.*, 936 F.2d 417 (9th Cir. 1991). The author was counsel to the PGA Tour in this action.

53. *Guth v. Loft*, 5 A.2d 503 (Del. 1939).

54. Ibid.

55. *Rogers v. Hill*, 289 U.S. 582 (1933).

56. *Heller v. Boylan*, 29 N.Y.S.2d 653, *affirmed*, 32 N.Y.S.2d 131 (1941).

57. *Donahue v. Rodd Electrotype Company of New England, Inc.*, 328 N.E.2d 505 (Mass. 1975).

58. *Meiselman v. Meiselman*, 307 S.E.2d 551 (N.C. 1983).

59. *Galler v. Galler*, 203 N.E.2d 577 (Ill. 1964).

60. *Ringling Bros.-Barnum & Bailey Combined Shows, Inc. v. Ringling*, 53 A.2d 441 (Del. 1947).

61. *Abercrombie v. Davies*, 130 A.2d 338 (Del. 1957).

62. *Oceanic Exploration Co. v. Grynberg*, 428 A.2d 1 (Del. 1981).

63. *Lehrman v. Cohen*, 222 A.2d 800 (Del. 1966).

64. *Sinclair Oil Corp. v. Levien*, 280 A.2d 717 (Del. 1971).

65. *Jones v. H.F. Ahmanson & Company*, 460 P.2d 464 (Cal. 1969).

66. *Perlman v. Feldmann*, 219 F.2d 173 (2d Cir.), *cert. denied*, 349 U.S. 952 (1955).

67. *Caplan v. Lionel Corp.*, 246 N.Y.S.2d 913 (1964), *affirmed*, 198 N.E.2d 908 (1964).

68. *Ross v. Bernhard*, 396 U.S. 531 (1970).

69. *Grobow v. Perot*, 539 A.2d 180 (Del. 1988).

70. Cary, "Federalism and Corporate Law," p. 663.

71. Tamar Frankel, "Corporate Directors' Duty of Care: The American Law Institute's Project on Corporate Governance," p. 705.

72. *Weinberger v. UOP, Inc.*, 457 A.2d 701 (Del. 1983).

73. *Unocal Corp. v. Mesa Petroleum Co.*, 493 A.2d 946 (Del. 1985).

74. *Revlon, Inc. v. MacAndrews & Forbes Holdings, Inc.*, 506 A.2d 173 (Del. 1985).

75. *Paramount Communications, Inc. v. Time, Inc.*, 571 A.2d 1140 (Del. 1989).

76. Ken Auletta, *Media Man*, p. 115.

77. *Paramount Communications Inc. v. QVC Network, Inc.*, 637 A.2d 34 (Del. 1994).

78. Bruce Orwall and Joann S. Lublin, "Suit Against Disney Over Ovitz Severance Chills Boardrooms."

79. *Revlon, Inc.*, 506 A.2d 173.

80. *First Union Corp. v. SunTrust Banks, Inc.*, 2001 WL 1885686 (N.C. Bus. Ct. August 10, 2001).

81. *Dodge v. Ford Motor Company*, 170 N.W. 668 (1919).

82. *A.P. Smith Mfg. Co. v. Barlow*, 98 A.2d 581 (N.J. 1953), *cert. denied*, 346 U.S. 861 (1953).

83. E. Merrick Dodd Jr. "For Whom Are Corporate Managers Trustees?"

84. *New York City Employees' Retirement System v. Securities and Exchange Commission*, 45 F.3d 7, 9 (2d Cir. 1995).

85. Ronald Coase, *The Nature of the Firm*.

86. Michael Jensen and William Meckling, "The Theory of the Firm."

87. Rutherford B. Campbell Jr., "Corporate Fiduciary Principles for the Post-Contractarian Era," p. 511.

88. *Jordan v. Duff & Phelps, Inc.*, 815 F.2d 429 (7th Cir. 1987), cert. dismissed, 485 U.S. 901 (1988).

Chapter 7

1. Lisa Endlich, *Optical Illusions: Lucent and the Crash of Telecom,* p. 156.

2. U.S. House of Representative Subcommittee on Oversight and Investigations of the Committee on Energy and Commerce, "Hearing on Capacity Swaps by Global Crossing and Qwest: Sham Transactions Designed to Boost Revenues?"

3. Ibid.

4. Ibid.

5. Ibid.

6. *Securities and Exchange Commission v. Adelphia,* 2002 SEC LEXIS 2891 (S.D.N.Y. Nov. 14, 2002).

7. Kenneth R. Timmerman, *Shakedown: Exposing the Real Jesse Jackson,* pp. 282–283.

8. *Securities and Exchange Commission v. WorldCom, Inc., Complaint,* p. 2.

9. Report of Investigation by the Special Investigative Committee of the Board of Directors of WorldCom, Inc., p. 13.

10. Ibid., p. 49.

11. Ibid., p. 1.

12. Ibid., p. 15.

13. Ibid., p. 223.

14. Ibid., p. 29.

15. First Interim Report of Dick Thornburgh, Bankruptcy Examiner, *In re WorldCom, Inc.,* p. 9.

16. Ibid., p. 11.

17. Ibid., p. 6.

18. Ibid., p. 50.

19. Richard C. Breeden, "Restoring Trust," p. 20.

20. Ibid., p. 31.

21. Ibid., p. 1.

22. Ibid., p. 146.

23. U.S. House of Representatives, Committee on Financial Services, "Wrong Numbers: The Accounting Problems at WorldCom," pp. 21–22.

24. Ibid., p. 95.

25. Ibid., p. 179.

26. Ibid., p. 23.

27. Mark Lander, "For Salomon, as Adviser, Millions Plus Revenge."

28. U.S. House of Representatives, Committee on Financial Services, "Wrong Numbers," pp. 62–63.

29. Ibid., p. 25.

30. Ibid., p. 97.

31. Shawn Young, "MCI Restatement Drops $74.4 Billion."

32. Editorial, "The Time Warner Shuffle," *New York Times,* July 20, 2002.

33. U.S. House of Representatives, Subcommittee on Oversight and Investigations, "Hearing on the Financial Collapse of HealthSouth," p. 5.

34. Report of Investigation by the Special Committee of the Board of Directors of Hollinger International Inc., p. 25.

35. Ibid., p. 29.

36. *Securities and Exchange Commission v. Parmalat Finanziaria S.p.A.,* 2003 SEC LEXIS 3078 (S.D.N.Y. 2003).

Chapter 8

1. *Carpenter v. Danforth,* 52 Barb. (N.Y.) 581 (1868).

2. *Goodwin v. Agassiz,* 283 Mass. 358, 186 N.E. 659 (1933).

3. William O. Douglas, "Directors Who Do Not Direct," p. 1306.

4. U.S. Senate Report. Report No. 73–1455, p. 113.

5. Ibid., p. 55.

6. *In re Cady Roberts & Co.,* 40 S.E.C. 907 (1961).

7. *Securities and Exchange Commission v. Texas Gulf Sulphur Co.*, 401 F.2d 833 (2d Cir. 1968), *cert. denied, sub. nom., Coates v. Securities and Exchange Commission*, 394 U.S. 976 (1969).

8. Daniel Fischel, *Payback: The Conspiracy to Destroy Michael Milken and His Financial Revolution*, pp. 43–44.

9. Thomas L. Hazen and Jerry W. Markham. *Corporations and Other Business Enterprises: Cases and Materials*, p. 757.

10. *Chiarella v. United States*, 445 U.S. 222 (1980).

11. *Securities and Exchange Commission v. Materia*, 745 F.2d 197 (2d Cir. 1984).

12. *Carpenter v. United States*, 484 U.S. 19 (1987).

13. *United States v. O'Hagan*, 521 U.S. 642 (1997).

14. *Securities and Exchange Commission v. Switzer*, 590 F. Supp. 756 (W.D. Okla.).

15. *United States v. Willis*, 737 F. Supp. 269 (S.D.N.Y. 1990).

16. Dirks v. Securities and Exchange Commission, 681 F.2d 824 (2d Cir. 1982), *reversed*, 463 U.S. 646 (1983).

17. Ibid.

18. *Securities and Exchange Commission v. Yun*, 327 F.3d 1263 (11th Cir. 2003).

19. Fischel, *Payback*, p. 41.

20. Ibid., p. 161.

21. Charles R. Morris, *Money, Greed, and Risk: Why Financial Crises and Crashes Happen*, p. 131.

22. Fischel, *Payback*, p. 7.

23. Ibid., p. 158.

24. Kevin G. Salwen and Laurie P. Cohen, "Getting Tough: SEC Under Breeder Takes a Harder Line on Securities Crime," *Wall Street Journal*, May 10, 1990.

25. *United States v. Chestman*, 947 F.2d 551 (2d Cir.1991), *cert. denied*, 503 U.S. 1004 (1992).

26. *United States v. Kim*, 184 F. Supp. 2d 1006 (N.D. Cal. 2002).

27. *Securities and Exchange Commission v. Adler*, 137 F.3d 1325 (11th Cir. 1998) and *United States v. Smith*, 155 F.3d 1051 (9th Cir. 1998).

28. 17 Code of Federal Regulations § 240.10b5–1.

29. Colleen DeBaise, "McDermott Knows Their Pain."

30. Jerry Oppenheimer, *Martha Stewart: Just Deserts: The Unauthorized Biography.*

31. Peg Tyre and Daniel Mcginn, "A Big House for Martha? A Tough Indictment Raises the Specter of Prison Time," p. 41.

32. "Proclaiming Her Innocence and Asking for Letters from Her Fans, Martha Stewart Published an Open Letter," *New York Post*, June 8, 2003.

33. Jeffrey Toobis, "A Bad Thing: Why Did Martha Lose?" *New Yorker*, March 22, 2004.

34. Ibid.

35. Constance L. Hays, "Martha Stewart's Sentence: The Overview," *New York Times*, July 17, 2004.

36. Benjamin Graham and David Dodd, *Security Analysis*, p. 17.

37. Ibid., p. 29.

38. Ibid., p. 30.

39. *Securities Industry Association v. Board of Governors of the Federal Reserve System*, 468 U.S. 207, 210, n.2 (1984).

40. *Securities and Exchange Commission v. Dirks*, 463 U.S. 646 (1983).

41. *In re Schering-Plough Corporation*, Securities Exchange Act Release No. 48461 (S.E.C. September 9, 2003).

42. U.S. Senate, Committee on Governmental Affairs, "Hearing on the Watchdogs That Didn't Bark: Enron and the Wall Street Analysts," p. 3.

43. Ibid., p. 54.

44. Simon English, "Grubman Still Going In at Citigroup," *Daily Telegraph* (London), August 19, 2003.

45. *State of New York v. Anschutz et al. Complaint*, Supreme Court of New York, September 30, 2002.

46. Ibid.

47. The description of these events is drawn from Citigroup Global Markets, Inc., New York Stock Exchange Hearing Panel Decision No. 03–72 (April 22, 2003).

48. Ibid.

49. *Friedman v. Salomon/Smith Barney,* 2000 U.S. Dist. LEXIS 17785 (S.D.N.Y. 2000), *affirmed,* 313 F.3d 796 (2d Cir. 2002), *cert. denied,* 157 L.Ed. 2d 43 (2003).

50. Jay R. Ritter, "The Hot Issue Market of 1980," p. 215.

51. *Friedman v. Salomon/Smith Barney, affirmed,* 313 F.3d 796, *cert. denied,* 157 L.Ed. 2d 43.

52. *Swarb v. Credit Suisse First Boston,* Fed. Sec. 1. (CCH) §92, 924 (D. Mass. 2004).

53. The description of these changes is based on the government's indictment. *United States v. Quathone* (S.D.N.Y. 2003).

54. U.S. Senate Committee on Governmental Affairs, "Hearing on the Watchdogs That Didn't Bark," p. 2.

55. Ibid., p. 115.

56. Ibid., p. 2.

57. Ibid., p. 22.

58. Ibid. p. 56.

59. Samuel Eliot Morison, *John Paul Jones: A Sailor's Biography,* p. 359.

60. U.S. Senate Report No. 73–1455, p. 339.

61. Clifford E. Kirsch, ed., *The Financial Services Revolution: Understanding the Changing Role of Banks, Mutual Funds, and Insurance Companies,* p. 382.

62. Paul F. Roye, Remarks Before American Law Institute/American Bar Association Investment Company Regulation and Compliance Conference.

63. Dennis Vacco, "Martin Act Martinet," *Wall Street Journal,* April 12, 2004.

64. Terry Pristin, "The 1998 Campaign: The Tactics: In a 'Virtual' Race, Politics Without Kissing Babies."

Chapter 9

1. Arthur Levitt, *Take on the Street,* p. 109.

2. Harvey Pitt was one of the author's supervisors at the SEC from 1972 to 1974, and the author acted as legal adviser to chairman Casey with respect to that inquiry.

3. Neal Batson, Court-Appointed Examiner, Second Interim Report, *In re Enron Corp.,* p. 51.

4. Joe Consan, "The George W. Bush Success Story: A Heartwarming Tale About Baseball, $1.7 Billion, and a Lot of Swell Friends," p. 42.

5. U.S. Senate, Committee on Banking, Housing, and Urban Affairs, "Accounting Reform and Investor Protection," pp. 1189, 1653.

6. Ibid., p. 1303.

7. U.S. House of Representatives, Committee on Financial Services, "Hearing on Accounting Under Sarbanes-Oxley: Are Financial Statements More Reliable?" p. 574.

8. The author acted as a consultant on certain aspects of those issues.

9. Robert W. Gordon, "A New Role for Lawyers? The Corporate Counselor After Enron," p. 1190.

10. Susan P. Koniak, "When the Hurlyburly's Done: The Bar's Struggle With the SEC," p. 1237.

11. Loren Fox, *Enron: The Rise and Fall,* p. 851.

12. The author was an attorney in the office of general counsel at the SEC at that time.

13. *O'Melveny & Myers v. Federal Deposit Insurance Corp.,* 512 U.S. 79 (1994).

14. Thomas Lee Hazen, "Administrative Law Controls on Attorney Practice: A Look at the Securities and Exchange Commission's Lawyer Conduct Rules," p. 325.

15. Theo Francis and Jonathan Weil, "AIG Could Face Criminal Charges."

16. Frank Partnoy, "The Siskel and Ebert of Financial Markets? Two Thumbs Down for the Credit Rating Agencies," p. 648, n. 139.

17. John A. Kouwenhoven, *Partners in Banking: An Historical Portrait of a Great Private Bank, Brown Brothers Harriman & Co. 1818–1968,* p. 125.

18. *Mallinckrodt Chemical Works v. Goldman Sachs & Co.,* 420 F. Supp. 231 (S.D.N.Y. 1976).

19. *County of Orange v. McGraw Hill Companies, Inc.*, 245 B.R. 151 (C.D. Cal. 1999).

20. U.S. Senate, Committee on Governmental Affairs, "Hearing on the Fall of Enron: How Could It Have Happened?" p. 73.

21. Ben Rand, "First Steps, Long Journey."

22. "Eliot's Insurance Policy."

23. William J. Holstein and Edward M. Kopo, "Spitzer's Climate of Fear."

24. Henry G. Manne, "Regulation in Terrorem."

25. Arthur Levitt Jr., "Money, Money, Money."

Chapter 10

1. Gregg Easterbrook, *The Progress Paradox: How Life Gets Better While People Feel Worse.*

2. Robert Dallek, *An Unfinished Life: John F. Kennedy 1917–1963,* p. 583.

3. "Europe vs. America," *Wall Street Journal.*

Chapter 11

1. Ralph Nader, Mark Green, and Joel Seligman, *Taming the Giant Corporation,* pp. 8–9.

2. Otis M. Smith, "The Consumer's Role in Corporate Governance."

3. Staff Report to the Senate Committee on Governmental Affairs, "Financial Oversight of Enron: The SEC and Private-Sector Watchdogs," p. 39, n. 137.

4. Securities and Exchange Commission, "Proposed Rules," Securities Exchange Act Release No. 42994 (July 12, 2000).

5. *Bily v. Arthur Young & Co.*, 834 P.2d 745 (Sup. Cal. 1992).

6. *Cenco, Inc. v. Seidman & Seidman*, 686 F.2d 449, 454 (7th Cir.), *cert. denied,* 459 U.S. 880 (1982).

7. *Kingston Cotton Mills Co.*, [1886] 2 ch. 279, 288.

8. *Bily v. Arthur Young & Co.*, 834 P.2d 745, 762.

9. Robert A. Prentice, "The Case for Educating Legally Aware Accountants," p. 612.

10. "Treasury Official Sees Need for Relevant Disclosure, Supports SEC Proposals," Fed. Sec. L. Rep. No. 2054.

11. U.S. Senate, Committee on Banking, Housing, and Urban Affairs, "Hearings on Accounting Reform and Investor Protection," p. 143.

12. Charles R. Morris, *Money, Greed, and Risk: Why Financial Crises and Crashes Happen,* p. 73.

13. "Wall Street Crash, Parallel Bars," *Economist,* p. 81.

14. Conrad Black, *Franklin Delano Roosevelt: Champion of Freedom,* p. 385.

15. Ibid., p. 393.

16. Ibid., pp. 394–395.

17. George Gilder, "America's New Jingoes."

18. H. Paul Jeffers, *Diamond Jim Brady: Prince of the Gilded Age,* p. 96.

19. Charles R. Geisst, *The Last Partnerships: Inside the Great Wall Street Dynasties,* p. 246.

20. Black, *Franklin Delano Roosevelt,* p. 497.

21. Patricia Beard, *After the Ball: Gilded Age Secrets, Boardroom Betrayals, and the Party That Ignited the Great Wall Street Scandal of 1905,* p. 94.

22. P.T. Barnum, *Humbugs of the World,* p. 143.

23. James G. Cannon, *Clearing Houses,* pp. 248–249.

24. U.S. House of Representatives, Capital Issues Committee, p. 2.

25. Joseph E. Stiglitz, *The Roaring Nineties,* p. 40.

26. Patricia A. McCoy, "A Political Economy of the Business Judgment Rule in Banking: Implications for Corporate Law," pp. 48–50.

27. John J. Byrne et al., "Examining the Increase in Federal Regulatory Requirements and Penalties," pp. 20–21.

28. *Kardon v. National Gypsum Co.*, 69 F. Supp. 512 (E.D. Pa. 1946).

29. *Superintendent of Insurance v. Bankers Life & Casualty Co.*, 404 U.S. 6 (1971).

30. *Cort v. Ash,* 422 U.S. 66 (1975).

31. *Cannon v. University of Chicago,* 441 U.S. 677 (1979).

32. Joel Seligman, "The Private Securities Reform Act of 1995," p. 718.

33. "Conflicted in California," *Wall Street Journal.*

34. Diana Henriques, "Enron's Many Strands: A Big Investor, Even a Watchdog Is Not Always Fully Awake."

35. "Pension Fund Shenanigans," *Wall Street Journal.*

36. Henry G. Manne, "The Case for Insider Trading."

37. *Basic Inc. v. Levinson,* 485 U.S. 224 (1988).

38. Ibid.

39. Mary O'Sullivan. *Contests for Corporate Control,* pp. 206–207.

40. Jon D. Hanson and Douglas A. Kysar, "Taking Behavioralism Seriously: The Problem of Market Manipulation," p. 640.

41. Securities and Exchange Commission, "Trading Practices Rules Concerning Securities Offerings," pp. 17, 108.

42. *Santa Fe Industries, Inc. v. Green,* 430 U.S. 462 (1977).

43. *Chris-Craft Industries, Inc. v. Piper Aircraft Corp.,* 480 F.2d 341, 383 (2d Cir. 1973).

44. Tom Barbash, *On Top of the World: Cantor Fitzgerald, Howard Lutnick, and 9/11,* pp. 92–93.

45. *Marowski v. Securities and Exchange Commission,* 274 F.3d 525 (D.C. Cir. 2001), *cert. denied,* 537 U.S. 819 (2002).

46. *United States v. Mulheren,* 938 F.2d 364 (2d Cir. 1991).

47. *In re Soybeans Future Litigation,* 892 F. Supp. 1025 (N.D. Ill. 1995).

48. Daniel Fischel and David J. Ross, "Should the Law Prohibit 'Manipulation' in Financial Markets?" p. 508.

49. Frank H. Easterbrook and Daniel R. Fischel, "Mandatory Disclosure and the Protection of Investors," p. 669.

50. Henry G. Manne, *Insider Trading and the Stock Market,* p. 159.

51. *Laidlaw v. Organ,* 15 U.S. (2 Wheat) 178 (1817).

52. Ibid., p. 194.

53. *Cipollone v. Liggett Group, Inc.,* 505 U.S. 504 (1992).

54. *Zobrist v. Coal-X, Inc.,* 708 F.2d 1511 (10th Cir. 1983).

55. *Wegerer v. First Commodity Corp.,* 744 F.2d 719 (10th Cir. 1984).

56. *Indosuez Carr Futures, Inc. v. CFTC,* 27 F.3d 1260 (7th Cir. 1994).

Selected Bibliography

A Note on Sources

The *Wall Street Journal* and the *New York Times* are the principal sources for market events, statistics, reports of indictments, trials, and other contemporaneous events in the text. The Houston papers were useful for reports on the Arthur Andersen trial. The Web site for the Securities and Exchange Commission was used to obtain descriptions of actions by that agency (http://sec.gov/). Numerous Web sites of companies involved in scandals or otherwise mentioned in the text were also used by the author as sources of information. Space prevents citation to the thousands of articles and Web sites used as sources, but they are readily accessible by LEXIS or Google searches. The Selected Bibliography contains several of the hundreds of other sources that were consulted.

Abercrombie v. Davies, 130 A.2d 338 (Del. 1957).

African-American Slave Descendants Litigation, In re, 304 F. Supp. 2d 1027 (N.D. Ill. 2004).

Ahrens, Dan. *Investing in Vice.* New York: St. Martin's, 2004.

American Law Institute. *Principles of Corporate Governance.* New York: American Law Institute, 1984.

Andersen & Co. *The First Fifty Years: 1913–1963.* New York: Garland, 1984.

A.P. Smith Mfg. Co. v. Barlow, 98 A.2d 581 (N.J. 1953), *cert. denied,* 346 U.S. 861 (1953).

Auletta, Ken. *Media Man: Ted Turner's Improbable Empire.* New York: Atlas, 2004.

Bajaj, Mukesh, Sumon C. Mazumdar, and Atulya Sarin. "Securities Class Action Settlements: An Empirical Analysis." Available at http://securities.stamford.edu/research/studies/2000//16ssrnboard.pdf, November 16, 2000.

Barbash, Tom. *On Top of the World: Cantor Fitzgerald, Howard Lutnick, and 9/11: A Story of Loss and Renewal.* New York: HarperCollins, 2003.

Barnes v. Andrews, 298 F. 614 (S.D.N.Y. 1924).

Barnett, George E. "The Securities Act of 1933 and the British Companies Act." *Harvard Business Review* 13 (1934): 1.

Barnum, P.T. *Humbugs of the World.* Reprint. Detroit: Singing Tree Press, 1970.

Basic Inc. v. Levinson, 485 U.S. 224 (1988).

Baskin, Jonathan Barron, and Paul J. Miranti Jr. *A History of Corporate Finance.* Cambridge: Cambridge University Press, 1997.

Bates v. Dresser, 251 U.S. 524 (1920).

Batson, Neal. Court-Appointed Examiner's First Interim Report. *In re, Enron Corp.* Case No. 01–16034 (AJG) (S.D.N.Y. Bankruptcy), September 21, 2002.

Batson, Neal. Court-Appointed Examiner's Second Interim Report. *In re, Enron Corp.* Case No. 01–16034 (AJG) (S.D.N.Y. Bankruptcy), January 21, 2003.

Batson, Neal. Court-Appointed Examiner's Third Interim Report. *In re, Enron Corp.* Case No. 01–16034 (AJG) (S.D.N.Y. Bankruptcy), June 30, 2003.

Batson, Neal. Court-Appointed Examiner's Final Report. *In re, Enron Corp.* Case No. 01–16034 (AJG) (S.D.N.Y. Bankruptcy), November 4, 2003.

Beard, Patricia. *After the Ball: Gilded Age Secrets, Boardroom Betrayals, and the Party That Ignited the Great Wall Street Scandal of 1905.* New York: HarperCollins, 2003.

Bell, Greory S. *In the Black: A History of African Americans on Wall Street.* New York: Wiley, 2002.

Berle, Adolf A. Jr. "Publicity of Accounts and Directors' Purchases of Stock." *Michigan Law Review* 25 (1927): 267.

Berle, Adolf A. Jr., and Gardiner C. Means. *The Modern Corporation and Private Property.* 1932. Reprint. New York: Harcourt, Brace, World, 1968.

Bernstein, Peter L. *Wedding the Waters: The Erie Canal and the Making of a Great Nation.* New York: W.W. Norton, 2005.

Bily v. Arthur Young & Co., 834 P.2d 745 (Sup. Cal. 1992).

Black, Bernard S. "Agents Watching Agents: The Promise of the Institutional Investor Voice." *UCLA Law Review* 39 (1992): 811.

Black, Conrad. *Franklin Delano Roosevelt: Champion of Freedom.* New York: Public Affairs, 2003.

Bloomberg News. "Jurors Were Divided Over Morgan's Lawsuit." *New York Times,* January 4, 2003.

Board of Governors of the Federal Reserve System. *Lending Functions of the Federal Reserve Banks: A History.* 1973.

Bogert, George, and George T. Bogert. *The Law of Trusts and Trustees.* St. Paul, MN: West, 1984.

Boies, David. *Courting Justice, From NY Yankees v. Major League Baseball to Bush v. Gore (1997–2000).* New York: Miramax Books, 2004.

Boraks, David. "After a Legal Taste Test, SunTrust Sticks to Coke." *American Banker,* June 16, 2003.

Brandeis, Louis D. *Other People's Money and How the Bankers Use It.* New York: Fredrick A. Stokes, 1914.

Breeden, Richard C. "Restoring Trust." Report to the Honorable Jed S. Rakoff, United States District Court for the Southern District of New York on Corporate Governance for the Future of MCI, Inc., August 2003.

———. "Thumbs on the Scale: The Role That Accounting Practices Played in the Savings and Loan Crisis." *Fordham Law Review* 59 (1991): 71.

Brehm v. Eisner, 746 A.2d 244 (Del. 2000).

Brewster, Mike. *Unaccountable: How the Accounting Profession Forfeited a Public Trust.* Hoboken, NJ: Wiley, 2003.

Brian, Denis. *Pulitzer: A Life.* New York: Wiley, 2001.

Brief, Richard P. *History of Public Accounting in the United States.* New York: Garland, 1988.

Brief, Richard P., ed. *Accounting Thought and Practice Through the Years.* New York: Garland, 1986.

———. *A History of Cooper Brothers & Co. 1854 to 1954.* New York: Garland, 1986.

Brinkley, Douglas. *Wheels for the World: Henry Ford, His Company and a Century of Progress (1903–2003).* New York: Viking, 2003.

Broome, Lissa L., and Jerry W. Markham. *Regulation of Bank Financial Service Activities: Cases and Materials.* St. Paul, MN: West Group, 2001.

Brudney, Victor. "The Independent Director—Heavenly City or Potemkin Village?" *Harvard Law Review* 95 (1982): 597.

Bryon, Christopher. *Martha Inc. The Incredible Story of Martha Stewart Living Omnimedia.* New York: Wiley, 2002.

Business Roundtable v. Securities and Exchange Commission, 905 F.2d 406 (D.C. Cir. 1990).

Byrne, John J., Douglas W. Densmore, and Jeffrey M. Sharp. "Examining the Increase in Federal Regulatory Requirements and Penalties: Is Banking Facing Another Troubled Decade?" *Capital University Law Review* 24 (1995): 1.

Cady Roberts & Co., In re, 40 S.E.C. 907 (1961).

Caiola v. Citibank, N.A., 295 F.3d 312 (2d Cir. 2002).

California Independent System Operator v. Federal Energy Regulatory Commission, 372 F.3d 395 (D.C. Cir. 2004).

California Power Exchange Corporation, In re, 245 F.3d 1110 (9th Cir. 2001).

Campbell v. Loew's, Inc., 134 A.2d 852 (Del. Ch. 1957).

Campbell, Rutherford, B. Jr. "Corporate Fiduciary Principles for the Post-Contractarian Era." *Florida State University Law Review* 23 (1996): 561.

Cannon v. University of Chicago, 441 U.S. 677 (1979).

Cannon, James G. *Clearing Houses.* London: Smith Elder, 1910.

Caplan v. Lionel Corp., 246 N.Y.S.2d 913 (1964), *affirmed,* 198 N.E.2d 908: (1964).

Carpenter v. Danforth, 52 Barb. (N.Y.) 581 (1868).

Carpenter v. United States, 484 U.S. 19 (1987).

Carter & Johnson, In re, 47 S.E.C. 471 (1981).

Cary, William L. "Corporate Standards and Legal Rules." *California Law Review* 50 (1962): 411.

———. "Federalism and Corporate Law: Reflections Upon Delaware." *Yale Law Journal* 83 (1974): 663.

Cassidy, John. *Dot.com: The Greatest Story Ever Sold.* New York: HarperCollins, 2002.

Cenco, Inc. v. Seidman & Seidman, 686 F.2d 449, 454 (7th Cir.), *cert. denied,* 459 U.S. 880 (1982).

Cendant Corp. Prides Litigation, In re, 51 F. Supp. 2d 537 (D.N.J. 199), *vacated in part,* 243 F.3d 722 (3d Cir.), cert. denied, 534 U.S. 889 (2001).

Central Bank v. First Interstate Bank, N.A., 511 U.S. 164 (1994).

Charlestown Boot & Shoe Co. v. Dunsmore, 60 N.H. 85 (1880).

Chatfield, Michael. *A History of Accounting Thought.* Huntington, NY: R.E. Krieger, 1974.

Chatfield, Michael, and Richard Vangermeersch, eds. *The History of Accounting: An International Encyclopedia.* New York: Garland, 1996.

Checkosky v. Securities and Exchange Commission, 139 F.3d 221 (D.C. Cir. 1998).

Chernow, Ron. *Alexander Hamilton.* New York: Penguin, 2004.

Chiarella v. United States, 445 U.S. 222 (1980).

Chris-Craft Industries, Inc. v. Piper Aircraft Corp., 480 F.2d 341, 383 (2d Cir. 1973), *cert. denied sub nom, Bangor Punta Corp. v. Chris-Craft Industries, Inc.,* 414 U.S. 910 (1973).

Choi, Stephen. "Regulating Investors Not Issuers: A Market Based Proposal." *California Law Review* 88 (2000): 279.

Cipollone v. Liggett Group, Inc., 505 U.S. 504 (1992).

Citigroup Global Markets, Inc., New York Stock Exchange Hearing Panel Decision No. 03–72 (April 22, 2003).

Clinger & Co., In re, Securities Exchange Act Release No. 39390 (S.E.C. 1997).

Coase, Ronald H. *The Nature of the Firm: Origins, Evolution and Development. 1937.* New York: Oxford University Press, 1991.

Coffee, John C. Jr. "Market Failure and the Economic Case for a Mandatory Disclosure System." *Virginia Law Review* 70 (1984): 717.

———. "Understanding Enron: 'It's About the Gatekeepers, Stupid.'" *Business Lawyer* 57 (2002): 1403.

Cole, Benjamin. *The Pied Pipers of Wall Street: How Analysts Sell You Down the River.* Princeton: Bloomberg, 2001.

Colloff, Pamela. "The Trick Is Not to Act Like a Lawyer." *Texas Monthly,* September 22, 2002, p. 157.

Colyar, A.S. *Life and Times of Andrew Jackson.* Vol. 2: *Soldier-Statesman-President.* Nashville, TN: Marshall & Bruce, 1904.

Commodity Futures Trading Commission. "A Study of the Nature, Extent and Effects of Futures Trading by Persons Possessing Material Nonpublic Information." Washington, DC: Government Printing Office, 1986.

"Conflicted in California." *Wall Street Journal,* May 11, 2003.

Consan, Joe. "The George W. Bush Success Story: A Heartwarming Tale About Baseball, $1.7 Billion, and a Lot of Swell Friends." *Harpers,* February 2000, p. 39.

Cort v. Ash, 422 U.S. 66 (1975).

Coulter, Ann. *How to Talk to a Liberal (If You Must).* New York: Crown Forum, 2004.

County of Orange v. McGraw Hill Companies, Inc., 245 B.R. 151 (C.D. Cal. 1999).

Cox, James D., Thomas Lee Hazen, and F. Hodge O'Neal. *Corporations.* New York: Aspen Law & Business, 1995.

Craig v. Anyon, 212 A.D. 55, 208 N.Y.S. 259 (N.Y. App. Div., 1st Dept. 1925).

Credit Suisse First Boston, In re, No. E-2002–41. Complaint. Office of Secretary of the Commonwealth of Massachusetts, October 21, 2002.

Dallek, Robert. *An Unfinished Life: John F. Kennedy 1917–1963.* Boston: Little, Brown, 2003.

D.E. & J. Limited Partnership v. Conaway, 284 F. Supp. 2d 719 (E.D. Michigan, 2003).

DeBaise, Colleen. "McDermott Knows Their Pain." *Wall Street Journal,* December 4, 2003.

DeCesaris, Michael, Amy Olitsky, and Douglas J. Zona. "Energy Trading Strategies in California: Pro-Competitive or Market Manipulation?" Paper presented at the Cornerstone Research Conference on Market Manipulation in the Electricity and Natural Gas Markets. Washington, DC, October 2, 2003.

Delaware v. New York, 507 U.S. 490 (1993).

Department of Enforcement v. Quattrone. Disciplinary Proceeding Nos. CAF030007–08 (N.A.S.D. March 6, 2003).

Dickson, Paul, and Thomas B. Allen. *The Bonus Army: An American Epic.* New York: Walker, 2005.

Dodd, E. Merrick, Jr. "For Whom Are Corporate Managers Trustees?" *Harvard Law Review* 45 (1932): 1145.

Dodge v. Ford Motor Company, 170 N.W. 668 (1919).

Donahue v. Rodd Electrotype Company of New England, Inc., 328 N.E.2d 505 (Mass. 1975).

Douglas, William O. "Directors Who Do Not Direct, *Harvard Law Review* 47 (1934): 1305.

Drucker, Peter F. *Concept of the Corporation.* New York: John Day, 1946.

Dura Pharmaceuticals Inc. v. Broudo, Civ. No. 09-932 (S. Ct. 2005).

Dunn v. Commodity Futures Trading Commission, 519 U.S. 465 (1997).

Dwyer, Jim, and Kevin Flynn. *102 Minutes: The Untold Story of the Fight to Survive Inside the Twin Towers.* New York: Times Books, 2005.

Easterbrook, Frank H., and Daniel Fischel. *The Economic Structure of Corporate Law.* Cambridge, MA: Harvard University Press, 1991.

———. "Mandatory Disclosure and the Protection of Investors." *Virginia Law Review* 70 (1984): 669.

Easterbrook, Gregg. *The Progress Paradox: How Life Gets Better While People Feel Worse.* New York: Random House, 2003.

Edwards, J.R. *The History of Accounting.* 4 vols. London: Routledge, 2000.

Eichenwald, Kurt. *Conspiracy of Fools: A True Story.* New York: Broadway Books, 2005.

"Eliot's Insurance Policy." *Wall Street Journal,* October 21, 2004.

Endlich, Linda. *Optical Illusions: Lucent and the Crash of Telecom.* New York: Simon & Schuster, 2004.

English, Simon. "Grubman Still Going In at Citigroup." Daily Telegraph (London), August 19, 2003.

Enron Annual Reports 1998–2000.

Enron Corp., In re, Complaint, Ch. 11, Case No. 01–16034 (AJG) (S.D.N.Y. 2001).

Enron Corp., In re, 2003 U.S. Dist. LEXIS 1668 (S.D. Texas).

Enron Corp., In re, 2003 U.S. Dist. LEXIS 7632 (S.D. Texas).

Enron Corp., In re, 2003 U.S. Dist. LEXIS 10686 (S.D. Texas).

Enron Corp., In re, 188 F. Supp. 2d 684 (S.D. Texas) 2002.

Enron Corp., In re, 235 F. Supp. 2d 576 (S.D. Texas) 2002.

Enron Corp., In re, 258 F. Supp. 2d 576 (S.D. Texas) 2003.

Enron Corp., In re, 284 F. Supp. 2d 511 (S.D. Texas) 2003.

"Enron: What Went Wrong?" *Fordham Journal of Corporate and Financial Law* 8 (2002): 1.

Ernst & Ernst v. Hochfelder, 425 U.S. 185 (1976).

Ernst & Young, In re, 2004 SEC LEXIS 831 (2004).

Escott v. Barchris Construction Corp., 283 F. Supp. 643 (S.D.N.Y. 1968).

"Europe vs. America," *Wall Street Journal,* June 18, 2004.

Eveson, Todd H. "Financial and Bank Holding Company Issuance of Trust Preferred Securities." *North Carolina Banking Institute* 6 (2002): 315.

Federal Reserve Board Staff. *A Review and Evaluation of Federal Margin Requirements.* Washington, DC: Federal Reserve Board, December 1984.

Figes, Orlando. *A People's Tragedy: The Russian Revolution (1891–1924)*. New York: Penguin, 1996.

Fileti, Thomas R., and Carl R. Steen. "Synthetic Lease Financing for the Acquisition and Construction of Power Generation Facilities in a Changing U.S. Energy Environment." *Fordham International Law Journal* 24 (2001): 1983.

Finch, Christopher. *In the Market: The Illustrated History of the Financial Markets*. New York: Abbeville Trust, 2001.

First Interim Report of Dick Thornburgh, Bankruptcy Examiner, *In re, WorldCom, Inc.*, Case No. 02–15533 (AJG) (S.D.N.Y. Bankruptcy), November 4, 2002.

First Union Corp. v. SunTrust Banks, Inc., 2001 WL 1885686 (N.C. Bus. Ct. August 10, 2001).

Fischel, Daniel. *Payback: The Conspiracy to Destroy Michael Milken and His Financial Revolution*. New York: HarperBusiness, 1995.

Fischel, Daniel, and David J. Ross. "Should the Law Prohibit 'Manipulation' in Financial Markets?" *Harvard Law Review* 105 (1991): 503.

Fischer v. Kletz, 266 F. Supp. 180 (S.D.N.Y. 1967).

Flanagan, William G. *Dirty Rotten CEOs: How Business Leaders Are Fleecing America*. New York: Citadel, 2004.

Fliegler v. Lawrence, 361 A.2d 218 (Del. 1976).

Foreign Corrupt Practices Act of 1977. Public Law No. 95–213, 91 Stat. 1494.

Fox, Lawrence J. "The Academics Have It Wrong: Hysteria Is No Substitute for Sound Public Policy Analysis." In *Enron Corporate Fiascos and Their Implications*, ed. Nancy B. Rapoport and Bala G. Dharan. New York: Foundation Press, 2004.

Fox, Loren. *Enron: The Rise and Fall*. New York: Wiley, 2003.

Fradkin, Philip L. *Stagecoach, Wells Fargo and the American West*. New York: Simon & Schuster, 2002.

Francis Theo, and Jonathan Weil. "AIG Could Face Criminal Charges." *Wall Street Journal*, October 22, 2004.

Frankel, Tamar. "Corporate Directors' Duty of Care: The American Law Institute's Project on Corporate Governance." *George Washington Law Review* 52 (1984): 705.

Frankfurter, Felix. "Securities Act—Social Consequences." *Fortune,* August 1933, p. 55.

Fraser, Steve. *Every Man a Speculator: A History of Wall Street in American Life*. New York: HarperCollins, 2005.

Friedman v. Salomon/Smith Barney, 2000 U.S. Dist. LEXIS 17785 (S.D.N.Y. 2000), *affirmed,* 313 F.3d 796 (2d Cir. 2002), *cert. denied,* 157 L.Ed.2d 43 (2003).

Fund of Funds, Ltd. v. Arthur Andersen & Co., 545 F. Supp. 1314 (S.D.N.Y. 1982).

Galbraith, John Kenneth. *The Great Crash, 1929*. Boston: Houghton Mifflin, 1988.

———. *The Affluent Society.* Boston: Houghton Mifflin, 1958.

———. *The Liberal Hour.* Boston: Houghton Mifflin, 1960.

———. *New Industrial State.* Boston: Houghton Mifflin, 1967.

———. *Economics and the Public Purpose.* Boston: Houghton Mifflin, 1973.

Galler v. Galler, 203 N.E.2d 577 (Ill. 1964).

Gasparino, Charles. *Blood on the Street: The Sensational Inside Story of How Wall Street Analysts Duped a Generation of Investors*. New York: Free Press, 2005.

Gateway, Inc., In re, 2003 WL 22683974 (S.E.C. 2003).

Gatton, T. Harry. *Banking in North Carolina: A Narrative History*. Raleigh, NC: Bankers Association, 1987.

Geisst, Charles R. *The Last Partnerships: Inside the Great Wall Street Dynasties*. New York: McGraw-Hill, 2001.

———. *Wheels of Fortune: The History of Speculation from Scandal to Respectability.* New York: Wiley, 2002.

Gilbert, Martin. *A History of the Twentieth Century, 1933–1951*. New York: William Morrow, 1998.

Gilder, George. "America's New Jingoes." *Wall Street Journal,* October 8, 2004.

Gilder v. PGA Tour, Inc., 936 F.2d 417 (9th Cir. 1991).

Gillers, Stephen. "The Flaw in the Andersen Verdict." *New York Times,* June 18, 2002.

Gilson, Ronald J., and Reinier Kraakman. "Investment Companies as Guardian Shareholders: The Place of the MISC in the Corporate Governance Debate." *Stanford Law Review* 45 (1993): 985.

Globe Woolen Co. v. Utica Gas & Electric Co., 121 N.E. 378 (N.Y. 1918).

Grobow v. Perot, 539 A.2d 180 (Del. 1988).

Goodheart, Lawrence. *Abolitionist, Atheist: Elizur Wright and the Reform Impulse.* Ohio: Kent State University Press, 1990.

Goodwin, Jason. *Greenback: The Almighty Dollar and the Invention of America.* New York: Henry Holt, 2003.

Goodwin v. Agassiz, 283 Mass. 358, 186 N.E. 659 (1933).

Gordon, John Steele. *An Empire of Wealth: The Epic History of American Economic Power.* New York: HarperCollins, 2004.

Gordon, Robert W. "A New Role for Lawyers? The Corporate Counselor After Enron." *Connecticut Law Review* 35 (2003): 1185.

Gouge, William M. "A Short History of Paper Money and Banking in the United States Including an Account of Provisional and Continental Paper Money to Which Is Prefixed an Inquiry Into the Principles of the System." 1833.

Graham, Benjamin, and David Dodd, *Security Analysis.* 2nd ed. New York: McGraw-Hill, 1940.

Grant, Adam. "Ziggy Stardust Reborn: A Proposed Modification of the Bowie Bond." *Cardozo Law Review* 22 (2001): 1291.

Grant Thornton LLP, In re, 2004 WL 85632 (S.E.C. 2004).

Great Atlantic & Pacific Tea Co., Inc., In re, 2004 U.S. App. LEXIS 14175 (3d Cir. 2004).

Guft v. Loft, 5 A.2d 503 (Del. 1939).

Hague, William. *William Pitt the Younger.* New York: Alfred A. Knopf, 2005.

Hanson, Jon D., and Douglas A. Kysar. "Taking Behavioralism Seriously: The Problem of Market Manipulation." *New York University Law Review* 74 (1999): 630.

Harvard College v. Amory, 26 Mass. (9 Pick) 454 (1830).

Hays, Constance L. "Martha Stewart's Sentence: The Overview." *New York Times,* July 17, 2004.

Hazen, Thomas Lee. "Administrative Law Controls on Attorney Practice: A Look at the Securities and Exchange Commission's Lawyer Conduct Rules." *Administrative Law Review* 55 (2003): 323.

———. *Treatise on the Law of Securities Regulation.* 4th ed. St. Paul, MN: West Group, 2002.

Hazen, Thomas L., and Jerry W. Markham. *Corporations and Other Business Enterprises: Cases and Materials.* St. Paul, MN: West Group, 2003.

Heller v. Boylan, 29 N.Y.S.2d 653, *affirmed,* 32 N.Y.S.2d 131 (1941).

Hemenway, David, *Prices and Choices: Microeconomic Vignettes.* 3rd ed. New York: University Press of America, 1993.

Henriques, Diana B. "The Brick Stood Up Before. But Now?" *New York Times,* March 10, 2002.

———. "Enron's Many Strands: A Big Investor, Even a Watchdog Is Not Always Fully Awake." *New York Times,* February 5, 2002.

Herman, Arthur. *To Rule the Waves: How the British Navy Shaped the Modern World.* New York: HarperCollins, 2004.

Hirschson, Stanley P. *General Patton: A Soldier's Life.* New York: HarperCollins, 2002.

Holstein, William J., and Edward M. Kopo. "Spitzer's Climate of Fear." *Wall Street Journal,* November 23, 2004.

Hopkins, Leon. *The Hundredth Year.* Plymouth, UK: McDonald & Evans, 1980.

Hunt, Edwin S. *The Medieval Super-Companies: A Study of the Peruzzi Company of Florence.* New York: Cambridge University Press, 1994.

Indosuez Carr Futures, Inc. v. CFTC, 27 F.3d 1260 (7th Cir. 1994).

Jeffers, H. Paul. *Diamond Jim Brady: Prince of the Gilded Age.* New York: Wiley, 2001.

Jenkins, Holman W. Jr. "Should the Stock Market Be the Sentencing Judge?" *Wall Street Journal,* March 31, 2004.

———. "Thinking Outside the Sarbox." *Wall Street Journal,* November 24, 2004.

Jensen, Michael C., and William H. Meckling. "The Theory of the Firm: Managerial Behavior, Agency Costs, and Ownership Structure." *Journal of Finance and Economics* 3 (1976): 305.

Jeter, Lynne W. *Disconnected: Deceit and Betrayal at WorldCom.* Hoboken, NJ: Wiley, 2003.

Johnson, Christian. "The Failure of Superior Bank FSB: Regulatory Lessons Learned." *Banking Law Journal* (November/December 2002): 927.

Johnson, Haynes. *The Best of Times: America in the Clinton Years.* New York: Harcourt, 2001.

Johnson, Jo, and Martine Orange. *The Man Who Tried to Buy the World: Jean-Marie Messier and Vivendi Universal.* New York: Portfolio, 2003.

Jones, Edgar. *Accountancy and the British Economy, 1840–1980: The Evolution of Ernst & Whinney.* London: B.T. Bratsford, 1981.

Jones v. H.F. Ahmanson & Company, 460 P.2d 464 (Cal. 1969).

Jordan v. Duff & Phelps, Inc., 815 F.2d 429 (7th Cir. 1987), *cert. dismissed,* 485 U.S. 901 (1988).

JPMorgan Chase Bank v. Liberty Mutual Insurance, 189 F. Supp. 2d 24 (S.D.N.Y. 2002).

Kador, John. *Charles Schwab: How One Company Beat Wall Street and Reinvented the Brokerage Industry.* Hoboken, NJ: Wiley, 2002.

Kardon v. National Gypsum Co., 69 F. Supp. 512 (E.D. Pa. 1946).

Karmel, Roberta. *Regulation by Prosecution: The Securities and Exchange Commission vs. Corporate America.* New York: Simon & Schuster, 1982.

Kaufman, Michael T. *Soros: The Life and Times of a Messianic Billionaire.* New York: Alfred A. Knopf, 2002.

Keating, Muething & Klekamp, In re, 1979 WL 186370 (S.E.C. 1979).

Keller, Elisabeth, and Gregory A. Gehlmann. "A Historical Introduction to the Securities Act of 1933 and the Securities Exchange Act of 1934." *Ohio State Law Journal* 49 (1988): 329.

Kingston Cotton Mills Co., [1886] 2 Ch. 279, 288.

Kirsch, Clifford E., ed. *The Financial Services Revolution: Understanding the Changing Role of Banks, Mutual Funds, and Insurance Companies.* New York: McGraw-Hill, 1997.

Klein, Edward. *The Truth About Hillary.* New York: Sentinel, 205.

Klein, William A., and John C. Coffee Jr. *Business Organizations and Finance: Legal and Economic Principles.* New York: Foundation Press, 2004.

Koniak, Susan P. "When the Hurlyburly's Done: The Bar's Struggle With the SEC." *Columbia Law Review* 103 (2003): 1236.

Korman, Richard. *The Goodyear Story: An Inventor's Obsession and the Struggle for a Rubber Monopoly.* San Francisco: Encounter Books, 2002.

Kouwenhoven, John A. *Partners in Banking: An Historical Portrait of a Great Private Bank, Brown Brothers Harriman & Co. 1818–1968.* Garden City, NY: Doubleday, Page, 1968.

Krass, Peter. *Carnegie.* Hoboken, NJ: Wiley, 2002.

Laidlaw v. Organ, 15 U.S. (2 Wheat) 178 (1817).

Lander, Mark. "For Salomon, as Adviser, Millions Plus Revenge." *New York Times,* October 3, 1997.

Lasser, William. *Benjamin V. Cohen, Architect of the New Deal.* New York: Century Foundation, 2002.

Lay, Kenneth. "The Politics of My Trial," *Washington Post,* September 1, 2004.

Lee, T.A., and R.H. Parker. *The Evolution of Corporate Financial Reporting.* Sunbury-on-Thames, UK: Nelson, 1979.

Leebaert, Derek. *The Fifty-Year Wound: The Price of America's Cold War Victory.* Boston: Little Brown, 2002.

Leeds Estate. 36 Ch. D. 787 (1887).

Lehrman v. Cohen, 222 A.2d 800 (Del. 1966).

Levin v. Metro-Goldwyn-Mayer, Inc., 264 F. Supp. 797 (S.D.N.Y. 1967).

Levitt, Arthur Jr. *Take on the Street, What Wall Street and Corporate America Don't Want You to Know, What You Can Do to Fight Back.* New York: Pantheon Books, 2002.

———. "Money, Money, Money." *Wall Street Journal,* November 22, 2004.

———. "The Numbers Game." Remarks at New York University Center for Law and Business, September 28, 1998.

Lewis, Michael. *Liar's Poker: Rising Through the Wreckage on Wall Street.* New York: Norton, 1989.

Lincoln Savings and Loan Association v. Wall, 743 F. Supp. 901, 920 (D.D.C. 1990).

Lindsey, Lawrence B. "I'm No Social Security Hypocrite." *Wall Street Journal,* May 26, 2000.

Loss, Louis. *Securities Regulation.* Boston: Little, Brown, 1961.

Louis K. Liggett Co. v. Lee, 288 U.S. 517 (1933).

Lovenheim v. Iroquois Brands, Ltd., 618 F. Supp. 554 (D.D.C. 1985).

Lowenstein, Louis. "Financial Transparency and Corporate Governance: You Manage What You Measure." *Columbia Law Review* 96 (1996): 1335.

Lowenstein, Roger. *Buffett: The Making of an American Capitalist.* New York: Broadway Books, 1995.

―――. *Origins of the Crash: The Great Bubble and Its Undoing.* New York: Penguin Press, 2004.

―――. "The Fall of the House of Regas." *New York Times Magazine,* February 1, 2004, p. 26.

Lucent Technologies, Inc. Securities Litigation, In re, 217 F. Supp. 2d 529 (D.N.J.) 2002.

Macey, Jonathan R. "Wall Street Versus Main Street: How Ignorance, Hyperbole, and Fear Lead to Regulation." *University of Chicago Law Review* 65 (1998): 1487.

Macey, Jonathan R., and Geoffrey P. Miller. "Kaye, Scholer, FIRREA, and the Desirability of Early Closure: A View of the Kaye Scholer Case From the Perspective of Bank Regulatory Policy." *Southern California Law Review* 66 (1993): 1115.

Mahar, Maggie. *Bull! A History of the Boom 1982–1999.* New York: HarperBusiness, 2003.

Mahonia v. West LB AG, [2004] EWHC 1938 (Comm), Royal Court of Justice London (August 3, 2004).

Malik, Om. *Broadbandits, Inside the $750 Billion Telecom Heist.* Hoboken, NJ: Wiley, 2003.

Mallinckrodt Chemical Works v. Goldman Sachs & Co., 420 F. Supp. 231 (S.D.N.Y. 1976).

Mann, Bruce H. *Republican Debtors: Bankruptcy in the Age of American Independence.* Cambridge, MA: Harvard University Press, 2002.

Manne, Henry G. *Insider Trading and the Stock Market.* New York: Free Press 1966.

―――. "The Case for Insider Trading." *Wall Street Journal,* March 17, 2003.

―――. "Regulation in Terrorem." *Wall Street Journal,* November 22, 2004.

Maremont, Mark et al. "Mistrial Scuttles Possible Guilty Verdicts in Tyco Case." *Wall Street Journal,* April 5, 2004.

Markham, Jerry W. "Fiduciary Duties Under the Commodity Exchange Act." *Notre Dame Law Review* 68 (1992): 199.

―――. "Privatizing Social Security." *San Diego Law Review* 38 (2001): 747.

―――. *A Financial History of the United States: From Christopher Columbus to the Robber Barons (1492–1900).* Armonk, NY: M.E. Sharpe, 2002.

―――. *A Financial History of the United States: From J.P. Morgan to the Institutional Investor (1900–1970).* Armonk, NY: M.E. Sharpe, 2002.

―――. *A Financial History of the United States: From the Age of Derivatives Into the New Millennium (1970–2001).* Armonk, NY: M.E. Sharpe, 2002.

―――. "Accountants Make Miserable Policemen: Rethinking the Federal Securities Laws." *North Carolina Journal of International Law and Commercial Regulation* 28 (2003): 725.

―――. "Super-Regulator: A Comparative Analysis of Securities and Derivatives Regulation in the United States, Great Britain and Japan." *Brooklyn Journal of International Law* 28 (2003): 319.

Markham, Jerry W., and Thomas L. Hazen. *Corporate Finance, Cases and Materials.* St. Paul, MN: West Group, 2004.

Marowski v. Securities and Exchange Commission, 274 F.3d 525 (D.C. Cir. 2001), *cert. denied,* 537 U.S. 819 (2002).

Martin, Dick. *Tough Calls: AT&T and the Hard Lessons Learned From the Telecom Wars.* New York: Amacom, 2005.

Mason, Christopher. *The Art of the Steal: Inside Sotheby's—Christie's Auction House Scandal.* New York: G.P. Putnam, 2004.

Mattessich, Richard. *The Beginnings of Accounting and Accounting Thought.* New York: Garland, 2000.

McCoy, Patricia A. "A Political Economy of the Business Judgment Rule in Banking: Implications for Corporate Law." *Case Western Law Review* 47 (1996): 1.

McDonald, James, *A Free Nation Deep in Debt: The Financial Roots of Democracy.* New York: Farrar Straus & Giroux, 2003.

McKean, David. *Tommy the Cork, Washington's Ultimate Insider from Roosevelt to Reagan.* South Royalton, VT: Steerforth, 2004.

McLean, Bethany. "Is Enron Overprices?" *Fortune,* March 5, 2000.

McLean, Bethany, and Peter Elkind. *The Smartest Guys in the Room: The Amazing Rise and Scandalous Fall of Enron.* New York: Penguin, 2003.

McNish, Jacquie, and Sinclair Stewart. *Wrong Way: The Fall of Conrad Black.* Woodstock, NY: Overlook, 2004.

Medical Committee for Human Rights v. Securities and Exchange Commission, 432 F.2d 659 (D.C. Cir. 1970), *vacated as moot,* 404 U.S. 403 (1972).

Meinhard v. Salmon, 249 N.Y. 458, 164 N.E. 545 (N.Y. Ct. App. 1928).

Meiselman v. Meiselman, 307 S.E.2d 551 (N.C. 1983).

Meltzer, Allan H. *A History of the Federal Reserve (1913–1951).* Chicago: University of Chicago Press, 2003.

Mepham, Michael J. *Accounting in Eighteenth-Century Scotland.* New York: Garland, 1988.

Merrill Lynch, Pierce, Fenner & Smith Inc., 456 U.S. 353 (1982).

Merritt-Chapman & Scott v. Wolfson, 321 A.2d 138 (Del. 1974).

Miller v. Asensio & Company, Inc., 2004 WL 792365 (4th Cir. 2004).

Michaels, Adrian. "KPMG Accused of Ignoring Xerox Warnings." *Financial Times,* January 30, 2003.

Minkow, Barry. *Cleaning Up: One Man's Redemptive Journey Through the Seductive World of Corporate Crime.* New York: Nelson Current, 2005.

Minton v. Cavaney, 364 P.2d 473 (Cal. 1961).

Mitchell, Lawrence E. "The Death of Fiduciary Duty in Close Corporations." *University of Pennsylvania Law Review* 138 (1990): 1675.

Morgenson, Gretchen. "Market Timing: A Longtime Practice Comes Under New Scrutiny." *New York Times,* November 10, 2003.

Morison, Samuel Eliot. *John Paul Jones: A Sailor's Biography.* New York: Barnes & Noble, 1959.

Morris, Charles R. *Money, Greed, and Risk: Why Financial Crises and Crashes Happen.* New York: Times Business, 1999.

Morris, Edmund. *Theodore Rex.* New York: Random House, 2001.

Munk, Nina. *Fools Rush In: Steve Case, Jerry Levin, and the Unmaking of AOL Time Warner.* New York: HarperBusiness, 2004.

Murio, Reid Anthony. "An Independent Auditor's Suit for Wrongful Discharge." *Albany Law Review* 58 (1994): 413.

Murphy, Bruce Allen. *Wild Bill: The Life and Legend of William O. Douglas.* New York: Random House, 2003.

Nader Ralph, Mark Green, and Joel Seligman. *Taming the Giant Corporation.* New York: W.W. Norton, 1976.

National Commission on Terrorist Attacks Upon the United States. *The 9/11 Commission Report.* New York: W.W. Norton, 2004.

New York City Employees' Retirement System v. Securities and Exchange Commission, 45 F.3d 7 (2d Cir. 1995).

New York Trust Company v. Eisner, 256 U.S. 345 (1921).

Nichol's Case, 3 Deg. & J. 387 (1859).

Nobes, C. *Landmarks in Accounting History.* London: ICAEW, 1979.

O'Brien, Creide. *The Development of Accounting in Ireland.* Kildare: National University of Ireland, 1979.

Oceanic Exploration Co. v. Grynberg, 428 A.2d 1 (Del. 1981).

O'Connor, Sean M. "Be Careful What You Wish for: How Accountants and Congress Created the Problem of Auditor Independence." *Boston College Law Review* 45 (2004): 741.

Office of the Vice President. *Blueprint for Reform: The Report of the Task Group on Regulation of Financial Services.* Washington, DC: Government Printing Office, 1984.

O'Melveny & Myers v. Federal Deposit Insurance Corp., 512 U.S. 79, 81 (1994).

Oppel, Richard A. Jr. "Enron Traders on Grandma Millie and Making Out Like Bandits." *New York Times,* June 13, 2004.

Oppenheimer, Jerry. *Martha Stewart: Just Deserts: The Unauthorized Biography.* New York: William Morrow, 1997.

Orwall, Bruce, and Joann S. Lublin. "Suit Against Disney Over Ovitz Severance Chills Boardrooms." *Wall Street Journal,* October 11, 2004.

O'Sullivan, Mary. *Contests for Corporate Control.* Oxford: Oxford University Press, 2000.

Paramount Communications Inc. v. QVC Network, Inc., 637 A.2d 34 (Del. 1994).

Paramount Communications, Inc. v. Time, Inc., 571 A.2d 1140 (Del. 1989).

Parker, Richard. *John Kenneth Galbraith: His Life, His Politics, His Economics.* New York Farrar, Straus and Giroux, 2005.

Parker, R.H. *The Evolution of Corporate Financial Reporting.* Sunbury-on Thames, UK: Nelson, 1979.

Partnoy, Frank. *F.I.A.S.C.O.: Blood in the Water on Wall Street.* New York: Norton, 1997.

———. "The Siskel and Ebert of Financial Markets? Two Thumbs Down for the Credit Rating Agencies." *Washington University Law Quarterly* 77 (1999): 619.

———. "Barbarians at the Gatekeepers? A Proposal for a Modified Strict Liability Regime." *Washington University Law Quarterly* 79 (2001): 491.

———. "The Paradox of Credit Ratings." In *Ratings, Rating Agencies and the Global Financial System,* Ch. 3, ed. Richard M. Levich, Giovanni Majnoni, and Carmen Reinhart. New York: New York University Press, 2002.

———. *Infectious Greed, How Deceit and Risk Corrupted the Financial Markets.* New York: Henry Holt, 2003.

"Pension Fund Shenanigans." *Wall Street Journal,* August 20, 2004.

Perlman v. Feldmann, 219 F.2d 173 (2d Cir.), *cert. denied,* 349 U.S. 952 (1955).

Pinter v. Dahl, 486 U.S. 622 (1988).

Piper Capital Management, Inc., In re, 2000 WL 1759455 (S.E.C. 2000), *affirmed,* 2003 WL 22016298 (S.E.C. 2003).

Plender, John. "Tame Pussies, Watchdogs, and Siamese Twins: Broker Abacus Needs Attention." *Financial Times* (London), April 8, 2002.

Powell, Jim. *FDR's Folly: How Roosevelt and His New Deal Prolonged the Great Depression.* New York: Crown Forum, 2003.

Prentice, Robert A. "The Case for Educating Legally Aware Accountants." *American Business Law Journal* 38 (2001): 597.

Previts, Gary J., and Barbara Dubis Merino, *A History of Accountacy in the United States: The Cultural Significance of Accounting.* Columbus: Ohio State University Press, 1998.

Ramo, Alan. "California's Energy Crisis: The Perils of Crisis Management and a Challenge to Environmental Justice." *Albany Law Environmental Outlook* 7 (2002): 1.

Rand, Ben. "First Steps, Long Journey." *Rochester Democrat and Chronicle,* May 16, 2004.

Reliant Resources, Inc., In re, Securities Exchange Act Release No. 47828 (S.E.C. May 12, 2003).

Remillard Brick Co. v. Remillard-Dandi Co., 241 P.2d 66 (Cal. 1952).

Remini, Robert. *Daniel Webster: The Man and His Time.* New York: W.W. Norton, 1991.

Renehan, Edward J. Jr. *Dark Genius of Wall Street: The Misunderstood Life of Jay Gould, King of the Robber Barons.* New York: Basic Books, 2005.

Report of Investigation by the Special Investigative Committee of the Board of Directors of Enron Corp., February 1, 2002.

Report of Investigation by the Special Investigative Committee of the Board of Directors of WorldCom, Inc., March 31, 2003.

Report of Investigation by the Special Committee of the Board of Directors of Hollinger International, Inc., August 30, 2004.

Resnick v. Touche Ross & Co., 470 F. Supp. 1020 (S.D.N.Y. 1979).

Reves v. Ernst & Young, 494 U.S. 56 (1990).

Reynolds, Alan. "Not Spitzer's Job." *Wall Street Journal,* October 22, 2004.

Ringling Bros.-Barnum & Bailey Combined Shows, Inc. v. Ringling, 53 A.2d 441(Del. 1947).

Ripley, William Z. *Main Street and Wall Street.* New York: Harper Brothers, 1939 edition.

Ritter, Jay R. "The Hot Issue Market of 1980." *Journal of Business* 575 (1984): 215.

Rogers v. Hill, 289 U.S. 582 (1933).

Rogers, Jim. *Hot Commodities: How Anyone Can Invest Profitably In the World's Best Market.* New York: Random House, 2004).

Rosenfeld v. Fairchild Engine & Airplane Corp., 309 N.Y. 168, 128 N.E. 291 (1955).

Ross v. Bernhard, 396 U.S. 531 (1970).

Roye, Paul R. Remarks Before American Law Institute of American Bar Association Investment Company, regulation and compliance conference, October 16, 2003.

Royle, Trevor. *Civil War: The Wars of the Three Kingdoms 1638–1660.* London: Little, Brown, 2004.

Salwin, Kevin G., and Cohen, Laurie P. "Getting Tough: SEC Under Breeder Takes a Harder Line on Securities Crime," *Wall Street Journal*, May 10, 1990.

Santa Fe Industries, Inc. v. Green, 430 U.S. 462 (1977).

Schecter, Barnet. *The Battle for New York: The City at the Heart of the American Revolution.* New York: Walker, 2002.

Schering-Plough Corporation, In re, Securities Exchange Act Release No. 48461 (S.E.C. September 9, 2003).

Schilit, Howard. *Financial Shenanigans: How to Detect Accounting Gimmicks and Fraud in Financial Reports.* 2d ed. New York: McGraw Hill, 2002.

Schwartz, Donald E. "A Case for Federal Chartering of Corporations." *Business Lawyer* 31 (1975): 1127.

Schwarz, Jordan A. *Liberal: Adolf A. Berle and the Vision of an American Era.* New York: Free Press, 1987.

Scott, Austin W. "Liabilities Incurred in the Administration of Trusts." *Harvard Law Review* 28 (1915): 725.

———. "The Progress of the Law, 1918–19: Trusts." *Harvard Law Review* 33 (1919–20): 688.

———. "The Trusts as an Instrument of Law Reform." *Yale Law Journal* 31 (1922): 457.

———. *The Law of Trusts.* Boston: Little, Brown, 1939.

Scott, Kenneth E. "Corporation Law and the American Law Institute Corporate Governance Project." *Stanford Law Review* 35 (1983): 927.

Securities and Exchange Commission. Form 10-K. Annual Report for the Fiscal Years Ending December 31, 1993–2000, of the Enron Corp.

Securities and Exchange Commission. News Release 03–70 (June 5, 2003).

Securities and Exchange Commission. "Proposed Rules." Securities Exchange Act Release No. 42994 (July 12, 2000).

Securities and Exchange Commission. *Report of the Special Study of the Securities Market.* H.R. Doc. No. 95, 88th Cong., 1st sess. (1963).

Securities and Exchange Commission. "Revision of Auditor Independence Requirement." Securities Exchange Act Release No. 43602 (November 21, 2000).

Securities and Exchange Commission. "Trading Practices Rules Concerning Securities Offerings." 68 Fed. Reg. 17,108 (April 12, 1996).

Securities and Exchange Commission v. Adelphia, 2002 SEC LEXIS 2891 (S.D.N.Y. Nov. 14, 2002).

Securities and Exchange Commission v. Adler, 137 F.3d 1325 (11th Cir. 1998).

Securities and Exchange Commission v. Dirks, 463 U.S. 646 (1983).

Securities and Exchange Commission v. Dynegy, Inc., SEC LEXIS 2415 (S.D. Texas Sept. 25, 2002).

Securities and Exchange Commission v. Fastow, Complaint, Southern District Texas (2002).

Securities and Exchange Commission v. Howey, 328 U.S. 293 (1946).

Securities and Exchange Commission v. Koenig, Cir. No. H-04-3370 (S.O. Tex. 2004).

Securities and Exchange Commission v. Lucent Technologies, Inc., 2004 SEC LEXIS 1007 (D. N.J. May 17, 2004).

Securities and Exchange Commission v. Materia, 745 F.2d 197 (2d Cir. 1984).

Securities and Exchange Commission v. National Student Marketing Corp., 457 F. Supp. 682 (D.D.C. 1978).

Securities and Exchange Commission v. Parmalat Finanziaria S.p.A., 2003 SEC LEXIS 3078 (S.D.N.Y. 2003).

Securities and Exchange Commission v. SG Ltd., 265 F.3d 42 (1st Cir. 2001).

Securities and Exchange Commission v. Spiegel, Inc., 2003 SEC LEXIS 22176223 (N.D. Ill. 2003).

Securities and Exchange Commission v. Stewart, Civ. No. 03 CV 4070 (S.D.N.Y. 2003).

Securities and Exchange Commission v. Switzer, 590 F. Supp. 756 (W.D. Okla).

Securities and Exchange Commission v. Texas Gulf Sulphur Co., 401 F.2d 833 (2d Cir. 1968), *cert. denied, sub. nom., Coates v. SEC*, 394 U.S. 976 (1969).

Securities and Exchange Commission v. WorldCom, Inc. Complaint. Civil Action (S.D.N.Y. N.Y. June 26, 2002).

Securities and Exchange Commission v. Yun, 327 F.3d 1263 (11th Cir. 2003).

Securities Exchange Act Release No. 17114 (Sept. 2, 1980).

Securities Industry Association v. Board of Governors of the Federal Reserve System, 468 U.S. 207 (1984).

Sedighim v. Donaldson, Lufkin, & Jenrette, Inc. 167 F. Supp. 2d 639 (S.D.N.Y. 2001).

Seligman, Joel. "The Private Securities Reform Act of 1995." *Arizona Law Review* 38 (1996): 717.

————. *The Transformation of Wall Street: A History of the Securities and Exchange Commission and Modern Corporate Finance.* Boston: Northeastern University Press, 1995.

Shafer-Pearson Agency, Inc. v. Chubb Corp., 237 Ill. App. 3d 1031, 606 N.E.2d 17 (1992).

Shiller, Robert J. *The New Financial Order: Risk in the 21st Century.* Princeton: Princeton University Press, 2003.

Shlensky v. Wrigley, 237 N.E.2d 776 (Ill. App. 1968).

Siebert, Muriel. *Changing the Rules: Adventures of a Wall Street Maverick.* New York: Free Press, 2002.

"Sinclair and Watergate." *Wall Street Journal,* October 29, 2004.

Sinclair Oil Co. v. Levien, 280 A.2d 717 (Del. 1971).

Skeel, David A. Jr. *Debt's Dominion: A History of Bankruptcy.* Princeton, NJ: Princeton University Press, 2001.

Smith, Adam. *An Inquiry Into the Nature and Causes of the Wealth of Nations.* 1776. New York: Modern Library, 1994.

Smith, Otis M. "The Consumer's Role in Corporate Governance." Address before the National Capital Assembly, Washington, DC, November 10, 1977.

Smith, Rebecca, and John R. Emshwiller. *24 Days: How Two Wall Street Journal Reporters Uncovered the Lies That Destroyed Faith in Corporate America.* New York: HarperBusiness, 2003.

Smith v. Van Gorkom, 488 A.2d 858 (Del. 1985).

Smitten, Richard. *Jesse Livermore, World's Greatest Stock Trader.* New York: Wiley, 2001.

Snell, Daniel C. *Ledgers and Prices in Early Mesopotamian Merchant Accounts.* New Haven: Yale University Press, 1982.

Sobel, Robert. *The Great Boom, 1950–2000: How a Generation of Americans Created the World's Most Prosperous Society.* New York: Truman Talley, 2000.

Sonde, Theodore. "Professional Disciplinary Proceedings." *Business Lawyer* 30 (1974): 157.

————. "'Up the Ladder' and Over: Regulating Securities Lawyers—Past, Present and Future." *Washington & Lee Review* 60 (2003): 331.

Soybeans Future Litigation, In re, 892 F. Supp. 1025 (N.D. Ill. 1995).

Space Controls, Inc. v. Commissioner, 322 F.2d 144, 148 (5th Cir. 1963).

Spacek, Leonard. *The Growth of Arthur Andersen & Co. 1928–1973: An Oral History.* New York: Garland, 1989.

Speed v. Transamerica Corp., 135 F. Supp. 176 (D. Del. 1955).

"Spitzer's Justice," *Vanity Fair,* January 2005, p. 118.

Squires, Susan E., Cynthia Smith, Lorna McDougall, and William Yeack. *Inside Arthur Andersen, Shifting Values, Unexpected Consequences.* New York: FT Prentice Hall, 2003.

State ex rel Pillsbury v. Honeywell, Inc., 291 Minn. 322, 191 N.W.2d 406 (1971).

State of New York v. Anschutz et al. Complaint, Supreme Court of New York, September 30, 2002.

Stewart, James B. *Disney War.* New York: Simon & Schuster, 2005.

Stiglitz, Joseph E. *The Roaring Nineties.* New York: W.W. Norton, 2003.

Stone, Amey, and Mike Brewster. *King of Capital, Sandy Weill and the Making of Citigroup.* New York: Wiley, 2002.

"Structured Financing Techniques Committee on Bankruptcy and Corporate Reorganization of the Association of the Bar of the City of New York." *Business Lawyer* 50 (1995): 527.

Sumitomo Corp. v. Chase Manhattan Bank, 2000 U.S. Dist. LEXIS 15707 (S.D.N.Y. 2000).

Superintendent of Insurance v. Bankers Life & Casualty Co., 404 U.S. 6 (1971).

Swarb v. Credit Suisse First Boston, Fed. Sec. 1. (CCH) §92, 924 (D. Mass. 2004).

Swartz, Mimi, with Sherron Watkins. *Power Failure: The Inside Story of the Collapse of Enron.* New York: Doubleday, 2003.

Sweeny, James L. *The California Electricity Crisis.* Stanford, CA: Hoover Institution Press, 2002.

Timmerman, Kenneth R. *Shakedown: Exposing the Real Jesse Jackson.* Washington, DC: Regnery, 2002.

Toffler, Barbara Ley. *Final Accounting: Ambition, Greed, and the Fall of Arthur Andersen.* New York: Broadway, 2003.

Toobin, Jeffrey. "A Bad Thing. Why Did Martha Lose?" *New Yorker*, March 21, 2004.

Touche Ross & Co. v. Securities and Exchange Commission, 609 F.2d 570 (2nd Cir. 1979).

Transnor (Bermuda) Ltd. v. BP North America, 738 F. Supp. 1472 (S.D.N.Y. 1990).

Treaster, Joseph B. *Paul Volcker: The Making of a Financial Legend.* Hoboken, NJ: Wiley, 2004.

"Treasury Official Sees Need for Relevant Disclosure, Supports SEC Proposals," (CCH) Fed. Sec. L. Rep. No. 2054 (2002).

Tri-State Developers, Inc. v. Moore, 343 S.W.2d 812 (Ky. 1961).

Truell, Peter, and Larry Gurwin. *False Profits: The Inside Story of BCCI, The World's Most Corrupt Financial Empire.* Boston: Houghton Mifflin, 1992.

"Trustees and the Commutation of East India Stock." *Law Times* 56 (1874): 193.

Trustees of Dartmouth College v. Woodward, 17 U.S. (4 Wheat) 518 (1819).

Tyre, Peg, and Daniel Mcginn. "A Big House for Martha? A Tough Indictment Raises the Specter of Prison Time." *Newsweek,* June 16, 2003.

Ultramares Corp. v. Touche, 255 N.Y. 170, 174 N.E. 441 (N.Y. Ct. App. 1931).

Unger, Harlow Giles. *John Hancock, Merchant King and American Patriot.* New York: Wiley, 2000.

United States House of Representatives.

    Capital Issues Committee. *Report of the Capital Issues Committee,* H. Doc. 1485, 65th Cong., 3d sess., 1918.

    Committee on Energy and Commerce. "Hearing on Lessons Learned from Enron's Collapse: Auditing the Accounting Industry." 107th Cong., 2d sess., February 6, 2002.

    Committee on Financial Services. "Hearing on Accounting Under Sarbanes-Oxley: Are Financial Statements More Reliable?" 108th Cong. 1st sess., September 17, 2003.

    Committee on Financial Services. "Wrong Numbers: The Accounting Problems at WorldCom." 107th Cong., 2d sess., July 8, 2002.

    Committee on Financial Services. "Rebuilding Investor Confidence, Protecting U.S. Capital Markets: The Sarbanes-Oxley Act: The First Year," 2003.

    Report No. 85, 73rd Cong., 1st sess. (1933).

    Report No. 722, pt. 1, 102nd Cong., 1st sess. (1992).

    Report No. 1383, 73rd Cong. 2nd sess. (1934).

    Subcommittee on Capital Markets, Insurance, and Government Sponsored Enterprises of the Committee on Financial Services. "Hearing on Mutual fund Industry Practices and Their Effect on Individual Investors."108th Con., 1st sess., March 12, 2003.

    Subcommittee on Employer-Employee Relations of the Committee on Education and the Workforce. "Hearing on Enron and Beyond: Legislative Solutions." 107th Cong. 2nd sess., February 27, 2002.

    Subcommittee on Oversight and Investigations of the Committee on Energy and Commerce. "Hearing on Capacity Swaps by Global Crossing and Qwest: Sham Transactions Designed to Boost Revenues?" 107th Cong., 2nd sess., September 24 and October 1, 2002.

    Subcommittee on Oversight and Investigations of the Committee on Energy and Commerce. "Hearing on the Financial Collapse of Enron: Part 1." 107th Cong., 2nd sess., February 5, 2002.

    Subcommittee on Oversight and Investigations of the Committee on Energy and Commerce. "Hearing on the Financial Collapse of Enron: Part 2." 107th Cong., 2nd sess., February 7, 2002.

    Subcommittee on Oversight and Investigations of the Committee on Energy and Commerce, "Hearing on the Financial Collapse of HealthSouth." Pts. 1 and 2, 108th Cong., 1st sess., October 16 and November 5, 2003.

United States Senate.

    Committee on Banking, Housing, and Urban Affairs, "Hearings on Accounting Reform and Investor Protection." 107th Cong., 2nd sess., March 5–6, 14, 19, and 20–21, July 8–12, 15, and 25, 2002.

Committee on Banking, Housing, and Urban Affairs. "Hearing on Recent Developments in Hedge Funds." 108th Cong., 1st sess., April 10, 2003.

Committee on Energy and Natural Resources. "Hearing on Enron Corporation's Collapse." 107th Cong., 2nd sess., January 29, 2002.

Committee on Governmental Affairs. "Hearing on the Fall of Enron: How Could It Have Happened?" 107th Cong., 2nd sess., January 24, 2002.

Committee on Governmental Affairs. "Hearing on Rating the Raters: Enron and the Credit Rating Agencies."107th Cong., 2nd sess., March 20, 2002.

Committee on Governmental Affairs. "Hearing on Retirement Insecurity: 401(k) Crisis at Enron."107th Cong., 2nd sess., February 5, 2002.

Committee on Governmental Affairs. "Hearing on the Watchdogs That Didn't Bark: Enron and the Wall Street Analysts."107th Cong, 2nd sess., February 27, 2002.

Committee on the Judiciary. "Hearing on Accountability Issues: Lessons Learned From Enron's Fall."107th Cong., 2nd sess., February 6, 2002.

Minority Staff Report of the Staff of the Permanent Subcommittee on Investigations of the Committee on Governmental Affairs. "U.S. Tax Shelters: The Role of Accountants, Lawyers, and Financial Professionals. 108th Cong., 1st sess. (2003).

Report No. 1455, 73rd Cong., 2nd sess. (1934).

Staff Report to the Committee on Governmental Affairs. "Financial Oversight of Enron: The SEC and Private-Sector Watchdogs." Senate Doc., 107th Cong., 2nd sess. (October 8, 2002).

Staff Report to the Senate Subcommittee on Reports, Accounting and Management of the Committee on Government Operations. *The Accounting Establishment.* Senate Doc. 34, 95th Cong., 1st sess. (1977).

Subcommittee on Financial Management, the Budget, and International Security of the Committee on Governmental Affairs. "Hearing on Mutual Funds: Trading Practices and Abuses That Harm Investors." 108th Cong., 1st sess., November 3, 2003.

United States v. Arthur Young & Co., 465 U.S. 805 (1984).

United States v. Chestman, 947 F.2d 551 (2d Cir.1991), *cert. denied,* 503 U.S. 1004 (1992).

United States v. Fastow. Indictment. Cr. No. H-02–0665 (S.D. Texas, October 31, 2002).

United States v. Fastow. Indictment. Cr. No. H-03 (S.D. Texas, April 30, 2003).

United States v. Fastow. Superseding Indictment. Cr. No. H-02–0665 (S.D. Texas, April 30, 2003).

United States v. Kim, 184 F. Supp. 1006 (N.D. Cal. 2002).

United States v. Kopper. Information. Cr. No. H-02–0560 (S.D. Texas, August 20, 2002).

United States v. Masten, 170 F.3d 790 (7th Cir. 1999).

United States v. Morgan, 118 F. Supp. 621 (S.D.N.Y. 1953).

United States v. Morton Salt Co., 338 U.S. 632 (1950).

United States v. Mulheren, 938 F.2d 364 (2d Cir. 1991).

United States v. O'Hagan, 521 U.S. 642 (1997).

United States v. Quattrone. Indictment. Cr. (S.D. N.Y. 2003).

United States v. Scrushy, Indictment. CR-03-be-0530-s (N.D. Ala. 2003).

United States v. Simon, 425 F.2d 796 (2d Cir. 1969), *cert. denied,* 397 U.S. 1006 (1970).

United States v. Smith, 155 F.3d 1051 (9th Cir. 1998).

United States v. Willis, 737 F. Supp. 269 (S.D.N.Y. 1990).

United States v. Winstar Corp., 518 U.S. 839 (1996).

United States v. Wolfson, 405 F.2d 779 (2nd Cir. 1968).

Unocal Corp. v. Mesa Petroleum Co., 493 A.2d 946 (Del. 1985).

Wachovia Bank & Trust Co. v. National Student Marketing Co., 650 F.2d 342 (D.C. Cir. 1980), *cert. denied sub nom., Peat, Marwick, Mitchell & Co. v. Wachovia Bank & Trust Co.,* 452 U.S. 954 (1981).

Walker, Stephen P. *Society of Accountants in Edinburgh.* New York: Garland, 1988.

Walkovszky v. Carlton, 223 N.E.2d 6 (1966).

"Wall Street Crash, Parallel Bars." *Economist,* October 27, 2001, p. 81.

Wallison, Peter. "Rein in the Public Company Accounting Oversight Board." *Financial Services Outlook,* American Enterprise Institute, February 2005.

Walt Disney Company Derivative Litigation, In re, 825 A.2d 275 (Del. Ch. 2003).

Wegerer v. First Commodity Corp., 744 F.2d 719 (10th Cir. 1984).

Weightman, Gavin. *The Frozen-Water Trade.* New York: Hyperion, 2003.

Weinberger v. UOP, Inc., 457 A.2d 701 (Del. 1983).

Weisberger, Bernard A. *America Afire: Jefferson, Adams, and the Revolutionary Election of 1800.* New York: William Morrow, 2000.

Weisman, Steven R. *The Great Tax Wars.* New York: Simon & Schuster, 2002.

Whittingham, Richard. *Boy Wonder of Wall Street: The Life and Times of Financier Eddie Gilbert.* New York: Texere, 2003.

Wilgus, H.L. "Purchase of Shares of a Corporation by a Director from a Shareholder." *Michigan Law Review* 8 (1910): 267.

Wilson, John Donald. *The Chase: The Chase Manhattan Bank, N.A. 1945–1985.* Boston: Harvard Business School Press, 1986.

Winans, R. Foster. *Trading Secrets: Seduction and Scandal at the* Wall Street Journal. New York: St. Martin's, 1986.

Wiswall v. The Greenville and Raleigh Plank Road Company, 56 N.C. 183 (1857).

Woodward, Calvin. "Listening to the Mockingbird." *Alabama Law Review* 45 (1994): 563.

Young, Michael R. "The Liability of Corporate Officials to Their Outside Auditor for Financial Statement Fraud." *Fordham Law Review* 64 (1996): 2155.

Young, Shawn. "MCI Restatement Drops $74.4 Billion." *Wall Street Journal,* March 15, 2004.

Zahn v. Transamerica Corp., 162 F.2d 36 (3d Cir. 1947).

Zobrist v. Coal-X, Inc., 708 F.2d 1511 (10th Cir. 1983).

Zuckoff, Mitchell. *Ponzi's Scheme: The True Story of a Financial Legend.* New York: Random House, 2005.

Name Index

Subject Index

A

ABS Securities, 10
Accounting abuses
  big bath write offs, 356
  capacity swaps, 317
  capitalizing expenses, 356–357
  channel stuffing, 218–220, 315
  co-borrowings, 326
  consulting, 185, 478–479
  continuing problems after Enron, 627
  cookie jar reserves, 217–218, 313
  deferred expenses, 357
  flash sales, 317
  gap closures, 315, 349
  line costs, 349
  mark-to-market accounting, 57–59,
    99–100, 491
  non-compete fees, 368
  office boy loans, 612
  retirement accounts, 477
  secret reserves, 216–217
  tax accounting vs. financial accounting,
    109, 334
  tax shelters, 480–482
  topside entries, 346
  travel expenses, 479–480
Accounting profession
  accrual accounting, 213–216
  adversarial relationships between auditors
    and clients, 468
  audit failures, 604
  audit process, 600–602
  as bloodhounds, 600
  cash accounting, 213–216
  certification of accounting statements, 161
  certified public accountants, 168
  channel stuffing, 218–220
  consulting business spin offs, 319
  consulting issues, 177–195, 479

Accounting profession *(continued)*
  cookie jar reserves, 217–218
  declining numbers, 603
  double entry accounting, 162
  expectations gap, 179
  failed audits before Enron, 180–182,
    185–186
  generally accepted accounting principles,
    159
  generally accepted auditing standards,
    161, 600
  goodwill, 355–356
  history of profession, 161–169
  independence issues, 189–192
  liabilities from failed audits, 186–189
  liability standards, 169–170, 188
  licensing requirements, 168–169
  limited liability partnerships, 195–196
  numbers leaving the profession, 454
  peer reviews, 189
  as policemen, 194–195
  pro forma results, 221
  real time information, 604
  reform efforts, 175–180
  risk based accounting, 363–364
  role of FASB, 160
  role of management, 603–604
  round trip trades, 231–232, 356
  savings and loan crisis, 182–185
  secret reserves, 216–217
  shortcomings, 170–174
  staleness of reports, 604
  standard setting, 159
  statement of cash flows, 220–221
  tracing, 601
  vouching, 601
  as watchdog, 601
  working for management, 603
Accrual accounting, 213–216
Affinity group frauds, 21

733

About the Author

Jerry W. Markham is a professor of law at Florida International University at Miami where he teaches corporate and international business law. He previously was a partner in the international law firm of Rogers & Wells (now Clifford Chance), chief counsel for the Division of Enforcement of the United States Commodity Futures Trading Commission, secretary and counsel for the Chicago Board Options Exchange, and attorney in the Office of General Counsel at the United States Securities and Exchange Commission. Markham taught as an adjunct professor of law at the Georgetown law school in Washington, DC, and was a professor of law at the University of North Carolina at Chapel Hill before moving to Florida. He holds law degrees from Georgetown and the University of Kentucky. Markham is the author of a three-volume *A Financial History of the United States*, published by M.E. Sharpe, and selected as a *Choice* Outstanding Academic Title for 2002. He is the author and coauthor of several other books on financial matters.